HISTORY OF

CONTRA COSTA COUNTY

CALIFORNIA

WITH

Biographical Sketches

OF

*The Leading Men and Women of the County Who Have Been
Identified with Its Growth and Development
from the Early Days to the Present*

ILLUSTRATED
COMPLETE IN ONE VOLUME

HISTORIC RECORD COMPANY
LOS ANGELES, CALIFORNIA
1926

TABLE OF CONTENTS

(Numbers refer to pages.)

HISTORY OF CONTRA COSTA COUNTY

CHAPTER I

Influence of tradition and mythology on discovery of America. SPANISH AND ENGLISH EXPLORATIONS AND DISCOVERIES (p. 33): Explorations and discoveries of Cortez and Alarcon. Explorations in Alta or Nueva California (p. 36): Discoveries by Cabrillo and Ferrolo on the Pacific Coast—Drake's voyages of discovery and plunder—New Albion—Drake circumnavigates the globe—Voyages and discoveries of Viscaino. Colonization of Alta California (p. 41): Missionary work of the Jesuits—Junipero Serra and the Franciscans succeed the Jesuits—Joint colonization by Church and State under Serra and Galvez—Expeditions by land and sea under Portola and Galvez—The nineteen missions, with dates of their founding. Aborigines of California (p. 44): Viscaino's description of the Indians of California—Their characteristics and mode of life—Superiority of Northern tribes over those of the South. THE PASSING OF SPAIN'S DOMINATION (p. 46): Visits of La Perouse and Vancouver to the Pacific Coast—Spanish monopoly of the fur trade—The American smugglers—Russian activities on the Pacific Coast—Fort Ross—The Mexican struggle for independence—El Ano de los Temblores—El Ano de los Insurgentes. THE FREE AND SOVEREIGN STATE OF ALTA CALIFORNIA (p. 49): The arbitrary administrations of Chico and Gutierrez—Alvarado and Castro raise the standard of revolt—The Free State of Alta California proclaimed—Recognition of Alvarado in the South, and his appointment as governor under Mexican authority. DECLINE AND FALL OF MEXICAN DOMINATION (p. 51): The government passes into the hands of native-born Californians—Growth of foreign population and influence—Arrest and imprisonment of foreigners—Capture of Monterey by Commodore Jones—Micheltorena's administration in Los Angeles and Monterey—Pico succeeds to the government—His troubles with Castro and the "foreign adventurers"—Marsh's letter to Cass. THE AMERICAN CONQUEST OF CALIFORNIA (p. 61): Fremont's expedition to California—The Bear Flag Republic—Making of the flag. Under the Stars and Stripes: Commodore Sloat raises the American flag at Monterey—Activities of Stockton and Fremont—Capitulation of General Pico at Cahuenga. Mexican laws and American officials—Peace established. GOLD! GOLD! GOLD! (p. 67): Viscaino's reference to gold—First discovered in 1841 at the San Francisco Ranch, or in 1842 at San Francis-

quito—Marshall's discovery of gold at Coloma in 1848—The controversy
over dates—Account of the great gold rush. MAKING A STATE (p. 77):
Organization of a provisional government and adoption of a State constitution—Election of State officials—The first legislature—Admission of California to Statehood.

CHAPTER II

ADVANTAGES OF LOCATION (p. 81): Area, boundaries, and population—
The water front—Fresh water anchorage—Most valuable river traffic—Fine
system of highways—Unsurpassed climate. EASTERN CONTRA COSTA COUNTY
(p. 83): Topography and products—The rich valleys—The sandy lands—
The tule lands—Dairying. MOUNT DIABLO (p. 85): San Francisco Examiner's account of its discovery and naming by the Spaniards in 1772—Legends
and description of the mountain—The Mount Diablo Estate. VALLEYS IN
CONTRA COSTA COUNTY (p. 88): Tassajara Valley—San Ramon Valley—
Alhambra Valley—Ygnacio Valley.

CHAPTER III

Division of State into counties, 1850—Original boundary of the county—
Present boundary—Acts of the court of sessions, 1850: assessments for county
expenses and public buildings; licenses levied—Board of supervisors created,
1852—Provision for $27,000 court house, 1854—Division of county into dis-
tricts, 1855—Assessed valuations in 1850 and 1875—Assessor's report, 1853—
Spanish families and early land claims—The Indians of Contra Costa County
—Old adobes. Transportation: Early ferries and passenger boats—Building
and extension of railroad lines—Bridges and ferries—Minerals and mining—
Important industrial concerns.

CHAPTER IV

OFFICERS OF CONTRA COSTA COUNTY, FROM ITS ORGANIZATION TO THE
PRESENT TIME: Senators—Assemblymen—District judges—County judges
and superior judges—Associate justices of court of sessions—Justices of the
peace—District attorneys—County clerks, recorders, and (after 1855) audi-
tors—County clerks—County auditors—County recorders—County sheriffs—
County tax collectors and treasurers—Tax collectors—County treasurers—
County assessors—Public administrators—County coroners—County surveyors
—Superintendents of schools—County commissioner and county physicians—
County supervisors.

CHAPTER V

Townsite laid out for Martinez heirs by Col. W. M. Smith, 1849—Grant
of Pinole and San Pablo Ranchos to Ignacio Martinez and Francisco Castro,
1823—William Welch secures Las Juntas Rancho, 1832—Early settlers—
Survey of the first addition, 1850-1851—Town incorporated and trustees

Lodges of the city—Churches—Schools—Banks—The Concord Sun—Incorporation of Concord as a city of the sixth class, 1905—Population—Streets and sewers—Light, power, gas, and water supply—Fire department—Fires—Modern buildings—Mount Diablo Union High School—Libraries—Chamber of Commerce—Products—Shipping facilities—Diablo Air Mail Field Base.

CHAPTER X

Location—Named in honor of Judge J. B. Crockett—Original townsite—California & Hawaiian Sugar Refining Company—Community center club house—Thomas Edwards, the founder of Crockett—The Edwards family home—Notes from the diary of John Edwards. Later Growth of the Town: The town in 1883—The California Beet Sugar & Refining Company—The California & Hawaiian Sugar Company—The Crockett Record and Crockett Signal—Population of the city—First National Bank and Bank of Pinole—Churches of the city—Growth of the schools—John Swett Union High School—Other modern buildings—The fire department—Crockett and Valona Business Men's Association—Citizens' Improvement Association—Lodges of Crockett—Veterans' Memorial Hospital.

CHAPTER XI

Founded by William F. Rust in 1888—Post office established at Rust—Incorporated as a city of the sixth class under the name El Cerrito in 1917—Establishment of schools and churches—Erection of modern school buildings—Population in 1926—Improvement of streets—City Hall—First board of trustees—Present city officials—Advantages of El Cerrito as a residential city—Clubs and associations—Assessed valuation of city property—Quarrying by Bates & Borland and the Hutchinson Company—The El Cerrito Journal—The fire department—Annexation election of 1926, and control of San Pablo Avenue.

CHAPTER XII

Bay Point (p. 159)—Danville (p. 160); Mount Diablo Country Club—Alamo (p. 162)— Pacheco (p. 164)—Brentwood (p. 166)—Byron (p. 168)—Clayton (p. 171)—Oakley (p. 172)—Rodeo (p. 173)—Tormey (p. 173)—Cowell (p. 174)—Walnut Creek (p. 174)—Lafayette (p. 174)—San Ramon (p. 175)—San Pablo (p. 176)—Morgan Territory (p. 177)—Avon (p. 177)—Hercules (p. 178).

CHAPTER XIII

MARTINEZ BRANCH LIBRARY (p. 178): Work of the E. Q. V. Society and the Martinez Free Reading-Room and Library Association—Library building—Yearly circulation of books. ANTIOCH BRANCH LIBRARY (p. 179): The Library Club—Mr. Williams' reading room for boys—Work of the Woman's Club and Library Association—Library building—Yearly circula-

CHAPTER XIV

CHAPTER XV

CHAPTER XVI

CHAPTER XVII

together with data of birth, marriage, and death—often under data line as given in the local press—and with the surnames arranged in alphabetical order, rather than chronological, for greater convenience of reference.

CHAPTER XVIII

A chronological presentation of excerpts from the complete set of bound volumes in the office of the Gazette in Martinez, covering the more important events, historical, political, and personal, that have occurred in Contra Costa County since the early days; tracing the gradual development and expansion of its varied interests; and recalling many interesting incidents in the lives of its pioneers.

PREFACE

In the compilation of the History of Contra Costa County for this work, the writer has pursued an uncharted course. The general State history, which introduces the story, has been taken from early publications, the accuracy of which cannot be questioned. The story of Contra Costa County has been gleaned from many sources, the earliest of which was the Slocum history of 1882. This book is regarded as being fairly correct, so far as it goes, to the time of its publication. The files of the newspapers have been a source of information, as have, also, interviews with many of the oldest inhabitants. The citizens of the various cities, towns and villages have kindly supplied material, when called upon, and this has been woven into the story of their localities; also, this information has been verified by scanning the files of the newspapers, to check up on items and dates.

One feature that has never appeared in former county histories is the chapter on the early settlers who have passed away. This will be of absorbing interest, for it mentions many whose names, even, would not otherwise have been mentioned, because no representatives of their families are now in the county. The files of the Martinez Gazette, dating from September, 1858, have yielded much of the data for this chapter, as also the data for the chapter of gleanings from the local press. The value of these files to the county and State can never be estimated in dollars and cents, and they should be safeguarded for the future.

To all those who have kindly extended a helping hand, the writer wishes to extend his hearty thanks. Especial mention is due the Martinez Gazette, Martinez Standard, Crockett Signal, Antioch Ledger, Brentwood News, Byron Times, Richmond Independent and Richmond Record-Herald. To Ed. W. Netherton the writer wishes to extend thanks for the irrigation articles; to Mrs. Alice Whitbeck, for her story of the library development; and to C. A. Odell, for his history of Richmond, the early data for which required much research work. To each and every one who has responded when called upon, acknowledgment is here given.

The publishers wish to thank the following photographers for their cooperation in supplying photographs: Lancaster Studio, Martinez; Smith Studio, Pittsburg; and Hartsook's Studios in Stockton, Oakland and San Francisco.

The biographies of many will be missed from the section devoted to the stories of the lives of the people, as will also their portraits; not because of the fault of the publishers of this book, but because it was impossible to impress upon many the importance of recording for posterity their life histories and family records. In other cases the life history has been omitted out of deference to the wishes of some member of the family.

The growth of Contra Costa County is so rapid, with its many and varied opportunities on every hand, that it has been impossible to give a fully detailed record of the achievements of the past few decades; it is to be hoped that these will be more amply recorded in some work of a future date, when what is now taking place shall have become settled history.

The publishers have asked no remuneration from any quarter, and have made no charge for printing any material; their only source of revenue has been from the sale of the history. To all those who have supported the work, thanks are here given. We feel sure that in the coming years this History of Contra Costa County will prove invaluable, and will be a source of gratification to the families of those mentioned herein.

HISTORIC RECORD COMPANY, Inc.

Los Angeles, Cal.,
December 16, 1926.

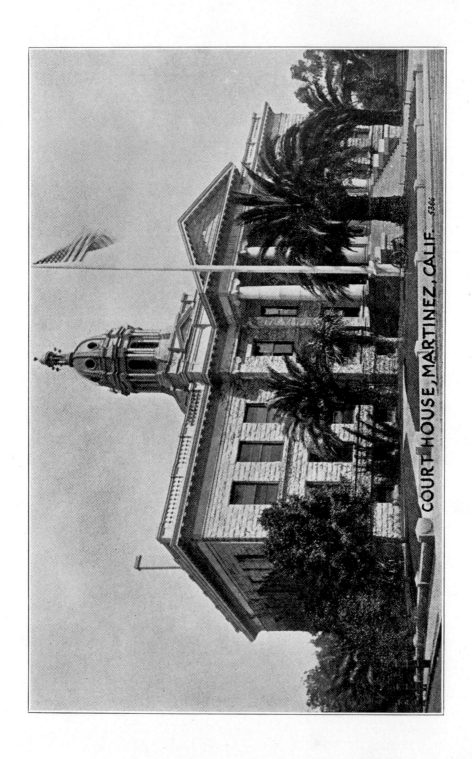

COURT HOUSE, MARTINEZ, CALIF.

CONTRA COSTA COUNTY

CHAPTER I

INTRODUCTORY: THE EARLY HISTORY OF CALIFORNIA

For centuries before the discovery of America, there had been a vague tradition of a land lying somewhere in the seemingly limitless expanse of ocean stretching westward from the shores of Europe. When Columbus proved the existence of a new world beyond the Atlantic, his discovery did not altogether dispel the mysteries and superstitions that for ages had enshrouded the fabled Atlantis, the lost continent of the Hesperides. Romance and credulity had much to do with hastening the exploration of the newly discovered western world. Its interior might hold wonderful possibilities for wealth, fame and conquest to the adventurers who should penetrate its dark unknown.

The fabled fountain of youth lured Ponce de Leon over many a league in the wilds of Florida; and although he found no spring spouting forth the elixir of life, he explored a rich and fertile country, in which the Spaniards planted the first settlement ever made within the territory now held by the United States.

When Cortez's lieutenant, Gonzalo de Sandoval, gave his superior officer an account of a wonderful island ten days westward from the Pacific Coast of Mexico, inhabited by women only, and exceedingly rich in pearls and gold, although he no doubt derived his story from Montalvo's romance, the "Sergas de Esplandian," a popular novel of that day, yet Cortez seems to have given credence to his subordinate's tale, and kept in view the conquest of the island.

SPANISH AND ENGLISH EXPLORATIONS AND DISCOVERIES

To the energy and enterprise of Hernan Cortez is due the early exploration of the northwest coast of North America. In 1522, Cortez established a shipyard at Zacatula, the most northern port on the Pacific coast of the country that he had just conquered. Here he intended to build ships to explore the upper coast of the South Sea (as the Pacific Ocean was then called); but his good fortune, that had hitherto given success to his undertakings, seemed to have deserted him, and disaster followed disaster. He finally, in 1527, succeeded in launching four ships.

Three of these were taken possession of by the king's orders for service in the East Indies. The fourth and the smallest made a short voyage up the coast. The commander, Maldonado, returned with glowing reports of a rich country he had discovered.

In 1528 Cortez was unjustly deprived of the government of the country he had conquered. His successor, Nuno de Guzman, president of the royal audiencia, as the new form of government for New Spain (Mexico) was called, had pursued him for years with the malignity of a demon. Cortez returned to Spain to defend himself against the rancorous and malignant charges of his enemies. He was received at court with a show of high honors, which in reality were hollow professions of friendship and insincere expressions of esteem. He was rewarded by the bestowal of an empty title. He was empowered to conquer and colonize countries at his own expense, for which he was to receive the twelfth part of the revenue. Cortez returned to Mexico, and in 1532 he had two ships fitted out, which sailed from Acapulco, in June of that year, up the coast of Jalisco. Portions of the crews of each vessel mutinied. The mutineers were put aboard of the vessel commanded by Mazuela; and the other vessels, commanded by Hurtardo, continued the voyage as far as the Yaqui country. Here, having landed in search of provisions, the natives massacred the commander and all the crew. The crew of the other vessel shared the same fate lower down the coast. The stranded vessel was afterwards plundered and dismantled by Nuno de Guzman, who was about as much of a savage as the predatory and murderous natives.

In 1533 Cortez, undismayed by his disasters, fitted out two more ships for the exploration of the northern coast of Mexico. On board one of these ships, commanded by Bercerra de Mendoza, the crew, headed by the chief pilot, Jiminez, mutinied. Mendoza was killed and all who would not join the mutineers were forced to go ashore on the coast of Jalisco. The mutineers, to escape punishment by the authorities, under the command of the pilot, Fortuno Jiminez, sailed westerly away from the coast of the mainland. After several days' sailing out of sight of land, they discovered what they supposed to be an island. They landed at a place now known as La Paz, Lower California. Here Jiminez and twenty of his confederates were killed by the Indians, or their fellow mutineers, it is uncertain which. The survivors of the ill-fated expedition managed to navigate the vessel back to Jalisco, where they reported the discovery of an island rich in gold and pearls. This fabrication doubtlessly saved their necks. There is no record of their punishment for mutiny. Cortez's other ship accomplished even less than the one captured by the mutineers. Grixalvo, the commander of this vessel, discovered a desolate island, forty leagues south of Cape San Lucas, which he named Santo Tomas.

Cortez, having heard of Jiminez's discovery, and possibly believing it to be Sandoval's isle of the Amazons, rich with gold and pearls, set about building more ships for exploration and for the colonization of the island.

He ordered the building of three ships at Tehauntepec. The royal audiencia having failed to give him any redress or protection against Nuno de Guzman, he determined to punish him himself. Collecting a considerable force of cavaliers and soldiers, he marched to Chiametla. There he found his vessel, La Concepcion, lying on her beam ends, a wreck, and plundered of everything of value. He failed to find Guzman, that worthy having taken a hasty departure before his arrival. His ships having come up from Tehauntepec, he embarked as many soldiers and settlers as his vessels would carry, and sailed away for Jiminez's island. May 3, 1535, he landed at the port where Jiminez and his fellow mutineers were killed, which he named Santa Cruz. The colonists were landed on the supposed island and the ships were sent back to Chiametla for the remainder of the settlers. The vessels became separated on the gulf in a storm and the smaller of the three returned to Santa Cruz. Embarking in it, Cortez set sail to find his missing ships. He found them at the port of Guayabal, one loaded with provisions, the other dismantled and run ashore. Its sailors had deserted and those of the other ship were about to follow. Cortez stopped this, took command of the vessels and had them repaired, and then set sail for his colony.

Finding the interior of the supposed island as desolate and forbidding as the coast, and the native inhabitants degraded and brutal savages, without houses or clothing, living on vermin, insects and the scant products of the sterile land, Cortez determined to abandon his colonization scheme. Gathering together the wretched survivors of his colony, he embarked them on his ships and in the early part of 1537 landed them in the port of Acapulco.

At some time between 1535 and 1537 the name California was applied to the supposed island, but whether applied by Cortez to encourage his disappointed colonists, or whether given by them in derision, is an unsettled question. The name itself is derived from a Spanish romance, the "Sergas de Esplandian," written by Ordonez de Montalvo and published in Seville, Spain, about the year 1510. The passage in which the name California occurs is as follows: "Know that on the right hand of the Indies there is an island called California, very near the terrestrial paradise, which was peopled with black women, without any men among them, because they were accustomed to live after the fashion of Amazons. They were of strong and hardened bodies, of ardent courage and great force. The island was the strongest in the world from its steep rocks and great cliffs. Their arms were all of gold and so were the caparison of the wild beasts which they rode, after having trained them, for in all the island there is no other metal." The "steep rocks and great cliffs" of Jiminez's island may have suggested to Cortez or to his colonists some fancied resemblance to the California of Montalvo's romance, but there was no other similarity.

For years Cortez had been fitting out expeditions by land and sea to explore the unknown regions northward of that portion of Mexico which he had conquered, but disaster after disaster had wrecked his hopes and impoverished his purse. The last expedition sent out by him was one commanded by Francisco Ulloa, who, in 1539, with two ships, sailed up the Gulf of California, or Sea of Cortez, on the Sonora side, to its head. Thence he proceeded down the inner coast of Lower California to the cape at its southern extremity, which he doubled, and then sailed up the outer coast to Cabo del Engano, the "Cape of Deceit." Failing to make any progress against the head winds, April 5, 1540, the two ships parted company in a storm. The smaller one, the Santa Agueda, returned safely to Santiago. The larger, La Trinidad, after vainly endeavoring to continue the voyage, turned back. The fate of Ulloa, and of the vessel too, is uncertain.

The only thing accomplished by this voyage was to demonstrate that Lower California was a peninsula. Even this fact, although proved by Ulloa's voyage, was not fully admitted by geographers for two centuries.

In 1540 Cortez returned to Spain to obtain, if possible, some recognition and recompense from the king for his valuable services. His declining years had been filled with bitter disappointments. After expending nearly a million dollars in explorations, conquests and attempts at colonization; fretted and worried by the indifference and the ingratitude of a monarch for whom he had sacrificed so much; disappointed, disheartened, impoverished, he died at an obscure hamlet near Seville, Spain, in December, 1547.

The next exploration that had something to do with the discovery of California was that of Hernando de Alarcon. With two ships he sailed from Acapulco, May 9, 1540, up the Gulf of California. He reached the head of the Gulf of California. Seeing what he supposed to be an inlet, but the water proving too shallow for his ships to enter it, he manned two boats and found his supposed inlet to be the mouth of a great river. He named it Buena Guia (Good Guide), not Colorado. He sailed up it some distance and was probably the first white man to set foot upon the soil of Upper California. He descended the river in his boats, embarked on his vessels and returned to Mexico. The viceroy, Mendoza, who had fitted out the expedition of Alarcon, was bitterly disappointed on the return of that explorer. The report of the discovery of a great river did not interest his sordid soul. Alarcon found himself a disgraced man. He retired to private life and not long after died a broken-hearted man.

EXPLORATIONS IN ALTA OR NUEVA CALIFORNIA

Juan Rodriguez Cabrillo, reputed to be a Portuguese by birth and dispatched by Mendoza, the viceroy, in command of the San Salvador and the Vitoria to explore the northwest coast of the Pacific, sailed from Navidad, June 27, 1542. Rounding the southern extremity of the peninsula of Lower California, he sailed up its outer coast. On August 20 he reached Cabo del Engano, the most northerly point of Ulloa's exploration. On the 28th of September, 1542, he entered a bay which he named San Miguel (now San Diego), where he found "a land-locked and very good harbor."

He remained in this harbor until October 3. Continuing his voyage, he sailed along the coast eighteen leagues, discovering two islands which he named San Salvador and Vitoria after his ships (now Santa Catalina and San Clemente). On the 8th of October he crossed the channel between the islands and mainland and anchored in a bay which he named Bahia de los Fumos y Fuegos, the Bay of Smokes and Fires (now known as the Bay of San Pedro). Heavy clouds of smoke hung over the headlands of the coast; and inland, fierce fires were raging. The Indians, either through accident or design, had set fire to the long dry grass that covered the plains at this season of the year.

After sailing six leagues further up the coast, he anchored in a large ensenada or bight, now the Bay of Santa Monica. It is uncertain whether he landed at either place. The next day he sailed eight leagues to an Indian town, which he named the Pueblo de las Canoas (the Town of Canoes). This town was located on or near the present site of San Buena-ventura. Sailing northwestward, he passed through the Santa Barbara Channel, discovering the islands of Santa Cruz, Santa Rosa and San Miguel. Continuing up the coast, he passed a long narrow point of land extending into the sea, which from its resemblance to a galley boat he named Cabo de la Galera, the Cape of the Galley (now called Point Concepcion). Baffled by head winds, the explorers slowly beat their way up the coast. On the 17th of November they cast anchor in a large bay which they named Bahia de los Pinos, the Bay of Pines (now the Bay of Monterey). Finding it impossible to land on account of the heavy sea, Cabrillo continued his voyage northward. After reaching a point on the coast in forty degrees north latitude, according to his reckoning, the increasing cold and the storms becoming more frequent, he turned back and ran down the coast to the island of San Miguel, which he reached November 23. Here he decided to winter.

While on the island in October, he had broken his arm by a fall. Suffering from his broken arm, he had continued in command. Exposure and unskilful surgery caused his death. He died January 3, 1543, and was buried on the island. No trace of his grave has ever been found.

Cabrillo on his deathbed urged his successor in command, the pilot Bartolome Ferrolo, to continue the exploration. Ferrolo prosecuted the voyage of discovery with a courage and daring equal to that of Cabrillo. February 28 he discovered a cape which he named Mendocino in honor of the viceroy, a name it still bears. Passing the cape he encountered a fierce storm which drove him violently to the northeast, greatly endangering his ships. On March 1, the fog partially lifting, he discovered a cape which he named Blanco, in the southern part of what is now the State of Oregon. The weather continuing stormy and the cold increasing as he sailed north-ward, Ferrolo reluctantly turned back. Running down the coast, he reached the island of San Clemente. There in a storm the ships parted company and Ferrolo, after a search, gave up the Vitoria as lost. The ships, however, came together at Cerros Island; and from there, in sore distress for provisions, the explorers reached Navidad, April 18, 1543. On the discoveries made by Cabrillo and Ferrolo the Spaniards claimed the territory on the Pacific coast of North America up to the 42nd degree of north latitude, a claim that they maintained for three hundred years.

The next navigator who visited California was Francis Drake, an Englishman. He was not seeking new lands, but a way to escape the vengeance of the Spaniards. Francis Drake, the "Sea King of Devon," was one of the bravest men that ever lived. Early in his maritime life he had suffered from the cruelty and injustice of the Spaniards. Throughout his subsequent career, which reads more like romance than reality, he let no opportunity slip to punish his old-time enemies. It mattered little to Drake whether his country was at peace or war with Spain; he considered a Spanish ship or a Spanish town his legitimate prey.

Drake sailed out of Plymouth harbor, England, December 13, 1577, in command of a fleet of five small vessels, bound for the Pacific coast of South America. Some of his vessels were lost at sea and others turned back, until when he emerged from the Straits of Magellan he had but one left, the Pelican. He changed its name to the Golden Hind. It was a ship of only one hundred tons' burden. Sailing up the South Pacific coast, he spread terror and devastation among the Spanish settlements, robbing towns and capturing ships until, in the quaint language of a chronicler of the expedition, he "had loaded his vessel with a fabulous amount of fine wares of Asia, precious stones, church ornaments, gold plate and so mooch silver as did ballas the Goulden Hinde."

From one treasure ship, the Caca Fuego, he obtained thirteen chests of silver, eighty pounds weight of gold, twenty-six tons of uncoined silver, two silver drinking vessels, precious stones and a quantity of jewels; the total value of his prize amounted to three hundred and sixty thousand pesos (dollars). Having spoiled the Spaniards of treasure amounting to "eight hundred sixty-six thousand pesos of silver, . . . a hundred thousand pesos of gold, . . . and other things of great worth, he thought it not good to return by the streight (Magellan) . . . least the Spaniards should there waite and attend for him in great numbers and strength, whose hands, he being left but one ship, he could not possibly escape."

Surfeited with spoils and his ship loaded with plunder, it became necessary for him to find the shortest and safest route home. To return by the way he came was to invite certain destruction to his ship and death to all on board. At an island off the coast of Nicaragua he overhauled and refitted his ship. He determined to seek the Straits of Anian, that were believed to connect the Atlantic and Pacific oceans. Striking boldly out on an unknown sea, he sailed more than a thousand leagues northward. Encountering contrary winds, and the cold increasing as he advanced, he gave up his search for the mythical straits, and, turning, he ran down the northwest coast of North America to latitude thirty-eight degrees, where "hee found a harborrow for his ship." He anchored in it June 17, 1579. This "convenient and fit harborrow" is under the lee of Point Reyes and is now known as Sir Francis Drake's Bay.

Fletcher, the chronicler of Drake's voyage, in his narrative, "The World Encompassed," says: "The 3rd day following, viz., the 21st, our ship having received a leake at sea was brought to anchor neerer the shoare that her goods being landed she might be repaired."

The ship was drawn upon the beach, careened on its side, caulked and refitted. While the crew were repairing the ship, the natives visited them in great numbers. From certain ceremonial performance Drake imagined that the Indians were offering him the sovereignty of their land and themselves as subjects of the English crown. He gladly accepted their proffered allegiance and formally took possession of the country in the name of the English sovereign, Queen Elizabeth. He named it New Albion.

Having completed the repairs to his ship, Drake made ready to depart, but before leaving he set up a monument to show that he had taken possession of the country. To a large post firmly set in the ground he nailed a brass plate on which was engraved the name of the English Queen, the date of his arrival, and the statement that the king and people of the country had voluntarily become vassals of the English crown; a new sixpence was fastened to the plate to show the Queen's likeness.

After a stay of thirty-six days, Drake took his departure, much to the regret of the Indians. He stopped at the Farallones Islands for a short time to lay in a supply of seal meat; then he sailed for England by the way of the Cape of Good Hope. After encountering many perils, he arrived safely at Plymouth, the port from which he sailed nearly three years before, having circumnavigated the globe. His exploits and the booty he brought back made him the most famous naval hero of his time. He was knighted by Queen Elizabeth and accorded extraordinary honors by the nation. He believed himself the first discoverer of the country he called New Albion.

The English founded no claim on Drake's discoveries. The land hunger that characterizes that nation now had not then been developed.

Fifty years passed after Cabrillo's visit to California before another attempt was made by the Spaniards to explore her coast. In September, 1595, just before the viceroy, Don Luis de Velasco, was superseded by Conde de Monte Rey, he entered into a contract with certain parties, of whom Sebastian Viscaino, a ship captain, was the principal, to make an expedition up the Gulf of California "for the purpose of fishing for pearls." There was also a provision in the contract empowering Viscaino to make explorations and take possession of his discoveries for the crown of Spain. In September, 1596, Viscaino sailed up the gulf with a fleet of three vessels, the flagship San Francisco, the San Jose, and á Lancha. The flagship was disabled and left at La Paz. With the other two vessels he sailed up the gulf to latitude twenty-nine degrees. He encountered severe storms. At some island he had trouble with the Indians and killed several. As the long-boat was departing, an Indian wounded one of the rowers with an arrow. The sailor dropped his oar, and the boat careened and upset, drowning twenty of the twenty-six soldiers and sailors in it. Viscaino returned without having procured any pearls or made any important discoveries. After five years' waiting, he was allowed to proceed with his explorations.

Viscaino followed the same course marked out by Cabrillo sixty years before. November 10, 1602, he anchored in Cabrillo's Bay of San Miguel. Whether the faulty reckoning of Cabrillo left him in doubt of the points named by the first discoverer, or whether it was that he might receive the credit of their discovery, Viscaino changed the names given by Cabrillo to the islands, bays and headlands along the California coast. Cabrillo's Bahia San Miguel became the Bay of San Diego; San Salvador and Vitoria were changed to Santa Catalina and San Clemente; and Cabrillo's Bahia de los Fumos y Fuegos appears on Viscaino's map as the Ensenada de San Andres, but in a description of the voyage compiled by the cosmographer, Cabrero Bueno, it is named San Pedro. It is not named for the Apostle St. Peter, but for St. Peter, Bishop of Alexandria, whose day in the Catholic calendar is November 26, the day of the month Viscaino anchored in the Bay of San Pedro.

Sailing up the coast, Viscaino passed through the Santa Barbara Channel, which was so named by Antonio de la Ascencion, a Carmelite friar, who was chaplain of one of the ships. The expedition entered the channel December 4, which is the day in the Catholic calendar dedicated to Santa Barbara. He visited the mainland near Point Concepcion, where the Indian chief of a populous rancheria offered each Spaniard who would become a resident of his town ten wives. This generous offer was rejected. December 15, 1602, he reached Point Pinos, so named by Cabrillo, and cast anchor in the bay formed by its projection. This bay he named Monterey, in honor of the viceroy, Conde de Monte Rey. Many of his men were sick with the scurvy, and his provisions were becoming exhausted. So, placing the sick and disabled on the San Tomas, he sent them back to Acapulco; but few of them ever reached their destination. On the 3rd of January, 1603, with two ships, he proceeded on his way. After sighting Cape Blanco, he turned and sailed down the coast of California, reaching Acapulco March 21, 1603.

Viscaino, in a letter to the King of Spain, dated at the City of Mexico, May 23, 1603, grows enthusiastic over California's climate and productions. It is the earliest known specimen of California boom literature. After depicting the commodiousness of Monterey Bay as a port of safety for the Philippine ships, he says:

"This port is sheltered from all winds, while on the immediate shores there are pines, from which masts of any desired size can be obtained, as well as live oaks and white oaks, rosemary, the vine, the rose of Alexandria, a great variety of game, such as rabbits, hare, partridges and other sorts and species found in Spain. This land has a genial climate, its waters are good and it is fertile, judging from the varied and luxuriant growth of trees and plants; and it is thickly settled with people whom I found to be of gentle disposition, peaceable and docile. . . . Their food consists of seeds, which they have in great abundance and variety, and of the flesh of game such as deer, which are larger than cows, and bear, and of neat cattle and bisons and many other animals. . . . They are well acquainted with gold and silver and said that these were found in the interior."

The object of Viscaino's boom literature of three hundred years ago was the promotion of a colony scheme for the founding of a settlement on Monterey Bay. He visited Spain to obtain the consent of the king and assistance in planting a colony. After many delays, Philip III, in 1606, ordered the viceroy of New Spain to fit out immediately an expedition to be commanded by Viscaino for the occupation and settlement of the port of Monterey. Before the expedition could be gotten ready, however, Viscaino died and his colonization scheme died with him.

COLONIZATION OF ALTA CALIFORNIA

A hundred and sixty years passed after the abandonment of Viscaino's colonization scheme before the Spanish crown made another attempt to utilize its vast possessions in Alta California.

The Jesuits had begun missionary work in 1697 among the degraded inhabitants of Lower California. With a perseverance that was highly commendable and a bravery that was heroic, under their devoted leaders Salvatierra, Kino, Ugarte, Piccolo and their successors, they founded sixteen missions on the peninsula.

For years there had been, in the Catholic countries of Europe, a growing fear and distrust of the Jesuits. Portugal had declared them traitors to the government and had banished them in 1759 from her dominions. France had suppressed the order in her domains in 1764. In 1767, King Carlos III, by a pragmatic sanction or decree, ordered their expulsion from Spain and all her American colonies.

The Lower California missions were transferred to the Franciscans, but it took time to make the substitution. At the head of the Franciscan contingent that came to Bahia, Cal., to take charge of the abandoned missions, was Father Junipero Serra. His success as a preacher and his great missionary zeal led to his selection as president of the missions of California, from which the Jesuits had been removed. April 2, 1768, he arrived in the port of Loreto with fifteen associates from the College of San Fernando. These were sent to the different missions of the peninsula. These missions extended over a territory seven hundred miles in length and it required several months to locate all the missionaries. The scheme for the occupation and colonization of Alta California was to be jointly the work of Church and State. The representative of the State was José de Galvez, visitador-general of New Spain, a man of untiring energy, great executive ability, sound business sense and, as such men are and ought to be, somewhat arbitrary. Galvez reached La Paz in July, 1768. He immediately set about investigating the condition of the peninsula missions and supplying their needs. This done, he turned his attention to the northern coloni-

zation. He established his headquarters at Santa Ana near La Paz. Here
he summoned Father Junipero for consultation in regard to the founding
of missions in Alta California. It was decided to proceed to the initial
points San Diego and Monterey by land and sea.

The first vessel fitted out for the expedition by sea was the San Carlos,
a ship of about two hundred tons burden, leaky and badly constructed. She
sailed from La Paz January 9, 1769, under the command of Vicente Vila.
In addition to the crew there were twenty-five Catalonian soldiers, commanded by Lieutenant Fages, Pedro Prat, the surgeon, a Franciscan friar,
two blacksmiths, a baker, a cook and two tortilla makers. Galvez in a
small vessel accompanied the San Carlos to Cape San Lucas, where he
landed and set to work to fit out the San Antonio. On the 15th of February this vessel sailed from San José del Cabo (San José of the Cape),
under the command of Juan Perez. On this vessel went two Franciscan
friars, Juan Viscaino and Francisco Gomez. Captain Rivera y Moncada,
who was to pioneer the way, had collected supplies and cattle at Velicata
on the northern frontier. From here, with a small force of soldiers, a
gang of neophytes and three muleteers, and accompanied by Padre Crespi,
he began his march to San Diego on March 24, 1769.

The second land expedition, commanded by Governor Gaspar de Portola in person, began its march from Loreto, March 9, 1769. Father
Serra, who was to have accompanied it, was detained at Loreto by a sore
leg. He joined the expedition at Santa Maria, May 5.

The San Antonio, the last vessel to sail, was the first to arrive at San
Diego. There she remained at anchor, awaiting the arrival of the San
Carlos, the flagship of the expedition, which had sailed more than a month
before her. On April 29, the San Carlos, after a disastrous voyage of 110
days, drifted into the Bay of San Diego, her crew prostrated with the
scurvy, not enough able-bodied men being left to man a boat.

On the 14th of May Captain Rivera y Moncada's detachment arrived.
The expedition had made the journey from Velicata in fifty-one days. On
the first of July the second division, commanded by Portola, arrived. The
four divisions of the grand expedition were now united, but its numbers
had been greatly reduced. Out of 219 who had set out by land and sea
only 126 remained. The ravages of the scurvy had destroyed the crew of
one of the vessels and greatly crippled that of the other; so it was impossible to proceed by sea to Monterey, the second objective point of the
expedition.

If the mandates of King Carlos III and the instructions of the visitador-
general, José de Galvez, were to be carried out, the expedition for the settlement of the second point designated (Monterey) must be made by
land; accordingly Governor Portola set about organizing his forces for
the overland journey. On the 14th of July the expedition began its march.
It consisted of Governor Portola, Padres Crespi and Gomez, Captain

Rivera y Moncada, Lieutenant Pedro Fages, Engineer Miguel Constanso, soldiers, muleteers and Indian servants, numbering in all sixty-two persons.

On the 16th of July, two days after the departure of Governor Portola, Father Junipero, assisted by Padres Viscaino and Parron, founded the mission of San Diego.

The San José, the third ship fitted out by Visitador-General Galvez, and which Governor Portola expected to find in the Bay of Monterey, sailed from San José del Cabo in May, 1770, with supplies and a double crew to supply the loss of sailors on the other vessels, but nothing was ever heard of her afterwards. Provisions were running low at San Diego, no ship had arrived, and Governor Portola had decided to abandon the place and return to Loreto. Father Junipero was averse to this and prayed unceasingly for the intercession of Saint Joseph, the patron of the expedition. On the 23rd of March, when all were ready to depart, the packet San Antonio arrived. She had sailed from San Blas the 20th of December. She encountered a storm which drove her 400 leagues from the coast; then she made land at thirty-five degrees north latitude. Turning her prow southward, she ran down to Point Concepcion, where at an anchorage in the Santa Barbara Channel the captain, Perez, took on water and learned from the Indians of the return of Portola's expedition. The vessel then ran down to San Diego, where its opportune arrival prevented the abandonment of that settlement.

With an abundant supply of provisions and a vessel to carry the heavier articles needed in forming a settlement at Monterey, Portola organized a second expedition. This time he took with him only twenty soldiers and one officer, Lieutenant Pedro Fages. He set out from San Diego on the 17th of April and followed his trail made the previous year. Father Serra and the engineer, Constanso, sailed on the San Antonio, which left the port of San Diego on the 16th of April. The land expedition reached Monterey on the 23rd of May and the San Antonio on the 31st of the same month. On the 3rd of June, 1770, the mission of San Carlos Borromeo de Monterey was formally founded with solemn church ceremonies, accompanied by the ringing of bells, the crack of musketry and the roar of cannon. Father Serra conducted the church services. Governor Portola took possession of the land in the name of King Carlos III. A presidio or fort of palisades was built and a few huts erected. Portola, having formed the nucleus of a settlement, turned over the command of the territory to Lieutenant Fages. On the 9th of July, 1770, he sailed on the San Antonio for San Blas. He never returned to Alta California. In 1777 this mission was moved to Carmel Valley, and here it became known as El Carmel Mission.

Then the following nineteen missions were established in order of dates as here given:

San Antonio de Padua, San Luis Obispo County, June 14, 1771.

San Gabriel d' Arcangel, San Luis Obispo County, September 8, 1771.

San Luis Obispo de Tolosa, San Luis Obispo County, September 1, 1772.

Dolores, or San Francisco de Assis, San Francisco, October 9, 1776.

San Juan Capistrano, Los Angeles County (now Orange County), November 10, 1776.

Santa Clara, Santa Clara County, January 12, 1777.

San Buenaventura, Santa Barbara County, March 31, 1782.

Santa Barbara, Santa Barbara County, December 14, 1786.

La Purisima Concepcion (Immaculate Conception), Santa Barbara County, December 8, 1787.

Santa Cruz, Santa Cruz County, September 25, 1790.

La Soledad (Our Lady of Solitude), Monterey County, September 29, 1791.

San Jose, Alameda County, June 11, 1797.

San Juan Bautista (St. John the Baptist), Monterey County, June 24, 1797.

San Miguel Arcangel, San Luis Obispo County, July 25, 1797.

San Fernando Rey de Espana (Ferdinand, King of Spain), Los Angeles County, September 8, 1797.

San Luis Rey de Francia (Louis King of France), San Diego County, July 13, 1798.

Santa Ynez, Santa Barbara County, September 17, 1804.

San Rafael Arcangel, San Rafael, Marin County, December 14, 1817.

San Francisco de Solano, Sonoma County, August 25, 1823.

ABORGINES OF CALIFORNIA

Whether the primitive California Indian was the low and degraded being that some modern writers represent him to have been, admits of doubt. A mission training continued through three generations did not, perhaps, greatly elevate him in morals. When freed from mission restraint and brought in contact with the white race, he lapsed into a condition more degraded and more debased than that in which the missionaries found him. Whether it was the inherent fault of the Indian or the fault of his training is a question that is useless to discuss now. If we are to believe the accounts of the California Indian given by Viscaino and Constanso, who saw him before he had come in contact with civilization, he was not inferior in intelligence to the normal aborgines of the country east of the Rocky Mountains.

Sebastian Viscaino thus describes the Indians he found on the shores of Monterey Bay three hundred years ago:

"The Indians are of good stature and fair complexion, the women being somewhat less in size than the men and of pleasing countenance. The clothing of the people of the coast lands consists of the skins of the sea-wolves (otter) abounding there, which they tan and dress better than is done in Castile; they possess also, in great quantity, flax like that of Castile, hemp and cotton, from which they make fishing-lines and nets for rabbits and hares. They have vessels of pine wood very well made, in which they go to sea with fourteen paddle-men on a side with great dexterity, even in stormy weather."

Indians who could construct boats of pine boards that took twenty-eight paddle-men to row were certainly superior in maritime craft to the birch-bark-canoe savages of the East. We might accuse Viscaino, who was trying to induce King Philip III to found a colony on Monterey Bay, of exaggeration in regard to the Indian boats, were not his statements confirmed by the engineer, Miguel Constanso, who accompanied Portola's expedition 167 years after Viscaino visited the coast.

The Indians of the interior valleys and those of the coast belonged to the same general family. There were no great tribal divisions like those that existed among the Indians east of the Rocky Mountains. Each rancheria was to a certain extent independent of all others, although at times they were known to combine for war or plunder. Although not warlike, they sometimes resisted the whites in battle with great bravery. Each village had its own territory in which to hunt and fish and its own section in which to gather nuts, seeds and herbs. While their mode of living was somewhat nomadic, they seem to have had a fixed location for their rancherias.

The early Spanish settlers of California and the mission padres have left but very meager accounts of the manners, customs, traditions, government and religion of the aborigines. The padres were too intent upon driving out the old religious beliefs of the Indian and instilling new ones to care much what the aborgine had formerly believed or what traditions or myths he had inherited from his ancestors. They ruthlessly destroyed his fetiches and his altars wherever they found them, regarding them as inventions of the devil.

From the descriptions given by Viscaino and Constanso of the coast Indians, they do not appear to have been the degraded creatures that some modern writers have pictured them. In mechanical ingenuity they were superior to the Indians of the Atlantic seaboard or those of the Mississippi Valley. Much of the credit that has been given to the mission padres for the patient training they gave the Indians in mechanical arts should be given to the Indian himself. He was no mean mechanic when the padres took him in hand.

Bancroft says "the Northern California Indians were in every way superior to the central and southern tribes." The difference was more in climate than in race. Those of Northern California, living in an invigorating climate, were more active and more warlike than their sluggish brethren of the south. They gained their living by hunting larger game than those of the south, whose subsistence was derived mostly from acorns, seeds, small game and fish. Those of the interior valleys of the north were of lighter complexion and had better forms and features than their southern kinsmen. They were divided into numerous small tribes or clans.

The Spaniards never penetrated very far into the Indian country of the north, and consequently knew little or nothing about the habits and customs of the aborigines there. After the discovery of gold, the miners invaded their country in search of the precious metal. The Indians at first were not hostile, but ill treatment soon made them so. When they retaliated on the whites a war of extermination was waged against them. Like the mission Indians of the south, they are almost extinct.

THE PASSING OF SPAIN'S DOMINATION

The Spaniards were not a commercial people. Their great desire was to be let alone in their American possessions. Philip II once promulgated a decree pronouncing death upon any foreigner who entered the Gulf of Mexico. It was easy to promulgate a decree or to pass restrictive laws against foreign trade, but quite another thing to enforce them.

After the first settlement of California, seventeen years passed before a foreign vessel entered any of its ports. The first to arrive were the two vessels of the French explorer, La Perouse, who anchored in the harbor of Monterey, September 15, 1786. Being of the same faith, and France having been an ally of Spain in former times, he was well received. During his brief stay he made a study of the mission system and his observations on it are plainly given. He found a similarity in it to the slave plantations of Santo Domingo.

November 14, 1792, the English navigator, Capt. George Vancouver, in the ship Discovery, entered the Bay of San Francisco. He was cordially received by the comandante of the port, Hermanagildo Sal, and the friars of the mission.

Through the English, the Spaniards became acquainted with the importance and value of the fur trade. The bays and lagoons of California abounded in sea otter. Their skins were worth in China all the way from $30 to $100 each. The trade was made a government monopoly. The skins were to be collected from the natives, soldiers and others by the missionaries, at prices ranging from $2.50 to $10 each, and turned over to the government officials appointed to receive them. All trade by private persons was prohibited. The government was sole trader. But the government failed to make the trade profitable. In the closing years of the century the American smugglers began to haunt the coast. The restrictions against trade with foreigners were proscriptive and the penalties for evasion severe, but men will trade under the most adverse circumstances. Spain was a long way off, and smuggling was not a very venal sin in the eyes of layman or churchman. Fast sailing vessels were fitted out in Boston for illicit trade on the California coast. Watching their opportunities, these vessels slipped into the bays and inlets along the coast. There was a rapid exchange of Yankee notions for sea otter skins, the most valued peltry of California, and the vessels were out to sea before the revenue officers could intercept them. If successful in escaping capture, the profits of a smuggling voyage were enormous, ranging from 500 to 1000 per cent above cost on the goods exchanged; but the risks were great. The smuggler had no protection; he was an outlaw. He was the legitimate prey of the padres, the people and the revenue officers. The Yankee smuggler usually came out ahead. His vessel was heavily armed, and when speed or stratagem failed he was ready to fight his way out of a scrape.

Each year two ships were sent from San Blas with the memorias—mission and presidio supplies. These took back a small cargo of the products of the territory, wheat being the principal. This was all the legitimate commerce allowed California.

The fear of Russian aggression had been one of the causes that had forced Spain to attempt the colonization of California. Bering, in 1741, had discovered the strait that bears his name and had taken possession, for the Russian government, of the northwestern coast of America. Four years later, the first permanent Russian settlement, Sitka, had been made on one of the coast islands. Rumors of the Russian explorations and settlements had reached Madrid, and in 1774 Captain Perez, in the San Antonio, was sent up the coast to find out what the Russians were doing.

Had Russian America contained arable land where grain and vegetables could have been grown, it is probable that the Russians and Spaniards in America would not have come in contact; for another nation, the United States, had taken possession of the intervening country, bordering the Columbia River.

The supplies of breadstuffs for the Sitka colonists had to be sent overland across Siberia or shipped around Cape Horn. Failure of supplies sometimes reduced the colonists to sore straits.

On the 5th of April, 1806, Count Rezanoff anchored safely in the Bay of San Francisco. He had brought with him a cargo of goods for exchange but the restrictive commercial regulations of Spain made it difficult for him to trade with the natives, although the friars and the people needed the goods Rezanoff brought to exchange. After Rezanoff's visit the Russians came frequently to California, partly to trade, but more often to hunt otter. While on these fur-hunting expeditions they examined the coast north of San Francisco with the design of planting an agricultural colony where they could raise grain to supply the settlements in the far north. In 1812 they founded a town and built a fort on the coast north of Bodega Bay, which they named Ross. The fort mounted ten guns. They maintained a fort at Bodega Bay and also a small settlement on Russian River. The Spaniards protested against this aggression and threatened to drive the Russians out of the territory, but nothing came of their protests and they were powerless to enforce their demands. The Russian ships came to California for supplies and were welcomed by the people and the friars if not by the government officials.

The Russian colony at Ross was not a success, however. After the decline of fur-hunting the settlement became unprofitable. In 1841 the buildings and the stock were sold by the Russian governor to Capt. John A. Sutter for $30,000, and the settlement was abandoned.

Notwithstanding the many changes of rulers that political revolutions and Napoleonic wars gave the mother country, the people of California remained loyal to the Spanish crown, although at times they must have been in doubt who wore the crown.

On the 15th of September, 1810, the patriot priest, Miguel Hidalgo, struck the first blow for Mexican independence.

Arrillaga was governor of California when the war for Mexican independence began. Although born in Mexico he was of pure Spanish parentage and was thoroughly in sympathy with Spain in the contest. He died in 1814 and was succeeded by Pablo Vicente de Sola. Sola was Spanish-born and was bitterly opposed to the revolution, even going so far as to threaten death to any one who should speak in favor of it.

As the revolution in Mexico progressed times grew harder in California. The mission memorias ceased to come. No tallow ships from Callao arrived. The soldiers' pay was years in arrears and their uniforms in rags. What little wealth there was in the country was in the hands of the padres. They were supreme. "The friars," says Gilroy, who arrived in California in 1814, "had everything their own way. The governor and the military were expected to do whatever the friars requested. The missions contained all the wealth of the country." The friars supported the government and supplied the troops with food from the products of the neophytes' labor. The crude manufacturers of the missions supplied the people with cloth for clothing and some other necessities. The needs of the common people were easily satisfied. Gilroy states that at the time of his arrival "there was not a sawmill, whip saw or spoked wheel in California. Such lumber as was used was cut with an axe. Chairs, tables and wood floors were not to be found except in the governor's house. Plates were rare, unless that name could be applied to the tiles used instead. Money was a rarity. There were no stores and no merchandise to sell. There was no employment for a laborer. The neophytes did all the work and all the business of the country was in the hands of the friars."

The year 1812 was the Año de los Temblores. The seismic disturbance that for forty years or more had shaken California seemed to concentrate in power that year and expend its force on the mission churches. The massive church of San Juan Capistrano, the pride of mission architecture, was thrown down and forty persons killed. The walls of San Gabriel Mission were cracked and some of the saints shaken out of their niches. At San Buenaventura there were three heavy shocks which injured the church so that the tower and much of the facade had to be rebuilt. The whole mission site seemed to settle and the inhabitants, fearful that they might be engulfed by the sea, moved up the valley about two miles, where they remained three months. At Santa Barbara both church and the presidio were damaged and at Santa Ynez the church was shaken down. The quakes continued for several months and the people were so terrified that they abandoned their houses and lived in the open air.

The other important epoch of the decade was El Año de los Insurgentes, the year of the insurgents. In November, 1818, Bouchard, a Frenchman in the service of Buenos Ayres and provided with letters of marque by San Martain, the president of that republic, to prey upon Spanish commerce, appeared in the port of Monterey with two ships carrying sixty-six guns and 350 men. He attacked Monterey, and after an obstinate resistance by the Californians it was taken by the insurgents and burned. Bouchard next pillaged Ortega's rancho and burned the buildings. Then, sailing down the coast, he scared the Santa Barbaranos; then, keeping on down, he looked into San Pedro, but finding nothing there to tempt him he kept on to San Juan Capistrano. There he landed, robbed the mission of a few articles and drank the padres' wine. Then he sailed away and disappeared. He left six of his men in California, among them Joseph Chapman of Boston, the first American resident of California.

THE FREE AND SOVEREIGN STATE OF ALTA CALIFORNIA

Governor Figueroa on his deathbed turned over the civil command of the territory to José Castro, who thereby became "gefe politico ad interim." The military command was given to Lieut.-Colonel Nicolas Gutierrez, with the rank of comandante general. The separation of the two commands was in accordance with the national law of May 6, 1822.

Castro executed the civil functions of gefe politico four months; and then, in accordance with orders from the supreme government, he turned over his part of the governorship to Comandante General Gutierrez and again the two commands were united in one person. Gutierrez filled the office of "gobernador interno" from January 2, 1836, to the arrival of his successor, Mariano Chico. Chico had been appointed governor by President Barragan, December 16, 1835, but did not arrive in California until April, 1836. Thus California had four governors within nine months. They changed so rapidly there was not time to foment a revolution.

Chico began his administration by a series of petty tyrannies. Exasperated beyond endurance by his scandalous conduct and unseemly exhibitions of temper, the people of Monterey rose en masse against him, and so terrified him that he took passage on board a brig that was lying in the harbor and sailed for Mexico with the threat that he would return with an armed force to punish the rebellious Californians; but it was only a threat; he never came back again.

With the enforced departure of Chico, the civil command of the territory devolved upon Nicolas Gutierrez, who still held the military command. Although a mild-mannered man, he seemed to be impressed with the idea that he must carry out the arbitrary measures of his predecessor.

He quarreled with Juan Bautista Alvarado, the ablest of the native Californians. Alvarado and José Castro raised the standard of revolt. They gathered together a small army of rancheros and an auxiliary force of twenty-five American hunters and trappers under Graham, a backwoodsman from Tennessee. By a strategic movement they captured the castillo or fort which commanded the presidio, where Gutierrez and the Mexican army officials were stationed. The patriots demanded the surrender of the presidio and the arms. The governor refused. The revolutionists had been able to find but a single cannon ball in the castillo, but this was sufficient to do the business. A well-directed shot tore through the roof of the governor's house, covering him and his staff with the debris of broken tiles; that and the desertion of most of his soldiers to the patriots brought him to terms. On the 5th of November, 1836, he surrendered the presidio and resigned his authority as governor. He and about seventy of his adherents were sent aboard a vessel lying in the harbor and shipped out of the country.

With the Mexican governor and his officers out of the country, the next move of Castro and Alvarado was to call a meeting of the diputacion or territorial congress. A plan for the independence of California was adopted.

Castro issued a pronunciamiento, ending with "Viva La Federacion! Viva La Libertad! Viva el Estado Libre y Soberano de Alta California!" Thus amid vivas and proclamations, with the beating of drums and the booming of cannon, El Estado Libre de Alta California (The Free State of Alta California) was launched on the political sea.

Notwithstanding this apparent burying of the hatchet, over the difficulties arising because of the insistence of claimants in the south for the capital at Los Angeles, rather than at Monterey, and notwithstanding considerable trouble that had arisen and several battles fought and won by Alvarado's forces, there were rumors of plots and intrigues in Los Angeles and San Diego against Alvarado. At length, aggravated beyond endurance, the governor sent word to the surenos that if they did not behave themselves he would shoot ten of the leading men of the south. As he had about that number locked up in the castillo at Sonoma, his was no idle threat. One by one Alvarado's prisoners of state were released from Vallejo's bastile at Sonoma and returned to Los Angeles, sadder if not wiser men. At the session of the ayuntamiento on October 20, 1838, the president announced that Señor Regidor José Palomares had returned from Sonoma, where he had been compelled to go by reason of "political differences," and that he should be allowed his seat in the council. The request was granted unanimously.

The surenos of Los Angeles and San Diego, finding that in Alvarado they had a man of courage and determination to deal with, ceased from troubling him and submitted to the inevitable. At the meeting of the ayuntamiento, October 5, 1839, a notification was received, stating that the supreme government of Mexico had appointed Juan Bautista Alvarado governor of the department. There was no grumbling nor dissent. On the contrary, the records say, "This illustrious body acknowledges receipt of the communication and congratulates His Excellency. It will announce the same to the citizens tomorrow (Sunday), will raise the national colors, salute the same with the required number of volleys, and will invite the people to illuminate their houses for a better display in rejoicing at such a happy appointment." With his appointment by the supreme government the "Free and Sovereign State of Alta California" became no more than a dream of the past.

DECLINE AND FALL OF MEXICAN DOMINATION

While the revolution begun by Alvarado and Castro had not established California's independence, it had effectually rid the territory of Mexican dictators. A native son was governor of the department of the Californias (by the constitution of 1836 Upper and Lower California had been united into a department); another native son was comandante of its military forces. The membership of the departmental junta, which had taken the place of the diputacion, was largely made up of sons of the soil, and natives filled the minor offices. In their zeal to rid themselves of Mexican office-holders, they had invoked the assistance of another element that was ultimately to be their undoing.

During the revolutionary era just passed the foreign population had largely increased. Not only had the foreigners come by sea, but they had come by land. Capt. Jedediah S. Smith, a New England-born trapper and hunter, was the first man to enter California by the overland route. A number of trappers and hunters came in the early thirties from New Mexico by way of the old Spanish trail. This immigration was largely American, and was made up of a bold, adventurous class of men, some of them not the most desirable immigrants. Of this latter class were some of Graham's followers.

By invoking Graham's aid to put him in power, Alvarado had fastened upon his shoulders an old Man of the Sea. It was easy enough to enlist the services of Graham's riflemen, but altogether another matter to get rid of them when no longer needed.

There were rumors of another revolution, and it was not difficult to persuade Alvarado that the foreigners were plotting to revolutionize California. Mexico had recently lost Texas, and the same class of "malditos extranjeros" (wicked strangers) were invading California, and would ultimately possess themselves of the country. Accordingly, secret orders were sent throughout the department to arrest and imprison all foreigners. Over 100 men of different nationalities were arrested, principally Americans and English. Of these forty-seven were shipped to San Blas, and from there marched overland to Tepic, where they were imprisoned for several months. Through the efforts of the British consul, Barron, they were released. Castro, who had accompanied the prisoners to Mexico to prefer charges against them, was placed under arrest and afterwards tried by court-martial, but was acquitted. He had been acting under orders from his superiors. After an absence of over a year twenty of the exiles landed at Monterey on their return from Mexico. Robinson, who saw them land, says: "They returned neatly dressed, armed with rifles and swords, and looking in much better condition than when they were sent away, or probably than they had ever looked in their lives before." The Mexican government had been compelled to pay them damages for their arrest and imprisonment and to return them to California.

The only other event of importance during Alvarado's term as governor was the capture of Monterey by Commodore Ap Catesby Jones, of the United States navy. This event happened after Alvarado's successor, Micheltorena, had landed in California, but before the government had been formally turned over to him.

The following extract from the diary of a pioneer, who was an eyewitness of the affair, gives a good description of the capture:

"Monterey, Oct. 19, 1842.—At 2 p. m. the United States man-of-war United States, Commodore Ap Catesby Jones, came to anchor close alongside and in-shore of all the ships in port. About 3 p. m. Captain Armstrong came ashore, accompanied by an interpreter, and went direct to the governor's house, where he had a private conversation with him, which proved to be a demand for the surrender of the entire coast of California, Upper and Lower, to the United States government. When he was about to go on board he gave three or four copies of a proclamation to the inhabitants of the two Californias, assuring them of the protection of their lives, persons and property. In his notice to the governor (Alvarado) he gave him only until the following morning at 9 a. m. to decide. If he received no answer, then he would fire upon the town.

"I remained on shore that night and went down to the governor's with Mr. Larkin and Mr. Eagle. The governor had had some idea of running away and leaving Monterey to its fate, but was told by Mr. Spence that he should not go, and finally he resolved to await the result. At 12 at night some persons were sent on board the United States who had been appointed by the governor to meet the commodore and arrange the terms of the surrender. Next morning at half-past 10 o'clock about one hundred sailors and fifty marines disembarked. The sailors marched up from the shore and took possession of the fort. The American colors were hoisted. The United States fired a salute of thirteen guns; it was returned by the fort, which fired twenty-six guns. The marines in the meantime had marched up to the government house. The officers and soldiers of the California government were discharged and their guns and other arms taken possession of and carried to the fort. The stars and stripes now wave over us. Long may they wave here in California!"

"Oct. 21, 4 p. m.—Flags were again changed, the vessels were released, and all was quiet again. The commodore had received later news by some Mexican newspapers."

Commodore Jones had been stationed at Callao with a squadron of four vessels. An English fleet was also there, and a French fleet was cruising in the Pacific. Both these were supposed to have designs on California. Jones learned that the English admiral had received orders to sail next day. Surmising that his destination might be California, he slipped out of the harbor the night before and crowded all sail to reach California before the English admiral. The loss of Texas, and the constant influx of immigrants and adventurers from the United States into California, had embittered the Mexican government more and more against foreigners. Manuel Micheltorena, who had served under Santa Anna in the Texas war, was appointed January 19, 1842, comandante-general inspector and gobernador propietario of the Californias.

Santa Anna was president of the Mexican republic. His experience with Americans in Texas during the Texan war of independence, in 1836–1837, had determined him to use every effort to prevent California from sharing the fate of Texas.

Micheltorena, the newly appointed governor, was instructed to take with him sufficient force to check the ingress of Americans. He recruited a force of 350 men, principally convicts enlisted from the prisons of Mexico. His army of thieves and ragamuffins landed at San Diego in August, 1842.

Micheltorena drilled his Falstaffian army at San Diego for several weeks and then began his march northward; Los Angeles made great preparations to receive the new governor. Seven years had passed since she had been decreed the capital of the territory, and in all these years she had been denied her rights by Monterey. A favorable impression on the new governor might induce him to make the ciudad his capital. After a stay of a month in the city Micheltorena and his army took up their line of march northward. He reached a point about twenty miles north of San Fernando, when, on the night of the 24th of October, a messenger aroused him from his slumbers with the news that the capital had been captured by the Americans. He spent the remainder of the night in fulminating proclamations against the invaders fiercer than the thunderbolts of Jove, copies of which were dispatched posthaste to Mexico. Then, with his own courage and doubtless that of his brave cholos aroused to the highest pitch, instead of rushing on the invaders, he and his army fled back to San Fernando, where, afraid to advance or retreat, he halted until news reached him that Commodore Jones had restored Monterey to the Californians. Then his valor reached the boiling point. He boldly marched to Los Angeles, established his headquarters in the city and awaited the coming of Commodore Jones and his officers from Monterey.

On the 19th of January, 1843, Commodore Jones and his staff came to Los Angeles to meet the governor. At the famous conference in the Palacio de Don Abel, Micheltorena presented his articles of convention. Next morning, January 21, Jones and his officers took their departure from the city amidst the beating of drums, the firing of cannon and the ringing of bells, saluted by the general and his wife from the door of their quarters. On the 31st of December Micheltorena had taken the oath of office in Sanchez's Hall, which stood on the east side of the plaza. Salutes were fired, the bells were rung and the city was illuminated for three evenings. For the second time a governor was inaugurated in Los Angeles.

Micheltorena and his cholo army remained in Los Angeles about eight months. The Angelenos had all the capital they cared for. They were perfectly willing to have the governor and his army take up their residence in Monterey. The cholos had devoured the country like an army of chapules (locusts) and were willing to move on.

Micheltorena, while not a model governor, had many good qualities and was generally liked by the better class of foreign residents. He made an earnest effort to establish a system of public education in the territory. Schools were established in all the principal towns, and territorial aid from the public funds to the amount of $500 each was given them. But he was unreliable and not careful to keep his agreements. He might have succeeded in giving California a stable government had it not been for the antipathy to his soldiers and the old feud between the "hijos del pais" and the Mexican dictators. These proved his undoing. The native sons under Alvarado and Castro rose in rebellion. In November, 1844, a revolution was inaugurated at Santa Clara. The governor marched with an army of 150 men against the rebel forces, numbering about 200. They met at a place called the Laguna de Alvires. A treaty was signed in which Micheltorena agreed to ship his cholos back to Mexico.

This treaty the governor deliberately broke. He then intrigued with Capt. John A. Sutter, of New Helvetia, and Isaac Graham to obtain assistance to crush the rebels. January 9, 1845, Micheltorena and Sutter formed a junction of their forces at Salinas—their united commands numbering about 500 men. They marched against the rebels to crush them. But the rebels did not wait to be crushed.

Another Mexican-born governor was deposed and deported, to join his fellows, Vitoria, Chico and Gutierrez. In accordance with the treaty of Cahuenga, and by virtue of his rank as senior member of the departmental assembly, Pio Pico was appointed constitutional governor of California, September 3, 1845, by President Herrera.

Castro gave Pico a great deal of uneasiness. He ignored the governor and managed the military affairs of the territory to suit himself. His headquarters were at Monterey, and doubtless he had the sympathy if not the encouragement of the people of the north in his course.

But the cause of the greatest uneasiness was the increasing immigration from the United States. A stream of emigrants from the western States, increasing each year, poured down the Sierra Nevadas and spread over the rich valleys of California. The Californians recognized that through the advent of these "foreign adventurers," as they called them, the "manifest destiny" of California was to be absorbed by the United States.

In the summer of 1845 a force of 600 veteran soldiers, under command of Colonel Iniestra, reached Acapulco, where ships were lying to take them to California; but a revolution broke out in Mexico and the troops destined for the defense of California were used to overthrow President Herrera and to seat Paredes. California was left to work out her own destiny unaided or drift with the tide—and she drifted.

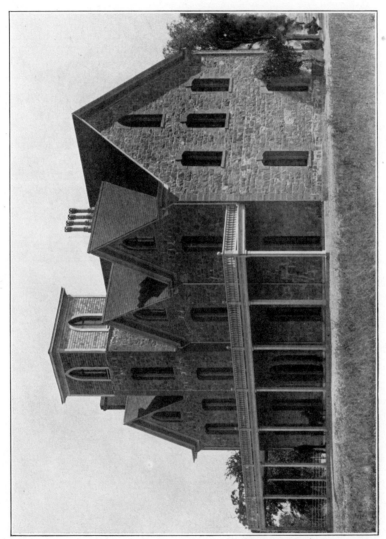

THE STONE HOUSE, BUILT BY DR. JOHN MARSH IN 1856

MARSH'S LETTER TO CASS

The following letter, which Dr. Marsh wrote to Hon. Lewis Cass, Secretary of War, in 1842, is so illuminative of the period and the situation, that we give it in full:

"Farm of Pulpines, near St. Francisco,
Upper California, 1842.

"Hon. Lewis Cass.

"Dear Sir: You will probably be somewhat surprised to receive a letter from an individual from whom you have not heard, or even thought of, for nearly twenty years; yet although the lapse of time has wrought many changes both in men and things, the personal identity of us both has probably been left. You will, I think, remember a youth whom you met at Green Bay in 1825, who, having left his Alma Mater, had spent a year or two in the 'far, far West,' and was then returning to his New England home, and whom you induced to turn his face again toward the setting sun; that youth who, but for your influence, would probably now have been administering pills in some quiet Yankee village, is now a gray-haired man, breeding cattle and cultivating grape-vines on the shores of the Pacific. Your benevolence prompted you to take an interest in the fortunes of that youth, and it is therefore presumed you may not be unwilling to hear from him again.

"I left the United States in 1835, and came to New Mexico, and thence traversing the States of Chihuahua and Sonora, crossed the Rio Colorado at its junction with the Gila, near the tidewater of Gulph, and entered this territory at its southern part. Any more direct route was at that time unknown and considered impracticable.

"I have now been more than ten years in this country, and have traveled over all the inhabited and most of the uninhabited parts of it. I have resided eight years where I now live, near the Bay of San Francisco, and at the point where the rivers Sacramento and San Joaquin unite together to meet the tide-water of the bay, about forty miles from the ocean. I possess at this place a farm about ten miles by twelve in extent, one side of which borders on the river, which is navigable to this point for sea-going vessels. I have at last found the far West, and intend to end my ramblings here.

"I perceive by the public papers that this region of country, including that immediately north of it, which until lately was the most completely a terra incognita of any portion of the globe, is at length attracting the attention of the United States and Europe. The world, at length, seems to have become awake to the natural advantages of California and Oregon, and it seems probable that at the same moment I am writing, their political destinies are about being settled, at least for a long time to come. I mention the two countries together because I conceive the future destiny of this whole region to be one and inseparable. The natural conformation of the country strongly indicates it, and a sympathy and fellow feeling in the inhabitants is taking place, which must soon bring about the consummation.

California, as well as Oregon, is rapidly peopling with emigrants from the United States. Even the inhabitants of Spanish origin, tired of anarchy and misrule, would be glad to come under the American Government.

"The Government of the United States, in encouraging and facilitating emigration to Oregon, is, in fact, helping to people California. It is like the British Government sending settlers to Canada. The emigrants are well aware of the vast superiority of California, both in soil and climate, and I may add, facility of access. Every year shorter and better routes are being discovered, and this year the great desideratum of a good and practical road for wheel carriages has been found. Fifty-three wagons, with that number of families, have arrived safely, and more than a month earlier than any previous company. The American Government encourages emigration to Oregon by giving gratuitously some five or six hundred acres of land to each family of actual settlers. California, too, gives lands, not by acres, but by leagues, and has some thousands of leagues more to give to anybody who will occupy them. Never in any instance has less than one league been given to any individual, and the wide world from which to select from all the unoccupied lands in the territory. While Col. Almonte, the Mexican Minister to Washington, is publishing his proclamations in the American newspapers forbidding people to emigrate to California, and telling them that no lands will be given them, the actual Government here is doing just the contrary. In fact they care about as much for the Government of Mexico as for that of Japan.

"It has been usual to estimate the population of Upper California at five thousand persons of Spanish descent, and twenty thousand Indians. This estimate may have been near the truth twenty years ago. At present the population may be stated in round numbers at seven thousand Spaniards, ten thousand civilized, or rather domesticated Indians. To this may be added about seven hundred Americans, one hundred English, Irish, and Scotch, and about one hundred French, Germans, and Italians.

"Within the territorial limits of Upper California, taking the parallel of 42° for the northern, and the Colorado River for the southeastern boundary, are an immense number of wild, naked, brute Indians. The number, of course, can only be conjectured. They probably exceed a million, and may perhaps amount to double that number.

"The far-famed missions of California no longer exist. They have nearly all been broken up, and the lands apportioned out into farms. They were certainly munificent ecclestiastical baronies; and although their existence was quite incompatible with the general prosperity of the country, it seems almost a pity to see their downfall. The immense piles of buildings and beautiful vineyards and orchards are all that remain, with the exception of two in the southern part of the territory, which still retain a small remnant of their former prosperity.

"The climate of California is remarkably different from that of the United States. The great distinguishing difference is its regularity and uniformity. From May to October the wind is invariably from the northwest, and during this time it never rains, and the sky is brilliantly clear and serene. The weather during this time is temperate, and rarely oppressively warm. The nights are always agreeably cool, and many of the inhabitants sleep in the open air the whole year round. From October to May the southeast wind frequently blows, and is always accompanied by rain. Snow never falls excepting in the mountains. Frost is rare except in December or January. A proof of the mildness of the winter this moment presents itself in the shape of a humming-bird, which I just saw from the open window, and this is in latitude 38° on the first day of February. Wheat is sown from October until March, and maize from March until July. As respects human health and comfort, the climate is incomparably better than that of any part of the United States. It is much the most healthy country I have ever seen or have any knowledge of. There is no disease whatever that can be attributed to the influence of the climate.

"The face of the country differs as much from the United States as the climate. The whole territory is traversed by ranges of mountains, which run parallel to each other and to the coast. The highest points may be about six thousand feet above the sea, in most places much lower, and in many parts they dwindle to low hills. They are everywhere covered with grass and vegetation, and many of the valleys and northern declivities abound with the finest timber trees. Between these ranges of mountains are level valleys, or rather plains, of every width, from five miles to fifty. The magnificent valley through which flow the rivers of St. Joaquin and Sacramento is *five hundred miles long,* with an average width of forty or fifty. It is intersected laterally by many smaller rivers, abounding with salmon.

"The only inhabitants of this valley, which is capable of supporting a nation, are about a hundred and fifty Americans and a few Indians. No published maps that I have seen give any correct idea of the country, excepting the outline of the coast.

"The Bay of San Francisco is considered by nautical men one of the finest harbors in the world. It consists of two principal arms, diverging from the entrance in nearly opposite directions, and each about fifty miles long, with an average width of eight or ten. It is perfectly sheltered from every wind, has great depth of water, is easily accessible at all times, and space enough for half the ships in the world. The entrance is less than a mile wide, and could be easily fortified so as to make it entirely impregnable. The vicinity abounds in the finest timber for ship-building, and in fact everything necessary to make it a great naval and commercial depot. If it were in the hands of a nation who knew how to make use of it, its influence would soon be felt on all the western coast of America, and probably through the whole Pacific.

"I think it cannot long remain in the hands of its present owners. If it does not come into possession of Americans, the English will have it. This port in their hands, what will Oregon be worth to the United States? They loudly threaten to get possession of Cuba as an offset against Texas.

Will they not be quite as likely to obtain California, as an offset against Oregon? A British ship of war was here last summer, whose captain was a brother of Lord Aberdeen, and one of her lieutenants a son of Sir R. Peel. The gentlemen declared openly that this port would soon belong to them. This I take to be only a slight ebullition of John Bullism; but that they want this port, and will have it if possible, there can be no doubt, a consummation most earnestly and ardently to be deprecated by every American. I hope it may direct your views to take an interest in this matter.

"The agricultural capabilities of California are but very imperfectly developed. The whole of it is remarkably adapted to the culture of the vine. Wine and brandy of excellent quality are made in considerable quantities. Olives, figs, and almonds grow well. Apples, pears, and peaches are abundant, and in the southern part oranges. Cotton is beginning to be cultivated and succeeds well. It is the finest country for wheat I have ever seen. Fifty for one is an average crop, with very imperfect cultivation. One hundred fold is not uncommon, and even one hundred and fifty has been produced. Maize produces tolerably well, but not equal to some parts of the United States. Hemp, flax, and tobacco have been cultivated on a small scale, and succeed well. The raising of cattle is the principal pursuit of the inhabitants, and the most profitable.

"The foreign commerce of Upper California employs from ten to fifteen sail of vessels, mostly large ships. Somewhat more than half of these are American, and belong exclusively to the port of Boston. The others are English, French, Russian, Mexican, Peruvian, and Hawaiian. The French from the islands in the Pacific and the Russians from Kamtschatka, and their establishments on the northwest coast, resort here for provisions and live stock. The exports consist of hides and tallow, cows, lard, wheat, soap, timber, and furs. There are slaughtered annually about one hundred thousand head of cattle, worth $800,000. The whole value of the exports annually amounts to about $1,000,000. The largest item of imports is American cotton goods. The duties on imports are enormously high, amounting on most important articles to one hundred and fifty per cent on the original cost, and in many instances to four or five hundred. Thus, as in most Spanish countries, a high bounty is paid to encourage smuggling. Whale ships visit St. Francisco annually in considerable numbers for refreshments, and fail not to profit by the facilities for illicit commerce.

"California, although nominally belonging to Mexico, is about as independent of it as Texas, *and must ere long share the same fate.* Since my residence here, no less than four Mexican governors have been driven from the country by force of arms. The last of these, Micheltorena, with about four hundred of his soldiers and one hundred employes, was driven away about a year ago.

"This occurred at the time that the rest of the nation was expelling his master, Santa Ana, although nothing of this was known here at the time. The new administration, therefore, with a good grace, highly approved of our conduct. In fact, the successive administrations in Mexico have always shown a disposition to sanction and approve of whatever we may do here, from a conscious inability to retain even a nominal dominion over the country by any other means. Upper California has been governed for the last year entirely by its own citizens. Lower California is in general an uninhabited and uninhabitable desert. The scanty population it contains lives near the extremity of the Cape, and has no connection and little intercourse with this part of the country.

"Upper California has a productive gold mine, and silver ore has been found in many places. A mine of quicksilver has been very lately found in this vicinity, which promises to be very valuable.

"I know not, since you have been so long engaged in more weighty concerns, if you take the same interest as formerly in Indian affairs, but since I have supposed your personal identity to remain, I shall venture a few remarks on the aborgines of California. In stature the California Indian rather exceeds the average of the tribes east of the mountains. He is heavier limbed and stouter built. They are a hairy race, and some of them have beards that would do honor to a Turk. The color similar to that of the Algonquin race, or perhaps rather lighter. The visage, short and broad, with wide mouth, thick lips, broad nose, and extremely low forehead. In some individuals the hair grows quite down to the eyebrows, and they may be said to have no forehead at all. Some few have that peculiar conformation of the eye so remarkable in the Chinese and Tartar races, and entirely different from the common American Indian or the Polynesian; and with this unpromising set of features, some have an animated and agreeable expression of countenance. The general expression of the wild Indian has nothing of the proud and lofty bearing, or the haughtiness and ferocity so often seen east of the mountains. It is more commonly indicative of timidity and stupidity.

"The men and children are absolutely and entirely naked, and the dress of the women is the least possible or conceivable remove from nudity. Their food varies with the season. In February and March they live on grass and herbage; clover and wild pea-vine are among the best kinds of their pasturage. I have often seen hunderds of them grazing together in a meadow, like so many cattle.

"They are very poor hunters of the larger animals, but very skilful in making and managing nets for fish and fowl. They also collect in their season great quantities of the seeds of various grasses, which are particularly abundant. Acorns are another principal article of food, which are larger, more abundant, and of better quality than I have seen elsewhere. The Californian is not more different from the tribes east of the mountains in his physical than in his moral and intellectual qualities. They are easily domesticated, not averse to labor, have a natural aptitude to learn mechanical trades, and, I believe, universally a fondness for music, and a facility in acquiring it.

"The Mission of St. Joseph, when in its prosperity, had one hundred plough-men, and I have often seen them all at work in one field, each with his plow. It had also fifty weavers, twenty tanners, thirty shoe-makers, forty masons, twenty carpenters, ten blacksmiths, and various other mechanics. They are not nearly so much addicted to intoxication as is common to other Indians. I was for some years of the opinion that they were of an entirely different race from those east of the muntains, and they certainly have but little similarity. The only thing that caused me to think differently is that they have the same Moccasin game that is so common on the Mississippi, and what is more remarkable, they accompany it by singing precisely the same tune! The diversity of language among them is very great. It is seldom an Indian can understand another who lives fifty miles distant; within the limits of California are at least a hundred dialects, apparently entirely dissimilar. Few or no white persons have taken any pains to learn them, as there are individuals in all the tribes which have communication with the settlements who speak Spanish.

"The children, when caught young, are most easily domesticated, and manifest a great aptitude to learn whatever is taught them; when taken into Spanish families, and treated with kindness, in a few months they learn the language and habits of their masters. When they come to maturity they show no disposition to return to the savage state. The mind of the wild Indian, of whatever age, appears to be a *tabula rasa,* on which no impressions, except those of a mere animal nature, have been made, and ready to receive any impress whatever. I remember a remark of yours some years ago, that 'Indians were only grown-up children.' Here we have a real race of infants. In many recent instances when a family of white people have taken a farm in the vicinity of an Indian village, in a short time they would have the whole tribe for willing serfs. They submit to flagellation with more humility than the negroes. Nothing more is necessary for their complete subjugation but kindness in the beginning, and a little well-timed severity when deserved. It is common for the white man to ask the Indian, when the latter has committed any fault, how many lashes he thinks he deserves. The Indian, with a simplicity and humility almost inconceivable, replies ten or twenty, according to his opinion of the magnitude of the offense. The white man then orders another Indian to inflict the punishment, which is received without the least sign of resentment or discontent. This I have myself witnessed or I could hardly have believed it.

"I fear the unexpected length of this desultory epistle will be tedious to you, but I hope it will serve at least to diversify your correspondence. If I can afford you any information, or be serviceable to you in any way, I beg you to command me. Any communication to me can be sent through the American Minister at Mexico, or the Commanding Officer of the Squadron of the Pacific, directed to the care of T. O. Larkin, Esq., American Consul at Monterey. I am, sir, very respectfully,

"Your obedient servant,

"Hon. Lewis Cass."   "John Marsh.

THE AMERICAN CONQUEST OF CALIFORNIA

The Mexican War marked the beginning by the United States of territorial expansion by conquest.

After the adoption of liberal colonization laws by the Mexican government in 1824, there set in a steady drift of Americans to California. At first they came by sea, but after the opening of the overland route in 1841, they came in great numbers by land. It was a settled conviction in the minds of these adventurous nomads that the manifest destiny of California was to become a part of the United States, and they were only too willing to aid destiny when an opportunity offered. The opportunity came and it found them ready for it.

Capt. John C. Fremont, an engineer and explorer in the service of the United States, appeared at Monterey in January, 1846, and applied to General Castro, the military comandante, for permission to buy supplies for his party of sixty-two men, who were encamped in the San Joaquin Valley, in what is now Kern County. Permission was given him. There seems to have been a tacit agreement between Castro and Fremont that the exploring party should not enter the settlements, but early in March the whole force was encamped in the Salinas Valley.

Castro regarded the marching of a body of armed men through the country as an act of hostility, and ordered them out of the country. Instead of leaving, Fremont intrenched himself on an eminence known as Gabilan Peak, raised the Stars and Stripes over his barricade, and defied Castro. Castro maneuvered his troops on the plain below, but did not attack Fremont. After two days' waiting Fremont abandoned his position and began his march northward. On May 9, when near the Oregon line, he was overtaken by Lieutenant Gillespie, of the United States navy, with a dispatch from the President. Gillespie had left the United States in November, 1845, and, disguised, had crossed Mexico from Vera Cruz to Mazatlan, and from there had reached Monterey. The exact nature of the dispatches to Fremont is not known, but presumably they related to the impending war between Mexico and the United States, and the necessity for a prompt seizure of the country to prevent it from falling into the hands of England. Fremont returned to the Sacramento, where he encamped.

THE BEAR FLAG REPUBLIC

On the 14th of June, 1846, a body of American settlers from the Napa and Sacramento valleys, thirty-three in number, of which Ide, Semple, Grigsby and Merritt seem to have been the leaders, after a night's march, took possession of the old castillo or fort at Sonoma, with its rusty muskets and unused cannon, and made Gen. M. G. Vallejo, Lieut.-Colonel Prudon, Capt. Salvador Vallejo and Jacob P. Leese, a brother-in-law of the Vallejos, prisoners. There seem to have been no privates at the castillo, all officers. Exactly what was the object of the American settlers in taking General Vallejo prisoner is not evident. General Vallejo was one of the few eminent Californians who favored the annexation of California to the United States. He is said to have made a speech favoring such a movement in the junta at Monterey a few months before. Castro regarded him with suspicion. The prisoners were sent under an armed escort to Fremont's camp. William B. Ide was elected captain of the revolutionists who remained at Sonoma, to "hold the fort." He issued a pronunciamiento in which he declared California a free and independent government, under the name of the California Republic. A nation must have a flag of its own, so one was improvised. It was made of a piece of cotton cloth, or manta, a yard wide and five feet long. Strips of red flannel torn from the shirt of one of the men were stitched on the bottom of the flag for stripes. With a blacking brush, or, as another authority says, the end of a chewed stick for a brush, and red paint, William L. Todd painted the figure of a grizzly bear passant on the field of the flag. The natives called Todd's bear "cochino," a pig; it resembled that animal more than a bear. A five-pointed star in the left upper corner, painted with the same coloring matter, and the words "California Republic" printed on it in ink, completed the famous Bear Flag.

Under the Stars and Stripes

The California Republic was ushered into existence June 14, 1846, attained the acme of its power July 4, when Ide and his fellow patriots burnt a quantity of powder in salutes, and fired off oratorical pyrotechnics in honor of the new republic. It utterly collapsed on the 9th day of July, after an existence of twenty-five days, when news reached Sonoma that Commodore Sloat had raised the stars and stripes at Monterey and taken possession of California in the name of the United States. Lieutenant Revere arrived at Sonoma on the 9th, and he it was who lowered the Bear Flag from the Mexican flagstaff, where it had floated through the brief existence of the California Republic, and raised in its place the banner of the United States.

Commodore Sloat, who had anchored in Monterey Bay July 2, 1846, was for a brief time undecided whether to take possession of the country. He had no official information that war had been declared between the United States and Mexico; but, acting on the supposition that Captain Fremont had received definite instructions, on the 7th of July he raised the flag and took possession of the custom-house and government buildings at Monterey. Captain Montgomery, on the 9th, raised it at San Francisco, and on the same day the Bear Flag gave place to the stars and stripes at Sonoma.

General Castro was holding Santa Clara and San José when he received Commodore Sloat's proclamation informing him that the commodore had taken possession of Monterey. Castro, after reading the proclamation, which was written in Spanish, formed his men in line and, addressing them, said: "Monterey is taken by the Americans. What can I do with a handful of men against the United States? I am going to Mexico.

All of you who wish to follow me, 'About face!' All that wish to remain can go to their homes." A very small part of his force followed him.

Commodore Sloat was superseded by Commodore Stockton, who set about organizing an expedition to subjugate the part of the territory which still remained loyal to Mexico. Fremont's exploring party, recruited to a battalion of 120 men, had marched to Monterey, and from there was sent by vessel to San Diego to procure horses and prepare to act as cavalry.

While these stirring events were transpiring in the north, Pio Pico had entered upon the duties of the governorship with a desire to bring peace and harmony to the distracted country. He appointed Juan Bandini, one of the ablest statesmen of the south, his secretary. After Bandini resigned, he chose J. M. Covarrubias; and later José M. Moreno filled the office efficiently.

The principal offices of the territory had been divided equally between the politicians of the north and the south. While Los Angeles became the capital, and the departmental assembly met there, the military headquarters, the archives and the treasury remained at Monterey. But, notwithstanding this division of the spoils of office, the old feud between the arribenos and the abajenos would not down, and soon the old-time quarrel was on with all its bitterness. Castro, as military comandante, ignored the governor, and Alvarado was regarded by the surenos as an emissary of Castro's. The departmental assembly met at Los Angeles, in March, 1846. Pico presided, and in his opening message set forth the unfortunate condition of affairs in the department. Education was neglected; justice was not administered; the missions were so burdened by debt that but few of them could be rented; the army was disorganized, and the treasury was empty.

On the 16th of June, Pico left Los Angeles for Monterey with a military force of a hundred men. The object of the expedition was to oppose, and, if possible, to depose Castro. To enlist the sympathy and more ready adhesion of the foreign element of Los Angeles, Pico issued the following circular. (A copy, probably the only one in existence, was donated some years since to the Historical Society of Southern California.)

[Seal of] "Gobierno del Dep. de Californias.

"Circular.—As, owing to the unfortunate condition of things that now prevails in this department in consequence of the war into which the United States has provoked the Mexican nation, some ill feeling might spring up between the citizens of the two countries, out of which unfortunate occurrences might grow, and as this government desires to remove every cause of friction, it has seen fit, in the use of its power, to issue the present circular.

"The Government of the department of California declares in the most solemn manner that all the citizens of the United States that have come lawfully into its territory, relying upon the honest administration of the laws and the observance of the prevailing treaties, shall not be molested in the least, and their lives and property shall remain in perfect safety under the protection of the Mexican laws and authorities legally constituted.

"Therefore, in the name of the supreme government of the nation, and by virtue of the authority vested upon me, I enjoin upon all the inhabitants of California to observe towards the citizens of the United States that have lawfully come among us, the kindest and most cordial conduct, and to abstain from all acts of violence against their persons or property; provided they remain neutral, as heretofore, and take no part in the invasion effected by the armies of their nation.

"The authorities of the various municipalities and corporations will be held strictly responsible for the faithful fulfilment of this order, and shall, as soon as possible, take the necessary measures to bring it to the knowledge of the people. God and Liberty. Pio Pico.
"José Matias Moreno, Secretary pro tem.
"Angeles, July 27, 1846."

When we consider the conditions existing in California at the time this circular was issued, its sentiments reflect great credit on Pico for his humanity and forbearance. A little over a month before, a party of Americans seized General Vallejo and several other prominent Californians in their homes and incarcerated them in prison at Sutter's Fort. Nor was this outrage mitigated when the stars and stripes were raised. The perpetrators of the outrage were not punished. These native Californians were kept in prison nearly two months without any charge against them. Besides, Governor Pico and the leading Californians very well knew that the Americans whose lives and property this proclamation was designed to protect would not remain neutral when their countrymen invaded the territory. Pio Pico deserved better treatment from the Americans than he received. He was robbed of his landed possessions by unscrupulous land sharks, and his character was defamed by irresponsible historical scribblers.

Pico and Castro left Los Angeles on the night of August 10, for Mexico, Castro going by the Colorado River route to Sonora. Pico, after being concealed for a time by his brother-in-law, Juan Foster, at the Santa Margarita and narrowly escaping capture by Fremont's men, finally reached Lower California and later on crossed the Gulf to Sonora.

Stockton began his march on Los Angeles August 11. He took with him a battery of four guns, mounted on carretas, each gun drawn by four oxen. He had with him a good brass band.

Major Fremont, who had been sent to San Diego with his battalion of 170 men, had, after considerable skirmishing among the ranchos, secured enough horses to move, and on the 8th of August had begun his march to join Stockton. He took with him 120 men, leaving about fifty to garrison San Diego.

Stockton consumed three days on the march. Fremont's troops joined him just south of the city, and at 4 p. m. of the 13th the combined force, numbering nearly 500 men, entered the town without opposition; "our entry," says Major Fremont, "having more the effect of a parade of home guards than of an enemy taking possession of a conquered town."

Squads of Fremont's battalion were sent out to scour the country and bring in any of the California officers or leading men whom they could find. These, when found, were paroled.

On the 17th of August, Stockton issued a second proclamation, in which he signed himself commander-in-chief and governor of the territory of California. It was milder in tone and more dignified than the first. He informed the people that their country now belonged to the United States. For the present it would be governed by martial law. They were invited to elect their local officers if those now in office refused to serve under the new order.

Four days after the capture of Los Angeles, the Warren, Captain Hull, commander, anchored at San Pedro. She brought official notice of the declaration of war between the United States and Mexico. Then for the first time Stockton learned that there had been an official declaration of war between the two countries. United States officers had waged war and had taken possession of California upon the strength of a rumor that hostilities existed between the countries.

The conquest, if conquest it can be called, was accomplished without the loss of a life, if we except the two Americans, Fowler and Cowie, of the Bear Flag party, who were brutally murdered by a band of Californians under Padillo, and the equally brutal shooting of Berryessa and the two de Haro boys by the Americans at San Rafael. These three men were shot as spies, but there was no proof that they were such, and they were not tried. These murders occurred before Commander Sloat raised the stars and stripes at Monterey.

On the 15th of August, 1846, just thirty-seven days after the raising of the stars and stripes at Monterey, the first newspaper ever published in California made its appearance. It was published at Monterey by Semple and Colton and named The Californian. Rev. Walter Colton was a chaplain in the United States navy and came to California on the Congress with Commodore Stockton. He was made alcalde of Monterey and built, by the labor of the chain gang, and from contributions and fines, the first schoolhouse in California, named for him Colton Hall. Colton thus describes the other member of the firm, Dr. Robert Semple: "My partner is an emigrant from Kentucky, who stands six feet eight in his stockings. He is in a buckskin dress, a foxskin cap; is true with his rifle, ready with his pen and quick at the type case." Semple came to California in 1845, with the Hastings party, and was one of the leaders in the Bear Flag revolution. The type and press used were brought to California by Augustin V. Zamorano in 1834, and by him sold to the territorial government, and had been used for printing bandos and pronunciamentos. The only paper the publishers of The Californian could procure was that used in the manufacture of cigarettes, which came in sheets a little larger than

3

foolscap. The font of type was short of w's, so two v's were substituted for that letter, and when these ran out two u's were used. The paper was moved to San Francisco in 1848, and later on consolidated with The California Star.

The capitulation of Gen. Andres Pico at Cahuenga put an end to the war in California. The instructions from the secretary of war were to pursue a policy of conciliation towards the Californians, with the ultimate design of transforming them into American citizens. Colonel Fremont was left in command at Los Angeles.

Mexican Laws and American Officials

Upon the departure of General Kearny, May 31, 1847, Col. Richard B. Mason became governor and commander-in-chief of the United States forces in California by order of the President. Stockton, Kearny and Fremont had taken their departure, the dissensions that had existed since the conquest of the territory among the conquerors ceased, and peace reigned. Mexican laws were administered for the most part by military officers. The municipal authorities were encouraged to continue in power and perform their governmental functions, but they were indifferent and sometimes rebelled. Under Mexican rule there was to trial by jury. The alcalde acted as judge and in criminal cases a council of war settled the fate of the criminal. The Rev. Walter Colton, while acting as alcalde of Monterey, in 1846-1847, impaneled the first jury ever summoned in California. "The plaintiff and defendant," he writes, "are among the principal citizens of the country. The case was one involving property on the one side and integrity of character on the other. Its merits had been pretty widely discussed, and had called forth an unusual interest. One-third of the jury were Mexicans, one-third Californians and the other third Americans. This mixture may have the better answered the ends of justice, but I was apprehensive at one time it would embarrass the proceedings; for the plaintiff spoke English, the defendant in French; the jury, save the Americans, Spanish, and the witnesses, all the languages known in California. By the tact of Mr. Hartnell, who acted as interpreter, and the absence of young lawyers, we got along very well."

The process of Americanizing the people was no easy undertaking. The population of the country and its laws were in a chaotic condition. It was an arduous task that Colonel Mason and the military commanders at the various pueblos had to perform, that of evolving order out of the chaos that had been brought about by the change in nations. The native population neither understood the language nor the customs of their new rulers, and the newcomers among the Americans had very little toleration for the slow-going Mexican ways and methods they found prevailing. To keep peace between the factions required more tact than knowledge of law, military or civil, in the commanders.

Peace Established

The treaty of peace between the United States and Mexico was signed at Guadalupe Hidalgo, a hamlet a few miles from the City of Mexico,

February 2, 1848; ratifications were exchanged at Queretaro, May 30 following, and a proclamation that peace had been established between the two countries was published July 4, 1848.   Under this treaty the United States assumed the payment of the claims of American citizens against Mexico, and paid, in addition, $15,000,000 to Mexico for Texas, New Mexico and Alta California.   Out of what was the Mexican territory of Alta California there has been carved all of California, all of Nevada, Utah and Arizona and part of Colorado and Wyoming.   The territory acquired by the treaty of Guadalupe Hidalgo was nearly equal to the aggregated area of the thirteen original states at the time of the Revolutionary War.

The news of the treaty of peace reached California August 6, 1848. On the 7th Governor Mason issued a proclamation announcing the ratification of the treaty.   He announced that all residents of California who wished to become citizens of the United States were absolved from their allegiance to Mexico.   Those who desired to retain their Mexican citizenship could do so, provided they signified such intention within one year from May 30, 1848.

The war was over; and the treaty of peace had made all who so elected, native or foreign born, American citizens.   Strict military rule was relaxed and the people henceforth were to be self-governing.   Americans and Californians were one people and were to enjoy the same rights and be subject to the same penalties.   The war ended, the troops were no longer needed, and orders were issued to muster out the volunteers. These all belonged to Stevenson's New York regiment. The last company of the Mormon battalion had been discharged in April.   The New York volunteers were scattered all along the coast from Sonoma to Cape San Lucas, doing garrison duty.   They were collected at different points and mustered out.   Although those stationed in Alta California had done no fighting, they had performed arduous service in keeping peace in the conquered territory.   Most of them remained in California after their discharge and rendered a good account of themselves as citizens.

GOLD!   GOLD!   GOLD!

Sebastian Viscaino, from the bay of Monterey, writing to the King of Spain 300 years ago, says of the Indians of California: "They are well acquainted with gold and silver, and said that these were found in the interior."   Viscaino was endeavoring to make a good impression on the mind of the king in regard to his discoveries.   The traditions of the existence of gold in California before any was discovered are legion.   Most of these have been evolved since gold was actually found.   Col. J. J. Warner, a pioneer of 1831, in his "Historical Sketch of Los Angeles County," briefly and very effectually disposes of these rumored discoveries. He says: "While statements respecting the existence of gold in the earth of California and its procurement therefrom have been made and published as historical facts, carrying back the date of the knowledge of the auriferous character of this State as far as the time of the visit of Sir

Francis Drake to this coast, there is no evidence to be found in the written or oral history of the missions, in the acts and correspondence of the civil or military officers, or in the unwritten and traditional history of Upper California that the existence of gold, either with ores or in its virgin state, was ever suspected by any inhabitants of California previous to 1841; and, furthermore, there is conclusive testimony that the first known grain of native gold dust was found upon or near the San Francisco ranch, about forty-five miles northwesterly from Los Angeles City, in the month of June, 1841. This discovery consisted of grain gold fields (known as placer mines), and the auriferous fields discovered in that year embraced the greater part of the country drained by the Santa Clara River from a point some fifteen or twenty miles from its mouth to its source, and easterly beyond Mount San Bernardino."

The story of the discovery as told by Warner and by Don Abel Stearns agrees in the main facts, though differing materially in the date. Stearns says gold was first discovered by Francisco Lopez, a native of California, in the month of March, 1842, at a place called San Francisquito, about thirty-five miles northwest from Los Angeles. The circumstances of the discovery by Lopez, as related by himself, are as follows: "Lopez, with a companion, was out in search of some stray horses, and about midday they stopped under some trees and tied their horses out to feed. They were resting under the shade, when Lopez, with his sheathknife, dug up some wild onions, and in the dirt discovered a piece of gold, and, searching further, found some more. He brought these to town, and showed them to his friends, who at once declared there must be a placer of gold. This news being circulated, numbers of the citizens went to the place, and commenced prospecting in the neighborhood, and found it to be a fact that there was a placer of gold."

Colonel Warner says: "The news of this discovery soon spread among the inhabitants from Santa Barbara to Los Angeles, and in a few weeks hundreds of people were engaged in washing and winnowing the sands of these gold fields."

Warner visited the mines a few weeks after their discovery. He says: "From these mines was obtained the first parcel of California gold dust received at the United States mint in Philadelphia, and which was sent with Alfred Robinson, and went in a merchant ship around Cape Horn." This shipment of gold was 18.34 ounces before and 18.1 ounces after melting; fineness .925; value, $344.75, or over $19 to the ounce, a very superior quality of gold dust. It was deposited in the mint July 8, 1843.

It may be regarded as a settled historical fact that the first authenticated discovery of gold in Alta California was made on the San Francisco rancho in the San Felicano Cañon, Los Angeles County. This cañon is about ten miles northwest of Newhall Station on the Southern Pacific Railroad, and about forty miles northwest of Los Angeles.

It is impossible to obtain definite information in regard to the yield of the San Fernando placers, as these mines are generally called. William

Heath Davis, in his "Sixty Years in California," states that from $80,000 to $100,000 was taken out for the first two years after their discovery. He says that Mellus at one time shipped $5000 of dust on the ship Alert. Bancroft says: "By December, 1843, two thousand ounces of gold had been taken from the San Fernando mines." Don Antonio Coronel stated that with the assistance of three Indian laborers, in 1842, he took out $600 worth of dust in two months. De Mofras, in his book, states that Carlos Baric, a Frenchman, in 1842, was obtaining an ounce a day of pure gold from his placer.

These mines were worked continuously from the time of their discovery until the American conquest, principally by Sonorans. The discovery of gold at Coloma, January 24, 1848, drew away the miners, and no work was done on these mines between 1848 and 1854. After the latter dates work was resumed, and in 1855, Francisco Garcia, working a gang of Indians, is reported to have taken out $65,000 in one season. The mines are not exhausted, but the scarcity of water prevents working them profitably.

It is rather a singular coincidence that the exact dates of both the first and second authenticated discoveries of gold in California are still among the undecided questions of history. In the first, we know the day but not the year; in the second, we know the year but not the day of the month on which Marshall picked up the first nuggets in the millrace at Coloma. For a number of years after the anniversary of Marshall's discovery began to be observed, the 19th of January was celebrated. Of late years January 24th has been fixed upon as the correct date; but the Associated Pioneers of the Territorial Days of California, an association made up of men who were in the territory at the time of Marshall's discovery or came here before it became a State, object to the change. For nearly thirty years they have held their annual dinners on January 18, "the anniversary of the discovery of gold at Sutter's sawmill, Coloma, Cal." This society has its headquarters in New York City. In a circular recently issued, disapproving of the change of date from the 18th to the 24th, the trustees of that society say: "Upon the organization of this society, February 11, 1875, it was decided to hold its annual dinners on the anniversary of the discovery of gold at Sutter's sawmill, Coloma, Cal. Through the Hon. Newton Booth, of the United States Senate, this information was sought, with the result of a communication from the secretary of the State of California to the effect that the archives of the State of California recorded the date as of January 18, 1848. Some years ago this date was changed by the society at San Francisco to that of January 24, and that date has been adopted by other similar societies located upon the Pacific and Atlantic coasts. This society took the matter under advisement with the result that the new evidence upon which it was proposed to change the date was not deemed sufficient to justify this society in ignoring its past records, founded on the authority of the State of California; therefore it has never accepted the new date."

Marshall himself was uncertain about the exact date. At various times he gave three different dates, the 18th, 19th, and 20th, but never moved it along as far as the 24th. In the past thirty years three different dates, the 18th, 19th and 24th of January have been celebrated as the anniversary of Marshall's discovery.

The evidence upon which the date was changed to the 24th is found in an entry in a diary kept by H. W. Bigler, a Mormon, who was working for Marshall on the millrace at the time gold was discovered. The entry reads: "January 24. This day some kind of metal that looks like gold was found in the tailrace." On this authority about ten years ago the California Pioneers adopted the 24th as the correct date of discovery.

While written records, especially if made at the time of the occurrence of the event, are more reliable than oral testimony given long after, yet when we take into consideration the conflicting stories of Sutter, Marshall, the Winners and others who were immediately concerned in some way with the discovery, we must concede that the Territorial Pioneers have good reasons to hesitate about making a change in the date of their anniversary. In Dr. Trywhitt Brooks' "Four Months Among the Gold Finders," a book published in London in 1849, and long since out of print, we have Sutter's version of Marshall's discovery given only three months after that discovery was made. Dr. Brooks visited Sutter's Fort early in May, 1848, and received from Sutter himself the story of the find. Sutter stated that he was sitting in his room at the fort, one afternoon, when Marshall, whom he supposed to be at the mill, forty miles up the American River, suddenly burst in upon him. Marshall was so wildly excited that Sutter, suspecting that he was crazy, looked to see whether his rifle was in reach. Marshall declared that he had made a discovery that would give them both millions and millions of dollars. Then he drew his sack and poured out a handful of nuggets on the table. Sutter, when he had tested the metal and found that it was gold, became almost as excited as Marshall. He eagerly asked if the workmen at the mill knew of the discovery. Marshall declared that he had not spoken to a single person about it. They both agreed to keep it a secret. Next day Sutter and Marshall arrived at the sawmill. The day after their arrival, they prospected the bars of the river and the channels of some of the dry creeks and found gold in all.

"On our return to the mill," says Sutter, "we were astonished by the work-people coming up to us in a body and showing us some flakes of gold similar to those we had ourselves procured. Marshall tried to laugh the matter off with them, and to persuade them that what they had found was only some shining mineral of trifling value; but one of the Indians, who had worked at a gold mine in the neighborhood of La Paz, Lower California, cried out: 'Oro! Oro' ('Gold! Gold!'), and the secret was out."

Captain Sutter continues: "I heard afterward that one of them, a sly Kentuckian, had dogged us about and that, looking on the ground to see what we were in search of, he lighted on some of the flakes himself."

If this account is correct, Bigler's entry in his diary was made on the day that the workmen found gold, which was five or six days after Marshall's first find, and consequently the 24th is that much too late for the true date of the discovery. The story of the discovery given in the "Life and Adventures of James W. Marshall," by George Frederick Parsons, differs materially from Sutter's account. The date of the discovery given in that book is January 19, 1848. On the morning of that day Marshall, after shutting off the water, walked down the tailrace to see what sand and gravel had been removed during the night. (The water was turned into the tailrace during the night to cut it deeper.) While examining a mass of debris, "his eye caught the glitter of something that lay lodged in a crevice on a riffle of soft granite some six inches under water." Picking up the nugget and examining it, he became satisfied that it must be one of three substances—mica, sulphurets of copper, or gold. Its weight satisfied him that it was not mica. Knowing that gold was malleable, he placed the specimen on a flat rock and struck it with another; it bent, but did not crack or break. He was satisfied that it was gold. He showed the nugget to his men. In the course of a few days he had collected several ounces of precious metal. Some four days after the discovery it became necessary for him to go below, for Sutter had failed to send a supply of provisions to the mill, and the men were on short commons. While on his way down he discovered gold in a ravine at a place afterwards known as Mormon Island. Arrived at the fort, he interviewed Sutter in his private office and showed him about three ounces of gold nuggets. Sutter did not believe it to be gold, but after weighing it in scales against $3.25 worth of silver, all the coin they could raise at the fort, and testing it with nitric acid obtained from the gun shop, Sutter became convinced and returned to the mill with Marshall. So little did the workmen at the mill value the discovery that they continued to work for Sutter until the mill was completed, March 11, six weeks after the nuggets were found in the tailrace.

The news of the discovery spread slowly. It was two months in reaching San Francisco, although the distance is not over 125 miles. The great rush to the mines from San Francisco did not begin until the middle of May, nearly four months after the discovery. On the 10th of May, Dr. Brooks, who was in San Francisco, writes: "A number of people have actually started off with shovels, mattocks and pans to dig the gold themselves. It is not likely, however, that this will be allowed, for Captain Folsom has already written to Colonel Mason about taking possession of the mine on behalf of the government, it being, he says, on public land."

As the people began to realize the richness and extent of the discovery, the excitement increased rapidly. May 17, Dr. Brooks writes: "This place (San Francisco) is now in a perfect furore of excitement; all the workpeople have struck. Walking through the town today, I observed that laborers were employed only upon about half a dozen of the fifty new buildings which were in course of being run up. The majority of the mechanics at this place are making preparations for moving off to the mines, and several people of all classes—lawyers, storekeepers, merchants, etc., are smitten with the fever; in fact, there is a regular gold mania springing up. I counted no less than eighteen houses which were closed, the owners having left. If Colonel Mason is moving a force to the American Fork, as is reported here, their journey will be in vain."

Colonel Mason's soldiers moved without orders—they nearly all deserted, and ran off to the mines.

The first newspaper announcement of the discovery appeared in The Californian of March 15, 1848, nearly two months after the discovery. But little attention was paid to it. In the issue of April 19, another discovery is reported. The item reads: "New gold mine. It is stated that a new gold mine has been discovered on the American Fork of the Sacramento, supposed to be on the land of W. A. Leidesdorff, of this place. A specimen of the gold has been exhibited, and is represented to be very pure." On the 29th of May The Californian had suspended publication. "Othello's occupation is gone," wails the editor. "The majority of our subscribers and many of our advertising patrons have closed their doors and places of business and left town, and we have received one order after another conveying the pleasant request that the printer will please stop my paper or my ad, as I am about leaving for Sacramento."

The editor of the other paper, The California Star, made a pilgrimage to the mines in the latter part of April, but gave them no extended write-up. "Great country, fine climate," he wrote on his return. "Full flowing streams, mighty timber, large crops, luxuriant clover, fragrant flowers, gold and silver," were his comments on what he saw. The policy of both papers seems to have been to ignore as much as possible the gold discovery. To give it publicity was for a time, at least, to lose their occupation.

In The Star of May 20, 1848, its eccentric editor, E. C. Kemble, under the caption "El Dorado Anew," discourses in a dubious manner upon the effects of the discovery and the extent of the gold fields:

"A terrible visitant we have had of late. A fever which has well-nigh depopulated a town, a town hard pressing upon a thousand souls, and but for the gracious interposition of the elements, perhaps not a goose would have been spared to furnish a quill to pen the melancholy fate of the remainder. It has preyed upon defenseless old age, subdued the elasticity of careless youth and attacked indiscriminately sex and class, from town councilman to tow-frocked cartman, from tailor to tippler, of which, thank its pestilential powers, it has beneficially drained (of tipplers, we mean) every villainous pulperia in the place.

"And this is the gold fever, the only form of that popular southerner, yellow jack, with which we can be alarmingly threatened. The insatiate maw of the monster, not appeased by the easy conquest of the rough-fisted yeomanry of the north, must needs ravage a healthy, prosperous place beyond his dominion and turn the town topsy-turvy in a twinkling.

"A fleet of launches left this place on Sunday and Monday last bound up the Sacramento River, close stowed with human beings, led by love of filthy lucre to the perennial yielding gold mines of the north. When any man can find two ounces a day and two thousand men can find their hands full, was there ever anything so superlatively silly?

"Honestly, though, we are inclined to believe the reputed wealth of that section of the country, thirty miles in extent, all sham, as superb a take-in as was ever got up to guzzle the gullible. But it is not improbable that this mine, or, properly, placer of gold can be traced as far south as the city of Los Angeles, where the precious metal has been found for a number of years in the bed of a stream issuing from its mountains, said to be a continuation of this gold chain which courses southward from the base of the snowy mountains. But our best information respecting the metal and the quantity in which it is gathered varies much from many reports current, yet it is beyond a question that no richer mines of gold have ever been discovered upon this continent.

"Should there be no paper forthcoming on Saturday next, our readers may assure themselves it will not be the fault of us individually. To make the matter public, already our devil has rebelled, our pressman (poor fellow) last seen was in search of a pickax, and we feel like Mr. Hamlet, we shall never again look upon the likes of him. Then, too, our compositors have, in defiance, sworn terrible oaths against type-sticking as vulgar and unfashionable. Hope has not yet fled us, but really, in the phraseology of the day, 'things is getting curious.' "

And things kept getting more and more curious. The rush increased. The next issue of The Star (May 27) announces that "the Sacramento, a first-class craft, left here Thursday last thronged with passengers for the gold mines, a motly assemblage, composed of lawyers, merchants, grocers, carpenters, cartmen and cooks, all possessed with the desire of becoming rich. The latest accounts from the gold country are highly flattering. Over three hundred men are engaged in washing gold, and numbers are continually arriving from every part of the country." Then the editor closes with a wail: "Persons recently arrived from the country speak of ranches deserted and crops neglected and suffered to waste. The unhappy consequence of this state of affairs is easily foreseen." One more twinkle, and The Star disappeared in the gloom. On June 14 appeared a single sheet, the size of foolscap. The editor announced: "In fewer words than are usually employed in the announcement of similar events, we appear before the remnant of a reading community on this occasion with the material or immaterial information that we have stopped the paper, that its publication ceased with the last regular issue (June 7). On the approach of autumn, we shall again appear to announce The Star's redivivus. We have done. Let our parting word be hasta luego." Star and Californian reappeared November 14, 1848. The Star had absorbed The Californian. E. C. Kemble was its editor and proprietor.

Although there was no paper in existence on the coast to spread the news from the gold fields, it found its way out of California, and the rush from abroad began. It did not acquire great force in 1848, but in 1849 the immigration to California exceeded all previous migrations in the history of the race.

Among the first foreigners to rush to the mines were the Mexicans of Sonora. Many of these had had some experience in placer mining in their native country, and the report of rich placers in California, where gold could be had for the picking up, aroused them from their lazy self-content and stimulated them to go in search of it. Traveling in squads of from fifty to one hundred, they came by the old Auza trail across the Colorado desert, through the San Gorgonio Pass, then up the coast and on to the mines. They were a job lot of immigrants, poor in purse and poor in brain. They were despised by the native Californians and mal-treated by the Americans. Their knowledge of mining came in play, and the more provident among them soon managed to pick up a few thousand dollars, and then returned to their homes, plutocrats. The improvident gambled away their earnings and remained in the country to add to its criminal element. The Oregonians came in force, and all the towns in California were almost depopulated of their male population. By the close of 1848, there were 10,000 men at work in the mines.

The first official report of the discovery was sent to Washington by Thomas O. Larkin, June 1, and reached its destination about the middle of September. Lieutenant Beale, by way of Mexico, brought dispatches dated a month later, which arrived about the same time as Larkin's report. These accounts were published in the Eastern papers, and the excitement began.

In the early part of December, Lieutenant Loeser arrived at Washington with Governor Mason's report of his observations in the mines made in August. But the most positive evidence was a tea caddy of gold dust, containing about 230 ounces, that Governor Mason had caused to be purchased in the mines with money from the civil service fund. This the lieutenant had brought with him. It was placed on exhibition at the war office. Here was tangible evidence of the existence of gold in California, the doubters were silenced, and the excitement was on and the rush began.

By the first of January, 1849, vessels were fitting out in every seaport on the Atlantic coast and the Gulf of Mexico. Sixty ships were announced to sail from New York in February and seventy from Philadelphia and Boston. All kinds of craft were pressed into the service, some to go by way of Cape Horn, others to land their passengers at Vera Cruz, Nicaragua and Panama, the voyagers to take their chances on the Pacific side for a passage on some unknown vessel.

With the opening of spring, the overland travel began. Forty thousand men gathered at different points on the Missouri River, but principally at St. Joseph and Independence. Horses, mules, oxen and cows were used for the propelling power of the various forms of vehicles that were to convey the provisions and other impedimenta of the army of gold seekers. By the first of May the grass was grown enough on the plains to furnish feed for the stock, and the vanguard of the grand army of gold hunters started. For two months, company after company left the rendezvous and joined the procession until for 1000 miles there was an almost unbroken line of wagons and pack trains. The first half of the journey was made with little inconvenience, but on the last part there were great suffering and loss of life. The cholera broke out among them, and it is estimated that 5000 died on the plains. The alkali desert of the Humboldt was the place where the immigrants suffered most. Exhausted by the long journey and weakened by lack of food, many succumbed under the hardship of the desert journey and died. The crossing of the Sierras was attended with great hardships. From the loss of their horses and oxen, many were compelled to cross the mountains on foot. Their provisions exhausted, they would have perished but for relief sent out from California. The greatest sufferers were the women and children, who in considerable numbers made the perilous journey.

The overland immigration of 1850 exceeded that of 1849. According to the record kept at Fort Laramie, there passed that station during the season 39,000 men, 2500 women, and 600 children, making a total of 42,100. These immigrants had with them, when passing Fort Laramie, 23,000 horses, 8000 mules, 3600 oxen, 7000 cows, and 9000 wagons.

Besides those coming by the northern route, that is, by the South Pass and the Humboldt River, at least 10,000 found their way to the land of gold by the old Spanish trail, by the Gila route, and by Texas, Coahuila and Chihuahua into Arizona, and thence across the Colorado desert to Los Angeles, and from there by the coast route or the San Joaquin valley to the mines.

The Pacific Mail Steamship Company had been organized before the discovery of gold in California. March 3, 1847, an act of Congress was passed authorizing the secretary of the navy to advertise for bids to carry the United States mails by one line of steamers between New York and Chagres, and by another line between Panama and Astoria, Ore. On the Atlantic side the contract called for five ships of 1500 tons burden; on the Pacific side, two of 1000 tons each, and one of 600 tons. These were deemed sufficient for the trade and travel between the Atlantic and Pacific coasts of the United States. The Pacific Mail Steamship Company was incorporated April 12, 1848, with a capital stock of $500,000. October 6, 1848, the California, the first steamer for the Pacific, sailed from New York, and was followed in the two succeeding months by the Oregon and the Panama. The California sailed before the news of the gold discovery had reached New York, and she had taken no passengers. When she arrived at Panama, January 30, 1849, she encountered a rush of 1500 gold hunters, clamorous for a passage. These had reached Chagres on sailing vessels, ascended the Chagres River in bongos or dugouts to Gorgona, and traveled thence by land to Panama. The California had accommodations for only 100, but 400 managed to find some place to stow themselves away. The price of tickets rose to a fabulous sum, as high as $1000 having been paid for a steerage passage. The California entered the Bay of San Francisco February 28, 1849, and was greeted by the boom of cannon and the cheers of thousands of people lining the shores of the bay. The other two steamers arrived on time, and the Pacific Mail Steamship Company became the predominant factor in California travel for twenty years, or up to the completion of the first transcontinental railroad in 1869. The charges for fare on these steamers in the early fifties were prohibitory to men of small means. From New York to Chagres in the saloon the fare was $150; in the cabin, $120. From Panama to San Francisco in the saloon, $250; cabin, $200. Add to these the expense of crossing the isthmus, and the Argonaut was out a goodly sum when he reached the land of the golden fleece; indeed, he was often fleeced of his last dollar before he entered the Golden Gate.

The first effect of the gold discovery on San Francisco, as we have seen, was to depopulate it, and of necessity suspend all building operations. In less than three months the reaction began, and the city experienced one of the most magical booms in history. Real estate doubled in some instances in twenty-four hours. The Californian of September 3, 1848, says: "The vacant lot on the corner of Montgomery and Washington Streets was offered the day previous for $5000 and the next day sold readily for $10,000." Lumber went up in value until it was sold at a dollar per square foot. Wages kept pace with the general advance. Sixteen dollars a day was a mechanic's wages, and the labor market was not overstocked even at these high rates. With the approach of winter, the gold seekers came flocking to the city to find shelter and to spend their suddenly acquired wealth. The latter was easily accomplished, but the former was more difficult. Any kind of a shelter that would keep out the rain was utilized for a dwelling. Rows of tents that circled around the business portion, shanties patched together from pieces of packing boxes, and sheds thatched with brush from the chaparral-covered hills constituted the principal dwellings at that time of the future metropolis of California. The yield of the mines for 1848 has been estimated at $10,000,000. This was the result of only a few months' labor of not to exceed at any time 10,000 men. The rush of miners did not reach the mines until July, and mining operations were mainly suspended by the middle of October.

New discoveries had followed in quick succession Marshall's find at Coloma until, by the close of 1848, gold placers had been located on all the principal tributaries of the Sacramento and San Joaquin Rivers. Some of the richest yields were obtained from what was known as "dry diggins." These were dry ravines from which pay dirt had to be packed to water for washing or the gold separated by dry washing, tossing the earth into the air until it was blown away by the wind, the gold, on account of its weight, remaining in the pan.

A correspondent of the Californian, writing August 15, 1848, from what he designates as "Dry Diggins," gives this account of the richness of that gold field: "At the lower mines (Mormon Island) the miners count the success of the day in dollars; at the upper mines near the mill (Coloma), in ounces; and here, in pounds. The only instrument used at first was a butcher knife, and the demand for that article was so great that $40 has been refused for one.

"The earth is taken out of the ravines which make out of the mountains and is carried in wagons or packed on horses from one to three miles to water and washed. Four hundred dollars is the average to the cart load. In one instance five loads yielded $16,000. Instances are known where men have carried the earth on their backs and collected from $800 to $1500 a day."

The rapidity with which the country was explored by prospectors was truly remarkable. The editor of the Californian, who had suspended the publication of his paper on May 29 to visit the mines, returned and resumed it on July 15 (1848). In an editorial in that issue he gives his observations: "The country from the Ajuba (Yuba) to the San Joaquin Rivers, a distance of one hundred twenty miles, and from the base toward the summit of the mountains as far as Snow Hill, about seventy miles, has been explored, and gold found in every part. There are probably three thousand men, including Indians, engaged in collecting gold. The amount collected by each man who works ranges from $10 to $350 per day. The publisher of this paper, while on a tour alone to the mining district, collected, with the aid of a shovel, pick and pan, from $44 to $128 a day, averaging about $100. The largest piece of gold known to be found weighed four pounds." Among other remarkable yields the Californian reports these: "One man dug $12,000 in six days, and three others obtained thirty-six pounds of pure metal in one day."

MAKING A STATE

Col. R. B. Mason, who had been the military governor of California since the departure of General Kearny in May, 1847, had grown weary of his task. He had been in the military service of his country thirty years, and wished to be relieved. His request was granted, and on the 12th of April, 1849, Brevet Brigadier General Bennett Riley, his successor, arrived at Monterey and the next day entered upon his duties as civil governor. Gen. Persifer F. Smith, who had been appointed commander of the Pacific division of the United States army, arrived at San Francisco February 26, 1849, and relieved Colonel Mason of his military command. A brigade of troops 650 strong had been sent to California for military service on the border and to maintain order. Most of these promptly deserted as soon as opportunity offered, and found their way to the mines.

A year had passed since the treaty of peace with Mexico had been signed, which made California United States territory; but Congress had done nothing toward giving it a government. The people were becoming restive at the long delay. The Americanized Mexican laws and forms of government were unpopular, and it was humiliating to the conqueror to be governed by the laws of the people conquered. The question of calling a convention to form a provisional government was agitated by the newspapers and met a hearty response from the people. Meetings were held at San José, December 11, 1848; at San Francisco, December 21, and at Sacramento, January 6, 1849, to consider the question of establishing a provisional government. It was recommended by the San José meeting that a convention be held at that place on the second Monday of January. The San Francisco convention recommended the 5th of March; this the Monterey committee considered too early, as it would take the delegates from below fifteen days to reach the pueblo of San José. There was no regular mail and the roads in February (when the delegates would have to start) were impassable. The committee recommended May 1 as the earliest date for the meeting to consider the question of calling a convention. Sonoma, without waiting, took the initiative and elected ten delegates to a provisional government convention. There was no unanimity in regard to the time of meeting or as to what could be done if the convention met. It was finally agreed to postpone the time of meeting to the first Monday of August, when, if Congress had done nothing towards giving California some form of government better than that existing, the convention should meet and organize a provisional government.

The confusion constantly arising from the attempt to carry on a government that was semi-military and semi-Mexican induced Governor Riley to order an election to be held August 1, to elect delegates to a convention to meet in Monterey September 1, 1849, to form a State constitution or Territorial organization to be ratified by the people and submitted to Congress for its approval. Judges, prefects and alcaldes were to be elected at the same time in the principal municipal districts. The constitutional convention was to consist of thirty-seven delegates. Instead of thirty-seven delegates, as called for, forty-eight were elected and seated.

Of the forty-eight delegates elected twenty-two were natives of the Northern States; fifteen of the Slave States; four were of foreign birth, and seven were native Californians. Several of the latter neither spoke nor understood the English language and William E. P. Hartnell was appointed interpreter. Dr. Robert Semple, of Bear Flag fame, was elected president; William G. Marcy and J. Ross Browne, reporters.

Early in the session the slavery question was disposed of by the adoption of a section declaring that neither slavery or involuntary servitude, unless for the punishment of crimes, shall ever be tolerated in this State. The question of fixing the boundaries of the future State excited the most discussion. The present boundaries were established by a majority of two.

A committee had been appointed to receive propositions and designs for a State seal. Only one design was offered. It was presented by Caleb Lyon of Lyondale, as he usually signed his name, but was drawn by Major Robert S. Garnett, an army officer. It contained a figure of Minerva in the foreground, a grizzly bear feeding on a bunch of grapes; a miner with an uplifted pick; a gold rocker and a pan; a view of the Golden Gate with ships riding at anchor in the Bay of San Francisco; the peaks of the Sierra Nevadas in the distance; a sheaf of wheat; thirty-one stars; and above all, the word "Eureka" (I have found it), which might apply either to the miner or the bear. The design seems to have been an attempt to advertise the resources of the State. General Vallejo wanted the bear taken out of the design, or if allowed to remain, that he be made fast by a lasso in the hands of a vaquero. This amendment was rejected, as was also one submitted by O. M. Wozencraft to strike out the figures of the gold digger and the bear and introduce instead bales of merchandise and bags of gold. The original design was adopted with the addition of the words, "The Great Seal of the State of California." The convention voted to give Lyon $1000 as full compensation for engraving the seal and furnishing the press and all appendages.

The constitution was completed on the 11th of October and an election was called by Governor Riley to be held on the 13th of November to vote upon the adoption of the constitution and to elect State officers, a legislature and members of Congress.

At the election Peter H. Burnett, who had been quite active in urging the organization of a State government, was chosen Governor; John McDougall, lieutenant governor; and George W. Wright and Edward Gilbert, Members of Congress. San José had been designated by the constitutional convention the capital of the State pro tem.

The people of San José had pledged themselves to provide a suitable building for the meeting of the legislature, in the hope that their town might be made the permanent capital. They were unable to complete the building designed for a State capital in time for the meeting. The uncomfortable quarters furnished created a great deal of dissatisfaction. The legislature consisted of sixteen Senators and thirty-six Assemblymen. There being no county organization, the members were elected by districts. The Senate and Assembly were organized on the 17th of December. The Governor and Lieutenant-governor were sworn in on the 20th. The State government being organized, the legislature elected John C. Fremont and William M. Gwin United State Senators.

On the 22nd the legislature elected the remaining State officers, viz.: Richard Roman, treasurer; J. I. Houston, controller; E. J. C. Kewen, attorney-general; Charles J. Whiting, surveyor-general; S. C. Hastings, chief justice; Henry Lyons and Nathaniel Bennett, associate justices. The legislature continued in session until April 22, 1850. Although it was nicknamed the "Legislature of a Thousand Drinks," it did a vast amount of work and did most of it well. It was not made up of hard drinkers. The majority of its members were above the average legislator in intelligence, temperance and patriotism. The members were not there for pay of for political preferment. They were there for the good of their adopted State and labored conscientiously for its benefit.

The State had set up housekeeping without a cent on hand to defray expenses. There was not a quire of paper, a pen, nor an inkstand belonging to the State, and no money to buy supplies. After wrestling with the financial problem some time, an act authorizing a loan of $200,000 for current expenses was passed. Later on in the session another act was passed authorizing the bonding of the State for $300,000 with interest at the rate of three per cent a month. The legislature divided the State into twenty-seven counties, created nine judicial districts, passed laws for the collection of revenue, taxing all real and personal property and imposing a poll tax of $5 on all male inhabitants over twenty-one and under fifty years of age.

California was a self-constituted State. It had organized a State government and put it into successful operation without the sanction of Congress. Officials, State, county and town, had been elected and had sworn to support the constitution of the State of California, and yet there was really no State of California. It had not been admitted into the Union.

On August 13th the bill for the admission of California finally came to a vote. It passed the Senate, thirty-four ayes to eighteen noes. In the House the bill passed by a vote of 150 ayes to fifty-six ultra Southern noes. It was approved and signed by President Fillmore September 9, 1850. On the 11th of September the California Senators and Congressmen presented themselves to be sworn in.

The news of the admission of California reached San Francisco on the morning of October 18, by the mail steamer Oregon, nearly six weeks after Congress had admitted it. Business was at once suspended, the courts were adjourned, and the people went wild with excitement. Messengers, mounted on fleet steeds, spread the news throughout the State. Newspapers from the States containing an account of the proceedings of Congress at the time of admission sold for $5 each. It was decided to hold a formal celebration of the event on the 29th and preparations were begun for a grand demonstration.

At the plaza a flag of thirty-one stars was raised to the mast head. An oration was delivered by Judge Nathaniel Bennett, and Mrs. Wills recited an original ode of her own composition. The rejoicing over, the people settled down to business. Their unprecedented action in organizing a State government and putting it into operation without the sanction of Congress had been approved and legalized by that body.

Like the Goddess Minerva, represented on its great seal, who sprung full-grown from the brain of Jupiter, California was born a fully matured State. She passed through no territorial probation. No State had such a phenomenal growth in its infancy. No State before or since has met with such bitter opposition when it sought admission into the family of States. Never before was there such a medley of nationalities—Yankees, Mexicans, English, Germans, French, Spaniards, Peruvians, Polynesians, Mongolians—organized into a State and made a part of the body politic nolens volens.

CHAPTER II

CONTRA COSTA COUNTY: GENERAL FEATURES

Contra Costa County will some day be called the "Hub" of California; and rightly so, for its strategic location at the crossing of the trade routes from the fertile valleys of the interior of the State, and from the great Northwest, where the captains of commerce meet and barter with the rest of the world, will in the near future, much more than in the past, compel the recognition of its peculiar and paramount advantages.

In writing about the county, the difficulty lies not so much in finding topics for discussion as in selecting among so multitudinous and so varied an array of facts those which will give a clear and distinct appreciation of the region as a whole, without overcrowding and confusing the understanding. The writer has had an intimate acquaintance with nearly every county in the State for over a quarter of a century, during which time a careful study has been made of each for the purpose of describing and illustrating its advantages. While recognizing the varied claims of the different sections of our State, this one for climate, that one for scenery, another for wealth of lumber, or mineral resources, and others for specialized horticultural, viticultural or agricultural opportunities, about which ample volumes might be written with justice to each, yet the writer feels that nowhere else in California is there to be found such a gathering together of material advantages, such manifold chances for advancement, such fertility of soil, balminess of climate, and beauty of scenery; nor such large-hearted hospitality of the people, linked with kindred social graces and a wide-awake spirit of business enterprise which, at last awakened, is now welcoming the coming of the new day of larger undertakings, of wider views, and of broader developments. Ours then be the pleasant task of recording a few of the reasons why there has gatherd within the confines of Contra Costa County, one of the smaller among the fifty-eight counties of the State, a population of some 60,000 of the most alert, open-eyed and far-seeing of its people.

ADVANTAGES OF LOCATION

Contra Costa County contains 877 square miles of territory, or, to be more exact, 561,873 acres of land, over three-fourths of which is cultivated, and the balance utilized for grazing and pasturage. It is situated almost midway between the north and south boundaries of the State, and near the western border and the Pacific Ocean, being thus placed by nature at the very center of things. The southwestern end of the county is within seven miles in an air line of the Coast's great metropolis, San Francisco. Then right adjoining are the growing cities of Oakland and Berkeley, with

almost a quarter of a million inhabitants, who are surging across the
county line in throngs and rapidly building up the interval between the
confines of Berkeley and Richmond, the banner city of the county, which
possesses the brightest future of any of the towns that front on San
Francisco Bay.

The Water Front

Beginning at Richmond, whose southern eminences are but eight miles
across the water from San Francisco, is the first deep water adjacent to that
city, and the beginning of what is probably the most incomparably valuable
asset of the county, a water front of seventy miles extent, comprising by far
the greatest amount of deep-water frontage on the Bay. Already this circumstance has been taken advantage of by many manufacturing establishments in various parts of the country.

Fresh Water Anchorage

An item of especial interest in regard to this water front is the fact
that in the upper portions, stretching from the Carquinez Straits, in
increasing ratio, to Antioch and the eastern end of the county, on the San
Joaquin River and its tributary channels, the waters are fresh, and as a
consequence afford a cheap and easy means for ocean-going vessels to get
rid of barnacles and other salt-water growths, which die in the fresh water
and drop off, leaving the vessel's bottom clear, thereby saving the expense
and delay of being dry-docked and scraped.

Most Valuable River Traffic

The traffic of the Sacramento and San Joaquin Rivers through the Delta
District of Contra Costa County amounts to $108,000,000 annually, a
larger traffic than that of any other river in the United States. Of this
vast sum, $52,000,000 originates in the Delta, the remainder coming from
points farther inland.

Included in the Delta are 525,000 acres—a small empire—where
enterprising farmers and horticulturists are annually producing millions
of dollars' worth of field and orchard products for the world's food supply.

Many companies receive their raw material by boat and ship out the
manufactured product by steamer and rail. The main lines of the Southern
Pacific, the Santa Fe, and the Sacramento-San Francisco Railroads traverse
the county, the first two having tracks that follow the coast line, reaching
all industrial centers.

There is regular ferry boat service from Contra Costa points. The
largest ferry boat in the world plies between Port Costa and Benicia, carrying trains as well as passengers.

River shipping is another transportation convenience. Three hundred
miles of navigable rivers terminate on the Contra Costa water front,
placing a wide and prosperous interior within easy access of the shipper.

FINE SYSTEM OF HIGHWAYS

The system of highways makes motor transportation to all parts of the county possible. Three transcontinental highways pass through Contra Costa County.

The county is the pioneer of the double track concrete highway, which adds comfort to motoring and makes collision accidents practically impossible.

A road test recently conducted in Contra Costa County by scientific experts was watched by road engineers from all over the country, who were interested in discovering the most durable materials and construction for heavy-traffic highways.

Auto trucks and stage lines offer convenient service when it is needed. It is a down hill haul from practically all the State to the Contra Costa water front.

UNSURPASSED CLIMATE

Contra Costa owes its favorable climate to its position and topography. Situated between the Golden Gate and the great San Joaquin Valley, it escapes the chill and fog that so often visit the former, and the high dry heat of the interior. The Contra Costa range of hills protects the county from the direct force of the constant trade winds, whose force proves unpleasant to all but the most rugged and robust. Deflected by this range, these winds blow up San Pablo Bay and, striking the northern shore of the Carquinez Straits, sweep eastward into the vast interior valleys. As a consequence, Contra Costa County receives the benefit of their cooling influence without being subjected to the effects of their direct onslaught. The mean annual temperature, determined by observations extending over many years, ranges from 52 to 60 degrees, except in the eastern portion, where the average is from 60 to 68 degrees. Winter frosts are rare, and are light and of short duration.

Droughts are unknown in Contra Costa County; the abundant winter rains, the absence of the intense evaporating heat of the interior, and the ozone and moisture-laden breezes from the ocean furnish abundant supplies of watery vapor for all forms of vegetation, without the use of irrigation.

Of course there are variations in the different sections of the county. The extreme western valleys fronting on San Francisco and San Pablo Bays are cooler and moister than the eastern, but both are equally well fitted, with some minor exceptions, for all classes of agriculture.

EASTERN CONTRA COSTA COUNTY

The eastern end of Contra Costa County is an empire of itself, a land of perennial richness and inexhaustible fertility. Its topography is varied. Along the northern and eastern portions, which lie on the San Joaquin and its channels, there is a level plain, which continues for its whole eastern face, fronted by a large area of tule delta lands, intersected by many creeks and sloughs. Its center, south and west, is extremely hilly, with fertile valleys lying between the ridges, while the canyons, through which flow smiling streams, gamboling on their way to the rivers, are shaded with a variety of fine trees and woods.

Lying in the northern foothills of Mount Diablo is the coal-producing region. From the mines opened here much mineral wealth has been extracted.

The plain lands of this section were formerly one of the most remarkable wheat and hay-raising districts of the State, but were partially cropped out. While hay is still a staple, the great reliance of this region is fruit, thousands of acres of which are just coming into bearing. These plains are in fact the commencement of the great valley of the San Joaquin, a country most fair to look upon. In time to come, when subdivided and intensively cultivated, these lands will, where properly watered, bear wonderful crops of grain, fruit, vegetables and other farm produce.

The Rich Valleys

Back of this plain land open up the smaller valleys, the chief of which are the Marsh, the Briones, and the Deer Creek valleys. These valleys are now largely devoted to general farming, fruit and the cultivation of grapes. There is here much deep alluvial soil, on the hills as well as in the valleys, and also many broad acres of that reddish soil, impregnated with minerals, which makes such wonderful land for grapes and fruits. From Antioch east there is a region where table grapes are a very profitable crop.

The Sandy Lands

There is a strange region lying between Oakley and Brentwood. The soil is sandy and was originally covered with chaparral and scrub oak. Useless land, said many men who tried to farm it and made a failure. About 1887, however, James O'Hara came to the region. He bought some of this land and was laughed at. But he had ideas. He planted fruit trees on this sandy land and in doing so transformed the region. Nowhere else does the fruit ripen so early or prove so sure a crop.

The Tule Lands

The tule lands are the wonder of the world. As fertile as the dyked lands of Holland and as inexhaustible as the plains which receive the annual floods of the Nile, there is nothing that they will not grow. Barley, potatoes, beans, onions, vegetables fit to grace the tables of kings, are grown, often two crops in the year, and especially asparagus and celery. Fruit trees grow here too, and bear amazing crops, but vegetables pay better and bigger returns.

Dairying

Dairying is another industry that is coming rapidly to the front, and is yielding splendid returns for the investment. The milk and cream are usually sent to the cities, where there is a great demand. A sign of the times is the fact that these are all "sanitary" dairies, where especial precaution is taken to insure absolute cleanliness in every department.

MOUNT DIABLO

This mountain is a distinctive possession of our county. Lying very near the geographical center, it seems almost the pivot about which swings every interest of the region and, in a sense, of the whole middle and northern portions of the State. Its singularly commanding position makes it the observed of all observers, and its beauty, both of contour and of surroundings, deepens its charm on closer acquaintance.

About it gather most of the traditions of the Indian aborigines, to whom it was a terror-striking divinity, loved or feared according to its brighter or more threatening mood; and associated with it are many incidents of special historic interest. The Indians called the mountain "Pupunia," and often took shelter in its many caves.

Says the San Francisco Examiner:

"The country . . . dominated by Diablo was first revealed to white men on March 20, 1772, when Capt. Don Pedro Fagis, Fray Juan Crespi, twelve leatherjackets (soldiers), a muleteer, and a Lower Californian Indian, attending the pack train, set out from Monterey to reach the old Port of San Francisco. The old Port of San Francisco had been variously described by Drake (1579), Cermenon (1597), Carbrera Bueno (1734), Gaspar de Portola (1769). But the Bay of San Francisco, as we today know it, had not been seen by white men until Portola's soldiers fell upon its southern arm in 1769. It was not until 1775 that the old name was transferred from the old Port of San Francisco (Drake's Bay) to the present Bay of San Francisco.

"On Friday, March 27th, with wondering eyes the motley band of Spaniards beheld for the first time the Golden Gate (it was not so named until 1848).

"On their march over San Antonio Valley, now Alameda and Oakland, great herds of deer, antelope and elk were encountered, and bear were daily camp visitors. In the evening smoke arose from hundreds of Indian campfires among the oaks, a picture hard to reconcile with the noisy cities of today. Continuing on over the Richmond hills, following the line of least resistance, they traveled over what is practically the route of the popular boulevard skirting the base of Mount Diablo.

"Fray Crespi gave a detailed account of the fertile country over which the party traveled and tells with much disappointment of encountering, after so long and tedious a journey, a body of water (Carquinez Straits), which prevented their going forward to Point Reyes (old Port San Francisco).

"A conference was held among the little band, and to push forward meant building boats; so the project was abandoned. On the return trip they crossed the present site of Antioch, going eastward along the southern shores of Suisun Bay to a point just north of Diablo. From these hills Captain Fagis and Fray Crespi beheld before them the great rivers of the great central valleys, and Fagis named the nearest one the San Joaquin.

"Thus, to that expedition of 1772 stands the credit of discovering the Golden Gate and the Sacramento and San Joaquin Rivers; the naming of the dominating landmark, Mount Diablo; and acquainting the world with the splendid region on the eastern shore which Fray Palou calls 'Great Sea of the Mediterranean'."

A legend of Mount Diablo runs as follows:

There was once a time when there were no human inhabitants in California. There were two spirits, one evil and the other good. They made war on each other, and the good spirit overcame the evil one. At that period the entire face of the country was covered with water, except two islands, one being Mount Diablo and the other Eagle Point on the north. There was a coyote on the peak, the only living thing there. One day the coyote saw a feather floating on the water. As it reached the island it turned into an eagle, which flew upon the mountain. The coyote was pleased with his new companion; dwelling in harmony together, they made occasional excursions to the other island, the coyote swimming and the eagle flying.

After some time they counseled together and concluded to make Indians, and as the Indians increased the water decreased, until where the water had been there was now dry land.

At that time, what is now known as the Golden Gate was a continuous chain of mountains, so it was possible to go from one side to the other without getting wet. Then there were only two outlets for all the waters on this side of the Sierras, the Russian River and the San Juan at Pajaro. A great earthquake later severed the chain of mountains and formed the Golden Gate. Then the waters of the ocean and Bay mingled and it was not long before the "pale face," or white man, found his way into California; and so as the waters decreased at the coming of the Indian, so have the Indians decreased at the coming of the white man, until the war-whoop is heard no more and the council fire is no more lighted. The Indians, like shadows, have passed silently away from the land of the coyote and the eagle.

The following legend of the naming of Mount Diablo is told by General Vallejo:

"In 1806 a military expedition from San Francisco marched against the tribe 'Bolgones,' who were encamped at the foot of the mountain. The Indians were prepared to receive the expedition, and a hot engagement ensued in the hollow fronting the western side. As the victory was about to be decided in favor of the Indians, an unknown personage, decorated with the most extraordinary plumage, and making divers movements, suddenly appeared near the combatants. The Indians were victorious and the incognito (Puy) departed towards the mountain. The defeated soldiers, on learning that the spirit went through the same ceremony daily and at all hours, named the mountain Diablo, in allusion to its mysterious inhabitant, who continued to make his appearance until the tribe was subdued by troops in command of Lieut. Gabriel Moraga, in a second campaign of the same year. In the Indian tongue, Puy means evil spirit; in Spanish, it means Diablo; in Anglo-American, Devil."

The mountain is also said to take its name from a phenomenon witnessed amongst its gorges at a time when Indians were numerous. The story runs thus: Once, in an expedition against horse-thief tribes, who inhabited the valley as far down as the base of the mountain, the native Californians came up with a party of freebooters laden with spoils of a hunt, and immediately gave chase, driving them up the steep defiles which form the ascent of the mountain on one side. Elated with the prospect of securing and meting out punishment to the robbers, they were pressing hard after them, when from a cavernous opening in their path there issued forth such fierce flames, accompanied by so terrible a roaring, that, thinking themselves within a riata's throw of the principal entrance to his infernal majesty's summer palace, the astonished rancheros forgot their hostile errand and, turning tail, went down the mountain faster than they went up. On reciting their adventure to their fellow ranchers, it was agreed that the Devil and his chief steward had fixed their abode in the mountain; and so they named it Mount Diablo.

The mountain itself is one of the most conspicuous and best-known landmarks in California, and as such was naturally selected as the basis of the survey systems of the State this side of the Tehachapi. It is not its great elevation which has given it its preeminence, for other peaks in the Coast Range are higher. Its height is only 3896 feet. But it is comparatively isolated and towers grandly up from the level of the sea almost unimpeded by foothills, save some on the south and west, where it is somewhat dwarfed. Its symmetry and its grandeur, its fine double summit and conical outline, all make it a mountain among mountains and the natural point of departure for eye and measurement.

From its summit there is spread a view that seems illimitable. The eye ranges over an extent of 400 miles from north to south, and to the east over the whole extent of the Sacramento-San Joaquin basin. Shasta and Lassen Buttes are visible in clear weather to the north, and to the south the vast uplift which culminates in Mt. Whitney. To the west, all that great tumble of ridges and valleys that make up the Coast Range, and even the streets of San Francisco, through a good glass, and beyond, the Pacific Ocean, are visible—truly a noble prospect. It is estimated that this comprehensive view embraces an area of 40,000 square miles and that of as interesting a country as lies anywhere under the sun and stars. Mount Diablo is worthy of a pilgrimage around the world to see.

Mount Diablo Scenic Boulevard, which winds through the Mount Diablo Estate, was built in 1916 by R. N. Burgess and associates. Its total length is twenty-three miles, in its two branches that run through the Mount Diablo Country Club and to Walnut Creek. The climb rises 3849 feet, with a seven per cent to eight per cent grade. The features are the Garden of Jungle Gods (giant freak rocks) and Devil's Slide. From the top of Mount Diablo, in favorable weather, can be seen the State's heart north and south, and the entire range of the Sierra Nevadas.

On October 25, 1926, in the presence of a large throng on the summit of Mt. Diablo, Glenn B. Ashcroft of Alameda, president of the Society of Engineers of San Francisco, dedicated the northerly pinnacle to the memory of Colonel Leander Ransome, pioneer engineer, who in 1851 established that point as the base meridian for all surveys in California.

The Mount Diablo Estate of 10,000 acres belongs to the Mount Diablo Park Club and to Mount Diablo Park, which is open to guests and members. This organization grew out of the Oakwood Park Stock Farm owned by Seth Cook, a retired miner and horseman. He was a royal entertainer and had a race course of his own, with a row of eucalyptus trees all around the track. It is now owned by the Country Club as a community farm of forty acres, with Diablo the business center of the community.

VALLEYS IN CONTRA COSTA COUNTY

The chief valleys in the county are known as the Alhambra, Pacheco, Ygnacio, Clayton and San Ramon. These actually constitute one valley, however, and are continuous for almost thirty miles, varying in width from one-half mile to fifteen miles. There are smaller separate valleys, known as Stone, Lone Tree, Pinole, Rodeo, Franklin and Briones, all well watered by running streams. In the eastern part of the county begins the great San Joaquin Valley, with an average width in Contra Costa County of twenty miles, and with a beautiful stretch of country sloping from Mount Diablo to the San Joaquin River.

Ygnacio Valley lies at the foot of Mount Diablo on the northwest, and reaches to the Sacramento River and Suisun Bay. Walnut Creek flows through this valley.

Diablo Valley is separated from Ygnacio Valley by Lime Ridge, and extends southeasterly. It contains about fifty square miles of arable land and is drained by a small creek which has its source in the ridge.

Stone Valley is a small valley east of and adjoining San Ramon.

Pacheco Valley lies on the northern side of Mount Diablo and extends to Suisun Bay. It is a central valley of the county and is six miles wide by fifteen miles in length. It merges into Ygnacio Valley and is watered by Walnut Creek. Mount Diablo Creek drains the eastern portion and, adjoining Walnut Creek, empties into Suisun Bay.

San Ramon Valley extends towards the south and merges with Livermore Valley in Alameda County. It is about one mile wide and twelve miles long, with Contra Costa hills on one side and on the other the spurs and foothills of Mount Diablo.

Alhambra Valley lies to the south of Martinez, where it opens up to Carquinez Straits, and is about six miles long and one mile wide. The famous Alhambra Mineral Springs are in this valley.

Franklin Valley, better known as Franklin Canyon, is a spur of Alhambra Valley and runs back into the Contra Costa hills about three miles. It is one of the show places along the Santa Fe Railroad.

San Pablo Valley, one of the largest in the county, faces San Francisco Bay and contains about 18,000 acres of land.

Briones, Pinole and Rodeo are smaller valleys that extend back into the hills. Deer Creek Valley is in the eastern part of the county.

TASSAJARA VALLEY

This extensive valley lies on the southeastern slopes of Mount Diablo, and is a beautiful region of more or less high ridges and large expanses. It is a land of cattle ranges and dairy farming, although much grain and hay are also grown.

This section is somewhat cut off from the rest of the county, and as a consequence much of the business of the region gravitates to Livermore and Pleasanton, nearby towns in Alameda County. It is a rich country, possessing resources of immense potential value.

This valley was settled by many Irish ranchers and is a grain-raising locality. Abner Pearson was one of the first American settlers. Then came Gillette Brothers in 1851; they raised the first grain in 1852. Mark Elliott, Wilson Coats, and Levi Maxey were also among the pioneers. Philip Mendenhall was a large property owner in the valley, as is also Thomas Carneal. There has been but little advancement made beyond grain-raising, although some fruit is being raised at this writing.

SAN RAMON VALLEY

The largest, the richest in natural resources, and one of the most favored valleys for the country homes of San Franciscans and other city dwellers is the San Ramon. It stretches from the waters of the Sacramento River at Suisun Bay to the southern extremity of the county, and ranges in width from fifteen miles in its lower part to a mile or less in some parts of its upper reaches. It possesses every variety of soil, and taken all in all, is considered one of the richest and most beautiful pieces of land in the State.

In point of scenic beauty, it is unsurpassed. On one side is the Contra Costa range, a rare aggregation of beautiful peaks and slopes, grand heights and deep, dark canyons, that present a kaleidoscope of changing loveliness with the procession of the seasons.

On the other side is Mount Diablo and its wonders, bright and glad when the sun shines bright, sombre and forbidding when shrouded with storm clouds, beautiful always.

San Ramon has many tributary valleys. In the early times San Ramon was a famous cattle country.

It is a region where horses and other animals thrive well. Some of the fastest and best horses in the country have been raised in this valley —horses that have carried off the biggest money.

But now-a-days fruit orchards, grape vineyards and intensive cultivation are coming to the fore.

Dairy farming, likewise, is an expanding industry and very profitable. People are adding to their herds every day, and prosperity is visible on every hand.

In San Ramon Valley are some of the most beautiful country homes in the West, where art and nature vie with each other to create a charmed environment.

ALHAMBRA VALLEY

Contra Costa County may be called a Jewel Box, containing gems of value, all beautiful, all brilliant, all blessed with perennial virtue, but of different qualities and possessing an endless variety of settings. Among these Alhambra shines with brightest luster, every acre of its length presenting a charm to sight and memory.

Alhambra Valley is all the lovelier because it is small. It is only five miles in length, and is nowhere more than a mile wide. The mountains crowd up close on every side. Trees crown their eminences often, and mark the course of their canyons; great oaks dot the landscape. The soil of the bottom lands is the richest loamy mold, and bears bumper crops. The hillsides have lighter, more pliable soils, which for some kinds of vines and trees are unexcelled. El Hambre Creek flows down through the valley.

On a knoll in the lower part of this valley John Muir, the famous naturalist and lover of the Sierras, made his home; and John Swett, premier educator of the State, also selected this valley for his home.

The famous Alhambra water, which is bottled at Martinez and shipped over the world, comes from copious springs about a mile below the head of the valley. It is piped to the bottling depot at Martinez.

Alhambra is the nearest valley to the city of Martinez, which in fact is built in its mouth. The Santa Fe railway crosses it, a mile or so up, over a viaduct that has been admired for its elegant and substantial construction.

YGNACIO VALLEY

This fertile valley has been aptly styled the Dreamland of California. the soil of this valley, which lies at the northwestern foot of Mount Diablo, is of that peculiarly rich, dark loam which has always been found the very best for fruits of every kind. There are large orchards here of pears, prunes, peaches, almonds, apricots and walnuts which yield unfailing crops. Where the valley has not been transformed into orchard and vineyard, it is still dotted with the great oaks that beautify so much of the county. Beautiful estates cover the whole area of this valley—the homes, most of them, of wealthy people who spend a portion of the year, at least, away from the distractions of the cities and the cares of business.

PIONEERS OF CONTRA COSTA COUNTY

NO. 1. ALBERT W. GLASS
NO. 2. JOHN KING
NO. 3. MILTON LABAREE
NO. 4. WILLIAM MEESE
NO. 5. LEVI MAXEY

NO. 6. EDW. McCAULEY
NO. 7. SAMUEL RAMAGE
NO. 8. LEE PARKER
NO. 9. EDWARD SHUEY
NO. 10. ALBERT STONE
NO. 11. SAMUEL MORE

NO. 12. C. G. GOOLD
NO. 13. J. P. CHRISMAN
NO. 14. MYRON HALL
NO. 15. DAVID GLASS
NO. 16. WILLIAM Z. STONE
NO. 17. NATHANIEL HOWARD

NO. 18. R. O. BALDWIN
NO. 19. JAMES BOONE
NO. 20. WILLIAM COX
NO. 21. GEORGE McCAMLEY
NO. 22. ELISHA C. HARLAN

CHAPTER III

EARLY COUNTY HISTORY

On December 15, 1849, an act was signed dividing the State into counties. It was passed on February 18, 1850, and confirmed on April 25, 1850.

The original boundary of Contra Costa (Opposite Coast) County was as follows: Beginning at the mouth of Alameda Creek and running northeasterly to the middle of the Bay of San Francisco; thence north or northwest following as near the middle of the bay as possible, to the Straits of San Pablo; thence up the middle of the straits to Suisun Bay and up the middle of said bay to the mouth of the San Joaquin River; thence, following up the middle of said river, to a place known as Pescadero or Lower Crossing; thence in a direct line to the northeast corner of Santa Clara County, which is on the summit of the Coast Range, near the source of Alameda Creek; thence down the middle of said creek to its mouth, the place of beginning, including the islands of San Pablo, Coreacas and Tesoro. The county seat to be at Martinez.

On March 25, 1853, an act was passed by the legislature creating Alameda County from the south portion of Contra Costa County, and a part of Santa Clara County.

The present boundary of Contra Costa County was then established, viz.: Beginning at the Bay of San Francisco at the northwest point of Red Rock, being the common corner of Marin, Contra Costa and San Francisco Counties, as established in Section 3950 of the Political Code of the State of California; thence up the straits and Bay of San Pablo, on the eastern boundary of Marin, to the point of intersection with the line bearing south 26½ degrees east, about 6¼ miles from the southwest corner of Napa County as established in Section 3958, Political Code, forming the common corner of Marin, Solano, Sonoma and Contra Costa Counties as established in Section 3955; thence to Carquinez Straits; thence up said straits and Suisun Bay to the mouth of San Joaquin River; thence up said river to confluence of the west and main channels thereof, as laid down in Gibbe's map; thence up west channel to a point about ten miles below Moore & Rhodes' ranch, at a bend where said channel, running downward, takes a general course north, the same being on the west line of San Joaquin County and forming the northeast corner of Alameda County and southeast corner of Contra Costa County; thence on the north line of Alameda County, as laid down in Higley's map and established in Section 3953, to the easterly line of San Francisco City and

County, as established in Section 3950; thence due northwest along the easterly line of San Francisco, 4½ miles, more or less, to place of beginning. The county seat to be at Martinez.

On May 13, 1850, by order of County Judge E. M. Warmcastle, the court of sessions convened at Martinez. There were present Judge Warmcastle; Absolom Peak and Edward G. Guest, associate justices; T. A. Brown, county clerk, and N. Jones, sheriff. It was ordered that there be assessed and collected for ordinary county expenditure from the real and personal property taxable by law to the amount of twenty-five cents on each $100; and that in the same manner a like sum should be levied for constructing public buildings for use of the county. The county clerk was ordered to procure a suitable building for location of the court house and clerk's office, to fit up same, and supply all necessary books and stationery. A State poll tax of $2.50 was made collectible from those whom the law required to pay it. On June 3, the county clerk was ordered to receive sealed proposals for the erection of a jail. On July 20, certain accounts for labor performed on temporary buildings were allowed. A sum not to exceed $50 was also allowed to procure an official seal.

On August 17 the following licenses were levied: To vend goods, wares, merchandise, with a capital of $5000 or less, $20 per year. To vend spirituous, malt and fermented liquors in less quantities than one pint, $50 per year.

An application was made and a license granted Oliver C. Coffin to establish a ferry between Martinez and Benicia upon his filing a $2000 bond. Fares limited by the court: Each man, $1; each man and horse, $2.50; each single horse or mule, $2; each wagon, $5; each carriage, $4; each head of sheep or hogs, etc., 50 cents.

On May 11, 1852, the court of sessions ordered one-half of the revenue collected for county purposes, fixed for the year at fifty cents on $100, should be set apart as a public building fund; also a call for bids to build a court house in court house square, Martinez. The latter was recalled by the supervisors on August 10.

On May 3, a board of supervisors was created for the county; an election was held on June 14, 1852, and William Patten, S. H. Robinson, Victor Castro, R. Farrelly, and T. J. Keefer were elected. Patten was chosen chairman. On July 5 committees were duly appointed and matters arranged for the full organization of the board, who at once assumed the reins of civil government. Their earliest order was the laying out of a road between Oakland and San Pablo.

In 1854, L. R. Townsend submitted plans; and H. J. Childers & C. Chipman a bid to build a court house for $27,000, which was accepted. The site chosen was on a hill fronting the bay, Lot 4, Block 2, Martinez.

On March 20, 1855, the county clerk, assessor and surveyor divided the county into three districts. On April 30 an election was called to choose a supervisor for each district. John H. Livingston was elected in the first district; L. E. Morgan in No. 2; and W. R. Bishop, in No. 3.

For the first fiscal year, 1850-1851, the assessed valuation of land within the boundaries of the county, as at present defined, was $408,756; value of improvements, $10,225; personal property, $237,266; total, $656,247. In 1875-1876 the assessed valuation of land had increased to $4,593,910; improvements, $522,973; personal property, $1,820,480. Value of town lots, $139,426; improvements, $211,448. Total valuation of property, $7,368,312.

In 1853, according to the assessor's report, there were 40,000 apple, 20,000 peach, 10,000 pear, 7000 plum, 4200 cherry, 1500 quince, 1250 apricot, 1000 fig, 3500 mulberry, 1000 almond, 500 prune, 1000 orange, 50 lemon and 100 olive trees in the county; and there were 600,000 grape vines, with a sprinkling of almost every other kind of fruit grown in the middle zone.

Spanish Families and Early Land Claims

In 1852 there were living in Contra Costa County the following Spanish families: Alvarado, Castro, Sepulveda, Estudillo, Moraga, Briones, Martinez, Sunol, Soto, Peralta, Altemerano, Amador, Miranda, Berryessa, Pacheco, Boca, Higuero, Alviso and Naviaga.

The following is a list of land claims in Contra Costa County:

Elam Brown for Alcalanes, 1 square league, granted August 1, 1834, by José Figueroa to C. Valencia. Claim filed February 2, 1852; confirmed February 14, 1853; appeal dismissed November 26, 1856. 3,328.95 acres, patented.

Salvio Pacheco for Monte del Diablo, granted March 30, 1844, by José Figueroa to S. Pacheco. Claim filed February 27, 1852, confirmed by district court January 14, 1856; appeal dismissed November 24, 1856. 17,921.54 acres; patented.

Robert Livermore, claimant for Cañada de los Vaqueros, granted February 29, 1844, by Manuel Micheltorena to Francisco Alviso et al. Claim filed February 27, 1852; confirmed by committee September 4, 1855; by district court December 28, 1857; appeal dismissed December 28, 1857.

Joseph Swanson, administrator of the estate of William Welch, for Las Juntas, 3 square leagues, 13,324.29 acres; granted February 9, 1844, by Manuel Micheltorena to William Welch. Claim filed March 23, 1852; confirmed by committee December 20, 1853; dismissed November 3, 1857.

Heirs of Juan Sanchez de Pacheco for Arroyo de Las Nueces y Bolbones, granted July 11, 1834, by José Figueroa to Juan Sanchez de Pacheco. Claim filed April 6, 1852; confirmed by committee April 11, 1853; by district court December 22, 1856. Decision of United States Supreme Court as to right to appeal in 20 Howard, 261. Decree of district court affirmed by U. S. Supreme Court in 22 Howard, 225. 17,734.52 acres.

Rafaela Soto de Pacheco et al. for San Ramon, granted June 10, 1833, by José Figueroa. Claim filed April 13, 1852; rejected by committee November 22, 1853; confirmed by district court February 8, 1858.

Teodora Soto for Cañada del Hambre and Las Bolsas del Hambre, granted May 18, 1842, by Juan B. Alvarado to Teodora Soto. Claim filed April 29, 1852; confirmed by committee May 15, 1855; by district court April 16, 1857; appeal dismissed August 11, 1857. Two square leagues, 13,312.70 acres.

John Marsh for Los Méganos, 4 square leagues, granted October 13, 1835, by José Castro to José Noriega. Claim filed May 3, 1852; rejected by committee March 14, 1854; confirmed by district court April 9, 1858, and later by the United States Supreme Court.

Maria Antonia Martinez de Richardson et al. for Pinole, 4 square leagues, 17,786.49 acres, granted June 1, 1842, by Juan B. Alvarado to Ygnacio Martinez. Claim filed July 8, 1852; confirmed by committee October 24, 1854; dismissed March 10, 1857.

Leo Norris for part of San Ramon, 1 square league, 4,450.94 acres, granted by Figueroa to José M. Amador. Claim filed September 20, 1852; confirmed by committee August 1, 1854, by district court Sept. 10, 1857.

Joaquin Ysidro Castro, administrator for San Pablo, 4 square leagues, 19,394.40 acres, granted by Figueroa June 12, 1834, to Francisco Castro, deceased, and to his heirs; and on the 13th, the surplus lands to Joaquin Ysidro Castro and the heirs of Francisco Castro. Claim filed October 9, 1852; confirmed by committee April 17, 1855; by district court February 24, 1858; appeal dismissed March 10, 1858.

Maria Manuela Valencia for Boca de Cañada del Pinole, 3 square leagues, 13,353.38 acres, granted June 21, 1842, by Juan B. Alvarado to M. M. Valencia. Claim filed December 13, 1852; rejected by committee August 10, 1854; confirmed by district court November 26, 1854, and by United States Supreme Court.

Joaquin Moraga for Laguna de los Palos Colorados, 3 square leagues, 13,318.13 acres, granted August 10, 1841, by Alvarado to Juan Moraga and Juan Bernal. Claim filed February 15, 1853; confirmed by committee January 23, 1855; by district court March 24, 1856; appeal dismissed April 8, 1858.

Jonathan D. Stevenson et al. for Médanos, 2 square leagues, 8,890.26 acres, granted November 26, 1839, by Alvarado to José Antonio Mesa et al. Claim filed February 24, 1853; confirmed by committee June 19, 1855; by district court October 16, 1856; appeal dismissed April 2, 1857.

Inocencio Romero et al. for land granted February 4, 1844, by Micheltorena to I. Romero et al. Claim filed February 4, 1844; rejected by committee April 17, 1855, and by district court September 16, 1857.

E. R. Carpentier, 10 square leagues, a portion granted by de Sola; another portion granted in 1841 to Juan, José and Victor Castro by Alvarado; another portion granted by Figueroa to Francisco Castro and regranted in 1844 by Micheltorena to Louis Peralta. Claim filed February 28, 1853; rejected by committee January 30, 1855; appeal dismissed for failure of prosecution, April 21, 1856.

H. W. Carpentier for 225 acres, granted by de Sola and Micheltorena to Louis Peralta. Claim filed February 28, 1853; discontinued by claimant January 23, 1855.

William C. Jones et al. for San Pablo, 3 square leagues, granted June 12, 1834, by Figueroa to Francisco M. Castro. Claim filed March 1, 1853; rejected by committee March 27, 1855; appeal dismissed for failure to prosecute April 21, 1856.

James Enright et al. for Médanos, 2 square leagues, granted November 26, 1839, by Alvarado to José Antonio and José Maria Mesa. Claim filed March 2, 1853; rejected by committee March 27, 1855; appeal dismissed for failure to prosecute April 21, 1856.

THE INDIANS OF CONTRA COSTA COUNTY

The Indians of Contra Costa County were the Jucheyunes, Alcalanes, Bolgones, and Carquinez. They were ignorant and went half naked, the men wearing a crude sort of loin cloth and the women an apron of tules, hanging from the waist to the knees, front and back, and open at the sides, as summer garb; in winter their garments were made from deer skin or feathers from water fowls. Their summer habitations were little more than shelters made from boughs, interwoven to hold together and keep off the sun. In winter they lived in their wikiups, "sometimes erected on level ground," as Bancroft describes them, "but more frequently over an excavation three or four feet deep and from ten to thirty feet in diameter. Round the brink of this hole willow poles are sunk upright in the ground, the top drawn together forming a conical structure; or the upper ends are bent over and driven into the earth on the opposite side of the hole, thus giving the hut a semi-globular shape. Bushes or strips of bark are then piled up against the poles, and the whole covered with a thick layer of earth or mud. In some instances the interstices of the frame are filled with twigs woven crosswise over and under between the poles, and the outside covering is of tule reeds instead of earth. A hole at the top gives egress to the smoke, and a small opening close to the ground admits the occupants. Each hut generally shelters a whole family of relations by blood and marriage, so that the dimensions of the habitation depend on the size of the family."

The Indians were short and stocky, broad-shouldered and strong. They were swarthy and had flat features and long, straight, black hair, coarse and unkempt.

Dr. John Marsh, writing to Lewis Cass in 1846, says "they are a hairy race, and some of them have beards that would do honor to a Turk. In some individuals the hair grows quite down to the eyebrows, and they may be said to have no foreheads at all. Some few have that peculiar conformation of the eye so remarkable in the Chinese and Tartar races, entirely different from the American Indian, or the Polynesian; and with this unpromising set of features, some have an animated and agreeable countenance."

For food they ate various kinds of roots, earthworms and grasshoppers. They made a bread from the pounded kernel of the acorn or buckeye, and used some kinds of fat worms for shortening. In fact they ate anything and everything, according to the season.

The Contra Costa Indians cremated their dead, the near relation of the deceased being given the honor of lighting the funeral pyre, which consumed all possessions that had been piled around the body. Afterwards the ashes would be mixed with pitch and smeared on the faces of the relations as a badge of mourning. They believed in a continued existence after death, and had a vague idea of the Great Spirit. They held certain rocks to be sacred, and would not eat grizzly bear meat, which they held in veneration. They were extremely docile and would willingly submit to punishment for faults committed, if shown kindness to start with. They were about the only laborers in California in the early days.

Old Adobes

In San Pablo is located what is left of the oldest adobe house in Contra Costa County. It was built in 1838 by Don Joaquin Castro, once governor of California under Spanish rule. The outer walls are of adobe (clay and grass to hold it together) three feet thick; the inner walls are two feet thick. The rooms were spacious and were the scene of many fashionable gatherings. This house, first occupied by the Castro family, was later the home of Juan B. Alvarado, also an ex-governer, and the father of Henry V. Alvarado, one of the superior judges of the county. This property is now a part of the Belding estate.

Adobe bricks were made by the Indians, who usually worked for the Spanish dons without pay. The bricks were made of clay, mixed with grass to hold the shape, molded into shape, and left to dry. First one side was turned to the sun, then the other, until dry all through. They were then laid into the wall with mortar made of mud, and again left to dry. To build an adobe house was a laborious task, and usually a year elapsed before the house was ready for occupancy.

At the county line, there is another adobe house, which was occupied by Victor Castro, a son of the former governor. In conncetion with it are two long buildings, one used as a stable and the other as a chapel for the Indians. Some of the Castro family are buried near this latter house.

On the Sobrante Grant is still a third adobe. This was occupied by a daughter of Castro. She married a Catterras. In the yard at this place members of the Catterras family are buried.

Transportation

The first mail ever carried up the Sacramento River was carried by Seth M. Swain, of Martinez, in the schooner John Dunlap, on July 24,

1849. He received $600 for his service, although the postage paid was less than $60 and the mail was all contained in one bag.

In 1849 Dr. Semple, of Benicia, established the first ferry running to a point now the site of Alhambra cemetery. The boat was propelled by oars at first; then a wheel was put on and run by horse power.

In 1851, Capt. O. C. Coffin put on the first flat-bottom boat, the Ione, and carried passengers from Antioch and Collinsville. He brought the boat to Martinez, remodeled it, as it had been run by horse power, put in an engine, and gave regular service between Martinez and Benicia until July, 1854. There was no ferry slip or wharf; an apron was used to land passengers and vehicles. The landing was at the foot of Ferry Street. Later the Ione became a float for a pile-driver; and when her days of usefulness were over she was run aground in the tules, and there her hull gradually rotted.

In 1853 a steam ferry was built in New York, brought via the Horn to Martinez and launched in the spring of 1854, and began regular service in July. It was owned by Capt. O. C. Coffin and Charles G. and Henry Coffin and was called the Carquinez. There was a large volume of business done in carrying stock across the straits. A large corral was built where the depot grounds of the Southern Pacific now are. It was composed of cordwood, which was used on the ferry to generate steam. The sticks were four feet long and the corral was built six feet high, and there was always enough wood on hand to keep a good corral. The charge was $1 per head for cattle. The ferry also carried mail and passengers, as there were many school children going to and from Benicia.

When the Carquinez was condemned, the Benicia was built and the engines were transferred from the old to the new boat. When the railroad put on the Solano, the Benicia failed to pay and was abandoned.

Vessels plying between San Francisco and up river points made Martinez a port of call daily.

In 1877 the railroad was built through Contra Costa County by the Central Pacific. The road was completed in 1878, at which time immigration began in earnest and the whole county benefited. Stage coach and sail boat were slow means of getting over the country, and freight teams soon disappeared.

Byron came into prominence on account of its mineral springs being visited by thousands from every part of the United States and abroad.

The San Ramon branch of the railroad was built in 1890 and opened up the best section of the county.

The Santa Fe, established early in 1895 as the San Francisco and San Joaquin Valley Railroad at a cost of $2,500,000, began operating at Stockton on July 22. It had been built by San Francisco capital. In 1899 the company sold out to the Santa Fe. On August 26 of that year the Santa Fe was completed to Pinole, and on March 3, 1902, the post office, Wells-Fargo Express, telegraph office and news depot opened, all in the

4

railroad station. In 1900 the line was completed between Stockton and Richmond, the shops being located in the latter place that year, and the service on cars being done in the open on side tracks until January 26, 1901, when permanent buildings were erected and the shops began functioning.

In January, 1909, the Oakland, Antioch & Eastern was incorporated, a 1200-volt electric line between San Francisco, Oakland and Sacramento, and passing through the Moraga Valley to Moraga, the Country Club, Burton and Lafayette, and through San Ramon Valley to Saranap. It branched off to Alamo, Danville and Diablo, Walnut Creek, Pacheco Valley, Concord, Bay Point, West Pittsburg, and again to Pittsburg. It was incorporated by A. W. Maltby, of Concord, W. Arnstein, of Alamo, and S. L. Napthaly and H. A. Mitchell, both of San Francisco. Work began at Bay Point in February, 1909; and in May, 1911, it was opened to Walnut Creek, and on to Oakland in April, 1913. On April 11, 1911, the Oakland, Antioch & Eastern incorporated to build to Sacramento from Bay Point, and in August, 1913, the line was put in operation between Bay Point and Pittsburg Landing. The new road leased the old Oakland & Antioch and the San Ramon Valley Railroad, and passenger and freight service are looked after carefully.

The county is traversed and served by several lines of auto stages running from Stockton, Oakland, and other Northern California points, so that no difficulty arises when a person wants to reach any given point at any time.

Bridges and Ferries

An aid to transportation through Contra Costa County from the east and north will be found in the two large toll-bridges now under construction by the American Toll Bridge Company, a $5,000,000 corporation. The one nearest completion is being built across the San Joaquin River three miles south of Antioch and connects with Sherman Island. This bridge will open up a quicker route to the bay cities through the richest farming sections of the county. It will cost $1,400,000 when completed, and will have a clearance of from 31½ to 70 feet from high water to the floor of the bridge, with a ninety-foot fairway between the piers supporting the causeway. The roadway will be wide enough for three automobiles abreast and cement walks for pedestrians.

The bridge, 3587 feet long, a concrete trestle, has one fixed steel span with seventy-foot clearance at high water, and one steel lift span with a minimum clearance of 136 feet when the span is open. Each span has 270 feet between the piers. Both the fixed and the lift span will accommodate the river traffic, and the lift span all sea-going vessels when open.

Thousands of tourists, routed over the Victory Highway from all eastern points through Sacramento, and on down past Courtland, Isleton and Rio Vista to Sherman Island, will pass through Antioch, Pittsburg, Concord and Walnut Creek on the concrete highways to Oakland and San Francisco.

The Carquinez Straits bridge will extend from a point near South Vallejo, in Solano County, to Valona, in Contra Costa County, and will be one of the largest bridges of its kind in the country. It will be 3350 feet in length and will cost $6,500,000. There will be a clearance of 135 feet for ships, a thirty-foot concrete roadway, space for sidewalks, and one track for electric trains.

Engineers who have studied the vehicular traffic in the State, particularly the present ferry receipts of the Rodeo Ferry, which is owned by the company building these bridges, estimate that the two bridges will carry more than a million vehicles during the first year they are in operation. The American Toll Bridge Company promises that both bridges will be completed and open for traffic before the expiration of the new time limit, which was fixed as February 5, 1927, a twelve-months extension of time having been granted by the board of supervisors.

At the expiration of twenty-five years the owership of the Carquinez bridge, by terms of the franchise, reverts to Contra Costa and Solano Counties. Until that time Contra Costa County will receive one per cent of the gross income from both bridges, which it is estimated will exceed $1,000,000 annually. Solano County will receive one per cent of the gross income from the Carquinez bridge, and Sacramento County a like per cent of the gross income from the Antioch bridge. In addition, this county will receive $100 per month for franchise rights.

Then there are the ferries: The Richmond-San Francisco ferry, from Richmond to San Francisco; the Richmond-San Rafael Ferry, from Richmond to San Quentin Point, opening up the coast counties of Marin, Sonoma, Mendocino, and Humboldt; Rodeo Ferry from Rodeo to South Vallejo, a short route through Napa and Solano Counties to Sacramento and the north; the Martinez-Benicia Ferry, also giving direct communication for Oakland and San Joaquin Valley points with Northern California and the coast counties; the Port Costa-Benicia Southern Pacific train ferry, with the largest ferry boat in operation in the world; and the ferry for the Oakland, Antioch & Eastern (Sacramento Short Line), near Pittsburg.

MINERALS AND MINING

In 1850 a lime quarry was discovered one mile from Pacheco. This was the first in the State and was owned by F. L. Such & Company.

On November 24, 1858, Rountree, Walker & Dickson discovered coal half way between the base of Mount Diablo and what is now Antioch, five miles from the San Joaquin River. That same year W. C. Israel discovered coal while cleaning out a spring on his land at Horse Haven. He, with his father and brother George, opened up the vein. Later they disposed of it to Watkins and Noyes. In 1861 the mine was abandoned.

On December 22, 1859, three and one-half miles from Horse Haven, Frank Somers and J. T. Cruikshank discovered the Black Diamond vein. Somers, Cruikshank, H. S. Hauxhurst, and S. Adams located lands that were later known as the Manhattan and Eureka Mines. George Hauxhurst, G. H. P. Henderson and William Henderson, and Frank Somers opened the Black Diamond and the Cumberland Mines. Noah Norton afterwards had the Black Diamond and Frank Such the Cumberland. Such sold out to C. T. Cutler, A. Tyler, J. Sturgis, and L. C. Wittenmyer of Martinez, who successfully worked the property and built the roads from Clayton and New York Landing. They also helped Norton to open the Black Diamond.

The Pittsburg Mine was located by G. H. P. Henderson. The Central Coal Mine was located by J. E. Wright, who later was joined by W. B. Stewart. The Union Mine was located by George Hauxhurst. Independence was purchased from R. Charnock by Greenwood and Newbauer.

The Empire Company opened in 1876. For many years coal-mining was the principal interest in the county. Somersville, Nortonville, and Black Diamond, or Pittsburg Landing, were built through this industry.

Copper was discovered in 1863, and its discovery created great excitement. Prices for land soared, and for a time hundreds prospected, but the excitement soon died down. Clayton was the center of this excitement, and the operations there brought on boom times. Lots sold for high prices, many companies were formed, shafts were sunk, and some ore was obtained. The first shipment was two tons of copper ore, and was made on September 19, 1863, when it was sent to San Francisco to be smelted. Later a smelter was erected at Antioch.

In March, 1860, L. W. Hastings discovered silver on the east side of Mount Diablo. Nothing ever came of it, however, except as a venture in which many people dropped their money.

Paint deposits were discovered in 1862 and were tested out by Dr. E. F. Hough. These deposits were found two miles from Martinez on the bank of the El Hambre Creek, and the colors were yellow, green, blue and red. In 1863 a mill for grinding was built, but the industry was never developed to the extent necessary to determine its real value commercially.

In 1862 petroleum was discovered near Antioch. Coal oil was also found near Pacheco in 1868.

The Cowell Portland Cement Company have 3000 acres at the base of Mount Diablo, where they have the greatest cement plant in the world.

IMPORTANT INDUSTRIAL CONCERNS

Among the industrial concerns of Contra Costa County we mention the following as the more important:

City	Firm	Value of Product	Number of Employees
Antioch—	Hickmott Canning Co.	$ 750,000	140
	The Paraffine Companies, Inc.	3,000,000	285
	Antioch Mill & Lumber Co.	200,000	25
Bay Point—	Coos Bay Lumber Co.	3,600,000	250
	American Foundry Co.	10,000	6
Brentwood—	Cal. Wharf & Warehouse Co.	8,000	5

Crockett—Cal. & Hawaiian Refining Corp. ....$70,000,000............2000
Cowell—Cowell Portland Cement Co. .... 3,000,000............ 235
Giant—Giant Powder Works .... 5,000,000............ 150
Hercules—Hercules Powder Works .... 10,000,000............ 250
Martinez—Shell Oil Co. .... 40,000,000............1200
    Associated Oil Co. (Avon) .... 25,000,000............ 850
    American Oriental Oil Co. .... 550,000............ 35
Nichols—General Chemical Co. .... 750,000............ 350
Oleum—Union Oil Co. .... 10,000,000............ 500
Pittsburg—Columbia Steel Corporation .... 7,000,000............1500
    Redwood Manufacturers Co. .... 4,750,000............ 400
    Pioneer Rubber Mills .... 3,000,000............ 400
    F. E. Booth Co. .... 2,500,000............ 500
    Great Western Electro Chemical Co. .... 1,000,000............ 250
    Pittsburg Fisheries .... 800,000............ 250
    Western California Fish Co. .... 500,000............ 25
    A. B. Davis Fisheries .... 300,000............ 100
    National Chemical Co. .... 85,000............ 45
    Alaska Fishermen 250
    Bundesen & Lauritzen, Shipbuilders 40
    C. A. Hooper Lumber Co. 60
    California Bean Growers 18
    Johns-Mannsville Co. 125
    Pioneer Dairy Co. 35
    Coast Counties Gas & Electric Co. 35
    Standard Oil Co. 50
    Union Oil Co. 20
Port Costa—Port Costa Brick Works 40
    Port Costa Warehouses 400
Richmond—Standard Oil Co. and 20 aux. plnts. 60,000,000............2850
    Pacific Sanitary Mfg. Co. .... 3,000,000............1100
    Certain-Teed Products .... 2,250,000............ 200
    Stauffer Chemical Works .... 1,250,000............ 50
    California Cap Works .... 685,000............ 120
    California Art Tile Co. 65
    Blake Bros. Quarry .... 500,000............ 50
    E. M. Tilden Mills .... 165,000............ 40
    Hutchinson Quarry Co. .... 190,000............ 30
    Pacific Vegetable Oil & Lead Co. .... 275,000............ 25
    Princeton Knitting Mills .... 250,000............ 45
    Pullman Car Shops 750
    Republic Steel Package Co. 20
    Richmond Pressed Brick Co. .... 250,000............ 50
    Santa Fe Railway Shops 700
    Standard Sanitary Manufacturing Co. 1000

Selby—Selby Smelting & Lead Co. ....$60,000,000............ 450
Stege—Wheeler, Reynolds & Stauffer 25
    Stege Lumber Co. 40
Walnut Creek—Cal. Walnut Growers' Assn. 35
    Walnut Creek Canning Co. 35
    Tilden Mill & Lumber Co., various plants 40
    Southern Pacific Railroad Co. 500
    Pacific Gas & Electric Co. 50

CHAPTER IV

COUNTY OFFICERS

The officers of Contra Costa County, from the time of its organization down to the present, are chronologically listed below under their official titles.

SENATORS

1850, W. R. Bascom; 1851, G. B. Tingley; 1852, Jacob Gruwell; 1854, W. H. McCoun; 1856, A. R. Meloney; 1858, G. W. Dent; 1860, A. Inman; 1862, C. B. Porter; 1867, J. J. Green; 1871, D. Goodale; 1875, Paul Shirley; 1879, W. H. Sears; 1882, W. B. English; 1884, Frank C. DeLong; 1886, J. P. Abbott; 1900, C. M. Belshaw; 1908, E. B. Martinelli; 1916, J. C. Owens; 1918, W. R. Sharkey.

ASSEMBLYMEN

1850, Elam Brown; 1851, N. B. Smith; 1852, H. W. Carpenter; 1853, F. M. Warmcastle; 1854, Warren Brown; 1855, A. R. Meloney; 1856, A. Inman; 1857, F. M. Warmcastle; 1858, B. S. Hines; 1859, C. Yager; 1860, C. B. Porter; 1862, T. B. Wright; 1865, T. A. Brown; 1869, J. H. Carothers; 1871, J. W. Galloway; 1873, A. W. Hammitt; 1875, Charles Wood; 1877, A. J. Young; 1879, D. N. Sherburne; 1880, J. P. Jones; 1882, G. W. Carter; 1886, D. N. Sherburne; 1890, G. W. Carter; 1892, H. Hook; 1894, C. M. Belshaw; 1900, M. B. Ivory; 1902, Henry Ells; 1906, P. C. Campbell; 1908, T. D. Johnson; 1910, M. R. Jones; 1916, T. D. Johnson; 1918, W. E. Calahan.

DISTRICT JUDGES

1850, J. H. Watson; 1851, C. P. Hester; 1853, E. W. McKinstry; 1863, T. A. Brown, 1865, S. H. Dwinnelle, who served until 1879, when the office was abolished.

COUNTY JUDGES AND SUPERIOR JUDGES

1855, R. N. Wood; 1856, T. A. Brown; 1863, Mark Shepard; 1871, C. W. Lander; 1875, T. A. Brown, who served until 1879, when the office was abolished and the superior bench was organized, to which he was elected, being continued in the office until 1886. He was succeeded by J. P. Jones, who served until 1900. W. S. Wells was appointed to succeed Jones, and in 1908 Fred V. Wood succeeded to the office, serving until 1914, when R. H. Latimer was elected. H. V. Alvarado was appointed upon the death of Latimer and is still in office. In 1915 Department 2 was organized, and A. B. McKenzie was appointed and later elected, and is still in office.

ASSOCIATE JUSTICES OF COURT OF SESSIONS

1850, A. Peak and E. G. Guest. Guest resigned and S. J. Tennent was appointed August 19, 1850. 1851, B. R. Holliday and A. R. Meloney; 1852, E. G. Weld succeeded Holliday; 1853, G. F. Worth and J. M. Blood; 1854, J. B. Richardson and L. S. Knowles; 1857, F. Vanderwenter and Thomas Russell; 1860, R. P. White succeeded Vanderwenter and that same year the office was abolished.

JUSTICES OF THE PEACE

The county started out in 1850 with six justices of the peace, viz.: B. R. Holliday, A. Peak, E. G. Guest, S. J. Tennent, J. S. Beemer and José J. Estudillo.

In 1851 Edson Adams succeeded Peak from Brooklyn, and A. R. Meloney succeeded Guest

In 1852 William Hillegass succeeded Holliday, G. M. Blake succeeded Adams, S. Baldwin succeeded Meloney, and A. W. Genung succeeded S. J. Tennent.

In 1853 the following justices were elected: M. Cole, G. F. Worth, P. M. Lea, J. M. Blood, G. W. Kimball, J. G. Perkins, A. R. Meloney, D. Hodges.

In 1854 two justices were elected from each newly made district, viz.: M. Bowen and G. F. Worth, district No. 1; G. W. Hammitt and H. B. Hale, district No. 2; A. B. Bates and L. S. Knowles, district No. 3; S. Stone and J. F. Alsop, district No. 4; F. Mitchell and S. Pacheco, district No. 5; and J. B. Richardson and S. Adams, district No. 6.

In 1855 R. A. Madison and G. M. Jones were elected in district No. 1, M. M. Mentlo and D. Meacham in district No. 2, W. Whipple and J. Huff in district No. 3, D. P. Smith and S. A. Reeves in district No. 4, R. Desty and B. Clark in district No. 5, F. Latture and William Wyatt in district No. 6.

In 1856 L. E. Morgan succeeded Jones in No. 1; L. C. Wittenmyer succeeded Meacham in No. 2, J. L. Bromley and F. Latture succeeded Whipple and Huff in No. 3, and the extra three townships were consolidated with the first three.

In 1857 George Christian succeeded Madison in No. 1, F. Vanderwenter succeeded Mentlo in No. 2, L. M. Brown succeeded Wittenmyer in No. 2, J. C. McMaster and Thomas Russell succeeded Bromley and Latture in No. 3.

In 1858 E. F. Weld and Thomas Reynolds were elected in No. 1, F. Vanderwenter and Joseph Venable in No. 2, J. H. Russell and C. E. Wetmore in No. 3.

In 1859 A. F. Dyer succeeded Reynolds in No. 1, and J. W. Maxey and L. M. Brown were elected in No. 2.

In 1860, in No. 2, R. P. White succeeded L. M. Brown and J. W. Venable succeeded J. W. Maxey; and John Osborne succeeded Russell in No. 3.

In 1861 H. M. Stanage was elected to succeed Venable in No. 2; P. Germain and William Girvan were elected in No. 3.

In 1862 the justices were as follows: W. K. Leavitt and George F. Pease, Twp. No. 1; G. W. Hammitt and James Foster, Twp. No. 2; J. T. Cruickshank and William Girvan, Twp. No. 3.

In 1864, in Twp. No. 1, O. F. James succeeded Leavitt, and A. F. Dyer was elected over Pease; H. M. Stanage succeeded Foster in No. 2, and C. P. Marsh and John Phillips were elected in No. 3.

In 1865 the justices were: O. F. James and A. F. Dyer in Twp. No. 1, G. W. Hammitt and A. W. Hammitt in Twp. No. 2, E. S. Sayles and J. J. McNulty in Twp. No. 3.

These officers held until the election in 1867, when John C. Dodd and T. D. Palmer were elected in Twp. No. 1, H. M. Stanage and James Foster in Twp. No. 2, and J. W. Hook succeeded E. S. Sayles in No. 3.

In 1868 C. W. Lander succeeded Dodd in Twp. No. 1, and the others were reelected in their various townships.

In 1869 H. Allen and S. C. Wilbur were elected in Twp. No. 1, John Slitz and Charles Woods in Twp. No. 2, D. Mayon and H. Ashbrook in Twp. No. 3.

In 1871 W. H. Ford and T. D. Palmer were elected in Twp. No. 1, and D. S. Carpenter succeeded Mayon in Twp. No. 3. In 1872-1873 Twp. No. 4 was created, with G. R. Oliver as the justice; the justices from the other three townships held over.

In 1873 J. R. Young and J. J. Kerr represented Twp. No. 2; G. R. Oliver and Samuel Bacon, Twp. No. 3; D. S. Carpenter and A. Pray, Twp. No. 4; and D. P. Mahan and D. K. Berry, the new Twp. No. 5.

In 1875 the list reads: W. H. Ford and T. D. Palmer, Twp. No. 1; John Slitz and J. J. Kerr, Twp. No. 2; G. R. Oliver and Samuel Bacon, Twp. No. 3; D. S. Carpenter and D. S. Woodruff, Twp. No. 4; A. Richardson and T. D. Uren, Twp. No. 5.

In 1877 A. Rumrill succeeded Palmer in No. 1, M. H. Turner and Henry Shuey were elected in No. 2, J. F. Harding succeeded Oliver in No. 3, James Rankin succeeded Woodruff in No. 4, J. E. W. Carey succeeded Richardson in No. 5.

In 1879 Henry Hurst succeeded Shuey, R. H. Latimer succeeded Bacon, A. W. Hall and H. Ingram were elected in No. 4, and J. P. Abbott and H. B. Jewett in No. 5.

In 1880 W. H. Ford and A. Rumrill held office in Twp. No. 1; M. H. Turner and Charles Woods, in Twp. No. 2; H. J. Wilson and R. H. Latimer, in Twp. No. 3; Robert Hastie and H. Ingram, in Twp. No. 4; R. Shipley and J. P. Abbott, in Twp. No. 5.

The list for the year 1881-1882 was: M. H. Bailhache and A. Rumrill, Twp. No. 1; M. H. Turner and S. F. Ramage, Twp. No. 2; H. J. Wilson and J. F. Harding, Twp. No. 3; Robert Hastie and A. W. Wall, Twp. No. 4; J. P. Abbott and J. E. W. Carey, Twp. No. 5. W. H. Ford, who had held office in Twp. No. 1 for many years, died and Mr. Bailhache took his place.

In 1882-1883 F. M. Smith succeeded Bailhache and D. D. Wills succeeded Carey. No. 6 was created and S. F. Ramage was elected.

1884 witnessed a change as well as additional justices. F. M. Smith held over in No. 1, W. M. Downey succeeded Rumrill, T. S. Braw and J. S. Warren were elected in No. 2, M. Turner and G. W. Hammitt in No. 3, S. F. Ramage and W. J. Perkins in No. 4, J. F. Harding and S. C. Nichols in No. 5, and R. Hastie and W. Parsons in No. 6; and F. Clifford and A. W. Wall were elected for the new district No. 7, D. D. Wills and J. O. Diffin in the new No. 8, J. E. W. Carey and W. K. Doherty in the new No. 9, and W. J. Duffy and J. Brunson in the new No. 10.

In 1886 the new men in office were: J. H. Livingston, No. 1; H. P. Edwards and J. Casey, No. 2; A. B. Harrison, No. 3; W. A. Hammitt and J. J. Burke, No. 5; P. Daley, No. 7; B. F. Haney, No. 8; and D. N. Williams, No. 10.

1890 saw many new faces among the justices. D. J. West succeeded Smith and J. B. Smith succeeded Livingston in No. 1; H. P. Edwards held over; M. W. O'Neill succeeded Casey in No. 2; F. E. Weston succeeded Harrison in No. 3; G. W. Hammitt held over in No. 3, as did S. F. Ramage in No. 4; J. A. Shuey was elected over Perkins in No. 4; W. A. Hammitt and J. J. Burke held over in No. 5; William Hawes and O. N. Rogers succeeded Hastie and Parsons in No. 6; Wall held over and F. Clifford succeeded P. Daley in No. 7; W. Gribble and C. F. Montgomery succeeded Wills and Haney in No. 8; J. E. W. Carey held over and T. E. Middleton succeeded Doherty in No. 9; Duffy held over and H. C. F. Dohrman was elected over Williams in No. 10.

In 1894 the following were elected: No. 1, F. M. Smith and J. B. Smith; No. 2, J. P. Casey and M. W. O'Neill; No. 3, F. E. Weston and J. M. Simpson; No. 4, S. F. Ramage and A. E. Clarke; No. 5, W. A. Hammitt and J. M. Goodale; No. 6, H. McDonald and O. N. Rogers; No. 7, William Thomas and G. R. Jones; No. 8, William Gribble and N. A. Tyler; No. 9, C. M. Chapman and L. Arnstroff; No. 10, John Wilcox and Henry Cocks.

In 1898 the following justices were elected: No. 1, D. S. Carpenter; No. 2, J. P. Casey; No. 3, N. B. Rogers; No. 4, W. C. Lewis; No. 5, J. J. Burke; No. 6, O. N. Rogers; No. 7, P. Brown; No. 8, E. Stinchfield; No. 9, C. M. Chapman; No. 10, W. Lindsey; No. 11, J. Garrity; No. 12, T. B. Pratt; No. 13, R. Hastie; No. 14, L. Arnstroff; No. 15, W. Hough; No. 16, Joel Harlan.

In 1902 D. S. Carpenter and J. P. Casey were reelected in Nos. 1 and 2; W. H. Hough was elected in No. 3; S. F. Ramage, No. 4; J. J. Burke, No. 5; J. Fitzgerald, No. 6; J. J. Dickinson, No. 7; A. C. Hartley, No. 8; C. M. Chapman, No. 9; E. B. Masterson, No. 10; J. V. Enloe, No. 11; M. W. O'Neill, No. 12; G. Goethels, No. 13; J. F. Carey, No. 14.

In 1906 the following were elected: C. H. Hayden, No. 1; J. P. Casey, No. 2; W. H. Hough, No. 3; A. E. Clark, No. 4; J. J. Burke, No. 5; J. Fitzgerald, No. 6; A. C. Hartley, No. 8; A. W. Callis, No. 9; E. B. Masterson, No. 10; J. V. Enloe, No. 11; M. W. O'Neill, No. 12; G. L. Goethels, No. 13; A. J. LeGrand, No. 14; John Roth, No. 15.

DISTRICT ATTORNEYS

1850, J. F. Williams; 1852, T. T. Bouldin; 1853, H. Mills; 1857, E. Parker. May 3, 1858, W. W. Theobalds was appointed, vice Parker. 1861, Mark Shepard; 1863, H. Mills; 1875, J. P. Jones; 1877, F. M. Warmcastle; 1879, Eli R. Chase; 1884, W. S. Tinning; 1894, C. Y. Brown; 1902, H. V. Alvarado; 1910, A. B. McKenzie, who resigned to become superior judge in Department 2, January 2, 1915; 1914, T. D. Johnson; 1918, A. B. Tinning, who is the present incumbent.

COUNTY CLERKS, RECORDERS, AND (AFTER 1855) AUDITORS

1850, T. A. Brown; 1855, C. Yager. In 1855 the office of county auditor was established and combined with those of county clerk and county recorder under Yager. 1857, L. C. Wittenmyer; 1863, G. P. Loucks; 1867, L. C. Wittenmyer; 1869, A. J. Markley; 1870, L. C. Wittenmyer, appointed vice Markley, deceased; 1871, G. J. Bennett; 1873, L. C. Wittenmyer, who served in the three offices combined until 1875, when each office was given a separate official.

COUNTY CLERKS

1875, L. C. Wittenmyer; 1890, F. L. Glass; 1892, L. C. Wittenmyer; 1894, F. L. Glass; 1898, J. E. Rodgers, who served until 1908, when J. H. Wells was appointed to fill the vacancy caused by his resignation. In 1910 J. H. Wells was elected, and is still in office.

COUNTY AUDITORS

1875, M. H. Bailhache; 1879, J. W. Darby; February 25, 1880, J. D. Darby, vice J. W. Darby, deceased; 1881, J. D. Darby; 1882, A. J. Soto; 1886, C. Ed. Curry; 1890, A. J. Soto; 1906, A. N. Sullenger, who still holds office.

COUNTY RECORDERS

1875, W. B. Russell; 1877, C. Ed. Miller; 1880, J. D. Darby; 1881, C. Ed. Miller; 1882, Charles S. Cousins; 1894, A. E. Dunkel; 1906,

M. H. Hurley, who held office until his death in 1924. On February 9, Flora Irene Hurley, his widow, was appointed, and still holds the office.

COUNTY SHERIFFS

1850, Nathaniel Jones; 1852, N. Hunsaker; 1853, J. F. S. Smith; 1855, N. Hunsaker; 1857, J. C. Hunsaker; 1861, J. J. McEwen; 1865, H. Clausen; 1867, R. B. Hard; 1869, W. Brown; 1871, M. B. Ivory; 1875, F. Wilkening; 1877, D. P. Mahan; 1884, James Rankin; 1890, C. W. Rogers; 1894, R. R. Veale, who has served to the present date.

COUNTY TAX COLLECTORS AND TREASURERS

1850, D. Hunsaker, who resigned April 23, 1853, B. R. Holliday being appointed in his stead; 1853, Robert E. Borden; 1857, H. Fogg; March 2, 1861, S. Swain, appointed vice Fogg, deceased; 1861, O. F. Alley; 1869, J. R. L. Smith. In 1873, the two offices were each supplied, each with an incumbent. J. R. L. Smith continued as treasurer until 1875.

TAX COLLECTORS

1873, M. B. Ivory; 1875, H. Gallagher; 1879, W. Shuey; October 3, 1881, D. S. Carpenter, vice Shuey, deceased; 1894, H. C. Raap, who served until G. E. Searcy was elected in 1906. In 1910, M. W. Joost was elected, and is still serving.

COUNTY TREASURERS

1875, A. Tyler; 1877, R. D. Hathaway; 1890, P. L. Roberts; 1894, J. O. Sherburne; 1898, R. L. Ulsh; 1902, T. A. Wiley, who served until 1910, when L. N. Buttner was elected. He died in 1913 and was succeeded by J. R. Baker, who in turn was succeeded by C. L. Dodge, the present incumbent.

COUNTY ASSESSORS

1850, N. B. Smith; 1852, L. H. Hastings; 1853, J. M. Jones; 1855, O. F. Alley; 1857, J. F. S. Smith; 1859, J. J. White; 1861, N. J. Clark; 1863, Philip Sage; 1865, F. A. Matthews, who resigned August 2, 1869, J. L. Bromley being appointed in his stead; 1869, James Foster; 1879, J. N. Stow; 1886, F. Williams; 1894, H. T. Jones; 1910, G. O. Meese, who is still serving.

PUBLIC ADMINISTRATORS

1852, W. W. Chipman; 1853, N. Jones; 1854, J. A. Morgan; 1855, George Langdon; 1857, M. R. Barber; 1859, B. R. Holliday; 1861, M. R. Barber; 1863, D. S. Woodruff; 1865, J. E. Stevens; 1867, D. Small. He resigned August 8, 1868, and B. R. Holliday was appointed. 1869, R. B. Brock; March 19, 1872, E. W. Heller, appointed vice Brock, deceased; 1881, J. W. Guy; 1884, E. W. Heller; 1886, G. H. Scammon; May, 1891, Charles Wood appointed vice Scammon, deceased; 1894, F. W. Gunther; 1898, J. Bendixen; 1902, M. H. Hurley; 1910, C. E. Daley; 1922, Raymond Johnson, who is still in office.

COUNTY CORONERS

In 1855 the office of county coroner was formally established and William Armstrong was elected. He resigned and L. H. Hastings was appointed January 14, 1856. These followed: 1856, W. A. J. Gift; March 2, 1857, J. F. S. Smith appointed to fill vacancy; 1857, J. M. Sutton; 1858, John Tennent; June 9, 1859, C. H. Ruggles appointed vice Tennent; November 8, 1859, E. T. Hough, appointed; 1860, J. L. Labaree; 1861, H. H. Fassett; 1863, E. T. Hough; 1866, J. H. Carothers; 1869, C. A. Ruggles; 1871, J. H. Livingston; 1875, E. W. Hiller. In 1875 the office was combined with that of public administrator and E. W. Hiller was elected to the two offices; he was succeeded by J. W. Guy in 1879. In 1884 the offices again became separated and J. W. Guy was succeeded by W. Dunnigan; 1886, J. W. Guy; 1890, H. J. Curry; 1892, J. C. McMaster; 1894, H. J. Curry; 1906, C. L. Abbott; May, 1918, Bert Curry appointed vice C. L. Abbott; 1918, C. F. Donnelly, who was succeeded by Aubrey Wilson in 1926.

COUNTY SURVEYORS

1850, W. Brown; 1853, T. M. Aull; 1855, D. Small; 1859, George Vosberg; January 2, 1860, J. B. Abbott, vice Dixon, resigned; December 2, 1861, K. W. Taylor was appointed, vice Abbott; 1861, John Doherty; 1862, K. W. Taylor; 1867, T. A. Talleyrand; 1871, Robert Hunt; 1873, R. Eddy; 1875, R. M. Jones; September 16, 1879, T. A. McMahon, vice Jones; 1880, T. A. McMahon; 1890, Elam C. Brown; 1892, T. A. McMahon; 1894, Elam C. Brown; 1914, R. R. Arnold, who still holds the office.

SUPERINTENDENTS OF SCHOOLS

1855, J. Vandermark; January 6, 1856, Thomas Ewing, vice Vandermark, resigned; 1856, J. M. Jones; 1857, E. H. Cox; 1859, A. F. Dyer; 1861, D. S. Woodruff; 1863, J. F. S. Smith; March 19, 1864, H. R. Avery, vice Smith, resigned; 1864, H. R. Avery; 1867, A. Thurber; 1871, H. S. Raven; 1873, A. Thurber; 1877, E. Wemple; 1879, A. A. Bailey; 1886, W. A. Kirkwood; 1894, A. M. Phalin; 1902, A. A. Bailey; 1906, W. H. Hanlon, who is still in office.

COUNTY COMMISSIONER AND COUNTY PHYSICIANS

In 1898 L. C. Wittenmyer was elected county commissioner.

On February 8, 1872, C. R. Holbrook was appointed county physician.

On August 5, 1874, J. H. Carothers was appointed county physician vice Holbrook.

In 1898 C. E. Brown was elected county physician.

There appear to have been no further elections to these offices until 1922, when E. Merrithew was elected county physician.

COUNTY SUPERVISORS

In 1851 the board of supervisors came into being, S. L. Robinson, Victor Castro, Robert Farrelly, William Patten, and T. J. Keefer being elected.

In 1852 C. Lund succeeded Castro, and E. W. Winn succeeded Farrelly.

In 1853 an entire new board was elected, viz.: A. W. Genung, Joseph Martin, C. W. Ish, I. Hunsaker and J. C. McMaster, who were to serve two years.

In 1855 the county was districted into three districts and two men were elected from each, viz.: No. 1, J. H. Livingston and T. A. Brown; No. 2, L. E. Morgan and N. Jones; No. 3, W. R. Bishop and C. E. Wetherbee.

In 1856 J. Emeric from No. 1, Ira J. True from No. 2, and A. Olmstead from No. 3 succeeded Livingston, Morgan and Bishop.

In 1857 J. L. Bromley succeeded Olmstead in No. 3; in 1860 J. T. Walker succeeded Bromley in No. 3; in 1861 G. H. Barrett succeeded Emeric in No. 1; in 1862 J. R. L. Smith succeeded True in No. 2; in 1863 R. G. Davis succeeded Walker in No. 3; in 1864 J. Tewksbury succeeded Barrett in No. 1; in 1865 D. N. Sherburne succeeded Smith in No. 2; in 1866 R. B. Hard succeeded Davis in No. 3; in 1867 John Tormey succeeded Tewksbury in No. 1; in 1868 R. H. Wright succeeded Hard in No. 3; in 1872 P. Walker succeeded Wright; in 1873 G. P. Loucks succeeded Walker in No. 3; P. Walker was elected from the new district No. 4, and J. C. McMaster from No. 5.

In 1877 Patrick Tormey succeeded John Tormey in No. 1, and W. Renwick succeeded Sherburne in No. 2. In 1878 W. B. English succeeded Loucks in No. 3; in 1880 D. N. Sherburne succeeded Renwick in No. 2; in 1882 T. E. Middleton succeeded Sherburne in No. 2, B. F. Beebe was elected over English in No. 3, and W. Nellis succeeded Walker in No. 4. In 1884 John Galindo succeeded Beebe in No. 3, P. Walker was again returned in No. 4, and Martin Flynn succeeded McMaster in No. 5. J. D. Bowen died in 1885 and P. Brown was appointed to fill the vacancy.

In 1886 J. Kelly succeeded Middleton in No. 2, and C. J. Clayton succeeded Walker in No. 4. In 1892 J. M. Stow was elected in No. 2 in place of Kelly, and M. B. Ivory in place of Flynn in No. 5. In 1894 A. Rumrill was elected over Tormey in No. 1, and D. F. Majors over Galindo in No. 3.

In 1896 William Hemme was elected in No. 1, Paul de Martini in No. 2, and J. D. Wightman in No. 3. In 1898 P. Tormey was elected in No. 1, William Hemme in No. 2, E. J. Randall in No. 3, Paul de Martini in No. 4, and J. D. Wightman in No. 5. In 1900 J. M. Stow was elected in No. 2, Paul de Martini in No. 4, and J. D. Wightman in No. 5. In 1902 P. Tormey was elected in No. 1, and E. J. Randall in No. 3. In 1904 R. Harrison was elected in No. 2, W. J. Buchanan in No. 4, and J. H. Trythall in No. 5. In 1906 V. Hook was elected in No. 3. In 1908 Charles Rihn was elected in No. 1, and J. P. Casey in No. 2. In 1914

Zeb Knott was elected in No. 1, and in 1918 C. H. Hayden was elected in No. 3. Casey served until his death in 1923, and in April, 1923, Oscar Olsson was appointed his successor.

The members of the board of supervisors at the present time (1926) are: For district No. 1, Zeb Knott; for No. 2, Oscar Olsson; for No. 3, C. H. Hayden; for No. 4, W. J. Buchanan; for No. 5, R. J. Trembath.

CHAPTER V

MARTINEZ

The town of Martinez had its beginning in 1849, when Col. William M. Smith, then acting as agent for the Martinez heirs, decided to lay out a townsite. As early as 1823, Ignacio Martinez and Francisco Castro applied for and were granted the Pinole and San Pablo Ranchos, comprising many leagues of land. They erected adobe houses and barns, began planting trees and vines, and became the first fruit and grape growers in Contra Costa County. There were no roads, only trails through the valleys and over the hills; however, other families followed the example of these two pioneers and established homes for themselves. These two pioneer families were the center of all local social gatherings, and a typical Spanish hospitality was always extended by them and their neighbors.

In 1832 William Welch secured title to a tract of land known as the Las Juntas Rancho, on which a portion of the city of Martinez now stands. In 1849 Col. William M. Smith secured the services of T. A. Brown to survey and lay out a town on 120 acres on the west side of El Hambre Creek. Lots sold rapidly, and soon buildings were in the course of construction. The first building was the house of Dr. Leffler, erected by Nicholas Hunsaker. T. A. Brown built the second structure and, with his brother Warren and N. B. Smith, opened and conducted the first trading post in the county. Boorman and Dana also had a store in 1849, as did Howard & Wells; the latter was managed by one Howard Havens. That same year the Bradley house was completed, and N. Jones erected a cottage next to the Berryessa adobe. Dr. Tennent was the first physician and Seeley Bennett the first livery stable man in the town.

In 1850-1851 T. A. Brown surveyed the first addition to the new town, under orders from the owners of the Welch Rancho, El Hambre Creek being the dividing line. There were over 500 acres in this tract, and the first buildings were the residences of Messrs. Lawless, Wise, Douglas, McMahon, and Bolton. It is well to mention that the Douglas home was the office of the first county clerk. There was also erected the office of the Contra Costa News, the first newspaper in the county.

VIEWS OF MARTINEZ IN 1868, TAKEN FROM TOP OF COURT HOUSE

In 1850 a negro named Jones opened the first eating house on the site of the Alhambra Hotel. In 1851 Teodoro Soto built an adobe home, later known as the Hickman adobe.

The first school was started in a house later occupied by T. A. Brown. The school room was also the meeting place of the court when in session; also church services were held in it on Sundays. The Masonic lodge met in the rooms in the second story. B. R. Holliday was the first school teacher in the town of Martinez, where he conducted a private school, and R. B. McNair is on record as the second teacher, and the first public school teacher.

In 1852 the Union Hotel was built. This was run by R. E. Borden, who was also the county treasurer.

A petition was circulated and presented to the court of sessions to have the town incorporated, which was done, and the election was held on February 5, 1851, for the first board of trustees. Not long thereafter the supreme court held that the act under which the incorporation was made was void; and as the costs necessary to another election were deemed excessive by the citizens, the matter was dropped, to be revived again in 1876, when the incorporation became an actuality.

On August 2, 1852, the first execution took place, when José Antonio was hanged for the murder of A. Morales on May 29, 1852. He was taken to the edge of the village and hanged from the limb of a sycamore.

The second execution in Contra Costa County was that of a man named Monroe, who murdered a Mr. Briggs near Marsh's Landing. He was hanged from the limb of a tree near the old Martinez school building in September, 1854. The third hanging took place in the jail yard at Martinez, when Manuel Juarez was executed for the murder of Elizabeth Robinson, an aged women who lived alone. He was hanged on July 28, 1867, declaring he was innocent.

The Methodist Episcopal church was established in 1854; the Episcopal in 1855; and in 1866 a Sunday school and library were established by the Episcopalians; and their church was built in 1869, as noted later.

On September 18, 1858, the Contra Costa Gazette was established as a weekly newspaper and the first paper was issued by W. B. Soule & Company. This paper withstood the ravages of time and never missed an issue in sixty-eight years. The complete files of the paper are the repository of much of the real history of Contra Costa County found in this book. W. B. Soule & Company were in turn succeeded by C. R. K. Bonnard and B. E. Hillman. On February 26, 1859, W. Bradford bought the paper; on April 28, 1860, he sold a half-interest to R. R. Bunker, and on March 23, 1861, sold the balance to W. W. Theobalds. The paper was moved to the fast-growing town of Pacheco in 1861, which was then the grain-shipping center. In 1865 C. B. Porter bought out Theobalds' interest. In 1871 a disastrous fire completely destroyed the plant, and in November, 1873, it was moved back to Martinez, its present site. On March 3, 1882, F. K. Foster purchased a third interest. On November 3, 1883, Porter sold out to Bunker and Foster, and on August 27, 1887, T. S. Davenport bought out Foster. It appeared as a semi-weekly on January 4, 1888. On October 3, of that year, James Foster purchased a half-interest from Davenport, but this was sold to W. C. Brown after Foster's death. On January 7, 1893, the paper was restored to a weekly. In 1898 Brown sold to G. E. Milnes, and in 1907 Milnes sold to W. A. Rugg, who had established the first successful daily paper in Martinez, the Daily Press, on March 1, 1900. Four years later the Press was sold to the Gazette Publishing Company and the name was changed to the Daily Gazette. Mr. Rugg still owns the paper.

The California Express was published in 1867 by Alex Montgomery, and continued for nearly two years.

J. W. Collier started the Enterprise in 1871. It was a Democratic sheet, printed in San Francisco. It only lived a short time.

The Contra Costa News was established in Pacheco in 1873, was removed to Martinez in 1877, and is now one of the influential weeklies of the county.

The Martinez Daily Standard and the Contra Costa Standard are published in conjunction by the Contra Costa Publishing Company. The daily was established in 1911.

Martinez and Benicia were joined by telegraph on April 8, 1859, and that same year Mette & Company established the first stage line between Martinez and Oakland. On September 17, 1860, the Martinez Engine Company was organized. In May, 1867, Coffin & Standish erected the first flouring mill. On February 4, 1871, the Martinez Hook & Ladder Company was organized, and on September 5 of that year the Martinez Water Company was incorporated. The new bridge over Alhambra Creek was opened to traffic on November 13, 1875.

Grace Episcopal Church was built in 1869, E. P. Gray serving as the first pastor. On June 18, 1874, the Congregational Church was organized with W. S. Clark as the first pastor.

In 1876 agitation was renewed for reincorporating the city, and on May 23 the election for city officers was held. The boundaries of the town as finally incorporated were as follows: "Beginning at a point where the fence dividing the lands of J. P. Jones and L. I. Fish touches the Straits of Carquinez, thence southwardly along said fence and continuing same course to the line of the homestead tract of H. Bush; thence westerly along the north line of Bush's homestead tract to Arroyo del Hambre; thence southerly along said Arroyo to the center of G Street, to the western boundary of the town of Martinez as originally surveyed; thence northwardly following the western boundary of the town plat to the Straits of Carquinez, to place of beginning." In July, 1880, the population of Martinez was 875.

In 1879 the Bush property was purchased for a Catholic college, which was later built by the Christian Brothers and given the name of De La Salle Institute. In 1850-1851 the Catholics used Brown's store for church services. They then began an adobe building, but never completed it. In November, 1858, they erected a church, which blew down in 1866; then another, the present building, was erected.

Shirley & Mizner operated a ferry between Benicia and Martinez, landing at the foot of Ferry Street, so named. In 1878 they sold out to the Northern Railway Company, and this company, with the San Pablo and Tulare Railway Company, constructed the first railroad through the city of Martinez.

In 1882 the Martinez Packing Company was established; and a salmon cannery was also operated by Joseph Black, both at a time when the fishing industry meant much to the town. The Pacific Coast Steel & Iron Manufacturing Company was built in 1884.

In 1887, B. Fernandez erected the Martinez Hotel on the site of the Morgan House, which had burned down; the property had been bought up by Fernandez. In 1887, also, the Martinez Electric Light & Gas Company was organized.

Several fires have devastated Martinez, and mention is here made of the more destructive ones. In September, 1856, the Union Hotel and Blum's, Lazar's and Hook's stores were burned. In July, 1867, fire destroyed the Gift mansion. On December 12, 1876, several buildings at the southwest corner of Main and Ferry Streets were burned; on March 16, 1877, the residence of Mrs. Chase; on January 6, 1878, Granger's Restaurant; and on March 8, 1880, the Alhambra schoolhouse. The next serious conflagration was the disastrous fire of August 19, 1904, when over half the business houses were burned and two entire blocks were laid in ashes, with the greatest financial loss the city ever experienced. Again, a fire occurred on July 16, 1925, that burned several business places on the corner opposite from the one above mentioned.

The earthquake of October 21, 1868, did considerable damage. It razed two walls of the Alhambra Hotel, threw down the walls of the court house, top and rear, and did minor damages to many smaller buildings. On April 18, 1906, slight damage was done to chimneys, but otherwise the city experienced no harm.

The buildings constructed in the last two decades have been modern in every respect. The county hospital building was built at a cost of $70,000, in 1910. The city hall was built in 1911. The court house, costing $600,000, was erected of granite in 1901. The Alhambra High School was erected in 1904, and the grammar school in 1909.

The Alhambra Water Company, established in 1903, began bottling water piped from the famous Alhambra Springs, and shipping to various parts of the country.

The Mococo, or Mountain Copper Company, established its smelting plant here in 1905. It employs 400 men, with a payroll of $500,000 annually. The California Transportation Company built a wharf and began making regular calls at Martinez in 1909. In 1911 the city established its municipal wharf under a bond issue.

In 1911 the Pacific Gas & Electric Company bought out the Contra Costa Electric Light & Power Company; and the Great Western Power Company entered this field in 1913. The Contra Costa Gas Company was established in 1915. The Martinez-Benicia Ferry was established in 1913.

In 1914 the city experienced its first real boom, when the Shell Oil Company chose Martinez as the site for the central base of their future operations. Hundreds of families settled in the town, homes began springing up everywhere, and the business district enlarged accordingly. The Shell Company bought the Cutler, Potter and Arnstein properties, comprising about 400 acres adjoining the city, and began by erecting a $5,-000,000 oil refinery and employing some 2000 men. From that date to the present time the policy of the company has been one of expansion, and this has meant prosperity for the entire city. The Shell Company was followed by the Associated Oil Company.

The streets are all paved, many miles of sidewalks built of cement have been installed, and the water mains have been extended to all the additions. The State Highway traverses the county via the Tunnel Road to Berkeley, and also via Franklin Canyon and Pinole.

CHAPTER VI

RICHMOND
By CLARENCE A. ODELL

The first inhabitants of Richmond and the surrounding country were of a prehistoric race, as we learn by investigation of the Indian or shell mounds, of which there are several located in this county. Among those in this vicinity is the one at the mouth of Wild Cat Creek; a larger one just behind the Mastersen Hotel at San Pablo, about 300 feet north from the old Alvarado Hacienda; and another that was occupied by the house of Antone Luis, not far from the San Pablo station of the Southern Pacific Railroad; but the most important of them all is the one at Ellis Landing. These shell mounds, or "kitchen middens," as they are sometimes designated by scientists, who are much interested in them because of the anthropological and historic facts which they disclose, are composed of the accretions of centuries of tribal life. All the offal, refuse and debris, as well as burials of generations succeeding generations, have, from the dead level, built up mounds that represent alike the abodes and the history of the dusky aborigines.

The Ellis Landing shell mound is situated east from Ellis Landing, on the northwest shore of San Francisco Bay proper, directly north of Brooks' Island. It is mostly submerged and imbedded in an average of about thirteen feet of fine silt, but rests on a firm gravel foundation. The mound has a roughly triangular outline. With the shore as a base, it stretches out about 300 feet. The greatest height above the marsh level

MACDONALD AVENUE, RICHMOND, 1925

RICHMOND IN 1900

was seventeen feet, and the greatest depth below the marsh level, about sixteen feet.

Scientists who have investigated this mound have been unable to fix its age. Some state that it is probably 3500 years old; others venture no opinion further than to say it is prehistoric. It is made up of charcoal ashes and shells, of which there were four hundred varieties. In it were found implements, weapons and ornaments already totaling some 630 specimens. Many skeletons have also been unearthed from it. In the graves of the males were found charm stones, obsidian blades and smaller weapons. In the graves of the women were found mortars, pestles and awls; while the infants' graves had in each a handful of disk beads made from the obivelle shell, or pendants of abalone shells.

This mound, like others, was built simply of refuse, and besides being a conspicuous archaeological feature, furnishes incontestible evidence of having survived considerable subsidence of the Bay country, which occurred subsequent to the arrival of primitive man; and it was for these reasons especially investigated by the Department of Anthropology of the University of California. It would seem that it was the custom of these early Richmondites to emigrate to the mountains during the summer to fatten on the berries, pine nuts, acorns and wild game then so freely supplied by nature; and that on the approach of winter they came back to their tepees along or near the bay shore and drew upon the sea for their winter food. From some unknown cause this race of people became extinct; and it is only from the mounds which they left as monuments in this region that we may have any conception of the story of their existence.

Richmond, with a population of 27,000 and an assessed valuation of $27,000,000, is the largest city in Contra Costa County. It is situate on the northeast of a low range of hills formerly known as the "Potrero de San Pablo" (pasture of the San Pablo Rancho), which forms the headland of a broad peninsula projecting from the easterly or mainland shore of the Bay of San Francisco. This peninsula and headland separates San Francisco Bay from San Pablo Bay and the bodies of water above it, viz.: Carquinez Straits, Suisun Straits, Suisun Bay and the deltas of the two great interior rivers of the State, the Sacramento and San Joaquin.

The earliest available record of Richmond and its immediate vicinity is contained in the diary of Rev. Father Crespi, the historian of the first expedition to explore the eastern shore of the Bay of San Francisco, in 1772. In this diary he states that the expedition camped on Cerrito Creek (the county line at El Cerrito, the boundary between Contra Costa and Alameda Counties), where they "killed a fat bear and enjoyed a supply of fresh meat"; the next day, marching on (through what is now Richmond), they "viewed the second arm of the sea or large round bay" (San Pablo Bay). There they noticed a large whale disporting itself, and "therefore infer that this bay is sufficiently deep for large vessels."

From 1772 until April, 1823, there seems to be little, if any, authentic history of this locality; but on April 15, 1823, Francisco Castro presented to the Provincial Assembly (Deputation) of Alta California a memorial stating, that "being the owner of large herds of horned cattle and horses," he finds himself under the necessity, in order to preserve the cattle which he now possesses, and may hereafter possess, and in order to provide for the maintenance of his numerous family, to solicit of the Assembly that a piece or tract of land be given to him for the purpose of fixing his establishment, and asking that it would be pleased to concede to him the "possession of three square leagues [sitios] in the place called 'Los Cuchigunes,' or 'San Pablo,' " and praying that there be given to him the "corresponding possession and ownership of this land, as it may be proper in the premises" for his protection and that of his succession; and thereon the Assembly made the following decree:

"Monterey, April 15th, 1823.

"The Honorable Assembly [Deputation] grants to the claimant the piece of land which he solicits, measuring three square leagues, considering the said claimant entitled to said favor for his services, his known probity and the abundance of stock which he possesses, for which purpose the Government appoints the Commander of the Presidio of San Francisco for the measurement, and giving him possession of the lands for which he petitions."

Said decree was signed "Arguello" and countersigned "José Joaquin de la Torre, Secretary."

On April 15, 1823, Louis Antonio Arguello, whose name is signed to the foregoing decree, was President of the Provincial Assembly (Deputation) of Alta California and was acting as Governor of California.

On January 1, 1827, the said Francisco Castro presented to the Commander-in-Chief (Señor Comandante General) of the Californias a petition stating that he had, on said 15th day of April, 1823, presented to the said Provincial Assembly the said memorial, and that the Assembly had made to him the said order or decree.

The said petition of January 1, 1827, further contained the following: "Considering that to the present time the foregoing decree has not been complied with, the reason therefor being unknown to me, I present myself to you in order that, making use of the powers with which you are invested, you will be pleased to give the orders necessary for the purpose of having the foregoing decree enforced. . . .

"Wherefore I respectfully pray that, taking my petition into consideration, you will be pleased to order all that which you will deem pertinent and reasonable, which favor will, I hope, be granted to me."

On the margin of this petition the following order was made by the Commander-in-Chief of the Californias:

"Port of San Diego, January 29th, 1827.

"The Commander of San Francisco will be pleased to report why the right of possession within referred to was not given."

On July 27, 1827, the said Francisco Castro presented a petition to the Commander-in-Chief and Political Chief (Comandante General y

Gefe Superior Politico) of California, which petition begins as follows:
"Francisco Castro, owner of the Rancho San Pablo, respectfully presents himself to you, and in due form of law exposes," and proceeds to
set forth, "that during four years he has been in possession of said place as
shown by the document respectfully presented to your Honor herewith;
and as in this document, issued by the Most Excellent Deputation, it
appears that it decrees and commands that due possession be given me,
and requires the Commander of San Francisco to do so; that though that
gentleman notifies me for the purpose of giving me said possession, as I
was at that time a member of said Deputation, and was then called to
Monterey on public service, I could not obey said summons, and as from
that day to this I have not as yet been able to settle this matter, I now
have recourse to the well known justice of your Excellency, requesting
that you should be plesaed to order that due possession of said tract of
land be given me."

The petition further states that he has "already built upon said land a
walled house, having a stone fence measuring 40 varas to the other
wooden ones, and planted a garden with many fruit trees therein and a
vineyard containing upwards of one thousand stalks of vines, built a mill,
and sowed thirty fanegas of wheat, and one-half a fanega of corn and
beans each"; that he has "six hundred head of cattle, and five hundred
horses, more or less"; that the tract of land "runs along the bank of the
creek [estero] and shores of the bay [mar] of San Francisco, from north
to northwest from where it bounds with the Rancho of the Sergeant Luis
Peralta."

The "walled house" above referred to was built on or near the southerly banks of Wild Cat Creek, just a little east of the present San Pablo
Avenue. The old adobe house, which has been more or less improved, and
is still standing east of San Pablo Avenue, just a little north of El Cerrito
Creek (the boundary between Alameda and Contra Costa Counties), was
built by Victor Castro, one of the sons of Don Francisco Castro.

On January 30, 1828, Castro again presented his petition to be placed
in possession of said land; and on May 10, 1830, he presented another,
his fifth petition to be put in possession of the land sought, and which
recites that he therefore renews his claim that due possession be given
him of the said tract, and that the amount expended, and the improvements made by his family on the said land "be taken into united
action—the same consists of a house measuring ten varas, and having good
foundations, one thousand stalks of vines, and sundry other plants.

"And in order that this claim be attended with full knowledge of the
facts, and justice rendered me in the present instance, I will add that I am
fifty-five years of age; am married and have ten children; was born in the
town of Cinaloa, in the District of Sonora, which was founded by my
father; that I was for thirteen years a soldier and corporal in the Mexican
artillery; and that I have belonging to me on the tract which I occupy one

thousand four hundred head of cattle, six hundred sheep and five hundred horses."

On this last petition the following marginal decree was made by the Political Chief of Alta California:

"Monterey, 26th May, 1830.

"Let claimant add to his petition a plan [diseño] showing the conformation, extent, and all other important particulars relating to the tract of land claimed by him."

Don Francisco Maria Castro died on November 5, 1831, before any other proceedings were had, leaving a widow, Gabriela Berryessa Castro, seven sons and four daughters surviving him.

On May 26, 1834, Joaquin Ysidro Castro, the son and first executor of the will of said Francisco Castro, presented to the "Political Chief" a petition, stating that in consequence of the death of his father, who had instituted him the heir (heredero) of a portion of his property and guardian of that of his brothers, "as results from the Testament, a copy of which is archived in this Capitol," . . . he solicits the lawful ownership of a tract of land named San Pablo.

The petition proceeds in the following words: "a plan of which I herewith present, together with a copy of the first petition for said tract, presented by my father, dated the 15th day of April, 1823, and copy of the Gubernatorial decree of the same date," and states, "the same having remained without effect, I hereby reiterate the petition, imploring of your Honor the proper documents for the security of the stock which occupies the aforesaid place."

Governor José Figueroa, on June 12, 1834, at Monterey, made a decree and grant, reciting: "Whereas the late Francisco Maria Castro has had granted to him [tiene concedido] by the Most Excellent Territorial Deputation, since the 15th of April, 1823, the land known under the name of Los Cuchigunes or San Pablo, bounded by the Ranchos of San Antonio and El Pinole, and by a portion of the Bay of San Francisco; and whereas, his successors [herederos] subsequently applied for the lawful ownership thereof. . . .

"Now, therefore, using the powers with which I am intrusted, and in the name of the Mexican Nation by decree of this day, I do grant to the said successors the above mentioned land, declaring the same to be their property," etc., subject to the usual conditions, the fourth one being as follows:

"Fourth.—The land of which mention is made is of three square leagues, more or less, according to the diseño which accompanied the expediente granted to them. The Judge who will put them in possession shall cause it to be measured according to law, so that the boundaries may be marked out, the surplus, if any, reverting to the Nation for such uses as may be proper."

On June 23, 1835, the said Joaquin Y. Castro presented to the "Political Chief" a petition for an augmentation of the San Pablo Rancho, reciting: "I have already solicited from your Excellency the legitimate possession of the Rancho San Pablo which we, the heirs of my deceased father, actually occupied, as I have already stated in my first petition, but through inadventence have neglected to ask for the extent of land included in the plan annexed thereto, and have said that I asked for the three square leagues which we anciently occupied. . . .

"This piece of land being rather small for the number of cattle grazing on the same, which number we are exerting ourselves to increase, I solicit you, in the name of the other heirs, and as their attorney in fact, that said petition be understood to include with the three leagues which we occupied the augmentation of the land described in the aforesaid diseño."

On August 14, 1835, Governor Figueroa made an order which recited that "Considering the petition at the beginning of this expediente, and the grant [concession] which was obtained on the 15th day of April, 1823, from the most Excellent Territorial Deputation, the subsequent petition which was made on the 23rd day of June of the present year, praying for the amplification of a little more than a square league according to the diseño marked No. 2, and also such other additional documents as were furnished in conformity with the law and regulations in such cases made and provided, I hereby declare Don Francisco Maria Castro the lawful owner in full property, and by his demise his successors, of the tract of land known under the name of Los Cuchigunes or San Pablo, bounded by the Ranchos of San Antonio and El Pinole, and by a portion of the Port of San Francisco. I order that a good and sufficient title be made out and that the same be registered in the proper record book; that it be delivered to the testamentary executor and heir, Joaquin Ysidro Castro, for all necessary purposes, and that the expediente thereof be archived."

"I, Don José Figueroa, general of brigade of the Mexican republic, commander in general, inspector, and political chief of the territory of Upper California, so order and decree, and in faith thereof hereunto affix my name.

"José Figueroa,
"F'co Del Castillo Negrete, Secretary."

On August 20, 1835, a grant was made by said José Figueroa in the same terms as said grant of 1834 for the whole property, including the augmentation, to the successors of Francisco Maria Castro, and declaring the same to be their property.

On May 22, 1840, the expediente was presented to the Departmental Assembly, and the same was approved by the Assembly on May 30, 1840.

On October 9, 1852, the said Joaquin Ysidro Castro, as "Administrator with the will annexed of the estate of Francisco Maria Castro," filed with the United State Land Commissioners to ascertain and settle private land claims in the State of California, under the Act of Congress of March 3, 1851, a petition for the confirmation of said grant. After other recitals in said petition appears the following: "Petitioner further represents that said Francisco was married to Gabriela Berryessa, and died in the year 1831, leaving surviving him his wife and eleven children, the issue of said marriage being Alvina, Maria de Jesus, Maria, Francisca, Martina, Antonio, Juan José, Gabriel, Victor, Jesus Maria, and petitioner, (Joaquin Ysidro Castro). That the said Francisco left a will signed, attested, and published according to law, whereby he devised and bequeathed to his wife one undivided half of his land and other property, the other half to his said children to be equally divided between them. That said Martina Castro has intermarried with Juan B. Alvarado." . . . "That since the death of Francisco first aforesaid, his said children, Alvina, Maria de Jesus, and Maria died without issue, and their share of said land descended to their said mother, who thereupon became the absolute owner of fourteen twenty-seconds (14/22) of all of said land.

"That afterwards, on the 4th day of August, 1851, said Gabriela Berryessa de Castro, by deed executed the day and year aforesaid, in consideration of the natural love and affection for her said daughter, Martina Castro de Alvarado, gave and conveyed to said Martina all the said interest (14/22) of her, the said Gabriela, to and in said land. That said Martina thereupon became entitled to fifteen twenty-seconds (15/22) of all the land aforesaid."

On April 17, 1855, the claim of petitioner was confirmed and adjudged to be valid. Such further proceedings were had that the claim was finally confirmed by the proper United States District Court, the land was surveyed and the final survey was approved on August 17, 1864, by Hon. Ogden Hoffman, United States district judge. According to this final survey the rancho contained 17,938.58 acres, a patent for which was on January 31, 1873, executed and issued by the United States.

The above-mentioned deed from the widow, Gabriela Berryessa de Castro, to her daughter Martina Castro de Alvarado was recorded on September 9, 1851, in the office of the county recorder of Contra Costa County. It was the cause of considerable dissatisfaction among the remaining heirs of Don Francisco Castro, and was one of the reasons for the protracted litigation which involved the title of this magnificent tract of land. A proceeding was begun in the Probate Court of Contra Costa County, to set aside and annul the will of Don Francisco, in August, 1852, more than twenty years after his death, and on October 30, 1852, a judgment setting aside the order admitting the will to probate was entered; but in 1856, on the second appeal to the Supreme Court, the will was again declared to be valid.

From time to time the various heirs sold off portions of their holdings, in some instances attempting to convey a complete title, while in others the conveyance called for an undivided interest. The title thus became so involved that none of those claiming an interest in the rancho knew exactly what he owned. There were various suits and disputes, and efforts made to effect a settlement; and in 1856 an agreement for or deed of partition was formally drawn up, between parties of nine parts. By it three disinterested parties, viz., James Alexander Forbes, John B. R. Cooper and

Nicholas Gray, were named and appointed to make partition of the rancho, and to that end to make the necessary survey, map, and report, which were to be filed for record among the land records of Contra Costa County "with this deed of partition and release, the whole to take effect when so filed and recorded, and not before."

This instrument purports to have been executed and acknowledged by nearly all the parties to it. The survey, map and report were made, and the deed, etc., were filed and recorded on August 28, 1857.

Nicholas Gray, one of the above named commissioners, was at that time a deputy United States surveyor, and the map and report he made, dated September 15, 1856, places the acreage of said grant at 29,941, of which 2,470 acres were marsh land; but the final report of the referees in partition of the San Pablo Rancho, which was incorporated in the final decree of partition, signed by Judge J. C. B. Hubbard, March 3, 1894, places it at 17,628.15 acres.

It may be of interest, in passing, to note that on October 10, 1853, one of Don Francisco's sons, Juan José Castro, and his wife mortgaged to Thomas J. A. Chambers all of their right, title and interest in and to the San Pablo Rancho, declaring in said mortgage that it was "one undivided eighth part of the whole of said rancho," to secure the payment of a promissory note for $633, payable on demand, with interest at the rate of five per cent, per month, compounded monthly, until paid. On July 3, 1856, their interest was sold under foreclosure proceedings; and on January 12, 1857, no redemption having been made and the time for redemption having expired, the sheriff of Contra Costa County, N. Hunsaker, issued a deed therefor to John H. Saunders and Hiatt P. Hepburn. The early part of this year, 1926, the Mercantile Trust Company paid $1,000 per front foot for their lot, 50 feet on the north side of Macdonald Avenue by 107½ feet on the east side of Tenth Street, where their new bank is now nearing completion.

Joseph Emeric had acquired the Jesus Maria Castro and Francisco de Moraga interests, amounting to a 2/22 interest in the rancho, but had not signed the agreement for the partition made by Gray, and interests of some of the minor heirs were not bound by that agreement. On November 19, 1867, Joseph Emeric and others brought suit in the district court of the Fifteenth Judicial District of the State for partition of the rancho. An interlocutory decree was rendered in that court on July 15, 1878. Several appeals were taken; and the judgment and order denying a new trial were reversed by the Supreme Court (Emeric vs. Alvarado, 64 Cal. Reports, page 529) and the case sent back to the lower court, where Judge James G. Maguire, on January 5, 1889, entered an interlocutory decree adjudging partition among the parties in interest according to their respective shares, as determined and set forth in the findings. There were several hundred parties to the action; and the findings of fact, conclusion of law, and interlocutory decree covered about 750 printed pages. From this last decision there were appeals taken by five sets of appellants to the

Supreme Court (Emeric vs. Alvarado, Cal. 90, page 444), but on August 7, 1891, that court rendered a decision covering the five separate appeals and affirming the judgment and interlocutory decree rendered by Judge Maguire, and also his order denying a new trial.

The final decree in partition was rendered on March 3, 1894, by Judge J. C. B. Hubbard; and the costs and expense of partition were fixed by that decree at $103,470.73. The cost of recording the certified copy of this final decree and of filing the certified copy of the map accompanying the same, in the office of the county recorder of Contra Costa County, was $300.

At the commencement of the suit in partition, Dr. Jacob M. Tewksbury claimed the ownership and possession of nearly 5000 acres of the rancho, but by said final decree this was cut to 2214.155$^1/_3$ acres. In the meantime he had built some levees across the marsh lands lying between the mainland and the Potrero, and ultimately acquired title to about 1200 acres of this "salt marsh and overflowed land." The south 400 acres was sold in 1905 by his widow to H. C. Cutting, who organized the Point Richmond Canal & Land Company. This company dredged a canal from near Ellis Landing on the slough to a point near where the Washington School now stands, and almost parallel to Cutting Boulevard, and with the material thus obtained filled and reclaimed about half the acreage bought, subdividing it into streets and lots, and sold many of the lots. The writer was told some years ago by John R. Nystrom that he, Nystrom, had frequently sailed in a bay sloop through the channel between the Potrero and the mainland, from San Pablo Bay to Ellis Landing, before Tewksbury built the levees that finally caused shoaling, and ultimately the closing of the sloughs.

Among other portions of the San Pablo Rancho acquired by Tewksbury, and confirmed to his widow, Emily S. Tewksbury, by the decree, was lot No. 48, as described by the decree and delineated on said map, said lot consisting of 392.12 acres. The southeasterly line of this lot was 100 feet northwesterly of the line of Washington Avenue and extended from the marsh on the north side of the Potrero across to San Francisco Bay. In 1901 Mrs. Tewksbury sold about half of this lot No. 48, and also a portion of the salt marsh and overflowed land, to the Standard Oil Company, and has since sold that company the larger portion of the northerly 800 acres of marsh. On these lands acquired from the Tewksburys the Standard Oil Company's mammoth refinery and its adjuncts now stand.

The easterly portion of this lot No. 48 was subdivided and sold off in lots, as is shown in the map of the Town of Richmond, Amended Map No. 1 of the Town of Richmond, and maps of Third Addition to the Town of Richmond, Fourth Addition to the Town of Richmond, and Bay View Addition to the Town of Richmond.

Dr. J. M. Tewksbury was the leading physician in San Francisco, where he died on February 4, 1877, leaving a widow, Emily S. Tewksbury, and a son and a daughter. By his will he left his entire estate to his widow. For some years he and his family lived across Wild Cat Creek from Francisco Castro's home, east of the end of San Pablo Avenue, where the road up San Pablo Creek joins the avenue.

Joseph Emeric was another owner of a large interest in San Pablo Rancho. The final decree in partition awarded his son, Henry F. Emeric, as his successor, 1991.132 acres. Among the parcels awarded to him was Lot 44, which contained 236.49 acres. Henry F. Emeric married Elizabeth Dover on May 10, 1899. He died in August, 1899, leaving all of his estate to his widow. She, in the early part of 1900, sold Lot 44 to John Nicholl for $50,000. The John Nicholl Company subdivided that portion of the lot lying northwest of the Santa Fe Railway, and on August 28, 1900, filed the map known as "Map of the Nicholl Subdivision of the Town of Richmond." As there was considerable hard feeling between Nicholl and the Tewksburys, the first subdivision map prepared by T. W. Morgan, C. E., for the company, made no provision for the opening of Richmond and Nicholl Avenue as they now exist, between the Tewksbury and Nicholl subdivisions, but was laid off in a continuous line of lots mostly 40 by 100 feet, backing up against the Tewksbury line and fronting on Washington Avenue.

John Nicholl came to this locality in 1857. He bought 200 acres of the San Pablo Rancho and built his house, which still stands and is occupied by his son, Joseph L. Nicholl, on the south side of Macdonald Avenue at 28th Street. The eucalyptus trees still standing in front of the house were planted in 1868, and are said to be the oldest in the county. This tract, in the decree of partition, is designated as Lot No. 55, and contains 191.76 acres. It extended from Road No. 14 (now 23rd Street) to 32nd Street on the east, and from the south line of the Oakland branch of the Santa Fe Railway to the vicinity of the Grant School. The easterly nineteen acres of the portion south of Macdonald Avenue was purchased by the city and is now being improved, and is known as Nicholl Park. It was here that John Nicholl, as captain, and a number of the earlier settlers, organized a small company known as a "Home Guard," which assembled and had "guard mount" and other drills during the Civil War.

Nicholl acquired other interests in the San Pablo Rancho prior to the partition, and on the advice of his attorney, John B. Moon, accepted Lot 45 of the San Pablo Rancho, containing 152.81 acres and including the promontory known as Point Richmond, now Ferry Point, Moon saying to him that some day it would be "valuable as a railway terminus." The truth of this prediction was proved when on February 26, 1897, Robert W. Watt, as vice-president of the San Francisco & San Joaquin Valley Railway, gave Mr. Nicholl a check for $80,000, dated on that day and drawn on the Bank of California, in payment for fifty-seven acres, including Point Richmond and adjacent land, which the Santa Fe Company now own. For some reason the deed was made out to Claus Spreckels. This, as we all now know, was the entering wedge for the Atchison, Topeka & Santa Fe Railroad to reach tidewater on the Bay of San Francisco. An interesting sidelight on its coming is found in an article by A. S. Macdonald written in 1910, entitled "The Beginning of the City of Richmond," from which the following is quoted:

"One November evening in 1895, I drove out from Oakland, bound for the San Pablo Marshes on a duck hunt. Leaving San Pablo Avenue, we passed the old Nicholl homestead and came to what is known as Twenty-third Street. Here the county road turned to the north, and then to the west again along Richmond Avenue. The only house on the road at that time belonged to Mrs. McGann, whose daughter was the first postmistress of Richmond. It was a muddy, treacherous road from her place to the Potrero, used only by a Swiss dairyman, tenant on the Tewksbury land, residing about where the Standard Oil Company's office now stands. Leaving our team at this place, we walked out on the dyke to blinds out at the mouth of the San Pablo Creek. It was a perfectly beautiful morning, sun shining brightly and not a breath of wind; consequently no ducks were flying, and after sitting five hours without a chance shot I concluded to quit, walk over the Potrero hill, and explore the Bay shore. On reaching the summit of the hill, a magnificent view greeted my eyes—Mt. Tamalpais looming up to the right, Berkeley to the left and, seemingly just across the way, San Francisco—without a sign of life to disturb the quiet and peaceful scene. I wondered why such a delightful spot had been neglected for either pleasure or profit, as not alone its beauty, but also its commercial possibilities, appealed to me at once and I determined to investigate.

"The government map and surveys showed a depth of sixty-five feet of water, the only point on the east side of the Bay where land and navigable deep water met. Aside from this, I discovered a saving of over twelve miles could be made by the Southern Pacific Railroad Company by a ferry from Point Richmond directly to San Francisco, instead of handling freight through Oakland to the shallow estuary of the Peralta Street slip.

"These facts I presented to Mr. Huntington with the idea of establishing the freight and overland traffic of the railroad company at that point. Mr. Huntington thought very favorably of the project and prepared to look over the proposition; but unfortunately, or rather fortunately, as it has since turned out, he had become entangled in some lawsuits and left the State.

"Not discouraged, however, as soon as the Santa Fe Railroad Company announced its intention of reaching San Francisco, I presented my scheme to them. To avoid attracting attention, the chief engineer, head officials and I went out by separate routes and carefully examined the water front, with the result that it was considered the most feasible and economical point on the Bay for a terminus, and was adopted.

"As soon as this question was definitely decided, I knew that a great city must grow up there, and the next thing was to find a proper location. The Potrero was rough and hilly, while the immediate surrounding land was low, flat and swampy; the next choice tract was that belonging to George H. Barrett, a pioneer resident. This we secured and named the

City of Richmond. The country was uninviting-looking enough at the time, except the homestead of Barrett, which stood on Tenth Street, just north of Macdonald Avenue.

"The subdivision of this hay ranch by myself and associates was quite a serious problem and, to begin with, rather discouraging, as streets had to be laid out, blocks graded, sewers constructed, water and gas mains secured, railroad stations established by both the Southern Pacific and Santa Fe Companies, and street car facilities acquired; but all of this and much more has been accomplished, thanks to the energetic, enterprising people who have taken up their residence there—and much credit must be given the Women's Improvement Club.

"The argument which I made to induce the railroad to build to Richmond is stronger and better today, since it has been proven, than when first used—to wit, that it was the only place on the East Shore and the most desirable place on San Francisco Bay where land and navigable water came together, giving shipping facilities unexcelled anywhere else on the whole Coast.

"In addition to this, now, with the Southern Pacific Railroad, Santa Fe Railroad, and belt line railroad for land connections, and the Standard Oil Company's immense plant and the cables of the great Electric Company affording cheap power, it is an ideal place for manufacturing, as is evidenced by the large manufacturing concerns already attracted to this locality.

"Richmond, with its fine climate, lying snugly behind the Potrero and sheltered from the prevailing westerly winds, its navigable harbor, overland railroads and cheap power, has a basis for growth possessed by few cities and, having all the improvements of a modern progressive municipality, is bound to be one of the most important cities on the Coast.

"I was laughed at in 1900 when I predicted a population of 10,000 in ten years. President Ripley stated that Richmond would have a population of 20,000 in fifteen years, and I have every confidence in his prediction.

"Augustin S. Macdonald."

In the early fifties the place at the foot of Tenth Street was known as Ellis Landing. Before that time this district was for ages the burial ground of prehistoric man. Scientists from all over the world have studied Ellis Shell Mound, and their researches unearthed much of value before modern improvements came. In 1849 Capt. George Ellis operated schooners between San Francisco and Ellis Landing. The channel ran from San Francisco past Ellis Landing to San Pablo Bay, through the present site of the Standard Oil refinery. The Potrero Hills formed an island subject to government occupancy. When this channel was closed, it made this section part of the mainland. In 1859 Captain Ellis acquired the property. He operated two schooners, Sierra and Mystery, carrying produce and freight between the landing and San Francisco. John Nystrom was manager of the landing. When Ellis died his children acquired the property, and the old Ellis home and ninety acres of harbor property were purchased from George and Selena Ellis, his sister, by the Ellis Landing & Dock Company; M. Emanuel was president of the company.

George H. Barrett once owned 420 acres in what is now the business district of Richmond. Barrett Avenue is named for him. A. S. Macdonald bought some of the Barrett property, Macdonald Avenue being named for him.

Owen Griffins was a large landowner in the south part of Richmond. Part of it was subdivided by Griffins and Watruss, who sold to John Nystrom, and he added Nystrom's Addition.

Benjamin Boorman came in 1859. A biographical sketch of Mr. Boorman will be found in another part of this history.

Bernard Schapiro bought 1500 acres of the Tewksbury property and subdivided it.

William H. Wood was another pioneer. His widow married Mr. Boorman. Her children were Robert N. Wood, Richard C. Wood, Lucetta Wood Dunlap, Ann Elizabeth Wood, and Frank G. Wood. By her second marriage there were two children, Adelaide Picton and Emily Axtell.

Under the guise of its being "the People's Road," the San Francisco & San Joaquin Valley Railroad was built from Bakerfield to Stockton, and then on to Point Richmond. The portion from Stockton to Point Richmond, now known as Ferry Point, was built during 1899 and the early part of 1900. When the writer came here in November, 1899, the rails had been laid this side of Pinole, although the grading was nearly finished, and the tunnel was through the Potrero Hills, but the fill across the tidelands from near Keller's Beach to the Point had not been completed. However, a few people had awakened to the fact that there would be a city here, or at any rate a chance to sell lots, for on June 3, 1899, the "Map of the Town of Point Richmond" was filed in the office of the county recorder of this county. This tract was handled and sold by Charles T. Rodolph, of Oakland, and was the first within what is now the City of Richmond to be subdivided. It comprised the land on the north side of Barrett Avenue (then Road No. 12) and designated on that map as Point Richmond Avenue, between Mrs. McGann's property at the east line of A Street (called Spreckels Avenue on that map) and the Santa Fe Railroad, and also included a triangular piece west of the railroad, cut into some five or six blocks. As the place where Point Richmond Avenue crossed the railroad was destined to become a very busy portion of the yards of the railroad, the company exchanged some of their ground east of the railroad south of Point Richmond Avenue for that portion of the Town of Point Richmond lying west of the railroad, as shown on said map. The streets now known as A, B, and C Streets, and Garrard Boulevard, were designated on the map as Spreckels, Santa Fe, Topeka, and Atchison Avenues, respectively. The propaganda setting forth that the San Francisco and San Joaquin Railway was to be "the People's Road," to deliver them from the bondage and monopoly of the Southern Pacific, which was then the only road reaching the Bay of San Francisco or traversing the great San Joaquin Valley, was a shrewd move on the part of the Santa Fe people, for they succeeded in getting quite a large popular subscription for the stock, and many advantages in the way of obtaining rights of way. The building of the road exhausted the funds raised by the sale of stock and bonds issued; and the Santa Fe Company very accommodatingly stepped in and furnished a ferry boat (the Ocean Wave, a stern-wheeler from somewhere up around Puget Sound), rolling stock, and other equipment, and took over the management of the road.

The first through train from Chicago, over the Santa Fe, arrived on July 3, 1900, about noon. Captain H. P. Lauritzen was in charge of the ferry boat, Ocean Wave, waiting for the train.

Prior to the arrival of that overland train, Lyman Naugle, Richmond's grocer, first newspaper publisher and first postmaster, had arrived from somewhere and had established himself and family in a small building on the north side of what is now Barrett Avenue, between A and B Streets. He and his family were the first and, for several weeks, the only settlers on this, the first part of the townsite platted. On April 15, 1900, he put in a few cases of old type, an old broken composing stone, and a small chase, and proceeded to set up the forms for the first newspaper published in this city, which he called the Richmond Record. In those days there was no Richmond depot on the Southern Pacific, only a three-sided shed with a long board seat in it, at the crossing of Road No. 12, now Barrett Avenue. This "flag stop" was then called Barrett Station, as Barrett's house, just east of Tenth Street between Macdonald on Nevin Avenues, was the nearest house to it, where the Southern Pacific trains stopped twice a day if "flagged." It was to this point Naugle carried the forms for his paper, and then on into Berkeley where the paper was printed. Soon after, he got a hand press; and on July 5, 1900, assisted by Frank Critchett (who now lives in Oakland and has the first copy of the paper printed, and who was the first subscriber, and the writer), began the actual publication of a newspaper in the young city. The first few issues of the Record were mailed from Stege, a little settlement with a railroad depot and post office, and called into being by the California Cap Works, the Stauffer Chemical Company's plant, and a match factory. Uncle Sam was not yet fully aware of the birth of this "Wonder City," but in August a post office was established in Naugle's store and print shop and he was appointed as our first postmaster.

The second subdivision of our city was known as the "Townsite of Santa Fe" and was owned and put on the market by McEwen Brothers, a corporation composed of George and Frank McEwen and some of their family. This tract extends from the south line of the A. T. & S. F. Oakland branch right of way, to the salt marsh lands, then owned by the Tewksburys on the south, and from a line 100 feet west of First Street easterly to Tenth Street. The map of this subdivision was filed in the office of the county recorder at Martinez on March 17, 1900.

The next plat filed was known as "Map No. 1 of the Town of Richmond," being a portion of Lot No. 48 of the San Pablo Rancho, owned by Emily S. Tewksbury, and covered a few lots facing on what was called Tewksbury Avenue (now Standard Avenue) from 100 feet west of Washington Avenue over about to Castro Street. This map was filed on June 30, 1900.

Then came the "Nicholl Subdivision of the Town of Richmond," a map filed on August 28, 1900; and after it, on November 10, 1900, was filed the "Amended Map No. 1, of the Town of Richmond," which took in more of Lot No. 48.

We'll step over again to Barrett Avenue, where, at the northwest corner of A Street (then Point Richmond Avenue and Spreckels Avenue), T. M. Ross (who had come down from Sacramento) had started the construction of the second building to be put up in Richmond. He had not yet got the roof on when along came Frank Critchett, from Tulare, who landed here about July 1, 1900, with his good wife Martha and her three sons: Elton Mason, Albert Mason and William D. Mason, the last named then about fourteen years of age. William D. Mason was afterward superintendent of the Standard Oil refinery. Critchett thought it would be a good place for business; so he bought the property and started to finish it. But the roof was barely done when he sold it to Henry Wanske, who opened, and for some time after operated, the Star Saloon. His reason for selling was that the writer had made a deal whereby Critchett was given by the John Nicholl Company the two lots at the north corner of Washington and Richmond Avenues (80 feet on Washington by 100 feet on Richmond) in consideration of his erecting, opening, and maintaining for not less than eighteen months, what they were pleased to term a first-class Mechanics' Hotel. The Tewksbury and Nicholl people also wanted Naugle, with his newspaper, grocery and post office. Naugle would not go without Critchett, nor would he go without Naugle; so as a part of the same deal we arranged with Naugle to move over to the hillside in consideration of Nicholl's giving him a lot 40 by 100 feet where the bank now stands, at the west corner of Washington and Richmond Avenues, and $300 to be used in the construction of a building, to house his grocery, print shop and post office, on the lot adjacent, 40 feet front on Richmond Avenue by 120 deep, given him by the Tewksburys, together with $300 in cash to be used in constructing that building. This building was started about September 1, 1900; and on the 10th, before he could get the roof completed, we secured a big dray and loaded on it Mr. Naugle's effects, including the Richmond Post Office, and brought the "whole cheese" over and established him in his new quarters. The post office did not stay long with the "bunch" at Washington and Nicholl Avenues. It was a hard blow to Rodolph and the others interested at the original location, which was for years known as "Old Town," to lose their most valuable advertising assets, other than the railroad, i. e., the grocery, newspaper and postoffice. Mr. Naugle had failed to get permission of the post office department to make the move, and having raised the ire of Mr. Laymance and his friends, soon had Mr. Bricker, United States postal inspector, hot on his trail with a very large demand from so diminutive a man, "to immediately take that post office back." Back it went; and Naugle, with his grocery and print shop on the hillside, had to trudge through the rain and mud of that winter over to Old Town to take care of his post office. The spring following Miss Lizzie McGann was appointed to succeed him, and was postmaster for many years, until Waverley Stairley was appointed, who in turn was succeeded by J. M. Long.

Frank Critchett, a small man with lots of energy and executive ability, soon got a crew of men together and started building operations at a lively rate. His hotel was started before we "stole" the post office. Then Miss McNally, who was boarding a lot of railroad men in a tent near where the roundhouse stands and was having difficulties with the winds and rain, prevailed on Critchett to put her up a hotel on the gore lot at the foot of Washington Avenue. Bill Richards came over from San Francisco and bought the lot adjoining Critchett's on the north, and he wanted a two-story building put up on it immediately. So Frank took over the management of that work and soon had Richards Hall, where were had many a dance and frolic, under roof. He must have had a preference for "Bills," as there were Bill Redding, Bill Falls and Bill Conn, all sawing and hammering away at the same time. Those were stirring times in the live town; in fact the wind during that winter "stirred" several of the unfinished buildings clear off their foundations. The John Nicholl Company had five cottages under construction—one at the south corner of Washington and Richmond Avenues, one on Washington on the second lot above Naugle's corner, one on Richmond opposite the end of Park Place, and two on Tunnel Avenue, between Richmond and Nicholl Avenues. During the earlier part of that season, P. M. (Pat) Dean and Mr. Wyatt had put up a two-story frame building on Tewksbury (now Standard) Avenue and were occupying it for a boarding house and saloon. And with so many other memories crowding along, I almost forgot what must have been a very important place during the railroad construction work around here—the old "Hunters' Home" saloon, that stood on the south side of Tewksbury Avenue opposite the end of the road that came up from the railroad yards. How long it had been there I do not know, but the building looked old when I first saw it. It was afterward moved across the street to its present location on the corner.

Road No. 12, of which Barrett Avenue is now the easterly portion, extended from Road No. 14, now Twenty-third Street, to a point a little west of the junction of Garrard and Barrett Avenues, and thence southwest to a junction with Road No. 26, now Standard Avenue, about 100 feet west of Washington Avenue. In January, 1901, the Santa Fe shops were

5

moved from Stockton to Richmond; urgently necessary repair work on cars and engines had, prior to that, been done in the open. It is rumored that, in making the blueprints for the layout of construction of shops and roundhouse, the tracing was inadvertently placed upside down, so that the plans as shown thereon provided for the shops and roundhouse to be westerly instead of easterly of the main line. At all events the roundhouse was built so that it was squarely on and across that portion of Road No. 12. In 1901 an abandonment of the portion of Road No. 12, from and across the railroad on down through the roundhouse and shops, was put through the board of supervisors, on condition that the Santa Fe give a new roadway, graded and graveled, and sixty feet wide, in exchange. That road was afterward abondoned to the Santa Fe Company's use in exchange for the present Garrard Boulevard, eighty feet wide. It was filled to grade and an oil macadam top put on by the company, and served for many years; within the past few months (November, 1926) the Santa Fe and the Key System have completed a fine job of paving the portion of the boulevard from Ohio to Macdonald Avenues with concrete base and bitumen top.

As is the case with all new railroad towns, the Santa Fe's first depot or station was a box car; then came a frame building on the east side of the track near where Ohio Avenue crossed the railroad. A reading room for the employees was also constructed there by the company. The station and reading room were maintained there until moved to their present location at the west end of Macdonald Avenue.

INCORPORATION AND ANNEXATION MATTERS

On October 5, 1903, the first petition for incorporation of the city was filed with the board of supervisors. The territory described and sought to be incorporated included all west of Twenty-third Street now within the present city boundary. The supervisors reduced the area so as to exclude about everything but the subdivided territory on the Potrero, but the sponsors for incorporation preferred not to have the proposition go to a vote that way. On September 6, 1904, another petition was filed describing a smaller portion than that described in the first. There were various delays by the supervisors in passing on the matter, and they finally lost jurisdiction; so on June 5, 1905, a third petition was filed. In this was described a small territory. On July 3, 1905, the board of supervisors made an order calling an election on Thursday, August 3, 1905. At that election 256 votes were cast in favor of and 52 against incorporation. On August 7 the supervisors canvassed the vote and made an order declaring Richmond duly incorporated as a city of the sixth class, under the General Incorporation Act.

The first board of trustees were: Edward J. Garrard, Frank Babcock, Samuel R. Curry, Frank Critchett, and Herman B. Kinney. The first meeting of the board was held in the main office of the Critchett Building, August 14, 1905. Samuel R. Curry was selected by the board as president; Wm. R. Satterwhite was appointed city attorney; Robert

G. Stitt was chosen as city recorder; and W. Stairley, as treasurer. Harry Livingston had been elected city marshal, and J. N. Galbraith, city clerk.

The boundaries of the new city were about as follows: Beginning on the east line of the wharf of the Pacific Coast (now Standard) Oil Company; thence northeasterly along line of the wharf and east line of the land of the oil company to a point about 450 feet north of Standard Avenue; thence southeast to intersection of north line of Ohio Street with easterly line of right of way of the Santa Fe Railway; thence northerly along right of way line to north line of Macdonald Avenue 100 feet west of First Street; thence south to Cutting Boulevard; thence southwesterly in a line running about 1000 feet northwest of the old road where it crossed the Potrero to the brickyard, over to the edge of the tide-land surveys; thence following the outer line of the tide lots to near the outer wharf; thence zigzaging around so as to leave Ferry Point out, and then following outer boundary of tide lots to place of beginning.

A census taken at that time showed a population of 2118.

On December 22, 1905, all the territory within the present city limits lying west of a point 170 feet east of Twenty-second Street was annexed. On October 12, 1908, a board of fifteen freeholders consisting of H. C. Wyatt, president, and Dr. C. L. Abbott, F. E. Adams, Levi Boswell, L. D. Dimm, J. A. Follett, E. J. Garrard, E. A. Gowe, I. E. Marshall, John Roth, H. H. Turley, E. M. Tilden, Dr. Chas. R. Blake, L. S. Higgins, and I. M. Perrin, were elected and prepared our present charter, which was ratified by vote of the people on February 9, 1909; was approved by concurrent resolution of the legislature and adopted by the assembly on February 17, 1909, and by the senate on February 25, 1909; was filed in the office of the secretary of state on March 4, 1909; and went into effect at noon of July 1, 1909. It provides for election of a city council of nine members, whose terms of office are six years each, these to be elected on the second Monday in May of each odd-numbered year. The council each year select one of their own members as presiding officer, designated as mayor, and also appoint a city manager, a clerk, and all other city officials.

The members of the first council under the new charter were: Edward J. Garrard, John N. Hartnett, James C. Owens, Edward McDuff, Otto R. Ludwig, Homer E. Wyatt, John J. Dooling, Joseph B. Willis, and Jerry A. Follett. Their first meeting was held on July 6, 1909. Willis was chosen as mayor; and the following appointments were made: T. Park Jacobs, city clerk; W. Stairley, treasurer; H. H. Tutley, auditor; I. E. Marshall, assessor and tax collector; Lee D. Windrem, city attorney; Orlin Hudson, engineer; Jas. P. Arnold, chief of police; Dr. H. M. Barney, commissioner of health and city physician; and Wm. Lindsay, police judge.

On October 17, 1911, an election was held for annexation of all the territory east of Twenty-third Street now within the city limits, and also the greater part of what is now El Cerrito, but failed to carry.

On May 28, 1912, an election for annexation of the territory east of Twenty-third Street was again held, and carried. The territory annexed did not include any east of San Pablo Avenue lying south of the Santa Fe Railway or Stege Junction, nor what is platted and known as Richmond Annex west of San Pablo Avenue.

THE STANDARD OIL COMPANY

The Standard Oil Company's refinery is the pioneer, and the largest of the city's industries, and might well be called the industrial backbone of the city of Richmond. In 1901 the Pacific Coast Oil Company, as this branch of the Standard was then known, with their refinery at Alameda, and W. S. Rheem as general manager, bought, on his recommendation, 117 acres of land from Mrs. Emily S. Tewksbury, and about November 1, of that year, began grading and other work for the construction of a new refinery, as they were abandoning the Alameda location for the more advantageous one in Richmond. This was the nucleus of their holdings of 1350 acres and their present immense oil refinery, the largest west of the Mississippi River. In this connection the following item from Martinez, dated November 29, 1926, is of interest:

"Martin W. Joost, Contra Costa County tax collector, today received the largest individual tax payment ever received in this county when the Standard Oil Company tendered its check for $376,143.21 in payment of the first tax installment on its Richmond refinery and the oil storage and pipe lands in this county.

"Joost, in reporting the record payment of a third of a million dollars by one concern, stated that this equals almost the total amount collected to date, $465,000. None of the other heavy payers of taxes have sent in their checks so far."

Luther D. Dimm was assistant superintendent; John C. Black, construction engineer; E. A. Gowe, cashier; Frank Babcock had charge of the pipe fitting department; Ed. Axelson, Sr., was head of the boiler department; G. B. Fredenberg was superintendent of the acid works; and Joseph F. Brooks, who is now manager of the refineries throughout California for the company, with offices in their twenty-two-story building in San Francisco, was in charge of the can factory.

As there are no producing oil wells in this vicinity, one might wonder where all the oil comes from to keep a plant of such capacity supplied. Great storage tanks and reservoirs were built in the apparently inexhaustible oil fields in the interior of the State, and a double pipe line nearly 300 miles long was laid to conduct the oil therefrom to Richmond. The oil was heavy and ran slowly; hence it was necessary to establish pumping stations at various points throughout its length, and it is even necessary to heat the oil at these stations so that it will flow more freely. This great pipe line transportation scheme was a vast experiment, for which many predicted failure; but the fact that millions upon millions of barrels of oil have been pumped through the stations, and that the company has since laid another line or two alongside of the first ones, and other companies have adopted the same system of oil transportation, is the best proof of its success.

The oil transported through these lines is stored in tanks and reservoirs on the hills about halfway between Pinole and Richmond, at what is known as the "Tank Farm"; from there the oil flows by gravity through about three miles of pipe to the refinery.

To give some idea of the immensity of this plant, we have but to say that for the five-year period from 1915 to 1920 the average daily run of crude oil through the refinery was approximately 50,000 barrels, and for the past year the average has been about 80,000 barrels per day. The daily average of men employed at the plant in 1915 was 1800; in 1919 it was 3400; in March, 1920, on account of the large amount of construction work going on, it was 4500; and for the past year the daily average has been about 2800 men.

In January, 1917, the company adopted the eight-hour day for their men, and while the number of employees from 1915 to 1920 increased about 100 per cent, the payroll increased to about $700,000, or about 300 per cent. In 1926 the monthly payroll averaged about $550,000.

In 1921 the company adopted a plan for giving the employees an opportunity to become stockholders in the company, permitting them to make installment payments of not to exceed twenty per cent of their monthly salary, the company agreeing to credit them with fifty per cent additional for each dollar so paid on the purchase price of the stock. A large number of the employees grasped this wonderful opportunity. The scheme was brought to a close in December, 1926; and the company issued stock to eighty-seven per cent of its men.

The products of this plant are many and varied, and are distributed all over the world. The company owns its own fleet of steamers and oil barges, thus adding to the convenience of delivery.

TRANSPORTATION AND POWER FACILITIES

The Richmond harbor, in point of tonnage, ranks among the great ports of the country, and ranks fourth among Pacific Coast ports. More than 5,480,000 tons of cargo, excluding lumber, passed over Richmond's docks in 1925. The city has sixteen miles of deep water front.

The Santa Fe Railroad's Pacific Coast Terminal is at Richmond, where are located its great freight yards and shops employing more than 750 men. The Southern Pacific's Ogden, Shasta, Sunset, and San Joaquin Valley Lines converge at Richmond. These two transcontinental carriers maintain an inter-switching agreement and operate in rotation the Richmond Belt Line. This service gives Richmond factories the most convenient and advantageous local and transcontinental shipping service on the Pacific Coast. Switching charges, on either line, on a car destined for a main-line haul, are absorbed by the carrier.

Richmond enjoys a trap-car or L. C. L. service based on a flat rate of $2.70 per car for the movement of L. C. L., provided the line-haul revenue equals $15. For this fee of $2.70, the Southern Pacific or Santa Fe will pick up carload lots of L. C. L. shipments at the plant and transfer them to freight warehouse, or handle incoming L. C. L. shipments from freight station to plant. Local switching charges are 34 cents per ton, $7.20 per car minimum.

Richmond is served by a belt line railway which is independently owned. It is operated over alternating five-year periods by both the Southern Pacific and the Santa Fe, connecting these railways with the wharves. The Richmond Belt Line operates 11.30 miles of track, 8600 feet having been added early in 1926.

Since 1921 the tonnage at Richmond has increased seventy per cent. In 1925 a total of 30,174 cars were handled over the Belt Line Railway, which is within the switching lines of both the Santa Fe and the Southern Pacific as regards a main-line haul. Passing through the most highly developed section of industrial Richmond, the services of the Belt Line Railway are a distinct asset to every manufacturing concern locating within the territory it feeds.

No city in the United States is more advantageously placed with respect to fuel and power than Richmond. The Western States Gas & Electric Company is the chief power distributor in the city, but the Pacific Gas & Electric Company and the Great Western Power Company also serve Richmond. The high-power transmission lines from the hydro-electric plants in the Sierra Nevada Mountains reach Richmond first of the Bay Cities, and Richmond thus has first call on the vast resources of the hydro-electric power projects. Rates are set by the California Railroad Commission, and have been characterized by Herbert Hoover as "the cheapest in the United States."

At Richmond are the Pullman Shops, the Standard Oil Refinery, the Republic Steel Package Company (head office, Cleveland), the Certainteed Products Company, the Santa Fe Shops, the Pacific Sanitary Manufacturing Company (4 plants), and more than fifty other industries, which in 1926 turned out $185,000,000 of manufactured goods.

A recent survey showed that Richmond possesses more than 106 miles of splendidly paved streets. By reason of their effect on traffic and transportation, good streets are a distinct asset to every city, and Richmond has followed a consistent plan of street improvement commensurate with her growth and industrial importance.

Schools of the City

A splendid system of public, high, and vocational schools serves the people of Richmond, and high standards of instruction prevail. Because of the industrial life upon which the city depends, especial emphasis is placed upon vocational and trade school work.

The first public school within the present boundaries of Richmond was held in a small frame building on the west side of San Pablo Avenue about 500 feet north of McBryde Avenue. This was the first school in the San Pablo school district, which included all of the territory comprised within the San Pablo Rancho. On February 2, 1903, the district was divided into three parts, forming the Richmond, Stege and San Pablo school districts. After the city of Richmond had grown, and had annexed the lands east of Twenty-third Street, and including Stege, by the election of May 28, 1912 (though the annexed territory did not include all of the Stege district), the Richmond and Stege districts were consolidated, and that is why the Fairmont, Kensington and Harding schools, all in the city of El Cerrito, are under the jurisdiction of the trustees, and form a part of the Richmond school district at this time.

The first building, with its additions, which housed as many as eighty pupils at one time, stood until quite recently, and in later days was used as a road house and saloon. The first teacher to preside there was a Miss Heniky, a woman of unusual ability, able to converse fluently in five different languages. After five years of service she resigned and married. Professor Skinner, then a teacher in the Berkeley school, accepted the position, as he was given a much larger salary than the then little hamlet of Berkeley could afford to pay. Miss Ruth Ann Nicholl was also one of those who taught in that building—and taught one of our present teachers, then Emily Boorman and now Mrs. Axtell.

The Richmond public schools proper had their beginning in March, 1901, when our city was a village of only a little more than 100 people— and most of these living in tents. The school opened in Richards Hall, on the northwest side of Richmond Avenue adjacent to the Critchett Hotel, with fifteen pupils, from the first to the sixth grade inclusive. A. Odell, a veteran of the school room, was the teacher. During his term and through his efforts the school was removed, as soon as the building would house them, to the basement of the old First Methodist Church, a frame building on Richmond Avenue near Martina Street. This building was later torn down to make room for a newer brick structure. Mr. Odell was stricken with typhoid fever and the last two weeks of the term were taught by Miss Calista Rumrill. Miss Emily Boorman (now Mrs. Axtell) opened the next term in July, 1901, with eighty-seven pupils, the school still being in the church basement.

The San Pablo school district, of which we were then a part, had voted bonds for the construction of a new school building for San Pablo, at its present location on Market Street, and one for the Stege section out on Potrero Avenue adjoining the Stege home place, now East Shore Park; but on account of the rapid growth of Richmond, a portion of the funds were diverted to the construction of our first school building—a two-room affair now used by the old volunteer firemen as a clubroom—on the half-block of property at the southwest corner of Standard Avenue and Castro Street, donated by Mrs. Emily S. Tewksbury for school purposes. In the fall of 1901 Miss Boorman, with her numerous flock, moved into this new building, and soon a Miss Henry was employed to assist her.

In June, 1901, the trustees of the San Pablo school district, viz., J. R. Nystrom, Harry Ells and John Peres, applied to the University of California for a man to take charge of their scattered schools. Walter T. Helms—who was born on January 3, 1877, near San Lorenzo, and had graduated at the Hayward High School and at the University of California and was taking postgraduate work there—was recommended and at once employed. He entered upon his duties in July, 1901, as principal of the three schools of the district. The one at San Pablo had its problems to solve, Richmond was in embryo, and the Stege school was inconvenient to reach; but Mr. Helms was equal to the occasion.

During 1901 the population had increased rapidly and the small quarters then occupied by the school were too small; also the children of the east side were handicapped by the long walk to the school on the west side. For their accommodation J. R. Nystrom, clerk of the board, secured the use of the loft in the barn on the Wicks property at the southwest corner of Sixth Street and Ohio Avenue, in the early part of 1902; and here the first school on the east side of town was held, with Miss Elizabeth Carpenter, now Mrs. James Cruickshank, as teacher. The school was afterwards moved to Henry J. Fitzgerald's building at the corner of Main and Haight (now Fifth) Streets. After the opening of Macdonald Avenue in the early part of 1902, it became necessary to provide more room; and a small frame building on the west side of Second Street, a little north of Macdonald Avenue (now occupied by a Chinese laundry), was secured for the purpose, and another teacher was added to the faculty.

Upon the division of the district in February, 1903, Mr. Helms remained as principal of the San Pablo schools at a salary of $100 per month. There were six other teachers—viz.: Ruby Roth, Nellie Jones, Susan Leonard, Ada Roth, Elizabeth Carpenter and Mrs. L. L. Johnson —at salaries of sixty-five dollars per month. For the year, the enrollment was 277 pupils, with an average daily attendance of 187. That year there was apportioned to the Richmond school district $2741 from State funds, and $3072.90 from the county funds, a total of $5813.90. A bond issue was voted that year for a new building, and the little building on Standard Avenue was shunted to one side and a six-room two-story building erected. This was sold in 1912, was moved west across Standard Avenue, and is now an apartment house.

The original Tenth Street school building was constructed with a part of that bond issue, on the west side of Tenth Street between Macdonald and Bissell Avenues, in 1903. It was a frame building of four rooms. Four more rooms were added, but the growth of the school was so rapid that even with these added rooms it was too small. This eight-room structure was sold in 1912 to Theo. Marcollo, moved to the east side of First Street, and converted into an apartment house. John E. Zumwalt was selected as the principal of the school (now Lincoln) in 1903, and continued till his death in 1924.

In 1907 Richmond had two elementary schools, the one on Standard Avenue and the Tenth Street School, with an average daily attendance of 577 pupils, and fourteen teachers. In October, 1926, there were ten elementary schools, one junior high school, one high school, and departments of part-time study, kindergarten, and Americanization. One hundred ninety-four teachers and supervisors are employed, and the total enrollment is 5484.

RICHMOND UNION HIGH SCHOOL

In 1907 the Richmond Union High School District was formed, and is made up of the territory originally comprising the San Pablo School District. William F. Belding, L. D. Dimm and B. B. McLellan were the original board of trustees. The first meeting of the board was had in the old Pioneer Club rooms. Professor Walter T. Helms was chosen as supervising principal, and thereupon organized the faculty, consisting of Prof. B. X. Tucker, as principal (he still is), and Miss Ruth Petersen (now Mrs. B. X. Tucker) and Miss Alberta Bell (now Mrs. A. H. Burnett). The school opened in the old unused original two-room school building on Standard Avenue. A bond issue was then put over for the purchase of the site now occupied by the school, on Twenty-third Street between Macdonald and Bissell Avenues, and the construction of the original building at a total cost of $85,000. Since that time various additions have been made to the grounds and building, at a total cost of about $100,000.

In 1924 the board purchased about twenty acres just beyond the city limits, on the east side of Twenty-third Street, at a cost of $60,000, and on October 29, 1926, awarded a contract for the construction of the new high school building at a total cost of $592,991. The linoleum for the building was contracted for on the same day at a cost of $8460.

ROOSEVELT JUNIOR HIGH SCHOOL

The Roosevelt Junior High School, on grounds taking in the entire block bounded by Eighth and Ninth Streets and Bissell and Chanslor Avenues, was built in 1920, costing with the grounds a total of $425,000. It has a capacity for 1200 pupils, and the auditorium built in conjunction with it has a seating capacity of 1500.

NEWSPAPERS

On July 7, 1900, the Record made its first appearance as a weekly, Lyman Naugle, editor. There was no postoffice and the papers were mailed from Stege. When the postoffice was established, Naugle was appointed postmaster. The Richmond Record made its appearance as a daily on February 8, 1902.

The Santa Fe Times was established in 1902 by W. B. Brown. He moved to Macdonald Avenue and published the Richmond Terminal. George Ryan succeeded to the ownership in 1913.

The Tribune was established in 1903, but did not long survive.

In 1910, J. L. Kennon established the Weekly Herald. This was merged with the Record under the name of the Record-Herald.

The Richmond Daily Leader was established in March, 1912, By G. A. Milnes. The Daily Leader and Daily Record-Herald were merged that same year, and F. J. Hulaniski was manager of the combined papers. He started the Contra Costan, a weekly, which was issued by the Record-Herald office.

In August, 1914, H. C. Cutting established the Thinkograph magazine, printed in San Francisco until 1916, when he brougt it to Richmond. He established the Richmond News in 1916.

The Richmond Daily Independent made its bow in 1910, J. N. Foss and M. J. Beaumont being the owners. John Galvin bought the Foss interest, and is still connected with the paper.

The Daily News was established in January, 1914, by the Daily News Company, Inc., backed by some twenty labor organizations. In 1916 it was reduced to a weekly, and that same year H. C. Cutting took over the paper and organized the Richmond Printing and Publishing Company. In 1917 the Daily News was resumed. The evening paper is the Richmond Independent; the morning paper, the Record-Herald; and the Richmond Terminal is the weekly.

Along in the early part of 1901 a post office was established on the west side of town, with Miss Lucetta Wood (now Mrs. Paul Dunlap) as postmaster. She continued in office for ten years. The post office department at first designated it East Yard, to correspond with what the Santa Fe Company there called their station, in contradistinction to their yards at Point Richmond, now Ferry Point. After a while the company was prevailed upon to change the station's name to Richmond, and ultimately the post office department changed the post office name to Point Richmond, as there was already a Richmond post office on Barrett Ave.

TABLES

CIRCULATION OF PUBLIC LIBRARY

	Main Library	West Side Branch Library	Stege Branch Library	23rd Street Station	Grant Station	Total
1910-11	16,596	4,216	....	....	....	20,811
1911-12	22,616	5,391	....	....	....	28,007
1912-13	33,043	5,895	....	....	....	38,939
1913-14	44,965	6,661	1,083	....	....	52,709
1914-15	66,497	10,318	3,058	....	....	79,873
1915-16	78,541	18,550	4,736	....	....	101,827
1916-17	84,233	18,300	5,854	....	....	108,387
1917-18	90,117	19,564	6,483	....	....	116,164
1918-19	100,877	14,374	5,646	....	....	120,897
1919-20	127,385	21,749	6,542	....	....	155,676
1920-21	158,278	24,997	6,934	....	....	190,209
1921-22	173,252	25,768	7,873	....	....	206,893
1922-23	194,123	28,669	9,512	320	....	232,624
1923-24	194,808	22,512	10,351	....	....	227,671
1924-25	238,228	24,016	11,566	....	1,306	275,116
1925-26	279,268	23,462	12,437	....	2,599	317,766

MEMBERSHIP

Borrowers' cards issued to July 1, 1925 8,953
Borrowers' cards added by new registration 1,464
Borrowers' cards cancelled 879
Borrowers' cards in force June 30, 1926 9,538

ESTIMATED VALUE OF CITY-OWNED PROPERTY

City Hall:
Furnishings and Equipment....$ 10,000.00
Police Department and Jail:
Land and Buildings................. 3,000.00
Equipment 2,000.00
Fire Department:
Land and Buildings................. 40,000.00
Apparatus, etc. 70,000.00
Garbage Dump:
Land 4,000.00
Library:
Land and Buildings................. 45,000.00
Furniture and Fixtures........... 12,000.00
Books 49,650.00
Land 25,000.00

Natatorium:
Land and Building.................$ 135,750.00
Furnishings and Equipment.... 3,300.00
Parks and Playgrounds:
Land 145,000.00
Equipment 13,000.00
Street Department:
Equipment 8,000.00
Wharves:
Buildings 425,000.00
Equipment 25,000.00
Water Front Land..................... 67,000.00

Total $1,082,700.00

ESTIMATED VALUE OF SCHOOL PROPERTY

School	Real Estate	Building	Furnishings and Equipment	Total
High School	$140,000.00	$270,000.00	$35,000.00	$445,000.00
Roosevelt Junior High School	60,000.00	310,000.00	25,000.00	395,000.00
Lincoln	140,000.00	125,000.00	15,000.00	280,000.00
Washington	45,000.00	85,000.00	7,000.00	137,000.00
Grant	40,000.00	70,000.00	8,000.00	118,000.00
Stege	35,000.00	75,000.00	8,000.00	118,000.00
Peres	70,000.00	40,000.00	5,000.00	115,000.00
Fairmont	25,000.00	45,000.00	3,000.00	73,000.00
Nystrom	35,000.00	40,000.00	2,500.00	77,500.00
Pullman	10,000.00	10,000.00	800.00	20,800.00
El Cerrito	10,000.00			10,000.00
North Richmond	20,000.00			20,000.00
East Richmond	28,000.00			28,000.00
Kensington	18,000.00	55,000.00	1,500.00	74,500.00
Harding	30,000.00	55,000.00		85,000.00
Total				$1,996,800.00

FINANCIAL STATEMENT, CITY OF RICHMOND
RECEIPTS, DISBURSEMENTS AND BALANCES
City Funds

	Balance July 1, 1925	Receipts	Disbursements	Balance June 30, 1926
General Fund	$123,592.74	$551,115.01	$563,024.40	$111,683.35
Compensation Insurance Fund	18,313.46	641.06	384.17	18,570.35
Library Fund	4,226.39	27,752.77	28,345.32	3,633.84
School Fund	6,101.56	10,659.68	10,798.84	5,962.40
Harbor Improvement Fund	87,769.71	27,347.11	102,706.75	12,410.07
Park and Playground Fund	18,442.09	72.00	2,715.01	15,799.08
Natatorium Building Fund	75,367.71		75,367.71	
1912 Bond Int. and Redemption Fund	20,042.57	69,287.93	68,375.00	20,955.50
1920 Bond Int. and Redemption Fund	3,128.75	34,801.64	35,180.00	2,750.39
1922 Bond Int. and Redemption Fund	6,191.30	7,994.75	10,100.00	4,086.05
1924 Bond Int. and Redemption Fund	5,970.52	5,329.84	6,687.50	4,612.86
Total	$369,146.80	$735,001.79	$903,684.70	$200,463.89

School Funds
Richmond School District

	Balance July 1, 1925	Receipts	Disbursements	Balance June 30, 1926
General Fund	$ 4,029.42	$ 43,937.22	$ 28,870.05	$ 19,096.59
Salary Fund		159,176.05	157,418.00	1,758.05
Special Fund	8,704.92	158,625.78	127,370.08	39,960.62
Building Fund	3,257.21	289,291.27	55,688.27	236,860.21
Library Fund	3,601.65	4,000.00	3,279.71	4,321.94
Kindergarten Fund	2,147.76	13,097.06	10,752.99	4,491.83
Total	$ 21,740.96	$668,127.38	$383,379.10	$306,489.24

CHAPTER VII

PITTSBURG

The city of Pittsburg has at present (1925) an estimated population of 7500. The site of what is now Pittsburg was brought into public notice when the United States Army and Navy engineers investigated it as a possible military and naval base, but little ever came of their investigations, though a townsite was surveyed and given the name "New York of the Pacific."

In his "Early Recollections of California" General Sherman says: "I made a contract to survey, for Col. J. D. Stevenson, his newly projected city of New York of the Pacific, situated at the mouth of the San Joaquin River. The contract also embraced the making of soundings and marking out of a channel in Suisun Bay. We hired a small metallic boat with a sail, in San Francisco, laid in some stores and proceeded to the United States ship Ohio. At General Smith's request we surveyed and marked the line dividing the city of Benicia from the government reserve. We then sounded the bay back and forth and staked out the best channel up Suisun Bay. We then made the preliminary survey of the city of New York of the Pacific, which we duly platted."

It is understood that General Sherman received $500 and ten lots in the new townsite for his services.

In 1850 a strong effort was made to remove the State's capital, then at San Jose, to New York of the Pacific.

When coal was discovered in commercial quantities the place became known as Black Diamond. The main support of Black Diamond was from the coal mines and the fishing industry; and the latter is quite an item in the present prosperity of the city. However, the present growth and development are largely due to the efforts of the late C. A. Hooper and the C. A. Hooper Company. When Mr. Hooper became owner of the Rancho Los Médanos, on which the town is located, he believed there was a great industrial future for the place, and in every way possible he aided in its upbuilding. He interested San Francisco capitalists and boosted for the town. Since his death, in July, 1914, his son-in-law, W. E. Creed, a well-known attorney of the metropolis, has managed the Hooper interests, carrying out the plans and ideas of Mr. Hooper so far as is possible.

The Los Médanos Rancho of 10,000 acres was granted by the Mexican government in 1835 to José Antonio Mesa and José Miguel Garcia. It was finally patented by the United States government, in October, 1872, to their successors, J. D. Stevenson and others. In 1849-1850 the Mesas and Garcia conveyed the rancho to Stevenson. The name Los Médanos is derived from the sand hills that come down to the river on the eastern boundary. Stevenson disposed of his interest to Pioche, Bayerque & Com-

PITTSBURG, CONTRA COSTA COUNTY. VIEW OF WATER FRONT

PITTSBURG, CONTRA COSTA COUNTY. VIEWING ENTRANCE TO CITY FROM THE WEST, ON TENTH STREET

pany, a banking firm in San Francisco. They sold to L. L. Robinson, one of the pioneer mining men and railroad builders. Upon his death it became the property of his sister, Mrs. Cutter, and she in turn disposed of it to C. A. Hooper. Robinson had divided the large acreage into smaller parcels and had rented it out to stockmen. The name Pittsburg was bestowed upon the city in 1911 because of its industrial possibilities.

The city has had a phenomenal growth through the concerted efforts of its leading citizens. In January, 1920, municipal bonds were voted and carried 9 to 1 for a water system, $140,000; city hall, $75,000; library, $7500; streets, $125,000; municipal wharf, $40,000; sewers, $20,000; storm sewer, $15,000; fire apparatus, $10,000; street cleaning apparatus, $7500.

The fire apparatus consists of two Seagrave engines. The service is motorized, and maintains two salaried men and a volunteer department. The fire engine arrived in October, 1920.

The city hall was dedicated April 14, 1923, and is valued at $75,000; the land upon which the building stands is valued at $25,000. In 1924 the Veterans' Memorial Building was completed at a cost of $25,000.

The schools of Pittsburg are without equal in the county. In 1915 the brick grammar school building was erected at a cost of $80,000. There is a kindergarten school, and the city is in the Riverview Union High School district. In April, 1921, bonds were voted, 329 for and 65 against, in the amount of $100,000 for a new school building, and it is a decided ornament to the city, though it is inadequate for the present attendance.

The municipal dock was completed in 1925. The Free Public Library was erected from a $20,000 bond issue. The sewer system is being gradually extended by the bond issue for $40,000. The Municipal Water System, valued at $140,000, is being extended. In 1919 the Black Diamond Water Company was taken over by the Pittsburg Water Company.

The Chamber of Commerce has 150 active members and there is an active Business Men's Association. In 1915 the Pittsburg Athletic Association was formed. Its membership includes all the leading business men and officials. A block of land, donated by the C. A. Hooper Company, was improved for a recreation park, and a grandstand was erected to accommodate 1000 people.

A tree warden was appointed in 1915 and trees were set out on all the principal streets. The work was carefully planned by the citizens. The trees comprise many California varieties. Property owners vie with each other in lawn and flower planting. All streets are paved. Railroad Street is the principal business thoroughfare.

Pittsburg is served by the Pacific Gas & Electric and the Great Western Power Companies; by the Southern Pacific, Santa Fe, and Sacramento and San Francisco Short Line railroads, with auto busses connecting with the Oakland, Antioch & Eastern electric. River boats run from the docks to and from San Francisco and river points, carrying fruit, produce, and passengers.

The Pittsburg Dispatch, a weekly newspaper, was started by A. P. Butterworth and H. C. Jackson, the first issue appearing on January 3, 1917. The Pittsburg Post is another live paper.

Banking facilities are provided by the Mercantile Trust Company and the First National Bank. The latter began business in 1919, C. Lepori, president.

The first brick building on Railroad Avenue was the post office building, and was erected in 1912. Hotel Los Médanos, a modern hotel, was built by the C. A. Hooper Company in 1917 at a cost of $60,000.

Principal Industrial Firms

The Great Western Electro-Chemical Company, the only plant of its kind west of Detroit, is incorporated for $2,000,000. Its first officers were Mortimer Fleishhacker, president; John F. Bush, vice-president; Arthur Lillienthal, secretary and treasurer. C. W. Schedler was superintendent until 1919, when he was made general manager. Some 300 men are employed at the plant.

The Pioneer Rubber Works, the largest west of Chicago, employ some 350 people and make a specialty of garden hose, 12,000,000 feet being manufactured annually. They also manufacture fire hose, belting, packing, auto tires, caustic soda and chloride of lime. They make conveyor belts, and in 1925 filled an order for the largest belts ever made. These were two belts, thirty-six inches wide and about a quarter of a mile in length, which were installed in the sugar refinery at Crockett. The plant covers fifteen acres of ground, and the company is capitalized at $2,500,000.

In June, 1910, ground was broken for the Columbia Steel Company's plant. On November 22 of that year, the first heat was poured at the foundry, and the original casting is still in use in the yard of the plant. The original foundry was 300 by 60 feet; the original open-hearth unit, 100 by 25 feet; and at present the total is about 618 feet in the main bay. In 1916 the second open-hearth was completed; and in 1917 the finishing department was put in operation. The present capacity is 10,000 tons per month. Some 1500 men are employed in the plant, more than ten times the first month's payroll.

The Redwood Manufacturers Company was the pioneer manufacturing concern to locate here. The plant gets its material from the Humboldt redwoods and manufactures tanks, pipe, doors, etc. Its products are shipped to all parts of the United States and Europe.

The Lanteri Shipbuilding Company was established by B. P. Lanteri. Here dredgers and ships are built. Some of the largest clamshell dredgers in the world have been built at this plant, which is now owned by Bundesen and Lauritzen.

The National Chemical Company; Booth's Cannery, the largest on the Coast, employing more than 1000 men in catching salmon, shad, striped

ANTIOCH FREE LIBRARY

bass and catfish, and 200 to 300 men in canning and packing fish; and the Western California Fish Company, are other important concerns.

FRATERNAL ORGANIZATIONS

Pittsburg Lodge No. 429, F. & A. M., was organized on January 20, 1912, with twenty-two Master Masons, mostly demitted from Antioch Lodge. The first meeting was held February 20, 1912. On October 10, 1912, its charter was granted; and on November 9, the lodge was instituted and officers installed. There is an Eastern Star Chapter also.

Other lodges are Pittsburg Lodge No. 436, I. O. O. F.; Los Médanos Lodge, Daughters of Rebekah, I. O. O. F.; Knights of Pythias; and Loyal Order of Moose. B. P. O. E. No. 1474 was organized in October, 1923. An Elks Hall Association was formed, and a lot was secured at the southeast corner of Los Médanos and Tenth Streets for a modern Elks hall. There is an Aërie of Eagles; and the Foresters and Improved Order of Red Men are represented, as are also the Native Sons (Parlor No. 246) and Native Daughters (Parlor No. 146). David Solari Post of the American Legion was organized and named in honor of one of those who made the supreme sacrifice in the Argonne. There are also many benefit lodges and societies represented in this fast growing city.

CHAPTER VIII

ANTIOCH

The city of Antioch was first known as New York of the Pacific, and sometimes was called Smith's Landing. Its founder, William W. Smith, with his brother, J. H. Smith, both preachers, had come to California via Cape Horn in 1849 and, landing in San Francisco, he found that men were wanted by J. D. Stevenson for carpenter work at a place about fifty miles away. Being an architect, and handy with carpenter's tools, he accepted a position at $14 per day and at once he and his brother embarked on the Rialto for that point, where J. D. Stevenson and Dr. William Parker had purchased a part of the Los Médanos Grant from José Antonio Mesa. Soon after the arrival of the Smiths at New York of the Pacific, they were called upon by Dr. John Marsh, who came down from his rancho and offered them the hospitality of his home.

W. W. Smith, who came from Maine, was appointed the first alcalde of the place and as such had charge of all sanitary, civil, criminal and judicial affairs of his district. In carrying out the duties of his office, Smith spent $2000 in time, money, and medicines, none of which was ever repaid.

In 1850, W. W. Smith, hearing of the arrival in San Francisco of a shipload of settlers from Maine, went down and found a number of families who wished to obtain land and settle in California. Among them were Capt. George W. Kimball and brother, a Mr. Douglass, several named

Hathaway, a Mr. Marshall and son Benjamin, and a Mr. Dennison. They came to Smith's Landing. A street was laid out running east and west, and each family who wished to settle was presented with a lot.

Pulsifer Brothers established a garden on the flat and watered it by means of a wooden pump fixed in the slough.

Smith erected the first building in the township, which was called the New York House, to which he later added a large oven for baking bread and cakes, and in which even an entire beef could be roasted. Besides earning $14 a day as a builder, Smith during the evening occasionally fried $50 worth of doughnuts, and baked bread, etc., the bread being worth $1 per loaf. Men working on the river boats often paid $1 for the privilege of sleeping on the floor of the New York House in their own blankets. Later, Smith leased the New York House to his brother's widow and moved to a ranch near where Antioch now stands.

The second house was erected by John Beemer, agent for Stevenson & Parker; and he was also the first postmaster and justice of the peace. The third building was built for Dr. Forejo of San Francisco, in which H. F. Toy opened a saloon.

In 1850 Howard Nichols purchased the ship Mt. Vernon and turned it into a receiving hulk, where steamers took on and discharged cargoes and passengers. In 1851 he fitted it up as a boarding-house.

A man named Lord; H. H. Hartley, a lawyer; and a Mr. Bodfish were among the early settlers. J. C. McMaster, a Forty-niner, with William Dupee, operated the Flying Cloud on the Sacramento and San Joaquin Rivers and located in Antioch. He later became a member of the board of supervisors.

On July 4, 1851, a basket picnic was held at the residence of W. W. Smith, which stood on the main street of the town. The principal topic discussed at the gathering was the naming of the town. There were between thirty and forty men, women and children present. A chairman was chosen, and several names were proposed, among them Minton, after a steamer that ran up and down the river. This name was suggested in the hope that by its adoption the Minton might be induced to stop at the landing. Another name proposed was Paradise. Deacon Pulsifer arose and said that there were many claimants to the lands in California, and they might lose their lands and it would then be 'Paradise Lost'." W. W. Smith then proposed that inasmuch as the first settlers were disciples of Christ, and one of them (his brother, Joseph Smith) had died and was buried on the land, that it be given a Bible name in his honor. He suggested Antioch, and so it was acclaimed.

The first school was established in the settlement in 1850 and was held in the galley of a ship owned by Captain Mitchell, which had been moved on shore. Adelia B. Kimball, a girl of twelve, daughter of Capt. G. W. Kimball, was the teacher. She later became Mrs. A. B. Schott. The second teacher was James Cruickshank, who was followed by Mrs. Woodruff. The next building used as a schoolhouse was a small one-room house near E Street. As the community grew and more room was needed, Joseph Galloway presented a site, the old grammar school lot, and a wooden building was erected. Then came a two-story brick with wooden additions which sufficed until 1890, when a substantial school building was erected. Later two grammar schools were provided through a bond issue of $91,000, the old building being used for a kindergarten and the first and second grades.

On June 23, 1883, Mrs. Annie Stinchfield opened a private school for children of the primary grade.

Bonds were voted for $74,000 in 1925, and a new grammar school building was completed in 1926. The old building was razed in September, 1926.

A religious gathering of people of the Congregational faith was early organized by a Mr. Morgan. Miss Adelia Kimball started the first Sunday school; she was assisted by Miss Drusilla Boobar and Annie Morrison. The school met in the town hall. On June 12, 1865, a meeting was held to organize a permanent church, Capt. G. W. Kimball being chairman and Rev. J. H. Warren, secretary. The following were charter members of the First Congregational Church: Mrs. R. H. Aldon, Mrs. M. H. Boothby, G. W. Brown, Mr. and Mrs. F. C. Barrett, G. C. Carmen, Isaac Hardy, G. W. Kimball, Almon Walton, S. C. Woodruff, Miss Ida Fuller, Mrs. J. C. O'Brien, David Woodruff, and William Utter.

The Catholic Church was organized in 1872, when Father V. Vinzes celebrated mass in the home of John Mulhare, where services were held for a year. In 1873 a church was built, and in 1875 Father Patrick Calahan came as the first resident priest. In 1880 he built the rectory. He died in 1902, and Father Antone Riley took charge; and in 1905 the new and commodious church was erected through his efforts. Records at Benicia show that the property on which the church and rectory stand was deeded to the Catholics in 1850.

The Advent Christian Church was organized September 25, 1877, by Mrs. M. J. Clark, an evangelist, with a charter membership of some thirty people, many of whom were members of the First Congregational Church. Among them were Mr. and Mrs. John Schott, T. N. Wills, Mr. and Mrs. H. F. Beede, Mr. and Mrs. Isaac Hardy, Louis A. Schott, and Dr. and Mrs. E. L. Wempler. Mrs. Clark served the church as pastor until Rev. W. R. Young was made the first resident pastor. He served until 1900.

The Methodist Episcopal Church was organized in September, 1899, by J. P. Abbott and Dr. W. S. George, at a meeting held in Hamburg Hall. They were assisted by W. Dunnigan, L. S. Lafferty, and Isaac Lafferty. Rev. James Blackledge was secured as the preacher, and he was succeeded by Rev. Brill. In 1890 he had secured sufficient funds to build a church building.

In 1910 the Church of Christ, Scientist, held their first meetings at the home of one of their members. In July, 1911, an organization, with fifteen charter members, was perfected, and in 1912 a lot was purchased at Fifth and D Streets. In 1915 a chapel was erected; and the first meeting in it was held on April 4 of that year.

San Joaquin Lodge No. 151, I. O. O. F., was instituted in Antioch on January 9, 1869. William Girvan was the first Noble Grand. Antioch Encampment No. 114 was organized October 9, 1908. J. T. Belshaw was the first Chief Patriarch. On June 28, 1888, Mizpah Lodge No. 102, D. of R., was instituted. The Odd Fellows own the old Union Hall.

Antioch Lodge No. 175, F. & A. M., was organized October 12, 1865. The First Master, under dispensation of May 21, 1865, was F. Williams, and he continued Master after the lodge received its charter. Ariel Chapter No. 42, O. E. S., was organized March 30, 1880. G. E. Wright was the first Worthy Patron, and Elizabeth Williams, the first Matron. The Masons purchased the Belshaw building in 1925.

General Winn Parlor No. 32, N. S. G. W., was organized July 26, 1884. The Native Sons are also represented by Mount Diablo Parlor No. 101, and the Native Daughters by Antioch Parlor No. 223. Antioch Aërie No. 785, F. O. E., was organized September 1, 1904, and Antioch Lodge No. 1612, L. O. M., was organized in February, 1915, with Dr. W. S. George as Dictator.

Besides these, there are the Y. M. I., No. 101; Pocahontas Lodge, I. O. R. M.; Antioch Pyramid No. 24, Sciots; and Antioch Chapter, Order of De Molay. There are also the Portuguese lodges, U. P. E. C., U. P. P. E. C., I. D. E. S., and S. P. R. S. I.

In 1859 coal was discovered in the hills south of Antioch, and the development of the mines added to the prosperity of the town. A railroad was built to the mines from Antioch. In 1863 copper was discovered in the hills, and a smelter was built in the town. The mining, however, was short-lived.

The first lumber yard was started in 1864 by J. W. Galloway and E. C. Boobar, who sold to Rouse, Forman & Co., in 1877. In February, 1907, the business was incorporated as the Antioch Lumber Company.

In 1865 I. Lobree started a pottery, and three years later I. Nicholson started the Albion Pottery.

In 1899 the Antioch Paper Mill was established by M. D. Keeney. In 1900 Peter and James Brown bought the mill, added new machinery, and increased the output. In March, 1912, this plant became the property of the Paraffine Paint Company, of San Francisco, and was incorporated as the California Paper and Board Mills. Numerous fires have occurred at the plant.

The Antioch Ledger, a weekly paper, was established by J. E. Townsend and Harry Waite, and its first issue was circulated on March 10, 1870. Since that date the paper has never failed to go to print. In August Townsend became sole owner; and in December J. P. Abbott bought a half interest, and Townsend sold the other half to E. G. Fuller, who sold to H. A. Weaver in 1872. The following year he sold to Abbott, who carried on the paper until 1881, when he leased it to C. H. Smith. Charles F. Montgomery succeeded to the ownership in 1884; and when he died his son, Curtis F. Montgomery, remained in charge until April 1, 1905, at which date C. F. McDaniel bought the paper. In 1921 A. W. Flaherty became the sole owner.

On September 12, 1891, the Bank of Antioch was organized; S. G. Little, president. Its capital stock was $100,000. In 1923 it erected a building costing $22,000.

On January 3, 1911, the First National Bank of Antioch and the Antioch Bank of Savings began to do business. The capital stock of the former was $25,000; and of the latter, $50,000. J. L. Harding was president.

F. L. Fulton operates a shipbuilding plant, constructing river barges, launches, etc.

In 1922 the R. Hickmott Canning Company was established, with James Glenn as manager.

Antioch has a population of 2500 within its corporate limits, and is a city of the sixth class. It was first incorporated in 1872. Later it was disincorporated, but was again incorporated in 1890.

On December 8, 1874, the fire department was organized; F. Williams, president; M. S. Levy, secretary; S. Jessup, foreman. The department developed with the times, and its equipment now includes a Ford truck chemical unit, at the central station, and four hose trucks in various parts of the city. A Gamewell fire alarm system is in operation.

The water supply of Antioch, for domestic and other purposes, is carried to the various parts of the town in 10-, 8-, 6-, and 4-inch pipes. The mains are so arranged that in case of fire the domestic supply can be cut off and the water pumped direct to the point where needed. There can be developed 300 pounds pressure if it is needed, but generally 110 to 115 pounds pressure is used. The water comes from the river and passes through a chlorinizing process before entering the mains. The chlorination plant, installed in 1916, and the water system, are owned by the city. The pumping plant cost $100,000. To develop the system, bond issues were voted: in December, 1903, of $22,000; in 1914, of $25,000; and in 1922, of $96,000. In 1926 the Antioch domestic water supply dam, made possible by the last bond issue, was completed. The reservoir, which has a capacity of 100,000,000 gallons, is located about three miles back in the hills. The bonds of this bond issue were sold at a premium of about $8000. The total sum enabled the city to construct the dam, to lay a fourteen-inch pipe line from the reservoir to the city, to install such pumps as were needed, and also to build a fence around the reservoir. This adjunct to the city's water supply insures adequate water for all purposes for many years to come.

The Pacific Gas & Electric Company and the Contra Costa Gas & Electric Company, of Pittsburg, supply electricity and gas for light and power.

On December 21, 1903, a bond issue of $8000 was voted for a sewer system. The later development of the system, which has been trebled, has been made out of the town's resources. The total assessed value of property in Antioch in 1912 was $539,000; in 1924, $1,500,000.

In 1919 a bond issue for $55,000 was voted for a city hall, which was erected that year on four lots, each 25 by 100 feet, valued at $1000 per lot. The assessed value of the new hall is $60,000 with its furnishings.

Forty-seven blocks of oil macadam were put in in 1914, under a street improvement act of 1911, at a cost of $84,000; in 1916-1917, fifty-four blocks of concrete base, one and one-half inches Topeka Top, were laid at a cost of $120,000 under the same act.

The city is served by the Southern Pacific and the Santa Fe railroads, and a great deal of hauling is also done by auto trucks. An auto stage line connects with the Sacramento-San Francisco Short Line hourly at Pittsburg.

Antioch is a port of call for all river boats. There is an average depth of sixty to eighty feet of water at the wharf. The country back of the city is a rich dairy section, and a great deal of grain is also raised. Fruit and nuts are another source of wealth to the back country. These products, together with the excellent docking facilities, make of Antioch a fine shipping point.

The Antioch Memorial Building was erected in 1925 at a cost of $22,000, by an apportionment by the board of supervisors from a tax levy of three mills on the property valuation, in honor of the men who participated in the World War.

The Antioch Free Library was erected from the Carnegie Foundation Fund.

The city officers in 1925 are: James D. Donlon, president of the board; R. M. Beede, treasurer; John E. McElheny, city clerk; members: W. A. Christiansen, H. A. West, George W. Harter, and R. A. Wall.

CHAPTER IX

CONCORD

In 1869 Salvio Pacheco, Fernando Pacheco, and Francisco Galindo laid out the town of Concord, platting lots and streets. There were nineteen blocks and a plaza. The laying out of the town was undertaken in order to afford people living at Pacheco, who were continually being flooded out, an opportunity to locate on higher ground, because every flood necessitated rebuilding, repairing or raising buildings that had been damaged by the water. The donor of the land suggested the name Todos Santos (All Saints). This is the name by which the town was recorded.

The Americans dubbed it "Drunken Indian," but the public finally gave it the name it now bears.

When the town was laid out it was decided by the founders that if those who lived and did business in Pacheco would locate in Concord, a certain number of lots would be given them free. Samuel Bacon was the first man to take advantage of this offer; and in June, 1869, he built a store and residence on the new townsite, at what is now the site of the American Bank. That summer Charles Lohse built a machine shop. Henry Loring erected the Klein Hotel, which later became known as the Concord Hotel. Several other business houses and homes were erected.

Among the first settlers were John Brawand, who had a livery stable; and George Gavin, who ran a blacksmith shop. H. Ivey also had a livery. J. H. Keller, a Forty-niner, opened the first butcher shop. Foskett & Elsworthy bought out Keller in 1869 or 1870. John Wiechers conducted the Mount Diablo Hotel until his death. This hotel stood on the site of the Concord Inn. The first bakery was opened by John Lambert, who, in 1889, erected a building of his own, more adequate for his business. Others were John Turney, B. Mahoney, John Denkenger, A. Gehringer, and Philip Klein. Klein ran the Concord Hotel; Charles Klein, his son, now conducts a drug store. F. C. Galindo, grandson of one of the founders of Concord, is proprietor of the Concord Department Store. M. Neustaedter, son of B. Neustaedter, with his sisters, runs a store in the town. M. S. Soares was another of the poineers. His sons, J. M. and George, own the Concord Ice & Fuel Company. Henry Bott, a blacksmith and wagon-maker, has been on the same corner with his plant for fifty years. He was a member of the first board of trustees upon the incorporation of the town and is still a member. In 1892, with a partner, Mr. Smith, he erected a new shop building.

Pacheco Lodge No. 117, I. O. O. F., was organized in 1863, with G. P. Loucks as first Noble Grand. On January 1, 1896, the hall was moved from Pacheco to Concord and dedicated.

Besides the Odd Fellows Lodge, there are the W. O. W., Neighbors of Woodcraft, I. O. R. M., U. P. E. C., and I. D. E. S.; Concord Parlor No. 245, N. S. G. W.; Mount Diablo Lodge No. 228, D. of R.; Concord Chapter, O. E. S.; Mount Diablo Lodge No. 448, F. & A. M., organized in 1915; and Y. M. I., organized July 31, 1887.

Concord has a Catholic church, a Presbyterian church, a Christian church, and a Church of Christ Scientist, organized in the order given. In 1873 a Catholic church was erected. In December 1882, a Presbyterian church was organized, with Rev. D. Monroe as pastor; and William Caven, John Brawand and E. A. Jaquith, trustees.

The first school was established in 1870 and was taught by Mrs. Henry Polley. A grammar school was built in 1892, and a high school in 1906.

Foskett & Elsworthy founded the First National Bank, now a branch of the American Bank.

The Bank of Concord was established in 1900 by M. E. Lyon, who also built the Concord Inn.

The Concord Sun was founded by S. Fargeon. Later the name was changed to the Concord Transcript and the ownership fell to H. A. Downer. He was succeeded by J. S. Taylor, who sold to H. E. Griffith. Griffith sold to Mrs. N. K. Cushing. In 1910 a corporation called the Transcript Publishing Company was organized and published a paper every Thursday. This corporation was dissolved in 1914, when Catherine Burke purchased the paper. She married J. M. Soares, and together they direct the paper's destinies.

On February 5, 1905, Concord was incorporated as a city of the sixth class. B. Elsworthy was the first president of the board; Joseph Boyd, the second; E. J. Randall, third; J. M. Finney, fourth; H. W. Bott, fifth; J. M. Soto, sixth; Charles Klein, seventh; and D. J. Baldwin the eighth president.

Since the incorporation of the town, which now has 2100 population, $200,000 have been spent for street work. The city issued bonds in the amount of $29,000 for a sewer system, and pays $1,000 a year interest on them. Concord was the first town of its size to have paved streets, which were put down in 1914-1915.

The P. G. & E. and the Great Western Gas & Electric Company supply electricity for power and lighting, and the Contra Costa Gas Company, in 1916, began to supply gas for fuel and domestic purposes. Port Costa Water Company supplies pure water for all purposes.

On April 12, 1879, a fire department was organized, and this has grown with the town and is now equipped with a La France chemical engine, purchased in 1925, at a cost of $6000. The old chemical engine is owned jointly by the town and the Farm Bureau.

On April 25, 1917, Concord was visited by a fire which destroyed the business portion of the town, including the Concord Inn, Concord Mercantile Company, B. Neustaedter's store, the office of Drs. L. Martin and Edward Johnson, and M. C. Meehan's hardware store, the law offices of A. S. Sherlock, and some apartments.

In 1912 the Oakland & Antioch Electric Railway entered the town, and then many of the old landmarks gave way to modern buildings.

Among the modern buildings in Concord are the M. E. Lyon Building, Bacon Block, Majestic Theater, J. J. January Building, Seifried Building, Concord Auto Service Station, Chevrolet and Ford, the new grammar school erected in 1924, and the high school. The new auditorium of the grammar school was opened in 1926.

The Mount Diablo Union High School in Concord is the second largest school in the county, having twenty teachers and a student body of 400. The district takes in a territory surrounding Concord that includes the towns of Walnut Creek, Lafayette, Bay Point, Clayton, Cowell, Avon, and Pacheco. The total assessed valuation of the district is over $13,000,000.

A Carnegie Library and a branch of the Contra Costa County Library serve the people of the locality with reading matter.

A Chamber of Commerce has been in continuous service since its organization in 1917.

There are heavy shipments of green and dried fruits, nuts, and all kinds of farm products sent out from Concord annually over the Southern Pacific and the Sacramento Short Line. The Concord Ice & Fuel Company and Russi & Somer have ample storage warehouses. There are four fruit packing-houses at Minert Station, a short distance from town.

In 1925 hangars were built near Concord for the Diablo Air Mail Field Base for air mail transportation. The following newspaper reference to this base appeared under the date of January 26, 1925:

"Six government planes detailed to the federal air mail will use the base as a test field for an indefinite period, starting today.

"In establishing the Concord trans-continental terminus the federal government has stationed fourteen air plane experts at the local base.

"The site is practically immune from the almost continual land and bay fogs of surrounding regions. Because of this and the adaptability of the ground formation for landing purposes, the experts declare it an excellent location."

CHAPTER X

CROCKETT

The town of Crockett, six miles below Martinez on Carquinez Straits, was named in honor of J. B. Crockett, a member of the Supreme Bench of California. The original townsite consisted of eighteen blocks divided into lots 50 by 100 feet each, with the streets running east and west.

The town is the location of the California & Hawaiian Sugar Refining Company, the largest plant of its kind in the world, representing an investment of more than $7,000,000 and employing about 2000 people. The fine water-front of Crockett permits vessels of the deepest draft to load and discharge cargoes. The Sugar Company is very liberal in civic affairs; it furnishes a playground for the children, and a club house for the grown-ups. This is recognized as a community center club house.

THOMAS EWDARDS, THE FOUNDER OF CROCKETT

"Thomas Edwards, founder of Crockett, was born in North Wales on April 5, 1812. At the age of fourteen he went to sea and continued before the mast for ten years. He then became mate on a Mississippi River boat, where he met J. B. Crockett and W. C. Ralston. On February 9, 1843, he married Mary Pugh, who was also born in North Wales, on July 20, 1819. In 1849 they started for California. They wintered in Council Bluffs and started the next spring with forty men and ten wagons for California, reaching the end of the journey in September, 1850. He came almost immediately to the Carquinez Straits and engaged in the stock business on 1800 acres of land. The rest of his life is the history of Crockett. He died February 15, 1883. Two sons, Thomas and David, still make their home in Crockett."

The above quotation, and the following data relative to the founding of the town of Crockett, were taken from the Crockett Signal of November 17, 1922, when there was published a special edition at the twenty-fifth anniversary of the founding of the California & Hawaiian Sugar Refinery.

Thomas Edwards, Sr., came to Carquinez Straits in 1866 and located in Bull Valley (Port Costa). J. B. Crockett, a practicing attorney and a friend of Mr. Edwards, came into possession of a strip of land one mile long on the straits and running three miles south, as counsel fees in settling a grant suit. Crockett and Edwards entered into a partnership on the land, but Edwards was unable to secure possession on account of squatters on the land. These men were living in a cabin, the present site of the A. H. Boucke home, and were cutting wood back in the hills and shipping by boat to the bay section. Watching their opportunity when the men were away from their cabin, Mr. Edwards and his sons took possession. When the men came back to their cabin and found themselves dispossessed, they went to the Fernandez ranch at Pinole, organized a band of sixteen men, and started back to oust the Edwards's. Mr. Fernandez, who knew the circumstances of Edwards' claim, hearing of the band of men leaving his ranch, mounted a horse and overtook them and succeeded in turning them back. The history of Crockett dates from 1867, when the Edwards family settled here, where they have since made their home. Thomas and David are the only survivors of the family.

Thomas Edwards erected his family home on the bay shore, in a little cove overlooking the water, the shore-line being just at the edge of his front yard. The shore-line has gradually receded until it is several hundred feet to the water's edge. There was an old Indian burying-ground in the immediate vicinity. The townsite comprised 115 acres. Edwards sold to J. L. Heald, who built a machine shop of brick and a foundry. He helped lay out the town. Edwards received $50 per acre, but reserved every other lot. The Edwards house is still standing in a grove of trees, most of which were planted by Mrs. Edwards.

Notes From the Diary of John Edwards

The following items are taken from the Signal, as copied from a diary kept by John Edwards. In 1877 the Southern Pacific was pushing its road along Carquinez Straits, construction having begun in 1876.

"Feb. 6, 1877—The engineers arrived; 300 men are working on the railroad.

"May 31.—Railroad men began driving piles for Edwards' wharf.

"June 5.—The carpenters began work. The graders commenced on the local water-front.

CROCKETT, CALIFORNIA—1920

CROCKETT, CALIFORNIA—1923-24

"June 12.—Construction work was halted on account of a dispute over rights of way over Donahue and Robinson's land.

"June 13.—A schooner carrying forty Chinese workmen for the railroad was nearly wrecked on the rocky point [where the sugar factory now stands].

"Aug. 22.—Hugh Edwards and a friend made a trip to San Francisco on the cars.

"Sept. 3.—Railroad men are stringing telegraph poles along the right-of-way; cars came up in sight of Edwards' house.

"Sept. 5.—Election day, and all went to Martinez, over the new county road for the first time, to vote. P. Tormey was elected supervisor.

"Sept. 11.—Rails laid past Edwards' house and cars passed. Engine 35 pulled a train of thirty-five cars and I rode on the train.

"Sept. 25.—The first passenger train, with Leland Stanford on board, went through to Martinez.

"Oct. 9.—The first morning newspapers were received by train.

"Dec. 16.—A jury brought in a verdict for $1600 in favor of Robinson in damage suit over rights of way.

"June 23, 1878.—Two engines hauling forty-three cars of lumber and iron for the tunnel came up.

"July 5.—Passenger trains began making regular stops opposite Edwards' house.

"July 18.—A letter was received from the railroad authorities, making Edwards' place a flag station.

"Aug. 30.—Overland trains began passing.

"Dec. 18.—Billings' Engine No. 28 ran into the morning emigrant train, telescoping three cars and injuring several people.

"Dec. 22.—A great quantity of lumber for Port Costa ferry ship arrived.

"March 20, 1879.—Mr. Gordon, telegraph operator, opened Valona station. He is stopping at Edwards' house.

"April 5.—Valona office abandoned.

"April 25.—Fire destroys James McHarry's store.

"Dec. 8, 1880.—Edwards opened negotiations to buy Judge Crockett's interest in the ranch for $30,000.

"Dec. 29.—A sidetrack was surveyed for the Edwards's.

"Dec. 30.—Mr. Heald of Vallejo arrived, looking for a foundry site.

"Feb. 12, 1881.—The Gazette says that J. E. Eckley transferred 250 acres to Frances Eckley and Carrie Adams for $5000.

"March 9.—A. D. Starr and partner of the Buckeye Mills in Vallejo are around looking for a site.

"May 20.—An express office has been established at Vallejo Junction.

"June 25.—Dr. Strentzel and Mr. Edwards view the franchise made with Lee for tidelands.

"July 29.—Mr. Edwards finished the survey for the outline of a town-site.

"Oct. 8.—Mr. Starr called to see about getting a mill-site.

"Nov. 7.—T. A. McMahon, of Martinez, came down to survey the town-site.

"Nov. 18.—Grading began for a hotel.

"Jan. 16, 1882.—The carpenters are putting up rafters on Heald's foundry.

"Feb. 17.—The Pinkerton House was opened to the public.

"Feb. 22.—The first load of machinery for Heald arrived.

"March 2.—Mr. Heald turned the first wheel in his foundry with a threshing engine.

"March 3.—The foundry is in operation. The whistle blew at noon for the first time.

"March 10.—A meeting was held with the Port Costans on the school question. They ran the meeting to suit themselves.

"March 11.—An election was held to elect W. S. Cown, Doyle and John Edwards trustees of Carquinez district.

"March 13.—A man named Welsh was around looking for a mill-site and seemed favorably impressed.

"May 23.—The lumber arrived for J. C. Glancy's house.

"May 27.—School trustees go to San Francisco and purchase $130.45 worth of supplies.

"June 5.—School began with eighteen scholars. Miss Lottie Bent is the teacher. James and Nellie Narbett and three Perrin children are among the pupils.

"July 20.—The first town water tank was set up by William Narbett for Mr. Edwards and a pipe line laid to it.

"Aug. 10.—The foundrymen gave their first ball; there were twenty-seven couples present.

"Aug. 16.—There are three Port Costa children in the Crockett school.

"Sept. 9.—Two freight cars ran off the Solano Ferry today.

"Nov. 18.—Starr & Company accepted the franchise offer of Edwards.

"Nov. 29.—The deed was signed by Edwards and the franchise turned over to Starr & Co.

"Dec. 31.—The heaviest snowstorm ever experienced; six inches of snow fell and stayed on the ground seven days.

"Jan. 18, 1883.—Starr got his quit claim deed to high land across the track. [Hotel Crockett is now on the site.]

"Feb. 4.—Pile driver arrived.

"Feb. 6.—The Mary Glover brought a load of piles for Starr's mill.

"Feb. 15.—Thos. Edwards, Sr., died. He was buried on the 18th at Martinez.

"April 7.—Legion of Honor organized. There are twenty members.

"April 12.—A wind storm scattered lumber for Starr's mill about the Straits.

"April 15.—The first church services were held in Crockett settlement. About thirty-five attended. Mr. Ballagh preached.

"April 23.—A site was chosen for a Congregational Church.

"April 29.—The first church services were held at Port Costa; twelve people attended. Rev. Drahms preached.

"May 4.—The Barkentine Restler was the first vessel to berth at the Starr wharf.

"June 15.—There was a postoffice established at Crockett.

"July 7.—The first load of groceries was received for Mr. Barnhisel. He has the first store in Crockett.

"July 14.—The school was reorganized. Miss Jones, teacher.

"July 21.—Dr. Strentzel gave A. D. Starr a block of land.

"July 31.—The lumber was put on the ground for the first house on Dr. Strentzel's town-site, Valona.

"Sept. 22.—Masons began laying brick for the flour mill."

Later Growth of the Town

At the close of 1883 Crockett contained: the Pinkerton place, now Deininger's; Heald's foundry; schoolhouse; postoffice; Barnhisel's store; Edwards Brothers' market; Daniel Brown's house, the first one built on the townsite; and the homes of M. A. Hayes, John Flood, J. C. Glancy, William Narbett, William Perrin, W. E. Parks, C. H. Gardiner, and a few others.

In 1897 the California Beet Sugar & Refining Company, R. P. Riblet, the first president, purchased the Starr Mill and converted it into a beet and cane sugar factory. The California & Hawaiian Sugar Company took charge in 1905, and began melting in March, 1906. That year they melted 67,000 tons. This company has grown into the largest refining company in the world, and has a melting capacity of 4,500,000 pounds.

April 22, 1899, the Crockett Signal says the Carquinez school district had an attendance of 166.

The first newspaper in Crockett was the Record, and the first issue was put out on Saturday, January 11, 1896. Hart A. Downer was editor and publisher. The Record was discontinued on December 19, 1896. On April 8, 1899, W. G. Howes founded the Crockett Signal, which lasted only a short time. In December, 1903, the Signal was revived, and it continued until November 19, 1904. In January, 1906, W. M. Laidlaw again revived the paper. He has since continued its management very successfully, building up a fine job-printing business in connection with the paper.

Crockett now has a population of 4000. It has a First National Bank, organized in 1919 with $25,000 capital, which was increased to $50,000. T. J. O'Leary was the first president and F. W. Hutchinson was president in 1926. There is also a branch of the Bank of Pinole, established in 1908.

The Congregational Church of Crockett, built in 1884, and the Presbyterian Church of Valona are combined under the head of the Crockett Community Church. There is also the St. Rose's Catholic Church.

The school has developed from the one first organized in June, 1883, with eighteen pupils, to a very modern institution containing twenty-six rooms, with 476 scholars and a principal and twenty-two teachers. The John Swett Union High School is also located at Crockett, and has 212 pupils and eighteen teachers. On Sunday, October 24, 1926, the laying of the cornerstone of the new John Swett Union High School building was observed with appropriate ceremonies. This is to be one of the finest and most modern high school buildings in the county.

In 1916 a Y. M. C. A. building was dedicated. The Carquinez Women's Clubhouse, the Loring Theater, Crockett Music House and Crockett Theater are among the modern buildings that ornament the town.

The town is amply protected from fire by its volunteer department with modern equipment. The Sugar Company maintains its own department, made up of its own employees. The Valona department is also a volunteer organization. One of the latest municipal developments in Crockett was the purchase, by the city, of the old Salvation Army barracks on the north side of Loring Street, between West and Bay Streets, for a permanent fire house. The building was remodeled after plans drawn at the suggestion of Lloyd Edwards, fire chief, who had visited many cities and made inspection of their fire houses. The plans were approved by the trustees and the building was completed and taken over by the department on March 29, 1926. The building has ample accommodations for the La France Triple Combination fire engine and a combination hose and chemical cart. The upper floor is fitted out with eight single, modernly equipped and furnished bedrooms for the volunteer firemen who wish to live there. There are also a kitchenette with all appurtenances, a meeting or dining room, a fine clubroom facing Loring Street and shower baths and toilets. There are thirty-one men in the department, all volunteers. The Crockett fire department cooperates with the fire fighters of the C. & H. at all times, as do the latter with the local department when needed.

As a means of promoting good-will, there is a Crockett and Valona Business Men's Association. There are also a Citizen's Improvement Association that works continually for civic betterment, and a Girl's Club.

Almost every lodge and fraternal organization is represented in Crockett, among them: Carquinez Lodge No. 337, F. & A. M.; Crockett Chapter No. 184, O. E. S.; Crockett Lodge No. 329, I. O. O. F.; Crockett Encampment No. 43; Carmel Lodge No. 150, D. of R.; Crockett Aërie No. 774, F. O. E.; Carquinez Tribe No. 98, I. O. R. M.; Selby Lodge No. 192, K. of P.; Court Carquinez No. 1001, I. O. F.; Neola Council No. 172, I. O. R. M.; Degree of Pocahontas; Carquinez Parlor No. 205, N. S. G. W.; Court Chris Bremmer No. 166, F. of A.; Alhambra Circle No. 205, Neighbors of Woodcraft; Crockett Post No. 33. American Legion; Camp Fire Girls; Boy Scouts; Carquinez Woman's Club; Contra

Costa Chapter, U. A. O. D.; Cavour Grove No. 192, U. A. O. D.; Cro-lona Circle No. 70, U. A. O. D.; Consello Florida do Esperanca No. 59, U. P. E. C.; Council Santa Rosa No. 29, I. D. E. S.; and Carquinez Par-lor No. 234, N. D. G. W.

The Veteran's Memorial Hospital was erected in 1925, by a tax levied by the supervisors, costing about $20,000.

CHAPTER XI

EL CERRITO

The beginning of what is now one of the best residential cities in Contra Costa County took place when, in 1888, William F. Rust, a blacksmith, located a shop on San Pablo Avenue in which to ply his trade. This was then the center of a good farming community; and in order to meet the demands of ranchers, Mr. Rust leased property and built his shop. The community grew apace, and in 1909 a postoffice was estab-lished, Mr. Rust being appointed the first postmaster, which position he occupied for three years; in fact, he was postmaster, blacksmith and general counselor to the settlers of this district, which was then known as Rust. Mr. Rust is now living retired, having invested his money wisely in real estate in this district. In September, 1917, it was found desirable to incorporate the town as a city of the sixth class, and it was given the name of El Cerrito (The Little Hill). At that time the population had grown to about 1500 souls.

In 1905 a school was established and soon after a community church, under the direction of a Methodist preacher. There was, however, a Catholic church established a short time prior to that of the Methodists. Both of these congregations have grown, and in 1925 both erected new edifices. In 1916 the school was taken into the jurisdiction of Richmond; and in 1924 a modern school building was erected, where eight grammar grades are carried on. In 1926 an extensive addition was made to the building to accommodate the increase in attendance; also a modern school building was erected on Fairmont Avenue.

The estimated population of El Cerrito, in 1926, is given as about 4000. Nearly all the streets in the town are paved. During the interval from 1917 to 1924 about forty blocks of paving were laid, and during 1924-1925 $500,000 was spent on street work. A new city hall was built in 1925, also to house the fire department, and a fire alarm system has been installed. This was done through a bond issue of $65,000 voted by the people.

The first board of trustees, elected in 1917, were: Kirk Gray, P. A. Lee, J. Sandwick, G. W. Adams and P. Larson. Mr. Gray was elected chairman of the board. This board of trustees held office until the regular election in 1918, when P. A. Lee was chosen chairman. George Conlon succeeded Mr. Adams at this election. Mr. Lee served as chairman until April, 1924. He was succeeded by George Conlon, who in turn was succeeded, in 1925, by Frank McDermott. In 1926 C. Zimmerman became the presiding officer.

The attractiveness of the city as a residential district is enhanced by its adequate street car service, with a one-fare rate to Richmond, ending at Sixteenth Street, and one fare to any Oakland point; its tax rate of ninety cents on every $100 valuation; its modern homes, with cheap rents; and its modern public facilities and conveniences. Ninety per cent of the residents outside of the Berkeley Country Club Terrace, own their own homes, all of modern construction and varying in price according to the demands of the owners. The city is in Sanitary District No. 7 and is served by the East Bay Water Company, the Western States Gas Company, and the Pacific Gas & Electric Company. The city limits extend along San Pablo Avenue from the Alameda County line three miles northerly, and the width averages about two miles, from the Avenue to the top of the Berkeley Hills. The Berkeley Golf Club is located at the northern boundary of the town. The city includes about one-half of the residences on the hill, in the Mira Vista district, a suburb of Richmond. The El Cerrito Improvement Club and the Berkeley Terrace Welfare Club have a distinct bearing on the civic development of the city; while the Parent-Teachers Association of El Cerrito looks after the educational interests of the young and growing generation. A branch of the Contra Costa County Free Library is located in El Cerrito, and housed in a comfortable building on Fairmont Avenue. The Berkeley Country Club Terrace Improvement Association, which was organized on August 25, 1923, became the El Cerrito Improvement Association March 4, 1924.

At the time of incorporation of the city the assessed valuation of property in El Cerrito was $1,125,000; in 1925 the estimated valuation was a little more than twice that amount. Business of nearly every description is carried on by enterprising merchants, who esteem it a privilege to boost their town and its advantages. The principal industry inside the corporate limits is quarrying. Bates and Borland and the Hutchinson Company have large quarries here. The city has one enterprising newspaper, the Journal, established in April, 1925, and published weekly by L. A. Sirard. In 1925 the old volunteer fire department was disbanded, a new department organized, and a new La France engine and chemical truck put in commission. In 1926 the fire department headquarters, along with other city offices, were moved to the new city hall.

On August 24, 1926, an annexation election was held at which territory was added to the city in order to control the San Pablo Highway. Starting on the highway at Bay View Avenue it runs west to Avila Street, then 100 feet south to San Diego Street, westerly to Panhandle Boulevard and southerly to the county line. This territory on the west side of San Pablo gives El Cerrito control of San Pablo Avenue for three miles.

CHAPTER XII

OTHER TOWNS OF THE COUNTY

BAY POINT

The town of Bay Point is situated on a tract of government land lying between the Los Médanos Grant on the east and the Monte del Diablo or Pacheco Grant on the south and west. The land was first patented to H. H. Smith by President U. S. Grant. Smith sold his preemption and homestead rights to Daniel Cunningham. This part of the tract bordered the bay shore. Where the Smith lumber plant now is, was the site of the old Cunningham homestead. The other part of the tract, where the business and residential parts of the town are located, was upon land patented by President Grant to Mr. Clark, who in turn sold to A. H. Neeley, a friend of Mr. Cunningham. The Cunningham heirs and Mr. Neeley sold to C. A. Smith, a large lumber manufacturer of Minneapolis, Minn., who had decided to locate his Western business in close proximity to San Francisco and manufacture and distribute his product. This was in 1907, when Bay Point was a tule bog.

Mr. Smith arranged to purchase 1500 acres with one and one-half miles of tidewater frontage from the heirs of Dan Cunningham and A. H. Neeley. The deal was consummated and the nucleus of the town was started on November 26, 1907. William Smith, from Pittsburg, started the first general merchandise store in 1908-1909. The first residence was erected by William Buholtz in 1908, the second by Samuel Gilroy that same year.

The original name of the shipping point was Seal Bluff. The Copper King Smelting Company erected a smelter and docks at a cost of $1,375,-000. They closed down February 15, 1903. In 1890 there was a warehouse built at that point, and this was the first and only warehouse ever located at Bay Point.

Bay Point is served by the Southern Pacific, Santa Fe and San Francisco-Sacramento Short Line railroads. The town is divided into two units. That part lying between the Southern Pacific and Santa Fe and the bay is devoted to manufacturing; and that between the two roads and the foothills, to residence property and business places. The main Pittsburg and Martinez highway passes through Bay Point, and also the main county highway to Oakland.

In 1918, as a war measure, yards were established by the Pacific Coast Shipbuilding Company to build ten emergency fleet ships, Diablo being the first built. Four hundred men were given employment. The town of Clyde was built to house the employees of the shipyard. It is now peopled by the employees of the Associated Oil Company at Avon, and by many of the Shell employees from Martinez.

At Bay Point are located the Coos Bay Lumber Co.'s plant; stores of all kinds; a postoffice; a graded school with 150 pupils attending, and five teachers (it is in the Mount Diablo Union High School district); Congregational, Catholic, and Swedish Lutheran churches; Bay Point Foundry; and the First National Bank, organized January 7, 1920, with $25,000 capital, a branch of the First National Bank of Pittsburg. There are also lodges of the Independent Order of Odd Fellows, the Rebekahs, the Woodmen of the World, the Royal Neighbors, and a Masonic Club.

The town has paved streets, cement sidewalks and curbs, an artesian water supply system piped into the town from the hills to the south, about one and a half miles from the Government Ranch. The population is about 800 people, and it is a thriving locality.

DANVILLE

The town of Danville, eighteen miles south of Martinez, is located in a horticultural district which was one of the early grain-raising sections of Contra Costa County. It has a population of about 400 people, and is enterprising and progressive.

Danville was started in 1858 when Daniel and Andrew Inman built a smithy. Inman sold out to J. E. Close, who carried on the blacksmith shop for years. In 1858 M. Cohen built the second building in the place for a branch establishment of the store at Alamo owned and conducted by Cohen & Wolf. This building stood for sixty years. The first hotel was kept by H. W. Harris in 1858, and he was also the postmaster. The mail came via stage from Walnut Creek. P. E. Peel conducted the second store. He was succeeded by John Conway, who carried on the business for many years.

There are two versions given regarding the naming of Danville. One is that it was named for Dan Inman, the man who built the first building. Another is that the honor was given "Aunt Sallie" Young, who named it Danville after Danville, Ky., her birthplace.

There had been a schoolhouse erected in the valley, about a mile from the townsite, in 1858; this was moved into the town in 1870 and put on a lot in the south end of the town, where the first grammar school was built in 1865. This building burned, and the country schoolhouse was moved onto the plat of ground. A new building was erected in 1895 and did duty until 1922, when the new building was erected at the north side of the town. This modern building was built from a bond issue of $15,000. In 1910 the Union High School was established at Danville, known as the San Ramon Valley Union High School, and school was held in temporary quarters until the present high school building was erected on a site adjoining the new grammar school.

In 1872 Granger's Hall was built. The Grange is still a live organization of the district.

Church services were first held in the vicinity in 1857, in a private house, by Rev. D. McClure, a Presbyterian preacher. After 1858 services were held in the schoolhouse. On October 1, 1875, the cornerstone was laid for the first church edifice, a Presbyterian church, and in June, 1876, the building was dedicated, after the indebtedness of $2500 had been fully paid. On January 1, 1876, Rev. R. S. Symington took charge of the church work, and to him is largely due the building and finishing of the church. Danville now has, also, a Catholic church.

There were a number of sturdy pioneers to whom great credit is due for the upbuilding of Danville and vicinity. Among them we mention Thomas Flournoy, who owned a ranch on the east side of the creek; J. E. Close, a blacksmith, who purchased the Inman shop; R. O. Baldwin, who owned a large ranch southwest of town; James Stone, a neighbor of Baldwin's; A. J. Young, who taught school for years; a Mr. Kerr, who owned 200 acres adjoining the town on the west, and who sold this ranch to James Stone, who sold to John Hartz; R. B. Love, a large rancher in this section; and W. Z. Stone, William Meese, Charles Wood, the Boone family, Dr. J. L. Labaree, D. N. Sherburne, A. J. Young, and Bruce Stone (who came in 1860), the last two named being still alive. Descendants of Flournoy, Close and Baldwin are still represented here; also Mrs. D. N. Sherburne is still here.

In 1891 the San Ramon branch of the Southern Pacific reached Danville, at which time new impetus was given the town. John Hartz surveyed and sold town lots in an addition which includes the southwest part of town. The Oakland, Antioch & Eastern Electric Railway came in 1914, but this road was abandoned in 1924 as unprofitable and the tracks were taken up.

The San Ramon Valley Chamber of Commerce was organized with A. S. Ormsby as its first president; Will Meese, secretary; Dr. Fred Booth, vice-president; and A. H. Cope, treasurer. The Chamber took in San Ramon, Danville, Walnut Creek, Alamo, Tassajara and Lafayette. In December, 1924, the Chamber was reorganized without Lafayette and Walnut Creek. At this time, 1925, E. C. Weister is president and Mrs. Jessie Higley, secretary.

Danville Lodge No. 378, I. O. O. F. was instituted on July 26, 1892. Other fraternal organizations are: Danville Lodge No. 123, Daughters of Rebekah; Danville Grange No. 85, P. of H., which has about 200 members and is a strong organization; the Foresters of America; the U. P. E. C.; the I. D. E. S.; and the Woodmen of the World. The Odd Fellows, in conjunction with the Patrons of Husbandry, erected a social and fraternal hall in 1912.

In 1923 a district fire company was organized with a fine motor chemical engine. The district covers Alamo, Danville and Tassajara, and the upkeep is paid by taxation.

The Veterans' Memorial Hall, one of the recent modern buildings,

6

was erected by a fund apportioned by the board of supervisors, and cost about $20,000. It is in honor of the soldiers of the World War.

The San Ramon Valley Bank is the financial bulwark of the town, and occupies its own building. It was organized in Walnut Creek in 1907, and the Danville branch was established in 1911. C. W. Close is resident manager.

The products of the country surrounding the town include walnuts, pears, and prunes in the valley; and on the sloping hills grain and hay are raised. These products are shipped over the Southern Pacific and by motor trucks to Sacramento, San Francisco, Oakland and Berkeley. A large business is done in trucking.

A bus line is operated during the summer season over a scenic boulevard to the top of Mount Diablo, which is one of the great attractions for tourists.

MOUNT DIABLO COUNTRY CLUB

The Mount Diablo Country Club was organized by George W. McNear and a number of his associates who were golf enthusiasts. Property was purchased in Contra Costa County in the foothills of Mount Diablo and extensive grounds were laid out on the 600 acres. Here is one of the best eighteen-hole golf courses with grass greens and fairways to be found in the State. Tennis courts and ample provision for other recreational games are also to be found here. One of the most modern club houses has been erected and is the scene of frequent and enjoyable banquets. There is a fine reservoir lake, with bath house and swimming pool; and black bass abound in this lake. A paved road leads to the club property, which lies three miles from Danville to the east. Besides being an ideal recreation center, it is also an ideal home place and some half-hundred fine homes are now built within the confines of the property. The club has its own water supply, which is adequate for all purposes, the water being piped four miles down to the grounds. The club membership is limited to 400 and is made up of people from the east bay cities. The officers of the club are: George W. McNear, president; W. S. Dinwiddie, vice-president; Roy L Pratt, secretary. The board of directors, in addition to the above named, are: William Dolge, Bernard Ransome, Hon. L. R. Weinmann and William Cavalier.

ALAMO

The village of Alamo, which means Poplar in Spanish, is a settlement two miles north of Danville and sixteen miles south of Martinez, on San Ramon Creek. In the early days this section of the county was settled by the Spanish families, Francisco Garcia being one of the pioneers living on the San Ramon Grant near this particular spot. On October 3, 1852, D. P. Smith settled east of the place. At that time there were but four houses between this place and Martinez. In 1852 David Glass started a small trading-post at his place.

Henry Hoffman opened the first store in the village, having bought David Glass' stock. This firm soon after became known as Wolf & Company, Mr. Hoffman retaining an interest. George Englemire opened the second place in 1852, and ran a shoe shop and general store. The post-office was established in 1853 at the home of John M. Jones, who was postmaster, assisted by his wife, Mary A. This was the only postoffice between Martinez and Mission San José, the carrier making a round trip once a week, with a horse and cart. In connection with their store, Wolf & Company opened a hotel. In due time other shops were opened, a harness shop, meat market and smithy. The third building was of brick and was occupied by Wolf & Company, who soon opened a hotel in connection with the store; Mr. Hoffman, retaining an interest in the store, was manager of the hotel. When Wolf & Company moved to Danville, Mr. Hoffman sold his interest in the store to remain as hotel-keeper of Henry's Hotel. He took a partner named William Maxey in the late fifties.

In 1857 James Foster opened a wagon and carriage shop. He also made furniture and coffins. The timbers in his shop were shipped from Maine around the Horn.

In January, 1858, Albert W. Stone arrived in the settlement; and that same year J. C. Peterson and F. L. Hamburg also came. Lomax & Smart had a general store, and overhead was the Masonic Hall where Alamo Lodge No. 122, F. & A. M., which was instituted in 1858, held its meetings. In 1860 a two-story brick building was built on the west side of the street by Wolf & Cohen, and the Masons moved their lodge room to the upper floor. The bricks in this building were made by G. W. Webster from clay on the Van Gorden place, the kiln being erected on Rancho El Rio, across the creek. The earthquake of 1868 damaged this building and it was torn down, and the Masons moved to Danville.

In 1854, a Cumberland Presbyterian church was erected south of town, and that same year the first school opened in the valley, with Richard Webster as teacher. For a time school was held in the home of Captain Wall, and it was known as the Wall School.

In 1859 the Contra Costa Educational Association built the Union Academy, a boarding and day school, which was opened in June, 1860, Rev. David McClure being the principal. This building was located between Alamo and Danville and was a three-story structure. John H. Braly succeeded McClure, and Robert King followed Braly. The building burned in 1868 and was never rebuilt.

In 1860 Daniel Selley located in Alamo.

In 1862 tobacco was first raised here by Stout and Peden.

In March, 1861, Rev. T. M. Johnston published the Pacific Cumberland Presbyter, a religious paper.

In connection with the activities of Rev. T. M. Johnston, we glean a few items from a diary kept by him and now in the possession of his granddaughter, Mrs. C. M. French, of Merced. It seems that Rev. Johnston came to California on account of ill health, as his diary starts back on February 21, 1859, when he writes from some point back in the East en route by stage to California:

"Albuquerque mail arrived early."

"March 6—Arrived at Ft. Smith, stopped at St. Charles Hotel."

"March 22—Passed Ft. Fillmore and crossed the Rio Grande."

"March 27—Arrived at Ft. Yuma."

"April 1—Passed Visalia last night."

"April 4—Arrived at What Cheer House in San Francisco."

"April 6—Started for Stockton, went to Napa City, took stage for Benicia, where took boat for Stockton."

"Sunday, January 20, 1861—Preached at Lafayette."

"Sunday, March 10—Preached at Alamo."

"May 29, 1861—Married John O'Brien and Mrs. Mary E. Crawford."

"June 8, 1861—Hail storm today."

"December 26—Rained excessively all day. Creek higher than I ever saw it."

"Friday, April 22, 1864—Preached funeral of James Foster's child today to a large congregation."

"December 21, 1864—Married Albert G. Wilks and Jane Toomey today at house of J. T. Walker."

"January 1, 1867—Mrs. Isaac Yoakum died about 5 p. m. today."

"February 26, 1871—Preached funeral sermon of Roxana Simpson at Sycamore school house."

"Sunday, March 8, 1874—Received this day by express a package containing books and apparatus of deputy assessor."

"March 10—Commenced assessing today."

"Saturday, April 4—Difficult to assess foreigners."

Rev. Johnston was a traveling preacher and missionary. He spent a great deal of his time traveling about from Visalia to Napa, Sacramento and Stockton, organizing congregations and helping to build up churches.

PACHECO

Located five miles south from Martinez is the village of Pacheco, once the most likely town in all Contra Costa County, but now a cross-road village. The first house to be erected in the vicinity was the residence of G. L. Walrath, which was built in 1853. This place was purchased by George Loucks in 1856. Lathrop, Fish & Walrath owned a warehouse, which afterwards became the property of Bray Brothers of San Francisco. In 1857, soon after locating in Pacheco, Mr. Loucks built a large warehouse, 150 feet long, and the next year added 125 feet to it. This stood about a mile from the townsite, on Walnut Creek. On account of the stream filling up with silt, in 1862, this warehouse was moved further down stream. In 1857, W. K. Hendricks bought some land from Mr.

Loucks and built a mill. The first sailing vessels to call at Loucks' wharf were the C. E. Long and the Ida. F. L. Such had a lime kiln, and the first vessels to enter the creek came for his products.

In 1860, Dr. J. H. Carothers, with Hale & Fassett, bought land and laid out a townsite. J. B. Abbott made the survey and Hale & Fassett erected the first store, which was occupied by John Gambs. Capt. Ludwig Anderson built his home in 1860. That same year Elijah Hook built a brick building; J. H. Fray's fireproof building was completed; and a man named Woodford started the first hotel. Thus the town was started.

In August, 1860, a fire destroyed several buildings; and on August 15, 1867, the Pacheco Flour Mills, owned by W. J. Ireland, were destroyed. In October, 1881, Wagner & Russi became owners of this plant, by purchase from Mrs. Ireland. On September 5, 1871, another fire ravaged the town, entailing a loss of more than $30,000, the heaviest loss falling on Elijah Hook, L. F. Moreno, Bunker & Porter of the Contra Costa Gazette, L. Anderson, J. H. Fray, and the Odd Fellows Hall.

The first church was of the Presbyterian denomination, and was organized in 1862. The next was the Catholic church, organized in 1867, and the third was a Congregational church.

On September 12, 1863, Pacheco Lodge No. 117, I. O. O. F., was instituted. In 1871 the lodge erected its own building, but it was destroyed by fire in September of that year. On April 26, 1872, their new hall was dedicated. The lodge was later moved to Concord.

The first school was established in 1859, and D. S. Woodruff was the teacher.

Capt. Ludwig Anderson started his lumber yard in 1860. P. Standish established the Pacheco Plow Works in 1859. He sold to H. M. Dalton in 1861, and first exhibited his plow at the Bay District Fair in 1862. In 1879 the plant was removed to Oakland.

In June, 1868, Lohse & Bacon built a warehouse at Seal Bluff Landing.

On October 21, 1868, the great earthquake did great damage to the buildings in Pacheco, and throughout Contra Costa County.

On June 19, 1869, Mohawk Tribe No. 20, I. O. R. M., was organized.

On May 29, 1869, the Western Union Telegraph Company completed their line to Pacheco and established an office in the store of Fassett & McCauley, appointing Barry Baldwin as their agent.

On December 29, 1870, the Contra Costa Savings & Loan Bank was organized, with a capital of $50,000.

On May 10, 1871, the following officers were selected for the new military company of forty members: George J. Bennett, captain; H. N. Armstrong, first lieutenant; and William Fassett, second lieutenant.

The Pacheco Tobacco Company was incorporated on February 6, 1871, with a capital stock of $10,000, for curing and manufacturing tobacco. The directors were W. K. Dell, D. F. Majors, B. Baldwin, S. W. Johnson and R. H. Cornell.

The Contra Costa News was established in Pacheco in 1873 by popular subscription; Mr. Chadwick was manager. In May, 1877, W. R. Crauna bought the paper, and in October moved the plant to Martinez.

Pacheco Grange was organized on February 5, 1876 with thirty charter members.

BRENTWOOD

Probably no section of California has made greater strides in agricultural development in past years than Brentwood. Up to a few years ago irrigation would have been considered not only impracticable, but unnecessary, in the country around Brentwood. It took the engineers and agricultural experts of the Balfour-Guthrie Company, owners of 13,000 acres, to discover the possibilities of the land, if irrigated. They laid their plans carefully and constructed an irrigation system which is now the finest in the State.

In 1837 the Los Médanos Rancho was sold to Dr. John Marsh, and that year marks the coming to Contra Costa County of the first American citizen. He established his residence in a small adobe, but later built the now famous Stone House, which was most of the time intact and unoccupied until the quake of 1868. Dr. Marsh met his death on September 24, 1856, while on his way to Martinez to take a boat to San Francisco. He was accosted by three Mexicans at Potter's Hill, on Pacheco Road, and was killed. Thus passed the man who first developed the Brentwood Irrigated Farms, and from whom the Marsh Grant derived its name. The development of the property was retarded many years, until the final settlement of the suit of Bergin vs. Sanford, which resulted in the partition of the grant, a small portion going to Sanford, while the Bergin interests got 95 per cent of the tract, and this was bought by the Balfour-Guthrie Company. For many years fine crops of wheat, oats and barley were harvested from these lands. Now, with the land under irrigation, English walnuts and alfalfa are being grown very profitably. It cost the Balfour-Guthrie Company $500,000 to bring about this change. A concrete ditch carries water from Indian River, and by means of laterals it is distributed by meter to all parts of the 13,000 acres.

On the ten-acre experimental farm maintained near Brentwood, the Balfour-Guthrie Company demonstrated that celery, asparagus, potatoes, and all sorts of vegetables, fruits and berries thrive and bring good returns in this section.

Brentwood, the center of this area, has grown apace with the development of the surrounding country. Its principal street is Oak Street, which was paved in 1915. Some of the principal buildings are Hotel Brentwood, built by the Balfour-Guthrie Company at a cost of $40,000, the Bank of Brentwood, the Liberty Union High School, and the Brentwood-Deer Valley Grammar School. This grammar school, which cost $40,000, was financed by a bond issue voted at the election in September, 1921; and the building was occupied in 1922. The school has four teachers and an enrollment of ninety-nine pupils. Other modern buildings are the Rolando, Jansse & O'Meara, W. W. Morgans, Brentwood Garage, and Shafer's Funeral Home.

Brentwood was started in 1874. That year Joseph Carey built the first building, a blacksmith shop. In 1876, E. Bacigalupi erected a building and opened a saloon. L. Grunauer opened a general merchandise store in 1880, in the third building erected in town. J. E. W. Carey was the first justice of the peace and notary. A postoffice was established November 9, 1878, C. R. Estabrook being postmaster. The Methodist Episcopal church was built in 1885, and the Christian church in 1889.

H. B. Jewett was the pioneer rancher, and lived on the grant of land now occupied by the northwest part of town. While the railroad was being built, Mrs. Jewett boarded some of the men.

The Balfour-Guthrie Company established the first water system on the east side of the town and put in a septic-tank sewer system on that side. The water supply is now furnished by the Eastern Contra Costa Irrigation Company.

The early agricultural products of this section were wheat and barley, and in 1890 Brentwood was the largest shipping point, for the shipment of these grains, between New Orleans and San Francisco.

The Brentwood Lodge of Masons, No. 345, was instituted in 1901, with fourteen charter members. William Jereslaw was the first Master; Aubrey Williamson, Master in 1925. There were 115 members in 1925.

Maspha Chapter No. 198, O. E. S., was instituted in 1901 with twenty-two charter members; Henrietta Stone, first Matron; Mrs. Hazel Kreim, Matron in 1925. In 1924 the Masons and the Eastern Star erected a Masonic Temple, costing $20,000, with furnishings.

The Independent Order of Odd Fellows organized a lodge in 1892.

Brentwood Grammar School was organized in 1882, and the building was inclosed in 1888; this building stood until 1923. The first high school was held in two rooms of the old grammar school until the high school was built. The first building burned and was replaced by the present structure.

Brentwood Courier was established in 1892. There was only one issue of the paper, as the plant burned. One bundle of the papers was saved, and they sold for fifty cents each.

Fred Eachus established the Brentwood News in 1897.

E. W. Netherton started the Brentwood Enterprise, having bought Eachus' plant.

Sam Hill became owner of the Brentwood News in 1920. The paper is a weekly, with a circulation of 650.

Brentwood Bank was established in 1913; president, R. G. Dean, who continued in that office until his death. The Balfour-Guthrie Company, through R. F. MacLeod, owned 210 shares, and local stockholders the rest; the capital stock was $25,000. This bank was sold to the Bank of Antioch in 1922. Robert Wallace is the only one of the original directors still in office. The institution is now known as the Brentwood Branch of the Bank of Antioch.

Among the early settlers of the town and vicinity are: C. J. Preston, who came in 1867, and is now deceased; and Mrs. Elizabeth (Pearce) Shafer, who came in 1868 and is still a resident. She crossed the plains in 1858, lived in Solano County for ten years, and married William Shafer, who came to the Los Médanos Grant and engaged in the stock business. R. G. Dean, now deceased, came in 1869; Mrs. Jerusha Dean, his widow, lives in Martinez. Robert Wallace came in 1869, was elected justice of the peace in 1900, and still holds that office.

The Southern Pacific serves the community as common carrier, as do also a regular Stockton-Brentwood auto stage and motor trucks. Half the hay and milk is hauled by trucks. What fruit is raised is hauled to Oakley, where two packing plants care for it, those of the Earl Fruit Company and the Stewart Fruit Company. When the large acreage now planted comes into bearing, packing houses and canning facilities will be provided, land already having been purchased by Hunt Brothers for that purpose. The present crops made possible by irrigation are alfalfa and fruit. Six thousand acres are in fruit trees—peaches, apricots, etc.— from one to three years old. There is still considerable stock raised and ranged in the hills, some 30,000 acres being devoted to pasture; and there is also considerable dairying.

John Williams organized the Brentwood Coal Company, backed by the Sanford family of New York. He secured two sections of land near Marsh Landing, where he had deep water, erected a wharf, and opened the coal vein, installing all necessary machinery and equipment, and building boarding-houses and bunk-houses. The coal, however, was found to be of inferior quality, and water flowed into the shaft in such quantity that it could not be handled, and consequently the whole project was abandoned. The property was sold for taxes, and was bought in by the Clay Street Bank of San Francisco; and M. B. Ivory was placed in the position of manager and superintendent. When the town was started, it was given the name Brentwood, after the name of the mine, as some claim. Others say that the town derives its name from Brentwood in Essex, England, whence originally came the family of Dr. John Marsh, and that the owner of the Marsh Grant donated the townsite.

BYRON

The name of this thriving town was given to it by the railroad company. It has a population of about 500 people and is located in the extreme eastern end of Contra Costa County, in the center of a highly developed, irrigated district, on the main line of the Southern Pacific Railway. It is two and a half miles from the world-famous Byron Hot Springs, and had its beginning in 1878, when the railroad began operating trains through this district.

The first building put up was erected by a man named Smith, a cobbler, who built a shack of rough boards where he mended boots and shoes. Henry Wilkening erected the first house, which was his family home and was also used as a hotel. He formerly ran the Red House at Point of Timber. On November 9, 1878, the postoffice was established and Mr. Wilkening was appointed postmaster. That same fall Charles Peers moved a house from the old Iron House to the new townsite and opened a saloon. Mr. Wilkening erected a building on a lot adjacent to his hotel, and in it opened the first saloon. This building is the only one of the pioneer structures still standing, all the others having been destroyed by the various fires that have ravaged the town. F. M. Holway came at the same time as Wilkening and entered his employ, and he is still doing business in the old pioneer building, where he has a soft drink emporium and a billiard hall. He bought the property in 1885 from the heirs of Wilkening, who died in 1883. The hotel, burned in one of the first fires to occur in the village, was rebuilt by Mr. Holway in 1885, and was rented to M. M. Grover for a term of five years. Again the structure was destroyed, but was not rebuilt. In 1878 Fish & Blum erected a large warehouse.

Fabian & Levinsky built the first store building in 1879. Peers & Dengels had the first meat market in 1882. Frank Phelps came in 1884 and started the first smithy. In 1883 the Congregational Church was built and Rev. W. H. Tubbs was installed as pastor. Rev. Tubbs was also considered an artist with the paint brush. In 1887 Byron Lodge No. 335, I. O. O. F., was instituted with five charter members, F. Rahnestorf, Noble Grand; there are now (1925) 195 members. In 1889 Florence Knight Lodge No. 264, D. of R., was organized. It was first known as Grace Darling Lodge. In 1903 the Odd Fellows erected their new hall, a two-story structure. In 1888 V. J. Engle started the first lumber yard on property sold him by F. M. Holway.

Prior to the activities mentioned above, this section was a vast cattle range, known as Point of Timber on the river, where there was a landing owned jointly by the neighboring ranchers, and as Eden Plain to the west. Here, where the range land had a wide scope, the hardy settlers did all in their power to build up a law-abiding community, and accumulate fortunes for themselves. Alonzo Plumley came in 1851; so did Ferdinand Hoffman, who owned 920 acres of land; and J. S. Netherton was the third settler in Point of Timber. H. C. Gallagher, J. E. Carey, J. F. Carey, A. Richardson, W. R. Wilder, C. J. Preston, D. Perkins, D. K. Berry, M. Berlinger, Thomas McCabe, J. P. McCabe, H. C. McCabe, George Cople, A. T. Taylor, J. Christensen, R. N. McEntire, W. J. Cotes, J. B. Henderson, R. G. Dean, M. A. Walton, J. H. Baldwin and others were among the number who laid the foundation for this thriving community.

The pioneers were stock-men and later came the raising of grain, mostly wheat. At one time Byron was the liveliest shipping point between Stockton and San Francisco.

In 1868 the Methodist Episcopal parsonage was built, and the following year A. E. Hertell took charge of the circuit, which included Eden Plain. In 1871 it was Point of Timber and Antioch, and in 1872 Somersville and San Joaquin were added to the charge. In 1875 Rev. E. Jacka went to Point of Timber. In 1897 the Methodists erected their building. Later the Seventh Day Adventists came into the field, and lastly, in 1917, the Catholics.

Excelsior Lodge No. 349, I. O. G. T., was organized on March 7, 1869; Point of Timber Lodge, A. O. U. W., was organized on April 12, 1870; and Point of Timber Grange No. 14, Patrons of Husbandry, was organized on May 21, 1873, as an outgrowth of the Farmers' Protective League. R. G. Dean was Master. These God-fearing, hardy pioneers had much to do with the early development of the whole eastern end of Contra Costa County.

James A. Salts kept a store at Point of Timber. Henry Tichenor ran the first hotel at the Hot Springs. After him came Henry C. Gallagher, who was the first man to advertise the curative powers of the water. This was in 1878, and at that early day he brought many sporting men from the bay cities and elsewhere to his hotel. Here they coursed dogs for amusement. Caswell & Durwood Wright, in 1870, ran a stage line from Banta to Antioch through Point of Timber, making the run twice a week, with a change of horses at the Red House.

The Odd Fellows formed an association and erected a building over the piles of lumber in Engle's yard for their lodge room. When this burned they bought the land of Engle & Peers and erected their own building, under the name of the Odd Fellows' Hall Association.

Byron Parlor No. 170, N. S. G. W., was organized on February 7, 1891. Then came Donner Parlor No. 193, N. D. G. W.; Mt. Diablo Camp No. 496, W. O. W.; and the Portuguese lodges: I. D. E. S., No. 96, organized on November 26, 1911, and U. P. E. C., No. 165, organized on October 27, 1920.

Soon after the founding of Byron a school was started. Ella McCabe was the first teacher. The Excelsior district had been organized some time before, with Miss Ida Hall as teacher.

In 1897 the old school building that had been used as the Grange Hall, in the Excelsior district, was moved to Byron.

In 1906 Harry Hammond established the Byron Times, which has done more, through its special editions, to advertise the whole delta section, than all other agencies.

In 1915-1916 the Byron-Bethany Irrigation project was started, and in 1917 water was running in the ditches. With the coming of water in suitable quantity to irrigate the land, the ranchers began putting in alfalfa, which has proved a very profitable crop, with five cuttings a year. Most of this is fed to dairy stock, and the milk and cream are shipped to Oakland.

In 1924 the Bank of Tracy, Byron Branch, which had well served the financial convenience of the community, was sold to the American Bank, Byron Branch; E. C. Hannum, president; Judson Swift, cashier.

During 1924 the Borden Highway was completed. This highway crosses the delta country to Stockton, traversing the entire length of Contra Costa County.

CLAYTON

The village of Clayton, located at the base of Mount Diablo, at the head of Diablo Valley, was named after Joel Clayton and was started in 1857, when he laid out one street and platted a few lots on either side. The prospecting for coal was the primary reason of founding a settlement. W. K. Taylor surveyed the site in 1858. The first house erected on the present site of the town was built in 1857 by Romero Mauvais, who erected a building and opened a tavern. This latter became the site of the Clayton Hotel. In 1858 George Chapman erected a hotel adjoining, and in 1858 James Curry opened a livery stable. In 1858 Charles Rhine moved his business from a point two miles distant, where he had started a store in 1856, into the town. A. Senderman opened a general merchandise store next to the Chapman hotel building that same year.

In 1857 a religious congregation was organized by a Presbyterian preacher in the home of Howard Nichols; this organization was later merged with a Congregational church, organized on February 1, 1863, by Rev. J. J. Powell. On November 10, 1867, a church was dedicated by Rev. James W. Brian.

On February 28, 1864, the town was nearly wiped out by a disastrous fire. On March 9, 1872, Joel Clayton died. In July, 1873, a temperance meeting was held in Clayton; and on May 6, 1876, three years later, Unity Lodge No. 11, I. O. G. T., was organized.

Some of the early settlers of Clayton and vicinity were: Capt. Howard Nichols, J. D. Allen, William Taynton, Milton Shepard, D. Fisher, Adolph Zophy, G. O. Chapman (who had crossed the plains with Fremont in 1846, and who died in 1920), Henry Polley, Isaac Mitchell, C. Ryan, John Collins, and the Duncans, Donners, Stranchans, Kirkwoods, Myricks, Claytons and Cowdles. C. E. Wetmore was the first justice of the peace, and William Morris also filled that position in 1862-1863.

When copper was discovered, Clayton was at its height of prosperity; but when the mining excitement diminished, the people began leaving and today there is but one general store, and only a few inhabitants remain in the once thriving town. The country round about is devoted to general farming and stock-raising. Members of the Chapman family are the only pioneers represented in the village, but on various ranches are descendants of several of the early settlers.

OAKLEY

Oakley is a growing town located on the Santa Fe Railroad in the heart of one of the most productive farming sections of Contra Costa County, through which runs the State highway. It is on the border of the reclaimed lands, upon which hundreds of acres of asparagus are raised every year; also the town is now surrounded by producing orchards and vineyards.

The town is located on section 25, township 2 north, range 2 east. The first settlers were James O'Hara, Andrew Walker, B. F. Porter and R. C. Marsh. Deeds of right of way were given to the Santa Fe (not sold) with the understanding that they erect a temporary shelter and that, when needed, a permanent depot and freight buildings be erected. On September 9, 1898, the postoffice was established, R. C. Marsh, postmaster, who received the first mail on November 1. The first eight months the mail was brought from Antioch daily, by cart; then it came from Brentwood in charge of the United States postal service. Prior to this it was handled by the drivers A. N. Norcross and Daniel Methven. The first passenger train stopped on July 1, 1900.

James O'Hara planted the first almond and fruit trees and the first store was run by J. A. Jesse. J. M. Augusto carried on the first blacksmith shop.

On July 4, 1905, the first Fourth of July celebration was held, with some 2000 guests present. In 1909 the first addition to the town was platted by Mr. O'Hara. Later R. C. Marsh added another. The building in the town kept abreast of the development of the country—stores, garage, machine shops, hotel, community hall and three packing plants, a bank, etc.

The first religious services were held under the branches of a tree. Then the Congregational Mission was established, with Paul Bandy the first preacher. The Methodists had a church a short distance out in the country; but it was soon moved into town, and in 1908 a new edifice was built. Next came the Baptist Church. In due time a school was opened; and when the occasion demanded, a modern building was erected.

The Ladies' Improvement Club is one of the important adjuncts to the growing town and has done much for civic betterment, as has also the Farmers' Club.

The Loganberry was introduced in the Oakley district in 1900 by Rev. C. S. Scott, who brought the plants from Southern California.

At the packing house of the Miller-Cummings Company of San Francisco, hundreds of tons of asparagus, tomatoes and grapes are shipped to Eastern points yearly. Apricots ripen earlier in Oakley than in any other section, on account of the sandy soil, and these apricots are in great demand in the Eastern States.

The Bank of Oakley, established in 1920, has been the financial guide in the community and has always fostered all upbuilding of the substantial sort. J. H. Shaw, the president, is a real banker and upbuilder.

RODEO

The thriving town of Rodeo is situated on San Pablo Bay, where a fine water front and excellent shipping facilities are to be found. Its name was derived from the rodeos that were held there by the Spaniards in the early days of the cattle barons. Patrick Tormey owned the townsite. The town was established in 1890. A man named Hawley built the first store and sold general merchandise, and was the postmaster in 1892. Jerry Mahoney in 1892 bought the first lots put up for sale and erected the first building, which he conducted as the Rodeo Exchange. A Mr. Graham bought the second lot and built the first hotel, and J. D. Smith erected two residences that same year.

In 1893 the first school was established, which in 1913 had seven teachers. The town has a Presbyterian church, established in 1911; and the Catholic church was built in 1918. That same year the First National Bank was established, T. J. O'Leary being the first president. S. J. Claeys is the present president. Their new building was erected in 1921. In 1921 the Bank of Pinole established their Rodeo Branch, with Mrs. Gertrude Bernard as manager.

The volunteer fire company was organized in 1895 with an ordinary hose cart; there is now a chemical truck, and there are four companies with seventy-five members. T. P. Lewis is the fire chief. The town owned its own water supply. S. J. Claeys put in the water system.

The plants of the Union Oil Company and Western Oil Company are located in the nearby town of Oleum; and the powder factories of the Hercules Company, the plant of the C. & H. Sugar Company, and the Mare Island Navy Yard supply many residents, who commute to the last-named place. The Standard filling station is located here. The Rodeo Ferry to Vallejo, which gives a twenty-minute service, has done much to advance the popularity of Rodeo.

The social and fraternal life of the town finds expression in the activities of Rodeo Rebekah Lodge No. 342, established on November 13, 1913; Rodeo Lodge, I. O. O. F., established on August 4, 1906; Rodeo U. A. O. D. No. 177; Rodeo Circle No. 54, U. A. O. D.; I. D. E. S. No. 69; U. P. P. E. C. No. 12; and S. P. R. S. I. No. 71.

The opening of Hotel Rodeo on April 30, 1892, was an auspicious affair. A special train of five cars was run from San Francisco and carried guests from the entire bay district to inspect the work done by the Rodeo Packing Company at its immense stock yards and plant. At the banquet 225 people were seated at one time in the dining room.

The estimated population in 1925 is 1000. The living pioneers are F. Furtado, John Mello, J. D. Smith, Mrs. Olinda Joseph, and Jeremiah Mahoney.

TORMEY

Tormey was the original station between Oleum and Rodeo. It was then moved and was known as El Ciervo (The Deer). When the Selby Smelting Company came, in 1886, the hotel was erected by Mr. Tormey, who also built five cottages. The public school was established in 1888. In 1900 the smelting company bought the townsite and property adjacent. Mr. Tormey died in May, 1907.

COWELL

The town of Cowell is located four miles from Concord, in the foothills of Mount Diablo, and was established by the Cowell Cement Company of San Francisco, in connection with their building the great cement works there, which were opened in February, 1908. This is the greatest plant of its kind in the world, and employs hundreds of men. The railroad was built by the company, connecting with the Southern Pacific, the Santa Fe and the Oakland, Antioch & Eastern. The first resident physician for the company was Dr. W. E. Bixby.

WALNUT CREEK

This town is one of the oldest, and also one of the most beautiful in the county. Situated on the Arroyo de las Nueces (Creek of the Walnuts), whose waters have eaten their way down through the rich alluvium to a depth varying from fifteen to thirty feet, and almost in the center of the great San Ramon Valley, its name does not belie its character. This lovely creek was given its name from the wild hard-shelled walnuts that grow along its course; and today both in town and all through the surrounding country, walnut trees abound—now, however, mostly the thin-shelled English walnut, which has been grafted on the hardy native stock. Many walnut groves are found in the vicinity, and many of the splendid country roads have walnut trees planted along the margin, affording delightful shade and presenting beautiful vistas where the giant trees overarch the roadway.

The central location of the town assures it a future of importance. It is a station on the San Ramon branch of the Southern Pacific, from which are made heavy shipments of fruit, grapes, nuts, and other products.

The street improvements in Walnut Creek represent an outlay of about $60,000. The streets are of concrete and oil macadam, and extend over the major part of the town. A new fire house costing $3000 has been built, and in it has been installed a new La France fire engine pumper with a capacity of 400 gallons per minute. The cost of the engine was $7000.

A Lions Club was instituted in December, 1925.

LAFAYETTE

Lafayette is a small town situated three miles west of Walnut Creek and fourteen miles east from Oakland. It is located on the Tunnel Road, a paved thoroughfare connecting Contra Costa County with the East Bay Cities. The town had its beginning when the owner of the Rancho Alcalanes, a Spaniard named Valencia, who owed W. A. Leidesdorff, of Yerba Buena, considerable money, arranged to sell the property to get the money owing him. On February 7, 1848, Elam Brown, who had bought the rancho, moved his family onto it, and thereafter it was the family home for many years. After concluding the purchase, Mr. Brown sold one-tenth of the holding to Nathaniel Jones for $100, both families settling on the tract about the same time. Brown and Jones erected the first two frame buildings. Brown moved his location twice before permanently settling. His last place was torn down in 1924.

In 1848 Mr. Brown sowed wheat, and when harvested the grain was hauled to San Jose to be ground into flour. In 1849 he bought a horse power mill in Benicia and erected it on his place. The families did their household shopping in San Jose, the nearest settlement. Mr. Jones was the first to set out trees and shrubs for family use and ornamental purposes.

In 1852 Benjamin Shreve came to the place, and then he and Mr. Brown gave the place the name of Lafayette.

In 1853 Milo J. Hough built the first hotel, and a cemetery was platted; also an interdenominational building was built by the people and church services were held. J. H. Gorham and George W. Hammitt were also making their homes in the new settlement.

On January 15, 1859, the Contra Costa Agricultural, Horticultural & Mechanical Society was formed, with L. I. Fish president. At the regular meeting on May 14, T. A. Brown was elected president; Elam Brown, treasurer; H. H. Fassett, recording secretary; N. Jones, corresponding secretary; W. Bradford, D. Small, E. H. Cox, W. T. Hendrick, J. O'Brien, J. A. Hamilton, D. Goodale, W. J. Caldwell, D. Carrick and José Martinez, vice-presidents. The first fair was held in Pacheco on October 11, 1859.

There was a library association organized in Lafayette in 1860, but it never functioned.

On June 6, 1859, near Lafayette, the home of R. S. Linville was burned and Mrs. Linville and two children lost their lives.

On March 8, 1863, occurred the death of Stephen Jones, father of Nathaniel Jones.

On October 8, 1864, Brown & Company opened a stage line between Walnut Creek and San Ramon, connecting with Oakland lines.

When the Tunnel Road and the Oakland, Antioch & Eastern Electric Railway were completed, a new era opened for this suburban district, and now there are many fine homes erected in the hills and valley sections surrounding Lafayette. An auditorium was built by public subscription and served for all public gatherings. In 1865 N. Jones started a newspaper, but it lived only two months. There is a postoffice at Lafayette, and a Methodist Episcopal church and an Improvement Club; and a new auditorium is being erected. Some of the most beautiful scenery in the county is to be found in the Lafayette section.

SAN RAMON

This little village was originally called Limerick, but the name was changed when the railroad came. It is surrounded chiefly by a region devoted to general farming and cattle ranges, although the growing of fruits and grapes has made great progress. It is the terminus of the San Ramon branch of the Southern Pacific and the most southerly town in the county, and when the road is continued on to Pleasanton, and thence to San Francisco, greater activity may be expected. Some splendid places are to be found in this vicinity.

SAN PABLO

The town of San Pablo, Contra Costa County, was named for the Rancho San Pablo that had been granted to Don Francisco Castro in 1823. It was his home until his death, in 1831. In 1838 a commodious adobe house was erected by the Castros on the property. Mrs. Castro died in 1851. Juan B. Alvarado, at one time governor of California, married a daughter of Castro and they moved into the adobe in 1849, and here he died in 1882. He donated to the Catholic Church three acres of land for church purposes, and in 1854 the first Catholic Church was dedicated by Archbishop Allemany. In 1864 a new church was erected at a cost of $300 and was dedicated to Saint Paul. The Catholic Church plans a very modern building in the near future. The resident priest is Father Porta, who is beloved by all his parishioners. The Baptists also built a church later on, and this was replaced by a modern structure in 1925. It is a large and commodious building, and the congregation is a large one. Weatherby & Poole kept the first store. In 1855 Peck & Dohrman opened the San Pablo Hotel in an adobe building. Dr. Goodale was the first physician. John Wilcox and John Nicholl were large land-owners in the vicinity, as was also Joseph Emeric. John Proviso was one of the early merchants of the village. W. F. Belding was another of the pioneer merchants. In 1860 a meeting of the citizens was called to raise money for the purchase of a steamer to use as a ferry to run to San Francisco from San Pablo. San Pablo Avenue goes through the town and is a good paved thoroughfare. There are now a town hall and several stores and garages in the town, and many modern cottages and bungalow homes occupied by employees of the various industrial plants in Richmond and vicinity. On account of the close proximity to Richmond, there is little to hope for as to the future of the town, but there are a number of good ranches in the district where dairying is carried on and fruit and hay are grown by the ranchers.

The oldest landmark now known in San Pablo is the Alvarado Hacienda, built in 1838 of adobe bricks. It is about ninety feet long and had broad porches on two sides, with great overhanging gables and an attic. It is now a part of the general mass of structure known as the Belding store, at the west corner of Alvarado and Church Streets. The porchway being boarded up, it now holds boxed goods, barley and pork barrels. Little heeds the purchaser who drops into the store for a few potatoes or to pay a bill, that some seventy or eighty years ago this present store room was the Mecca each fall, after the grand rodeos, for all the Dons,

Donnas, Senors, Senoritas, vaqueros and peons that gathered around the homes of Don Ygnacio Martinez, S. J. Tennent, Briones, Pacheco, Moraga, Castro, Galindo and other pioneers of the time.

It was customary in very early times for ships to anchor off shore from what is now San Pablo and Richmond, there to receive from the barges the hides, horns and tallow produced in this vicinity and adjacent interior country. There being no sale for the meat, vast herds were slaughtered for the products mentioned. The tallow was reduced in great kettles, poured into forms dug in the soil, and then taken to the ship's hold.

The fall rodeos or round-ups were followed by the great social event of the year—the Spanish fandango. In all these festivities San Pablo was the rallying point for all the grandees, with their families and attendants, throughout this entire section. For a week these gatherings were devoted solely to sports, dancing and unlimited hilarity, only to move on—a great cavalcade of horsemen, horsewomen, wagons, bedding and camp outfits—to Pinole, there to repeat the performances and then again to move on to other ranchos.

MORGAN TERRITORY

In 1856 Jeremiah Morgan, familiarly called "Jerry" Morgan, located in this section. He came from Ygnacio Valley, where he had settled in 1853. He had been on a bear-hunting expedition on Mount Diablo and in its vicinity discovered a tract of land that struck his fancy, and as a result he settled upon a tract of 2000 acres. It is situated in a productive section of the county. After he had located his family in the new home he called it Morgan Territory, and it is still known by that name. It took Morgan three days to get into the territory with his wagons in 1856. Marsh Creek has its source here. In 1857 Alonzo Plumley acquired a possessory title to half the original tract. A school was established in 1858 and William Ellis was the first teacher. In 1859 Ransome Woods, Solomon Perkins, John Gibson and C. Leeming settled in the territory. In 1860 Edward Curry bought out Gibson and Leeming.

Jerry Morgan was born in the Cherokee Nation, Ala., in 1819, and came to California across the plains in 1849 from Illinois. He died at his home on January 23, 1906.

AVON

The Associated Oil Company is responsible for the founding of the town of Avon. The company erected their refinery here and have spent many millions of dollars to build up a large plant. They have direct water transportation, and both the Santa Fe and the Southern Pacific Railroads also serve the town. The oil company was incorporated in 1901, acquired the property of the National Oil Transportation Company in 1905, and have direct pipe lines from Coalinga, Kern River and

McKittrick oil fields to tidewater at Monterey Bay. In 1906 they completed a line to Port Costa. In 1913 they erected their refinery on 620 acres they had purchased at Avon, as they named the town. Since that date they have been continually expanding.

HERCULES

Hercules, in Contra Costa County, is an incorporated city of the sixth class and was built up by the Hercules Powder Company in the locality of the plant where they manufacture explosives. It is adjacent to Pinole. Many of the employees of the powder works live in the town, and others reside in the nearby towns and cities. During the World War the city took on new life and there were several hundred men working in the manufacture of war materials.

CHAPTER XIII

LIBRARY DEVELOPMENT

By Mrs. Alice G. Whitbeck, County Librarian

Previous to the establishment of the Contra Costa County Free Library in 1913, the record of the efforts of small communities to supply themselves with books and magazines through clubs or personal subscriptions is all that we have of the early history of the library movement. These pioneer efforts met with many obstacles, but the earnest and unflagging zeal of a few enthusiastic workers held the clubs and associations together until the final achievement of a county-wide library system.

The struggle of each community is a story in itself, the recording of which brings back the names of many early residents now held in memory and of many more who still hold the same interest in the larger library that they did in the one of small beginnings.

Martinez Branch Library

The Martinez Library dates back to October 24, 1883, when a little club was formed with five charter members, the Misses Julia Fish, Jane Grey Frazer, Marion Taylor, Carrie Cutler, and Louise Corbert, for the purpose of working for a free reading room. They called themselves the E. Q. V. Society, but kept steadily before them the idea of a reading-room whenever they might be able to accomplish it. In 1885 a book social was given, netting 150 books. Immediately the Martinez Free Reading-Room and Library Association was organized, officers elected, and the public invited to become members by paying dues of twenty-five cents a month. This membership grew and great interest was shown. The use of a room had been given by Dr. John Strentzel in a building owned by him on Main Street, and the room was prepared for use by the young people of the town. Generous contributions of time, money, and talent were given

MARTINEZ, FROM HILL BACK OF MISS JULIA FISH'S HOME

freely in many entertainments and benefits that were devised for this purpose. In 1893 a lot on a prominent corner on Main Street was donated by Mrs. John Strentzel and her daughter, Mrs. John Muir. The lot was of thirty-two feet frontage by ninety-six feet in depth, and was deeded with the provision that the building placed thereon must be always devoted to library purposes.

The association now filed articles of incorporation, and a deed was shortly afterward executed, which contained a provision that a two-story brick building covering the entire lot be placed there within two years, or the property would revert to the Strentzel estate. A canvassing committee was immediately appointed, and by May reported more than $1700 pledged.

Byron Brown offered free of charge his services as architect and supervisor of the building, a generous gift, since it left all funds to go to actual work of construction. Everybody was interested, and the town agreed to lease the rear portion of the lower floor—a room for town meetings and offices and a large room for the fire apparatus. The upper floor was to be leased for a term of years to the I. O. O. F., thus insuring an income with which to meet interest and reduce the debt that must be incurred to erect the building. When the bids came in, the lowest, $6371, was found to be that of C. H. Ludden, who thus became the builder. In the latter part of February, 1896, the building was completed, furnished, and occupied, with a debt of $3800 to be paid by the efforts of the association, represented by a board of seven trustees, elected annually. This debt was reduced in ten years by entertainments of all kinds to a little over $800. When the earthquake caused damages to the amount of $1400, again the people, in their interest for the welfare of the library, collected $900; so the whole debt then stood at $1300. This was paid off in the next five years. On its twenty-fifth anniversary the association's fifteen-year note of indebtedness was burned.

With the establishment of the County Library, it was not possible to keep up the subscriptions. The town trustees then came to the aid of the institution and supplied the means of upkeep, while the County Library supplied the library service. Figures from the County Library report of 1924-25 show that a total of 43,017 books were circulated during the year. The collection of books varies in number of volumes, as a constant exchange is maintained between it and the County Library, located on the upper floor of the library building.

Antioch Branch Library

The first efforts in Antioch toward providing reading for the public were made by a library club, each member of which contributed five dollars as purchase price of two books. The books were exchanged at house-to-house meetings.

About 1904 Mr. Williams, with the idea of helping the boys of the town, started a small reading room in a store on Main Street, but later built a gymnasium and library-room on the corner of Third and F Streets. A small fee was charged for the use of the books; and with his mother, he kept this reading-room open for five or six years.

In 1911 a part of the membership of the Woman's Club started a library association, each contributing one dollar a year and as many books as she could spare from her shelves. The books were kept in the clubhouse and were distributed each week by one of the members. Later Miss Carrie Williamson was appointed librarian, and she has had charge continuously. When the County Library was established in 1913, Antioch cooperated at once and gave the use of its clubhouse for the County Library books, which, together with those accumulated, were circulated freely. Miss Williamson continued in charge.

Through the efforts of Mrs. Mary L. Fulton, Mrs. Keeney, and Mrs. Frederika J. West, funds were raised to buy a corner lot for the building which the Carnegie Corporation donated to the county. This building, costing $2550, was planned by Frances Reid. Though small, the building has proved adequate to the demands. As in all the county branches, an exchange of books constantly keeps the collection alive. The 1924-25 County Library report shows that 16,518 volumes were circulated during the year. Miss Williamson has served continuously with great satisfaction to the public.

CONCORD BRANCH LIBRARY

On October 29, 1906, a mass-meeting was called and met in Odd Fellows Hall for the purpose of organizing a public library and reading-room. Dr. George McKenzie was elected chairman and Miss G. R. Crocker secretary, with the additional names on the committee of Joseph Boyd, W. A. Kirkwood, and Mrs. F. F. Neff. At the next meeting the following permanent officers were elected: President, W. A. Kirkwood; vice-president, Mrs. H. H. Elsworthy; secretary, Miss G. R. Crocker; treasurer, Joseph Boyd; directors, Mr. Pingree, Mr. Gehringer, Mr. Spencer, Mr. Randall, and Miss Skinner.

The first location was in the Fire Hall; and books received by donations, with others borrowed from the State Library and Oakland Club, were circulated. Miss Skinner was the first librarian and Mr. Martin the first assistant, the latter receiving ten dollars a month. Dues were twenty-five cents a month. Frequent entertainments were given to provide for the new books and maintenance.

A strong interest has always been felt by the library association in the welfare of its reading-room; and when the County Library was formed, it was among the first to grasp at the idea of enlarging its usefulness and joined immediately. Mrs. Ballenger, who had been a most interested and faithful librarian for a number of years, was forced to give up the work from ill health, and Mrs. H. Elise Williams was appointed. A pleasant room in the Foskett building was rented by a continuation of this same library association, and the books and magazines were supplied by the County Library.

A donation of $2500 from the Carnegie Corporation enabled the county to erect a small building in 1917, in the town park. Mrs. Williams was succeeded by Mrs. Ellen Thurber, the present custodian. The circulation of books for the year 1924-25 was 16,143 volumes.

CROCKETT BRANCH LIBRARY

In 1908 the Crolona Men's Club was formed in Crockett, the membership composed largely of men from the California and Hawaiian Sugar Refining Company. The company and a number of men interested donated about 600 volumes and provided the clubhouse. In 1910 the Y. M. C. A. assumed control of the Crolona Club. When the County Library was established, the collection housed in the Y. M. C. A. rooms became a part of the County Library. The books were accessioned and a charging system installed. After it became apparent that the club house was too small for its purpose, a new building was started in 1914 and was completely furnished and equipped by the sugar company. The building that had been occupied was remodeled for the Crockett Girls' Club and a County Library collection placed there under the charge of Mrs. Edith Powers. Because of the use made of the larger men's clubhouse, all the books for the use of the town residents were placed in the Girls' Club clubhouse.

In 1918 the California and Hawaiian Sugar Company moved and fitted up the old Pinole Bank for a town library. This building has been entirely fitted to the needs of the company, and Mrs. Charlotte Standish has been the custodian continuously. The circulation from this branch for the year 1924-1925 was 16,143 volumes. In addition to this number of books circulated from the branch, many books are housed in the library of the Community Center and are used by the men exclusively.

WALNUT CREEK BRANCH LIBRARY

At the time of the establishment of the County Library, the members of the Woman's Club of the town were contemplating a reading-room in their clubhouse and had gathered a number of books together. They realized the great help that the County Library would be to them and put off the opening of their reading-room until the County Library could help in preparing and adding to their collection. For the first year a committee of ladies kept the library open and distributed the books. Later Mrs. Hempstead was appointed, and she was succeeded by Mrs. Caroline Gamble.

The library moved its quarters twice before the new Carnegie building was ready for occupancy. The lot for the building was donated by the Burgess Company, a corner on which a very delightful bungalow library was erected in 1916.

Mrs. Robinson, the present custodian, has been in charge since the resignation of Mrs. Gamble.

Pittsburg Branch Library

There had been no move to start a library in Pittsburg until a gift from Mr. Sumner Crosby of several hundred volumes made it apparent that there must be some place to house them. A room was fitted up in the town hall and locked book cases provided. Mrs. Theresa Minaker was appointed custodian and has held the position since the opening.

The library soon outgrew its quarters, and when the new town hall was built a room was planned on the second floor. This room also was soon found too small, and bonds were voted to build a building on a site donated by Mr. Wiggington E. Creed. A building designed by Mr. A. W. Cornelius will be ready for occupancy February 1, 1926. The circulation of the Pittsburg Branch for the year 1924-1925 was 19,503 volumes, a large number of books to be given out, considering its very crowded quarters.

Richmond Library

The Richmond Library Club was formed on August 16, 1907, with Mrs. W. W. Felch as chairman of the library committee. The club rented a small room on the corner of Sixth and Macdonald Avenue, and the library was kept open by a committee of women, among whom were Mrs. W. W. Felch, Mrs. E. K. Smallwood, Mrs. C. Smith, Mrs. Clarence Jenkins, and Mrs. C. B. Evans. Books were donated and entertainments given to meet the expenses. In 1908 a request was made to the Carnegie Corporation for a library building, the Woman's Improvement Club having given five lots in a central location on Nevin Avenue for a site. A gift of $17,500 was granted upon the usual conditions, and in June, 1909, the first meeting of the trustees was held. Mrs. E. B. Smallwood was elected president; Harry Adkison, secretary; and as directors, Mrs. George W. Topping, L. D. Dimm, and J. C. Bedwell. Mrs. Alice G. Whitbeck, of Berkeley, was appointed the first librarian, May 2, 1910. The library was dedicated with appropriate exercises on August 17, 1910.

Great interest was shown in its development, generous and adequate support was given by the city trustees, and after three successful years, in which the library became a vital part of the community, Mrs. Whitbeck resigned to take charge of the County Library, and Miss Della M. Wilsey, of Pomona, was appointed librarian. Several changes at that time were made in the library staff. At the time of the resignation of Mrs. Whitbeck plans were made and partially carried out to install a children's room in the basement, the three years' growth proving the inadequacy of the room originally planned as such. This room, very pretty and complete in all its appointments, was finished, but another two years' growth showed the necessity of using the still larger assembly room for the children, and turning their room into a cataloging and work room.

In December, 1917, Miss Wilsey was married to James A McVittie and Miss Norah McNeill, of Berkeley, was appointed librarian. The growth and expansion of the library have been continuous. The Point Richmond library, which was established on July 7, 1908, became a branch of the Richmond Public Library on January 1, 1910. It is now known as the West Side Branch, occupies commodious quarters at Washington Avenue and Park Place, and has a yearly circulation of more than 20,000 volumes.

The Stege Branch, established in July, 1913, was located on Potrero Avenue, and for nine years was under the charge of Mrs. Florilla Brown, a well known and widely loved local resident. Mrs. Brown was eighty years old when she resigned the position a few months before her death in 1922. The library is at present located on South Wall Street, where it is much used by the children of the neighborhood and has a yearly circulation of 10,000 volumes.

The Grant Branch, a small neighborhood branch library located in the Grant School building, was opened in 1924, the school authorities giving free use of the room occupied.

On account of the crowded condition at the main library, a special building tax was levied in 1921, and a $42,000 addition was completed in March, 1924. By this addition the main library was increased to almost double its original size; double-deck steel book stacks were installed, and the boys' and girls' department was very much enlarged.

From the original collection of a few hundred books, the library's stock now numbers over 48,000 volumes, and for the year 1924-1925 the combined circulation of books, magazines and pictures was 275,116.

From its inception, the Richmond Library has given special attention to work with children. The large and well-equipped boys' and girls' department at the main library is in charge of a specially trained children's librarian, and includes a well-organized picture collection of over 23,000 pictures, and a special school department from which libraries are sent to all of the classrooms of the nine elementary schools of the city.

Mr. George B. Fredenburg is president of the Board of Library Trustees, the other members being Mrs. W. B. Trull, Mrs. T. T. Cramer, Mrs. B. X. Tucker, and Mr. Carl R. Alexander.

At the time of the establishment of the County Library, and for three years thereafter, the Richmond Library was a part of the County Library system; but in January, 1916, it withdrew, and is now the only library not affiliated with the County Library.

THE COUNTY LIBRARY SYSTEM

The accounts of the inception and growth of the branches already given embrace, as far as is known, the efforts of the different communities towards establishing a library in their midst. The Contra Costa County Free Library was established in 1913, and has recently rendered to the supervisors its twelfth annual report, which shows that 184,081 volumes were circulated from forty-four branches, and 52,935 books sent to fifty-five schools.

The early history of the County Library is interesting, as it was so largely pioneer work. The work began with Mrs. Whitbeck as librarian and one assistant, Miss Anne Weyand.   A room was rented from the Martinez Library Association, and immediate steps were taken to help the struggling places noted in the brief histories and to establish other branches; also, to bring in as many schools as possible.   As a result of rapid and well-organized work, books were sent to twenty-eight places the first year.   Some of these were the reading-rooms already mentioned; others were merely deposits in stores, post offices, private homes, and isolated schools.

The growth from year to year was so rapid that three moves were made in office quarters, until finally the large lodge room on the upper floor of the Martinez Reading Room Association building was vacated and fitted up as County Library office and library.   This growth has necessitated an increased office force, embracing a school department, a branch department, a cataloging department, and a records department.   At the present time, nine full-time assistants are employed to process, catalog, ship and exchange books to ninety-nine different points.

The policy of the County Library has been to have each town supply its own library room or building in whatever way it may.   Many times these have been started in a very small way, only to find out in a year or two that they wanted better quarters.   This has been especially noted in the cases of the towns of Brentwood, Byron, Danville, El Cerrito and Lafayette.   Improvements are constantly taking place, and there is a general effort to have larger and better reading-rooms.

The work with the schools has grown enormously, and has been made possible by the assistance and cooperation of County Superintendent of Schools Mr. W. H. Hanlon, and by the very full measure of appreciation shown by the teachers served.   The citizenship classes have come in for much help in the way of books, pictures and musical records.   Besides furnishing books to the schools, the County Library circulates maps, globes, charts, pictures, music records, and films.   More and more the teachers are realizing what the County Library means to them.   The county is almost entirely covered by service to branches or schools.   What remains to do is to increase and improve this service.

CHAPTER XIV

LODGES OF THE COUNTY

It has been very difficult to gather material for the compilation of a history of the various secret societies in Contra Costa County.   This has been due in part to lack of whole-hearted response, on the part of some, to calls and correspondence intended to elicit the needed information, though others, both officers and members of organizations, have freely cooperated in securing the necessary data; and we thank them kindly.   It has been the purpose of the compiler to give, in this chapter, an account of the organizing of the local societies, especially as regards the granting of dispensation and charter, and the names of the charter members and original officers. It is to be understood that many other local societies (as also, indeed, most of those mentioned here) will be found listed in the chapters devoted to the cities in which they are located. Here follows the record, so far as we have been able to secure the information.

Masonic Lodges

Martinez Lodge No. 41, F. & A. M., was granted a dispensation on July 26, 1852, continued upon application on August 3, 1853; a charter was ordered May 3, 1854; and the following were the officers and members: Robert N. Woods, M.; J. Mitchell, S. W.; H. Mills, J. W.; D. Small, Treas.; J. S. Days, Sec.; J. Tucker, S. D.; E. T. Weld, J. D.; S. Russell, Tyler; Masons, S. G. Briggs, A. Hooper, J. T. Trippen, J. S. Walls. In 1859 the lodge erected its own hall by subscription of the members.

Antioch Lodge No. 175, F. & A. M., was granted dispensation on June 15, 1865; was constituted on October 12, 1865; and the charter members were: Francis Williams, Rozwell Hard, J. P. Walton, D. H. Cleaves, N. Adams, S. Jessup, J. J. McNulty, J. C. O'Brien, J. E. Wright, R. Charnock, Jackson W. Ong, Thomas Cryan, E. T. Mills. The officers under dispensation were F. Williams, M.; S. W. Bedford, S. W.; J. C. O'Brien, J. W. Upon the charter being granted, these were elected: F. Williams, W. M.; S. W. Bedford, S. W.; J. C. O'Brien, J. W.; J. E. Wright, Treas.; M. Kline, Sec.; N. Adams, S. D.; S. Jessup, J. D.; E. T. Mills, Tyler.

A petition was sent in to form a lodge at Crockett on December 20, 1898; dispensation was granted for Carquinez Lodge No. 337, F. & A. M., on April 26, 1899; and the first meeting was held on April 29, of that year. A charter was granted on October 12, 1899, and the lodge was constituted on October 28, 1899.

Brentwood Lodge No. 345, F. & A. M., was organized in February, 1902; its charter was received on October 15, 1902. The lodge had thirteen charter members.

A petition was sent from Richmond, signed by sixteen Masons, to organize a lodge in that city. This resulted in the organization of McKinley Lodge No. 347, which received dispensation on April 5, 1902. The first meeting was held April 12, 1902, with Harry Ells as Master. On November 8 the lodge was regularly constituted.

Pinole Lodge No. 353, F. & A. M., held its preliminary meeting on November 11, 1902; its charter was granted on February 17, 1903, and it had eighteen charter members.

Pittsburg Lodge No. 249, F. & A. M., was organized on January 20, 1912, with twenty-two Master Masons as charter members, most of them demitting from Antioch Lodge No. 175. The first meeting was held under dispensation on February 20, 1912, and on October 10 of that year a charter was granted. On November 9 the lodge was instituted.

On June 4, 1912, Alpha Lodge No. 431, F. & A. M., was organized in Richmond, on account of the wide territory covered, by twenty-five charter members. The first meeting was held under dispensation on May 24, H. A. Stiver, Master. A charter was granted on October 10; and on November 12, 1912, the lodge was duly instituted.

Mount Diablo Lodge No. 448, F. & A. M., was granted dispensation on May 21, 1916; the first meeting was held on May 30, and on October 17, 1916, a charter was granted, when twenty-three men signed the roll.

Harbor Lodge No. 502, F. & A. M., was organized on March 3, 1921, C. W. Duncan, Master.

Point Lodge No. 503, F. & A. M., was instituted on March 3, 1921, C. J. Peterson, Master. The organization of the last-named lodge gives the city of Richmond four lodges.

ROYAL ARCH CHAPTERS

Antioch Chapter No. 65, R. A. M., was issued a charter on April 29, 1885. On May 13 the chapter was constituted and C. H. Frink was elected High Priest.

Richmond Chapter No. 42, R. A. M., was granted a charter on December 21, 1912, Harry Ells being elected High Priest.

EASTERN STAR CHAPTERS

Ariel Chapter No. 42, O. E. S., was instituted at Antioch on March 30, 1880, with twelve charter members, by Grand Worthy Patron C. L. Thomas. The members were: Elizabeth Williams, Alice Parkinson, Kate Forman, Malvina G. Abbott, Alice Rouse, Mrs. T. B. Jacobs, Annie McKillips, Alyszan R. Jessup, Mary E. Frink, N. W. Smith, C. H. Frink, G. Rouse and J. P. Abbott.

Occidental Chapter No. 64, O. E. S., was organized on October 15, 1881, with the following charter members at Martinez: Elizabeth Williams, L. C. Wittenmyer, Francis Williams, Eva Bissell, Clara K. Wittenmyer, Lizzie T. Russell, Emma Moore, Helen C. Carothers, Margaret E. W. Thompson, Mary Brown, Narcissa H. Woodruff, Caroline J. Hollenbeck, H. M. Hollenbeck, Clara L. Wittenmyer and Leontine Blum.

Miramar Chapter No. 205, O. E. S., was organized in Richmond on September 5, 1902, Mrs. P. C. Campbell, Worthy Matron.

Crockett Chapter No. 184, O. E. S., was organized on September 7, 1900.

Almona Chapter No. 214, O. E. S., was organized at Walnut Creek on September 5, 1903.

Pinole Chapter No. 220, O. E. S., was organized at Pinole on February 23, 1904, with fifteen charter members.

Los Cerritos Chapter No. 234, O. E. S., was organized in Martinez on July 22, 1905.

Acantha Chapter No. 249, O. E. S., was organized at Richmond on September 7, 1906, Mrs. F. Schoen, Worthy Matron.

Beacon Chapter No. 383, O. E. S., was organized in Richmond on September 9, 1921, Mrs. J. Burdon, Worthy Matron.

Point Chapter No. 394, O. E. S., was organized in Richmond on July 6, 1922, Mrs. H. G. Stidham, Worthy Matron.

Odd Fellows Lodges

Pacheco Lodge No. 117, I. O. O. F., was instituted at Concord on September 12, 1863. The officers installed on July 6, 1864, were: L. B. Farish, N. G.; E. Hook, V. G.; William Gieraw, Rec. Sec.; W. A. Smith, Fin. Sec.; G. W. Johnson, Treas. There were fifty-one members reported on July 31, 1863.

Mount Diablo Lodge No. 128, I. O. O. F., was organized on October 27, 1866, with John H. Williams, N. G.; T. S. Jones, V. G.; A. E. H. Stover, Sec.; William Prosser, Treas.; J. Jones, Rec. Sec.; W. R. D. Reese, Conductor; J. Lightowler, Guard.

San Joaquin Lodge No. 151, I. O. O. F., was instituted with eleven men, at Antioch, on January 9, 1869. The following officers were installed: William Garvin, N. G.; M. S. Levy, V. G.; George Thyarks, Rec. Sec.; R. Eddy, Treas.

Martinez Lodge No. 297, I. O. O. F., was instituted on July 20, 1882, with the following charter members: Paul Shirley, J. Borland, John Leffler, R. N. Doyle, S. W. Johnson, E. W. Hiller, Barry Baldwin, C. H. Ludden, M. B. Ivory, James Stewart, S. Blum, and W. S. Tinning. The first officers were: Paul Shirley, N. G.; C. H. Ludden, V. G.; W. S. Tinning, Rec. Sec.; E. W. Hiller, Sec.; R. N. Doyle, Treas.; S. Blum, John Leffler and Barry Baldwin were trustees.

Crockett Lodge No. 329, I. O. O. F., was instituted in Crockett on February 3, 1887, with the following charter members: John A. Glick, J. O. Marsh, S. H. Barnhisel, Steve Cowin, Robert Howe, Axel Nord, W. G. Short and John L. Heald.

Byron Lodge No. 335, I. O. O. F., was instituted at Byron on November 23, 1887, with the following charter members: U. J. Engle, M. Grunauer, T. E. Callin, W. J. Casselman and Fred Rahmstorf.

Danville Lodge No. 378, I. O. O. F., was instituted at Danville on July 26, 1892. The following were officers and charter members: E. A. Bunce, Treas.; B. W. Stone, Rec. Sec.; B. W. Bennett, N. G.; J. M. Huckins, V. G.; W. Z. Stone, Edw. Griffith and M. L. Simpson.

Rodeo Lodge No. 196, I. O. O. F., was instituted at Rodeo on May 4, 1906, by Grand Master Theodore Bell; and among the charter members were: J. E. Slade, C. D. Ambrosia, J. M. Ownes, T. J. Francis, S. H. Cunningham, E. B. Catt and C. E. Mancrief. There were thirty charter members all told. The lodge was given No. 196, which had been the number of Relief Lodge at Stony Point, until Relief Lodge was consolidated with other lodges.

Giant Lodge No. 400, I. O. O. F., was organized at Pinole on October 2, 1907, with these charter members: B. C. Mawes, H. H. W. Randall, Leander Smith, W. C. Gerrish, S. E. Mackey, E. E. Randall and Leonard Garroutte. On June 30, 1908, it had twenty-nine members.

Eclipse Lodge, No. 403, I. O. O. F., was instituted at Richmond on July 20, 1908, by Grand Master John E. Raker, with the following charter members: F. W. Heckman, D. S. Tyler, J. P. Philpott, I. L. Dearborn, S. C. Swanson, Theodore Iversen, Lester Follett and V. W. Poulsen. On June 30, 1909, it had thirty-three members.

On the night of February 1, 1902, Twilight Lodge No. 119, I. O. O. F., the pioneer Odd Fellow Lodge of Richmond, was organized. Delegates came from Berkeley, Oakland, and various towns in Contra Costa County, and despite the stormy night there was much enthusiasm at the hall in Point Richmond. The following were the charter members: John Murray, J. A. Whiteside, D. DeBarrows, T. A. Tipp, E. J. Summerfield, E. Nelson, John Swanson and I. V. McCoy. On September 16, 1908, a communication was received by Eclipse Lodge from Twilight Lodge for a conference regarding consolidation. On January 6, 1909, the conferences resulted in consolidation and the name became Eclipse Lodge No. 403. C. B. Clarenback, N. G.; J. B. Hunt, V. G.; J. W. Shell, Rec. Sec.

Bay Point Lodge No. 443, I. O. O. F., was instituted at Bay Point on August 15, 1914, with thirty-three members having the degrees conferred upon them by members from Pacheco Lodge No. 117, San Joaquin Lodge No. 329, and Byron Lodge No. 335. The charter members were: F. L. Lindquist, C. H. Counch, J. Buckholtz, L. Ludgren, C. Johnson, William Mattson, A. H. Erickson, Carl Hanson, Henry Roman, M. Caragliotti, J. L. Olsen, D. P. Alden, M. Percival and Charles Brauner.

Odd Fellows' Encampments and Cantons

Social Encampment No. 150, I. O. O. F., was instituted at Nortonville on December 18, 1874, with the following charter members: James Rankin, T. S. Brown, J. H. Smith, Samuel Brown, John Trengrove, G. H. Scammon and Evan Thomas.

Contra Costa Encampment No. 99, I. O. O. F., was instituted with twenty-eight members on May 13, 1905. The following were the first officers: R. G. Erskine, C. P.; Charles Johnson, H. P.; W. A. Leight, S. W.; John Westfall, J. W.; N. B. Tiller, Scribe; George K. Drew, Treas.

Canton Richmond No. 40, Patriarchs Militant, I. O. O. F., was organized and mustered in by C. H. Kornbeck, Deputy Commander, on March 21, 1924. The first officers elected were: Frank Rhoads, Commandant; Charles Washburn, Lieutenant; D. W. Poulsen, Ensign; M. G. Cofer, Clerk; J. A. Shaffer, Accountant. There were twenty-two charter members.

Odd Fellows' Hall Association

In 1914 a movement was started to organize an Odd Fellows Hall Association in Richmond, and it was brought to fruition on February 16,

1916, when the association was incorporated. The directors were: J. G. Gerlach, Frank Rhoads, R. E. Todd, T. Edgar, Charles Johnson, L. B. Hutchins, Robert Dornan, Mae Sutton and Thomas Handley. Several sites were offered; but it was not until February, 1921, that a site was selected and purchased. In October, 1925, a fine building was completed, which was dedicated with appropriate ceremonies on October 24 of that year.

REBEKAH LODGES

Richmond Lodge No. 206, D. of R., was organized April 22, 1907, with the following members: Mrs. Rose Michell, Mrs. Emma Tyer, Miss Minnie Tyer, Mrs. Mary E. Donoho, Mrs. Hattie Horstman, Mrs. Mary A. Tiller, Mrs. Stella Milroy, Mrs. Mae S. Bedwell, Mrs. Ella Heckman, Bessie Woods, Mrs. Abbie Oakes, Adolph Horstman and Daniel Tyer; and there were six new members initiated at the first meeting.

Zephyr Lodge No. 263, D. of R., was instituted in Richmond on April 5, 1902, in Fraternal Hall, with the following charter members: Sadie DeBarrows, Daniel DeBarrows, George Galbraith, John Murray, Lottie Murray, Elva Summerfield, E. J. Summerfield, Linda Whiteside and James Whiteside. The officers were: Emily Walker, N. G.; Emma Galbraith, V. G.; Laura Farnell, Sec.; and Nellie Adams, Treas. At the end of 1903 the lodge had eighty-one members.

Danville Lodge No. 123, D. of R., was instituted September 22, 1894, with the following charter members: Margret Boydston, Lillian Coats, Lydia Stone, Lucy Stark, Ennetta Botts, B. W. Stone, William Stark, William Hayden, W. N. Coats and B. W. Bennett. This lodge was given the number of Banner Lodge No. 123, which had surrendered its charter in January, 1893.

Mizpah Lodge No. 102, D. of R., was organized at Antioch on June 28, 1886.

Los Médanos Lodge No. 116, D. of R., was instituted at Pittsburg with the following charter members: Nellie A. and Fred Carter, Jennie C. and John H. Gallant, Nannie Cottrell, Mae E. Wright, and A. Betterworth. Los Médanos took the number of Fern Leaf Lodge of Forestville, which had surrendered its charter in May, 1895.

Mt. Diablo Lodge No. 228, D. of R., was instituted on October 12, 1897, at Concord, with the following charter members: Jennie D. and F. L. Loucks, W. E. Clanton, J. W. Haberly, Ency and Joseph Boyd, Jasper H. Wells, H. A. Rowley, W. C. Railsback, Anna and F. F. Neff, Mary A. and C. H. Clayton, Lillie and Eva Wells, and Carrie Bibber.

Florence Knight Lodge No. 264, D. of R., was instituted at Brentwood on April 12, 1902, with the following charter members: Ida L. Morgan, Abbie and Ruth LeMoine, M. Alice Collins, and Frank P. Baker. This lodge was later moved to Byron.

Carmel Lodge No. 150, D. of R., was organized at Crockett on October 1, 1889, with the following charter members: Stephen Cowin, Fred

C. Larsen, Robert Rowe, Ella Petersen, Wm. Cowin, Susan Edwards, Henry H. Hita, Rosetta Cowin, John D. Jones, Flora M. Jones, J. E. Petersen, Alice M. Trask, J. J. Smith, Stella Trask and Frank A. Starr.

Rodeo Lodge No. 342, D. of R., was instituted at Rodeo on November 22, 1913, with the following charter members: Mae Priscilla, Louis Priscilla, Charles Pomber, Luna B. Clarke, Hannah M. Owens, and Stella L. Olsen. On June 30, 1914, it had fifteen women and thirteen men members.

Twin City Lodge No. 321, D. of R., was instituted at Pinole on June 18, 1921, and was given the number of Presidio Lodge, San Francisco, which had consolidated with other lodges. These were the charter members: Cecil and Henry C. Pake, Carrie and Charles Stevens, Goldie E. and Fred Allison, Ella L. Gerrish, and August E. Person.

Alhambra Lodge No. 292, D. of R., was instituted December 14, 1906, at Martinez, with the following charter members: Pearl J., Emma, and Charles Ball, Annie E. Rice, Bertha and Joseph Bickel, Sarah J. Jennings, Margaret A. Crilley, Walter S. Evans and A. E. Selmer.

Carquinez Lodge No. 352, D. of R., was organized at Bay Point on November 21, 1914, with nine members, viz.: Mamie Ritter, Isabel A. Nay, Christine and Henry Henrickson, Clara Parker, F. L. Linquist, Antone Anderson, Carl Hanson, and Charles Brauer.

KNIGHTS OF PYTHIAS AND PYTHIAN SISTERS

Black Diamond Lodge No. 29, K. of P., was organized on October 24, 1874, with thirty charter members, Watkins P. Morgans, P. C.; F. J. Deeman, C. C.; A. A. Paul, V. C.; and Robert Prutton, Prelate.

Richmond Lodge No. 13, K. P., was instituted in 1903 with the following charter members entering on the night of institution: Chas. Carpenter, A. J. Timmons, J. W. Johnson, C. B. Gregory, Chas. V. Adams, H. L. Sharrer, Geo. Welsh, Richard Paasch, Emil Anderson, H. Silverthorn, A. F. Silva, A. S. Lilly, John McCann, Andrew Erskine, A. B. McVicker, G. W. Lamley, Lyman Naugle, J. McI. Morrison, J. H. Partrage, A. W. Keeler, W. F. Belding, Jr., Geo. B. Hinds, Wm. N. Sutherland, Chas. L. Easton, W. M. Laidlaw, J. C. Bly, Wm. A. Thomas, Chas. Desmond, O. B. Graves, Fred Walworth, Wm. A. Light, J. S. Woods, Fred Ormand, Frank Meredith, M. Dicely, L. W. Dicely, Jas. Verges, W. E. Holmes, Emil Mino, H. H. Burner, Frank Lucas, S. L. Hartman, J. Tarro, F. H. Brownell and Chas. Malmstead.

Pythian Castle was the first lodge building put up by any of the lodges in Richmond. It was erected in 1903 on Fifth Street, just south of Macdonald Avenue. Pythian Sisters No. 86 also meet in this building.

BENEVOLENT PROTECTIVE ORDER OF ELKS

Richmond Lodge No. 1251, B. P. O. E., was organized on May 2, 1911, with twenty-nine members, and was granted dispensation on August 1. The Elks Hall Association was incorporated on January 26, 1912.

The first meeting of its directors was held February 3, 1912 and on February 14 two lots were purchased on which to erect a building. These lots cost $12,000. Excavation began on October 31, 1912, and the building was completed on January 26, 1914. The cost of the building was $78,000, and of the furnishings, $22,000. It is one of the modern business blocks of Richmond.

Pittsburg Lodge No. 1474 was organized at Pittsburg on October 20, 1923, with 107 charter members. The first Exalted Ruler was Dr. T. B. Blackshaw. An Elks Hall Association was incorporated on March 1, 1924, and a lot was purchased at a cost of $8500; but no building has been erected to date.

IMPROVED ORDER OF RED MEN

Mohawk Tribe No. 20, I. O. R. M., was organized on June 19, 1869, in Martinez. The order is also represented by Carquinez Tribe No. 98 and Neola Council No. 172, I. O. R. M., both of Crockett.

NATIVE SONS OF THE GOLDEN WEST

The first Parlor of the Native Sons of the Golden West was organized on July 26, 1884 at Antioch, with twenty-five members. It was given the name of General Winn Parlor, No. 32. C. F. Montgomery was named the first President and C. M. Belshaw, Secretary.

On February 7, 1887, a charter was asked for Mount Diablo Parlor No. 101, at Martinez, and seventeen members signed the roll. T. A. McMahon was the first President, and F. L. Glass, the first Secretary.

Central Parlor No. 140, at Walnut Creek, was the next Parlor to be organized, the date being June 19, 1889. E. B. Anderson was President and J. A. Black, Secretary. There were thirty-nine members to start this Parlor, but it was dissolved on April 25, 1896.

The Native Sons of Byron and vicinity were next to apply for a charter; and on February 7, 1891, Byron Parlor No. 170 was organized with H. W. Johnston, president; W. H. Lewis, secretary; and twenty enthusiastic charter members.

Sunrise Parlor No. 204, of Pinole, was launched on August 4, 1899, with thirty-three members. J. W. Wilson was president and J. Wunderlich was Secretary. This Parlor was dissolved on April 27, 1907.

Carquinez Parlor No. 205, of Crockett, was the next. It was organized on August 5, 1899, with forty-four members. W. H. McDonald was President and H. T. Smith, Secretary.

On January 6, 1903, Richmond Parlor No. 217 was organized with twenty-one members. C. F. Grant was the first President and J. D. Grant was the first Secretary.

Concord Parlor No. 205 was organized on November 2, 1908, with thirty charter members. A. C. Gehringer was President and C. Hook, Secretary.

Diamond Parlor No. 246 was organized at Pittsburg with twenty-seven members on February 4, 1909. W. G. H. Croxon was President and L. H. Schmalholz was Secretary.

San Ramon Valley Parlor No. 249 was organized at Danville on April 10, 1909, with twenty-three members. C. G. Goold was President and S. H. Flournoy, Secretary. This Parlor was later dissolved.

Native Daughters of the Golden West

The first Parlor of Native Daughters was organized in Martinez on December 10, 1887, and was given the name of Ramona Parlor No. 21. Mrs. Lizzie Russell was the first President.

Richmond Parlor No. 147 was organized on December 2, 1905, with thirty-two charter members. The officer presiding was Mrs. A. C. Lang, Past President; Mrs. R. H. Spiersch, President.

Donner Parlor No. 193, N. D. G. W., was organized on November 4, 1911, at Byron. Mrs. A. Alexson was Past President and Mrs. H. T. Hammond, President.

Carquinez Parlor No. 234 was organized at Crockett in 1926.

Patrons of Husbandry

Alhambra Grange, Patrons of Husbandry, was organized on September 12, 1874, with Dr. John Strentzel, Master; W. Frazer, Secretary; H. Raap, Overseer; B. R. Holliday, Lecturer; J. McHarry, Chaplain; J. C. McHarry, Treasurer; E. Barber, Steward; L. Smith, Assistant Steward; J. Stewart, Gatekeeper; Mrs. A. Boss, Ceres; Mrs. H. Raap, Pomona; and Miss Louise Strentzel, Flora.

American Legion Posts

The American Legion is represented in Contra Costa County by the following Posts: Henry A. McNamara Post No. 29, Martinez; Roy Freirichs Post No. 200, Brentwood; Harding Post No. 161, Antioch; David Solari Post No. 151, Pittsburg; Crockett Post No. 33, Crockett; Richmond Post No. 10, Richmond; Walnut Creek Post No. 115, Walnut Creek; and Mount Diablo Post No. 246, Danville.

CHAPTER XV

BANKS AND BANKING

In the early days of Contra Costa County there were no local banks, and the banking business was for the most part carried on by and through the general merchants, who usually had a safe for their own convenience and, when so requested by their customers, would accept money of their surplus funds. They were sometimes given the money in a sack or some other kind of receptacle, with instructions to pay out sums of money upon written orders for various amounts as needed. This, however, was the custom only under unusual cricumstances. It was usual for the customer to take a receipt for what money he turned over to the merchant, and that money was mixed with the merchant's and he would keep strict account of disbursements and receipts. It was not an unusual thing for the merchant to pay a certain rate of interest for the use of the money entrusted to him.

The first bank in the county was organized at Pacheco by Hale Brothers, general merchants, who were often asked to make loans on good mortgage security for their customers. It was on December 29, 1870, that the Contra Costa Savings & Loan Bank of Pacheco was organized with $50,000 capital. The directors were W. K. Dell, G. M. Bryant, John Gambs, Barry Baldwin and W. M. Hale. Two years later, on March 27, the Contra Costa Bank was incorporated to do a general banking business.

On October 7, 1873, the Bank of Martinez was incorporated, its board of directors being L. I. Fish, W. W. Cameron, S. Blum, H. M. Hale, W. M. Hale; L. I. Fish, president; W. M. Hale, cashier. Its capital stock was $50,000. On May 26, 1875, its capital stock was increased to $100,000. In July, 1890, L. C. Wittenmyer bought L. I. Fish's interest and became president, holding the office until 1899, when he sold out. James Rankin was his successor as president, and he was succeeded by W. S. Tinning in January, 1902. W. A. Hale was the next president and is still serving in that office. J. E. Rodgers is vice-president; Frank Jones, cashier; P. D. Butcher, assistant. The directors are J. E. Rodgers, A. B. Tinning, W. A. Hale, E. W. Merrithew and T. B. Fernandez. The policy of the bank has always been constructive and helpful.

The Bank of Antioch was organized on September 12, 1891, with $100,000 capital stock, $70,000 paid up; S. G. Little, president; R. Harkinson, secretary. C. M. Belshaw succeeded Mr. Little as president.

Contra Costa County Bank, in Pittsburg, began business on January 1, 1904, with capital stock of $50,000; D. A. Bender, president. This bank was taken over in 1924 by the Mercantile Trust Company of San Francisco as one of their chain of banks.

Bank of Pinole was established on October 25, 1905, by E. M. Downer, with a capital stock of $25,000; J. Bermingham, Jr., president; P. Tormey, vice-president; Lou Hart, secretary; E. M. Downer, cashier. The board of directors were J. Bermingham, Jr., P. Tormey, E. M. Downer, L. Kavanagh, W. A. Ray, Mrs. Sara Bermingham and Henry Boysen. In 1908 a branch was established at Crockett, and in 1910 the capital stock was doubled. It erected its own building in 1915, and in 1916 the branch bank building was built.

The First National Bank of Contra Costa County was organized in Martinez on May 16, 1907, and began business on June 7. Its officers

7

were E. A. Majors, president; N. E. Gluckman, cashier. Its capital stock was $25,000, which was doubled on May 2, 1908. Its board of directors were: E. A. Majors, A. E. Blum, E. J. Randall and W. K. Cole. This was taken over by the American Bank of California in 1924. Leslie Alt, cashier.

The San Ramon Valley Bank was organized on June 28, 1907, at Walnut Creek; John Hackett, president; A. H. Cope, first vice-president; A. Burton, second vice-president; Joseph Silveira, cashier and manager. On the same day that this bank was organized the private bank conducted by J. L. Silveira at Walnut Creek was incorporated with the San Ramon Valley Bank; John Hackett, president; Ralph Harrison, F. V. Wood, A. P. Borges, W. K. Cole, directors. The Danville Branch of the San Ramon Valley Bank was established in May, 1911, C. W. Close, manager. On October 21, 1912, the San Ramon Valley Bank opened a branch at Concord; Guy E. Green, cashier; directors, Eli Hutchinson and M. Frank Russi.

The Mechanics Bank of Richmond, formerly the Iversen Banking Company, was organized in 1905 by Josias Iversen. It was reorganized August 15, 1907, under its present title with a capital stock of $25,000, which was doubled on October 12, 1912; and this was again doubled on July 27, 1916. The original stockholders were: L. I. Cowgill, Charles Nelson J. Iversen, H. C. Morris, S. C. Denson, L. N. McDonald, and F. W. Judson. L. I. Cowgill was president and W. L. Ballenger, cashier. The bank building was built in 1906 by B. H. Griffins at Eighth Street and Macdonald Avenue.

The First National Bank of Richmond was organized on May 24, 1910, with a capital stock of $100,000. C. E. Worden, of San Francisco, was the first president; C. J. Crary, cashier.

On July 1, 1911, the Richmond Savings Bank was organized by the officers and directors of the First National Bank.

The First National Bank of Concord was organized on March 20, 1911, with a capital stock of $25,000; F. W. Foskett, president; H. H. Elsworthy, vice-president; and W. L. Brown, cashier. The first directors were: P. Roche, J. Sutton, E. H. Shibley, A. C. Gehringer, C. L. Devereaux, J. M. Lovazzola, J. V. Enloe and William Ford. In 1912, L. A. Stevenson became cashier, and on January 1, 1917, the capital was doubled.

The Bank of Byron was organized on May 11, 1911, as a branch of the Bank of Tracy. There is also a branch of the American Bank at Byron.

The First National Bank of Walnut Creek was organized in September, 1912, with capital stock of $25,000. Its officers were A. H. Cope, president; J. H. Stow, vice-president; H. G. Flint, cashier; Elmer Cameron, assistant. The directors were: A. H. Cope, J. H. Stow, H. G. Flint, P. Thompson and R. N. Burgess. The bank first opened its doors in the Brooks realty offices on October 28, 1912.

The Bank of Brentwood was issued articles of incorporation on April 4, 1913, and began business on July 15, with a capital stock of $50,000, $25,000 paid up. R. G. Dean was president; Robert Wallace, Jr., vice-president; and Lee Durham, cashier. The directors were: R. G. Dean, Alex Burness, Robert Wallace, Jr., R. F. MacLeod and Frank H. Ludinghouse. This is a Balfour-Guthrie concern. The first day it was opened $22,138 was deposited.

The First National Bank of Antioch was organized on January 3, 1911, capital stock $25,000. Its officers were: J. L. Harding, president; J. A. West, vice-president and manager; J. A. West, cashier. The directors were J. L. Harding, J. A. West, E. C. Werrell, J. Arata, W. C. Williamson, J. G. Prewett, and M. Baeta. At the same time the Antioch Savings Bank was opened with the same directors and officers, and with an authorized capital of $50,000, of which $25,000 was paid up.

The National Bank of Martinez was organized in April, 1924, and opened in May, 1924. Fifty-two of the fifty-four stockholders live in Martinez. The bank moved into its new home, Estudillo and Main Streets, in 1925. It is capitalized for $50,000, and has resources of $200,000. R. B. Borland, president; P. Ferrarini, vice-president; A. J. Heald, cashier.

The Bank of Oakley was organized on August 23, 1920, with capital stock of $25,000. The first officers were: O. M. Champlin, president; J. H. Shaw, vice-president; F. C. Anderson, secretary; and P. A. Anderson, cashier and treasurer.

The Bank of Richmond was organized on April 25, 1902; William Minzer, president; W. F. Belding, vice-president, and W. Stairley, cashier. This bank is now a branch of the Mercantile Trust Company of California, having been taken over in 1924.

The First National Bank of Crockett was issued a charter on March 19, 1919, and opened for business on June 1. Its capital stock was $25,-000. In 1922 this was increased to $50,000. The bank had a surplus of $10,000 in 1926; deposits, $588,062.23. The original directors were: P. Murphy, C. P. Thomas, C. Gemignani, B. H. Zuppan, G. W. Likens, M. D., G. M. O'Malley, M. D., F. W. Hutchinson, A. Berger, P. Lucey, T. J. O'Leary, and A. Aljets. T. J. O'Leary was president; G. W. Likens, vice-president; and J. B. Leadbetter, cashier. In 1926 F. W. Hutchinson was president; A. Aljets, vice-president; and Mrs. M. D. Parker, secretary and cashier.

CHAPTER XVI

IRRIGATION

The following editorials from the local press afford a first-hand account of the growth of sentiment in favor of irrigation, and the increasing demand for an equitable distribution of the available water resources to the irrigable lands of the county.

Editorial, January 1, 1876.—"That any irrigation measure can be adopted by any legislature which will be wholly satisfactory to all who are demanding action in the matter, is not to be supposed. It should not fail, however, to adopt some measure that will prohibit the acquisition of water rights by private corporations or persons, and will condemn such of these rights as have been acquired, wherever and whenever the larger public interests are to be subserved by such condemnation. Provision should also be made for determining the available water supplies for irrigation and domestic or manufacturing requirements, and the institution of means that may ultimately secure their economical and equal distribution for such purposes. There is urgent need in many sections of some immediate available means of irrigation, and if the legislature can provide for these wants without putting obstacles in the way of such a general plan as it may ultimately be desirable to adopt, it should certainly do so. But it is clear enough that as yet we have not enough data for the adoption of such a general system as will answer the future needs.

"It may be a question, too, whether with our sparse population and limited markets for our staple products, we could at present command the capital or fair terms that would be required for carrying out a satisfactory system for irrigation works. And if such works are undertaken upon means to be raised by bond issue at large discount, there would be much probability that bondholders might ultimately come to own the works and the land instead of their remaining the property of the farmers of the State."

Editorial: An Irrigation Policy Demanded by the Farmers, May, 1879.—"The time has come when the State will be called upon to adopt some policy with reference to the utilization of its surplus waters where practicable, for irrigation of soil. Its first care should be to prevent the water being seized and made private property of speculating monopolists, and to extinguish such claims as have unjustly been asserted to them. It will be its duty to see how they can be fairly and economically distributed where they are needed and furnished to consumers at a rate not oppressive. . . .

"It would seem to be the duty of the State to institute a commission or board of engineers to determine sources and the amount of supply of water for irrigation, and also the best plan of distribution where required. The State might, authorized by special amendment to the constitution, construct main conduits and enable, by bond guarantee, the landowners of such districts as might be organized to construct their own work. The general advantages would justify a tax on all property in the State for payment of interest and redemption of bonds for portion of work done by the State on this plan, with water rents and special district taxes levied and collected for the interest and redemption of ranchers' bonds. Any system that will meet the requirements will meet with more or less objections, and even if it prove perfect in every detail, there would be objections made by those who cannot monopolize its benefits."

EAST CONTRA COSTA IRRIGATION COMPANY

East Contra Costa Irrigation Company is a mutual company, and its development work was the first irrigation project in the county. All of the stock has since been taken over by the Knightsen Irrigation District, the Lone Tree Irrigation District and the Brentwood Irrigation District, one share of stock being issued for each acre of land represented in the various districts. The three districts mentioned were each organized under the State law known as the Wright Irrigation Act.

The rights to water of the East Contra Costa Irrigation Company are based on appropriation and use (not riparian), by which means it obtained legal rights to as much water as can be supplied by its plant.

The waters for irrigation in this district are diverted from the head of a dredged canal forty feet wide, seven feet deep, and one mile long, starting at Indian Slough near Point of Timber Landing, a natural channel extending inland from Old River, one of the main delta channels of the San Joaquin River. The delta channels of the Sacramento and San Joaquin are all inter-connected, so that the water supplied for irrigation comes from the combined flow of both rivers.

The system consists of a series of seven pumping plants lifting water from the river level in successive stages to a maximum of 144 feet. It is very generously designed and of permanent construction, and is capable of watering 25,000 to 30,000 acres. From the main canal, which runs east and west, main laterals extend north and south, dividing the territory into north-and-south zones. The slope of the country is west and east.

The seven pumping plants lie along the main canal, one above the other. The canal is divided into seven steps, each plant lifting the water through one step. The intake station lifts all the water required for the entire system and discharges it into the first step; the balance flows to No. 2, which lifts it into the second step, where the water is diverted to irrigate that level; and so on through the seven steps or zones.

The main canal is concrete-lined through its entire length. The pump plants are of the highest grade of electrically driven power equipment, all of the most permanent and enduring character, and had been constructed prior to the present era of high cost of labor and material. The system could not now be duplicated for less than two or three times its original cost.

The company was organized in 1913. Construction was begun that same year, and the pump plants were carried to completion; the main canal and main laterals were constructed during 1913, 1914 and 1915. Since then the sub-laterals have been under construction as necessary to meet the demands of the system. Also some additions have been made to the main canals and the plants.

In his report to the Brentwood Irrigation District, Engineer Woolley, who was also engineer for the Knightsen and Lone Tree Districts and formerly assistant engineer for East Contra Costa Irrigation Company, states:

"Much anxiety has been manifested in times past with reference to the encroachment of salt water in the Delta Channels and possibility of the condition reaching that where the water would be unsuited for irrigation use. Late in 1919 tests for salinity were begun by the East Contra Costa Irrigation Company on water from the intake tunnel; there was also installed an automatic recording gauge for registering continuously the level of the water at the same point. These salinity tests have been carried forward continuously. The maximum degree of salinity thus far recorded was 33.4 parts per 100,000, this being much below even the danger point, and occurring for short periods as water requirements were at a minimum.

"A continuous record of the water level at the mouth of intake tunnel shows that at no time was there a depth of water less than 3.3 feet over the sill of the intake tunnel; also that this condition prevailed only for very limited periods and at such times as the demand for water was low.

"The irrigation season of longest duration for this system was that of 1917, when during 285 days 13,143 acre-feet were pumped to irrigate 3733 acres, at the rate of 3.5 acre-feet per acre. With a water right of 200 cubic feet per section and 285 days' irrigation season, the total volume of water available would be 114,000 acre-feet, or on a basis of 2000 acres an average gross duty of 5.7 acre-feet per acre, an amount far in excess of actual requirements. It may, therefore, be conceded with certainty:

"(1)   That the water is of suitable quality at all times.

"(2)   That there will always be sufficient water at the intake to supply the needs of the system.

"(3)   That the water right is ample as to volume for the supply of the total acres to be included under this project."

KNIGHTSEN IRRIGATION DISTRICT

During 1912-1913, a period of sub-normal rainfall, the East Contra Costa Irrigation Company, a mutual service corporation, was formed to irrigate certain lands which embrace what is now the northern portion of the Byron-Bethany Irrigation District, the East Contra Costa Irrigation Company's holdings, and the main portion of the Lone Tree and Knightsen Districts.

The pioneering and financing were done by Balfour-Guthrie Irrigation Company, which firm had bought the Marsh grant of 13,000 acres. It was evident that, if the water was to be delivered to many holders of tracts who were desirous of taking stock in the Contra Costa Company, some means of securing rights of way would be necessary, a mutual service company not having the right of eminent domain then. The Wright Irrigation Act provided not only the necessary right of eminent domain and an excellent method of financing, but the protection of the Bond Commission, and this was the plan advanced by the local branch of the Contra Costa Farm Bureau, which had carried on an educational campaign for years.

The petition for the organization of the Knightsen Irrigation District was presented to the supervisors on November 17, 1919; it received seventy signatures out of 115 on the assessment roll of the district at that time. The original signers represented 70 per cent of the value of the lands included in the proposed district. The election on the formation of the district and for the officers was held January 19, 1920. The vote on the formation of the district was 94 for to 23 against. Directors: Division No. 1, Joseph Minto; No. 2, E. B. Sellers; No. 3, H. W. Heidorn; No. 4, Frank Estes; No. 5, Byron Grigsby; assessor, I. M. Bailey; collector, A. H. Shafer; treasurer, A. E. Bonnicksen.

Due consideration of the construction of an independent plant occupied the directors and officers during the winter of 1920. After considering the preliminary report of W. F. Woolley, chief engineer, and A. C. Wilson, consulting engineer, of San Francisco, it was the unanimous opinion of the board that the purchase of stock in the East Contra Costa Irrigation Company not only prevented a great economic waste in building two plants designed to serve practically the same territory, but would be less expensive in first cost to the district, providing earlier delivery of water and economy in operation, and a water-right of great value. A contract for 10,000 shares of stock was made after the legality of the step had been considered by E. A. Bridgeford, attorney for the district, and the purchase was made.

The feasibility of irrigating the lands included in the Knightsen District had been demonstrated in the irrigation of adjacent lands. The splendid remuneration received from such irrigation is a matter of common knowledge in Eastern Contra Costa County; and with frequent recurrence of dry years the absolute necessity for irrigation, if the section was to develop, was conceded by all interested.

There being little data on rainfall in the Knightsen section, conclusions were arrived at by Woolley, in making his report to the board of directors, from Antioch records on the one side and Tracy records on the other. The records showed that the mean seasonal rainfall in 1879 was 10.37 inches at Tracy, while at Antioch it was 12.97 inches. "It is usually conceded that the rainfall at Knightsen and vicinity is less than at the other two points, due to the sheltering effect of Mount Diablo, which is due west of the district."

The Knightsen District is unusually well supplied with transportation facilities. The maximum distance to track within the irrigated district is less than two miles. The Southern Pacific passes on the west; the Santa Fe, on the east. Brentwood is on the Southern Pacific; and Knightsen, on the Santa Fe. A concrete highway running the entire length of the district is the main and direct highway connecting San Francisco and the Bay cities with the valley. The bulky crops of the district are hauled by river boats, the delta channels being deep enough for boats. This district is the closest of eastern Contra Costa districts by rail, highway and water to the markets of the Bay cities. The Pacific Gas & Electric Company and the Great Western Power Company serve electricity for lights and power. Rural delivery serves the greater part of the district, and many telephones give the conveniences of urban life.

The principal slope of the district is towards the east; and there is a slight fall to the north, the direction of the principal drainage canal, Marsh Creek, which follows the entire length of the district on the western boundary, cutting off the flood waters from the Diablo hills and carying off such drainage water as is led into it by users of water in the district. On the east side the sloughs of the San Joaquin care for drainage of excess irrigation.

The soil of the district is Yolo clay-loam, with a capping of fine sand in large areas. In places, the sand knolls project above the average levels; and most of these are planted to trees, almonds principally. The Knightsen and Oakley sections are the best almond districts in California, Oakley being the center of packing. At the time of the organization, 115 were on the roll. The average size of the ranches was eighty-five acres. The assessed value, $856,611.50. Almonds, grapes, and alfalfa are the products of the district; and dairying is also carried on.

LONE TREE IRRIGATION DISTRICT

The Lone Tree Irrigation District, organized under the State law know as the Wright Irrigation Act, embraced 2167 acres lying along the line of the Southern Pacific, northwest of Brentwood. In 1918 certain of the lands now included within the district endeavored to secure water from the East Contra Costa Irrigation Company and landowners. Some 600 acres were signed to take stock in this company contingent upon securing the necessary rights of way. These could not be secured by negotiation and the plan was abandoned.

In 1919, when the Knightsen Irrigation District was under way, there was some discussion of including these lands; but when the district boundaries had been finally settled upon, they were left out. In April, 1920, the landowners held a meeting to formulate some plan to secure irrigation, and it was finally decided to organize a district, such pro-

EARLY DAYS IN EASTERN CONTRA COSTA

cedure permitting the securing of rights of way by condemnation if necessary, and offering every material advantage of financing by means of bond issue. A petition was circulated, and was presented to the supervisors on May 3, 1920, and approved by them the same day. On July 14, 1920, the State engineer advised the supervisors that the plan was feasible and recommended that they grant permission to form the district. This the supervisors did on August 2, 1920, calling an election for September 10th. The vote was unanimously in favor, and the district was organized on September 24th, the directors and officers taking office at their first regular meeting that day.

Assistant State Engineer S. C. Whipple, after a survey of the district, says in a report made to W. F. McClure, on which he based his recommendation to form the district:

"The general slope of the land is toward east and northeast, elevations ranging from 150 feet in the southwest corner to about 50 feet at the eastern limit. The soils are highly productive and free from alkali and hardpan. According to reconnoissance survey of the Bureau of Soils, four types are represented; these in order from the east are: Oakley sand, Yolo clay-loam, Yolo adobe, and Diablo abode.

"The topography affords good natural drainage. Ground water reported from forty to eighty feet below the surface. There is little danger of its rise, inasmuch as irrigation water will be supplied by pumping against a considerable head, with consequent economy in use."

The entire acreage is gradually being set to orchard. At the time of the formation of the district, 612 acres were in trees, the balance being grain land. Since that time much of the grain land has been set to trees.

BRENTWOOD IRRIGATION DISTRICT

The newest of the East Contra Costa irrigation projects was organized under the Wright Act for the purpose of taking over the stock of the East Contra Costa Irrigation Company that had not been disposed of to the Knightsen and Lone Tree Districts. Of the 20,000 shares, Knightsen got 10,001, Lone Tree 2095, and Brentwood 7904, each acre of land in the three districts representing one share of stock.

The East Contra Costa Irrigation Company had been operating plants and conducting the business of water distribution to Knightsen and Lone Tree and to the individual owners in what is now Brentwood District. It is the intention of the three districts—stock, water and property rights of the East Contra Costa Irrigation Company having all been secured by due process for that purpose—to consolidate and dispose of the mutual company, with the following advantages:

1. Elimination of three boards of directors and officers.
2. More direct, economic and efficient apportionment of water distribution.
3. Elimination of possible overlapping among the employes and conflict between districts.

4. All rights, privileges and advantages enjoyed by an irrigation district over a mutual water company.

5. Better money rates for land owners and more readily available capital for further development.

The Brentwood district embraces 1904 acres of land surrounding Brentwood and east of Mount Diablo. The main line of the Southern Pacific traverses the tract. The soils are uniform in the district and are classified as Yolo clay and Yolo adobe, both types being suitable for irrigation.

In 1922 the crops planted in the district were: Trees, 1600 acres; grain, 3000 acres; nurseries, 55 acres; grapes, 200 acres; but these figures have been materially changed, trees and alfalfa gradually supplanting all grain acreage. The varieties of trees are prunes, apricots, walnuts, almonds, peaches, figs, and cherries.

The seasonal rainfall in the district is practically the same as in Knightsen. No accurate record had ever been kept. At Tracy, twenty miles southeast, it was 10.37 inches in 1879; at Antioch, 15 miles northwest, 12.97 inches.

The lands of the Brentwood district had been served for several years by the East Contra Costa Irrigation Company. The sufficiency and value already established, the change from a mutual company met no opposition in forming the district. On July 11, 1922, a meeting of the landowners was held to form an organization. Petitions were circulated and signatures representing 6046 acres were secured, the balance within the boundaries belonging to non-resident owners and not represented. On December 24, 1922, the supervisors approved; and Mr. Eaton, representing the State engineer, reported favorably. On January 17, 1923, the State engineer reported favorably to the supervisors. An election was held on March 20, 1923, the result of which was 106 for, none against. The following officers and directors were elected: Robert Wallace, Jr., president; J. W. Cooper, secretary; J. M. Trembly, assessor, tax collector and treasurer; W. F. Woolley, engineer; A. D. MacKenzie, Walter Moffatt, William Dainty and Byron D. Swift.

The Byron-Bethany Irrigation District

The development of irrigation in California on a permanent basis began about 1887. It is based upon the Wright Act, which provided municipal forms of organization and construction in farming communities, including right of eminent domain and the right to issue bonds and levy taxes for construction purposes. Bonding provisions of a district are safeguarded by the establishment of a State Irrigation Commission, composed of the attorney general, State engineer and superintendent of banks. They investigate and make report on water supply, feasibility of the system, soil conditions and value of lands embraced in the proposed district. The maximum amount of property indebtedness will not exceed 60% of the aggregate value of the lands and complete water system. State supervision is also provided for.

The Byron-Bethany project is the result of the efforts put forth by the late Volney Taylor of the Byron district. The great increase in land values and production in other districts where irrigation had been introduced led Mr. Taylor, Charles Cople and others to interest their friends, and meetings were held to consider the formation of a large irrigation enterprise south of Tracy and Byron. It was proposed to divert water from the San Joaquin River at Tuolumne City and at a slough near the intersection of the San Joaquin, Alameda and Contra Costa County lines. Differences of opinion developed at these meetings which resulted in the withdrawal of the lands of the present Byron-Bethany Irrigation District from the larger enterprise and the organization of a portion of these lands to be served by a cooperative irrigation company.

By 1914 surveys, plans and estimates of costs of works were made which amounted to between $9 and $10 per acre, exclusive of rights of way; and the Byron-Bethany Irrigation Company was duly organized and construction work was begun, pumps installed, and ditches sufficiently completed to be in operation for the 1917 irrigation season. Water rights and rights of way had not been settled prior to this work, and the company was brought into legal difficulties for the reason that a private or cooperative company could not exercise the right of eminent domain. To meet this situation the company secured from the State Railroad Commission a certificate as a public utility; then they brought suits of condemnation to establish their water rights and secure rights of way.

By 1917 the cost of work, partly because of war conditions, had exceeded their original estimates and had reached the sum of $25 per acre for the 8000 acres then under service. In 1918-1919 it became necessary to organize a district under the Wright Act. The petition was filed with the board of supervisors on September 15, 1919, with 122 signers out of the 187 on the assessment roll of the district. The vote was 173 for, 14 against. The original signatures represented $130,000 in excess of a majority of the value of the lands. It was the announced policy of the district to acquire, at a fair value, the property of the Byron-Bethany Irrigation Company, and then to reconstruct and extend the plant to cover all the lands within the district with sufficient water for general irrigated, diversified farming, the district to build laterals to each, or for large ownerships, to each quarter-section.

The original officers and directors of the company were: District No. 1, J. D. Rosa; No. 2, R. R. Houston; No. 3, M. Grunauer; No. 4, A. Peterson; No. 5, W. Saxouer, all directors. The officers: R. R. Houston, president; M. G. Preston, assessor, tax collector and treasurer; L. L. Dennett, attorney; A. F. Donaldson, secretary; B. H. Grover, manager; F. H. Tibbetts, engineer. The present officers and board of directors are: W. J. Livingston, president; Robert Armstrong, assessor, tax collector and treasurer; G. A. Howard, secretary; V. L. Wooley, manager; L. L. Dennett, attorney. Directors; W. J. Estes, W. J. Livingston, M. J. Pimentel, M. C. Monroe and William Saxouer.

The Byron-Bethany Irrigation District comprises about 17,600 acres lying about twenty miles west from Stockton. The land covers portions of Township 1 north; Townships 1 and 2 south, Range 3 east; portions of Townships 1 and 2 south, Range 4 east, Mount Diablo Base and Meridian, east of and behind Mount Diablo. The junction point of San Joaquin, Alameda and Contra Costa Counties is within the district boundaries, about 58% of the district being in Contra Costa County, 25% in Alameda County, and 17% in San Joaquin County. The West Side Irrigation District joins it on the south and the Balfour-Guthrie Irrigation Project on the north. Included in this is the town of Byron. The total assessed valuation for 1926 is over $1,500,000, exclusive of improvements. The improvements, which include alfalfa and orchards, are about $1,000,000. As this is a history of Contra Costa County, one-third of the above amounts can be deducted, two-thirds of the district being in Contra Costa County. Byron town property would be about $50,000. The total cost per acre amounts to approximately $50 per acre.

The original bond issue was $550,000, of which $3000 were retired in 1924; $4000 in 1925; $5000 in 1926. An additional bond issue of $100,000 was issued September 1, 1923, to complete the work as outlined by the engineer's report made in 1919 for additional concrete ditch lining and concrete pipelines, and an additional electric pump at Station No. 4 with a 40-h.p. motor and a 10¼ second-feet capacity. This bonded indebtedness is carried by about 13,000 acres out of the original 17,600, the balance of the land being either too poor or too high to irrigate, and assessed at a very low figure.

The sources of supply are the Delta branches of the San Joaquin River; the main pumping plant is on a dredged channel 5120 feet long, connecting with the upper end of Italian Slough, which is a navigable waterway about two miles in length, and connecting with Old River near the southern end of Victoria Island. Old River connects with the main San Joaquin River at the head of the Delta about eleven miles from Bethany. There are four pumping plants with a combined capacity of considerably more than 115 second-feet of water and a total horsepower of 1655 electric motors.

The main canal divides the district into two sections, Byron on the north and Bethany on the south. All of the water for the Byron section runs northerly through a canal seven miles in length. The district covers a tract of irregular shape, in length about twelve miles north and south, with a width of from one mile in the center to three and one-half miles at the northern end and about three miles at the southern. The main pumping plant is near the center. The Southern Pacific Railroad runs through the length of the entire district; the Santa Fe is about two miles distant from the northern end, and the Western Pacific about two miles from the southern. There are deep navigable sloughs and delta branches of the San Joaquin River extending to the district, and steamers are supplied with numerous landings to facilitate shipping of the products raised. The county highway also passes through the entire tract. The southern part of the district is chiefly adobe, and the balance is clay loam 18 to 30 inches deep. The drainage is a natural slope favorable for the run-off. Alfalfa and fruits are raised in abundance; while the higher land is given over to grain and grain hay. With this fourth irrigation district the entire eastern part of Contra Costa County is made one of the most productive sections in the entire State.

Growth of Irrigation, as Reflected by the Press

The following news items from the issues of the local press, here presented for the most part in chronological order, even though sometimes without date, afford additional interesting data regarding the history of irrigation in the county.

June 19, 1886.—An irrigation club has been organized at Antioch with the following officers: J. B. Abbott, president; C. F. Montgomery, vice-president; George Fowler, secretary; H. F. Beede, treasurer.

1911.—The great irrigation scheme for Eastern Contra Costa, which was brought to light this week, is creating considerable discussion throughout the county, especially in the eastern section. The residents are hoping that the plan may be carried out. A company of capitalists from the bay region has been organized and R. L. Dunn, engineer, has been engaged to draw up plans. These plans provided for pumping water from the San Jose near Oakley to a large storage reservoir. From this point the water will be run over 3500 acres through laterals over twenty-five miles in length. The distance will extend from Bay Point to the San Joaquin County line and to the slopes of Diablo.

December 2, 1911.—Reclamation District No. 779 was declared valid by the court. A fight which has been carried on before the supervisors and the supreme court for three years over this district came to a close when Judge Latimer handed down a decision in the Portman case.

March 27, 1912.—Four hundred acres will be put into alfalfa by Wilhoit & West and cut up into small tracts and sold. A complete irrigation system is to be installed, and from 400 to 600 acres more will be put into alfalfa next spring.

August 24, 1912.—The great Marsh Grant is to be cut into small tracts by the Balfour-Guthrie Company. Rights of way for a great irrigation system have been secured. The water will be taken from Old River and raised by electrical pumps to a sufficient height to permit it to flow over the vast acreage, which will rival Imperial Valley in productivity.

November 9, 1912.—The district around Walnut Creek is becoming an irrigation center. Roleb McPherson is pumping water from a fine well onto his alfalfa. He will cut seven crops this year. The Bancroft place has a fifty-horse-power motor in their well, which has been used to irrigate their trees. W. H. Leahy has installed a small plant and is able to irrigate his orchard and garden.

November 29, 1912.—By a judgment handed down by Judge R. H. Latimer in the superior court, Reclamation District No. 800 in Contra Costa County, commonly known as the Wilhoit District, was declared legal and valid. This ends the contention in regard to the swamp lands, which included land owned by the Bairds.

January 25, 1913.—Ground was broken for the Marsh Grant irrigation system by Edward Malley, a contractor of San Francisco.

The F. X. Smith ranch of 160 acres near Brentwood was sold to Balfour-Guthrie Company. These holdings will be included in the big irrigation district.

March, 1913.—The contract for the dredger-cut from Indian Slough through Point of Timber landing, and also for concrete construction on the Eastern Contra Costa Irrigation Project, was awarded March 6th. The dredging, which will require the moving of 100,000 cubic yards of earth and will cost $4500, was awarded to the Golden State Miners Iron 'Works. The State Contsruction Company, concrete contractors, are to receive $17,000 for concrete work. Work on both contracts is to begin at once. All this work to be done on the Marsh Grant, or Los Médanos Rancho.

March 15, 1913.—When the reclamation of the Sand Mound tract is complete, all the land lying between Taylor and Sand Mound Sloughs and False River, which had formerly been a part of the mainland by the damming up of Dutch Slough, will be converted into an island. The old dams on Dutch Slough have been cut away; and the flood water of False River, which had no outlet by that course and which had flooded the lands mentioned, will be allowed free passage through Sand Mound, Taylor and Dutch Sloughs. This also makes the big Jersey Tract an island.

May 17, 1913.—Peter G. King, of Oakland, sells 500 acres adjoining the Marsh Grant to Balfour-Guthrie Company, and this will be added to their other holdings and come under the irrigation project.

August 16, 1913.—A party of engineers are in the field making preliminary surveys for the irrigation system considered by C. A. Hooper for his property, the Los Médanos Rancho near Pittsburg.

October, 1913.—A big irrigation project was launched at Byron; 8000 acres will be watered, extending from Italian Slough, where the water will be taken along the hill section of McCabe's, crossing to Hoffman's, thence to Peterson's, Cople's, and Henry McCabe's, and taking in all the land east to the Wilhoit-West holdings. There will be three lifts of twenty feet each. The main ditch will be six miles long, with fifteen miles of laterals.

March 7, 1914.—The Byron-Bethany Irrigation Company, with a capitalization of $100,000, has been organized by ranchers in the vicinity of Byron, and articles of incorporation were filed Monday. The plan is to build an irrigation system to furnish water to the farms in the vicinity of Byron. Work will be begun at once. The incorporators are: August Alexson, Charles Cople, R. R. Houston, J. A. Modin, C. F. Peterson, William Saxouer and V. Taylor.

January 9, 1915.—A project for the formation of a new reclamation district in Contra Costa County is on foot, and the supervisors will act on the petition at their next meeting. The district embraces 3516.54 acres, some of the finest Delta land in the county. The owners are the Standard Investment Company, 100 acres; W. H. Maxson, 465.18 acres; J. H. Prince, 184 acres; J. I. Parsons, 274 acres; F. K. Houston, W. J. Hotchkiss, L. Friedlander, 1440.95 acres; W. T. Session, W. T. Jeter, H. E. Irish, C. W. Purrington, 516 acres; E. A. Bridgeford, 370 acres.

September 15, 1916.—The big irrigation ditch of the Byron-Bethany Irrigation Company is completed. Water is now the problem, as the Sproule & Driscoll interests served an injunction and want compensation.

March 2, 1918.—A project which aims to put many thousands of acres of farming land near Knightsen under irrigation is being agitated.

Recently there were placed on record deeds by which the California Delta Farms Company made valuable reclamation of drainage and irrigation rights to Districts 2029, 2027, and 2026; and the Boulder Land Company to District 576; the considerations named were $327,650, $375,140, $449,000, and $321,398.

The California Delta Farms Company was the recipient of $1,000,000 from Districts 2024 and 2026 when that amount was paid for the levees surrounding the new irrigation and reclamation project in Eastern Contra Costa County. The cost of the levees was assessed to the entire district; and the county, while retaining the land, received that amount for the levees alone.

1919.—The irrigation plan at Knightsen has again been revived by the Farm Center. A total of twenty-four landowners have already signed the petition, and seventeen more have signified their intention to do so.

August 9, 1919.—As the petition for the 9000-acre Knightsen Irrigation District is completed, it will be presented to the supervisors. The Farm Bureau is now turning its attention to other irrigation projects, which, when completed, will add 40,000 acres to the irrigated area of the county. The new districts contemplated are: Oakley-Antioch, 6000 acres; Pittsburg, Concord and Walnut Creek, 9000 acres; between Antioch and Bay Point, and 20,000 acres around Concord and Walnut Creek; and Danville District of 1500 acres in San Ramon Valley near Danville.

January, 1920.—The Knightsen Irrigation project was carried at the election January 19th, by a vote of 94 to 23. The directors of the five districts included are Joe Minto, 1st; E. B. Sellers, 2nd; H. W. Heidorn, 3rd; Frank Estes, 4th; Byron Grigsby, 5th; Dr. I. M. Bailey, assessor; A. H. Shafer, tax collector; A. E. Bonnicksen, treasurer.

At a meeting of the board of supervisors Monday, the Knightsen Irrigation District was declared officially organized as the result of the recent election held there.

February 28, 1920.—A meeting was held to consider the Oakley-Antioch Irrigation project by the Oakley Farm Center.

April 17, 1920.—The Byron-Bethany Irrigation Company has applied for authority to sell its holdings to Bryon-Bethany Irrigation District for $265,000.

September 27, 1920.—The directors of the recently formed Lone Tree Irrigation district met at the Lone Tree schoolhouse Friday night for the purpose of mapping out the ditches, etc.

January, 1921.—With the approval of the proposed Knightsen Irrigation District by Assistant State Engineer Whipple, plans are being made for the establishment of an irrigation system in that section of the county.

At the election ordered for April 6 in the Knightsen Irrigation District, to vote on bonds in the amount of $650,000 for a system that will water 10,000 acres, the bonds carried, 99 to 21.

A recent report of the Department of Commerce of the United States shows an increase of 66 per cent in the amount of irrigated lands in Contra Costa County. In 1910 there were 32,640 acres under cultivation; in 1920, 49,125 acres. The irrigated acreage was 26,856 in 1909, and 44,833 in 1920. The amount of land capable of irrigation in the county is 46,472 acres.

June, 1921.—A petition has been filed for a dissolution of the Byron-Bethany Irrigation Company.

The Byron-Bethany Irrigation Company was formally dissolved by Judge Latimer on August 9, 1921. The concern was organized a few years ago for the purpose of constructing an irrigation system, which is now in full operation, and the work of the company is completed.

December 9, 1922.—The Brentwood Irrigation District has been approved by the supervisors. There are 7855 acres included in the district.

January, 1924.—Jersey Island Reclamation District No. 830 has made application to the State Department of Public Works for use of water from San Joaquin River and tributary streams for irrigating purposes.

Directors for Brentwood and Knightsen Irrigation Districts elected January 25: Robert Wallace, Jr., and A. D. McKenzie, for Brentwood, vice R. F. MacLeod; H. O. Abbott, P. J. Moody and H. W. Heidorn so succeed E. B. Sellers, F. H. Estes, and B. L. Grigsby of the Knightsen District.

CHAPTER XVII

THE PIONEERS: NATIVITY, NECROLOGY, BRIEF MENTION

In this chapter brief mention is made of some of the more important of the pioneers who have lived in Contra Costa County, together with data of birth, death, and marriage—often under date line as given in the local press. For convenience of reference, the alphabetical arrangement has been followed rather than the chronological. Much additional information regarding the pioneer settlers of the county will be found in a later chapter of "Gleanings from the Contra Costa Gazette," in which the chief events of interest in the county's history are presented in chronological order from 1858 to the present time.

J. P. Abbott was born in New Hampshire in 1840, came to California in 1863, located in Antioch in 1867, and published the Antioch Ledger for eleven years. He married Melvina G. McMaster, June 25, 1872. His death occurred in 1912.

Mrs. Encarnacion Altemarino, of Pinole, daughter of Ygnacio Martinez, for whom the town was named, died at Pinole, aged seventy-five.

Don Juan B. Alvarado was born in Monterey in 1908. He was governor of California from 1836 to 1843, and collector of customs from 1843 to the American occupation. In 1836 he raised the standard of independence and proclaimed the "Free and Sovereign State of Alta California." He died in San Pablo in 1882. He was called the "Napoleon of California."

February 19, 1926.—On Saturday night, Mrs. Honora Anderson, widow of Capt. Ludwig Anderson, succumbed to the infirmities of old age, and breathed her last in the home she had occupied as a young wife and mother. She was born in Ireland on September 29, 1835, and came to California when a young girl. For seventy-four years she lived in this State, sixty-eight of that time in Contra Costa County.

On November 20, 1910, Capt. Ludwig Anderson died at Pacheco after more than half a century of activity as a business men of the county. He was eighty-five years and three months old at the time of his death. He was born in Denmark, August 26, 1825, went to sea when sixteen years old, later sailed to the United States, arriving in New York in 1848, and in 1850 came via the Horn to California on the Oregon, the vessel that brought news to California that she had been admitted to Statehood. He engaged in the coasting trade until 1860, and then engaged in the lumber business in Pacheco. He established the firm of L. Anderson & Company there, and later established the business in Martinez. In 1858 he married Honora Troy in San Francisco, and they had seven children. He was survived by his widow and six children.

Smith Ashley was born in Ohio in 1822, came to California in 1853 via Nicaragua, and in 1861 located at Pacheco, where he was a farmer. In 1846 he married Sally L. Call.

April 8, 1907.—A. E. Austin, a pioneer of 1886 in Contra Costa County, died aged eighty years. He was a blacksmith and wheelwright. His first shop in Martinez was on Escobar Street, where Johnson's Machine Shop is located.

F. S. Bacon was born in Massachusetts in 1833. He came to California across the plains in 1852, and the next year came to Bay Point and pre-empted land. In 1860 he came to Pacheco, but soon moved to Concord, where he was the first merchant.

January 7, 1891.—Samuel Bacon, born in Barre, Mass., died in Concord, aged fifty-seven years. He was a pioneer of 1852. He served as postmaster of Pacheco and was one of the original settlers of Concord, where he was in the mercantile business.

On July 6, 1907, A. A. Bailey died at Vine Hill. He was born in Wisconsin in 1844 and came to California in 1874. In 1877 he came to Contra Costa County as principal of the Antioch schools, and he was elected superintendent of schools in 1879, and also for the succeeding four terms. In 1906 he took up the real estate business in Richmond. He was a Democrat.

Died, in Martinez, December 4, 1891, M. H. Bailhache, a native of Illinois, aged fifty-three years. He was an old and highly respected citizen of this county, where he resided since 1870, and was a member of General Canby Post, G. A. R. He was serving as postmaster.

H. W. Baker, a pioneer of the county, died at his home in Antioch on December 17, 1898. He was foreman for L. L. Robinson of the Los Médanos Grant, and was a member of the Odd Fellows.

Died, December 20, 1922, J. Rio Baker, aged seventy-three years. He was born in Utah and came to California in the early seventies and settled at Antioch. He was in the drug business, served as postmaster, and was appointed county treasurer to succeed L. E. Buttner, deceased. He was a Mason.

John Baker was born in Pennsylvania in 1819, crossed the plains with oxen in 1853, and located on a ranch near Walnut Creek. In 1848 he married Martha Ann Glass; they had four children.

Robert O. Baldwin passed away on April 26, 1908, at his home near Danville, aged eighty years, just one month and one day after the celebration of his Golden Wedding anniversary. He was born in Ohio in 1828 and in 1850 came to California, crossing the plains with mule-teams and pack-animals. In 1852 he came to Contra Costa County to visit and was so impressed that he remained, locating on a ranch one and a half miles southeast of Danville. He married Mary Cox in 1858, and for fifty years lived in the same house. Five of their six children survived him.

Died, in Martinez, July 21, 1891, Matthew R. Barber, aged seventy-five years. Matthew Barber was born in Ohio in 1815, crossed the plains in 1849, worked in the redwoods near San Antonio (then in Contra Costa County), and while there wrote the tickets for the first election for officers of the new county. Later he built several of the first houses in Martinez, and then farmed two miles from town. He located permanently in the county in 1852, and served as public administrator four terms. He married Orpha Bean in 1837, and had five children.

October 12, 1912.—J. P. Bernard, a pioneer, died in Martinez, aged seventy-six years. He was born in Massachusetts in 1836, and came to California as a young man. He had made his home in Martinez for twenty-seven years.

Benjamin F. Beebe was born in New York in 1830, came via Panama to California in 1863, located in Contra Costa County and farmed near Concord. He served on the board of supervisors. In 1869 he married Fannie C. Kuble, and they had two children. His death occurred in May, 1901.

Died, on January 27, 1913, William F. Belding, pioneer merchant of San Pablo, president of the Bank of Richmond, and a member of the board of education. He left a widow, Mrs. Emma Belding; a son, W. F. Jr., and two grandchildren. Mr. Belding was a prominent Mason.

January 16, 1926.—Mrs. Virginia Belding, widow of William F. Belding, passed away at her home in San Pablo Tuesday morning. She was the sole survivor of a pioneer family and had resided in San Pablo and San Francisco since 1860.

C. M. Belshaw and wife were killed in an automobile accident November 23, 1919, when their Packard touring car plunged over a 400-foot cliff between Rockaway and Moss Beaches on the Pedro Mountain grade. Mr. and Mrs. J. D. Sherwood of Seattle, who were with them, were also killed. C. M. Belshaw was one of the best-known men in Contra Costa County. He was born in Amador County in 1861, was reared in San Francisco, graduated from Harvard in 1883, and was elected to the Assembly on the Republican ticket in 1894. He was an Elk and a Native Son.

January 23, 1926.—John Bendixon, at one time public administrator of Contra Costa County, died at the Martinez hospital Friday morning, following an illness extending over a period of two years. He was born in Denmark and was eighty-three years old.

May 20, 1905.—Seeley James Bennett, one of the pioneer stage men of the county, died last Sunday, aged seventy-one years. He was born in Ohio in 1833 and came to California via the Gulf of Mexico in 1859. Coming to Contra Costa County, he engaged in the livery business in Pacheco, in 1860. In 1861 he started and operated the first stage line from Pacheco to the Mount Diablo coal mines. In 1862 he came to Martinez, and that year he married Jane Hough. They had one son. Mr. Bennett was a Mason.

Mrs. Harriet A. Bent died on February 19, 1899, aged eighty years. She was born in Vermont in 1819, was married in 1838, and in the early fifties came to California. She was one of the first white settlers in Alhambra Valley.

Mathias Berlingen was born in Prussia in 1830, came to America in 1861 and to California via Panama in 1863, and in 1867 located in Contra Costa County at Point of Timber. In 1874 he married Else K. Schnoor.

Died, in Martinez, February 2, 1888, Dr. Hermann Bernett, a native of Germany, aged fifty years.

Simon Blum, pioneer merchant prince of Contra Costa County, died Saturday evening, November 30, 1913, at his residence in Martinez at the age of seventy-nine years. He was born in the North of France in 1834; in 1850 he left for New York; and in 1852 he came via the Isthmus on the steamship Uncle Sam, boarding the Sierra-Nevada for San Francisco and arriving there in February, 1853. In 1854 he removed to Martinez, where he bought the mercantile business of Captain Fogg, and thereafter this was his home and the scene of his operations. He became a very prominent citizen, and wealthy. His brother, Gabriel Blum, was associated with him. He married Leontine Alexandre in 1861, and they had five children. He was a Mason and an Odd Fellow. In 1911 Mr. and Mrs. Blum celebrated their Golden Wedding anniversary.

Henry Blume was born in Prussia in 1837, came to California in 1856, located at Pinole in Contra Costa County in 1859, and engaged in ranching. In 1867 he married Frederika Gohunning, and they had five sons.

Joshua Bollinger was born in Missouri in 1810, crossed the plains in 1850 with ox-teams, and in 1855 came to Contra Costa County and farmed at Bollinger's Canyon.

Mrs. Sophie Boone, a resident of San Ramon Valley for years, and prominent in the Danville section, died January 16, 1921, aged seventy-two years.

Mrs. Boots, one of the first school teachers in Martinez, died in the spring of 1918, at her home in Niles, Alameda County, aged ninety-nine.

Mrs. Elitha Boss, who came to Contra Costa County in 1851 and for sixty-six years made her home here, died in Pleasant Hill on May 24, 1917. She was the mother of six children.

On May 21, 1923, at her home in Martinez, occurred the death of Mrs. Amelia M. Bowen at the age of eighty-three years. She was born in Mexico, and came to California in 1850 and to this county in 1856, since which time she had lived in Martinez. She was survived by three sons.

John D. Bowen, supervisor of the fourth district, residing at Stewartsville, died on September 7, 1885, aged sixty-six years. He was a native of South Wales, born April 9, 1819.

February 28, 1920.—Joseph Boyd, a pioneer of Concord, died of injuries received when an explosion occurred while he was welding a large piece of pipe taken from a water-pump. He was a native of Canada and had been a resident of Concord for thirty years, where he owned considerable property and operated a blacksmith and machine shop.

Died, February 26, 1915, at his home in Alhambra Valley, Fred Brackman, aged forty-nine years. He was born in Ygnacio Valley, but for thirty years prior to his death was a resident of Alhambra Valley. He left a widow and four sons.

Thomas W. Bradley was born in Tennessee in 1818 and crossed the plains in 1843 under the guidance of Joel Walker. He served in the Bear Flag War under Captain Grigsby. In 1849 he came to this county and farmed near Lafayette. He married Rebecca Allen in 1846, and had nine children.

Died, in Martinez, December 25, 1895, Frank D. Briare, a native of New York, aged seventy-five years. He was born March 22, 1820, came West in 1850, and in 1852 came to Martinez. For years he was in the restaurant business.

Mrs. Mary Ford Briare, wife of Frank D. Briare, died in Martinez, June 26, 1885. She was born in Ireland in 1834, and came to Boston in 1849, and arrived in California the day of the Terry and Broderick duel. Since 1859 she had lived in this county.

January 27, 1906.—The death of Louisa Briones, the oldest native daughter in the State, occurred at Oakland last Tuesday. She was born in the old Mexican garrison in San Francisco, June 21, 1816, a daughter of Joaquin Moraga. In 1844 she married Ramon Briones, of Briones Valley, Contra Costa County.

John L. Bromley was born in Maryland in 1820, served in the Mexican War, came to San Francisco in 1852, and in 1853 located on Mount Diablo Ranch. He served as justice of the peace, associate justice of the court of sessions, supervisor and assessor. In 1851 he married Anna Levering, and they had eleven children. He moved to Oakland in 1873.

Died, January 9, 1901, in Martinez, C. Y. Brown, a native of Contra Costa County, aged forty years. He was born in Lafayette in 1861, educated in the Martinez schools, admitted to the bar in 1883, elected district attorney in 1891 on the Democratic ticket, and reelected in 1894 and 1898. He was a member of Mount Diablo Parlor, No. 101, N. S. G. W.

On January 14, 1922, Mrs. Caroline T. Brown, widow of Judge T. A. Brown, answered the final summons at her home in Martinez, aged eighty-eight years. She was born in Illinois and knew Lincoln when he worked in a grist mill for her father. In 1849 she came to California, and in 1850 to Martinez. In 1850 Rev. Cameron, her father, built the first brick building in Martinez. She married T. A. Brown in 1851. She was survived by two sons.

Elam Brown (see his biographical sketch on another page).

Died, at Lafayette, January 18, 1884, Mrs. Margaret Brown, wife of Hon. Elam Brown, aged eighty-nine years and twenty-eight days.

The death of Mrs. Minnie Andrew Brown, wife of Elam C. Brown, occurred in Martinez in the summer of 1922, at the age of fifty-five years. She was born in Ohio in 1867, and came to California and accepted a position in the Martinez school.

Laura A. Brown, widow of Warren Brown, died at Lafayette on April 9, 1914, aged eighty years, six months. She was born in Ohio in 1833, and crossed the plains in 1853 with her mother, Mrs. Lois Hastings, and party. That fall she came to Martinez. She married Warren Brown in 1854, and had been a resident of Lafayette over fifty years.

Hon. Thomas A. Brown was born in Illinois in 1823, crossed the plains to Oregon in 1843, in 1847 came down to California, and in 1849 located in Martinez. In 1849 he was appointed alcalde for the district; and in 1850 he was elected the first county clerk and recorder. He was then elected supervisor, and in 1856, county judge. He served in the State Assembly in 1865, was elected county judge in 1874, and superior judge in 1879.

Wallace Brown died at the age of sixty-three years in Martinez on December 3, 1921. He was the son of the late Judge T. A. Brown, and was born in this city.

Hon. Warren Brown was born in Illinois in 1826 and came with his father, Elam Brown, to California in 1846. He was elected county surveyor in 1850, served as a member of the State Assembly in 1854, and in 1869 was elected sheriff. He died in 1889.

James Bryant, a native of England, died in Martinez November 8, 1908, over eighty-six years of age. He came to California via the Horn, being 112 days on the voyage, and came to this county in 1862. He mined at Nortonville, and five years prior to his death he came to Martinez to live.

William H. Buckley died at his home in Walnut Creek at the age of ninety-nine years. He was born in the State of New York, came to California from Mexico in 1849, and in 1854 bought land near Walnut Creek, where he died.

Died, in Martinez, January 3, 1898, R. R. Bunker, a native of Massachusetts, aged seventy-five years. He was a pioneer of 1850 in California. In 1860 he came to Martinez and bought an interest in the Gazette, and until 1861 it was published by Bradford & Bunker. That year Bradford sold to W. W. Theobalds, the firm becoming Bunker & Theobalds. In 1861 the paper was removed to Pacheco. In 1865 C. B. Porter bought the Theobalds interest, and in 1873 the paper came back to Martinez. In March, 1882, F. F. Foster bought a one-third interest in the paper, and the firm became Bunker, Porter & Foster. Porter and Foster retired, and Bunker and Davenport published the paper, and later Bunker and Needles. In 1892 W. G. Brown and Bunker formed a partnership, and in 1895 Mr. Bunker retired.

Louis N. Buttner, county treasurer, died suddenly at 12:30 Saturday morning, July 5, 1913, aged forty-seven years. He was born at

Sunol, and in 1889, in San Francisco, was married to Mary Hendry, who with two sons was left to mourn his passing. He was a prominent Mason and Past Master of No. 41, and was a member of the Native Sons of the Golden West at Crockett.

W. E. Calahan, Assemblyman, dropped dead in his drug store at Antioch, December 26, 1919.

Joseph F. Carey, one of the very early settlers of eastern Contra Costa County, died Tuesday, May 24, 1910. He was born in New York in 1833, moved to Wisconsin with his parents, and in 1853 crossed the plains to California. Settling in Contra Costa County in 1865, he engaged in ranching, and had a blacksmith shop at Brentwood. In 1866 he married Laura Ann Welch.

Dr. J. H. Carothers was born in Pennsylvania in 1824 and graduated at Miami Medical College. He located at Martinez in 1854, laid out the town of Pacheco in 1857, and was elected to the legislature in 1869.

July 8, 1905.—After a life of unusual activity, D. S. Carpenter died in Martinez, aged seventy-four years. He was a prominent Odd Fellow. He was born in New York in 1833, came to California in 1852, and in 1856 located in Contra Costa County. He served as justice of the peace and as county tax collector. In 1863 he married Sarah Travers Curry, and they had eleven children.

April 6, 1924.—J. P. Casey, of Port Costa, was summoned by death, at the age of seventy-nine years. A native of Ireland, he came to the United States fifty years ago, and to Port Costa forty years ago. Mr. Casey served sixteen years as a member of the board of supervisors. He left three children.

Patricio Castro was born in Contra Costa County in 1843; he farmed five miles south of San Pablo. He married Harriet O'Neil in 1875, and they had three children.

John Cavanaugh was born in County Cork, Ireland, in 1811; he came to California via Panama in 1862 and located in San Ramon Valley, but later moved to Mount Diablo Valley.

John G. Chase was born in New Hampshire in 1837; came via Panama in 1856, and in 1858 located in this county at Antioch, when there was only one house there, and engaged in the livery business. He married Elmira A. Johnson in 1868, and had two children.

February 16, 1918.—J. H. Chichester, a pioneer of Richmond, died at his San Pablo home Thursday evening, aged sixty-five years. He was born in New York in 1853, and married Miss Alice Pabb in 1876. He taught school and soon after his marriage moved to San Pablo.

May 19, 1906.—John P. Chrisman, a pioneer resident of Contra Costa County, died at Danville Saturday, aged eighty years.

Died, in Martinez, May 27, 1901, George W. Christian, a native of New York, aged seventy-three years. Mr. Christian was born in 1828 and came to California across the plains in 1849. In 1852 he moved to this county, where he had since lived.

Daniel Clancy was born in Ireland in 1822, came via Panama in 1859, and in 1860 located in this county. He married Mary A. Falvey in 1851, and had nine children.

On March 16, 1913, in San Pablo, Charles Henry Clark, the oldest voter in the county, died, aged ninety-seven years and eleven months.

R. J. Clark, a pioneer of Contra Costa, died at his residence in Martinez, March 27, 1885. He was born in Nantucket, November 20, 1815, and in 1851 came to California at the solicitation of Captain Coffin, who desired his services as engineer of the ferry plying between Martinez and Benicia. He remained at his post thirty years.

May 26, 1906.—Mrs. Susan Classen, who came to California in 1853 to join her father, Seth M. Swain, died in Martinez, aged seventy-four years.

Joel Clayton was born in England. He came across the plains to California in 1850, located land near Black Diamond coal mines in 1859, and established the town of Clayton. He died in 1872.

Felix G. Coats was born in Missouri in 1828, crossed the plains by prairie schooner in 1849, and located with his parents in Contra Costa County in 1852. On February 23, 1860, he married Lovina Doggett, and they had six children. He died on June 10, 1916.

Died, January 4, 1886, Wilson Coats, a native of Tennessee, born in 1802, who came to California, crossing the plains with oxen in 1849. He located in Contra Costa County about 1852, settling in Tassajara Valley, being then the only settler there.

August 21, 1915.—Mrs. Ann Coleman, one of the oldest pioneers of Martinez, died Monday, aged ninety years. She had lived in Contra Costa County fifty-two years.

Died, May 14, 1918, at the home of her daughter, Mrs. Mary A. Armstrong of Byron, Mrs. Rebecca Conner, aged ninety-six years and six months. She was born in Ireland in 1821, came to the United States in 1847, and for forty-four years had lived in Byron.

John Conway was born in Ireland in 1830 and was brought to America an infant. He came via Panama to California in 1860, located near Danville, and farmed. Later he engaged in mercantile business in San Ramon, having bought out P. G. Peel. He married Nora O'Brien in 1858, and they had two children. He died on January 24, 1915, at Danville, aged eighty-five years.

Died, near Alamo, December 27, 1891, Henry Cook, pioneer, aged seventy-four years. He was born in Pennsylvania in 1817, crossed the plains to Oregon in 1847, and came on to California in 1848. He located in Contra Costa in 1874.

June 10, 1922.—This week, in Seattle, was held the funeral of George W. Cormack, a native of Contra Costa County, whose discovery of gold on Bonanza Creek in the Klondike, August 17, 1896, sent 60,000 prospectors hurrying to Alaska, visited up to that time only by trappers and missionaries.

March 13, 1926.—Herman Costa, for over fifty years a resident of Martinez, died at his home on Thompson Street on Tuesday night, aged sixty-nine years. For thirty-two years he had been a member of the Odd Fellows Lodge.

January 15, 1921.—Died, at Concord, J. C. Costa, aged eighty-four years. He was born in Portugal and when a young man came to California. He was survived by ten children.

November 12, 1898.—Thursday morning at 9 o'clock, Charles S. Cousins, a highly respected resident of the county, died at his home in Martinez. He was born in New York in 1830, came to California in 1859, and located in Contra Costa County. In 1861 he became a clerk in the United States mint at San Francisco; in 1870 he came to Pinole and farmed; in 1882 he was elected county recorder, and held the office until 1895, when he retired.

William Cowan, Sr., one of Contra Costa County's oldest residents, died at his home near Brentwood on February 3, 1910, aged eighty-two.

William Wilson Cox, of San Ramon Valley, died Friday, April 15, 1910, at the family residence. He was born in Indiana in 1833. In 1852 he went to Missouri with oxen, and on May 2, 1853, started on the five-months journey to California, crossing the plains and coming to this county upon his arrival. He had lived here ever since. In 1865 he married Mary E. Grist, and they had six children.

Died, in Byron, December 13, 1896, Samuel Crawford, a native of Scotland, aged sixty-seven years.

Died, February 21, 1908, James Curry, an old pioneer, born in Tennessee, in 1835, who came to California in 1851. He crossed the plains with ox-teams and located in Contra Costa County in 1852, when he settled in Moraga Valley, and later moved to Curry's Canyon; still later, in 1860, he went to Clayton and engaged in the butcher business and afterwards in the livery business. He drove the stage from Antioch to Oakland. He married, in 1861, Ella Callahan; and they had eight children.

September 26, 1925.—William Dainty, pioneer of eastern Contra Costa and one of the best-known ranchers of the Brentwood section, passed away Tuesday night about eight o'clock at Merritt Hospital, Oakland, after a short illness. He was a native of Brentwood and was about sixty years of age. He is mourned by a widow, Mrs. Ella Dainty, one son, Leonard, and three daughters, Mrs. Esther Moody, and Misses Velma and Wilma Dainty, all of Brentwood. A particularly sad feature of the death of the pioneer is that one of his daughters was to have become a bride next Saturday. Mr. Dainty was a nephew of Mrs. H. L. Howard of Martinez, and was well known here, where he frequently visited.

Thomas Dake, for more than thirty years a resident of Martinez, died on September 10, 1919, ninety-one years of age. He had been a resident of California about forty-five years.

Died, on March 27, 1921, Mrs. Marie Elizabeth Daley, one of the pioneer women of Martinez, who came here with her father, Cornelius S.

Whitcomb, when she was four years old, and settled near Lafayette. She had lived in the county over sixty years, and was an active worker in the Methodist Episcopal Church.

March 30, 1907.—Died, aged seventy-nine years, David Davis, a pioneer miner of Nortonville. He was a native of Wales, born in 1828, and in the early sixties came to this county.

John Davis was born in Dalmatia in 1825, came to California in 1849, and in 1851 located in Contra Costa County. He married Anna Connor and had six children.

March 19, 1911.—Died, in Pinole, David Dean, a pioneer of Contra Costa County and a native of New York, aged eighty-two years.

January 28, 1925.—One of the pioneers of Richmond, Peter W. Dean, passed away at his home at 829 Fifty-sixth Street, Oakland, last night at about 8 o'clock. He was forty-three years old and was a native of Berkeley. He was the brother of Patrick M. Dean of Richmond, the man who became famous about twenty years ago by the promotion of the Nelson and Wolgast fight at Point Richmond.

R. G. Dean, a pioneer of the county, passed away at Brentwood April 12, 1920, in his ninetieth year. He was born in New York in 1831, was orphaned at sixteen years of age, and left for California when he was eighteen years old. He married Miss Jerusha H. Martin in San Francisco in 1864. He was the man who named Lake Tahoe.

John Denkinger was born in Germany in 1830, came via Panama in 1858, and in 1863 located in this county east of Concord. He married Emilie Balz in 1863, and had four children.

January 28, 1911.—With the death of Mrs. Carmen de Soto in Concord last Saturday, there passed the last of the Spanish pioneer settlers who came to Contra Costa County following its admission to Statehood. She was born at Warm Springs Rancho, near the Mission of San Jose, in 1830, a daughter of Don Valentine Higuera. In 1852 she married Silveria de Soto, and in 1853 they moved to Contra Costa County with their personal property in a carreta. Mr. de Soto died in 1906.

Died, August 10, 1885, in Martinez, Mrs. Eyiaca de Briones de Soto a native of California, aged eighty-one years.

Silveria de Soto, one of the last of the early pioneers, died on October 13, 1906, aged seventy-six years. He was born at San Jose and came to Contra Costa County in 1853, settling at San Ramon, and later in Ygnacio Valley, where he lived until his death. In 1852 he married Carmen Higuera. He was survived by his widow and seven children.

Andrew Diffenbach was born in New York in 1832, came via the Horn on the Empire in 1852, located in this county at Brentwood in 1867, and was a rancher and butcher.

November 17, 1883.—Austin Dohrmann, one of the oldest and best-known Contra Costa citizens, died at his home near Concord.

Theodore Downing was born in Michigan in 1826, came to California across the plains in 1854, and engaged in the butcher business in Martinez: in 1859 he was in the hotel business in Pacheco, and later farmed. He married Mary Quackenbush in 1852, and had two children.

William Hall Dukes, pioneer of 1852, of Pleasant Hill, passed away at his home July 5, 1917. He was born in Tennessee, and on coming to California engaged in mining for a short time; later he located in Contra Costa County, where he bought a farm, built a house, and lived the remainder of his days. He and his wife, who died eight months before his death, had five daughters and one son.

A. E. Dunkel, vice-president of the Bank of Martinez and a prominent Contra Costa citizen, died at his home in Martinez on June 13, 1922, aged sixty years. He was born in Angels Camp, Calaveras County, in 1862. He came to Contra Costa County as a young man and located at Pacheco, but later came to Martinez. He was county recorder for twelve years and resigned to take over the management of the Contra Costa County Abstract & Title Company. He was survived by his widow and a son.

Capt. J. E. Durham, for many years a resident of Ygnacio Valley and an active citizen of the county, died December 12, 1919, aged ninety years. He was born in 1829 in Tennessee, came to California in 1850 with a government train as teamster to Fort Laramie, and then made his way to Salt Lake and on to California in 1851. He came to Contra Costa County in 1870.

Leonard Eddy, a pioneer resident of the county, died in Martinez June 12, 1885. He was born in New York, January 15, 1828, and came to California from Illinois in 1849. He located at the base of Mount Diablo in 1850.

Thomas Edwards was born in North Wales in 1812, crossed the plains to California in 1849, and in 1867 moved to Carquinez Straits and engaged in stock-raising. In 1881 he arranged with Mr. Heald to establish a foundry on his place, and the town of Crockett was laid out.

Charles H. Ellerhorst, aged eighty-three years, and for fifty years a resident of Pinole, died on Thanksgiving Day, November 30, 1922. He was born in Germany and came to California fifty years ago. He was a Mason.

Mark Elliott, one of the oldest residents of this county, died at his home in Sycamore Valley, December 7, 1884. He was born in Ohio in 1826, crossed the plains in 1850, and in 1852 located in the Sycamore district. Coal was struck on his property on Alamo Creek. In 1864 he married Martha Dempster, and they had two children.

The death of H. F. Emeric, at his ranch at San Pablo, is recorded August 14, 1899. He was born in New York, and in 1854 came with his parents to California. He served in the legislature from Contra Costa County in 1894-1895, and was appointed on the Fish and Game Commission by Governor Budd. He was fifty-one years of age at the time of his death.

Died, at his residence near Walnut Creek, July 24, 1883, Capt. Orris Fales, native of Wales, aged sixty-six years.

May 19, 1912.—Bernardo Fernandez died at Pinole, aged eighty-three years. He was born in Portugal and from the age of thirteen followed the sea until 1853, when he came to San Francisco via the Horn. He bought land at Pinole in Contra Costa County that same fall, freighted to San Francisco, and added to his holdings as he prospered until he came to be the owner of 3000 acres, and one of the wealthiest and most prominent men in the county. He was active up to the time of his death. In 1859 he married Charlotte Caudra, and they had six children.

March 27, 1918.—Died, at her home in Pinole, Mrs. Carletta Fernandez, for over fifty years a resident of the county. Mrs. Fernandez was born in Chile in 1840 and came to Pinole in 1859; she was a member of the California Pioneers.

Harrison Finley was born in Missouri in 1837, crossed the plains in 1860 with oxen, and in 1863 located in Tassajara Valley. In 1862 he married Lavina Ray, and they had eight children.

February 28, 1911.—Died, Charles Fish, one of the oldest settlers of Martinez, aged ninety-two years. He was born in New York in 1818 and came via the Horn to California in 1853, and the next year to Contra Costa County. In 1857 he became associated with S. Blum; and he was associated with S. Blum and W. A. Hale in the organization of the Bank of Martinez. In 1876 he married Mary Elizabeth Grimes.

August 29, 1925.—One of the few remaining pioneer women of early days in Contra Costa County died Saturday morning when Mrs. Mary Elizabeth Fish, widow of the late Charles Fish, breathed her last at her home in Berkeley. Mrs. Fish had been in failing health for some time, and for several days members of her family had realized that the end was rapidly approaching.

As Mary Elizabeth Grimes, the pioneer matron was born in Bethany, N. Y. She became Mrs. Charles Fish before Mr. Fish came to California in the early fifties; and they resided for many years in Martinez, the Fish homestead being one of the oldest pioneer habitations in the county seat. One son, Charles Stanley, and two daughters, Misses Grace Emily and Blanche Ellen Fish, mourn the passing of their pioneer mother.

October 13, 1900.—The funeral of Lafayette I. Fish, a pioneer of California of 1850, was held last Thursday afternoon from his residence. He was born in New York in 1824, came to California in 1850, and in 1852 located in Contra Costa County and bought some land. He was the first president and one of the organizers of the Bank of Martinez in 1873.

Mrs. Laura Flournoy, a native of Kentucky, but a resident of California from girlhood, died near Danville, January 15, 1921, aged sixty-five years. She was an active worker in the Presbyterian church.

Erastus Ford was born in Michigan in 1830, crossed the plains in 1849, and in 1850 located in this county.

William R. Forman was born in Missouri in 1821, came via Panama to California in 1851, and in 1857 located in this county and farmed; he also was a member of the firm of Rouse, Forman & Company, lumber dealers. He married Malinda E. Highland in 1843, and they had a family of four children.

F. W. Foskett, president of the First National Bank and a capitalist of Concord, died on September 11, 1919. He came to Concord many years ago and engaged in the butcher business with H. H. Elsworthy. When they sold out they established the First National Bank. He left a widow, three sons and one daughter.

Died, in Walnut Creek, December 26, 1891, James Foster, aged sixty-seven years. Mr. Foster was born in Maine on October 31, 1824, and came to California in the middle fifties and the following year to Alamo, where he conducted a wagon shop. He was postmaster and justice of the peace; served five terms as county assessor, being elected in 1869; studied law, making a specialty of Spanish grants; and was appointed referee for subdividing lots in Martinez. He became interested in the Gazette in 1887, and his ability contributed much to its success. A short time before his death he deeded his half-interest in the semi-weekly Gazette to his granddaughter, Edna Needles. He married Nancy A. Prescott in 1852, and they had three children.

August 7, 1918.—Mrs. Melvina Abbott Franks, the first white girl born in Antioch, died at Mount Zion Hospital, San Francisco, Tuesday night. She was a daughter of J. C. McMaster, one of the first supervisors of the county back in 1853, and had lived in Antioch all her life. She married J. P. Abbott after her graduation from Mills College. He died in 1912, and in 1917 she married Arthur Franks.

R. R. Fuller was born in Massachusetts in 1818, came via the Horn to California in 1853, and located on a farm near Antioch. He married Sarah A. Pierce in Massachusetts and had four children.

Died, in Concord, May 25, 1892, Antonio Galindo, at the age of sixty-seven years.

April 10, 1926.—Concord, April 3. Descended from one of California's oldest Spanish families, and a resident of this community for over seventy years, Mrs. Marina Galindo, granddaughter of Salvio Pacheco, one of the earliest Spanish settlers in Contra Costa County, and on her mother's side the granddaughter of Valentino Amador, one of the first Spanish officers at the San Francisco presidio, died at her home at the age of seventy-seven years. She was born in Santa Clara on May 25, 1848, and when seven was brought to Contra Costa County by her parents, and had lived here ever since.

John Gambs was born in Germany in 1827 and came to the United States in 1847 and to California via the Horn in 1848. In 1861 he located in Pacheco, and engaged in merchandising. He married Helen Ohl and had five children.

Lawrence Geary was born in Baden, Germany, in 1827, came to the United States in 1848, and in 1852 crossed the plains and located in Contra Costa County. In 1854 he married Jane Wallace, and they had five children.

Col. W. W. Gift was born in South Carolina in 1796, came to California in 1849, and was sergeant-at-arms in the Assembly when the first legislature met at Monterey. In 1853 he was appointed registrar of the land office and later he was custom house inspector at Panama Straits. In 1854 he came to Martinez. He married Elizabeth Dodson in 1819, and had eight children. Colonel Gift was a lover of fine horses, and raced Twilight. He died in 1881.

Died, near San Ramon, September 9, 1897, David Glass, a native of Pennsylvania, aged seventy-nine years. He was born in Pennsylvania in 1818, and moved to Ohio with his parents. In 1841 he went to Iowa, where he built the first house in Ottumwa. He married Elizabeth J. Hall, and in 1850 they came to California. In Placerville Mr. Glass engaged in the mercantile business, but that same year he came to Contra Costa County and lived near Walnut Creek for a time. Later he bought 700 acres south of San Ramon. The deceased left a widow and seven children.

J. B. Greer, a pioneer of Point of Timber, where he conducted a warehouse, died at the home of his daughter, Mrs. R. H. Caven, near Concord on Monday, July 10, 1905, at the age of ninety-five years and six months.

Munson Gregory was born in Ohio in 1828, crossed the plains in 1850, and in 1857 bought a ranch near Mount Diablo. In 1858 he married Laura Knox, and they had three children.

Louis Grunauer was born in Prussia in 1854; he came to America in 1868, and direct to California, via Panama. In 1878 he located in this county and erected the first store in Brentwood, and was the first postmaster.

Died, in Martinez, Friday, January 13, 1899, Henry M. Hale. He was born April 4, 1833, in Ohio, and in the late fifties came to California, direct to Pacheco, where he entered the employ of his brother. In 1873 they came to Martinez and organized the Bank of Martinez.

April 7, 1906.—A county pioneer, Mrs. Mary E. Hale, died Sunday evening, April 1, 1906. She was born in Detroit, Michigan, seventy-three years ago, and crossed the plains with her father, James E. Lyon, in the fifties. She married Henry M. Hale in 1861.

Died, in Martinez, August 20, 1883, William M. Hale, aged fifty-one years and eleven months. Mr. Hale was born September 20, 1831, in Ohio and came to California in 1853. In 1858 he removed to Pacheco and carried on a business under the name of Hale & Fassett and the Hale Brothers until 1873, when the business was closed out on the organizing of the Bank of Martinez, both brothers being large stockholders and William becoming cashier. In 1863 he married Mary L. Lyon, and they had a son and a daughter.

Mrs. Mary E. Hall, a pioneer of 1859 in Contra Costa County, died at her home in Alamo on February 23, 1917. She was born in Pennsylvania and came to California and Contra Costa County in 1859, where she had since lived. She left five children.

Myron W. Hall, the father of the walnut industry in this county, died at San Ramon, December 16, 1910. He was born in Pennsylvania in 1831. At the age of eighteen he came West with Lysander Stone, who was bringing a large band of stock to California. In 1857 he came to Contra Costa County, locating in Green Valley. In 1859 he went back East and married Lucy E. Dorman, and returned to California with her. In 1870 Mr. Hall bought land near Alamo. In 1872 he planted the first native walnuts, and the trees have borne ever since. Six children were born to Mr. and Mrs. Hall.

Henry M. Hallenbeck died in Martinez, November 6, 1918, aged eighty-seven years. He was born in New York in 1831, crossed the plains in 1851, and came direct to Martinez, where he had since lived. He left a widow and five children.

Austin W. Hammitt, one of the pioneers of the county, died at Concord on December 10, 1897, aged seventy-four years. He was born in Ohio, crossed the plains with oxen to Oregon in 1849, mined for a time, and then returned East. In 1851 he returned to Oregon as captain of a train, and in 1857 came to Contra Costa County and located at Walnut Creek, engaging in the mercantile business and in farming. He was justice of the peace from 1865 to 1867 and was elected to the Assembly in 1873. In 1849 he married Samantha Shaffer, and they had four children. He left a widow and three children.

F. A. Hammitt, pioneer of Contra Costa County and resident of Lafayette and later of Concord, died at Martinez Hospital Thursday morning, November 8, 1917. He was a native of Wisconsin, was seventy-three years of age, and had lived in the county sixty years.

Died, in Lafayette, February 17, 1896, G. W. Hammitt, a native of Kentucky, aged seventy-three years.

Capt. James T. Harding, one of the oldest residents of Pacheco, died November 28, 1886. He was born in Massachusetts in 1810, and was a resident of the county since 1858.

March 22, 1907.—Died, Hiram P. Hardy, a native of New Hampshire born in 1825. In 1849 he came via the Horn to California, and in 1853 came to Contra Costa County, where he worked for Dr. Strentzel and ranched. Mr. Hardy furnished molding sand to foundries in California, Oregon and Washington for over forty years.

Died, in Port Costa, February 17, 1890, Charles Harkins, aged sixty-nine years. Mr. Harkins was formerly a butcher in Martinez, and was an old settler of the county.

July 4, 1925.—On Tuesday evening, June 30, Robert Harkinson died at the family home in Antioch, aged seventy years. He was born in Pittsburgh, Pa., came to California in 1874, and took employment with the Bank of Dixon, with which institution he remained until 1883, when he went to San Luis Obispo. In 1891 he moved to Antioch and was instrumental in founding the Bank of Antioch and became its first cashier, which position he retained continuously until 1920, when he retired from active business. Mr. Harkinson married Alice Brinkerhoff in Dixon and leaves one daughter, Mrs. Maude Robertson of Berkeley, his wife having passed away several years ago. Interment will be made in Antioch.

Joel Harlan was born in Indiana in 1828, crossed the plains with his parents in 1846, and bought land in Amador Valley in 1852; but when Alameda County was formed, his house was one of the points defining the boundaries of the counties, and he was left in the new county. He was married in 1849 in Sonoma, by ex-Governor Boggs, to Minerva Fowler, and they had nine children. He died in 1875.

Died, at Danville, May 13, 1922, Isabella MacLeod Harrison. She was born in Washington, D. C. in 1837. She married A. B. Harrison in 1869 and came to California in 1872, settling at Walnut Creek; in 1887 they moved to Danville, where she had since lived. She had a family of four boys.

On June 28, 1920, John Hartz, one of the Pioneers of Contra Costa County, died at his home in Danville. He was born in Germany in 1847. In 1865 he landed in California and began as a ranch-hand in Alameda County; in 1888 he bought 280 acres of James Stow. He married Catherine Johnson in 1877, and they had three children. He was treasurer of the Odd Fellows at Danville for twenty years.

Died, in Martinez, April 3, 1909, Roswell B. Hathaway, a native of New York. Mr. Hathaway was born in 1826 and came to California in 1854, locating in Contra Costa County. He was a rancher, later was in the butcher business in Pacheco and Concord, and in 1876 was elected county treasurer, which office he held for three terms.

George W. Hawxhurst, one of the oldest and most progressive citizens of the county, died September 2, 1890. He was a native of New York, born in 1827; came to California in 1850, and to this county in 1855; and with Mr. Somers located the Black Diamond claim and the Cumberland. He also located the Union Mine.

Died, at his home in Martinez, April 7, 1897, E. W. Hiller, aged sixty-eight years. She was born in Massachusetts in 1828; came via the Horn to California in 1849 on the Aurora, a whaling ship; and in December, 1852, came to San Pablo, and in 1854 to Martinez. He served in an official capacity several times, was appointed public administrator in 1872, and held office until he was stricken with paralysis. In 1858 he married Mary C. Burdett.

Died, February 24, 1915, in Martinez, Mrs. Agnes M. Hittman, widow of the late Frederick Hittman, a native of Germany, aged seventy years. She left five daughters and three sons.

October 19, 1916.—James Hoey, a pioneer of Martinez and secretary of the Democratic County Central Committee over thirty years, passed away aged sixty-three years. He was born in Ireland in 1854 and came to America in 1870, and that same year to Martinez. He married Mary Tormey on November 9, 1880, who survived him with three daughters.

Died, in Byron, October 12, 1899, Ferdinand F. Hoffman, aged seventy-two years and six months. He was born in the Rhine Province in 1826 and came to America in 1847 and to California in 1850, crossing the plains. He located in Contra Costa County in 1858 and engaged in the tannery business. In 1861 he located on a ranch near Byron. In 1870 he married Elizabeth Nolling; and they had three children.

Died, in Martinez, July 22, 1891, William Hoffman, aged seventy years. Mr. Hoffman was born in Prussia, June 21, 1821. He came to the United States in 1847, and in 1849 to California via Cape Horn. He located in Contra Costa County soon after, and in 1855 bought a residence in Martinez and established a tannery.

After a residence of seventy-two years in Martinez, Mrs. Cornelia Jane Hollenbeck died at the home of her daughter, Mrs. R. V. Lytton, at the age of eighty, on November 1, 1923. She was born in Iowa, came to California in 1849 with her parents, and settled in Martinez in 1851. She left five children.

On August 15, 1908, in the Alhambra Valley, Beverly R. Holliday passed over the Great Divide. He was a pioneer of 1849 and the first educator in Martinez, where he opened the first seminary in 1850. He was born in Warren County, Ky., December 22, 1823. From 1840 to 1849 he taught school in Illinois. In March, 1849, he set out across the plains with ox-teams, and in January of 1850 he came to Contra Costa County. He was elected justice of the peace in 1850 and was chosen as one of the associate judges of the Court of Sessions in 1854. In 1853 he engaged in farming, and he was a pioneer in fruit culture. In 1858 he subscribed funds to help found the Gazette. He married Jane A. Holliday, August 19, 1855, and left six children.

April 26, 1902.—Mrs. Miranda Hook, relict of William Hook, died last Wednesday at her home in Ygnacio Valley. She was one of the oldest residents of the county. She came across the plains with her husband in 1850. In 1854 Mr. Hook bought land in Contra Costa County, and this has been the family home ever since. She was eighty-three years old.

Dr. E. F. Hough was born in New York in 1823, graduated from Ohio Medical College, crossed the plains in 1852 from Illinois, settled in Ygnacio Valley in 1853, came to Martinez in 1855, and built Hough's Hotel, which he ran for twenty-five years. He was one of the first to discover mineral paints in this county. In 1842 he married Sibyl Marsh, and they had two children.

Died, near Byron, May 30, 1899, R. G. Houston, a native of Ohio, aged sixty-six years. He was born in 1833, came to California in 1852, and two years later located in Contra Costa County. He had always taken an active part in politics.

8

C. E. Howard, a pioneer of San Ramon Valley, died May 23, 1912, in Danville. He was born in Massachusetts in 1826, came to California in 1849, and in 1856 came to Contra Costa County.

Nathaniel S. Howard, of Walnut Creek, died Wednesday, January 25, 1899. He was born in Plymouth County, Mass., in 1819 and came to California in 1849 via Cape Horn, on the Howard. In September, 1856, he came to this county and bought a farm near Danville.

Benjamin Hughes died at Walnut Creek October 18, 1908, aged eighty-three years. He was born in Illinois in 1825 and came to California in 1852, crossing the plains with ox-teams and locating in Contra Costa County on his arrival. In 1857 he bought a ranch near Walnut Creek, where he resided until death. He married Miss Emily Seeley in 1851, and they had two children.

M. F. Hurley, aged fifty-five years, died at his Martinez home on January 30, 1924. He was born in Massachusetts in 1868, and was educated in Martinez, where his parents moved in 1878. In 1902 he served a term as public administrator, and in 1907 was appointed county recorder, which office he held until his death. He married Flora Irene Morford in 1912. Mr. Hurley was survived by his widow and three children.

October 3, 1925.—Mrs. Josephine Inman, widow of the late Daniel Inman, founder of the town of Danville, and for whom that community was named, passed away Thursday at her home near Livermore at the age of seventy-eight years. Mrs. Inman came to the San Ramon Valley in early days, her husband's family coming to the valley in 1846 and residing there continuously from that time on.

M. B. Ivory was born in Pennsylvania in 1831; came to California in 1858, and located in Green Valley; was elected sheriff in 1871; and was reelected in 1874.

November 27, 1923.—Clark Jaquith, for fifty years a resident and business man of Concord, died at the age of seventy-five years. He was a native of Canada. He is survived by a son and a daughter.

Mrs. Elizabeth Johnson died on May 22, 1910, at her home. She was born in England, and came with her mother, Mrs. Vaughn, to America. She married Thaddeus Johnson in 1856. They settled near Walnut Creek, where Mr. Johnson farmed. In 1890 they moved to Martinez, and here Mr. Johnson died in 1895.

Sampson W. Johnson was born in Virginia in 1828. He started for Oregon in 1846; but at the Sink of the Humboldt he changed his mind and came to California, joined Fremont, and remained till 1847. In 1859 he came to this county and established a livery business in Martinez. In 1850 he married Annie McClellan, and they had four children.

December 1, 1912.—The oldest woman voter in Contra Costa County, Mrs. Catherine Williams Jones, one of the pioneers of California and the county, died on November 30. She was born in Wales in 1821, and came to New York in 1849 with her parents. She married John N.

Jones, who died in 1910. They had been residents of California about fifty years and of Nortonville since the early seventies.

Elizabeth C. (Allen) Jones, wife of Nathaniel Jones, died at Crockett on January 19, 1907. She was born in Missouri and married Mr. Jones in 1842. They came West in 1846, and in 1847 to Contra Costa County, and settled on a part of the Alcalanes ranch. Mrs. Jones was eighty-four years old at the time of her death.

John N. Jones died at Nortonville Saturday night, August 6, 1910. He was born in Wales in 1819, and came to America in 1848. He was married in Philadelphia in 1849 to Catherine Williams, who came from Wales to join him. About fifty years prior to his death they came West, and about two years later moved to Nortonville. Mr. Jones was ninety-one years old at the time of his death.

On May 12, 1905, John W. Jones, a pioneer resident of the county, died at the age of eighty-three years. He was born in Kentucky in 1822; in 1853 he crossed the plains with ox-teams to California, coming to La-fayette on his arrival here. In 1855 he bought a ranch, upon which he lived until he moved to Martinez. He had one son, Henry T. Jones.

January 13, 1900.—Joseph P. Jones, who served on the bench as superior judge in Contra Costa County for thirteen years, was buried last Friday. He was born in Indiana in 1844, and accompanied his parents to Oregon in 1853. In 1865 he returned to Indiana and entered the University of Bloomington, graduating in law in 1867. He came to Mar-tinez in 1869; was elected district attorney in 1873, serving two years; and then served in the legislature. In 1886 he was elected superior judge. He was a prominent Mason.

Mrs. Mary A. Jones died on July 23, 1918, at her home in Alamo, aged ninety-three years. She was born in Tennessee in 1825, and came to California before the days of the gold rush, via the Oregon route, reaching Napa on November 10, 1846. She moved to San Jose in 1847, and in 1851 came to San Ramon Valley, where she had since made her home.

The death of Nathaniel Jones, who had been a resident of the county since 1847, occurred on January 31, 1899, at Walnut Creek. He was born in Eastern Tennessee in 1820. He moved to Missouri and in 1842 married Elizabeth C. Allen. In 1846, with fifteen or twenty others and their families, he crossed the plains, bound for Oregon, but changed his course and came to California, arriving here November 2, 1846. He served in the battle of Santa Clara under Capt. Julius Martin. He settled in this county in 1847. His was the first wagon to cross Carquinez Straits on Dr. Semple's ferry propelled by oars. At his death he was seventy-nine years of age.

Martin Joost, last of the pioneer Joost family, died at his Vine Hill home Sunday, November 11, 1917, aged seventy-four years. He was born in Germany, and came to California in the pioneer days. For eighteen years before his death he made his home with his sister.

February 27, 1926.—Infirmities due to advanced age closed the long life of Mrs. Mary Jane Joselin at her home at Antioch, Friday night. She was eighty-five years old and had resided in Antioch for fifty-nine years. She was born at Middle Point, Wis.

June 27, 1925.—The last of the old '49ers in Contra Costa County, and one of the best-known and most highly respected pioneers of Central California, passed on to his reward Saturday evening at 8 o'clock when John Henry Keller of Concord succumbed to an attack of the heart. While members of the family realized that his passing might come at any time, on account of his advanced age, Mr. Keller's death was sudden and came as a shock to his sons and daughters and legion of friends throughout the county.

John H. Keller was a pioneer of California and a '49er in every sense of the term. Born in New Albany, Ind., July 2, 1844, he would have reached the advanced age of four score and one in another ten days. When a boy of five years he crossed the plains to California with his parents, a journey which took seven months and brought the family to Marysville in the fall of 1849. There they settled and resided for many years when Mr. Keller was growing to manhood. As a young man he joined that collection of fearless and intrepid men who made early-day history, as a Pony Express Rider.

Fifty-four years ago Mr. Keller came to Contra Costa County, and for more than a half century has resided in or near Concord and the Clayton Valley. He engaged in the butcher business, following that pursuit until his retirement a few years ago. He was one of the guests of honor at the '49 celebration held in Sacramento recently, and with the passing recently of Charles Lohse of Ygnacio Valley, Mr. Keller was left the sole surviving member of the hardy '49ers in Contra Costa County. Now he too has passed on.

Nine daughters and sons mourn the passing of their pioneer father, the wife and helpmate of the years, Mrs. Celestia Keller, having died a little over a year ago. The funeral will be held in Concord Tuesday. Burial at Clayton.

Mrs. Harriet Baird Kellogg, a resident of Martinez for many years, died at the home of her daughter, May 15, 1918, aged eighty-two years. She was born in Pennsylvania in 1836, came to California in 1887, and for several years was president of the Women's Chamber of Commerce of San Diego. She came to Martinez in 1899.

Died, at Vine Hill, April 30, 1910, James Kelly, aged seventy-three years. He was born in Belfast, Ireland, in 1837, and came to the United States in 1847 with his father, and in 1854 came to California, crossing the plains with his brother Samuel. Arriving in Contra Costa County, the brothers engaged in the dairy business at Pinole. In 1864 James Kelly went back to Wisconsin and married Margaret Dowd, and in 1887 he bought a ranch near Martinez. He served as supervisor from 1887 to 1891.

Capt. George W. Kimball, one of the Forty-niners of Antioch, died November 18, 1879. He had been a resident of Antioch since his arrival as captain of a ship built in Maine, of which State he was a native, born in 1806.

Died, at his home near Clayton, January 7, 1918, Nicholas Kirkwood, aged eighty-seven years. He was born in Scotland and came to California via the Horn in 1852, and to this county in 1857. He had never married.

On April 9, 1921, W. A. Kirkwood, former superintendent of schools of Contra Costa County, died in Oakland, aged sixty-three years. He left a widow, one son and three daughters.

March 5, 1926.—Concord, March 2. Charles W. Klein, prominent business man and resident of Concord for many years, and mayor of this city for a number of years, passed away at his home this morning. He was born and reared in this valley and was one of the successful and substantial citizens. He was about fifty-three years of age. He leaves a widow and two daughters.

John C. Kouse was born in New York in 1828; came via Panama in 1853; and in 1861 located in this county, where he mined, ran a hotel, and engaged in the lumber business. He died in 1907.

November 8, 1923.—E. R. Lamb, for forty-three years a resident of Ygnacio Valley, passed away at the age of seventy-five years. He was born in Connecticut, came to California via Panama when he was twenty-one years of age, locating in Napa County for a short time, and then came to Contra Costa County. A widow and two children survive him.

Mrs. M. B. Lander, one of the best-known and most highly respected women of Martinez, died on December 10, 1903. She was born in Illinois and came to this county very early. She was sixty-five years of age.

October 15, 1921.—B. P. Lanteri, owner of the Lanteri Shipyards at Pittsburg and ex-mayor, met death by drowning on October 9, while returning from a duck-hunt. He was riding in the bow of his launch, which was operated by William Whitlied, and as they approached Dutton's Landing a cable used in drawing a barge was suspended, and as the launch passed underneath it it caught Mr. Lanteri and hurled him into the stream. He was killed by the blow from the cable. He was thirty-eight years old.

Died, near Walnut Creek, August 4, 1891, John Larkey, aged sixty years. He was born in Ohio in 1831, came to California across the plains with horse teams in 1853, and in 1857 located on his 730-acre ranch near Walnut Creek and engaged in farming. In 1864 he married Martha E. Spore, and they had six children.

May 29, 1923.—Judge R. H. Latimer passed away after being stricken with paralysis while trying a case in his chambers. He was born in Missouri in 1854 and came to California in 1879, locating in Concord. Later he moved to Walnut Creek and engaged in the drug business, during which time he studied law, and was admitted to the bar in 1884. In

1886 he moved to Martinez and engaged in the practice of law, and in 1909 he was elected superior judge. He was survived by his widow. Judge Latimer was a member of the Masonic lodge.

December 13, 1924.—Charles H. Lohse, pioneer of Contra Costa County, died at the home of his daughter, Mrs. H. C. Thomas, in Oakland. He was over the century mark, having celebrated his 100th anniversary on April 27, 1924. He came to Ygnacio Valley over fifty years ago.

Died, January 5, 1915, Henry Loring, pioneer of Contra Costa County, first hotel-keeper of Pacheco, and builder of the first hotel in Concord. He was born in Germany, and came to Contra Costa County in 1852. He was eighty-one years of age.

George P. Loucks was born in New York in 1819; married Ann Liebre in 1841, and had four children; came to California in 1851, and in 1857 located in Contra Costa County, where he engaged in farming and warehousing. He served as county clerk and as supervisor.

Peter G. Loucks, pioneer of Pacheco, died at the home of his son in Sonoma, July 4, 1917, aged seventy-three years.

October 1, 1921.—After being a resident in California for seventy-five years, J. G. Lucas passed away at Richmond at the age of ninety-three years. He was born in the Azores. When eighteen years of age he went to sea and made his first visit to California, in 1846, on the sailer Magnet; he returned in 1850, and in 1863 bought land of the old San Pablo Grant.

June 30, 1921.—C. H. Ludden, a pioneer of 1876, died at the age of sixty-seven years. He was born in Massachusetts and engaged in the contracting business. He is survived by a widow, one daughter, and three sons.

Mrs. Mary Lynch, a resident of Contra Costa County for sixty years and owner of one of the largest ranches in the San Ramon Valley, died at her home December 26, 1915, aged seventy-eight years.

William Lynch died on August 28, 1910, at his home in San Ramon Valley, aged eighty-two years. He was born on Long Island in 1828, and came to California in 1849, and in 1850 to Contra Costa County, where he worked at the carpenter's trade and at farming.

September 16, 1899.—The funeral of the late Joseph McCabe, who died in Oakland, was held at Brentwood on September 2, 1899. He came to California in his early boyhood, crossing the plains. He left a wife and three children.

Thomas McCabe was born in Ohio in 1810, crossed the plains in 1850 as captain of a train, located in this county in 1865, and died in 1910.

Died, July 8, 1915, at Walnut Creek, Daniel McCullough, aged seventy-three years.

Thursday evening, October 17, 1901, James McDermott, an old and highly respected resident of Somersville, was struck and killed by the east-bound train at Martinez. He had come down to attend the funeral of his friend, James Rankin.

William P. McGuire, one of the pioneers of the county, died Monday, December 28, 1914, aged eighty-one years. He was born in Kentucky and came to California in the early days. He left a widow, Mrs. Sarah McGuire, and seven children.

James McKenna died at his home at Vine Hill, April 8, 1913, aged sixty-five years. He was born in Ireland in 1848 and had been a resident of the county thirty years.

T. A. McMahon, well-known county official and business man of Martinez, died on April 28, 1914. He was born in this county in 1856, and was educated in the Martinez grammar school and in the University of California. He served sixteen years as county surveyor. In 1890 he was elected mayor, and served for six years.

Job C. McMaster was born in Maine in 1822, came to California on the brig Forest in 1849, located where Antioch stands in 1851, and with W. W. Smith laid out the town of Antioch. He was one of the first to engage in the dairy business, and in 1852 organized a company to make brick. In 1853 he was elected supervisor, and again in 1873.

George W. McNear, the grain king, who had large warehouse interests in this county, died in Oakland December 31, 1909, aged seventy-two years. He was the owner of a large part of Port Costa and built and owned the Port Costa Water Works.

December 16, 1922.—J. J. McNamara, ex-mayor, the moving spirit of the Martinez-Benicia Ferry & Transportation Company, and an active spirit in the development and progress of Martinez, died at his home at the age of fifty-five years. He was born here and engaged in the mercantile business for a number of years. He left a wife and two daughters.

Died, on August 16, 1913, Mrs. Mary McNamara, a native of County Louth, Ireland, aged sixty-five years.

December 31, 1904.—On Monday, D. R. McPherson, a pioneer of the county, where he lived for over fifty years, passed away at Walnut Creek. He was a native of Kentucky and crossed the plains in 1849. He leaves eleven children, four sons and seven daughters.

W. A. Maltby, a capitalist of Concord, died November 29, 1919.

On May 7, 1922, at his home in Martinez, O. L. Marsh died at the age of eighty-one years. He was born in Pennsylvania in 1841, and served in the Civil War with the 105th Ohio Volunteer Infantry. In 1876 he came to Martinez and followed the carpenter's trade. He left a widow and three children.

April 19, 1924.—Mrs. Elizabeth O. Marshall died, aged seventy-five years, at Antioch. She was born in Maine in 1849, married Perry Marshall in 1869, came to California in 1875, and since then has resided in Antioch. She leaves three children.

Died, in Martinez, February 16, 1894, Vicente Martinez, a native of California, aged seventy-five years. He was born in Santa Barbara in 1818, and in 1838 came with his father to Contra Costa County, the latter having been granted the Pinole Rancho. In 1849 he came to Martinez.

March 13, 1926.—Walnut Creek, March 11. Vicente Martinez, scion of one of the oldest families in the county, the county seat being named for his father, died last night at 10 o'clock. He was born at Pinole seventy-two years ago.

June 17, 1916.—L. R. Mead, thirty-five years owner of Byron Hot Springs, died in San Francisco, aged sixty-eight years. He was born in Michigan and came to California in 1860. In 1881 he bought Byron Hot Springs.

Died, at San Ramon, May 27, 1899, William Meese, a native of Ohio, aged seventy-four years, nine months and twenty-five days. He was born in 1824. In 1850, with eight others, he came by pack-mules to California; and in 1852 he located in Contra Costa County, in the San Ramon Valley. He married and raised a family.

Felix J. Mette, retired mining man and operator of the first stage line between Martinez and Oakland in the early days, died in Oakland on May 6, 1912, aged eighty-three years.

December 12, 1925.—On Monday death claimed Mrs. Isabella Mills, ninety-three years old. The third white woman to settle in San Pablo, she came from Michigan in 1857 and was one of the earliest settlers to develop the soil in the San Pablo section. She was the widow of Walter Mills, and is survived by four generations of descendants, all of whom were born, reared and educated in Contra Costa County.

January, 1921.—Died, near Clayton, Isaac Mitchell, aged ninety-two years. He came here in 1849. Mitchell Canyon, at the base of Mount Diablo, is named for him.

The pioneer editor of Contra Costa County, Charles F. Montgomery, of the Antioch Ledger, died in that town on February 17, 1899. He was the oldest male white child born in Shasta County, his birth taking place on April 24, 1851. He learned the printer's trade in Chico when sixteen years of age, and came to Antioch in 1884 and revived the Ledger. He served as justice of the peace and as secretary of the Democratic convention at San Francisco that nominated J. H. Budd for Governor. He was a member of the Native Sons of the Golden West, Masons, Odd Fellows, and the California Press Association.

April 16, 1921.—At ten o'clock Saturday morning, Edwin Morgan, a pioneer merchant of Contra Costa County, died at his home in Martinez, aged seventy-one years. He was born in Texas in 1850, came overland in the sixties, located in Ygnacio Valley, and in 1870 came to Martinez, where he opened a hardware store. He left six children. Mr. Morgan was an Odd Fellow.

Died, in Martinez, June 2, 1884, Elizabeth Morgan, widow of Daniel Morgan, a native of County Louth, Ireland, aged seventy-eight years, two months and three days.

Jeremiah Morgan died on January 23, 1906. Jerry, as he was familiarly known, was born in the Cherokee Nation, Alabama, in 1819, but later became a resident of Illinois. In 1849 he crossed the plains with oxen to California. He returned to his Illinois home and again crossed the plains in 1853 and located in Ygnacio Valley. In 1856 he located in what is known as Morgan Territory, where he had 2000 acres of land.

Watkins P. Morgans was born in Wales in 1842, came via Panama in 1864, and in 1868 located at Nortonville.

Died, in Brentwood, May 4, 1895, Dr. H. V. Mott, a native of New York, aged seventy-three years. He was born in 1822, came to California in 1850, and settled in Contra Costa County in 1866, where he followed his profession until his death.

John Muir, the world-famed naturalist, was buried from his Alhambra Valley home at Muir Heights, Contra Costa County, on Sunday, December 27, 1914. The short, simple but impressive sermon was delivered by Rev. William F. Bade. Mr. Muir's principal books are "The Mountains of California," "Our National Parks," "Stricken," "The Story of a Dog," "My First Summer in the Sierras," and "The Yosemite." He was an enthusiastic writer and speaker on the preservation of American forests. In 1880 he married Louise, daughter of Dr. Strentzel, who owned a large tract of land near Martinez. It was on this ranch that Mr. Muir lived the last thirty years of his life. He was born in Dunbar, Scotland, in 1838.

Dr. F. E. Neff, for thirty-two years a physician of Concord, and well-known throughout central Contra Costa County, was instantly killed at seven p. m., June 18, 1923, at Minert Station in Ygnacio Valley. He was riding alone in a Chevrolet coupe, and as he was crossing the electric track his car was hit by the Sacramento-San Francisco flier. He was born in Pennsylvania in 1862, and in 1896 married Miss Anna Williams who survived him. He also left five sons and one daughter.

June 18, 1921.—At the advanced age of eighty-eight years, John S. Netherton died in Santa Cruz. He was born in Missouri, April 30, 1833, crossed the plains in 1850 with oxen and mined for a time, then came to Contra Costa County and settled down to ranching in the Tice Valley in Point of Timber. He was the third settler east of Mount Diablo and west of Stockton, the other two being A. Richardson and C. J. Preston. In 1859 he married Matilda Estes, and they had nine children.

Mrs. Matilda Netherton, one of the pioneer residents of the Byron district, died at the home of her son Delbert, October 30, 1912. She was born in Missouri in 1839, crossed the plains in 1850 with her parents, Mr. and Mrs. Joel Estes, and settled in Moraga Valley. In 1859 she married J. S. Netherton, and they moved to Point of Timber, where they lived for fifty years. They celebrated their fiftieth wedding anniversary in 1909. She left five sons and her husband.

John Nicholl, one of the founders of Richmond, died in the fall of 1914 at the age of ninety-one years. He was born in 1822 in Ireland and came to America in 1849, and to California in 1853. He accumulated $6000, with which he bought 200 acres of the San Pablo Rancho, and later added several hundred acres more. He started the first school in his district and hauled the lumber for it. He left a fortune of between $3,000,000 and $4,000,000.

Howard Nichols was born in Massachusetts in 1799; came to California in 1849 via the Horn in the ship Oscar, of which he was part owner; settled at New York of the Pacific in 1850, and bought a ranch at Mount Diablo in 1852. In his house was established the first Congregational congregation in the district.

John R. Nystrom, founder of Richmond and a pioneer of Contra Costa County, died December 24, 1913, just as he was declared winner of an important lawsuit. He, was born in Finland, and was sixty-five years of age. He came here in 1871 and settled near Stege, and began to build up a fortune. He acquired land, now the present site of Richmond, and when the town was founded began to sell off his property.

Died, in Antioch, November 4, 1885, John C. O'Brien, a native of Ireland, aged sixty-three years, nine months and twenty-nine days. Mr. O'Brien had been a prominent resident of the county thirty-two years. He was born January 6, 1822, came to California in 1849, and in 1853 came to this county. He was a member of the Odd Fellows and Masons.

James O'Hara, a pioneer of the Sand Lands district, died in Oakley on September 8, 1912, aged seventy-two years. He was born in Maine and came to California when young, and later to Contra Costa County.

Died, at Concord, May 11, 1884, Fernando Pacheco, a native of California, aged sixty-five years, eleven months and nineteen days. He was a son of Don Salvio Pacheco, who died in August, 1876, and who had filled every position of trust, except that of Governor, under the Mexican government.

At his home in Ygnacio Valley, October 8, 1907, H. P. Penniman died aged eighty-three years. He was one of the earliest settlers in the Valley, coming in 1852. He left a wife and three children.

Charles Bruce Porter, for many years a resident of this county, and for seventeen years one of the publishers and the chief editor of the Gazette, died in San Francisco on November 15, 1894, aged seventy-seven years. He was born in Massachusetts in 1817 and came to California in 1849, and to this county in 1855. He served in the Assembly in 1860, and was also elected to the Senate. He left a widow and six children.

Henry Raap, born in Germany in 1830, died July 3, 1914, at the residence of his daughter, Mrs. V. Hook. Mr. Rapp came to America in 1851, and to California via Nicaragua in 1854. In 1862 he went back to Germany and married Marie Magdalene Classen. Four sons and one daughter were born to them. They settled in Alhambra Valley very early. In 1863 he bought a farm near Martinez.

Peter Raap, for fifty years a resident of Alhambra Valley, was found dead in his bed Sunday morning, October 12, 1919. He was born in Germany and was seventy-six years of age. In 1866 he came to California, and settled in Alhambra Valley.

F. Rahmstorf, for over forty years a resident of the Byron district, died April 27, 1918, aged seventy-eight years. He was born in Germany. He was a member of the Odd Fellows for forty-five years.

S. F. Ramage was born in Ohio in 1836; he came via Panama in 1856 and located in this county, where he ranched and teamed and served as justice of the peace. He was married twice and had five children.

Died, at Lane Hospital, San Francisco, October 15, 1901, James Rankin, a native of Scotland, aged fifty-three years. Mr. Rankin was born in 1848, came to America in 1865, and arrived in Contra Costa County in 1870, where he made his home. He was elected sheriff in 1884 and served two terms. Then he was interested in coal mining at Somersville. In 1899 he was elected president of the Bank of Martinez. He was a Mason.

Dr. Frank Rattan, a pioneer physician of Antioch and Martinez, died January 3, 1917. He practiced in Antioch twelve years and then came to Martinez, where he bought the W. K. Cole drug business. He was fifty-six years of age at the time of his death.

Died, December 27, 1904, at Alamo, Hamilton S. Raven, sixty-five years of age. He was born in New York and reared in Michigan. Coming to California, he taught school for thirty years, twenty-five years in Contra Costa County, near Walnut Creek. In 1870 he married Almira Baker, who died in 1891. They had five sons and one daughter.

Charles Rhine was born in Poland in 1838; came via Panama in 1856; located in this county in 1857; opened a store near what is now Clayton in 1858; and in 1859 was one of the first to open up a business in Clayton, in partnership with Joel Clayton. In 1868 he married Celia Lobree, and they had eight children.

William Rice, a pioneer of 1860 of the county, passed away near Walnut Creek November 6, 1885, aged seventy-one years. In 1862 he built a schoolhouse and opened a private family school on his place.

Died, May 17, 1915, at Pleasant Hill, E. A. Rodgers, one of the oldest residents of the district, who came to California in 1859 and had lived on his ranch for forty-five years. He was born in Ireland and was seventy-six years of age. He left four children and a widow.

C. W. Rogers, former sheriff of Contra Costa County and constable of Walnut Creek, died at his Martinez home on February 21, 1912, at the age of fifty-nine years. He was born in Amador County in 1853. In 1874 he married Martha Leich. He was a member of the Native Sons and the Woodmen.

Died, in Walnut Creek, April 5, 1897, Mrs. E. J. Rogers, aged fifty-nine years, eleven months and twenty-five days.

On November 16, 1907, at Berkeley, John C. Rouse, a pioneer of California, passed away. He was born in New York in 1828; in 1853 he came to California, and in 1861 to Contra Costa County as foreman of the Pittsburg Coal Mine. He continued the mining business as owner for many years, and also was identified with the lumber and banking interests of Antioch. He was a Mason.

July 28, 1917.—Mrs. W. A. Rugg, wife of the editor and proprietor of the Gazette, passed away at their home in Martinez Saturday evening, aged fifty-three years. As Jessie Baird Kellogg, she was born in Wisconsin in 1864. She married W. A. Rugg in Missouri in December, 1882. Coming to California in 1887, they located in San Diego; in 1898 they came to Martinez. One daughter survived her besides her husband.

Died, in Martinez, June 16, 1894, Mrs. Nancy Russell, relict of Capt. Thomas Russell, a native of Massachusetts, aged ninety-five years. Mrs. Russell was born in 1799. She came with her husband to California in 1849; later they bought a ranch in Ygnacio Valley. For many years Mrs. Russell made her home in Martinez.

George Russi, Sr., prominent mill owner and manufacturer, owner of the Pacheco Flour Mill, died at Pacheco November 12, 1910. He was born in Switzerland in 1854, and came to California about 1880, and started the Pacheco Flour Mills. He left a widow and five children.

September 19, 1925.—One of the foremost real estate operators in Central California, one who of late years has been active in Martinez and who was one of the men who founded the city of Richmond, passed to his final rest Sunday morning when W. H. Sanford breathed his last at his home in Martinez. He was a native of Tennessee, aged sixty-five years. He leaves a widow, Jennie E. Sanford, and was the father of Mrs. Grace Hansel and Mrs. Era Holmes of Oakland, W. H. Sanford Jr. of San Francisco, and Miss Hazel Sanford of Martinez.

Died, in Port Costa, March 14, 1891, George H. Scammon, aged fifty-seven years. He was born in Maine, came to California in 1859, and made his home in Walnut Creek. He then moved to Nortonville, remaining there until the decline of coal mining, when he moved to Port Costa. He was serving his second term as public administrator at the time of his death. He was a member of the Odd Fellows.

Died, March 17, 1915, at Brentwood, William Shafer, a native of Pennsylvania, aged seventy-nine years. For over fifty years he had been a resident of Brentwood, where he engaged in farming. He left a widow, three daughters and two sons.

Died, April 7, 1906, Albert Sherburne, aged seventy-three years. He was a native of New York, a pioneer of 1852 in California, whither he came via the Isthmus, and located in Contra Costa County in 1856.

Died, near Danville, August 19, 1897, David N. Sherburne, a native of New York, aged seventy-five years. He was born October 14, 1822, went to Illinois when twelve years old, and in 1850 crossed the plains on horseback and arrived at Placerville on August 26. He mined until 1856 and then came to Contra Costa County, locating near Danville. In 1856 he was elected supervisor, and filled the office four terms. In 1879 he was elected to the legislature, and in 1880 he was again elected supervisor.

Benjamin Shreve was born in Pennsylvania in 1828, crossed the plains in 1852, and in 1853 engaged in business and ran a hotel in this county. In 1857 he petitioned Congress to establish a postoffice at his place, which was named Lafayette, and he was the postmaster.

Charles Sickal, a native of Kentucky and for sixty years a resident of Martinez, having crossed the plains with oxen in 1855, died at his home on April 24, 1918, aged eighty-two years.

December 12, 1925.—C. A. Smith, seventy-three, president of the Coos Bay Lumber Company at Bay Point and one of the most prominent lumber men in the West, died at his home in Berkeley. Smith moved to the Pacific Coast from Minnesota in 1884. He founded the C. A. Smith Lumber Company, now the Coos Bay Lumber Company, owned lumber properties in Humboldt County and Southern Oregon and had large mills at Marshfield, Ore., and Bay Point, Cal., the latter one of the most complete in the world.

Died, in Martinez, October 18, 1895, John B. Smith, a native of New Bedford, Mass., aged fifty-six years. He came to California when thirteen years of age, in 1852, and the next year came to Martinez, which had since been his home. He was justice of the peace several years.

John F. S. Smith was born in Georgia in 1821; served under Col. Jack Hays in the Indian troubles, and later in the Mexican War; came in 1850 via Panama to California and to Martinez, where his brother had laid out the town; settled on Bull Head Ranch in 1852; and in 1853 was elected sheriff. He also served as assessor.

Napoleon B. Smith was born in Ohio in 1818; crossed the plains with his brother, Henry C., in 1845, being piloted by L. W. Hastings to Fort Laramie, and from there by Captain Bridger through the Indian country; engaged in business in Martinez in 1849; was elected first county assessor; and in 1852 was elected to and served in the legislature. He was a member of the Bear Flag party and participated in the events of June 14, 1846, and was a farmer in the Alhambra district. Francis M. Smith, his son, supposed to be the first American male child born in Contra Costa County, was born on January 25, 1848.

Rev. W. W. and Rev. Joseph H. Smith came to California via the Horn in 1849 on the brig Forest, and to New York of the Pacific on July 11 of that year as carpenters. W. W. Smith entered the ministry of the Christian Church in 1840. He was the first appointed Alcalde of New York of the Pacific, and gave the name Antioch to the town, which had been called Smith's Landing after him. W. W. Smith died on October 16, 1899, at the age of eighty-seven years. Joseph H. Smith died in 1850.

June 26, 1916.—A. J. Soto died at his Martinez home on Court Street. He was born on San Miguel Rancho in 1858, graduated from St. Mary's College in 1882, was elected county auditor, and with the excep-

238 CONTRA COSTA COUNTY

tion of two years held that office until 1907. He was assistant district attorney and inheritance tax appraiser. He left a widow and two girls.

September 5, 1903.—James Stewart, a resident of Contra Costa County since 1856, died last Monday. He was born in Ireland in 1825 and came to America in 1847, and in 1853 to California, crossing the plains. He farmed in Rodeo Valley until 1879, and then came to Martinez and engaged in mercantile pursuits.

Mrs. J. M. Stow, a pioneer resident of Walnut Creek, died on July 29, 1910. Her maiden name was Alice Glass. She was born in Walnut Creek, and in 1873 married J. M. Stow.

James M. Stow, pioneer capitalist and public-spirited citizen of Contra Costa County, died on August 17, 1919, in San Diego. He was born in Illinois in 1847, and came with his mother to California in 1850, via Panama, to join his father in California. In 1860, after the death of his father, the family settled in Contra Costa County, and from his twelfth year young Stow was reared in this county. In 1873 he opened a store in Walnut Creek. In 1880 he was elected county assessor, and served seven years. He was one of the chief promoters of the first telephone company, which came into existence in 1881. He was the owner and proprietor of the Martinez Gazette and vice-president of the Bank of Martinez. He built the Contra Costa part of the Oakland and Contra Costa County tunnel. He was agent for the Wells-Fargo Express Company, and the holder of Alhambra Springs. Mr. Stow was a Mason and a Methodist.

Died, on September 24, 1897, in Alhambra Valley, where she had been a resident since 1853, Mrs. L. E. Strentzel, aged seventy-six years.

Died, at his home in Alhambra Valley, October 31, 1890, Dr. John T. Strentzel, aged seventy-seven years, a native of Lieben, Poland.

Died, in Martinez, February 7, 1884, Eliza Reddell Sturgis, wife of Josiah Sturgis, aged sixty-four years and nine months, a native of Nantucket, Mass. "She was one of the pioneer women of 1857, who, with her children, joined her husband on the Coast."

John Sturgis died April 22, 1886, aged seventy-nine years. He was known as "Uncle John" and was one of the earliest settlers of Martinez, having come here in 1850.

January 15, 1910.—Mrs. Elizabeth (Lawrence) Swain, the last of the earliest English-speaking residents of Martinez, passed away Saturday evening at her home. Elizabeth Lawrence was born on the Island of Nantucket in 1839. At the age of twelve she left with her mother to join the husband and father in California, coming via the Nicaragua route. The steamship North America, on which they were passengers, was wrecked and they were detained a month at San Juan del Sur, at which point they were picked up by a vessel and brought around the Horn, arriving at San Francisco July 7, 1852. George A. Lawrence had located in Martinez, and the daughter and wife came here. Mrs. Swain had lived here fifty-eight years.

On August 22, 1913, John Swett, a pioneer educator of California, died at the age of eighty-three years, at his Alhambra home, "Hill Girt." He was the founder of the State school system, a teacher, author, pioneer educator, and most highly respected citizen. He was born in New Hampshire July 31, 1830, and began teaching when seventeen years of age. He came via the Horn to California and was 135 days on the water, arriving here in 1853. He mined for a time and then returned to San Francisco and began teaching. In 1853 he became principal of the Rincon School, and remained there until 1862. One of the first graduates of the University of California was one of Swett's pupils at Rincon. Mr. Swett served as State superintendent of public instruction from 1863 to 1867, and then again took up teaching, holding fine positions in San Francisco and later in Contra Costa County.

Mrs. Mary L. Swett, relict of the distinguished educator, John Swett, died November 14, 1919, at her Alhambra Valley home in her eightieth year. She was the daughter of Judge E. P. Tracy, who drafted the platform on which Abraham Lincoln was first elected to the Presidency. She began teaching in San Francisco at the age of eighteen. She was born in 1839 in Connecticut and in 1854 came to California via Panama with her parents. She married John Swett in 1862, and they had seven children, four of whom grew up.

February 27, 1926.—John Tarpley died at the local hospital Monday morning, aged seventy-eight years. He had resided in San Ramon many years and leaves a son there.

Gabriel Tarwater, a pioneer of Contra Costa County, died at his home in Ygnacio Valley, Saturday afternoon, November 9, 1912, aged eighty-three years. He was born in Missouri, came to California in 1849, and had resided here sixty years. He left a widow and four children.

January 16, 1926.—For seventy years a resident of Contra Costa County, and having approached to within three years of the century mark, Mrs. Martha J. Tarwater, one of the few remaining pioneers of the early fifties, breathed her last at her Ygnacio Valley home, where she had lived for half a century. Mrs. Tarwater was born in Missouri and came to California in 1852. With the exception of four years, 1852 to 1856, she had lived in Ygnacio Valley.

Alex Taylor came to California in 1868, and located at Point of Timber. He died in 1912.

On August 25, 1923, at 5:30 p.m., Volney Taylor passed away at his home in eastern Contra Costa County. He was born in Canada in 1851 and came to California with his parents. In 1878 he married Agnes E. Andrew. In 1868 he moved to his place in eastern Contra Costa County and built a fine country home, and here he accumulated a fortune. He was a member of the Methodist Episcopal Church, and for thirty years had been a trustee of the Good Templars' Home at Vallejo.

Died, in Martinez, September 30, 1858, Archibald Tennent, Sr., aged seventy years.

Died, near Pinole, August 16, 1886, Dr. S. J. Tennent, M. D., a native of England, aged sixty-eight years. Dr. Tennent had practiced in the Sandwich Islands. He was a California pioneer of the first mining days, in 1848, and had settled at Pinole soon after, where he farmed the Pinole Ranch. In 1849 he married Rafaela Martinez, and they had ten children.

Died, at Providence Hospital, Oakland, March 20, 1915, Mrs. Angenette Thompson, a pioneer of Lafayette, where she had lived for fifty-nine years. Mrs. Thompson was sixty-eight years of age. She married Peter Thompson on March 23, 1862. She left three sons and three daughters.

Peter Thompson died on July 31, 1914, aged seventy-six years. He was born in Canada in 1837, came to California in 1859, and located soon after at Lafayette, where he continued to reside until his death.

March 27, 1926.—A pioneer matron of Contra Costa County, Mrs. Charlotte Thompson, of the Lafayette section for many years, passed away at an Oakland hospital on Monday. She was a native of California and was seventy-two years of age. Mrs. Thompson was the wife of Robert Thompson, roadmaster of the Lafayette section.

January 5, 1924.—The death of W. S. Tinning occurred at his home in Martinez shortly after midnight, at the age of seventy-two years. He was born in New York in 1852 and when a young man came to California and Martinez. From 1885 to 1893 he was district attorney. On January 13, 1902, he was made vice-president of the Bank of Martinez, and he succeeded James Rankin as president. He is survived by his wife, Mrs. Miriam Porter Tinning, and six children.

The death of John Tormey of Bay Point occurred at St. Francis Hospital, San Francisco, in 1908. He had been a resident here for thirty-five years. He was a native of Ireland and was fifty-four years of age at the time of his death. He left a wife and three children.

January 25, 1890.—The funeral of General M. G. Vallejo, last Thursday, was largely attended.

February 26, 1908, Mrs. R. R. Veale passed away in Martinez. She was born in San Francisco in 1865 and was married in 1884. She left six children.

Died, at Brentwood, June 5, 1886, Richard R. Veale, a native of Illinois, aged forty-seven years and eleven months. Mr. Veale had been a resident of the county since 1868, when he located in Eden Plain, and of California since 1857, when he came to this State via Panama. In 1880 he married Malinda Sexton.

John Tormey was born in Ireland in 1825, crossed the plains in 1850 with oxen, and in 1865 located in this county and bought an interest in the Pinole Grant in partnership with his brother Patrick. He served as supervisor from Township No. 1 for years. In 1859 he married Anna Waterhouse, and they had nine children. He died in 1877.

Patrick Tormey, supervisor, passed away on Tuesday, May 7, 1907. He was born in Ireland in 1840 and came to New York in 1858, and to California that fall, landing in San Francisco on October 31. He joined his brother John, and together they bought 7000 acres of the Pinole Ranch. In 1877 he was elected a member of the board of supervisors, and with the exception of 1894 to 1898 had since served the county. He married Mary Matthews in 1875.

Died, in Martinez, March 19, 1891, Mrs. Mary B. Tucker, relict of the late Capt. John Tucker, aged seventy-nine years. She had been a resident of Martinez since 1851. Captain Tucker died in 1881.

Died, on April 3, 1902, James Walker, a native of Tennessee, born in 1825. He came to California in 1847, crossing the plains with oxen and arriving in 1848. He was a nephew of Joel Walker, scout and guide. In 1853 he came to Ygnacio Valley and farmed until 1890, when he sold out and bought a home in Walnut Creek. Mr. Walker served as a county supervisor three years. He was seventy-six years old when he died.

Standing in the cemetery of Martinez is a monument bearing the inscription: "Capt. Joseph R. Walker. Born in Roane County, Tenn., December 13, 1798. Emigrated to Missouri in 1819, to New Mexico in 1820, Rocky Mountains in 1832, California in 1833. Camped at Yosemite, November 13, 1833. Died October 27, 1876. Age, 77 years, 10 months, and 14 days."

Captain Walker passed his last years with his nephew, the late James T. Walker, in Ygnacio Valley, near Martinez. He made his first trip across the plains in 1820 to New Mexico, on a trapping and trading expedition, but at Prescott Lake troops were dispatched by the Governor of New Mexico to order their return. In 1832 Walker determined to make a visit to California. The best maps he could get of the country represented a river flowing from Salt Lake to the Pacific Coast. He determined to follow this route and early in the spring set out at the head of thirty experienced trappers, well mounted and well outfitted. Arriving at Salt Lake, he made a circuit of it, only to be disappointed in his attempt to find the river. Nothing daunted, he struck west and in October reached the Sierra Nevadas, which he crossed and attempted to descend near the headwaters of the Tuolumne, but failing, went farther south, struck the Merced, and got into the San Joaquin. His were the first white man's eyes that ever looked upon the Yosemite, which he then discovered. His party camped and trapped until spring. In the meantime Captain Walker, with a few men, explored the principal valleys of California. In 1833 he went south along the foothills, looking for a pass to the east. Guided by his unfailing instinct, he came to what he considered the only true pass through at 35½ degrees north latitude, and named it Walker's Pass. He kept on the thirty-fifth parallel and passed through Colorado. In 1859 he acted as guide to troops sent up the Colorado River to Fort Yuma. He had been down the Colorado but never up it, but each day he would draw a map showing where the mountains approached the river, where the valley widened, etc., from memory, as he had seen it in 1833. Captain Walker was cotemporary with Jedediah Smith, Kit Carson, Jo Bridger, Bill Williams, Fitzpatrick, the Sublettes, and all the noted frontiersmen of the early days. In 1843, while Captain Walker was at Fort Hall, Captain Childs, the Yount family, Julius Martin and family, and Frank McClellan came along and wanted him to pilot them over the mountains. Walker was afraid they could not make it that winter. Captain Childs was sent ahead and was to return and meet the party at Walker's Lake. The party started, but missed Captain Childs, who was to have provisions for them, and they were in sore straits. They traded horseshoe nails for fish from the Indians on Walker's River. Winter was closing in on them, and beyond the lake they killed their cattle, cached their wagons and goods, and after much suffering got into Tulare Valley. The women and children's sole dependence for food was placed on the rifle of Captain Walker. Captain Walker was a brother of Joel Walker.

Died, December 30, 1919, at his home in Antioch, Joseph Wallrath, aged seventy-one years. He was born in Germany in 1848 and came to America in 1865, locating in Ohio, where he married Carolina Wendeln, who died there. In 1883 he came to California, locating at Brentwood, where he married Anna Lohse. In 1885 he located at Antioch.

Mrs. Almira Walton, a pioneer of Brentwood, died on March 17, 1908, aged ninety-two years. She was born in Georgia and came to California in 1856, and to Contra Costa County in 1862.

F. W. Warmcastle was born in Pennsylvania in 1815; served as first lieutenant of Captain Crieg's Missouri Mounted Volunteers; came to California in 1849; was elected county judge in 1850; and served in the Assembly in 1853 and again in 1857, and in the Senate in 1877. He also served as district attorney.

Mrs. Arthur Webb, for thirty-four years a resident of Crockett, died January 2, 1920, aged sixty-nine years. She was born in New York and had been a resident of California forty-six years.

Frank Webb, a native of Maine, born in 1833, and a pioneer of 1858 in California and of 1859 in Contra Costa County, died Thursday, April 5, 1906.

I. Weiss, a pioneer of 1859 in California, and of 1860 in Martinez, died May 15, 1896. He was born in Prussia in 1831. In 1862 he embarked in business in Martinez, and in 1877 erected a building, which he had since occupied. He was a Mason; and it became known, upon his death, that he was the donor of the Bear Flag donated to the Native Sons of the Golden West and carried by them at the celebration in San Francisco in 1890. So modest was he that he did not want his name mentioned in connection with the furnishing of the flag.

Died, near Clayton, September 29, 1894, Chauncey E. Wetmore, a native of Connecticut, aged seventy-six years, nine months and one day. Mr. Wetmore arrived in California in 1847, before the discovery of gold. He engaged in business in San Francisco, and then in Benicia, and later

CONTRA COSTA COUNTY

removed to Contra Costa County. His next move was to Oakland, but eventually he returned to this county and made his home near Clayton. He was an independent thinker.

Died, in Walnut Creek, July 7, 1893, Cornelius S. Whitcomb, a native of Canada, aged eighty years. Mr. Whitcomb came to this county in 1851, and settled near Lafayette.

C. N. Wight, for over fifty years a resident of the county, died at Pittsburg, April 17, 1913, aged seventy-nine years. He was born in New York and came to Contra Costa County in 1852, via Panama.

In December, 1919, at the age of ninety-two years, Randolph H. Wight, a pioneer of Contra Costa County, died at the home of his daughter in Berkeley. Mr. Wight was born in New York in 1827 and came to Oregon in 1847. In 1848 he arrived in California, and in 1852 came to Contra Costa County for the first time. He married Orfa Durfee in 1848.

December 17, 1921.—The death of Mrs. Frances E. Wilder, daughter of Capt. George Donner, at Byron recently, recalls the tragic story of the Donner Party's trials of 1846-1847 while en route to California. Of all those who came across the plains, the Donner Party suffered the greatest loss of life. Out of eighty-eight, forty-two perished.

Arthur Williams, pioneer butcher of Walnut Creek and one of the oldest peace officers in the county, died at his home on September 21, 1915. He was born in New York and was a soldier in the Civil War at sixteen years of age. Mr. Williams had been a resident of California for forty-four years. He was a Mason and an Odd Fellow.

December 10, 1898.—Francis H. Williams, public administrator of Contra Costa County, was suddenly stricken with heart disease in the office of Dr. E. E. Brown. He was born in Denmark in 1829; in 1846 he came to New York, thence went to New Orleans, and in 1850 sailed via Cape Horn for San Francisco, settling in Solano County. In 1864 he came to Contra Costa County and located at Antioch until coming to Martinez in 1878. In 1886 he was elected county assessor, and served until 1894. In 1896 he was appointed public administrator to succeed Francis Gunther, who had been adjudged insane. He married Mrs. Elizabeth J. Emmons in 1862.

Died, September 29, 1885, Jesse H. Williams, in Moraga Valley, aged seventy years, four months and sixteen days. Mr. Williams was born in Virginia in 1815; he came across the plains in 1850 with ox-teams, and in 1854 came to Contra Costa County with his wife and five children.

January 27, 1925.—William P. Williamson, Antioch pioneer, aged ninety-six years, passed away at his home there on Tuesday, January 27, 1925, after a brief illness. He was a native of New Jersey and had come to California sixty years ago via the Isthmus of Panama. He is survived by two daughters, Miss Carrie Williamson and Mrs. Bertha Brewer of Antioch, and two sons, Everett and Chester Williamson of San Francisco.

Died, in Martinez, April 11, 1898, Thomas Z. Witten, a native of Virginia, aged eighty-four years. Mr. Witten was born in Virginia in 1816. He went to Missouri in 1838, and in 1849 came to California, crossing the plains. In 1856 he came to Contra Costa County and settled near Pacheco. He left six children.

Lewis Cass Wittenmyer, one of the most prominent and public-spirited men of the county, was born in Indiana in 1828, and came across the plains from St. Joseph, Mo., with mule teams in 1849, and mined for a time. In 1851 he took up 160 acres on San Lorenzo Creek. He returned East in the fall of 1852, but came to California the next summer, bringing a band of cattle and horses, and settled in Sycamore Valley. In 1857 he came to Martinez, where he lived until the time of his death, which occurred in the fall of 1904. He held many offices of public trust and was highly honored by all who knew him. He served as justice of the peace several terms, and was county clerk for thirty-two years. In 1872 he married, and he became the parent of four children. He was a prominent Mason.

March 19, 1911.—Died, at San Pablo, Frederick Wolf, a native of Germany, born in 1833 and a pioneer of 1859 in California. In 1860 he came to San Pablo. At his death he was seventy-eight years of age.

On Monday morning, May 20, 1907, Charles Wood died at his Danville home. He was born in 1830 in Massachusetts, came to California in 1852, and in 1862 removed to Sycamore Valley, Contra Costa County.

December 18, 1918.—Mrs. Charles Wood, a resident of Sycamore Valley for fifty years, died this morning at the home of her son, Charles J. Wood, at the old family homestead. She was born in New York and was eighty-seven years old. She married Charles Wood in 1857 and in 1862 came to Sycamore Valley to live. Two sons and two daughters are the survivors of her family.

Died, March 25, 1915, at Woodside in San Ramon Valley, George Wood, aged seventy-eight years. He was born in Massachusetts and came to California in the early fifties.

David S. Woodruff was born in New York in 1829. He came via Panama in 1858, located in Bay Point and taught school; and in 1861 he was elected superintendent of schools. He also served as public administrator and was justice of the peace at Nortonville two years. He opened a drug store in Antioch, and moved to Martinez in 1880.

CHAPTER XVIII

GLEANINGS FROM THE FILES OF THE CONTRA COSTA GAZETTE, 1858-1926

The establishment of a newspaper in Contra Costa County was an important factor in its upbuilding and development. On September 18, 1858, W. B. Soule & Company, of Martinez, printed the first copy of the Contra Costa Gazette, a weekly paper of four six-column pages, issued every Saturday. From that date, sixty-eight years ago, up to September 18, 1926, the paper did not miss an issue. A complete set of bound volumes of the paper is to be found in the Gazette office in Martinez. The following data, historical and personal, gleaned from the files of the paper, will serve to chronicle the main events in the early history of the county, trace the gradual development and expansion of its varied interests, and recall many interesting incidents in the lives of its pioneers.

In the extracts given, side-head dates are for the most part to be understood as dates of the weekly issues. Undated paragraphs follow in chronological sequence, as a rule, between those with dates, but often are not to be assigned to the preceding dated issue. It has seemed unnecessary to use quotation marks, especially as the matter given has often been condensed.

Some of the advertisers whose names appeared in the issue of September 18, 1858, were:

Charles A. Ruggles, M. D.

Solano Hotel, Benicia, F. W. Weimann, proprietor.

E. H. Bryan, copper, tin and sheet iron wares, stores, pumps, lead pipe, etc.

L. H. Hastings, dealer in beef, pork, hides, tallow and all kinds of produce.

A. Hersey, painter, glazier, paperhanger, whitewasher, and all kinds of imitations of wood and marble.

J. W. Sanborn, Benicia, "where can be found papers from all the principal Atlantic cities; also an assortment of stationery, periodicals, etc."

S. Blum & Brothers, dealers in groceries, clothing, drygoods, boots shoes, etc.

E. Lasar, dealer in dry goods, clothing, groceries, boots, shoes, etc.

George F. Worth, notary public.

Martinez Lodge No. 41, F. & A. M.; T. A. Brown, W. M.; John F. S. Smith, Secretary.

Hale & Fassett, dealers in drygoods, groceries, crockery, hardware, clothing, etc., Pacheco, Cal.

Walter Lopez, shaving saloon.

Alhambra Hotel and Restaurant, meals at all hours. Horses and carriages to let. Josiah Sturgis, proprietor, Martinez.

Cornelius Connelly, 500 bushels Australian Red Seed Wheat for sale.

Bella Union Hotel and French Store, L. Dutil, dealer in groceries, etc. He recommends himself for superior wines and liquors.

September 18, 1858.—A slight earthquake shock was felt here Sunday evening about 8 p. m. [As Saturday was the day of publication, the Sunday mentioned fell on September 12.]

The through mail to Memphis and St. Louis starts from San Francisco at 1 o'clock tomorrow morning, and it is calculated by the contractor that it will get through in twenty-five days. Preparations have been made to transport promptly any number of passengers that may offer, or any amount of mail matter. One hundred miles per day is the distance to be traveled, which, if the stages are able to perform, will cut the time considerably under twenty-five days. We fully expect that in the course of a year this southern mail will be run regularly through in from fifteen to twenty days.

The steamer Sonora arrived in San Francisco on Thursday, at 11 a. m. She brings highly interesting and important news. The Atlantic telegraph wire has been successfully laid. Congratulatory messages have been exchanged between Europe and America. The Queen of England sent the first dispatch to Mr. Buchanan and was immediately replied to. The cable was spliced in mid-ocean July 29. On August 4 the Niagara arrived with one end at Trinity Bay, New Foundland. On the 5th the cable was landed and connected with the American station. On the 16th the first message was flashed along the wires.

On Monday evening the overland mail coach, which left Salt Lake September 1, arrived at Placerville with two passengers.

The 6th Infantry has left Fort Bridger for California via the Humboldt.

General Harney and a number of troops are en route to Oregon.

Notice: The stock-owners of this county can have facsimile brands of their own inserted in this paper by paying cost of engraving and the usual price of advertising.

Born, in Martinez, on September 23, 1858, to the wife of Henry Bush, Jr., a son.

San Ramon.—There is no law laid down in the statutes in relation to hogs running at large in this county.

September 25, 1858.—We are indebted to Henry Rich of the Knickerbocker, of Benicia, for his gentlemanly treatment towards us and our friends on Sunday last. We would state that he has on hand a full supply of mussels and a fine glass of brandy on which those who are waiting for the river-boats would do well to regale themselves. May success always attend him.

October 2, 1858.—Total value of property assessed for the year 1857 was $1,842,405; but for 1858, $2,536,617, an increase of $694,212. This difference is in part due, no doubt, to the increasing activity and thoroughness of our efficient assessor.

October 9, 1858.—A company of eighty men is organized at Weaverville to fight the Indians, and another is about forming.

The Los Angeles Vineyard reports that gold and ores of silver and copper have been found in the mountains north of Los Angeles.

The steamer Golden Gate, which left San Francisco on Tuesday last for Panama, carried away 420 passengers and $1,850,120 in treasure.

The law prohibiting the immigration of Chinese went into effect on the 1st inst. The last arrivals were per the ship Frowning Bird, the 28th ult.

First dispatch over the Placerville and Humboldt Telegraph was sent October 7, 1858. Messages are now being sent hourly from Placerville east.

Advertisement:—Ambrotypes, melancotypes, and portraits on leather. Also for sale, gilt mouldings and picture frames. J. W. Jones.

October 16, 1858.—The overland mail arrived yesterday from San Francisco via Los Angeles, from Memphis and St. Louis, with four days later news from the East. The mail left St. Louis on the same day that the mail steamer left New York, and was detained thirty-seven hours at Fort Smith, Ark., waiting for the mail from Memphis; but still, with this drawback, the overland mail arrived in San Francisco before the mail steamer.

San Francisco Markets: Flour, $9 to $10.25, slight decline; wheat, $2.75 to $3, as to quality; barley, $1 to $1.02½; oats, $1.50 to $1.55, as to quality; butter, Atlantic States, from 18 cents to 23 cents. Dealers. will pay 65 cents per dozen for eggs. Fresh butter, 80 cents per pound; cheese, 21 cents; spring chickens, $5 to $8 per dozen; old hens, $10.50; tame geese, $5 per pair; turkeys, 30 cents to 32 cents per pound; apples, jobbing at 15 cents to 20 cents per pound; Spanish cattle, 6 cents to 7 cents per pound, live weight; calves, 12 cents; American cattle, 8 cents to 11 cents per pound, live weight.

October 30, 1858.—The Gazette comes out, with Bonnard & Company, editors and proprietors, who announce that they will "make it a paper worthy of the support of the citizens of the county, and not a vehicle to advance the interests of any clique of men or party, but an independent journal soaring above and toadying to none of the latter interests."

January 1, 1859.—Contra Costa Agricultural Society formed at Lafayette.

First County Fair was inaugurated October 11, 1859, and an excellent exhibit took place. In September, 1861, a pavilion, 60 by 40 feet, was built at Pacheco.

The first officers of the above were: L. I. Fish, president; Daniel Small, vice-president; H. H. Fassett, recording secretary; L. M. Brown, corresponding secretary; John M. Jones, treasurer.

February 26, 1859.—W. Bradford appears as editor and publisher of the Gazette, and in his editorial he says: "It is usual for editors to set forth the manner in which they will conduct their paper and to enlarge upon the advantages their accession to the editorial corps will be to the community, giving in detail the course they intend to pursue. Now, we do not propose to do anything of the kind. We shall endeavor to so conduct the Gazette as to make it a welcome weekly visitor to the family circle, the farmer, the mechanic and the merchant."

February 26, 1859.—Ferryboat Carquinez will make regular trips between Martinez and Benicia, leaving Martinez at 8 a. m., 10 a. m., 11 a. m., 1 p. m., 3 p. m., 5:30 p. m.; leaving Benicia at 8:30 a. m., 10:30 a. m., 11:30 a. m., 1:30 p. m., 3:30 p. m., and 6 p. m. Coffin & Swain.

Born, April 30, 1859, in San Ramon Valley, to the wife of Jacob Reid, a son; May 1, to the wife of R. O. Baldwin, a daughter.

April 7, 1860.—Overland Pony Express. The first Central Overland Horse Express for St. Louis left San Francisco on Tuesday afternoon. It carries 85 letters at $5 each, amounting to $425. It is calculated to make the trip to St. Louis in nine or ten days. At the same time the express leaves Sacramento, a courier leaves St. Joseph, Missouri, and if the project is a success at the start we may look for the announcement, at Carson City, of news only nine or ten days old, say on the fourteenth of this month. Mr. Wm. W. Finney, the agent of Russell, Majors & Company, has placed his station three hundred miles from Sacramento, towards Salt Lake, in order for the start. Another division extends out from Salt Lake to meet him, and from the latter city, eastward, the stations of the mail from St. Joseph to Salt Lake will be used.

April 28, 1860.—The Pony Express. The Pony Express last arrived was nine days and seventeen hours from St. Joseph, Missouri. The Express passed through this place on Monday morning in charge of Mr. Thomas J. Bedford of Benicia. By previous arrangements, the ferry boat Carquinez was at her berth in Benicia at an early hour, in anticipation of its arrival, and not a moment of time was lost in conveying it to this place. As the boat touched this side, the horse sprang from her deck, and dashing up the wharf was soon lost to sight as he and his gallant rider went flying on their way to Oakland. The distance from Martinez to Oakland is about twenty-five miles. The Express left here at 7:33 a. m. and arrived at Oakland as reported to us at 9:32, which, if correct, makes the time occupied one hour and fifty-nine minutes. According to the city papers, however, it was accomplished in one hour and forty-five minutes, which was probably the swiftest riding on the whole route.

On April 28, 1860, the Gazette is published by Bradford & Bunker. "R. R. Bunker, having purchased a half interest in the Gazette establishment, will hereafter be associated and equally authorized with the undersigned in the publication of this paper. W. Bradford."

On June 9, 1860, in San Francisco, a trial run was made with a steam wagon that arrived from England. It was guided with an appliance like on a boy's velocipede.   It was loaded with fifty tons and moved along briskly enough where the road was firm enough to bear the weight. Now that our Yankee machinists have a model, they may succeed in making improvements until perfection is reached. For the present we do not believe that the steam wagon will run our horses and mules off our common roads.

July 7, 1806.—Pacheco Engine Company, No. 1, has the following officers and members: W. J. Caldwell, fireman; J. McDermott, assistant; John Phillips, secretary; W. T. Hendrick, treasurer; Elijah Hook, Nelson Howe, J. H. Troy, Henry Miller, S. J. Gould, Gus Wilson, J. C. Fish, John Thorn, S. Dubois, R. S. Brown, G. P.Sanford, J. Babbatt, Edw. Doane, Peter Pons, J. A. Littlefield, John Cerf, George Zogbaum, George Eminett, H. R. Hicks, S. Bacon, W. Henry, S. Standish, W. K. Dell, George Sturtevant, W. H. Boss, A. Wortheimer, H. Lord, G. F. Rupert, P. H. Standish, G. W. Doane, W. E. Woodford, G. S. Tate, J. Clark, T. Downing, J. W. Baker.

July 13, 1860.—The non-arrival of the pony express at the expected time was a source of deep regret to all who felt an interest in the success of the enterprise. The delay is probably caused by the breaking up of stations during the Indian troubles and the necessity of re-stocking the route with horses. A number of animals have been purchased in this vicinity for that purpose, and we may soon expect regularity in its movements.

March 16, 1861.—"I have disposed of my interest in the Gazette office to W. W. Theobalds, who, in connection with Mr. Bunker, will continue the publication of the paper, and who together are authorized to collect all outstanding accounts of the office.   W. Bradford."

The paper thereafter was issued by Bunker & Theobalds.

January 4, 1862, it began raining, and on the 11th the valleys, farming regions, hills, mountains and mining districts suffered; flumes and structures of all kinds used in mining were swept away, also bridges, miners' cabins, etc. Snow fell to a depth of six inches at the coal mines, and there were also landslides.

In 1862 the Hot Springs near Byron were brought to the notice of the public, though they had been discovered years previously.

Stockraisers of the early sixties in Contra Costa County, with registered brands, included the following in or near the places named:

Martinez: J. Strentzel, Dr. F. E. Hough, Dr. John Tennent, M. R. Barber, B. R. Holliday, S. M. Swain.

Alamo: M. B. Mitchell, A. Ford, A. Hemme, B. Hall, S. A. Carpenter, James Foster, F. A. Bonnard, A. W. Hammitt, S. Stone, U. Huntington, W. Z. Stone, W. C. Chapman, D. P. Smith, W. Hayes & Bro., S. Wolff & Co., E. H. Cox, Joel Harlan, J. M. Jones, Golder Field, D. Glass.

Danville: John Smith, R. O. Baldwin, J. Flippin, D. L. Spencer, J. Steme, J. M. Jones, J. L. Labaree, T. Flournoy.

Pacheco: James Hoyt, S. Pacheco, J. L. Bromley, D. Boss, J. T. Walker.

November, 1862.—The Postmaster General has ordered the discontinuance of the Antioch postoffice, as being of the class deemed unnecessary.

December 20, 1862.—Dr. E. F. Hough discovered deposits of red, green, yellow and blue paints near Martinez on El Hambre Creek and has associated himself with M. R. Barber and N. B. Smith, and two capitalists of San Francisco, to develop the property.

January 10, 1863.—Walnut Creek has had a postoffice established. The postmaster is J. R. McDonald.

March 21, 1863.—Two years ago hardly a solitary house could be seen where Antioch now stands, and now there are some sixty buildings, all occupied, and more needed. There are two stores, express office, and saloons. The Stockton steamer stops there on its way up and down the San Joaquin River, so the people can get the papers from San Francisco and Stockton the day of issue. Religious services are held on Sunday, and a school of from twenty-five to thirty pupils is established.

May 23, 1863.—Mining companies include: Ypsilanti Gold, Silver & Copper Company, Clayton district, Contra Costa County, capital stock, $420,000, 4200 shares at $100; Cayuga Copper Mining Company, Clayton district, Contra Costa County, 3300 shares at $100 each; Bay County Gold & Silver Mining Company, Contra Costa County, capital stock $530,000, 1860 shares. Other companies are: Contra Costa Mining Company, Oriental Copper Mining Company, Pine Tree Mining Company, Georgiana Mining Company, Rock Oak Mining Company, Peerless Mining Company, Bay State Mining Company, and Bunker Mining Company; and in the San Ramon district: Cold Springs Mining Company, Buena Vista Mining Company, Golden Spear Mining Company, Silver Spear Mining Company.

The following have been included since the last issue of the Gazette, to work copper mines in Contra Costa County: The Keokuk Gold, Silver & Copper Mining Company, capital stock $600,000, 12,000 shares at $50 each; and Contra Costa Copper, Gold & Silver Mining Company, capital stock $420,000, 8400 shares at $50 each.

Twelve more were included during the week ending May 30, 1863.

August 1, 1863.—Adjutant General Kibbe has prepared and published a list of electors, residents of California, in the military service of the United State, entitled to vote at the next election. Here is the list from Contra Costa County: C. N. Ashley, M. Toumy, J. Neal, James E. Mason, J. Eichenburger, R. Hutchinson, P. F. Lawrence, W. H. Watrous, O. M. Coombs, Hopkin Hopkins, Charles Myer, N. B. McGill, Thomas Howell, G. R. Hosmer, Henry Andrews, B. Sharpless, James Baron, M. S. Loomis, William Whitney, F. O. McGuire, I. B. Sheppard, R. Haskell, G. Lawson, T. Scott, J. McConliff, P. Smith, William Crawford, A. J. Dexter, John Ulric, V. Abbey, Dr. George Gwyther, M. A. Meisenheimer.

September 19, 1863.—The first shipment of copper ore from the Mount Diablo mines, about one ton of rock from the Mount Zion, and a ton from the Pioneer, passed through Pacheco to San Francisco to be smelted.

January 23, 1864.—The Federal officials, in completing the work of enrollment in Contra Costa County, report 1560 men liable for military duty.

March 5, 1864.—A fire in Clayton on February 23 wiped out the Clayton Hotel, Rhine & Clayton's store, Union Hotel, A. Senderman's store, Perry Cram's livery, Dell's House; about $15,000 loss, one-fourth insured.

1867-1868.—Mrs. Jane C. Smith planted some mulberry trees and raised some silk worms near Somersville.

Mrs. Sarah C. Sellars, in the Iron House district, had some 3000 trees. A cocoonery was built near the grove, on scientific principles.

Mrs. Lafferty, Mr. Betteheim and Mr. Mills also raised cocoons.

April 1871.—James Steele and Isaac Yoakum were arrested in the Moraga Valley for assault upon the Moraga family. Some fifteen or twenty shots were fired from rifles; one horse, ridden by a Moraga, was killed. The affray was a dispute over the possession of land, originally owned and occupied by the Moragas but claimed by Carpentier and Yoakum under judicial decrees.

April 27, 1871.—Isaac Yoakum was shot, the affair taking place in Alameda County, while he and an assistant were driving some cattle to Yoakum's ranch in Moraga Valley. [Later Silverio Moraga was killed by George Steele, July 8, 1871.]

June 4, 1873.—Miss Gumecinda Moraga sued Isaac Yoakum in the Third District Court for $10,000 damages, for an alleged assault committed during the difficulties incident to the Moraga feud.

November 2, 1872.—The following statistics of the county were compiled from returns made to the surveyor general by the county surveyor, January 1, 1871, to January 1, 1872:

Land enclosed in 1871: 125,940 acres; land cultivated in 1871, 69,790 acres.

	Acreage	Harvested
Wheat	51,140	701,720 bushels
Barley	15,400	310,030 bushels
Oats	1,800	48,900 bushels
Rye	670	2,000 bushels
Corn	200	5,320 bushels
Buckwheat	30	570 bushels
Peas	20	410 bushels
Beans	225	4,560 bushels

	Acreage		Harvested	
Potatoes	90		16,890	tons
Sweet potatoes	6		30	tons
Onions	28		3,810	bushels
Hay	13,700		14,300	tons
Beets			1,800	tons
Turnips			700	tons
Pumpkins and Squash			2,000	tons
Butter			194,200	pounds
Cheese			38,900	pounds
Wool			110,620	pounds
Honey			6,200	pounds

January 25, 1873.—Isaac Lobree, general grocer and provision merchant at Antioch, was arrested on complaint of the town marshal, Mahon, convicted and fined $5, on a charge of violating the Sunday law, by keeping his place open. He paid the fine, thereby signifying his acceptance of the law. This is the first conviction under the law.

January 25, 1873.—The Martinez public school, which has been closed the past two months, will reopen in the Masonic Hall, January 27. It is to be hoped that the new school building will be completed by May 1, for the summer term.

April 5, 1873.—H. W. Carpentier has instituted suits in ejectment against many of the settlers and occupants of the Castro Sobrante lying between and surrounded by Pinole, San Pablo, Moraga, San Ramon, El Hambre and Welch ranchos. Most of the parties are living on the upper end of the tract claimed and, as they have reason to believe, upon what are public lands, if the Sobrante is not stretched beyond its proper limits.

April 5, 1873.—By requirement of the new code, Contra Costa County, with some 8000 inhabitants, must be apportioned into five supervisoral districts at the next meeting of the Board; and at the next general election the people of each district will elect a supervisor, if the district has not already an official.

First District: Martinez, Pinole, San Pablo; about 400 votes.

Second District: Lafayette, Walnut Creek, and Danville; about 400 votes.

Third District: Pacheco, enlarged by San Miguel and part of Welsh, Concord, Bay Point and part of Black Diamond; about 300 votes.

Fourth District: Clayton, Nortonville with Landing and part of Black Diamond, and Somersville; about 350 votes.

Fifth District: Antioch, Point of Timber; about 390 votes.

July, 1873.—J. S. Hill contemplated building Hotel Mount Diablo. Articles of incorporation were filed November 4. Capital stock $25,000, shares $10 each.

September 27, 1873.—Danville Grange, P. of H., with thirty charter members, was organized at Danville today.

November 22, 1873.—The certificate of incorporation of the Bank of Martinez was filed in the county clerk's office October 6, 1873. Directors: L. D. Fish, W. W. Cameron, S. Blum, H. M. Hale, W. M. Hale. Capital stock $50,000; 500 shares at $100 each. The new bank building is now completed and the bank is already proving a great public accomodation and has been doing a brisk business. This is the second week it has been open for business.

January 10, 1874.—On December 29, 1873, Antioch Grange, P. of H., was instituted with J. P. Walton, Master.

Judge C. W. Lander died very suddenly, on January 16, 1874, of congestion of the brain, on the veranda of the residence of Mrs. Jane E. Chase, about midway between the village center and his own residence. He was a graduate of Waterville College, Maine.

January 23, 1874.—Marshall Martin was hanged in the inclosure of the jail yard in Martinez, for the murder of Valentine Eischler, committed about a year ago on Marsh Creek, since which time he has been in the county jail. Verdict of the coroner's jury at time of execution: "We, the jury, find that Marshall Martin was born in Tennessee, was about fify-eight years old, and that he came to his death by being executed by the sheriff and his deputies of Contra Costa County at Martinez under warrant issued out of the Fifteenth District Court of the State of California. We also find that the arrangements for the execution were perfect in every particular; and that any fall that would have broken the neck would have severed the head from the body on account of the muscular development being soft and flabby. D. W. Swain, Wm. Hanna, T. McMahon, J. W. Fish, David Powell, F. M. Smith, A. B. Hamblen, T. Redfern, B. V. Merle, A. Altamerano."

The Governor, on Wednesday, issued a communication to T. A. Brown, as county judge, to fill the vacancy caused by the death of Judge Lander.

February 18, 1874.—Articles of incorporation of Green Valley and Mount Diablo Summit Road Company were filed to construct and maintain a turnpike road from a point on the Green Valley Road to a junction with Mount Diablo Summit Road; stock $5000; shares $10 each.

February 21, 1874.—Among the mail contracts for four years, from July 1, awarded by the Postoffice Department, was one to L. A. Miller for daily service on the Martinez to Oakland route, which includes Lafayette, Walnut Creek, Alamo, Danville and Pacheco, for $1685 per year; and one to John Eads for daily service on the Pacheco-Antioch route, embracing Concord, Clayton, Nortonville and Somersville, for $1180 per year. The mail between San Pablo and Martinez was awarded to N. P. Ingalls.

April 4, 1874.—Within a week the mountain grade of the Diablo Summit Road will be completed and the crossings of the canyon portion made passable for any description of vehicle, so that the ascent to the summit may be quickly and pleasantly made.

April 18, 1874.—The coach line for the Diablo roads, the one from Martinez through Pine Canyon, and that from Haywards through Green Valley, will have the finest carriages and teams ever employed for coach passenger conveyances on this Coast. Fifty fine horses have been purchased. The carriages are being built by the Kimbal Carriage Company and are especially designed for style, strength, lightness and elegance.

The Martinez and Pine Canyon line will be run by J. Seeley Bennett; the Haywards line, by W. S. Low.

April 25, 1874.—The residents of Ygnacio Valley, San Ramon, Lafayette and Walnut Creek are making a laudable effort to establish a high school in the vicinity of Walnut Creek. $5000 in subscriptions have already been secured on further subscription of $10,000.

May 2, 1874.—This has been a noteworthy day, not only for Martinez, but for all lovers of outdoor travel in California. The carriage road from Martinez to the summit of Diablo was thrown open to the public. Last summer J. S. Hall made the ascent alone on horseback from Clayton, and knowing something about mountain roads, conceived the plan of building a scenic road to the summit. He enlisted the support of others, and the road is the result.

September 26, 1874.—The Danville Grange celebrated the opening of their new hall today with a festal meeting. A very pleasant time was enjoyed by all.

The Alhambra Grange was organized December 4, 1874.

March 13, 1875.—A fire company has been organized at Antioch, and apparatus consisting of four poles, three hooks, two ladders, and four axes, has been ordered.

December 18, 1875.—The new church at Danville is rapidly nearing completion, and it is expected it will be ready for occupancy in the early spring. Rev. Symington is to serve as pastor.

January 15, 1876.—The survey of the Moraga Rancho in two separate tracts, one of 12,800 acres and the other of about 500 acres, excites some remarks and conjectures. If the quantity, to which the title of a grant presumed to be in one body has been confirmed, can be located in two parts, within the exterior limits, why not in ten to twenty or more to cover all the choice spots? Mr. Carpentier has run the 500-acre strip through the Redwood Canyon, and the larger acreage embraces all the best portion of Moraga Valley.

April 28, 1876.—The Central Pacific Railway depot was located at Martinez.

June 3, 1876.—Frederick Langenkamp, of Ygnacio Valley, is the pioneer hop grower of the county. Three years ago he planted ten acres. This year his prospects are fine for a large yield. He has a furnace, drying house and packing rooms constructed on approved plans, and is going into the business as a source of good profit.

August 30, 1878.—Antioch Ledger announces that Henry C. Galla-gher has taken a five-year lease of the hotel at the Point of Timber Hot Springs.

September 7, 1878.—There is a fever created by the survey of the Sobrante Grant, begun some weeks ago under the direction of the United States Surveyor General, and many people in the western border of Contra Costa County and about Oakland have been much excited in hopes of getting a grab at what may prove to be government land, after the location and restriction of the Sobrante.

The land is all in the possession of settlers who have purchased the grant title and who hold mostly in large tracts; but the privileged few, armed with the inside information, have located University script on every foot of the ground except 160 acres to each settler. In addition the hills teem with squatters who are busy selecting their locations without any regard to the grant title or the University script. The squatters are ignorant as to the lines of either survey, and annoy the farmers whose titles are not affected as much as they do those whose lands lie in the disputed belt.

The grant owners hope to have the survey rejected; the script holders hope and expect that it will not be; and the squatters hope to acquire some right by being early in the field. The script locators are entirely dependent upon the ruling of the courts in their favor, and are willing to await the turn of events; but the squatters are persistent and not disposed to remain quiet, for fear they might waive some right which they otherwise might acquire. The settlers are determined to defend their rights and are quietly arming. Nearly every house on the disputed ground is a citadel stored with arms and ammunition. It is to be regretted that this entangle-ment could not be gotten over without resort to arms, either to assert or defend the rights of any man.

September 7, 1878.—K. W. Taylor is now engaged in making the partition surveys of the San Pablo Rancho for the commissioners appoint-ed under the partition decree and judgment of the court.

September 7, 1878, the postoffice was established at Pinole and Bernardo Fernandez was appointed postmaster.

September 21, 1878.—The occupants of the Sobrante lands excluded from the recent survey, and of lands on previously finally located grants that have been included in the late Sobrante survey, are in an unpleasant state of worriment; and those of the excluded Sobrante lands are forced to the extremity of resisting the invasion of script locators and preemptors with death-dealing arms, or of surrendering their possessions. There have been as yet no fatal encounters, but shots have frequently been exchanged between the two forces. There is a possibility that there may be consid-erable bloodshed for possession of some of these lands.

Rancho el Sobrante finally confirmed to J. J. & Victor Castro, surveyed by William Minto in August, 1878, containing 20,563.42 acres, which area covers 10,375.69 acres included in the final survey of Rancho La Boca de la Cañada del Pinole and 221.09 acres included in the final survey of Rancho Laguna de los Palos Colorados.

October 12, 1878.—Ejectment suits begun by several owners under Sobrante Grant title whose lands have been jumped upon claim that they are public lands by the recent survey. Most of these claimants have been in possession for years. Among the suits of ejectment are: one by Felix Brisac against some twenty-three or twenty-four alleged tresspassers, one by Daniel Clancy against four or five, one by Mrs. Mary Baden against four, one by N. Thode against four, one by Herman Hadler against four, one by Julius Reiners against four.

Married at the residence of the bride's parents near Point of Timber, October 22, 1878, by Rev. L. H. Meade, of Clayton, Volney Taylor and Miss Agnes E. Andrews.

November 23, 1878.—The thriving village of Walnut Creek has been improved the past summer by a large addition to the schoolhouse; half a dozen cottages; the two-story building of J. M. Stow, postmaster, store below and Masonic Hall above; the new store of Shuey & Pittman; an enlargement of D. N. Sherburne's store, which has been provided with a fireproof safe. Walnut Creek has the aspect of a thrifty business village. The fine climate and attractive surroundings are likely to insure a constant future gain of population.

November 30, 1878.—An anvil salute was fired under the direction of the Workingmen's Club in honor of Dennis Kearney, when he passed through Martinez on his way East on the Overland last Tuesday afternoon. The great agitator bowed his acknowledgements from the rear platform.

In the several suits brought in the District Court by Sobrante owners under grant title to eject trespassers, judgment of ejectment was given for the plaintiffs with cost of suit; and in the case of Brisac against Twomey et al., the judgment included damages of $1000.

December 7, 1878.—The owners of the Briones Grant were notified by telegram from Washington, D. C., last Tuesday, that their patent had been issued and recorded in the general land office and would be mailed to their order on Friday of this week.

January 25, 1879.—The Union Cemetery, controlled by a corporation, George Fellows, president, has been located on four acres on a quarter section of C. J. Preston's land leading from Point of Timber to Brentwood.

April 12, 1879.—The Concord fire department has been fully organized and a committee appointed to report on apparatus. $134 was subscribed to further the objects of this committee. Officers: H. J. Nelson, foreman; Charles Bente, assistant; S. Bacon, treasurer; B. J. Murphy, secretary; Charles Navas, P. Klein and Paul Lohse, trustees.

May 17, 1879.—The board of supervisors purchased the south half of the vacant portion of the town block east of the court house, of L. C.

Wittenmyer, for $500, and are negotiating for the other half for the same sum, which has been declined.

July 12, 1879.—James Stewart announces the opening of his new cash grocery and provision store at the corner of Castro and Locust Streets.

July 26, 1879.—The beginning of a sewerage system for Martinez has been made in the line of an 8-inch iron-stone pipe laid through four blocks up from the bay on Las Juntas Street, with provision for constructing side drains on either side.

Married, at Point of Timber, September 3, 1879, by Rev. William Gaffney, Wells N. Moore and Olive A. Plumley; also on September 3, Henry Sedge and Sarah E. Plumley.

September 6, 1879.—On September 1, 1879, Walnut Creek was alive with people from the houses of the town and country, thronging the main street to witness the golden wedding of Milo H. Turner and Caroline M. Clark. They were married in Troy, N. Y., in 1829; came to California in 1852; came to Contra Costa County and located at Walnut Creek in 1874. The wedding ceremony was again enacted, after which congratulations were in order. Many beautiful presents were given the couple.

September 30, 1879.—Gen. U. S. Grant was greeted by about 300 people and the firing of a salute, when the train on which he was a passenger made a two-minute stop at Martinez. He stood on the platform of the rear car and after three cheers had been given, courteously raised his hat in acknowledgment.

November 24, 1879.—The great railroad ferry-boat Solano, of the Northern Railway Company, for service from Benicia to Bull Valley, made her trial trip November 24 from Oakland to Benicia slip, and thence across the straits to Bull Valley, where she lies ready for service. The boat is the largest in the world ever built for such service, and all the resources of the builders have been employed with a view to strength and efficiency.

Married at Clayton, December 20, 1879, by D. S. Carpenter, justice of the peace, Joseph A. Houston, of Byron, to Miss Isabel McLane of Lake County.

January 10, 1880.—Judge T. A. Brown presided at the opening of the new Superior Court last Monday, January 5. No business offering, he declared a recess. There is much doubt as to the regularity and validity of any proceeding in the Superior Court under the present practice, Acts and Codes. An early act of the legislature is looked for, which will enable them to go on without the raising of any questions as to the validity of their proceedings.

September 9, 1882.—The Port Costa Flouring Mills Company has filed articles of incorporation with the county clerk of San Francisco County for the purpose of carrying on a general flouring mill business at

9

Port Costa. Capital stock $150,000. Directors: F. M. Brown, William M. Given Jr., W. B. English, Barry O. Baldwin, and E. J. Coleman.

At Port Costa wharf building is progressing rapidly and track laying will soon commence on the wharf recently surveyed. Soon tracks will be laid all around the houses built on the piles at this place.

September 16, 1882.—A Legion of Honor is about to be instituted at Clayton.

September 23, 1882.—Since September, 1858, we do not remember that we have had so early a considerable rain throughout so large a portion of the State as that of last Saturday. . . . In this county there was a heavy fall at Antioch, which seems to have been confined to the river margin. In the evening it showered heavily at Martinez, while in the vicinity of Pacheco and Concord the fall of rain and hail was heavy, but did not extend to Walnut Creek.

Port Costa.—The coal bunkers have been started, and work from this source has brought about sixty men to this place. The wharf will be 800 feet long, and from 30 to 40 feet wide.

The hotels of Port Costa are full to overflowing. Rooms are in great demand; beds are at a premium. There is a good chance for some energetic person to start a lodging house here.

Concord.—The telephone line between Pacheco and Clayton was completed last week.

October 7, 1882.—The Port Costa Warehouse & Dock Company has incorporated with a capital stock of $500,000. The directors are: A. Cheesebrough, E. B. Cutter, A. E. Mosby, J. H. Freeman and A. R. Church. The object is to do a general storage business.

October 28, 1882.—H. O. Beaman of Pinole is having a new residence constructed.

A. K. P. Nason has filed a declaration of homestead in Block 23 in the town of Antioch. The value of the property is estimated at $2000.

New powder works are being erected near Pinole by the Granite Powder Company. Some day we expect to hear that the west end of the county has entirely gone to blazes.

O. F. James, for nearly twenty-two years postmaster of Martinez, has resigned and will soon retire from his long business career.

December 2, 1882.—The Concord boys are talking about organizing a brass band.

The coal market is so brisk at present that the Mount Diablo mines are unable to fill all the orders that come in.

December 9, 1882.—A Presbyterian church has been organized at Concord with Rev. D. Monroe as pastor; William Caven, John Brawand, and E. A. Jaquith, trustees. There has been $500 appropriated by the Presbytery, $600 by the citizens for a building, and S. Bacon has given a lot.

December 23, 1882.—A Good Templars Lodge, with forty-two members, was organized at Lafayette, with officers elected and installed. A

Good Templars Lodge with 23 members was organized at Martinez, and officers elected.

December 30, 1882.—A Good Templars Lodge was organized at Danville December 16, with thirty-seven members.

January 6, 1883.—The snow-storm on Sunday last was a surprise and a novelty, although it was general throughout the Bay counties, where snow is seldom experienced. Contra Costa seems to have received more than her share. There fell at least five inches in our county and the west valleys, and east of Diablo the fall in places amounted to a foot.

January 13, 1883.—Last week the British ships Minnie Burrell, Argonaut and Cernga left Port Costa for Europe, and the Glendarnel arrived.

J. D. Peters of Stockton estimates that there are 400,700 tons of wheat in the State on December 31, of which 30,000 tons are in Contra Costa County.

January 20, 1883.—A brass band was organized at Antioch.

A certificate of co-partnership has been filed by L. Levinsky, P. Fabian, and M. Grunauer, who will conduct a merchandise business at Byron under the name of P. Fabian & Company.

January 27, 1883.—The Antioch Lodge of Good Templars has now 105 members. It is the banner lodge of the county.

The Concord Literary and Dramatic Club has been organized with A. Thurber, president; Dr. E. Bragdon, secretary; Mrs. R. H. Caven, treasurer; and with a membership of twenty-five.

February 24, 1883.—The citizens of Walnut Creek have made a commendable movement in the organization of a Hook & Ladder Company; foreman, W. B. Rogers; secretary, J. M. Wilson; treasurer, M. Kirsch.

. Scammon's Hotel is now completed at Port Costa. For the last few months the hotels at Port Costa have been crowded to utmost capacity.

March 3, 1883.—The thermometer at the Martinez postoffice Thursday reached 78 degrees in the shade. A little more of that snow, please.

The recently erected railroad coal bunkers at Port Costa are finished and ready for use and the tracks were laid to bring the trains under the chutes, of which there are fifty, from which a train of twenty-five cars can be loaded in a few minutes. The capacity is about 12,000 tons of coal.

Port Costa.—The first pile was driven Monday for the erection of the Nevada Bank's large wharves and warehouses, which, when completed, will be 2300 feet long. At the present rate, our town will soon be a solid structure for a distance of three miles.

March 17, 1883.—Excelsior Lodge, I. O. G. T., of Byron, which was organized March 7, 1869, with eighteen charter members, celebrated its fourteenth anniversary with 160 present, visitors coming from many neighboring lodges.

At a meeting of the citizens of Martinez at the Court House Monday evening for the purpose of organizing a water company to supply Martinez and Port Costa with water, R. R. Bunker was elected chairman, and

C. Ed. Miller, secretary. A committee was appointed to draw up articles of incorporation, also one to see where water could be obtained. The former committee was composed of I. E. Marshall, S. Blum, S. J. Bennett, Thos. McMahon, J. O'B. Wyatt; the latter: T. A. McMahon, I. E. Marshall, and W. S. Tinning.

March 31, 1883.—A slight earthquake shock was felt in Martinez at ten minutes of eight o'clock yesterday morning.

The Congregational church at Eden Plain has been removed to Brentwood, where it will be occupied by the Methodist Episcopal congregation, who bought it.

The Antioch Lodge of Good Templars now has a membership of 150 and is about to establish a reading-room for the public.

Articles of incorporation of the Nevada Warehouse & Dock Company, capitalization $500,000, were filed this week.

Murphy & Cavanaugh will open their new store at Concord on April 2, with the greatest display of goods ever exhibited in the town.

April 7, 1883.—The Antioch Town Hall was ready for occupancy this week.

A Council of the American Legion of Honor will be instituted at Crockett this evening by Deputy Grand Commander S. B. Thompson of Martinez.

May 5, 1883.—Starr & Company, milling corporation, are building a 4000-barrel mill and large wharves for wheat shipping, and a warehouse to hold over 100,000 tons at the wheat port on the south side of Carquinez Straits.

May 5, 1883.—The first annual meeting of the Contra Costa County Grangers' Warehousing and Business Association, under new articles of incorporation, was held last Wednesday at the Alhambra Grange Hall in Martinez, and was attended by nearly all the stockholders who represent Alhambra, Walnut Creek and Danville granges.

May 19, 1883.—A meeting of the Martinez Gun Club was held in the office of Justice F. M. Smith last Saturday evening, with President H. Weatherby in the chair. A constitution and by-laws were adopted.

June 2, 1883.—A fine stream of water was struck in the tunnel of the Martinez Water Company Tuesday, a distance of twenty-seven feet from the mouth of the tunnel. There are now two streams running from the tunnel and the indications are that a still greater abundance will be found. The water is of fine quality and comes out through the rock crevices with a force that indicates an immense pressure behind it.

June 9, 1883.—A brass band has been organized by a number of young men at Point of Timber and Byron.

The first direct rail shipment for the Grangers' Warehouse by new switch connection, was made to Port Costa, of 150 tons of wheat stored and sold by R. O. Baldwin of San Ramon Valley.

Another fine stream of water was struck in the tunnel of the Martinez Water Company. There are now three streams of excellent water.

At a meeting of the Contra Costa County Agricultural Society held at Pacheco last Saturday, it was resolved that the society become a member of the National Trotting Association. This will give the society an opportunity to govern the conduct of drivers and parties entering horses for races.

June 16, 1883.—Nelson Peterson, of Antioch, has been granted a patent for an improved road cart.

E. W. Hiller started out his ice wagon this week through Pacheco, Concord, Walnut Creek, Alamo and Danville.

Over 30,000 gallons per day is now running from the tunnel of the Martinez Water Company, and prospects are good for doubling that amount in a few days.

A recent census of the Martinez School District shows 126 boys and 117 girls between the ages of 5 and 17, nine less than for last year.

June 23, 1883.—A barn on the ranch of N. W. Smith, near Antioch, was struck by a whirlwind one day last week and completely destroyed, one piece of the roof being carried forty yards.

July 14, 1883.—The results of wheat-threshing in the county, so far reported, indicate a shrinkage and loss of forty per cent from effects of the early June hot spells.

July 28, 1883.—George W. McNear has purchased the El Hambre Ranch interests of W. A. Piper for $100,000.

The Nevada Dock warehouses took their first grain for storage a few days ago.

Report of grain production in Point of Timber shows the turnout of a few fields:

A. Richardson	165 acres	1,500 lbs.
A. Porter	75 acres	1,900 lbs.
S. M. Wills	110 acres	840 lbs.
J. Geddes	400 acres	850 lbs.
George Cople	200 acres	840 lbs.
A. V. Taylor	78 acres	1,725 lbs.
J. S. Netherton	47 acres	1,350 lbs.
J. M. Baldwin	300 acres	1,650 lbs.
Volney Taylor	125 acres	1,720 lbs.

The larger returns are the result of thorough cultivation, the shallow plowing giving the best returns in quality and quantity.

W. P. Netherton, after his harvest vacation, has returned to Oakland to continue his high school studies.

September 1, 1883.—The first ship to load at Nevada Dock warehouses, the Euterpe, 1197 tons, was docked there last Tuesday. The second ship docked Thursday.

The Grangers' warehouses at Martinez are filling up with grain, and nearly all storage room has been engaged.

September 8, 1883.—The twentieth anniversary of Pacheco Lodge No. 117, I. O. O. F., will be held at the Fair Grounds next Wednesday at ten o'clock a. m.

September 15, 1883.—R. O. Baldwin, of San Ramon, took first prize at the Golden Gate Fair in the "horses of all work" class for his stallion, "Gold Hill." Capt. J. E. Durham, of Pacheco, took one of the premiums in the Roadster Stallion class for his colt, "McVeagh."

September 15.—Two church services were held for the first time last Sunday at Port Costa.

October 6, 1883.—There is much reason to fear that our Mount Diablo coal mines, that have for the past twenty years furnished so large a portion of the steam-making fuel of the State, will be unable much longer to maintain a competition with the fine large coal veins of Oregon and Washington.

It is understood that orders were received at Somersville to discontinue all mining in the Pittsburgh Mine and take out all underground machinery and tracks. In the Black Diamond Mine at Nortonville work has been retarded by a heavy inflow of water, which overtaxes the pumping machinery, and the owners are making no move to remedy the situation as it now exists.

A deplorable lack of interest was shown by the farmers in the slim attendance at the Twenty-third Exhibition of the Contra Costa County Agricultural, Horticultural, and Mechanical Society at the Fair Grounds near Pacheco.

October 13, 1883.—The pumps of the Black Diamond coal mine have got the heavy flow of water reduced and under control so that work has been resumed in full force.

The earthquake of last Tuesday morning was the liveliest since 1868. It occurred a few minutes after one o'clock a. m., lasting three seconds.

October 27, 1883.—The Contra Costa Telephone Company have let the contract to run an extension of their line through Nortonville, Somersville, and Stewartville to Antioch. It is but a few weeks ago that their line was extended to Oakland and San Francisco, giving direct connection with those cities and with San Leandro, San Lorenzo and Haywards.

A Sabbath school was successfully organized at Port Costa last Sunday. Preaching was held in the evening and is to be continued regularly.

November 3, 1883.—The Pittsburg coal mine has been closed permanently.

A lamp-post and large lamp have been placed at the corner of the Court House lot near the entrance on Main Street.

November 10, 1883.—A telephone has been ordered placed in the sheriff's office by the board of supervisors for the use of the county.

Walnut Creek Hook & Ladder Company now possess a fine cart fully equipped.

The business portion of the town of Port Costa was almost entirely destroyed by fire. The business portion was a line of wooden buildings along the water's edge, every building resting on piles. Fire rapidly spread towards McNear's warehouse, taking every building in its path.

The wharf was also damaged, and several thousand bushels of wheat and eight cars. The loss is only partly covered by insurance. Four hotels, three saloons, eight freight cars and eighty tons of wheat were destroyed.

November 17, 1883.—Mr. Ipswich, late purchaser of the Centennial Hotel, has had a force of carpenters and painters repairing and renovating the building.

The Hook & Ladder Company of Concord have appointed a committee to receive bids for the erection of a handsome hall.

December 1, 1883.—Charles B. Porter, for eighteen years editor of the Gazette, has disposed of his interest in the paper.

The Pacific Coast Steel & Iron Manufacturing Company desire to locate in Martinez if they can sell $50,000 of stock here, which is offered at half-price.

The California Redwood Company filed notice of application for a wharf franchise. They have bought twenty acres near Pinole for their yards. They desire a franchise on the water's edge.

December 8, 1883.—The Petroleum Refining & Developing Company has incorporated for the purpose indicated by the title. The principal place of business is Haywards. It is claimed that first-quality petroleum has been discovered in the Livermore Mountains and development work is soon to begin.

The Commercial Hotel was opened to the public Monday evening, and a large number of people took advantage of the occasion to inspect the establishment. There is certainly no hotel in the county superior to the Commercial. The proprietor, J. Ipswich, spread a sumptuous supper for his guests.

From 3500 to 4000 tons of coal per month are being taken out of the Empire Mine.

December 13, 1883.—This week's weather has been cold, foggy and disagreeable. Ice and fog is a condition we seldom have in Martinez.

D. P. Griffin has bought a half-interest in the Pacheco Flour Mills.

The farmers of the Danville section look for a dry year and have stopped plowing, as the ground is very hard.

A. C. Tichnor, of Los Angeles, claims to have invented an electrical process which will do away with telephone and telegraph wires and poles. [Query: Was this an early experiment in wireless telegraphy?]

December 22, 1883.—A meeting of subscribers and others interested in the proposed new steel works at Martinez will be held at the Exchange Hotel this afternoon at two o'clock.

The total amount of real estate sales for the last five months of 1883, through the office of Matthews & Sayre, amounted to $167,450.

December 29, 1883.—Rainfall to date 2.13 inches. The farmers generally have resumed plowing.

At a meeting of the State Teachers' Association in San Francisco this week, D. J. Sullivan of San Pablo was placed on the Committee of Nominations.

Port Costa is being rapidly rebuilt. Several houses have been erected and others are going up. The new Catholic church is nearly completed.

The Point of Timber Landing Company are engaged in constructing a canal, thirty-six feet wide and four and a half feet deep, from a point in the slough near their old wharf, where their buildings are located. It is to be about 4000 feet long. At the ordinary high tide this will furnish over six feet of water, and at low tide two feet.

Ninety-six trains per day run over the road between Port Costa and Oakland.

January, 1884.—The year 1883 was ushered in by a remarkable snowstorm; New Year's Day, 1884, was mild and pleasant.

Contra Costa County began the new year with $118,946.76 in its treasury.

The tunnel of the Martinez Water Company is now in 300 feet, and prospects for additional water grow gradually better.

January 26, 1884.—The American Exchange Hotel, corner Main and Wyatt Streets, in Antioch, was entirely destroyed by fire early last Monday morning. John Griffin, son of the owner of the hotel, and Patrick Hines, a section-hand, perished in the flames. The hotel was built in 1871 by Patrick Griffin, but was destroyed by fire the same year. It was rebuilt of brick, being the only brick hotel building in the county.

February 2, 1884.—Rainfall to date, 6.12 inches.

St. Patrick's Church, at Port Costa, will be dedicated tomorrow.

Everybody is smiling this week on account of the rain. The farmers and merchants are all happy. Up to Friday noon of this week 3.36 inches of rain had fallen at Martinez. Other sections benefitted in like manner.

February 9, 1884:—The following notice was presented and adopted at a meeting of the Pacific Coast Steel & Iron Manufacturing Company, held at Melrose:

"Notice is hereby given to all whom it may concern, that in pursuance of the written consent of the stockholders of two-thirds of the capital stock of the Pacific Coast Steel & Iron Manufacturing Company, and which consent is in writing and duly filed in the office of the said company, that the office and the principal place of business of the Pacific Coast Steel & Iron Manufacturing Company will be changed from Melrose, Alameda County, to the town of Martinez, Contra Costa County, California, and that hereafter said office and place of business of said Company will be at Martinez aforesaid."

February 9, 1884.—The Catholics of Lafayette, Moraga Valley, Alamo and Walnut Creek are preparing to erect a church not far from Walnut Creek.

February 23, 1884.—A large force of men and teams are at work on the foundation of the new steel works. The buildings and machinery are to cost over $110,000.

During the past week there have been eight ships loading at the Nevada Docks, and seventeen at Port Costa.

The Antioch Ledger was revived last week as a Democratic paper, Charles F. Montgomery being its new editor and proprietor. The Ledger makes a good showing on its local page, and its editorial columns are original and interesting.

Vincent Hook has purchased the Fish Ranch between Martinez and Pacheco, containing over 1000 acres.

March 8, 1884.—Up to ten o'clock Friday afternoon the rainfall at Martinez had amounted to 1.68 inches, making a total for the season of 12.19 inches.

March 15, 1884.—The total rainfall for the season is now 16.25 inches.

March 15, 1884.—The Gazette has purchased another job press, making four now in operation.

The efforts of the Martinez Water Company have been rewarded. Now 62,000 gallons daily come from Maraschi Canyon, six miles from town. The tunnel is in 360 feet. Five or six miles of pipe will be required, and its fall will be 800 feet. A reservoir will be built on the hills near Martinez and the water piped into town.

March 22, 1884.—The damage to crops on Roberts Island by the breaking of the levee is estimated at $500,000.

Six thousand sacks of wheat were shipped by car this week from the Grangers' warehouse here to the Grangers' warehouse on the Straits.

Treat & Whitman, experienced horticulturists, are setting out from eighty to one hundred acres in fruit trees and vines on their place in Ygnacio Valley.

March 29, 1884.—A severe earthquake was felt in this county on Tuesday, at seventeen minutes to five o'clock p. m., followed by a slight shock one hour later. The quake seems to have been quite general throughout the State. In San Francisco brick buildings were cracked in many places.

April 5, 1884.—A question now before the citizens of Martinez is that of incorporating. It is believed the proper time has arrived for such a move.

The month of March had 8.50 inches rainfall.

April 19, 1884.—The new El Dorado Hotel at Antioch opened last week.

The Concord Sun has gone into an eclipse; whether partial or total is not known.

E. W. Hiller has secured the Antioch ice-house for this season and is now prepared to furnish ice at that point.

May 10, 1884.—Martinez is to be incorporated under the general laws.

Today the first run of steel will be made at the works to test the cupolas and to see that everything is in running order.

The new Presbyterian church at Walnut Creek is going up rapidly.

The Steel Company is making molds and shells for castings. The men engaged in the work are experienced and skilful.

It seems to be definitely settled that Moore & Smith will locate their extensive lumber yards here in Martinez during the summer.

Work progresses on the California and Nevada narrow gauge, and it will reach Walnut Creek this summer.

May 31, 1884.—Oakland and Carquinez Railway Company filed articles of incorporation with the county clerk of Alameda County, with a capital of $500,000. The projected road will run from Oakland harbor over the San Antonio range of hills to Moraga Valley, Contra Costa County, and thence to the Straits of Carquinez.

News from Crockett and Wheatport state that the Sunday school has an average attendance of forty; the public school, an attendance of thirty-five. Two dwellings have been erected, a variety store opened, and a new butcher shop put in operation. Heald's Agricultural Warehouse is going full blast, and Starr's Mill is completed to the second story.

The assessment roll of the county will probably foot up between $12,000,000 and $13,000,000 this year.

A new tannery is about to be started near Martinez by two Benicia men. The schooner Columbus is here with a cargo of bark for the enterprise.

The new officers of Martinez, elected May 31: F. M. Warmcastle, Samuel Robin, Dr. H. Bernett, Dr. John Leffler, trustees; John O'B. Wyatt, clerk; J. J. Jones, treasurer; Frank Pitts, marshal. There was a tie vote for the fifth member of the board of trustees between J. H. Borland and Henry Potter, and it was declared neither was elected.

June 14, 1884.—The rainfall brought the total up to 24.23 inches.

San Ramon Hotel will be opened today as a first-class country hotel, with Joseph Kaster, proprietor; Joseph Willard will be the manager.

The rain damaged the hay crop of the entire State, and much of the heavy grain is badly damaged. The loss in the State will run up into the millions.

June 21, 1884.—J. H. Borland was declared elected the fifth member of the board of trustees of Martinez at a special election.

A run of 10,000 pounds was made at the steel works last Monday.

Matthews and Sayre sold during the last twelve months more than 8049 acres, totaling $372,500, and making an average price of $46 per acre. This means the development of ranch property and new settlers.

July 12, 1884.—The new Congregational church at Stewartville will be ready for occupancy in ten days.

The old and new fire organizations of Martinez were consolidated at a meeting Tuesday evening at the court house. President, L. C. Wittenmyer; foreman, Neal Hurley; treasurer, James Braire; treasurer, J. H. Borland; secretary, J. O'B. Wyatt.

Report of Superintendent Borland, of Contra Costa Telephone Company: 54 miles of line; 34 instruments; balance on hand, $384.08.

August 9, 1884.—The board of supervisors have engaged William Minto and T. A. McMahon to draw a correct county map.

August 16, 1884.—The dedication of Bennett's new hall was a grand success.

Blaine and Logan Clubs are being organized all over the county.

September 6, 1884.—The display of fruits, vegetables, cereals, etc., from this county in San Francisco made by Matthews & Sayre equaled any display ever made there and was in many respects superior to similar exhibits from other counties heretofore made, and yet the fruit represented but a few of our best orchards. Among those who contributed were Messrs. Raap, McBride, Dr. Strentzel, Fish, Dudley, Sickal, Thomas, John Gambs, Dick and Dukes. Following is a list of the products exhibited: Grapes—seedless, Sultanas, Sweet Water, Rose of Peru, Flaming Tokay, Zinfandel, Muscat, Palestine, Mission, Victor, Black Hamburgs, and Golden Chasselas; numerous varieties of peaches, pears, plums, apples, oranges, lemons, cucumbers and melons; wheat, seven feet high; barley and oats, nine feet high; rye; chestnuts; corn with six ears to a stalk and fourteen feet high.

The Twenty-fourth Annual Fair of Contra Costa County Agricultural, Horticultural and Mechanical Society was held at Pacheco September 8 to 13.

The county was treated to a fine rain Sunday night. Very little damage was done, as the threshing was practically finished.

Thirteen schooners were loaded with hay and grain at Antioch this week by W. A. Brunkhorst.

Bray Brothers have shipped 2557 bales of hay this week.

September 27, 1884.—The fleet of the Pacific Yacht Club will visit Martinez today.

The amount of wheat received at Bray's each day amounts to from forty to fifty tons.

October 4, 1884.—There was a sharp frost in the San Ramon Valley Thursday morning.

October 18, 1884.—Construction work on the new Congregational church building at Crockett has begun.

During the past week the rainfall in the county has been 1.13 inches.

November 22, 1884.—Over sixty men are at work excavating and grading for the site of the new Selby's Lead Works, a short distance below Vallejo Junction. This large enterprise will add to the business and wealth of the county.

December 6, 1884.—Eight street lamps were placed in position this week in Martinez at advantageous points. These lamps will give sufficient light for all present purposes, as there are several private street lamps which will continue to be used.

The great event at Point of Timber last week was the opening of the Landing Company's Canal, which is three-quarters of a mile long cut through the tules from Indian Slough to the company's yard on the mainland. The stock is all owned by residents of Point of Timber. A schooner with 50,000 feet of lumber is expected in the canal in a few days.

The first new sidewalk on the official grade in Martinez was constructed this week by Robin & Maloche in front of their blacksmith shop on Main Street.

December 17, 1884.—William P. Netherton, oldest son of J. S. Netherton, graduated from Oakland High School last week.

On December 17 the Byron Hotel burned; insurance, $7000.

December 20, 1884.—It is stated that the Black Diamond coal mine will shut down within a few weeks owing to operating expenses.

January 3, 1885.—A new sidewalk has been placed, leading to the Court House.

January 17, 1885.—Articles of incorporation of the Antioch & Mendocino Lumber Company have been filed with the Secretary of State; paid up capital, $200,000. Antioch is to be made the forwarding point for all kinds of lumber on the Southern Pacific.

January 24, 1885.—The Martinez Water Company has proved a success. An abundance of water, sufficient to supply a city of 20,000, has been obtained. The work has been carried on by John and Harry Porter, who back their faith by their work. The tunnel is 900 feet long and is situated 840 feet above Martinez.

January 31, 1885.—Rainfall to date, 8.19 inches.

At Port Costa all the wharves are lined with ships, and wheat is being poured out of car, warehouse and barge for nine hours daily, six days of the week. Many of the ships work three gangs at once.

February 21, 1885.—The Empire Mine is shipping 125 tons of coal per day.

A tax was voted at Crockett for a new school building; fifty votes solid.

The Three Brothers, the second largest ship afloat under sail, loaded 45,000 sacks of wheat this week at Port Costa.

March 7, 1885.—The marriage certificate of W. P. Netherton and Maggie M. Glassford was filed this week.

The new Catholic church at Pinole will be dedicated March 8 by the Most Reverend Archbishop Riordan.

March 14, 1885.—Lumber is being hauled for a new large "Cash Store" building in Martinez, to be built for L. M. Lasell, of Nortonville.

March 28, 1885.—A meeting for the organization of a N. S. G. W. Parlor at Martinez was called for Monday evening at the office of Justice F. M. Smith.

General Canby Post No. 78, G. A. R., organized in Martinez, is the first organized by Civil War soldiers in the county. G. W. Bowie is Commander; M. H. Bailhache, Senior Vice; O. L. Marsh, Junior Vice; R. N. Doyle, Q. M.; Dr. H. Bernett, Surgeon; Harry Heinz, Chaplain; George H. Wellington, Officer of the Guard; and A. L. Gartley, Adjutant.

The first passenger train on the narrow gauge left Oakland at nine o'clock Sunday morning with a number of officials and invited guests on board, and made the trip to San Pablo and return. All were pleased with the smoothness of the road.

April 18, 1885.—A communication of the Water Company, offering to sell its works to the town for $25,000, was received and laid over until April 28.

The Martinez Warehouse property, the warehouses and real estate on Pacheco Creek, schooners Martinez and Melrose, and the steamship Tulare, now located in Martinez, all being a portion of the assets of the estate of W. A. Bray (Bray Brothers), will be sold at 226 Clay Street, San Francisco, today to the highest bidder. The sale is under the direction of assignees, C. A. Knox and Frank Otis.

April 25, 1885.—At the sale of the Martinez Warehouse property, Blum & Company of Martinez put in the highest bid, and the property was sold to them. They will soon remove their offices to the old Bray offices.

May 16, 1885.—The following schooners arrived at Martinez this week for Blum & Company: The Christina Stephens, with a cargo of 7500 posts; the John McCullough, with 120,000 feet redwood; the Martinez, with a load of bricks; and the Melrose, with a load of coal, lime and lumber.

The furniture and fixtures of the late Good Templars Lodge in Martinez were sold at auction on May 23 by W. A. J. Gift.

A Chapter of R. A. M. was recently instituted in Antioch.

The dedication of the new Pythian Castle of Black Diamond Lodge No. 29, K. of P., of Martinez, will take place on June 5, upon which occasion a grand ball will be given. This lodge has erected a fine two-story structure on Main Street.

The Martinez Cash Store and Wholesale Grocery, Lasell & Company, proprietors, will be opened to the public Monday morning.

Mr. Norris, of Concord, is laying a real city sidewalk around his premises, constructed of cobblestones from the quarry near town. Other property owners please take the hint.

William Thomas has had erected, at his own expense, a water-fountain on Main Street at the Knights of Pythias corner for the benefit of the public. The water comes from a spring on his father's premises and is of good quality.

June 6, 1885.—The thermometer reached 100 degrees in the shade Friday, the 29th of May, at Walnut Creek.

July 4, 1885.—Of the $38,000 bonded indebtedness of the county, $9000 has been paid, leaving $29,000 still outstanding.

The residence of John Murphy, near Concord, was burned Sunday morning, with a loss of $3000.

The firm of Matthews & Sayre has dissolved, Mr. Sayre going to Lakeport. Mr. Matthews has united with Easton & Eldridge of San Francisco under the firm name of Pacific Coast Land Bureau, and will remain in Martinez as agent of the bureau. Since coming here Mr. Matthews has been active in selling lands for his company. The first year 8049 acres passed through their hands and sold for $372,500. The second year 14,973 acres were sold for $838,532.

July 25, 1885.—The Gazette is dressed in mourning out of respect to General Grant.

August 1, 1885.—Up to yesterday forty-five schooner-loads of hay, 12,000 bales, had been shipped this season from Blum & Company's warehouse.

Preparations are under way for the Twenty-fifth Annual Exhibit of the County Fair. The Grangers of Contra Costa are discussing the propriety of combining for making a general display of farm products.

The Martinez postoffice has been raised to the dignity of a third-class salaried office.

Our warehouse capacity is shown in the subjoined table, which includes all the warehouses in the county except that of the State Grangers' Business Association located on the Straits:

G. W. McNear, Port Costa	42,000	tons
Contra Costa County Grangers', Martinez	6,200	tons
Starr & Company, Crockett	50,000	tons
Blum & Company, Martinez, (two grain warehouses)	2,700	tons
Blum & Company, Martinez, (two hay warehouses)	900	tons
Blum & Company, Pacheco, (two grain warehouses)	2,550	tons
Blum & Company, Pacheco, (two hay warehouses)	500	tons
Blum & Company, San Pablo	1,500	tons
Blum & Company, Brentwood	2,500	tons
Blum & Company, Byron	1,500	tons
B. Fernandez, Pinole	3,400	tons
Nevada Warehouse & Dock	90,000	tons
Contra Costa County Grangers', Crockett	10,000	tons
Total warehouse capacity for County	213,750	tons

August 29, 1885.—The bell for the Congregational church arrived a few days ago. It weighs 900 pounds.

September 5, 1885.—The County Fair will open Monday on the grounds of the society near Pacheco.

September 12, 1885.—Dr. Strentzel shipped this week a large assortment of fruit to the Louisville Exposition and will continue shipments during the Fair.

The Alhambra Grange of Martinez will celebrate its eleventh anniversary at Grange Hall next Saturday afternoon by a harvest festival.

Entries at the County Fair were almost one-half less than last year.

September 19, 1885.—A small distillery outfit was captured above Antioch by United States officers.

M. Cohen, of Danville, announces that on account of ill health he will sell his business and retire.

September 26, 1885.—Patrick Brown was appointed supervisor for District No. 4, to fill the vacancy caused by the death of John D. Bowen.

The sale of delinquent steel stock took place Saturday at the office in the Gazette Building. . . . The amount received on the assessments will pay all debts of the county. An offer has been accepted from a Stockton man to rent the building for a foundry, but he has not qualified as yet.

Thomas & Baldwin have fitted up a drug store in the new Fernandez Hotel building.

October 3, 1885.—Dr. Strentzel has succeeded in getting grapes to Eastern markets safely. The fruit was carefully packed in carbonized bran, which appears to have answered the purpose. He packed four boxes in a different manner and shipped them as an experiment.

The Cook ranch stock, which has won premiums at the Golden Gate, State and Stockton Fairs, were returned to the ranch Monday.

The board of directors of Martinez Free Library and Reading Room met last Tuesday evening, organized, and elected the following officers: A. Tait, president; Miss Maggie McMahon, treasurer; Miss Alice Bush, secretary; John L. Chase, librarian. It was determined to open a reading room at once, and the public was invited to make use of its privileges.

There are but few residents remaining in Nortonville. Somersville is a little better situated, as the Rankin mine is still working. Just now the outlook for coal is not very bright.

At Selby's Smelting Works about $30,000 in gold and 30,000 ounces of silver are being handled each day. The well at the works is now down 620 feet.

On the night of October 6, the Orinda Park School was destroyed by fire, the work of an incendiary, no doubt.

Martin Bonzagni has purchased the interest of his partner in the soda works at Pacheco and will conduct the business alone.

November 14, 1885.—The new Congregational church was dedicated Sunday at Martinez, and C. S. Vaile was installed as pastor.

November 21, 1885.—The warehouses at Port Costa are about filled with wheat, most of which is being loaded into ships direct from the cars.

Point of Timber rejoices over another rain.

The Landing Company have gotten through the first year of their canal, as boats come and go without getting stuck in mud.

Byron Hotel, built on the ruins of the old one, is about completed and adds much to the appearance of the town.

D. R. Thomas, of Martinez, will soon commence tunneling for water in the hills on his own premises near town. He already has two tunnels, one 184 feet and the other over 200 feet long, and during the summer he has supplied several with good water. He proposes to extend the tunnels and run two more. If he can furnish Martinez with one-fourth of the water required, it will be a benefit.

The new county map was completed a few weeks ago and accepted by the supervisors. It is an admirable work and will prove valuable for reference and general information regarding the outlines of the county, its water-front, roads, rivers and creeks, boundaries, grants, towns and general topography.

The marriage of Miss Baudelia Soto and A. J. Galindo, Jr., was celebrated December 13, 1885.

December 26, 1885.—Martinez Cornet Band has been organized with the following members: A. E. Blum, G. Shirley, T. A. McMahon, J. L. Chase, A. J. Soto, F. Berryessa, W. A. Hale, R. Harvard, F. M. Smith, Henry Curry and W. R. Matthews. Prof. Fred Schmidt, of Stockton, was engaged as instructor.

January 1, 1886.—Rainfall to date, 13.83 inches. The farmers in the county are anxiously waiting for the ground to get dry enough to plow.

Business transacted at the Depot in Martinez for December: Shipped to San Francisco, 81,700 pounds of barley, 2 cows, 2 calves, 2 horses, 1000 pounds dried fruit, 3980 pounds wine, 11,500 pounds grape fruit, 719,186 pounds wheat; to Port Costa, 146,200 pounds barley; to Oakland, 5 bulls; to San Jose, 83,120 pounds general merchandise. Received, 360,000 pounds general merchandise.

January 9, 1866.—The Fernandez Hotel has been leased by H. R. Wright for five years.

W. R. Matthews is canvassing the town to see what chance there is of the citizens' subscribing for a gas company, with proposed capital of $50,000. If that amount is raised, M. G. Elmore of San Francisco will subscribe $20,000.

The Martinez Free Library and Reading Room opened October 7, and began with 130 books; there are now 300 books, in addition to magazines and other periodicals. The room used is donated by Dr. Strentzel.

Walnut Creek has the honor of starting the anti-Chinese movement in this county. A meeting was held on January 27.

John Gambs, of Pacheco, has over 13,000 gallons of wine stored in his cellar.

Selby's Smelting Works use over 400 tons of coal per month.

Antioch's new postmaster, ex-Sheriff D. P. McMahon, took charge of the office on January 25.

February 6, 1886.—The Martinez Hotel, in the Fernandez Building, was opened to the public Tuesday evening. A grand ball was held Friday evening.

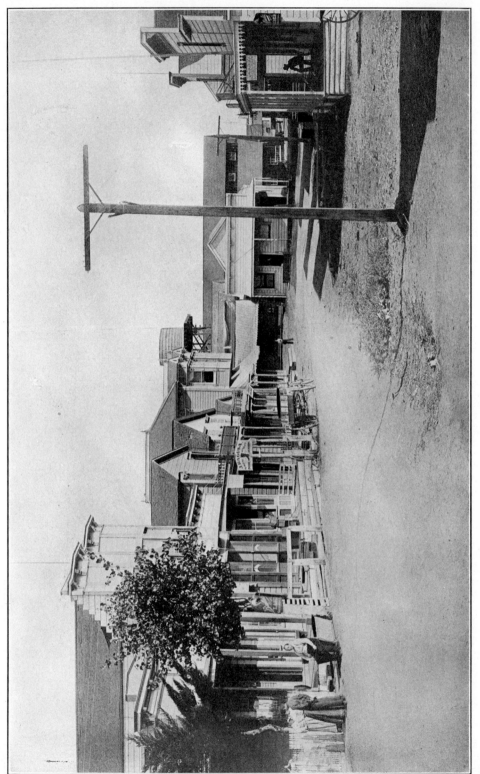

EARLY DAYS, PITTSBURG, CALIFORNIA

February 13, 1886.—An anti-Chinese meeting is called for Monday evening at the Court House.

There was a slight earthquake felt Wednesday evening at nine-thirty o'clock.

Charles Ludden is making a lot of gymnasium apparatus for the Martinez schoolyard, for the boys and girls. The children should be supplied with all needful appliances for obtaining healthful exercise.

Contra Costa County is destined to become a paradise of vineyards and orchards, of which Ygnacio and Diablo Valleys will be the central portion.

Mrs. Corbett, the postmistress, has decided to move into the new Martinez Hotel building, and a large corner room is being fitted up for the office.

March 30, 1886.—Brentwood is booming right along and will be a lively town this summer.

Dr. H. V. Mott has been appointed postmaster at Brentwood.

A branch of the Y. M. I. is being organized in Martinez. Father Aerden has been made temporary president, and Will Lawlers, secretary.

Curry & Jones have secured the contract for carrying the mail over the route from Martinez through Pacheco, Concord, Antioch, Judsonville, Stewartville, Somersville, and Nortonville, for the next four years.

The California and Nevada Railroad Company have put on trains between San Pablo and Oakland. They will soon connect up San Pablo Creek with the Walnut Creek stage.

April 3, 1886.—The new Methodist Episcopal church at Lafayette will be dedicated tomorrow.

The fare from San Francisco to Stockton is ten cents via the river boats. The fare from Port Costa to Stockton via the Southern Pacific is $2.30.

April 10, 1886.—An exciting baseball match took place at Martinez Sunday between the "Courthouse Gang" and the "Down Town Chumps." Seven innings were played and the final score was 35 to 18 in favor of the Chumps. The game was enjoyed by both participants and spectators.

April 17, 1886.—Y. M. I. No. 25 was organized Sunday at the Catholic church, with 50 charter members. James Kenna was elected president.

Up to May 1, 1886, the seasonal rainfall is 23.48 inches.

B. J. Murphy has been appointed postmaster for Concord, and Mrs. A. Guyeth for Walnut Creek.

W. R. Matthews has started a movement for holding a fair in Martinez during the stay of the G. A. R. visitors in San Francisco, about the middle of August, for the purpose of displaying the various resources of the county. At the conclusion of the fair the exhibits are to be taken to San Francisco and displayed there. Every farmer in the county is requested to make exhibits of everything raised from the soil.

May 22, 1886.—The Pacific Yacht Club will sail up to Martinez tomorrow.

Ninety degrees in the shade Sunday.

John Conway has been appointed postmaster at Danville.

Justice of the Peace F. M. Smith and Miss Libbie Tibbetts were united in marriage Thursday morning, May 20, 1886, by Judge A. Van R. Paterson.

A new warehouse for Blum & Company is being erected at Bay Point, upon the site of the old one that was blown down two years ago. The new building is 150 by 44 feet. They will also erect a small station house, as Bay Point is a flag-station.

May 29, 1886.—W. B. Thomas has purchased E. W. Hiller's ice business.

Vessels at Nevada Dock are storing away grain at the rate of 100 car-loads per day. The accumulation of cars on Tuesday was 450.

June 12, 1886.—The El Cierbo Hotel at Selby was opened on Saturday, June 5, with a grand ball. The proprietor, Mr. Pickford, is to be congratulated on his well-appointed place.

June 19, 1886.—Mrs. B. J. Murphy has been appointed postmaster at Concord.

An interesting game of ball was played Sunday at the new recreation grounds in Martinez between the Haymakers of Clayton and the 2nd nine of the Martinez club. The score was 16-17 in favor of Martinez.

June 26, 1886.—The new schoolhouse at Port Costa is finished, and reflects credit on Mr. Casey, chairman of the board of trustees, and Mr. O'Donnell, the contractor. It is located near the old building on a lot 75 by 100 feet.

Amount of tax levied $3,750.00
Losses from various sources 1,102.00
                                                                    _____
                                                                    $2,648.00
Cost of building $1,600.00
Cost of lot 1,000.00
Fencing, etc. 298.00

July 10, 1886.—For the first time since 1854, when Colonel Baker delivered a thrilling oration, the Fourth of July was celebrated in Martinez in a manner worthy of the day and its associations. Nearly every building in town was decorated and every individual exerted himself to add to the temporary attractions. A fine procession wended its way through the principal streets, headed by Grand Marshal L. C. Wittenmyer and his aides, A. J. Soto, Myrtel Blum, Frank Glass and James Briare. The floats were numerous and well named. The principal address was made by General G. W. Bowie. An oration by Judge Paterson was also delivered. Two baseball games were played: One between Clayton and Martinez, with a score of 21 to 15 in favor of Martinez; and one between the

Martinez Club and the Hofberg Club of Pacheco, with a score of 4 to 5 in favor of Hofberg. The day ended with fire works and a grand ball.

July 17, 1886.—The Concord postoffice made a Money Order.

The narrow gauge has bought six new passenger coaches and two locomotives, which are to be put on the new lines from Oakland to Temescal.

The losses sustained from the extensive grain fires in Sycamore Valley were: Charles Wood, $2000; D. Sherburne, $300; J. D. Smith, $100; John Camp, $250; besides damages to pastures of the first two named.

July 31, 1886.—The new wagon road was completed July 30 from Martinez to Port Costa at a cost of $668 per mile. The contractor lost $137 on the job. The road will be continued on to Crockett.

August 7, 1886.—On Tuesday Judge T. A. Brown sent his resignation to Governor Stoneman, to take effect October 1, 1886. In July, 1885, he was stricken with paralysis while attending to the duties of his office.

September 4, 1886.—Work began on macadamizing Main and Ferry Street, of Martinez, Tuesday morning. It will take from sixty to seventy-five days to complete the contract.

The California raisin crop for this year is estimated at 600,000 boxes.

September 18, 1886.—The Fair was very successful and reflects credit upon Contra Costa County.

The delegates of the Congregational churches of Solano and Contra Costa Counties held their conference in the Congregational church at Martinez.

J. J. Jones, of the Alhambra Poultry Yards, received premiums at the State Fair for the best breeding hens of Dark Brahmas, Buff Cochins, Plymouth Rocks, Brown Leghorns, White Leghorns, one male and four females each; the best Brown Leghorn cockerel and pullet; the best White Leghorn cockerel and pullet; and the best Houdan cock and hen.

October 2, 1886.—The first shower of the season occurred Thursday.

Port Costa, October 9, 1886.—McNear is building a warehouse, 100 by 100 feet, between Burke's Hotel and the railroad. It is intended tor storing hay, potatoes, etc., and will be fireproof.

Brentwood Lodge, No. 243, A. O. U. W., was installed Saturday evening in Wristen's Háll by District Deputy Grand Master Frank Coleman and State Deputy Frank S. Poland.

Pierce Ryan, of Byron Hot Springs, is having an addition to the hotel erected. It will be 150 feet long and two stories high.

October 23, 1886.—Judge Warmcastle received his commission Saturday and opened court Monday morning.

There will be a grand turnout this evening at Martinez to listen to Hon. James McKenna and J. P. Abbott at Bennett's Hall. The Concord Brass Band has been engaged for the occasion.

The Martinez town trustees have purchased a hook and ladder truck for $225, the original cost of which was $600. About $30 will put it in fine order.

November 13, 1886.—The Terry residence, near Clayton, was totally destroyed by fire; estimated loss, $20,000, half of which is covered by insurance.

A special election was held in Township No. 5. J. J. Burke was elected.

January 15, 1887.—The lower portion of Ferry Street is being repaired by the railroad company.

The Port Costa Lumber Company is located at Valona, having acquired Smith & Moore's business and franchises, one from Dr. Strentzel, and one from Prof. John Muir, which includes the entire water-front from Starr's Mills at Crockett to Vallejo Junction. A contract for 1500 feet of wharf, 200 feet wide, has been let. The company is a combination of all the Oregon pine lumber interests of the Coast, and the new yards will be the general coast distributing point.

January 22, 1887.—3.68 inches of rain have fallen, as against 15 inches for 1886.

Feburary 5, 1887.—Mount Diablo Parlor No. 101, N. S. G. W., was organized in the Odd Fellows Hall this week by C. M. Belshaw, of Antioch. The following were elected: A. E. Dunkel, Past President; T. A. McMahon, President; W. T. Wallace, Jr., C. Y. Brown, and James Johnston, First, Second and Third Vice-Presidents; F. L. Glass, Recording secretary; Guy Shirley, Financial Secretary; A. E. Blum, Treasurer; H. E. Curry, Marshal.

The twelve instruments for the new Cornet Band of Martinez arrived Thursday.

February 12, 1887.—The snowstorm of Saturday was a surprise. Up to yesterday noon we have had 7.47 inches of rain for the season. In the interior of the county the rainfall has been much heavier.

The first ball of the Black Diamond football club will be held in the Black Diamond Hall Tuesday evening.

Quite an exodus from the coal mines of this county to Washington Territory has recently taken place.

That portion of Main Street one block below the bridge has been macadamized and is now in fine shape.

March 5, 1887.—A Board of Trade was organized in Martinez by an enthusiastic assemblage held in the courthouse Saturday evening. The organization was fully perfected the following Thursday with 170 members. The following officers were elected: President, E. B. Smith; vice-president, S. Blum; treas., Bank of Martinez; sec'y, Will Acton.

The following communication speaks for itself:

Los Angeles, Calif., March 8, 1887.

L. I. Fish, Esq., Martinez, Calif.

Dear Sir: The box of fine navel oranges, lemons, and limes came this forenoon and are now doing duty in our show windows for Contra Costa County. Have labeled them as you desire and given them the center front of the window. They are very fine—no better anywhere. . . . Am glad you thought to send limes in all stages of growth, as it effectually disposes of the "frozen and snow-bound" business. . . . A good many come in and ask about them, etc. . . . Many say they will go north, where they can get soil at a reasonable price, with rainfall and climate thrown in.

Yours truly,
(Signed) E. W. Giddings,
Agent, Central and Northern California
Immigration Association.

Over $2000 have been subscribed to make known our resources. A general interest is manifested. The windows of the Board of Trade room are gradually being filled with displays of products of the county. Every variety of temperate and semi-tropical products is grown in Contra Costa County—wheat, barley, alfalfa, fruit and vegetables. It has a climate that is unexcelled. The tide of immigration is setting this way. The Board of Trade numbers 200 members.

April 9, 1887.—The Board of Trustees of Martinez have determined to take steps to recover the block in the eastern portion of the town known as the Plaza. The block in question is claimed by S. Blum. The object of the board is to have the court definitely determine the ownership. The Plaza was a portion of the William Welch ranch. In 1851, when the town was platted by the heirs through Joseph Swanson, their agent, F. M. Warmcastle, Elam Brown, N. B. Smith, J. F. Williams, T. A. Brown, and others, purchased lots adjoining the square, which was known as the Plaza up to 1870.

April 16, 1887.—(Antioch Ledger)—N. W. Smith, of Lone Tree Valley, has 1600 almond trees, five to seven years old; also, 400 French prune, 600 apricot, 150 peach, 100 plum, sixty fig, sixty apple and pear, and twelve cherry trees.

May 7, 1887.—The old toll road from Redwood Canyon to East Oakland may now be traveled free of charge, the franchise having expired.

3000 tons of rails will be required for the new double track between Oakland and Port Costa. The track will be twenty-two miles long.

R. D. Thomas has purchased a tract of land in the flat south of town for the purpose of boring for water. He is of the opinion that he can furnish ample water for private and public use. He also believes that he can furnish electric lights.

May 28, 1887.—The trustees of the town met Tuesday evening and granted a permit to D. R. Thomas to lay four-inch pipes in the streets for supplying the town with water for a term of twenty years.

The annual meeting of the Contra Costa County Agricultural Society was held in Concord on Saturday and plans for reorganization were made.

June 4, 1887.—Express offices were opened this week by Wells-Fargo & Company in John Conway's store at Danville and in H. C. Hurst's store at San Ramon.

Why use tugs? To the surprise of everybody in Martinez, the large bark-rigged ship "Roswell Sprague," capacity 1000 tons, came up the

Straits last Sunday under full sail in a spanking breeze and dropped anchor off the head of Grangers' Wharf, having on board 600,000 feet of cedar plank and timber for railroad bridges, tunnels, culverts, etc., being constructed along the line.

Mr. Thomas is now actively engaged in supplying the town with water. He has seven wells on his tract in the flat, 5½ to 7 inches bore, all connected with one main. His 50,000-gallon tank at the wells is full, and his engine is at work every day pumping to the main reservoir. He expects to have water in the town mains within a week.

July 2, 1887.—During the present week Mr. Thomas has placed about 1500 feet of pipe leading water to the residences of E. R. Chase, O. L. Morgan and Alexander Tait.

July 30, 1887.—Water rate fixed at $3.75 per month, per hydrant, to be paid D. R. Thomas by the town of Martinez.

July 30, 1887.—Concord is to organize a Y. M. I. tomorrow.

Things are booming at Nevada Docks, Port Costa, Crockett, Valona and Selby.

The postoffice at Moraga has been discontinued and its business transferred to Oakland.

A slight idea of the vast quanity of wheat going into the warehouses may be gathered from the fact that 580 carloads arrived at Port Costa in one night last week.

West Hill Water Works, owned by D. R. Thomas, will supply 20,000 gallons daily to the Southern Pacific Railway.

August 20, 1887.—The Martinez Hook & Ladder Company, headed by the band, paraded the streets last evening and made a fine showing.

August 27, 1887.—The Martinez Gas Company will commence building their works Monday. A lot has been purchased from S. Blum & Company of ample dimensions for their requirements. The stock of the company is about all taken, and gas for Martinez is assured at three dollars per thousand cubic feet.

Contra Costa wants telegraphic facilities.

September 10, 1887.—The boom has reached Byron and extensive improvements are being made in that wide-awake and rapidly progressing town. A new Congregational church, a commodious schoolhouse, and a fine lumber yard have been erected, and the contractors have just completed the finest town hall in Contra Costa County.

The boom has struck Danville; two real estate offices have been opened, and several of the old residents have sold out.

September 17, 1887.—The San Francisco and San Joaquin Valley Railway Company was incorporated last Saturday, capital stock $10,000,-000, for the purpose of carrying freight and passengers from a point at or near Antioch, Contra Costa County, to a point near Rogers, Kern County, 380 miles.

Work is being pushed rapidly on the gas works. A force of men are engaged in laying pipe mains through the streets.

October 1, 1887.—On Monday some twenty of the Martinez sports-men signed their names for the purpose of organizing a gun club. The following names were enrolled: Ed. Morgan, W. A. Hale, A. P. Nelson, W. J. Douglas, George Gill, L. D. Anderson, E. J. Summerfield, T. S. Davenport, A. E. Blum, George McMahon, J. P. Briare, Charles Hewitt, Charles Wright, C. E. Curry, F. A. Hodapp, T. A. McMahon, R. A. Fraser, Harry Moore, Frank Prairo and Steve Bennett.

The new Methodist Episcopal church at Byron is rapidly nearing completion.

Semi-annual report of Librarian:
Number of books in library..............................601
Number of paper-covered books....................301
Number of books purchased since April.........84
Number of books donated since April............10
Average attendance at Reading Room............25
(Signed) Martha C. McMahon
Cash on hand for fiscal year ending on October 4, 1887 ....$ 37.05
Total expense for year.............................$284.10

October 22, 1887.—Sixty-two teachers attended the Institute at Concord.

The first meeting for the purpose of the organization of the stock-holders of the Martinez Gas Company was held October 20. Dr. J. Strentzel was elected president; R. R. Bunker, vice-president; Alex Bad-lam, secretary; R. R. Thomas, treasurer.

November 5, 1887.—On Sunday evening, for the first time in its history, gas was lighted in Martinez for public use.

The main streets have been macadamized. The West Hill Water Works provide ample water. A fine fire company has been organized; also the Martinez Brass Band.

November 19, 1887.—The fiftieth anniversary of the marriage of Mr. and Mrs. Matthew Barber was celebrated November 14, 1887, when about 140 of their personal friends, old and young, assembled at the family homestead. Lunch tables were spread and filled with good things to eat. A pleasant time was enjoyed by all.

The Thanksgiving ball given by the Martinez Military Band was a so-cial and financial success. Tasty and elaborate decorations were made. A novel grand march was a feature of the evening. A large attendance enjoyed the sumptuous feast.

December 3, 1887.—The new string band recently organized in Martinez has begun practicing and soon will be able to furnish excellent music for dances. Max Blum, first violin; A. E. Blum, second violin; Professor Leroy, cornet; C. H. Wright, double bass. Two more pieces are soon to be added.

December 17, 1887.—The Native Daughters of the Golden West, Ramona Parlor No. 21, was duly initiated at the Knights of Pythias Hall last Saturday evening. List of officers: Mrs. Lizzie Russell, President; Mrs. C. K. Wittenmyer, Past President; Mrs. Emma Case, First Vice-President; Babe Jones, Second Vice-President; Jennie Fraser, Third Vice-President; Kate Potwin, Recording Secretary; Cora Hough, Financial Secretary; Mame Jones, Treasurer; Maggie Carrigan, Inside Sentinel; Ella Swain, Outside Sentinel.

The California Steamship Navigation Company has bought the Walker, and now the fare, by river, from San Francisco to Stockton is seventy-five cents.

December 24, 1887.—The twenty-fifth anniversary of the marriage of Mr. and Mrs. Henry Raap was remembered by their numerous friends at their home on the outskirts of Martinez.

January 4, 1888.—The Gazette appears today in a new form as a semi-weekly paper with a new dress.

January 7, 1888.—M. Cohen, formerly of Danville, has opened a store in the Martinez Hotel building.

January 11, 1888.—During the past three or four days the weather has been cold about Martinez; in fact, the coldest since 1854. The thermometer has been down as low as 26 degrees. Ice over an inch thick has been taken out of troughs, and every puddle is frozen over.

January 14, 1888.—Twenty-two degrees was reported at the depot at 6:30 a. m.; 18 degrees at Pacheco; 14 degrees at Walnut Creek. Water pipes burst in a most extravagant manner and plumbers were in great demand.

January 18, 1888.—The new hose cart ordered for the county arrived Sunday and is a beauty.

February 25, 1888.—The opening of coal mines at Somersville has been the means of employing many men at that place, and it is now one of the liveliest in the county.

February 29, 1888.—The Steamer Julia was blown up at 6:10 Monday, as it was leaving the wharf at South Vallejo with seventy passengers on board, about forty of whom were killed. The steamer was burned to the water's edge. Fire was communicated to the petroleum tank on the wharf, and soon the whole structure was in flames.

April 4, 1888.—The Town Improvement Commission met last Saturday at the courthouse and endorsed the movement for roads, bridges, town hall and other improvements.

A Leap Year Ball was given by the Native Daughters of the Golden West and was largely attended. Splendid music was rendered. The grand march was led by Mrs. L. T. Russell, president, and A. T. Gartley.

April 7, 1888.—The ninth anniversary of the Concord Hook & Ladder Company, No. 1, was celebrated Thursday, April 5. The Concord and Martinez bands were in evidence, and the Martinez Fire Department was out in full force. A grand ball was held, followed by a grand feed. The celebration was a grand success.

May 26, 1888.—A fine new Cottrell cylinder press has just been installed in the Gazette office. It is a fine piece of machinery.

September 18, 1889.—The work of clearing away debris and rebuilding the burned portion of Port Costa is progressing rapidly. The new warehouse will be 1500 by 100 feet, and much more spacious than before.

The new residence erected for C. S. Cousins, of Pinole, is now completed.

The Twenty-ninth Annual Fair of the Contra Costa County Agricultural Society, but in reality the first of Agricultural District No. 23, will open Monday, September 23.

October 2, 1889.—John L. Heald, of Heald's Foundry at Crockett, has finished putting in the wine-making machinery at Senator Hearst's place in Sonoma.

October 9, 1889.—The first rainfall of the season, that of Monday, was phenomenal; 1.50 inches fell during the day, which is remarkable for the first rain.

October 9, 1889.—The extensive agricultural works at Crockett owned by J. L. Heald have been incorporated. Mr. Heald started the business originally at Vallejo. Under the new management the works will be enlarged.

October 12, 1889.—Thursday afternoon the last blow was struck by the contractor on the new bridge. That evening the band turned out to celebrate the event.

The old zinc warehouse at Ferry Wharf, an old landmark built in 1850, in Martinez, is being torn down by George T. Bush. The older residents will remember that steamers landed at this warehouse and discharged their cargoes.

October 26, 1889.—The Walnut Creek Library will be opened on Monday evening, October 28, under the name of the San Ramon Valley Library.

November 2, 1889.—A company has been formed in St. Paul to operate an extensive cannery at Martinez, and will occupy the old steel plant.

A paper mill for Antioch is about to be established.

November 6, 1889, a heavy frost was felt at Danville.

December 7, 1889.—The Ramona Parlor, Native Daughters of the Golden West, will give a fancy dress ball on their anniversary, next Tuesday evening.

Mrs. L. M. Willis has sold the Antioch Ledger to Mr. Gill, of Lemoore, and is going to retire.

December 18, 1889.—On Monday afternoon, about three o'clock, the 50,000-gallon water-tank of the West Hill Water Company, which was filled to overflowing, suddenly burst, throwing water, splinters and iron hoops in all directions.

January 18, 1890.—Twenty-eight years ago last Saturday, January 11, 1862, occurred the great flood in California, an event which has served as a date from which to determine the period of other occurrences. In the season of 1861-1862 there was 10.80 inches of rain previous to January 1. In January, 15.36 inches of rain fell, and that heavy fall caused the devastating flood. This season there was 20.58 inches before January 1.

January 22, 1890.—Eight carloads of fruit were shipped from Martinez during the season of 1889.

At a meeting of the citizens of Pacheco, January 13, a club called the Pacheco Social Club was organized. P. G. Loucks was elected president; George Holmes, secretary; and R. Angelo, treasurer.

The new depot at Crockett is now covered.

The great storm, general all over the State, caused damages in every section. In Visalia boats were plying up and down Main Street Saturday noon. Stockton was flooded and the city plunged in total darkness Saturday night. Heavy snow-slides were reported at Downieville and Sierra City. Los Angeles and San Bernardino suffered severely. In Contra Costa County, Pacheco Valley was one sheet of water, and it invaded Concord for the first time. Stages were delayed. Telegraph and telephone wires were down. There were heavy slides between Martinez and Port Costa. The inclemency of the weather has been a detriment to business in general.

February 1, 1890.—We now have had 29.41 inches of rain.

Danville, Brentwood and Walnut Creek all report isolation on account of bad roads and storms.

February 26, 1890.—The season's rainfall is 35.41 inches. The heaviest recorded was for 1852-1853, when 36.36 inches fell at Sacramento. This season is pretty sure to pass that record.

Briones Valley takes the lead in the county in rainfall, 47.50 inches. Snow fell to the depth of an inch Thursday.

March 8, 1890.—There is now a really fair prospect of an amicable division of the San Pablo ranch. Nearly all of the claimants have agreed upon the terms of the division.

May 14, 1890.—Thursday morning the rain gauge added enough to bring the total to 40.53 inches as against 17.32 inches for 1889.

The Pinole Packing Company, after a considerable time, is at last assured. It is a syndicate represented by Garretson and Hetches of Sioux City, Kans. They will slaughter and pack meats and establish an industry for working up hides, etc.

April 19, 1890.—Steam was got up in the cannery on Thursday to put the machinery in motion and adjust the same.

April 30, 1890.—The new bell, weighing 2700 pounds, for the Catholic church, arrived at Martinez Saturday and was hauled to the churchyard, blocked up and rung for the first time. It has a deep tone.

May 17, 1890.—Strawberries have made their appearance in local markets and meet with ready sale. The first cherries of the season were received from H. Raap in Martinez.

The Alamo bridge is completed on the Green Valley Road in the Walnut Creek district.

July 12, 1890.—A large warehouse belonging to S. Blum & Company goes up in smoke; loss $2500; insurance $1500.

August 13, 1890.—A handsome flag, 6 by 8 feet in size, having a large bear painted thereon, together with a staff, was presented to Mount Diablo Parlor No. 101, N. S. G. W., by some kind but unknown man.

September 6, 1890.—A fire at Brentwood destroyed Moody's & Brewer's smithy, Shafer's livery, and the entire printing establishment of Mr. Humphrey. The local paper was being issued, and only a few copies had been run off.

The Smith Mineral Springs in Alhambra Valley have been fitted up with bath tubs and are now open to the public.

Frank L. Glass announces himself a candidate for county clerk.

On September 22 the second fair under the new organization of Agricultural District No. 23 will open at the fair grounds.

September 24, 1890.—H. H. Markham, candidate for Governor, is announced to speak at Antioch September 26. He will be tendered a reception in Martinez between 10 and 12 o'clock that morning.

October 1, 1890.—Destruction of the saloon of Nicholas King by fire, in which King was fatally burned, and of the butcher shop of Minor Slater and the brick building occupied by James Morrow, occurred on Saturday. On account of no water pressure it was with difficulty that other buildings were saved.

Contra Costa County Improvement Association organized, and drew up by-laws for "The Contra Costa Association"; John Swett, president; E. B. Smith, secretary; J. H. Borland, vice-president, District No. 1; W. B. Rogers, vice-president, District No. 2; W. A. Patterson, District No. 3; M. Sickal, District No. 4; A. C. Hanley, District No. 5; Mrs. M. H. Bailhache, treasurer.

The condition of the monster ferry boat, Solano, is worrying the railroad authorities. She has never been out of the water since launched, and there is no dry dock in the State large enough to receive her. She must soon be repaired or sunk.

December 10, 1890.—Work on the San Ramon branch railway is progressing very satisfactorily. The ground is being graded for a depot. Rails a mile from Concord.

January 14, 1891.—The county census gives the population of the county as 13,515: whites, 12,978; Chinese, 468; Indians, 4; colored, 57; and Japanese, 8.

Fifteen new buildings have been erected in Pinole in the last year.

February 25, 1891.—Wheat is coming into Port Costa at a lively rate. There are now 500 cars in the yards.

Owing to another heavy landslide east of Nevada Dock last Monday, traffic via Martinez was shut off for several hours.

March 7, 1891.—A meeting of the Alhambra Cemetery Association was held. M. H. Bailhache called the meeting to order and trustees were elected to fill vacancies. The organization now stands: M. H. Bailhache, president; G. A. Sherman, vice-president; L. C. Wittenmyer, secretary, superintendent and treasurer: trustees, M. H. Bailhache, G. A. Sherman, L. C. Wittenmyer, L. S. Davenport and E. Morgan.

March 11, 1891.—A baseball club was organized in Martinez Saturday evening, with Real Sharp, manager; George Woolbert, captain; Albert Hickman, secretary and treasurer.

March 28, 1891.—The four-masted schooner Kitsap arrived Saturday with 950,000 feet of lumber and lath for Port Costa Lumber Company at Vallejo Junction. In docking her, the wharf was rammed and damaged to the extent of several hundred dollars.

Last Sunday the first service was held in the new church at Port Costa.

According to the census returns, Mount Diablo district still furnishes the greater portion of coal produced in California. There has been a revival, to some extent, in mining operations.

April 15, 1891.—Dunham, Carrigan & Company have bought the Heald Mill at Crockett and have made Mr. Heald manager.

April 25, 1891.—President Harrison's train made a short stop at Martinez. An anvil salute was fired by A. Grimes. A delegation of leading citizens met the train. The school children were out in full force and presented him with a fine basket of flowers, and the Native Daughters presented another to the President's wife; other bouquets were presented by individuals. James McKenzie was one of the Presidential party.

April 25, 1891.—Papers of the incorporation of Contra Costa Gas & Water Company have been completed and sent to Sacramento for filing. Prospects for obtaining both water and gas seem to be very good.

Railroad graders have passed Danville and track-laying is under full swing.

April 29, 1891.—Brentwood turned out in full force to greet President Harrison's train. After a short speech and hand-shaking, the train departed amid cheers for the President.

On April 22, 1891, the Golden Wedding anniversary of George P. Loucks and his wife was fittingly celebrated at their residence by their many friends.

The construction train was run upon the Walnut Creek depot grounds April 21; the gravel train arrived April 29. The grounds for the depot were donated by Mr. and Mrs. Botillo. Two trains daily run from Emery Station to Orinda Park.

At the Monday session of the board of supervisors, Charles Wood of Danville was appointed public administrator to fill the vacancy caused by the death of Mr. Scammon.

May 27, 1891.—Articles of incorporation have been filed in the county clerk's office by the Gas & Water Company.

A destructive fire at Crockett last Monday evening destroyed Ed. Summerfield's drug store, Lasell & Brothers' dry goods store, Eckley & Bartlett's butcher shop, and Cavanaugh's saloon. Total loss, $35,000, only partly insured.

May 30, 1891.—Four locomotives at Danville at one time impart a lively appearance to the neighborhood.

The Martinez school census showed the following results for children between the ages of five and seventeen years: Boys, white, 151; girls, white, 159; Negro boys, 4; Negro girls, 6; Indian, 1. Total, 321.

June 6, 1891.—Commencing Sunday, the 7th, the San Ramon Branch organization will open for freight and passenger business. The opening marks an era in the history of Contra Costa County. Trains leave San Francisco at 7:30 a. m., arrive in Martinez at 9:29, leave Martinez at 5:10 p. m., and arrive in San Francisco at 6:45 p. m. Quite a number of residents of Martinez availed themselves of the opportunity of inspecting the line. There was also a delegation from San Francisco.

July 4, 1891.—The Signal Service Reports state that the temperature for June has been the highest for many years, if not the highest ever recorded in California.

At the conclusion of the day's festivities there will be a grand ball at Bennett's Hall under the auspices of Mount Diablo Parlor No. 101, N. S. G. W.

The railroad company has had another well bored near the depot at Concord. An artesian flow was struck at a depth of fifty-seven feet, flowing 1000 gallons per minute, four feet over the top of pipe. A valuable artesian belt has been opened.

July 15, 1891.—The late fire on the east side of Mount Diablo inflicts a heavy blow on the stockmen, the feed having been entirely destroyed over a large area.

Deeds by the following persons to the Southern Pacific for right of way of the San Ramon Railroad have been filed at the recorder's office: J. D. Smith, J. A. McGovern, Mrs. A. Love, D. P. Smith, W. W. Cox, Manuel Sherman and Maria Sherman, C. Waite, William Meese, R. O. Baldwin, Eli R. Chase, J. B. Moraga and L. P. Moraga, John Baker, M. D. Young, John Wilhelm, Felipa Soto de Welch.

The Nevada Docks will be quite deserted as soon as Eppinger & Company leave. There will be only one shipper, William Dresbach. It would not be surprising if the Nevada Bank were to ship wheat on its own account.

July 29, 1891.—The county's wealth is estimated as follows: Real estate, $9,226,600; improvements, $1,805,010; city and town lots, $460,-

957; improvements thereon, $605,000; telephone and telegraph lines, $20,087; money, $50,428; solvent credit, $34,000; other personal property, $3,310,569; total, $15,571,651.

The mortgages in Antioch and Martinez amount to $50,984; on farm and other town property, $2,550,597; value of property affected by mortgage, $4,299,618; and assessed value of trust deeds and mortgages, $2,-601,581.

Acres sown to crops in 1891: Wheat, 44,500; oats, 1600; barley, 28,-400; corn, 2200; hay, 48,400. Acres planted to grapes, 4350; to fruit and nuts, 264,770.

August 8, 1891.—The Antioch Philharmonic Club has been organized with a membership of thirty-five. O. E. Swain is president.

August 29, 1891.—Twenty cars of fruit passed through Martinez on Thursday from San Ramon Valley, and large shipments are being made every day.

The Home Orchestra was organized on Thursday evening in Martinez. Its members are: Mrs. T. A. McMahon, Max Blum, Gustave Weiss, Miss Jennie Fraser, A. E. Blum, and Prof. W. B. Bartlett, who acts as leader.

The school districts composing the central portion of the county having voted for a Union High School, a meeting of the trustees of the several districts is called to meet at Walnut Creek on September 26. It is desired that parties having eligible sites submit their propositions to the trustees.

October 10, 1891.—On Tuesday evening, 3200 boxes of grapes were shipped from Martinez.

The Lumbermen's and Longshoremen's Association will give their first ball at Crockett on October 17.

October 14, 1891.—Decidedly the most severe earthquake shock experienced in this vicinity since 1868 occurred on Sunday evening at 10:30 p. m., lasting thirteen seconds. Clocks were stopped and light articles thrown from shelves, etc. In Napa the Masonic building was badly damaged, and at the State Asylum the inmates became almost uncontrollable.

Mahoney & Ivey have been awarded the contract for carrying mail from Martinez to Pacheco, and will run a stage twice a day.

October 28, 1891.—At the last meeting of the town trustees an order was made contracting to take gas for five months from November 1, the gas company furnishing burners at their own expense.

November 7, 1891.—The board of supervisors on Wednesday made an appropriation for one-third of the actual cost of the proposed Pacheco Canal to give relief to farmers of overflowed lands. This leaves $2000 to be contributed by those benefited.

December 26, 1891.—A disastrous fire visited the town Wednesday morning, about three o'clock, starting in a Chinese wash-house. It spread to the Commercial Hotel and the James Rankin building. The loss amounted to about $12,000.

January 16, 1892.—The Starr Mill began making flour last week.

January 16, 1892.—The new fire engine is expected to arrive today. More than ten times the cost of the engine would have been saved had it been on hand at the last fire. It is hoped it will prove satisfactory when the time comes to use it.

January 30, 1892.—The Martinez Military Band has been reorganized. A number of new musicians have been added, and their prospects for performance and efficiency are better than ever.

The "Boys' Brigade" being organized at Brentwood is very popular with all the boys from twelve to seventeen years of age. They have a regular uniform. The object is to produce habits of reverence and respect for authority.

February 3, 1892.—At a meeting in the town hall Monday evening the Martinez branch of the Merchants' Retail Commercial Agency was organized, with the leading merchants as members. There are agencies all over California, and now a branch at Antioch, Concord, Crockett, and all towns of the county.

February 24, 1892.—The Contra Costa Herald is a new eight-page paper at Brentwood. It is published by E. W. Netherton and is to be independent in politics.

March 3, 1892.—Brick is being manufactured at Pacheco at Blum's brickyard. This is the beginning of what promises to be an important industry for Contra Costa.

The country adjacent to Brentwood, known as Eden Plain, is rapidly being set to almonds and is destined to become a great center for that industry. William Shafer, Thomas Murphy, P. J. Moody, and E. W. Steading have set out twenty acres or more each.

March 16, 1892.—The foundation for the packing house is now laid at Rodeo. The building is to be of brick, four stories high, 150 by 175 feet. Work will also commence on the canning department.

The new hotel is now opened for business and is handsomely furnished, while the bar-room is the finest in the county.

April 13, 1892.—Over a year ago the Gazette published extracts from more than fifty papers about the ten-block system of naming roads and numbering county houses. Thus far no criticism has been made. Recent dispatches from Washington say that the postmaster general has become interested, as it remains the only obstacle to rapid and accurate service in the country. These dispatches have been published all over the country, and Contra Costa County has been mentioned in all of them.

David Bush and A. L. Bancroft are now at work interviewing Contra Costa people about money with which to measure our roads and block them off preparatory to numbering the country houses.

Hon. Joseph McKenna has presented each school in the county with a fine large map of the United States. In retiring from public office Mr. McKenna cherishes a feeling of kind regard for those whose confidence he has enjoyed.

April 23, 1892.—The Martinez Free Library Association has been compelled to vacate the place so long occupied and will be placed in the room formerly occupied by Mrs. Hollenbeck on Ferry Street.

The violence of the quake was felt here quite enough to satisfy almost everybody. At Dixon the Masonic Hall was badly damaged and will have to be taken down. The Odd Fellows' building at Vacaville is also in ruins.

On May 7, 1892, the Contra Costa Fruit Growers' Association was organized, with George Frazer, president; H. M. Bush, vice president; H. Raap, secretary; G. A. Putnam, treasurer.

Married, in Martinez, May 12, 1892, by Rev. D. W. Calfee, Edward W. Netherton of Brentwood and Miss Alice M. Carpenter of Martinez.

May 28, 1892.—A kiln of brick will soon be ready for the market from S. Blum's yard at Pacheco.

Martinez Steel Manufacturing Company: I will pay five cents per share for assessment-paid stock in this company. D. J. West.

July 6, 1892.—The day was made to order for the Antioch celebration of our national anniversary. The weather was ideal; a fine parade was had, including a number of floats, the Fire Department, and the Native Sons of Antioch and Martinez. Two bands furnished the music. The oration was delivered by Col. J. P. Irish. The day closed with a grand ball in the evening.

July 13, 1892.—The Giant Powder Works at Fleming's Point, West Berkeley, met with destruction in some five or six separate explosions about 9 a. m. Saturday. The concussions caused destruction to adjacent buildings, and to windows in Oakland, San Francisco and Berkeley. The shock was plainly felt in Martinez.

Danville Lodge No. 378, I. O. O. F., was organized July 26, 1892, with seven charter members; twenty-two new members were initiated.

August 13, 1892.—Last week parties leased 1000 acres in Briones Valley and are now prospecting for oil.

Nathaniel Jones and wife celebrated their Golden Wedding anniversary at Walnut Creek, Wednesday, August 10, 1892.

October 1, 1892.—The water question is getting to be a serious question in Martinez. A number of families are entirely dependent on the water-works for their supply and are cut off without a drop. The Water Company is under contract to supply the railroad; and as there is not water enough within reach of the shallow wells, the town is likely to be shut out entirely until the winter rains set in.

October 26, 1892.—Columbus Day was celebrated at Orinda Park by the teachers, pupils and parents of Mount Pleasant and Orinda Park school districts. The Alhambra School also celebrated the day with appropriate ceremonies.

Alamo and Port Costa held fitting exercises in honor of Discovery Day, October 21, 1892. Liberty, Byron, Oak Grove, Pacheco and Green Valley also held their celebrations in proper observance of the day.

November 23, 1892.—The work of measuring and blocking off the roads of the central part of the county, on the ten-block system, has been under way for some time. The committee on rural affairs are L. C. Wittenmyer, W. A. Kirkwood and A. L. Bancroft. H. M. Gregory has charge of the field work. Considerable money has been subscribed by San Francisco people.

November 30, 1892.—The Lafayette Hotel was totally destroyed by fire Sunday evening; also the stable and entire contents.

More than 100 miles of road have been measured off thus far in the new system of blocking.

January 14, 1893.—At a meeting of the town trustees Tuesday evening, an ordinance was introduced providing for a special tax levy to purchase a chemical engine for protection against fire.

January 21, 1893.—On Gwin Ranch, four miles east of Martinez, a flowing well is reported at eighty feet, yielding an inch stream. Shallow flowing wells are reported in Pacheco Valley; also at Concord, on the east side of Walnut Creek, at 160 feet.

A map of Contra Costa County is on exhibit at the Mechanics' Institute in San Francisco, showing the ten-block system of numbering houses and naming roads.

January 28, 1893.—The fine warehouse of J. A. Shuey at Danville was totally destroyed by fire Tuesday night, together with all its contents. There were 4000 tons of hay in storage. The contents and the building were well insured.

The Rodeo Daily News made its expected appearance on March 1, 1893. Ernest Hymens is the publisher and editor. It is an eight-page folio newspaper.

April 29, 1893.—The California & Nevada Railroad is completed to within three miles of Lafayette. This branch line is a private affair of the Grant Brothers.

Work will progress from now on upon the new ferry piers at Emeryville. It is proposed to construct two steel ferry boats.

May 13, 1893.—A local camp of the W. O. W. will be instituted at Masonic Hall Saturday evening, with thirty charter members. The name of the camp will be Laurel Camp No. 145.

The new owners of the Narrow Gauge have organized and elected officers as follows: J. S. Emery, president; E. A. Phelps, secretary; Abner Doble, J. J. Souvenir, George W. Schell, A. H. Clough, and William Thomas, directors. The road will be made a broad-gauge.

May 30, 1893.—The Rodeo Daily News suspended publication.

June 17, 1893.—E. W. Netherton and family have removed to Santa Cruz, where Mr. Netherton will be employed in the office of the Sentinel.

August 5, 1893.—The Rodeo Packing Company suspended on account of the present financial stringency.

10

Frank T. Swett, of Alhambra Valley, has just returned to Martinez after an extended visit to the East. He describes the stagnation in business and hard times among the laboring classes as deplorable. He happened to be in Manchester, N. H., when the great Amoskeag Mills closed. They are the largest in the world and had run continuously for thirty years. 8000 people are out of employment.

The Antioch Ledger goes from the control of C. F. Montgomery & Son to Prof. G. F. Foster, who has given ample evidence of ability in the editorial chair.

December 30, 1893.—Chris Evans, the train robber, who had been sentenced to prison for life for murder, made his escape from the Fresno County jail last Thursday evening.

March 10, 1894.—On Saturday last Judge J. C. B. Hubbard signed the decree for the partition of the San Pablo Ranch. It is a formidable document of 500 pages and will cost $300 to record. This ends a case that will go down in history as one of the most noted land contests in California. The amount and value of the land in dispute, the ability and repute of the counsel employed, and the length of time extended, have given it wide notoriety. Parties secure in the possession of their premises can now improve with security. A large increase in population can now be looked for, and general advancement of the whole section may be realized.

March 17, 1894.—Byron has a brass band of fifteen pieces, and it is very liberal with its services.

On Friday evening the Lafayette Improvement Club gave its initial party at Corvillo Hall. It was organized some weeks ago, with Ed. J. Brady, president. A sumptuous repast was served at midnight.

March, 1894.—Concord now has the fair grounds of the Agricultural Society, a fine railroad station, the Klein and Mount Diablo Hotels, the firms of Novas & Beebe, Randall Brothers, Henry Soto, Gambs & Kaliski, general merchants; M. M. Brackenridge, hardware; Maggie Soto, B. Neustaedter, dry goods; two harness shops; one bakery; two blacksmiths; three grain warehouses; one livery; one meat market; one drug store; the Weekly Sun; two doctors; the I. O. O. F. lodge; express office and postoffice; a hook and ladder company; a free reading room; a $15,000 school; three churches; a firemen's hall, and a hall for public meetings.

May 5, 1894.—Work was commenced Monday on the new sewer to run from Howard Street, near Dr. Tennent's residence, down Talbert to Main, and thence down Main to Castro to connect with the sewer laid last year.

The guide posts erected by the county are a great public convenience, and if they suffer at the hands of vandals it will go hard with the offenders. The Lasell Company have supplemented the useful work by placing distance posts along the highways out of Martinez.

June 2, 1894.—The machinery for the manufacture of gas has been placed in position and new rates will soon be announced.

July 14, 1894.—Ferry wharf is the most lively place in town. Since the tie-up of trains the mail, express, freight and passenger traffic is all handled by the California Transit Company.

July 26, 1894.—The Black Diamond Cannery, erected seventeen years ago, was burned to the ground. The cannery was owned by the Sacramento River Packers' Association, and was one of the best and most completely equipped on the coast.

Besides the cannery, the Southport Land and Commercial Company's wharf works, and a sloop owned by Gus Smith, and a plunger of the Sacramento River Packing Company were burned.

The board of supervisors has arranged the judicial townships and made provision so that but one justice and one constable be allowed to each township.

September 22, 1894.—The Lawless Block was destroyed by fire. A crowd gathered and worked to save Miss Shuey's millinery stock and the contents of the Free Reading Room in the Rankin Building.

The most successful fair held in many years, with an unprecedented attendance, was held this year by the Agricultural Society.

On September 22, a Rebekah Lodge was instituted at Danville by Grand Master J. H. Simpson, with twelve charter members. The degree of Rebekah was conferred on fifty-six new members by the Livermore Rebekah team. Mrs. Boydston was elected Noble Grand. After the usual speech-making, about 150 gathered around the banquet table.

September 29, 1894.—The thermometer ranged from 104 degrees to 110 degrees in the shade for the closing days of the week.

The town well for sprinkling purposes has been sunk to a depth of twenty-five feet and is eight feet square. It is quite likely to prove adequate for the purpose.

November 10, 1894.—The Walnut Creek Sentinel suspended publication with last Saturday's issue. The publishers found too small a field for their enterprise.

A ferry between Martinez and Benicia is now assured. It will make use of the Grangers' wharf and will be a great convenience to the public.

December, 1894.—A committee has been appointed to solicit subscriptions for the erection of a fireproof building for the Free Reading Room and Library.

January 5, 1895.—A heavy rain fell, flooding the country; rivers of water filled the city streets. The whole flat on the oustkirts of the town was a sea of water, and water came tearing down the city streets a foot or more deep. Smith, Castro and Las Juntas Streets carried a torrent. It was impossible to cross Main and Castro without high gum-boots. The storm is unprecedented since 1862.

The storm washed out several thousand feet of the Southern Pacific tracks, east of town, and there was a bad break in the embankment between Concord and Walnut Creek.

An earthquake shock on Thursday, the 24th, which lasted ten seconds, was the most severe experienced here for several years.

As a result of the severe rainstorm the county wagon-road to Oakland is blocked by a landslide of about 200,000 tons of earth and a detour is necessary. The slide covers an area 100 by 150 feet and is located about three miles from Oakland.

February 2, 1895.—A bell has been hung in the schoolhouse tower at Byron.

February 16, 1895.—There will be a mass meeting of citizens of Martinez and vicinity in the town hall on February 20 to take steps to induce the projectors of the San Joaquin Valley Railroad to make Martinez a station on the new line.

March 30, 1895.—The Mountain House on Mount Diablo is closed for lack of patronage.

April 6, 1895.—The San Pablo News made its first appearance.

April 20, 1895.—The Sunset Telephone & Telegraph Company has introduced the new long-distance system in Martinez. New wires will be strung through the streets, and the new phones will replace the old-style boxes. Some forty subscriptions have been received.

May 11, 1895.—Hart A. Downer has sold the Contra Costa News to A. Dalton, Jr., and last Wednesday's issue was circulated under the new management.

June 15, 1895.—180,000 tons of wheat, owned by the Fair interests, is being loaded at Port Costa for Liverpool. Two hundred men are employed and sixty-five ships will be required.

The Union Oil Company has purchased the real estate and wharf of the California Lumber Yard Company at Rodeo and intends to erect an oil refinery. The investment is about $100,000.

The Antioch High School was declared lapsed, in accordance with the law, on account of not being used for school purposes the allotted length of time.

Martinez is to have an academy where higher branches are taught and students prepared for the university. Revs. E. W. Stoddard and Hamilton Lee will have charge. It will open Monday, August 5, in Guild Hall of the Episcopal Church.

The roads of Contra Costa County are all named, and the ten-block system of numbering the country houses was adopted by ordinance No. 56 of the board of supervisors; and it now becomes the duty of the board to erect sign-posts and guide-boards. The roads are: No. 2, Contra Costa Highway; No. 3, Alhambra Way; No. 4, Franklin Road; No. 6, Hillsdale Local; No. 13, Camino Diablo; No. 16, Willow Pass; No. 62, Vista Ygnacio; No. 63, Valley Center Local; No. 63a, Ogontz Road; No. 64, Concord Lateral; No. 65, Via Concordia; No. 66, Linne Ridge Crossing; No. 78, Paso Nogal; No. 81, Granville Way; No. 85, Kent Road; No.

103, Golden Gate Way; No. 104, Walnut Way; No. 105, LaGrange Road; No. 106, Garden Annex; No. 110, Locust Way; No. 112, Sara Connex.

August 24, 1895.—C. H. Ludden was awarded the contract for the new library building, at $6371.

At their session Tuesday evening the town trustees passed resolutions to contruct cement sidewalks on the business sections of Main and Ferry Streets.

The town of Oleum is to be established on property owned by the Union Oil Company, and will mark the advent of a new industry in the county.

According to County Auditor Soto, under the present system we have paid out $1,700,000 for county roads during the past forty years.

The library, conceived in 1883, now has 1800 bound volumes and hundreds of volumes of unbound magazines, etc., and will soon be housed in its own building.

Establishment of a creamery at Walnut Creek opens up another industry for Contra Costa County.

The output of the coal mines of Contra Costa County during the year 1894 was valued at $94,000.

December 7, 1895.—R. R. Bunker, after thirty-six years as associate proprietor and editor of the Gazette, severs his connection, and W. C. Brown succeeds as sole editor and proprietor. He has been associated with the paper the past two and a half years.

On Monday evening, December 24, a meeting was held at Concord of some thirty men of Ygnacio Valley, to form an independent military company. A committee was appointed.

Simon Blum offers one or all of three tracts for the new site of the County Hospital.

January 4, 1896.—The Odd Fellows dedicated their hall at Concord on New Year's Eve.

Brentwood Lodge, A. O. U. W., has consolidated with the Point of Timber Lodge at Byron, making that the banner lodge of the county, with more than sixty members.

The furniture of the Antioch High School was sold at auction by Superintendent Phalin.

January 11, 1896.—Contra Costa Tent, K. O. T. M., was organized in Martinez Tuesday evening, with twenty charter members.

On Tuesday evening, January 9, a public installation of officers of the Court Todos Santos, A. O. F., was held in the Odd Fellows Hall.

March 14, 1896.—J. P. Briare has succeeded Mrs. E. L. Bailhache as postmaster. Mrs. Josie McCann will be retained as assistant.

April 3, 1896.—Members of the Martinez Board of Trade and Development Association held a meeting in the town hall and elected directors for the year: James Rankin, W. K. Cole, W. S. Tinning, F. A.

McMahon and R. H. Latimer.   James Rankin was elected president and W. A. Hale, secretary.

Milk was delivered to the Walnut Creek Creamery for the first time Monday, and their first churning was done on Wednesday.

The new officers elected at the town election Monday were: W. J. Douglas, treasurer; M. H. Hurley, clerk; J. J. Anderson, W. A. Hale, J. J. McNamara, W. R. Matthews, Mr. Blum.

May 26, 1896.—The campaign for woman suffrage was opened in Contra Costa County on Tuesday in the opera house. The meeting was called to order by Mrs. L. D. Fish, who introduced the national organizer, Miss Mary G. Hay. Rev. Anna Shaw and Elizabeth Upheim Yates also delivered addresses.

The celebration on July 4th was the best ever held in the county. The parade, over a mile long, was a feature deserving much praise, and the games were a pleasing feature. J. L. Geary was orator of the day. Ed. Randall was grand marshal; aides, Reese Jones, W. A. Hale and Theodore Moiles. L. C. Wittenmyer was president of the day. W. K. Coles and the Benicia ball teams played a good game, won by Martinez, 28 to 19. The visiting yachtsmen were tendered a barbecue and lunch. Fireworks in the evening were much enjoyed and the Native Sons ball was largely attended. Concord and Martinez bands furnished excellent music. Everybody had a good time.

August 8, 1896.—Free mail delivery for Contra Costa County.

November 7, 1896.—The Salvation Army has named their new farm for ex-convicts "Knights of Hope Farm." It consists of 300 acres near Pacheco, forty acres in fruit trees. The use of the farm has been given the Army by Mr. Montgomery, of San Francisco, with an option to purchase.

November 28, 1896.—Parlor No. 92, N. D. G. W., was instituted at Pinole with thirty-five members. First Past President, Nellie E. Barry; First President, Marie Fernandez.

December 5, 1896.—Morello, the horse that won the futurity stakes and Chicago Derby, died on the J. O. Rees ranch in this county November 29. He had been suffering from paralysis three months. He was valued at $100,000.

December 19, 1896.—It is rumored that two strangers dug up a bag of gold back of Rogers Hotel at Walnut Creek, last week, which had been buried several years ago by a murderer.

January 7, 1897.—A local lodge of the Knights of the Maccabees was organized.

January 11, 1897.—The Pinole Times and the Crockett Record were established.

January 30, 1897.—Simon Blum has an account book that is of interest, as it contains considerable information regarding the cost of laying out the town of Martinez and a list of those who purchased the first lots sold. The town was laid out and surveyed in blocks and lots in 1849.

Cost of Survey	$2500	Sails and work on boat	$ 300
Cost of map	100	Iron safe	50
Recording power attorney	6	Old power attorney	16
Stakes	150	Acknowledging deeds	187
Witnessing documents	50	Six cans paint oil	105
Lawyer's fees	12	Flat book	250
Printing deeds	240	Lawyers' fees, new deed form	400
Printing deeds	727	Acknowledging three deeds	6
Agent's salary	750	Anchor	14
Boat for town	250		

Lots 1, 2, 3, and 4, Block 2, A. Van Horne Ellis $400
Lots 1, and 2, Block 3, C. H. H. Cook 200
Lots 1 and 2, Block 8, W. M. Smith 200
Lots 1, 2, 3 and 4, Block 9, G. C. Wood 400
Lots 1 to 8, Block 10, T. Shilleber 800
Lot 1, Block 13, W. H. Taylor 100
Lots 1 and 2, Block 17, Thomas Smith 200

Then appear the names of other purchasers: Nicholas Hunsacker, Nathaniel Jones, Moses Wells, William Hendricks, Charles Johnson, M. D. Rickey; the latter paid $300 for Lot 8, Block 12.

Lots 3 and 4, Block 17, J. P. Stark $600
Lots 2 and 3, Block 19, O. D. Paulson 600
Lots 5 and 6, Block 20, G. W. Tucker 600

The Walnut Creek Creamery began operation March 10, 1897.

March 13, 1897.—Messrs. Stoddard and Lee have decided they cannot continue the Martinez Academy after the close of the present term. With the closing of the Academy, Martinez and vicinity will have no facilities beyond the grammar grades.

March 20, 1897.—H. H. Whitman, of Ygnacio Valley, is in receipt of his returns from New York of his pear shipment. Out of 780 boxes of Winter Nellis but five boxes were lost, netting him clear $739.74, or $147.95 per acre for five acres.

The Martinez Board of Trade was organized March 21, 1897.

March 27, 1897.—Married, in Antioch, March 22, 1897, by Rev. W. J. Brier, Jr., Mr. A. B. McKenzie of Martinez and Miss Melvina I. Durham of Concord.

April 24, 1897.—The Walnut Creek Hall Association has incorporated, and 5000 shares at par value of $20 have been subscribed. The Association will build a hall, which will be occupied by the Mount Diablo Lodge of Workmen and Central Parlor, Native Sons. The following leading citizens were elected to the board of directors: James M. Stow,

V. Hook, A. Legrecht, J. T. Breneman, C. Sharp, M. Kirsch and H. T. Jones.

On May 23, a barbecue was held at the William Buckley ranch, along which the road will wind to the mouth of the proposed tunnel that will pierce the hills, connecting Alameda and Contra Costa Counties. An inspection of the tunnel, which began twenty years ago and pierced the hill about 100 feet on the Contra Costa County side and 200 feet on the Alameda side, revealed the fact that it was completely filled with debris. Representative people were present from Alameda and Contra Costa Counties. Subscriptions were taken and $1600 was subscribed by Alameda citizens and $1200 by Contra Costa County—J. M. Stow, $500; J. O. Miner, $40; E. J. Hutchinson, $100; W. B. Rogers, $100; and A. Hemme, $100.

July 17, 1897.—The Martinez High School Association was organized with the following officers: Mrs. L. I. Fish, president; Mrs. T. A. McMahon, secretary; Mrs. L. M. Lasell, treasurer.

July 24, 1897.—The Martinez High School will occupy rooms on the ground floor of the Sherman homestead, the house recently vacated by Judge and Mrs. George F. Worth.

August 7, 1897.—The Martinez High School opened with an attendance of twenty-two pupils. The course is the same as at the Oakland High School. Prof. and Mrs. R. C. Bentley, of Nebraska, have been engaged to teach. It is to be hoped that a public high school may be established before the beginning of another school year.

August 21, 1897.—Papinta, the vaudeville favorite, has purchased a $15,000 ranch in Contra Costa County, 100 acres in Ygnacio Valley, four miles from Concord. Fifteen acres are in paper-shell almonds, fifteen acres in French prunes, and fifteen acres in vineyard.

October 17, 1897.—A local Parlor, N. D. G. W., was organized at Antioch.

November 20, 1897.—The Concord Courant is the new paper issued by H. A. Downer.

November 27, 1897.—This issue of the Gazette is published under the new ownership of G. E. Milnes, he having become editor and proprietor on this date.

January 15, 1898.—The News has changed hands, and under the new management of C. F. Montgomery will be called "The County Paper." It is an eight-page paper.

April 2, 1898.—The worst earthquake Martinez has experienced since 1868 occurred at 11:42 Wednesday night. Vibrations from northeast to southwest lasted forty seconds. There was another at 5 o'clock Thursday morning. It damaged the court house, cracking the wall in three places, and twisted and strained it. The library building was also damaged. James Stewart's store had everything, jams, jellies, etc., piled on the floor. In Alhambra Valley the shock was more severe. In Port Costa every saloon was wrecked.

The Women's Improvement Club elected permanent officers Tuesday evening: President, Mrs. E. L. Bailhache; first vice-president, Mrs. E. M. Taylor; second vice-president, Mrs. F. L. Glass; secretary, Mrs. M. B. Lander; assistant secretary, Mrs. Charles Curry; treasurer, Mrs. O. L. Marsh.

April 16, 1898.—After fourteen years of litigation in the courts of the State, Mrs. Kelly loses her suit in connection with the purchase of stock in the old steel works.

April 23, 1898.—Tuesday night a train bearing soldiers, horses and artillery passed through Martinez, and Wednesday evening two more went by, taking the soldiers to New Orleans and Key West.

May 28, 1898.—Martinez is patriotic. A company of volunteers is being formed and already fifty names have been placed on the muster roll.

The Martinez Red Cross held an enthusiastic meeting at Bennett's Hall on June 1.

June 4, 1898.—The Martinez High School Association has been organized for the ensuing school year: President, Mrs. James Rankin; vice-president, G. A. Sherman; treasurer, Mrs. L. M. Lasell; secretary, Mrs. T. A. McMahon. Mr. and Mrs. Bentley will remain as teachers. Pupils from outside the district will be welcome at a tuition of $5 per month. The home pupils' tuition will be $10 per month, as heretofore.

June 4, 1898.—The ladies of Walnut Creek and vicinity met at the home of Mrs. C. R. Leech and organized a Red Cross Society: Mrs. C. R. Leech, president; Mrs. Durham, vice-president; Mrs. E. Anderson, recording secretary; Mrs. Esther Williams, financial secretary; Mrs. James Hook, treasurer; Miss Zora Barry, corresponding secretary. The society held its first regular meeting at the home of Mrs. Arthur Williams, number 64.

June 11, 1898.—The ladies of Concord and vicinity have formed a Red Cross Society. The following officers were elected: President, Mrs. Dr. McKenzie; recording secretary, Mrs. Dr. Neff; financial secretary, Mrs. J. J. January; and treasurer, Mrs. James Boyd.

Joe Boyd, of Concord, proved his loyalty by paying the railway fare from Concord to San Francisco for every Concord recruit. He is rustling for members of the Red Cross, which now has fifty. Concord has ten young men in the army.

July 30, 1898.—An explosion in the nitroglycerine house at the California Powder Works at Pinole resulted in the death of four and the wounding of fifteen. There were two separate explosions about three and one-half hours apart.

September 3, 1898.—The occasion of the opening of the Town Hall at Walnut Creek caused quite a ripple of excitement in the social life of Walnut Creek and adjacent valleys. A splendid program was given, which was enjoyed by all present, including people from Oakland, San Francisco and Martinez, besides those living in and near Walnut Creek.

The hall was made possible through the generosity of Mrs. F. X. Hill and the A. O. U., and the untiring work of the women of Walnut Creek and vicinity.

September 7, 1898.—After an official canvass of votes of the election held to establish a Union High School, it was found that the proposition was defeated by fourteen votes.

September 17, 1898.—At the home of Mr. and Mrs. O. W. S. Burpee of Walnut Creek, the Golden Wedding anniversary of Mr. and Mrs. Albert Sherburne was celebrated. Two hundred invitations were issued.

December 10, 1898.—On December 5, the gelatine house of the Judson Powder Works was blown to atoms. C. D. Kennedy, the superintendent, and four Chinese were instantly killed.

On January 7, 1899, the Gazette was changed to a five-column eight-page paper under the ownership of G. E. Milnes.

It was decided in 1899 that the bridging of Carquinez Straits was impracticable. This was a subject that had been discussed for ten or more years by both the railroad company and various bridge companies of California. When the Solano was built, the railroad company asked the Government for a permit to build a bridge, which was denied.

February 25, 1899.—Considerable progress is being made on the Valley Road between Point Richmond and Stockton. The tunnel near Pinole will be completed in ninety days. It will not be long before the State will be reaping the advantages of the new railroad.

February 25, 1899.—A pressed brick and terra cotta depot is to be erected at Pacheco Landing by the railroad.

March 14, 1899.—The California and Nevada Railroad will pass into the hands of the Santa Fe. Capt. C. K. King is now in charge of the California and Nevada.

April 22, 1899.—The body of Hugh P. McClellan, one of the ten Contra Costa boys who early answered the call to arms, and who gave his life for his country, was brought back from the Philippines on the Ohio and laid to rest at Concord. He was born near Concord twenty-one years ago, the only son of Mr. and Mrs. Charles McClellan, and was a member of Co. I, 14th U. S. Infantry. He was shot in battle on February 5 at Manila and died from wounds. A military funeral was accorded him by the citizens of Concord, Pacheco and vicinity, and never in the history of the county has a more fitting tribute been paid to the memory of anyone.

May 6, 1899.—Attorney Hartley was appointed justice of the peace at Antioch.

May 13, 1899.—Holler & Company's fruit and salmon cannery at Black Diamond was burned to the ground last Wednesday evening.

The boring of the Pinole tunnel of the Valley Railroad, 18 feet square and 1045 feet long, is completed.

May 27, 1899.—Crack shots of the State are to assemble at Antioch for a two days' tournament of California Inanimate Target Association.

July 8, 1899.—Shortly after midnight Friday the big tunnel at Franklin Canyon was pierced by crews working from opposite sides.

July 22, 1899.—The almond growers of Contra Costa County met at Brentwood to organize a Contra Costa County Almond Growers' Association. William Shafer, of Brentwood, was elected president; J. W. Thomas, of Oakley, vice-president; R. J. Trembath, secretary; James O'Hara, S. C. Scott and A. M. Graves, executive committee.

C. K. King was succeeded as receiver of the California and Nevada Railroad by A. A. Grant.

During the recent National Educational Association convention held in Los Angeles, the exhibit of Contra Costa County schools received much praise. It was prepared under the supervision of Superintendent Phalin. The Los Angeles Record Says: "The Contra Costa County display represented the daily work of the pupils collected by the superintendent without the knowledge of the pupils or of the teachers. It compared very favorably with work prepared especially for the exhibit."

August 5, 1899.—The last six grand juries have condemned the court house, and there is a strong movement for a new county building. The present building was erected in 1854 and cost $27,000.

August 12, 1899.—The board of supervisors have voted to erect a new court house.

August 19, 1899.—Timbers are being smashed every day in the Franklin Canyon tunnel by the shifting of the earth on account of its peculiar formation.

August 26, 1899.—The welcome that is being given the California Volunteers who returned from Manila this week is the greatest affair ever held in the State. Over $60,000 was raised for the occasion. The California boys have all seen hard service and are all worthy of the ovation being given them.

September 23, 1899.—The annual session of the County Teachers' Institute was held in Martinez and was a success, many teachers being present.

October 14, 1899.—The town trustees have granted an electric light franchise to Joseph Mayo.

December 2, 1899.—The steel viaduct across Alhambra Valley, just back of Martinez, will be completed in a few days. It is 1680 feet long. On Monday the first train passed over the Point Richmond section to Cornwall, five miles from Antioch.

January 13, 1900.—W. S. Wells was appointed by Governor Gage to serve as superior judge of Contra Costa County, to succeed Judge Jones, deceased. He came to Contra Costa County in 1887.

February 16, 1900.—The Contra Costa Oil & Petroleum Company organized last week. They have control of 1200 acres near Antioch where oil was found thirty-five years ago at a depth of 122 feet in paying quantities.

F. L. Glass has been appointed postmaster for the next four years.

April 14, 1900.—Last Thursday the doctors of the county met at Antioch and organized the Contra Costa County Medical Society. Six physicians were present. The officers are: President, J. S. Riley; first vice-president, J. T. Breneman; second vice-president, Dr. F. Rattan; secretary, George McKenzie; treasurer, W. S. George.

The residence of Supervisor Paul DeMartini was destroyed by fire at Clayton.

Last Monday the town trustees elected were W. A. Hale, Reese Jones, J. G. Duane; treasurer, W. J. Douglas; clerk, M. H. Hurley; marshal, George Woolbert. Total votes cast, 223.

June 30, 1900.—There is a general enthusiasm for the monster celebration to be held on July 4 at Martinez, and contributions are readily coming in to make it a success. The ladies are to aid in securing funds for the celebration. A monster crowd of people from all of the county is expected. The celebration will last two days. W. H. Bowen, of Cornwall, has been selected grand marshal. There will be many forms of amusement. Everything is in readiness for the two-day celebration.

July 7, 1900.—The monster celebration was termed a grand success. Over 7000 people enjoyed the festivities. Miss Mamie Walsh of Valona represented the Goddess of Liberty; the maids of honor were Edith Barnard, Clara Mills, Nellie Casey and Daisy Collins. W. S. Tinning was president of the day. H. C. Raap represented Uncle Sam; Miss Florence Carpenter, Fire Queen; Miss Emma Bernard, Angel of Peace, on the N. D. G. W. float. The decorations were fine; the parade, unexcelled and there were also splendid literary exercises and races of all kinds.

July 11, 1900.—Wednesday was the sixtieth birthday and the thirteenth wedding anniversary of D. G. Muir, the well-known fruit-grower of Alhambra Valley. This fact was not forgotten by his wife, and while he was absent in town she planned a surprise. It was a five o'clock tea. When Mr. Muir returned home in the afternoon he was met by his many friends. All sat down to the festal board and spent pleasant hours recalling old scenes and incidents.

Quite a force of men are at work on the Randall tract for the Peyton Chemical Company's plant.

July 21, 1900.—The Union Stock Yards Company property at Rodeo, which cost $700,000, was auctioned off for $23,000 to A. Alper, representing the Great Western Smelting & Refining Company of San Francisco. The sale was confirmed by Judge Ogden of Oakland.

August 18, 1900.—Work on the new electric line for which a franchise was granted to Henshaw and McDonald last Monday by the board of supervisors will begin at once.

August 25, 1900.—An enthusiastic meeting of the Martinez Republican Club was held last Thursday. A large crowd was in attendence.

The new ferry steamer San Pablo, owned by the Santa Fe, was launched last Saturday afternoon at Union Iron Works and christened by Miss Payson, daughter of the president of the road. This will be the finest ferry boat on the bay and will run between Point Richmond and San Francisco. The vessel has a length of 225 feet, 64 feet beam, and draws 17.6 feet of water. It has 2000 horse-power and 15-knot speed.

September 1, 1900.—The twelfth anniversary of the organization of the Dante Society will take place this year at Concord, September 15 and 16.

The ticket nominated by the Republican Convention at Martinez last Saturday was: Superior judge, W. S. Wells; senator, C. M. Belshaw; assemblyman, B. M. Ivory; supervisors: District No. 2, J. M. Stow; No. 4, W. J. Buchanan; No. 5, E. D. Grigsby.

The Democrats in convention at Concord nominated Arthur Williams of Walnut Creek for assemblyman; supervisors: District No. 2, James Daley; No. 4, Paul DeMartini; No. 5, J. D. Wightman.

October 13, 1900.—The result of the vote for the removal of the county seat from Martinez to Concord stood 2112 for Martinez and 1228 for Concord.

November 17, 1900.—The board of supervisors decided to accept plans and specifications for the new courthouse, to cost $100,000.

The officers of the Martinez Library Association to serve the following year are: G. A. Brick, president; A. A. Lobree, vice-president; Mrs. Tinning, secretary; and Jessie L. Hale, librarian.

December 1, 1900.—The "Owl" train from Los Angeles to San Francisco was ditched between Cornwall and Antioch last Sunday. The car was derailed and thrown on its side, but all passengers escaped uninjured. The track was badly torn up.

January 5, 1901.—The bids for the construction of the new court house were opened by the board of supervisors, and the final result was the rejection of all offers, as none of them came within the limit prescribed by the board.

January 12, 1901.—With this issue of the Gazette, G. E. Milnes buys the interest of J. M. Stow and James Rankin, and becomes sole owner and proprietor. Mr. Milnes has had sole management of the Gazette for the past three years.

January 26, 1901.—Dr. Frank Rattan purchased the drug business of W. K. Cole and will remove to Martinez and take up the practice of Medicine. He has been located at Antioch for the past ten years.

April 13, 1901.—Plans are selected for the new court house. Havens & Toepke, architects of Sacramento, are the successful bidders.

April 20, 1901.—At the election held Saturday in the districts of Concord, Pacheco, Mount Diablo, Oak Grove, Bay Point, Lime Quarry, and Pleasant Hill, for the purpose of determining whether a Union High School should be maintained, it was decided by a vote of 311 to 76 that such a school should be established. It is to be located at Concord.

May 4, 1901.—The smelter of the Copper King, Ltd., located at Seal Bluff, is in full operation. Large quantities of ores are arriving from Fresno County daily.

The Oakwood Stock Farm, owned by John F. Boyd, comprising 6000 acres near Mount Diablo, has been sold to a syndicate of Montana and Eastern capitalists. The farm has a world-wide reputation for the breeding of trotters and other stock. Some of the finest cattle in the United States were bred on this farm.

The court house plans were finally adopted and a building authorized not to exceed in cost $145,000.

May 25, 1901.—President McKinley's train will pass through Martinez about noon today, but will not stop.

A communication from W. H. Penniman of Walnut Creek says in part, regarding the automobile: "In your issue of the 11th inst., I noticed in the column devoted to the doings of the supervisors pertaining to the running of autos on the public roads of the county that J. O. Miner and John Devlin appeared before the board and asked for an ordinance to prohibit the running of autos upon the public roads because they frighten horses. . . . It does not seem possible that in this progressive age any person or people could be found so unprogressive as to wish to retard the fulfilling of one of the greatest wishes of the past generations, to be able to glide smoothly and more swiftly over the roads with power other than the horse. . . I tell you that the auto has come to stay, even more so than the bicycle. . . . What scares one horse will not scare another, and an auto is no worse, if as bad, as many other things that could be enumerated."

June, 1901.—Residents of the town of Richmond are to form a sanitary district; the object of the move is to put in a complete system of sewers.

Alameda County is in line for the tunnel road. At a meeting of the board of supervisors they obligated themselves to levy a tax to raise $10,-000 to be paid as Alameda County's share of the cost of building the' proposed tunnel.

July 6, 1901.—The bid of the Pacific Construction Company was accepted by the supervisors for the new court house building, to be constructed of granite at a cost of $177,383. Luke Bulger was appointed superintendent of construction.

Fourth of July was celebrated in Concord and Crockett, both places drawing large crowds and having fine parades, speech-making, games, races, fireworks and dancing. At Crockett, Theodore Moiles was grand marshal; Judge T. B. Pratt, president of the day; and J. E. Hughes, speaker. At Concord, Arthur Williams was grand marshal; J. M. Oliver, speaker of the day; and E. J. Randall, president of the day.

July 13, 1901.—The results of the election held last Saturday to determine the question whether a high school should be maintained or not, were: Martinez, 188 for, 0 against; Vine Hill, 6 for, 12 against; Alhambra, 18 for, 2 against; Franklin, 5 for, 0 against; Briones, no election. The board comprised: J. E. Rodgers, Martinez; L. Brockman, Briones;

George Frazer, Franklin; Mrs. M. R. Kelly, Vine Hill; John Swett, Alhambra. Mrs. M. R. Kelly was elected president; J. E. Rodgers, secretary. E. I. Rowell was elected as principal.

July 20, 1901.—A permanent organization of the board of trustees of Mount Diablo Union High School was effected last Saturday. E. J. Randall, of Concord, was elected president; M. T. Sickal, of Ygnacio, secretary; John Sutton, of Lime Quarry, third member of the executive committee. The full board consists of E. J. Randall, M. T. Sickal, John Sutton, John Parkinson, W. A. Kirkwood, Miss Annie Loucks, George Putnam. G. W. Wright was elected principal. The high school will open on August 5 with one teacher, and so continue until its growth warrants additions. [The school opened with thirty-two pupils, and with Miss M. L. Grover as teacher.]

The people of Oakland went before the legislature and secured the passage of an act that would enable the Supervisors of Alameda and Contra Costa Counties to complete and build the tunnel road.

July 27, 1901.—About 400 men along the water-front go on strike over wages. The men ask $3 per day for nine hours' work, and time and a half for overtime. The employers offered 30 cents an hour straight, with no extra pay for overtime. The men accepted the above wage and time and a half for overtime.

July 27, 1901.—Work on laying out the grounds for the new court house commenced last Wednesday, and excavating will soon start.

Flames of unknown origin wiped out Byron Hot Springs Hotel with a loss of $85,000. The buildings destroyed were the main hotel, 300 by 30 feet, with two wings 50 by 100 feet each, a cottage of twenty rooms, the laundry, and the gas and ice plants.

August 3, 1901.—The school districts of Carquinez, Port Costa and Selby are determined that they shall have a union high school; and petitions have been circulated, the required number of names secured, and an election called for August 10.

Gold bullion valued at $320,000 was stolen from the Selby Smelter last Tuesday morning. John Winters, formerly an employee of the plant, was captured as a suspect and made a confession and showed where he had hidden the bullion. There is a squabble over the $25,000 reward.

The election on August 10 for a union high school for Carquinez, Port Costa, and Selby was a success; ninety-one voted for the school, and one against. The number of heads of families in the district is as follows: Carquinez, 301; Port Costa, 91; Selby, 40.

August 31, 1901.—A petition embracing Brentwood, Iron House, Sand Mound, Eden Plain, Excelsior, Byron, Hot Springs, Liberty, Deer Valley, Lone Tree and Live Oak has been presented to the county superintendent, who has called an election.

Carquinez District selected J. J. Davis, of Crockett; N. McNamara, of Selby; and L. M. Buttner, of Port Costa, as trustees of the new high school district.

On account of no final settlement of the strike along the water-front, the warehousemen are putting in electric appliances to take the place of stevedores.

September 7, 1901.—A dispatch from San Francisco says that President McKinley was shot twice at the Exposition Grounds at Buffalo, N. Y., by an assassin. [Upon his death, memorial services were held in Curry & Jones Hall, which was packed to overflowing.]

President Ralston, of the Selby Company, says that those who will share in the $25,000 reward for the capture of Winters, who got fifteen years at San Quentin, are R. R. Veale, Pete Donaldson, Ex-Chief of Police Lees, Captain of Detectives Seymour, and Detectives Tom Gibson, Crockett, and Silvey of Morse's agency. The Pinkerton Agency declines to accept any reward other than pay for their services.

September 21, 1901.—The Standard Oil Company purchased 117.66 acres at Richmond and will erect immense storage tanks.

October 5, 1901.—The public schools closed as a precaution to prevent the spread of scarlet fever, which seems to have secured a strong hold in Martinez.

A special agent of the United States Government is here to investigate the establishment of a rural free delivery route in Alhambra Valley, Franklin Canyon, Vaca Creek and Vine Hill districts for mail-delivery every day except Sunday.

November 8, 1901.—The car shops of the Santa Fe at Richmond were destroyed by fire. The loss to the company amounted to $125,000.

December 14, 1901.—Ceremonies for the laying of the cornerstone of the new court house take place today. The Grand Masons of the State are to lay the stone. A procession will form at Masonic Hall and march to the court house site. J. D. Wightman will give an address, inviting the Grand Master to commence ceremonies; and W. S. Wells, Grand Master of the State of California, will respond. Napa Commandery No. 34, K. T., will be in attendance.

February 8, 1902.—Twilight Lodge No. 129, I. O. O. F., was instituted at Richmond last Saturday night with thirty-four members. John Murray, Noble Grand; J. A. Whiteside, Vice-Grand; A. Bishop, Treasurer; T. A. Tipp, Warden; E. J. Summerfield, Conductor; John Swanson, Inside Guard; F. Kennedy, Outside Guard.

San Pablo Water Company secured 200 acres at the mouth of Wildcat Creek and will sink wells and pipe water to Richmond.

April 5, 1902.—The Contra Costa Chamber of Commerce was organized on Saturday, March 29. W. S. Tinning was elected temporary chairman; G. E. Milnes, secretary; and A. Beam, treasurer.

April 10, 1902.—The McKinley Masonic Lodge No. 347, F. & A. M., of Richmond, was instituted by Grand Master W. S. Wells. The officers elected were: Harry Ells, W. M.; W. A. Walker, S. W.; Dr. J. McI. Morrison, J. W.; W. Stitt, Treasurer; W. O. Shaw, Secretary; W.

H. Smith, Senior Deacon; John Murray, Junior Deacon; R. R. Thornton, Marshal; William Richards, Tyler. There were seventeen charter members.

May 3, 1902.—At a meeting of the Chamber of Commerce, President Tinning presided. W. A. Hale, the new secretary, was in his place. A pamphlet descriptive of the county is to be issued as soon as all the data are available.

May 3, 1902.—The town of Concord went out to get the site of the Fair Grounds and raised $3000. The board of directors of the Agricultural Society conceded that good work had been done and deserved support. There will be a good race track, and the grounds will be put in first-class shape. All buildings, etc., will be moved from Walnut Creek to the new site of seventy acres in the Galindo tract.

May 17, 1902.—As a result of the protracted fight for the location of the union high school building in the eastern section of the county, the second election gave Deer Valley 121, Brentwood 122. The new district will be known as Liberty Union High School District. The school opens at Brentwood on August 25, with Mr. I. Wright as principal.

The Contra Costa Driving Club have filed articles of incorporation and have been granted a charter. The directors are: W. S. Wells, F. W. Paskett, P. J. Horgan, W. S. Burpee and George A. Wiley. A. B. McKenzie is secretary. Capital stock, $10,000.

June 7, 1902.—As the result of a fire in Byron today, the business section of the town was wiped out. The town not being equipped with fire fighting apparatus, the buildings were at the mercy of the flames.

A special election is to be held on August 11, 1902, for the purpose of submitting the proposition to incur a bonded indebtedness of $71,000 for the completion of the court house, $20,000 for the jail, and $70,000 for the complete furnishing of the court house.

The high schools of the county are: The John Swett High School, of Crockett; Louis P. Webb, principal; Miss A. Hutton, vice-principal; thirty-two students. The Alhambra Union High School; F. A. Cooley, principal; Miss Amanda McComb, vice-principal; forty-three students. The Mount Diablo High School of Concord; G. W. Wright, principal; Miss Maude Grover, vice-principal; Miss G. Crocker, assistant; fifty-one students. The Liberty Union High School, of Brentwood; I. Wright, principal; Miss B. Hagmayer, vice-principal; twenty-one students.

All bids for the construction of the tunnel between Alameda and Contra Costa County have been rejected, and the work is to be done by day labor. The work is to begin at once. The portion in Alameda County is 436 feet, and that in Contra Costa County, 616 feet. Superintendent Stow now has the road finished to the face of the tunnel on this side.

The bonds for finishing and furnishing the court house and jail were carried by a large majority.

December 27, 1902.—Bay Point Smelter was closed down.

January 10, 1903.—At a meeting of the board of supervisors the salaries of the justices of the peace were fixed as follows:

District	Name	Population	Salary
1	D. S. Carpenter	3096	$100
2	J. P. Casey	1258	40
3	W. H. Hough	1310	40
4	S. F. Ramage	1322	40
5	J. J. Burke	2080	45
6	J. H. Fitzgerald	1301	40
7	J. L. Dickinson	466	15
8	A. C. Hartley	1515	40
9	C. M. Chapman	1416	40
10	E. B. Masterson	3000	100
11	J. V. Enloe	2285	45
12	M. W. O'Neill	3020	100
13	G. L. Goethels	531	15
14	J. F. Carey	750	15

March 21, 1903.—The first session of the board of supervisors to be held in the new court house was held on March 14. All the various officers are now installed in their new quarters.

March 28, 1903.—What the tunnel road means to that section of the county is shown by the following: Property held at $20 per acre now sells easily at $100 per acre.

The torrent of oil from the wells baptized the Standard Oil Company's great new pipe line Saturday at Bakersfield, and 20,000 gallons of that murky fluid are on the way to the water's edge at Point Richmond. The oil is now plunging on its way towards Pond, the first pumping station out of Bakersfield, twenty-eight miles away. It is expected to reach there in thirty-six hours. There it will be led into a receptacle big enough to hold the whole 20,000 gallons, whence it will be pumped to the next station, and so on until it has been passed by ten stations, twenty-eight miles apart on the 280-mile pipe line. It will be at least two weeks before the oil will reach Point Richmond.

May 2, 1903.—The corner-stone for the new schoolhouse at Byron was laid with appropriate ceremonies last Saturday.

May 30, 1903.—The supervisors of the State held their annual convention at Martinez on May 26, 27 and 28, and all the visitors seemed pleased with their visit. After the usual business sessions, trips were made to various places of interest in the county. J. D. Wightman was elected chairman; and County Clerk J. E. Rodgers, secretary.

The new court house was dedicated on May 29 with impressive ceremonies. Much credit is due the volunteer firemen for the success of the day's program. President of the day, G. E. Milnes; Ruth Dow, Fire Queen; orator of the day, J. P. Abbott, of Antioch. Judge Wells made the dedicatory speech. There was a parade formed on Ferry Street near the depot, including the grand marshal and his aides; Martinez Band; president of the day, orators of the day and chaplain in carriages; hook and ladder truck, conveying the Fire Queen and maids; Ramona Parlor, N. D. G. W.; a company of sailors in uniform, from merchant ships in the harbor; the Dante Society, in uniform; Laurel Camp No. 145, W. O. W.; chemical engine; citizens in carriages; and Tug-of-War float. After the services there was a barbecue and sports, and in the evening a banquet and dance.

Decoration Day was fittingly observed in Martinez on May 30. The fire company and ships in the harbor took part in the ceremonies. Judge W. S. Wells was chairman, and Judge E. M. Gibson was orator of the day.

June 13, 1903.—After a period of five years at Crockett, W. G. Hawes, editor of the Crockett Signal, has decided to suspend the publication of his paper and to move his plant to East Oakland.

Eppinger & Company, of San Francisco, owners of the Pacific Coast Works at Crockett, have been forced to the wall; their liabilities were $1,500,000, and assets $750,000. The failure is one of the worst in the State, but the losses fell heaviest upon banks that are able to stand them, not on the farmers.

June 11, at 5:15 a. m., the residents of the town were awakened by a violent earthquake shock. It made the houses rock like small pieces of cork bobbing on a wave.

The terrible wreck on the Southern Pacific at Byron last December, in which over thirty persons lost their lives in the wreck of the Stockton Flyer and the Owl trains, is recalled in a suit filed in supreme court this week for $20,000 damages. The plaintiff in the case is Ella A. Sessions, widow of Charles Sessions, a capitalist of Oakland, who was crushed in the wreck.

June 20, 1903.—Elections were held in the towns of Black Diamond and Pinole last Monday to determine the question of incorporation, which was carried by overwhelming majorities. The vote was 50 for and 1 against at Black Diamond. Clerk, T. M. Donovan; treasurer, V. G. Viscasco; marshal, T. M. Rogers; trustees, W. G. H. Croxon, W. J. Buchanan, J. A. Junta, D. Israel, and V. D. Maggio. At Pinole the vote was 106 for and 5 against. Clerk, E. M. Downer; treasurer, A. Greenfield; marshal, H. A. Christian; trustees, J. A. Fraser, S. J. Stotts, J. P. Barrett, Joseph Walton, and Thomas Shimmins.

July 4, 1903.—The Copper King, Ltd., filed a petition in involuntary insolvency Wednesday in San Francisco; liabilities, $614,223; assets, $306,704.

Eppinger & Company were declared insolvent. The creditors will not realize more than ten per cent.

July 25, 1903.—The pipe line of the Standard Oil Company from Bakersfield to Richmond, 283 miles, is a success. The first oil was pumped into the tank at Richmond Saturday at nine o'clock; during the first hour 800 barrels were pumped. The enterprise involves an investment of $3,000,000, and together with the local plant, $6,000,000. Seven hundred people are employed in and about Richmond.

R. N. Frick gets a franchise for an electric railroad to the peak of Mount Diablo. The franchise calls for an electric railway from the intersection of the Alameda-Contra Costa County line to the top of Mount Diablo, also branching off at Walnut Creek and running through Ygnacio Valley to Martinez.

The supreme court ends the Sobrante Case, which has been in the courts for more than twenty years and involves title to 19,000 acres of land in the west end of the county, valued at $4,000,000. The land can now be divided among the various parties interested.

October 17, 1903.—Oil that has been sought by an enterprising company for years, has at last been discovered on the Minor ranch. As the murky fluid shot up into the air it caught fire from lanterns hanging on the derrick, and workmen barely escaped with their lives. Much valuable machinery was destroyed by the flames.

December 5, 1903.—The Brentwood Hotel, the leading hotel of the town and a landmark for years, was burned to the ground Sunday night.

January 30, 1904.—Contra Costa County has had prepared, under the supervision of H. C. Raap, a splendid exhibit of its products and resources. At the proper time this exhibit is to be sent to the St. Louis World's Fair. The good results that will accrue from such an exhibit will be many. Anyone seeing it can not help being convinced that Contra Costa County is a good place in which to cast his lot. Contra Costa County has over 500 jars containing as nice specimens of fruit as can be found, and should maintain her individuality.

January 30, 1904.—The Vallejo Junction Hotel, located at Vallejo Junction, was destroyed by fire at an early hour Friday morning.

February 13, 1904.—The Gazette has just installed the Simplex oneman typesetter machinery, which is almost human in its workings.

March 12, 1904.—The flood of last Thursday was the worst the town has experienced for the past fourteen years. The water backed up on Main Street so that foot travel, except in a limited area, was out of the question. North of Main Street everything clear to the water-front was one mass of water, in places four feet deep. Portions of the railroad track were washed out and trains were delayed several hours. At Pacheco several buildings were washed away.

March 26, 1904.—The exhibit for the St. Louis Fair was shipped, and H. C. Raap will leave in about a week to see that it is properly installed. There was more than a big furniture car would hold.

May 28, 1904.—The Martinez Aerie of Eagles was instituted by Hon. Charles Nagle, State Deputy Grand President.

June 4, 1904.—After a visit of six weeks at the St. Louis Fair, where he superintended the placing of the Contra Costa County exhibit, H. C.

Raap is home. He says that this county's exhibit is by far the best seen at the Fair.

July 2, 1904.—The first graduating exercises of the Alhambra Union High School were held Friday, July 1, at Curry & Jones Hall. The colors of the school are Blue and Gold. Diplomas were given Aileen Murphy, Laura M. Mellerup and Francis J. Kelly.

School Superintendent A. A. Bailey's report shows 6860 children in the county between the ages of five and seventeen.

July 9, 1904.—Celebrations of the Fourth were held in various places in the county. In Antioch R. R. Veale was grand marshal and C. M. Belshaw orator of the day. At Mitchell Canyon some 1200 enjoyed the exercises. Gus L. Goethals was president of the day and E. J. Randall orator. At Orinda some 400 attended a barbecue held under the auspices of Mr. and Mrs. J. Harris. Judge McGraw made an address, followed by Mr. Burke of San Francisco.

August 27, 1904.—A devastating fire on August 19 consumed a large portion of Martinez's business district. It was first seen in the Ottman Refrigeration Plant, but by reason of delayed service in coupling hose the fire secured such headway that it could not be checked. The Curry & Jones livery, in fact the whole block of the Commercial Hotel, was ablaze. Efforts were then directed to save the property on the opposite sides of the streets.

Help came from Benicia by boat, and even from Concord. The following sustained losses:

	Loss	Insurance
McNamara & Winkleman	$ 6,500	$1,250
A. P. Nelson	6,000	2,000
M. L. Biess	4,000	
C. C. Gill	2,000	500
J. W. Douglass	3,000	700
Martinez Hotel	500	
Bank of Martinez	1,000	1,000
J. Ipswich	2,000	1,000
M. Bergamini	3,500	1,750
McMahon Bros.	7,000	2,000
C. C. Swain	200	200
E. Morgan	5,000	2,250
Mrs. S. Rankin	10,000	3,600
W. J. Johnson	3,000	1,500
Curry & Jones	1,000	300
Sunset Telephone Co.	500	
J. W. Ottman	3,000	1,000
J. Dahlstrom	5,000	
M. Lawless	3,000	1,500
G. W. Reed	500	

There were many minor losses besides.

September 17, 1904.—C. E. Ertz, of the Bull's Head Oil Company, has named his subdivision, laid out on the Frazer ranch, East Martinez.

February 11, 1905.—At a hotly contested election last Saturday Concord fought out the incorporation question and elected, as trustees, H. W. Bott, M. N. Breckenridge, H. H. Elsworthy, M. E. Lyon, and James Boyd; clerk, G. P. Keller; treasurer, F. W. Foskett; marshal, J. W. Guy.

February 25, 1905.—The directors of the Bank of Martinez have let the contract for a new modern building of brick and stone, and costing $10,666, to Wilson-Lyons Company. Other buildings being constructed are the pressed-brick building of Mrs. Rankin, costing $11,000, which will be ready for occupancy on May 1; the Bergamini Block, which is about completed, a two-story brick and stone building, costing $5000; and that of T. A. McMahon and J. J. McNamara, which will cost $10,000.

March 4, 1905.—The coal yards and grain depot of A. M. Coleman & Company, at Point Richmond, were totally destroyed by fire, and the coal sheds of the Richmond Supply Company were partially burned. Coleman's loss amounted to $3500 and Black's to $500.

June 10, 1905.—The board of supervisors granted the request that a new township be created to include Richmond, Santa Fe, Stege, San Pablo and Grant, and appointed Frank Hull justice of the peace.

June 17, 1905.—John Zimmerman was found guilty of the Stege robbery of the Central Bank of Oakland of $10,000. The jury was out nineteen hours.

July 15, 1905.—Charles H. Hayden has been appointed justice of the peace to succeed D. S. Carpenter, deceased.

July 29, 1905.—Los Cerritos Chapter, O. E. S., was instituted at Martinez Saturday night with a membership of thirty. The following officers were appointed: Worthy Matron, Mrs. R. B. Borland; Associate Matron, Mrs. O. E. Haywards; Patron, W. A. Hale; Secretary, Mrs. A. B. Wilson; treasurer, George A. Wiley; Conductress, Mrs. E. Pasch; Associate Conductress, Mrs. W. A. Hale.

Mr. and Mrs. T. McMahon celebrated the fiftieth anniversary of their marriage on August 6, 1905.

The Alhambra Union High School opened Monday with thirty-one students enrolled. E. W. Stoddard is the principal; Miss Ruth I. Swett, vice-principal; and Miss Florence N. Ewing and Miss Rosalind Wulzen, teachers.

August 19, 1905.—The trial jury sitting in circuit court before Justice Beatty in the case of Sessions vs. the Southern Pacific Railway, in which Mrs. Sessions sued for $20,000 because Charles A. Sessions was killed by collision of trains on December 20, 1902, brought in a verdict in favor of the railway company, holding that Sessions was a trespasser on the train because he was traveling on an old pass given him by Conductor William Doland.

A Lodge of the Fraternal Brotherhood was organized in Martinez on August 12. One hundred and twenty-four were elected to membership by ballot.

The Alhambra Cemetery Association met and elected E. Morgan president, to fill the vacancy made by the death of L. C. Wittenmyer, and C. H. Hayden to fill the vacancy on the board. The board of directors are E. Morgan, M. R. Jones, C. C. Swain, Elam Brown, and C. H. Hayden.

August 26, 1905.—John Zimmerman was sentenced to forty-five years for the Stege robbery. He held up and robbed John Dailey and Frank Roche near Stege in March, relieving them of $10,000 belonging to the Central Bank of Oakland which was being taken to Richmond to be used in paying the help of the Standard Oil Company.

November 4, 1905.—Sterling Parlor No. 146, Native Daughters of the Golden West, was organized at Black Diamond, with twenty-two charter members. Mrs. Joseph McAvoy, Past President; Mrs. W. H. Diffin, President.

December 2, 1905.—Richmond Parlor No. 147, Native Daughters of the Golden West, was organized at Richmond with thirty-two charter members. The officers installed were: Past President, Mrs. A. C. Lang; President, Mrs R. H. Spiersch; first Vice-President, Mrs. Julius Shiefwater; Second Vice-President, Mabel Roth; Secretary, Mrs. G. A. Dimick; Treasurer, Mrs. W. S. Bennison; Marshal, Miss Effie Rihn; Trustees, Miss Belle Johannsen and Miss Mable Kohnhoff.

A Knights of Pythias Lodge was instituted on December 9 at Martinez; 175 visitors from various lodges were in attendance. Thirty-one candidates received the three ranks, and nine were admitted by card. The officers installed were: P. C. Commanders, W. M. Laidlaw, C. R. Hayes, R. B. Borland, G. W. Sweetser; C. C., George Elder; Vice-C. C., A. E. Goyette; Prelate, C. H. Ludden; Master of Work, L. F. Osborne; Master at Arms, A. J. Soto; Inner Guard, L. M. Tubbs; Outer Guard, A. W. Large; Keeper of Records, C. H. Hayden; Master of Finance, Walter Morgan; Master of Exchequer, R. B. Borland; Physician, Dr. G. W. Sweetser; Trustees, Dr. G. W. Sweetser, E. Osborne, Dr. M. N. Mitchell.

March 10, 1906.— The water-front town of Stege is experiencing a building boom. The Stauffer Chemical Works soon to be erected will be one of its largest concerns. Another important industry is that of the U. S. Briquette Company. The Metropolitan Match Company is improving its plant.

April 7, 1906.—Papers are filled with accounts of the terrible earthquake and fire in San Francisco.

April 28, 1906.—The lack of glass caused by the conflagration in San Francisco necessitates the repair of windows with boards.

The Martinez Library Association will have to incur a $1500 debt to repair the damage to their building in the earthquake. They also lost fifty volumes in a bindery in San Francisco.

The following is the essay given by W. E. Stoddard on graduating night, June 8, 1906:

"The first school in Martinez was taught by B. R. Holliday, in the early part of 1850; his school consisted of five or six pupils gathered in the Blossom, now known as the Gift house, standing at the foot of Thomas' Hill. The school increased from six to twenty-six during the two terms. He received $75 per month. In the fall of 1850 he was succeeded by McLaughlin.

"In 1851 there was a school taught in an old house across from D. Calahan's furniture store by a Mrs. Rice, who had twelve or thirteen pupils.

"Mr. Hinckley was the next teacher, who taught a three-months term in 1852 in a house that stood on Mills Street near Main.

"In 1853 Mr. More taught in a small brick building on the corner of Main and Ferry.

"In the latter part of the same year Mrs. Phoebe R. Alley taught in a house owned and now occupied by Mr. and Mrs. C. C. Swain. Mrs. Alley lived upstairs and used her kitchen for a school-room. Rough seats were made and a curtain was drawn to hide the cook-stove and utensils. It was during her term that the school first received aid from the State.

"Hiram Burns was the next teacher and taught six months in 1854 in the brick building on Ferry Street already mentioned.

"In 1854 Rev. Sanbourne taught in a house, later Mrs. Henry Hale's residence, but afterwards in a building on Main Street.

"J. Vandermark was the first superintendent of schools of the county.

"In 1856 Dr. Holmes taught in a house which might be termed the Public Building of Martinez, as it was used as a church, court house and Masonic Lodge hall.

"In 1856 Miss Gregory, a graduate of Oberlin, also taught in this building. She had twenty or thirty pupils and Miss Charlotte Worth was an assistant.

"In 1857 Miss Jane Lyon succeeded Miss Gregory. There were twenty pupils taking high school studies and twelve in intermediate grades. On account of the building being too small, Miss Lyon taught primary classes at noon while eating her lunch and at odd times when the older ones were not reciting. Her time was fully occupied from eight in the morning until late in the evening. She had to buy the apparatus needed, out of her own pocket. In winter a stove was borrowed and the pupils furnished fuel. The pipe was of three different sizes, which the teacher and pupils put together with wire and mortar.

"In the early part of 1858 Miss Lyon accepted a call to Sacramento and Miss Eliza May took her place. She taught two terms.

"On September 4, 1858, S. H. Bushnell was employed. One of his pupils told the following: 'Two boys were to be whipped, and one of them was sent to get a switch. He obeyed, went to the creek, cut a fine green poison-oak switch, and brought it to the teacher. The boys got their whipping, also a week's vacation, as the teacher was nursing a bad case of poison oak.'

"There were forty-eight scholars, twenty-eight girls and twenty boys. A new Masonic Hall had been completed in 1860, and the public school moved into it, where Mr. Bushnell taught two years.

"The school gradually grew, and in 1873 the citizens of Martinez had erected a two-story wooden building, which was completed May 1st.

"D. T. Fowler was the last teacher in the Masonic Hall and the first in the new schoolhouse. Mrs. Fowler and Miss Connors were his assistants. There were only eight months of school yearly, on account of funds. The ladies of the town organized an Educational Aid Society, with Mrs. Alley president. They gave entertainments and solicited subscriptions to pay the teachers for two more months, so that a ten-months school could be maintained. This society also bought desks and a piano, and laid a two-plank sidewalk from Main Street to the schoolhouse."

Contra Costa County's subscription towards rebuilding the schools in San Francisco was between $500 and $600.

The plans and specifications for the repair of earthquake damages to the new court house were placed in charge of A. A. Cantin, architect.

August 25, 1906.—Recent reports from the Copper King Mining Company, Ltd., of London, with mines in Fresno and a smelter here, which was forced into bankruptcy, indicate that all creditors will be paid in full. The trustee of the concern has been given permission to work the mine, and says there is plenty of ore in sight to pay all liabilities.

September 15, 1906.—The Pinole Aerie of Eagles was instituted Wednesday, September 14, with fifty-six charter members. The officers are: Sam Bermingham, Past President; J. Doughty, President; W. G. Hays, Vice-President; J. V. Enloe, Secretary; T. J. Stats, Treasurer; F. Lockyer, Chaplain; George Floyd, Conductor; N. G. Scanlon, Inside Guard; J. Clancy, Outside Guard; H. W. Baldwin, Physician; J. Silva, J. A. Lewis and John T. Silva, Trustees.

September 15, 1906.—There was a big fire at Richmond on Tuesday night, the 11th, which destroyed almost an entire block, including the undertaking parlors and furniture store of E. B. Smallwood, the Eureka Lodging House, Mrs. Jacka's restaurant, and the fruit stand of F. Huston. There was no fire department and the blaze was fought by bucket-brigade. The loss was $25,000.

The estimated loss in a fire at Black Diamond was $10,000, with $4000 insurance. The buildings burned were: C. Lepori's store, residences of J. R. Nichols and G. Crivello, and the warehouse of W. J. Buchanan & Company. The fire started in the barn of C. Lepori. The firemen worked well and with good results.

The Gazette has installed a Mergenthaler Linotype machine. Mr. Milnes will welcome visitors and will see that the workings of this wonderful machine are explained to them.

November 3, 1906.—Work on the pottery plant buildings at Richmond is being pushed rapidly. The new concern will manufacture all kinds of porcelain ware and will employ 150 men.

The California Wine Association has commenced work on its new warehouse and winery at Point Molati on Richmond Island. When completed, the plant will cost a half million of dollars; 10,000,000 gallons of wine will be stored in vats, and the plant will handle 25,000 tons of grapes. The wharf is already completed and deep-water transportation assured.

February 9.—L. N. Buttner was appointed county treasurer to fill the vacancy caused by the death of G. A. Wiley.

February 23, 1907.—The Antioch Lumber Company incorporated with a capital stock of $100,000; A. M. Simpson, president; J. P. Abbott, vice-president; R. M. Beede, treasurer; H. F. Beede, secretary.

March 16, 1907.—The Richmond Chamber of Commerce was organized with H. C. Cutting, president; L. D. Dimm, vice-president; J. Q. Black, secretary; H. L. Boswell, assistant.

On March 14 there were fifty-five fishing boats between Port Costa and Martinez. As many as seventy were counted from a court-house window.

March 30, 1907.—The Henley-Tyler Lumber Company of Richmond has been incorporated with a capital stock of $50,000.

April 15, 1907.—The Richmond Union High School is located in Block 99, Macdonald Avenue, on a site of twenty lots.

April 26, 1907.—Mr. and Mrs. Charles Wood of Danville celebrated their Golden Wedding anniversary at their "Woodside Home."

The First National Bank of Contra Costa County opened its doors June 7, 1907, with Ed. Majors, president; A. E. Blum, vice-president; E. J. Randall and W. K. Cole, directors; M. E. Gluckman, cashier.

June 29, 1907.—The private bank conducted by J. L. Silveira at Walnut Creek has been incorporated, and will be known as the San Ramon Valley Bank, Inc., capital stock, $25,000. They will have a branch at Danville. John Hackett is president; A. H. Cope, first vice-president; A. Burton, second vice-president; J. L. Silveira, cashier and manager; C. W. Close, manager of the Danville branch. Ralph Harrison, F. V. Wood, A. P. Borges, and W. K. Cole make up the directorate.

July 27, 1907.—The supervisors place the increase in valuation on property in the county at $3,275,862, which will bring the total up to $27,122,288 as against $23,846,426 in 1906.

August 15, 1907.—Two passenger trains came through Franklin tunnel on Thursday morning, the first trains since January 26, when the tunnel was blocked by slides and caving in.

December 7, 1907.—The Gazette changed hands. W. A. Rugg bought out G. E. Milnes. From 1900 to 1904 Mr. Rugg was editor of the Daily Press, which paper was later changed into the Daily Gazette. Mr. Rugg has always been a fearless writer and is out for a square deal.

January 18, 1908.—C. J. Preston, owner of a farm two miles out of Byron, Contra Costa County, lays claim to the record alfalfa yield on land that is not irrigated. He has just cut the sixth crop on his sixty acres of field, which has netted him a clear gain of $80 an acre. His total profits exceed $4000.

February 20, 1908.—Twenty-four persons were killed, four white and twenty Chinamen, at the explosion at the powder works in Pinole. Destruction to property amounted to $100,000.

The last of the Richmond Union High School bonds have been sold.

On May 9, 1908, the Martinez Gun Club held a regular shoot, each member having a chance at twenty blue rocks:

G. E. Searcy	16	J. Mayo	8
G. McDonald	15	M. Joost	4
A. E. Blum	9	C. Daley	13
F. Joost	7	W. Morgan	15

On May 20, 1908, the Oregon Express was wrecked near Pinole; five were killed.

The total number of children of school age in the county is 9222, as follows:

Alamo	68	Alhambra	55
Antioch	442	Bay Point	78
Black Diamond	911	Brentwood	111
Briones Valley	50	Byron	80
Carquinez	791	Central	143
Concord	405	Danville	81
Deer Valley	30	Eden Plain	53
Excelsior	47	Franklin	45
Green Valley	25	Highland	50
Hot Spring	36	Iron House	68
Jersey	34	Lafayette	105
Liberty	37	Lime Quarry	66
Live Oak	94	Lone Tree	40
Martinez	702	Moraga	49
Morgan Territory	33	Mt. Diablo	116
Mt. Pleasant	32	Oak Grove	71
Oakley	90	Orinda Park	14
Pacheco	125	Pinole - Hercules	395
Pleasant Hill	61	Port Costa	249
Richmond	1830	Rodeo	193
San Pablo	254	San Ramon	111
Selby	160	Sand Mound	39
Sobrante	25	Somersville	21
Stege	378	Summit	16
Sycamore	66	Tassajara	81
Vasco	29	Vine Hill	81

Willow Springs 56

June 6, 1908.—Martinez is to have a garage for the motoring public. W. J. Johnson plans an up-to-date auto-repair shop, with motor cars for sale and for rent.

Pinole was visited by a conflagration that destroyed six buildings; loss, $40,000.

July 11, 1908.—The Selby Smelter has been ordered to close, by order of Superior Court Judge Harrier of Solano County, until some device has been installed which will consume the deadly mineral fumes.

August 29, 1908.—There are fifty-eight schools in the county, 135 teachers, and six union high schools in addition to the district schools; that is, at Concord, Richmond, Brentwood, Crockett, Martinez and Antioch. There are fifty-seven school buildings in the county. The school census for the year showed 5990 pupils, with an average attendance of 3358. The average cost of primary instruction was $21.97 per scholar; for high school instruction, $93.22. In 1907 the county paid for school purposes $43,470.12.

On Tuesday, September 1, 1908, John N. Jones and his wife celebrated the fifty-ninth anniversary of their marriage. They came to California in 1853.

October 30, 1908.—Fifty years ago, the school marshal of District No. 1 (Martinez) gave the following item: Number of children between the ages of 4 and 18 in his district, 371.

Fifty years ago, on October 10, 1858, the first overland mail from San Francisco arrived at St. Louis, having made the trip in twenty-four days, eighteen hours and twenty-six minutes. Mr. Butterfield was received at St. Louis with a triumphal procession. He telegraphed the news of his arrival to Washington from Jefferson City, and on the 9th received the following reply:

"Washington City,
"October 9, 1858.

"John Butterfield,
    "President Overland Mail Co.

Sir: Your dispatch has been received. I cordially congratulate you on the result. It is a glorious triumph for civilization and the Union. Settlements will follow the course of the road and the East and West will be bound together by a chain of living Americans which can never be broken.

(Signed) "James Buchanan."

[Note: Today (1925) the trip is made in thirty-two hours from San Francisco to New York with fourteen stops by aeroplane.]

October 24, 1908.—$1,000,000 will be expended by the Standard Oil Company at Point Richmond on reclamation of a large tract of marsh land for the erection of additional refinery machinery.

October 31, 1908.—Two large warehouses at the end of Berryessa Street, used for the storage of lumber by the Martinez Lumber Company, were burned in a spectacular fire this morning about 1 a. m.

February 10, 1909.—Richmond's new charter carried, 582 for and 269 against. The Board of Freeholders began work on a new governing instrument last October, calling for nine elective councilmen to serve for a term of six years.

March 13, 1909.—This morning at ten o'clock, on the front steps of the Court House, a portion of the Bull's Head Oil Works' property was sold under the sheriff's hammer for $7318.56.

On April 21, 1909, the Golden Wedding of Mr. and Mrs. Myron W. Hall, of Alamo, was celebrated at Danville.

The John Swett Union High School was dedicated April 30, 500 being present. It is safe to say that there is no more modern or better equipped school building in the State.

May 15, 1909.—George Barnovich, who was convicted of dynamiting the home of Superintendent Hartman of the California & Hawaiian Sugar Refining Company, February 5th, was sentenced by Judge Latimer to serve life imprisonment in San Quentin.

June 5, 1909.—The graduating class of Alhambra Union High School: Leila Veale, Hazel Soto, Florence Morris, Ida Hale, Nellie Glass, Villani Hoey, Lydia Bulger, Orpha Domnaugh, Agnes Mayo and Alma Honegger.

July 10, 1909.—The Supreme Court affirmed the decision by Judge W. S. Wells for the partition of the Marsh ranch at Brentwood. The decision brings to a close a legal battle that has waged for forty years. The ranch, 13,000 acres, was originally patented to John Marsh. His heirs sold it to J. P. Sanford in 1871, partly for cash and partly on credit. Sanford was caught in the panic of 1873 and was unable to meet the requirements, so the property was foreclosed in 1875. The division will be as follows: George Davidson, 2829 acres; A. G. Moseley, 2829 acres; T. I. Bergen, 1680 acres; C. N. Ellinwood, 1414 acres; C. E. Sanford, J. E. M. Sanford, Mariah E. Robertson and A. M. Sanford, 707 acres each; heirs of H. McAllister, 399 acres; Garrett W. McEnerney and W. B. Treadwell, 333 acres each; heirs of T. P. Stoney, 222 acres; heirs of J. A. Stanley, 222 acres.

September 4, 1909.—A fountain was unveiled in Richmond Saturday at the intersection of Park Place and Washington Avenue by the West Side Women's Improvement Club. One thousand were present to see the bronze fountain unveiled. The exercises opened with music by Fisk's band of Oakland, after which Mrs. Luther Dimm lifted the veil. Mrs. S. R. Curry made an appropriate address.

The Martinez Grammar School was dedicated on September 25.

October 30, 1909.—The election held Monday in Martinez, for annexation, resulted in 229 ballots for and 13 against.

January 1, 1910.—With the coming of the Pullman car works to Richmond, it has taken another boom.

April 2, 1910.—One of the largest transactions in real estate in this section was the sale, by the Canadian Bank of Commerce of San Francisco, of Jersey Island to D. W. Carmichael and A. L. Shinn. The island contained 4000 acres and the purchase price was $200,000.

April 9, 1910.—H. T. Jones, county assessor, resigned and George Meese was appointed by the supervisors to fill the vacancy.

April 21, 1910.—The immense oil reservoir of the Standard Oil Company, west of Pinole, is burning. A force of 200 men and 100 teams are desperately at work to prevent the spread of the flames to the large tanks a short distance south. The reservoir is 100 feet from the Santa Fe Railway, and all trains are being run over the Southern Pacific between Richmond and Bay Point.

April 30, 1910.—The Oakland & Antioch Railway Company, incorporated January 8, 1910, with a capital stock of $3,500,000, plan to begin construction at once on a line from Oakland to Bay Point.

The Oakwood Park Stock Farm, comprising 5800 acres in San Ramon Valley, has been sold to Col. H. D. Loveland, S. L. Bright and A. P. Holland. A recent valuation of $450,000 was placed on the property. The land and improvements represent an outlay originally of $800,000.

May 28, 1910.—Bull's Head Oil Company has been reorganized and is now known as the American Oriental Company. The new company will soon begin active operations.

An auto stage line has been established between Walnut Creek and Oakland and will soon be extended to Danville. There will be three round trips daily. The operating company will be known as the California Transit Company.

Work on the Pullman shops is progressing rapidly at Richmond. The company intend to make this plant one of the largest in the country. The Southern Pacific and Santa Fe Railways have built spur tracks to the shops from their main lines.

Roads recommended for improvement by the highway commission appointed by the supervisors under the act of March 9, 1907, are:

(1) Byron-Knightsen Road, from the county boundary line between Alameda and Contra Costa County through Byron and Knightsen to the Brentwood-Oakley Road, 15.02 miles.

(2) Brentwood-Oakley Road, from the Byron-Knightsen Road to the Southern Pacific, through Brentwood and to Oakley, 8.72 miles.

(3) Oakley-Antioch Road, from the Brentwood-Oakley Road, through Oakley to the Santa Fe Railway and to the limits of Antioch, 6.40 miles.

(4) Antioch-Black Diamond Road, from the western limits of Antioch to the eastern limits of Black Diamond and Eighth Street, 3.39 miles.

(5) Black Diamond-Bay Point Road, from the western limits of Black Diamond to Bay Point, 7.73 miles.

(6) Bay Point-Martinez Road, from Bay Point to crossing of Mount Diablo Creek, through the Government ranch and Vine Hill to Martinez, 8.20 miles.

(7)   Martinez-Crockett Road, from the western limits of Martinez, through Port Costa and Crockett, 5.16 miles.

(8)   Crockett-Pinole Road, from Crockett through Valona, Tormey and Rodeo to Hercules and Pinole, 7.65 miles.

(9)   Pinole-San Pablo Road, from the western limits of Pinole through San Pablo, 5.97 miles.

(10) San Pablo Avenue, from San Pablo to the county boundary, 4.22 miles.

(11) San Pablo Station Road, from the intersection of Alvarado Avenue and Church Street to Market and on Market Street to the Station, 1.16 miles.

(12) Tenth Street, from Station Road to the northern limits of Richmond and Tenth Street, 0.59 miles.

(13) Twenty-third Street Road, from San Pablo Station Road to Twenty-third Street and the limits of Richmond, 0.28 miles.

(14) Macdonald Avenue, from San Pablo Avenue Road on Macdonald Avenue to Richmond limits, 1.29 miles.

(15) Stege Road, from San Pablo Avenue and Potrero Avenue on Potrero to Bay, and on Bay to Stege, 0.83 miles.

(16) Potrero-Pullman Avenue, from Potrero and Bay on Potrero to Pullman and on Pullman to Cutting Boulevard, 0.80 miles.

(17) Cutting Boulevard, from Pullman Avenue across the Southern Pacific right of way on Cutting to the limits of Richmond, 0.44 miles.

(18) San Ramon Valley Road from the county boundary through Danville, 7.83 miles.

(19) Tassajara Road, from Danville to Tassajara, 8.06 miles.

(20) Danville-Walnut Creek Road, from Danville through Alamo and Walnut Creek, 6.43 miles.

(21) Tunnel Road from Walnut Creek through Lafayette to the county line, 10.78 miles.

(22) Walnut Creek-Concord Road, from Walnut Creek to Concord, 6.27 miles.

(23) Clayton Road, from the limits of Concord to Clayton, 5.34 miles.

(24) Concord-Martinez Road, from the limits of Concord to Bay Point-Martinez Road, 2.04 miles.

Estimated mileage, 124.60. Estimated cost, $1,460,000, including grading, paving, bridges, culverts, overhead, engineering, etc.: Bridges and culverts, $409,600; grading and paving, $1,051,000.

The bond election called for deciding upon the building of the roads is set for August 2. The success of the movement means more for the county than any other project. The board of supervisors adopted the report of the highway commission, and sounded the slogan in the cause of prosperity by calling an election for a bond issue of $1,460,000 for 124 miles of roads.

July 14, 1910.—Assessed valuation of the county, $35,231,648.

Successful rallies being held throughout the county for good roads have created great enthusiasm.

Directors elected on July 29 for a joint ferry company were: J. H. Glendon, Benicia; Gus Gnauf, Ed Kuhland and L. A. Stevens, Martinez; J. W. McClellan, L. M. Lasell and J. J. McNamara. President, J. J. McNamara; vice-president, J. H. Glendon; secretary, H. K. White; treasurer, Bank of Martinez.

The highway commission bonds were defeated by 256 votes.

September 17, 1910.—Pacheco Mills move their office and warehouse to Concord. The big mill remains at Pacheco. Work on the storage warehouse near the Southern Pacific depot in Concord is being pushed rapidly.

On October 7, 1910, fire broke out in the Burlington Hotel at Port Costa, causing a damage of $1000.

October 8, 1910.—The Pinole Hotel was totally destroyed by fire on Friday, the 7th, together with a cottage owned by Mrs. Frater; loss was $10,000.

The greatest real estate deal in the history of the county, from the standpoint of acreage and money, was made on October 7, when R. N. Burgess, of San Francisco, purchased the holding of Foskett & Elsworthy, stock raisers and butchers of Concord, thus coming into possession of 3700 acres. The tract consists of seven ranches: Government, Murphy, part of Galindo, Ayres, Webster, Samuels and Clier ranches.

With a charter membership of over sixty, the Concord Chamber of Commerce was organized October 15, 1910, at a meeting held in the I. O. O. F. Hall. A. W. Maltby was elected president; George W. Wilson, secretary; M. E. Lyon, treasurer. Board of Directors: H. Helsworthy, G. W. Whitman, E. U. Leland, and M. Neustaedter.

November 5, 1910.—Three autoists were killed and two injured in an accident on Pacheco Road, Sunday night, when a large roadster plunged into the ditch being excavated by the Port Costa Water Company two miles from Martinez. The dead are: Clarence E. Kline, J. P. Mahoney, and Peter Pacheco; the injured, J. McKay and Antonio Fortado.

November 12, 1910.—J. M. Stow has completed a fine business block in Walnut Creek, and another is in course of construction.

On November 22, 1910, at one p.m., the first rails of the Oakland & Antioch Electric were laid at Bay Point. One hundred men are engaged in the work.

The Postoffice at Somersville is to be discontinued. At one time this was the only office in the county to do an international money order business. When the coal mines closed, the business gradually decreased. It is also said that the Nortonville office is to be closed.

February 13, 1911.—The Oakland & Antioch Electric operated its first car from Bay Point Monday afternoon at three o'clock, and amid the tooting of horns and the blowing of whistles made its run from Bay Point to Concord. A splendid banquet was held in Concord.

February 25, 1911.—Miss Emilie Haywood, daughter of Mr. and Mrs. O. E. Haywood of Alhambra Valley, is now playing the leading part in the "Madame Sherry" Company in the East, after playing understudy one season with the New York Company. Wherever they go, Miss Haywood is making a hit with the critics.

March 11, 1911.—The new County Hospital building has been completed within the estimates and has been accepted by the supervisors.

The opening of the R. N. Burgess holdings, which have been subdivided near Concord, occurs next Sunday. Electric cars will be operated from Bay Point to Concord, and special trains will be run over the Southern Pacific from Oakland, San Francisco and Berkeley.

The election in Black Diamond to change the name to Pittsburg was carried 80 to 30.

The Oakland & Antioch Electric Railway Company have reincorporated as the Oakland, Antioch & Eastern Railway, with a capital stock of $10,000,000, of which $80,000 is paid up.

On May 6, 1911, a grand barbecue was held at Walnut Creek to welcome the advent of the Oakland, Antioch & Eastern Railway.

June 3, 1911.—Three thousand dollars were subscribed in one hour towards the building of the highway between Bay Point and Martinez.

June 6, 1911.—Walnut Creek voted $20,000 bonds for a new grammar school building, the bonds carrying 68 to 8.

The Woman's Improvement Club was formed at Walnut Creek on July 5. Mrs. H. Spencer was elected president; Mrs Hackett, vice-president; Mrs. George Crompton, secretary; Mrs. Joseph Silveira and Mrs. R. L. Nougaret, trustees.

September 16, 1911.—R. N. Burgess and his associates are considering opening a National Bank at Walnut Creek. It has been rumored for some time that a branch of the Concord Bank would be started at Walnut Creek.

October 15, 1911.—Sixteen families were rendered homeless and the town hall was destroyed by a fire in Rodeo, through the overturning of a lamp in a barn while a woman was milking a cow. Lack of water hindered the work of the fire-fighters.

November 4, 1911.—Point of Timber Parlor, Native Daughters of the Golden West, was instituted at Byron. Mrs. H. T. Hammond was elected president; Mrs. A. Alexson, past president; Mrs. C. Cople, first vice-president; Grace Blum, second vice-president; Viola Holway, third vice-president; Mrs. L. Richardson, secretary; Mrs. A. Plumley, treasurer; Maud Plumley, financial secretary; Mrs. M. Gaines, marshal; Minnie Steding, inside sentry; Lottie Hudson, outside sentry; Mrs. W. Frey, Mrs. A. Pitou and Mrs. Stone, trustees.

11

The Town Hall site was purchased by the trustees for $5000, and the remainder of the property was purchased for $4000, from the general fund for park purposes.

January 6, 1912.—The Martinez-Benicia Ferry Company will be incorporated with capital stock of $50,000, shares $10 each.

January 20, 1912.—Contra Costa Chamber of Commerce is launched at Concord. Over 100 boosters gathered at the banquet to work for all Contra Costa County. The members present Friday night, January 19, are determined that the people of the county shall learn and the world shall know that the old saying, "Joined hands and united efforts can win and build an empire," is applicable to this county as well as any other part of the State. A feature of the speeches was the good-roads bond issue.

During 1911 Contra Costa County was second in the State in the production of barley, which was over 3,000,000 bushels worth over $1,500,000.

February 17, 1912.—The old Veale tract of 1700 acres, about five miles northeast of Brentwood, was sold to the California Realty Company of San Jose for $140,000.

February 24, 1912.—The work on the loading station and oil refinery at Martinez will begin at once, was the statement of J. C. Van Eck manager of the Rothschild interests in the Royal Dutch Shell Oil Company. The initial appropriation is $500,000.

On Thursday, February 22, officials of the Associated Oil Company visited Martinez and Avon and inspected the site for their proposed refinery at Avon. If building operations begin soon, 500 men will be employed in construction work.

On March 14, Bay Point Chamber of Commerce was organized with sixteen charter members. The following officers were elected: President, S. W. Cunningham; vice-president, W. L. Cleveland; secretary, S. Shideler; treasurer, A. W. Smith.

March 16, 1912.—Contra Costa Chamber of Commerce was organized and officially launched today. Following are the officers: President, C. J. Rihn, of Richmond; first vice-president, E. J. Randall, of Concord; second vice-president, F. C. Macgurn; third vice-president, C. S. Dodge, of Crockett; secretary, F. E. Brooks, of Walnut Creek; treasurer, W. A. Hale, of Martinez. Directors: L. R. Mead, of Byron; Sumner Crosby, of Pittsburg; W. McBryde, of Pinole; Mrs. E. H. Shibley, of Martinez, president of the Women's Improvement Club; Mrs. C. W. Keeney, president of the Antioch Women's Club; Mrs. G. S. Gibson, president of the Richmond Women's Improvement Club. Charter members: W. A. Rogers, Joseph McCann, Julia A. Barry, John Rosa, A. N. Paterson, G. L. Putnam, C. L. Pingree, G. P. Upham, D. C. Ray, C. M. Bulger, R. R. Veale, Cecil Hall, H. J. Kammerer, F. C. Gill, S. M. Dodge, J. H. Martin, C. L. Dodge, D. J. Lucey, R. L. Clancy, J. R. Nystrom, L. N. Buttner, J. O'B. Wyatt, H. M. Stone, C. G. Goold, N. S. Boone, J. Kent, E. H. Shibley, Lillian V. Shibley, Mildred

L. Crampton, Leila E. Veale, S. Y. Shideler, W. R. South, J. M. Christen, F. P. Munson, L. H. Enloe, G. D. Young, H. Hall, I. B. Saliture, W. J. Love, W. Eggleston, T. S. Newson, T. B. Duery, W. G. Shaw, M. T. Sickal, E. J. Randall, L. Anderson Company, M. R. Jones, J. H. Trythall, J. W. McClellan, F. H. Upham, W. H. Penniman, P. H. Cunningham, C. Macgurn, H. A. West, A. C Gehringer, G. T. Crampton, F. L. Glass, W. A. Rugg, W. A. Hale, W. R. Sharkey, J. J. McNamara, J. P. Allen, J. F. Hoey, W. B. Williams, L. L. Levinson, G. O. Duncan, Nellie K. Cushing, Aga D. Lander, E. B. Barber, P. Douglas, W. S. Burpee, M. W. Joost, J. H. Coulter, A. B. Coleman, G. E. Green, F. E. Brooks.

March 27, 1912.—On March 23, 1912, Mr. and Mrs. Peter Thompson celebrated the fiftieth anniversary of their wedding at Lafayette.

May 18, 1912.—R. N. Burgess buys Lyons' interest in Concord Bank. This may mean that he will not open another bank as planned.

June 8, 1912.—The Pacheco Flour Mills are to suspend milling

June 11, 1912.—The Concord Warehouses were destroyed by fire. The losses were as follows: A. E. Blum, $5000, insurance, $1500; Mt. Diablo Commercial Co., grain, $7000, well insured; Mt. Diablo Commercial Co., hay, $3000, well insured; home of Miss Barrett, $1500.

July 13, 1912.—A crew of fifty workmen with tools arrived at Danville Wednesday night to begin work on the new road to the summit of Mt. Diablo, starting at Oakwood Park Stock Farm. The work has been started by the R. N. Burgess Company. Over 150 cars of rock and gravel has been ordered and will be delivered over the Southern Pacific.

On July 18 the famous Byron Hot Springs Hotel was burned to the ground. There were 100 guests in the hotel, but all escaped. Eight years ago the old hotel building was destroyed.

July 20, 1912.—The Dutch Shell Company have awarded the contract for ten steel tanks for storage of oil and the steel gas holders for the Asiatic Petroleum Company or Indian Oil Company, for $57,350, to the Western Pipe & Steel Company.

C. A. Hooper, Pittsburgh millionaire, has purchased the Moraga Grant at a cost of $1,000,000.

August 10, 1912.—The Mount Diablo Company will exploit Oakwood Farm. The club-house is being remodeled for occupancy.

August 10, 1912.—The town trustees awarded Murry-Elwell Company the contract to improve the water-front; their bid being $31,340, including the architect's and engineer's fees.

The charter for the Walnut Creek National Bank has arrived, and the R. N. Burgess Company will erect a new building for bank purposes.

October 12, 1912.—Great crowds were present at the Concord Walnut Carnival.

October 21, 1912.—The branch of San Ramon Valley Bank at Concord opened for business at nine o'clock a. m., this Monday. Guy E.

Green is cashier; J. H. Coulter, assistant; Eli Hutchinson and M. Frank Russi, resident directors.

The Corcoran ranch between Benicia and Selby, bordering Carquinez Straits, directly in the so-called funnel zone of the Selby Smelter, has been sold by the owners, Dan, John and Michael Corcoran, to the Selby Company for $100,000.

Bay View Pavilion, the only dance and entertainment hall in Martinez, was destroyed by fire on October 27. It was built in 1905 by J. J. McNamara and Reese Jones.

The First National Bank of Walnut Creek, founded by R. N. Burgess Company, opened for business in the Brooks real estate offices at Walnut Creek on October 28. J. A. Flint is cashier, and Elmer Cameron, assistant cashier.

November 2, 1912.—The John Nicholl Company sold to J. H. T. Watkinson 112 acres in the city of Richmond for $500,000. A $400,000 mortgage was given to Nicholl by Watkinson. Nicholl purchased the tract a few years ago for $100 per acre.

November 16, 1912.—The property of the Judson Dynamite & Powder Company, near Stege, has been sold to the E. I. du Pont de Nemours Powder Company of Pinole.

The Antioch paper mills, one of the most extensive industrial enterprises in the county, and the property of the Paraffine Paint Company, were totally destroyed by fire Tuesday afternoon. The fire started in Mill No. 5 when an oiler threw a quantity of oil on a hot roller used in slicking the paper. The oil blazed to the ceiling and set fire to the mill before aid could be summoned. The costly machinery in all the mills was entirely destroyed. The loss to the company is $500,000. About 130 men are thrown out of employment. During the last few months work has been under way, enlarging the plant to double its former capacity, and was about completed.

November 23, 1912.—The old Tule Ranch will be known hereafter as the Knightsen Ranch. It was purchased by W. J. Hotchkiss, of Berkeley, and comprises 3000 acres, part of which was at one time under cultivation, only to be destroyed by the great Jersey break several years ago. Three clamshell dredgers are working night and day on the reclamation project. When the levees are completed, a drainage pump, which cost $7000, will be installed.

The cottages and hotel at Byron Hot Springs are to be rebuilt at once.

December 4, 1912.—The town trustees accepted the new City Hall built by G. W. Boxton at a contract cost of $12,990. The hall is a fine two-story brick building, and is a credit to the town.

December 14, 1912.—The rebuilding of the tunnel road is now in progress. About twenty men and teams are working from the Fish ranch towards the tunnel.

December 21, 1912.—The California Delta Farms Company, capitalization $7,500,000, with an authorized bond issue of $3,500,000, acquired by purchase 39,337 acres of delta lands at an estimated value of $12,000,-000. Lee A. Phillips, of San Francisco, is president of the company. Twenty-two thousand acres are now under cultivation and leased. The lands involved are the Roosevelt and King Edward islands, owned by Holland Land & Water Company, and the Palms & Orwood tracts, owned by Orwood Land Company. On the latter's tract, 1000 acres are in asparagus, 5600 acres in potatoes, and 1400 acres in onions.

Lee Dyer received the appointment as postmaster at Avon and will open the office to accommodate the Association employees at work on the Marsh lands.

A head-on collision in dense fog wrecked two locomotives and injured several trainmen and passengers on the Santa Fe in Rodeo Valley near Luzon, Tuesday, the 17th of December. The injured passengers and trainmen, except those eastbound, were taken in a relief train to Richmond. Greater disaster was averted by the action of Dave Hopkins, on the west-bound train, who slowed down at the curve to comply with orders, saw the smoke of the on-coming train, and had his train at almost a stand-still when the collision occurred.

January 9, 1913.—Martinez people awakened to find a blanket of snow over two inches deep covering the ground. Young and old promptly took part in the greatest snow carnival ever held here. Snowballing and tobogganing were in order. The grammar and high schools were dismissed for the morning, so that all could enjoy the sport.

Ground was broken for a $1,000,000 refinery at Avon by the Associated Oil Company.

The Associated Oil Company asks for a wharf franchise; $10,000 is the estimated cost of the wharf.

Lacking just one week of being two years after the first Oakland & Antioch electric car was run over the line from Bay Point to Concord, the first electric train passed through Redwood Canyon tunnel Friday, February 21, onto the Oakland side and ran to Lake Temescal.

March 1, 1913.—The Western Pipe and Steel Company have been awarded the contract to erect twenty-five steel oil tanks, each of 55,000-barrel capacity, for the Associated Oil Company at Avon. The Nevada Dock Station will be maintained as terminus for their pipe lines.

The Oakland & Antioch line is opened from Bay Point to Oakland. The golden spike was driven Saturday, March 2, at midnight, by General Manager H. A. Mitchell.

Balfour-Guthrie Company was awarded the contract for a modern two-story reinforced concrete forty-room hotel building at Brentwood, to cost $41,000.

April 5, 1913.—The Associated Oil Company awards the contract for the erection of machine shops, boiler and pump houses, and drum sheds at Avon, to MacDonald & Kahn, at a cost of $19,489.

Articles of incorporation for the Bank of Brentwood were filed on April 4; capitalization, $50,000; $25,000 paid up. This is a Balfour-

Guthrie concern.   R. F. MacLeod, secretary of the company, holds 210 shares; R. E. Dean, 10 shares; F. H. Ludinghouse, 10 shares; Robert Wallace, Jr., 10 shares; and Alex Burness, 10 shares.

A Farmers' Institute was held at Oakley, April 17 and 18, and proved to be a big affair.

May 10, 1913.—With the placing in position of the forty-fifth five-foot section of concrete, on May 5, the great concrete chimney of the Mountain Copper Works in this city, the largest chimney of its kind in the State, was practically completed.   When the last bucket of concrete was deposited the American flag was raised, 300 feet above sea level.

On June 3, fires were built in the first of the three furnaces at the Mountain Copper Company's smelter, and the other two are to be connected up during the week.   The mammoth chimney proved a success.

May 17, 1913.—Warren McBryde was appointed supervisor in District No. 1 to succeed C. J. Rihn, resigned.

May 24, 1913.—The "Liberty Bell," the student body annual of the Liberty Union High School of Brentwood, is off the press in the Gazette office, and is one of the handsomest high-school annuals ever issued in the county.   It is a book of seventy-eight pages, with a large advertising section and with pictures of the graduating class: Myra Pearce, Elaine Wallace, Edith Cakebread, Richard Wallace and Judson Swift.   The cover design is a Liberty Bell; the colors, purple and gold; and it is dedicated to Balfour-Guthrie Company.   Myra Pearce is the editor-in-chief, and Elaine Wallace, business manager.

The finest annual ever issued by the students of the Alhambra High School, "The Torch," is now off the press.   It is a book of 100 pages, replete with interesting stories, bright and snappy notes, and fine cuts, and is bound in alligator skin, embossed in gold.   Credit for the book is given J. K. Cushing, the editor, and M. B. Veale, the business manager, and their staffs.

June 28, 1913.—The tunnel road is now open, as the road from the Fish ranch to the tunnel is completed.   While the road was closed, the supervisors of Alameda and Contra Costa Counties lowered the floor two feet and macadamized it.

The first electric train from Sacramento to the Bay over the O. A. & E. was operated Wednesday, July 3, when the officials and promoters made their first official tour.   The ferry boat Brigit, which will ferry the trains across Suisun Bay, was delivered to the company Tuesday evening and carried its first train of cars Wednesday morning.

J. Rio Baker was appointed county treasurer to succeed L. N. Buttner, deceased.

July 12, 1913.—The ferry boat, City of Seattle, which is to be put on the Martinez & Benicia run, arrived at Benicia Sunday after a successful trip from Seattle in tow of the steamer Wm. Chatham.   As soon as the boat has been inspected and a number of changes made, it will be put in operation.

July, 1913.—The property valuation of Contra Costa County is given as $48,000,000:

Alamo	$300,265	Nichols	$ 610,340
Alhambra	204,865	Orinda	119,460
Antioch	412,590	Oak Grove	797,430
Antone	77,455	Oakley	167,950
Ambrose	238,155	Pinole	176,315
Briones	224,370	Pacheco	403,565
Brentwood	511,445	Pittsburg	840,485
Byron	335,115	Pleasant Hill	359,440
Concord	842,515	Port Costa	462,325
Cowell	467,210	Rodeo	446,230
Cunningham	430,490	Richmond	1,944,730
Carquinez	1,506,820	Sobrante	839,920
Danville	359,550	Selby	956,810
Deer Valley	207,755	Summit	38,125
Eden Plain	652,165	Sycamore	368,160
Excelsior	524,655	San Pablo	1,284,510
Green Valley	218,245	Somersville	71,270
Franklin	74,780	San Ramon	526,455
Highland	121,600	Sand Mound	509,730
Hot Springs	307,525	Sheldon	167,305
Iron House	293,735	Tassajara	196,475
Jersey	234,055	Vine Hill	218,590
Lime Quarry	317,445	Vasco	89,065
Live Oak	238,400	Walnut Creek	597,765
Lone Tree	240,545	Willow Springs	315,380
Lafayette	418,800	Richmond	14,843,795
Liberty	211,785	Pittsburg	657,455
Mt. Pleasant	150,995	Martinez	1,151,510
Moraga	206,785	Antioch	547,165
Morgan Territory	87,050	Concord	298,075
Martinez	213,255	Pinole	158,075
Mt. Diablo	269,855	Hercules	652,715

July 19, 1913.—Stock subscription for the Martinez-Benicia Ferry & Transportation Company has been closed. About $23,000 in all has been subscribed.

The Bank of Brentwood threw open its doors on July 15. R. G. Dean is president and Lee Durham is cashier. The deposits the first day amounted to $22,138.

Traffic via the Martinez-Benicia ferry is very heavy. Sunday, July 27, the receipts amounted to $200.

August 4, 1913.—Work has started on the addition to the California-Hawaiian Company's refinery at Crockett. About $2,000,000 will be expended to bring the output to 40,000 tons of refined sugar annually.

Byron Hot Springs Hotel is to be rebuilt, and the specifications call for a concrete structure.

August 22, 1913.—A franchise has been sold whereby all towns in Contra Costa County will have gas. S. Waldo Coleman, to whom the franchise was granted, will soon be laying mains throughout the county.

The eight new wells of twelve-inch diameter and from forty to 100 feet deep, which have been sunk during the past few weeks at the Galindo Water Station of the Port Costa Water Company, are soon to be connected with the main line pipe, and water will be drawn from them to supply Martinez, Port Costa, Crockett and Rodeo, in addition to the manufacturing establishments which are steady patrons.

August 30, 1913.—Two aerial electrical stations of the P. G. & E. in Concord and Walnut Creek were wrecked by dynamite and the two towns plunged into darkness about midnight, August 23. The work was done by experts. The dynamite was placed so that the upper portion of one of the tall supporting poles was blown away and the cross-beam so shattered that it dropped, throwing the heavy transformers to the ground, where they were broken. There have been several threats over the employment of non-union men.

The C. A. Smith Lumber Yards at Bay Point were swept by flames on August 26, and over 40,000,000 feet of the most expensive lumber in the yards destroyed; $1,000,000 is the estimated loss. The mill and box factory were saved. Calls for help were sent to Concord, Richmond, Martinez, Pittsburg and Antioch. A special train over the O. A. & E. brought fire-fighters from Pittsburg; a special over the Santa Fe from Richmond arrived about midnight; and about one o'clock a Southern Pacific train came from Oakland. The fire tug Crolona of the California & Hawaiian Sugar Company was brought out and did valiant service in saving docks and wharves. Orders were sent out to do everything to stop the fire, and a dynamiting crew blew up several large lumber piles before the flames could be checked. While over 1000 men were fighting the flames, the women of Bay Point prepared hot coffee for them.

On August 27 an aerial transformer of the P. G. & E. in Richmond was blown up at the corner of Cutting Boulevard and Kearney Street, which wrecked the lines carrying current for electric light to Pullman, Stege and East Richmond.

On September 3, 1913, the Oakland, Antioch & Eastern began regular train service over their line from Sacramento to Oakland. The event was celebrated by a luncheon at Hotel Oakland at which city officials, boosters and others from Sacramento joined with Oaklanders in lauding the possibilities of the new road.

September 17, 1913.—The San Ramon warehouse burns, and 850 tons of hay are a total loss. Bishop Brothers and ranchers of the valley were heavy losers.

The 4000-foot wharf at Avon was finished this week. It has a frontage of 200 feet on Suisun Bay and is fifty feet wide.

A gala event was the presenting of the band stand to the city by the Women's Improvement Club Saturday night. The band concert was a big drawing card of the evening.

At a meeting of the board of directors of the Bank of Concord, held on October 3, the Burgess and Whitman interests in the bank were sold to W. K. Cole and his associates of the San Ramon Valley Bank. The Concord branch will be discontinued.

Mr. and Mrs. George W. Yoakum celebrated their fiftieth wedding anniversary Saturday, November 1, 1913, at their home in Martinez.

On November 30 the Pacheco postoffice was discontinued. It was established fifty years ago. All mail hereafter will designate Martinez or Concord as postoffice.

The Brentwood Hotel formally opened its doors Monday night for a grand ball. The hotel cost Balfour-Guthrie Company $60,000.

January 3, 1914.—Pacheco was inundated and two feet of water was on the main highway to Concord. Considerable road-work was washed away, caused by over-flowing of Walnut Creek. Near the slaughter-yards eleven of the telephone poles were blown down on the Martinez-Concord road. At Vallejo Junction the high cliff began to slide and crews were rushed there to protect the railroad. The O. A. & E. suffered from the storm in Moraga Valley, where tracks were undermined.

Rainfall up to January 1, 1914, 9.23 inches.

The Army Board approves the Richmond Harbor project, according to information sent by Congressman C. F. Curry.

The Martinez-Benicia Ferry makes a splendid record. Its financial standing is excellent, as shown by the secretary at a meeting of the stockholders. Total receipts from July 20 to January 1, $36,788; 24,032 passengers were carried, and 4352 autos, 566 motorcycles and 705 teams.

March 7, 1914.—The first trains over California's first community railway were operated Monday on the new line of the San Ramon Valley Railway, extending from Walnut Creek to Danville. The seven and a half miles of road was built by subscription and is the property of the farmers who own the property over which the road operates. The rolling stock and equipment are furnished by the Oakland, Antioch & Eastern Railway.

Henry J. Curry has just completed a new theater building at a cost of over $30,000, which was formally opened on April 17. The theater is a handsome building and fills a long-felt need in Martinez.

The Associated Oil Company is to double its capacity at Avon. They are running full capacity now and are unable to supply the demand for their refined products. The work of grading for the new stills and tank bottoms is under way.

May 23, 1914. — The world's greatest ferry, Contra Costa, was launched in the West Oakland shipyards Saturday morning. It is to be used in ferrying the Southern Pacific trains across the Straits from Benicia to Port Costa. The length of the ferry is 433.4 feet; over guards, 420 feet; beam, 66½ feet; depth moulded, 19.5 feet; depth amidships, 19 feet 9 inches. It will carry four train tracks with a capacity of thirty-six freight cars and two engines. It has fourteen bulkheads; and 2,000,000 feet of lumber, thirty tons of spikes, seventy-six tons of round iron, and 16,600 treenails entered into its construction. The Contra Costa will be put into service on June 1 and will handle the passenger trains through the new steps, while the Solano will handle the freight trains.

St. Mark's Catholic Church in Richmond was totally destroyed by fire on May 22. The rescue of the Blessed Sacrament and the vestments by Rev. O'Connor was one of the incidents which will long be remembered. The church was built in 1911 at a cost of $8000.

June 6, 1914.—An order was placed by the Shell Oil Company for 172 miles of pipe for a line between Coalinga and Martinez. This is pretty good proof that the Shell Company intends to establish their long-talked-of refinery here.

Contra Costa County, not including Richmond, receives annually hundreds of millions of feet of lumber; millions of pounds of wood pulp for paper manufacture; thousands of cars of ores to be smelted, hundreds of carloads of sand, scores of cars of manganese ore and silica, millions of tons of raw sugar to be refined, thousands of cars of grain to be handled at its ports, and thousands of carloads of other raw materials for use in its factories. Contra Costa County produces and ships annually thousands of cars of celery, asparagus and river fruits; and thousands of cars of manufactured articles are produced in the factories.

July 25, 1914.—A new pipe line, to cost $4,234,685, and an oil refinery are assured for Martinez.

August 1, 1914.—Martinez lost the tide-lands case and thereby has no right or title to the municipal water-front. Suit was begun in Superior Court in 1911 against eighty or more defendants.

November 18, 1914.—Russi & Sonner Flour Mills at Pacheco were destroyed by fire. The mills were about to be reopened after being idle several years.

Seven hundred cars of material are to be shipped to Martinez for building the Shell refinery.

December 24, 1914.—The giant ferry, Contra Costa, made her first trip today.

A. B. McKenzie resigns as district attorney to accept the position of superior judge, Department 2, that has just been authorized for Contra Costa County. This will save holding extra sessions of court when there is a full calendar.

The new library and reading room at Brentwood was opened to the public on January 5. Brentwood can claim the distinction of being the first town in the field to put up its own building. Entire credit is due the Library Association which was formed last February, with Mrs. Andrew Bonnickson at its head and an executive committee of earnest and progressive women.

1914 was a big year for the Martinez and Benicia Ferry; it carried 13,659 autos and 62,000 passengers.

The Lacy Manufacturing Company of Los Angeles has the contract for building forty-one steel tanks of 55,000 gallons capacity each, for the Shell Oil Company at Martinez. The work is to be completed by April 1.

The hull of the Oakland, Antioch & Eastern ferry boat Bridgit, which burned in the Mallard Island slip several months ago, has been lifted from the bay, and the entrance to the slip on the Contra Costa Mainland is now open.

On February 3, 1915, Antioch Lodge, L. O. M., was instituted with a charter membership of seventy-two.

On February 5 the Mountain Copper Company, Ltd., resumed operations in its plant at Martinez. The plant will operate to fifty-per-cent capacity.

April 3, 1915, was Contra Costa County Day at the P. P. I. E., and all the county turned out, with over 400 automobiles in line and about 1000 people walking. The parade was over three miles long and went up Market Street, San Francisco, headed by the Richmond Band. Every town and every industry of any importance in the county were represented in the procession, as were also the schools. It was the greatest dedication day since the exposition opened and will be long remembered by those who participated.

April 10, 1915.—The city of Martinez has made an appropriation of $50 per month to the Free Library, and it will be known as the Martinez Municipal Library. The appropriation is for the next ten months, and thereafter $30 per month, unless a tax levy is made to support the library.

On April 12, 1915, the Contra Costa County Bar Association was organized at a meeting of the attorneys of the county held in Department No. 1 Courtroom. W. S. Tinning, of Martinez, was elected president; J. E. Rodgers, of Martinez, vice-president; T. H. DeLap, of Richmond, secretary; Leo F. Tormey, of Martinez, treasurer. Members of the executive committee: M. R. Jones, A. S. Ormsby, of Martinez; and D. J. Hall, of Richmond.

April 24, 1915.—A deal aggregating over $3,000,000 was announced today, when it became known that an Eastern syndicate had agreed to take over 30,000 shares of outstanding capital stock of the Giant Powder Company at $110 per share.

The Richmond-Marin ferry service opened May 1 and 2 with a monster two-day celebration. The first boat to cross from the Marin County shore to the Point Orient wharf was met by a welcoming committee. A luncheon was given and on May 2 the Richmond people were guests of Marin County at San Rafael, where a barbecue was held.

On May 15, the board of supervisors inspected the new addition to the County Hospital, which was erected at a cost of $30,000. The addition gives accomodations to bring the total to 120.

The Union Oil Company is increasing its capacity at Oleum and spending $25,000. They will build fifteen new storage tanks and increase the size of their wharf.

June 5, 1915.—The Shell Company starts operating the American Oriental plant. G. W. Geear to be superintendent at Bull's Head Point. The Shell lease became effective Tuesday and fires were relighted, with all the American-Oriental force at their former places.

The Valley Pipe Line Company, of Coalinga, has started oil through the pipes to test the lines. There are eleven stations between the tank farm and Coalinga. The capacity of the line is 30,000 barrels every twenty-four hours.

The first auto party over the new Mount Diablo scenic boulevard, built by the R. N. Burgess interests, has reached the 2500-foot level, to which point the road is completed. There the inn and toll-house are to be built. The toll rates as fixed by the supervisors are: 2-passenger automobile, $1.00; all others, $1.50; 2-horse vehicle, $1.50; 4-horse vehicle, $2.00; 6-horse vehicle, $2.50; individual persons, 25 cents; cow, horse, etc., 10 cents each; sheep, 2½ cents.

On Wednesday, June 8, the Antioch Paper Mills suffered a $50,000 fire. The entire stock of paper-making material was lost, in the destruction of the rag pile.

The Contra Costa Free Library is the first library in the State which is in line for aid from the Carnegie Library Fund. The appropriation will be $2500; the city to contribute $250 each year towards its maintenance, which is the only condition.

The new $10,000 hospital erected by the Standard Oil Company, adjoining its refinery at Richmond, will be officially opened on June 12 by the Contra Costa County Medical Society.

July 19, 1915.—The Boulevard District election for commissioners was held in the two polling places, Moraga and Alamo; Arthur Burton, Edw. R. Williams, and Josiah Boucher were elected. The next step is to organize and lay out the course, which has practically been decided upon.

June 26, 1915.—Stills are completed, tanks filled, and actual operation hinges on the completion of the power station, is the progress announced by the Shell Oil Company. The plant, as laid out, will give employment to 150 men, all skilled mechanics in their line.

The board of supervisors, on Monday, voted their intention of levying a direct tax of 25 cents on every $100 assessed valuation of property for the next fiscal year, to start the building of public highways from the tunnel through the county to Byron.

Increase in assessed valuation of property from 1906 to 1915:

1906	$21,590,845	1911	$39,700,914
1907	27,122,288	1912	42,631,665
1908	29,405,603	1913	47,731,341
1909	32,472,408	1914	52,204,930
1910	35,399,378	1915	54,488,451

On July 12 an entire block of business places at Rodeo was gutted by fire; the loss was $25,000.

August 14, 1915.—The third fire which has visited the Antioch Paper Mills has been burning two days, with a loss of over $60,000.

The most disastrous grass fire in the county was that of Tuesday afternoon, when 3000 acres of pasture and stubble in the Rodeo Valley were destroyed by flames. Hundreds of men were fighting the blaze. The Santa Fe sent a special train of fire fighters.

The supervisors on Monday awarded the contract for the construction of the drawbridge over Pacheco Slough at Avon, and for pile trestling along the Martinez-Bay Point road, and for the first link of 3.01 miles of the permanent county highway from the tunnel to Bryant Station. The contract price is $35,625.75.

On September 4, 1915, an explosion occurred at the Hercules Powder Plant in Pinole, killing two men. Following is a list of previous explosions at this plant: July 27, 1892, nitro-glycerine house; four killed and nine wounded. May 21, 1894, nitro-glycerine house; five men killed. September 1, 1897, mixing and packing house; four men killed. May 3, 1899 nitro-glycerine house; two killed. June 4, 1904, gelatine mixing house; four men (2 Chinese) killed. Two small explosions in 1905; two men killed. July 1907, nitro-glycerine; four Chinese killed. February 1, 1908, quinine packing house and three cars of dynamite; four white men and twenty-three Chinese killed. September 30, 1909, nitro-glycerine explosion; four killed.

September 30, 1915. — This is the fiftieth anniversary of the founding of the Antioch Congregational Church.

On October 5, 1915, a business block in Brentwood was burned, causing a loss of $20,000, to the following property: Tremley's Hardware Store, Peter Olsen's building adjoining, the residences of Frank Golden, Hercules Logan and M. Sargent, two barns, and the tank and tank-house owned by the Balfour-Guthrie Company.

The Contra Costa Gas Company's plant at Pittsburg, which supplies gas to Antioch, Pittsburg, Concord and Martinez, is being enlarged by adding a 20,000-cubic-foot storage tank and machines that will double the capacity. The plant represents a $200,000 investment. The main office of the company is located at Martinez.

January 27, 1916.—Concord experienced a light fall of snow this morning.

February 19, 1916.—During 1915 the Martinez-Benicia Ferry carried 78,895 passengers, 16,893 automobiles, 1183 motorcycles, 1439 teams. The directors of this corporation are W. H. George, J. J. McNamara, J. W. McClellan, H. Likas, P. B. Fry and L. V. Cooper. Total disbursements for the year, $18,666; received from all sources, $30,045.48; sinking fund, $4000.

The early settlers of Contra Costa County, those men and women who came in the early days, held a reunion on February 23 at the home of

Mrs. Mary Gilpatrick in honor of Mrs. J. H. Carothers, who celebrated her eighty-eighth birthday.   Those present were:

Year Came		Year Came	
Charles Lohse (age, 91 yrs.) 1849		Mrs. L. C. Wittenmyer	1865
Mrs. Jane E. Bennett	1852	Mrs. Caroline Brown	1849
Mrs. Hathaway	1853	Mrs. H. Hale	1859
Mrs. Leontine Blum	1859	Mrs. Manuel Taylor	1866
Mrs. C. Bower	1850	Mrs. Dora Ludden	1850
Miss G. Miranda	1851	Mrs. Margaret J. Kelly	1864
Mrs. Charles Lohse	1850		

March 18, 1916.—Contracts were awarded for a clubhouse, garage and cottages at Avon by the Associated Oil Company, at a cost of $38,000.

The Contra Costa Free Library was established on July 21, 1913. Work began on October 1 in a small room rented from the Martinez Free Reading Room Association. Mrs. Alice Whitbeck, librarian of the Richmond Public Library, was appointed librarian, with Miss Weyand as assistant. They started in a very small way a system that has been far-reaching in influence. Through the cooperation of Mr. Hanlon, county superintendent of schools, the majority of schools over the county are in close touch with and receive every benefit of the librarian and library. Miss Weyand resigned and Miss Hale was appointed assistant. Later Miss Coulter and Miss Halliday were added to the force. There were eighteen branches the first year and sixty-six in 1915. In addition to her library work, the librarian has given talks at schools and clubs in the various towns.

April 7, 1916.—Charles E. Bibber was elected a member of the board of directors of the Bank of Concord to succeed J. D. Silveira, who resigned. Mr. Bibber purchased Silveira's interest in the bank.

May 24, 1916.—The Matson liner, Wilhelmina, yesterday completed her eighty-second voyage from Honolulu, bringing 119 cabin and 87 steerage passengers, 77,000 bags of raw sugar, 12,000 bags of refined sugar, 500 tons of molasses, 28,000 cases of canned pineapples, 3000 bunches of bananas, 650 cases of fresh pineapples, and 280 bags of coffee. The liner was docked at Crockett this morning to discharge the cargo of raw sugar.

June 24, 1916.—The Gazette, always first with the latest, has secured the United Press News Service and is now the only paper in the county with direct wire news service daily.

July 15, 1916.—The Tunnel Road is now open to traffic. Automobiles are allowed to travel the highway, the first time in a year.

On July 30, 1916, the new chapel of the Martinez Christian Science Society was formally opened and dedicated. Its seating capacity of 200 was filled. The chapel is located on Mellus between Las Juntas and Court Streets, and is of a Swiss bungalow type.

The first Carnegie Library in Contra Costa County was opened and dedicated at Walnut Creek on August 22, with appropriate ceremonies. This is also the first library to be built, with funds obtained through the Carnegie Foundation, after the bungalow type particularly adapted to the needs of smaller places, where the cost of maintaining a larger building would be burdensome.

The Antioch branch of the County Library opens on September 16. The building was built with funds from the Carnegie Foundation.

September 17, 1916.—Mount Diablo Parlor No. 101, N. S. G. W., unfurled the American flag on a pole forty feet above the peak of Mount Diablo, and 3849 feet above sea level. A staff built of cement and rock quarried from the flank of the mountain itself was dedicated to the "Pioneers of Contra Costa County." Mr. and Mrs. Robert G. Dean, of Brentwood, who came here in 1850, pulled the cord which released the flag. The flag was made by Mrs. J. H. Martin, formerly of Concord, and Miss Loretta Collins of Vallejo, and was presented to Mount Diablo Parlor. The staff from which it is to fly was built by W. H. George, of the Cowell Portland Cement Company, and was presented to Mount Diablo Parlor. The construction work was handled by H. B. Morey & Sons, of Menlo Park.

On September 30, 1916, the new Hotel Martinez was thrown open to the public with a grand ball. The hotel has been remodeled and rebuilt, and also refurnished, and is steam-heated throughout. On the roof a dancing platform has been built and provision made for afternoon and evening parties.

January 6, 1917.—The six big realty companies with which B. Schapiro and his associates in land development and promotion in Contra Costa County are interested, have been consolidated into one holding company known as the Contra Costa Realty Company. Articles of incorporation are on file. The capitalization is $1,000,000, with the principal place of business at Richmond. The directors are: Ben Schapiro, R. R. Veale, J. E. Bouquet, F. A. Cascioni, H. A. Johnston, E. M. Downer and E. D. Armstrong.

January 13, 1917.—In a lengthy opinion in the case of Henry Cowell Cement & Lime Company vs. the various ranchers in that vicinity, Judge R. H. Latimer holds that dust is a private nuisance and not a public evil. Thus comes to a close a suit which has extended over many years and cost thousands of dollars. The suit was filed in 1910 in the name of the people of the State of California vs. Cowell Portland Cement Company to abate a nuisance.

January 16, 1917.—Alhambra Creek was frozen over at seven o'clock this morning for the first time in over twenty years.

March 3, 1917.—The Union Oil Company is to increase the capacity of its asphalt and lubricating oil plants at Rodeo.

March 10, 1917.—The first shipment of material arrived for the construction of Unit Three of the Trumble system at the Shell refinery.

On March 6, the new ferry, City of Martinez, was christened as she glided down the ways at Pittsburg. As soon as she is fitted up she will be put on the Martinez-Benicia run.

March 17, 1917.—The Associated Oil Company reclaims a sixty-acre tract near Avon for additions to the big plant. The addition will be for lubricants particularly.

The Standard Oil Company has purchased 100 acres of the Mizner estate and will at once begin the work of filling, grading and preparing for the extension of its mammoth plant at Richmond. When completed, the plant will be the largest of its kind in the world.

The California Cap Works at Stege were destroyed by a blast on March 12. Two Chinese were killed and three seriously injured. The explosion was caused by a Chinaman dropping a tray of caps.

The Associated Oil Company is preparing to operate the American-Oriental property. The lease held on the property by the Shell Oil Company expired some time ago.

The San Ramon High School was dedicated on March 10, when a large crowd gathered to witness the ceremonies.

March 13, 1917.—Unusual precautions are being taken by the Shell Company in guarding its big refinery and tank farm at Martinez during these days and weeks of strained relations with Germany. A strict guard has been maintained ever since the plant has been in operation. Day and night guards patrol the property. No passes are issued except to employees and persons whose business calls them to the plant.

Searchlights and machine guns will protect the Standard Oil refinery at Richmond. Sixteen giant searchlights, formerly used at the Exposition, have been secured; and 100 new guards have been put on.

April 7, 1917.—Two tall towers on which will be mounted two powerful searchlights, and which will be operated during the night and throw their powerful beams of light to all parts of the $5,000,000 refinery, will be in place in a few days.

Company B, 2nd Infantry, N. G. C., of Richmond, was mustered into Federal service at the Presidio in San Francisco Tuesday afternoon.

Twenty-three special deputy sheriffs were sworn in this week to guard the property of the Associated Oil Company at the Avon Refinery & American-Oriental works. The men were nearly all employees of the company.

Practically all the big plants on the bay shore are guarded. The Standard Oil at Richmond, Giant & Hercules Powder Works, Union Oil at Oleum, American-Oriental, Associated Oil and Great Western Electro-Chemical are guarded day and night by armed guards.

The Contra Costa County Council for Defense has been named by Governor Stephens. It includes Judge R. H. Latimer, Sheriff R. R. Veale, District Attorney T. D. Johnson, and J. H. Trythall, chairman of the board of supervisors. These will name three private citizens.

April 28, 1917.—A food-conservation mass-meeting was held in Martinez and was attended by over 300 citizens from various parts of the county; it was held under the auspices of the County Council of Defense.

The Concord business district was swept by fire, including the Concord Inn, Post Office, Mercantile Company, Bank of Concord, B. Neustaedter & Son, general merchandise, and the offices of L. L. Martin, D. D. S., E. E. Johnson, D. D. S., A. S. Sherlock, attorney, and Mrs. S. A. Fletcher, modiste. Nearby towns sent assistance, including Martinez, Antioch, Avon, Cowell, Walnut Creek and Oakland.

May 5, 1917.—Judge O. Duncan, of Walnut Creek, first commissioned officer from Contra Costa County, was called to the colors as first lieutenant this week.

The Martinez Red Cross Auxiliary was organized, with 163 members, to handle the work in Martinez; chairman, W. H. Hanlon.

The veterans of the Spanish-American War stand ready, and members of Fitzhugh Lee Camp No. 9 pledged themselves to the Government, giving notice that they stand ready to answer a call to arms.

On his twenty-fourth birthday, R. W. Netherton, son of E. W. Netherton of Martinez, left Sunday to enlist in the aviation corps of the United States Army.

June 2, 1917.—Following is a list of the Mount Diablo High School graduates: W. B. Bliss, Mary W. Bott, Joseph Brazil, Minnie M. Carpenter, Laura E. Dunn, M. L. Frandsen, F. Freitas, J. W. Graves, Marjorie Holman, Charles Jennings, Dorenda Maltby, A. K. Matheson, Clara M. Morken, Ida I. Myrick, Zelma I. Myrick, F. W. Neff, E. L. Parker, Julie H. Prettyman, J. A. Randall, J. J. Salazar, A. Sibrian, Ethel C. Smith, Beatrice A. de Soto, C. L. Thomson, H. H. Titcomb, Helen G. Welch, Hazel B. Wetmore and N. F. Wilson. This is the largest class to be graduated in the history of the school.

A fast Oakland, Antioch & Eastern train crashed into an automobile near Moraga on May 27. Four women and one man were instantly killed: Miss Gladys Mortimer, Mrs. A. E. Richmond, Miss Eva Walker, Mrs. F. J. Canin, and A. J. Hawkins, all of Oakland.

A recruiting station for Company H, 2nd California Infantry, was opened on May 30. Lieut. M. O. Ballard is in charge, with Captain Sutherland as assistant. They aim to bring their company up to its maximum strength.

Mortimer Veale, Cullom Hadapp, Malcolm Borland, Earl Soto, and Ralph West, on the eve of their departure for war service, were banqueted by Martinez citizens.

Home Guards ready for any emergency: E. W. Jensen, Martinez; J. N. Feeley, Hercules; E. H. Shibley, Port Costa; Otto Hasenpuch, Valona; W. Matheson, Cowell; W. R. Wood, Walnut Creek; G. B. Putnam, Pleasant Hill; Alex Burrick, Brentwood. Eighty men have signed the Home Guard roll.

June 9, 1917.—6298 young Contra Costa County citizens sign the roll for the draft, the various towns being represented as follows:

Walnut Creek	68	Selby	46
Concord	109	Richmond	1907
Avon	18	Rodeo	146
Alamo	22	San Pablo	167
Martinez	393	San Pablo Creek	24
Moraga	34	Hercules	143
Clayton	39	Pinole	157
Lafayette	50	Vine Hill	35
Cowell	68	Giant	48
Danville	107	Alhambra	76
Tassajara	28	Stege	128
Port Costa	94	Nichols	102
San Ramon	23	Bay Point	105
Crockett	363	Valona	190
Pacheco	28	Pittsburg	390
Antioch	326	Lone Tree	70
Oakley	91	Jersey	110
Knightsen	89	Orwood	17
Brentwood	94	Byron	130

June 16, 1917.—Contra Costa County subscribed $856,350 to the first Liberty Loan call.

On Saturday, June 23, the Concord Library, the third of the Carnegie Foundation Fund buildings for this county, was opened to the public.

The entire county is now thoroughly organized in all departments for the work of winning the war.

July 7, 1917.—As a member of Ambulance Unit No. 2 of the University of California, Malcolm McKenzie, son of Judge and Mrs. A. B. McKenzie of Martinez, left with 118 other members of that unit for Allentown, Pa., Wednesday afternoon, the first Martinez boy to start on the journey across the seas to the battle front.

The ferry boat City of Martinez made its first regular run in the Martinez & Benicia service on July 6.

August 11, 1917.—John Hansen, of Jersey, was the first man from Contra Costa County who successfully passed all requirements of the draft board and was passed into the conscription army of the United States.

By order of the board of supervisors District No. 17 was created, which includes Knightsen and Oakley.

September 8, 1917.—Monday's fire record in Martinez: National Hotel; S. Barlettani, blacksmith shop and residence; Mrs. M. Brosch, residence; S. Barlettani, cottage; G. Stewart, grocery; J. W. McClellan, residence; L. Bulger, residence. The loss was $30,000, partly covered by insurance.

October 20, 1917.—The regimental organization of the Contra Costa Home Guards has been completed and the captains of the three most proficient companies in the organization have been elevated to higher rank. Captain E. W. Jensen has been made Lieutenant Colonel; Captains Long of Richmond, Jack Kasch of Cowell, and Frank Thompson of Lafayette have been elevated to the rank of Major.

Election of officers was held Thursday for the Martinez company. First Lieut. B. E. Stotts was made Captain; Second Lieut. Gould was made First Lieutenant; and First Sergeant Richmond was made Second Lieutenant.

December 8, 1917.—A deal was closed Monday in Martinez for the transfer of the Wallace water-front lands lying west of the Grangers' wharf to George W. McNear, Inc.

January, 1918.—Justice of Peace C. H. Hayden resigned. Rex L. Boyer was appointed as his successor for township No. 1.

January 19, 1918.—Raymond F. Gavin, the first Contra Costa boy to make the supreme sacrifice, was laid to rest beside his parents in Sunset View, Richmond.

February 2, 1918.—Three lost their lives in the fire which destroyed Miller's Hotel at Fairview.

The Martinez sewer and water bonds were carried by a majority of over three to one; $200,000 was the amount voted on.

The first Martinez boy to give up his life in France was Private Henry A. NcNamara, who died accidentally. He was buried at Suresnes, France, April 3, 1918.

A letter from a Richmond boy, J. M. Masiel, private, Company D, 6th U. S. Engineers:

"My regiment has been attached to the British for two months, and we have been in the active service ever since, from the third line up to the front, where we were lucky to have our first chance with the British to prove our ability. If you have heard anything about the engineers helping to hold back the wild bull-headed Hun, it was us (cut by censor). Believe me, we sure knocked them over while they lasted.

"The Tommies, Australians, Canadians and all of them will never forget us, being engineers, doing what we did. We built steel bridges across the Somme so fast it made their heads swim. We took prisoners and killed the enemy like a mowing machine cuts grass. I never saw such a mess in my life. It will take him a good many nights to bury them.

"They came over ten to one. We were in the front line seven days and nights. We gave him his! If you see my mother, ask her to let you see the thanks we received from the Fifth Army General of the British.

"I've seen everything over here. An American aviator brought down a Fritz two-seater yesterday, that dropped about two Richmond blocks from us. The pilot and observer were both lucky they did not get killed.

"We wear our steel helmets all the time, day and night—so much shrapnel about when we start shooting at his planes.

"I think I'm the first Richmond boy to be in the front line at the right time, and also the first one to get a Fritzie. I've got a souvenir from him for luck."

June 8, 1918.—Bert Curry of Richmond was appointed coroner by the board of supervisors to fill the vacancy left by Dr. C. L. Abbott.

June 15, 1918.—The San Francisco Milling Company's local plant at Pittsburg was totally destroyed by fire last night, with all the machinery, raw and finished products, one car of wheat, and one car barley.

The first Contra Costa boy to meet death in action on the battlefields of the Marne was Private Sidney Severns, U. S. Marine Corps, who was killed on June 7. The message was received by his mother in Martinez the same day she received a "Mother's Day" note from her boy, which said, "Don't worry about me. I have not been anywhere near the great drive yet. I have not fired a shot out of my rifle since I have been in France."

Martinez pays $34,004.53 for a water system from the Port Costa Water Company, including the system, pumping plant, site, excepting the main pipe-line to Port Costa and Crockett. The deeds were delivered to the trustees, and the plant will be turned over on July 25.

Reclamation projects in the great San Joaquin island delta region have been set afoot since January 1, amounting to $3,000,000. Foremost of these have been the Delta Farms Company, and the Lee Phillips and subsidiary interests.

July 27, 1918.—The Martinez Canning Company's plant, on the Martinez water-front between the C. T. and Grangers' wharves, is ready for business with the first season's run. The building and equipment cost about $300,000.

The first Crockett man to make the supreme sacrifice on the battle-fields of France was Corporal Ora Alfred Sweet, Company D, 26th Infantry. He was killed in action on the French front on July 21.

On August 20, the old Briones home, on the corner of Estudillo and Thompson Streets, was destroyed by fire. It was one of the oldest existing landmarks in Martinez, having been erected sixty years ago by Casmido Briones.

At the age of eighty-six years, Mrs. Ingraham, of Vine Hill, is proud of the work she has done for the Red Cross.

September 14, 1918.—On Thursday the Liberty Union High School at Brentwood was totally destroyed by fire, starting from chemicals in the school laboratory. The building and annex were well insured, but the loss of books to the pupils will be heavy. School opened two weeks ago.

November 9, 1918.—Corporal Peter Byer, Jr., of Tassajara, and Simon Anderson, of San Ramon, made the supreme sacrifice on the field of battle in France. They were among the first Contra Costa boys to enter service.

November 30, 1918.—2,000,000 tins is the 1918 pack of the Martinez Cannery.

January 11, 1919.—The gelatin plant at the Hercules Powder Works blew up on January 7, killing four men.

On January 6, the news flashed over the country of the death of Ex-President Theodore Roosevelt.

The Martinez-Benicia Ferry & Transportation Company bought from Mrs. Helen Muir Funk nine acres and the old wharf of the Grangers' property at the foot of Berrellessa Street for $10,000.

February 22, 1919.— United States Congress appropriates $64,500 for widening and deepening of Suisun Bay and the San Joaquin River channel from Antioch to Martinez. This was obtained through Congressman C. F. Curry.

During 1918 the Martinez-Benicia Ferry transported 83,280 automobiles, 296,574 passengers, 965 teams and 3115 motorcycles. The directors reelected are: J. J. McNamara, J. W. McClellan, of Martinez; W. H. George, of Cowell; and A. J. Pementa, J. R. Chisholm, R. H. Mann, and Gus Gnauck of Benicia.

On Sunday, March 9, the reorganized Martinez Band of twenty-six pieces gave a very enjoyable concert at the City Hall Park.

May 3, 1919.—At the recent reorganization of the Gazette Publishing Company, the following officers were elected: W. A. Rugg, president and general manager; B. E. Stotts, vice-president and assistant general manager; J. K. Cushing, secretary and general news editor.

May 24, 1919.—John Weaver, an aged recluse living near Clayton, was found murdered on Friday morning. He lived alone in a small cabin. Robbery is believed to have been the motive, for he was in the habit of keeping money and valuables in his cabin. He was over sixty, and a pioneer of this section.

July 12, 1919.—Practically the entire central portion of Brentwood was destroyed by fire Tuesday morning, when a blaze started in the store of O. H. Jansee. The loss was estimated at $15,000.

July 19, 1919.—The bond issue for $125,000 for the high school building was carried at Wednesday's election.

July 26, 1919.—A phenomenal vote was cast throughout the county in favor of the $2,600,000 good-roads bond issue. The vote showed 3852 for and 169 against—22 to 1.

Andrew Carnegie died at his home in Lenox, Mass., August 11, 1919.

Three hundred people were present at the opening of the Concord Farm Center Club-house on August 16.

August 30, 1919.—Life imprisonment was given Peter D'Amico, who was found guilty of the killing of Frank Bradon in a Pittsburg saloon several months ago.

In one of the most blood-curdling wholesale murders that has ever been committed in Contra Costa County, three Hindoos were chopped to pieces in their cabins on Jersey Island early Tuesday morning, Bran Singh, Bhetan Singh and Iber Singh. The report of the murder was made by Lachman Singh, who was occupying the same cabin with one of the murdered men. According to his story, he was in the hut with Bran Singh at Camp 8 on the property of the Jersey Island Company, on the opposite side of the island from the headquarters of the company. He said he heard someone trying to force entrance to their cabin, and fled through the back window to another Hindoo camp. He summoned his friends and together they went back to the cabin and found Bran Singh dead. They went at once to Camp 13, where other friends were, and found the other two men in the same shape. Lachman Singh reached headquarters about daybreak, and officers were summoned.

September 27, 1919.—The Oakland, Antioch & Eastern Railway will hereafter be known as the San Francisco-Oakland Railroad.

The Contra Costa County Exposition, which continued for eight days, was participated in by many exhibitors from various localities in this part of the State. The Tommasino Royal Italian Band was hired for the duration of the big show. The attendance broke all records for the first day's attendance.

Estimated cost of the proposed concrete highways to be constructed out of the $2,600,000 bond issue is as follows:

Bay Point to Pittsburg	8.46	miles	$261,800
Martinez to Bay Point	5.50	"	156,000
Martinez to Dublin	23.00	"	687,816
Pacheco to Concord	1.50	"	66,600
San Pablo Creek	12.00	"	390,664
Franklin Canon	9.00	"	296,748
Crockett Straits	1.50	"	50,000
Richmond to Giant	5.00	"	140,000
Knightsen	3.25	"	51,000
Brentwood East	3.70	"	92,372
	72.91	"	$2,223,000

PROPOSED SECONDARY ROADS

Ygnacio Valley	5.50	miles	$55,000
Concord to Clayton	5.50	"	55,000
Clayton East	12.50	"	125,000
Tassajara Road	10.00	"	100,000
Old River		"	27,000
	33.50	"	$362,000

SUMMARY

Maintenance Equipment	$ 15,000
Concrete Highways	2,223,000
Secondary Roads	362,000
	$2,600,000

The Associated Oil Company starts preliminary work at Avon to double the size of its plant at the cost of $2,000,000. The company has gone to considerable expense the last few years in providing recreation for the employees with a fresh-water swimming pool, bowling alleys, billiard and ball-rooms.

The contract has been let for the Brentwood High School to Hannah Brothers, of San Francisco, for $63,795.

The closing of the first annual Contra Costa County Exposition, October 13, marked the sixtieth anniversary of the closing of the first County Fair ever held in Contra Costa County.

The success of the Exposition is largely due to the various Farm Bureaus of Contra Costa County; 10,000 attended the big show Sunday.

October 18, 1919.—John Tait, of San Francisco cafe fame, and his associates purchased Byron Hot Springs Hotel Thursday, October 16. It is said that $100,000 will be spent in refitting the hotel. C. J. Brun has been installed as manager.

December 20, 1919.—Active work has been started by the Foundation Company, one of the largest concerns of its kind operating in this country, upon the construction of mechanical shops for the Standard Oil Company which will cost $1,000,000.

On Wednesday, December 24, Charles Butters purchased the site of the old Peyton Chemical Company, including 127 acres of land, for $65,000.

John Barleycorn passed away peacefully on January 23, 1920, at 10 o'clock. His death struggles were not overly hard, but in Martinez there are many mourners.

On January 26, in a Byron bank robbery, $50,000 in currency, liberty bonds, jewelry and securities were stolen from 154 safe-deposit boxes. The robbers burned a hole through the Bessemer steel plates around the combination to the safe-deposit vault.

January 24, 1920.—The Oakland, Antioch & Eastern Railway was sold at public auction today on the courthouse steps by Sale Commissioner A. E. Dunkel. The purchasers of the road were the members of the reorganization committee composed of the directors of the Oakland, Antioch & Eastern Railway. The price was $1,200,000.

January 31, 1920.—Improvements on a large scale will be made by the San Francisco-Sacramento Railroad Company, according to General Manager H. A. Mitchell. $90,000 for ballasting rock will be spent; and other improvements are a branch line from Clyde to the shipyard of the Pacific Coast Ship Building Company at Bay Point, reconstruction of the tunnel between Shepherd Canyon and Redwood Canyon, erection of additional substations, and new electrical motor equipment for installation on passenger cars.

At Brentwood, January 31, the board of directors of the Bank of Brentwood elected R. Wallace Jr., president; F. Ludinghouse, vice-president; Alex Burness, treasurer; R. G. Dean and R. F. MacLeod, directors.

The Building and Loan Committee of the Chamber of Commerce of Martinez, consisting of D. L. Hilson, chairman, L. Bonzagni and Ralph Wight, enlarged the committee to include E. A. Majors, R. H. Latimer, J. H. Wells, M. W. Joost, J. R. Baker, A. N. Sullenger, M. H. Hurley, G. O. Meese, Dr. E. W. Merrithew, T. B. Swift, Frank Roberts, Joe Sparacino, J. W. McClellan, E. R. Lasell, J. J. McNamara, G. P. Keller, F. L. Glass, E. R. Colvin and J. E. Colton. The committee as a whole met and selected Hilson, Wells, Bonzagni, Colvin and Wight to prepare by-laws for a Martinez Building & Loan Association.

F. Rolandi, contractor, who was awarded the job of constructing the Martinez-Dublin highway, has started work; and O'Brien Brothers, who have the contract for the Franklin-Canyon road, are placing equipment on the ground.

March 8, 1920.—Antioch's new city hall was formally accepted by the trustees.

The Brentwood Post of the American Legion was organized on March 20; W. F. Wooley, president; R. J. Wallace, secretary-treasurer; Charles Forbes, first vice-president; Fay Donaldson, second vice-president.

April 3, 1920.—A complete confession of the triple murder on Jersey Island last September has been made by Maher Singh, who was arrested in San Francisco. Sheriff Veale took Singh into custody as he was about to board the liner Korea Maru for Calcutta, India.

March 27, 1920.—Thursday was a red-letter day in the history of the Columbia Steel Company, when the great rolls, together with the majority of the units of the new rolling mill, were put in action for the trial run.

April 24, 1920.—J. E. Colton, for the past four years mayor of Martinez, was reelected to that office.

May 1, 1920.—Crockett Encampment No. 43, I. O. O. F., was instituted April 8, with fifty-three charter members.

May 1, 1920.—The Antioch Bank buys the controlling interest in the Bank of Brentwood, when the entire stock held by the Balfour-Guthrie Company, C. and R. F. MacLeod, and Alex Burness was purchased. MacLeod and Burness have been succeeded on the board of directors by R. E. Davis and Mr. Mahaffey.

May 8, 1920.—The theatre constructed by Enea Brothers in Pittsburg was opened to the public on May 4, when a large crowd of local people attended the dedication ceremonies. The new building cost $100,000.

June 18, 1920.—L. A. Crowell, a banker of North Dakota, and P. Henitz of Minneapolis, Minn., took over the controlling interest of the First National Bank at Bay Point. L. A. O'Brien, vice-president, retains his interest and will become field auditor for Crowell. The new directorate will be C. B. Johnson, L. A. Crowell, L. A. O'Brien, A. E. O'Brien, and C. E. Howes.

Richmond gets big $2,000,000 plant of the National Products Company, which has bought an entire block on the inner harbor for plant and warehouse purposes.

July 12, 1920.—J. A. McVittie, for eight years city auditor of Richmond, was appointed city manager at a salary of $4000 per year.

September 25, 1920.—The new $60,000 high school at Brentwood was opened with a large attendance. The district from which students are drawn are Byron, Byron Springs, Excelsior, Deer Valley, Brentwood, Knightsen, Oakley and Lone Tree.

September 27, 1920.—Maher Singh was sentenced to death by Judge McKenzie, for the killing of the three Hindus on Jersey Island. December 17 was set for the day of the execution at San Quentin. The last murderer to be sentenced to death and executed in Contra Costa County was Marshal Martin, January 23, 1874, by Sheriff M. B. Ivory. Martin was convicted of murdering Valentine Eischler of Brentwood on November 16, 1872. At that time executions were not conducted at the penitentiaries; the hanging was held in Martinez in the presence of the sheriff, district attorney, a local preacher, and a few residents.

October 2, 1920.—The bond election in Richmond for progressive harbor policies was carried by an overwhelming majority. For completing the harbor at a cost of $400,000, the vote stood 2872 for and 459 against; for the construction of warehouses at a cost of $150,000, the vote was 2781 for and 459 against. The adoption of the second proposition makes available at once the sum of $328,000 appropriated by Congress to assist in the development of Richmond Harbor. The city has already spent $100,000 on a municipal wharf.

October 9, 1920.—Robert Clark, wharfinger and agent for the Martinez-Benicia Ferry Company, and his family, narrowly escaped death from drowning Thursday morning when the warehouse and a portion of the Benicia municipal wharf collapsed from the effects of teredos undermining the piles.

October 30, 1920.—The county superintendent of schools, W. H. Hanlon, appointed Rachael K. Miller as county nurse, who will have charge of health conditions in all schools of the county. She will be paid by the county and by the Red Cross organizations, furnishing her own transportation about the county.

November 1, 1920.—W. K. Cole, of Concord, has sold his stock in the Concord Bank to B. G. Ensign, of Berkeley, and Albert Smith, of Rodeo.

February 19, 1921.—There are 100 stockholders in the Martinez & Benicia Ferry & Transportation Company.

The board of trustees of Benicia have granted the Ferry Company a forty-year franchise for East Fifth.

The affairs of the Ferry Company have been satisfactorily arranged, with J. J. McNamara, president; Grant R. Allen, general manager.

March 5, 1921.—The board of trustees of the local Martinez High School opened bids for the construction of a new building, for which bonds had been voted in the amount of $175,000.

Through reorganization of the sugar firm of Crockett, the California & Hawaiian Sugar Refining Company will hereafter be known as the California & Hawaiian Sugar Refining Corporation. The directors of the new corporation met in San Francisco and purchased the physical properties and assumed all liabilities. The capitalization is $20,000,000; $5,000,000 is 8 per cent preferred stock, the balance common stock. The stockholders will provide $10,000,000 for readjustment.

On March 24, ground was broken for the new $175,000 high school building on Smith Street. Munson Brothers, of San Francisco, have been awarded the contract.

The ferry steamer Avon J. Hanford, of the Rodeo-Vallejo Ferry Company, entered service March 29, and made her first trip in eleven minutes. She is 186 feet long and can carry sixty-five automobiles. A half-hour service will be maintained.

May 3, 1921.—The Bank of Martinez increased its capital stock from $100,000 to $125,000, and also increased its surplus to $281,500.

June 16, 1921.—Antioch dedicated her $100,000 grammar school building with appropriate ceremonies Thursday evening. Addresses were made by Superintendent W. H. Hanlon and R. J. White.

July 9, 1921.—Dedication ceremonies for the opening of the new I. O. O. F. building in Martinez were held on July 6 with the joint installation of Odd Fellows and Rebekahs.

An increase of $2,405,070 in the assessed valuation of Richmond property is shown by the City Assessor, J. O. Ford. The assessment this year is $26,722,370.

The Episcopal Church work was organized April 2, 1862, by Mrs. Martha Coffin and Miss Caroline Fish in Martinez, with six women and five men. The first recorded services of the Episcopal Church were held in Benicia by Major Townsend, U. S. A., September 24, 1854. On Sunday, July 10, 1870, Grace Church of Martinez was consecrated by Bishop Kipp. The fifty-first anniversary of the founding of the church will be held on July 10, 1921.

August 10, 1921.—A fund of $25,000 to erect a memorial building on a site near the city hall, purchased last year by the city for $30,000, was appropriated by the Richmond city council. The memorial will be erected in honor of Richmond's service men.

On August 21 the Franklin Canyon Highway was opened for travel. Miss Margaret Tinning christened the road with a twenty-year-old bottle of champagne. Many people from the surrounding towns were present.

August 27, 1921.—In 1912 the assessed valuation of Antioch was $538,000; it is now, 1921, $1,199,325.

A $100,000 exploitation campaign for Richmond through the East and Middle West, covering a year and including motion pictures, lectures, newspaper articles and display advertisements setting forth the industrial and home building opportunities of the city, is to be carried on. The result will mean great industrial and commercial growth for Richmond.

Engineers and road-builders from every section of the country gathered at Pittsburg on November 9 for the formal opening of the experimental highway constructed here by the Columbia Steel Company to determine the most durable type. The highway is built a quarter of a mile in length in circular form, with sixteen different types of construction. The tests have been in progress for several weeks with delicate instruments, in tunnels and under the road, where the effects of atmospheric changes on concrete have been recorded. Today thirty-six Government trucks, each weighing 14,500 pounds, were put in operation on the road. These machines will be operated over the road until the slabs of concrete have been destroyed. When the test is finished that section of the highway which best withstood the tests will be selected as the most durable. There were about 500 present.

December 17, 1921.—The fleet of trucks engaged in wrecking the test highway at Pittsburg have traveled 57,908 miles and have subjected the circular track to 1,896,560 tons, according to the report made by the Good Roads Bureau of the California State Automobile Association. The total weight passing over each section from December 4 to the 10th was 636,300 tons, the trucks traveling 17,538 miles. There has been no section to give way thus far, but all show signs of cracking. On December 14, the weight of the trucks was increased from eleven tons to thirteen and a half tons, and the weight is to be increased until thirty-ton loads are carried over the road, and the speed increased to twenty miles. The engineers say these tests will result in a lasting benefit.

January 16, 1922.—Classes will begin in the new $185,000 high school building just completed. The bonds were voted two years ago by the citizens. The building is designed in Romanesque style of architecture, walls of reinforced concrete, with red tile roof. The auditorium will seat 850; the main building is 250 feet long and two stories high.

January 28, 1922.—After three months, the wheels of heavy traffic will cease rolling over the concrete slabs at Pittsburg. The testing will continue in the spring. The ditches around the road will be kept flooded and be drained in the spring when tests are resumed.

Former records for snowfall were broken here Sunday, January 29, when snow fell the entire day. In some places in the county it was ten inches deep. Old trees on the highway were broken by the weight of the snow. The fall was general throughout the county and in the bay cities. In Berkeley it was a foot deep in places, and in Martinez about eight inches on the average.

On March 21, ground was broken for the $12,000 Women's Club building at Las Juntas and Mellus Streets in Martinez.

May 6, 1922.—Concord voted 117 for and 1 against the issue of $70,000 bonds for the construction of a new grammar school building.

On May 14, 1922, Martinez was accorded the honor of having broadcasted the first complete Sunday religious service from a radio station on the Pacific Coast. The services were conducted by Rev. N. F. Sanderson, who delivered his sermon from the Rock Ridge Station in Oakland. In the Congregational Church a magnavox had been installed, and the entire services were enjoyed.

June 3, 1922.—By a vote of 166 for and 15 against at Brentwood, and 11 for and 2 against at Deer Valley, the bond issue was carried to build a $40,000 grammar school at Brentwood.

June 24, 1922.—The Shell Oil Company has purchased, for $4500, one and one-half acres of land from James Dent, adjoining their present holdings.

July 8, 1922.—The board of supervisors purchased the Fernandez Estate on Court and Ward Streets in Martinez for $12,500, as a site for the prospective Hall of Records.

July 22, 1922.—Construction was started by Cahill Brothers on the first $125,000 unit of the half-million-dollar warehouse and processing plant for the California Bean Growers' Association. It will be 80 by 326 feet, part of it five stories high. It is located on a four-acre tract purchased by the Association between Antioch road and the bay, west of the Redwood Lumber Yard. The association has a private wharf with 104 feet frontage.

Work has begun on the enlargement of the Pioneer Rubber Company's Mills of Pittsburg, it being a part of the $500,000 development program authorized by the directors.

Pittsburg will have the first Junior High School in the county with the completion of the $12,000 building, which will be ready for occupancy September 1. The equipment will cost $7000.

On July 29, 1922, two thousand acres of range land was swept by flames on the eastern side of Ygnacio Valley and the south side of Mount Diablo. There was serious damage to cattle ranges.

August 5, 1922.—On August 3, at a meeting of the directors of the First National Bank and the San Ramon Valley Bank in Walnut Creek, the two banks were merged and the stock liquidated. Officers and directors: E. B. Ensign, president; Arthur Burton, vice-president; W. S. Burpee, C. R. Leech, N. S. Boone and F. A. Marshall, directors.

August 19, 1922.—The almond crop of Contra Costa County for 1922 is valued at $2,500,000 and has been signed to the California Almond Growers' Exchange by 110 growers. Contra Costa County is third in the State in almond production.

The First National Bank of Richmond has merged with the Mercantile Trust Company of San Francisco. The banking-house of the old Bank of Richmond at Macdonald and Eighth will be closed, but the parent bank at Point Richmond will be maintained. C. S. Downing and W. K. Cole have sold their interests.

Fifteen hundred Klansmen from all parts of Northern California were initiated into the K. K. K. on Saturday night in West Pittsburg, in the marsh lands between Mount Diablo and the Carquinez Straits.

W. K. Cole committed suicide in San Francisco on September 14, 1922, when sixty years of age. He had been in ill health for some time and had spells of despondency. He was a prominent druggist of Martinez at one time, but sold out his drug business and engaged in banking; he was a director of the Bank of Martinez.

December 9, 1922.—E. A. Majors, president of the First National Bank of Martinez, announces that the controlling interest in the bank has been sold to the American Bank of Oakland. There will be no change in the directorate or in the personnel of officers. The bank will be conducted as a National bank; later it may be changed into a State bank.

December 23, 1922.—Crockett and Valona vote $240,000 bonds for the purchase of several acres of land and the erection of a grammar school building.

March 3, 1923.—The Bay Point business district was damaged to the extent of $35,000 when several stores and other buildings were destroyed by fire.

March 10, 1923.—A large section of the business district of Byron was destroyed by fire. The loss is estimated at $200,000. The buildings destroyed were the Byron Times, postoffice, Santos Hotel, L. V. Plumley's merchandise store, Ellis Howard's butcher-shop, barber-shop and shoe-shop in the S. M. Cabral building.

April 28, 1923.—The Pioneer Rubber Company of Pittsburg has doubled its capitalization, raising it from $1,000,000 to $2,000,000.

One of the heaviest and finest fruit crops in Alhambra Valley and Pleasant Hill in years, is reported this year. The pear crop alone is valued at $187,000; and the total valuation of the crop, for all fruits, is nearly $500,000.

July 14, 1923.—"One of the best auto-camp parks in the country," is the verdict of the motor-tourist campers that enjoy the privileges of the Martinez Auto Park, operated by the Chamber of Commerce.

The people of Martinez have spent about $600,000 for new streets in four years.

Richmond expended a total of $132,461.38 during the past fiscal year, ending June 30, for the paving of streets.

July 20, 1923.—Ground was broken in Pittsburg by the C. A. Hooper Company for the first twenty of 250 bungalow-homes to be constructed by that firm.

July 24, 1923.—The Pacific Cellouis Mills at Walnut Creek, makers of artificial silk, received a car of machinery from Germany this week. It will be installed at once, and they expect to begin operations September 1.

August 2, 1923.—Without interruption in business, the American National Bank ceased to exist today and became the American Bank, under a California charter.

September, 1923.—The grape crop in Alhambra, Ygnacio, San Ramon and other valleys in this part of the county, will be worth $250,000.

September 15, 1923.—Thomas Carneal, who owns many acres of land in the Tassajara district, conceived the idea of providing an up-to-date school building for the pupils of the community. He set aside an ample tract of land for playgrounds, then had a fine concrete building erected, and equipped the building throughout with the latest in fixtures and furniture, and also an automatic player-piano. The whole investment amounted to $13,000, which he donated to the district. The Highland district is in a rather isolated section, and Mr. Carneal thought the school children would like to know what was going on in the outside world; so he added a modern radio-receiving set to the equipment.

On September 17, 1923, a terrible fire in Berkeley burned over thirty square miles. A number of Contra Costa County families reside in Berkeley. Local students attending the University of California were victims of the fire, which destroyed sixty blocks.

October 7, 1923.—The fiftieth anniversary of the founding of the Bank of Martinez was observed fittingly today by the bank's officers. On October 7, 1873, the Bank of Martinez opened for business with a capital stock of $50,000; L. I. Fish, president; W. M. Hale, secretary and cashier; H. M. Hale, teller and accountant; L. I. Fish, William W. Cameron, Simon Blum, Henry M. Hale, and W. M. Hale, directors. The town then had a population between 500 and 600. On May 26, 1875, the capital stock was increased to $100,000. L. I. Fish was succeeded by L. C. Wittenmyer in 1890. James Rankin succeeded to the presidency in 1899, and in 1902 W. S. Tinning. W. M. Hale was cashier from 1873 to 1883; H. M. Hale, from 1883 to 1899; W. A. Hale, from 1899 to date. The original building burned in 1904; an annex was added in 1915.

October 13, 1923.—The Bank of Concord held a meeting and Albert Smith was elected vice-president, succeeding B. G. Ensign, resigned, he having purchased Ensign's stock. J. H. DeMartini, also a new stockholder, was elected cashier.

Over 2000 attended the institution of the Pittsburg Lodge of Elks on October 20. The lodge was instituted by District Deputy Exalted Ruler George Rucker, of San Jose. After the ceremonies of institution the officers took their chairs and initiated seventy-one members.

Over 700 autos have registered at the auto camp since the opening on June 1. Figuring four passengers to a car, this makes 2800 people who spent from one night to a week here. Of this number twenty have bought homes in Martinez or have made permanent homes in the county.

November 24, 1923.—The consolidation of the Contra Costa County Bank with the Mercantile Trust Company of California has been approved. By this act the bank will become a unit of an institution with resources in excess of $130,000,000, with offices in thirteen San Francisco Bay cities. Officers and directors of the Bank are: W. E. Creed, president; W. J. Buchanan, vice-president; A. S. Sbarbaro, vice-president; G. Todaro, cashier; Armand Stow and N. Canevaro, assistants; C. J. Wood, Otis Loverage, W. E. Creed, A. S. Sbarbaro, W. J. Buchanan, G. Todaro and N. Canevaro, directors. The resources of the bank are over $1,300,000.

December 11, 1923.—Pittsburg business property was sold by James Fitzgerald for $22,000, according to the deed filed in the office of the county recorder. The property included a building in the business section.

December 15, 1923.—The furnaces of the Mountain Copper Company at Bay Point are closed down, throwing 125 men out of employment.

January 5, 1924.—Richmond has a population of between 22,000 and 25,000. East Bay Water Company has 4800 services. The manager of the company estimates that the total number of connections in the town is 5300. The phone company has 2975 connections. The Western States Gas & Electric Company has 6353 consumers. The average daily attendance in school is 3924.

Bulding permits in Pittsburg for 1923 totaled $190,723; seventy-five per cent of this amount was for homes. This is exclusive of Creed Tract No. 2, where buildings represent $150,000.

The Pinole Times is twenty-nine years old. It was established by E. M. Downer and Dr. M. L. Fernandez and was the third paper in the county. Downer & Fernandez published it till the latter withdrew. John Birmingham took his place, continuing until 1916, when Ed. Ebsen bought the paper.

The Union Ice Company starts work on their $30,000 ice plant at the corner of Escobar and Pine Streets.

Property loss by fire in San Ramon Valley: Total alarms, 56; loss, $53,500; inside limits, $11,525; outside limits, $41,975.

January 19, 1924.—Rural free mail delivery began at Brentwood, extending to Marsh Creek, Deer Valley and Antioch Road, 25.6 miles. The service includes 115 homes. Will Coates is the temporary carrier.

W. A. Hale, was made president of the Bank of Martinez, to succeed Mr. Tinning, deceased; F. R. Jones, cashier; A. B. Tinning, director.

February 2, 1924.—The Pacific Gas & Electric buys thirty acres of the Amos Graves ranch at Antioch, where they will establish a substation.

February 9, 1924.—Mrs. Flora Irene Hurley was appointed by the board of supervisors to fill out the balance of her husband's term as county recorder.

On June 18, the fiftieth anniversary of the founding of the Congregational Church in Martinez will be observed by a three days' program.

March 22, 1924.—The plague of the hoof and mouth disease in several parts of Contra Costa County is discovered, and immediate steps taken to quarantine the places where discovered. Some of the most valuable herds in the county are in San Ramon Valley, and extra precautions are being taken to protect the stock.

March 22, 1924.—Every herd in Pinole Valley is to be killed in the hoof and mouth disease war. There are twenty-seven exposed herds near Richmond; 266 cattle were killed and put under the ground today. It was then decided by Government experts that every animal in and around Richmond and Pinole has been exposed.

Protective quarantine was placed on ranches from Danville to the county line.

A charter for the National Bank of Martinez has been granted by the comptroller of currency, and steps are under way to establish the new bank by April 15. It will have a capital stock of $60,000, and has 100 per cent local capitalization. The plans include the erection of a building on the Joost property, at Main and Mill, and until the building is completed the bank will be housed in the rear of the library building. The officers are: R. B. Borland, president; Primo Ferrarini, vice-president; A. J. Heald, secretary and cashier.

The Contra Costa Golf Club was organized on Wednesday, April 2. A. B. Tinning was elected president; George Nees of Crockett, vice-president; C. A. Withington of Martinez, secretary; W. A. Hale, treasurer. The board of directors: Dr. E. Todd, Concord; R. V. Davis, Antioch; H. Lamond, Pittsburg; W. H. Hanlon, Martinez; Mrs. H. T. Silver, Walnut Creek. M. W. Joost was chosen chairman of the membership committee. A site near Pacheco was decided upon, 311 acres for $21,770. The membership fee is $100. A nine-hole sand-green course can be constructed for $3000.

April 12, 1924.—The largest cofferdam in the world has been sunk in the Carquinez Straits for the construction of the Carquinez bridge by the American Toll Bridge Company.

Mount Diablo High School takes many first prizes in the Fifteenth Annual Track Meet of the Contra Costa High School League, with a score close to 100 points over Alhambra High of Martinez.

April 19, 1924.—Oscar Olsson was appointed to succeed J. P. Casey, deceased, on the board of supervisors.

Up to date, $400,000 has been the loss in Contra Costa County in the slaughter of cattle in the hoof and mouth plague.

The State of California, on May 17, completed the payment of $180,000 to Contra Costa County cattlemen as compensation for herds destroyed in connection with the hoof and mouth disease. A like amount is yet to be paid by the United States Government.

May 24, 1924.—Under the first apportionment of taxes collected from the sale of gasoline, Contra Costa County received $29,402. The total apportionment was $5,533,943.03. Los Angeles County drew $1,094,-625.11, and little Alpine County $83.84.

The Richmond-San Rafael ferry boat City of San Rafael was launched at the Robertson Shipyards, Alameda, Saturday night. The City of San Rafael is the largest and fastest of the company's three ships; it has a 750-horsepower engine and a capacity of seventy automobiles. The ship was christened by Miss Athalie Clark of Richmond. The launching was attended by many citizens of Richmond and San Rafael. The new slips, wharves and terminals at Castro Point are nearing completion. The boat and improvements represent almost a million-dollar investment.

May 31, 1924.—The Pioneer Rubber Company of Pittsburg had a $20,000 fire on May 25.

Pier No. 1, on the Solano side of Carquinez Straits, is practically completed for the big bridge across the Straits. It is on dry land and is of reinforced concrete. On the Crockett side the cofferdam, 150 feet long and 52 feet wide, is being driven deeper and deeper into the earth. The outer part of the dam is built like a ship and is water-tight. It will be driven 55 feet into the earth, after which 225 concrete piers will be driven inside. Each pier, reinforced, weighs fifteen tons. There will be four similar dams, forty feet square. There will be two spans, each of 1100 feet, the central tower pier 150 feet wide, anchor span each side 500 feet long, and 135 feet clearance for ships. The bridge will be completed early in 1927, when the six-minute ferry owned by the same company will be abandoned. For twenty-five years the bridge will be a toll-bridge, which will provide dividends on the capital stock.

The Contra Costa County Golf Club is now certain to become a reality. A large gathering of enthusiastic golfers met in Department 2, Tuesday evening, at which representatives from every part of the county were present. The limit of membership at $100 is 200.

August 16, 1924.—Contra Costa stock losses from hoof and mouth disease amount to $426,844.57.

September 8, 1924.—Contracts totaling $1,200,000, and calling for completion of the Antioch-Sherman Island bridge within twelve months, were let to the American Toll Bridge Company; $850,000 for concrete work and foundations went to Duncanson-Harrelson Company, of San Francisco; and $350,000 for steel, to the Golden West Iron Works, of San Francisco.

September 20, 1924.—California Wharf & Warehouse at Port Costa burned early this morning. The loss in grain is estimated at $450,000; and in buildings, $400,000. The concern is owned by the Balfour-Guthrie Company, who had just renewed their franchise for the wharf for twenty-five years.

November 1, 1924.—Martinez was advanced to city delivery of mail on November 1, 1924. On March 1, 1924, it was allowed three carriers and given the status of a village delivery. There are still three carriers.

January 8, 1925.—Cost of government in Contra Costa County has increased 81.28 per cent the last two years, but the duties of the various officers have been doubled in the same time, according to the report of J. O. Ford, grand jury expert, on file today with the inquisitorial body. According to Ford's report the offices of the district attorney, county clerk and probation officer have seen the greatest increase of duties. In-

12

crease in crime has been the cause of the bulk of the additional work demanded of the district attorney and the probation officer, according to the expert's report. A considerable portion of the increase in government cost is represented in the funds expended in enforcement of the prohibition law, the expert declares.

January 8, 1925.—Two huge conveyor belts, weighing seven and one-half tons each, considered the largest on the Pacific Coast, were delivered to the C. & H. Sugar Refinery at Crockett, the past week. The belts, manufactured at the Pioneer Rubber Works near Antioch, are each 950 feet long, three feet wide, and one inch in thickness, made of seven-ply duck with a heavy coating of rubber on either side. It took three weeks to manufacture the conveyors, at a cost of $10,000. A single flat car was used in their transportation to the Crockett refinery.

January 8, 1925.—The Delphian Club of Martinez, starting with thirty-one members, was brought into being last night at a meeting of the Martinez Woman's Club of virtually the entire membership.

January 13, 1925.—The regular and annual meeting of the East Contra Costa Chamber of Commerce was held in the banquet room of Hotel Brentwood, January 13, more than fifty members being present, among whom were a number of ladies. The dinner served by Landlord Crawford was greatly enjoyed.

President Roy Davis called the meeting to order and the minutes of the previous meeting were approved as read by Secretary George Upham. Roy Davis was reelected president and Paul Anderson, treasurer. At this time three directors from each of five towns were elected as follows: Antioch, M. B. Veale, Thomas Milan, A. Flaherty; Oakley, Jim S. Crandell, O. M. Champlain, Bill O'Hara; Knightsen, D. D. Watson, Ed. Sellers, W. A. Fotheringham; Brentwood, Jerry O'Meara, C. B. Weeks, George Shafer; Byron, L. Z. Richardson, Harry Hammond, H. C. Hannum; and in addition, from Lone Tree, O. C. Prewett; from Live Oak, E. J. Vieria; and from Knightsen, G. Somerhalder.

January 17, 1925.—Growth of Richmond from a few scattered shacks on an expanse of wheat fields and marshland in 1900 to a thriving industrial city of approximately 30,000 inhabitants in 1925, was reviewed in a pioneer day program given yesterday by the Richmond Rotary Club. Dr. C. L. Abbott and Walter T. Helms made fifteen-minute addresses concerning the early history of Richmond. Dr. Abbott told of coming to the old town of San Pablo in 1900, when Richmond was just starting, of the struggles to get Richmond incorporated, and how a committee composed of Frank Hull, J. Q. Black, Frank Crichett and himself finally arranged a plan that won out, resulting in the election of E. J. Garrard as the first mayor of the little city. Walter Helms narrated how he came here while studying law, to take over the schools of the San Pablo school district, which included what is now San Pablo, Richmond and El Cerrito.

Among the pioneers of Richmond who were present as guests of the Rotarians were Ben Boorman, Harry Ells, A. C. Lang, Lee D. Windrem,

C. A. Odell, Robert Fernald, Rebus Lipe, Edward Hoffman, V. A. Fenner, O. L. Wright, Chris Theis and Dr. P. C. Campbell.

January 31, 1925.—Of the scores of chamber of commerce secretaries in the thickly populated bay region, only half a dozen are women, and two of these reside in Contra Costa County. They are Miss Catherine Beam, secretary of the Martinez chamber, and Mrs. Jessie Higley of the Danville chamber. In the Association of Bay Chamber of Commerce Secretaries both women are known as "live wires," always looking out for the interests of their communities.

January 31, 1925.—The Rodeo-Vallejo Ferry Company, holder of the franchise to construct the Carquinez Straits bridge, has sold two lots and a tract of 2.71 acres at the bridgehead at Crockett to the American Toll Bridge Company for $40,500, according to a deed filed yesterday with the county recorder. The Toll Bridge Company was organized for the purpose of constructing the bridge.

Almond blossoms in January is the record of Martinez this year. A tree resembling a huge popcorn ball burst into bloom last week on the ranch of L. Brackman.

February 7, 1925.—During the year 1924, $14,264,000 was spent in Contra Costa County for major building.

Walnut Creek's new Memorial Hall will be dedicated Sunday afternoon, February 8, when Supervisor C. H. Hayden will make the memorial address. A large program has been planned by the American Legion Post at Walnut Creek. All ex-service men and the general public are invited to attend the ceremonies, which will be held in the main auditorium.

The contract for the construction of the Brentwood Memorial Hall was awarded to George H. Field Company of Antioch by the board of supervisors, on their bid of $16,860. This contract covers the construction of the last of the seven memorial halls to be built by the county. The Brentwood building is being erected under the direction of the Roy Frerichs Post of the American Legion.

Antioch's celery-shipping season, through Santa Fe docks, is about ended, with a total of 1550 cars. Last year 1628 cars were shipped, but in dollars and cents this year's crop will bring greater returns.

A forty-eight-room three-story annex is to be added to Hotel Oehm in Martinez, the new addition to cost between $50,000 and $75,000. It will be built on the 50 by 100-foot lot adjoining the hotel on Alhambra Avenue.

Diablo Air Mail Terminal will be formally opened this afternoon. Mayor Klein of Concord has declared a holiday for business houses and schools of that city. C. A. Richardson, manager of the western division of the transcontinental air mail service, will be present.

February 14, 1925.—A Board of Commerce is being organized in Pinole, with forty business firms signed up. A meeting will be held in the near future to elect officers and directors and secure quarters.

"Contra Costa County is notable among the counties of the State in its memorials to World War veterans. When the doughboys started over seas they were promised that when they returned they could have 'anything they wanted'. Making good this promise, the board of supervisors has built a veterans' memorial hall in each town in the county where there is an American Legion Post. These are now being finished and dedicated. Walnut Creek dedicated its hall last Sunday. Danville hopes to open its building on Washington's Birthday.

"The buildings were paid for by a small direct tax, all of which has already been raised. On the threshold of each one is a brass plate reading 'Dedicated to those who served'. While the halls are nominally in the custody of the American Legion, they are open to all veterans' organizations. The Legion men have gone further and offered their use free to any and all patriotic, civic and welfare associations, such as the Boy Scouts, Red Cross, farm bureau, chamber of commerce and improvement clubs. They will be, in a manner, community halls. The building in Danville is to house the public library and the chamber of commerce. In Martinez there is to be a public swimming pool. The structures are designed to serve as substantial memorials to the men of Contra Costa county who served their country at the time of its need, and mark the towns containing them as having a full quota of patriotic citizens."—*Editorial in San Francisco Chronicle.*

February 14, 1925.—The growth of El Cerrito is evidenced by the fact that building permits representing a total of $37,000 were issued last month.

The ferry boats of the Martinez-Benicia Ferry & Transportation Company are undergoing their annual repair and overhaul, which will be completed within two weeks.

The first consignment, seven crates of asparagus, shipped this year, left Antioch last Friday, February 13, for the California Corporation markets in New York. This is thirteen days in advance of the first shipment made in 1924.

Congratulations were showered upon Mr. and Mrs. John B. Green, of Richmond, last Sunday, in honor of the sixtieth anniversary of their marriage, which was solemnized in England, February 8, 1865.

February 21, 1925.—According to the survey filed with the harbor engineers, Contra Costa's population has increased in the last five years from 53,900 to 62,800.

Armand Stow of Pittsburg, formerly of Walnut Creek, has been promoted to be manager of the Pittsburg branch of the Mercantile Trust Company.

February 28, 1925.—With asparagus bringing $1 a pound in New York and a carload a day being shipped East by express from Antioch and the Delta country, prospects for a good season among the "grass" growers are looming up. This spring delicacy is selling for 25 cents to 35 cents a pound in San Francisco, at the present time. It is expected that larger shipments will be forwarded within the next few days, as the crop is rapidly maturing.

The name of Governor Alvarado, father of Superior Judge Henry V. Alvarado, one of the last Spanish chief magistrates, will be honored by the naming of Richmond's principal park after him, according to action of the Richmond council Tuesday evening, February 24. The late Governor Alvarado owned a typical Spanish home in the Contra Costa hills not far from the park.

February 28, 1925.—Directors of East Contra Costa Chamber of Commerce of the five towns in Diablo Valley met in regular session Tuesday evening and voted an appropriation of $200 to sign the roads in Diablo Valley along all of the main highways. This appropriation will probably be extended to cover all cross-roads in the district later.

May 16, 1925.—Mrs. Julia Michaels, of Richmond, on Wednesday filed a petition in the Superior Court here for letters of admission in the estate of her husband, Max Michaels, who died a few days ago at his late residence in Richmond.

May 16, 1925.—At a recent meeting of the electors of the John Swett Union High School at Crockett, it was decided to call an election to vote on a $400,000 bond issue for the purpose of erecting and equipping a new building to supplant the one now in use. Plans for the building, which, according to County Superintendent of Schools William H. Hanlon, will be one of the finest and most up-to-date in the State, are now being drawn by a San Francisco architect; and it is expected that the election will be called as soon as the plans are complete.

Crockett now has one of the best-equipped elementary schools in the State and, with the proposed new high school, will take a leading place as an educational center.

May 23, 1925.—The 11,700-ton Norwegian freighter Talabot, largest steamer ever to navigate the straits and up-river region, weighed anchor and started down stream late Wednesday, carrying more than a million feet of lumber from the yards of the Redwood Manufacturers Company, where she has been loading since Monday. A stop was made at Point San Pedro to take on a load of case oil, after which the Talabot will proceed up coast to Noyo, Mendocino County, to complete her lumber cargo, and then will sail for Australia with a cargo equivalent to 5,600,000 feet.

Despite the size of the craft, which is 428 feet long with a 56-foot beam, Captain Larson and crew of forty-two men navigated the narrow up-river channel without difficulty and made a landing at the Redwood Company's docks under the Talabot's own power. A landing was made at 7 o'clock Saturday evening, and Sunday the big ship was open to visitors, hundreds of interested sight-seers going aboard during the day. The Talabot is said to be the largest boat ever to visit the Pittsburg waterfront, and the ease with which a landing was effected augurs well for the future of Pittsburg's deep-water harbor.

May 30, 1925.—O. H. Klatt, of the American Toll Bridge Company, was in Martinez Friday for the purpose of filing with the office of the county recorder the plans, specifications, and contract for construction of the unfinished portion of the foundation of the Carquinez bridge, together with the completion bond supplied by the National Surety Company. The contract is between the American Toll Bridge Company and the Missouri Valley Bridge and Iron Company and is signed by Avon J. Hanford as president of the Toll Bridge Company and T. S. Tullock, president of the Missouri Valley Bridge and Iron Company.

The contract price for the completion of the foundation of the bridge is $1,419,700, and the bond to secure the completion of the work within sixteen months from last February 1st is for the same amount. Approximately $1,000,000 has already been spent for the foundation work done by Duncanson and Harrelson, San Francisco contractors.

May 30, 1925.—Harvesting of barley began in the Byron section early this week, a number of crews being in the field. Threshing began Wednesday on the Winegar ranch, where there are 250 acres of Golden Oregon Mariout. The yield will run from twenty-five to thirty-five sacks to the acre. Here there is also 100 acres of early Baart wheat that promises twenty sacks to the acre. Stanley Cabral began threshing operations this week in the Bethany country. The Cabrals have considerable fine barley and wheat in the Vasco territory, southwest of Byron, where the promise is for a good yield. There is considerable barley in the Byron-Tracy-Delta sections, and the yield in almost every instance will be the highest in recent years.

June 13, 1925.—In honor of three birthday anniversaries, Frank Higuera of Pinole entertained at a barbecue picnic held at the V. Martinez ranch near Walnut Creek, Sunday. The guests whose birthday anniversaries it was were: Frank Higuera, Virgie Bronestadt and V. Martinez.

June 27, 1925.—Asparagus is still being harvested at some of the tracts in the delta, but the end of the season is near. Asparagus ranks second in California for canned vegetables. Ninety per cent of the canned asparagus of the United States is grown in the delta districts of the San Joaquin and Sacramento rivers. The San Joaquin delta is rapidly becoming a large asparagus producer. Some of the large acreages in the delta are located on the Bishop tract, Webb Island, Bouldin Island, and Terminus tract.

June 27, 1925.—A handsome $10,500 clubhouse for Carquinez Golf Club members is under construction at the club's grounds at Giant. The building, according to present estimations, will be thrown open to members October 1.

The building with furnishings will represent an outlay of $15,500. The furnishings committee estimates the luxurious furnishings for the club will cost $5000.

The Carquinez Golf Club has shown steady growth and progressiveness since its organization last year.

The directors of the Carquinez Golf Club are: Dr. U. S. Abbott, president; Grant Miner, Jr., vice-president; Ira R. Vaughn, treasurer; Arthur A. Alstrom, secretary; Frank Gordon, T. H. DeLap, A. P. Hill and R. H. Stratton.

July 4, 1925.—The Martinez Home Builders' Association, organized here by local business men and capitalists several years ago to promote the erection of homes for contract sale in this city, formally and officially passed out of existence Monday when Judge McKenzie ordered the dissolution of the corporation.

The association has disposed of all of the dwellings which it had built on property lying south and west of Susanna and Pine Streets, as well as all of the unimproved property, and as the promoters did not intend to continue operations, dissolution of the corporation was ordered.

July 4, 1925.—With the filing of certificate of extension of corporate existence for an additional fifty years, it was revealed Tuesday that the California Transportation Company, operating between San Francisco and Stockton, has been in existence for half a century. It was fifty years ago June 19th last that the company began operations on the bay and rivers, and it has continued uninterrupted freight and passenger service ever since.

July 4, 1925.—Mrs. Alice G. Whitbeck, head of the Contra Costa County public library system for the past twelve years, was on Monday reappointed by the board of supervisors for her fourth term of four years. During Mrs. Whitbeck's administration, the county library system has developed from humble beginnings to a high degree of efficiency, and it ranks today as one of the leading county libraries of the State. Much of this success may be directly attributed to Mrs. Whitbeck's untiring efforts and ability to administer the affairs of the county library.

July 4, 1925.—Justice Glass' monthly report filed Thursday shows a total collection in fines and fees last month of $4691. Of this total violators of the Wright Act contributed $4450, motor vehicle rule breakers $75, the fees from civil matters $6 and miscellaneous fines $185.

Byron, July 8, 1925.—The 100-foot bridge over Big Slough on Victoria Island, on the Borden road to Stockton, went out early Wednesday morning, presumably breaking under a heavy truck, many of which have been using this highway. Engineer Quail of Stockton was immediately notified and it is expected the bridge will be replaced within forty-eight hours. In the meantime travel over the Borden road is held up.

July 11, 1925.—Banner Refining Company, one of the large oil operating syndicates in California, on Monday closed the deal for the purchase of the lands of the old refinery which has been operated at various times for years past at Rodeo. The sale was made by the Union Petroleum Corporation, and the revenue stamps indicate a $35,000 deal involving a little over thirteen acres of waterfront lands.

The last operators of the plant were the Sinclair interests, operating under a lease on the lands and plant.

July 11, 1925.—Fire, which raged a week ago Tuesday evening near Muir Station and was thought at first to be merely one of many grass fires, has proven to have been a blaze causing considerable destruction and heavy loss on the Phillips ranch, where a large quantity of fruit, packed and ready for shipment, was destroyed and where a part of the orchards was fire-swept, about 250 fine almond trees being damaged by the flames.

The fire spread from the Santa Fe Railway's right of way, where a crew of men was burning dry grass and weeds, to the adjoining lands of the Phillips ranch. H. Wilson, operating the ranch, claims a loss of over $800 in ripe fruit entirely exclusive of trees, all of which were fine, healthy trees and bearing well.

Adjusters for the Santa Fe are expected here Thursday to make an adjustment with Wilson to cover the loss sustained.

July 11, 1925.—Bent Bros., Los Angeles contractors, started work Monday on the grading and construction of two of the largest oil reservoirs in the world at the plant of the Shell Company in Martinez. The reservoirs, which will hold over a million barrels of oil each, both larger than the heretofore largest storage tank at Avon, are to be rushed to completion to increase the oil storage facilities at the Martinez refinery.

July 11, 1925.—With an increase in assessed valuation of city property, improvements and industries of more than $600,000, Martinez has the proud distinction for this year of showing the greatest percentage of valuation increase of any corporated city or town in Contra Costa County. Martinez' assessment for 1925 reaches the grand total of $3,426,910, which incidentally puts this city in second place among Contra Costa municipalities, being topped only by Richmond.

July 18, 1925.—Contract for the erection of the new manual training building as a part of the plant of the Alhambra Union High School was awarded by the trustees Wednesday morning to F. H. Cress. The new building and alterations to the gymnasium building, a part of which has been used for the manual training shop, will cost in the neighborhood of $15,500.

The new manual training building will be approximately 60 by 96 feet and will be completely equipped for manual training and mechanical drawing classes. The gymnasium building, from which the former department will be removed, will be altered to provide for a change of location of the boys' showers and the enlarging of the gymnasium proper for the better accommodation of athletic activities.

July 18, 1925.—Federal hunters in the predatory animal control division have killed 167 coyotes, 72 wildcats and three other animals in Contra Costa, according to a detailed report of six months' operations ending June 30, submitted to the board of supervisors by Charles G. Poole, leader of the hunting division.

The county, State and federal governments are dividing the cost of hunting down predatory animals. Poole's report shows that the federal government has paid $260, the State government $1135, and Contra Costa County $1036 for maintaining a corps of hunters over the six months' period.

July 18, 1925.—The oldest double-ender side-wheel ferry boat on San Francisco Bay, the veteran El Capitan, which carried passengers from Oakland pier to San Francisco in the early eighties and which for years was on the Vallejo Junction-South Vallejo run, will spend her last days in the movies.

Like humans, the ferry boat had to wait until it was ready for the "boneyard" to achieve world-wide renown and to get into the public eye. The old ferry that was always ready to operate, and which for a quarter of a century, despite its advanced age, relieved the newer and more modern ferries when they went out of commission, was sold last week to Thomas Crowley for $750, far below the actual "junk" value, and will in the future be used in motion picture production, in the filming of marine scenes.

July 18, 1925.—A fire of unknown origin partly destroyed the plant of the Stauffer Chemical Company at Stege on Monday, damage of which is estimated at between $20,000 and $30,000.

Both the Richmond and El Cerrito fire departments were summoned to help extinguish the blaze, which was confined to the "tower" where considerable nitric and sulphuric acid was stored.

Officials of the company estimated that sixty days would be required to repair the damage. In the meantime the men employed in this part of the establishment will be out of work.

July 25, 1925.—With the business of the local post office increasing nearly $1000 during the first six months' period of the current year, over that of last year, the outlook for a record year is bright.

The total amount of business transacted the first six months of 1925 in the post office was $11,656.87, as against $10,704.24 for the same period in 1924, and this in a year that is not inflated with election mail and voters' ballots, as was last year.

July 25, 1925.—That the pear crop of the Alhambra Valley orchards this year is the heaviest and of the best grade of all pear-producing sections of the State is the unqualified statement made this week by Frank T. Swett, general manger of the Pear Growers' Association and the man in the best position of all to know the status of crop conditions locally and throughout the State.

July 25, 1925.—With the aid of Antioch Red Cross, War Mothers, Camp Fire Girls, Boy Scouts and Harding Post, American Legion, Memorial Hall, recently erected at an approximate cost of $20,000, has been completely furnished.

August 8, 1925.—Contra Costa chickens are in demand in Chile. A second order has just been received by cable by James Dryden from the Chilean experimental station for a shipment of high-egg-record White Leghorns. The first order was shipped to Chile in January, which was received in good condition after a five weeks' voyage.

August 8, 1925.—One of the largest second mortgages and deeds of trust ever recorded in Contra Costa County went on record Friday afternoon when the American Toll Bridge Company gave a two-million-dollar second mortgage on its Carquinez and San Joaquin bridges to the American Bank of San Francisco.

This is to secure an additional loan in the above amount, to the $4,750,000 negotiated with the Bank of California as trustee, to complete the two bridge structures. The papers were filed here by the Contra Costa Abstract & Title Company.

August 8, 1925.—Checks amounting to $2,239,106 including one for Contra Costa County for $233,764.72, have been mailed by the State Department of Agriculture to farmers who lost livestock in the campaign, about a year ago, to check the foot and mouth disease. The money needed for indemnification purposes was appropriated by the last legislature.

Los Angeles County losses, totaling $897,443.23, were the heaviest; Merced was second, with a total of $508,319.56, and Contra Costa third with a near quarter-million loss.

The disbursement of the fund by counties was as follows:

Alameda $99,618.43; Contra Costa $233,764.72, Fresno $19,657.25, Kern $4,058.48, Los Angeles $897,443.23, Madera $148,285.60, Mariposa $43,957.64; Merced $508,319.56; Orange $28,972.56, San Bernardino $8,125.18, San Francisco $141.71, San Joaquin $9,157.15, San Mateo $51.25, Stanislaus $3,319.21, Tulare $16,110.35, Tuolumne $190,-329.19.

August 15, 1925.—School funds allocated to this county from the State amount to $348,236.00, according to notification which has been received in the office of Superintendent of Schools William H. Hanlon from State Superintendent of Public Instruction Will C. Wood.

Division of these funds, with the attendance, is as follows:

Nine thousand forty-one average attendance, elementary schools—$269,105.50.

Two thousand two hundred twenty-three, average attendance, high schools—$79,130.50.

Various other methods of apportioning funds are also used. Each high school district receives $550 for each year it is maintained. Special day and evening classes receive from the State $7,240, and the part time classes of the county $2,600, for their maintenance.

August 15, 1925.—Tremendous recent increase in the demand for higher education in Crockett has far outstripped the capacity of the John Swett High School in that community, with the result that the school trustees and prominent citizens of Crockett are planning a campaign for the voting of $450,000 in bonds for the building of a new high school.

The proposed new John Swett High School will be a vocational institution equipped with workshop, automobile repairing department, and a department for household economics, in addition to the usual subjects embraced in a high school course.

Crockett only recently voted $300,000 in bonds for the erection of a new grammar school.

August 22, 1925.—Crops in the San Joaquin delta this year will aggregate in value about $2,000,000 more than in 1924, according to latest estimates. The 1925 yield is estimated at $20,000,000, with last year's $18,000,000. The leading delta crops this year are potatoes, onions, beans, corn, barley, asparagus and sugar beets. Practically all the sugar beets grown in the lower river district are consumed at the sugar manufacturing plant at Tracy.

September 5, 1925.—One of the two ancient oaks that have stood for a century or more—at least they were massive trees when the first settlers came to the San Ramon Valley—on the Flournoy ranch, collapsed two weeks ago and in falling was shattered to bits. When the white man first came to the San Ramon Valley the companion oaks stood as majestic sentinels overlooking the beautiful sweep of valley and hill, but the ravages of time and the passing of the years so deadened and weakened the oaks that during the recent heat wave in the valley one of the trees collapsed, leaving the other "standing guard" until such time as it too must succumb.

September 5, 1925.—Regarded as an assurance of development of the Burgess Tract lands from Concord to the United States mail base and Clayton Valley sections, Lee Harris, Concord rancher, brought in a 118-foot well, proving the possibilities of the district for irrigation projects. Well borers struck gravel strata at ninety-five feet. The short distance of good water surprised farmers of the entire section.

September 5, 1925.—With a sugar content of twenty per cent, the vineyard of Harold Bloomfield near Knightsen will yield forty tons, according to estimates just made. Bloomfield has sixteen acres in the Tokay vineyard, of which ten are three-year-old vines and six acres, two years old.

September 26, 1925.—The Associated Chambers of Commerce of Contra Costa County have published a booklet which extols the agricultural wealth and industrial activity of the county. Each section of the county is adequately described, and the articles are profusely illustrated. The booklet has been issued primarily to interest prospective settlers in Contra Costa County. The booklet is prefaced with the following:

"Whether in agriculture or in industry, human effort seeks its maximum activity. Contra Costa County, bordering on the great Bay of San Francisco, and with seventy miles of its own water front, offers a wide range of selection to those who desire to live and work amid pleasing surroundings and under conditions that are well-nigh ideal. Practically all fruits, grains and garden crops of the temperate zone are profitably raised in Contra Costa County; live stock is an important industry, and the total value of manufactured products runs over $425,000,000 a year.

"It is the combination of industry and agriculture, with unusually attractive living conditions, that has made so great an opportunity not only for financial advancement, but also for comfort and contentment."

Contra Costa County leads all counties in the United States in per capita wealth. There is an average of $5418 for every person in Contra Costa County, as opposed to the next highest county, with a per capita wealth of $3300.

Walnut Creek, September 29, 1925.—Again has Walnut Creek's prize walnut tree contributed the limit of one-tree production. It produced this year 282 pounds of nuts, the production last year being the record up to that time, 274 pounds. Nuts from this tree won sweepstakes and seven first prizes at the State fair.

Port Costa, September 30, 1925.—The steamer Alchiba is docked at the Port Costa warehouses, taking on 8000 tons of barley for European points. This is one of the largest single grain cargoes to be shipped this year.

October 3, 1925.—Smith Brothers, Incorporated, of Dallas, Texas, will build the three-mile Lafayette Tunnel of the East Bay Municipal Utility District, running from a point near the town of Lafayette to the San Pablo Creek in the hills back of Berkeley. They were awarded the contract for $1,101,822. E. H. Reeder, chief engineer for Smith Brothers, will have general engineering supervision on the Lafayette Tunnel. The Smith Brothers Company is one of the large contracting firms of the country. Their largest California jobs have been for the State of California on the Sutter By-Pass Levee.

The time limit of the Lafayette Tunnel is eighteen months. The contractors will work from both ends and from headings from one or more shafts simultaneously. They will employ from 600 to 1000 men and will drive the job through on three eight-hour shifts.

October 10, 1925.—Construction of the mammoth million-barrel oil storage reservoir at the Shell refinery in Martinez has progressed to a point where the largest and most needed of the reservoirs being constructed will be ready for use within a fortnight. Bent Brothers are building two reservoirs at the Shell, one of a million barrels capacity and the other half that amount. The same contracting firm is building the first of twelve proposed two-million-barrel storage reservoirs for the Standard Oil between Pittsburg and Antioch.

October 7, 1925.—The harvesting of over eighty tons of cucumber seed in Diablo Valley started Tuesday. Three hundred and fifty acres of cucumbers have been planted in Diablo Valley, being grown exclusively for seed. These are grown as an intercrop in the young orchards and, with 350 acres planted producing better than 500 pounds of seed per acre, will bring in a revenue of crop close to fifty thousand dollars.

This is the first year cucumber seed has been grown in Diablo Valley, and it is expected several times this acreage will be planted in 1926. The principal growers are: George Allan, R. C. Christiansen, and the Kirkman Nurseries.

In harvesting the seed the cucumbers are picked from the vines and thrown in windrows, after which a separating machine drawn by horses pulps the cucumber and separates the seed, which is afterwards washed and dried. Many of the cucumbers grown are weighing in excess of five pounds each.

October 17, 1925.—With the granting of a contract by the Richmond City Council to the Tibbetts Pacific Company for $64,770 for the construction of an open wharf on the inner harbor, a program of harbor improvement adopted in 1920 was finally put into effect. The contract calls for the construction of an open wharf with creosoted piling on property owned by the City of Richmond on the inner harbor channel. This channel, dredged as a part of the United States government program of development of Richmond harbor, was recently improved by the City of Richmond, which dredged a turning basin at the site of the wharf. Bonds for the present wharf construction were voted by the city at an election in 1920.

October 17, 1925.—Firmly convinced that the business interests and citizens are a unit in supporting their compliance with the fire department's request for additional fire fighting equipment of the most advanced type, the city trustees at a special meeting Monday night unanimously voted the purchase of a $12,500 American-La France fire engine, a 750-gallon pumper fully equipped.

October 23, 1925.—The steel lift span of the Antioch-Sherman Island Bridge has been completely installed and with a few minor adjustments will be ready for service within a fortnight. O. H. Klatt, general manager of the American Toll Bridge Co., in Martinez Wednesday afternoon en route to the bridge site, stated that the company expects to have the bridge completed and handling traffic early in December.

October 23, 1925.—The dreaded puncture vine, so deadly to automobile tires and destructive to farm land, which some years ago ravaged one of California's counties and which has been found in three places in the eastern part of this county, was detected this week getting a start beside the Southern Pacific tracks at Pittsburg. Farm Advisor A. M. Burton was immediately notified and a determined war on the pest with the aid of kerosene is being waged.

October 17, 1925.—P. D. Busch, superintendent of the Concord airmail base, returned from an extensive tour of inspection, covering the entire western division of the federal air-mail service.

"No two air stations are operated the same," declared Busch, "and we are endeavoring to unify the entire western section." Mechanical operations are to be improved here, he said. Additions will be made to the machine shop at the Concord terminal.

Reports have been received from Japan, stating that messages over low-wave radio station in Concord were heard the last week. Dante Cordano and T. K. Johnson are in charge of the Concord sending station.

November 7, 1925.—David Macartney, pioneer of Antioch, who confesses to having weathered seventy-six winters, became a bridegroom Friday in Martinez when Mrs. Rebecca Davis of Los Angeles became his wife. For nearly a half century "Uncle" Dave Macartney has resided in Antioch, where he conducts a stationery and notion store and where, being a stanch disciple of Thomas Jefferson, he has served as postmaster for numerous terms. His friends in eastern Contra Costa are numbered by hundreds, and from each and every one congratulations and best wishes will be forthcoming.

November 7, 1925.—Pinole has had some banner natal days, and discovers claim to distinction in the fact that ten sets of twins have been born in the town from 1914 to 1924, inclusive, as follows:

To Mrs. Antone Light, March 4, 1914; Mrs Manuel Marcos, July 25, 1914; Mrs. John Chattelton, August 17, 1914; Mrs. William Quill, April 14, 1915; Mrs. Thomas Atkinson, January 23, 1917; Mrs. C. H. Drysdale, October 29, 1918; Mrs. Frank Maddox, September 7, 1920; Mrs. Burton F. Wills, May 19, 1923; Mrs. M. F. Goularte, December 23, 1923; Mrs. John Catrino, November 29, 1924.

November 7, 1925.—Breaking all records for the production of fruit, growers of central Contra Costa County sent out upward of 6500 tons of pears, grapes, peaches and apricots during the season just closed, according to a report by L. H. Rodebaugh, traffic manager of the Sacramento Short Line, to the directors of the company. Rodebaugh's report showed that in all 500 cars of fruit had been shipped over his line. Of this total 283 cars were pear shipments. There were 197 cars of grapes, twelve cars of apricots and eight cars of peaches. Most of the shipments were from Walnut Creek, Concord, Meinert, Alamo and Moraga. Practically the entire crop went to the east, where Contra Costa fruit is eagerly sought in the better markets, the report stated, though some of the crop was disposed of to the local canneries. The shipment shows a decided increase over that of last year.

December 5, 1925.—For over two years Grant D. Miller, coroner of Alameda County, has been boring hole after hole in hope of striking water on his ranch near Lafayette, but without results until Monday, when at a depth of 308 feet, the borers struck a flow which for three days has shot three feet over the top of the well.

December 5, 1925.—Workmen engaged in clearing the old McNamara property on Main Street, preparatory to erecting a new building for the J. C. Penney Company, on Monday uncovered one of the town's oldest drinking founts, where the town pump may have stood in the olden days. The old plank sidewalk hid a deep well of clear, cold water. The well is encased with rock and doubtless gave way to the modern water system. It will be filled in and abandoned.

December 19, 1925.—Crockett, December 14, 1925.—Free city delivery of mail, numbering of houses and naming of streets, a new railroad depot and lower fire insurance rates are the major projects which the Crockett-Valona Business Men's Association has mapped out for consummation the coming year.

December 19, 1925.—Rodeo to vote on $80,000 issue of bonds for new school at the January election. The school conditions in Rodeo are in a deplorable state, owing to the overcrowded condition of the class rooms, and it is hoped that the bond issue will carry.

January 2, 1926.—Deed of the Lanteri shipyards at Pittsburg from Annie Lanteri to H. F. Lauritzen and H. F. Bundesen was filed in the county recorder's office Thursday, the consideration being $25,000.

January 2, 1926.—Crockett Signal, January 1—With 119 cabin passengers and a heavy cargo, the Matson liner Matsonia, Capt. John T. Diggs, arrived Tuesday morning from Honolulu. She had 112,926 bags of the 1926 sugar crop for the Crockett refinery.

The Matson freighter Mauna Ala is due to arrive Wednesday with 119,285 bags of raw sugar; the Mahukona with 53,840 bags; and the Enterprise, with 22,983 bags.

The opening days of 1926 have been the coldest in the memory of old-timers, who unhesitatingly state that for sixty years they have not experienced such penetratingly cold weather. For eleven straight days a miserable cold tule fog sent its chilling mists o'er land and water, day and night. A light fall of rain broke this up, only to let the ocean fog hold sway. And when the ocean fog is not operating, there is an east wind which brings down piercing cold blasts from the mountains.

January 16, 1926.—John Miller, of Richmond, stated that at the top of Barry Hill, on the Franklin Canyon Highway, ice formed on the telephone wires fully an inch in diameter. He stated that north and east winds were meeting at the top of the hill and the heavy fog was freezing to whatever it touched. Icicles several inches long hung on the trees and bushes, where the fog had drifted in.

January 16, 1926.—Crockett Signal, January 15—Weighted down with ice, which incrusted the poles in some places fully six inches thick, the transcontinental lines of the Pacific Telephone and Telegraph Company, for a distance of two miles across the hills between Crockett and Luzon station in Rodeo Valley, have been wrecked, the weight of the ice bearing down so heavily on the wires that the poles have been snapped off, leaving the ninety individual wires through Contra Costa County a mass of tangled wreckage. Four extra crews are rushing the work of repairing the lines. It may be days or even weeks before the circuits are restored and service resumed.

January 23.—Crockett Signal, January 22.—The steamer Monoa, of the Matson Line, arrived Wednesday from Honolulu. She brought 65,720 bags of raw sugar for the refinery.

Hawaii's 1926 sugar crop is ripening so fast that every vessel of the Matson Line's fleet, with the exception of the motor ship Annie Johnson, is being placed into service again.

The big 14,000-ton freighter, Manukai, is en route from Hawaiian Island ports to San Francisco with 203,492 bags of raw sugar, which comes to Crockett.

January 23, 1926.—Sixty-four industrial plants in Contra Costa County annually produced manufactured or plant products conservatively valued at $404,123,620, two and a half times the production valuation of ten years ago, when the totals were only $161,332,100, figures thought at that time to be stupendous. These sixty-four plants employ 17,428 men and women, and each year pay these workers the sum of $26,424,500 in salaries.

February 13, 1926.—What engineers say will be the highest electric transmission tower in the world is being erected by the Pacific Gas and Electric Company as a part of the new 220,000-volt line now being built from Vaca-Dixon substation to Antioch. The record-breaker, which will be at the crossing of the Sacramento River, near Rio Vista, will be 459 feet high, rising thirty feet higher than the new telephone headquarters, San Francisco's tallest building.

To get its lines across the Sacramento and San Joaquin Rivers and at the same time comply with the Federal Government's clearance requirement for navigable streams, the company must put up five steel towers ranging in height from 269 to 459 feet, two at the Sacramento crossing and three at the San Joaquin crossing. The tallest tower of the latter span will be 359 feet.

Without a splice in the wire, six copper-clad steel cables will stretch from anchorage to anchorage, 7029 feet, nearly a mile and a third, across the Sacramento, 8835 feet, more than a mile and two-thirds across the San Joaquin. Supporting towers will be necessary to maintain the prescribed clearance height, but there is to be a single unbroken span of 4135 feet over the Sacramento River and one of 3175 feet over the San Joaquin.

The line will end three miles south of Antioch, where the company is building its Contra Costa substation. With the new line operating at world's record voltage it will be possible to carry directly a larger block of power to the industrial district centering around Pittsburg and Antioch.

February 19, 1926.—Did you know that Martinez was at one time, and for many years, the principal place of business of the Pacific States Telephone Company? It was; and to the central exchange, built over twenty years ago at Ferry and Ward Streets, the directors and stockholders of the company came once a year to hold their annual meeting. A special train was chartered annually to bring the party to Martinez, where Manager P. B. Borland was always waiting to receive the high officials of the company.

February 19, 1926.—Pittsburg — A smokestack weighing nearly twelve tons and standing 145 feet high, the largest ever erected in a single unit on the Pacific Coast, was hoisted into position at the blooming mill of the Columbia Steel Works on Monday. Crews are rushing work day and night to complete the mill, which will cost $380,000.

Record-Herald, February 24.—The new Methodist Episcopal Church at El Cerrito was dedicated Sunday. The handsome new structure at

Stockton and Everett Streets was officially opened when morning, afternoon and evening services were held.

Walnut Creek, March 4, 1926.—Walnut Creek's first playground commission was appointed Wednesday by the city trustees. The members are Mrs. Herbert Vaughn Brooke, Mrs. J. McGeehon, S. Quigley, C. P. Howard and William Miles.

Crockett Signal, March 5, 1926.—The Carquinez Women's Club will be twelve years old Wednesday, it having been organized March 10, 1914. It has prospered under its various presidents, but no set of officers has ever achieved more in the way of beautifying the town than the first of the organization. May continued success attend the workings of the Women's Club.

March 5, 1926.—For the first time in the history of the municipality, Martinez is about to foreclose and sell a piece of property for taxes. It is Lot 3 in Block 3, Fairview Addition, and is assessed in name of Maria Berterini. The taxes have not been paid on the property for five years, and a deed was recorded to the town "for taxes." The amount of the tax bill is $4.41.

March 5, 1926.—Concord, March 2—Airplanes constructed at the Douglas airplane plant at Santa Monica, assembled here, and later tried in Chicago, will be used in the air service between San Francisco and Eastern points. The new planes have a capacity of 1000 pounds, as against 350 pounds of the army ships. Service between Los Angeles and Seattle, with Concord as a base, is expected to be in operation by April 1.

March 13, 1926.—Pinole, March 8—The first building of the civic center planned for Pinole was dedicated Saturday afternoon and evening, when the fire house and library were accepted by Mayor E. M. Downer.

March 10, 1926.—Crockett Signal—Simultaneously with the floating of Old Glory from the flagpole at the top of the seven-story refinery this morning at 10:25, the machinery of the mill was set in motion as the converting of the first charge of raw sugar into the marketable article was commenced. Passing river crafts, and train and church bells joined in making a din. It is three years since the refinery closed. It is estimated the output of the refinery during the ten months will reach 180,000 tons. Before this the output ranged between 60,000 and 70,000 tons.

March 13, 1926.—The largest single deal in Martinez business property in recent years was negotiated Friday afternoon when a number of Oakland men headed by C. L. Philliber, George A. Lewis and A. R. Mitchell acquired title, by purchase, to the entire Fernandez estate holdings in the Court Block, bounded by Main, Las Juntas, Escobar and Court Streets, for $32,500, and at the same time obtained agreement for the purchase of the Brown property, southwest corner of Main and Las Juntas Streets, for $17,500.

March 27, 1926.—Regarding the recent survey of social and industrial conditions in the county, we find that of the 65,000 population, 44,000 reside in the cities. There are estimated to be 16,774 foreign-born whites and 43,787 native-born, of whom thirty-one per cent are of foreign parentage. Approximately 15,000 people live on farms, 5000 being distributed on the 2000 individual farms, of which 1561 are owned by the men who are occupying or farming them. There are estimated to be 28,000 head of cattle, worth $7,815,084, in the county, and in 1924 the poultry industry represented an investment of $396,517.

March 27, 1926.—Crockett, March 23—A total of 394,916 bags of sugar will be received at the California & Hawaiian Sugar Refining Corporation this week. On Sunday the Manukai arrived with 188,405 bags of raw sugar; Tuesday the Maui arrived with 103,311 bags; and Friday the Lurline is due with 103,200 bags.

Crockett Signal, April 3, 1926.—The first truss span of the long approach for the viaduct of the Carquinez bridge was swung into position yesterday, marking the starting of the actual steel erection on the largest highway bridge in the West. In eighteen minutes the giant mass of steel work was swung into place, after being assembled on the ground. The steel and other materials that are arriving daily are taxing the warehouse and storage facilities.

April 8, 1926.—Sixty-seven years ago today, on April 8, 1859, the first telegraph cable was laid across Suisun Bay between Martinez and Benicia, and California's second capital and Contra Costa's county seat were joined by wire for the first time. Laying down of the submarine telegraph cable at that time was a notable feat.

April 9, 1926.—Martinez Standard—The fertility of Contra Costa soil was shown when it became known that at the wharf of the Martinez-Benicia Ferry Company, where piling was driven into salt water several months ago, shoots several inches in length are developing on the piling made of eucalyptus trees. D. Joselin of Martinez made the discovery. "Some fertile land, I'll say," Joselin commented. "But what I can't understand is that the piles are all driven root end up, and that's no April-fool joke either."

Pinole, May 6, 1926.—The old Alvarez homestead was destroyed by fire Monday night. This building was one of the old landmarks of Pinole, having been built about seventy years ago.

Brentwood, May 28, 1926.—Mrs. Elizabeth Shafer celebrated her eighty-third birthday at her home in Brentwood on Wednesday by entertaining a number of friends who called during the day. Mrs. Shafer crossed the plains in a prairie schooner when about sixteen years old and has resided in Contra Costa county for the past fifty-eight years.

June 5, 1926.—Twenty Contra Costa pioneers gathered over the holidays at Pacheco's pioneer schoolhouse to glimpse for the last time scenes and associations of childhood days before the structure is torn down to make way for the modern school recently authorized by the school trustees and for which $14,000 bonds have been voted. Mrs. Edna D. Thurber of Concord and Mrs. S. J. de Soto were hostesses at the affair, which has been an annual event since the organization of the reunion five years ago by Mrs. Robert Wallace of Brentwood.

Those invited to the reunion included: Mrs. Nannie Oliver Thiel, Mrs. Maud O. Wentworth, Miss Ella Ashley, Mrs. Julia V. Thurber, Mrs. Ella Eimonson, all of Berkeley; Mrs. Lottie H. Standish, of Crockett; Mrs. Fannie Dager, Mrs. Carrie Anderson, Mrs. Nellie R. Gorham, Miss Jessie Rowley, Mrs. Belle Loucks Sears of Porterville; Mrs. Alice M. Wallace of Brentwood; Miss Dollie Anderson and Miss Annie Loucks of Pacheco; Miss Ida Hall of Alamo; Mrs. Mary Hendricks Alexander of Napa (whose father built the first flour mill in Pacheco); Mrs. Martha S. de Soto, Mrs. Lena McLean, Mrs. Mary Gehringer, Mrs. Nellie Dunn Thurber, Mrs. Margaret Anderson Randall, and Mrs. Susan Dunn de Soto, all of Concord.

July 10, 1926.—Announcement of the purchase of the Lauritzen Ferry Company operating between Contra Costa County and Sherman Island, just east of Antioch, was made by the American Toll Bridge Company. Frank E. Reynolds, engineer for the bridge company, stated that the sale includes all franchises, good will, etc., of the ferry company. The ferry immediately parallels the new Antioch-Sherman Island bridge. Ferry service has been discontinued.

July 10, 1926.—The opening to travel of the widened and much improved tunnel road between Oakland and Walnut Creek and the existence of the new steel bridge at Antioch, which eliminates all ferrying between the bay and Sacramento, stimulated holiday travel between the bay cities and Sacramento. During the three days a mechanical count of machines crossing the bridge showed a total of 6500 cars.

Topping last year's Fourth of July traffic record by 540 automobiles, the Martinez-Benicia Ferry carried more than 5200 cars on Saturday, Sunday and Monday. Manager A. J. Pometta stated that none were forced to wait longer than forty minutes at any time.

July 17, 1926.—Last Monday, jelly boiled over at Danville, causing a $20,000 fire. The buildings destroyed are: Danville Emporium, owned by the Fosters; residence of N. A. Andreasen, occupied by Ed. Fingersen and family; residence of Mrs. Ella Case; and residence of A. B. Cabral.

July 31, 1926.—Working three eight-hour shifts a day, contractors are rushing the construction of the $1,375,000 Claremont tunnel, the longest underground link in the Mokelumne water project. Extending for three and one-half miles in a straight line, from Orinda to Rockridge, the bore is being cut through hills which are 1650 feet above sea level at the highest point. Starting at a height of 340 feet above sea level at Orinda, the tunnel will gradually slope to the 328 foot level at Rockridge, giving a daily flow of 200,000,000 gallons.

Workmen will have to remove 100,000 cubic yards of dirt in order to complete the bore. These men will be closely followed by another gang which will construct the concrete pipe line, nine feet in diameter.

Twenty-two thousand cubic yards of concrete will be required to complete this phase of the work.

The contract for the Claremont tunnel was signed June 15, and work on the project was begun immediately. It is estimated by engineers that it will take 950 days to completely finish the work.

July 31, 1926.—For the first time since the old Martinez-Clayton horse-drawn stage suspended and abandoned its service, Martinez and Concord are to be linked by direct stage commencing next Sunday, when Robert Miller inaugurates a daily automobile stage service.

August 7, 1926.—With a vote of seventy-two to fifty-four in favor of the proposition, residents of San Pablo decided to form a fire district to protect their buildings. As the result of the election equipment including hydrants, hose and ladders will be purchased to be used by the volunteer fire department.

August 7, 1926.—Brentwood, August 4—By an overwhelming vote the residents of Brentwood yesterday established the first Contra Costa County water district to serve the town with a domestic water supply. With 122 registered voters a total of 107 votes were cast, of which 101 were in favor of a $20,000 bond issue to purchase existing equipment, install complete fire protection, and develop new wells for local supply. This is the first district in Contra Costa County under the county water district act.

Martinez Standard, August 9, 1926.—The Martinez-Benicia Ferry Company transported 438,023 passengers in the fiscal year ending June 30, according to a ferry traffic report just made public by John K. Bulger of San Francisco, United States inspector of steam vessels. Bulger's figures show that more than 58,000,000 persons were transported across San Francisco Bay and its branches during the year, and that 29,310,985 passengers were handled by Southern Pacific lines. The Rodeo-Vallejo Ferry Company handled 1,437,527 passengers and the Richmond-San Rafael Ferry Company 736,644.

August 12, 1926.—Brentwood, August 12—The election called for the purpose of consolidating the Lone Tree, Knightsen and Brentwood districts cast a heavy vote Tuesday for the consolidation. The new district will be known as the East Contra Costa Irrigation District; and by this election the East Contra Costa Company, which formerly supplied the water for the three districts, will cease to exist, as will the Brentwood, Knightsen and Lone Tree Irrigation Districts. The new district will maintain its headquarters in Brentwood. The consolidation will reduce the operating expense of the district by close to $5000 annually.

August 7, 1926.—Sale of the Port Costa Water Company, founded and operated for many years by the George W. McNear interests, to a group of investors represented by the bond house of Pierce, Fair & Co., was announced jointly Tuesday afternoon by E. H. Shibley, manager of the system for years, and Harry Reinhardt of Berkeley, who succeeds Shibley as manager of the water company. Neither Shibley nor Reinhardt was in a position to make public the price paid the McNears for their controlling interest in the water company, but it is understood to have been a sum of sizeable proportions. The deal involves all lands, wells, pumping plants, pipe lines and storage reservoirs owned, controlled or operated by the Port Costa Water Company.

September 18, 1926.—The Contra Costa Gazette, the first newspaper established in Contra Costa County and one of the few of the early-day newspapers of the State to have continued without change of name through all the years from 1858 to the present day, and never having missed a single issue, today celebrates its sixty-eighth birthday.

And on this, its sixty-eighth birthday, it is with pardonable pride we announce the passing of the old reliable Contra Costa Gazette from the weekly to the daily field, thus taking the place of the Daily Gazette which holds the distinction of being the oldest daily newspaper now published in Contra Costa County. Hereafter the Contra Costa Gazette will be published daily, excepting Sundays and legal holidays.

On September 18, 1858, Vol. 1, No. 1 of the Contra Costa Gazette made its appearance in Martinez, then a village of a mere handful of souls. Some years later, when Pacheco became the principal business center of the county, the Gazette was moved to that town and published there for a number of years, returning to Martinez when the county seat again took precedence and became the principal seat of business for the central part of Contra Costa County.

The management of the Gazette points with justifiable pride to the long career and enviable reputation which this old-established pioneer journal has enjoyed for more than half a century and still holds. And in announcing this change in publication policy the Gazette celebrates its birthday by the installation of a specially built press room of the latest model Goss-Comet perfecting web press, shipped directly from the factory in Chicago. The Gazette's new Goss-Comet press operates at high speed, being fed from great rolls of print paper, and has a capacity of four, six or eight pages printed simultaneously, and being delivered from the press folded and ready for the carriers at a speed of several thousands an hour.

With its new press and two of the latest model linotype machines, with other modern equipment, the Gazette finds itself on this, its sixty-eighth birthday, in a position of being able to give to the people of Martinez and all Contra Costa County a newspaper chronicling local and county events, second to none in its field, it being the aim of this newspaper in future as in the past to furnish the reading public with a true, accurate and dependable account of the events of the day and concerning people and affairs in which they are most interested.

The Contra Costa Gazette, published daily, will be a bigger and better paper than ever before in its history, if the ambitions of the management and staff meet with successful fulfillment. All the news that's fit to print all the time will continue to be found in the Gazette with such features as are aimed to please and interest both young and old.

"GOLD STAR" HEROES OF THE WORLD WAR

Following are the names of the seventy-six from Contra Costa County who gave their lives in the World War:

Anderson, Simeon M.
Bauer, Adolph C., Jr.
Beyer, Peter
Brandon, Hazel L.
Brown, Elmer B.
Brown, William J.
Carroll, J. R.
Catelini, B. L.
Crowley, Dennis
Damiano, Leo L.
Davidson, John T.
Del Zotto, Caesar
Depianti, Domenico
Dias, Edward M.
Dingman, R. L.
Doglio, Joseph J.
Duncan, Henry C.
Dunn, V. L.
Dunn, W. E.
Eryavich, Joseph F.
Fleming, William J.
Flinn, Roy E.
Franco, John
Freitas, George
Freml, Wesley, Jr.
Frerichs, Melvin L.
Gatto, Pietro
Gavin, Raymond F.
Glum, William
Granzella, Agripino
Hagen, Louis C., Jr.
Hampton, Robert B.
Harding, Stacy L.
Harper, Richard J.
Hartnett, James
Henegar, Hugh M.
Hoey, Matthew J.
Johnstone, William H., Jr.

Keenan, Patrick J.
Kennedy, Lawrence S.
Lacey, Howard F.
Latkoski, Joseph
Lee, George M.
Lorentson, Oscar
Luchsinger, Fred W.
McNamara, Henry A.
McQuarrie, John E.
MacDiarmid, Orvis R.
Magreil, Thomas
Miller, James P.
Morgan, Albert J.
Nesbitt, R. J.
Parenti, Ameda
Parkinson, Royal A.
Peterson, William
Prestridge, John B.
Redding, Earl W.
Remani, Frederick W.
Ross, G. W.
Roveda, Pompeo
Rumble, Ernest
Secor, B. A.
Sievers, M. H.
Severns, Sydney
Solari, David A.
Spears, Matthew J.
Springer, Charles E.
Stone, William E.
Studebaker, Floyd A.
Sweet, Ora A.
Trelut, Frank
Turner, Guy A.
Vargus, George B.
Walsh, Martin
Wilkinson, Charles
Wood, Lloyd

BIOGRAPHICAL REVIEW

PIONEERS, PAST AND PRESENT

Thomas A. Brown

BIOGRAPHICAL REVIEW

PIONEERS, PAST AND PRESENT

THOMAS ALLEN BROWN.—A pioneer of the Pacific Coast country, Thomas Allen Brown first came to Oregon in 1843, and it was he who laid out the city of Portland in 1844, before gold was discovered in California. He was born on October 16, 1823, in Greene County, Ill., and was the oldest of four children born to Squire Elam Brown, a sketch of whom appears on another page of this history. When he was fourteen years of age the Brown family settled in Platte County, Mo., and six years later, when he was twenty years old, young Brown joined a party of emigrants and crossed the plains and mountains to Oregon. He had had the advantages of a good education and had chosen the profession of the engineer, which he followed in Oregon. When he was only twenty-one he was chosen to make the original survey and plats of the city of Portland.

His advent to California came in 1847, when he made a visit to his parents, who had come to California in 1846 and stopped at Mission San Jose until Squire Brown could find a location for a home, which was soon found in the Moraga Valley. In 1848 T. A. Brown went back to Oregon to settle up his affairs, and then at once returned and for a short time was in the mining districts, after which he came direct to what is now the city of Martinez. In 1849 he was appointed alcalde of this district, and held office till April, 1850, when he was elected county clerk and recorder under the new county government. In 1849, before California was admitted as a State, Mr. Brown was selected by Col. William Smith, agent for the Martinez family who were owners of all the land lying west of Alhambra Creek, to survey a townsite and lay out 120 acres. The lots were quickly sold, and then the heirs of the Welch Rancho, on the east side of the creek, employed Mr. Brown to survey and plat about 500 acres, which he did in 1850-1851, and this is known as the Additional Survey. Mr. Brown erected a building that stood about on the spot where the present Scott Hotel is located, and here, with his brother Warren and N. B. Smith, he conducted the first store in Martinez, the town being named after the owners of the grant on which it was located. He next served as a supervisor one year, and then took up the study of law while acting as county clerk. He was admitted to practice in 1860, and from that date until his death he was considered one of the brightest men in the legal profession in Contra Costa County.

Mr. Brown was elected county judge in 1856 and served until 1864. In 1865 he was elected to the State Assembly, and served during two sessions. He practiced his profession in Martinez; and in 1874, upon the death of Judge Lander, he was appointed county judge, and held that office until the State constitution went into effect and created the superior court, when he became the first superior judge. He remained in this office until he resigned a very short time before his death.

Thomas Allen Brown was united in marriage in 1851 with Miss Caroline Thelia Cameron, born in Fulton County, Ill., on January 5, 1834. She was the daughter of Rev. John M. and Polly Cameron, and came with them to California across the plains with ox-teams in 1849 and located for a short time in Sacramento. The family then came to Contra Costa County and Mr. Cameron erected the first brick house in Martinez, at the corner of Las Juntas and Green Streets. There were eleven girls in the Cameron family and one son, Thomas M. W. W. Cameron, who married Alice Marsh, daughter of Dr. John Marsh, was the son of this Thomas M. Cameron. Later, after his family had all married, Rev. and Mrs. Cameron went to Sonoma County and settled near Sebastopol, where they both passed away. About the time of his marriage to Miss Cameron, Thomas A. Brown erected a brick house just north of the creek, above what is now the State Theatre, and this was their first home here. Three sons were born of their union: Elam C., who is mentioned on another page of this history; Wallace, born in 1857, who died in 1921, unmarried; and Byron Brown, now the only survivor of the entire Brown family.

Thomas Allen Brown was one of the most public-spirited citizens of this county, and was always doing his share to advance the best interests of his fellow citizens. His wife was an accomplished woman, and was endeared to her family and a large circle of friends. Mrs. Brown died on January 14, 1922; and Judge Thomas A. Brown died on August 5, 1889. As surveyor, engineer, merchant, lawyer and jurist, he was recognized as the leading citizen of Contra Costa County, and was known and respected throughout the entire State.

DR. JOHN MARSH.—The most conspicuous character of Contra Costa County was the late Dr. John Marsh, the first white man to locate within the county, and here to begin farming and stock-raising. He it was who first extolled the wonders of this far western country as a farmer's paradise and, as the pioneers wended their way across the plains in search of gold or a home, he made it a particular duty to welcome all of those that came within his boundaries. Dr. Marsh had about 6000 head of cattle on his broad acres at all times and their increase was about 1500 head each season. His only help were the Indians of this region and these he taught to speak English so they could be understood. He found them very willing to do whatever tasks they were set to perform and he was always humane in his treatment of them.

John Marsh was born in Danvers, Mass., on June 5, 1799, and was a son of John and Mary (Brown) Marsh. He prepared for college with the Reverend Doctor Eaton, of Boxford, Mass., and finished at the Phillips Academy at Andover. At the age of eighteen he entered Harvard University and while attending college taught in his native town to defray his expenses. As a youth he was fond of hunting and trapping. After he had graduated he went to Fort Snelling (now St. Paul), Minn., where he had been appointed instructor to the children of the officers at that post. Leaving there after two years, he went to Detroit, Mich., and with Governors Schoolcraft and Cass, he went to Prairie du Chien, Wis., and for three years was Indian agent at Fort Crawford, near there. From 1828 to 1835 he was engaged in the mercantile business at St. Joseph, Mo., then he sold out and started West on horseback, with an exploring expedition. He entered California at its southern end and stopped for a time in the pueblo of Los Angeles. It was while there that he obtained from the Mexican government a grant of land at the base of Mount Diablo, in northern California. Immediately proceeding to this location he made a settlement and began raising cattle, his only assistants being the native Indians. He was the first white man to raise grain in what is now Contra Costa County.

The land secured by Doctor Marsh was known as the Los Meganos Rancho and was ten by twelve miles in extent. He settled there in 1837 and named his ranch "Rancho de los Pulpunes." With the aid of the Indians be built an adobe house and after carrying on farming with success for several years, began to write to his friends in the East, and to the newspapers, describing the wonders and possibilities of the soil. In fact his were the first letters that "boosted" California lands. In later years when settlers began coming into the State he always extended to them the hospitality of his home and did what he could to show them a welcome fitting his position.

Upon the discovery of gold his lands advanced in value, and soon afterward his property was confirmed to him by the United States government. He had a landing on the San Joaquin River above what is now Pittsburg, then known as New York of the Pacific. His land was dotted with live-oak trees, and Marsh Creek traversed the entire length of the property. From plans drawn by Thomas Boyd, he began the construction of a stone house 60 by 40 feet in dimensions and three stories high. It was made from the native stone found on the ranch, which when exposed to the air materially hardened. There was a piazza on three sides that was ten feet wide. The cost of the building was about $20,000. The house stands to this day, but Dr. Marsh never lived to enjoy his new home for he was killed the year it was completed, 1856. He experimented with fruits of all kinds, had several vineyards, and orchards of apples, plums, figs, almonds and pears. The famous stone house was damaged by the earthquake of 1868, but was restored.

Dr. Marsh was married on June 24, 1851, to Miss Abbie Tuck, born in Massachusetts, who left her home in 1850, and upon arriving in California located in Santa Clara. She passed away leaving one daughter Alice, who married W. W. Cameron, of Martinez. Dr. Marsh met his death at the hands of Jose Olivas, Juan Garcia and Felipe Moreno, on September 24, 1856, while en route to San Francisco to meet with his attorney there. He was intercepted before reaching Martinez and brutally murdered. His driverless horse continued into Martinez and was found by some citizens who went back and found his body a few miles out of town. The Doctor was a man of commanding appearance, a keen observer of men and things, and a man of wide information gained through his extensive travels. He was a good French and Spanish scholar and was familiar with the habits and manners of each race. In the report of the U. S. Exploring Expedition he was considered the best authority for information of the country traveled over. He had made several private expeditions into various parts of the country. To Dr. John Marsh all honor is due for the early settlement and development of the resources of Contra Costa County and his name will ever be held in reverence by posterity.

HON. ELAM BROWN.—The second American in Contra Costa County was Hon. Elam Brown, who was born in Herkimer County, N. Y., on June 10, 1797. His father was a farmer and had married a Miss Lyons, both of whom were of Scotch descent. They had three sons and four daughters, Elam being the oldest son. When he was one year of age, his parents moved to Berkshire County, Massachusetts, and six years later they migrated to Ohio, which was at that time a vast timbered wilderness. It was a long hard journey of 700 miles, through a thinly settled country, but after many days of weary traveling through the rugged Alleghany Mountains, and being almost worn out by fatigue and exposure, they came in sight of the broad Ohio River. As they stood upon an elevation and looked upon the grand scene before them, they forgot for a time all about the pleasant home they had left; they thought no more of their weary traveling, but gazed with pleasure upon the beautiful scene spread before them. Below them, on the bank of the beautiful river, stood the little village of Wheeling, while far beyond extended the wild forests of the land to which they were bound. From Wheeling they crossed the river into Ohio. There was at that time but one house on the river opposite Wheeling.

Leaving the river at that point, and traveling thirty miles through the dense forest, they reached Zanesville, a village of eight or ten cabins; thirty miles from Zanesville was Newark, which consisted of only four or five cabins; and about five miles from Newark they came to a cabin on the spot where Granville now stands. There they came to a stop, for twenty-five miles of dense forest lay between them and the destined settlement, with not so much as a dim trail through it. The only chance they had to reach the settlement was to open a road, which was a hard undertaking; but the pioneer knows no discouragement. They opened the road and reached the settlement in safety. Their family increased the settlement to nine families, four of which were from Berkshire County, Massachusetts, and from that it was named the Berkshire settlement. The nearest white settlement north of them was on Lake Erie, about 100 miles distant, and fifteen miles south was the Worthington settlement.

There it was, at seven years of age, that Mr. Brown entered upon a frontier life, with all its hardships and pleasures. There he learned all the inconveniences to be encountered by the pioneer. The first school building in the settlement was a log cabin furnished with seats and desks composed of logs split, and the flat sides hewn off smoothly. It was there that Mr. Brown and his brothers received their first lessons in school. Elam being the oldest son, had to give so much time to the labors of the farm that his educational advancement was very much retarded. Early in life he became deeply interested in history and geography, and made those branches his chief study.

His father died in 1815, and the care of the estate rested on this son, who discharged this duty until 1818. He then left Ohio and went to St. Louis, at that time a French trading post. From St. Louis he traveled on foot 100 miles up the Missouri River, but becoming dissatisfied, he returned, and in company with Charles Gregory, went to Madison County, Ill., where he remained one year, then went fifty miles north to a new settlement on Apple Creek, afterwards organized into Greene County. He married, January 10, 1823, Sarah Allen, the daughter of Thomas Allen, and settled on the first farm he ever owned. He soon sold his farm and moved forty miles north to a new settlement, afterwards organized into Morgan County, Ill., where he resided for fourteen years, twelve of which he served as justice of the peace. He spent the summers of 1826-1827 in the lead mines of Wisconsin. It was not known at that time whether they were in Illinois or in an unorganized territory. The children of Elam Brown and his wife were: Thomas Allen, born in 1823; Warren; Margeline Smith; and Lawrence Myers.

In 1837 Mr. Brown moved from Illinois to the Platte Purchase, a tract of land bordering on the Missouri River, purchased by the United States from the Indians in 1836. There he located and cleared a farm of 180 acres, upon which he resided until 1846, and here his wife died in 1845. He sold his farm and made preparations to emigrate to the Pacific Coast. Early in the spring of 1846 a company of fourteen families, including sixteen wagons, was organized, with Mr. Brown as captain. On the first day of May, 1846, the company crossed the river at St. Joseph, moving forward as rapidly as was consistent, with nothing to interrupt their progress until they reached the South Platte. They had in the meantime fallen in with other companies, so the train at that time consisted of about thirty wagons.

They had been travelling up the river and had camped at the junction of the two tributaries. Soon after dark the cattle stampeded and after a delay of one week spent in searching for them, they succeeded in finding all except 120 head, of which 62 were oxen. This was a serious loss. It left their teams very much broken up, but they managed to buy some cows from other trains, and by working those and what cows and oxen they had, they were enabled to proceed on their journey.

When they came within a few miles of Fort Laramie, Mr. Brown, with five companions, started on ahead of the train in order to make some arrangements for more oxen, and to have some blacksmith work done at the fort by the time the train came up. They had gone but a short distance when an Indian met them and seemed very anxious to communicate something to them, but they were unable to understand him, so he turned and accompanied them. They had gone but a short distance when they reached an elevation from which they could look down on the Platte, about two miles distant; there, to their amazement, they saw about three hundred well mounted Indians. The Indian with them waved his blanket as a signal and the others advanced towards them in solid column, on a cavalry trot, their arms and dress glittering in the bright sunshine.

Mr. Brown says that he never saw a better parade by well trained cavalry than he witnessed by those red men of the plains. He judged the signs to be favorable, and on being asked by Mr. Crowly, who exhibited considerable fear and anxiety, what it all meant, told him to go back and give instructions to the trains to come up in two lines, so that they could swing together in case of an emergency, and to look well to their arms. Mr. Brown was left with one companion, Mr. Scott, the others having gone back on the first appearance of the Indians.

When they came within twenty-five feet of Mr. Brown he raised his hand as a signal for them to halt; they did so. The chief dismounted from his horse and walked back and forth in front of the line, addressing them. After he finished he advanced and extended his hand to Mr. Brown; then eleven others came forward and presented their hands to him. By this time the train had almost reached them, and Mr. Brown sent for some tobacco; when it was brought he sat down on the ground and motioned to the chiefs to be seated; they did so, forming a circle. He handed the tobacco to the head chief, who distributed it and lighted a pipe, and after taking a whiff, he passed it to Mr. Brown, who did the same, and passed it to the next, and so on until it was passed around the circle. The oxen became very restless and Mr. Brown motioned to the chief to have the lines opened so that the teams could pass on. The request was immediately granted, and the train passed on by the fort and camped on the North Platte. The Indians came on and camped near the emigrants. Other trains, on hearing of the appearance of Indians, pushed forward as rapidly as possible to join Mr. Brown's train. During the evening some of the Indians came into camp and began to meddle with things in the wagons. Complaint was made to the chief, who mounted a wagon and made a speech, and the Indians left the camp of the Americans and bothered them no more.

Mr. Brown was informed by a French trader that the Indians desired the emigrants to give them a feast, claiming it as a tribute for passing through their country and destroying their game. The emigrants could not do so that evening on account of the wind; but the next morning plenty of provisions were prepared and taken out a short distance from the camp and placed upon some logs; then the Indians were invited to partake of it, when, unexpectedly, only the chief and eleven others came forward and partook of the feast. After it was over the emigrants had, through an interpreter, a friendly conversation with the Indians, and made them a few presents, and all separated good friends.

The next morning the emigrants left for Fort Laramie and traveled up the river all day. They camped by a spring about half a mile from the river. About dark the cattle took a stampede, going back the road they had come, but on reaching the river they plunged in and swam to an island about eighty rods from the shore. Two young men, Joseph Stillwell and George Marsh, doffed their clothes, swam the river and followed the cattle to the upper end of the island, and succeeded in getting them back to camp about midnight.

The train passed through the Black Hills, crossed the North Platte, then traveled up the Sweetwater, crossed over the mountains on to Green River, with nothing but sickness to interrupt their progress. They crossed Green River and traveled on to Fort Bridger; there Mr. Brown had to leave his son, Warren, who had been sick twenty days with typhoid fever. They traveled on over to Bear River, and to Fort Hall on the Snake River, thence down the Snake River about forty miles, and turned south over on to the Humboldt. They went down the Humboldt to the sink, thence west across the eight-mile desert on to the Truckee. They traveled up the river, crossing it twenty-seven times with much difficulty, on account of the large rocks and swift current, and arrived near the summit. The mountain reared its summit far above them, and the ascent was so steep that their weary teams could not draw the wagons up it. They knew something had to be done; winter was near, starvation with it. After considerable trouble they managed to get fifteen yoke of oxen to the top of the mountain. They then extended a chain from the teams to the wagons, which were 200 feet below, but to prevent the chain from bearing too heavily upon the ground they placed on the summit a large roller made of a log, over which they passed the chain, and by that means they were enabled to draw up one wagon at a time. All the wagons and the sick and convalescent were safely landed on the summit by sunset. There was a joyful company around the camp fire that night. They had surmounted the great barrier and anticipated an easy down grade. Their joy was well founded, as was proven by the fate of the Donner train, but a few days behind them, which was caught in a snow-storm and most of them perished.

In all this long journey from St. Joseph on the Missouri River to the Pacific shores, there was not a bridge or a ferry for the crossing of any stream.

The emigrants traveled on and camped on the spot where Sacramento City stands, only a rancheria then. About one mile and a half up the American River stood Sutter's Fort, and from there they procured fresh beef and flour. Fresh meat and bread were highly appreciated, for these had long been desired.

Mr. Brown concluded, after a few days' rest, to go to Santa Clara, but feared that his teams would not be able to take his wagons, for many of his oxen had fallen by the way. He made arrangements with Captain Sutter to take one of his wagons on a boat to Yerba Buena, as he supposed that place to be close to Santa Clara. The only house between Sutter's and San Jose Mission was one in Livermore Valley. Mr. Brown spent one week in San Jose Mission, and then went to Santa Clara, where all the families south of the Bay had assembled for safety, for it had become manifest that the country was hostile. When he arrived at Santa Clara he found thirty families, with only about fifteen men to protect them, the others having gone to join Captain Fremont.

Mr. Brown went into the San Antonio redwoods, where there was plenty of hard work, and spent the summer of 1847 in whip-sawing lumber. He hauled his lumber to San Antonio Creek, and boated it over to San Francisco. During that time he was making every effort to find a farm that he could purchase. The Californians were bound by a pledge not to sell, or even give any information in relation to the lands. They said, "If we can't fight these heathens out, we can starve them; for we can keep them from a permanent settlement here." In the fall he learned that Leidsdorff, a trader in San Francisco, had a ranch for sale, that he had secured from Vallencia, a Spaniard. Mr. Brown purchased the ranch and 300 cows that Liedsdorff had bought of Vasques, of Half Moon Bay. He built a strong corral on the ranch and engaged an American and his vaqueros to bring the cattle up to the ranch. The cattle were herded through the day and corralled at night for a few months, after which they gave no further trouble. They increased rapidly and were good beef at all seasons of the year.

But there was something more to look to than the raising of stock. There was no government except the military authority, vested in Colonel Mason, and he manifested much delicacy in using that authority. The confusion of national affairs, caused by the close contest in Congress on the slavery question, one party opposing and the other favoring its extension, prevented any action by that body towards a law for organizing a territorial or state government. Colonel Riley, who superseded Mason in 1848, issued a proclamation for the people to hold an election to elect delegates to a Convention. What a relief to those who had lived in the country for some time without any courts or legal tribunals and government. Hope revived in those who fully realized the condition of things.

The Convention, which consisted of thirty-seven members, convened and organized in Monterey on the first day of September, 1849. The members were mostly immigrants from almost every State in the union, with many of the preferences and prejudices of those days. Yet sound sense prevailed. Mr. Brown was a member of the Convention that framed the State Constitution, and also of the first two legislatures after its adoption. He often attended mass meetings, but was never a delegate to a political convention. He was always free to speak his mind, and allowed others the same privilege. He said: "Amid all the various surroundings and positions through life I have never struck or been struck, never run for or from man or boy. I have had but few lawsuits or contentions. I have never bet a cent on a race or cards, and have never dealt in stock. I was never intoxicated by liquor although I was raised in a tavern, but I have never dealt in the article since. I have never cheated a man, knowingly, out of a dollar, but the reverse has occasionally occurred. I do not intend this as a boast but as an acknowledgment of the blessing bestowed on me through a long life, by my good and benevolent Creator. Discouragements have seldom crossed my path. But allow me to relate one instance. While on guard one cold, rainy night in Santa Clara, during that memorable week of the siege, expecting every moment that the Spaniards would charge in from the north or south—and to make the surroundings more gloomy, the Mission Indians were howling over a dead comrade, and as many dogs as Indians were engaged in the howling—amid all that there came into my mind this thought: I had committed an error that had involved my children as well as myself. I had brought them from a good home and a land of safety; had left a sick son at Fort Bridger, doubting his recovery; had a son and daughter in the Mission, likely to be butchered by the Spaniards. The fate of Travis and Fanning came fresh in my mind; for half an hour or more I was a homesick man strolling up and down the muddy streets of Santa Clara. Sound reason and resolution came to my assistance and I became my own man again. I have been blessed with buoyant spirits and a strong resolution. These properties have added much to my comfort of mind and success in business."

Died at Lafayette, Contra Costa County, California, August 10, 1889, age ninety-two years.

13

JUAN B. ALVARADO.—Among the best known men of the Spanish period in Alta California, the name of Juan B. Alvarado will ever stand out prominently for his recognized ability and public spirit. He was honored as a patriot and statesman throughout his long career, and was chosen governor and served from 1836 to 1843. A native of California, he was born at Monterey in 1809, of pure Castilian blood, and was carefully reared by his mother and early in life displayed a taste for learning and culture. He was a man of great natural talent and these striking qualities attracted the attention of Governor Sola, who assisted him with his studies in acquiring a knowledge of political and military science. Notwithstanding this aid he was compelled to depend on himself to a great extent and was what would be called a self-made and -educated man. He was very broadminded and was a great reader. It is stated that he was excommunicated by the priests for reading Fenelon's Telemaque. He entered political life as a young man and became secretary of the Territorial Deputation or California Legislature, and from that time down to the American occupation he held some kind of office.

In 1836 Juan B. Alvarado raised the standard of independence and proclaimed the Free and Sovereign State of Alta California in opposition to what was then known as the existing Centralist Government of Mexico. By this act and the ability displayed by him in encouraging the revolution, and the success with which he carried it through, he was often called "The Napoleon of California," which was evidently far from his ambition. He was a great student of the life of George Washington and it is more than likely he wished to emulate his example more than anything else. There were difficulties enough for him to overcome as head of the revolutionary movement and he had to meet and overcome a rival governor in the person of his uncle Don Carlos Carillo, of Santa Barbara, whom he made prisoner in his own house and later aided in escaping. In 1838 the government of Mexico recognized Alvarado as Governor intercino, and in 1839 appointed him governor proprietario, or Constitutional Governor of the Californias, both lower and upper California, which office he held until the accession of Micheltorena, in January, 1843. Alvarado was a sort of autocrat but it was never known that he was ever actuated by motives other than those which he conscientiously believed to be for the good of the country and the trust reposed in his hands. From 1843 to the American occupation he served a portion of the time as collector of customs at Monterey; and for a part of the time in military service as colonel of the militia of the department known as Defensores de la Patria, Defenders of the Country.

In 1845, when Governor Micheltorena was expelled, Alvarado made an able and successful military campaign, during which he and Gen. Jose Castro made a successful march, famous among Californians of those days, but about the only active service he ever saw. When the Amer-

H. F. Beede.

icans raised the Stars and Stripes in 1846 he was far-seeing enough to know the struggle against them would be futile and he took no active part in the events which succeeded.

In 1839 Juan B. Alvarado married Dona Martina Castro, daughter of Don Francisco Maria Castro, of San Pablo and he lived there with his family in the old adobe house until his death on July 13, 1882. His wife died in 1875, aged sixty-five years. He was survived by three sons and two daughters: John C., an attorney of San Francisco for years, died in 1907 in London, England, at the time he was connected with the Anglo-Mexican Mining Co.; Maria Victoria Delphina Carrick, died in Berkeley in 1893; Augustus F., died in New Mexico in 1891; Henry V., who is mentioned on another page in this history; and Adelina Tedford, resided in Chicago for years. In the history of California, as time rolls on, the things which Alvarado stood for and the things which he did, the measures which he advocated and the laws which he passed, his official as well as his private life will shine forth with increasing brightness and will constitute an instructive and interesting chapter.

HENRY FULLER BEEDE.—A man of strict integrity and sterling worth, who is held in high esteem throughout the community in which he has lived since 1868, and has filled all of his obligations as an enterprising citizen and genial neighbor, is Henry Fuller Beede, of Antioch, who has proved in many ways a helpful factor in local affairs. A native of Maine, he was born at Farmington, Franklin County, on November 16, 1850, and represents the fifth generation of the family in America. According to a record book kept by Thomas Beede, grandfather of our subject, the progenitor of the family was Eli Beede, who came from the French Island of Jersey in 1705, when a lad of fourteen years, his object being to gratify his curiosity and to verify the many stories he had heard of the New World. His father had been lost at sea and his widowed mother did not want to trust her son to the dangers of an ocean voyage, but his entreaties won her consent and soon an opportunity came that looked favorable. A ship was about to sail for Boston, commanded by his father's brother, and as this captain was considered a suitable person to be given charge of the lad, arrangements were made for his passage. The mother expected that in a few months she would see her son again, but this was their final parting, for he never went back. On the voyage the lad was so seasick that he then declared he never would undertake another sea voyage. It then became the duty of his uncle to make satisfactory arrangements for the lad to remain in Boston. This was a hard task, for the lad could speak nothing but French; and in this unhappy condition he left him. Eli Beede did not long remain in Boston, for he was put out to a man named Shaw, a farmer in the town of Hampton; and hence he grew up to the age of twenty-one on the farm, after which he selected farming as his life work and settled down at Kingston, N. H. He married a Miss Sleeper, and they had four sons and two daughters, all of whom, except one daughter, became the parents of large families, and all lived to ripe old ages.

Eli Beede, although holding the ease and pleasantry of the French, was naturally of a morose temper and was stern with his family. He was considered, however, to be an honest man, a good neighbor and a sincere Christian. His education was limited but he could read the Bible and cipher enough to keep his accounts, and even with this handicap he accumulated a large estate in the town of Kingston. By strict adherence to right living in every way, he was physically able to control his own affairs until just a few months prior to his death, which occurred in 1782, at ninety-one years of age. His religious tendencies in later life leaned towards the Friends, but he never joined their society and was a member of the Congregational Church in Kingston. Thomas Beede states that he was present at the funeral, which was largely attended, the sermon being preached by Rev. Dr. Shepard, of Brentwood, on the doctrine of the resurrection as taught by St. Paul in the 15th Chapter of I Corinthians. The sermon seemed to be well received by all except the Friends, who had other views on that subject. He was buried near Rev. Doctor Thayer's meeting-house, and his grave was left, according to the custom of the Friends, without any mark or monument. One circumstance in the story of his life is considered very singular, and that is that he never received a letter from, nor wrote a letter to, his mother or any members of the family from the time he sailed from his home shores.

Those following Eli Beede in line of descent were Thomas Beede; another Thomas Beede, an excellent scholar, writer, mathematician, draftsman and eloquent speaker. He was a fellow student with the noted Rev. Doctor Channing, the great Unitarian minister, and had in his possession many letters from that Divine. He served as a member of the board of Dartmouth College for many years and was a Grand Secretary of the Masonic order in New Hampshire. A third Thomas, born in New Hampshire, owned and operated a stage line between Farmington and Portland, Maine. He came to California via the Isthmus of Panama in early days, ran a livery stable in Stockton from 1851 to 1853, then went back to Maine and thence to Kankakee, Ill., and then back to California, where he and his wife died at Antioch.

This brings us down to Henry Fuller Beede, the fifth in line of descent from Eli Beede. He came to California when he was eighteen years old. His father was Thomas and his mother was Lucia Sarah (Merrill) Beede, born in New Hampshire and Maine, respectively. From the age of five years Henry Fuller Beede lived in Illinois, where he secured his education in the schools of that period. Upon coming to Antioch, Cal., in 1868, he worked for his brother, George, a merchant in this city at that time; and when he was twenty-one he found employment with Galloway and Boobar, lumber merchants in Antioch and the originators of the present concern known as the Antioch Lumber Company, of which Mr. Beede is now the president and manager. In 1877 Mr. Galloway retired and the business was carried on under the title of Rouse, Ferman & Beede, continuing thus until Mr. Rouse sold part of his interest to Capt. Asa Simpson, of San Francisco, and the firm name was changed to the Antioch Lumber Company. Mr. Beede is the only one of the original stockholders in the corporation, which is capitalized for $100,000. The concern does a general lumber and jobbing business, having a well-equipped planing mill in connection with the plant, where all kinds of building material are finished and delivered to the trade. This establishment is one of the oldest mercantile firms in Antioch, and has seen a gradual growth from a small concern to its present proportions under the ever-watchful eye of Mr. Beede, who has given his time and attention to the business. Besides being president and manager of the Antioch Lumber Company, Mr. Beede is president of the Bank of Antioch, which also owns the Bank of Brentwood, with aggregate deposits of over $1,000,000. He was one of the founders and is a trustee of the Congregational Church in Antioch, and in every way has been a leading factor in the building-up of this city and county.

The marriage of Henry Fuller Beede and Margaret Ellen McNulty, daughter of J. J. McNulty, took place on April 14, 1872. The McNulty's came to California in the mining days and settled at Columbia, Tuolumne County, later moving to Contra Costa County, where J. J. McNulty was justice of the peace for many years. Margaret Ellen taught school at Nortonville, and her marriage occurred at the age of nineteen. The union of Mr. and Mrs. Beede resulted in the birth of eleven children: Harry McNulty, born April 13, 1873 (see his sketch); Charles Frank Tyler, born October 15, 1874, who married Edith Little, a native of England and became the parent of four children: Nancy Belle, Charles Austin, Frank McNulty, and Olive; Mary Lucia, who married E. P. Rapp, deceased July 10, 1916; Ralph Merrill, born January 14, 1879 (see his sketch); Olive, who married Roy V. Davis, cashier of the Bank of Antioch (see his sketch), and became the mother of two children: Margaret Olive, the wife of Ole Berg, of Oakland, and William K.; LeRoy Wemple, born January 21, 1883, who married Winnifred Bassett, a native of California and has three children: Carrol, Winnifred and Margaret Ann; Nellie Geraldine, who married W. J. Kelley, and has two children, Patricia and Gerald, and resides in San Francisco; Arthur Chamberlain, born September 13, 1885, deceased September 2, 1891; Ramona Bell, wife of J. E. Cortner, of Oakland, and mother of two children: Jacob and Jane Ellen; Frank R., born April 30, 1897 (see his sketch); and one daughter who died at the age of six months.

Henry Fuller Beede served as a member of the board of trustees of Antioch for many years; and also served on the Republican County Central Committee for Contra Costa County. He was president of the Eastern Contra Costa Promotion Club, and with Hon. J. P. Abbott was largely responsible for the building of the Santa Fe Railway through Contra Costa County into Antioch. They were the owners of the water front property and for a nominal sum deeded over sites for warehouse, depot and right of way. He is a stockholder in the Robert Dollar Steamship Company in San Francisco. Fraternally, Mr. Beede is a Mason, being a Past Master of Antioch Lodge No. 175, F. & A. M.; a member of Antioch Chapter No. 65, R. A. M.; and also a member of the Eastern Star. Mr. Beede has tried to so regulate his life that his example will be worthy of emulation by his descendants; and he has worked for all projects that had for their end the greatest good for the greatest number of people. It is to such men as he that Contra Costa County owes a debt of gratitude.

(Since the above was written, Mr. Beede passed away, on April 13, 1926, mourned by his family and a wide circle of friends.)

COLBURN JOHNSON PRESTON.—A successful pioneer rancher of the Point of Timber section of Contra Costa County and one who always willingly did his full share towards the upbuilding of his section of the county was the late Colburn Johnson Preston, who passed away on March 17, 1925. He was a man of enterprise and keen foresight and was looked upon as one of the leaders in the development of eastern Contra Costa County. He was born in Bradford County, Pa., on July 16, 1837, attended the common schools of his home locality and grew up on a farm. In 1864 he came West, crossing the Isthmus, and found employment on a ranch in Nevada. In the fall of that same year he came to California, and in 1865 located in Point of Timber and developed a ranch home. At that time there was not a house between his place and Antioch and the country was in an almost primitive condition. He worked hard and was granted a satisfactory degree of prosperity so that he was able to retire in 1904. He lived in Berkeley, Stockton and Antioch and finally moved to Brentwood.

Mr. Preston was united in marriage in October, 1859, with Melissa Woodard, also a native of Pennsylvania, and they had seven children: Francis M., born January 23, 1861, married Ida Burress of Bay Point and had two children, Marion and Lloyd; Eva Sarah, born October 23, 1869, married Frank M. May and their children are Marjorie and Evelyn; Rosa May, born February 13, 1872, married George G. Daunt of Petaluma and they have a daughter, Dorothea; Ida, born November 20, 1873, married William H. Engle of Oakland; Jennie, born November 10, 1875, passed away on September 8, 1902; Bertha Ann, born March, 1879, married Leslie V. Richardson and had two children, Reginald, now deceased, and Gwendolyn; Mott C., born July 16, 1882, married Winifred Shafer and is mentioned on another page of this history. Mrs. Melissa Preston died February 1, 1917. Mr. Preston was one of the first men to grow alfalfa in this section of the county; and in 1867 he harvested all the grain on the West Side from Bay Point to Visalia. His political views were Republican and he served as a school trustee of the Excelsior and the Liberty Union High School districts.

HENRY BASCOM REED.—Numbered among the pioneers of California who braved unknown dangers and many hardships to lay firm the foundation of our commonwealth, was Henry Bascom Reed, who came to Antioch, Contra Costa County, in 1869. Some of his descendants are still living in this county. He was born on May 20, 1828, at Kanawha Saline, Va., and at the age of fourteen accompanied his parents to Iowa, then a frontier State, and settled on the west bank of the Mississippi River. Black Hawk, the Indian war chief, was located on the reservation of Samuel Reed, father of H. B. Reed. Both parents died in Iowa.

H. B. Reed went back to Virginia and in 1851 came from that State to California with a saddle cavalcade. There were five Reed brothers and each had two saddle horses, and side arms for each member of the cavalcade. Besides, they carried their provisions, equipment and munitions in two wagons drawn by mules with negro drivers. These drivers were family slaves. They left Virginia in the spring of 1851 and arrived at Marysville, Cal., that same fall, with money and provisions all gone. The brothers sold their equipment, except the mules; and these they used as pack animals and freighted supplies to the mines in Sierra County, carrying on the business until the fall of 1853. That fall they embarked in the lumbering and logging business on the American River near what is now the site of Folsom. They got out some 2,000,000 feet of lumber, when a storm and cloudburst wiped out their entire mill and product. The eldest brother then remarked, "The devil take the hindmost," and they then separated. Henry Bascom, with Fred, who was later the first train dispatcher on the Union Pacific out of Council Bluffs and Wilber, went into Sierra County and began mining and prospecting, and were fairly successful.

Henry B. Reed had made enough so that he felt safe in returning to Virginia to marry the girl of his choice; so he went to San Francisco and took passage on the Yankee Blade for the East. The vessel was wrecked off the Santa Barbara coast, and he and some of the passengers were rescued from a watery grave by the Goliath and returned to San Francisco. He again found himself almost broke and back in California. With what money he had he bought a saddle and bridle in San Francisco and got a rowboat to take him across the bay to Peralta (now Oakland), where he bought a horse and went by way of San Pablo and Antioch across the San Joaquin River and through Stockton and Sacramento to Marysville, to join his relatives who were located there. Here he entered an apprenticeship to learn the trade of the harnessmaker, and when he had mastered it he went to Vacaville and engaged in the business for himself. While there he met and married Mrs. Katherine (Brezee) Wightman, widow of Oscar Wightman. She had one son, Joel David Wightman. Katherine Brezee was born in Dover, Delaware County, N. Y., on December 14, 1832, and when a small child was taken to Lockport, Ill., and there grew up and married Mr. Wightman. In 1852 the Wightmans crossed the plains in a covered wagon, and Joel D. was born at Council Bluffs, Iowa.

This incident delayed the party and prevented them from getting to California that year, but they arrived in San Jose in October, 1853. In the Santa Clara Valley they farmed till 1857, when they settled in Vacaville, and there Mr. Wightman died in 1858. The following year Mrs. Wightman married H. B. Reed, who had established himself as a harnessmaker in Vacaville. They had four children. Frank Putney Reed was born in Sierra County on March 11, 1861, and now lives in Antioch. G. C. Reed, born in Carson City, Nev., on October 3, 1862, married Miss Alice Davidson, a member of a pioneer family of Antioch, and died leaving three children: Arthur, of Sacramento; Inez, who died aged twenty-seven; and Alice Evelyn, Mrs. R. L. Stevens, of San Francisco. Jessie Maria married Frank George, and both are now deceased. Katie Brezee died at the age of eighteen months. They also reared a girl, Mollie Nicholson, from the age of three months until her marriage to E. P. Spangler, of San Francisco.

In 1869 H. B. Reed came to Antioch and engaged in contracting and building; later he opened an undertaking parlor, which he carried on till he died. He was a highly respected man and a loyal citizen. Politically he was a Democrat. He was a devout Christian. The Reed family are descended from Persian ancestors and have records extending back to 2000 B. C., and a Reed genealogy is treasured in the archives of California. The family kept migrating westward, to Italy, to England, to Virginia, and finally to California. Members of the family are found prominent in church and state, especially in Virginia, being ministers and statesmen. Samuel Reed, father of H. B. Reed, served with Admiral Perry on the Great Lakes in the War of 1812; and his last campaign was with Gen. Samuel Houston in Mexico. On the maternal side, the Brezees came from French Huguenot stock and settled in New York State early in the nineteenth century.

WILLIAM JOHNSON.—The brave pioneers of the Golden State are fast passing away, and in the archives of the land which they settled, and out of its crudity evolved the present-day civilization, should be preserved the story of their trials and triumphs. The subject of this sketch, William Johnson, the father of Mrs. Charles G. Goold, of Danville, was an honored pioneer of California. When a lad of sixteen he accompanied his father, James Johnson, across the Indian-infested Western plains and rugged mountains from the State of Michigan to California, in 1852; the father started with his family on April 6, 1852, and arrived in Sycamore Valley, Contra Costa County, Cal., on September 11 of the same year. William Johnson was born in Cass County, Mich., July 11, 1836, a son of James and Elizabeth (Mendenhall) Johnson. Mrs. Johnson's brother, William Mendenhall, had preceded the Johnsons to California and had settled in the Sycamore Valley, Contra Costa County, and built the original home on the place now occupied by C. J. Wood. Upon arriving in California, James Johnson and family stopped for a short time with the Mendenhalls and then they visited in Santa Clara County, where Mr. Johnson had relatives. Then he moved to Contra Costa County, took up 320 acres of land, and followed farming for years. He was a blacksmith by trade and opened the first shop in Danville, and made the first plow ever made in this county, by hand. He passed away in 1892 at the age of seventy-two; his wife survived him until August, 1900, dying when eighty-four years of age.

William Johnson, when a young man, took up a quarter-section of government land adjoining the ranch of his father and there followed raising grain and stock. He improved the place with a substantial house, barns and outbuildings, hauling the lumber used to construct the buildings from the redwoods in Moraga Valley. The timbers were not sawed, but were split, and the buildings were so well constructed that some of them remain standing until this time, 1926. Mr. Johnson also bought 640 acres in the Livermore mountain district.

William Johnson was united in marriage with Annie Shimpf, a native of London, England, of German descent; and they were the parents of three children: Almira, who married Charles G. Goold, the well-known and successful farmer and banker of Danville; Emma, now deceased; and Clara, Mrs. Ralph Harrison. William Johnson, during his operations as a farmer, ploughed the present route of San Ramon Creek. Heavy rains set in and washed the ditch through the newly ploughed land and it continued to grow larger and larger until it reached its present proportions. In the early days, wild Mexican cattle and horses were roaming these valleys at will, and wild oats and mustard grew so high that it was necessary for a man to go on horseback to look over their tops.

ELAM BROWN BARBER.—A son of a Contra Costa County pioneer, Elam Brown Barber still resides on the home ranch near Martinez. He was born on June 13, 1846, near Jacksonville, Ill., the son of Mathew Root Barber. The latter was born in Ohio on August 7, 1813, and when two years of age was taken to Bond County, Ill., where the family settled as pioneers in that prairie country. At an early age Mathew's father died and the lad was taken into the home of Elam Brown, at Lafayette, Ill. He attended the pioneer schools in Illinois, and on November 14, 1837, was married in Pike County, Ill., to Orpha Bean who was born on March 15, 1814. They had five children: Mrs. Maria Lander, William H., Daniel N., Elam Brown and Mrs. Clara E. Goodall. Mathew Barber farmed, raised stock and made wagons in Illinois until 1849, when on March 15 he started across the plains with an emigrant train and in September of that year arrived at Hangtown, Cal. He mined a short time and then came to Contra Costa County, where Elam Brown was living at Lafayette, which was named after the town he came from in Illinois. For a time Mr. Barber worked in the redwoods, and while thus employed he wrote the tickets for the election of the first officials of this county. Later he worked at the carpenter trade and helped build many of the first homes in Martinez. On February 14, 1851, he left San Francisco for the East on a vessel, crossed the Isthmus, and arrived in Illinois, where he had left his family. They started back across the plains with covered wagons, driving a large band of stock, and arrived in Martinez on August 22, 1852, after an uneventful journey. He then purchased a ranch two miles from the town and began making a home, and during that time he was elected and served four successive terms as public administrator. Mathew Barber and his family were highly respected, and he always showed his public spirit in advancing the prosperity of the county. He died July 21, 1891, and Mrs. Brown passed away on December 2, 1899.

Elam Brown Barber started with the family across the plains when he was five years old. One incident he recalls was the overtaking of a train that had been massacred by Indians, and the men of their train buried the victims. He received his education in the public schools and Heald's Business College in San Francisco. When he had finished school he returned to the home ranch and ever since then has carried on the work there, keeping abreast of the times in all things. While he represents an old family, he has also made a name and place for himself and has a wide circle of friends.

JOHN NICHOLL.—Many lives have entered into the foundation of the State of California, but none more worthy to be considered in a history devoted to the biographies of its citizens than the late John Nicholl. Those who have come to California more recently, to enjoy the superior advantages now offered, do not always realize what a great debt they owe the pioneers who faced dangers and endured hardships to lay firm the foundation of a greater civilization and a permanent prosperity.

John Nicholl was born in County Antrim, Ireland, on November 19, 1822, a son of Hugh and Mary (Aiken) Nicholl, of Scotch-Irish descent. His schooling was limited; but he was taught hard work on the farm, and after reaching the age of twenty-five decided to seek his fortunes in the New World. He arrived in New York in 1849 and worked as a laborer for a time. It was in New York that he married Agnes Booth, a friend of his youth, who had come to America in 1850. In 1854, with a party numbering thirteen, Mr. and Mrs. Nicholl boarded the George Law for the Isthmus of Panama. They crossed the Isthmus, Mrs. Nicholl riding a mule while Mr. Nicholl walked. Reaching the Pacific side they boarded the John L. Stephens en route for San Francisco, where they arrived on January 16. Mr. Nicholl paid one dollar to cross the bay to San Leandro Creek, where he leased a ranch and began general farming. He worked hard and prospered, and in 1857 came to Contra Costa County, bought 200 acres of the San Pablo Rancho, and here began developing a home for his family. He raised grain, hay and stock, and for many years operated a threshing machine within a radius of six miles of his ranch. He added to his holdings some 400 acres east of his home place and increased the volume of his production. The first school here was started by Mr. Nicholl, who hauled the lumber in his own wagon. For forty years he served as an elder in the Presbyterian Church at San Pablo, and he was one of the founders of the First Presbyterian Church in Oakland. He also erected the first brick building on Washington Street, Oakland. Later he was one of the large bean raisers in Ventura County, where he owned considerable land.

It was for a time impossible to get a clear title to grant lands, and for a great many years those who had bought land from the Spanish settlers were engaged in expensive litigation. Finally, when it was possible to secure a title, Mr. Nicholl was advised by his attorney, Mr. Moon, to let the 400 acres go and take 150 that had been offered in exchange, at Point Richmond. This he did, and he later began the building up of the town. He sold to the backers of the Santa Fe Railroad fifty-three acres for $80,000, receiving the money in one check drawn on the Bank of California. From this time and until his death Mr. Nicholl was intensely interested in the building up of Richmond. He owned some thirty or forty houses, organized and was president of the John Nicholl Company, and was a stockholder in the First National Bank of Richmond.

On May 13, 1895, Mrs. Nicholl passed away, and the following month Mr. Nicholl took up his home in Oakland. There he died in 1914, mourned by a host of friends made during his long and busy career.

THOMAS EDWARDS.—It seems eminently fitting that the names of early pioneers should be perpetuated in such manner that their labors in the days of trial and suffering may remain an inspiration and encouragement to others of the present day period. Great honor is due the pioneers of the Golden State and their descendants possess a heritage of which they may well be proud. Thomas Edwards was a pioneer of 1850 in California. He was born in North Wales on April 5, 1812, and at the age of fourteen went to sea, continuing for ten years, at which time he secured a position as mate on river steamers plying the Mississippi River. He worked for Captain Roe, who later became a large pork-packer in St. Louis, as first mate for five years. It was while he was working on the Mississippi River that he met J. B. Crockett, for whom Crockett, Cal., is named, who was then a law student in Cincinnati. On account of the news of the discovery of gold in California, in 1849 Mr. Edwards gave up steamboating and arranged to come to the Pacific Coast. The winter of 1849-1850 was spent in Louisa County, Iowa, then with his wife and three children he went to Council Bluffs and joined a party of forty men with ten wagons for the overland trip via Fort Hall and Lassen's Cutoff to California. After a few hundred miles travel with this party, in which there were but two women, Mr. Edwards stopped at the

Platte River to rest his stock. The rest of the train continued West as fast as they could go, thus the balance of the long and tiresome journey to California was made alone. They arrived on Mormon Slough, near Stockton, in September, 1850. Going to Tuolumne County Mr. Edwards rented a hotel building at Green Springs for $500 per month and opened a hotel. In a few months the owner raised the rent and he quit, moved about ten miles away and began business at Owen House; he also began raising stock. He sold out in 1856 and bought a place at Knights Ferry, the former residence of John Dent, brother-in-law to General Grant; he also bought a ranch and continued the stock business and ranching. He had settled at this place on account of the school advantages for his children. In 1863 he transferred his range over the Sierras to Owens Valley and was the second settler there. He butchered and furnished the government with meat until 1865. The town of Independence was laid out on his ranch.

In 1867 Mr. Edwards and family came to Contra Costa County and on Carquinez Straits ranched on 1800 acres. In 1881 he arranged with Mr. Heald for the location of a foundry on the bay frontage. Later with Mr. Heald he laid out the town of Crockett, naming it after the friend he had met while steamboating on the Mississippi and who had come to California and secured possession of this land in payment for a lawyer's services to a client. Mr. Edwards gave two lots for the public schools on the hill, but when the school house was moved the lot was sold for an apartment house site; he also gave a lot 50 by 140 for a church and parsonage, which is still used for those purposes. Thomas A. McMahon was the surveyor who plotted the townsite. Mr. Edwards gave the right-of-way to the Southern Pacific, and land for their depot and freighthouse. His one condition was that it must be called Crockett, although the first depot was located at Valona, only a short distance away. Reaching an agreement with Dr. John Strentzel, the founder of Valona, and A. D. Starr of the Starr Milling Company, the depot was moved to Crockett to be near the flouring mill owned by Mr. Starr. When Mr. Heald located in Crockett with his foundry he bought forty-seven acres on the water front and reserved seven acres for his own plant; and every other lot was owned by him because of his help in laying out the town. Mr. Edwards sold the water frontage to Mr. Heald for fifty dollars an acre. Mr. Edwards was so closely connected with every movement in this vicinity that it would be hard to mention any improvement that did not feel his guiding hand. His circle of acquaintances was a large one and he was highly respected by all who ever had the opportunity to meet him.

Thomas Edwards, Sr., and Mary Pugh were married in Cincinnati, Ohio, on February 19, 1843, by the Rev. John H. Jones, pastor of the Welsh Congregational Church. Mrs. Edwards had come to the United States from the same part of Wales as had Mr. Edwards, in charge of Rev. B. W. Chidlaw. She was born on July 20, 1819. Of this marriage

the following children were born: Hugh P., named for his grandfather Edwards who died in Wales on October 2, 1844, was born in St. Louis on August 13, 1844; John, who was born in Iowa on April 7, 1847; Thomas, born December 4, 1849, and died April 3, 1851, the funeral services being read by John Dent at Knight's Ferry; Thomas (II), born August 19, 1851, in Tuolumne County, is living in Crockett; David, born December 29, 1852, in Tuolumne County, is mentioned on another page in this history; Edward, born October 8, 1854; Susan Jane, born June 10, 1858, died February 9, 1893. The original Edwards homestead is still standing at Crockett. It was built on a mound of shells on the bank of the bay and was an ideal home site. Mrs. Edwards planted many of the trees now seen on the place. Mr. Edwards, after a long and useful life, passed to his reward on Febraury 15, 1883, at Crockett, and his funeral sermon was preached by Rev. A. Drahms, a Congregational preacher from Martinez, who afterwards became chaplain at San Quentin. The mother died at the age of seventy-four in 1893. David and Thomas Edwards are the only survivors of their family.

JOHN J. McNAMARA.—Perhaps no man was better known, nor more prominent in the upbuilding of Contra Costa County, than John J. McNamara, whose entire career was spent in the county, and whose life record is that of an honored and upright citizen, and a thoroughly intelligent, patriotic and useful man. A native son of Contra Costa County, he was born on December 28, 1867, the son of Michael and Catherine McNamara, both natives of Ireland. Michael McNamara came to the county in the early sixties and engaged in farming, and later in the grocery business in Martinez. John J. McNamara was associated with his father in the grocery business at one time, and later he engaged in that business for himself, conducting a grocery store in Martinez for twenty-eight years. He also engaged in the liquor business at the corner of Ferry and Main Streets, and another of his business interests was that of the Palm Garden Grill, of which he was the owner.

Mr. McNamara was one of the most progressive citizens Martinez has ever had, a "booster" and a builder. He served as mayor for many years, and for twenty years was on the board of trustees of the city; and during his incumbency of both offices, many improvements were made in Martinez. During his term as mayor, the new city hall was built, and his name is engraved on the cornerstone. The bridge across the creek was also built during this time, and is one of the most important factors in the growth of Martinez. Mr. McNamara did not stop at encouraging public building. He also erected many buildings on his own account, among them the Alhambra Market building, where he owned a half interest in the business; and he built in Martinez eight residences, which he sold, and two double houses now owned by Mrs. McNamara. Seeing the need for accommodating newcomers to the city, he erected the first apartment house in Martinez, known as the City Hall Apartment Building, in which he retained a one-third interest. He also owned ranches at various times, which he sold. When a young man of eighteen years, he was foreman of the McNear ranch, and thus gained a thorough knowledge of the agricultural resources of this part of the State; and he never wavered in his firm belief in the future prosperity and advancement in store for Contra Costa County. Perhaps one of his most important works for the district was the organizing of the Martinez-Benicia Ferry, of which company he was president up to the time of his death. This ferry system has been of inestimable benefit to Martinez and Contra Costa, and will always be a monument to the foresight and public spirit of the man. He promoted the new theatre building, now sold to the West Coast Theatres, Inc. For thirty years, also, he carried on an insurance business.

By his marriage Mr. McNamara was united with Annie E. Hitmann, also a native of this county, and the daughter of John and Catherine Hitmann, early settlers here. Two girls blessed the union of Mr. and Mrs. McNamara: Mildred L., wife of Albert Bonnel; and Beatrice W. The death of Mr. McNamara occurred on December 9, 1922, and left a place vacant which can never be filled. His work here came at a time when men of foresight and public spirit were most needed to lay a sure foundation for future generations, and he willingly took up the burden and fulfilled the obligation in the loyal spirit of his pioneer parents. Fraternally prominent, he was a member of the Loyal Order of Moose, the Knights of Columbus, the Eagles, the Red Men, the Young Men's Institute, and the I. D. E. S. In politics, he was a Republican.

CHARLES A. SWEENEY.—The city marshal and tax collector of Antioch, Contra Costa County, is Charles A. Sweeney and he is one of the oldest city officials who have held office continuously in that city. He came to this city in June, 1880, and was foreman for a hog buyer, having charge of fattening the animals for market. He was appointed town marshal in 1914 and served ever since; and for a quarter of a century served as constable, having been elected to that office soon after settling in Antioch.

Mr. Sweeney was born in San Francisco on August 14, 1857, and is a son of the late William B. and Nora (Hartnett) Sweeney, both natives of Ireland. The father came to California via Cape Horn in a sailing vessel in 1849, and his wife joined him here in 1850. He started teaming in San Francisco and carried on that business many years. He died in Antioch in 1909; and his wife passed away in 1906. Charles A. attended the public schools in San Francisco and at an early age served an apprenticeship to learn the butcher's trade, which he followed until coming to Antioch in 1880. He has always been a Democrat and served as a deputy sheriff many years, also as constable and city tax collector. For many years he served as secretary of the Eagles lodge, of which he is a member; and he belongs to the Native Sons, the Foresters of America and the Young Men's Institute.

In 1879 Mr. Sweeney married Mary J. Curtis, a native of San Francisco and they had three children: Estella J., Mrs. William J. Beasley; Charles D.; and Edward S. Mr. Sweeney holds the respect and esteem of his fellow citizens and always shows his public spirit when it comes to the development of his community.

LAFAYETTE IRVING FISH.—One of the pioneers of Contra Costa County, L. I. Fish was born in Batavia, N. Y., on October 27, 1824, the son of Libbeus and Polly (Holcomb) Fish, the former born in Townsend, Windham County, Vt., in 1781, and the latter a native of Rochester, N. Y. They were married on January 1, 1805. Next to the youngest of eleven children born to his parents, Mr. Fish was reared in Batavia, N. Y., where he attended the public schools. Later, in 1839, he attended Mr. Emmert's school for boys; and two years later still, on going to Jackson, Mich., he there attended school for two years. Upon finishing his schooling, he entered C. W. Penney's general merchandise store in Jackson, and from there went to Monticello, Miss., remaining for a time. Returning then to Michigan, he was again with Mr. Penney until he decided to come to California. In August, 1849, he left Jackson, Mich., and in January, 1850, he arrived via Panama in San Francisco. When he left New York, Mr. Fish purchased a quantity of butter in firkins, knowing that such a commodity was scarce in California and that if he could get it through safely it would sell for a good price. When he got to Panama he had an opportunity to dispose of it at a good price and the man to whom he was going to sell it asked for a sample. He bored a hole into one of the firkins and found the butter liquid; so he stopped up the hole and refused to sell. He brought it to San Francisco, where he sold it for $1.05 per pound. He often related this story as an amusing example of the trials of the pioneer. Mr. Fish came on to Marysville to join a company to engage in mining, and they proceeded by ox-teams to Slate Creek. Here he found the miners leaving for Feather River; he joined the rush, and opened a store at Nelson Creek, on the north fork of Feather River, where he built a log house for store and home and often kept lodgers.

In 1852, Mr. Fish came to Contra Costa County, and soon after purchased an interest in the Welch grant, and there he engaged in farming for many years. He turned the virgin soil and kept at work against all obstacles—and there were many in those pioneer days, and were a real test of manhood and of the survival of the fittest. In 1853 he returned East and spent one year purchasing sheep and building wagons; and in the spring of 1854 he started across the plains with a band of 5000 sheep and a small band of cattle. With the drivers of the stock on saddle horses, and the balance of the party in covered wagons, they made their way overland, and being well armed and exceedingly watchful, they arrived safely in the Sacramento Valley, in October, 1854, and succeeded in bringing 3000 sheep and 141 head of cattle. These Mr. Fish sold at a handsome profit, receiving from $7 to $10 per head for his sheep, which had cost him $1.50. He continued ranching on the Welch Ranch, and later raised grain with a Mr. Lathrop until they dissolved partnership. Mr. Fish thereafter continued alone, and was one of the successful grain growers in the San Joaquin Valley. He was one of the first to summer-fallow the land, which proved such an important factor in subsequent grain raising in the State. In his operations he farmed very large tracts, producing great quantities of wheat and barley, and was one of the first men to ship grain from San Francisco to the Eastern markets. As early as 1855 he had sent East for a reaper, mowing machine and other machinery.

In 1873, with Hale Brothers, Mr. Fish founded and opened the Bank of Martinez, of which he served as president until he retired, in 1890, on account of his physical condition, after having made a decided success of the bank. As early as 1878 he entered the wholesale grain business with Simon Blum and Barry Baldwin, buying and shipping grain. His first-hand knowledge of the resources and opportunities for developing land in California gave him absolute confidence in its future productiveness, and he purchased ranches in various counties in the State, some thirteen pieces of property all told; and his faith has been more than justified.

The marriage of Mr. Fish, occurring in San Jose, Cal., in 1881, united him with Miss Frances Webster, born in Stockholm, N. Y., April 10, 1853. She was educated in that State and attended the normal school at Potsdam, after which she was sent, together with five men, to Cedar Falls, Iowa, where they established a normal school, now known as the Iowa Teachers' College. In 1878 she became a teacher in the San Jose State Normal School, and it was in California that she met Lafayette Fish. They made their home in Martinez, where Mr. Fish built a residence for his family. Two children were born to this worthy couple: Irving Webster and Anne Holcomb. Irving Webster married Miss Clare Bristol in 1910. No children were born of this union. He was engaged in business in Honolulu, but returned to California and engaged in ranching at Ukiah until his death, in June, 1922. Anne Holcomb was born in Martinez and finished her education at Miss Head's school, in Berkeley, after which she attended the New England Conservatory of Music in Boston, Mass. In company with her mother and brother, she then traveled for a year, making a trip around the world and visiting the different countries en route. In 1909 occurred her marriage to Robert Noble Burgess. Mr. Burgess was born in St. Johns, N. B., and came to California with his parents when a boy, settling in Berkeley. Among other development projects with which he has been connected was the establishment of the Mount Diablo Country Club. Five children have come to them: Robert Noble, Jr., and Frances Webster, Suzanne Fish, Nancy Fish, and

Polly Holcomb. The family reside at "The Homestead," near Walnut Creek.

Lafayette Irving Fish died in October, 1900, and his death marked the passing of an eminently worthy man, one who had done his full share in the building up and developing of the State in which he had pioneered in the early fifties, and in whose growth he had remained to share a part. His widow survived him until August 25, 1923. Her last days were spent at her Berkeley home. A truly wonderful woman, mentally alert and of cultured mind, Mrs. Fish will long be remembered for her thorough understanding of human nature, her helpful charity, and her many unostentatious benefactions. She was interested in music and art, and withal was a very good business woman, being of great aid to her husband during his life, and ably managing the affairs of the estate after his passing. Her worth was deeply appreciated by all who came in contact with her, and many lives were made brighter through her gracious ministrations. She was a devout member of the First Congregational Church.

CHARLES MORTIMER BELSHAW.—One of the most popular native sons of California and a man held in highest esteem by all who knew him was the late Charles M. Belshaw. He was born at Fiddletown, Amador County, on March 11, 1861, a son of Mortimer W. and Jane E. (Oxner) Belshaw, both natives of Herkimer County, N. Y. The former died on April 28, 1898; and the latter in 1900, after having rounded out lives filled with great usefulness to their fellow citizens and to their adopted State, where M. W. Belshaw was a prominent figure in mining and business circles for many years.

Charles M. was a student at the City College and University Mound College in San Francisco, and in 1879 took a preparatory course under the late Prof. George Bates of San Francisco, after which he entered Harvard University at Cambridge, Mass., and was graduated with the Class of 1883. His college course completed, Mr. Belshaw came back to California and became timekeeper, paymaster and wharf clerk to the Empire Coal mines, in which his father was heavily interested, and thus relieved his father from a great deal of responsibility. He also became owner of the Antioch Water Works, formerly established by his father. The first water was sold from house to house and was carted about in barrels. Upon the death of M. W. Belshaw he succeeded to his mining interests and served as president of the California Miners' Association. In 1894 he was elected to the State assembly on the Republican ticket and served three full terms. He was then elected State senator in 1900 and served his constituents with distinction. He took a very active interest in every movement for the upbuilding of the best interests of his native state and was looked upon as one of its Republican leaders.

Mr. Belshaw was twice married. His first wife was Miss Miriam E. Waite, daughter of Tyler K. and Marietta Waite, and was born in De Kalb County, Ill. In 1915 he was married a second time, Maude Spencer, a native of California, becoming his wife. Both he and his wife met accidental deaths in an automobile accident on November 23, 1919, while motoring south of San Francisco on the Ocean Shore road. He was a Past Master of the Masonic Lodge; Past High Priest of the Royal Arch Masons; a Knight Templar and a Shriner; and Past Patron of the Eastern Star Chapter. He belonged to the Elks, and was a Past President of Antioch Parlor, N. S. G. W., and a trustee of the Grand Parlor of the State. Charles M. Belshaw had many friends and was a friend of nearly everybody.

HON. HENRY V. ALVARADO.—Perhaps no man now living in Contra Costa County is better known than Hon. Henry V. Alvarado, judge of Department One of the superior court of the county. He is a native of the State, born in Oakland, on July 15, 1857, the son of a former Governor of California, Juan B. Alvarado, mentioned in another sketch in this history. Our subject received his education in the schools of San Francisco and after his school days were over entered the law office of his brother, John C. Alvarado, and read law under him for a time. In 1896 he was admitted to the California Bar and at once opened an office in Martinez, where he began to build up a clientele. In 1902 he was elected district attorney of Contra Costa County, was reelected in 1906 and served until 1910, a period of eight years. In 1911 Mr. Alvarado went to Richmond and opened an office there with B. H. Griffins as a partner, the firm being Alvarado and Griffins. Perhaps the most important litigation with which Mr. Alvarado was connected was the case of Joseph Emeric vs. Juan B. Alvarado et al. This case occupied the courts in California for thirty years. During the run of the suit the original plaintiff and defendant both died, Joseph Emeric's son, Henry F. Emeric, being substituted as plaintiff, and Henry V. Alvarado substituted for his father as chief defendant. The final decree in the case was rendered by Judge J. C. B. Hubbard in 1894. This litigation proved ruinous on account of the long time and tremendous expense in trying it. It settled, however, many points of law pertaining to the partition of estates and to this day remains California's greatest partition suit. Henry V. Alvarado was appointed to the superior bench by Governor Richardson, to fill the vacancy caused by the death of Judge R. H. Latimer, on June 15, 1923, and now presides over Department One in Contra Costa County.

Judge Henry V. Alvarado was united in marriage in August, 1879, at San Pablo, with Miss Annie V. Chevesich, a daughter of Don Carlos Chevesich, and born in California. They have two children: Lucile, who married Frank W. Skinner, of Whittier, an employe of the Standard Oil Company, and has a son Francis; Grace, married W. M. Sahlberg, of Sacramento, a construction engineer. Judge Alvarado is a member and a Past Master of Martinez Lodge No. 41, F. & A. M.; is a Scottish Rite Mason, and belongs to Aahmes Temple, A. A. O. N. M. S. of

Oakland. An excellent lawyer, well versed in the law, Judge Alvarado is making good on the bench by his wise and learned decisions and his keen sense of justice and interpretation of the law. He is intensely interested in California history, as well as the history of Contra Costa County, and contributes to newspapers and magazines articles on early-day history of the State.

WILLIAM ALEXANDER FRAZER.—One of the well-known and highly honored pioneers now living in the county is William Alexander Frazer, the second son and fourth child of the late pioneer, William Beverley Frazer, who was born in North Carolina in 1824 and came across the plains in 1843 to Oregon, where he stopped a short time, and then came down into California and built one of the first sawmills in Santa Cruz County. He next went to Sonoma County, and while there was taken prisoner by the Mexicans and held a short time. Returning to Oregon as captain of a train of homeseekers, he settled near Turner, in Marion County, until he came again to California and settled in Contra Costa County in the fall of 1859. In the month of February, 1860, he moved to Martinez and bought about a half section of land, situated where the Shell Oil Company refinery is now located. Here he became a general rancher, also raising horses and cattle, until his death in September, 1868, which occurred at the early age of forty-four years at his ranch home, one mile east of Martinez. He was survived by his widow and nine children: George M., Jennie, William Alexander, Ellen, Sarah, Frank M., Thomas J., Isaac, and Louise. Jennie Frazer became the wife of the late Judge J. P. Jones, for sixteen years superior judge of Contra Costa County; she lived to be seventy-one years old, and died in Oakland, in September, 1921. M. R. Jones, the well-known attorney of Martinez and Oakland, is her son. Ellen Frazer resides in San Jose. Sarah married Dr. W. P. Mauzy of Oakland, and is deceased. Frank M. Frazer is a retired rancher and stockraiser, residing in Oakland. Dr. Thomas J. Frazer resides in Oakland and practices in San Francisco. Dr. Isaac Frazer is a retired dental surgeon, residing in San Jose. Louise is the wife of H. M. Bush, realtor of Martinez. Mrs. Frazer died in San Jose, on April 24, 1916.

William Alexander Frazer was born in Marion County, Ore., on January 21, 1854, and from six years of age, when he came with his parents to Martinez, his early life was passed on the home ranch. He attended the common schools and later studied at Heald's Business College in San Francisco. With the exception of five years spent in Kings County and six months spent in traveling and sightseeing in the Eastern and Southern States, he has passed his entire life in Contra Costa County, engaged in ranching. In 1910 he purchased his present home place of twenty acres, and here he raises fruits and almonds successfully.

Mr. Frazer's first marriage, occurring in Martinez on March 3, 1880, united him with Miss Lizzie Hardy, a native of Martinez and daughter of the late P. Hardy, early Martinez pioneer. Three children were the result of this union: Hiram H., residing in Berkeley; Elam B., who died at the age of ten years; and William B., who married Beulah Lea, and is the father of two children, Ruth and Donald. He is a marine engineer and machinist, and enlisted in the navy during the World War.

The second marriage of Mr. Frazer, occurring on December 19, 1916, united him with Mrs. Emma (Parrish) Trisket, a native of Harford, Pa., who came to California in 1916. Both being of literary tastes, Mr. and Mrs. Frazer have a large and well-selected private library, one of the best in the county, and they are an unusually well-read and well-informed couple. Mr. Frazer became a member of the Christian Church when twenty-one years old, and he and his wife attend that church at Concord. He is a Republican in politics.

The entire Frazer family have always been looked up to as among the leading people in Contra Costa County, especially in point of character and unquestioned integrity. Thorough Americans, they are of Scotch-Irish blood. Mr. Frazer's father, William Beverley Frazer, was born in North Carolina and came across the plains from Missouri to Oregon in 1843, in a covered wagon; while his mother, Delilah (Cook) Frazer, was born in Tennessee in 1832 and with her parents came across the plains in 1845 from Missouri to Oregon, where the two brave young pioneers met and were married.

R. H. WALL.—The pioneer shoe merchant of Antioch is R. H. Wall, proprietor of the Antioch Shoe Store in that city. Mr. Wall is a native of Contra Costa County, born in Somersville on February 14, 1865, the son of R. J. and Jane (Macartney) Wall, honored pioneer settlers of this county. They were natives of England and Scotland, respectively, and the father was a coal miner after settling in Somersville.

R. H. Wall grew up in Antioch and attended the public schools of the county. He began clerking in a shoe store in Antioch when a mere boy, and when he was old enough he started a store for himself, beginning on a modest scale and continually increasing his patronage until he now does the leading business in his line in the city, where his honest dealings and straightforward methods have gained for him the respect of all who know him. He has taken an active part in the official life of Antioch, serving as a member of the board of trustees, and for ten years as city clerk, and that at a time when the salary of the clerk was but ten dollars a month. In 1923 he received the appointment as a trustee to fill a vacancy caused by the resignation of G. B. LaMontagne, and was elected to the same position in 1924.

On March 13, 1897, in San Francisco, R. H. Wall and Miss Eliza Gambs, a native of the State and a lady of fine attainments, were united in marriage. They have two children: Mrs. Fred W. Swain, of Berkeley;

John Muir

and R. H. Wall, Jr., a graduate of the Antioch High School, class of 1926. Mrs. Wall is a member of the Eastern Star and the Rebekahs, while Mr. Wall is a member of the Native Sons. Whatever is good for Antioch is sure to have his stanch support, whether it concerns the water supply, good streets, parks, industrial concerns, schools or churches. He backs the best men and measures regardless of party lines. Mr. Wall was brought up in the Congregational Church.

JOHN MUIR.—The American naturalist and explorer, John Muir, late of Contra Costa County, was born in Dunbar, Scotland, on April 21, 1838, and in 1849 accompanied his parents, Daniel and Ann (Gilrye) Muir, to America. They settled on Fox River, Wisconsin, where his father cleared a farm and taught his son to work amidst pioneer surroundings for twelve years. The lad had very little opportunity to get an education after coming to Wisconsin; consequently he educated himself, following in the footsteps of the Great Emancipator. Every book that he could get hold of he read with avidity, storing up knowledge of all kinds, and he was thus able to pass the examinations necessary for entrance into the University of Wisconsin in 1861. His pioneering experience led him to be a student of nature and after two and one-half years in the university he left to pursue his chosen life study and for several years he roamed the woods of Wisconsin and Canada. With this initial experience he resolved to go to Florida and he walked from Indiana, through a thousand miles of the forests of the South. While in Florida he had an attack of malarial fever which almost proved fatal and he then resolved to come to California.

John Muir arrived in the Golden State, coming by way of Panama, early in 1868. San Francisco had no charms to induce him to stop there long. He immediately set out on foot for the Yosemite Valley and for the next five years made that locality his home, summer and winter, working part of the time herding sheep and in a sawmill to give him funds with which to pursue his explorations and investigations of that region. He proved that the Yosemite was actually chiseled out of the granite mountain by glacial action instead of by having been split by an earthquake shock, as had been generally believed. His wonderful literary gift for the portrayal of nature soon made him famous. During the years he spent exploring the Sierras he discovered sixty-five residual glaciers.

Mr. Muir made his first trip to Alaska in 1879, discovered and named Glacier Bay and Muir Glacier, and explored some of the upper courses of the Yukon and Mackenzie Rivers. In 1880 he accompanied the De Long search expedition into the Arctic on the steamer Corwin; and in 1903 and 1904 traveled in the Caucasus, Siberia, Manchuria, Japan, India, Egypt, Australia and New Zealand. In 1874 he had settled in San Francisco and there spent his winters in writing. He wrote considerably for newspapers and periodicals and urged the formation of national parks, and both the Sequoia and Yosemite are in part due to his efforts. He published his first book in 1894, The Mountains of California; and in 1901 issued Our National Parks. Various other editions were published by him to the number of ten, all of absorbing interest, and are to be found in almost every public library in California.

In 1880 John Muir was united in marriage with Miss Louise Wanda Strentzel, daughter of Dr. John Strentzel, pioneer fruit-grower of the Alhambra Valley, Contra Costa County. Wanda, Mrs. Thomas Rea Hanna; and Helen, Mrs. Buel A. Funk, of Daggett, Cal., were the two children born to John Muir and his wife. Mrs. Muir passed away in August, 1905.

Although he traveled widely after his marriage, he had made a permanent settlement in this county, which remained his home until his death on December 24, 1914, at the age of seventy-six years. He was world-famous as an exponent of the beauties of nature. He was a member of the American Academy of Arts and Letters; member of Washington Academy of Sciences; fellow A. A. A. S.; Honorary A. M. of Harvard University, 1896; LL. D., University of Wisconsin, 1897; L.H.D., Yale University, 1911; president of the Sierra Club, and of the American Alpine Club. John Muir's life was full of adventure and rich in varied experiences. He was a most talented letter writer and it is through the medium of his letters that his life history has been written. His mountaineer experiences were full of adventure and at times he suffered untold hardships. His influence was strong in winning public support for conservation of National Parks and reservations. He was a warm friend of Theodore Roosevelt when he was president, and is spoken of frequently in Roosevelt's writings. The president often consulted Mr. Muir on the subject of forest preservation and the formation of new national parks for the American people.

Mr. and Mrs. Muir are buried in the private burial ground on the ranch that was located by Dr. Strentzel in 1853, and which he gave to Mrs. Muir at the time of her marriage. The Muirs lived on this ranch until the death of Dr. Strentzel, when they went to reside with Mrs. Strentzel, and it was there Mr. Muir passed away.

JULIA FRANCES FISH.—California as a State owes much to the women who have come here and helped build up a great commonwealth. To the agricultural and business progress of the different communities they have added educational and cultural advancement, founded art centers, made possible music studios, and above all, have founded libraries and gathered together books for the education of the growing generation and the further advancement of the entire population. And Contra Costa County has been fortunate in the representative women who have aided in such work here.

Miss Julia Frances Fish has been a resident here for the past fifty years, and during that time has left a deep impress for good in the community where she has made her home. Born in Batavia, N. Y., on

January 3, 1835, a daughter of Libbeus and Rebecca Carter (Vaughn) Fish, she is of old Colonial stock, her great-grandfather, Josiah Fish, having served in the Revolutionary War. Her father, Libbeus Fish, was born in Vermont and came with his parents to Rochester, N. Y., and there his marriage to Polly Holcomb occurred on January 1, 1805. The young couple then removed to Batavia, N. Y., where he became a man of affairs and also served as justice of the peace. Polly Holcomb Fish passed away, and Mr. Fish married again, becoming united with Mrs. Rebecca Carter Vaughn, a native of Massachusetts. They made a visit to Michigan, and liked the country there so well that they decided to make it their home, locating at Jackson in the late thirties. In 1859 Mr. Fish went to Batavia, N. Y., on a visit, and there he passed away that same year. Rebecca Carter Vaughn Fish died in Jackson in 1872. Eleven children were born to Libbeus and Polly (Holcomb) Fish, of whom nine grew to mature years: John, Josiah, Eli, Charles, Lafayette, Caroline, Minerva, Mary and Cornelia, all now deceased. Of the second union with Rebecca Carter Vaughn, four children were born and two, Albert and Julia, grew up.

Julia Fish was reared in Jackson, Mich., where she pursued her studies in the public schools, afterwards finishing with a course at the Batavia Seminary at Batavia, N. Y. She then returned to her home in Jackson, and for the next two decades passed through many interesting phases of life there. Her father, Libbeus Fish, was one of the organizers of the Republican party, under the Oaks at Jackson, Mich. At the time of the organization, in 1854, Miss Fish, stirred by patriotic enthusiasm, made a large bouquet, or floral piece, in red, white and blue and presented it to the men at the meeting, and it was placed on the speaker's stand. She was an interested observer of the trying times during the Civil War, from the declaration of war until its close. She saw the first regiment of "Boys in Blue" leave Jackson for the front, and was among the noble band of women who cheered them on their way.

In 1874, after the death of her mother, Miss Fish came to Martinez for a visit to her brothers, Lafayette, Charles and Josiah Fish, who were very early settlers and prominent business men in Contra Costa County, and a sister, Miss Caroline Fish, who was also here. This visit proved to Miss Fish that she would never again be content to live in the East, and in 1875 she settled her affairs there and came to California to live. She presided over her brother's home until his marriage, and then built her own residence on Willow Street, Martinez, and there she has since made her home. She has made successful investments, and devotes her time these latter years to looking after them, and to enjoying her books and her many friends in Martinez.

Miss Fish is frequently called the founder of the Martinez Library. Many years ago, sensing the lack of reading matter available in Martinez for public use, she proposed a reading club for the young men of the city. They met each Wednesday evening at her home, and were so faithful in attendance and showed such marked interest that she suggested that they start a public library. An effort had been made some years before, but had not been successful. Miss Fish was sure, however, that there would be no failure this time, and so filled the workers with her enthusiasm that they all put their shoulders to the wheel and took the first step, which was a book social. Giving a musical and entertainment, they made a book the price of admission—old or new, paper or leather cover, but a book—and this first social was so successful that it netted them over 100 books as a nucleus for their library and the beginning of the present institution. Dr. Strentzel gave them a building which had been an old saloon. They had to clean it, and this proved quite a task; but nothing daunted, they set to work, and Rev. Mr. Tubbs gave his time and services to paint and paper the building and did much to improve the place. In the beginning, as was natural, they met with some opposition, but Miss Fish made the meetings at her house so interesting and attractive that the young people flocked to the work, and this time there was no failure, but an actual library was started, from which has sprung the splendid Martinez Public Library of today, an institution of inestimable value to the people of Contra Costa County and one which is much appreciated. Because of her active part in its conception and consummation, Miss Fish is today known as the Mother of the Martinez Library.

Her father had started a genealogy of the Fish family before his death, and after Miss Fish came to California she spent much time very pleasantly in tracing the family history and finally published a small book on the Fish family, which is traced back to 1644. Miss Fish is a true pioneer, and it would be hard to find a more thoroughly interesting and broadminded woman, always willing to give of her time and means for the advancement of the common good. She is a member of the Episcopal Church.

CHARLES E. CHAPMAN.—In the annals of Contra Costa County mention must be given to the Chapman family, members of which were among its pioneer settlers and, up to the present day, have had no small part in its up-building. The father of Charles E. was the proprietor of the Clayton Hotel, which stood on the site of the present store, during the wild days of the copper excitement of the early sixties. George O. Chapman, the father, was a native of New York, became a Mexican War soldier and came to California with the hordes of '49. In 1851 he joined Walker's Expedition into Central America, which resulted in disaster, most of the men being killed. Mr. Chapman, with a few others, escaped into Mexico and remained there until 1853, when he returned to Contra Costa County, after disposing of his Mexican holdings. He engaged in ranching on what is now known as the Dilwood ranch (it having been purchased by Dilwood at a later date.)   In 1862 he married Miss Nancy Ione Larsen, a native of Kentucky, who came to Stockton in 1850 and attended the public school there.   After their marriage the couple resided in Pacheco, where G. O. Chapman engaged in the lumber business with Walter K. Dill.   In 1863 he built the Clayton Hotel, a three-story frame building, there being about 5000 people residing in Clayton at that time.   It was in this structure that Charles E. Chapman was born on November 6, 1864, the eldest of a family of seven children.   G. O. Chapman lived to be eighty-nine years old, his death occurring in Clayton in 1914.   Charles E. Chapman's maternal grandmother died at the venerable age of ninety-nine years in February, 1926.   At one time there were five generations on both sides living of this remarkably long-lived family.

Charles E. Chapman grew up in Clayton and was one of the pupils in its early public school.   His father was the owner of a ranch one and one-half miles east of Clayton and it was there that Charles was employed up to the time that he was twenty years old.   Then for eight years he worked in the Mount Diablo winery, after which he was employed for seven years as wine maker at Glen Terry.   Removing to a ranch near Stockton he became a bean raiser for two years, going from there to the Cowell Portland Cement Company, where for more than seven years he was a valued worker in the chemical laboratories.   On account of his failing eyesight he was obliged to resign from this position in 1921 and then returned to his home in Clayton.

In addition to other employment, Mr. Chapman was a constable for a period of twenty-two years and was noted for the fearlessness with which he discharged the duties of this, at times, perilous office.   In 1912 Mr. Chapman had a narrow escape from death at the hands of a man whom he had arrested, one John Lincoln.   The prisoner attacked Mr. Chapman, who was unarmed, and endeavored to shoot him.   Mr. Chapman, with quick presence of mind, grabbed him by the throat and was choking him as he fired.   The bullet went wild and shot the prisoner himself in the head.   In 1920 he was fired at twice by one Frank Tutt on whom he was attempting to serve a warrant of arrest.   Tutt was shooting to kill and it was not until after the second shot had been fired that Mr. Chapman was obliged to shoot and kill his assailant in self-defense.

Mr. Chapman was married October 17, 1888, to Miss Sally Naoma Mitchell, a native of Lake County, Cal., and they are the parents of four children.   Wilda is the wife of Ed. Stafford of San Jose, and they have three children, Verndon, Lysle and Neill.   Dr. Herbert Samuel Chapman is a successful physician and surgeon of Stockton, is married and has two children, Duff Gordon and Barbara.   He served in the navy during the war, enlisting and being commissioned a lieutenant.   Later he was transferred to a hospital in France, where he became chief surgeon; also in this capacity he served on the S. S. Prinz Frederick Wilhelm, and made twenty-seven trips during the war and afterwards during the return of troops. He received a commission as captain before his discharge. Clarence, who was a member of the Third Division with General Liggett's 18th Field Artillery in France, went over as a corporal and came back a lieutenant. Victor B. is now a student at Stanford University, where he is taking a course in civil engineering and drafting.

ISAAC N. MORGAN.—Until the survey of Contra Costa County was made a vast territory was controlled by Jerry Morgan, father of the subject of this sketch. Jerry Morgan was born in Cherokee Nation, Ala., in 1819, and removed to Illinois while a young man, and later became a member of one of the first bands of intrepid souls that braved the perils of forest, plain and desert in their journey to California in 1849, with ox-teams and with mules. After his arrival he worked for one year in the gold mines on the American River. His father was called to the Mexican War and was killed in one of the engagements. After his father's death Jerry returned to Illinois and married Miss Sarah Ellis. In 1853 the young married couple made the long journey across the plains in a big wagon train bound for California. They first settled in the Ygnacio valley and it was while on a hunting trip, in search of bear and elk, that Mr. Morgan was attracted to the territory which was afterwards to bear his name. He said to his wife, "I think I will go over there and settle."

With his eight yoke of oxen he hauled lumber from the Santa Cruz mountains to build his home, which was erected in 1856. For a time he controlled considerable land of the county until a survey was made and he was alloted 2400 acres in the section still known as Morgan Territory Precinct in Contra Costa County, which was so named in his honor. Jerry Morgan was one of the friends of Dr. John Marsh and well known among the other early settlers of the county. He died January 23, 1906, having been the father of fifteen children.

Isaac N. Morgan, youngest son of Jerry Morgan and fourteenth child, was born in Morgan Territory on March 5, 1862. His education was received in the early pioneer schools and he grew up in the business of farming and stock raising. When eight years old he rode the range with his saddle horse, and a few years later he became a plow boy, doing all kinds of work on the ranch with the assurance of a veteran. He has developed into one of the substantial citizens of the county, is a successful farmer and stock grower, a man of broad and liberal views who is highly esteemed by all who know him. He is the owner of 180 acres of rich land in Morgan Territory Precinct and is a public spirited individual. He has served on numerous grand and trial juries, but has never run for public office although often solicited to do so. His father, Jerry Morgan, was a prominent Odd Fellow, having donated $500 toward the building of the first Odd Fellow building in Pacheco.

When twenty-one years old Issac N. Morgan was married to Miss Jane E. Howard, daughter of Robert Howard, a steamship engineer who lived in San Francisco and was employed on the line running from San Francisco to Panama and return. Mrs. Morgan was born in England but was brought to this country while an infant, living in New York and Panama before her arrival in San Francisco at the age of ten. Mr. and Mrs. Morgan attended the same school as children. They are the parents of fourteen children. Robert R., a government trapper, makes his home in Morgan Territory; Sadie, wife of Jacob P. Ackerman, a farmer near Brentwood, has four children; Alice, wife of Henry C. Hansen, a farmer near Brentwood, has six children; Albert J. died from pleuropneumonia and influenza at Camp Lewis in 1918 at the age of twenty-three; Jerry married May Hansen, resides on a ranch near Brentwood, and they have four children; Elizabeth, wife of Burnett McNamara, rancher and horticulturist near Knightsen, has one child; John Howard spent more than a year in France and two Fourths of July on the ocean; he married Lillian Van Buren, and is a foreman for the Balfour-Guthrie Company at Brentwood, and they have four children; Willard J. served a year at Camp Kearny during the World War; Ada, wife of Valentine Hansen, rancher and vineyardist of Marsh Creek, has three children; Marian, wife of Hector Logan, near Brentwood, machinist for Balfour-Guthrie Company, has one child; George F., single, helps run the home ranch; Charles Ellis works for the Associated Oil Company at Avon; Edith is at home; and Howard also works for the Associated Oil Company at Avon.

EDWARD WALLACE NETHERTON.—A native son of Contra Costa County, newspaper man, and representative citizen of the State, Edward W. Netherton, known to his intimate friends as Ed. Netherton, was born at Point of Timber, now Byron, on July 20, 1869, the son of pioneer parents. His father, John Smith Netherton, a direct descendant of Capt. John Smith of Pocahontas fame, was born near Liberty, Clay County, Mo., in 1834, and crossed the plains in a covered wagon drawn by oxen and landed in California in the summer of 1850. He went at once to the mines in the vicinity of Hangtown, in the Mother Lode section, and followed mining on the American, Cosumnes and Mokelumne Rivers, and in other sections of the Sierras until 1856. Deciding that he could better his condition at some other occupation he quit mining and came to Contra Costa County and engaged in ranching in Moraga Valley.

In 1858 John Smith Netherton married Matilda J. Estes, daughter of Joel and Jane Estes, all of whom had come to this State, across the plains with an ox-team train from Ray County, Mo., in 1850, and located first in Solano County, later moving to Moraga Valley. The Estes had come from an adjoining county in Missouri and had crossed the plains about the same time as had Mr. Netherton, but had never met until they had all located in Moraga Valley, this county. This valley is now the home of many wealthy people of the bay counties. Mr. Netherton was one of the men who did real things to make this state what it now is.

John Smith Netherton and his wife reared a family of nine children: Carrie Luella; William Price, prominent attorney and banker of Santa Cruz; Frethias J., an attorney and former state superintendent of public instruction of Arizona, and a delegate to the U. S. Congress from the then territory of Arizona; Edward W., of this review; George E., business man of Martinez; Walter E., retired rancher; Delbert W., rancher; Elmer E., who was killed in an accident when he was seven; and Clara Belle, who died at the age of fifteen. The father died at the age of eighty-nine years, after living a life rounded out to the full and filled with results of good works for the benefit, not only of himself and family, but for the good of the general public and State. He was the third settler in the Point of Timber district of this county and there became a prosperous farmer and large land owner. The mother died in 1913 at the age of seventy-five years.

Ed. Netherton received his education in the public schools of Contra Costa County and in the Oakland High School, supplemented in the school of hard knocks, and experience, thus fitting him for the tussle for a livelihood. His first work was with the Oakland Tribune, owned by William C. Dargee. With John P. Cooper, Ed. was the first man to get the news of the insurrection in the Hawaiian Islands when the Queen Lilioukalani government was overthrown; he was the first to get the news by boarding an incoming vessel from the islands, there being no cable or wireless at that period. The entire story was published in the Examiner, no other paper in the world having the story until later.

Under the Wilson administration Ed. Netherton was chief of the sales tax division in the Internal Revenue service with headquarters at the custom house in San Francisco, directing a force of forty-five men and making a collection of federal taxes of more than $2,000,000 per month. This position he held during Wilson's administration, 1917 to 1922. The balance of his life has been spent in newspaper work.

The marriage of Ed. Netherton with Alice Carpenter, daughter of Daniel S. and Sarah (Curry) Carpenter, was celebrated in Martinez on May 12, 1892, on the same street in which they now live. They have one son, Raymond Wayne Netherton. Mrs. Netherton's father was among the first settlers in this county and served as tax collector for sixteen years. The mother crossed the plains in the early fifties and settled in Moraga Valley and is still living. Mr. Carpenter died at the age of seventy-five years. Their family consisted of thirteen children, seven of them being girls and all of them living with their families in Martinez. Mr. Netherton is a Democrat, having served his party as Chairman and Secretary of the County Central Committee and as a member of the State Central Committee. He is a member of the International Typographical Union. His recreation is found in hunting and fishing and doing politics. He is a staunch friend, a hale fellow well met and has hosts of friends in this and adjoining counties, all wishing him the best of luck.

ALFRED SEYMOUR ORMSBY.—One of the leading attorneys of Contra Costa County, and a man of unusual attainments, Alfred Seymour Ormsby came of a long line of legal and professional men, and it was but natural that he should reach success in life through keen mental ability, coupled with an integrity of character which endeared him to all who came in contact with him, both as a man and as a help in legal difficulties. A native Californian, born at Petaluma on December 23, 1871, he was the son of Alfred Walter and Lucy Grace (Price) Ormsby, who were married in San Francisco on October 14, 1868, and became the parents of three children: Elon A., a physician and surgeon at Centerville; Alfred S., of this review; and Arthur Walter, a merchant at Walnut Creek. The wife and mother still lives at Walnut Creek, aged seventy-eight years.

The Ormsby family is of Norse origin. About the year 1706, they left Norway and emigrated to the north of Ireland, where during the course of the centuries many members of the family rose to prominence in the legal and medical professions. The progenitor of the Ormsby family in America was John Ormsby, who settled at Tecumseh, N. Y., in Colonial times, and from him the line ran to his son, Benjamin; grandson, Elijah; great-grandson, Alfred Walter; and great-great-grandson, Alfred Seymour Ormsby.

Elijah Ormsby was born in Buffalo, N. Y., and was graduated from an academy in New York State in 1841. He became a lawyer, practicing in his native state for a time, and then removed to Chicago, where he continued in his profession. He was a strong abolitionist and was a personal friend of Abraham Lincoln; and his voice was heard in political campaigns, for he was a distinguished public speaker, with the courage of his convictions. He was a graduate of the University of Michigan, class of 1861, and during the Civil War served as captain in Company M, 16th Michigan Volunteer Infantry.

After the war, in the fall of 1865, Elijah Ormsby came to California and resumed the practice of law; and when his son, Alfred Walter Ormsby, reached manhood, the law firm of Ormsby and Ormsby was formed, and became widely known as successful attorneys in the Bay region. In connection with their law business they became largely interested in the planing-mill business, and owned and operated planing mills at San Francisco, Oakland and Petaluma. Elijah Ormsby died in San Francisco in 1887, having attained the advanced age of eighty-six years. Alfred Walter Ormsby died at the early age of thirty-four years, in Oakland.

Alfred Seymour Ormsby was reared in Oakland, mainly, and attended the public schools of that city. When only seventeen years old, in partnership with his oldest brother, Elon A., he took over a stock of jewelry and ran a store until after he graduated from the Oakland High School in 1889. After his graduation he pursued a law course in Oakland, and was admitted to the bar in 1898. After some years spent at Walnut Creek, he moved to Martinez, on August 1, 1911, and became one of the leading trial lawyers in Contra Costa County, enjoying an exceptionally large general practice; in later years he gradually began to specialize in real estate law. He was a prime mover in the organization of the Contra Costa Bar Association. His long and honorable connection with the legal profession in the county gained him the confidence of the entire community.

The marriage of Mr. Ormsby, which occurred on November 30, 1893, united him with Miss Alice A. Waite, a native of Hannibal, Mo., and daughter of Cornelius and Ann (Pocklington) Waite, both natives of England, the former born in Leicestershire, and the latter in Lancashire, that country. Cornelius Waite followed contracting and building in Oakland after coming to this country. He was a noted singer, and for many years sang in London Cathedral; in Oakland he sang with the Hughes Quartette and in the Orpheum Club. Mrs. Ormsby was reared in Oakland, where her parents were great social favorites. Her mother likewise was a person of artistic tastes and ability. Both Cornelius Waite and his wife reached the age of eighty-six years, and then Mrs. Waite was called to her last resting place, dying in Walnut Creek in 1924. Mr. Waite still resides in that city, making his home with a daughter. Three children came to bless the union of Mr. and Mrs. Ormsby. Dorothy Mildred, the oldest, died at the age of eight years. Walter Arwin is a graduate of Stanford University, class of 1922. He married Margaret Swift, a graduate of the University of California and a teacher of English and music in the Alhambra Union High School in this county. Walter is the assistant manager, at Martinez, of the Richmond-Martinez Abstract Company, Inc. Alice Marion was graduated from the Martinez High School, class of 1925, and is now attending the State Teachers' College of San Francisco.

In Fraternal relations Mr. Ormsby was prominent. He was a member of Alamo Lodge No. 122, F. & A. M., in Walnut Creek; belonged to Richmond Commandery No. 59, K. T.; and was a member and a Past Patron of Almona Chapter No. 214, O. E. S. He belonged to the Native Sons; to Richmond Lodge No. 1251, B. P. O. E.; and to Martinez Loyal Order of Moose. In politics he was a staunch Republican. While living in Walnut Creek he served as justice of the peace. He served for two terms as chief deputy district attorney under A. B. McKenzie and Thomas Johnston, the latter succeeding A. B. McKenzie in that office, and proved to be an able and fearless prosecutor. In religious belief he was an Episcopalian. In all walks of life he was an honorable and upright man, one who won the respect of his fellow men and who was sincerely mourned at his passing. His death occurred in Martinez, on January 15, 1925. He was buried with full Masonic rites; and the funeral, one of the largest ever held in Contra Costa County, attested to the high esteem in which he was held in the hearts of his countless friends in the community.

LOREN MARCELLUS LASELL.—The merchant prince of Contra Costa County, L. M. Lasell, founder of "The Emporium of Contra Costa County," now the largest department store in this section, with its four-teen completely stocked departments, is easily recognized as the leading figure in commercial circles in Martinez. In 1885, when Mr. Lasell began hauling lumber for his Martinez store from Nortonville, he little dreamed that inside of forty years he would have the largest store in Martinez, nor that his trade would come from such a wide radius as it now does, due to the wonderful system of highways and the hundreds of automo-biles that travel over them; yet he was far-sighted in locating here, be-cause of the natural advantages Martinez had to offer even in the early days when nearly all of the grain of the State was shipped from this county, both by rail and water, and the fact that his early expectations have been surpassed by actual realizations is proof of his stick-to-it-iveness and also of his faith in the people—and their faith in him, for "Once a customer of Lasell, always a customer of Lasell." In the historical sec-tion of this history mention is made of the erection of the first store building Mr. Lasell occupied. The location at that time was thought to be out of the business zone, but Mr. Lasell had faith in his business and knew he could draw the people to him by offering goods at the right prices. This he did, and has always done; and as a consequence his store has had a gradual growth from a small general merchandise store to the present modernly equipped and completely stocked establishment which would be a credit to any city.

L. M. Lasell was born at Birch Ridge, half way between St. Albans and Lake Champlain in Vermont, on April 12, 1851, the son of Smith and Sarah (Skinner) Lasell, farmers in Vermont. They had a family of nine children. Merrill was born on January 10, 1847, enlisted in the Union Army for service in the Civil War, and was honorably discharged at close of the war, after which he married and reared a family. He died in Plattsburg, N. Y., January 17, 1917. Haskell was born on August 15, 1849, is a carpenter by trade, and is still living in Plattsburg, N. Y. Loren Marcellus is our subject. Marshall was born on May 15, 1853, farmed in Clinton County, Vt., and is still living. Fred A. was born on June 10, 1854, came to California and worked in the store owned by L. M. Lasell, later had a store of his own at Crockett, and died December 20, 1918, in San Francisco. Alvah S. first saw the light on October 23, 1856, was an exceptionally able business man, and ran flouring mills for the Sperry people. He died on January 15, 1917. Henry was born on July 20, 1858, and is a farmer in Clinton County, Vt. Erastus P. was born on May 7, 1860, and is a dealer in musical merchandise in Rich-mond, Cal. The only daughter is now Mrs. Jennie S. White. She was born on December 13, 1862, and lives at Plattsburg, N. Y. The father, Smith Lasell, was born May 6, 1822, in Vermont, served in the Union Army during the Civil War, suffered great hardships and endured severe privations in the swamps in Florida and was honorably discharged, but never regained his health nor arose from his bed. He died at his farm home near Ellenburg Depot, N. Y., November 4, 1878. The mother, Sarah (Skinner) Lasell, was born on January 16, 1824, and died on April 21, 1901.

L. M. Lasell was reared on the Vermont farm of his Grandfather Skinner and obtained but a limited schooling, having to start out for himself at the age of twelve as a farm hand on his uncle's farm, for twelve dollars per month, working from four A. M. until after dark much of the time. For the most part, therefore, he is self-educated; but he took delight in attending the old-time spelling schools and often spelled down the whole neighborhood. He was also fond of arithmetic and liked to study; nor was he afraid of hard work. After some years he entered the employ of the J. G. Rodgers Iron Company, at Au Sable Forks, N. Y., manufacturers of a variety of things in iron and steel for blacksmiths and buildings; and while with this company, because of his expertness in figures he became examiner of the bookkeepers' work and was sent to Jay, Essex County, to take charge of the weighing up of the iron at the forge, and also the grain at their gristmill at Jay. Desiring to see California, he came out here on a sight-seeing trip and never returned East. He became bookkeeper for G. K. Smith, merchant at Biggs, Butte County; and the following spring he went to San Francisco and met Conro & Dodge, who wanted him to go to Nortonville in Contra Costa County and take charge of their store at that place, then a thriving mining town, but now defunct. Mr. Lasell accepted the position and met with very good success in his work for nine years. He then came to Martinez and built a frame building, which is still standing, put in a stock of general merchandise, used the newspapers for liberal advertising, and began rapidly to build up a very substantial business, for he bought and sold goods and produce right. His strict attention to details inspired his customers with confidence in him, and as the country began to be settled he enjoyed an increase in his business from year to year until the ultimate result of this small beginning is shown in the up-to-date store building in Martinez and the many other interests Mr. Lasell has in Contra Costa County. He was one of the organizers of the First National Bank, served on the board of directors, and was a pillar of strength to the institution. This is now known as the Martinez Branch of the American Bank of San Francisco. He owns the Alhambra Springs property of 300 acres, from which pure mineral spring water is piped to Martinez and there bottled and shipped to many places from their bottling plant adjacent to the Southern Pacific Railroad tracks and water transportation. Alhambra Pure Spring Water is widely known and has a wide distribution from its offices in Oakland and San Francisco, as well as from Martinez. Mr. Lasell is a heavy stockholder in the American Toll Bridge Company, now building bridges across Carquinez Straits from South Vallejo to Crockett and from Antioch to Collinsville, both of which will prove a boon to autoists, all of whom are now obliged to ferry across. The company is now running a steam ferry as an aid in transporting autos until the bridges are completed.

Mr. Lasell has been twice married. His first wife, whom he married in Contra Costa County on January 22, 1878, was Miss Sarah E. Wight, born in California, a granddaughter of the late Harry Randolph Wight, who made his first trip to California in 1848, from New York. He became a prosperous rancher in New York Valley in this county and lived to be ninety-four years of age. Mr. and Mrs. Lasell had three children: Cora Lasell Craft, of San Francisco; L. Wight Lasell, of Berkeley; and Ernest Randolph Lasell, who is mentioned on another page in this history. Mrs. Lasell died in August, 1915. The second marriage of Mr. Lasell, which occurred on January 12, 1918, united him with Miss Sadie Davenport, who is connected with the best pioneer families of California, and who capably presides over the home which they purchased at the head of Green Street. She is interested financially in the L. M. Lasell Company copartnership. Mr. Lasell has never sought public office, although he has served as a member of the board of city trustees and has always been in favor of civic betterment and has exerted his influence for the upbuilding of Contra Costa County in general and Martinez in particular. He is a staunch Republican, and leans towards the Christian Science faith. In summing up his life, it can be said that there has never been a more public-spirited man in the county than L. M. Lasell.

MRS. ROSA SOLARI.—A pioneer business woman who has many good friends is Mrs. Rosa Solari, of Pittsburg, Cal., who has by good management successfully conducted her grocery business on Black Diamond Street for twenty-two years. She is the widow of John Baptiste Solari, an honored pioneer of Pittsburg who was well and favorably known by the old settlers of this community. Mrs. Solari is a native of Italy, born January 11, 1865, in Chiavari, County of Genoa, and on April 28, 1884, was united in marriage with Mr. Solari, who had lived in America for twelve years before he returned to be married. Soon after their marriage the young couple sailed for America, landing at New York City in May. They continued their journey to California, arriving May 25. Locating at Redwood City, Mr. Solari operated a vegetable garden until in 1889, when the family removed to Contra Costa County. For two and a half years he had a vegetable garden located in the Marsh Creek country, where he grew vegetables for the market and developed a vineyard. Later on, moving nearer to Black Diamond, he there cultivated a six-acre tract of land. This is now a part of the land occupied by the Redwood Manufacturers Company in Pittsburg. Mr. Solari raised vegetables for the market, selling them in Antioch
14

and Pittsburg. He died in Black Diamond, now Pittsburg, March 24, 1902, aged fifty-one years.

Mr. and Mrs. John B. Solari were the parents of four children: Louis, deceased; Mary, now the wife of Salvatore Enea, proprietor of the California Theater in Pittsburg, by whom she has four girls, Stella Rosa, Frances and Virginia; Priscilla Aida, the wife of Antonio Ferrante, of Pittsburg, and the mother of three children, Edmund, David and Aida; and David A., a patriotic soldier who gave his life for his country during the World War. He served in France with the American Expeditionary Force, as a private in Company G, Regiment No. 362, United States Infantry, and was killed in action at Gesnes in the Argonne. Three years later his body was returned by the Government to Pittsburg, and was buried with military honors at Colma, San Mateo County. David A. Solari was the only soldier from Pittsburg that was killed in battle, and as a tribute to his memory the American Legion Post at Pittsburg bears his name. He was Pittsburg's pioneer moving picture theater owner, and was associated with his brother-in-law Salvatore Enea in that business. They established a circuit of theaters which include The Palace at Pittsburg, The Strand in Stockton, one at Napa, and one at Hayward.

Mrs. Rosa Solari is a noble, generous-hearted woman, and has accomplished what few women could have accomplished under the circumstances; she successfully managed a business and at the same time reared and educated her family. Her sterling personal characteristics, accompanied by thrift and executive and financial ability, aided her in overcoming the obstacles that beset her pathway in life after the death of her husband, and today she is accorded well-merited praise from her many friends for the accomplishment of so noble a task.

DAVID EDWARDS.—The representative of his pioneer father, David Edwards, of Crockett, is worthy of the respect and esteem of the citizens of this community for the part he has taken since reaching manhood's estate. He is the fifth son in the family of Thomas and Mary (Pugh) Edwards, who are mentioned at length on another page of this history, and was born at Knight's Ferry, Stanislaus County, on December 29, 1852. He received his early education in San Francisco and was honor boy in his class of thirty-three, his brother Thomas standing second; Alexander Morrison, who later became a leading attorney in San Francisco, was third. David also graduated from the Pacific Business College in June, 1873.

After finishing school work, David Edwards came back to the ranch operated by his father and which had been leased from Judge Crockett, and he remained on the ranch until the town of Crockett was started. His first employment was with the Port Costa Lumber Company, their yards being located at the place selected for the abutment of the new toll bridge. At that time the waters of the bay were clear and fresh and wooden piles would last twenty years; now the toreda destroy them in one year as there is not enough fresh water to kill them off, for they cannot live in fresh water. Mr. Edwards is in favor of the project of building a dam to keep back the tidewater so the waters of the rivers can come closer to the bay shores. Upon leaving the employ of the lumber company, Mr. Edwards took up work with Wells Fargo and Company Express in 1906 and ever since he has been in the express service and is now with the American Railway Express. He well remembers when the railroad was built through here in 1876, also when Mr. Starr built his flouring mill, and knows flourmilling was profitable until the wheat crop ran out and George W. McNear bought the mill, which site was later purchased by the California and Hawaiian Sugar Refining Company. Many changes have taken place since those early days and during these changes Mr. Edwards has watched them with a great deal of interest, and has helped all worthy projects for the best interests of the people. He has many friends who esteem him for his worth as a friend and citizen.

David Edwards has been married twice. His first wife was Miss Livia Labaree of Danville, Contra Costa County, and they were married at Hollister on December 8, 1886, the ceremony being performed by Rev. R. L. Symington, who came from Missouri and was preaching at Danville and elsewhere. Mrs. Edwards's father was the first doctor to locate in this county, having come from Kokomo, Ind., with his family. She was a very popular woman and had many friends. She was a sister of Mrs. S. D. Bishop and sister-in-law of Mrs. Alice Labaree, teacher in John Swett Union High School. The second marriage united Mr. Edwards with Mrs. Annie J. Evans, and took place in Porterville in 1912. She came from Pittsburgh, Pa. Upon her advice, her niece, Mrs. Elizabeth M. Thomas, came to Crockett. She was prominent in fraternal and club life, and died in July, 1922. Mr. Edwards was the first deacon of the Congregational Church, serving for twenty years, and took an active and sincere interest in church work. He is a member of the Odd Fellows, and for many years was treasurer of the Crockett Lodge; he is a member of Golden Gate Encampment in San Francisco; and belongs to the Franklin Hospital Society, a benefit organization in San Francisco.

ALBERT WILLIAM GLASS.—One of the native sons of California, and a man who takes a great deal of interest in the cultivation of his fine 180-acre ranch located in the San Ramon Valley, is Albert William Glass, a breeder of fine Shropshire sheep, Holstein cattle and Duroc-Jersey hogs, and at one time an extensive breeder of fine horses. Born in a tent near Walnut Creek, on February 25, 1852, he is a son of David and Eliza Jane (Hall) Glass, the former a native of Kentucky and the latter of Ohio. In 1851 the family crossed the plains to California and settled at Marysville, where the father at first engaged in mining as a means of livelihood. Coming to Walnut Creek, he farmed for several years and then purchased 820 acres of the Amador Grant. This ranch was three miles long; and there the parents lived and died, the father on September 9, 1898, and the mother on December 12, 1899. They had nine children, viz.: Albert W., of this review; Mrs. Clara I. Ivory, deceased; Laura, Mrs. Fred B. Wood, of Oakland; Percy; Anita I., deceased; Loretta I., unmarried; Frank L., of Martinez; Fred L., deceased; and Rolla Clement, deceased.

Albert W. Glass received his education at McClure's Military Academy in Oakland. His first farming experience was obtained in Sycamore Valley, where he farmed 400 acres of land for about twelve years. Then he bought 180 acres of the old homestead, which is his present home place; and besides this, he leases land and raises grain and stock.

On June 25, 1889, A. W. Glass married Miss Lillie B. Feidler of Oakland, daughter of Nathan and May (Fleming) Feidler. Nathan Feidler died in Texas in January, 1906; and Mrs. Feidler passed away on September 7, 1900. Of their five children, Mrs. Glass is the only one living. Of the union of Mr. and Mrs. Glass three children were born. Harry Clifford, an abstractor in Martinez, is married and is the father of three children: Donald A., Harry C., Jr., and Leland Fairchild. Claude L., an orchardist in the San Ramon Valley, is married and is the parent of a daughter, C. Lucille. Arthur D. died when he was twenty-one years old. Mr. Glass has been a trustee of the San Ramon school district for many years. He belongs to the Woodmen of the World and to the Native Sons of the Golden West; formerly he was an active member of the Grange.

VOLNEY TAYLOR.—In a history devoted to the biographies and personalities of the pioneers of Contra Costa County there is none of them more worthy of mention than the late Volney Taylor. He was born June 20, 1851, in the Province of Quebec, Canada, a son of Alexander T. and Louisa (Bruce) Taylor, the former a native of Bolton, Canada, born September 15, 1821; the latter was a native of Vermont. Alexander Taylor, at the age of twenty-three, rented a farm in Canada which he afterwards purchased and operated eleven years. Selling his land he left Canada with his family and journeyed to New York City, from where he sailed on November 6, 1866, for California by the way of the Isthmus of Panama, and just one month later they landed safely in San Francisco. He later located near Vallejo, in Solano County. The family consisted of four children: Valeria, Avyette, Alexander V., and Volney the subject of this sketch. In 1868 the family moved into Contra Costa County, where Alexander Taylor bought 320 acres of land near Point of Timber, where he followed farming for years. He passed away in 1912.

Volney Taylor received his early education in the public school at Vallejo, which he supplemented by a course in the Pacific Business College at San Francisco, from which he was graduated in 1872. After leaving school he engaged in farming, later purchased his father's ranch at Point of Timber, and still later bought two other ranches, making in all a total of about 800 acres. He devoted his land to raising grain and

W. H. Sanford.

alfalfa, being one of the first to specialize in the production of alfalfa. Mr. Taylor was one of the original promoters of the Byron-Bethany Irrigation District. After bringing much of this land under a high state of cultivation he subdivided much of his own land and in 1896 moved to Oakland, but still retained his ownership of the old home place of 200 acres. In the fall of 1923 Volney Taylor, a man beloved by a legion of friends, passed away. His life's ambition had been to do good and many are the persons who have cause to remember his friendship and benevolence. His charities were many, yet never given as such, but always extended in that quiet and unostentatious way so characteristic of this truly good man. The marriage of Volney Taylor occurred in October, 1878, when he was united with Agnes E. Andrews, a native of Illinois. This union was blessed with one son, Everett B. Taylor, now a resident of San Francisco.

WILLIAM H. SANFORD.—Among the men who helped to develop Richmond and Martinez, in Contra Costa County, was the late William H. Sanford, who passed to his reward on September 13, 1925, after a busy and eventful career. He was born at Springfield, Tenn., February 3, in 1860, a son of George and Mary (Browning) Sanford. Grandfather Browning was a slave owner in the South before the Civil War; and George Sanford was the owner of a large plantation in Tennessee upon which he grew tobacco and cotton. Both parents are deceased.

William H. Sanford received his education in the public schools and in college. He was always interested in agriculture and made a careful study of soil and climate. He studied for the law and was admitted to practice, but gave it up to enter the nursery business, which he followed in Missouri and Kansas for eight years. He came west and engaged in the real estate business in Washington, Oregon and other States. Arriving in California in 1891, he located in Los Angeles and engaged in the advertising business for a time, and also was in the employ of the Pacific States Savings & Loan Company for seven years, traveling for this concern and advertising their advantages. In 1905 Mr. Sanford came to Richmond, Cal., became a partner in the New Richmond Land Company, and helped to lay out and develop the present city of Richmond, soon selling off the company's holdings. To induce settlers to come here and invest their money, he and Mrs. Sanford started on a tour of the United States and Canada, even going into Mexico. On this tour they gave lectures with illustrated moving pictures showing the wonders of the State of California, her mining industry, her timber, and many of her leading industries, especially featuring Contra Costa County. They also featured songs of California, and by this means of special advertising did more than any other agency to bring in money and people to help build up Contra Costa County. One of the important real estate projects was the opening of Shell Heights in Martinez, in 1915. Mr. and Mrs. Sanford were instrumental in bringing to Richmond the Certainteed

Roofing Company and the Pullman Car Shops, and many other firms and corporations located within the boundaries of this county through the influence of their advertising and personal solicitation. Mr. Sanford was very much interested in seeing Richmond grow, and in every way showed his public spirit in forwarding that end. Since his death Mrs. Sanford ably carries on the business in accordance with his sound policies.

William H. Sanford was united in marriage at La Veta, Colo., on December 11, 1887, with Miss Jennie El Maud Richardson, a native of Ohio and a daughter of Leroy and Eleanor Richardson. Her father was a veteran of the Civil War, in which he served as a Union soldier. He was an architect and builder, and after the Chicago fire in 1871 he went there and helped to rebuild the city. From there he went into Kansas and experienced some of the pioneer life in that State, and he was also in Colorado in the early days. He came to Los Angeles during its early boom years and witnessed much of the growth of the southern part of the State. Both he and his wife have passed away. Of the marriage of Mr. and Mrs. Sanford four children were born. Mrs. Grace Sanford Hanush was born in La Veta, Colo., and educated in the schools of California; she now lives in Oakland. Mrs. Charles S. Holmes was born in Bellingham, Wash.; she is a musician and resides in Berkeley. Mr. Holmes is connected with the Western Union Telegraph Company at Oakland. William H. Sanford, Jr., was born in Los Angeles and educated in the Richmond schools; he is a display artist in San Francisco. Miss Azalea E. Sanford was born at Redding, Cal., and is associated in business with her mother at 2221 Macdonald Avenue, Richmond; she belongs to Acantha Chapter No. 249, O. E. S. Mr. Sanford was a life member of Richmond Lodge No. 1251, B. P. O. E.; held membership in the Odd Fellows in Bellingham, Wash., and belonged to Alpha Lodge of Masons in Richmond. He was a member of the Industrial Commission of Richmond and the Chamber of Commerce. In politics he was a Republican. Mrs. Sanford belongs to the Eastern Star, and Amaranth Court in Richmond. She is a member of the Richmond Realty Board, the State Realty Board, and the National Realty Association. She organized one of the first Parent Teachers' Associations in the State in Shasta County, and served as its president. She enjoys the great out-of-doors and finds pleasure in clean sports. As a business woman she has shown her ability to handle difficult problems, and takes an active interest in all civic movements in Richmond. In politics she also is a Republican. She attends the Methodist Church.

C. J. O'NEILL.—The pioneer merchant of Port Costa, C. J. O'Neill, has been here since 1883 as proprietor of the leading grocery store, and he has ever since that early date been an active factor in the growth and development of Port Costa City and Contra Costa County. A native Californian, he was born at San Francisco on February 19, 1857, the son of John O'Neill, who was a native of Ireland and came to California via the Isthmus of Panama in 1850, and was married in San Francisco to Ellen Cunningham. She also was a native of the Emerald Isle, a woman of motherly qualities and great worth, who lived to be eighty-seven years old. The father was a house painter and grainer, and young C. J. O'Neill's first work was done in assisting his father on painting jobs.

The oldest of eight children born to his parents, C. J. O'Neill's early years were spent in San Jose, where the family moved from San Francisco, and when he was eight years old they moved to Vallejo; so he attended the public schools in both cities. In May, 1883, Mr. O'Neill came to Port Costa, and shortly thereafter embarked in the grocery business. In the beginning he continued to take occasional painting contracts, but after several months he confined his entire attention to the store, and his painstaking methods and courteous attention to the wants of his customers built up for the Pioneer Grocery a successful business and won the trade of a large number of satisfied patrons.

The marriage of Mr. O'Neill, at Port Costa in 1909, united him with Miss Josephine Drechsler, a native of Texas and a daughter of Wolfgang and Teressa (Sadler) Drechsler, natives of Germany. This union has been blessed with the birth of three children: John F., Cornelius, and Elsa. In his business Mr. O'Neill is ably assisted by his wife, who for many years was a teacher in the Port Costa school. She holds a life diploma and is a woman of unusual character and ability. She was a member of the first class to graduate from the Port Costa school, and her studies there were supplemented by a course in Gilson's private school in Oakland, after which she obtained her certificate to teach and for eleven years was connected with the Port Costa school. She is a trustee of the John Swett Union High School at Crockett. The family are members of the Catholic Church.

Interested since his first settling here in the further advancement of his home city and environs, Mr. O'Neill has always given his support to the correct public policies and to the men best fitted to carry them out. Though given opportunity on several different occasions to become a candidate for public office, he has declined in favor of giving his undivided attention to business affairs, but has done his share by working for civic betterment as a private citizen. He is a member of the Contra Costa County Grocers' Association.

ANDREW C. GEHRINGER.—The ideals which enter into the making of a true Californian and the high type of American citizenry are found harmoniously blended in Andrew C. Gehringer, who resides on his well-cared-for ranch near Concord. Mr. Gehringer comes from one of the earliest of the pioneer families, has lived an industrious and useful life, and reared a family of children who are following occupations that contribute greatly to the civic welfare; and, in addition, he has not neglected to give much of his own time and thought to those things which are essential to community development. His father was a native of the province of Wurtemburg, Germany, where he was born on January 12, 1823, and christened Andrew George Gehringer. He was a weaver by trade, but in his early youth he heard such glowing reports of the land of opportunity and freedom across the seas that he emigrated to the United States in the early forties. After he landed in New York he worked for a time in a stone quarry; and he hauled the massive slab of stone, forty feet long and six feet wide, which was placed in front of the state house in Albany. It had been a difficult matter to get a man to undertake the contract of handling this stone, but the sturdy young German accomplished it safely. Later he joined the National Guard of New York, 1st Infantry, Company H, which left Albany on July 31, 1846, for active duty in California during the Mexican War. He was standing guard duty in the Presidio in San Francisco when gold, discovered in California in 1848, was brought in to be assayed and proved to be twenty-three-carat gold. At the conclusion of the Mexican War he was given a land warrant calling for 160 acres of land. For a time he did some mining at Dutch Flat, which was so named in his honor. Later he settled in Santa Clara Valley, where he remained until 1863, at which time he came to Contra Costa County, locating near Pacheco. Concord was not in existence at that time. He purchased land from the Pacheco Grant and carried mail from Sacramento to Sausalito. Andrew George Gehringer was twice married, the second marriage occurring in 1860, to Mrs. Henrietta (Rengstorff) Ballmann. Of this union two children were born: Andrew C., the subject of this sketch, and his sister Lena, now Mrs. J. McKean of Concord.

Andrew C. Gehringer was born in Santa Clara, November 29, 1862, and was an infant when his father removed to Contra Costa County. His education was received in the local grammar school. He assisted his father as a boy and, at the age of seventeen, commenced to work for his brother. At the age of twenty-one he leased his father's farm and began work on his own responsibility. In 1895 he bought 100 acres of land and erected the home in which he is now living and where his family has been reared. Meantime he continued to look after his father's farm until the latter's death, which occurred on April 19, 1896. After his father's death more land was added to his possessions, and today he is owner of 200 acres devoted to various kinds of farm products, stock and fruit. His principal crops are grain, hay and nuts. He has been a director in the First National Bank of Concord (now the American Bank, Concord Branch), trustee of the high school, and foreman of the grand jury, and has fulfilled other important civic duties pertaining to the general community welfare. He is a member of the Farm Bureau, in which he has served as an officer, and is also a member of the Native Sons of the Golden West and the Independent Order of Odd Fellows.

Mr. Gehringer was married on November 27, 1887, to Miss Marie L. Denkinger, daughter of John and Emily Denkinger, both deceased, of whose four children Mrs. Gehringer is the only survivor. To Mr. and Mrs. Gehringer five children were born: Linda G., now Mrs. F. L. Dodd of Berkeley; Carl G., who is married and who is a school teacher at Oakley and lives with his father; Elaine L., now Mrs. P. Olivera of Concord; Hilda T., at home; and Andrew Narbert, attending the University of California. The high scholastic ability of this family is shown by the fact that all are teachers. Mr. and Mrs. Dodd conduct the Western Normal in Berkeley, a school for certified teachers. Mr. Gehringer likes to fish and hunt, and occasionally attends ball games. He occasionally speaks in public meetings, and an article which he wrote on the subject of water conservation appeared in "The Orchard and Farm," and won a prize. The contest was a discussion of the most important topic concerned in the welfare of the community. Mr. Gehringer believes the most important question of today is the conservation and replenishing of the underground water supply. The water level in the valley, for example, has lowered twenty-five feet in the past twenty-seven years, which is a smaller decrease than is found in many other places. He believes that the ideals of the present generation could be improved by the elimination of selfishness and a consistent regard for the welfare of humanity at large. Mr. and Mrs. Gehringer are members of the Christian Church. He is independent in politics.

PATRICK FLEMING.—Among the earliest settlers in what is now the Richmond district was Patrick Fleming, for he settled here with his mother in 1858. He was born in County Kildare, Ireland, in 1830, and came to the United States when about twenty-eight. His father having died, he was accompanied by his mother and they stopped in Boston six months, then came around the Horn to San Francisco, where an older sister, the wife of a Captain Bloomfield, had already located. Their stay was short in the metropolis and Mr. Fleming came to Contra Costa County and established a home in Potrero Gap and there engaged in ranching. He often stated that he could have bought the whole of what was later known as Point Richmond for $200, but he could not see the value and so hid his coin in a can and buried it, later to have his hogs root it up. His mother died at the age of ninety-four.

In 1864 Mr. Fleming married Bridget Beahan, born in the same county and grew up there with him, and also accompanied the Flemings to Boston, where she remained until he sent for her. They had ten children, five of them growing to maturity, viz: Edward, living in Oakland and the father of two boys and four girls; Thomas, in Richmond; Mary, making her home with Thomas; Sarah, died aged twenty-three; and Joseph, met an accidental death in the California Cap Works in 1922, when forty-eight. The children were reared on the Tewksbury ranch in Wild Cat Creek, whither the father had moved in the late sixties. The mother died in

1888 at the age of fifty-five. Mr. Fleming continued to farm and raise grain and stock until he was forced to retire on account of old age and he then made his home in East Richmond with his children. He died in 1917 at the age of eighty-seven, respected and beloved by a wide circle of friends. He often said that he gave the first $20 towards building St. Paul's Catholic Church in San Pablo, and for over fifty years enjoyed passing the collection box in that church. As a citizen he did his duty on the jury many times, was public spirited and enjoyed the close friendship of many of the old settlers in and about San Pablo. At his passing the county lost one of its highly respected citizens.

BENJAMIN BOORMAN.—The oldest man now living in the Richmond section of Contra Costa County both in years and residence is Benjamin Boorman, who lives on Cutting Boulevard, Richmond. This venerable citizen, now past ninety-four years of age, is hale and hearty and delights to recount the days of long ago to his many friends and visitors. A native of New York, he was born in Chautauqua County, on March 27, 1832, the son of Benjamin and Sarah (Hosmer) Boorman, both born, reared and married in England. They came to the United States and located in New York State where they were farmers and there they spent their last days, both passing away at the age of ninety-four years. After many years of hard work on the farm the elder Boorman sold the place to our subject and his brother who carried on the work for a time. When Benjamin was twenty he decided to go to Wisconsin and after five years spent in that state took Horace Greeley's advice to "Go West and grow up with the country" and went to Kansas where he followed the trade of carpenter, he having learned the rudiments of that calling while living in New York State; he had also worked at blacksmithing and at the harness-maker's trade in his home state. Settling in Leroy, Coffey County, Kans., Mr. Boorman followed his trade of carpenter and also took up eighty acres of land there. He became active in politics in that frontier state and served as a deputy sheriff and constable; was also a delegate to the county convention that was to select the county seats of the various counties.

Still following Greeley's advice, Mr. Boorman disposed of his holdings in Kansas and joined a government train going to Camp Floyd, then located near Salt Lake City. He later joined some friends and they started from Fort Leavenworth for California, Mr. Boorman being selected to captain the train, and he was the first man to drive a team over Simpson's Pass in Nevada. Coming direct to this county, where he had an old friend named Charles Mayburn, a farmer on the San Pablo Rancho, Mr. Boorman leased land and began raising hay and grain and some good stock, for he always has been a lover of good horses. His operations did not pan out as he expected; so he went to Nevada and bought a wood ranch, cutting the wood and hauling it to Virginia City; his first contract for wood was made with Governor Blaisdell. He did very well in this venture but put his savings into mining property and promptly lost them. This was in 1862-1863. He then made a visit to California, but went back to Nevada and bought lumber in the Sierra Valley, California, for $20 per thousand, hauling it to Austin, Nev., where he sold it for $500 per thousand. The year 1864 was spent in Montana where he worked as drifter at mining in Alder Gulch; he soon got another job as drifter, which paid him nine dollars per day, soon being increased to ten dollars. At one job he worked three months and averaged $500 per day for his employer. His wages were paid in scrip, which proved to be worthless; so he went on to British Columbia and bought an interest in a claim, continuing until in 1865, when he decided California was good enough for him and he came back to Contra Costa County and leased 600 acres from the Castro family and raised hay, grain and stock, supplying the former products to the feed stores in Oakland. He raised some very fine draft horses which he exhibited at various fairs in Oakland, and out of six specimens exhibited took five first premiums. He made some money and became a substantial citizen of the county.

In 1893 Mr. Boorman bought ten acres of land upon which he erected his present residence. Part of this tract he laid out in town lots, and he was the first man to sell the right-of-way to the Southern Pacific Railway when they came through here. At that time the population of San Pablo, West Berkeley, Oakland and Brooklyn was only a few more than 500 souls. He has lived to see the wonderful changes wrought in this section and has always taken a keen interest in the events from day to day. For sixteen years Mr. Boorman served as a deputy county tax assessor, his territory extending from the county line on the south to the Union Oil works on the north. He was assessing here when Richmond came into being and he knew everybody in this section and everybody knew Benjamin Boorman. He has the record of collecting poll taxes, in this section, collecting from 1800 employees of the Standard Oil Company refinery and 500 persons from Hercules Powder Works; that was at the time when the collector received a percentage of collections and of course was very active in getting hold of the men who had to pay. For nine years he served as a trustee of the San Pablo school district.

In 1875 Mr. Boorman was united in marriage in Contra Costa County with Mrs. Anne (Cross) Wood, born in Liverpool, England. She was the widow of William Wood, an Englishman, by whom she had six children, three of them now living, viz.: Robert, Frank and Luceta, wife of Paul Dunlap. Mrs. Boorman had come to California from England in 1856. Of the union of Mr. and Mrs. Boorman three children were born, two of them living. Mrs. Adelaide Picton, living in Richmond on Twenty-eighth Street, has five children. Mrs. Emily B. Axtell makes her home with her father and is engaged in educational work. All his life Mr. Boorman has been a Republican. He is a Mason, holding his membership in McKinley Lodge, and was the first man to join this lodge in Richmond. Mrs. Boorman died on July 23, 1919, at the age of eighty-two years. Now at the age of more than ninety-four years Mr. Boorman can look back upon a life well-spent and forward without fear for he has done what he could towards the development of this county he selected for his permanent home. He has bought and sold some real estate and made a success of whatever he undertook. His friends are legion and he is an interesting conversationalist, covering many points of early history of this country.

BLOOM B. ROGERS.—One of the best-known men of Contra Costa County, where he has lived practically all of his life, Bloom B. Rogers is a native son, and both his father and mother were also natives of California, for Grandfather Rogers crossed the plains in an ox-team train in 1850, founding the family here in that early day. Born in Walnut Creek, Contra Costa County, June 2, 1875, Bloom B. Rogers is a son of C. W. and Martha (Leach) Rogers, the former a native of Drytown, Amador County, and the latter of Ione, in the same county.

C. W. Rogers, son of the old pioneer, was born during the stirring pioneer times, and received his education in the famous old Lincoln School in San Francisco. Coming to Contra Costa County in 1860, he engaged in the butcher business in Walnut Creek, and later built the Ala Costa Inn at that place, which is still standing and is now owned by his brother, W. A. Rogers. He also operated a liquor establishment in connection with the hotel, as did practically all country hotel-keepers in those days. The old oak tree which stands in front of the Oak Center Cafe was one of the landmarks of the town, land surveys being made from the tree, and other community happenings starting or ending there. Held in high esteem by his friends in the county, C. W. Rogers was elected constable, and served in the days when land squatters caused much trouble for the settler. He later was elected sheriff of Contra Costa; in 1888 he moved to Martinez, and served six years in that office. At the end of that period he was elected constable and appointed night watchman of that city, and later he had charge of the pumping and water testing station of the Southern Pacific Railway. After a life too short in span of years, but full of kind deeds and long public service, this old settler of Contra Costa County passed to his reward in 1910, survived by his devoted helpmate and six children: Bloom B., of this review; Mrs. Viola Larkin; Mrs. Harriett McCann; Charles A.; Mrs. Noami Youney; and Mrs. Ruth Miller. Prominent fraternally, he was a charter member of Central Parlor, N. S. G. W., of Walnut Creek, and a charter member of the Martinez Camp, Woodmen of the World. In political affiliation he was always a stanch Republican.

Bloom B. Rogers was educated in the schools of Walnut Creek and Martinez. He worked for the Southern Pacific Railway when a boy, and later learned the printer's trade in the composing room of the Martinez Enterprise. For a time he was engineer with the Port Costa Water Company, and he was also in the employ of the Peyton Chemical Company, the Pacific Gas & Electric Company, the Standard Oil Company, and the General Chemical Company. During the World War he went East and was a lead-burner with the Du Pont Powder Company in Wisconsin. He was in charge of the lead plant for that concern in Butte, Mont., and he also was superintendent of the lead plant for the New Cornelia Copper Company at Ajo, Ariz. One of the best-known men in the county, with friends in every section of it, from the country districts to the larger cities, he was elected constable of Martinez in 1922, taking office in 1923, and is now most ably filling the position held by his father before him, for which he is most admirably fitted.

The marriage of Mr. Rogers, occurring on April 18, 1898, united him with Annie Devery, a native of Ireland. A man of unusual public spirit, he is actively interested in advancing the interests of his home county, both socially and economically. Fraternally, he is a member of the Blue Lodge of Masons; the Sciots, of Antioch; Martinez Parlor, N. S. G. W.; the Woodmen of the World; the Loyal Order of Moose; and the Phoenix, Ariz., lodge of Elks.

HON. ROBERT WALLACE, JR.—He who seeks to promote the cause of justice, and in the course of a long life advances directly or indirectly the educational, commercial and agricultural interests of his community or county, is entitled to mention in the pages of its history as a public benefactor. Such is the record of Judge Robert Wallace, a native son and an early pioneer of Contra Costa County, whose efforts have always been directed towards the county's betterment and welfare. He was born on September 28, 1859, at San Francisco, a son of Robert and Ann (Shepard) Wallace, both natives of Northshields, England. The father was reared in England, where he learned the trade of the ship caulker. He emigrated to America, and locating in San Francisco, Cal., in 1857, worked at his trade until he retired. The mother died in 1892. Robert Wallace, Sr., invested his savings in real estate, and in 1870 purchased 160 acres in Contra Costa County, south of Brentwood.

Robert Wallace, Jr., was reared on his father's ranch and after leaving school managed the home place; later he purchased 160 acres adjoining and became a very successful agriculturist. In 1903 he was elected justice of the peace of Township Nine, Contra Costa County; and through his able, conscientious and just decisions he has so won the confidence of the community that he has been re-elected to this important post ever since.

Judge Wallace was united in marriage with Alice J. Murphy, a daughter of John Murphy of Concord, and this union has been blessed with four children: Robert H., Ray L., Elaine A. (Mrs John P. Brewer), and Richard J. The family home is now located at Brentwood. Fraternally, Judge Wallace is a member and Past Master of Brentwood Lodge No. 345, F. & A. M., and a Past Patron of the Eastern Star. He is a trustee of the Masonic Temple at Brentwood, and much credit for the conception, erection and completion of this new and beautiful building is due to the enthusiasm, untiring efforts and wise counsel of Judge Wallace. He is a member of the Contra Costa County Agricultural Association and of the Point of Timber Cemetery Association, being the only surviving member of the original board. He is vice-president of the Bank of Antioch. The name of Robert Wallace, Jr., will be long and honorably associated with the history of Brentwood and Contra Costa County.

ALFRED FRANK.—A native son of Contra Costa County and now a farmer in the San Pablo district, Alfred Frank was born on October 20, 1867, a son of August Frank, who was born in Germany and was there educated until he came to California. He first located in the Eden district near Hayward, and then came to San Pablo and bought 160 acres of Juan B. Alvarado and began making improvements. He married Annie Hennings, also born in Germany, and they had two children: August, now in Hayward, and Alfred, our subject. The father died in 1868 at the age of thirty-eight. Mrs. Frank married for her second husband Frank Wrede, and they had four children: Christina, Mrs. L. Miller; Fred, deceased; Matilda, Mrs. Henry Phillips; and Miss Anna, all born on the Frank ranch in this county. In 1876 the family moved to the Eden district in Alameda County, and there the mother died in 1907 at the age of seventy-one.

Alfred Frank attended the public schools and worked at ranch work on the farm until about of age; then he came back to Contra Costa County and took charge of the old ranch where he was born. He and his brother had fallen heir to the property, which in the settlement of the Spanish grant diminished to eighty acres. This property he has improved with an orchard of apricots and peaches in commercial quantities. There had been a family orchard set out by his parents at an early period. He also erected the present buildings on the place, and has been prosperous in his undertakings.

Mr. Frank was married on December 16, 1897, to Miss Alvina Thode, born and reared on San Pablo Creek, where her father, Nicholas Thode, was one of the pioneer farmers. Her father and mother were born in Germany, came to the United States single, and were married in San Francisco. The father came as a young man, being accompanied by his father. For some time he engaged in dairying in South San Francisco, and then came to this county and farmed on the adobe lands for a time, after which he bought land on the creek and improved a fine farm. The Sheldon ranch, which he bought, was a part of the Sobrante Grant, and when that was settled he lost all but twenty-nine acres, upon which he lived until his death, in 1911, at the age of sixty-nine. His good wife, Emma Thode, died in 1924 at the age of seventy-six. They had seven children, viz.: Fred and Alvina, twins; Adelle, Mrs. Nels Engelbret;

John Geddes

Clara, Mrs. William Hughes; Emma, Mrs. James Connor; Rudolph; and one son, Otto, who died in infancy in 1880. The children were born, reared and educated in Contra Costa County. Mr. and Mrs. Frank have two girls: Alice, now the wife of Stanley Bergesen of Pittsburg; and Zetta, the wife of E. B. Jones of Richmond. Both girls are graduates of the Richmond High School. Mr. Frank is a very public-spirited man, doing all he can to aid in the development of this section. He is a booster for Contra Costa County, believing there is no other place in the State its equal for opportunities to make good. The family have a host of friends and are highly respected by all who know them.

JOHN GEDDES.—Among the earliest pioneers in eastern Contra Costa County was the late John Geddes, for over forty years identified with the agricultural development of the section known as Byron Precinct. He was a native of Halifax County, Nova Scotia, and was born on a farm on June 23, 1837, the son of William Putnam and Elizabeth (Blackie) Geddes, both natives of Nova Scotia, where they lived and passed away.

John Geddes helped his father with the farm work and went to school when he could be spared. In the winter time the snow would at times be six feet deep, and young John often had difficulty in getting to school; besides, he was obliged to help earn a livelihood by working in the woods, and therefore his education was meager. While still in young manhood he and his brother, Charles B. Geddes, sailed from Halifax via Boston and New York, and thence via the Isthmus of Panama, to San Francisco, arriving there in December, 1868. The brothers went to Stockton and engaged in work on the railroad then in course of construction from Tracy to Livermore. The next fall they rented a section of land in San Joaquin County. The first two years were too dry to raise crops, but the third year made up for it in a bumper crop of wheat and barley. They had three sections in wheat and a half-section in barley; altogether they farmed there for fourteen years.

On November 9, 1875, Mr. Geddes was married to Miss Jessie Carroll, born in Colchester County, Nova Scotia; and they became the parents of eight children: Emma, now the wife of Robert Clark, residing at Knightsen; Elizabeth, at home with her mother; Henry, who died at the age of three years; George, who married Mabel Shafer and lives at Knightsen; Herbert, who married Lola Masterton and lives in Brentwood, and farms a portion of the Geddes homestead; Harry, who married Ruth Ellsworth and is a farmer near the home place; Lloyd, who married Edith Chadwick and resides in Brentwood; and Marguerite, the wife of E. J. Lang, chief chemist for the Associated Oil Company, residing in Long Beach. The Geddes family removed to Contra Costa County and purchased 320 acres of land, which has been continuously farmed to good advantage. While Mr. Geddes gave most of the old home place to his sons, he continued to live there the balance of his life, content to grow old on the place which had been his home for so many years; and there he died on July 9, 1926.

ANSON STILES BLAKE.—Born in San Francisco on August 6, 1870, Anson Stiles Blake is the son of a Forty-niner in California. His father, Charles Thompson Blake, became a very prominent factor in the early development of the Northwest. The public schools of San Francisco furnished the early education of our subject, which he supplemented with a course at the University of California at Berkeley, graduating therefrom in 1891 with the A. B. degree. Upon leaving college he first worked as secretary of the Bay Rock Company on Sheep Island for two years, and then one year was spent in the mercantile trade in his native city. In 1894 he joined his father in the Oakland Paving Company in Oakland, continuing with that concern until 1913, when he sold out the interest. In 1904 the Blake & Bilger Company had been organized, and at the time of the earthquake and fire in San Francisco they were prospecting for rock deposits on the hill at Castro Point, Contra Costa County. These were found satisfactory, and thereupon they purchased from John and Luke Fay the entire property fronting the Bay and began operations, getting out rock for various purposes. In 1914 the interests held by Mr. Bilger in the corporation were sold to Blake Brothers Company. Since 1907 there has been quarried some 4,000,000 tons of their manufactured products, and this has been sold within a radius of 100 miles of the Bay cities. In the days of sailing vessels the ship took crushed rock for ballast, and it was carried to various ports of the world. A. S. Blake is president of this concern and has offices in San Francisco at 593 Market Street. E. T. Blake is vice-president and engineer, looking after the operations of the quarry. They employ some seventy men the year round and furnish a superior product to the trade. Both brothers erected modern and commodious homes in Contra Costa County in Kensington precinct, on the hill overlooking the Bay of San Francisco and the cities fronting the Bay.

Mr. Blake is in reality a pioneer of this section of the county, having been interested with George Schmidt, in 1897, in the purchase of the Ann Galvin property on the hills and on the flats. They paid for the first-mentioned the sum of $17 per acre, which included $7 court fees in settling the grant; and this they subdivided and sold at $80 per acre. The flat land they bought for $65 per acre, divided it into fifty-foot lots, and sold them for $50 per lot.

Mr. Blake is much interested in the gathering and preserving of California historical data, and is a member and a director of the California Historical Society. Blake Brothers Company is a member of the Richmond Chamber of Commerce.

In 1894 Anson S. Blake was united in marriage with Anita Day Symmes, born in San Francisco the daughter of Frank J. Symmes, a navy

officer, and granddaughter of Thomas Day, a pioneer of the Golden
State. They occupy their home in Kensington precinct, which Mr. Blake
erected in 1922. As a man and citizen, Mr. Blake is held in the highest esteem by all who know him, and is always ready to do his full share
towards assisting any enterprise for further developing his State.

WILLIAM F. RUST.—The actual founder and first citizen of
what is now the city of El Cerrito, is William F. Rust, better known
to the older generation in this locality as "Uncle Billy" Rust, now living
retired and enjoying a well-earned competency. He was born in Hanover, Germany, on November 27, 1857, and attended the schools in
his native land until he was sixteen, when he began an apprenticeship as
a blacksmith in Hanover. After serving the required number of years
he became a journeyman and in 1877 came to America, landing in Chicago, where he remained a little over a year. During this time he became
familiar with American methods and with enough of the language so
that he had no trouble in making himself understood and understanding
others. After visiting a sister who lived in Kansas City, Mo., where
she was one of the very early pioneers, he went to Cheyenne, where he
was employed by the U. S. Government as a blacksmith, at Camp Carling.
When the soldiers were ordered to Arizona at the time of the Apache
uprising, he was regularly enlisted in the service and remained with the
command for two years, when he was discharged.

In 1883 Mr. Rust came to California, stopping in San Pablo, then a
town boasting of a dozen saloons and about an equal number of houses.
It was a regular stopping place between Oakland, Point Isabella and
Martinez and was a lively place. He was engaged at his trade, and
while there became acquainted with Henry V. Alvarado, now superior
judge of Contra Costa County. In 1888 he made a trip to Europe to
visit his relatives, and when he came back he decided he would look for
a location and engage in business for himself. Looking about for a suitable location, he concluded that if he could get a site for a shop
he would locate on San Pablo Avenue, near the Contra Costa line. Mr.
Castro, the pioneer of this section, owned a great deal of land, which was
leased to tenants for crop rent, and from one of these, Henry Albertsen,
he leased a plot of ground for $20 per year. After he had built his
shop, hauling the lumber from Berkeley, he was called upon by Mr.
Castro, who made no objection to his shop but considered that inasmuch
as he owned the land he ought to have some rent for it, not knowing
that Mr. Rust had already bargained with Mr. Albertsen. He readily
agreed with Mr. Castro, and they decided that $5 per year would be
ample compensation. As this was a likely farming country, his trade
grew gradually, much of it being drawn from among his friends in the
San Pablo district, and he decided that he would engage in the implement business. In 1902 he made a trip back to Germany, taking his
family; and in 1903, after his return, he erected a store building, having

in the meantime been able to buy the land upon which his shop and house were built, and secured a clear title to 200 feet on the avenue. He then built another building, which was leased to a butcher, rented his shop and gave his attention to the hardware and implement trade. In 1909 it was deemed advisable to establish a post office, as the population had grown to such numbers that mail facilities were unhandy for the people. The post office was located in his store, and he was the postmaster at what was then called Rust, after him. Three years later he resigned the office and in 1914 sold the hardware business and retired; but after four years he again took over the hardware store and ran it for two more years, until in 1919, since which time he has been looking after his property interests and living retired. When the City of El Cerrito was incorporated in 1917, the new post office was changed to that name and was moved across the street, the old site and Mr. Rust's property being in the Annex, now a part of El Cerrito.

In the pioneer days the settlers were always extended credit by Mr. Rust, material for homes such as came from a hardware store being supplied to them and every assistance extended that was possible, to help along the growth of the community. His material for his shop and for his hardware store was all hauled from Berkeley, Oakland and the landing by his old white horse, which became a well-known sight on the avenue before automobiles became the fashion. To help out the farmers who had broken some piece of machinery, his ringing anvil could be heard far into the night and from a very early hour after midnight, in order to have the parts mended and not inconvenience the farmers. He remembers when the first automobile was driven to his place by a hardware salesman, who often sold direct to the ranchers such machinery as Mr. Rust did not carry. The first trip to a certain rancher met with disappointment, for the salesman was driven off the place because he drove a car. The farmer raised hay, and the auto did not consume that commodity!

Mr. Rust was married in 1886 to Lina Wagner, also born in Hanover, and two children blessed this union. William G., now a plumber in Portland, Ore., is married and has a son, Robert. Herman, an electrician in El Cerrito, is married and has two children, Serena and William. On June 13, 1914, Mrs. Lina Rust passed away at the age of fifty-six years, mourned by a wide circle of friends. On April 24, 1918, Mr. Rust was again married, Minna Voges becoming his wife. She was born in Germany, but came to America in 1902, and after spending four years in Indianapolis came to this State. Her mother passed away in March, 1926. Mr. Rust and his wife plan to take a trip to Europe in May, 1926, to visit friends. Fraternally, Mr. Rust is a member of the Sons of Hermann, in which order he is a Past Grand Master. When the final pages of history for Contra Costa County are written, there will be a page reserved for Uncle Billy Rust, in memory of the good he has done his fellow citizens in this end of the county.

MRS. ANNE BEIER.—Mrs. Anne Beier, widow of the late Soren A. Beier, and for thirty-six years a resident of the Pleasant Hill district of Contra Costa County, is a native of Sonderjylland, Denmark, and a daughter of Christen Peter and Anna Katrina (Skovdal) Toft. She was reared in Denmark and brought up in the Lutheran Church there, and when twenty-one years of age came to San Francisco, in June, 1876. There she was married to Soren A. Beier on August 25, 1883, the ceremony being performed by the Reverend Mr. Gronsberg.

Soren A. Beier was also a native of Sonderjylland, Denmark, born on February 19, 1849, and reared in his native land. Mr. and Mrs. Beier resided in Oakland for seven years following their marriage, both being employed by a prominent millionaire family of that city. On November 20, 1890, they came to Contra Costa County and invested their savings in a home ranch of fifty-four and one-half acres, which together they improved and planted, converting a wilderness into a productive ranch and making a cozy home for themselves. Theirs was a most happy wedded life, and after the death of Mr. Beier, on October 24, 1914, Mrs. Beier continued to make her home on the place; but in 1924 she sold the ranch to a nephew, Alfred Toft, who made a visit to Denmark that year. Mrs. Beier's many excellent qualities of mind and heart have won the respect of the entire community.

MRS. MARY FRAZER.—One of the best-loved and most highly honored pioneer women of Contra Costa County is Mrs. Mary Frazer, widow of the late George M. Frazer, a descendant of William Beverley Frazer, one of the earliest settlers in Contra Costa County and a well-known rancher and stock man. George M. Frazer, after a lifetime of great usefulness and activity, passed away at his ranch at Glen Frazer on June 20, 1923. He was the oldest in a family of ten children born to William Beverley and Delilah (Cook) Frazer, both of whom crossed the plains with ox-teams in the early forties. They lived for a time in Oregon, where they were married, and in 1859 came to Contra Costa County and in time became extensive ranchers and landowners. Here they reared their family of nine children.

As the oldest in the family, George M. was brought up to work on the home ranch and shared its responsibilities from youth. He was born near Turner, Marion County, Ore., on June 21, 1848, and came to Martinez with his parents in 1859, and the large ranch holdings of his father, about one-half section of land, purchased shortly after their arrival, afforded him ample opportunity to learn the rudiments of ranch work and also how to overcome the obstacles placed in the way of ranching in those pioneer days, when only the sturdy survived. He continued as his father's right-hand man until his marriage, at Danville, September 4, 1874, to Mary Nicholson, a native of that place, her birth occurring on August 13, 1855. As a bride she came to the Frazer place, one mile east of Martinez, and there her husband became the owner of several hundred acres of land, built his ranch home, and reared his children. The young pioneer couple prospered as farmers and stock raisers. Mr. Frazer raised blooded Durham cattle and registered hogs, often exhibiting his stock at the Contra Costa County fairs, where he was usually awarded first premiums for the excellence of his stock. They were heart and soul in the development of the county, especially in the matter of educational and moral uplift, good roads, and the general advancement of the district. Mr. Frazer was one of the prime movers in making possible the building of the Santa Fe Railway through Contra Costa County, donating the right of way through his land, and also donating twelve acres of land for a depot and station purposes, the station being named Glen Frazer, in his honor. As they prospered, Mr. Frazer had bought land about three miles west of Martinez, in Franklin Canyon, which is now the Frazer home place and is developed into a splendid ranch comprising 700 acres, situated near Glen Frazer station, and one of the show places of the county and there Mrs. Mary Frazer makes her home. The 320-acre ranch upon which Mr. and Mrs. George M. Frazer originally located near Martinez was sold and in 1914 became the property of the Shell Oil Company and is now the site of their great refinery.

Mary Nicholson Frazer was one of a large family of children. Her father, John Nicholson, was born in Delaware, and came to California in 1853, crossing the plains in a train of covered wagons from near Quincy, Ill. He settled at what is now Danville, Contra Costa County; the old Spanish settlement of Pacheco was then the nearest town, riverboats being then able to reach that point. John Nicholson married Frances Fields, born in Illinois of southern extraction; both the Nicholson and Fields families were of English ancestry. The mother died in Danville, at the age of eighty-three, after which the husband and father came to live with his daughter, Mrs. Frazer, in Franklin Canyon. Ten children were born to this pioneer couple: Henry, a rancher in Monterey County, died at the age of seventy-nine; George, a rancher near Danville, passed away at the age of forty-eight; Isabella Frances, widow of Theodore T. Ramsay, resides in San Jose; John William, died at the age of forty-two; Mary D., of this review; Martha Ann, married Charles Nelson and lived in Oakland until her death in 1925; Golder Andrew, died when reaching young manhood; Joseph, died in infancy; Adena, widow of Frank Wedgewood, resides in Oakland; and an infant, died unnamed. John and Frances (Fields) Nicholson were among the honored pioneers of the Danville section of this county and their lives were of worth to the community where they aided in building for posterity.

Mr. and Mrs. Frazer became the parents of six children who grew to maturity. Marion died at the age of twenty-four years. Charles B. is a rancher on the home place, part of which he owns; he married Mabel Coats and they have four children: James, George W., Clarence, and

Luella, Mrs. Carbean, who has two children, Betty and George Walter. Laura married, for her first husband, Frank Wolcott, by whom she had three children: Oliver Frank; Marian, who married Harry Johnson, a dentist in San Francisco, and has a son Francis and a daughter Betty; and Ruth, now Mrs. Elvin Nicholson and the mother of two children, Robert and Patricia. Frank Wolcott died and his widow married an older brother of his, Willard M. Wolcott, and they now have two children, Sarah Jane and Georgia. Hugh L., a graduate of the San Jose State Normal School, is a surveyor in the employ of the Pacific Gas and Electric Company; he married Esther Dyer and they have a home in Vallejo. Alexander McG. married Olive Julian, of Franklin Canyon, and they have two children, Julian and Ralph, and live on part of the home ranch, part of which he owns. Ethel is the widow of Barney Swearingen and makes her home in Richmond. Mrs. Frazer makes her home on the old home ranch in Franklin Canyon, and is surrounded by her children and grandchildren and a host of devoted friends.

ELISHA C. HARLAN.—In all sections of the world the pioneer is highly honored, especially in California, where the present generation realizes that the marvelous development that has characterized the early decades of the twentieth century is due to the determination of those hardy and fearless pioneers who with heroic fortitude faced the hardships of an overland journey and the greater hardships connected with the transforming of an unknown and sparsely settled region into one of the greatest commonwealths in the United States of America. The subject of this sketch, Elisha C. Harlan, is a worthy son of an honored pioneer of California, and is himself a native son, having been born in San Francisco, June 9, 1850, a son of Joel and Minerva (Fowler) Harlan.

Joel Harlan was born in Wayne County, Ill., on September 27, 1828. He was a son of George Harlan, who was born on January 1, 1802, in Lincoln County, Ky., and who married Elizabeth Duncan in 1823. In 1846 George Harlan outfitted for the trip across the plains, having covered wagons drawn by oxen. He brought his wife and son Joel with him, and was accompanied by William and Henry Fowler. The two last named had come to this State in 1843 and Henry worked on the General Vallejo home in Vallejo. They soon returned to their home, only to decide to come again to California with the Harlan train. George Harlan's train was the very first train to cross the great desert south of Salt Lake. The following were the children of George Harlan: Rebecca, Mrs. Ira Van Gorden, died in 1847; Mary, Mrs. Henry C. Smith, died in 1923; Joel; Nancy, Mrs. L. B. Huff; Elisha, deceased; Jacob, died in 1848 in Santa Clara. Elizabeth Duncan Harlan died in Santa Clara County in 1846. The second wife of George Harlan was Catherine (Fowler) Hargrave. Their children were Sarah Ann, Mrs. J. H. Farley; and George. George Harlan, the father, died on July 8, 1850, at Mission San Jose.

Joel Harlan and other members of the family were stopping at Mission San Jose prior to locating in San Francisco in 1846. He conducted a livery stable and ran a dairy, milk being delivered on horseback in those days. San Francisco had only a little over 250 population at that time. When gold was discovered he sold his livery business and other interests, went to Coloma, and opened up a general store, which he operated for a year. He then moved to San Lorenzo, bought a place and remained a short time, and then bought a ranch on the county line between Alameda and Contra Costa County in 1852. Some time later he exchanged that ranch for 1040 acres located where Elisha C. Harlan, our subject, now lives, in the San Ramon Valley. To this he added until he owned 1756 acres. This land has never been divided among the heirs of Joel Harlan.

Joel Harlan was married in 1848 to Minerva Jane Fowler, at Sonoma, Cal., the ceremony being performed by ex-Governor Boggs, of Mississippi. He and his wife had the following children: Elisha C., of this review; Laura M., deceased; Mary, Mrs. William Llewellyn, deceased; Helena, Mrs. Fred Osborne, of Oakland; Horace, deceased; Henry, deceased; Fred, of Pittsburg; and Addie, Mrs. Fred A. Stolp, of Piedmont.

Elisha Harlan attended school at Oakland and supplemented his studies with a course in Heald's Business College on Post Street. At one time, also, he attended a military school for one and one-half years. After leaving the business college he returned to the home ranch and helped with the managing of the place until his father's death. After the death of his father he purchased a ranch for himself from the heirs of Major Russell, and here he made his home for twenty-five years, and also operated the old home place. At the request of his mother he finally moved back to the old home ranch, where he now resides. He is engaged in cattle-raising, and even now, though seventy-six years old, rides his horse every day to superintend the 1200 acres of the Harlan Ranch.

On November 14, 1872, Elisha C. Harlan was united in marriage with Elmina Plamondon, the daughter and only child of Euzebe and Eleanor (Fillbrook) Plamondon, the former of French descent, the latter from Canada. She was reared and educated in Portland, Ore., and at Notre Dame in San Jose, where she specialized in music, finally graduating in Salem, Ore., under her old teacher. Mr. and Mrs. Harlan were blessed with two children: Mabel P. and Joel A. Mabel P. married Frank Davidson and now resides in Oakland. She has one son, Harlan W., a graduate of Oakland High School and the University of California. He is married and has a son, Harlan W., Jr. Joel A. is deceased. Mr. Harlan is a lover of life in the great out-of-doors and is especially fond of deer-hunting and fishing. He has inherited from his father and grandfather a fondness for cattle-raising, and it can be said to his credit that he maintains the splendid record of the Harlans for good cattle. Fraternally he was a member of Danville Parlor, N. S. G. W., and also

of the Grange. He has manifested his interest in educational matters
by serving as a school trustee of his district. Possessing a cheerful and
optimistic spirit, Mr. Harlan has a wide circle of warm friends and is
highly esteemed in the community where he has resided for so many years.

HENRY ALBERTSEN.—One of the oldest settlers in El Cerrito
is Henry Albertsen, now retired from all activity and living in the enjoyment of a well-earned competency and fairly good health. He was born in
Schleswig-Holstein, Germany, then a part of Denmark, on September 21,
1843, grew to manhood there and attended the schools of his neighborhood. During the war between Denmark and Austria he served as a teamster; he had a brother who also saw service in the same struggle and after
the war both came to America. They stopped in Davenport, Iowa, for
three years and in 1867 arrived in California.

Soon after landing in California our subject went to San Pablo and
found work on ranches, continuing till 1869, when with a partner he began baling hay on the various ranches from Golden Gate to Pinole and
met with very good success; one season was spent in the vicinity of Antioch. Mr. Albertsen leased land from the Castro family and raised hay
on it. He continued baling hay for twenty-eight years and made and
saved considerable money. At that early day the ferry boat plying between Oakland and San Francisco made only four trips daily, and so
few were the buildings that Oakland was plainly seen from this section
with the naked eye. The sidewalks were made of wood and the streets
were not paved, only sandy stretches of thoroughfare composed the principal streets of that city. Wild ducks, rabbits and other game were in
abundance, no one taking the trouble to shoot them for use.

Some eighteen years ago Mr. Alberstén bought a lot and erected a
cottage in what is now El Cerrito and here he is still living. He knew
almost every person in this section of the country at that time, now he is
practically a stranger, as almost all of the pioneers are dead. He has always been favorable to all methods that spelled progress for this county
and assisted so far as he has been able.

PAUL DE MARTINI.—A splendid type of the substantial Italian-
American citizenry of Contra Costa County is found in Paul de Martini
the subject of this sketch. As a county official and as an enterprising
individual Mr. de Martini has consistently labored to be of service to
the country of his adoption. He was born in the historic city of Genoa,
Italy, September 15, 1844, the son of Andrew and Catherine de Martini.
In 1861, at the age of seventeen, Mr. de Martini embarked from the
same city from which Columbus had once set out on a memorable voyage
and, like the famous navigator, he too found a new land of opportunity.
He had been lured by the tales of gold to be found in California and he
first engaged in placer mining in Calaveras County. After four strenuous
years at that work, in 1865 he came to Contra Costa County, settling

in Concord. He first engaged in market gardening on the Galindo tract. From there he moved to Nortonville, where for more than two years he conducted a boarding house. He then came to Clayton, which has since been his home. He bought land from Joel Clayton and planted a vineyard of wine grapes and until the time of the passage of the Volstead act Mr. de Martini conducted a winery and engaged in the manufacture of high-grade wines. Now that this has become one of the obsolete occupations his lands are planted to almonds, from which he annually secures fine crops.

Mr. de Martini has been honored by his fellows with the office of county supervisor for two terms serving from 1896 to 1900 and from 1900 to 1904. In politics he is a Democrat and takes a keen interest in the political happenings of the day. Despite his advanced years he is still active and vigorous mentally and physically. He was married in Concord, January 10, 1869, to Ansonia Maria Bartano, also a native of Italy who came to this country when one year old. Mrs. de Martini died in 1881. Four children resulted from this union: Walter, a successful attorney of San Francisco, is married and the father of two children; Henry is a prosperous farmer and stockman; Paul, a court interpreter, is married and the father of two daughters; Lillian Monia died at the age of twenty-four, unmarried.

THOMAS EDWARDS.—The two survivors of the Edwards family, that was the first to settle in what is now the town of Crockett, are Thomas and David, two brothers, who are still making Crockett their home and the scene of their activities. The family consisted of six boys and one girl. Thomas was born at Knight's Ferry on August 19, 1851, and was educated in the schools of the State and was associated with his father in the settlement of Crockett. This has been his home since boyhood and he has been interested in every phase of its growth and progress. The old Edwards home is built on an Indian mound fronting the bay and this was an ideal location for a home. This mound has yielded many relics and skeletons of the Indians of the country surrounding. "They have gone, they have vanished and cold is their clay; For the steel of the white man has swept them away."

Thomas Edwards was married in Crockett on April 20, 1892, to Annie Ashby, and they have had the following children: Edith E., now Mrs. A. G. Dyer of Crockett and the mother of a daughter, Violet; Stanley P., who married Lucy Chapin and has a daughter, Patricia; Thomas A., employed in the sugar refinery; Arnold B., valuation engineer at the C. & H.; and Grace Crockett, attending the State Teachers' College in San Jose.

Mr. Edwards was graduated from the grammar school in Martinez in 1867, and from the Pacific Business College in San Francisco in 1873. He has lived in Crockett all his adult life. He was one of the organizers of the Congregational Church in 1884, and served as postmaster from 1905 to 1915, during which time the parcel post and Postal Savings Bank

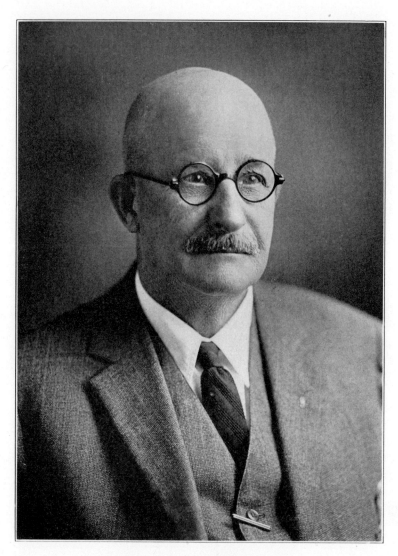

H. W. Bott

went into effect. He is a member of Crockett Lodge No. 329, I. O. O. F., and a member and Past Master of Carquinez Lodge No. 337, F. & A. M. For twenty-five years he has represented the American Railways Express Company, and for twenty years has handled the news agency for the San Francisco papers. He is highly respected by all who know him, and has had the best interests of Crockett at heart at all times.

HENRY W. BOTT.—A descendant of parents who were among the early settlers in the State, Henry W. Bott is one of the most highly respected citizens of Concord, Contra Costa County, where he has repeatedly served as chairman of the city board of trustees. Born in Tassajara Valley, Contra Costa County, on September 18, 1855, he is the son of George and Mary (Alcorn) Bott, the former a native of Germany, while the latter was born in St. Louis, Mo., and crossed the plains to California in 1849. The father left St. Louis, Mo., in 1849, lured by the gold discovery in California, and crossed the plains with a train of covered wagons drawn by ox-teams, encountering many hardships and dangers, for their train was attacked by the Indians at several places on the long overland journey. Arriving in Sacramento in the spring of 1850, George Bott first went to the mines in Calaveras County, and later to Nevada County. Four children were born to him and his good wife: Mrs. Mary Harmon, residing at Pine City, Whitman County, Wash.; Emma, the wife of Chief of Police Cook, in San Luis Obispo; Henry W., of this review; and Francis, deceased at six years of age. By a former marriage the father had one child, George Bott, Jr., now the janitor of the courthouse at Martinez. The mother died in 1861, when Henry was only six years old. The father reached the advanced age of ninety-eight years, and for many years before his death made his home with Mr. Bott at Concord.

After the mother's death the children were scattered, and Henry W. Bott started out to make his own living while yet a boy. He worked on ranches at Walnut Creek, and in the Pacheco and Alamo Valleys. In 1874 he was working with a threshing machine, and about this time he decided to learn the blacksmith's trade. Starting on May 24, 1874, to work for the pioneer blacksmith, William Bowman, on the same corner where the blacksmith shop now stands, he continued to work for Mr. Bowman for nine years and three months, and then went to Santa Cruz, where he worked at his trade for one year. Returning to Concord, he bought out his former employer and took for a partner Thomas G. Smith; and for the past forty-five years, under the firm name of Bott & Smith, they have conducted the leading blacksmith shop in Concord and the surrounding country. Both master blacksmiths and wagonmakers, their shop is well equipped with machinery for that work, and they have a long and honorable record for efficient service and square dealing.

Mr. Bott has been twice married. His first wife was Miss Cynthia Harmon of Pacheco, who became the mother of two boys, both of whom died with the "flu." His second marriage united him with Miss Nellie Welch, and their union has been blessed with two daughters: Madeline, widow of Robert Skinner, a lieutenant in the Marines during the World War who died in November, 1925, leaving a son, Robert Skinner, Jr., now with Mr. and Mrs. Bott; and Winnetta, now Mrs. William Davis, of San Francisco.

Always deeply interested in civic affairs, Mr. Bott took an active part in the incorporation of the city of Concord. He was elected to its first board of trustees, has been repeatedly reelected, serving for many years as chairman, and is still a member of the board. He stands for the best interests of the people and is justly popular, being able and honest and fair. During the World War Mr. Bott served on all the Liberty Bond drives and helped Concord go over the top in each drive. A consistent Democrat, he is opposed to all "sumptuary legislation." He is a member of the Odd Fellows Lodge at Concord, has been through all the chairs, and is a Past Grand of the order.

HANS A. MILLER.—None of the men now living in and around Crockett, in the western part of Contra Costa County, have a better conception of the growth of the industries hereabouts than has H. A. Miller, now living retired in the enjoyment of a competence well and honorably earned. A native of Denmark, he was born on December 12, 1871, the son of Jens Andrew and Petra (Holm) Miller, both born, reared, married and died in their native land of Denmark, where Jens Miller followed the building business. Hans A. attended the grammar and high schools of his native country up to the age of seventeen, also taking a technical course in the building trade. He had a strong desire to visit America and in 1889 he and a group of his friends were discussing the possibilities of America for young and energetic men and some of the boys decided they would try their luck in that foreign land. Hans A. wanted to go but on account of his youth his father would not give his consent when the matter was talked over with him. At this point a sister's persuasion won the day and after a promise to his father that after a period of five years he would return to his home, he embarked to make his own way in the world, arriving in New York on Easter Sunday in 1889. The place of his destination was San Francisco, Cal., where he arrived on June 9, of the same year.

Among the acquaintances here were Otto Johnson, with whom Mr. Miller roomed and who conducted a restaurant in San Francisco; he soon secured his young friend a job as a carpenter. Then there was M. A. Therkelsen, who turned out to be a son of the woman who did washing for Mr. Miller's mother back in Denmark. He had been a cook on a British ship but had taken up the life of a landsman upon arriving in California. Johnson and Therkelsen later undertook to raise chickens out on the Mission Road, leasing four acres of land for fifteen dollars for the purpose. Owing to disease getting among the fowls their venture was a failure and Therkelsen secured a job in the Selby smelter at Selby. This was during the winter of 1889-1890, the worst winter ever seen in this part of California. During all these changes among his friends Mr. Miller worked as a carpenter in San Francisco, where he later met Louis Miller, a maker of musical instruments and a musician of note. The carpenter's trade did not suit young Miller very well and Therkelsen told him to come to Selby and try for a job in the smelter, which he did when he was about eighteen years old. His qualifications as a leader of men and his ability to handle the job given him with dispatch, soon were rewarded and he was promoted to be foreman of fifty men and he continued in this position until 1909, when he was advanced to be the general foreman of the entire plant and this position he held, to the entire satisfaction of his employers and the men under him, until 1923, when he resigned to look after his own affairs. During the many years Mr. Miller was connected with the smelter he witnessed many changes in the methods of handling the materials and products of the plant, also the coming and going of thousands of men.

H. A. Miller was united in marriage on June 24, 1896, with Miss Alice Muth, born at San Pablo, Cal., the daughter of pioneer parents. Two children have blessed this union: Mrs. Ruth B. McGrath, living with her husband in Crockett Heights; and Clarence Alfred, who married Miss Ingrid Hartman, by whom he has one child, Constance Annette. Mr. Miller owns his own home in Valona and other property in this community, thereby showing his faith in the future of Crockett, where he has been prominent in the community's growth and development. He has served as a school trustee; is a Republican and has been selected as standard bearer many times. He a charter member of Selby Lodge Knights of Pythias, the oldest Knights of Pythias lodge in the county; and also belongs to the Odd Fellows. He was reared in the Lutheran faith. His motto is "Do unto others as you would have them do unto you."

FRED M. HOLWAY.—Having spent nearly half a century of his life at Byron, Cal., perhaps there is no other resident of the vicinity more familiar with the resources of eastern Contra Costa County, nor one who has witnessed more of the transformation wrought by present day civilization than Fred M. Holway. He is the oldest living business man at Byron, having continuously engaged in some business since 1883. At present he is proprietor of a pool hall and soft drink parlor, and sells fire insurance.

Fred M. Holway was born in Somersetshire, England, May 12, 1856, emigrated to Ameria when fifteen years of age, accompanied by his cousin Annie Pierce, now Mrs. Meinken. After arriving in New York City he continued his journey westward and located for a while in Chicago, where he attended school for a short time, then he visited St. Louis, but soon returned to Chicago, where he lived until the latter part of 1874, when he moved to Denver. In 1875 Mr. Holway arrived in San Francisco, and the year 1878 found him located at Antioch, Cal. Later in the same

year he came to what was then known as the Point of Timber district of
Contra Costa County, the stopping point of the stages between Banta and
Antioch. When the first railway was built through this place the station
was given the name Byron, and the postoffice was also located there. The
first hotel business was conducted by a Mr. Wilkening, but that building
was destroyed by fire in 1884. In 1885 Mr. Holway built the second
hotel which bore the name of Byron Hotel; this was destroyed by fire in
1917 and was never rebuilt.

On May 12, 1883, Fred M. Holway married Miss Emma Luhrsen, a
daughter of pioneer settlers near Tracy. They were the parents of ten
children, nine of whom are living; Eva, Percy M., Raymond, Herman,
Viola, Geraldine, Irene, Martha and Elvira. Aurora died when she was
twenty-three months old. Mrs. Holway died in 1912. Mr. Holway is
a charter member and Past Grand of Byron Lodge No. 335, I. O. O. F.,
Byron, and is a member of the Rebekahs. His jovial disposition and sterling character have won for him a host of warm personal friends and it
is safe to say no one in Byron is more highly esteemed than Fred M.
Holway.

MISS LOUISA A. SCHOTT.—Miss Louisa A. Schott is a native of
Antioch and the daughter of the late John and Adelia Barrett (Kimball)
Schott. Her grandfather, George W. Kimball, organized a company of
men who agreed to purchase shares at $101 each to build and equip a ship
to carry passengers and their belongings from Maine to California. These
passengers were the families of the shareholders in the vessel and they
were coming to California to establish homes in a new country. Even in
the days of '49 there were boosters for California, as is evident from a
memorandum of their agreement drawn up in 1849 from which we quote:
"We, the undersigned, are desirous of engaging in an enterprise on the
golden shores of California, the paradise of America, where summer
reigns perpetually, while the fertile soil is yielding its increase abundantly,
fruits growing spontaneously, fishes sporting most plentifully, and where
wild game is most prolific, on the shores of the Pacific. Our object is to
settle a township, or effect a permanent settlement on the Coast of California, at some central point, in some capacious harbor, where the salu-
brity of the climate, the fertility of the soil, mill privileges, timber for
ship building and other purposes, conveniences for the fisheries, for coasting, and other natural advantages, shall warrant a healthy and rapid
settlement." The reasons given for leaving their Eastern homes were:
"1st, the land has nearly all passed from the government into the hands
of speculators, who exact more for the soil than we are able to pay; 2nd,
the lumber is nearly all gone and the fishing business is uncertain; 3rd, the
land fails to yield its usual increase, the potato and some other crops being almost an entire failure; 4th, the summers are so short, and the winters so long, that we have to become the humble servants of our cattle
about eight months in the year; 5th, the despotism of fashion is so op-

pressive, and its exactions so insupportable, that like our Puritan Fathers, in order to preserve our integrity, we flee into the wilds of the far distant West; 6th, at this trying moment, Providence has opened to us a door of mercy and hope, and we gladly accept the proffered favor; 7th, we go because a continual summer, a salubrious climate, a fertile soil, and other natural advantages, open to us an unbounded field for industry and enterprise in that region." The ship was named the California Packet and was lying at Central Wharf, Boston, February 4, 1850. The circular from which the above was copied contains some interesting data of the intentions of the shareholders, and has been preserved by Miss Schott. George W. Kimball came to California in the days of gold and settled at the place now known as Antioch. He was of English ancestry, and of that sturdy type who are ever looking for new worlds to conquer. He had French, Irish, Welsh and even Greek blood in his veins, through the intermarriages of past generations.

Miss Schott's mother, Adelia Barrett Kimball, was the first public school teacher in Antioch when only twelve years of age. She was a woman of marked ability, a correspondent for various newspapers and magazines, and was well versed in the early history of Antioch, where she had a great influence for good. She lived to reach the age of seventy-seven years. John Schott was born in Pennsylvania, was a tailor by trade, and after serving in the Mexican War came out to California. He died at Antioch at the age of fifty-six from the rigors of army life. Miss Schott has two brothers living: George L., a carpenter by trade, living in Antioch; and Franklin T., an employe of the Oregon Short Line Railroad, living in Salt Lake City.

Miss Schott was reared and educated in Antioch. She is a musician, and for many years was organist in the Congregational Church. She is an Adventist in religious belief and takes an active interest in the activities of this denomination. The material in the historical department of this book relating to Antioch tells more of the family history and need not be repeated here. Miss Schott resides in the old home place at No. 415 Third Street, and is highly respected by all who know her.

MRS. AQUILINA VISCUSO.—The oldest living resident of Pittsburg, Cal., is said to be Mrs. Aquilina Viscuso, the widow of the late G. Viscuso, who came to California about fifty years ago and was one of the pioneers of New York Landing, afterwards called Black Diamond, and now Pittsburg. G. Viscuso was a pioneer in the fish business at Pittsburg. He was a native of Catania, Italy, where he was born on June 24, 1851, and his death occurred in Pittsburg, Cal., in 1918.

Mrs. G. Viscuso in maidenhood was Miss Aquilina Murzi, a native of Tuscany, Italy, where she was born on March 28, 1860. On September 1, 1882, when she was twenty-two years of age, Miss Murzi arrived in Pittsburg. On November 20, 1882, a little more than two months after her arrival, she was united in marriage with G. Viscuso.

They built the house where she now resides, and she has lived in it continuously for forty-four years. This happy union was blessed with nine children, six of whom are still living, three having died with the flu. The children in order of birth are: Sarah, wife of Dr. Gregory, of San Francisco; Theresa, wife of Casper T. Cautiello, the hardware merchant of Pittsburg; Joseph, who died in 1921; Mary, the wife of Harry H. Summer, who is in the lumber business at Pittsburg; Bert, a resident of San Francisco; Attilio, who married Erechetta Valoni of Pittsburg; John, who passed away in 1922; Susie who died in 1921; and Emma, the youngest. The four sons saw service during the World War. The Viscuso family are highly esteemed in the community and are consistent members of the Catholic Church at Pittsburg.

During her long residence of forty-four years in Contra Costa County, Mrs. Viscuso has witnessed marvelous changes both in the city of Pittsburg and in the county. Those who have come more recently to California to enjoy the highly improved conditions materially, socially and commercially that exist today, do not always realize what a great debt they owe to the pioneers who faced the hardships of existence when only the strong and brave could remain and by their fortitude helped to lay the foundation for the great commonwealth on the Pacific.

BETHEL S. COATS.—The son of an old California pioneer and himself a pioneer by birth, Bethel S. Coats is a fine representative both of the true Californian and of the rancher in the Tassajara section of Contra Costa County, where he was born on April 16, 1868. His father was Felix Grundy Coats, who was born in Missouri, there grew to manhood, and crossed the plains with ox-teams in 1849 with his father, Wilson Coats. Grandfather Wilson Coats was born in Smith County, Tenn., on August 10, 1802, and when fifteen went to Callaway County, Mo. On May 1, 1849, with his son and some others, he came across the plains to California, arriving on September 7, that same year. They mined in Placer and Nevada Counties till 1851. Wilson Coats went back to Missouri, via Panama, and joined his family; and they came back to California and settled in Contra Costa County, where he bought 160 acres of land. His was the only family in the Tassajara Valley for some time. His wife, whom he married on December 25, 1823, was in maidenhood Miss Mary Philipp; she was born in Tennessee, and died in California on November 27, 1875. Wilson Coats died aged eighty-four years. There were ten children in the Coats family. The great-grandfather was Rev. William Coats; he was born in Tennessee, was a Baptist preacher, and moved from Tennessee to Missouri in 1817. He died at the age of seventy years. Coats Prairie in Missouri was named for the Coats family, as they owned almost all the land in it.

Felix Grundy Coats was born in Callaway County, Mo., on August 9, 1828, grew to manhood there, and came with his father to California in 1849. He mined till the fall of 1851 and then gave up mining to come to the Tassajara Valley, Contra Costa County, to engage in ranching. He took up 160 acres of land and added a school claim and later purchased 640 acres where Bethel S. Coats now lives. He added to his holdings until he owned about 1200 acres. This he devoted to stock and grain and during his many years of actual work made a decided success. He married Leona Doggett, who was born in Arkansas and rode horseback from her native State to Oregon when she was a girl of eleven, in 1852. They were married on February 23, 1860, at Tassajara, she having come south from Oregon with her people in 1859 and settled about one mile from the present Coats ranch. The house built in 1855 by grandfather Wilson Coats was burned, but Bethel S. Coats has the bricks built into a chimney in his own home, which he put up in 1917. Of the family of children born to the Coats family we mention Nolen, now deceased; James, living in San Francisco; Bethel S., of this review; Ella, who married E. Seiler of Stockton; May, the widow of Marion Horton, residing in San Francisco, and Jennie, the wife of Thomas White, also in San Francisco. Felix G. Coats died on June 9, 1916, aged eighty-seven years and ten months. The wife and mother died on December 25, 1893, aged about fifty-two.

Bethel S. Coats attended the Tassajara school and for a short time went to the Livermore College conducted by J. D. Smith. He began his career as a rancher on the old home place and remained there until his children were ready for an advanced school and the family moved to San Jose, where he conducted a store for three years and carried on an orchard for about four. He continued to look after his property in Tassajara, where he has 320 acres. Since returning to the ranch after his stay in San Jose, he has resided here, raising hay, grain and cattle; and he also carries on dairying on a small scale. Mr. Coats is a member of the Woodmen of the World, Neighbors of Woodcraft, and the Grange.

On December 30, 1891, Bethel S. Coats and Miss Phoebe Bowles were united in marriage. She was born in San Luis Obispo County, a daughter of Caleb and Ellen (Patton) Bowles, both natives of Missouri. Caleb Bowles came to California and mined for a time, after which he settled in San Luis Obispo County and engaged in ranching, later moving to Tassajara, where he continued farming. Mr. Bowles was related to the late Senator George Hearst, and Mrs. Bethel S. Coats was named for Mrs. Hearst. Three children have been born of this union: Eunice, Mrs. William Rowe of San Gabriel, and the mother of four children: Phyllis E., Doris E., W. Bethel and Roberta E.; Bernice, a professional nurse in Stanford Hospital in San Francisco; and Doris, Mrs. Victor Morton, who lives near San Jose and is the mother of two children, Victor J. and Marcia B. Mr. Coats is a Presbyterian. The family enjoy motoring, and each year take an extended trip for their vacation. In 1923 Mr. and Mrs. Bethel S. Coats took an automobile trip back East over practically the same route as that covered by his father in six months with ox-teams in 1849. They spent seventeen days on their journey, and had a very enjoyable time.

HARTLEY M. BUSH.—Closely associated with the advancement of the commercial prosperity of Contra Costa County is Hartley M. Bush, who owns and operates the oldest real estate business in Martinez, together with considerable property in Contra Costa County, including valuable city property in Martinez. Well educated, talented and of undoubted business sagacity, he has attained to a place of influence in the community and has established himself in the confidence of his friends and fellow-citizens, who hold him in high regard and favor. He was born at Rochester, N. Y., at the old Bush family home, on April 15, 1868, while his mother was there on a visit to relatives. His father, David Bush, was also born in Rochester, N. Y.; his mother, Ellen (Morgan) Bush, was a native of Ohio.

Grandfather Henry Bush was a native of New York and came to San Francisco in 1851 via the Isthmus of Panama. Soon after his arrival he built the first fire-proof building in San Francisco, which was located on Clay Street; and Bush Street was named after him. Grandfather Bush had a large consignment of fruit trees sent him the following year, consisting of apples, pears, cherries and peaches, and these were planted on what was known as the Bush Homestead in Martinez. This site is now occupied by the de la Salle Institute, and many of the trees that the pioneer Henry Bush planted are still in full bearing.

David Bush, the father of our subject, was sixteen or seventeen years old when he arrived in San Francisco; here he grew up and was educated and became one of the most influential and prosperous business men of the Bay City. He organized the real estate company of David Bush and Son in San Francisco, maintaining a branch office in Martinez. He was one of the promoters of Golden Gate Park and helped develop it. During the panic of 1873 he raised money by popular subscription from the well-to-do citizens in San Francisco and hired men who were out of work, paying them one dollar per day for their labor in the park, continuing until times assumed a more stable aspect. There were four children in the Bush family: Brightie, now Mrs. J. O. Low, who resides in San Francisco; Alice, for years a physician in Oakland, who died in Shanghai, China, while on a world tour in March, 1926; the third child, a son who died in infancy; and Hartley M., the subject of this sketch. The father died in 1914 in San Francisco. He was a member of the Vigilance Committee, and he served as tax collector for San Francisco for eight years. He was a member of the Ohio Society in that city for many years.

Hartley M. Bush grew up in San Francisco and Martinez and attended the public schools at both places, graduating from high school in San Francisco. He entered the University of California, but was unable to graduate as his father needed his help in looking after the extensive properties he owned. He engaged in orcharding on the home place in Martinez and was successful from the start.

In 1890 Mr. Bush was married to Miss Louise M. Frazer, daughter of William and Delilah (Cook) Frazer, another pioneer family of Martinez, who crossed the plains to Oregon in a covered wagon in the forties and later came to California to educate their children. Mr. and Mrs. Bush are the parents of four children: Barbara is the wife of Robert Myers, and they live in San Francisco. David Frazer married Aila Holm and they have two children, Dorothea and Hartley; he is now an attorney at Oakdale. In April, 1917, before he had graduated from the University of California, he enlisted for service in the World War. From the Presidio he was sent to Camp Lewis; he became captain and was honorably discharged at the signing of the Armistice. Beverly F. is a dental student at the Affiliated Colleges in San Francisco. Arlien Louise, who was formerly employed with the Shell Oil Company in Martinez, is now Mrs. Dudley Henry of Long Beach.

Mr. Bush specializes in locating large business concerns. Among many others he located the Shell Company of California refinery at Martinez and the General Chemical Company. Mr. Bush owns the Bush tract on the eastern side of town, one of the finest residence districts in Martinez; his fine residence is located on this tract. Politically, Mr. Bush is a Republican with progressive tendencies, being a great admirer of the late Theodore Roosevelt.

MRS. MARY A. DICKINSON.—Among the prominent women in Contra Costa County is Mrs. Mary A. Dickinson, proprietor of Hotel Melrose at No. 463 Los Medanos Street, Pittsburg. She was born at Somersville, Contra Costa County, a daughter of James and Sarah (Brazil) Hobson. James Hobson was born in England in 1833, and his wife was born in Australia in 1837. He went to Australia and was there married, and with his wife came to California in 1862. They first went to Somersville for a short time, then returned to San Francisco, but in 1863 again came to this county, and in 1869 he bought a ranch of 240 acres near Somersville and raised wheat. For many years Mr. Hobson was in the employ of the old Clay Street Bank, prospecting in various parts of this State for coal, he being an experienced coal miner by trade. He was an honest and upright man, always trying to do a good turn for his friends. There were seven children born to Mr. and Mrs. Hobson: Mrs. C. H. Oders, of Oakland; Mrs. Mary A. Dickinson, of Pittsburg; Mrs. A. F. Portman, of Antioch; James F. and Edward F., both in Antioch; Mrs. Emma Lowery, of Los Angeles; and Charlotte, deceased. By a former marriage Mr. Hobson had two boys: Sampson, of Antioch; and W. J., of Santa Cruz. By her first marriage Mrs. Hobson had a

15

CONTRA COSTA COUNTY

daughter, Mrs. John Watkins, now deceased. After a long and useful life Mr. Hobson died in 1907 at the age of nearly seventy-five; Mrs. Hobson passed away on February 19, 1923, aged eighty-six years, both dying in this county.

Mary A. Hobson was reared on her father's ranch and attended the public schools near by. On September 14, 1886 she was married to James Isaac Dickinson. Mr. Dickinson was born in Newcastle, England, and was an expert miner by occupation. He was superintendent of the Stewartville Mine at the time of their marriage. In 1891 the family went to Antioch and Mr. Dickinson built the Dickinson Hotel and ran it for a time. It is now known as the Arlington Hotel. In 1893 he went back to Somersville and was superintendent of the mine there for a number of years. Two children were born of this union: Charles G., who married Gertrude Sippel, born in San Francisco, the daughter of Henry and Joan Sippel, natives of Canada and Wales, respectively; and Rowena Emma, wife of Dr. Edward Love of Colfax, Cal., and the mother of a daughter, Marilyn Jean. Mr. Dickinson died on December 21, 1923, in Pittsburg. In 1923 the Dickinsons came to this city, and here Mrs. Dickinson embarked in the hotel business, in a building that had been purchased by A. F. Portman; and she is building up a good and substantial business. She shows her public spirit in many ways, and cooperates in all progressive movements.

JOHN LOVE.—California numbers among her native-born citizens many men of excellent business ability who, as farmers, have done their part toward making the State famous for its grain and its live stock; and to this class of citizens belongs John Love, a prominent rancher in the Lone Tree District, Contra Costa County. Mr. Love has the honor of being the oldest white male born in this section of the county. On his present ranch of 160 acres he was born on August 5, 1869, the fifth child in a family of eight born to the honored pioneers, Robert and Elizabeth (McKinnon) Love, both natives of Scotland. Robert Love came to California in a covered wagon in 1852 and tried his luck at mining for gold, but his success was only limited. He then turned his attention to farming, first in Napa County. Then, in 1865, he preempted 160 acres of Government land, which is now occupied by our subject. Robert Love was seventy-three years old when he died and the mother passed away at the age of sixty-seven years, both dying on the old homestead. He served as a school trustee for many years. Fraternally, he was a Mason.

John Love is the only survivor of eight children. He was brought up to work on the home ranch and what schooling he received was obtained in the country schools of his neighborhood. At Napa, in 1920, Mr. Love was married to Miss May McGill, born in St. Joseph, Mo., a daughter of Alexander and Margaret (Schaffel) McGill. Mr. Love is a consistent Republican in politics, and fraternally he is a member of Antioch Lodge No. 161, I. O. O. F., in Antioch.

BYRON L. GRIGSBY.—A well-known business man of Brentwood, and also a rancher in the vicinity of that city, Byron L. Grigsby ably represents the pioneer California family whose name he bears. He was born at Grayson, Cal., on March 2, 1872, and was a son of the late Erasmus D. Grigsby, born in Pike County, Mo., and a farmer there, who married Miss Elmira Miller, a native of Illinois, after having settled in this State. They both came as pioneers in their young and vigorous days and became progressive members of the community where they lived and labored. After he came to California Erasmus D. Grigsby operated a 1000-acre grain ranch. In 1879 the family removed to Contra Costa County and located on leased land, where he farmed successfully and eventually became the owner of 800 acres. He operated a threshing machine during the harvest season in the eastern part of this county. Later he and his good wife left the ranch and retired to Berkeley; and there they both died, the father in 1914, aged seventy-two; and Mrs. Grigsby in 1922, at the age of seventy-three years. They had four children. Laura is the wife of W. W. Collis, a rancher in the Brentwood district. Warren is a miner and lives in Calistoga. Lilly married O. B. Palmer, a wholesale grocer of Oakland. Byron L. is the subject of this review. The family are of English origin.

Byron L. Grigsby grew up on the home ranch near Brentwood and went to the public schools. He learned to drive the thirty-two head of animals on the Holt combined harvester and thresher, and also became an expert sack-sewer and worked both for his father and for others during the harvesting season. He had the usual pioneer experiences of the boys of his age and time. At the Eden Plain School he was a schoolmate of R. R. Veale, sheriff of this county, and had to go four miles to school every day. Later he attended the grammar schools and a business college in Oakland to better fit himself for the career ahead of him. After his father retired from active work, Byron and his brother ran the home place for years. He now owns fifty acres of fine land in Brentwood Precinct No. 1, where he raises fruit and alfalfa. In 1925, with Louis Planchon as a partner, Mr. Grigsby engaged in the hardware and agricultural implement business at Brentwood. They handle the International Harvester Company's line of goods and in 1925 sold thirteen McCormick-Deering 10-20 tractors and two 15-30 tractors to Balfour-Guthrie Company. They carry a full line of agricultural implements, windmills and belting, and are fast building up a good paying business. Mr. Planchon is in charge of the mechanical part of the business and Mr. Grigsby has charge of the sales department. They operate under the name of Planchon & Grigsby.

Mr. Grigsby was married at Red Bluff, in 1905, to Miss Alice Eaton, daughter of George Eaton, owner of a large stock farm in Tehama County. He crossed the plains in 1852 with his parents when a lad of thirteen and near Salt Lake City the Indians drove off and killed all their cattle during a skirmish. Mr. and Mrs. Grigsby have a daughter, Virginia, now aged twelve years. Mr. Grigsby is president of the Eastern Contra Costa County Irrigation Board, of the Knightsen Irrigation Board, and of the Brentwood Grammar School Board. He serves as a deputy sheriff under R. R. Veale. Fraternally he is a Past Master of the Brentwood Masonic Lodge. In politics he is a Republican. He and his family are highly esteemed for their sterling qualities, and have a wide circle of friends in their locality. Mr. Grigsby has in his possession a diary and memorandum book kept by his grandfather when he crossed the plains to Oregon, which contains some very interesting statistics.

DANIEL DENEHY.—A booster for Crockett for many years and now a substantial citizen of that city and one of its well-known business men, Daniel Denehy was born at Smartville, Yuba County, Cal., on August 21, 1870. His father, Cornelius Denehy, was born in Ireland in 1842 and came to the United States in 1864 and is still living, making his home in San Francisco. His active career was spent in mining. The mother of Daniel Denehy was Mary Dunning Denehy, also a native of Ireland, but died when her twin sons were only eighteen months of age. The brother John lived to be fourteen, when he passed away. Cornelius Denehy married a second time, Miss Mary O'Brien becoming his wife in November, 1875. This couple celebrated their golden wedding anniversary in November, 1925. One son Neal, now in the drygoods business in San Francisco, and a daughter, Mrs. Mary Consiglieri, also in the Bay city, were born of this second union.

Daniel, better known among his friends as "Dan" Denehy, attended the public schools in Yuba County and when he was old enough to strike out for himself his first occupation was as a glass-worker in the Pacific and Illinois Glass Works, then he spent about eleven years in the employ of the Pacific Rolling Mills, both in San Francisco, and in 1898 opened a saloon in Crockett, continuing in the liquor business until the Eighteenth Amendment prohibited the sale of liquors, when he closed the doors of his establishment and quit the business for all time. Later he fitted up his former place of business and opened an up-to-date candy store, where he is to be found during business hours, and where he has built up a fine retail trade. He enjoys the confidence and esteem of the citizens of Crockett and has been connected with the civic development of the city by his connection with the Crockett-Valona Business Men's Association. His faith in Crockett has been shown by his investing in real estate and by his service as one of the fire commissioners of the city. He endorses the candidates of the Republican party and has been more or less active in political affairs. He is satisfied to remain in Crockett where his best days have been passed and believes in the future of this Straits district.

On August 23, 1905, Mr. Denehy was united in marriage with Mrs. Alice E. Story, a native of Tennessee. He adopted a daughter of his wife by a former marriage, who is now Mrs. Katherine Van Vankenburg, residing in Honolulu.

CLARK C. KRATZER.—A prominent citizen and successful business man of Richmond, Clark C. Kratzer is a self-made man who has made his way unaided by capital or influential friends and has worked his way to the top of the ladder of success and become a man of large and varied business affairs. Mr. Kratzer was born in Brown County, Ohio, on March 3, 1875, a son of Lewis and Nancy Kratzer, well-known and highly respected farmer folk of Mount Orab. The original Kratzer family in America is a pre-Revolutionary one, and its descendants are numerous. Great-grandfather Kratzer was one of the pioneer settlers of Mount Orab.

Clark C. Kratzer attended the local public school and grew up on his father's farm. Early in life he determined to make his own way in the world, and his life story to date is full of interesting events and has that fascination which attaches to the lives of all men whose careers had small beginnings and attained to large achievements. At the age of seventeen, in 1892, he left home and enlisted in the United States Army, being assigned to Battery E, 5th Heavy Artillery. He saw service in Cuba, being with the first detachment to land at San Juan, Porto Rico, and was in the Santiago campaign, serving under General Shafter, acting as his orderly sergeant and fighting side by side with the famous Roosevelt Rough Riders. Mr. Kratzer was personally acquainted with both General Shafter and Colonel Roosevelt. He was discharged at Porto Rico, after which he bought 160 ponies and began carrying mail over twenty-four different lines; later he entered the mail service and remained in it two years. He then went back to New York and again enlisted in the army and was sent to San Antonio, Texas, with a field artillery regiment. From here he was transferred to Fort Worden, Wash., and in 1904 he was discharged. During his military career he received five honorable discharges.

After leaving the army Mr. Kratzer came to Coalinga, Cal., and worked in the oil fields as a common laborer for a year, then became a driller, and eventually was made superintendent for the Commercial Oil Company on the Nevada Petroleum Oil Company's lease. He has the distinction of being the first man to use an automobile in the delivery of milk at Kingsburg, Fresno County, using an old two-cylinder Buick. Selling out the milk route, he took over the Buick agency at Coalinga, remaining from 1906 until 1918, when he sold out to come to Richmond, where he is now the general agent for the Buick for Contra Costa County. In point of service Mr. Kratzer is the third oldest Buick agent in California. Besides being the general agent for the Buick in the county and having nine sub-agencies in the various cities, he is proprietor of the new modern Buick Garage at Tenth Street and Bissell Avenue. In 1921 Mr. Kratzer became a partner in the undertaking business with Aubrey Wilson, and they have one of the most modern and best-equipped funeral homes in the county, located at Seventh Street and Bissell Avenue and known as the Wilson and Kratzer Funeral Parlors.

Mr. Kratzer is also a director in the First National Bank in Richmond, and he owns a very fine dairy farm in Tulare County, where he keeps a herd of registered Holstein cattle.

In 1904 C. C. Kratzer was united in marriage with Miss Belle Livermore, born in Selma, Fresno County, a daughter of a pioneer family of that county. Mr. Kratzer is prominent in civic, social and religious circles in Richmond. He belongs to the Eagles and the Red Men, has served as president of the Rotary Club, and is a deacon and the treasurer of the Christian Church. The sterling personal characteristics of C. C. Kratzer, accompanied by unquestioned financial and executive ability, have placed him among the foremost business men of Richmond.

GEORGE SELLERS.—The son of pioneer parents, and himself a pioneer of California, George Sellers is among the most prominent citizens of Eastern Contra Costa County. He was born in Fruitvale, now a part of the city of Oakland, on March 1, 1854, the son of Samuel and Sarah (Abbott) Sellers. They left New York and sailed around the Horn to San Francisco, where they arrived in 1850, after a voyage of six months, during which time Mrs. Sellers was a great sufferer from seasickness. Arriving in the Golden State Mr. Sellers went to the mines in the Mother Lode district and tried his luck at prospecting and mining in Mariposa County. He moved to Contra Costa County in 1860, bought 160 acres of land, and began farming, at which he continued with good success until his death in 1900. Mrs. Sellers died about 1897. The grandfather of our subject was a pioneer of California and was among those who named the town of Fruitvale. Two sons of the Sellers family are living: George, of this review; and S. A. Sellers, of Berkeley.

George Sellers attended the first public school in Oakland and in 1860 was brought by his parents to Contra Costa County, where he continued his studies. He finished his education in Heald's Business College in San Francisco, after which he came back to the home ranch, and ever since then he has been among the representative men of this part of the county. He owns forty acres of the choicest land in this section and has improved a fine home place. He is widely and favorably known throughout the eastern part of the county and for a time carried on a real estate business at Brentwood. His specialty is horticulture, to which he devotes close attention with correspondingly excellent results. His orchard is devoted to walnuts, apricots, and general fruits. Mr. Sellers is a man of commanding presence, standing six feet and three inches in height, and is an indefatigable worker.

Mr. Sellers was married on April 8, 1872, to Miss Adaline L. Buckley, of Contra Costa County, and they have had the following children: Henry Abbott, connected with the Hotchkiss Dairy for a time and now engaged in growing cotton at Fairbault, Cal.; Edwin Buckley, owner of sixty acres of the old Sellers homestead on Sellers Avenue, named in honor of the family; and Edith A., wife of H. L. French, a high school teacher in San Francisco, where she is a court stenographer. The Buckley family came to California in 1852. Mr. Sellers is active in the ranks of the Republican party, and served as a deputy sheriff for five years. He has been a stanch friend of the public school and has served as a trustee for many years. Mr. Sellers has been interested in some important litigation in this section of the county, and has always interested himself in all the progressive movements for the county's upbuilding. He favors co-operative marketing and has given much time and thought to that branch of the fruit-growing industry. He belongs to the Prune and Apricot Association of California.

ALONZO L. STONE.—A pioneer of Contra Costa County by birth and a successful rancher and walnut grower of the Alamo district, Alonzo L. Stone owns and occupies a thirty-eight-and-one-half-acre ranch called Walnut Home in Stone Valley, named in honor of his family, who at one time owned nearly all the land in this valley. The old adobe house in which he was born is still standing on the old home place on which his father settled in the pioneer days.

A. L. Stone was born on July 29, 1860, the son of Albert W. Stone, who was born in Erie County, Pa., on September 18, 1821, and died August 27, 1900. The years between these two dates were filled with many changes of environment and much hard labor, which finally brought success and a respite from arduous business responsibilities. When he was a lad Albert W. Stone went with his parents to Kalamazoo, Mich., and remained there until 1838. Then the family moved to Van Buren County, Iowa, where he learned blacksmithing and worked at the trade a short time. He had married Miss Alice Ward, who died in 1851, leaving him a son, Edward A., born in 1848, and who is now living in Washington and is the father of eight living children, seven of them girls and all teachers, while his only son is attending the University of Seattle. After the death of his wife, Albert Stone and his father outfitted with ox-teams and wagons and started on the journey of six months across the plains, arriving in California on September 1, 1852. Remaining but a short time, he returned to Iowa and married for his second wife Miss Martha Smith, born in England on February 18, 1829. Three weeks later, with his son Edward A., they were en route for California with a band of stock, and some relatives and friends who wanted to come West and who helped with the stock. They arrived safely in Colusa County, where Mr. Stone began the stock business on a portion of the old Dr. Glenn ranch. He was known as Colonel Stone by his many friends in the East, for his activities during one of the Indian wars in his section. In 1858 the family came south to Contra Costa County, whither Silas Stone, his father, and his wife Susanna Stone, two daughters and a son had emigrated in the middle fifties and had settled on a ranch and built the house where A. L. Stone is now living. Silas Stone was elected alcalde of this district. When he retired he went to live in Haywards with his daughter, Mrs. William Meek, and there he died. His widow died at the home of her son, Lysander Stone, in San Leandro. A. W. Stone soon moved into the old adobe house which he had bought with 100 acres of land from William Comstock. To this land he added from time to time until he owned some 900 acres, which he devoted to general farming and stock-raising. The children born of this second marriage are: Martha Jeannette, widow of Edward A. Bunce, lives on the old home place near the adobe; she has two daughters, Olivette, Mrs. A. C. McMillan of Stockton, and Mrs. Martha Johnson of Alamo. William J. Stone died in March, 1923, unmarried. Elwin L. resides in Berkeley and has five children: Robert, Harry, Alonzo, Rix and Agnes. Alonzo L., of this review. Flora M. is the wife of J. C. Jones and the mother of a son Alden; they live at Alamo. Susie G. married George Trevetts; she died in September 1904, leaving a daughter, Susie S. Annie A. is the widow of August Humburg and the mother of two children, Friedericke (Mrs. R. F. Jackson) and Lorenz, and lives at Alamo. Mrs. A. W. Stone died on July 2, 1910.

Alonzo L. Stone attended private and public schools at Alamo and had one term in Livermore College, finishing his education with a course at Heald's Business College in San Francisco. In 1880 he took a trip to Mexico, expecting to do some mining; but the depredations of the Indians prevented his carrying out his plans and after one year there he came home. In 1900 he went on a mining expedition to Alaska, but the hardships he had to undergo precluded any profit and he decided to return to California and take up farming; and ever since then he has devoted his energies to ranch life and work. Most of his place is set to walnuts; but he has sixteen varieties of grapes on his ranch, and some of his grape arbors are things of beauty. He has made a success of the work to which he was trained from boyhood and is content to live in comfort and ease at his home one mile east of Alamo.

Alonzo L. Stone was married on October 25, 1883, to Miss Minnie Berring of San Francisco, daughter of Rudolph and Sophie (Margroff) Berring. Her father was a bookeeper by occupation, and died many years ago. Mr. and Mrs. Stone have three children living. Lilias is at home. Bertha first married O. A. Towsley and has a son, Berring. Mr. Towsley died and she later married A. Ross, of Gonzales. Albert is married and lives at San Ardo. Mr. Stone is a member of the Woodmen of the World, Danville Camp, organized over thirty-two years ago, and has passed through the chairs, and is also a member of the Neighbors of Woodcraft. He is a director of the Farmers' Association of Walnut Creek, belongs to and for three years served as president of the Walnut Growers' Association of Contra Costa County, and is one of the board of managers of the Alamo Cemetery. He is active in all progressive projects that are brought forward to advance the best interests of his county and State, and has a large circle of friends.

JOSEPH T. ARATA.—An Italian-American citizen who has made good in California is Joseph T. Arata, of Antioch. He is the builder of and owner of the Commercial Hotel, a three-story brick structure, modern in all its appointments and a credit to the city. He has been a resident of Contra Costa County since 1878 and for many years ran a market garden and supplied the surrounding towns and country with fresh vegetables, and made a financial success. He was born on February 1, 1858, in the province of Genoa, Italy, in the little town of Chignia, near the village where Christopher Columbus was born. His father and mother were Nicholas and Angelina Arata, who had a family of six sons, of whom Joseph is the youngest. All of them came to America, and Louis is now in Crockett. The father died when he was eighty-four, and the mother at seventy-four.

Joseph Arata was the last of the boys to leave home for the new country across the sea, leaving after he had attended the schools of his native village and grown to manhood. He was married in Italy on January 17, 1876, to Rosa Arata, of the same name but no relation, and she was born just three days after he first saw the light. They celebrated their golden wedding anniversary on January 17, 1926, in fitting style at Antioch. Theirs was a school-day romance, as they both attended the same school and the same church in Italy. In his native land Mr. Arata followed farming for two years after his marriage, and then came to America before he could be drafted into the army. This marriage has resulted in the birth of eight children. Jennie, born in Italy, is the wife of John McEravy, a rancher near Chico; Nicholas, also born in Italy, works for the Antioch Lumber Company; Louis, born at Antioch, died in 1922 at the age of forty years; John is a farmer in Deer Valley, Contra Costa County; Lena, the widow of John Zappatini, lives in San Francisco; Julia married Tony Pavolini and died at Martinez in 1917; George is a butcher in Oakland; and Annie died in 1892 aged two years and four months. There are fifteen grandchildren and three great-grandchildren.

Mr. Arata left Italy for the United States just three days before his second child was born, and traveled by way of Havre, France, to Liverpool, England, and thence to New York, arriving at Castle Garden on October 25, 1878. His destination was Antioch, Cal., and he came via Chicago and San Francisco, arriving on November 19, 1878, and has lived here the past forty-eight years. He became a naturalized citizen in 1887 at Martinez in the court of Judge P. Jones. As soon as he reached Antioch he began market gardening in partnership with his brother Louis, renting land from L. S. Robinson, for twenty years. He was joined by his wife and babies on July 9, 1879. Quitting market gardening, he engaged in mixed farming for seventeen years, and at the same time ran a grocery store and sold vegetables in Antioch. In 1907 he erected his brick hotel building. This he still owns, and also has four residences in town. He is a stockholder in the Bank of Antioch and also in the First National Bank here. The family are members of the Catholic Church, and in politics are Republicans. He is a charter member of the Sons of Italy Columbus Society. Fraternally, he is a member of the Red Men and of the Odd Fellows Lodge and Encampment in Antioch. Mr. Arata is very public spirited and supports all movements that tend to help the people and benefit the city and county.

WAVERLEY STAIRLEY.—Now living retired from business cares and looking after his own private interests, Waverley Stairley is enjoying his ease at his comfortable home in West Richmond. His has been a busy life and now he enjoys his well-earned competence. He was born on August 3, 1845 at Greenville, S. C., a son of Benjamin F. and Elizabeth K. (Stone) Stairley, the latter a daughter of Col. Banister Stone, of Virginia. Great-grandfather George Stairley was born in Virginia and married Elizabeth Lester, daughter of Archibald and Elizabeth (Grymes) Lester, the latter a sister of Lucy Grymes, who was the mother of Light Horse Harry Lee, father of Gen. Robert E. Lee, of Confederate fame.

When twelve years of age Waverley Stairley accompanied his father to California, coming via Panama. He remained here but seven months, when he was returned to school in New York City, where he attended the New York City College on Forty-seventh Street. While attending school the Civil War broke out, in 1860, and our subject, then but fifteen years old, enlisted in the cavalry of Wade Hampton's Legion and rendered gallant service in the army in Virginia. During the war he had his horse shot from under him, and his regiment was reduced to seventy-two men, but young Stairley went through the rigors of war unscathed. When peace was declared he returned to New York and finished his education.

In 1866 he received the offer of a position in San Francisco and he again came West by the Panama route and ever since then has considered himself a western man. In 1868 Mr. Stairley became ticket auditor of the northern division for the Southern Pacific Railway Company and continued with this company for several years. In 1875 he became associated with the banking house of Belloc and Company, later engaged in the stock brokerage business in San Francisco under the name of Stairley and Haverstick, and during 1880 and 1881 was connected with the Madera Flume and Trading Company in the San Joaquin Valley. Mr. Stairley was engaged in the lumber business for many years, being associated with Moore and Smith of San Francisco; later was with the Sierra Lumber Company, on January 1, 1884, taking charge of their plant and yards at Red Bluff. In January, 1894, he was appointed Internal Revenue Collector of the Fourth District of California and was located in Sacramento for four years.

In 1902 Mr. Stairley came to Richmond to engage in the banking business. At that time there was only an old barn on Barrett Street, and a grocery store had been started near by. The East Yard postoffice had been created by the Santa Fe at what is now Richmond. When the Standard Oil Company located at Point Richmond there was no bank to handle their pay roll and men from the Standard and from the Santa Fe were sent to San Francisco to pack money over here to meet the demands of the employees. On April 25, 1902, the Bank of Richmond was established with William Mintzer, president, William F. Belding, vice-president, and Waverley Stairley, cashier, manager and secretary. The bank filled a natural place in the order of things and did a thriving business. He continued his connection with this bank until 1915, when he disposed of his interest to become postmaster of Richmond, to which position he had been appointed, and he served from 1916 until 1921. During his term in the office he instituted many projects for expansion to meet the needs of the fast-growing city. Since the above date he has lived retired.

Mr. Stairley was united in marriage with Miss Mary Ridgley Tilden, born in Maryland and a relative of Samuel J. Tilden of national repute. This union has been blessed with two children: Marmaduke Hamilton; and Louise Elizabeth, wife of George Lee, a financial broker of Richmond. There is one grandchild, Virginia Louise Lee, to brighten the family circle. Mr. Stairley is a member of the Legion of Honor, Sixth Degree. He has always taken an active interest in the upbuilding of Richmond and Contra Costa County and has won a very large circle of friends.

GEORGE PETERS.—A pioneer of 1881 in California, George Peters has seen a wonderful growth in the Pacific Coast country since that date. He was born in Germany on September 29, 1853, the son of Frederick William and Elizabeth Peters, the former a grocer. There were seven sons in the family, of whom our subject is the only one who came to America. Three of his brothers were living when he left home in 1877. As a young man he followed the sea and landed in San Francisco in 1881 and worked as a longshoreman and on vessels plying up and down the coast for several years. In 1887 he left the water and came to work in the Selby smelter, in the department where the gold is separated from the silver, continuing until 1918, when he was pensioned off by the company after many years of faithful service. He is now living retired in Crockett. He belongs to Selby Lodge, Knights of Pythias, and to the Woodmen of the World, having held minor offices in both lodges. He was formerly a member of Valona Fire Department No. 1.

On June 29, 1882, Mr. Peters was united in marriage with Miss Anna Sturneburg, a native of the same part of Germany as her husband and who came to California in 1882 to marry Mr. Peters. Her father was Peter William Sturneburg, manufacturer of tobacco, and her mother was Amelia Revenda in maidenhood. This marriage resulted in the birth of three children. William Frederick, a machinist with the California and Hawaiian Sugar Refinery, learned his trade at the Selby Smelter and was there four years; since then has worked his way up in the refinery. He is a member of Carquinez Tent No. 98, I. O. R. M., having passed through the chairs and represented his lodge at the Grand Lodge; he also belongs to Crockett Lodge No. 329, I. O. O. F., having joined in 1911;

and a member of the Valona Fire Department No. 2, and of the C. & H. Fire department. The second child was Arthur George, who died in early childhood. The only daughter is Mrs. Elsie Ravenda Vondercheer of Los Angeles; she has two children, Louise and Alfred. The Peters family have many friends in Contra Costa County and are among the most highly respected citizens of Crockett.

JOHN BAPTISTE GEMETTI.—One of the best-known men in the Alhambra Valley is John B. Gemetti, a foreman on Hill Girt, the historic ranch founded by the late Prof. John Swett. Since 1897, when Mr. Gemetti came here, he has proven a distinct adjunct to the development of this part of the county, and his knowledge has always been at the disposal of his friends and neighbors, to aid them with their problems in horticulture and viticulture. Born in Canton Ticino, Switzerland, on August 12, 1871, he is the son of John B. and Margaret (Rigoni) Gemetti, farmers of that country and both now deceased, the father after having reached sixty-seven years of age, and the mother having died on the old home place in Switzerland, aged eighty-three, in 1926.

John Baptiste Gemetti grew up on his father's farm in the old country, and there learned horticulture and viticulture, farming and stock-raising, dairying and cheese and butter making, as did many other youths in Switzerland. The oldest of four children born to his parents, he stayed and helped on the home ranch until nineteen years old, when he came to the United States, with San Francisco as his destination. Upon coming to the Alhambra Valley, in 1897, he was soon singled out by John Swett and son, Frank Swett, themselves horticulturists of note, and was induced to enter their employ. Mr. Gemetti became a foreman in 1901, and it is needless to say that his work has done much towards making Hill Girt the finest and most productive of all the excellent ranches in the Alhambra Valley. He is an expert in viticulture and understands the making of wine, and had charge of the winery on the ranch as well, operating it successfully until the days of war prohibition, when all wine-making ceased on this ranch. Mr. Gemetti continues as a foreman of the property, which is now the residence and under the management of John F. Swett, son of the old pioneer teacher, author and rancher.

The marriage of Mr. Gemetti, at Santa Rosa on August 25, 1900, united him with Miss Delia Cotta, daughter of James and Modesta (De Carli) Cotta. The mother is still living near Nicasio, Marin County, where they owned a large cattle ranch; the father passed to his reward in 1918, aged eighty-seven. Five children blessed the union of Mr. and Mrs. Gemetti. Robert Eugene is a graduate of the Alhambra Union High School and is now employed by the Shell Company; he married Miss Dora Mantel, of Oakland, and has one child, Robert Eugene, Jr. Walter is a graduate of Alhambra Union High School and is working with his father on Hill Girt ranch. Adeline married Russell Lake and resides at Menlo Park. Flora was chosen May Queen for the May Day Festival at Mar-

John Swett.

tinez in 1925; and she and Elsie are attending the Alhambra Union High School in Martinez. All of the children were born at Hill Girt with the exception of Robert Eugene, who was three months old when the family came to the ranch. They are exceptionally intelligent young folks and are all favorites in the community life.

Fraternally, Mr. Gemetti belongs to the Ancient Order of Druids and to the Swiss Mutual Benevolent Society at San Francisco. While registered as a Republican, he votes for the right man for the right place in local affairs, having cast his first vote for McKinley in 1896 in Martinez, after being naturalized in Judge Angelotti's court, in San Rafael, California.

JOHN SWETT.—American educator and author, John Swett was also recognized as the "Father of the Public School System of California." He was born in Pittsfield, N. H., on July 31, 1830, and grew up in the environment of a New England home. His parents were also born there amidst the hills and rolling swells of glacial morraines, where the land was hard to clear, but when so cleared was productive. Lumbering was the principal industry, and the tall white pines were used for masts and ship timbers.

In tracing the genealogy of the family it is found that John Swett, of Devonshire, England, was admitted to the freedom of the Massachusetts Bay Colony on May 18, 1642, and was granted tracts of land in the town of Newbury, Mass. His son, Benjamin Swett, was chosen one of the selectmen, and he drilled the militia and fought the Indians. He was killed in 1677 in Maine. He left five boys and six girls, among them Joseph Swett, who was elected to the provincial assembly in 1708. He married and had three children, of whom the next in line of descent was Thomas Rogers Swett. When he was three years old his father died and the lad was put out to learn the trade of the clothier and fuller. He served in the militia when he was sixteen, in the Revolutionary War under Captain Joseph Parson's command in a New Hampshire regiment, and was mustered out in January, 1779. Going to Pittsfield, he operated a mill and later farmed. He was twice married, having two children by his first wife and eight by his second wife, Betsy Knowlton Swett. He died in 1847 at the age of eighty-eight. Eben Swett, father of our subject, was the fifth child, and was born in 1799. On the maternal side, Abraham French, grandfather of our subject, was born in Stratham in 1758, was a carpenter, served in the Revolutionary War, married Hanna Lane and died in 1850.

John Swett attended the schools of his day and in 1836 moved with his parents into Pittsfield, where his mother ran a boarding house and his father continued farming. The boarding house was unprofitable and the family returned to the farm. The lad was surrounded by liberal home influences; his father always looked upon the sunny side of life, but trained his boys to work, never failing to give them ample time to play.

He served as town clerk of Pittsfield and as a selectman. The family lived on the products of the farm; even their clothing was of domestic make, the mother being an expert with the spinning wheel. Young John lived on the farm, went to school and tended the cattle in winter. He entered Pittsfield Academy in the fall of 1844, and studied reading, arithmetic, algebra, grammar, composition and declamation. Later he had one term at Pembroke Academy, after which he was offered a position as a teacher in the Buck Street school at ten dollars a month "and board 'round." He was now seventeen. In 1848 he began a three-months course in manual training on the farm. Always a great reader, he bought what books he could and borrowed whenever possible. In 1849-1850 he taught at West Randolph, Mass., for sixteen dollars a month, and during this time he made up his mind to come to California, but failed twice to make it possible.

On September 15, 1852, he bought passage, for $200, on the Revere, sailing from Boston Harbor, and after 135 days landed in San Francisco on February 1, 1853. Here he met Rev. S. H. Willey, a Presbyterian minister, then went to Marysville by water, outfitted for the mines and prospected and mined five months. Finding mining was not his forte; he returned to San Francisco and secured a position in the Rincon school in November, 1853. He entered into the spirit of the times and soon had built up a fine school system, and took an active part in educational affairs. During all this time he had been contributing to Eastern newspapers to help out with his finances. At an expense of $250 he made a trip back East via Panama, taking passage on the Golden Gate from San Francisco. After a visit with his family and friends he returned to California. In 1860 he became superintendent of the First Unitarian Society Sunday School in San Francisco.

The first political campaign entered into by John Swett was when he ran for superintendent of public instruction of California in 1862, being elected by a majority of 139 votes. He began his work in December and worked strenuously for the advancement of the public school system in California. For four years he edited the California Teacher. In 1867 he entered upon his duties as a teacher in the Denman School in San Francisco, and one year later was elected a teacher in the Lincoln Evening School, where he built up a fine system. He was appointed deputy school superintendent in 1869 by J. H. Widber. During this period in office he wrote Swinton's Word Book of written and oral spelling, receiving a one-half interest in the copyright; and also wrote Swinton's Word Primer, but did not have any interest in the copyright.

Upon leaving the office of deputy superintendent he became the principal of the Denman School. In July, 1876, he became principal of the Girl's High School and Normal Class in San Francisco, which had 400 pupils and twelve teachers. In 1875 he had published the first school history of California, an edition of 1000. From 1876 to 1889 he was the principal of the San Francisco High School, but resigned and went to

Contra Costa County and settled on a farm, where he remained two years. He was again induced to enter the political arena and was elected the superintendent of the city schools of San Francisco by an overwhelming majority, taking office on January 11, 1891, continuing until 1895.

His mother had died on March 5, 1896, at the age of ninety-two years. In 1898 he made a trip back East over the Canadian Pacific and thoroughly enjoyed the relaxation. Returning to his Contra Costa home he gave up educational work and devoted himself to raising fruit and farming on his Hill Girt Ranch, which he had bought in 1881, paying $7000 cash for 185 acres. In 1901 he was active in organizing the Alhambra Union High School; in 1906 he was appointed trustee of the San Francisco State Normal School by Governor Pardee. During his term as State superintendent of public instruction he had the law passed creating the State Board of Education, providing for teachers' institutes, organizing schools into grades and establishing school libraries; and he had the tuition charges abolished, making California schools absolutely free. Since then the trend of the school system has been upward, characterized by better buildings and with modern equipment, complete curriculum and competent teachers.

On May 8, 1862, John Swett and Miss Louise Tracy were united in marriage, the ceremony being performed at the Methodist Church on Powell Street, by Rev. M. C. Briggs. Mrs. Swett was the daughter of Frederick Palmer Tracy, a prominent lawyer and politician in the Bay city and a close friend of the late Leland Stanford. He came from a well-known California family, the town and station of Tracy on the main line of the Southern Pacific and the State Highway being named after Judge Tracy. He was an able lawyer and was a member of the committee on platform, and submitted the first draft of the Republican platform which was adopted at the convention in Chicago, and which nominated Abraham Lincoln for President. Mr. and Mrs. John Swett became the parents of four children who grew to maturity, viz.: Emily Tracy, who married John W. Parkhurst and died in April, 1892, aged twenty-nine, leaving a daughter Ruth Emilie, who was reared by the grandparents; Frank Tracy, president of the Pear Growers' Association of California and a resident of Berkeley; Helen Swett Artieda, a resident of Oakland and secretary of the Public Welfare League of that city; and John French, of Hill Girt Ranch. Mrs. John Swett died in 1919 at the age of seventy-nine years.

Among the many interesting facts in the life of John Swett was one concerning himself and John Muir, his neighbor and most intimate friend, when in May, 1913, they were both given the degree of Doctor of Law at the commencement exercises at the University of California by Benjamin Ide Wheeler, president of that institution. These two life-long friends were often referred to as the "Two Johns." This honor, coming just a few months before the death of Mr. Swett, was a fitting finale to their years of ideal friendship. Mr. Swett passed to his reward in August, 1913, at the age of eighty-three years.

JOHN J. SULLENGER.—In Contra Costa County there are many enterprising agriculturists who bring to their calling good business methods and excellent judgment, and whose labors are crowned with success. Conspicuous among this number is J. J. Sullenger, who owns and occupies a finely improved ranch lying about seven miles from the town of Brentwood, in a rich and fertile district known as the Lone Tree Precinct. He is a native Californian, his birth having occurred on January 7, 1858, in Oakville, Napa County, on the farm of his father, John C. Sullenger.

A native of North Carolina, John C. Sullenger went to Missouri when a boy, and in 1852, when eighteen or nineteen, crossed the plains via the Oregon Trail with a covered wagon train, and about that same year came on a schooner to San Francisco. He went to the mines and searched for gold, but not being especially successful in his quest he settled in Oakville, Napa County, where he was later married to Miss Annie Donahue. Our subject was the oldest of five children born of this union. His mother passed away when he was only eight years old; the father lived to be ninety-one years and eight months old, and died in Antioch.

John J. Sullenger was brought up by a stepmother, and his early education was acquired in the public schools of Rutherford, Cal. In 1882 he graduated from Heald's Business College in San Francisco. Then he engaged in farming in Napa County and later in Colusa County. After this he took up surveying as a livelihood and for a number of years did surveying work in Colusa, Butte, Mendocino and Sonoma Counties. In 1884 he came to Antioch, and four years later he purchased his present ranch of 206 acres, where he has since resided. He was in Brentwood before there was any town; the property was then a wheat field and the railroad had then just been completed.

In 1897 Mr. Sullenger was married to Miss Annie E. Love, a daughter of the pioneer Robert Love, who settled in Napa County in 1852. Mr. and Mrs. Sullenger became the parents of four children: John, Archie, Robert, and Elsie, a teacher at the Iron House School. Mrs. Sullenger passed away on December 30, 1924, mourned by a large circle of friends. In politics Mr. Sullenger is a Democrat.

OTIS LOVERIDGE. — As superintendent of the Los Medanos Rancho, with his head office in Pittsburg, Otis Loveridge is making his personality felt constructively in the development of the city and the surrounding country. His long association with the C. A. Hooper interests, and his close contact with Mr. Hooper himself, brought Mr. Loveridge into an intimate understanding of the scheme of things as outlined by Mr. Hooper, and he has been carrying out the program thus formulated ever since the death of his friend. A native of Oregon, Otis Loveridge was born at Molalla, Clackamas County, on April 18, 1877. His father, Newton Loveridge, crossed the plains with his father and settled in Oregon in 1865. The mother was in maidenhood Miss Amanda Robbins, and was born in Breckenridge County, Ky., where her father was a planter. Grandfather Robbins first crossed the plains in 1848 in a covered wagon, later returning East only to come out again in 1852. Both Mr. and Mrs. Newton Loveridge died in Los Angeles, the latter in 1923 and the former in 1924, when he was eighty-three years old.

Otis Loveridge grew up in eastern Oregon, whither his parents had removed to engage in the cattle business. He was raised on a stock range, with but slim opportunities for going to school. When a mere youth he came to California, in 1900, and entered the employ of Governor Pierce of Oregon, on his ranch on Victoria Island in the delta country. From laborer he gradually rose to the position of superintendent, giving satisfaction to his employer and holding the confidence of those under his direction. In 1908 he came to Black Diamond to become superintendent of the Los Medanos Rancho for C. A. Hooper. After the death of Mr. Hooper, Wiggington E. Creed, his son-in-law, became managing head of the property. Through close contact with Mr. Hooper, Mr. Loveridge caught his clear vision of the future in store for this section of the country, and is gratified to see many of his plans brought to a successful termination. Ever since locating in this vicinity Mr. Loveridge has worked for the benefit of the community at large, and he is counted among its active and public-spirited citizenry.

Otis Loveridge was married on Victoria Island to Miss Oliver and they have two children, Helen and Fay. Mr. Loveridge is chairman of the Pittsburg High School and Grammar School boards, of which he has been a member for years. He was one of the organizers of the present Union High School district and has watched its development with keen interest. Mr. Loveridge is a member of the board of directors of the Pittsburg Chamber of Commerce. Fraternally he is a Royal Arch Mason and a member of the Sciots.

FRED STEMMLE.—A pioneer of the Crockett-Valona section of Contra Costa County, Fred Stemmle recalls that when he first came to this place Valona had only four houses and one eight-room hotel; the latter had 150 boarders, some having to sleep out on the hillside, in barns or any kind of a place they could find. Oftentimes they were chased out by the coyotes, which were very numerous in this section at that time. He landed here on May 18, 1885; and he secured work at the Selby smelter on July 5, of that year, and continued with that corporation, except five years, when he served as constable, until he was retired on a pension in October, 1923. Not many men so regulate their lives that they remain with one concern thirty-two years as did Fred Stemmle. He worked through various positions and was a foreman for twenty-four years, during which time he discharged only two men.

Fred Stemmle was born in Massillon, Ohio, on February 11, 1862, and was a son of Joseph and Tacklaw (Kemper) Stemmle, both born and reared to their young man- and womanhood in Germany, leaving there in 1849 for the New World. They were married in Ohio and are both now deceased. Mr. Stemmle had a sister, Mrs. Josephine Shepherd, who died in Ohio in the fall of 1925. He attended the public schools in Ohio and when old enough to be self-supporting began working in coal mines until he came to California in 1885. His work here covers a long period and during that time many changes have been wrought in the communities in the entire state as well as in the business followed by our subject.

Mr. Stemmle was married on April 8, 1886, being united with Miss Mary Lovall, a native of Brazil, Ind. They had one child, John William, who married Miss Daisy Berryman, of San Francisco, and they have two children, Beth and Kenneth. Mrs. Stemmle died on November 2, 1925. Mr. Stemmle is a Democrat and a very progressive citizen and identified with the best interests of his community at all times. He is a close friend of ex-Senator Phelan and was influential during the Wilson administration in securing the present post office at Crockett. He was a member of the Democratic Central Committee of Contra Costa County for several years. His recreation is found in out-of-door sports and especially fishing and duck hunting. He recalls when some of the early hunters would kill some farmer's tame ducks and usually have to pay for them. He is now retired and enjoys a good story and usually can tell some of his own.

WILLIAM M. PENNINGTON.—Soldier, patriotic citizen and enterprising business man—these are prominent characteristics of William M. Pennington, the well-known and successful cement contractor of Richmond, Cal. He was born on November 6, 1871, in Scott County, Tenn., a son of Daniel and Susie (Slaven) Pennington, natives of Tennessee, as were also Grandfather George and Grandmother Pennington; and all were farmer folks. The children are: George Pennington; Mrs. John West, the mother of ten children; and William M. Mrs. Daniel Pennington, the mother of William M., was married twice, her second husband being a Mr. Owen, who was the father of several children; and so William Pennington had several half-brothers and half-sisters.

William Pennington attended the local public schools in Tennessee and when twenty-one years of age enlisted in the United States Army, in 1892, at Cincinnati, Ohio. During his time spent in the Army he saw active service in the Spanish-American War as a member of the division in which Colonel Roosevelt commanded a regiment, and was a member of General Wheeler's Corps of the 6th United States Cavalry, Troop F, which was engaged in the Battle of San Juan Hill, fourteen days and nights. Mr. Pennington has an enviable reputation as a sharp-shooter. By the time he reached the age of twenty-two he was the proud possessor of many medals which he had won for superior marksmanship, and was recommended for others; and at the age of fifty he was presented with a coat-of-arms and won another medal. He served his country loyally and was honorably discharged in 1899. Locating at San Francisco, Cal., he was appointed provost marshal for the Presidio, remaining there two years and nine months. In 1902 Mr. Pennington located in Richmond,

Cal., where he found employment with the Standard Oil Company for four years, being fireman in the refinery, where he had charge of eighteen men. Being anxious to enter business for himself, he became a cement contractor, in which work he has been successful both as a foreman and as a contractor. Prominent among the buildings for which he did the cement work are the City Hall and the Mechanics Bank at Richmond, and he was foreman of construction for the municipal wharf, for the Pullman Company's shops, and also for bridge work on the State Highway.

On October 15, 1899, William M. Pennington was united in marriage with Miss Mary Lawdermilk, the daughter of Doctor Lawdermilk, a graduate of the Medical University of Illinois, and also of the Medical University of Louisville, Ky. Doctor Lawdermilk has to his credit, as a literary effort, the History of Greene County, Mo., of which Springfield is the county seat. Mrs. Pennington's mother died when she was three years old. One brother is living at Weed, Cal. Mr. and Mrs. Pennington are the parents of four children: Gusta, who is now Mrs. J. R. Jackson, residing at Hercules, Cal., where her husband is employed with the powder works; Barney Nathan, an employee of the Union Oil Company, in the labor department; Carl Alfred Alexander, also employed by the Union Oil Company, and greatly interested in music; Minnie, a student in the Junior High School, where she is taking a business course. Fraternally, Mr. Pennington is a member of the Modern Woodmen, and also belongs to the Spanish-American War Veterans. For eighteen years he has had the distinction of being the person selected to fire all salutes over the graves of veterans, both G. A. R. and Spanish-American War Veterans. In 1925 he took an extended trip in his auto, going back East and South as far as his old home state of Tennessee, where he visited his mother. The trip consumed nearly three months extending from June 29 to September 22. He took all of his family except his married daughter. Among the places of interest visited outside of the larger cities was the monument to Lincoln, at Springfield, Ill. During his journey he was in fifteen States and had a view of twenty-three States.

Mr. Pennington stands for the highest principles in all business transactions and is a firm believer in obedience to law, which he ably upholds through his position as deputy sheriff of the county. He served as a member of the building committee when the City Hall was built at Richmond. His successful career is the reward of industry, thrift, persistency of purpose, and judicious management of financial affairs.

EDWARD HOWE HARLOW.—A pioneer in railroad service with the Santa Fe, the late Edward Howe Harlow of Richmond, came to this locality when what is now known as West Richmond was called East Yard, and helped to build the first car shops in order that the necessary repair work on engines and cars need not be done in the open. This was in June, 1900. In September of that same year his family joined him and have lived here almost continuously ever since. These shops burned down and were immediately rebuilt more substantially. Mr. Harlow was installed as master mechanic and remained in charge of the shops until 1907, when he was sent to Albuquerque, N. M., and for eighteen months was in charge of the shops at that place. Returning to Richmond he was in charge of the Valley Division, which extended as far as Bakersfield, but as the business of the company increased he was later made master mechanic of the terminal and at the time of his death, on January 26, 1922, was superintendent of shops. He was always working for the advancement of his community and was largely instrumental in selecting the site of the Pullman Company when they decided to establish a branch for the Pacific Coast. He took an active part in church circles and helped establish the first Episcopal Church at Point Richmond, also he and his wife helped organize St. Edmund's Church in Richmond and he served as warden for many years. He was a Mason, belonging to the Lodge, Chapter, Commandery and Shrine, the latter of Oakland; was also a member of Richmond Lodge No. 1251, B. P. O. E. No matter how busy he was he always found some time to assist with all progressive movements for the betterment of conditions.

E. H. Harlow was born in Janesville, Wis., on September 1, 1856, and is descended directly from Richard Warren, who came over in the Mayflower, a descendant of this Warren having married a Harlow. Mr. Harlow was educated in the Episcopal school in Janesville and at the age of sixteen entered the Chicago and Northwestern Railroad shops there and finished an apprenticeship as a machinist in their Chicago shops. After he had mastered his trade he worked as a journeyman until he was sent to the shops of that company at Harvard, Ill., where he was a foreman. He went from place to place for the Chicago and Northwestern, finally going with the Santa Fe in 1889 and spending seven years, from 1893 until 1900, at Gallup, N. M. In the latter year he was sent to Richmond. He was a thorough master of all branches of his trade and was held in high esteem by his superiors.

In Janesville, Wis., Mr. Harlow was married to Annah Cummings on July 15, 1890. She was born in Chemung Township, McHenry County, Ill. Her grandmother, Mary Bentley Smith, was descended from Capt. Caleb Bentley of Revolutionary fame. Mary Bentley Smith was born and married in Massachusetts, then went to Horseheads, N. Y., with her husband, pioneering that section, thence went to McHenry County, Ill., in 1836, when that was the frontier. Grandfather Smith had the honor of naming Chemung Township in Illinois, they having come from Chemung County, N. Y. Mrs. Smith was four years old when George Washington was inaugurated president of the United States and she had the pleasure of living under the administration of every president from Washington to McKinley. She died in Los Angeles in 1901, aged 106. She was the mother of thirteen children. Mrs. Harlow is a member of the Daughters of the American Revolution, has taken an active part in church and Sunday School work and was a teacher in the Sunday School in Richmond, and a member of the Ladies' Aid.

Mr. and Mrs. Harlow had five children, two of whom died in childhood. Philip L. was born in Janesville, Wis., graduated from the Richmond High School, married and has two children, Edward and Elthea, who, with their father, reside with Mrs. Harlow; he is foreman in the experimental laboratory at the Standard Oil refinery, is a Mason and an Elk, and belongs to the Carquinez Golf Club. E. George was born at Gallup, N. M., and also graduated from the Richmond High and is employed with the Standard Oil Company; he is deeply interested in Y. M. C. A. work in Richmond, and is a Mason. He has a son Paul. A. Page Harlow was also born at Gallup, N. M., and went to the Richmond High; he served with General Pershing on the Mexican border and with his company enlisted for service in the World War, and was a bugler with the replacement troops. He learned the trade of machinist at the Standard Oil refinery; was graduated from the A to Zed school in Oakland and is now preparing for secretarial work at the Y. M. C. A. college in Chicago. He takes a great interest in young boys. He also belongs to the Masonic order. Both Mr. and Mrs. Harlow were very active in civic affairs in Richmond and did their full share to make the city a better place in which to live and rear families. The family home has been located on Florida Street since 1905.

NUMA SIMS BOONE.—Among the most successful farmers and stock-raisers of San Ramon Valley is Numa Sims Boone, who has been a resident of the county since his birth. He is a son of the early pioneers, James O. and Sallie (Sims) Boone, who were both natives of Missouri, the former born February 28, 1828, and the latter November 7, 1841. James Boone first came to California in 1846 with ox-teams and located at what is now Dutch Flat, Placer County. While living in that locality he hauled, with his ox-team, the lumber for building the first house in that place, and also carried on a freight business between Sacramento and Dutch Flat, for which he received twenty dollars per day. James Boone had two brothers, Wellington and John, who came to California by way of Cape Horn. After James' arrival John was taken sick and the three brothers started back East by vessel, and while on the way he died and was buried at sea. The two brothers continued their journey and after arriving at New Orleans took a boat up the Mississippi and Missouri Rivers to Saint Joseph, Mo. James bought a farm and afterwards married Sallie Sims, and for two or three years they lived in Missouri, until Mrs. Boone's health failed and he decided to take her to California. They came by way of the plains and were six months in making the trip. Upon arrival in California they located in Yolo County, in the Putah Creek section, but as this place did not suit Mrs. Boone, after residing there three years he took his horse and wagon and started in search of a place that he thought would make a satisfactory home for his wife. Upon arriving at Danville in 1852, Mr. Boone said, "This is where I wish to locate," and having purchased 160 acres of land, he then returned to Yolo County for his wife. Here they made their home until Mrs. Boone's death on April 16, 1895. He spent his last years with his daughter, Mrs. Dr. Moore, in Benicia and passed away at her home on May 24, 1902. Their family consisted of three children: Lina, who married C. E. Dingle; Cora, an artist residing in Oakland, where she is supervisor of oil drawings in the public schools, and where her paintings are so highly prized by art lovers that the city has reserved one room in the City Auditorium for the exhibit of her pictures; and Numa Sims Boone, of this review.

Numa Sims Boone was born in Danville, Cal., on May 14, 1867, and began his life work as a farmer on the old home place; but later he engaged in stock-raising for himself. He has been very successful and at present superintends 2400 acres, raises grain and hay, has various kinds of stock, and has on the old home place a twelve-acre pear orchard which he helped set out when he was sixteen years of age, and from which he receives an annual rental of $1200. In stock-raising he keeps only full-blooded sires. At present he has only thirty-five horses, and he plans for the future to use tractors for all of his work. Mr. Boone has been very successful in raising hay, some seasons selling from $30,000 to $50,000 worth. In 1926 his yield of barley was thirty-five sacks to the acre, and his lands produce a phenomenal crop of tomatoes and cucumbers. The ability and resourcefulness of Mr. Boone as a progressive farmer, his good judgment in business affairs, and his wise management of financial matters are widely recognized. He was elected to the important office of president of the San Ramon Valley Bank at Danville, a position he held for ten years, but has since sold his interests in the bank.

On August 31, 1899, Numa S. Boone was united in marriage with Miss Minnie Thorn of Alameda, a daughter of Capt. Charles and Jeanette (Travis) Thorn, both natives of the State of New York. Captain Thorn was a seafaring man and ran the first passenger steamer boat from San Francisco to Alviso, the fare being eighteen dollars one way. He brought the lumber for building the first house in Santa Clara from New York. He had it set up, and it was in this house that Mrs. Boone was born. Mrs. Boone as a young lady attended the Denman School in San Francisco, after which, for some years, she was a business woman. Mr. and Mrs. Boone are the parents of two children: Travis Moore, who is a graduate of the technical school at Oakland, and now is the manager of the home ranch; and Eleanor Sims, who graduated from Mills College, class of 1926, and contemplates studying medicine. Fraternally, Mr. Boone is a charter member of the Woodmen of the World at Danville.

Thos. S. Duane

THOMAS S. DUANE.—One of Central California's successful nurserymen is Thomas S. Duane, who has been engaged in horticultural work
since a boy of ten years. Since coming to Contra Costa County, in 1884, his
work here has been of inestimable value to this part of the State. Born in
Genesee County, N. Y., on February 5, 1862, he is the son of Patrick and
Margaret (Daily) Duane. He was reared in the State of New York and
attended the grammar school at Dawes Corners, Genesee County; but his
schooling was limited, for when only ten years old he went to work in a
nursery for Nelson Bogue, a nurseryman in that State, and remained
with him for twelve years, during which time he was thoroughly grounded
in the rudiments of horticulture.

After having worked in leading nurseries in the Empire State, Mr.
Duane came to California in 1884, first stopping in Los Angeles for a
short time and then coming to Oakland and from there to Martinez. He
was welcomed to Contra Costa County by the late Prof. John Swett, John
Muir, and Mr. Heffner, who were engaged in fruit culture here. Mr.
Duane leased fifteen acres of Henry Raap the day he arrived in this
county, and immediately started a nursery; and he has been in the nursery
business ever since, selling his products all over the State. He has a wide
acquaintance in every section where fruit is grown, and his advice is
sought by hundreds who contemplate the planting of orchards. Besides
his home ranch of 100 acres two miles from Martinez, in Franklin Canyon, where he is proprietor of the Martinez Nursery, he holds under
lease the Rodeo Valley Nursery. He has established an enviable reputation as a nurseryman and horticulturist and has a wonderful variety of
nursery stock, among which are twenty varieties of apples and about the
same number of varieties of peaches; Kadota, Smyrna and black figs;
Bartlett, Beaury Boss, and Beaury Hardy pears; Japanese persimmon;
Concord walnuts; almost every variety of grapes; Royal Ann, Black Republican, Chapman and Bing cherries (he having developed the latter
variety, on which he took the gold medal at the St. Louis Exposition);
loganberries, blackberries and raspberries; three varieties of currants; and
fourteen varieties of plums, among them the Duane plum, propagated by
himself, and which is known as the French Prune No. 1. Besides these
he has practically every variety of fruit grown in California which he has
found favorable to the soil of Contra Costa County, for which section he
is a great booster at all times. He has planted and cared for several
orchards. The Busbee orchard of seventy acres of olives, ten acres of
almonds, and twenty acres of walnuts was planted by Mr. Duane and
brought into bearing from the bare land. He had a five-year contract
with Mr. Busbee, which singularly was only a verbal contract, his word
being recognized as sufficient even in a business contract. This was also
the case in his contract with James Sutton, when he planted and cared for
sixty acres for a period of three years; and also the same arrangement was
made in planting the Jackson place, of twenty acres; and thirty acres for
Mr. Doyle.

The marriage of Mr. Duane, which occurred in Martinez on July 17, 1894, united him with Miss Sarah Jane Rodgers, born at Pleasant Hill, Contra Costa County, a daughter of Patrick Rodgers, the well-known pioneer rancher of that place, who fifty-six years ago bought a ranch at Pleasant Hill and became identified with early life in the county. Four children blessed the union of Mr. and Mrs. Duane. Ruth Margaret is the widow of John Kellogg Cushing, former city editor of the Martinez Gazette, who died on May 20, 1924. William died in childhood. Joseph James married Miss Mildred Sliger of San Francisco, who was born and reared in Bedford County, Pa. They make their home with Mr. Duane, and he assists his father in operating the nursery. The fourth child, Verna Mary, is the wife of George Dewey Welch, proprietor of the Alhambra Motor Company of Martinez. She is a graduate of the Martinez-Alhambra Union High School and attended the State Teachers' College in San Francisco. Mrs. Welch majored in music at the College of the Holy Name in Oakland.

Public-spirited and actively interested in the betterment of his community, Mr. Duane has served as foreman of the Grand Jury and is a strong believer in law observance and law enforcement; and while he has declined public office, he supports the men he deems most capable of efficiently administering the county's affairs. During the World War he served on Liberty and Victory Loan drives, helping to put Franklin Canyon over the top in each instance, and also was active in Red Cross work. Before the day of paved highways in the county, he hauled 1100 tons of rock for roadwork, donating his services for the cause of good roads, especially the Franklin Canyon road. Mr. Duane was the means of having the first sewer system installed in Martinez, about 1893. He is a stockholder in the Martinez Bank, and a large property owner, owning a block of residence property on Alhambra Avenue in Martinez. He is a Democrat in politics, and a Catholic in church membership.

Hard work and an intense interest in horticulture, applied with business sagacity, have been the secret of Mr. Duane's success. During his years of work here he has been associated with Prof. John Swett, proprietor of the "Hill Girt" Ranch, and with John Muir, naturalist and botanist, in various horticultural ventures, and together they accomplished some wonderful things for Contra Costa County. Mr. Duane, a big man physically as well as mentally, has been in the nursery business fifty-four years. He knows the soil and climatic conditions of this region thoroughly, and has been a real factor in the development of the county, demonstrating its possibilities along horticultural lines and paving the way for future intensive development by new settlers, attracted to the locality by the results of his work. He is a friend of education and has served as a member of the Alhambra Union High School Board since 1904; and he was one of the first to start the agitation for the consolidation of the grammar schools, believing that the country children should have the same advantages that are enjoyed by the children in the cities. Besides being a fruit grower and nurseryman, he is a manufacturer of a pure olive oil that holds the highest test of any olive oil in the world. This he makes under the most sanitary conditions and markets under the name of the Thomas S. Duane Brand.

MANUEL BAETA.—How eastern Contra Costa County rewards those who intelligently till the soil and pursue agricultural pursuits is strikingly illustrated in the case of Manuel Baeta who owns two large and valuable ranches, one of about 300 acres adjoining Pittsburg, devoted to grain and hay, and the other of 320 acres, two and a half miles east of Brentwood, being in the heart of the alfalfa growing section of the county. For many years Mr. Baeta, as a young man, worked with the threshing crew of Mr. Grigsby, a pioneer thresher of that section. By hard work and strict economy he was able to purchase the home farm of 320 acres from Mr. Grigsby, which is mostly in alfalfa, although there is a forty-acre vineyard of choice table grapes on the property. This ranch lies east of the thriving city of Brentwood and is fast becoming very valuable owing to the rapid growth of that city as an agricultural center. Manuel Baeta was born on the Island of Flores, in Azores group, in 1865, and when a little over seventeen years old resolved to come to California and reached here in 1883. His native land failed to provide him a fortune or even to give him the rudiments of an education, a loss which he has keenly felt; but through business and general reading he has become a practical man of affairs and is a thorough farmer.

Mr. Baeta was married at Antioch to Miss Margaret Jacinta, a native of Antioch. For seventeen years Mr. Baeta rented land and farmed successfully until his naturally thrifty nature enabled him to ultimately buy his fine ranch properties. To Mr. and Mrs. Baeta have been born five children: Oliver runs the 320-acre home farm located two and a half miles east of Brentwood; Margaret, Edith and Grace are students at the State Teachers' College in San Jose, Cal., and Mabel is in the public school. In the fall of 1925 Mr. and Mrs. Baeta removed to San Jose, where they now reside. Fraternally, Mr. Baeta is a member of the I. D. E. S. and the U. P. E. C.

MANUEL VIERA.—Among the early settlers in eastern Contra Costa County is Manuel Viera, now living retired on his productive ranch on the State Highway near Antioch. He was born on the Island of Pico, Azores group, on April 10, 1854, and attended the schools in his neighborhood until he was fourteen. With a brother he then came to America, arriving in New Bedford, Mass., and remained for a time with an uncle, Antone Viera, working for him in his boarding house and going to night school to learn the English language. In 1870 he and his brother John came on to California. Here Manuel sought his uncle, Charles Smith, who was farming the Oakley ranch in Contra Costa County near Antioch. Wheat was the principal crop, and after it was harvested it was hauled

to Antioch for shipment by rail and boat.   As soon as he could look about
a little, young Viera found work on Sherman Island.   It was while he
was there that the late Charles McLaughlin, who was owner of considerable land and was irrigation agent for the Southern Pacific Railway, was
attracted to him and offered to assist him in getting a start.   He rented
some 800 acres of the Marsh tract, near the landing, and met with a fair
degree of success.   This gave him a start and soon he began buying land;
he also began the sheep business, and in time his flocks increased until he
had some 2000 head.   He also engaged in threshing and baling hay, running two threshing outfits with about twenty men each.   He threshed all
over this section of the county and down into Alameda County as far as
Livermore.   He worked hard himself and kept investing in land.   His
first purchase was 480 acres, which he developed into a comfortable home
place, and later added 368 acres of the Marsh tract, where he now lives.
This ranch was covered with large live-oak trees, and these he had to
clear off to set out his vineyard.   In time he came to own some 850 acres
of good farming and fruit land in this vicinity.   He also invested in property in San Francisco, but lost the buildings at the time of the fire in 1906,
and then sold his lots.   He was always progressive and has kept abreast
of the times, using more modern agricultural implements to facilitate his
ranch work.   He met with some bad luck with his sheep in the early days.
One of the dry years he sent his flocks south into Fresno County, hoping
to find feed for them, but he did not find it, and in driving them back to
Contra Costa County lost about 1000 head.   He pastured his sheep in
the Berkeley Hills and Moraga Valley, before these sections were built up.

Manuel Viera was fortunate in choosing for his life partner a woman
who has worked shoulder to shoulder with him and has given him every
encouragement possible in his efforts to attain success.   The wedding of
Mr. Viera and Miss Elizabeth Whelihan, a native daughter of California, born in San Francisco, occurred on April 17, 1882.   Her parents were
John and Dorothy (Flynn) Whelihan, who were born in Ireland and
came to New Orleans when they were young, and there grew up and were
married.   One daughter was born in New Orleans.   In 1854 they decided to come to California and took passage via the Isthmus of Panama.
John Whelihan settled in Contra Costa County and became a well-known
and prosperous rancher, but died in 1871 leaving six children: Mary,
Elizabeth, Julia, John, Eugene and David.   Of these, four are living.   As
a girl, Elizabeth Whelihan learned dressmaking, for her mother believed
in bringing her children up to become useful citizens.   Of the marriage of
Mr. and Mrs. Viera eight children were born.   John F. runs the home
ranch and is the father of four boys: John F., Jr., George, Robert and
Richard C.   Eugene J. is a rancher and has four children: Edward, Dorothy, Donald and Bettyjean.   Francis is also interested in ranching and
real estate.   May is an auditor in the quartermaster's department in San
Francisco. Cyril, a graduate from the University of California, was made
manager of the magnesite mine in which Mr. Viera is heavily interested

in Stanislaus County, but died at the age of twenty-two. Elizabeth died at the age of eight months. Joseph G., a rancher in Antioch Precinct No. 5, has four children: Joseph G., Jr., Howard, Bernard and Catherine. He saw service in the World War. William, now in the automobile business in San Francisco, was in five major engagements during the World War. He is married and has had three children: William, Jr., Stanley and Wallace, who died in infancy. Mr. Viera has distributed his property among his children, to give them a start in life, and they have all become useful citizens. In politics Mr. Viera is a Republican. He has given liberally towards all public improvements and believes in living up to the Golden Rule. The family are members of the Catholic Church and have a large circle of friends in eastern Contra Costa County.

JAMES LEROY EAKLE.—The efficient manager of the Tilden Lumber Company's yards at Richmond is James Leroy Eakle, who is also a director in the First National Bank of Richmond. He was born at Woodland, Cal., on July 23, 1884, a son of Christian and Margaret (Edrington) Eakle, both natives of Kentucky. Christian Eakle crossed the plains with an ox-team and settled in Yolo County, where he was later married. There were twelve children in the Eakle family, James Leroy being the youngest. He received his education in the public schools of Yolo County, graduating from the high school and then entering business college to better prepare him for the activities of life. His first work upon leaving school was in the lumber business of Tilden and Eakle at Knights Landing; his next move was to Nevada where he was employed by the Mazuma Lumber Company for a year. Returning to California he worked in a hardware store in San Francisco for Dunham and Hayden. In 1910 Mr. Eakle went to Pullman for the Tilden Lumber Company and remained there two years, then came as yard foreman to the plant of which he is now manager, having been promoted in 1915. The territory served by this lumber yard extends from Rodeo to the county line of Alameda County and twenty men are required to handle the volume of business. Mr. Eakle first came to Point Richmond in 1901, being employed here two months, but since 1903 he has practically made this his headquarters. In 1907-1908 he managed the first hardware store established on Macdonald Avenue, at Second Street, remaining for two years.

On November 19, 1912, Mr. Eakle and Miss Ethel Farnell were united in marriage at Richmond. She is a daughter of William and Elizabeth (Scott) Farnell, natives of Nova Scotia and California, respectively. The family settled in Mendocino County for many years. There are two children in the Eakle family, Jean Elizabeth, aged twelve; and James L., Jr., aged five. Mr. Eakle is a member of the Masons and the Elks. He belongs to the Chamber of Commerce and the Builders Exchange, serving as a director in the latter organization. He takes an active interest in community work and for recreation enjoys golfing, being a member of the Carquinez Golf Club.

COWELL PORTLAND CEMENT COMPANY.—The site where the Cowell Portland Cement Company is located was for many years part of the Rancho Monte del Diablo, the great grant owned originally by the Galindo family. Part of these lands bore lime rock and were acquired many years ago by Henry Cowell. He added to these from time to time and the property was leased out for grazing purposes.

In 1906 the Cowell family conceived the idea of building a cement plant in Contra Costa County, and the Cowell Portland Cement Company was incorporated by E. V. Cowell, S. H. Cowell, I. M. Cowell, H. E. Cowell, and W. H. George. Ground was broken and the construction of the Cowell Portland Cement Company was started.

The plant covers nine acres of ground and was completed and in operation early in 1909. It has operated continuously ever since, and has a daily capacity of 5000 barrels of Mt. Diablo Cement. Mt. Diablo Cement is distributed all over the States of California, Oregon, Nevada, the Hawaiian Islands, Central and South America. It was awarded the gold medal for quality at the Panama-Pacific International Exposition.

The Cowell Portland Cement Company is fortunate in the fact that almost all of its raw materials are found on its own property and the supply is inexhaustible. The Cowell Portland Cement Company operates its own store, hotels and boarding houses for its employees at Cowell, Contra Costa County, Cal. On the property is a good graded school which is attended by the children of the employees.

The parent company, Henry Cowell Lime and Cement Company, operates branches at Sacramento, Oakland, San Jose, Santa Cruz, San Francisco and Portland, Ore., which help in the distribution of Mt. Diablo Cement and other products manufactured and handled by this company.

At the present time S. H. Cowell is president, Miss Helen E. Cowell is treasurer, and W. H. George is secretary and general manager.

The products of the Cowell Portland Cement Company are carried to market by a railroad owned by the same stockholders, known as the Bay Point and Clayton Railroad Company, which has connections with the San Francisco-Sacramento Railroad Company at Clyde, Cal., and the Southern Pacific Company and the Atchison, Topeka and Santa Fe Railroad at Bay Point, giving it unsurpassed facilities for making prompt deliveries to its customers.

WALTER W. HOFFMAN.—Among the prosperous farmers of eastern Contra Costa County is Walter W. Hoffman, a man of ability, intelligence and good business capacity, whose property lies a short distance north of Byron in Byron Precinct No. 1. He is a man of liberal views and of strict integrity, energetic and capable, and throughout the community is held in high regard as a man whose word is as good as his bond. Of German ancestry, he was born July 15, 1871, the eldest of four children born to Ferdinand and Eliza (Knowlton) Hoffman, early settlers in the Byron section of Contra Costa County. Ferdinand Hoffman came to California from St. Louis, Mo., in 1852 and engaged in gold mining in El Dorado County, then upon removing to this section he and his brother Christian engaged in the sheep business. Ferdinand Hoffman became the owner of a section and a half of land in the Byron district. Most of this acreage is now in the Byron-Bethany Irrigation District, fifty acres are in the Diablo Valley, while 300 acres is pasture land and lies in the hills. The portion of the Hoffman estate now under irrigation has been distributed to the heirs and is in a high state of cultivation, is excellent alfalfa land and much of it has been planted to trees and vines. The other children of the Hoffman family are Mrs. Emily Fry; Byron F. married Miss McIntyre; and Mrs. Clara Houston, all farmer folk living in the Byron section. The father passed away in 1905; and the mother in 1924, aged seventy-two years.

At Brentwood in 1904, Mr. Hoffman was married to Miss Olive Wills, a daughter of pioneer Byron settlers, and to them have been born three children; Ferdinand W., a partner with his father in farming, saw service during the World War; Thelma, a graduate of the chemical department of the University of California, now in charge of the chemical laboratory at the University in Berkeley; and Elise. Mr. Hoffman operates ninety acres mainly devoted to alfalfa and grain; has twelve acres in young apricots and fourteen acres in table grapes. He is a director in the recently organized shipping association which gives a shipping point for farming products.

MRS. MARGARET BELSHAW.—A prominent place among the women who have left their impress on the development of Antioch and vicinity must be accorded Mrs. Margaret Belshaw, widow of the late John T. Belshaw, one of the foremost merchants and citizens of Antioch in his day. Although her name does not show on the roster, yet she aided her husband in the performance of his varied business affairs and was an inspiration to him at all times. Before her marriage she was Margaret Raap, born at Rome, N. Y., sixty-nine years ago, a daughter of Anthony and Julia (Shears) Rapp. They were both natives of Germany and there were married, Mr. Rapp being aged twenty-one and Mrs. Rapp, nineteen. He was a millwright and cabinet-maker, a trade he followed after arriving in America soon after their marriage. They became the parents of twelve children, the only survivors being Mrs. Belshaw and her sister, Mrs. Sarah DeWitt, of San Anselmo, Cal.

The progenitor of the Belshaw family in America was Thomas Warren Belshaw, a native of Ireland who came to the New World in 1755 with his wife Elizabeth and four children and settled in Connecticut. In 1793 they moved to Fort Herkimer, N. Y.; but soon after he and some others took up 1000 acres of land at Jordanville, and there he died in 1827, aged ninety-two. David Belshaw came next in line of descent.

David Belshaw was born in Connecticut, near Hartford, in 1777. He was twice married, his first wife being Lydia Isham; and she had seven children: Rose E., Erastus, William T., Flavilla, Lydia, Orilla and Sally. His second wife was Betsy Bennett. David Belshaw died in 1868.

William T. Belshaw, father of John T., was born in Herkimer County, on October 19, 1804. He married for his first wife Mary Rhodes, and they had two children, Mortimer W. and Rosetta McLaughlin. His second wife was Huldah Durfee, and she had four children: John T., Mary C. Dye, Lucy J. Starkweather, and Violetta H. Purchase. The mother of John T. Belshaw died on April 17, 1887.

John T. Belshaw was born at Jordanville, Herkimer County, N. Y., on June 4, 1834, and received his education in the common schools of his locality. He grew up in Jordanville and there, in 1876, was married to Margaret Rapp, and that same year he and his bride came to California and to Inyo County, where he became associated with his brother, Mortimer W., as superintendent of the Cerro Gordo mine, which he owned. In 1880 John T. Belshaw went to Judsonville, Contra Costa County, and bought an interest in a general merchandise business, the firm becoming Landow, Belshaw & Company. He continued with this firm till 1883, when he located in Antioch and engaged in the same line of business, having for his partners Mortimer W. and Jay P. Belshaw. This business occupied his time and attention for many years. Mr. Belshaw served as a member of the board of trustees of Antioch, and also of the public school. He died on July 1, 1908, after a busy and useful career.

Of the marriage of John T. Belshaw and Margaret Rapp three children were born. William Walter married Miss Ada Shreve on September 19, 1909, and they had a son Charles M., now living in Berkeley with his mother. William Walter Belshaw was a Mason, and belonged to the Sciots, the Eastern Star and to General Winn Parlor, N. S. G. W. He was one of the founders of the East Contra Costa Chamber of Commerce. He died at the home of his aunt in San Anselmo on August 22, 1925, having gone there for rest and to try to recuperate from an illness. John T. Belshaw, Jr., is purchasing agent for Contra Costa County and lives in Martinez. He married Grace Valentine Critcher on November 25, 1906, and they have four children: Cornelia Margaret, John T. Jr., Virginia Miriam, and Mortimer W. Imogene Violetta is the wife of Corning De Saules and resides in Sacramento. They were married on March 25, 1911, and have two children, Corinne Belshaw and Margaret Elizabeth.

Mrs. Belshaw is an active worker in the Women's Improvement Club of Antioch, and in every way tries to do her best to assist in the upbuilding of the city. She conducts an apartment house on G Street, leasing the southeast corner of the property to the Shell Oil Company for an oil service station. She is a good business manager and has drawn around herself a large circle of friends who esteem her for her many charitable acts and her high Christian character. She is a Christian Scientist. Fraternally, she is a member of the Eastern Star, and the Rebekahs at Antioch.

JOHN RICHARD NYSTROM.—In the annals of Contra Costa County, where so many years of his life were spent, the name of John R. Nystrom, the honored pioneer of Richmond, Cal., should be especially mentioned. He was a native of Finland, where he was born on August 24, 1848, the oldest child of four sons and four daughters of John and Johanna (Kalis) Nystrom, who spent their entire lives in that country. John was reared on a farm and was educated in the public schools of Finland. At the age of eighteen the spirit of adventure within him asserted itself and led him to sail on a sea-bound vessel as a deck hand. He soon became a capable sailor, mastering the nautical laws and regulations, and eventually became an adept in the intricacies of guiding a ship in safety to the various ports of the world. He was advanced to the position of an able seaman in less time than most sailors, and during his career as a seaman visited practically all of the important seaports of the world.

In 1870 Mr. Nystrom arrived in San Francisco harbor. He did not wait to receive his regular discharge from his vessel, but began sailing on San Francisco Bay and adjacent rivers. Desiring to abandon seafaring life, he located at Ellis Landing, Contra Costa County, and was employed by Ellis & Smith. After a time Mr. Nystrom, with Mr. Smith, went to Stege and there continued the business. In 1881 he purchased seventy acres of the San Pablo grant, which he improved and continued to farm until 1903, at which time he realized the value of his land as a residential section for the fast growing city of Richmond, which it adjoined. He subdivided his farm into city lots, with the exception of five acres which he retained as a home place, and called the tract the Nystrom Addition to the City of Richmond. In company with others he purchased the El Cerrito Land Company's property of forty-three acres, and with Harry Ells bought the Suarez Tract of forty acres. These tracts were subdivided and sold in city lots, the transaction being regarded as one of the largest real estate sales of that period.

On December 1, 1881, John R. Nystrom was united in marriage with Miss Mary Griffins, daughter of Owen and Kate (Evans) Griffins, natives of England, in which country the parents were married. Later Mr. and Mrs. Griffins emigrated to Australia, where Mr. Griffins was a merchant; and about 1856 he came to San Francisco. There the family remained until they locatetd at Alameda for a short time, after which they came to the Richmond district, as it is now known. Mr. and Mrs. Nystrom became the parents of the following children, now living: Alfred John and Edwin, both living in Richmond; Mary E., wife of C. E. Linville, of Lake County; Mabel E., wife of H. Mason, of Richmond; Alice, Mrs. L. E. Schrader, of Pittsburg; William H., of Richmond; Louise E., Mrs. F. M. Van Ness, of Pittsburg; Hazel E., a graduate of the Richmond High School, living at home; Edna M., also at home; and Raymond, who was educated at the Hitchcock Military Academy in San Rafael and is now in Berkeley. Mrs. Nystrom is a native daughter and was born on the Griffins ranch adjoining the property of her late husband. She has a brother, Evan Griffins, and a sister, Mrs. Kittie Crews, both in Richmond, the latter residing on the old home place at the corner of Ohio and Fifteenth Streets. Two other sisters are Mrs. Charles Berry, of East Oakland, and Mrs. C. L. Watrous, in Santa Clara County. A brother of J. R. Nystrom makes his home in Richmond.

J. R. Nystrom was an enthusiastic promoter of the best interests of Contra Costa County, and became prominent in the civic affairs of Richmond. He served fifteen years as school director, and in 1905 was elected to the office of city councilman. He passed away on December 23, 1913, at Richmond, where he was held in highest esteem as a constructive factor in the material, educational, and moral upbuilding of the city. Fraternally, he was a member of McKinley Lodge No. 347, F. & A. M., and of the Order of the Eastern Star, at Richmond, and was also a Knight Templar and a Shriner. The Nystrom family removed from Richmond to Berkeley in August, 1922, and now reside at 2970 Magnolia Avenue.

ERNEST WILLIAM REHNERT.—The memory of the early California pioneer is always held in reverence by the succeeding generations; for to his steadfastness of purpose and willingness to face danger, privation, and often death, to reach a new and undeveloped region in order that he may build a home for himself and help found a commonwealth for posterity, is due the success we now enjoy in this great State. Such a man was the late Ernest William Rehnert, who met an accidental death in 1892, when his team ran away. He was born in Prussia on September 6, 1824, and attended the Lutheran schools until he was confirmed. He then served an apprenticeship to learn the trade of the blacksmith, after which he worked as a journeyman in various cities in Europe, finally arriving at Hamburg, Germany. In 1847 he decided he would seek his fortune in the New World and accordingly embarked for America. In due time he arrived at Galveston, Texas, and there worked a year at his trade. He then entered the service of the United States Government as a veterinary surgeon and served during the Mexican War. On December 16, 1851, he arrived in San Francisco with his wife, whom he had married on June 15, of that year. She was Barbara Miller in maidenhood, and was a native of Germany.

Upon arriving in San Francisco, Mr. Rehnert worked two years at his trade and then established a business for himself, continuing at it for six years more. He went to the gold mines during the Fraser River excitement, but soon returned to California. The first home he owned was located at No. 310 Fremont Street in San Francisco. Later he bought a place in Oakland on Second Street, between Harrison and Alice Streets, in which the children still have an interest. In 1859 he came up into Contra Costa County and bought a squatter's claim to 125 acres in San Pablo, which was eventually lost through litigation. Here he improved a home and raised grain, hay and stock until he died. He also operated a threshing machine throughout the western end of the county,

John M. Walker

and threshed grain where the city of Richmond now stands. He was the first man to run a traction engine in this section and always kept abreast of the times in all things. He liked California and did all he could to foster projects for its upbuilding. He also conducted a blacksmith shop on his ranch.

Mr. Rehnert and his good wife became the parents of five children, two of whom are living. Charles W. Rehnert lives in Oakland with his wife, whom he married in 1893, and whose maiden name was Hattie Ward. They had three children, one of whom met an accidental death. Cecil Ward Rehnert is employed by Whitthorn & Swan, and Thelma Eleanor Rehnert is employed in the Farmers & Merchants Bank. Miss Louise Rehnert is engaged in the fire and auto insurance business, representing the Connecticut Fire Insurance Company; she also sells liability insurance and has been in business for fifteen years, operating under a State license. She lives at No. 440 Thirty-eighth Street, Oakland. Annie was a school teacher and died at the age of twenty-one years. A pair of twins died in infancy. Mrs. Rehnert died at the age of sixty-eight, in 1898.

After the death of Mr. Rehnert, his widow and his daughter Louise bought the old homestead place, which up to that time had been in litigation as part of the San Pablo Grant. Some time after, they built a modern and comfortable house; and here they made their home until the mother died, and Miss Rehnert lived there until 1923. Miss Rehnert is a member of the Lutheran Church. She takes an active interest in civic and community welfare.

JOHN M. WALKER.—An old settler held in highest esteem for the many qualities which have distinguished his long residence in this part of the State, is John M. Walker, one of California's native sons, born in Contra Costa County, on April 10, 1862, the only son of James T. and Mary C. (Vaughan) Walker. James T. Walker was a native of East Tennessee, born in 1820, and with his parents migrated to Missouri. His father, Joseph Walker, came to California in 1833 with the celebrated Kit Carson company; they trapped and hunted throughout California. He was the first white man to camp in the Yosemite, which he did in 1833. In 1844 James T. Walker organized a company of his own and the same year set out for the far West from Independence, Mo. He trapped and hunted until the discovery of gold, and then engaged in mining, locating a number of placer mines in Amador County in the early days. With a good stake he returned to Missouri and with his family and 500 head of cattle again started across the plains. The company started in 1849, but that winter was spent on the eastern side of the Rocky Mountains. In 1850 he located in Contra Costa County, where he spent the remainder of his days. He purchased part of the Rancho Las Nueces y Bolbones, a Spanish grant of 6000 acres, from Juana

16

Sanchos Pacheco, a widow, but a great deal of the land was afterwards subjected to much litigation and was lost; the balance was sold as a subdivision. James T. Walker engaged in farming and stock-raising and became very influential in the community. He was a county supervisor in the early days, and a staunch Democrat. The Vaughan family were also early settlers in California, coming from Missouri in 1857 and settling at Sutter's Fort. Later the father located on Dry Creek in Sonoma County, where he raised cattle and horses and engaged in general farming. There were three children in this family: Louise, now Mrs. Joel M. Walker, of Walnut Creek; Josephine, Mrs. Porter Claire, now deceased; and John M., our subject. The father passed away in 1902, aged eighty-two years; the mother lived to be eighty-four years old and died in April, 1922, in Walnut Creek.

The education of John M. Walker was received at the Pleasant Hill school and in the school of experience. When he became of age he naturally drifted into the cattle business, in which he was engaged for about thirty-two years; his herd numbered 1500 and more, most of the time. During the hard times about ten years ago, Mr. Walker lost heavily. He now owns eighty-five acres of homestead land on Mount Diablo.

At Concord, Cal., May 13, 1886, Mr. Walker was married to Miss Margaret McDonald, daughter of W. L. and Artimesia (Stinson) McDonald. The McDonald family came to California from Missouri in the sixties and settled in Napa County. W. L. McDonald was a breeder of fine horses and raised a number of winners. Mr. and Mrs. Walker have had seven children. J. R. Walker is a veterinarian in South San Francisco. Ambrose T. is superintendent of the McCreary Estate in San Benito County. Gertrude is now Mrs. Oren Chamberlain and resides in Oakland. Grace, Mrs. Ed. Forestier, makes her home in Burlingame. Jack lives in San Francisco. The other two children passed away in infancy. These children were all born on the Spanish grant settled on by James T. Walker when he came to the county. In politics Mr. Walker is a Democrat.

ERNEST G. GRIFFIN.—Descended from an honored pioneer family, and himself a well-known and highly esteemed citizen of Richmond, Cal., Ernest G. Griffin is a native son, having been born at Woodland, Yolo County, on September 26, 1874, the son of George W. and Anna C. (Brown) Griffin, pioneers of that county.

The grandfather, Joseph Griffin, was one of the early settlers of the Golden State, having crossed the plains in a covered wagon train in 1850, and for a time engaged in mining. Not finding the mining business as remunerative as he expected, he returned to Missouri, where he planned to remain. Circumstances, however, changed his plans and in 1857 he again crossed the plains, accompanied by his family and a brother-in-law, Ben. Ely. The second trip across the plains was not as peaceable as the first, for the Indians were hostile, and not only did they lose some of their stock, but on many occasions they narrowly escaped with their lives. After his arrival in California Mr. Griffin operated his ranch in Yolo County and in 1867 purchased more land, and by subsequent purchases accumulated about 1000 acres in Yolo County and 180 acres in Lake County. He was born in Virginia on February 6, 1818, a member of an influential family of that State. His mother died while he was yet at an early age, and, being left without the care of a mother, he was reared in the family of an older sister. In early days he migrated to Missouri. There he became a farmer, and from that State he journeyed overland to California, where he achieved success as a stockman and farmer. When he died on December 12, 1885, he left a large estate, and an enviable record as a man of sterling character who had led an exemplary Christian life and was a faithful member of the Christian Church.

George W. Griffin, the father of the subject of this sketch, was born in Ralls County, Mo., September 20, 1847, and has made his home in Yolo County since he was ten years of age. In 1872 he was united in marriage with Anna C. Brown, a native of Ohio, at the home of her mother in Woodland, Cal. George W. Griffin followed in the footsteps of his father and became a very successful farmer and large landowner, purchasing at one time over 1300 acres of land. In 1894 he was elected sheriff of Yolo County; and through his firm allegiance to the principles of law and justice, his resolute and daring spirit, he so pleased the voters of the county that he was elected four times to the office. George W. Griffin is the head of the G. W. & M. Quicksilver Mining Corporation of Colusa County.

Ernest G. Griffin started his career as a deputy, or under sheriff, in 1894, and in 1906 commenced his services in the employ of the Standard Oil Company. In 1916 he joined the United States Army and was stationed for a time at the Mexican border. During the World War Mr. Griffin served over seas and was in charge of the 3rd Battalion, 159th Regiment, United States Infantry, and while in France saw active service on the offensive at the Battle of the Somme, which continued from August 8 to Armistice Day, November 11, 1918. Mr. Griffin remained with the same battalion throughout his entire service in the World War, and when they returned to the United States he mustered them out at the Presidio in San Francisco. He then resumed his work with the Standard Oil Company, where he had formerly been employed since 1906 until he organized the first guard for the identification of the employees of the corporation and protection of the oil industry. After his return from the war and to the employ of the Standard Oil Company, he was promoted to the post of general foreman of labor at Richmond, where he is still located.

On September 6, 1900, Ernest G. Griffin was united in marriage with Miss Geraldine M. Delano, of Sacramento, a daughter of Joseph P. Delano, master mechanic of the Southern Pacific Railway. Her mother, whose maiden name was Jane Stanton, a native of Michigan, died when Mrs. Griffin was a little child. Mr. and Mrs. Griffin are the parents of one child, Blossom Griffin, a graduate of the University of California, Class of 1926, and now a teacher in the Richmond schools. Mr. Griffin is a fine marksman, and while a member of the National Guard of California won the United States championship for superior marksmanship. He is very fond of hunting and the life of the great out-of-doors.

ROBERT B. LOVE.—A representative of one of the pioneer families that helped to make history in California and Contra Costa County is R. B. Love, who was born at Somersville in 1868, the son of John and Margaret (Thomas) Love, natives of Illinois and Scotland, respectively. The father was one of the pioneer stage drivers and was well known to all the old timers in this section of the county. He came to California in the late fifties and was interested with his brother in the cattle business in Inyo County. Later he took up ranching and cattle-raising in the Diablo Valley and on Marsh Creek, where he had valuable holdings. Both parents have passed away, Mr. Love in 1876, and Mrs. Love in 1912, both in Contra Costa County.

R. B. Love attended the common schools and at the age of eleven began working with stock on his father's ranch. He became an adept with the rope and could ride with the best of the vaqueros on the range, and he practically lived in the saddle for many years. He next tried mining coal; but for the past twenty-five years he has lived in Antioch, where he owns the Santa Fe Hotel and has run it for many years. He has always been a booster for Antioch and has great faith in its future prosperity.

Mr. Love was united in marriage with Miss Anna Lewis, born at Tacoma, Wash., and they have had four children: Dr. E. L. Love, a dentist of Colfax, Cal.; Mrs. Arthur Manter, of Hayward, Cal.; Clyde, a machinist in Berkeley, Cal.; and Jessie, wife of Stanley Marlin, of Hayward, Cal. There are several grandchildren to brighten the Love home circle. Mrs. Love belongs to the Eastern Star and the Rebekahs of Antioch. Mr. Love erected one of the most beautiful country homes in the county, out of the native stone, on Marsh Creek. It was for many years the show place of the section. Both Mr. and Mrs. Love have always been hard workers for the upbuilding of the county. They have made many friends and are highly esteemed.

JOHN THEOPHIL STRENTZEL, M. D.—A man whose name will go down in the annals of Contra Costa County as the pioneer orchardist, is Dr. John Strentzel, who located in what is now the Alhambra Valley and for the balance of his life made this his home. He was born in Poland in 1813 and received his schooling in that country and in Hungary, obtaining his M. D. degree in Budapest. Early in life he decided to take up the profession followed by his father, that of medicine, and accordingly all his energies were thereafter bent in that direction. The breaking out of the Polish revolution in 1830 changed his outlook, and when the Polish army was disbanded a year later he was given the choice of joining the Russian army or exiling himself in some foreign land. Like thousands of his countrymen he chose the latter course, and his first thoughts were of America. He landed in New Orleans, stopping but a short time, and then pushed westward to Texas with the Peterson Colony that was formed in Louisville, Ky. In 1840 he built his cabin on land now the site of Dallas, Texas; and after several years spent on the Trinity River he purchased a homestead in Lamar County and practiced medicine and surgery for several years.

On December 31, 1843, Dr. Strentzel was united in marriage with Miss Louisiana Erwin, daughter of a prominent Kentuckian who had moved into Tennessee and later into Texas. The glowing reports of the wonderful Pacific Coast region so fired Dr. Strentzel's enthusiasm that he caught the fever of the Forty-niners and with a company of thirty-five persons set out across the plains, leaving his Texas home on March 22, 1849. For 800 miles the little party had to fight their way through an unknown country, as no pathfinder up to that time had blazed a trail to El Paso. The party suffered from lack of water many times, and upon reaching El Paso Mrs. Strentzel was taken ill from the effects of drinking alkaline water on the desert. They spent July 4, 1849, in El Paso, where the party broke up, some returning to their homes, some remaining in El Paso, and the remainder coming on to California. The trip of these last took them through the Apache Indian country. The Strentzels and party floated down and across the Rio Grande River above El Paso on a raft, and then by easy stages made their way westward. After crossing the Colorado River they struck out across the Mojave Desert and weary and worn arrived in San Diego, the gateway into California for their little band of Argonauts.

Dr. Strentzel had intended taking a boat at this port for San Francisco, but he was unable to sell his horses for what he deemed them to be worth and hence decided to take the trail overland. This brought him through the great San Joaquin Valley, and when he got to the Tuolumne River they were so thoroughly in love with the country that they decided they would remain. He established a store and ferry about two miles south of La Grange, which he conducted for two years. It is said that one day Dr. Strentzel would entertain John C. Fremont or General Miller and other noted personages of those days, and the next he might act as host to a band of desperadoes who were plundering the countryside. As a result of the hardships Mrs. Strentzel had undergone, her health was greatly impaired and for three years she was confined to her bed, requiring her husband's almost constant attention, in consequence of which he gave up his business to take care of his wife. He bought 600 acres of land along the Merced River below Snelling and took up cattle raising and ranching until the floods of the winter swept away the work of years in a single night, flooded his home, and subjected him to exposure from which he never fully recovered. As soon as he was able to travel, Dr. Strentzel left the Merced River country for good.

From Stockton the Strentzels traveled to Santa Cruz and then to Benicia, at that time the capital of the State, with the legislature in session. Here the Doctor met a former neighbor from home, who was living in Martinez, and was so impressed with his friend's glowing account of the wonderful climate that he visited the Cañada del Hambre Valley, which lay nestling in the hills and basking in the summer sun. He reasoned that here he had found the proper spot for indulging in his hobby of orcharding and growing flowers and shrubs; and on April 4, 1853, he came to Martinez and purchased twenty acres of land two and one-half miles south of Martinez, paying fifty dollars an acre for it. Mrs. Strentzel did not like the name borne by the valley, and christened the Strentzel home "Alhambra"; and the valley soon adopted and has since been known under that name, taken from Irving's description of the Moorish paradise. On this twenty acres Dr. Strentzel gave full play to his hobby and began the propagation of fruits and vines. He secured trees, plants and vines from Eastern sources, even importing some from Scotland, and planted them on his ranch. He set out the first pear orchard in Central California, which later contained sixty varieties of pears, and at this writing some of the trees are still bearing fruit profusely. With the help of his wife he raised fruits of all kinds. Some of the first Muscat grapes in the county were grown on his place, and it was through his success along these lines that the owners of the vast areas back in the hills and valleys that had been given over to grain and stock soon began to follow the Doctor's lead, so that grapes became one of the principal products.

Instead of succumbing to ill health, Dr. and Mrs. Strentzel regained their health and lived to enjoy themselves in their Alhambra Valley home. Their one child, Louise Wanda Strentzel, later became the wife of John Muir, world-famed naturalist, lecturer and traveler, from whom Muir Woods in Marin County were named. The home they first established in 1853 remained their home until the marriage of their daughter. After her marriage they gave the old homestead to her and moved nearer Martinez. On the commanding knoll in the center of the valley, this pioneer couple erected a comfortable home; and there they spent their declining years, surrounded by their many friends.

Dr. Strentzel was the founder of the first Grange in the county, a branch of the Patrons of Husbandry, and took a very active interest in the Grange movement in the State. He was a Republican in politics. Of a saving nature, he accumulated considerable property, both in the country and in Martinez, which, upon his death in 1890, passed to his wife and daughter. Some years after he died his widow gave to the city the site for the Martinez Free Library building. After her death the Strentzel property passed to the two daughters of the Muirs, one of whom, Mrs. Wanda Muir Hanna, lives in the original Strentzel homestead. The name of Strentzel is one to conjure with in Contra Costa County, and ranks along with the names of Sutter, Bidwell, Broderick, Terry and other strong and forceful Western characters.

MRS. ELIZABETH M. SHAFER.—The life of Mrs. Elizabeth M. Shafer has been so closely interwoven with the pioneer history of Contra Costa County that her name calls up to the old generation a past replete with incidents, the events which laid the foundation of the county's present prosperity, the hardships, the trials, the dangers and privations which accompanied every effort of the first settlers of this then practically unknown section. When William Shafer brought his bride to Contra Costa County in 1867, the wild oats grew in profusion and the wild cattle and horses roamed at will over the vast domain; wild flowers of every hue and variety grew upon the hillsides and in the valleys. Life in a new country is not all pleasure, however; but the indomitable spirit of the pioneer prevailed and for fifty-two years this pioneer couple labored and their courageous spirit was rewarded in seeing the wilderness of 1867 turned into a veritable garden spot. To the present generation Mrs. Shafer is equally well-known, and her interesting description of her life in the early days is listened to with rapt attention, for she still retains her wonderful memory for details of the pioneer settling of eastern Contra Costa County.

The parents of Mrs. Shafer were John T. and Sarah J. (White) Pearce, both natives of Ohio. Their parents removed to Indiana in 1842, and in that State Mr. Pearce met and married Miss White. The week after their marriage they moved by horse and wagon to Illinois, settling ten miles southwest of Chicago; and there, on May 26, 1843, their daughter Elizabeth M. Pearce was born. The following June her parents moved to a farm near Knoxville, Iowa, where she grew up and attended the country schools. On April 6, 1858, when she was fifteen years old, the family began their journey across the plains to California in a covered wagon, reaching their goal in September of the same year. The journey was not accomplished without hardships and privations, but owing to the courage and fortitude of the leaders and captain of the train, they crossed the plains successfully, with no serious results. The family first settled in Yolo County, where they remained for one year, and then moved to Rio Vista, Solano County, where Elizabeth M. attended school.

On January 26, 1861, Elizabeth M. Pearce was married to William Shafer, who was born on February 8, 1836, in Pennsylvania. Mr. Shafer grew to young manhood in his native State and when nineteen years old came to California and settled near the present site of Isleton, on the Sacramento River. The young couple farmed on the Sacramento River from 1861 to 1867, when they came to Contra Costa County and took up their residence in what is now the Eden Plain school district, so named by Mr. Shafer; this section is now known as Knightsen. Mrs. Shafer today relates the incident of crossing the river by means of scows and bringing their house with them. They settled in eastern Contra Costa County and became successful farmers and stock raisers; finally owning about 900 acres of tillable land. Mr. and Mrs. Shafer became the parents of five children: Adrian H., a rancher near Marsh Creek, Contra Costa County; George H., of Brentwood; Hannah J., who married Cyrus Harris, and passed away in 1922; Mabel E., the wife of George Geddes, a rancher in the Knightsen Precinct; and Winifred, the wife of Mott C. Preston, of Brentwood. Mr. and Mrs. Shafer retired from active farm life in 1913, after a happy and successful life of fifty-two years on the farm. They removed to Brentwood, where they built a fine residence and where Mrs. Shafer now resides. Mr. Shafer passed away at the family home on March 10, 1915, after a very useful life. He had been an Odd Fellow for many years, affiliating with Antioch Lodge. To such people as the Shafers, California, and Contra Costa County in particular, owe much, for their courage and industry helped to bring to eastern Contra Costa County its present prosperity.

ELAM C. BROWN.—No man in Martinez was better posted on Contra Costa County history of the early days than Elam C. Brown, who died on December 30, 1925, at his home in Martinez. His father was the pioneer of Martinez, and his grandfather was the second American farmer to locate in Contra Costa County and actually till the soil; the first man to do this was Dr. John Marsh. Our subject was named after his grandfather and, like him, had always taken an active interest in the preservation of historical material and relics pertaining to the pioneer days. He was a native son of Martinez and was born on February 5, 1853, a son of the late Hon. Thomas A. Brown, who is mentioned at length in another page in this history.

Elam C. Brown grew to young manhood and attended the public schools in Martinez, and afterwards took a classical course for a time at the University of California in Berkeley. His desire was to be a surveyor and civil engineer, and for one year he studied with and worked under M. C. King, at one time a surveyor of Oakland, before entering the university. After leaving college, equipped with a theoretical and practical knowledge of engineering, Mr. Brown did some of his first work in the mountain sections, and soon became interested in mining at Quincy, Plumas County. Returning to Martinez, he was elected county surveyor in 1892, took office January 1, 1893, and served over twenty years, retiring December 31, 1914. At each election he succeeded himself in office, performing his official duties to the satisfaction of all concerned. He also followed stock-raising in Briones Valley in this county, having 1700 acres of land at one time which he acquired from his father. His father helped to organize two of the early banks of Martinez, and Elam C. Brown remained a stockholder in the Martinez Bank until his death.

In Denver, Colorado, Elam C. Brown was united in marriage with Miss Minnie Andrews of Minnesota, a lady of culture and refinement. Mrs. Brown had a wide circle of friends, who mourned her passing in 1921. Mr. Brown lived in the old Brown residence at 825 Ward Street and had a host of warm personal friends.

J. D. Wightman.

JOEL DAVID WIGHTMAN.—Among the pioneers of Contra Costa County was Joel David Wightman, who made his influence felt for the best interests of the county he selected for his home and the scene of his activities. He was born at Council Bluffs, Iowa, on April 1, 1853, while his parents Reuben Oscar and Kate (Brezee) Wightman were en route to the West in covered wagons drawn by oxen. Mrs. Wightman had a brother living at Council Bluffs and about a week after their arrival there the baby was born. Mr. Wightman was not entirely satisfied with the train he had been with and decided to wait at Council Bluffs until another came along, and it was during 1854 that the family reached California. He had three brothers in the Santa Clara Valley, who had preceded him to California and thither he went to see them and to look about the country for a location. From there he went to Dutch Flat, Placer County, thence to Vacaville, Solano County. It was while they were living in the latter place that the father died in February, 1859, when his son was only five years of age. Soon afterwards Mrs. Wightman was married to Henry B. Reed, a harnessmaker of that town. Later they went to Carson City, Nev., where Joel attended school for about seven years, in the meantime making himself useful to his stepfather.

Coming back to California the Reed family located in Vacaville and there Joel started to learn the trade of wheelwright with a Mr. Ewing. Some time later Mr. Ewing went to Antioch, taking Joel with him, and the lad was so well impressed with the place that he induced his stepfather and mother to join him there. He completed his trade, then clerked in a store and worked at other employment until he went back to Carson City and helped to build the roundhouse for the railroad company, remaining a year. It was while there he met the woman whom he afterwards married. Returning to Antioch he took up carpentering and in time began taking contracts. Many of the early homes in and about Antioch were marks of his craft. He became interested in politics and was a successful candidate for supervisor and served two full terms. Although he was a Democrat he received the endorsement of the Republicans as well. He was a member of the building committee when the present courthouse at Martinez was erected. During his terms in office he gave his best energies to promote the interests of his constituents. He served two terms as justice of the peace in Antioch and was fair in dispensing justice as he saw it. He was a member of the Antioch Lodge No. 175, F. & A. M., and held the esteem of all who came to know him.

Joel D. Wightman was united in marriage at Antioch on March 5, 1874, with Mrs. Sarah (Snead) Osborne, a native of New Jersey, but living in Carson City, Nev., where she first met Mr. Wightman. She had two daughters by her first marriage: Mrs. Adelia Sterm and Mrs. Helena Swinburne, both now living in San Francisco. By her union with Mr. Wightman the following children were born: Carleton E., contractor and rancher of the Oakley district; Charles Budd, operator of a service station at Diablo Auto Park; and Ray Snead, all three mentioned elsewhere in this volume; Bessie B., wife of Fred Jasmann, of Dorris, Cal.; Percy S., in the garage business at Greenville, Cal.; and Minerva, a trained nurse and acting head of a hospital on the Island of Kaui, Hawaii. The family all grew up in this county and have made names and places for themselves upon growing to maturity. Mr. Wightman was an invalid about twelve years prior to his death, on March 5, 1917. He was superintending the raising of a flagpole at the Live Oak School when the staff slipped and pinned him to the ground, fracturing his spine, and for twelve years he was a patient sufferer. He was a man of high ideals and his passing was a great loss to the county. Mrs. Wightman makes her home with her son, Carleton E., near Oakley and is hale and hearty at the age of seventy-seven years.

CHARLES J. WOOD.—A native son of the Golden State whose life occupation has been that of a farmer is Charles J. Wood, the representative of a pioneer family in the Danville vicinity. Since an early period in the history of Contra Costa County, the Wood family has been identified with the agricultural interests of this locality, and it was on the ranch that he now owns and occupies that Charles J. was born, on November 9, 1868. His parents were Charles and Cynthia A. (Rice) Wood, natives of Concord, Mass., and Syracuse, N. Y.

In 1852 Charles Wood, Sr., came to California by the Nicaragua route, and immediately upon his arrival engaged in mining. Later, he, with his brother William, established a pack train between the mines and Marysville, where he was interested in the mercantile business. Mr. Wood was married in Marysville on April 26, 1857, to Miss Cynthia A. Rice, and five years later they, with two children, removed to Sycamore Valley, Contra Costa County, which place has remained the Wood home until the present day. Two children were born here, completing the family of four, William Louis, Sarah Elizabeth, Charlotte E., and Charles J. all of whom, excepting Sarah Elizabeth, still survive, she having passed away January 13, 1924. Mr. and Mrs. Wood, Sr., celebrated their Golden Wedding anniversary in April, 1907, only three weeks before the passing of Mr. Wood on May 20. Mrs. Wood survived until December 17, 1918. These pioneers were charter members of Danville Grange, instituted in 1873, Mr. Wood serving many years as Master. He was a progressive citizen, associated with various projects for the development of his locality and county, representing this district as assemblyman for two terms at Sacramento, and filling various offices of trust in Contra Costa County.

William Louis Wood lived for many years in Davis on the site of the present University Farm. He was married in 1900 to Miss Bertha Gaddis, of Woodland, and now resides with his family in Berkeley. He has two sons and one daughter: Henry C., Everett L., and Mrs. Remington Wood, all graduates of the University of California. Sarah Elizabeth, for fifteen years secretary of Danville Grange, was gifted with a genial, self-sacrificing disposition which endeared her to a host of friends, in whose memory she will long live for her cheery words and unselfish deeds. Charlotte E. Wood, who lives on the home place, is a woman of much culture, and for thirty years was teacher in the Sycamore school. She is unusually gifted with the pen; her verses and writings are much appreciated by the community, and she has been specially chosen "poet laureate" of the Grange, at Danville.

Charles J. Wood early in manhoood assumed the management of the home ranch. Following the footsteps of his father, he has been active in various enterprises that have had for their object the improvement and upbuilding of the community. He and his wife have been specially interested in providing for and encouraging better education. On October 24, 1897, Charles J. Wood and Kate F. Howard, daughter of Nathaniel S. and Elizabeth S. (Hitch) Howard, were married in Walnut Creek, Cal. Mr. Howard, a native of Massachusetts, came around Cape Horn, arriving in San Francisco on January 1, 1850. He proceeded at once to the mining districts, but soon returned to San Francisco, where in 1852 he was joined by his wife, also from Massachusetts. Here he was engaged in contracting until 1856, when he and his family moved to a farm in Green Valley. In 1887 he sold his farm and purchased a home in Walnut Creek. There were three daughters in the Howard family: Elizabeth, Mrs. William Smith, of Alamo; Amelia S., Mrs. Ridgway, of Walnut Creek; and Kate F., Mrs. Charles J. Wood, of Danville. Mrs. Howard passed away in June, 1876; and Mr. Howard in January, 1899.

Mrs. Charles J. Wood graduated from the Normal School in San Jose, and for ten years taught in the Contra Costa schools. She has been untiring in educational and Grange work, having served most successfully as Grange lecturer for many years. Although devoted to her family and home, she has always found time to aid in Red Cross and similar benevolent work when occasion required. Mr. and Mrs. Wood have three sons. Howard C. graduated from the University of California with his B. S. degree as civil engineer in 1923, and is now actively engaged in this work. George C. received his B. S. degree from the same university in 1922, graduating with honors from the College of Agriculture. He has been director of the local farm bureau, and is at present engaged in operating the home farm near Danville. Waldo E. is a senior in the University of California College of Agriculture, specializing in forestry. He was awarded the McDonald scholarship in 1926 for his high standing. These young men have been elected to various honor societies, and are a credit to their parents, their country and their Alma Mater. The Wood family are respected wherever known, and dispense a true California hospitality at their "Woodside" home.

JOHN F. SWETT.—A native of California, John F. Swett was born in San Francisco on August 1, 1879, a son of John and Mary L. (Tracy) Swett, and at the age of six was taken by his parents to their newly-acquired country home near Martinez to secure the advantages of rural life. He attended the Alhambra Grammar school from which he was graduated in 1892. One year later he returned to San Francisco and entered the Lowell High School, graduating in 1897. He then entered Stanford University that same year, taking a course intended to prepare him for the legal profession. In the midst of his college course, however, he suffered a severe attack of measles, which so weakened his eyesight and impaired his health, that he was compelled to give up all thought of a professional career. He returned to his home near Martinez and with his father and elder brother took up the management of Hill Girt Ranch, which consists of one hundred acres of orchard and vineyard situated in Alhambra Valley, four miles south of Martinez.

In 1918 John F. Swett was united in marriage with Miss Aileen Morrow, daughter of Stuart Morrow, a prominent business man of San Francisco.

After the death of his father and the retirement of his brother, Frank T. Swett, who became president of the Pear Growers' Association, Mr. Swett has managed the ranch property alone. In spite of his handicap of ill health he has been successful in a business way and Hill Girt Ranch has been one of the best-kept up and most prosperous of the fruit ranches of Contra Costa County.

DAVID MACARTNEY.—A veteran Odd Fellow and a pioneer of Antioch, David Macartney was born in Belfast, Ireland, on March 8, 1849, and when a babe in arms was taken to Australia, where his father went to work in the gold mines. Some years later the family, consisting of the father, mother, three sisters and our subject came to California. David being the youngest member of the family was then fourteen years old, and is now the only living member of the family. After a short stay in San Francisco the Macartneys came to Antioch, where his father, who had begun as a cabin boy and worked his way to master mariner, died.

Owing to the death of his parent our subject had to go to work, being the only son he became the head of the family. He became an employee of the Union Coal Company at Black Diamond, at a time when the coal was hauled from the mouth of the mines with four and six-horse teams. He was first in charge of the coal at the wharf where it was loaded onto two-masted, flat-bottomed schooners at Antioch, taken to San Francisco and other places for distribution. Five years at Antioch and one year at Black Diamond were spent by Mr. Macartney, then he worked at various kinds of business, and served two terms as postmaster during Cleveland's and McKinley's administrations, till 1901. He has been engaged in business in Antioch for many years and is about the oldest shopkeeper now doing business in that city. He has been a member of the

Odd Fellows for over fifty years, a member of the Encampment, of which he is treasurer. He has been a member of the Congregational Church in Antioch for sixty years; has served as a member of the school board for many years, part of the time as secretary.

On October 30, 1925, David Macartney married Miss Rebecca Davis, the ceremony being performed at Martinez. She was born at Winchester, Ill. There she taught school, as also at White Hall, Ill., and in Athens, Texas. She came to Los Angeles in 1909 as private secretary to her aunt, Mrs. Faithful Ebey. Mrs. Macartney is eligible to membership in the Daughters of the American Revolution by virtue of her great-great-grandfather George Ebey, serving as a member of a company of 100 picked men who fell at Stony Point on the Hudson, under command of Mad Anthony Wayne.

CHARLES W. HORNBACK.—There is no finer market to be found in Contra Costa County than the Community Market in Antioch, presided over by Frank J. Silva and Charles W. Hornback, the subject of this sketch. He is a native son and was born at Somersville, Cal., on February 21, 1892, the son of William and Annie (Wallace) Hornback, the latter born near Antioch. The father was born in Napa County, a son of James Hornback, a Kentuckian, who came to California in the early fifties and followed ranching near Napa. The father, now seventy years old, is still living and one of the trusted employees of the Paraffine Companies, Inc., in Antioch. These worthy parents have two children; Charles W., of this review; and Maybelle, employed in the Community Market.

Charles W. Hornback went to the local schools and had eighteen months in the Riverview Union High. He began as a clerk in the stores in Antioch when he was thirteen and when eighteen was employed with L. Meyer and Company, continuing until he formed his present partnership with Frank J. Silva in 1920. They bought out Walter H. Weeks, successor to Ross & Serpa. The latter had bought out G. C. Carman, a pioneer merchant. The present location of the concern is in the C. M. Belshaw building. All business of the company is conducted on a cash basis and they give their customers the benefit of the saving of bookkeepers' salaries. Four persons are employed in the market.

Mr. Hornback was married in San Francisco on July 26, 1920, to Miss Ruth V. Shears, a native of Nebraska. They have two children; Ramona and Robert Charles. Mr. Hornback is a member and a Past President of the Native Sons of the Golden West; belongs to the Masonic Lodge and to the Sciots, of Antioch. He enlisted for service in the World War in San Francisco and served in Motor Truck Train 406, saw fourteen months service in France and when the armistice was signed returned to the United States and was discharged at the Presidio in June, 1919. He is a charter member of the American Legion, Harding Post at Antioch. Mrs. Hornback belongs to the Eastern Star and the Rebekahs. They are Republicans.

JOHN N. CANEVARO.—The title of pioneer is justly merited by John N. Canevaro, for few men now living in Pittsburg located in this section of the county before Mr. Canevaro. When he came there were only four houses in the settlement, which was then called Black Diamond. During his long residence here Mr. Canevaro has witnessed the marvelous development of this community from a bare settlement to an up-to-date city of 9000 population.

John N. Canevaro was born near Genoa, Italy, on August 26, 1851, a son of G. B. and Catherine (Solari) Canevaro, and fourth in a family of eight children. His father was a farmer; and his mother, as a young woman, was a weaver of velvets and silks. When John N. Canevaro was twenty-five years of age, he was united in marriage with Miss Geronirna Piaggo, who also was born near Genoa. This union was blessed with two children before the parents emigrated to America in 1878. They sailed from Havre, France on the French Line Steamship Canada, arriving in New York City the latter part of July. From there they continued their journey by railway to San Francisco, Cal., arriving there on August 14, 1878. Mr. Canevaro at first engaged in the fishing industry. Later he was employed by the Nortonville Railroad, a road used in those early days to haul coal from the Black Diamond mines to New York Landing, and afterwards he was made section boss of the Somersville Railway, which was formerly known as the Nortonville Railroad.

Five children were born to Mr. and Mrs. Canevaro: Baptiste, who lives in Pittsburg; Frank, who was born in Italy and died in San Francisco at the age of twenty-four years; Nicholas, a florist in San Francisco; Kate, a teller in the Pittsburg branch of the Mercantile Trust Company of California; and Narciza, assistant cashier of the same company at Pittsburg. The two sisters in the bank are very efficiently discharging their duties, and have proved to the general satisfaction of their employers that women can and do successfully manage important business affairs. The Canevaro family are highly esteemed in the community and enjoy the fellowship of a large circle of friends. On August 22, 1926, Mr. and Mrs. Canevaro celebrated their fiftieth wedding anniversary in a very fitting manner.

DANIEL OLDHAM.—Since 1900 Daniel Oldham has been a resident of California, most of the time residing in Crockett and vicinity. He is a native of Ireland, born January 6, 1874, the son of Richard and Julia (Manning) Oldham, who have always resided in their native Ireland. After obtaining such schooling as he could at his home young Daniel decided he would come to America and accordingly in 1900 made the necessary arrangements and landed in San Francisco after an interesting trip across the continent by rail from New York. His first work was on the railroad for a year; by that time he had become used to the ways of the west and then he went to work for a water company in the mountains, again returning to railroad work. In 1902 he arrived at the Selby smelter and worked for a while. His roving disposition led him to go to Salt Lake City to accept employment with the Bamburger Mining Company, which he secured through an uncle. While so employed he was the victim of a premature blast and then decided he had had enough of mining and so returned to San Francisco, and later to work at the smelter in Selby, where ever since 1904 he has had steady work, though he ranched for a very short time.

In August, 1904, Mr. Oldham married Abbie Creedon, also a native of Ireland and who came here in 1902. She has one brother and six sisters all residents of the United States. Mr. and Mrs. Oldham have three children: Richard, who had two years in high school; John, who graduated from the high school; and Julia Rita, who is a senior in the high school and plans teaching as a vocation. Mr. Oldham had two brothers who came to America, but returned to Ireland, where they are living; and he has a sister in Berkeley, and two in San Francisco.

Mr. Oldham is of a jovial disposition, looks on the bright side of life and thoroughly enjoys life in California, where he expects to end his days. The family are Catholics in religious faith. He is a member of the I. D. E. S. and Woodmen of the World and carries some insurance in the company fostered by the smelter management.

JOHN G. REGELLO.—A pioneer of San Pablo, who came here in 1880, when he was but seventeen years old, John G. Regello has witnessed the great advancement of Western Contra Costa County since that time. He was born in Portugal on March 3, 1863, and at the age of seventeen made up his mind he would try his luck in California. His first work upon arriving here was found in the grain warehouses at Port Costa where he worked for a few years. He saved his money, and as soon as he could he leased land and began ranching, for eight years raising hay and grain on the Nicholl and Mintzer estates. He was successful and bought the Alvarado tract, continuing his ranching operations. He raised some fine cattle and horses, having some race horses that won renown. For twenty-three years he lived on this tract and then he sold it to B. Schapiro, who subdivided it into city building lots. Mr. Regello retained his home site, where he has lived ever since. He then bought thirty-six acres of the Ghirardelli property and sold an interest to the late Herbert Brown, but still retains some of the land. With others Mr. Regello bought the Rivers-Andrada tract, located in North Richmond, which contained about 100 acres, and this has been subdivided and sold. He has been a public-spirited man and has done his part to make it possible for people to make their homes in Richmond. Mr. Regello owns 147 acres of alfalfa in Merced County, bordering the Merced River. He was at one time a director of the Bank of Richmond.

In 1891 Mr. Regello married Miss Beatrice Lucas, also a native of Portugal, who came here when a young girl. They have had four children: Mary, Mrs. M. A. Perry, of Concord; Frances, Mrs. A. F. Rose, now living at Atwater; John, assistant cashier of the Mercantile Trust Company in Richmond, living at home; and Elizabeth, Mrs. Lawrence P. Vim, of Richmond. Mr. Regello and his wife are still living retired in the enjoyment of their hard-earned money, but they believe in doing all the good they can to as many as they can. Mr. Regello belongs to the U. P. E. C. of California. He spends much time in his garden.

John Regello, the son, was born on August 1, 1898, in Richmond. He attended the San Pablo Grammar School, and in 1916 was graduated from the Richmond High School. In 1915 he began working in the Mercantile Trust Company Bank of Richmond as messenger boy, was advanced to bookkeeper, and then teller in the Savings Bank, and later was advanced to teller and then to assistant cashier. He is apt at figures, and in school made a specialty of arithmetic, thus preparing himself for the work he is now doing. He is a member of the American Institute of Banking at Oakland, and belongs to the Elks, Knights of Columbus, and U. P. E. C., and to the Kiwanis and the Carquinez Golf Clubs. He stands high in the estimation of all who know him, and is rapidly forging his way to the front in banking circles.

HENRY TIMM.—Among the pioneers of El Cerrito is Henry Timm, now living retired in his comfortable home on Schmidt Lane. He has been a resident of the State since 1884, and of Contra Costa County since 1902, when he located on San Pablo Avenue and engaged in business. A native of Schleswig-Holstein, he was born March 21, 1858, and was educated in the public schools of his native country and also learned the nursery business, which he followed while in Europe. In 1878 he left home and came to America, and located in Pottawattamie and Carroll Counties, Iowa, and there worked as a farm hand four years. Then he drifted about the Northwest, working for the Great Northern Railroad during its construction through Idaho, Washington and Montana, and during that time saw some of the "wild and woolly West." For some time after coming to the West he worked as a camp cook for a pack-train outfit.

On July 1, 1884, he landed in San Francisco with considerable money. He wanted to see something of the life of a large city and did so, much to his regret in later years. He drove a wagon for a large brewery in Oakland for several years and became acquainted with a large range of country about that city and Berkeley. He then opened up a grocery store and saloon in Berkeley, continuing thus until 1900, and then retiring for a couple of years. In 1902 he came to San Pablo Avenue and Schmidt Lane and bought property, where he built a house and store building and opened a liquor business, which he conducted until the Eighteenth Amendment went into effect, since which time he has been retired. During his active years in this vicinity he made the acquaintance of nearly every one of importance, as his place was a general stopping place for travelers. He

A. J. Young.

Mary A. Young.

remembers early conditions, when the school house stood where the St. John's Catholic Church now stands, when farming was the only industry in this section of the country, and when the Italians had their extensive vegetable gardens here.

Mr. Timm was naturalized in 1885 in San Francisco, and since then he has voted with the Democrats. He is a member of the California Aerie of Eagles No. 1423, and of the Sons of Hermann in San Francisco. For recreation he likes camping in the mountains. He has never married.

ALBERT JEFFERSON YOUNG.—The twilight of a busy career finds Albert Jefferson Young retired from life's activities and living in a comfortable home on ten acres of land one mile from Danville, where he is enjoying the competency earned by years of diligent application to the duties of life. He was born at Independence, Mo., on June 24, 1841, the son of Thomas J. and Sarah J. (Patton) Young, natives of Kentucky and Missouri, respectively. His grandmother, Sarah (Smart) Young, was born in Danville, Va., and it was she who named the town of Danville, Cal. Her husband, James Patton, removed from Murfreesboro, Tenn., to Independence, Mo., in 1817, and it was while there that Sarah J. Patton was born. After one year spent in Independence, James Patton returned to Tennessee, but later he again settled in Missouri, and there he died in 1871. Thomas J. Young died while still a young man, but his widow reached the age of sixty-five years, passing away at Danville, Cal., in 1883. Mr. Young has a brother, Thomas Young, eight years his junior, now living in Turlock, Cal.

Albert J. Young attended the schools in Independence, Mo., and in 1856 was graduated from the Buchanan and Taylor Academy there. He then went to Council Bluffs, Iowa, and three years later was graduated from the high school of that city. While attending the high school he had the honor of meeting Abraham Lincoln in the home of a citizen of Council Bluffs and had the opportunity of talking with him there. In December, 1859, Mr. Young entered the office as a deputy clerk of the circuit court of Jackson County at Independence. Here he remained till the summer of 1861, when he resigned on account of ill health caused by the malaria. Following a long and severe illness of typhoid fever, his physician advised him to equip himself with an outfit and take a trip overland to California. Through the advice of an uncle at Council Bluffs, who had been an old freighter, he secured the proper outfit for the journey across the plains. On May 31, 1862, accompanied by his mother, her sister, and his brother Thomas, he started on the long journey, and after a very enjoyable trip they eventually landed at Sacramento. They met many Mormons, among them being Jeremiah Folsom, one of the architects on the great Tabernacle then being erected in Salt Lake City, the foundation of which was then being laid. In 1898, when Mr. and Mrs. Young were making a trip East to attend a Presbyterian Assembly, they stopped in

Salt Lake to visit Amelia Folsom, whom he had known in Council Bluffs, Iowa, and who was the last and favorite wife of Brigham Young. While there they learned many interesting facts about the Mormon activities in Salt Lake City. After their arrival in California, Mr. Young and his party settled in Napa, where his grandmother Young and other relatives were living. Here he rented land and he and his brother farmed; his brother looking after the ranch work while our subject was employed as a bookkeeper in a warehouse in Napa. An uncle from the San Ramon Valley in Contra Costa County paid the family a visit at Napa and advised them to move to this county and settle in the San Ramon Valley. This they did, and the two young men leased 100 acres of land from William Lynch in San Ramon and farmed for the following seven years. In 1869 Mr. Young bought 240 acres from T. T. Ramsey, where he now lives, and erected his present house. In 1884 he sold off all but ten acres to William Stone, retaining the house and ten acres for their home place.

In the spring of 1865, the trustees of the San Ramon school, knowing his qualifications, asked Mr. Young to teach their school, which he did for the next four years. This was the beginning of his educational work in this State. His next four years were spent in the Sycamore school, and then he returned to San Ramon and taught another four years. In 1877 he was elected to represent Contra Costa County in the State legislature as the assemblyman from this county. Returning again to the school room, he was four years in the Tassajara school, from 1879 to 1883. Then for the following seventeen and one-half years he taught in the Danville school without interruption, retiring from active school work in 1900. For twenty-five years he served as a member of the board of education of Contra Costa County. Mr. Young takes much pleasure in receiving as his guests many of his former pupils, who enjoy their visits to their old instructor.

In 1868 Albert J. Young was united in marriage with Miss Mary A. Shuey, daughter of John Shuey, a native of Mendon, Ill., and a pioneer farmer of the Fruitvale section of Alameda County. Her mother was Lucinda Stow before her marriage. Mrs. Young was born on February 24, 1850, and came to California via the Isthmus of Panama when she was six years old. She is a graduate of Miss Blake's Seminary in Oakland and is a gifted musician. She taught school in Contra Costa County for ten years. This union resulted in the birth of three children. Alice married J. L. Geddes, resides in Fresno and has one daughter, Florence. A remarkable coincidence is that Mrs. Geddes was born on March 18, 1871, the day her grandfather Patton passed away. Sarah L. Young is a graduate of the grammar schools of Contra Costa County, the Oakland High School, and the San Francisco Teachers' College and now is the principal of the Dewey Grammar School in Oakland. The only son, Robert S., died in 1900 at the age of twenty-four years. Mr. Young is a member of the Presbyterian Church and has served as an elder and clerk of the

Danville church for fifty-three years. At the expiration of fifty years of service as clerk, he was honored by a meeting of the Presbytery of San Francisco, which met in Danville to celebrate the event. He has served as superintendent of the Sunday School for half a century, and is now (1926) in active service as superintendent and teacher of a class in the Sunday School at Danville. Mr. and Mrs. Young are cheerful and happy in their comfortable home, and at the ages of eighty-five and seventy-six, respectively, are active in mind and body and enjoying life to its full. Mr. Young gives full credit for his long life and happy disposition to his mother's training and to his connection with religious work in the church and Sunday school.

FRED FRANK BREWEN.—One of the well-known and successful contractors of Richmond is Fred Frank Brewen, who has been active in many movements for the building up of the city in which he lives, and which he believes has a great future. He was born in California in a town that was first called Limerick, but later San Ramon, on November 6, 1871. His father was Eli Brewen, a blacksmith by trade, who died many years ago. The mother was in maidenhood Carrie Davis, and she is also deceased. Their family consisted of five boys and two girls. One son and one daughter live in Oregon, two reside in Martinez, and one died in Sonoma County. The parents were both born in Missouri and crossed the plains in an ox-team train in 1851. The father made a trip across the plains in 1849, and was so much impressed with the country that he went back for his wife and family.

Fred Frank Brewen attended the public schools and grew up to ranch work, after which he went into the lumber camps and to a shingle mill at Fortuna, Humboldt County, and got considerable experience in both places. He then went back to ranching. Being handy with tools, he worked at the carpenter's trade at various times and in 1892 entered the employ of what is now known as the Santa Fe Railroad Company as a carpenter. The road was known as the San Joaquin Valley Road and the People's Road until the rights of way were secured, and then the actual building and financing were done by the present company. Mr. Brewen was employed by the company for seven and one-half years, coming to Richmond in their employ. His ability to do various kinds of work and do it well made him a very valuable man, for he could do blacksmithing as well as carpentering. He first saw Point Richmond in 1901, when there was little to forecast the future of the community. For years it was called East Yard, and then Point Richmond, and is now known as West Richmond. Mr. Brewen began working as a journeyman carpenter with Mr. Way, and was foreman during the building of the house Mr. Brewen now occupies. He worked on the Critchett Hotel, the Matson and Baker houses (these being among the early structures here), and the McNally Hotel, now occupied by Thomas Kinney. In 1905 Mr. Brewen concluded he would take up the contracting and building business for himself, and his first contract was for a two-story building on Nicholl between Martina and Santa Fe Streets. During the year 1915 he ran a restaurant, but then reentered the contracting business, which he is now following with well-deserved success. Mr. Brewen was a member of the early volunteer fire department, and when it was changed to a paid department he continued for three years with the rank of lieutenant. He served as sanitary inspector for the city and for the government at the same time, and was in this office when the city was cleaned up from the rat pest. He has done police duty and is at present a deputy sheriff, serving under R. R. Veale. He was one of the men who were actively interested in starting the building trades organizations.

On May 29, 1900, Mr. Brewen married Miss Sophie Fowl, a native of Greenberg, Ind., and daughter of George Fowl, a carpenter. Mr. and Mrs. Brewen have had five children: Stellma, a graduate from the high school and business college, employed by the Santa Fe; Carl, who finished high school and is now a machinist with the Standard Oil Company; Fowl, who finished high school in Richmond and is working as a pattern maker in Oakland; Abbott, a pupil in the high school; and a daughter who died in infancy. Mr. Brewen is independent in politics, supporting the men he considers best fitted for office regardless of political policies. His recreation is found in hunting and camping, and he enjoys all kinds of healthful games. In his younger days he played baseball and still is an enthusiastic fan. He belongs to the Eagles.

GEORGE E. MURRAY.—An experience of many years in railway affairs has abundantly qualified George E. Murray for the responsible position of station agent for the Santa Fe Railroad Company at Pittsburg, Cal. Mr. Murray is a thorough railroad man and among the oldest in the employ of the Santa Fe system in California. He was born at Little Rapids, Wis., on May 8, 1889, a son of Robert and Eva (Childs) Murray, the former a native of New Brunswick and the latter of Wisconsin. The father was station agent at various places in Wisconsin. He passed away at Oshkosh, Wis., aged seventy years. The mother now makes her residence in Pittsburg, Cal. Of this union were born three sons. T. F. is on the ocean liner Pallas; he is a competent telegrapher and an S. O. S. man. J. D. is now employed with the Redwood Manufacturers Company at Pittsburg; he was formerly in the Navy Yards at Vallejo. George E. is the subject of this review.

George E. Murray attended grammar school in his native city and then entered the high school at De Pere, from which he was graduated in 1905. The family then came to the State of Washington, and there he worked at the mining camp of Silverton. In 1909 he came to Berkeley, Cal., where he became a student operator for the Santa Fe Railway. Later he was agent at Muir, Cal., and was there for three years, when he was called to the superintendent's office at Fresno. He came to Pittsburg in 1915. This station was at first called Diamond, but later, in 1911, the name was changed to Pittsburg. This thriving industrial city boasts of the only "joint facilities switch" in the State. This switch was laid in 1902 to accommodate the Redwood Manufacturers Company. Then an agreement was entered into by the Southern Pacific Railroad Company and the Santa Fe system whereby the Santa Fe Company was to do all the switching for both companies at Pittsburg, and the Southern Pacific Company was to do all the switching for both companies at Bay Point. This amicable agreement has proven of great benefit to both companies and was a wise move for all concerned.

At Muir, Cal., on September 16, 1912, Mr. Murray was married to Miss Esther Johnson, a native daughter of California; and to them have been born four children: Robert, William, Marjorie and Marian, the two last being twins. Mr. Murray is a member of the Pittsburg Chamber of Commerce and a charter member of the Rotary Club; and fraternally he is a member of the Masons and a charter member of the Elks, both of Pittsburg.

JOHN PETER BARRETT.—A pioneer of Pinole who has seen the growth and development of the town is John Peter Barrett, who came to California in 1875 and has been closely identified with this section of the State ever since. He was born in Brooklyn, N. Y., on January 6, 1853, the son of Henry and Jane (Brandon) Barrett, both now deceased. Henry Barrett was born in England but came to the United States when a young man and saw service in the Civil War. He was a stone cutter by trade.

John Peter Barrett attended school in different places where he lived as a boy growing to young manhood and at the age of twenty-two came to California and worked as a carpenter on the old Palace Hotel, just then being erected. He followed the carpenter trade several years. On account of dull times in San Francisco Mr. Barrett went to Prescott, Ariz., then the capital of the territory, and engaged in general sawmilling for three or four years. Coming again to San Francisco he applied for a job at carpenter work and was offered one dollar and fifty cents for his labor, as he was told that was all that was being paid to able bodied men. He refused and found a job with A. Lusk & Company as a fruit hauler for three dollars per day and he stuck to it for nearly three years. He then came to Contra Costa County and leased some land from his father-in-law and raised stock for four years and met with fair success. He then entered the California Powder Works, but made his home in San Pablo, going back and forth every morning and night with a two-wheeled cart and horse, reporting for work every morning at 6:30. He was made foreman of the nitric acid department, then promoted to the sulphuric acid department, with a satisfactory raise in wages, and given charge of all the acid works, a position of much responsibility. He hired and fired employees. He still lived in San Pablo and the superintendent proposed that he come to live nearer his work, which he decided to do and erected one of the first homes in Pinole and is still living in that same house, which is in good state of repair. He continued steadily at work and was gradually advanced from time to time, and when Mr. Burns, the superintendent, died, Mr. Barrett succeeded him in the department and increased the output from 20,000 tons of sulphuric acid to 100,000 tons. After twenty-three years of service with his company Mr. Barrett was pensioned at the age of sixty by Mr. Birmingham. He is now looking after his personal interests and ranch of thirty-five acres, part of which is in the limits of Pinole. He has some cows and chickens and raises garden truck. He enjoys being in the open and is a strong booster for the climate of this district, which he says "can't be beat."

Mr. Barrett was married on March 28, 1883, to Miss Eleanor Elizabeth Inwood, daughter of Henry and Elizabeth Eleanor (Buges) Inwood, English people. The following children have come to bless their home circle. The first died in infancy. William Henry, aged forty-three, is a bricklayer in San Francisco. John P., also a bricklayer, lives at home, is married and had one child, Ruth; his wife is deceased. Charles met his death in a coal mine in 1924; he had married and had a son, Charles. Nellie Elizabeth married Gus Weisman, an engineer at the Hercules Powder Works. For many years Mr. Barrett served as a school trustee; also one of the town trustees when the sewers were installed. He became a stockholder in the bank when it was organized and has favored every enterprise that has come to Pinole. He has seen the growth of schools, the commercial houses, the establishment of the newspaper, the postoffice, in fact every place of business and the residences have been erected since Mr. Barrett came here to live. He is a member of the Masonic fraternity and was one of the promoters of the lodge hall in the town. He belongs to the Chamber of Commerce. Mr. Barrett is fond of fishing and camping and takes a vacation whenever possible. It is to such men as Mr. Barrett that the county owes a debt of gratitude, for he never has hesitated when it comes to doing good for his home community.

C. W. JENSEN.—The success which has met the efforts of C. W. Jensen since he made his purchase of land in Contra Costa County has left him no reason to regret his removal from his native land. He was born in Denmark, March 8, 1887, the sixth child in a family of nine children born to Christian and Mary (Christensen) Jensen, both born in Denmark. The father is still living at the age of seventy-eight; the mother was seventy-five when she passed away.

Mr. Jensen attended the common schools in his native country and when old enough learned the butter and cheese making trade. He came to America in 1906, going to Triplett, Mo., for a year, after which he came to San Francisco, where he followed his trade. Later he went to Idaho and there worked at his trade until he was drafted into the World War on January 24, 1918. He was transferred to San Francisco and served with the 127th Infantry of the 32nd Division. He was on the Meuse-Argonne

J. P. Casey

front and was gassed twice, but not seriously. After the armistice was signed he was sent to Germany with the Army of Occupation and remained for five months. Returning to the United States, he was honorably discharged at the Presidio, San Francisco, in May, 1919. In August, 1919, he came to his present ranch home, consisting of ten acres which is planted to almonds, apricots and wine grapes. Besides his farming activities, Mr. Jensen does a general drayage business in Brentwood, and is also the agent for the Union Ice Company.

On January 1, 1923, Mr. Jensen was married to Miss Pauline Abbel, a native of Belgium. Mr. Jensen is a member of the Roy Frerichs Post, No. 202, of the American Legion and of California Lodge No. 1, I.O.O.F., at San Francisco. Mr. Jensen is a naturalized American citizen and is most loyal in his support of all measures for the advancement of his home section of Contra Costa County.

HON. JEREMIAH P. CASEY.—The late Judge J. P. Casey served many years as a justice of the peace and as a supervisor of Contra Costa County. He was born near Macroom, in County Cork, Ireland, in November, 1848, the son of Patrick and Margaret (Buckley) Casey, farmer folk in Ireland. The father took part in the wars between Ireland and England, lived to be ninety-three years old, and died in 1889. The mother died in 1901. The records of the family go back for many generations and show that the ancestors of our subject lived in the vicinity of Macroom, County Cork, and were farmers.

Jeremiah P. Casey grew up on the home farm and helped with the work on the place, and in the meantime attended the common schools. In 1873 he came to America in the hope that he could better his condition, arriving in San Francisco on May 13, of that year. Going to Davis, Yolo County, he secured work with the Southern Pacific Railroad Company in winter months and worked in the harvest fields in Solano County in the summer. He continued at various kinds of labor in various places in the State until 1879, when he landed in Port Costa and bought a saloon, which he rented for six months, and then opened a hotel; he also owned and operated a brewery. He held the office of justice of the peace for twenty years. In 1908 he was elected a member of the board of supervisors from the second supervisorial district of the county, and served until his death on April 6, 1924. The success he met with in his official capacity is shown in that he served continuously in office, at each election succeeding himself although being opposed by good and strong men politically in his district. He was one of the most progressive men in his section of the county, and his constituents knew their interests were safe when placed in the hands of Judge Casey. He was strong for good roads and worked untiringly to place Contra Costa County in the forefront of the counties of the State in this respect. He was a friend of education and served for years as a member of the board of trustees of the Port Costa district, and was instrumental in the erection of the first schoolhouse in Port Costa. In politics he was a Democrat. He belonged to the Hibernians in Vallejo, and to the Foresters of America and the Young Men's Institute in Port Costa, having served as first president of the latter.

Judge Casey was married in Vallejo, Cal., in June, 1890, being united with Mary Boyle, a native of County Cork, Ireland; and they had four children: Patrick, deceased; Margaret M., an employee of the Port Costa Water Company; Jeremiah, who married Catherine Murphy, has two children, Margaret and Catherine, and resides in Oakland; and John, an employee of the Southern Pacific, residing in Port Costa. Mrs. Casey died on August 20, 1907, aged forty years, and Miss Casey has practically reared the two boys from their youth. The family are Catholics.

GEORGE H. SHAFER.—A native of California, George H. Shafer has been a constructive factor in the development of eastern Contra Costa County and has at all times done his share toward the upbuilding of the community in which he has so long made his home. Every movement calculated to be of material benefit to the State or county has received his support, and today he is honored and respected by all who know him. He was born at Rio Vista, Cal., on February 26, 1866, a son of William and Elizabeth (Pearce) Shafer. His father was born in Bedford County, Pa., and came west across the plains about 1855. The family settled in Contra Costa County in 1867, where the father became an extensive agriculturist, owning and operating 900 acres of land. Elizabeth Pearce came across the plains with her parents in 1852 and in Contra Costa County she was married to William Shafer. Of this union five children were born: Adrian H., a rancher near Brentwood; Mabel, Mrs. George Geddes; Winifred, Mrs. Mott Preston; Hannah; and George H., of this review. The father was one of the early river men on the Sacramento, bringing vegetables from up the river to the coal mines; and later he became identified with the stock business and ranched on a large scale. He was active in politics, but never aspired to public office, although he was often a delegate to county conventions. He was a great temperance worker and did much to further the cause in his vicinity. William Shafer was seventy-nine years old when he passed away at Brentwood on March 11, 1915; Mrs. Shafer has now reached the age of eighty-one, and makes her home at Brentwood.

George H. Shafer worked on his father's ranch until sixteen years of age, and then went to Stockton and entered the normal school and business college, from which he was duly graduated. After finishing school he accepted a position with the C. A. Shaw Hardware & Implement Company and remained with them for some time. Returning to Contra Costa County, he purchased the livery business of P. J. Moody, at Brentwood, which he successfully operated for about twenty-five years.

On August 20, 1888, Mr. Shafer was married to Miss Martha C. Bainbridge, a native of Missouri, daughter of Dr. James A. and Mary Ellen (Herold) Bainbridge, both natives of Missouri. Dr. Bainbridge passed away at his daughter's home in Brentwood on April 5, 1914, aged eighty-one years, while the mother was only forty-eight years old when she passed away. Eight children were born of this union, of whom Mrs. Shafer is the sixth.

In 1888 Mr. Shafer was elected constable, an office he has held continuously ever since, excepting four years when he did not run for office owing to other matters that occupied his time. In 1888 he was appointed deputy sheriff. His present appointment is under Sheriff R. R. Veale, who was his schoolmate and a warm personal friend. In 1905 Mr. Shafer engaged in the undertaking business at Brentwood, at first in association with his only son, Earl B. Shafer, who is now superintendent of the Grower's Fertilizer plant at Stockton. Earl B. Shafer married Miss Emma Goodman of Oakley; and they have one daughter, Lelah, and make their home in Stockton.

Mr. and Mrs. Shafer have complete command of their occupation and dignify it with consideration and reliability, backed by a thoroughgoing technical knowledge. They maintain an attractive establishment, which was enlarged in 1923, and their growing business necessitates another addition in the near future. Mr. Shafer owns seventy acres of land adjacent to Brentwood. This is planted to almonds, fruits and wheat. In politics Mr. Shafer is a stanch Republican. Fraternally, he stands high in the Masonic, Odd Fellows and other orders in eastern Contra Costa County. He is a Past Patron of the Eastern Star at Brentwood. He has served as president of the East Contra Costa County Chamber of Commerce, and is now a director. Mrs. Shafer is a member of the Brentwood Public Library Association, which she helped establish. She is Past Deputy of the Foresters and Past Matron of the Eastern Star, and is now Deputy Grand Matron of the Grand Chapter, 17th California District, I. O. O. F. Mr. and Mrs. Shafer enjoy the esteem of a large circle of friends who justly honor them for their worth and ability.

FRANK J. PEACOCK.—A skillful mechanic and capable stationary engineer, well-known in Byron Precinct No. 1, is Frank J. Peacock, who is now serving as chief engineer at the McCabe Pumping Station on the pipe line where he has been continuously employed for the past twenty-two years. He has to his credit a quarter of a century of service as a steady and efficient engineer for the Standard Oil Company, and for ten years he was a locomotive engineer for the Southern Pacific Railroad Company, running from Rocklin to Truckee. Although sixty-four years old, he enjoys good health and is able to attend to his responsible duties daily.

Mr. Peacock is a native son and has witnessed many of the interesting events that have transformed the great State of California. A son of pioneer parents, he was born in Eldorado County on November 17, 1862, at old Pilot Hill, nine miles from the spot where John Marshall discovered gold in 1848. Benjamin Franklin Peacock, his father, was born in Pennsylvania and crossed the plains to California via the old Santa Fe trail in 1848, and for several years was engaged in gold mining. He was married, in California, to Frances Littlefield, who was born at Wells, Maine, but was reared in Lynn, Mass. Frank J. Peacock is the only living son of their family, but there are three daughters, the eldest being now seventy-two years old. The father lived to be ninety-six years old, and the mother was sixty-six when she passed away.

Frank J. Peacock grew up in Eldorado County and received his education in the public schools. He left home when he was only thirteen years old and tried his luck at gold mining and various other pursuits, with a varying degree of success. For several years he was deputy sheriff of Placer County. Having a penchant for machinery, he took a job as fireman for the Southern Pacific Railroad Company, and rose to be a locomotive engineer, working steadily for ten years. Then he entered the employ of the Standard Oil Company as engineer for the pipe lines, serving at the Vernalis, Tracy and Los Medanos pumping stations before coming to the McCabe station in 1906.

At San Francisco, in 1905, Frank J. Peacock was married to Miss Mary Miller. Mr. Peacock is a Democrat.

ANDREW NELSON.—An experienced smelterman, Andrew Nelson is now a resident of Contra Costa County and enjoys the esteem of a wide circle of friends. He was born in far-off Norway in 1859, the son of Jonathan and Aasa Mary (Anderson) Nelson. The schooling of Mr. Nelson was limited for at an early age he went to work in the smelter in his own country, continuing until coming to America in 1887. First he went from Norway to Australia and after some time spent in that country decided the new world held out a more hopeful prospect for a man of energy and consequently came to California and Crockett. With his previous experience he found no difficulty in getting work in the Selby smelter and he continued in that employment until 1920, when he was retired with a pension for long and faithful service as a furnace man. Although retired, Mr. Nelson is called for work occasionally at the sugar refinery. He is a member of the Independent Order of Odd Fellows and of the Woodmen of the World.

On July 18, 1889, Andrew Nelson married Mrs. Hellene Jorgenson, daughter of Jorgen Anderson and Tole Hellene Halvorson, both born in the old country. This union has been blessed with two children; Yorgan, born June 8, 1890, married Florence Falk and they have two sons, Andrew and George, Jr.; the only daughter and second child, Alma Louisa Nelson, was born April 22, 1896, and died in early childhood. Mrs. Nelson is one of ten children, several of whom came to America and are now living in the East. The Nelson home is one of the show places of Crockett and is a bower of flowering plants and shrubbery. Their home shows the touch of an expert housewife, such as Mrs. Nelson, and reflects the refinement of its occupants. They are kindly and hospitable folk and have a large circle of friends.

HENRY LEXON.—As the proprietor of the Pullman Bakery at No. 3061 Cutting Boulevard, Henry Lexon is gradually extending the scope of his business in Richmond and surrounding territory. He was born in Potsdam, Germany, the son of Henry and Frieda Lexon, the father a cabinet-maker by trade. As a lad he attended the schools of his native country and learned the trade of the baker. In 1898 he came to America and landed in Vancouver. One summer was spent in Alaska, and then he came to Seattle for six months. His next location was in San Francisco, where he engaged in business and was prospering until the great fire and earthquake of 1906 destroyed all he had gathered together, and with little insurance. He worked in Fairfield, Solano County, three years, and in 1912 came to Richmond; bought property at Pullman, on Cutting Boulevard, erected his present building, equipping it with modern appliances; and established the Pullman Bakery. Since that time his business has been steadily growing and he caters to a particular trade. He is assisted by his good wife, and gives his personal attention to the preparing and baking of his bread and pastries.

On December 13, 1905, Mr. Lexon married Miss Clara Wanderer, born at Vincennes, Ind., a daughter of Antone and Lena (Bohnert) Wanderer, both natives of Germany. She is one of eight children, all of whom are in San Francisco. Their children are: Henry, driving a delivery wagon for his father, and Clara, Alice, Margie, Lillian and Raymond. Mr. Lexon lends his influence to help promote all worthy projects for the betterment of his community.

ANDREW FRANCIS PORTMAN.—One of the successful grain raisers in Contra Costa County is Andrew Francis Portman, residing near Antioch. He is a native of this county and was born on September 2, 1876, a son of Andrew and Johanna (Babbe) Portman. The father was a large rancher, operating some 1240 acres near the Veale Tract in the eastern part of the county, in Knightsen precinct. In the Portman family there were six children, viz.: Fred, of Vallejo; Sophie, who married William Penland and also resides in Vallejo; Will, residing in Colusa County; Andrew F., of this review; Mary, Mrs. Ira Sullivan, of San Jose; and Hannan, Mrs. Alfred Gosney, also in San Jose. Mrs. Portman is still living, and at the age of seventy-eight is hale and hearty. She makes her home in San Jose. Andrew Portman lived to be ninety years of age, and died on July 3, 1923. The children were all born and reared in Contra Costa County, whither their mother came with her parents, Mr. and Mrs. Fred Babbe, from her birthplace in Germany, when she was a girl of seven years. Mr. Babbe had come to California in search of gold soon after the news of its discovery had been heralded to the world, had mined for a time, and then went back East and later brought his family to the Coast.

Andrew F. Portman was reared to farm work and received his schooling in the public schools of his neighborhood, working on the home place with his father and learning the various branches of agriculture. The home ranch contained a large Indian mound, from which many specimens left by the Indians were obtained as the mound was leveled to make levees, etc. There were skeletons, skulls, arrow heads, beads, Indian jewelry and their coins, making an interesting collection. After reaching manhood, Mr. Portman began ranching for himself. He has been very successful, is the owner of considerable land and also owns the Melrose Hotel in Pittsburg. He is considered one of the large grain raisers in the county, operating 1000 acres of the C. A. Hooper estate besides his own ranches.

On June 27, 1906, at Snelling, Merced County, Mr. Portman was united in marriage with Miss Jennie Hobson, daughter of the late James Hobson, an early settler in Contra Costa County who had a ranch adjoining the mining town of Nortonville, a settlement springing up on his land and named Hobsonville in his honor. There were nine children in the Hobson family, and the family is mentioned at length in the sketch of Mary A. Dickinson on another page in this history. Mr. Hobson died in March, 1905, aged seventy-five years; and Mrs. Hobson passed away on February 19, 1923, when eighty-six years old. Mrs. Portman belongs to the Eastern Star and Rebekahs in Antioch. Both she and Mr. Portman are Republicans.

JOHN E. McELHENEY.—A citizen of whom any community might well be proud is John E. McElheney of Antioch, Cal., the present city clerk who has been elected to the office by the votes of the citizens seven times in succession, a record seldom equalled by any official in Antioch, and a remarkable testimony to his efficiency and popularity. He is one of the oldest of the city officials of Antioch, having filled his position since March, 1912. He was born in Watsonville, Cal., on December 12, 1864, a son of James Rathbone and Amanda (Adams) McElheney, natives of New York State and Indiana, respectively. The father came to California in 1857 and mined for gold near Marysville, but later moved to Santa Cruz County on account of ill health, and became interested in stock raising. He later leased the agricultural park in San Jose and with the assistance of his son John carried on ranching.

John E. McElheney attended the public schools in San Jose and Santa Cruz, and then supplemented his studies by taking a commercial course at the San Jose High School, fitting himself to be an accountant. He began his career in this capacity, but found such work too confining for one who had been used to out-of-door life, and so looked about for a suitable opening. This he found at the Antioch paper mill, then owned by Brown Brothers. He worked in this plant for eighteen years, or until he was appointed city clerk of Antioch. Many large and valuable city improvements have been installed since Mr. McElheney has been in office. The new City Hall was erected at a cost of $60,000; the city water system has been rebuilt; extensive street paving has been prosecuted; and in 1926 the immense reservoir for storing water for use of the city was completed in the hills about three miles from town, with its pipe lines and pumps to handle the water. The reservoir has a capacity of 100,000,000 gallons and will insure an ample supply for years to come. The water is obtained from the Mount Diablo district.

On December 21, 1888, Mr. McElheney was united in marriage with Miss Annie Jane Roberson; and they have had eight children: Carl R., an insurance broker of Antioch; Ray Edward, with a chemical company in Pittsburg; Ethel A., Mrs. Arthur Doyle of Los Angeles; Thelma, a graduate nurse in Los Angeles; Peter Ellis, of Walnut Creek; Belva E., of Antioch; Ruth A., a graduate of the Antioch High School, Class of 1926; and Donna Marie, a high school pupil. Fraternally, Mr. McElheney is a member of the Moose and of the Foresters of America in Antioch. The family is most highly esteemed in the community and has a wide circle of friends.

WINFIELD SCOTT McRACKEN.—The name of Winfield Scott McRacken has stood for quality merchandise for nearly a quarter-century in Richmond, and it has been due to just such progressive business methods as have characterized the enterprise of this local merchant that this city has made such rapid strides in the past few years and has grown from a crossroads country town to a metropolitan city. On January 11, 1904, Mr. McRacken opened his first little store at Point Richmond, and from this modest beginning his business gradually grew up with the city, keeping abreast of the times, until today the store occupied at 1011 Macdonald Avenue is a retail establishment that would grace a city many times the size of Richmond. In 1906 Mr. McRacken took in a partner, incorporated the business, and opened another store on Macdonald Avenue between Second and Third Streets, which was then the main business district of Richmond. The Point store was still operated under the name of W. S. McRacken, and the downtown store was known as McRacken, Parker & Co. About a year and a half later Harry Adkinson bought out Mr. Parker's interest, and in 1910 they moved near the corner of Sixth Street and Macdonald Avenue, keeping in the heart of the business district as the city built eastward. In 1919 Mr. McRacken bought Harry Adkinson's portion of the business and the firm was again changed back to W. S. McRacken. Later the store at the Point was closed, and Mr. McRacken has devoted his entire efforts to the main store ever since. On March 1, 1926, the business was moved to the present location at 1011 Macdonald Avenue, which is the very center of things in Richmond today. Here Mr. McRacken is conducting one of the most up-to-date men's stores in the East Bay district.

W. S. McRacken was born in Iowa on August 16, 1861, a son of Andrew J. and Jane (Caldwell) McRacken, both natives of Pennsylvania. The father was of Scotch descent. Coming to America, the McRacken family had settled in Pennsylvania; Andrew J. McRacken, however, met his future wife in Iowa, and there they were married and reared their family. W. S. McRacken went to the public school until he was sixteen years old. In 1880 he came West to Nevada, where an uncle was in the mining business. He remained there for twenty-three years, and then came to California, settled at Richmond, and established the mercantile business so long and honorably connected with his name.

In October, 1891, Mr. McRacken was married to Miss Amy Blundell, a daughter of Dick Blundell. Her father and mother were natives of London, England, but she was born in Wyoming. Mr. and Mrs. McRacken have had three children: Ward, president of the Merchants' Association of Richmond and a partner in the store with his father; Hazel; and Harold Wayne, who was accidentally killed in San Francisco. Mr. McRacken was at one time a director in the old Bank of Richmond. He is a member of the Chamber of Commerce and the Merchants' Association of Richmond, and fraternally is a Mason.

JAMES HENRY MARTIN.—One of the pioneer merchants of Crockett and Valona, James Henry Martin has watched with interest the development of the industrial city that means so much to Contra Costa County. He is a native son, born in Porterville, on October 27, 1862. His parents were Thomas Leighton and Sarah Elizabeth (Nelson) Martin, natives of Kentucky and Tennessee, respectively, but early settlers in the San Joaquin Valley, which the elder Martin helped to develop from its virgin state.

James H. Martin attended school in Tulare County and came to Vallejo, where he engaged in mercantile pursuits for one year; then he returned to Tulare County and in Tulare carried on business two years. It was about thirty years ago that he decided to locate in Crockett and that decision he has never regretted. The development and growth of this town has been within his memory, and like all good citizens he has cooperated with every movement that has brought Crockett to its present enviable position with her sister cities in Contra Costa County. He has witnessed the growth of the schools, the commercial enterprises, the industrial development and now enjoys the confidence and esteem of nearly the entire citizenry of this end of the county. He has been a leader in financial circles and is a director in the Bank of Pinole; has served as a trustee of the grammar schools for more than sixteen years; and it is largely due to his efforts that the grammar schools of Crockett and Valona were merged into one institution and a fine school building was erected with modern equipment, and installation of the best corps of educators to be found anywhere. From five teachers the number has increased to twenty-three, and is still growing. He is a member of the Crockett-Valona Business Men's Association; and was a charter member of the Maccabees and has passed all the chairs in the local tent.

J. H. Martin was united in marriage on May 24, 1894, to Miss Emma Roth, born in Indiana, a daughter of Christian and Marie (Oligher) Roth, and a sister of Judge Roth, of Richmond. Mr. and Mrs. Martin have had seven children, viz.: Louise, at home; Lemuel Francis, married

Ethel Holly and resides in Crockett and they have two children; James W., married Helen Rogers and resides in Turlock and they have two children; Harold, employed by the Southern Pacific Railway at Crockett; Catherine E., at home; Roth L., and Elizabeth, are both attending high school. For many years Mr. Martin was located at Valona and during the heydey of that town's activities played a prominent part in mercantile life. Now that the two towns have been solidified and their interests in nearly every line of activity have been made one, he has located in Crockett. No man is better liked in this section than is J. H. Martin.

WILLIAM H. HANLON.—The able superintendent of schools of Contra Costa County, William H. Hanlon, is an educator of note, and is so recognized both in California and in other States where he is known. He is a native son, having been born at New York Landing, now known as Pittsburg, on October 25, 1880, a son of James and Ellen (Daley) Hanlon, both natives of Massachusetts, in which State they were married, at Cambridge. Fifty-six years ago, Mr. and Mrs. James Hanlon migrated to California, where he homesteaded a farm site of 160 acres adjoining the Rancho Los Medanos, located about three miles south of Pittsburg, and here he farmed for many years.

William H. Hanlon was reared on his father's ranch and attended the country schools, after which he entered the State Normal School at San Jose in September, 1896, pursued the regular pedagogical course, and graduated with the Class of 1900. In the fall of the same year he accepted the position of principal of the school at Pittsburg, which post he filled so efficiently for six years that in November, 1906, he was elected to the important office of county superintendent of schools for Contra Costa County, which position he still holds. Mr. Hanlon has the oversight of all high, junior high, grammar, elementary and kindergarten schools, both in the cities and in the country districts. This office requires the services of a broad-minded man of sterling character, extensive learning, and good executive ability; such a man the county has found in Mr. Hanlon. During the period of his tenure of office, he has done much to advance the cause of education, to which he is deeply devoted.

On December 5, 1908, at Oakland, W. H. Hanlon was united in marriage with Miss Winnifred Grace Carpenter, a daughter of Daniel W. Carpenter, for twenty years county tax collector, and a pioneer gold miner. He arrived in Placerville in the early fifties, but afterwards settled in Clayton, Contra Costa County; and it was here that Mrs. Hanlon was born. Mrs. Hanlon attended the San Francisco Teachers' College, specializing in music and voice culture. She possesses a pleasing soprano voice, and often delights her many friends at Martinez with her beautiful soprano solos. The Hanlons have been blessed with two children, Howard and Marjorie.

W. H. Hanlon is a member of national, State and county educational associations. He passed the State Bar examinations and was admitted to

practice in 1917. Like all good leaders in educational work, Mr. Hanlon
believes that the future of our nation depends on the capacities developed
and the good ideals inculcated in the minds of the young and growing
generation. He is in accord with the spirit of progress and is keenly alive
to the great opportunities awaiting the children who are now being
moulded by the public schools of the United States into intellectual, moral,
and loyal citizens of our great commonwealth.

ANDREW J. McMAHON.—A native son of Contra Costa County,
and one of its substantial business men, Andrew J. McMahon was born
in Martinez, on September 22, 1870, the son of Thomas and Adelaide
(Gibbings) McMahon, both natives of Ireland. The parents both came
to the United States in 1852, and were married in New York City in 1854,
leaving the next day for California by way of the Isthmus of Panama.
Cholera broke out on board the vessel, and they were two of the 146
survivors (out of 386 passengers) that arrived in San Francisco about
Christmas time, in 1854. They soon moved to Martinez, and Thomas
McMahon became a brick mason and plasterer, which trade he followed
the balance of his life, until retiring from active business just ten years
before his death, which occurred in April, 1912, on the ranch where he
first worked in the county, known as the Donohue Ranch, and now owned
by his son and daughter. He was eighty-one years of age when he died
and his good wife survived him until 1921, when she passed on, having
also reached eighty-one years in life's span.

Of the six children born to this worthy pioneer couple, Andrew J.
McMahon was the youngest. He grew up in Martinez and from the
age of sixteen to nineteen years worked on the newspaper, then called the
Daily Item, but later renamed the Argus, and now known as the Contra
Costa Daily Standard. On leaving this work, he established the Mc-
Mahon Brothers' Grocery, which he conducted until 1904. That year he
started in to do road work as a contractor, and thereafter built many
of Contra Costa County's roads. He dealt in large quantities of sand,
gravel and cement, and gradually became a dealer in road material,
leading to his present large business in that line now managed by his son,
Albin A., with the firm name of Andrew J. McMahon. In 1908 Mr.
McMahon was appointed probation officer for Contra Costa County by
Judge Latimer, and for sixteen years he held that position with ability
and credit, resigning in 1924.

The marriage of Mr. McMahon, occurring in Martinez in 1893,
united him with Miss Asilee Williams, born at Antioch, a daughter of
Francis Williams, who for many years was county assessor of Contra
Costa County. Three children have blessed their union: Albin A., man-
ager of the business, who married Margaret Berling; Francis, civil
engineer for the Shell Company, at Martinez, who married Miriam E.
Veale, daughter of Sheriff R. R. Veale; and Margaret, wife of Dr. Victor
Henny, chemist of London, England. Fraternally, Mr. McMahon is

Geo A. Putnam

a member of the Richmond Lodge No. 1251, B. P. O. E., and of the Martinez Parlor of Native Sons. In his years of service in the county as a public official and as a business man, he has taken an active interest in the moral, economic and business advancement of the community, working with the other representative men toward that end, and his foresight and knowledge of the county's resources have been of great value. In 1916, Mr. McMahon built a new family home, at 1011 Willow Street, Martinez, a large and beautiful concrete house, which is the center of much social activity.

GEORGE A. PUTNAM.—The successful ranchers of Contra Costa County have no better representative than George A. Putnam, who holds an assured position among the thrifty farmers and business men who are conducting the affairs in this part of California. Since 1912 he has been associated with his brother, Guy L., in the real estate business in Walnut Creek. A native son, he was born in Fruitvale, Alameda County, on June 3, 1860, the second child in a family of eight born to John H. and Elizabeth (Shuey) Putnam, natives of New York and Illinois, respectively.

In young manhood the elder Putnam left his native State, in 1853, bound for California via the Isthmus of Panama. Upon his arrival he went to the mines around Placerville and followed prospecting and mining until he contracted rheumatism, and then came to Lafayette and worked for Squire Elam Brown. He was married in 1856 to the daughter of John W. Shuey, a pioneer resident of Moraga Valley. They then went to Humbolt County, settled on Eel River and farmed there till the trouble with the Indians forced them to leave in 1858. Trading his land for a band of stock, Mr. Putnam drove them overland to Contra Costa County. En route he stopped for the night in the Russian River country in Sonoma County and negotiated with a resident for grazing for the night for his herd. The man had a large cornfield about half a mile back of the place where Mr. Putnam planned to keep his stock, and he told the owner he would put a herder between the grass plot and the corn to keep the animals from damaging the latter. The man replied that he'd stand any loss from the stock eating his corn. Next morning, when they came to get their cattle, none were in sight and they were traced to the cornfield; but when Mr. Putnam arrived there he realized what the owner had meant when he said he'd be responsible for damage, for the stalks were twenty feet high and a man would have to be on horseback to reach the lowest ear on the stalk. Arriving here, Mr. Putnam located in Pacheco, built the first hotel in the place, in 1858, and operated it for about eight months. Ranching appealed to him more strongly, however, and he went to Fruitvale, Alameda County, where his wife's father had settled in 1860. Returning to Contra Costa County later, he was superintendent of the Alcalanes Grant for a time, at Lafayette, for Squire Brown. From 1866 to 1872 he operated an express line between San Leandro and San Francisco, making his

17

home in San Leandro; and he served as the first marshal of that town. He was next in the general merchandise business in Walnut Creek for seven years. In 1879 he moved to Washington and farmed there for some years, finally dying at Seattle, where he had retired.

Of the marriage of John H. and Elizabeth Putnam eight children were born: Emma Daisy, Mrs. J. W. Stevens, who resides in Washington; George A., of this review; Minnie A., Mrs. T. Fagan of Copperopolis; William H., a miner in Siskiyou County; Charles A., Mrs. Mary Gau, and Victor Ray, all residing in Seattle; and Guy L., who lives in Oakland and carries on a real estate business in Walnut Creek in partnership with our subject. During the last years of their lives Mr. and Mrs. John H. Putnam made their home with their daughter, Mrs. Gau, in Seattle, both passing away in 1907 of pneumonia, aged eighty-four and seventy-four, respectively.

George A. Putnam attended public school at Pleasant Hill, near Walnut Creek, later taking an advanced course of study at the San Ramon school. After finishing school he went to work for his father in the general merchandise store and remained there until 1879, when he removed to Walla Walla, Wash., and engaged in farming until 1882. Returning then to Contra Costa County, he worked for his uncle as a clerk in his grocery store in Walnut Creek.

At Astoria, Wash., on January 16, 1886, Mr. Putnam was married to Miss Grace Brackett, born at Pacheco, Cal., a daughter of Rufus and Amanda (Hook) Brackett, natives of Massachusetts and Missouri, respectively. Rufus Brackett settled in Benicia, Cal., in 1849, and there became a successful merchant and rancher. Mrs. Brackett was born in 1842 and crossed the plains with her parents in 1850; she was educated in Martinez and Benicia and graduated from the Young Ladies' Seminary in Benicia. Mr. Brackett passed away in August, 1889. Mrs. Brackett makes her home with her daughter, Mrs. Putnam.

Since 1889, Mr. Putnam has resided in Walnut Creek. For a number of years he operated a dairy supplying milk and cream to the county hospital at Martinez, meantime farming quite extensively. He now owns and operates a sixty-acre walnut grove and is interested in the real estate business with his brother. Mr. Putnam served for two terms on the board of trustees of the Concord High School and was a member of the first board of directors of that institution. Mr. and Mrs. Putnam are the parents of five children: George Blalock, who married Miss Frances Vessing, a native of New York State, by whom he has two children, Claire and Robert; Miss Grace Bell, who resides in San Francisco; Marian Bernice, now Mrs. Charles Beattie, who lives in Stockton; John Van Alstine; and Dorothy Hazel. George Blalock, the oldest son, was born on May 17, 1888. After graduating from the Concord High School he entered the University of California, from which he was graduated in 1911 in agriculture. He enlisted in the U. S. Army on May 8, 1917, and was commissioned first Lieutenant in the Officers' Reserve, and went into active service with the 60th C. A. C. at Fort Scott, California, as first Lieutenant, serving two months before his discharge at the Presidio. He is now serving as first Lieutenant in the 860th Motor Transport Reserve, a Walnut Creek Company which he organized; and he is past commander of the Walnut Creek Post, No. 115, of the American Legion, and also a past commander of the Contra Costa Council of the Legion, and has the honor of being one of its founders. He in now salesman for the Western Sulphur Company of San Francisco. George A. Putnam is a Republican in politics. He is recognized as a thrifty and conservative business man in the community where he has continuously resided for the past thirty-seven years.

WALTER W. & NORTON J. MORGAN.—Among the representatives of old pioneer families who are carrying on, under more promising conditions, the work established by their sires, mention is due Walter W. and Norton J. Morgan, young men of energy and resource, and among the well-known business men in Contra Costa County. By right of inheritance they became owners of the E. Morgan Hardware & Plumbing Company, located at the corner of Ferry and Escobar Streets, Martinez. This is the oldest hardware establishment in Contra Costa County and was formed fifty-six years ago by Edwin and Oliver Morgan, brothers.

Edwin Morgan, the father of Walter and Norton Morgan, was born at Dallas, Texas, and sprang from the noted Southern family of Morgans, being closely related to General Morgan, famous as leader of Morgan's men during the Civil War. Edwin Morgan's parents were William and Lucinda Morgan. They crossed the plains to California when Edwin was four years old, settling first in San Jose, but remained there only for two or three months, when they removed to Contra Costa County. Here William Morgan worked for a time on the Pacheco Ranch, and then the family located in the Pleasant Hill district, where the Morgan Ranch was located. William Morgan became an extensive farmer and stock-raiser and at one time owned the larger part of the valley. Edwin Morgan worked with his father until he reached his majority; then he learned the tinner's trade at Pacheco. After learning his trade he moved to Martinez and opened a tin shop on Ferry Street, in 1875. Soon he branched out and added a stock of hardware, and this business he continued successfully until his death.

At Martinez, in 1878, Edwin Morgan was married to Miss Mary Abbie James, born at Martinez, Cal., a daughter of Oliver James, the first postmaster of Martinez. The James family was of Puritan origin, a representative settling in America in 1629. On her mother's side, Miss James was descended from a branch of the Winslow family, her mother having been Miss Abagail Cartwright. Miss Cartwright was a second cousin of the Cartwright who introduced the game of baseball in New

York State. To Mr. and Mrs. Edwin Morgan were born six children: Mabel M., now the wife of George Russi, a grain broker living in Portland, Ore.; Walter W., born in Martinez in 1882; Amy I., who makes her home in Martinez, and is married to Harry Seyers; Norton J., of this review; Emmalyn, a graduate of Stanford University Hospital and now a trained nurse in Martinez; and Edwin H. Morgan, Jr.

Edwin Morgan was a school teacher for many years; and he was also a city trustee and mayor of Martinez. Fraternally, he was a charter member of the Independent Order of Odd Fellows of Martinez and had passed through all the chairs. He was a Republican in politics. His death occurred on April 9, 1921, seven months after the decease of his wife.

Walter W. and Norton J. Morgan grew up in Martinez, and as soon as they were old enough went into the business with their father. The business has grown steadily until they employ six men besides themselves. This firm figures on jobs of plumbing such as for school buildings, residences and business blocks. In August, 1905, fire destroyed the original building, and the same year a modern building of pressed brick was erected to take its place.

Walter W. Morgan married Miss Dee C. Cottrel, and they have one child, Jean. The family reside in their own residence, located at 1134 Escobar Street. Mr. Morgan is a member and Past Consul of The Woodmen of the World, and also belongs to the Native Sons.

Norton J. Morgan married Miss Teresina Burger, born in the City of Mexico. They make their home in the old Morgan homestead at Martinez. Fraternally, he is a member of the Masonic order. Both brothers are Republicans.

JAMES M. STOW.—The late James M. Stow will be remembered as a man of unusual public spirit and enterprise who for more than four decades was actively identified with the industrial, social and politiacl advancement of Contra Costa County, and who substantially aided the growth and development of Walnut Creek. He was born in Illinois on August 29, 1847, and was a son of Josephus Stow, a native of Massachusetts, who married Miss Susan Dodd and established a home in Springfield, Ill. Josephus Stow left his farm in competent hands and joined the gold-seekers coming overland to California. Arriving in the Golden State, he engaged in mining with fair success, and in 1856 sent for his wife and three children, who came via Cape Horn. The family resided in Nevada County until 1859, when they removed to San Francisco, and there Josephus Stow passed away in 1860. Afterwards his widow settled at Danville, where she married John Perham. Later the family removed to Walnut Creek, and here Mrs. Perham died in 1886 at the age of sixty-six years.

James M. Stow was twelve years old when the family settled in Contra Costa County, and here his death occurred on August 17, 1919, at the age of nearly seventy-two years. In 1911 Mr. Stow removed to Pacific Grove. He erected one of the finest homes of that city; and while residing there he served as one of the city trustees and was mayor of the city, but resigned to return to Walnut Creek to look after his extensive real estate holdings in Contra Costa County.

James M. Stow attended public school in Oakland, and his early business training was gained in a general merchandise store in Walnut Creek; later he became owner of the business, which he conducted until elected to the office of county assessor on the Republican ticket in 1880. This office he filled to the entire satisfaction of the people of the county for a period of seven years. In 1887 Mr. Stow disposed of his store and engaged in the real estate and insurance business, becoming one of the county's foremost promoters. He was appointed postmaster of Walnut Creek and was a faithful government servant; and at the same time he was the agent for the Wells-Fargo Express Company. He was a notary public, was one of the chief promoters and organizers of the first telephone company of the county, and for a time owned and operated the Martinez Gazette. He was a stockholder in the Bank of Martinez, the Bank of Walnut Creek, and the Bank of Pacific Grove. When a tunnel was projected through the mountains, making a direct outlet to Oakland from Contra Costa County, a distance of 1026 feet, there were several bids from contractors to build the part belonging to Contra Costa County, but the county voted to have the work done by the supervisors. Mr. Stow superintended the work and saved the county over $17,000 on the construction of the road.

James M. Stow was twice married, the first union, which occurred on April 22, 1873, uniting him with Miss Alice Glass, a daughter of Joseph Glass, one of Contra Costa County's respected pioneers. Her death occurred on July 22, 1910. The children of this union are: Dr. Eleanor Stow Bancroft, resident physician at Mills College; Harriett, who died in infancy; Carrie, the wife of L. R. Palmer, of Walnut Creek; Garfield, engaged in the real estate business in Oakland, Cal.; Rufus, residing on the home place and employed at Mare Island; Pearl, the wife of Joseph E. Lawrence, of Walnut Creek; Orville, engaged in the ice business in Walnut Creek; Harry, constable of Walnut Creek; Armand, in Pittsburg; Blanche Eleen, who died in infancy; Russell, of Walnut Creek; and Forrest Chadbourne, in the Alhambra Valley. The second marriage of Mr. Stow occurred on March 20, 1912, uniting him with Mrs. Lillie (Berring) Gardner; and of this union was born one child, Berring.

Fraternally, Mr. Stow was a Mason and for a number of years served as secretary of Alamo Lodge at Walnut Creek. He was a member of the Methodist Church and served as trustee of the church at Pacific Grove. He purchased the pleasantly situated estate of Captain Fales near Walnut Creek, which he improved, making it an attractive and comfortable home place. Mr. Stow's extensive real estate holdings amounted to about 5000 acres of land. During his last term as supervisor he was an important factor in the building of the new courthouse at Martinez. He was a Republican, always took a keen interest in State and county politics, and enjoyed the esteem of all who knew him.

FRED N. MYRICK.—A well-known member of the old pioneer family of Myricks, which has made its impress on Contra Costa County, is Fred N. Myrick, owner of a fifteen-acre ranch in Clayton Precinct, of which locality he is a native. Mr. Myrick and his wife are of that brand of God-fearing, substantial citizens who are an asset to any community, and their many friends are glad to testify as to their sterling worth. Mr. Myrick's well-cared for ranch is devoted to the growing of almonds, apricots, grain and hay and is one of the most fertile spots in that section.

Fred N. Myrick was born on the old Myrick ranch in Clayton Precinct on December 27, 1862, the son of Christopher Mitchell Myrick, that rugged New England pioneer, a native of Nantucket, Mass., who came to California by way of Cape Horn during the gold rush days of Forty-nine. After trying his hand at mining, but with indifferent success, he came to San Francisco where he worked as a carpenter. Later he went back to Massachusetts and married his first wife, Lydia C. Joy, whom he brought back to San Francisco and then engaged in the water business, selling it from door to door to the residents at twenty-five cents per bucket. The city then had a population of about 500 souls. There were no children of this union that lived. His second wife was Mrs. Jane (Barstow) Loring, who had a daughter, now Mrs. Annie Matheron, of Martinez. Their children were five in number, viz.: Stanley G.; Fred N.; Walter A.; Lydia C. Clayton, of Oakland; Imogene, Mrs. William Benson, died at the age of twenty-one. In 1859 Mr. Myrick came to Clayton Precinct and bought 160 acres of land which he farmed the balance of his life. He died on April 18, 1915, aged eighty-seven. He was successful in spite of an expensive lawsuit over 247 acres of land that was claimed by the railroad company, but he held the property and farmed it for about forty years, making his home on the land, in a shack, to hold possession. He was well-liked by all who knew him for his integrity of character and uprightness.

Fred N. Myrick's early schooling was meager, as was that of most of the boys of that locality in that day. He worked on his father's ranch and developed the sturdy physique of the pioneer. At the tender age of nine he was able to drive a team, milk cows and do many other of the tasks usually assigned to a full-grown man. At the age of twenty-one he left his father's ranch and commenced working on other ranches.

Fred N. Myrick was married in Concord on November 17, 1889, to Miss Phoebe Lewis, born in Wales, the daughter of William D. and Mary (Bowen) Lewis, both born in Wales, and there married, whose children were as follows: Mrs. George Bloching, deceased, and Mrs. F. N. Myrick, both born in Wales; Martha and Seth, both deceased, were born in

George Van Gorder

Missouri; Martha 2nd, married Andrew Rumgay and died aged twenty; David, died aged four; Mrs. Margaret Llewellyn, of Washington; Edith, widow of M. Costello, of Oakland; and William C., of Washington. Mrs. Lewis died on September 8, 1925. Mr. Lewis was a miner and worked at Nortonville and Somersville in Contra Costa County, when the mines were flourishing here; also for the past thirty-eight years he has been mining in Washington. Mr. and Mrs. Myrick have had three children: Lottie B., married J. N. Wilson and lives in Martinez; Zelma I., became the wife of Thomas Bradshaw and lives in Oakland; and William, died in infancy.

GEORGE VAN GORDEN.—Of those who were drawn to California in the forties and early fifties, but few persons who journeyed across the plains and over the mountain passes can now be found among the living. Yet among those who accompanied the undaunted pioneers of California, before the discovery of gold, there is one still living, George Van Gorden, now in his eighty-second year and a resident of the San Ramon Valley near Danville, Contra Costa County. He was born in Detroit, Mich., on September 8, 1845, a son of Ira and Rebecca (Harlan) Van Gorden. The father was a native of Kings County, New York, and followed farming and cattle raising. Their family consisted of two boys: George, the subject of this sketch; and Jerome, now deceased. In the fall of 1845 the family left Michigan for Lexington, Mo., where they passed the winter, awaiting the coming of spring, when they anticipated making the overland journey through to the Golden State, accompanied by Grandfather George Harlan. The family joined a company consisting of 200 covered wagons bound for the Pacific Coast country, most of them expecting to locate in Oregon. As was the custom in those days of large migrations, the large wagon-train was divided into several divisions, and one capable man was chosen as leader of each party. Grandfather Harlan was chosen for their party. Another party in the same train was known as the "Donner Party," which originally started from Springfield, Ill., and was headed by George and Jacob Donner and James K. Reed, and consisted of their families. Each party was enlarged by additions and combinations as they journeyed along.

A new route over the mountains had been found and announced by Lansford W. Hastings prior to the starting of this train and it was said to save 300 miles. The Harlan party took this short-cut through Echo Canyon to what is now Ogden, over Hastings cut-off, named for Hastings. The Donner party went over the old Oregon Trail via Salt Lake, but on account of the longer route their decision proved very disastrous and the party was left snowbound in the high Sierra Mountains with scant provisions. They built cabins at a lake, now called Donner Lake, and sent a party of four men and four women on snowshoes in search of help and provisions. The party left December 16, 1846, with provisions for six days but the journey consumed thirty-two days and re-

sulted in the death of two of the men. The survivors arrived at Sutter's
Fort, where they were cared for, and relief parties were sent out to aid
the distressed snowbound immigrants. About half of the Donner party
died from starvation and exposure before assistance reached them.

George Van Gorden was a little baby when he was brought across the
plains and mountains to the Golden State, but during his life in California he has often heard his parents and relatives narrate the interesting
incidents of that long and dangerous trip. In crossing the San Joaquin
River, Mr. Van Gorden says, the party had to make rafts of bundles of
tule, as that was the only way the Indians had of navigating the river.
He is one of the very few persons now living who crossed the plains during
those perilous years in the forties. He is now in his eighty-second year
and believes he has resided longer in California than any other white man
now living. He is hale and hearty, and recently drove an automobile to
Los Angeles in one day, a distance of 400 miles. Mr. Van Gorden says
he has gone through all of the Indian uprisings without receiving a
scratch. These pioneers who have survived to the present day find in the
comforts of the present time ample compensation for the deprivations
of the past. Mr. Van Gorden has lived to see marvelous developments
and transformations wrought in California during his eighty years of residence in the State. He lived in Alameda County when Alvarado was the
county seat, and in 1858 removed from that county to Visalia. In 1865
he moved to San Luis Obispo County, where he made his residence for
thirty years.

About 1901 Mr. Van Gorden moved to Contra Costa County, settling
near Danville in the San Ramon Valley, where he owns 237 acres of land
upon which he raises fruit to some extent; he has a twenty-five-acre pear
orchard that he considers one of the best in the State. He also owns 450
acres in Trinity County upon which he has a gold mine, having found
nuggets to the value of eight dollars and upwards; the mine is paying
well. His chief occupation is stock-raising, especially race horses. On his
ranch he has raised some of the best horses that have ever graced a track;
some of them have been in the winning in every race in which they have
been entered. Among the horses that have been raised by him are:
Captain John, that took first premium in 1920 at Madison Square Gardens
in New York as the best thoroughbred stallion exhibited; and Durward
Roberts, that sold for $15,000 when nine years old, a hunter standing
seventeen hands high. Besides these, Sir Edward, Van Patrick, Florence
Roberts, Barbara Lane, Silvery Light and Judge Sanderson, all have
spread the name and fame of Contra Costa County to the world. He
has a colt that he refused $2000 for when two months old, a fine animal.

On September 24, 1868, George Van Gorden and Miss Anna Steiner
were united in marriage. She was born in Mariposa County but was
living at Visalia when they were married. Three children blessed their
marriage. Anita is the wife of Dr. H. S. Kergan, of Oakland, and the

mother of two children, Marian and Janice; Marian married Edwin L. Bruck of San Francisco and has two children, Ann and Edwin K.; Janice is the wife of William S. Street, of Oakland. George Maurice, Mr. and Mrs. Van Gorden's only son, died at the age of thirty-nine years, unmarried. Laura married F. W. Grunig and passed away six months after her son Durward was born; Mr. Grunig died three months later, and Durward was adopted by his grandparents, who reared him. He is married and has a son, Maurice Edward.

Mr. Van Gorden has seen the original gold nugget, known in history as the Marshall nugget, the one that heralded to the world the discovery of gold in California. In narrating the history of this nugget he said that Mrs. Peter Wimmer, a member of the overland party, was making soft soap when one of the boys found the nugget in a ditch under construction by Mr. Marshall, and gave it to Marshall, who in turn gave it to Mrs. Wimmer to test it and ascertain whether it was pure gold or not; she put it in the lye and soft soap kettle, and when taken out it proved to be pure gold. It was originally worth about eight dollars, but by handling through the years intervening it has been worn away until now its value is reduced to about six dollars.

ANDREW WATERMAN JOSSELYN.—Among the oldest and most active contractors and builders of Richmond and vicinity is Andrew Waterman Josselyn, who lives at No. 342 South Seventh Street, Richmond, to which city he came in 1904, when most of the district now covered by good homes and business houses was a grain and hay field. He has been actively connected with its upbuilding, and many of the buildings in Richmond and the surrounding territory are the result of his labor and intelligence. He was born at Boston, Mass., on January 24, 1849, the son of John Henry Josselyn, a contractor and builder of that city. The family trace their lineage back to the landing of the Pilgrims, and the succeeding generations have been prominent in business and civic affairs ever since. The mother, in maidenhood, was Miss Elizabeth Sawtelle; she died when Andrew W. was twelve years old. His father passed on when the young man was eighteen. Besides Andrew W. there were the following children in the Josselyn family: George Henry, John Hatch, Marcus H., Mary Elizabeth, and Horace, all of whom are deceased.

After attending the public schools of Boston, Andrew W. Josselyn served an apprenticeship at the trade of the carpenter, and in 1873 he came out to California to seek his fortune in the land of gold. Arriving in Oakland he followed his trade about eighteen months while he was a resident of that city, and then went to Mariposa and followed the building business about eight years, after which he made his home in Tulare for about eight years. Coming to Richmond in 1904 he began working at his trade here. Soon he began taking contracts, and among the buildings he constructed was the Milwaukee Hotel. He mentions that many new advantages not known in early days are now in vogue, that simplify building construction, and he takes advantage of all innovations in his line. For several years he made a specialty of stair-building, at which he was an expert.

Mr. Josselyn was married on May 1, 1900, being united with Miss Lila Forsythe, who was born in San Francisco. Her father was Samuel Forsythe, born in Belfast, Ireland. He married Helena Mullins, of Queenstown, Ireland, whose father, John Mullins, was connected with the Coast Guard Station of Ireland and for sixty-five years drew pay from the government, being pensioned with full pay. Mrs. Josselyn taught school in Mill Valley and Mariposa County, having graduated from the John Swett High School of San Francisco and from the San Jose State Normal School, now the San Jose State Teachers' College. She is also an accomplished musician, an honorary member of the Club Mendelssohn, and has taught music. She has been a member of the Rebekahs for thirty-six years and has passed all the chairs of the order. Her birthday is Bunker Hill Day, June 17, and the year was 1868. Mr. Josselyn is a member of the Ancient Order of Foresters and a life member of the Richmond Builders' Exchange. He believes in sticking to any job he has in hand till that job is completed, and attributes his success to that habit. In his political affiliation he is a Democrat, and when in Tulare County he served as secretary-treasurer of the County Central Committee of his party. Mr. and Mrs. Josselyn belong to the Episcopal Church. Both are fond of domestic animals. They have a wide circle of close friends in Richmond, and always show a true public spirit in supporting progressive movements for the public good.

LOUIS BRACKMAN.—A native son, successful dairyman and self-made man, Louis Brackman, who owns 179 acres in the Alhambra district, just beyond the city limits of Martinez, is the sixth child of the family of seven born to the late William Brackman, a native of Germany, who came from the East across the plains to California in 1849. He mined for a short while, then engaged in business in San Francisco, and from there moved to Moraga Valley, in Contra Costa County, finally locating at Pinole. Louis Brackman was born there on February 11, 1863, and was reared on the home ranch, having only the educational advantages offered by the early district school. He began to work when a lad, and early learned the rudiments of ranch work. He has owned and farmed several ranches before coming to his present place, and has made a success of horticulture as well as of dairy farming. He owned and operated a 300-acre fruit and grain ranch, and also another ranch in the Alhambra Valley, before making his selection of his present place. Here he has built a comfortable ranch home and substantial barns, and milks twenty-five cows, supplying fresh milk to the County Hospital, and separating the balance of his output and disposing of his cream to the Martinez Creamery. His dairy barn is a model of sanitation and cleanliness, as it is thoroughly cleaned twice daily, being flushed and washed with water every morning; for he takes great pride in the excellence of his product and in the healthful conditions surrounding his dairy herd.

The marriage of Mr. Brackman, occurring at Martinez in 1895, united him with Miss Nellie Carpenter, a daughter of a Contra Costa County pioneer, the late Daniel Carpenter, who served the county as tax collector. Mrs. Brackman was born at Clayton, Contra Costa County, and with her husband is interested in the upbuilding and development of their native county. They attend the Congregational Church at Martinez, and are representative citizens of their district.

JASPER H. WELLS.—An efficient and popular public officer, Jasper H. Wells, county clerk of Contra Costa County, was appointed on November 21, 1908, to fill the vacancy caused by the resignation of J. E. Rodgers; and that he is highly regarded by the citizens of the county is attested to by the fact that he has now continuously held the office for eighteen years. Mr. Wells is a native son, having been born at Santa Rosa, January 27, 1871, a son of Philip and Margaret Wells, the former born in Kentucky, the latter a native of Illinois. The family of Philip and Margaret Wells consisted of six children: Eva, who married C. A. Tarwater of Concord; Myrtle, who became the wife of John Sutton of Berkeley; Lillie; Ernest, of Portland, Ore.; Samuel, of Martinez; and Jasper H. The parents of Mrs. Philip Wells settled on Government Ranch, Contra Costa County, in 1853, afterwards removing to Sonoma County.

Jasper H. Wells was educated in the public schools and completed a course in the San Francisco Business College, graduating with the class of 1898. After his father's death in 1890, he managed the home ranch for eight years. After completing his business course he entered the office of the county clerk, filling the position of deputy clerk so efficiently that when J. E. Rodgers resigned to enter the practice of law Mr. Wells was appointed to the position of county clerk, which office he has filled so acceptably ever since.

On January 8, 1902, Jasper H. Wells was united in marriage with Miss Anna Ardelia Webb, a daughter of Frank and Phebe Webb, of Walnut Creek. This union was blessed by a son, Melvin Thomas Wells. Fraternally, Mr. Wells is a member of Pacheco Lodge No. 117, I. O. O. F., of Concord; Mt. Diablo Parlor No. 101, N. S. G. W.; and Richmond Lodge No. 1251, B. P. O. Elks. Mrs. Wells, who is an active worker in religious and fraternal circles, is a graduate of San Jose State Normal School and taught school for a number of years at Concord. Mr. and Mrs. Wells have an ever widening circle of sincere friends and are among the most highly esteemed citizens of Martinez and Contra Costa County.

LOUIS FONTANA.—A well-known citizen of Pittsburg, who has many varied interests in and around this city, is Louis Fontana. Mr. Fontana owns a vineyard of forty acres which he has developed into an income property, is proprietor of Fontana's Grocery Store at No. 203 Black Diamond Street, and also owns five other business buildings, besides the $26,000 garage building at the corner of Cumberland and Third Streets, now occupied by the Pittsburg Motor Company. As he has succeeded financially he has reinvested his money, for he realized Pittsburg would soon become one of the leading industrial cities of the East Bay district. He believes in advancement and shows his public spirit when called upon to help all projects that mean a bigger and better Pittsburg.

Mr. Fontana was born in Naples, Italy, on October 8, 1881, a son of Raffael and Maria Fontana. There were eighteen children in this family and seventeen of them are still alive. One brother died in Africa during his service in the World War. Both parents are deceased. Louis went to the local schools in his native city and was the first member of the family to come to America. He arrived in Pittsburg on April 27, 1907, and ever since has been closely identified with the best interests of the city. He believes in going ahead, keeps up with the times in all his business projects, and is counted among the well-to-do men of the county he has selected for his permanent home.

On November 24, 1913, Louis Fontana was united in marriage with Mrs. Kate Crevallo, whose maiden name was Di Maggio. By her first husband she had a son, Joe Crevallo, now nineteen years of age, who lives with his mother. Mrs. Fontana is of great help to her husband and is deserving of much praise for looking after the store while her husband is taking care of his ranch and other interests. By careful management they have become very prosperous and they have a wide circle of friends in this part of Contra Costa County. Mr. Fontana is a member of Pittsburg Lodge No. 78, I. O. O. F. Both he and his good wife are looked upon as honest and industrious citizens.

PATRICK LUCEY.—A pioneer hotel man of Crockett, Patrick Lucey has seen this part of Contra Costa County grow from practically its virgin state to the best industrial town in the county. In all movements for its growth Patrick Lucey can always be counted upon to do his share. He was born in Cork, Ireland, in 1869, one of a family of three boys and two girls who are still living. The parents both passed away when Patrick was only six years old, and in 1885 he came to America with three brothers who hoped to better their condition in the New World. What education he secured from books was in his native land, but his education in the school of bitter experience has meant more to him than all he could get from books. When he struck California he worked as a laborer until he saved enough to start in the hotel business. This has continued to occupy his time, with the exception of eighteen months that he spent in Martinez, where he was interested in the Martinez Ferry. To assist in the development of his town Mr. Lucey has been connected with banking interests and with lodges, having helped to organize the Eagles in Crockett with fifty members. Mr. Lucey believes in boosting for his home town in every way he can.

Patrick Lucey was married to Miss Mary Crowley, of San Francisco, and they have had seven children. The two oldest died in early childhood; the others are John Lucey, a machinist; Patrick Jr., a graduate from the Crockett High School who took a course in college and is a surveyor; Bernard, a graduate from the high school and employed by the gas company; Aileen, a high school graduate now attending normal school at San Francisco; and Rose, in the high school. In politics Mr. Lucey supports the men he considers best qualified to serve the people rather than stick to party lines in local affairs, but in national affairs he leans toward the Democratic party. He is a whole-souled gentleman and tries to do his duty as he sees it.

HANS A. M. HANSEN.—Another of the early settlers in what is now El Cerrito is Hans A. M. Hansen, living at 406 Schmidt Lane and conducting a small dairy there. He came to this locality in 1897, about the time the partition had been made on the San Pablo Grant, and began raising chickens and hogs on six acres that he leased. In 1903 he purchased two acres and in 1906 added two more, making all the improvements on the place except the three-room house that was already on the land. He has been an interested spectator of the growth and development of this part of the county and has willingly done his share to promote all forward movements for the good of all the people located here.

Mr. Hansen was born in Schleswig-Holstein, Denmark, March 4, 1860, and attended the public schools when he could be spared from work, for at the age of eight he worked among the cattle in the farming country where he was born, attending school an hour each day, and that was usually the noon hour. When he was old enough to enter the army he offered his services but was rejected and put back three years on account of being much under weight, weighing less than 100 pounds. At the age of twenty-three he came to the United States, intending to go to Nebraska; but on account of there being no such town shown on the map of that state as the one where his letter showed his nephew lived, he was sold a ticket to a town of the same name in Minnesota. Being unable to understand a word of English, he did not know where he was being sent. It was necessary to get a job and he did so, working on the construction of the railroad to Grand Island. He soon found trace of his relative and at once joined him for a visit, spending one winter with him. He then went to Wyoming, again working on railroad construction or on section work, until he had worked his way to California, landing in San Francisco in 1884. He liked the city life with its continual variety and change, and for thirteen years followed teaming for wages; and dur-

CONTRA COSTA COUNTY

ing this time he came to know almost every corner of that city. In 1897 he began to look about for a place to make a home. Coming to Contra Costa County, he found his present location, then a farming section, leased six acres, and began for himself. This has continued to be the family home. During the World War, Mr. Hansen was employed at the ship yards in Oakland, but afterwards he engaged in the dairy business.

In 1903 Mr. Hansen was united in marriage with Mrs. Johannah Welte, a native of Germany and the mother of two boys by her marriage with Mr. Welte. The boys were small at the time their mother married Mr. Hansen, and they took the Hansen name. Harry is married and lives in Berkeley. The other is named John. By this second marriage, Mrs. Hansen also has two boys: Christian, of Richmond; and Andrew, a graduate of Heald's Business College at home. Fraternally, Mr. Hansen is a member of the Fraternal Order of Eagles of Berkeley. Politically, he is independent in his views, supporting the men he deems best suited for the offices. He is an interesting conversationalist, and is well posted on early times and conditions in his locality.

CALVIN W. MINAKER.—A rancher of Antioch Precinct No. 5 of Contra Costa County worthy of mention in this volume is Calvin W. Minaker, whose productive fifty-two acre ranch is located on Wilbur Avenue about one mile east of Antioch. In 1902 Mr. Minaker located in the vicinity of Antioch and at first leased thirty acres from his cousin, Will E. Minaker, who is now a commission merchant in San Francisco. He made his first purchase of land, twenty acres, in 1905 and by subsequent purchases he has added to this until he now has fifty-two acres all planted and bearing, mostly in table grapes, but a few acres remain planted to hay. Mr. Minaker also owns another small ranch of five acres near Antioch.

Mr. Minaker was born in the Province of Ontario, Canada, on June 10, 1867, a son of Thomas and Christine Minaker, farmer folk in the Province of Ontario, Prince Edward County. Both parents are now dead. Calvin W. Minaker grew up on his father's farm, remaining there until he was twenty years old. He came to California, locating in Humboldt County, where he was employed by the Pacific Lumber Company at Scotia doing all kinds of work connected with a lumber mill.

Returning to his home in Canada he was married on April 26, 1899, at Bloomfield, to Miss Mabel C. Hudgin, also a native of Canada. They returned to Humboldt County where they resided until they came to San Francisco, remaining until 1902. In 1905 they acquired their present home place where they have since resided. Mrs. Minaker is a practical nurse and finds plenty to do in Antioch and vicinity. They have four living children: Maude L., the wife of Melvin H. Cavanaugh, resides in San Francisco; T. Alfred works for the Columbia Steel Corporation in Pittsburg; Gertrude C. and Prudence E. are at home. Mr. Minaker is a member of the Eel River Lodge of Odd Fellows at Rohnerville, Cal., and in politics is a Republican.

C H Hayden

CHARLES H. HAYDEN.—Among the leading citizens of Contra Costa County, Charles H. Hayden has been identified with the growth of both Martinez and the county since his arrival here in 1896. He is a native of Iowa, born in Calhoun County on June 29, 1870. His education was obtained in the public schools of his locality, and there he grew to manhood. From a youth he had always had a desire to visit the Pacific Coast country and in due time he landed in Portland, Ore., where he found employment with W. S. Ladd, of Ladd & Tilton, Bankers. He rapidly developed into a keen business man and in 1896, severing his relations in Portland, came to California and soon after located in Martinez, where he was employed in the hardware and plumbing establishment of E. Morgan, remaining there for eight years. His agreeable manners and clean-cut personality soon attracted the attention of some of the leading men of Martinez, and when the time came to fill the vacancy of the unexpired term of D. S. Carpenter as justice of the peace, Mr. Hayden was selected and thereafter gave his time to the duties of the office. So satisfactory were his services that he was elected at the following election and each succeeding one until he had served for thirteen years, when he resigned. His close attention to details, and the success with which he carried out the plans outlined, soon led to the proffer of further responsibilities, and for sixteen years he was a member of the board of trustees of Martinez, four years of that time serving as mayor. He helped put over the campaign for city ownership of the water supply; and he served as chief of the fire department for six years and assisted in its reorganization, scrapping the obsolete equipment and motorizing the entire department in order to bring it to its present efficiency. Always interested in the cause of education, Mr. Hayden has served for five consecutive terms as a school trustee, during which time modern buildings have been built and equipped, and thirteen acres purchased for a new grammar school site. He was elected a member of the board of county supervisors in 1918 and is now serving his second term. He has been prominently associated with the good roads movement in this county and believes that the best is none too good for a county that stands at the head of all the counties of the State in progress and wealth. Mr. Hayden is a firm believer in the future growth of Contra Costa County and Martinez, and backs that faith by investing in real estate. He opened up a real estate office many years ago and has steadily built up a name for himself as a man whose word is as good as his bond. He buys and sells property in any part of the county, does an insurance business to accommodate his patrons, and also loans money to help people establish themselves in the county. He helped to organize the Plywood Products Company in Martinez, and was one of the organizers of the Schlage Lock Company in San Francisco, both of which are concerns with great possibilities. It would be difficult to find a man that has been more interested in the development of California's interests than he, or more ready to boost every worthy project for the betterment of his home city and county. It is to such men that the present growth of the West is largely due.

Charles H. Hayden was united in marriage on December 28, 1898, with Miss Letta M. Cottrell, a native of Texas. They have had three children born to them, namely: Hoyt H., born August 31, 1903, now employed in the Jackson County Bank at Medford, Ore.; Hilda H., born May 25, 1907; and Ruth M., who died in early childhood. Mrs. Hayden belongs to the Woman's Improvement Club of Martinez, the Women of Woodcraft, and the Pythian Sisters. Mr. Hayden is a member of the Knights of Pythias and Woodmen of the World. Both Mr. and Mrs. Hayden are popular in social, civic and educational circles in Martinez, and are very public-spirited. During the World War they both took an active part in promptly putting Contra Costa County over the top in all the allied drives for the good of the cause.

DAVID A. GATTO.—Conspicuous among the pioneer business men of Pittsburg, Cal., is David A. Gatto, a man of enterprise and splendid business judgment who possesses a genial disposition, uprightness of character and a kindly heart towards all in need. He is the junior member of the firm of Gatto Brothers of Pittsburg. He and his brother Louis built the frame building at the corner of Black Diamond and Front Streets in 1902, and still occupy it as a place of business. The Gatto Brothers have been residents of Pittsburg for many years and have aided very materially in the upbuilding and advancement of the city by building business blocks and residences.

David A. Gatto was born in San Francisco, February 7, 1878, a son of Michael and Theresa (Gatto) Gatto, natives of Genoa, Italy. Although Miss Gatto bore the same surname, she was no relative. Soon after their marriage the young couple emigrated to America, settling for a time in New York City, but later removed to California, locating at San Francisco about October, 1874. Michael Gatto engaged in the wood and coal business and died in San Francisco when David was an infant. Their family consisted of five children: John, born in New York City, died in 1924; Louis, born in New York City, July 2, 1872, now a pioneer business man of Pittsburg; Charles, born in San Francisco, now deceased; David A., the subject of this review, and a twin brother Frank, who died in infancy. The widow of Michael Gatto married Giuseppe Guaragnella, a pioneer fisherman of New York Landing, later called Black Diamond and now Pittsburg. After her second marriage the mother removed with her family to the home of her husband at Pittsburg, and here passed away on November 21, 1911, at the age of sixty-two years. The stepfather, Mr. Guaragnella, still lives at Pittsburg and was ninety years old on February 12, 1926. He is well and favorably known in the bay region, having built a home at New York Landing, in 1876, a residence still standing and occupied by him as his home. By the second marriage of Mrs. Gatto, she had a son, T. J. Guaragnella, who is now a broker in San Francisco.

David A. Gatto attended the early schools in Black Diamond and assisted his stepfather in his fishing and other business enterprises. In 1897 he began the barber business here, being the pioneer barber of what is now Pittsburg, and he has been very successful in all that he has undertaken ever since. He early saw the great future for Pittsburg and in 1911, with his brother Louis, erected the first substantial brick block, located at the corner of Black Diamond and Front Streets, a two-story structure used for stores and lodge rooms and occupied by the Masons, Odd Fellows and Knights of Pythias. This building is a decided adjunct to the business blocks in Pittsburg and a credit to the builders of it.

Mr. Gatto has always taken an active interest in local politics. He is a leader among the Italian people, and it is the opinion of many that he has more friends and is stronger politically than any other person in Pittsburg. His counsel is eagerly sought by business men, laboring men and women, and candidates for office, and his judgment is highly regarded in matters pertaining to the welfare of Pittsburg and the community. He was appointed deputy city treasurer of Black Diamond by his stepbrother, T. J. Guaragnella, and so efficiently did he discharge his duties that he was regularly elected to the office at a subsequent election and afterwards it was said of him, "Gatto was the best city treasurer we ever had." For many years he has been a deputy sheriff under R. R. Veale. He has always stood for the advancement of education, and his stepson, Dave Irwin, was sent to Heald's Business College at Stockton and is now the accountant at Leland Stanford Junior University.

In October, 1901, at Pittsburg, David A. Gatto was united in marriage with Miss Jennie Junta, who died on July 19, 1904. This union was blessed with one child, Theresa, who is now with the Redwood Manufacturers Company at Pittsburg. The second marriage of Mr. Gatto took place at Pittsburg, March 27, 1907, when he was united with Mrs. Pauline Irwin, a sister of his first wife, who had one child, David Irwin. Of the present union there are two children: Jennie, now a student at San Francisco Normal School; and Michael, attending the local public school. Fraternally, Mr. Gatto is a member of Roma Lodge No. 147, K. of P., San Francisco, which he joined in 1899; a trustee of Diamond Parlor, N. S. G. W., of Pittsburg, and the designer of its seal, being a charter member of the Parlor; and a member at large of the Ancient Order of Foresters.

SABATINO BARLETTANI.—As a natural result of his thrift and industry, Sabatino Barlettani has become a prosperous citizen of Martinez, Contra Costa County, which has been his home for the past twenty years. His birthplace was Florence, Italy, where he was born on January

29, 1877, a son of Antonio and Marie Barlettani, both natives of the same country. He was reared and educated in his native country and there learned the blacksmithing trade, which he has followed persistently and successfully since. He came to America in 1907 and established his home in Martinez, where he has continuously resided and is now running his third blacksmith shop. Because of his reliability and adeptness he has built up a splendid trade in general blacksmithing and horseshoeing. The family residence and blacksmith shop are located on his own property at 516 Ward Street, besides which he owns other valuable real estate in the city.

The marriage of Mr. Barlettani united him with Miss Amelia Guinasso, who was born and reared in the vicinity of Genoa, Italy, and as a young woman came to America and to Martinez only one week later than the subject of this sketch. In Mrs. Barlettani are found the same qualities of thrift and industry which are outstanding characteristics of her husband. Their union has been a happy one. They are the parents of six children: Norma, Antone, Ardo, Frank, Woodrow and Sabatino. The family are communicants of the Catholic Church. Mr. Barlettani is a member of the Woodmen of the World and the Societa Operia Italiana di Muto Soccorso, both of Martinez. In politics he is a Republican.

GEORGE H. WRIGHT.—A well-known rancher of the Pacheco district, where he has lived since coming to Contra Costa County, on January 24, 1910, George H. Wright comes of old American stock, and in his life has adhered to the principles instilled through generations in the traditions of his family. Born in Elkhart, Ind., March 2, 1845, he is a son of Henry S. and Orilla (Smith) Wright, the former, who lived to be eighty-seven years old, being a native of Cattaraugus County, N. Y., and a founder and ironworker by trade; the latter, who lived to be seventy-four years of age, being a native of Geauga County, Ohio, of English extraction. Her ancestors settled in Massachusetts in 1620, and some of them served in the Revolutionary War. Grandfather Wright, father of Henry S. Wright, was of Welsh stock, and took an important part in the industrial life of New York in the early days.

Henry S. and Orilla Wright moved to Elkhart, Ind., in 1842, and there our subject's father built the first blast-furnace in northern Indiana. This furnace was located on the banks of the St. Joseph River, upon which stream Charles Crocker, the father of the family of California Crockers, boated iron ore to Wright's furnace; and Mr. Oliver, of the great Oliver Plow Works, there served his apprenticeship in the iron works. It was there that Henry S. Wright discovered the art of putting cold chilled points on cast iron, an art which was further developed by Mr. Oliver, who became the patentee and manufacturer of the celebrated Oliver Cast Chilled Plows, and thus became one of America's foremost millionaire manufacturers. In that vicinity the Studebakers started their first wagon shops, which during the Civil War grew to such importance that the plant covered ten acres of ground, and is now one of the great automobile manufacturing plants of this country.

George H. Wright received his schooling in a little log schoolhouse, rough as well as rustic, and studied his early lessons out of the New Testament and Webster's spelling book. He grew up in an abolitionist neighborhood, and when the Civil War broke out he volunteered at Kalamazoo, Mich., enlisting in Company B, 11th Michigan Infantry, in March, 1863, his younger brother, Edwin, then but fifteen, enlisting with him. Being a fairly good penman and scholar, he was detailed to do office work at headquarters, serving under both General Thomas and General Sherman. He was mustered out at Nashville, Tenn., at the close of the war, and honorably discharged at Jackson, Mich., in September, 1865.

Returning home to Indiana, the young soldier realized his lack of education, and entered high school at Bristol, Ind. There he was married on June 13, 1869, to Miss Annie Williamson, a native of Columbiana County, Ohio, and daughter of William and Ellen (Neidig) Williamson, the former a wagonmaker and millwright of note, who helped to build the Pillsbury Flouring Mills, at Minneapolis, and lived to be past eighty years of age. Satisfactorily passing the examination for a teacher's certificate in 1868, Mr. Wright taught three winter terms in Indiana, and then, in 1871, with his wife, first child and meager belongings, moved out to Sumner County, Kans., and there homesteaded 160 acres in South Haven, where their second child was born, the first white child born in that vicinity. The Indians were hostile, however, and the blizzards and scourge of grasshoppers so discouraged the young pioneers that they abandoned their homestead and came to California in 1873. Locating in Oakland, Mr. Wright engaged as a clerk for Gurnett Brothers, and later became an employee of the West Coast Manufacturing Company, in San Francisco, though still residing in Oakland. This firm manufactured furniture from white mahogany for the old Palace Hotel, and also made the seats for the old California Theatre, two chairs of which were presented to Mr. Wright, who remodeled them and has them in use in his home.

He next became manager of Kimball's horse and dairy ranch at San Rafael, for Mr. Kimball, of the then prominent and wealthy firm of Kimball & Ralston, at that time one of San Francisco's wealthiest companies. They failed, however, and Mr. Wright went across the Bay to San Pablo and there, after 1876, was with Henry Benson for three years. He then engaged successfully in the grocery business in Oakland for one year. About this time, Mr. Wright interested himself in the candidacy of J. C. Mellen for councilman, and after his election Mr. Mellen appointed him a member of the Oakland police force, where he was soon detailed to do office work. This position he held for three years, after which he served as deputy license collector for one year, and then for the next two years as deputy county assessor for Alameda County, under Tom Malloy. Following this, he went to South Berkeley, and successfully conducted a grocery business for fourteen years.

At the end of these various activities Mr. Wright decided to retire to ranch life, and in 1910 came to his present home place of some twelve acres on the Pacheco Road, two and one-half miles south of Martinez, where he has a comfortable home, built by the former owner, then a banker of Martinez. He devotes his acreage to fruit-growing, raising peaches, pears, apricots, grapes, and olives. With his family he has resided here for the past sixteen years, dispensing true California hospitality and taking an active part in the community life.

Five children were born to Mr. and Mrs. Wright: Lillian I., wife of G. J. Icard, residing at Baguio, P. I.; Minnie Alice, widow of William Kirkman, residing at Tacoma, Wash.; Albert P., who married Daisy J. Baird and resides in Martinez; George O., who married Genevieve Cornwall, and resides in Berkeley; and W. Merrill, who served in the navy during the World War and is now in charge of a Standard Oil station at Martinez. There are nine grandchildren in the family. Besides their own children, Mr. and Mrs. Wright reared Fred LeMar, now employed with the Shell Oil Company in Martinez. Mr. Wright is a charter member of Lyon Post No. 8, G. A. R., of Oakland. A Republican, he cast his first vote for General Grant, and his last vote for La Follette.

PERRY O. ROSS.—One of the real pioneers of Richmond is Perry O. Ross, a trusted and efficient employee of the Santa Fe Railroad Company. He built the seventh building in what is now the city of Richmond proper, in 1903, at No. 324 Sixth Street. When he bought the property he could have had the corner where Basham's drug store is now situated for $350, but he was given to understand that Macdonald Avenue was going to be a business street and he decided he would get back from the main artery to a quiet place where he could keep a cow and chickens. He paid $450 for two lots, erected his present house, and has lived here ever since. For $630 he sold a strip of nine feet for an alley when the post office association located the post office at Sixth and Macdonald, and later he moved his house to the north end of his lot and built a shop, which he leases. The property he now owns is valuable as a business lot. Where the Santa Fe depot stands, an old sawmill was located, and at that point was a fine place to dig clams. This part of the town was in disfavor with those who were living at East Yard or Point Richmond, and those who bought property and erected buildings here were called "clam diggers," and the location was known as the "mud flats."

Perry O. Ross was born at Brownsville, Ore., on April 10, 1869, and he received a common-school education there. His mother was Julia Blue before her marriage, and was a daughter of Rev. Newton Blue, who was sent to California from Oregon, where he had been laboring as a missionary, to continue his work in California. He died on board the ship that was bringing him to San Francisco and is buried on Alcatraz Island. Mr. Ross' mother was born in Oregon, and there she was married to William Ross, a harnessmaker by trade. He is now aged eighty-one and makes his home at Lankershim, Cal. On the maternal side the ancestry is traced to the family of James A. Garfield, former president of the United States.

After leaving school Mr. Ross worked in the woolen mills for fourteen years, reaching the position of assistant superintendent of the mill. He began railroading for a wage of $1.25 per day of eleven hours; at the time he was paying $12 per month rent for the house he lived in. In 1900 he began with the San Joaquin Valley Railroad as a fireman, running from Stockton to Bakersfield and Fresno. He had an opportunity to come to Richmond and take a job in the yards and decided he would benefit by so doing, as he did not like the heat of the San Joaquin Valley. He accordingly gave up his road rights and went into the yards as engineer. At that time there was only one engine used to do all the switching, and it did double duty. The first unit of the present shops was just begun at that time. Mr. Ross is now the oldest man in the yards, in point of service as engineer.

Perry O. Ross was united in marriage at Brownsville, Ore., on February 1, 1893, with Ada Lockwood, an English woman. They have two children. Grace, born in Oregon, married Ebon Stubblefield and has two sons, James and Edward R.; the family live in Los Angeles. Frances was born in Richmond and is a member of the Class of 1926 in the Richmond High School. Both children are musically inclined, specializing on the piano. Mrs. Ross' mother, Maria Jackson Lockwood, died in 1906 in Richmond at the home of a daughter, aged seventy-six. Mr. Ross is a member of Richmond Lodge No. 13, K. of P., and belongs to Camp No. 637, W. O. W. He is a musician, and while living in Brownsville, Ore., played E-flat cornet in the band and was agent for C. G. Conn's band instruments. He belongs to the Fresno Brotherhood of Locomotive Firemen, and to the Brotherhood of Locomotive Engineers.

GEORGE H. SOUTH.—An honored veteran of the Civil War and a resident of Contra Costa County, George H. South is counted among the highly respected citizens of Pittsburg and vicinity. A native of New York, he was born in the town of Clay, Onondaga County, April 19, 1843, the son of Richard and Elizabeth South, both born, reared and married in England. They were farmer folk who emigrated to America at an early date and settled in Onondaga County, later removing to Dane County, Wis., when their son George was a babe. This was at a time when there were no railroads to facilitate travel, and it was in the pioneer environment of Dane County that he grew to young manhood. There were seven children in the South family, five of whom grew to years of maturity. The oldest son, Matthew South, came to California in 1852 with an ox-team train. While in Salt Lake, Matthew South met with a young lady who wanted to get away from that city, and arrangements were made for her to do so. She was taken in charge by an old man, who was sent ahead of their train, both riding the same horse. When the train started, it was halted and searched by the Mormons, but the woman was not to be found. Upon reaching California the woman secured a position as a school teacher through the help of members of the train. Matthew South went to Texas in 1859 and became a large stockman. In 1861 George H. South went to the Lone Star State and was employed by his brother on the ranch. It was during this employment that he was captured by some Mexican bandits, together with his brother-in-law, Ezra Day, and forced to walk 300 miles over the desert into Mexico and imprisoned. Mr. Day was executed by the Mexicans, but our subject was able to get a note smuggled to the American consul, who succeeded in obtaining his release. In 1863 Mr. South joined the 1st Texas Cavalry and served under Gen. Phil Sheridan. This command marched through Texas to drive out Maximilian, and it is his boast that during his two years in the service "he never took a prisoner." He received an honorable discharge at San Antonio in 1865.

After having seen service in Tennessee, Alabama and Louisiana, it is no wonder that he was not content to settle down until he had seen more of the world. His first job was cutting wood on a steamboat for his passage up the Missouri River. Then three years were spent at mining in Helena, Mont., for which he was paid in scrip, which brought him only twenty cents on the dollar. In 1868 he arrived in Salt Lake City after a 500-mile trek across the plains with a pack-mule. He secured work on the construction of the railroad, and was present at the driving of the golden spike when the Central and Union Pacific lines were joined at Promontory Point. He was then given transportation to Sacramento, Cal., on a flat car. When Pittsburg was known as New York Landing, Mr. South was here and was working in the coal mines at the foot of Mount Diablo. He bought coal at the mouth of the mine for $2.50 a ton and hauled it to the town, where he sold it for $3.75 per ton. He still has two of the old wagons he used in this work and points to them with pride, for they were the beginning of his prosperity. When New York Landing became known as Black Diamond, Mr. South predicted great possibilities for the town, and he has lived to see his prediction come true. He has seen the advent of the automobile and air plane, declares that both will prove ruinous to the nation if given a "free rein" as at present, and says he would not own an automobile if he could afford to have an entire factory, and that too many men own machines to the detriment of their families. He declares that recent years have brought just two things worth while, "prohibition and moving pictures"—for he is a "movie fan."

In 1874 Mr. South was united in marriage with Miss Mary Whitney, daughter of William E. Whitney, pioneer of the Mount Diablo district,

P. Irene Hurley.

who burned the first lime here and who later entered the coal-mining industry at Nortonville. In the coal mines of his father-in-law at Nortonville Mr. South spent much time. The marriage of Mr. and Mrs. South was blessed with two children: William R. South, of Pittsburg, Cal., and Gertrude, wife of Thomas E. Kermode, of the Mount Diablo district. Mrs. South passed away in 1922, since which time Mr. South has lived alone on his ranch. Now in his eighty-fourth year, he is hale and hearty and enjoys living his particular way. He has many friends and delights to recount to them his varied experiences in the past.

MRS. F. IRENE HURLEY.—A native daughter of the State, who, like many of her sisters in California, is making good in the official circles of her community, is Mrs. F. Irene Hurley of Martinez, the efficient county recorder of Contra Costa County. By reason of her fitness for the position, through previous experience, she was appointed to her office by the board of supervisors on February 2, 1924, to fill the vacancy occasioned by the death of her husband, the late M. H. Hurley, whose death occurred on January 31, 1924.

Mrs. Hurley was born at Alviso, Santa Clara County, the daughter of Anderson and Harriet R. (Messersmith) Morford, natives of Ohio and Indiana, respectively, and both early pioneers of Santa Clara County. Her grandparents, John and Irene (Powell) Messersmith, were Eastern folks. Harriet R. Messersmith was only six years of age when she was brought to California across the plains behind slow-moving oxen from Indiana by her parents. Reared to the age of ten in Santa Clara County, F. Irene Morford went to the public schools there; then she came to Martinez, and in time was graduated from the John Swett Union High School at the town of Crockett, being a member of the first class to be graduated from the new building. In 1912 she was united in marriage with M. H. Hurley, who was born in Lowell, Mass., on September 29, 1868, and at the age of ten was brought to California. He grew up in Martinez, where he became a very popular citizen and served the people in various capacities, first as town clerk of Martinez and then as public administrator of Contra Costa County. Then, in 1907, he was elected county recorder, and was reelected in 1911, 1915, 1919 and 1923, each succeeding election attesting to his popularity in the county as shown by the majority of votes cast. He was a dependable official, and only once did he have an opponent for the office. By trade he was a printer and worked on both the Gazette and the Standard in Martinez. Mr. and Mrs. Hurley had three children: William M., Margaret C., and Lowell Neil.

For several years Mrs. Hurley was employed by the Contra Costa County Abstract & Title Company under A. E. Dunkel; and when she was called upon to assume the responsibilities of the office of county recorder, she was well qualified for the task and was able to demonstrate her ability to manage the affairs of the office with dispatch. She has as her chief deputy C. M. Bulger, and as second deputy, J. E. Fahy, and has four copyists and two index clerks.

Mrs. Hurley has always taken a prominent place in the social circles of Martinez, and is a member of Las Juntas Parlor No. 221, N. D. G. W. She is also a member of the State County Recorders' Association. When the women of California were granted suffrage, Mrs. Hurley was the first woman registered in the State, and she is also the first woman to hold an elective office in Contra Costa County.

FRANK MATHERON.—Of all the varied occupations followed in Contra Costa County, no other one has played such an important part as that of the agriculturist. And it is men of the sturdy type of Frank Matheron that form the solid bulwarks of their communities. Within his lifetime he has witnessed the growth of a rich coastal territory, a development in which he has materially aided.

Mr. Matheron was born in St. Hilaire, France, on January 4, 1854. His parents, Frank and Virginia Matheron, were hard-working, frugal peasant farmers who through industry and careful planning had been able to acquire the farm property on which they lived. As a boy young Frank worked on his father's farm and was only able to attend school four months a year. He did, however, receive a great deal of sound instruction in the growing of grain and breeding of cattle, a schooling which was to be of great value to him in later years.

In 1875 Mr. Matheron, then a youth of twenty-one, came to America. His first employment was with a sheep grower near Los Angeles. From there he went to Bakersfield, Kern County, where he was similiarly employed for about four years. In 1882 he was attracted to Clayton, in Contra Costa County, and made that vicinity his home for a number of years. He successfully farmed the Tilton ranch for many years, and also the Donner ranch. Later he became proprietor of what was known as the Matheron ranch, of forty acres near Clayton. In 1908 he sold the ranch and removed to Martinez, where the family home is now located, at 905 Henrietta Street. Mr. and Mrs. Matheron also resided in Oakland for eight years.

In 1888 Mr. Matheron was married to Mrs. Annie T. (Loring) O'Connor. She was born in San Francisco on July 19, 1858, and came with her parents to Clayton when she was about two and one-half years old. Her father, Samuel N. Loring, was one of the pioneer Forty-niners. He and his wife, Jane G. (Barstow) Loring, were both natives of Yarmouth, Maine. Samuel Loring was one of the heroic horde who were attracted by the cry of "Gold" in 1849, and he made the hazardous trip via the Isthmus. After making a substantial stake he went back to Maine, where he married his childhood sweetheart, and they returned to California together, crossing the Isthmus. He secured employment with Bray Brothers in San Francisco and became one of their trusted employees.

While on a business trip to British Columbia he was accidentally shot in loading a gun. Some time later his wife married Christopher M. Myrick, a member of one of the well-known pioneer families of Contra Costa County. He was born in Nantucket, Mass., on December 7, 1827, and also came to California as one of the Forty-niners. For a time he engaged in mining on the American River, but finally returned to San Francisco, where he engaged in carpentering, a trade which he had learned in his youth in Massachusetts. At times he carried and sold water in San Francisco at "two bits" per bucket, often making an average of twelve dollars per day in this manner. Soon after his marriage he removed to Clayton with his wife and infant son, Stanley Myrick, and his stepdaughter, Annie T. Loring, who received her education in the local school there. C. M. Myrick became the owner of 160 acres of land in Clayton Precinct, which he successfully farmed up to the time of his death. One of the interesting incidents of his life was a bitter litigation in which he engaged with a railroad company over 240 acres of land. The case was in the courts for forty years and, as might be imagined, the costs were tremendous.

Mrs. Annie T. O'Connor, nee Loring, met Mr. Matheron in Clayton, where they were married on March 1, 1888. They became the parents of five children: Joseph F., a sketch of whose life appears elsewhere; Leone Adella, wife of George Hendrickson, an employee of the Shell Oil Company, residing in Martinez; Ellie Loring, also employed by the Shell Oil Company in Martinez; Frank Charles, employed by the Great Western Power Company and residing in Pittsburg; and Percy Raymond, residing in Oakland, where he is engaged in business. Mrs. Matheron is also the mother of a daughter by her marriage with Mr. O'Connor, Henrietta Christine, wife of William T. Davis, a prosperous rancher of the Clayton Precinct. Mrs. Matheron has seven grandchildren. She is a member of the Congregational Church of Clayton. Both she and her husband are Republicans. Mr. Matheron has retired from active life since the sale of his farm.

JAMES T. NARBETT.—That California is developing a distinctive type of architecture which is attracting the attention of, and being copied in the East, is the sincere belief of James T. Narbett, well-known architect of Oakland and Richmond. Mr. Narbett himself has taken no small part in this development and his work will compare favorably with any to be found in this section of the West. He is a gentleman of many parts and he and his charming wife are ranked with the leaders of their community.

Mr. Narbett's adventurous career started in 1874, that being the year of his birth, which occurred at Rangoon, British Burmah, on that celebrated "Road to Mandalay" of which Kipling sings. He was born aboard a sailing vessel of which his father, William Narbett, was the owner and captain. His mother was Eleanor (Davis) Narbett, and both parents were natives of Wales and pioneers of 1881 in Contra Costa County. In 1877 the family came to America and located first in Washington, and then were in San Francisco for about one year. After a short residence in Oakland they removed to Benicia, crossing over to Contra Costa County in 1881 and settling at a location about one-half mile north of Crockett, before that town was established. Mr. Narbett had several brothers and sisters. One sister is Mary Sullenger, the county auditor's wife. A brother, Walter, is a pharmacist in Susanville. Martha is Mrs. W. E. Lewis of Crockett; and another sister, Irene, is Mrs. Dr. Gruenig of San Francisco.

James T. Narbett's early education was received in the grammar school of Crockett, and he also spent two years in the high school and in attendance at the Van Der Nailen School of English in San Francisco. In addition to this he has since taken other educational courses. After his grammar school days he learned to be a machinist during the period from 1890 to 1893. After one year of carpentering he became a contractor and followed that calling until 1907, at which time he branched out into the architectural profession, becoming a member of the American Institute of Architects in 1922. He has twice been a delegate to the national conventions of this organization. His business has prospered and he maintains a suite of offices in the Syndicate Building on Tenth Street, Richmond, where he employs three assistants, and he also maintains an office in the Richfield Oil Building at Oakland.

Many of the largest and handsomest buildings in Richmond have been designed by Mr. Narbett, including the Elks Building, Mechanics Bank, Alberts store, Richmond Independent office building, I. O. O. F. building, practically all the schools, fire houses and the Richmond Natatorium. His work in other cities includes the Campus Theatre in Berkeley, Masonic Temple in Hayward, and many other buildings of similar importance in this and other counties. In addition to his architectural work Mr. Narbett is interested in a number of other activities, including: The Prudential Mortgage Investment Company, capital of $5,250,000; the General State Life Insurance Company, of Oakland; vice-president of the Yerxa-Steves Holding Co., Inc., and the Bacon Land Co., Inc., both of Oakland; a director of the Richmond Syndicate Company, of Richmond. He has also served on important committees and is active in various city organizations, being a member of the Chamber of Commerce and Rotary Club. Mr. Narbett is architectural adviser of the Prudential Mortgage Investment Company of Oakland, and his office there is operated in conjunction with their offices. He has heavy investments in Richmond, Oakland and Berkeley. His home in Richmond, at 11th Street and Roosevelt Avenue, is one of the show places of that city, being of a particularly beautiful Spanish design.

Mr. Narbett volunteered for service immediately after the entry of the United States into the World War in 1917, and was commissioned captain of engineers in June and sent to Camp Lee, Va., the latter part of that year and remained there until called to the Hercules Powder

Company to design and supervise the construction of important work at that plant. This camp was recognized as being one of the best constructed and laid out camps in the country. He never had military training but, due to the fact that he passed with a very high percentage an examination in psychology, he was chosen to command a troup for over seas service, but just before the close of his camp was returned to Hercules Powder Company. He is a member of practically all of the Masonic bodies and is now Patron of Court Amaranth. He has been an active member of the Odd Fellows for twenty-nine years; and belongs to the Elks lodge, Athens Athletic Club of Oakland, and the Carquinez Country Club, and is a member of both the National and San Francisco Chapters of the American Institute of Architects.

During the gold rush to Alaska in 1898 Mr. Narbett went there and had an exciting time. While there he was stricken with pneumonia at Sheep Camp and overheard his comrades say that they were going to ship him out by boat. But with exceptional determination he arose the next morning at five o'clock, made a cup of coffee and ate cold beans, then walked to Dyea, where he consulted a doctor and walked back to camp that night, a total distance of thirty-one miles, crawling the last five miles over dark canyons and steep roads. At that time they had no dogs but hitched themselves to the sleds. He was one of the volunteers on March 8, 1898, to rescue some men buried by a huge snow slide in which eighty perished. Although he was reported to be among the killed, he and his companions were unharmed. They built a boat and went down the Yukon River to a point where they took the contract to furnish saw logs for a Dawson City sawmill. Before leaving for Dawson they shot two moose and sold them in the Dawson market. On the first of September they located their cabin on the Klondike River but Charles Jewell, the partner of Mr. Narbett, was taken ill and they returned to the United States.

On February 2, 1902, Mr. Narbett was united in marriage with Miss Gussie B. McDowell of Crockett, daughter of Oliver and Mary (Nichols) McDowell. Mrs. Narbett is a popular after-dinner speaker and is a leader in the Unity Center. She is an active club worker, a member of the Eastern Star, Daughters of the Nile, and is greatly interested in art and particularly in china painting. They have one son, Keith Oliver Narbett, age twenty-one, who is attending the University of California, studying architecture, which he decided to make his life's work.

Devoted as he is to his home life Mr. Narbett's strongest hobby is traveling; he delights in driving a car and travels about 20,000 miles a year. His advice to young men is to follow the Golden Rule, avoid snobbishness, feel yourself worthy of the best and strive to attain it, create a borrowing power in financial circles, and a good moral standing; then use, but don't abuse them. Plunge when you know you are right, but keep a reserve in the bank and live so as to not be afraid of anything, particularly work.

IRWIN ROSE.—The able day foreman of the wire mill of the Columbia Steel Corporation, Irwin Rose, has had years of experience in the steel and wire industry in the United States, and has been a resident of California since 1916. He was employed at the E. H. Edwards wire plant in South San Francisco until August 1924, when he came to Pittsburg and entered the employ of the Columbia Steel Corporation.

Born in Johnstown, Pa., on April 20, 1878, he is the son of James and Mary (Thomas) Rose, both now deceased. He attended the grammar and high schools in Johnstown, and his first employment after leaving school was at Braddock, Pa., with the Consolidated Steel and Iron Company, now the American Steel and Wire Company. For several years he worked in various steel and iron mills in Pennsylvania, Ohio and Illinois, and for four years he was in the employ of the Colorado Fuel and Iron Company, at Pueblo, Colo. From the latter place he came to San Francisco and entered the employ of E. H. Edwards Company. In all of his moving about Mr. Rose has been a keen observer and has acquired a vast fund of information that he puts to good advantage in his work.

In 1914, in Denver, Colo., Mr. Rose was united in marriage with Miss Nettie Jenkins, a native of Kansas, although she grew up in Denver. The family home is in Antioch at 808 G Street, Mr. Rose going daily to and from his work in the steel mill. Politically, he is a Republican.

WILLIAM E. YOUNG.—The efficient justice of the peace at Port Costa, Contra Costa County, is William E. Young, who is also one of the pioneers of 1885, the year he landed in this county. He was born in County Cork, Ireland, on December 4, 1859, a son of William and Jane Young, who lived and died in Ireland, as did their parents before them. Our subject attended school until he was seventeen. Then he sailed from Hull, England, for California, and after a stormy voyage around Cape Horn landed in San Francisco. His first work was as a sailor before the mast on vessels plying up and down the coast out of San Francisco. He came to Port Costa, when that port was the principal grain-shipping point in the State, as an employee of a firm of stevedores, and became superintendent for Herriman and Mills. When they quit business to go to the Alaska gold fields in Nome, Mr. Young was engaged as superintendent for the San Francisco Stevedore Company, and continued in their employ until 1924. In 1889 he made a visit back to his home in Ireland, returning to Port Costa that same year.

In 1889 Mr. Young was united in marriage, in Ireland, with Miss Sarah Jackson, born in County Carlow, Ireland, and they have had five children. William J. is an employe of the Standard Oil Company in Richmond. He married Miss Amy Russell and has two children: Amy J. and William. Frank N. is working for Balfour-Guthrie in the grain business; he volunteered his services during the World War. Jane is a graduate of the University of California and is now a teacher in the Horace Mann High School in San Francisco. Tennant died soon after his graduation from the high school; and Adelaide is a student at the State Teachers' College in San Jose. In his political affiliations Mr. Young is a Democrat. In 1916 he was elected a justice of the peace in Port Costa. He served four years and succeeded himself at the election in 1920 and again in 1924. He is serving the public faithfully in that office, dispensing justice as he sees it in cases that come before his court. He is looked upon as one of the old-timers of Port Costa and this section of Contra Costa County.

WILLIAM V. KELTZ.—Since 1904, William V. Keltz has been an eye-witness to the gradual growth and development of Richmond, taking an intelligent part in community affairs and doing his duty whenever called upon. When he arrived in Richmond to enter the employ of the Standard Oil Company he was not impressed with the outlook and thought if he could stand it one month that would be about the limit of time he would spend here. At that time he little thought that he would enter into the spirit of the new community and remain to profit by his wise investments here. Mr. Keltz was one of the organizers of the Pioneer Club, which was the nucleus of the Elks Club. Some of the business and professional men at Point Richmond, and several of the employees of the refinery, would meet at the noon hour and discuss topics while eating luncheon. Many matters of moment to the growing town were talked over and decided at these meetings. There were no street lights and people carried lanterns to see when going out at night. Even after electric lights were installed many carried a candle in their pocket to see to finish a meal, for the electric lights had a faculty of going out. Mr. Keltz was the first signer for the present Elks Lodge and circulated a petition to further its organization. His growing confidence in Richmond was so strong that when the Elks building was being planned he advocated that it be built at Twenty-third and Macdonald; and when Twenty-third Street was opened he suggested a wide street and gave twelve feet from lots he had bought, together with $100, to signify his interest in the matter. When the Soito tract was opened Mr. Keltz bought the first lots; he had an option on five and finally settled on three, and this was at a time when the entire locality was a pasture. People told him he was crazy to buy so far out in the country, but he said he was satisfied and he now feels amply repaid. While he was living at Point Richmond he paid the first assessment levied for street work done by Flynn and Tracy on Washington Street; and he was one of the men who led in having a sewer installed on that street. With his family he is living in the first house erected in the northeastern part of the city; it was built by Herbert Brown, who opened the tract. In every way that he could, Mr. Keltz has helped plan and carry out progressive movements.

William V. Keltz was born in St. Louis, Mo., on October 6, 1875. He received an academic education, and just as he had finished school the Spanish-American War broke out and he enlisted in Company A, 13th

Infantry, at Kansas City, Mo., and was sent to Buffalo and thence to Cuba. He was one of the youngest of the soldiers in his company; A. B. Scott was his captain and H. T. Ferguson, first lieutenant. He went through the siege at San Juan Hill, at which time their second lieutenant was killed while still in his cadet uniform, not having had time to change it. Out of his company fourteen were killed and twenty-eight wounded. After the war was over he was discharged in December, 1898. He then had an attack of typhoid, but in May, 1899, reenlisted, came to San Francisco, and from there went to the Philippines and served five years in the regular army. When his term expired he decided to come to San Francisco, and liked the climate so well that he decided to remain. It was then he came to Richmond and entered the refinery, where he is continuing as a valued employe of the Standard Oil Company.

In 1914 Mr. Keltz and Mrs. Mae (Ryan) Jette were united in marriage. She is descended from pioneer stock and was born in San Francisco, a daughter of James D. Ryan, who came to California via Cape Horn and was first assistant manager of the San Francisco Call for years. He died in 1915. His wife, Mary Catherine Maloney before her marriage, was also born in San Francisco. Grandfather David Maloney, who married Johanna Butler, was a native of Ireland and a scholar, being a graduate of Dublin College. He came to California and was present at the raising of the flag over Monterey in 1847. Mr. Maloney erected one of the first homes on Van Ness Avenue in San Francisco. Mrs. Keltz received a good education and married Arthur Jette, of San Luis Obispo County. His parents crossed the plains with a covered-wagon train and settled near Arroyo Grande, that county. The family were from Connecticut and of French ancestry. They were connected with the woolen mills in Connecticut. Mrs. Jette had three children by her first marriage. Arthur, born in San Luis Obispo, is a graduate of a vocational school in Berkeley and is employed by the Tilden Lumber Company; Mary Ethel, born in Arroyo Grande, was one of the first pupils to attend the Grant School in Richmond, and is now attending the State Teachers' College in San Francisco Class of 1927; and Harman Hall, born in Richmond, is attending the Roosevelt Junior High School. He was named for the Hall family of Ventura County, and for the Harman family of Staunton, Va. After the death of Mr. Jette in Richmond, where the family had located, Mrs. Jette married Mr. Keltz. They have an attractive daughter, Inez Josephine Gertrude Keltz. This is the first birth in a Keltz family in forty-seven years, and she and her father are the only known Keltz's living. Mrs. Keltz is president of the P. T. A. of the Grant School, and is active in educational and philanthropic work in Richmond, as also in the work of the Episcopal Church. Mr. Keltz belongs to Richmond Lodge No. 1251, B. P. O. E. Since settling here he has never missed voting at a local election, and he supports those who stand for the principles he considers best suited for the good of the people in general.

JOSEPH B. OGBORN.—Richmond has been exceedingly fortunate in the personnel of its residents, and that, perhaps, is the most important factor in what has been such rapid growth in the past decade. Both men and women who have located here have proven to be unusually progressive and public-spirited, and with the executive ability to carry their plans to success. Among the representative citizens must be mentioned Mr. and Mrs. Joseph B. Ogborn. Joseph B. Ogborn was a native of Ohio, born near Zanesville, of Scotch ancestry. His father died when he was a small child and he was obliged to start to work at the age of fourteen to help in the support of his mother and sisters. At that early age he started to learn the trade of carpenter, and later took up architectural drawing, and also the trade of millwright.

Coming to California about 1889, Mr. Ogborn was in Placerville, and Grass Valley, supervising the building of stamp mills in the mines. He later followed his profession as architect and builder in various places in the State; in San Francisco, before the earthquake and fire; in San Mateo, where he drew plans and superintended the construction of the Masonic Hall and other buildings; in Placerville, El Dorado County, where he built the Odd Fellows' block and the hotel; and in Oakland and Southern California, where he planned and erected several apartment houses.

When he decided to locate permanently, Mr. Ogborn came to Richmond, in 1910, and for a short time after his arrival followed his profession of architect. He drew up a building ordinance for Richmond, which was adopted by the city and is still in effect. Following this he was appointed city architect and building inspector, which position he held for two years. His ability as an architect was known all over the State. Among other buildings, he drew the plans for the Hotel Richmond; the Pillow Block; the old Germania Hotel; the Lincoln, Peres, and other schools, and many fine homes.

A Republican in national politics, Mr. Ogborn was an advocate of municipal ownership, as are most far-seeing men. He was elected a member of the city council of Richmond in 1916, and held that office until the time of his death, on April 21, 1919. Known as a friend of the workingman, he received the largest number of votes at his election of any candidate at that time, and his untimely passing cut short a career of more than ordinary usefulness to his fellowmen. Prominent in Masonry, Mr. Ogborn belonged to three branches of that order and was a member of Albert Pike Memorial in San Francisco and also of the Eastern Star. He was a member of Richmond Lodge No. 1251, B. P. O. E.; Loyal Order of Moose; and the Knights of Pythias.

The marriage of Mr. Ogborn, on February 17, 1899, at Monterey, Cal., united him with Miss Marie L. Rafetto, daughter of Dominick and Anna (Pence) Rafetto, pioneers of California. She owns the ranch in El Dorado County settled upon by her parents in an early day. Two daughters were born of this union: Aileen, who died in 1903, aged eighteen months; and Ieda V., still at home. The latter was born in San Francisco and graduated in May, 1926, from the University of California. While attending the university Miss Ogborn was president of the Theta Sigma Phi, woman's national journalistic honor society; a member of the English Club, four art honor society; Junior editor on the Daily Californian; member of Prytanean, an activity and scholarship honor society; and she took part in three Partheneia and was their publicity director.

Mrs. M. L. Ogborn is a member of the Richmond city council, elected to fill the unexpired term of her husband, May 21, 1919, and polling the largest vote of the nine members elected. A woman of keen perception and brilliant mind, she is an acknowledged leader, and her women friends were active for her in the campaign, which she won against strong opposition. She has since been twice reelected to the office, which is the best criterion that her services have given entire satisfaction. Fraternally, Mrs. Ogborn is a member and Past President of the Richmond Club, a woman's organization, holding that office two years. She is active in the Eastern Star, and is also a member of the Native Daughters of the Golden West. She is a director of the Social Service Bureau, third vice-president of Contra Costa Public Health Association, and local representative of the Travelers' Aid.

WILLIAM P. HUGO.—The position of assistant general superintendent of the Avon Refinery of the Associated Oil Company, located at Avon, Contra Costa County, is filled by William P. Hugo. The assistant bears an equal amount of the responsibility for the operation of this great plant, and he has been an important factor in the promotion of the company's work, which has proved of such importance in the development of this section of California. The Associated Oil Company is the third largest tax-payer in Contra Costa County, being exceeded in this respect only by the Standard Oil Company at Richmond and the California and Hawaiian Refining Company located at Crockett. The Associated Oil Company is a gigantic concern, with its many miles of pipe lines, refineries, warehouses, tanks, wharves and sea-going oil tankers. In 1912 this company began breaking ground for their great plant; and when operations were started in 1913, Mr. Hugo became chief chemist. He is now one of the three oldest employees of this corporation.

William P. Hugo was born on his father's farm twenty miles from Des Moines, Iowa, on July 6, 1887, a son of Carl and Anna (Swanson) Hugo, farmer folk of Iowa, who removed to California in 1893, when our subject was only six years old. The family settled at Kingsburg, where he first attended school; then he entered the high school at Selma, from which he was graduated in 1906. His father is now deceased, but his mother is still living. Mr. Hugo matriculated in the Chemical En-

gineering course of the University of California and was there from 1906 until 1910, when he was engaged as chemist by the Union Oil Company at Oleum for one year. Thereafter, for two years he was with the Spreckels Monarch Oil Refinery at West Berkeley, and then, in 1913, as before stated, he entered upon his duties as chief chemist with the Associated Oil Company at Avon, where he has so efficiently filled the position of assistant to the general superintendent of this concern.

At Los Angeles, Cal., in 1912, Mr. Hugo was married to Miss Elsie Johnson of Fresno, a daughter of S. G. Johnson, now deceased; and they are the parents of one child, Katherine.

WILLIAM A. RUGG.—A veteran newspaper man who has spent nearly a half century in the newspaper game in various parts of the country, and since 1907 has been owner and proprietor of the Martinez Gazette, is William A. Rugg, of Martinez. If the history of his life were written in detail it would fill a large volume, for he has had many interesting experiences, worked under disadvantages at times, and seen much of the country; but he has enjoyed his work, has always been optimistic, and has met with deserved success in his calling.

He was born on a farm in Winnebago County, Ill., on April 18, 1854, attended the public schools, and early in life learned to be self-reliant. In early manhood he went to Iowa and at Rockford was employed in the post office and express offices. In 1879 he went to Rockwell, Cerro Gordo County, Iowa, and established a newspaper which he named The Phonograph, and which is still in existence. After building up the newspaper he sold out, went to Kansas City, and became a reporter on the Kansas City Journal; and there he was married in 1882.

That same year he went to Chicago and worked on the Chicago Tribune; and the following year he was with the Omaha Bee, in Omaha, Nebr., and later took charge of a newspaper in Wichita, Kans. He came West to San Diego, Cal., in 1888, just at the close of the boom. While in the southern city Mr. Rugg was variously engaged. After one year there he established the Anaheim Independent at Anaheim, but soon returned to San Diego and started the Illustrated Magazine, a weekly. In 1898 he decided that Northern California held out better opportunities, and that year he arrived at Martinez and soon after started the Daily Press. This he published and put in circulation without type or press, and ran it until he sold out to the Gazette Publishing Company. In 1907 he bought out the plant of the Gazette, and has since issued a daily and a weekly paper. There is no branch of the printing game that Mr. Rugg does not know, and he takes great pride in the advancement of the city he selected for his home and in every way supports those movements which have for their object its improvement and upbuilding.

In 1882, while in Kansas City, William A. Rugg was united in marriage with Miss Jessie Kellogg, a native of Madison, Wis.; and they had

18

two children. Harriett became the wife of A. E. Lindsay, and they have a son, Jack Lindsay, who graduated from the Martinez Grammar School in 1926. The only son, Freddie, died when four years of age. Mrs. Rugg passed away in 1918, sincerely mourned by a wide circle of friends, and by her family. Mr. Rugg is a member of the Contra Costa Golf Club, and takes a very active interest in the game.

JOHN HENRY GRIBBIN.—A resident of Contra Costa County since 1898, John Henry Gribbin has made a host of warm friends throughout various sections since that year. He has seen much of the actual development of the western end of the county, and in Crockett has assisted every worthy project so far as his means would permit. He and his family are highly respected citizens of this thriving community. A native of Pennslyvania, John Henry Gribbin, better known to his intimates as "Johnny," was born on July 19, 1861, in Philadelphia. He has a brother and a sister still living in that city.

When a lad John H. Gribbin attended the public schools in his native city, but for various reasons his attendance was limited. He spent his time, until he arrived at Crockett, much as did the average boy and young man in his community. He arrived here in 1898 to take charge of the branch store started by L. M. Lasell, the pioneer merchant of Martinez. After one year he returned to Martinez and with samples of merchandise made trips throughout the county with team and wagon selling the goods to the citizens interested. After a short time as a clerk for A. Rumelsberg, he engaged in the general merchandise business for himself in the Strentzel Hall building at Valona, and built up a very satisfactory business until the closing of the sugar refinery three years later, which caused a severe depression in business circles in this section of the county. Mr. Gribbin then took up work in the Selby Smelter. On December 5, 1905, he had the misfortune to fall from a stack and break his left leg, which laid him up for some time. When he recovered he entered the employ of the C. & H. Sugar Refining Company in Crockett on April 10, 1906, and for thirteen years boiled soft sugar and ran the evaporation plant. For the past seven years he has served as watchman of the office gate and has made many warm friends and has the confidence of all who know him.

John Henry Gribbin was united in marriage on December 16, 1894, with Miss Verena Spuhler, a native of Zurich, Switzerland. She came to America in 1890 and after a year in New York City, two years in Seattle, Wash., and one year in San Francisco, has lived here ever since. Of her six brothers, only one ever came to America. Of this marriage the following children have been born. John H. Jr., who was born January 14, 1897, and known to his fellow-workers at the refinery as "Jack," finished the high school and after taking a special course, entered the refinery where he is a controller; he is married and the father of three children: Burton, Elaine Mila, and Jack, Jr. Emma Louise was born August 30, 1900, finished high school and then entered the refinery; she married

Ruskin Aughinbaugh, a boiler in the refinery, and has a son, Russell William. George W. was born February 22, 1906, and is in the electrical department of the refinery. J. H. Gribbin is a member of Golden Gate Camp No. 64, W. O. W.; is a charter member of the Fraternal Order of Eagles, Aerie No. 774, served as chaplain for seventeen years and is now treasurer, and at several sessions of the Grand Aerie has represented the local Aerie. He is a Republican but never aspired to office. The family are members of the Congregational Church, he being a trustee of the local congregation. The family reside in their own home in Valona and are enjoying all the comforts of modern civilization.

NEBUZARADAN B. TILLER.—As foreman of the boiler house for the Standard Oil Company at their Richmond refinery, N. B. Tiller, who lives at No. 146 Second Street, Richmond, has earned the good-will and confidence of those he serves and those who serve under his direction. He came to Richmond in May, 1903, when the ground now covered with homes and business houses was a grain field, and it has been his pleasure to see the city grow to its present place in the industrial life of the bay district. Mr. Tiller was born on May 27, 1858, near St. Joseph, Mo., a son of John Henry Tiller, a Kentuckian by birth and a blacksmith by trade. He moved from Kentucky to Missouri and then to Kansas, where he homesteaded 160 acres and farmed until his death in 1862. The mother, before her marriage, was Sarah Coffey of the Blue Grass State, and there she was married. There were five children in the family: William Thomas, of Missouri; N. B., of this review; Eliza, Mrs. Bowen, now deceased; Wallace Eugene, in Colorado; and Moses, a stockman in Oklahoma.

N. B. Tiller grew up in Kansas until he was about six, and then accompanied his mother to Missouri, where he grew up. He farmed near San Antonio, and also was a general merchandise dealer and postmaster in San Antonio. He came to California in 1895, locating in Los Angeles, where he was in railroad work for two years. Then he made a trip to Oregon, but not liking the country very well, came back to California. Going to Placer County he camped in Auburn Ravine one night, and the next morning went to Lincoln and sought employment with the pottery plant of Gladding and McBean as a common laborer. He was familiar with the work about such a plant and in a week was promoted to be a foreman, and he continued with that company until 1902. He then went to Stockton and was employed there until in May, 1903, when he located in Richmond and entered the refinery, with which he is still connected as foreman of the boiler house.

N. B. Tiller has been married three times. His first wife was Miss Florilda Blakeley, and they had six children. John Henry is married and has a large family, and resides in Missouri. Oliver is the father of four children and has a home in Missouri. Charles B., a painter in Los

Banos, Cal., has two children. Myrtle May married William Sears and lives in Merced County. Frank is married and has one girl, and resides in Richmond. Grover is deceased. By his second marriage, which took place in March, 1901, there were no children. On April 28, 1912, Mr. Tiller and Mrs. Beulah W. Tomlin were united in marriage, and they have a son, Grover Daton, aged thirteen.

Mr. Tiller is prominent in fraternal circles. He joined the Odd Fellows in 1894, in Clarksdale, Mo., and is a Past Grand; he also belongs to the Encampment and has gone through the chairs of that branch of the order. After locating in Richmond he joined Twilight Lodge, the first lodge organized here, transferring from Oro Lodge No. 115, I. O. O. F., at Whittier, Cal. With the assistance of John Westfall, George Drew and Charles Johnson, Mr. Tiller organized Contra Costa Encampment No. 99, I. O. O. F., and he is the only charter member left. In January, 1923, he was elected vice-president of the Odd Fellows Hall Association, serving two years; and he is still interested in the association. He is also a member of the Rebekahs and is a Mason, belonging to Alpha Lodge No. 431, F. & A. M. The family attend the First Christian Church in Richmond.

CHARLES E. ADAMS.—A Richmond pioneer of 1901, Charles E. Adams is also a native son of the Golden State, having been born near Santa Rosa, Sonoma County, on December 5, 1869. His father was John Adams, a native of Missouri, who crossed the plains with ox-teams in 1849 and, after remaining in this State for a time, went back to Missouri via Panama, bought up a band of cattle and started back with them across the plains, arriving safely after a hard journey. He settled on a ranch between Calistoga and Santa Rosa and for many years took an active part in all matters pertaining to the settlement and development of the new country he had selected for his home. He was a direct descendant from Sir Francis Drake, who was the first white man to touch the borders of California, dropping into what is known as Drake's Bay, Sonoma County, to make needed repairs on his ship. The noted singer, Lotta Crabtree, was a member of the train in which John Adams crossed the plains. After locating in Sonoma County Mr. Adams established a home and married Miss Holly Hudspeth, who crossed the plains with her parents in 1849 and settled in Sonoma County. The Hudspeths became prominent in the early settlement of that county, and many of their descendants still live there. The father of Mrs. John Adams served in the Mexican War and was also present at the raising of the Bear Flag in Sonoma. They settled in the Bodega Bay section and developed valuable farming properties. After some years on the ranch along the foothills, the Adams family moved to a ranch about two miles north of Santa Rosa on the Fulton road, and there Mr. Adams died at the age of sixty-eight years. His good wife lived to reach the age of eighty-three ere she answered the final call. She died at the home of a daughter in Napa, Cal. There were eleven children in the

Adams family, six of whom are living. Among the children we mention Lynchburg and Charles, living in Richmond; Henry, who died at Los Angeles in January, 1915, and who was the oldest man in point of service with the Valley Division of the Santa Fe at the time of his death; Press M., who met an accidental death on September 23, 1901, at Ferry Point; and Robert L., who was a fireman, but who quit railroading after his brother's death and went to ranching in Fresno County. Great-great-grandfather Isaac Drake served in the War of the Revolution, and when the two oldest sons of Charles Adams were small they went to Jackson County, Mo., to visit relatives, and while there attended the unveiling of a monument to Isaac Drake by the Daughters of the American Revolution from Omaha, Nebr., the address being made by James Monroe Adams, father of Mrs. Charles E. Adams.

Charles E. Adams attended the common school near his home, worked on the farm as a young man, and also played ball with the teams organized in the community. In 1889 he began working with a pile driving gang on the Northwestern Pacific, remaining with them for two years. In 1891 he went to Kansas City, Mo., to visit his father's relatives, and after coming back to California returned to Kansas City and worked on the electric railway until 1895. While there he was united in marriage, in 1895, with Miss Avonia Adams, daughter of James Monroe Adams, who married Miss Ann Nottingham. The parents of Mrs. J. M. Adams came to California as pioneers, and Grandmother Nottingham is buried in the Martinez cemetery. Mrs. Adams' mother is still living and has eleven children; and there are sixteen grandchildren. The only death in the family is that of the father. The Nottinghams became prominent citizens in Contra Costa County. Mr. and Mrs. Charles E. Adams have four children. Press M., born in Santa Rosa, is a graduate from the Richmond High School. He enlisted in the Masonic Ambulance Corps, served twenty-two months over seas, and was in action nine days during the World War. He is now employed by the Western Electric Company in Los Angeles. Roy L. was born in Stockton and also graduated from the Richmond High School. He served twenty-two months in France at the Base Hospital and after his return married Miss Lucille Metzner; and they have two children, Wanda Lee and Keith. He is conducting a grocery store at St. Helena. Mrs. Uldine Ross, of Richmond, is the eldest daughter and has two children, Trefry and Ted Adams Ross; Mrs. Ross graduated from the Richmond High School and from the Vocational High School in Oakland, in 1921, Argyle Ted graduated from the Richmond High School and is at present employed in the Mercantile Bank in San Francisco.

In April, 1896, Mr. Adams went to Stockton, where he was fireman in the yards of the Santa Fe for three years. He also fired between Stockton and Bakersfield, and between Stockton and Richmond. In 1900 he was promoted to be an engineer, and from 1901 to date he has piloted his train out of Richmond on a passenger run. When he began working here, there was but one passenger train; now there are eleven. In 1901 he came to Richmond and worked on the work train on the fill to connect with the Southern Pacific Railroad. He was the first man to settle his family at East Yard, as it was then called, and in 1902 he erected his present home at 122 Martina Street, where there was then a hay field. While running into Bakersfield he saw the first bottle of oil that was taken from the Kern River fields. In 1918 he joined McKinley Lodge, F. & A. M., and he has been a member of Riverbank Brotherhood of Locomotive Engineers No. 839 for twenty-four years. He finds diversion in attending a baseball game and in fishing, and in working in his flower plot adjacent to his house, where he has converted a blind street into a beautiful flower garden.

Mrs. Adams has taken an active interest in all civic affairs in West Richmond. She worked to establish the first religious services held in East Yard, when an old passenger car was used for a meeting house. The first church of the Methodist denomination was built up through the ministrations of W. N. Younglove, although it was really a community church. Rev. D. W. Calfee, who was the means of building fourteen churches during his lifetime as a preacher, erected the present Methodist Church at West Richmond. Mrs. Adams is active in the Ladies' Aid Society and one of the outstanding accomplishments of this body of energetic women, not only through the church membership, but in cooperation with the entire community, was the raising of the necessary money for the church by running a lunch counter near the Standard Oil works. The stand was built with lumber furnished by the Standard Oil Company and was erected by the husbands of the women of the community; and during the few years the women operated it they took in $36,000, the net profits of which went towards furnishing the parsonage and into the church fund. Mrs. Adams is a member of Mira Mar Chapter, O. E. S.

JOHN J. BRENNAN.—For many years connected with the Southern Pacific Railroad Company in the capacity of section foreman, John J. Brennan has seen much of the development of the San Joaquin Valley and is now a highly esteemed resident of Antioch, where he is serving the city as recorder and at the same time dealing in real estate and writing fire insurance. Mr. Brennan was born in Limerick, Ireland, on July 19, 1864, and grew up there until he was eighteen, when he came to America to try his fortunes. He stopped in New York State and held down a job as a shoe clerk until February, 1887, and then came to California, the "State of Opportunity" for industrious and energetic young men. He entered the employ of the Southern Pacific Railroad at Merced and later served as section foreman of an extra gang in Merced and Fresno, and in other places as far south as Bakersfield, meanwhile witnessing the wonderful changes in that great section of country. In 1898 he was transferred to Antioch as section foreman, continuing in this capacity until 1920, when he quit railroading to enter the real estate and insurance busi-

Stanley G. Myrick

ness in Antioch, where he had made many good friends. He had always been saving and was able to purchase a comfortable home for his family at the corner of Third and I Streets. He carries on a profitable business and takes an active interest in all movements for the upbuilding of Antioch. In 1922 he was appointed city recorder, and he is capably filling the office, by virtue of which he has jurisdiction of all misdemeanors committed in the city.

When Mr. Brennan came to marry he chose Miss Rosetta Spagnola, a native of Mariposa County, to be his wife. She represents a pioneer family of the Mother Lode country. They have three children: Helen, Madeline and Imelda. The family move in the best circles in Antioch and vicinity.

STANLEY G. MYRICK.—One of the important problems which the pioneer settlers of Contra Costa County had to solve was the question of water distribution. Under the spur of necessity they became skilled in drainage and the reclamation of waste lands. One of the well-known native sons of the county, born during this pioneer period, is Stanley G. Myrick, the larger part of whose life's labors have been devoted to this work. He is the oldest son of the late Christopher Mitchell Myrick, an early settler of the State. Christopher Myrick came to California in 1849 and mined for a time, before settling in San Francisco, where he worked at the carpenter trade until he decided to return East to marry Lydia Joy, the girl of his choice. After his marriage he came back to California and located in San Francisco, and was there engaged for seven years in the water business, selling by the bucket, from door to door. His wife died in San Francisco, and later he was united in marriage with Mrs. Jane G. (Barstow) Loring, who had a daughter by her union with Mr. Loring. She is now Mrs. Frank Matheron, of Martinez. Of this second union there were four children: Stanley G., Fred N., Mrs. Lydia Clayton, and Mrs. Imogene Benson, the latter now deceased.

Stanley G. Myrick was born in San Francisco on July 17, 1860, and when he was a year old the family came to Contra Costa County and located upon the ranch of 160 acres that the father had bought in Clayton Precinct, together with about 100 head of stock, from a Mr. King. Here the family settled and the father began raising stock, hay and grain. During this period of hard work for everybody, young Stanley's services were greatly needed at home, especially as he was the oldest child in the family. Owing to that fact, and the primitive methods of schooling available, the book learning he obtained was very limited. He was hardly more than a child when he was put to work at farming and stock raising, and learned to ride the range and to do skilfully many things which books cannot teach. Among other things, he became expert in building levees and reclaiming tule lands. For nineteen years he was a trusted and highly valued employee of Charles Gordon on Jersey Island, where his thorough knowledge of farming and drainage were of great service.

Mr. Myrick is a most trustworthy and capable citizen, and has a reputation for sterling honesty and dependability. In politics he is consistently Republican. Coming, as he does, from one of the pioneer families, he knew all the early settlers of the county and takes a keen interest in everything pertaining to local history. Although he is now sixty-six years old, he is active physically; and despite the strenuous existence which he has led, he looks much younger than his years. He is now practically retired, making his home on the Parker ranch. He recalls the time when wild geese came to this valley in thousands and covered acres of ground; deer abounded also, and elk horns were still numerous, showing that there were many elk here in early days.

HON. A. B. McKENZIE.—As judge of Department Two, superior court of Contra Costa County, Hon. A. B. McKenzie has shown his ability as a lawyer and jurist by his impartial and just interpretation of the law. A native of Canada, he was born at Goderich, in the Province of Ontario, on March 21, 1861. His parents, George and Mary (Bailey) McKenzie, were also Canadians. The father, who was born near Toronto, was a storekeeper at Goderich and held minor offices in his locality such as town and school trustee. The mother was also born near Toronto. There were six children in the McKenzie family, A. B. McKenzie being the second in order of birth. He attended the schools of his locality and assisted his father in his store until he was eighteen, and then worked as a clerk in a mercantile establishment in Toronto. In 1881 he went to New York City, as he believed better opportunities were awaiting him in the United States than he could find in Canada, and while there he was employed in the mercantile store of Lord & Taylor, and at the same time attended night school. Ambitious to make a name and place for himself in the world, he remained with the firm of Lord & Taylor for some years, saving his money, and pursued his studies at every opportunity, for he had determined to become a lawyer and his own boss.

In 1891 young McKenzie came to California and soon thereafter matriculated at the Hastings College of Law in San Francisco, this college being affiliated with the University of California. He pursued the regular law course for three years and was graduated with the Class of 1895. He was admitted to the California Bar that same year and coming to Martinez began the practice of his profession. His ability was soon demonstrated, and he built up a large clientele and made a large circle of friends. Such was his success that his friends prevailed upon him to become a candidate for the office of district attorney of Contra Costa County, and at the general election in 1910 he was elected, and thereafter served for four years with marked ability. In 1914 he became a candidate for judge of the superior bench, was elected, and took his office on January 1, 1915; and ever since he has served in that high office with great credit to his county and to himself. Ever since coming to Martinez to make his home, Judge McKenzie has shown his public spirit in many ways and has taken an active part in all movements for the betterment of the city and county.

On March 22, 1897, at Antioch, A. B. McKenzie was united in marriage with Melvina Durham, born in California, the daughter of the late Capt. Joshua E. Durham, owner of a fine ranch and also captain of a ferry boat. He was born in Tennessee; and in California he was married to Miss Sherman, a native of this State and the descendant of an old pioneer family. Of this union of Mr. and Mrs. McKenzie nine children have been born: Malcomb D., a graduate of the University of California, Class 1924, with the degree of B. A.; Norma, who graduated from the Alhambra Union High School in Martinez, and is now with the Associated Oil Company in San Francisco; Lorilee, employed in the Bank of Martinez; Maitland, a law student at Columbia University, New York; Roma, a student in the University of California; George, attending the University of California; Ross and Marian, pupils in the Alhambra High School; and Kathleen, in the grammar school. Judge McKenzie is essentially a home man and gives strict attention to his business. He was reared in the Presbyterian faith, is highly esteemed by all who know him, and with his wife enjoys a wide circle of friends and acquaintances. Fraternally, he is a member of Richmond Lodge No. 1251, B. P. O. E. In political belief he is a stanch Republican.

THOMAS R. BALL.—A prosperous rancher of Contra Costa County, where he has been engaged in fruit-raising for the past thirty-five years, Thomas R. Ball is an excellent example of the self-made Scotch-American. His success in life has come to him through hard work and through business acumen and foresight in choosing the fertile soil of Contra Costa County for his agricultural development work. Born at Paisley, Scotland, on September 9, 1869, he is the son of John and Martha (Harris) Ball, both natives of that country and the parents of eight children, of whom Thomas R. was the third in order of birth. He had three sisters and four brothers, most of whom came to the United States, though the parents lived and died in Scotland. One brother, George, is a retired railway conductor living at Hayward; John, a rancher of Contra Costa County, is deceased; David, who went to Australia, fell in the World War; and the others are James; Mary Ann Hunter, residing in Pittsburgh, Pa.; Mrs. J. C. McGill; and Sarah Elizabeth, who died at the age of two years.

Thomas R. Ball had but limited schooling, as he started out to make his own way in the world while still young, working at various occupations. After putting in some time as clerk in a dry-goods store in Scotland, he came to America in 1887, when eighteen years old, and spent the first year in the new country in Massachusetts. Next he went to Jersey City, and then to Yonkers, N. Y., where he worked in a shoe factory.

In 1889 he came to California, and for three years ran a milk wagon in San Jose. Then, after a year spent in Portland, Ore., he came to Contra Costa County; and here, renting a ranch at Pleasant Hill, for ten years he operated the land. In 1906 he bought his home ranch of fifty acres, upon which he has made all improvements, building a fine country home and planting the acreage to Bartlett pears, peaches and grapes. Five years later he bought twenty acres near Muir Station, now in grapes, almonds, and table grapes; this ranch was later sold to his brother John, but on his death in 1924, Mr. Ball re-purchased the land from his heirs. His third ranch, purchased in 1919, consists of twenty-five acres at Pleasant Hill, and is devoted to grapes and prunes. Mr. Ball operates all three ranches. He is an up-to-date horticulturist and viticulturist, using a Cle-Trax tractor and other modern implements in carrying on the ranch work. A man of mental poise and sturdy character, he continues to work early and late and is known as one of the most successful fruit-raisers in the county.

Mr. Ball found a true helpmate in his wife, to whom he was married on October 27, 1895, at Pleasant Hill. Mrs. Ball was Miss Jane Rodgers before her marriage. She is a daughter of the late Edward Rodgers of Pleasant Hill, and a cousin of Attorney James E. Rodgers of Martinez, and also of Mrs. Thomas S. Duane. Two children have blessed the union of Mr. and Mrs. Ball: Edward John, who married Mildred Lockard and is the father of one child, Jane; and Letitia, attending the Martinez Union High School.

Besides his ranch interests, Mr. Ball was for some time the local agent for the Pioneer Fruit Company. This agency is now being carried on by his son, Edward John. Mr. Ball is a stockholder in the Martinez National Bank. He is a highly respected man in the community, noted for his Scotch characteristic of good, hard common sense. He is a practical progressive in all matters, and a man whose opinion is given consideration. He was naturalized in San Francisco in 1895, and in politics is a Republican, while in all civic and community affairs he favors the men and measures best calculated to advance the county's best interests.

JACKSON H. MISNER.—A self-made man in every sense of the word, Jackson H. Misner, harbor manager for the City of Richmond, was born in Dayton, Ohio, and from there went to Oregon and Washington, where he attended school, graduating from the high school in Tacoma, after which he attended the Willamette University, a Methodist institution, for four years, taking the arts and science course. In 1894 he left Tacoma and went to Arizona, where he was employed by the Copper Queen Mining Company in various capacities until the breaking-out of the Spanish-American War. He enlisted and joined Roosevelt's Rough Riders, and after a time in training in Texas went with his command and took an active part in the campaigns. After the war he returned to the

United States and for several months was sick in a hospital in the East. When he received his discharge from the service, Theodore Roosevelt made an indorsement on the back of the document as follows: "A gallant and trustworthy soldier, one of the men whose courage and zealous performance of every duty made him an honor to the regiment." Returning to his home in Tacoma he remained there until called by Capt. Z. J. Hatch of the Monticello Steamship lines to come to California, and he remained in the employ of that company until 1911.

In 1914 Mr. Misner was called to Richmond to take charge of the building up of the harbor, as manager. He accepted the position, and by dint of hard work and taking advantage of his wide acquaintance with the shipping trade, he has created something the city is proud of. There was no deep water when he came to take control, but with the appropriation from the city and from the Federal Government a channel was dredged and the first boat came to dock in 1918. Now Richmond is a regular port of call for many lines of steamships, and the housing and docking facilities are inadequate for the volume of business. The tonnage passing through in 1925 was 278,671 tons, ninety-five per cent of which was for export; and it is estimated the tonnage for 1926 will exceed this amount, for the present docking facilities are being worked over capacity. During the time he has been in charge of this post, Mr. Misner has built the levees of the inner harbor.

When Mr. Misner married he chose Miss Florence Winton, of Vallejo, for his wife, and this union resulted in the birth of twin girls, Doris de Camp and Jeanne de Winton, graduates from the Richmond High School now attending the University of California at Berkeley. A Mason, Mr. Misner belongs to Alpha Lodge No. 431, F. & A. M.; Richmond Chapter No. 113, R. A. M.; Richmond Commandery No. 59, K. T.; and Aahmes Temple, A. A. O. N. M. S., of Oakland. He is also a member of the Sciots. His recreation is found in the mountains, away from the noise and bustle of work. His influence is helpful for every progressive movement, and he enjoys the confidence of many friends in the bay region.

EDWIN T. BLAKE.—The vice-president of Blake Brothers Company of San Francisco and Contra Costa County, Edwin T. Blake, is a native son of the Golden State, born in San Francisco on June 25, 1875, the son of a Forty-niner, Charles Thompson Blake, who came via Nicaragua to California in search of gold. Charles Thompson Blake was married in California to Miss Harriet W. Stiles, and they had four children. The father died in 1897; the mother is now living with her son, Edwin T. Blake, at his home in Kensington precinct.

Edwin T. Blake received his education in the public schools in San Francisco, and at the University of California, where he was graduated with his engineering degree. He was associated with the Oakland Paving Company, which his father had helped to organize in the early days; but in 1904, with his brother and Mr. Bilger, under the name of Blake &

Bilger Co., he began prospecting for rock deposits in Contra Costa County at Castro Point. Finding the desired quality of rock, they bought from Luke and John Fay the property embraced by the frontage on San Francisco Bay and began operations, developing with the passing of the years a very valuable property. In 1917 the corporation became Blake Brothers Company. The operation of the plant is under the direction of our subject, and some seventy men are kept busy the year round. The company's products are shipped to places within a radius of 100 miles of the bay cities. The plant is located near deep water and much of their output is shipped to points on the Sacramento and San Joaquin Rivers, as well as to bay points. In the early days of development work there were no paved roads, and during the stormy season, when Mr. Blake drove his automobile, he had to leave it at the county line where he could get it out of the mud, and take the street cars to their plant. Mr. Blake tells of coming through this district as a lad, hunting ducks, when there was nothing here but a place known as Castro Point.

Mr. Blake was united in marriage in San Francisco on January 12, 1904, to Miss Harriet W. Carson, a native of California. They reside in their home, erected in 1922, in Kensington precinct, overlooking the bay and the cities lying along its shores. Mr. Blake is a member of the American Institute of Mining Engineers. Politically he is a Republican.

GEORGE F. BLACK.—As city councilman of Richmond, Contra Costa County, and also one of the city's successful business men, George F. Black is well known throughout the bay section. A native Californian he was born in Sierra City, Sierra County, on November 17, 1870, the son of F. J. and Anna (Curley) Black, the former a native of Denmark, and the latter of Ireland. F. J. Black was an early California pioneer miner, who came West to try out his fortune on the new frontier.

George F. Black attended the schools of Sierra County, and at the age of twenty-one left home and started in life for himself. His first venture took him to Orange County, where he located in Santa Ana and engaged in the orange-growing industry, securing employment with Bishop & Company, and the Glassell Company, in the growing, packing and shipping of oranges. After a number of years in that work he became associated with the Copper Queen Consolidated Mining Company, in Arizona.

Coming to Richmond in 1912, Mr. Black became associated with his brother-in-law, Arno Fisher, in the grocery business. This company has grown and expanded, and now maintains three stores in Richmond, operated on the cash-and-carry plan, which has proven very successful and popular in the community, for their patrons know that they are getting an absolutely square deal and the choice of a fresh and large stock, made possible by the amount purchased in stocking the three stores.

The marriage of Mr. Black, occurring November 17, 1897, at Orange, Cal., united him with Carrie Bennett, a native of Humansville, Mo., and four sons have been born to them: Walter and Carl, both students at the University of Oregon; Leroy, a student at the University of California; and Neal, attending the Richmond High School. The three eldest boys are showing their mettle by working their way through college.

Fully alive to the possibilities of Richmond, and recognized as a loyal and progressive citizen, Mr. Black was elected a member of the Richmond city council in May, 1923, taking office in July of that year. An active worker for the further advancement of his home city, he is in favor of all practicable projects which have that end in view. He is a member of the Lighting, Ordinance, Building and Fence Committees. Fraternally, Mr. Black is a member of Twilight Lodge No. 119, I. O. O. F., and of the Woodmen of the World. In politics he is a Republican.

CHARLES B. DOUGLASS.—One of the prominent ranchers and fruit growers of Eastern Contra Costa County is Charles B. Douglass, who is located near Antioch and the Sherman Island bridge. He has worked intelligently and with a persistency of purpose to demonstrate that this section is adapted to almost any kind of vine, tree or seed put into the ground, and that when given proper care they will produce many fold. He has demonstrated that the Tokay grape ripens for market about three weeks earlier here than in any other part of the State, and therefore brings higher prices. It has a high sugar content and the proper coloring for early marketing. Mr. Douglass owns three ranches: the home ranch near the Sherman Island bridge, of thirty-five acres, which is devoted to Tokay grapes and to Walnuts; the Lone Tree ranch of eighty acres, where he has forty acres of cling peaches, twenty acres of Bartlett pears, and twenty acres of Tokay grapes; and the Knightsen ranch, in which Mrs. Douglass is also interested, of forty acres, devoted to Bartlett pears now three years old. In this orchard he is proving out the Caldwell process, which brings the trees into bearing at three years.

Charles B. Douglass was born at Westport, N. Y., on May 2, 1862, a son of William and Marian (Havens) Douglass. The father was born in Clinton County, and served with distinction throughout the entire Civil War in the 77th New York Volunteer Infantry, rising to be a first lieutenant. For many years he conducted a blacksmith shop at Westport. He served as a justice of the peace for twenty-five years, and was also postmaster. He died at the age of eighty-four years, and his wife passed away at the age of sixty-seven. Of their ten children Charles B. Douglass is the only survivor. On the paternal side the family is of Scotch ancestry, and emigrants of the family early settled in Massachusetts. Charles B. Douglass attended the public schools and learned the machinist's trade. On account of his health he was compelled to come to California, and here he began growing fruit and experimenting with soil production. He has worked in several fruit-growing counties and finally decided that here in Contra Costa County he had found ideal conditions, and his prophecy has proved to be correct. He is always ready to give aid and suggestions to those wishing to engage in fruit culture, and believes this section has just begun to be appreciated.

Besides his work as a producer, Mr. Douglass has given much study to marketing of the products of the ranches, and the Lone Tree Shipping Company was organized in February, 1926, with the following officers: C. B. Douglass, president, and J. L. Claghorn, secretary, who, with the following members, make up the full board of trustees: Andrew DeMartini, W. J. O'Hara, C. L. Lindquist, J. A. West, C. O'Brien, E. A. H. Prewett and Fred Heidorn. The board was authorized to purchase eighteen acres of land, construct a spur track on the Southern Pacific, erect a shipping and packing shed, and prepare dry yards. The association is cooperative. Already 1300 acres of fruit land and 800 acres of grapes have been pledged to the association, and this movement bids fair to make of this section a very important shipping point for the best fruit ever sent to the markets of the world.

Mr. Douglass was married at Fresno in 1893 to Miss Elizabeth Byer, who was born in Napa County but was reared and educated in Contra Costa County. They purchased their present home place in 1896. Two children have come to brighten the home circle, Esther and Robert. Esther is the wife of C. J. Painter, a machinist in San Francisco, and has two children, Douglass and Betty Ann. Robert assists his father with the ranch work. Both Mr. and Mrs. Douglass are highly esteemed by all who know them, and take an active interest in all problems for the betterment of their community and the State in general. They are Republicans in principle and action.

JAMES FRANK MAUZY.—When James F. Mauzy went to Walnut Creek, Contra Costa County, in 1914, there was little to suggest the prosperity which it has since been his privilege to help bring about. In 1924 he erected a modern Class A building, 40 by 100 feet, where he conducts a lucrative plumbing business, carrying a complete line of up-to-date plumbing fixtures, together with pumps and general equipment for same. He was born in Springfield, Mo., June 14, 1884, a son of William Elliott and Margaret (Patterson) Mauzy, natives of Indiana and Tennessee, respectively. The family left their Eastern home in 1897 for California. William Elliott Mauzy made a business of purchasing soldier claims and selling them; he is now living retired in Los Angeles, Cal.

The schooling of James F. Mauzy consisted of seven years in the grammar school; he then was obliged to go to work to help support the family and was apprenticed to a plumber, taking a full four-years course. He spent one year as a journeyman plumber, and then went to San Francisco and was there during the great earthquake and fire, remaining there until his removal to Walnut Creek in 1914.

The marriage of Mr. Mauzy united him with Miss Ina F. Lewis, a native of Ohio, daughter of Selvin and Mary (Miles) Lewis. Her father

Fred Meyer

Louise Meyer

is a chemist and drug manufacturer in Los Angeles, Cal. Mr. and Mrs. Mauzy are the parents of three children, Jessie, Elliott, and Elizabeth Jane. During the World War, Mr. Mauzy was a member of the Walnut Creek Home Guards. He is a Republican in politics, and serves as chairman of the board of town trustees and a member of the executive board of the Chamber of Commerce. He belongs to the Lions Club.

FRED MEYER.—A Richmond pioneer who has had much to do with street development in the early days is Fred Meyer, well-known and successful contractor for streets, highways, sewers and cement work; in fact all heavy contracting of that kind is his specialty. He was born near Minden, Germany, on September 16, 1869, and at the age of fourteen accompanied his mother to California, settling in San Leandro, Alameda County. She died on November 11, 1919. Besides Fred there were the following children in the Meyer home circle: Minnie is living in Masport, N. Y. Herman is in Brooklyn, N. Y. William is in the employ of the government at the Brooklyn Navy Yard; he was employed at the Panama Canal zone at times, and between times he was a Pinkerton detective. Mary is at Pittstown, N. J. Christ, who died in an auto accident in Richmond, was employed by his brother Fred for eighteen years. Fred is the subject of this review. Ferdinand accompanied the mother to California, but returned to Germany. He was a sea captain and died in 1920. The father, William Meyer, was a teamster and freighter in Germany and died in 1880.

Fred Meyer had meager educational advantages and at the age of thirteen worked in a glass works in Germany. He had an uncle, Ferdinand Meyer, in San Leandro who crossed the plains in 1851, and when the mother came to California she brought her three boys, leaving Fred and William here when she went back to Germany. Fred worked in San Lorenzo for fifteen dollars per month for five years for Stenzel Brothers. He worked on a threshing machine and from 4 A. M. to 8 P. M. for about six years; one season the run lasted 110 days. His contact with the world as a dry-goods peddler, driving his team through Alameda and Contra Costa County for two years, gave him a first-hand schooling in meeting people and has been of untold advantage to him in later life. In 1891 he began teaming and hauling, with headquarters in San Leandro, until moving to Richmond in 1901, at the solicitation of Laymance Brothers, to do some grading work on the streets of a tract just laid out in lots. He graded the first four streets of the town, viz.: First Street, Second Street, Third Street and Fourth Street. His first residence was on Fourth Street, between Nevin Street and Macdonald Avenue. His second residence was where the Stanley blacksmith shop now is located, and here he bought two lots and erected a house and stable. John Nicholl came to see him and told him he would have to get a boat or go swimming in such a location; but fortunately he was not called upon to do so, for there has been no high water since he has lived in this section, though he says he has seen Mr. Nicholl literally swimming in $20 gold pieces because he was so fortunate as to sell land for $5000 per acre that at one time could have been bought by Mr. Meyer for $75 per acre. The twenty acres through which Mr. Meyer graded the first streets was sold by Walter Laymance of Oakland in sixty days, in twenty-five foot lots.

In 1909 Mr. Meyer bought an acre in the Richmond Tract and erected the buildings suitable to his needs, and he has since lived upon it. He has done all kinds of street, road, sewer, cement and sidewalk work wherever he got a contract. He has a complete equipment for all work of the kinds mentioned and employs many men at times, according to the size of the contract. Besides his contracting work, Mr. Meyer owns the Pullman Water Company. This he developed from one well and one customer; now he has sunk seven wells to an average depth of 137 feet, and one well is 187 feet deep. He has laid water mains, from one-inch pipe to five-inch, all over the districts of North Richmond and Pullman and has 465 customers. Between the Nicholl home and San Pablo, where now stand fine homes and many business blocks, he has seen as many as three threshing machines at one time.

Mr. Meyer was married in San Leandro in 1899, at the home of Dr. Mason, to Louise Neindick, who was born and reared in San Francisco. This union has resulted in the birth of seven boys and one girl, viz.: Herman, Fred, Raymond, August, Henry, Harry, Lester and Doris. The older sons are associated with their father in business, and the others are attending school. All were born in Contra Costa County except Herman. Mr. Meyer stands for good schools, good roads, good government and all modern improvements for the bettering of conditions and the welfare of the people. In his political affiliations he picks the man he considers best fitted for the office regardless of party lines. He is well and favorably known throughout Contra Costa and Alameda Counties as a liberal-minded man.

GEORGE S. TANDY.—An expert carpenter and builder is found in the person of George S. Tandy, a native son of California and now a resident of Richmond, who, under a partnership arrangement with C. L. Theis, is carrying on a successful contracting and building business in western Contra Costa County. Mr. Tandy was born at Capay, Yolo County, on January 11, 1893, one of eleven children born to George W. Tandy, a harnessmaker by trade and a native of South Carolina. Grandfather George Tandy came around the Horn with his family in 1851. He was from County Cork, Ireland, and in his family were two children, George W. and a sister. The mother of G. S. Tandy was named Anna Faure before her marriage to Mr. Tandy, and was born in Germany. They were married in June, 1887, and had the following children: Catherine, deceased; Josephine, who married C. E. Armstrong and lives in Richmond; George S., of this sketch; May, deceased; William B., a petty officer in the United States Navy; Earl, of Richmond; Thomas, a real estate man in San Francisco; Ann, a trained nurse and a missionary in China; Clyde, employed by the Standard Oil Company in Richmond; Marie, a student in the University of California; and Pearl, deceased. The parents are living at Capay.

George S. Tandy remained at home and attended school, and worked at various jobs until 1915, when he came to Richmond and worked at the carpenter's trade until 1917. He then enlisted in the United States Army and was assigned to the quartermaster's department with the rank of first lieutenant. He worked on construction at Camp Lewis, Washington; the Presidio, in San Francisco; Camp Kearney, San Diego; Camp Johnson, Florida; Camp Meigs, Washington, D. C.; Fort Benjamin Harrison, in Indiana; and Fort Sill, Oklahoma. He was then sent back to the Presidio and there received his honorable discharge. Returning to Richmond, he was employed at the refinery for a short time and then began taking contracts to build homes in the city of Richmond. Among the buildings he has constructed are the Traverso, Sixteenth and Macdonald; Veale Hotel, 1514 Macdonald; Persico, Eleventh and Macdonald; the Black at Fourteenth and Macdonald; and the Whitesides, at Point Richmond. In 1921 he formed a partnership with C. L. Theis and they work harmoniously together on all contracts, both being expert workmen. As he has prospered Mr. Tandy has invested in the California Guarantee and Loan Association, and he is a stockholder in the Carquinez Hotel in Richmond. He is an active member of the Chamber of Commerce and the Builders' Exchange.

On September 27, 1917, Mr. Tandy was united in marriage with Miss Sylva Morrin, of Rumsey, Yolo County, the daughter of James M. and Estella (Chittenden) Morrin, both natives of Kansas. Her father was a physician and a very successful man in his profession, as well as a typical pioneer of the Rumsey section of Yolo County, and is still living at the age of ninety-two years. Two children have blessed the marriage of Mr. and Mrs. Tandy, Daire Albert and Robert Kent. Mr. Tandy is a member and a Past Commander of the American Legion Post in Richmond, and takes an active interest in the affairs of the Legion. He believes in fostering the Boy Scout movement, and says there is not a man in San Quentin who was ever a Boy Scout. His recreation is found as a baseball fan; and he also likes to hunt deer and ducks. Both himself and wife are highly esteemed by their many friends.

GEORGE SKOGEN.—Norway has given to the United States many good citizens, men who have become very successful and influential in the localities where they have settled. To the list of names of Norwegians who have aided in the agricultural development of Contra Costa County must be added that of George Skogen, the efficient superintendent of the Central Creameries Company in the Knightsen precinct and foreman of their 454-acre ranch. George Skogen was born on July 1, 1880, at Kongsberg, Norway, a son of Olaus and Mariana Skogen, well-to-do farmer folk of Oever Eker parish. His father died in 1908, aged sixty-five, but his mother still resides in the old home place. Their family consisted of twelve children, George being the third child in order of birth and the only one residing in California. Two sisters, Dagmar and Signe, reside in Oregon, while two brothers and one sister are still residents of Norway.

On March 20, 1902, George Skogen sailed from Christiania for America, landing at Halifax, N. S., and from there continuing his journey to Balfour, N. Dak., where he found work on a wheat farm. In 1904 he left Dakota and located in Minneapolis, Minn., and secured a position with the Soo Railroad Company as a fireman in their roundhouse. Mr. Skogen made a trip back to the old homeland in 1906-1907, being away about four months, and upon returning to America came again to Minneapolis. The following year he located at Kendall, Mont., where he went to work in a quartz mill. A second trip was made to Norway in the spring of 1911, which consumed about five months, and after returning to the United States he located at Fort Benton, Mont., where he worked one year.

On May 15, 1913, at Great Falls, Mont., George Skogen was united in marriage with Miss Bertha Skagen, a native of Norway, born at Goel, in Hallingdal, a daughter of Herbran and Joran Skagen. Three days later the happy couple left Montana for California, arriving at Stockton on May 21. After visiting San Francisco they finally settled at Menlo Park, San Mateo County, where Mr. Skogen became caretaker on the estate of a San Francisco wholesale coffee dealer.

In the fall of 1913 Mr. Skogen returned to San Francisco and had an interview with E. H. Fox, who at that time was part owner and manager of the Central Creameries, near Knightsen. The splendid record Mr. Skogen had already established as a dependable employee, his sterling character and efficient service won for him the confidence of Mr. Fox and in 1914 he was engaged as foreman of the 300-acre ranch belonging to the Central Creameries in Contra Costa County. His ability to manage men and his untiring efforts in behalf of the creamery company so pleased the management that on October 1, 1924, he was appointed superintendent of the creamery in addition to his duties as foreman of the ranch. This creamery is perhaps the largest of its kind in Contra Costa County and owns some 300 milch cows, four registered Holstein bulls, and considerable young stock. In addition to the 454 acres owned by the company they rent 800 acres. Mr. Skogen has seventeen men under his supervision, and eight milking machines are operated in the dairy. The milk is shipped to Oakland by truck, where it is pasteurized and bottled, and sold in Oakland and Berkeley.

Mr. and Mrs. Skogen are the parents of three children: Jerdece, Dorothy and Jorgen. Mrs. Skogen is distantly related to the late Congressman Berg from Goel, Norway, and also to Syver Olstad, a music dealer of Minneapolis, and agent for the White Star Line Steamship Company. Knut Olstad, of Oslo, Norway, who was the first president of the electric railroad at Christiania, Norway, is her second cousin. Fraternally, Mr.

Skogen is a member of Covenant Lodge No. 62, I. O. O. F., at Minneapolis. Mr. and Mrs. Skogen hold memberships in a Rebekah Lodge in San Francisco.

THOMAS McKEOWN.—For over a quarter of a century Thomas McKeown has been one of the large ranch operators of Contra Costa County. He came to California from his home in Ireland while still a youth, and has since that early day been a part of the agricultural growth and development of the central part of the state. Born in County Louth, Ireland, on June 22, 1875, he was the third in a family of twelve children born to Patrick and Margaret (Sands) McKeown, who were honest and upright farmer folk back in the old country, where the father died at the age of seventy-six, and the mother is still living, now seventy-six years old. One brother and three sisters of Mr. McKeown are living in California.

Growing up on his parent's farm, Thomas early learned the care of sheep, cattle and horses, and the hardships of farm life. When eighteen years of age he came to California, an older sister, Mrs. Mike White, having preceded him, and on arriving in San Francisco, July 2, 1893, he went to the Suisun Valley and there engaged in ranch work. Returning to San Francisco, he entered the employ of the Union Iron Works and for five years worked there steadily. At the end of that period, he came to Port Costa, and in association with his brother-in-law, Mike White, became a tenant on the McNear Ranch, which originally contained 3000 acres, from which has been taken the site for the Port Costa Brick Works, and sites for two different oil companies, leaving approximately 2750 acres of land. The partnership continued for several years, and for the past thirteen years Mr. McKeown has operated the land alone, his lease extending to the pasture, hay and grain lands. A large undertaking, it of necessity has involved much forethought and hiring of a number of men during the busy seasons. Mr. McKeown has proven the right man on the job, his hard and intelligent work having been rewarded with success, except during the seasons of the heavy drouth which were so hard on all California ranchers, and when the ranch had to be operated at a loss.

The marriage of Mr. McKeown, which occurred in San Francisco, united him with Miss Delia Kelley, also a native of Ireland, and who has been a true helpmate of sterling worth. Mr. McKeown has been a member of the Y. M. I. since he was twenty years old. They both are members of St. Patrick's Church at Port Costa, and are highly respected as hardworking, straightforward, generous-hearted people, who have the general welfare of the community at heart and work toward that end, voting for what they consider the correct principles of government and the men best suited to officially carry them out. Contra Costa owes much to just such people as Mr. and Mrs. McKeown, who settled here as young people and have woven their lives in with the steady advancement of their home community.

JOSEPH MINTA.—The hard-working Portuguese-American vine-yardist and asparagus grower, Joseph Minta, owns thirty-two acres of as fine land as can be found in Contra Costa County, which he has brought to a very high state of cultivation. On his ranch he has five acres of trees that he has set out and that are now in fine condition. He was born in Contra Costa County on November 12, 1876, the son of Manuel and Philomena (Joseph) Minta. Manuel Minta came from the Azores Islands in 1852 and settled in California, and from that time until he died, he was a hard-working and honored farmer. Both parents are now deceased. They had six children in their family, three boys and three girls.

Joseph Minta married Miss Rose Jacinta, born in Alameda County, who died in 1909 leaving three children: Ethel, wife of George Livira, a garage man in Knightsen; Elmer, in the high school; and Loretta, also in the high school. One child died at the age of nine years. Mr. Minta was reared in this county and has continued to farm ever since he has been old enough. He is a member of the I. D. E. S., at Antioch, the Odd Fellows at Byron, and the Eagles at Antioch. For many years he has served as a trustee of the Iron House school district, and he was one of the organizers and for three years a director, of the Knightsen Irrigation District. Politically he is a Republican. He has many friends in this section of the county, who esteem him as a high-minded citizen.

WILLIAM A. WARD.—The famous Blackhawk Ranch, known to high-grade cattle breeders throughout the world, is an institution which not only Contra Costa County, but the entire State of California may feel justly proud to have within its boundaries. The importance of the work being done on this ranch cannot be overestimated, for the high place accorded it in the annals of cattlemen everywhere has been justly merited. William A. Ward, one of the owners of this ranch and a recognized authority on all phases of cattle breeding, was born in Cambridgeshire, England, on August 19, 1881. His father, William, was a farmer and stock breeder of considerable note in that country. The mother's name was Caroline Ward, and there were two boys in the family, William of this review, and a brother who continues to reside in England. In 1905 Mr. Ward came to America, on a contemplated tour of the world, and landed in San Jose. After remaining there for six months he received a flattering offer to manage the estate of A. M. Easton at Burlingame, which he did for about five years. He returned to England in 1910 and remained for about two months, but the urge to return to California was insistent. Accordingly he came back, decided to become an American citizen and took out naturalization papers. In connection with A. M. Easton he established the Blackhawk Ranch, which contains about 1500 acres, and made it one of the most noted institutions of its kind in the world.

On the Blackhawk Ranch corn and hay are raised to feed the cattle, although most of the land is in pasture. The valleys are being set to walnuts; about 200 acres, it is contemplated, will be used for this purpose, which offers great possibilities. But the product which has made Blackhawk Ranch noted is its wonderful cattle. Highest honors were awarded cattle from this ranch at the American Royal at Kansas City and at the International Cattle Show in Chicago. In 1925 Blackhawk Ranch won more first prizes on bulls than have ever before been won by any breeder in a single year on cattle of his own breeding. Mr. Ward is an authority on pedigrees. Since he took up permanent residence in America he has made several trips to England, importing cattle and horses, particularly Shire horses and Shorthorn cattle. Mr. Ward's brother is the owner of a herd of Shorthorns in England. The breeding herd of Easton & Ward represents an investment of about $250,000, and it bears the reputation of being the best-bred herd of Shorthorns in America. One calf sold recently for $3500 and $10,000 was refused for the prize-winner at the American Royal.

The genius of Mr. Ward in his line was undoubtedly partly hereditary, for his father was a noted breeder of Shorthorn cattle and Shire horses. Mr. Ward was educated in an English high school and had a tutor in Cambridge and also since his arrival in America, although he never went to school here. He has always been in the cattle and horse business. Despite the high honors which he has attained as a breeder, he states that he has never yet been able to produce what he would consider a perfect bull. For the Blackhawk Ranch the best cows and bulls to be had anywhere are purchased, and the high-bred cattle produced by this ranch are in great demand in the East and elsewhere.

Mr. Ward was married on March 18, 1914, to Miss Louise Easton, daughter of A. M. and Louise (Adams) Easton, of Burlingame, the father being partner of Mr. Ward in the ownership of Blackhawk Ranch. Mr. and Mrs. Ward are the parents of four children: Elizabeth, Sally, John Adam and William Easton. Mr. Ward is a member of Alamo Lodge No. 122, F. & A. M. He is fond of athletic games, and of hunting, fishing and camping in the mountains. He is deeply interested in his work.

RICHMOND-SAN RAFAEL FERRY.—In the Bay transportation world, the name of Charles F. Van Damme stands out as a monument to a man with an idea that was founded on a correct interpretation of the needs of the bay region, with a trained mind that builded slowly and substantially on that idea. In the latter part of 1914, Mr. Van Damme was struck with the needs for the connecting link between the great East Bay region and the northern Bay counties and he investigated thoroughly.

The Richmond and the San Rafael Chambers of Commerce, under the leadership of James C. Owens, pioneer of Richmond, had interviewed the existing railway companies operating ferry lines on the bays, but the heads of these corporations scorned the idea of an automobile ferry between Richmond and Marin County. Mr. Van Damme stepped into the breach and, with a few friends and business associates, organized the Richmond-San Rafael Ferry and Transportation Co. in March, 1915. On May 1 of that year the corporation inaugurated their first service with the old ferry boat Ellen, one of the pioneer craft on the bay, and with a capacity of eighteen automobiles. The Ellen had been used as the relief boat by the Mare Island Ferry Company.

A contract was given to build the steamer Charles F. Van Damme, and this boat was put in commission July 23, 1916. It had a capacity for forty-five automobiles, and was believed to be large enough for many years to come. In 1921 the City of Richmond was put in commission. This was an especially built boat for automobile transportation. On June 26, 1924, the third boat of their fleet, the City of San Rafael, was put on the run between San Quentin Point and Castro Point. From ten employees in 1915, the company have increased their payroll to seventy-five.

In 1922 the company purchased forty acres in Marin County for its Marin terminal; and in 1922 leased the property at Castro Point and began building roads and blasting away hills and embankments to make way for landings, piers and the necessary buildings, and to provide ample parking space and the extension of street car lines. Over 4,000,000 of people have ridden on the steamers of this company since it inaugurated its service, and over 2,000,000 automobiles have been carried. Two hundred thousand machines and 700,000 passengers were carried by this company in 1923. The personnel of the corporation is Charles F. Van Damme, president; A. F. Mahoney, vice-president; H. T. Gill, auditor and secretary; O. J. Olson, treasurer; Mose Moch, manager; Henry A. Jacobs, attorney. The company give a 20-minute service when needed, and maintain a regular summer schedule until November, when their winter schedule goes into effect. The company show an investment in ships, piers, roads and terminal facilities of nearly $1,000,000. What this service has meant to the traveling public cannot be estimated in dollars, but it is conceded by all who know that no one interest has accomplished as much for the good of the bay cities as has the Richmond-San Rafael Ferry and Transportation Co., and their watchword is progress at all times, which also means service.

JOSEPH ROLANDO.—The owner of the Rolando Block in Brentwood, Joseph Rolando, has erected one of the best structures in Brentwood, most modern in all its appointments. It is of brick and stucco finish, is 50x100 feet in dimensions, and cost $20,000. It houses the post office, the Brentwood Electrical Company, the Brentwood Drug Store, and the Rolando Billiard Hall.

Left an orphan by the death of his parents before he was eighteen months old, Joseph Rolando was brought from France to Calumet, Mich., as a babe of one year and there he grew to boyhood. His schooling was neglected and at an early age he went to work in the Calumet and Hecla Mine. From the age of twelve until he was twenty-five he showed the stuff he was made of and satisfied his employers. He saved his money and embarked in business on his own account, being located in Duluth, Minn., and in Wisconsin and Illinois, until coming to California in 1913. He

landed at Brentwood and engaged in business, and now conducts an up-to-date refreshment parlor, giving it his personal attention. He leases his billiard parlor to others.

Mr. Rolando was married at Calumet, Mich., to Miss Felicina Guaia, born at Savoy, France. Mr. and Mrs. Rolando dispense a liberal hospitality to their many friends in Brentwood and vicinity, where both are well known.

EDWARD J. BURG.—In Edward J. Burg of Richmond, Contra Costa County has a man whose faith in the possibilities of this section of the county are unbounded. The real estate field in Richmond has called forth the most creditable ambitions of a few men whose resourcefulness, executive ability, keen business judgment and foresight have been the direct means of building up one of the finest cities on the Pacific Coast, with unlimited possibilities as an industrial center. These men have become leaders in all projects for advancing the varied interests of the citizens who have sought homes within the boundaries of the city.

Conspicuous among these men of vision is Edward J. Burg, president of Burg Brothers, Inc., pioneer realty dealers of Richmond. Mr. Burg was born in Sweden on January 12, 1868, a son of John and Augusta Burg. The mother died in 1873, and the father in 1879, leaving their family of three children to shift for themselves at an early age, our subject being but eleven years old when the father died. When he was twelve he accompanied his brothers, C. H. and G. F. Burg, to America, and for a short time stopped in Illinois. In 1881 he came on to California, locating in San Francisco. He first attended school in this country at Alamo, Contra Costa County, and the old schoolhouse is still standing. He then went to Oakland and worked his way through the California Military Academy, said to be the oldest private school in the State. Graduating from this institution, he took up newspaper work and traveled over the country extensively. In 1884 he was in the Indian campaigns in Montana as a member of the United States Cavalry. During his travels he visited South America and Central America, and was in Chili in 1889 during the revolution between the army and navy in that country; he also was interested in a coffee plantation in Central America for a time. If the complete life history of Mr. Burg were to be written, it would fill a volume; but we can only touch upon the most important events in his life.

In 1898 Mr. Burg went to Seattle, Wash., and joined the rush to the Alaskan gold fields; but he returned to San Francisco in 1900, and in 1902 began operating in Richmond real estate, having an office in San Francisco. His faith in the future of this city was built upon a firm foundation and he prospered so well that in 1906 he organized the Bay Cities Land Company, which was incorporated in 1912. The firm of Burg Brothers, Inc., was consummated in 1910; and afterwards he organized the Burg Brothers Lumber and Building Company, and later disposed of its interests. An example of what energy and resourcefulness can accomplish is furnished in the development of the following tracts in Richmond: Central Richmond Tract, Pullman Townsite Tract, Key Tract, Grand View Terrace Tract (a high class, fully restricted residential section of Richmond), and the Spaulding-Richmond-Pullman Townsite Tract. In 1912 Mr. Burg purchased from John Nicholl 112 acres, which he subdivided into the now famous Nicholl Macdonald Avenue Civic Center Tract upon which he caused a fine city hall to be built; and that, with two half city blocks, he presented to the city of Richmond as a civic center. It might be of interest to mention that in 1898 Mr. Nicholl tried to sell his 200-acre farm for seventy dollars per acre and was unable to find a purchaser; but in October, 1912, Burg Brothers paid $725,000 for 112 acres of it and in 1912 one lot 50 by 100 feet in size sold for $15,000, just $1000 more than the amount for which Mr. Nicholl offered the entire property less than fifteen years earlier. In 1926 part of this same property sold for $500 per front foot, thus showing the great advance in price of property on Macdonald Avenue and Twenty-third Street, now acknowledged to be the center of the future city. When Mr. Burg negotiated for the large acreage, the price paid was said to be the highest amount paid for that amount of land anywhere in the United States. In laying out the streets in these subdivisions Mr. Burg personally supervised the work, and to him must be given the credit for the fine wide streets that traverse the various properties.

On November 30, 1893, Edward J. Burg was united in marriage with Miss Beatrice M. Ramus, born in England but a resident of San Francisco at the time of their marriage. This union has been blessed with nine children, five boys and four girls. Edward A. married Miss Grace Cox, of Waco, Texas, and they have a daughter, Martha Ann. Edward is associated with his father and resides in Richmond. Dorothea is the wife of B. F. Edwards, a banker in Oakland, and they have three children, Robert, Benjamin and Dorothea. Ada married Basil L. Spurr, who is associated with Mr. Burg. They have two children, Patricia and Basil, and the family live in Richmond. The others are Cecil, John, Helen, Mary Lillian, Grant Lee, and David. Mr. Burg is intensely interested in the welfare of Richmond, and no other citizen is better qualified to judge of its potential possibilities than he. He believes sincerely in its future and declares that there is no other city on the Coast so ideally situated for industrial plants and transportation facilities, and that there is nothing to obstruct its growth, or to prevent it from becoming one of the greatest cities on the Pacific Coast. Mr. Burg belongs to Durant Lodge of Masons, in Berkeley; Berkeley Commandery; Aahmes Temple, in Oakland; Berkeley Lodge No. 1002, B. P. O. E.; and the Woodmen of the World.

HENRY EDWARD BOLTZEN. — Thoroughness has been the watchword of Henry Edward Boltzen; in whatever he has attempted to do he has labored persistently and untiringly for that success which today places him among the deserving agriculturists of Contra Costa County.

He farms forty acres belonging to Mrs. C. W. Lent, 130 acres belonging to Mott C. Preston, and the E. W. Netherton ranch of forty acres, all lying in the same neighborhood in Precinct No. 2 north of Byron, and all devoted to the growing of alfalfa. He was born on his father's ranch near Bethany, San Joaquin County, August 20, 1892, a son of Henry and Emma Boltzen, both natives of Schleswig-Holstein, Germany. The mother has been dead for twelve years. The father, now sixty years old, has a ranch of 160 acres near Bethany where he is a pioneer farmer.

The education of Henry Edward Boltzen was limited to the grammar school, but by diligent application he has become a well posted man. In 1920 Mr. Boltzen was married to Miss Virginia Lent, born in Oakland, Cal., and they are the parents of three children: Donald Lent, Virginia May and Henry Le Roy. In politics Mr. Boltzen is a Republican and fraternally, is a member of the Woodmen of the World. His wife is a member of the Native Daughters of the Golden West.

ALICE G. WHITBECK.—As librarian of the Martinez Free Library since 1913, Alice G. Whitbeck has filled a most important and really county-wide position in the way of education through good reading as supplementary to the regular school work, and also for those who have done with school days but are still reaching out for more mental work and advancement. A native daughter, Mrs. Whitbeck was born in San Francisco, a descendant of California pioneers on both sides of the family. Her father, William A. Grover, was born in Connecticut, in which state he studied medicine and received his degree as an M. D., before coming around Cape Horn to the Golden State. Arriving in San Francisco in 1849, he was a prominent physician and surgeon there during the pioneer years of the state's history. Much interested in education, he served for many years on the San Francisco board of education; and he was a member of California's first State Board of Medical Examiners. His marriage, in San Francisco, united him with Miss Marietta Osborn, of Sacramento, who also came around the Horn with her father's family.

Alice G. Whitbeck, after finishing her primary education, entered the University of California and graduated with the class of 1887, with her degree of B. L. This training she supplemented with the State Library course, at Albany, N. Y. Her first position was in the Mechanics-Mercantile Library in San Francisco, before the earthquake and fire, where she was assistant cataloguer. She was chosen as children's librarian of the Berkeley Public Library in 1905, and served there until 1910. She founded and started the Richmond Public Library in 1910-1913; and in the latter year she came to Martinez and became county librarian for Contra Costa County, which position she has admirably filled since that date. The library has been built up until it now has ninety-eight distributing points, the headquarters being at Martinez, with a county-wide library service, embracing all but two schools in the county. One of the most important pieces of educational work was done by the librarian in

1924-1925 when she supplied a very carefully selected list of books for general reading in the seventh and eighth grades, which was followed by the giving of certificates, supplied by the superintendent of schools, to the pupils who had read eight books from the assigned lists. During that period 457 such certificates were given out, thus showing the value of such suggestions in connection with the regular school courses, and its realization by the pupils who are endeavoring to gain the best results possible from their years in the schoolroom. Although this reading course entailed the purchase of a great many new books, with the necessary cataloging and extra statistical work, the result was so satisfactory as a whole that there is no doubt as to its worth, and as soon as possible it should be extended to the lower grades.

It is a fortunate county which can have at the head of its library work one so thoroughly in harmony with the spirit of the times; with broad vision, and at the same time competent to look after the detail work necessary to carry plans to a successful culmination. Continuous cooperation has been maintained with the County Farm Home demonstrator in furthering her nutrition projects by supplying books to the different centers on the subject; with the two directors of Citizenship classes by furnishing them with easy texts, pictures and foreign records; with the county nurse by supplying the necessary books on health instruction; with the Boy Scout and Sunshine Camps by sending to the camps books for their use; with the County Federation of Woman's Clubs and the Parent-Teacher organization by having exhibits of books and art pictures; and with every project which can be helped by the public library.

A clear and forceful speaker, Mrs. Whitbeck gives talks on books and reading whenever asked to do so by the different organizations. She stands for progress in library work throughout the county, and her work is much appreciated by the community at large, who recognize her as a woman of high ideals and fine executive ability.

Her marriage, occurring in 1892, united her with James L. Whitbeck, a native of New York State, and a graduate of the University of California, class of 1891. His death occurred in 1908, at Berkeley.

OTTO KRESSE.—Among the many artisans and expert workmen whose knowledge and workmanship contributed to the successful construction of the great steel plant of the Columbia Steel Corporation, at Pittsburg, Cal., none are more worthy of mention than Otto Kresse, superintendent of its open hearth furnaces. Mr. Kresse built and installed the first open hearth furnace for this plant, and is the oldest employee in the operative department.

Otto Kresse was born at Milwaukee, Wis., January 10, 1886, a son of Arnold and Theresa Kresse; his father is deceased, but his mother is still living and resides at Milwaukee, Wis. Otto's boyhood days were spent in Milwaukee, and after finishing his elementary education he attended the Milwaukee University, where he specialized in chemistry and metallurgy, graduating with the Class of 1904. During the next two years he was employed by the Dutcher Steel Casting Company of Milwaukee, following which he accepted a position with the Wellman-Seaver-Morgan Company, of Cleveland, Ohio, during the years of 1906 to 1910. Most of his work with this firm was the installing of steel furnaces in the plants to which the company had sold machinery equipment. Mr. Kresse built furnaces at Menominee, Mich.; Marion, Ohio; Milwaukee, Wis.; and Bucyrus, Ohio.

In September, 1910, Mr. Kresse was sent as the representative of the Wellman-Seaver-Morgan Company to Pittsburg, Cal., for the special purpose of building the first steel furnace at the plant of the Columbia Steel Corporation. It required four months to build the first furnaces and install the necessary equipment. This plant has had a phenomenal growth and has gained a nation-wide reputation for the execution of orders for extra large steel castings. During the World War the officers of the United States Navy and United States Merchant Marine were greatly surprised when they found that the Columbia Steel Corporation's work compared favorably with the best steel foundries of the East. Castings weighing as high as 80,000 pounds have been poured here, and some steel castings as large as 56,000 pounds have been shipped East. Keels were cast for several battleships and merchant vessels, and some of the steel keels were shipped as far East as Newport News and the Brooklyn Navy Yard. Credit is given to Mr. Kresse for his part in the execution of these orders.

On June 5, 1913, Otto Kresse was united in marriage with Miss Maud Minaker, of Pittsburg, Cal., the daughter of George A. Minaker, well-known former constable who served in that capacity for twenty-five years and is now a retired citizen of Pittsburg. This union has been blessed with two children, Georgia Jean and Doris May. Fraternally Mr. Kresse is a member of Pittsburg Lodge No. 429, F. & A. M., and was the first member of this lodge to be made a Master Mason, to which position he was raised in 1912. He has served as treasurer of the city of Pittsburg, first by appointment and afterwards by election for another term, and is an active member of the Pittsburg Chamber of Commerce. Mr. Kresse is a man of high ideals and stands for all movements that make for good citizenship.

EDWARD PETERSON.—The position of yard foreman for the Coos Bay Lumber Company, formerly the C. A. Smith Lumber Company at Bay Point, is one that requires native force and ability, coupled with patience and good judgment. In Edward Peterson the corporation has a valued employee, and in point of years of service with this concern he ranks among the very oldest, having entered the employ of the original company in 1908. To show the responsibility that falls upon the man in this position, we will state that the plant and yards cover 460 acres of ground, 260 acres of which are actually covered with lumber, mainly Douglas Fir and Port Orford Cedar, the latter a high-grade finishing lumber coming from the Coos Bay district in Oregon, in the southwestern part of which State this company owns seventy-five per cent of the standing timber. It is one mile from the dock to the offices of the company.

Edward Peterson was born in Christianstad, Sweden, on January 6, 1867, and was brought up and educated in his native land, serving in the army for two years. His father, Peter Abrahamson, is a farmer and is still living at the age of eighty-two, and his mother is also of that same age. Of the nine children in the family, our subject is the eldest. At the very early age of nine he started working on neighboring farms, doing such work as a child of his years could handle, receiving his board and clothes at first, and later being paid 125 crowns per year. In time he was married in his native land, and there his oldest child, Herman, was born. When the babe was only six months old Mr. Peterson sailed from Malmo, in the latter part of February, for the United States, arriving in March, 1893, with but one dollar to his name, and this a part of the sum he had borrowed to pay his passage. Being only twenty-six years old, and having a sturdy constitution and willing hands, he began work and earned enough to take him to Brainard, Minn., where he had intended becoming a farmer. This was the year of hard times, however, and for three months he could find no work to earn any money and was compelled to work for his board and room. When at last he secured employment he was paid $1.25 per day as a common laborer for the Northern Mills Lumber Company, remaining with them until they went broke, when they paid off their help with due bills. He realized he could not make headway in this manner and struck out for the country and found work on a farm for his board and twenty-six dollars a month. That winter he spent in the lumber woods at eighteen dollars a month and board, and worked from daylight till dark, in Cass County lumber camps. In the summer time he worked in the saw mills, and thus he came to be interested in the lumber and milling business instead of farming. Three years he continued at this employment. Then, having saved enough money to take him back to Sweden, he returned to his native country, where he farmed on rented land three years.

The call of the New World was too strong to be resisted any longer, however, and Mr. Peterson, with his wife and two children (Edwin having been born in the meantime), embarked for New York and landed there in April, 1900, going direct to Brainard, Minn. He took up his old line of work in the lumber industry. In 1908 he went to Potlatch, Idaho, and engaged with the Weyerhouser Lumber Company for two years, passing from one position to another until he was in charge of the sorting shed. There he became acquainted with S. W. Rodgers, who came to Bay Point in 1908. Mr. Rodgers sent for Mr. Peterson and he came out to join him in Bay Point and became his right-hand man. He helped to plan the yards, which cover 260 acres; helped lay the rails; and helped build the wharf, with the two traveling cranes, which now unload as high as 1,500,-000 feet of lumber a day from the ships. Three Fordson tractors and fourteen horses are used in the yards, where some 120,000,000 feet of lumber are handled annually. There are eighty men under his supervision, his chief assistants being Oscar and Axel Anderson. In 1914 a fire destroyed 40,000,000 feet of lumber, tracks, etc., so that our subject has practically rebuilt the entire yards.

After coming to this country, two more children were born to Mr. and Mrs. Peterson: Hilma, and Ida, a stenographer in San Francisco. Mr. Peterson is a member of the Lutheran Church in Bay Point. He helped to build the church and to organize the congregation, he being a deacon in the church. He helped also to organize the First National Bank in Bay Point. Politically, he is a Republican. There is no man in Bay Point in the lumber business better known than is Mr. Peterson, and he has hosts of friends.

MARY A. RIDGWAY.—Among the business women who occupy a position of prominence in the esteem of the citizens of Walnut Creek is Mary A. Ridgway, who since 1908 has been connected with the San Ramon Valley Bank, and since 1919 has occupied the responsible position of assistant cashier. She has also served as city clerk for three terms, and has won a wide popularity for the sterling traits which distinguish her character.

The Ridgway family has been identified with Contra Costa County ever since the seventies, and Mary A. was born at Walnut Creek, a daughter of Frazier and Amelia (Howard) Ridgway, the former a native of Shawneetown, Ill. The mother was born in San Francisco, Cal., and taught school for a number of years in Contra Costa County. Grandfather John Ridgway was also a native of Illinois, while Grandmother Ridgway, whose maiden name was Mary Alexander Posey, was a native of Kentucky. The grandparents on the mother's side were Nathaniel S. and Sarah Elizabeth (Hatch) Howard, both natives of Massachusetts. Nathaniel S. Howard came to California in 1850 via the second clipper ship that came to the Coast, and he landed in San Francisco on January 1 of that year; two years later he sent for his wife, who came via the Panama route. In 1856 the Howard family settled in Green Valley, Contra Costa County, where Nathaniel S. Howard became one of the substantial citizens of the county.

Frazier Ridgway is one of two brothers, and the only one to come to California. He settled in Contra Costa County some fifty years ago. For many years he was secretary for Daniel and Seth Cook, and now makes his home in San Francisco. There are two daughters in this family, Mary A. and Ruth Howard Ridgway, also of Walnut Creek.

Mary A. Ridgway attended grammar school in Walnut Creek, and when ready for high school she entered Mount Diablo Union High School at Concord, remaining until she entered the employ of the San Ramon Valley Bank some eighteen years ago, where as above stated she has held the responsible position of assistant cashier for the past seven years.

CARLETON E. WIGHTMAN.—One of the well-known men of the Oakley district of Contra Costa County, where he is a successful contractor and rancher, is Carleton E. Wightman, better known to his friends as Carl Wightman. He was born at Antioch on August 2, 1880, the oldest son born to Joel D. and Sarah (Snead) Wightman, mentioned at length on another page of this history.

Carleton E. Wightman spent fourteen years of his life in Antioch and there attended the public schools; then with his parents he went to the ranch home consisting of twenty-five acres half a mile west of Oakley, where he now lives. Twenty-two acres of this ranch is planted to olives. In addition to his ranch work, Mr. Wightman has built many buildings and residences in Antioch, Knightsen, Oakley, Brentwood and Byron.

At Brentwood on August 18, 1901, Mr. Wightman was married to Miss Lillian Lindsey, a native of Illinois, but brought up since twelve years of age in the Oakley precinct. Of this union eleven children were born, ten of whom are still living: Helen Minerva, graduate of the University of California hospital and now working at her profession in San Francisco; Joel David, mechanic in the paper mill at Antioch; Maude Lillian, a bookkeeper in San Francisco; Forest Pearl, at home; Frederick William, who died in 1918, aged nine years; and Frances Evelyn, Eugene, Bessie B., Wallace, Ruth Merle, and Barbara Ann. Mr. Wightman is serving as a school trustee for the Oakley school district.

WILLIAM M. McNEIL.—Ever since starting out for himself at twenty-one years of age, William M. McNeil has been a resident of Walnut Creek, where he engages in business as a well-driller and conducts a pump-supply establishment. He is a native of Contra Costa County, born at Lafayette on March 29, 1898, the fourth child in a family of five born to Robert E. and Gertrude (Thomson) McNeil, both natives of California. His great-grandfather, Andrew Allen, brought the first Durham cows to California and Contra Costa County, coming from Missouri, and spent the remainder of his days farming in this section. Robert E. McNeil was in the grocery business in Lafayette for twenty years, and for a time was engaged in farming in that vicinity. There are five children in this family: Stuart C., in the employ of the Standard Oil Company at Walnut Creek; Ruth, now Mrs. P. P. Draper, of Oakland; Alice; William M., our subject; and Bertha, now Mrs. D. D. Dean, of Lafayette.

The education of William M. McNeil was obtained in the grammar school in Lafayette; and at an early age he began helping on the farm and in the store. Since 1919 he has been in business for himself in Walnut Creek, and by hard work and persistency of purpose has met with gratifying success.

At Oakland, Cal., on October 25, 1920, Mr. McNeil was married to Miss Dolly May Neff, a native of Kansas, and a daughter of John Neff; and to them have been born two sons, William Lewis and Richard. Mr. McNeil is a Republican in politics. He is a member of the Lions Club of Walnut Creek.

Sarah J. Pearson

MRS. SARAH J. PEARSON.—A resident of California since 1876, and of Walnut Creek since 1877, Mrs. Sarah J. Pearson has been identified with the business, church and social life of Contra Costa County since that early day. She has wielded an influence for good in the community which is widely recognized and much appreciated by her many friends. Born in Scotter, Lincolnshire, England, she is a daughter of George and Ann (Conyer) Atkinson, both natives of England, where their lives were spent. Of their seven children Sarah J. is the youngest, and she is the only member of the family to come to California. She was reared in England, and received a good education in the public schools in that country.

In 1873 Mrs. Pearson came to the United States. She had a sister Mrs. Harris, residing in Leydan, Cook County, Ill., and came to make her home there, and it was there she met Joseph E. Pearson and was united in marriage with him in 1874. Mr. Pearson was born in Livingston County, N. Y. Though reared as a farmer's boy, he was a graduate from a medical college in Tennessee. During the Civil War he served in an Indiana regiment of cavalry, and after the close of the war he studied medicine, and practiced his profession in the South until coming to Illinois. There he taught school for a time, and in 1876 the young couple came to Bay Point, Contra Costa County, where he also taught for one year. In March, 1877, they located in Walnut Creek, and for two years thereafter Mr. Pearson taught in the local school. In the meantime the people in the community, learning that he was a physician, urged him to take up the practice of medicine. This he did, and his practice grew so rapidly that he was obliged to give up teaching and devote his entire time to his profession. In 1878 he bought two lots in the city, one on a corner, paying only seventy-five dollars each—an interesting item, showing the low value of real estate in those days. He built his residence on one of these lots in 1878, and in 1879 built the drug store. In 1888 Dr. and Mrs. Pearson bought residence property on Telegraph Avenue, Oakland, as an investment, and this she still owns. In 1886 he had the first cement sidewalk in town laid in front of his place of business and home. Dr. Pearson practiced medicine here for twenty years; then his health became impaired and he gave up the practice.

From the time they started the store Mrs. Pearson entered heartily into the management of it, and in 1892 she was registered as a pharmacist, being the first woman pharmacist registered in the county. Since the death of her husband, the pioneer doctor, which occurred in 1898, she has continued to manage the store and to reside in the old home, and in point of years of practice she is the oldest pharmacist in the county. She has been a member and active worker of the St. Paul's Episcopal Church in Walnut Creek ever since its organization and served as its treasurer for over thirty years. A Republican in politics, Mrs. Pearson has always taken an active interest in the upbuilding and advancement of her home community, more especially lending her aid to those movements which make for economic and social betterment. For a hobby and outdoor interest she has made a considerable study of botany and agriculture, and takes great pleasure in her garden. Of talented and cultured personality, Mrs. Pearson can be called a representative of the best type of Contra Costa's pioneer women.

GEORGE ALBERT BROCKHURST.—It is pleasing to note the large number of descendants of those who were attracted to California during the gold rush days of 1849 who are now engaged in the most productive of all occupations—tilling the soil. George A. Brockhurst, a successful and highly respected agriculturist located near Lake Orinda, is one of this number. His father, Henry Brockhurst, was a native of England who became one of the Forty-niners and located in Oakland. From there he went to Napa, where he resided for ten years, after which he removed to Orinda, and here his family was reared. He married Martha Summer, a native of Maine, and they became the parents of eleven children, nine of whom, five boys and four girls, are still living. Their eldest child, Samuel, died at the age of six months. The other children are: Annie, now Mrs. Sparhawk, who resides in Berkeley; William, living in Yonkers; George Albert, the subject of this sketch; Mary Elizabeth, now Mrs. Sundstrom, residing in Pasadena; Charles, who died in infancy; Emma, now Mrs. R. Ehlers, residing in Berkeley; Lottie, Mrs. E. Silva, also in Berkeley; Benjamin, in Walnut Creek; Eddie and James, both in Berkeley.

George Albert Brockhurst was born in Oakland, on Brockhurst Street, January 5, 1871, and received a common school education. He became thoroughly familiar with farming through practical experience on his father's farm, and at the age of thirty-one engaged in ranching on his own responsibility, renting 600 acres devoted to growing hay and feeding cattle. During the World War he raised wheat. In 1917 he became the owner of 200 acres of this same ranch; and now he grows red oats and hay and raises cattle. He has also done some teaming and road contracting. For the past seven years Mr. Brockhurst has been a school trustee. He is one of the most highly esteemed citizens of his vicinity.

George Brockhurst was married on April 26, 1917, to Mrs. Bertha Jorgenson Hansen, of Orinda. She was born in Denmark on a farm, a daughter of Thomas and Boddill (Gibsen) Jorgenson, one of nine children, of whom eight are still living. Seven of the children came to America and settled in San Francisco, but the parents remained in Denmark. Mrs. Brockhurst is the mother of two children by her first husband: James Hansen, aged sixteen, and Bernice Hansen, aged thirteen. Mr. Brockhurst is a fine, clean type of citizen; he does not use tobacco in any form. He is fond of outdoor life, his chief recreation being motoring; he has made a trip to New York City. He owns the family home site and several lots on Lake Orinda.

ALLISON BYER.—To have lived more than half a century in Contra Costa County is the distinction accorded to Allison Byer, the honored pioneer rancher of the Byron-Brentwood section. When but six years of age he accompanied his parents, the late John R. and Elvira (Bogges) Byer, across the plains from Illinois to California in 1863, coming by the covered wagon route. Upon arriving in the Golden State John Byer rented a farm in Yolo County, but owing to the drought of 1864 he removed to Napa County, where during the next two years, the family were nearly drowned out by the excessive rains. In the fall of 1869 they moved to Contra Costa County, where Mr. Byer bought 160 acres on Marsh Creek. During the season of 1870-1871 they experienced another drought which he managed to survive, and he afterwards purchased 160 acres in the Knightsen district and engaged in raising grain. John Byer lived to be eighty-seven years old, and died in 1921, being one of the oldest and most highly honored pioneers in east Contra Costa County; his wife died when sixty-nine years old, the mother of six children, four of whom were born in California.

Allison Byer was born on December 22, 1858, at Girard, Ill., and was six years old when he arrived in California, and ten years of age when his parents settled in the Knightsen district of Contra Costa County. After finishing his school days he rented land and raised grain; later he purchased 200 acres one-half mile north of Byron, and in the nineties moved there. After the death of his father in 1921, and division of his estate between the children, Allison received forty-two acres in Brentwood precinct and the Knightsen Irrigation District, upon which he built a modern house in 1925, where he now resides. Allison Byer sold 110 acres of his ranch to his two sons, Eugene and Virgil. Eugene Byer is mentioned on another page of this work. Virgil built a home on his portion and put ten acres in walnuts and peaches, the remainder is given to the raising of alfalfa.

In 1873 Allison Byer was united in marriage with Ida Plumley, a member of the well-known pioneer family of Byron, and they were the parents of four children: Virgil, Ethel, Eugene, and John R. Mrs. Byer died in 1897. The second marriage of Mr. Byer occurred in 1900 at San Francisco and united him with Mrs. Amanda (Wolf) Myers. Mr. Byer is a man of sterling worth and is held in high esteem throughout the county where he has resided for so many years.

DOMINIC MURCHIO.—For many years the Murchio Ranch has been one of the landmarks of Clayton Precinct in Contra Costa County. Even the casual passerby cannot fail to be impressed by its well-kept appearance and substantial buildings. Its 480 acres are devoted to the raising of hay, grain and stock, and it has been exceptionally productive. Dominic Murchio, progenitor of a large family and a highly respected citizen and neighbor, was the founder of this homestead, which has long

19

been noted for the hospitality of its inhabitants and the cheery social life within its walls. He is now deceased, but the traditions of the old home are still maintained by his widow and sons, who still live there.

Dominic Murchio and his wife, Julia Murchio, who survives him, were both born amid the vine-clad hills of sunny Italy. He was born on July 22, 1849, and his wife on August 15, 1859. They were married in California in 1879 and at once settled in Clayton Precinct. By the exercise of thrift and industry they prospered and became owners of one of the finest ranches of that vicinity. They were the parents of thirteen children, of whom eleven are still living. Two died in infancy. The eleven living are: Albert, who is married and has two children, Jack and Iola, and who lives in Berkeley; John, working for the Shell Oil Company; Joseph, a rancher in Clayton Precinct; Lena, now Mrs. Bouve of Oakland, and the mother of a daughter, Carol; Dolly, wife of Albert Foubert, of Oakland; Dominic, born on July 4, 1888; Louis, of Clayton; Frank, a farmer of Clayton; Azalia, wife of Victor De Martini of Lone Tree, Contra Costa County, who has three children, Donald, May and Victor; George, professional ball player residing at home; and Dewey, also at home. Mr. Murchio died in March, 1916.

Dominic Murchio, Jr., married Mary Garaventa, a native of Contra Costa County. He operates the old home ranch, under lease from his mother, growing hay, grain and cattle as formerly. Joseph Murchio is the owner of a fine farm nearby and, being unmarried, continues to reside at the old home place. The parents were pioneers highly honored by all who knew them, and all members of the Murchio family are highly respected as substantial, industrious and progressive citizens.

MRS. CARRIE L. PALMER. — Among the most worthy and highly esteemed native daughters of Walnut Creek, Cal., is Mrs. Carrie L. Palmer, a woman of strong personality, enterprising and persevering, who has won success in her active career by sheer persistency of purpose. Her father, James M. Stow, was only a small boy of nine years when he came to California from his native State of Illinois. The family settled in the LaFayette district of Contra Costa County, where he grew to young manhood. Later, when he removed to Walnut Creek, he was married to Miss Alice Glass, who was born at Alamo, Contra Costa County. Her parents, Joseph and Harriett (Stone) Glass, crossed the plains to California in 1850. James M. Stow became a prominent factor in the business life of Walnut Creek and Contra Costa County. For many years he held the position of county assessor, and he represented his district as supervisor. He was also postmaster of Walnut Creek, and throughout his entire residence was engaged in the real estate and mercantile business.

Carrie L. Stow attended the grammar school in Walnut Creek and the high school at Martinez. She then took a nurse's training course at the Waldeck Hospital in San Francisco, spending four years there. On October 2, 1905, she was united in marriage with Lewis R. Palmer, a native son of California, born October 29, 1874, at Jackson, Amador County, a son of Eliphalet Charles and Laroka (Turner) Palmer. When Lewis R. Palmer was one year old the family moved to the Reliez Valley, where his father farmed; and later still they moved to San Francisco, where the father conducted a livery business. Lewis R. Palmer received his education at Trinity College, and later studied in Heald's Business College in San Francisco. He then went to Winters, Yolo County, as bookkeeper for Griffith & Hazelrigg. In 1894 he came to Walnut Creek and worked in a warehouse, later engaging in the livery business with his father, and still later with Joel Harlan, to whom he sold out. He is a member of the undertaking firm of Guy, Palmer & Ford, in Concord. With Mr. Ford he bought the old Dias ranch near Walnut Creek. On this ranch they carry on general farming and are also engaged in raising fruit.

Both Mr. and Mrs. Palmer are Republicans. Fraternally, he is a member of Alamo Lodge No. 122, F. & A. M., of Walnut Creek; and Mrs. Palmer belongs to the Eastern Star Chapter of Walnut Creek. Two sons have been born to Mr. and Mrs. Palmer, Whitney Griffith and Harlow Baker.

ROY V. DAVIS.—As the efficient cashier and manager of the Bank of Antioch, Roy V. Davis, has made every effort to serve the people of his community by extending to all worthy projects the assistance of the financial institution of which he is the main guiding spirit, having the close cooperation of his associates in all matters concerning the upbuilding of both bank and community. The Bank of Antioch owns its own building, which is modern in every detail, and it caters to the growing patronage it so well deserves. For the convenience of its patrons there are 200 safety deposit boxes; and there is always someone in authority to lend a helping hand to those seeking information and advice. This bank maintains a branch in Brentwood, and the combined resources are $1,500,000. The slogan of the bank is "Service," and service is rendered to all who ask it. The officers of this institution have ever been ready and willing to encourage all legitimate movements for the upbuilding of eastern Contra Costa County in transactions large or small. The needs of the patrons are studied with the object to better serve them. Ranchers, manufacturers, merchants and builders have felt the influence of this financial institution and its large list of depositors shows the confidence in which it is held in the community. For twelve years Mr. Davis has been closely connected with the Bank of Antioch and during this time he has worked for the interests of bank, county and people to the best of his ability.

W. W. Morgans, Sr., is president; James Gunn, first vice-president; Robert Wallace, Jr., second vice-president; Roy V. Davis, cashier and manager; L. W. Mehaffey, assistant cashier, who with M. B. Veale and George Nunn, make up the board of directors. The Brentwood branch is under the management of Lee Durham.

Mr. Davis was born in Seneca, Mo., and had the advantage of a good education, which he has supplemented with a broad study of finance that has made him one of the best-informed bankers in Northern California, being recognized by the banking fraternity as a dependable and constructive man. The following communication shows the trend of Mr. Davis' constructive service slogan:

"Bank of Antioch
Antioch—Brentwood
To Our Depositors:

"The business of this bank has largely grown through our ability to assist and serve the people of the community. We aim for increased capacity to help in the practical affairs of our patrons—To give them a definite sense of direction—without criticism—To take personal interest in our depositors and friends—To maintain their friendship—To merit their confidence—To give information and—To be increasingly helpful— Is our constant aim.

"Roy V. Davis, Cashier.

"Bank of Personal Service."

Not alone in banking circles is Mr. Davis well known, but as president of the Associated Chambers of Commerce of Contra Costa County has his influence been felt for the good of the entire county. He believes in conducting the Chamber of Commerce as he does the bank, giving personal service and helping in every way to provide helpful information to all who ask it.

Mr. Davis had one of his dreams come to a reality when the Antioch Bridge was completed that joined the Sacramento Valley with Contra Costa County. Defeat did not discourage him; when he failed in one place he sought another angle until the $2,000,000 bridge was started and it was great satisfaction to him when it was formally opened to traffic at one minute after twelve o'clock on January 1, 1926, he being a passenger in the first automobile that officially crossed and recrossed the structure. It is conceded that to Roy V. Davis, more than to any other one man, is due the credit for the building of this wonderful piece of engineering that links the Sacramento Valley with this county and the Bay Cities.

WALTER G. REED.—Highly respected in business circles, and closely identified with church and Sunday school work in Martinez, Walter G. Reed's influence has always been given for the betterment of conditions in Martinez and Contra Costa County. He is the proprietor of a stationery and confectionery store at 724 Main Street, and there carries in the line of supplies a stock of such things as are necessary to the school pupils, office men and merchants of the city, together with a well-stocked candy case with standard makes of sweets.

Mr. Reed was born in Emerson, Ill., on February 19, 1865, the son of Franklin and Elizabeth (Keefer) Reed, who came to Illinois from Pennsylvania and located in Emerson. He is the youngest of the family of six children and is the only one in California. After his school days were over he worked at various employments until 1887, when he made his first trip to California, remaining one year. On account of the ill health of his mother he went back home, where she passed away when she was sixty-two years old. In 1889 Mr. Reed came again to California and worked on a ranch near Winters. Later he bought land and farmed on his own account, developed an orchard, and was engaged in fruit-growing for several years near Winters. In 1901 he came to Martinez, and here he has worked up a fine business in his retail lines, at the same time taking an active interest in social and civic affairs.

At Winters, Mr. Reed and Miss Olive Wilson, also a native of Illinois, were united in marriage in 1895. Mrs. Reed was reared in California and attended the schools of this State. Their fortunate union has been blessed by two children: Howard W., now cashier at Camp Curry, in Yosemite, and Charlotte, a graduate of the University of California and now a teacher in the Martinez High School. Mrs. Reed is a member of the Eastern Star Chapter, and is an able assistant to her husband in his business. He has been superintendent of the Congregational Sunday School for more than fifteen years, and is a pillar of that church. Since establishing himself in Martinez he has built up his trade by careful attention to the wants of his customers, and by always giving a square deal to all.

FRANK RUTHERFORD.—Near Danville, San Ramon Valley, Contra Costa County, lies the fifty-two-acre ranch owned and operated by Frank Rutherford, one of the enterprising and popular ranchers of this section. He is particularly well known as one of the first commercial walnut growers, having planted a large acreage on the Bishop ranch many years ago, all now in full bearing and bringing a substantial profit each season. He was born near Edinburgh, Scotland, on September 13, 1865, and is one of the fourteen children of William and Jessie (Balmer) Rutherford, farmer folk who lived in Scotland, where the father died. The mother came to California and died at Santa Barbara, aged eighty-eight years.

Mr. Rutherford was a young lad when he came to America. He settled in Santa Barbara County and farmed there until 1904, when he came to the Bishop ranch, his present home, in Contra Costa County. In 1919 he purchased his highly improved property here, near Danville. Besides walnuts, there are cherries and prunes on the place. Mr. Rutherford is superintendent of the Bishop ranch consisting of 2680 acres, which he has developed from a grain field and on which he has introduced diversified farming, planting on the place 300 acres to walnuts, 280 acres to pears, fifty acres to vineyard, twenty to prunes and twenty to peaches; moreover, some 400 hogs and 100 cattle are raised on the place annually. The company have their own warehouses for shipping their products.

On April 30, 1892, Mr. Rutherford was married to Miss Susan Grant, born at Aberdeen, Scotland, a daughter of David and Christina (Middleton) Grant, who had six children in their family. The parents came to California in 1892, and died in Santa Barbara, the father in 1902, the mother in 1921. Mr. and Mrs. Rutherford are the parents of six daughters: Daisy B., now Mrs. H. H. Steinmetz, living in San Francisco and mother of one child, George Edward; Florence G., Mrs. Frank Roy, residing in Danville; Christina J., also of Danville; and Frances S., Edith I., and D. Helen, who are at home. Mr. Rutherford is a director in the San Ramon Valley Bank and vice-president of the Walnut Growers' Association of Contra Costa County.

GEORGE LEE.—One of the most highly esteemed citizens of Richmond is George Lee, a financial broker with offices at the corner of Seventh Street and Macdonald Avenue. Mr. Lee was born in England on December 27, 1881, the son of William Lee, a scientist in horticulture, who married Miss Sarah Craddock. George Lee received his education in the English schools and lived in his native country until 1901, when he went to the Hawaiian Islands and for three years was in the employ of the Theo. H. Davies Companies. He came to Richmond in June, 1904, and entered the Bank of Richmond as assistant cashier; he was also one of the directors. In 1915, in association with John H. Nicholl, E. M. Tilden and J. F. Carlston, he came over to Richmond proper and reorganized the Mechanics Bank and put it on a sound basis. Mr. Lee was associated with the bank until the United States entered the World War. He then offered his services to the financial department of the Young Men's Christian Association and took his training at Stanford during August and September; but while at Ft. Barry, waiting for passports, the armistice was signed, and he returned home. Mr. Lee then established his present office in December, 1918, and acts for the John Nicholl Company in an advisory capacity. He has had a rapid increase in his investment business and is an especial friend of the foreign element in Richmond, many of whom seek his advice in business matters. Mr. Lee is proud to say that he has never lost a dollar for one of his clients. At the time of the building of the city hall he was given custody of the funds.

Mr. Lee was united in marriage on August 2, 1911, with Miss Louise Stairley, daughter of Waverley Stairley, founder of the first bank in Richmond and former postmaster of the city. She is related to Gen. Robert E. Lee, and to Senator Bankhead, of Alabama. They have a daughter, Virginia Lee, a student in the Richmond High School. Mr. Lee is a charter member of the Kiwanis Club and a member of Richmond Lodge No. 1251, B. P. O. E., and the Chamber of Commerce. He owns considerable property in Richmond and vicinity and has great faith in the future of the city. A conservative investor, he has confidence in what he undertakes and inspires confidence in those who seek his advice. He takes an active interest in civic affairs and believes in progression, and to such men as George Lee the community's interests can be safely entrusted.

Patrick Formey

PATRICK TORMEY.—Patrick Tormey, whose death occurred on May 7, 1907, was one of Contra Costa County's leading men, having efficiently and faithfully served the county as supervisor for thirty years, and was one of its large landowners, a rancher and stockman. He was born in Westmeath, Ireland, in the month of March, 1840, the son of Patrick and Mary (Rooney) Tormey; and he was reared and lived in Ireland until September, 1858, in which year, after completing three years of academic training, he sailed with three sisters and a brother, from Galway to the United States. Arriving in New York on September 29 of that year, he remained in that city only a short time, and on the 7th of October, in company with Hon. D. N. Sherburne, of Syracuse Valley, sailed for the Isthmus of Panama in the steamer St. Louis. From the Isthmus the journey to San Francisco was continued on the Louisa, which landed on the last day of October, 1858.

Arrived in California, Mr. Tormey at once joined his brother, John Tormey, at Suscoe, in Napa County, and there engaged in ranching for a year. In the fall of 1859 he moved to Stockton and for six months was employed in the California Flour Mills at that place, after which he came to Contra Costa County and for eighteen months was engaged in herding cattle for his brother on the Pinole Rancho. In June, 1861, he drove stock to Nevada. Returning at the end of four months, he leased a portion of the ranch which he later purchased, and here he engaged in agricultural pursuits for two years. At the end of that period he went to Sonoma County, and there for four years he ran the Adobe Ranch, near Petaluma.

Returning to Contra Costa County, together with his brother John, Mr. Tormey purchased 7000 acres, a portion of the Pinole Grant comprising the interests of Mesdames Estudillo, Merle, Berryessa, and Richardson, and a third share of the interest of Mrs. Castro. This property had a three-mile frontage on San Pablo Bay, and on it is located Tormey Station, originally on the line of the San Pablo and Tulare Railroad, later the Central Pacific, and now the Southern Pacific Railway. The lands advanced in value, and while carrying on the ranch work, Mr. Tormey built a fine residence and ranch buildings and made many improvements. The Union Oil gas refinery at Oleum is now located on a portion of this land, Mr. Tormey having sold that portion to a lumber company, which in turn sold to the Union Oil Company for a refinery.

In the fall of 1877, Patrick Tormey was elected to a place on the board of supervisors, the office having been made vacant by the death of his brother John, who had held it for nine years previously. Patrick Tormey was repeatedly reelected and held the office some thirty years, until his death. He was a most faithful and efficient public servant, and to know him was to appreciate his manly worth.

Mr. Tormey's marriage, which occurred in May, 1875, united him with Miss Mary Matthews, a native of Boston, Mass., and eight children blessed their union; John P., who died in 1924; Leo. F., a leading attorney at Martinez; Mary; Louis, deceased; and Clement, Ruth, Linus, and Verda, the latter a graduate of the Dominican College at San Rafael. The other sisters are graduates of the College of the Holy Name, at Oakland; while the brothers are graduates of St. Mary's College of that city. The good wife and mother died on March 21, 1906, having reached fifty-six years of age. She was a highly respected and much loved woman. This worthy couple may be called representative of California's pioneer men and women. Patrick Tormey more than did his share in building up his part of the Golden State, devoting his time unsparingly to his duties as a public officer; and Mary Tormey proved herself a capable helpmate, rearing a large family to carry on the work begun by their forebears, and carrying her share of the burden with the spirit which has made our pioneer women famous throughout the country.

JAMES DUNBAR KEITH.—The manager of the personnel department of the California and Hawaiian Sugar Refining Corporation at Crockett, "Jimmie" Keith, as he is familiarly known to his friends, is a native son, born in Oakland on December 4, 1887. His father, Samuel F. Keith, is also a native son, having been born in San Francisco. He married Lillie Bovee, who was born in Grass Valley, Nevada County, and is a representative of another pioneer family in California. James Bovee, her father, is mentioned in the story "The Gray Dawn" by Frank Norris and his picture hangs in the Golden Gate Park museum in San Francisco.

It was with this background that J. D. Keith was reared. He went to the public schools in San Francisco and did much the same as other boys of his time. He took a special course to fit himself for such work as he might find to do when he was through with his studies. As office boy he entered the employ of the California and Hawaiian Sugar Refining Company, kept the stock records, was assistant purchasing agent, accountant, manager of the insurance department, in fact was instrumental in organizing this department and was the first manager of same. After working his way through these various positions his ability and fidelity were rewarded by his appointment to his present position of trust and much responsibility. In fact Mr. Keith is a busy man with an enormous amount of detail to look after, but he accomplishes his tasks with a smile and enjoys his work. He came to live in Crockett in July, 1924.

Mr. Keith has made a special study of his department and it falls to his lot to look after housing conditions for employees, whereby the company investigates the man and sells him a home on suitable terms. Employment and fitting the man to his job is another duty entrusted to Mr. Keith and in this way the company obtains the best results from the labor and at the same time compensates its employees adequately. Administration of plant safety and health, employees' disability and death benefits and the C. and H. Employees' Mutual Benefit Association with its provision which pays two-thirds of normal earnings while the employee is disabled, fall under his supervision. It is the human interest that appeals to Mr.

Keith and by which he gets such excellent results. Other duties of his involve oversight of clubs for men and women, the nursery from which plants are distributed to the people for beautifying lawns, parkings, etc.; contact with churches, schools, clubs; educational work inside and outside of the plant in conjunction with the public schools; part time school to fit the employee, evening classes to train the employee the better to serve the company; and the technical library in the plant. One of the most important things which Mr. Rolph considers of benefit to the company is the hospitality program, which includes entertainment of guests and students who visit the plant, for which highly trained guides are supplied to answer all questions propounded. The Camp Fire Girls, Bluebirds, Boy Scouts, and Wolf Cubs, gardeners to maintain and develop the parks and playgrounds, are all maintained for the benefit of the young and others by the company. All this and many other lines of activity in and out of the plant come under Keith's watchful eye and he performs his duties with satisfaction to all.

On September 19, 1922, James D. Keith was married to Miss Fern E. Myers, born in Stillwater, Okla., daughter of Alonzo Myers, who married Stella Boatman. They have two daughters, Virginia and Carol Jean, and a son, Earl Douglas.

CHARLES J. RICHARDS.—A veteran employee of the Selby Smelter, Charley Richards, as he is familiarly known by his many friends, is one of the reliable men in the employ of the Selby Company and is general foreman of the ore room. In addition to his work at the smelter he has rendered good service to his community, especially in the line of maintaining good public schools, serving as trustee of the Selby Grammar School for more than thirty years, and is now clerk of the board; also for the past seven years he has been a member of the board of trustees of the John Swett Union High School. In many other ways he has served for the public good. He was born in England, on January 16, 1868, the son of Albert and Sarah (Morse) Richards. The elder Richards was a glove maker and always made his home in England. There are still a brother, Arthur, and a sister, Louise, living in England.

The public schools of England gave Mr. Richards his early education. In 1885 he landed in San Francisco and with William G. Davis came to Selby and secured a job. He began as a laborer and shoveled coal, then was promoted to be an electrical helper, next was made foreman of the ore-sampling department, in all having been in the employ of the company forty-one years.

Mr. Richards was married on February 6, 1895, to Miss Agnes McDonald of San Francisco. He belongs to the Knights of Columbus, Independent Order of Foresters and the Eagles. His politics are in accord with Democratic policies but he tries not to be narrow. He is heartily interested in the development of this region and during his long residence here has done his part to bring it to its present condition.

FRED ULYSSES NORTON.—The Norton family, of British ancestry on both sides, has been identified with American soil since the first days of the Revolutionary War, and are well known on the Atlantic coast, especially in New England. A genealogy of the family, making up a large volume, was published some years ago. Like most old New England families, they were mostly seafaring men in the early days, though in later years finding different occupations: some being of strong artistic tendencies, others devoting their lives as ministers of the Gospel, but all having strong convictions and carrying the family name untarnished through the succeeding generations.

Fred Ulysses Norton was born on July 27, 1863, in Falmouth, Maine, a son of Randall and Vienna (Branscomb) Norton, both natives of Maine, as were all the Nortons for several generations back to Great-grandfather Ichabod Norton, who was an ancestor of Lillian Nordica, the great American opera star, whose real name was Lillian Norton. Of Scotch-Irish blood, the Nortons became one of the leading families in the Pine Tree State, all strictly Protestant in faith and sturdy pioneers. Grandfather Rev. Lemuel C. Norton was a sea captain before he became a Methodist Episcopal minister, and it was he who established the first State hospital for the insane in Maine. Randall Norton, father of our subject, was also a sea captain; on one of his voyages to Savannah, Ga., he contracted the yellow fever, from which sickness he died at the age of forty years. His wife, Vienna (Branscomb) Norton, was of English ancestry, her grandfather having been brought to America as an English soldier in the Revolutionary War; but he favored the Revolutionists and, deserting the English ranks, joined the American army. After the close of the war he settled upon Mt. Desert Island, Maine, and became a seafaring man.

Just nine years old at the time of his father's death from yellow fever, Fred Ulysses Norton was the sixth child and a twin in a family of seven born to his parents, six boys and one girl, of whom the sister and three brothers are living. He completed the common schools, and had passed the examination for admission to the high school when, at fourteen years of age, he went to sea as a sailor before the mast on the brig Ernestine, of which his brother, Edmund Randall Norton, was captain. He sailed to the West Indies, Malagas, Santiago, and to Havana, for cargoes of sugar and molasses, and continued to follow the sea for six years, the last voyage being to the Rio de la Plata, in South America. On leaving the sea, he put in one year as clerk for his brother-in-law, William E. Wilson, in his general store at Cumberland Center, Maine; and with him he came to Los Angeles, Cal., in 1889. After his arrival there he worked on ranches for two years, and then for the following five years ran a butcher shop in Los Angeles. He next went to work in a brickyard for several years, most of his time being spent in construction and carpenter work incident to a large brickyard, installing machinery and so forth. On January 1,

1906, he came to Port Costa to take a similar position with the Port Costa Brick Company, and has worked as a general mechanic and carpenter with that concern almost continuously ever since.

The marriage of Mr. Norton, occurring in Los Angeles, on November 19, 1891, united him with Miss Mary Leuzinger, a native of Abilene, Kans., and daughter of John and Verena (Durst) Leuzinger, the parents both being natives of the same canton in Switzerland and of Swiss-German blood. They came to the United States and settled in Abilene, Kans., in 1863, and there John Leuzinger became a farmer, owning 240 acres of land, 160 acres of which they homesteaded. Eight children were born to John and Verena Leuzinger, four in Switzerland and four in Kansas, Mrs. Norton being the fifth child in order of birth and the first one born in America. She was reared in Kansas until thirteen years old, and then came with the rest of the family to Los Angeles in 1883, and in 1891 her marriage occurred. Eight children have blessed their union: Ralph, with the Associated Oil Company at Port Costa; Everett, with the same concern; Wallace, salesman for the California Clay Products Company in Los Angeles; John, who died when nine years old; Edward, attending the Polytechnic Engineering College in Oakland; Esther; John, and Marion, a graduate of the John Swett Union High School at Crockett and now attending the University of California at Berkeley. Mrs. Norton has always done her share in helping out the family fortunes, in addition to raising her large family; for years she had charge of the cook house for the Port Costa Brick Works, and has cooked for as many as twenty men, besides her family. Her youngest brother, who settled in Los Angeles, is the Rev. John A. Leuzinger, assistant pastor of the Emanuel Presbyterian Church of that city. Both Mr. and Mrs. Norton are Democrats in politics. Mr. Norton belongs to Tent No. 2, K. O. T. M., in Los Angeles.

O. PETER OLSEN.—One of the successful contractors and builders of Contra Costa County is O. Peter Olsen, who is aiding materially in the growth of Martinez and surrounding territory. A native of Denmark, he was born April 20, 1878, the son of O. Nilsen and Kjerstine Olsen. The father was a dairyman and farmer in the old country. Both parents are now deceased, and of their family of three boys and four girls only four are still living, O. Peter being the only son left to bear the family name.

Receiving a very thorough education in his native land, Mr. Olsen attended both the high and polytechnic schools there, and also was brought up and confirmed in the Lutheran Church, which is considered a part of the education of children in that country and undoubtedly has much to do with the sturdy character of the race. On finishing his schooling, for the following four years he served an apprenticeship in the carpenter's trade in Denmark, during which time he also studied drafting and architecture.

One of his brothers, Christian Olsen, came to the United States in 1882, and became a farmer in Iowa, where he carried on agricultural work for thirty-five years before his death occurred. His success inspired his younger brother to seek the newer country for greater opportunities than were offered in his home land, and O. Peter Olsen sailed from Esbjerg, Denmark, to England, and from Liverpool took passage on the liner Lucania, landing in New York in March, 1905. His first move was to visit his brother in Iowa, and from there he went to Sioux City, that State, and there worked at his trade in 1905-1906. After this he went to Chicago and there continued the same work for nine months. In the fall of 1906 he came to the West Coast, and for the following nine months did carpenter and building work, helping in the rebuilding of San Francisco after the disastrous earthquake and fire of April, 1906. In the spring of the following year he moved to Seattle, Wash., and worked on the Exposition buildings there for a short time. He then went to Dagmar, in what is now Sheridan County, Mont., and for the following six years continued at carpentry in that locality, and while there proved up on a homestead. Returning in the fall of 1914 to San Francisco, he worked on the buildings for the Panama-Pacific International Exposition for one year.

In October, 1915, Mr. Olsen came to Martinez, and since that date he has followed contracting and building for himself, and has met with deserved success. Among the buildings to his credit here are the Christian Science Church, the Women's Club building, and the J. H. Wells residence. In 1920 he purchased a thirteen-acre tract one mile southeast of Martinez, formerly known as the De Lacy tract, which he is subdividing and building up, having already built and sold seven houses at the date of this writing. This subdivision, which is on the Pacheco Road, is a distinct addition to the city and county, and Mr. Olsen deserves great credit for his foresight and faith in the present and future growth of Martinez and Contra Costa County.

The marriage of Mr. Olsen, which occurred at Medicine Lake, Mont., on April 2, 1912, united him with Miss Christine Mortensen, also a native of Denmark, though she has spent practically her entire life in this country, as she was brought here by her parents, Mr. and Mrs. L. C. Mortensen, when only three years old. One child has been born to Mr. and Mrs. Olsen, a son, Everett Lawrence. The family reside in Rose Cottage, a part of their new subdivision. An excellent mechanic and a man of sound business intelligence, Mr. Olsen is energetic and progressive in his work and ideas, and believes in building for the future. He became naturalized as an American citizen in Glasgow, Mont., in the fall of 1912 and in politics he is non-partisan, giving his support to the men and measures he deems most favorable to the general good. He belongs to the Martinez Chamber of Commerce.

REV. EDWARD G. McMULLAN, O. P.—St. Peter's Catholic Church, of Pittsburg, Cal., is especially fortunate in having as its pastor such an able minister and devout disciple of Christ as Father E. G. Mc-Mullan. He was born in San Francisco on March 30, 1886, and as a boy attended St. Patrick's School in his native city. Afterwards he became a student at St. Patrick's Seminary, at Menlo Park., Cal., where he completed the studies of the academic department, which included two and one-half years study of philosophy and theology. To further advance his education in preparation for his life work he entered the Dominican House of Studies, Washington, D. C., graduating with the Class of 1917, and was ordained on May 17, 1917. Father McMullan has a vigorous mentality and well-trained mind. He is eloquent in the pulpit, and his theological and scholastic attainments are of an unusually high order, in keeping with the educational advantages provided by the Church.

His first assignment was as assistant to the pastor of St. Vincent's Parish at Vallejo, Cal., where he served for three years. From Vallejo he was appointed assistant pastor of St. Dominick's Church in San Francisco, where he remained three years, afterwards assuming the pastorate of St. Dominick's Church, Eagle Rock, Los Angeles, for one year. With each succeeding pastorate he gained valuable experience and increased in spiritual power, which fitted him for larger responsiblities and tasks in the work of the Church and the salvation of souls.

In August, 1924, Father McMullan was called to the pastorate of St. Peter's Catholic Church at Pittsburg, Cal., which is a very large and strong congregation. The parish of St. Peter's comprises approximately sixty-five per cent of Pittsburg's 7000 population, giving an estimated membership of over 4500. In the great work of this parish he is ably assisted by the Holy Family Sisters from San Francisco, who come to Pittsburg twice a week to teach the catechism.

Father McMullan is wielding an inestimable influence for righteousness by his exemplary daily life before his parishioners, perpetuating in the minds of young and old the precepts and principles of Jesus. To administer to the spiritual, mental and material welfare of 4500 people is no small matter, and requires the grace of a strong Christian character—a character like that of Father McMullan, whom all delight to honor.

JUDGE WADE W. MOORE.—The present incumbent of the office of justice of the peace for township No. 6, Contra Costa County, is Attorney Wade W. Moore, of Pittsburg. Judge Moore has an enviable reputation for sterling character; and being well versed in legal lore, his decisions are wise and just and he possesses the ability to inspire his clients with the greatest confidence in his judgment. He was born at Paris, Stark County, Ohio, on October 26, 1889, the son of Albert and Rosella (Jackson) Moore. The father was a native of Pennsylvania; the mother was born at Cincinnati, Ohio. Seven children were born of this union, six of whom are still living. The father, Albert Moore, was a veteran oil driller, having conducted operations in many States and lands, including Peru, Brazil, Siberia, Canada, Mexico, and in the Eastern and Mid-Western States. The family formerly resided in Ashtabula, Girard and Hubbard, Ohio, but in 1904 migrated to San Francisco, Cal.

Wade W. Moore, the youngest boy of the family, attended high school in San Francisco and was graduated from the Wilmerding High School in the Class of 1908. Possessed of an aptitude for learning and a natural penchant for legal lore, he became a student of the San Francisco Law School and after a four-year course was graduated with the Class of 1916. While a law student he was employed by Jordan, Rowe, & Brand. He was admitted to the Bar in 1917 and began his practice in San Francisco. On April 2, 1918, he became a resident of Pittsburg, and opened an office for the practice of his chosen profession; and in November, 1922, he was elected for a term of four years to the office of justice of the peace for Township No. 6, Contra Costa County. Judge Moore is an active and enterprising citizen of Pittsburg, foremost in supporting every worthy movement which has as its aim the advancement of the civic, moral, and commercial interests of the county and community. He is a member of the Chamber of Commerce of Pittsburg, was one of the organizers of the First National Bank of Pittsburg, and is now a director of this bank as well as a director of the First National Bank of Bay Point.

The marriage of Wade W. Moore was solemnized at San Francisco, on October 23, 1919, when he was united with Miss Amy Jann, a native daughter of California. Fraternally Mr. Moore is a member of Pittsburg Lodge No. 429, F. & A. M., and is a charter member of Pittsburg Lodge No. 1474, B. P. O. E. Politically, he is a Republican in national affairs. His legal practice extends to the State and Federal courts.

ARTHUR CLIFFORD FOOTE.—In 1925 Arthur Clifford Foote established the Richmond Auto Wrecking Company, which is now located at San Pablo Avenue and Alameda Streets, El Cerrito, and which since the day of its inception has gradually been expanding. He was born in Rives Junction, Mich., a son of Wallace Henry and Aetna A. (Green) Foote, the father a well-known and successful real estate man in Iowa. When a small child our subject was taken to Emmet County, Iowa, where he grew up and attended school. The other members of the family are: Grace, Mrs. J. A. Cain; Wallace Clyde, in Los Angeles; and Claire Idell, the youngest son.

After completing his education at the high school Arthur Clifford Foote began his career as an express messenger and gradually worked his way into the hardware business. He went to Wilbur, Wash., where he was connected with Hay Brothers for four years. Next he was with the Holly-Mason Hardware Company in Spokane for five years. In 1912 he came to San Francisco and went to work in the Southern Pacific yards,

after which he spent five years in the employ of the Santa Fe in train service, continuing until 1925, when he embarked in his present enterprise. He still holds his membership in the Brotherhood of Railway Trainmen.

In 1912 Mr. Foote was married to Miss Georgie Jeanette Zims, of San Francisco, in which city her father was connected with the Stock Exchange. The family home is located at 2022 Burbeck Avenue, Richmond. Mr. Foote tries at all times to do his duty as a citizen, and shows his public spirit in many ways. He has many friends.

BERNHARD SCHAPIRO.—It is probable that there is no other one man living today who has contributed as much toward the growth of Richmond and surrounding territory as has Bernhard Schapiro, the well-known and popular real estate operator of that city. Mr. Schapiro's dealings have always conformed to the highest ethical standards of his calling, and he has been a city and home builder in the truest sense. The honor and esteem in which he is held in his community are conclusive evidence of the upright character of his transactions and his success has been entirely due to his extraordinary foresight, business integrity, and constructive aggressiveness. He was born in Prussia on January 11, 1865, the son of Elias Schapiro, a grain merchant and a native of Prussia who never came to America. The mother was Johanna Wakawsky, also of Prussia, and there were seven children in the family, four of whom died early in life. One brother, George, had a son Maurice, whom Bernhard Schapiro brought to America; he later became one of the leading music composers and publishers of New York, the compositions issued by Schapiro & Company being popular among musicians all over the country.

Mr. Schapiro received his early education in the schools of his native country. Leaving home at the age of thirteen, he became an apprentice in a mercantile establishment of Eastern Prussia, remaining there for four years. From there he went to the manufacturing town of Lodz in Poland, a short distance from Warsaw. In 1886, at the age of twenty-one, he came to the United States, landing in Philadelphia, where he secured employment at four dollars per week and remained there for about a year. His next experience was had in the tobacco fields of Pennsylvania. He traveled for a while through the Southern States selling cigars, which he declares were as good as the ten-cent ones of the present day, for $10 per thousand—which would now sell for at least $60 per thousand. His home in Pennsylvania was among the "Pennsylvania Dutch," and he remembers them with much affection, and with appreciation for their teachings and for the training which they gave him. He became associated with the local minister, who taught him the spirit and ideals of Americanism, thus influencing his entire life. Finally he quit cigar-selling and went to Chicago, where he met an European oculist who traveled from Chicago to San Francisco, and he accompanied him as an assistant until 1893, when they settled in San Francisco and opened a small optical store. In connection with this Mr. Schapiro conducted a sheet music store, distributing the publications of his nephew, who had attained a notable success in the music world. In 1901 he came to the site of the present city of Richmond and engaged in the real estate business with McEwen Brothers, one of the very first subdividers of Richmond property. He remained with this concern one year, and then started in business on his own responsibility, forming a partnership with George Henley, the firm being known as Schapiro & Henley. Mr. Schapiro maintained an office in San Francisco and Mr. Henley had an office at Point Richmond, there being no town known as Richmond at that time. Mr. Schapiro erected the second building located on Macdonald avenue.

Then a most remarkable change took place. An auditor of the Standard Oil Company, a Mr. Gow, and associates, purchased twenty acres of land between Fifth and Sixth Streets. Mr. Schapiro was selected as general agent for this tract, which was known as the Richmond Park Tract. At that time the present city, from Ohio Street northward, was a ranch; the Santa Fe had its station at The Point, then called East Yard. In 1903 Mr. Schapiro formed the San Pablo Land Company, which subdivided fifty acres; then he organized the Queen Land Company and subdivided the Sampson ranch land, then considered only a waste covered with morning glory plants. Joseph Grondana, a marketman in Oakland, paid $24,000 for sixty acres; and this he still owns, it being one of the richest garden plots in this section. It was about this time that Mr. Schapiro became associated with John Boquet, an old settler here. The next move was to buy the San Pablo Villa Tract of forty acres. In this he was associated with Messrs. Rheem and Dimm, and other men connected with the Standard Oil Company. Colonel Rheem built a street car line along Twenty-third Street out to this tract, which made the property more valuable. Mr. Schapiro next secured the Alvarado Tract, named in honor of H. V. Alvarado; and the next was the Schapiro Central Tract, lying to the south of the Alvarado property, and also on the car line. During this period he formed the East Richmond Land Company, Mr. Schapiro being the one who named the East Richmond section of the city. The purchase at that time was 1400 acres, extending from a line joining Mira Vista on the south and San Pablo Avenue, to the undivided property on top of the hill, thence north and east to McMahon's dairy. Again the street car line was extended to the entrance of Alvarado Park. In the meantime the 1400 acres had been subdivided, 400 acres into home lots and 1000 acres, together with 250 acres that had been added, for villa sites or acreage holdings; and the city bought forty-two acres for Alvarado Park, this being an idea conceived by Mr. Schapiro before his company bought the property.

In 1911 East Richmond was well established, and Mr. Schapiro made a trip to Europe. Upon his return he secured 450 acres, 100 acres on the south being set aside for a restricted section now known as Mira

Vista. The East Richmond Heights Land Company (out of the 1400-acre deal) was formed, and it bought 125 acres extending from the Mira Vista line to Clinton Street, and this was subdivided into lots and villa sites. The company also bought 400 acres east of Mira Vista, near the Country Club property, and 500 unsold lots in Mira Vista.

In Martinez Mr. Schapiro bought 250 acres now known as the Mountain View Addition and built some 200 houses; and there are 400 families residing in this tract at this time. In developing this tract he was assisted by R. R. Veale and J. E. Rodgers. He also bought 5000 acres in the Sacramento Valley. This tract is now known as the Richfield Colony, and consists of twenty- and forty-acre farms. His associate in this deal was Louis Titus, former president of the People's Water Company. His next venture was 5000 acres near Tracy, now known as Tracy Garden Farms.

The outbreak of the World War caused a cessation of land buying, and all of these various companies became consolidated under the name of the Contra Costa Realty Company. In 1919 Mr. Schapiro organized the Bay City Home Builders Company and immediately began erecting houses in Mira Vista, and he is continuing active operations and making one of the finest residential districts in the East Bay district. He is president and manager of the Contra Costa Realty Company and also of the Bay Cities Home Builders. He also heads the Western Home Builders, for the construction of larger business houses, etc., and B. Schapiro & Company is an organization which handles the business interests of a number of concerns, as well as for B. Schapiro personally.

On November 3, 1895, Mr. Schapiro was married to Miss Birdie Stern of San Francisco, daughter of A. Stern, a jeweler, and Sarah Stern. Both mother and father are now deceased. Children born from this union are: Esmond, a graduate of the University of California and now an attorney of San Francisco, associated with Jones & Doll; Zara, who attended the University of California and is now the wife of L. H. Shapiro, a successful San Francisco attorney; and Dorothea Schapiro, at home.

Mr. Schapiro is a member of the Chamber of Commerce, the Union League in San Francisco, and the Commonwealth and Press Clubs. He was also a charter member of the Berkeley Country Club, but no longer holds membership. Fraternally, he is a Scottish Rite Mason and a Shriner, and a member of the Elks. He is fond of hunting, fishing and swimming, and of other outdoor sports.

AUGUST FRED RIEMKE.—No citizen of Crockett has taken a more active and intelligent interest in building up an adequate fire department for the protection of the property of its people than has August Fred Riemke, one of the trusted employees at the sugar refinery. He was born in Germany on August 15, 1877, the son of Herman and Minnie Riemke. His father was killed in a railroad accident, and in 1879 Mrs.

Riemke brought her son to America. They landed in New York and there our subject attended the public schools and grew to manhood. He went to work at an early age, to buy his own clothes and to assist his mother, in Arbuckle Brothers sugar refinery and continued there in various capacities until 1906. Coming that year to Crockett, Mr. Riemke entered the refinery as a sugar boiler, became head of the department and later apparatus inspector.

In 1907 he became connected with the fire department and served four years as chief of the Crockett Fire Department. During these years many changes were made, from a Ford truck to a modern La France engine costing $12,500; eight-inch water mains with six-inch hydrants installed; remodeling of the firehouse by popular subscription at cost of $700. Mr. Riemke worked with the Improvement Club for street lighting and street signs, and in getting a permanent place for the fire apparatus by the fire commissioners from the Salvation Army. This move was begun about eight years ago.

On January 3, 1905, Mr. Riemke and Miss Grace Virginia Gamble, of Brooklyn, N. Y., were united in marriage. She is the daughter of Henry Elder and Jennie (Allan) Gamble, the latter of Scotch descent. Her father was a newspaper man employed on the New York Tribune; he died in 1893 at the age of thirty-two. She has a brother who is in the recorder's office in Brooklyn. Five children have been born to Mr. and Mrs. Riemke; Grace Wilma, employed in the office of the C. & H.; Alice Genevieve, in the high school; Hazel Margaret, also in high school; Anna Florence and Allan Fred, in grammar school. Mr. Riemke belongs to the Odd Fellows and Knights of Pythias, in which he has held offices. He owns his own home and is satisfied with life in general. The family are held in high esteem by their neighbors and friends.

DAVID RAMPOLDI.—A leading business man and honorable citizen of Martinez, David Rampoldi owns some very valuable city property in the city of his adoption. A native of Italy, he was born in Genoa, on March 17, 1866, a son of Louis and Mary (Pezzolo) Rampoldi. Louis Rampoldi was a blacksmith by trade. In 1866 he came to America because of the better wages offered here to men of his ability. Landing in San Francisco he went from there to the mines in Amador and Tuolumne Counties, where he acquired some valuable mining claims. He had left his wife and children in Italy, and while he was away his wife died, when our subject was eleven years old, and the lad was reared thenceforth by his grandmother Pezzolo and an older brother. He attended the schools of his native city, making good use of the advantages offered him, and when he was old enough he made up his mind that he would seek his fortune in the United States. Bidding good-bye to friends and relatives, young Rampoldi embarked for the New World from Havre, France, and landed in New York City on March 21, 1886. He was headed for California, where his uncle, Peter Rampoldi, was running a market garden at Pacheco. Upon his arrival, however, he went to work in Bertola's winery and remained there for seven years, and later worked in Raffeto's Vegetable Gardens for six years. Saving what he could from his earnings, he was enabled to buy a tract of land near Martinez well suited for market gardening, and he threw himself into making the most of his purchase by hard and persistent effort. Continuing along these lines, he laid the foundation for his present prosperity and financial position. In 1916 he started in the grocery business at 500 Main Street, in his own building, dealing in staple, fancy, domestic and imported groceries; and here he has built up a large patronage by his honest dealings, by giving every one of his customers a square deal and courteous attention.

In 1901 Mr. Rampoldi made a trip back to Italy and was there married to Mary De Benedetti, and they returned to his home in Martinez. They had three sons: Louis, Henry and John. The wife and mother died of the flu at the age of thirty-five, mourned by all who knew her. The two oldest boys are proprietors of Rampoldi's Confectionery, also located at 500 Main Street, and are doing a good business. Mr. Rampoldi became a citizen of the United States in 1890, and is a Republican. He owns valuable residence and business property, and is a stockholder in the First National Bank of Martinez.

THOMAS J. PATTERSON.—The efficient superintendent of the steel foundry of the Columbia Steel Corporation at Pittsburg is Thomas J. Patterson, known to his intimates as "Tom" Patterson. He has been connected with this great corporation's plant since 1912, coming here on January 12 of that year to take the position of foreman of the store-keeping room under the superintendent of the foundry. So well did he acquit himself in the performance of his duties that in 1916 he was promoted to the superintendency of the foundry and has since held that responsible position. During the World War this corporation filled some of their largest contracts, and the foundry handled the largest castings ever poured getting out one set of upper and lower rudders for the United States Merchant Marine per day for the United States Shipping Board, which were sent to the various ship-building plants on the West Coast; also some castings for battleships that were sent to Norfolk, Va., and to the Brooklyn Navy Yards, and that weighed approximately thirty tons. All of this was done under the personal supervision of Tom Patterson.

Tom Patterson was born in Eldred, McKean County, Pa., on June 12, 1879, a son of Thomas Dan and Josephine (Dritzel) Patterson. The father was formerly a painter and decorator, but later in life worked in the oil fields of Pennsylvania, and is now boss painter at the Columbia Steel Corporation's plant in Pittsburg and active for his years. The mother of our subject died when he was but five years old. Tom attended the public schools in McKean County and served an apprenticeship to the blacksmith's trade. In January, 1903, he went to Depew, N. Y., and worked at the foundry business as a common laborer, remaining there until

1912, during which time he rose to the position of foreman in the finishing department. He had 538 men under him. While there he was a co-laborer with Mr. Botsford, now managing director of the Columbia Steel Corporation, and it was through the influence of Mr. Botsford that Mr. Patterson came to Pittsburg.

Mr. Patterson was married at Depew, N. Y., May 16, 1907, to Miss Emma Liskoff, a native of New York State, and they have had four children: Beatrice Louise, a student in the State Teachers' College in San Francisco; Thomas J. Jr., in the Pittsburg High School; D. Herbert; and Jack Albert. Mr. Patterson is a member of Pittsburg Lodge No. 429, F. & A. M.; Stockton Council No. 10, R. & S. M.; Antioch Chapter No. 65, R. A. M.; and of the Loyal Order of Moose, the Knights of Pythias, the Pittsburg Elks, and the Sciots. In politics he is a Republican. His motto is "Be a Man."

CASPER PEDERSEN.—Those sterling traits of character, honesty, integrity and thrift, so characteristic of the Danes, are exemplified in the life and business affairs of Casper Pedersen, the senior member of the firm of Pedersen Brothers, proprietors of the Pedersen Brothers' Planing Mill, Richmond, Cal. Casper Pedersen was born on December 23, 1882, at Ribe, Denmark, a son of Niels and Katherine Pedersen, farmer folks at Ribe, where they owned thirty acres. The family consisted of eight children, seven now living, Casper being the oldest. The father died in 1921; Mrs. Pedersen, the mother, lives in Esbjerg, Denmark.

Casper Pedersen was reared at Ribe and attended the local school. While a youth he was apprenticed for four years to learn the trade of cabinet maker and mill worker. Realizing that America offered to young men of character and ability a greater degree of financial prosperity and independence than his native land, in his twenty-fourth year he sailed from Copenhagen for New York City, landing there on July 12, 1906. His first employment was secured in New Jersey, but he remained there only six months, and then migrated to California, arriving at Oakland on December 1, 1906. In 1915 Mr. Pedersen located at Richmond, where he became mill foreman for J. A. Fagerstrom, the former owner of the mill now owned by the Pedersen Brothers. After he had held this responsible position for about three years, the Pedersen Brothers leased the mill for two years and then, in 1919, purchased the plant.

The firm of Pedersen Brothers is composed of Casper and his brother Peter; a third brother, Jannik, is employed in the mill. The Pedersen Brothers' Mill is noted for its excellent workmanship and especially for its fine quality and artistic designs in finishing lumber for interior work. This mill has contributed much to the development of the building industry of this vicinity, not only at Richmond but also in the towns and country throughout this section of the State. From among the many fine buildings that have been furnished with finishing lumber by this mill mention is made of the Winter's Building, California Market, Albert's Store, and the J. C.

Penney Company at Richmond. Work from this mill has been shipped to Berkeley, Oakland, Santa Rosa, Alameda, San Rafael and even to San Francisco, where lately the New Mandarin Theatre was finished by the product of the Pedersen Brothers' Planing Mill of Richmond.

On November 30, 1907, Casper Pedersen was united in marriage with Miss Alice Jensen, and this union has been blessed with three children: Valborg, the wife of Charles Smith, of Alameda; Axel; and Henry.

Casper's brother and business partner, Peter Pedersen, was born at Ribe, Denmark, February 10, 1888; his marriage occurred at Richmond, Cal., on February 9, 1920, when he was united with Miss Susan Petersen. They have had three children: Robert, Catharine, and Gertrude, who died in infancy.

Fraternally, Casper Pedersen is a member of Harbor Lodge No. 502, F. & A. M.; of the Richmond Sciots; and of Eclipse Lodge No. 403, I. O. O. F.; and with his wife he is a member of the Acantha Eastern Star. He belongs to the Richmond Chamber of Commerce, the Lions Club, and the Contra Costa County Builders' Exchange. The Pedersen Brothers are enterprising and progressive business men, and lend their aid to those movements that are working for the betterment of Richmond's moral, educational, civic and financial interests.

FRANK C. SILVA.—From among the large number of employees of the F. E. Booth Cannery Company at Pittsburg, Cal., special mention is made of Frank C. Silva, a loyal, capable, and intelligent employee who has charge of the steam cooking of the great variety of products canned and shipped by this immense plant. This is a very responsible position and requires constant and intelligent attention.

Frank C. Silva is a native of the Island of Flores, one of the Azores group, where he first saw the light of day on June 12, 1877, as a son of Joseph and Anna Silva; he being the seventh child of a family of ten, eight of whom grew up. During his boyhood days Frank attended school and helped his father with the work on the farm, remaining at home until seventeen years of age. Following the example of many of his fellow countrymen, he then decided to see America, and sailed from Flores to New Bedford, Mass., where he arrived April 3, 1894. He secured employment as a farm hand at Little Compton, R. I. There he remained three years and then went to Marlborough, Mass., and obtained employment in a shoe factory, remaining there four years.

In 1901, at Providence, R. I., Mr. Silva became a naturalized citizen of the United States of America, after which he returned to his old home to visit his mother, his father having died after Frank left home. In 1902 he sailed again for America, this time landing on July 5 in New York City, whence he continued his journey to California, leaving the Southern Pacific Railroad train at a station known at that time as Cornwall, but which today is Pittsburg. At first he worked for his brother William Silva, who farmed about 800 acres of the C. A. Hooper estate near Pittsburg. Desiring to get into business for himself, Frank Silva then engaged in growing asparagus near Oakley, but that season the San Joaquin River broke over its bounds and the high water overflowed the land and entirely destroyed the crop. Going to Pittsburg, then called Black Diamond, Mr. Silva found work with the Redwood Manufacturers Company, beginning as a laborer. His loyal service and intelligent efforts were rewarded by his being appointed foreman, which position he held the last two years he was with the company. In 1916 Frank Silva accepted a position with the F. E. Booth Cannery Company, at Pittsburg, which ranks among the largest canneries on the Pacific Coast and is said to be the second largest cannery of asparagus in the world. Being a very intelligent and industrious employee, Mr. Silva rose to the important post of fireman and cooker for this great industry. He has charge of generating the steam by means of which the various products are cooked and sterilized. Among the various products canned by this plant are: asparagus, pears, peaches, apricots, plums and fish. Mr. Silva has a very responsible position, one requiring constant attention, and the company is to be congratulated that they have such an able and loyal employee to watch their interests at this vital point in the canning business.

LOUIS BECKMAN.—Although scarcely past middle age, Louis Beckman is a veteran railroad engineer with a certificate, recently granted, showing an honorable record of a quarter of a century of continuous faithful service for the Santa Fe Railway. He was one of the first arrivals in Point Richmond, at a time when it had nothing but a tentative boarding house and a few inhabitants that were sleeping in railroad cars. Mr. Beckman also bears a record of never having had a serious accident during his years of service, and feels that the public is generous toward railway engineers. He states that when he started work here there was but one freight train to every four now, and the trains have been lengthened from thirty cars to sixty. Then there were three or four passenger coaches, where now they have twelve or fifteen to each limited train, this having been made possible by larger engines and better road-beds.

Mr. Beckman comments on the risk that many otherwise sane individuals will take in crossing railroads, taking most hazardous chances with their lives. He mentions also that on one lap of his run there are seventy-eight crossings in a distance of twelve miles.

Mr. Beckman was born in Sweden on February 18, 1878, the son of Peter Beckman, a carpenter. At the age of ten, in 1888, he landed in New York, in care of his uncle, and they went on to Dubois, Pa. He received his education in the public schools there, and his first employment was in a power plant at the mines as a stationary engineer. In October, 1900, he came to Point Richmond and started to work for the Santa Fe as a fireman. In 1906 he was promoted to the position of engineer. He is a member of the Brotherhood of Locomotive Engineers, and belongs to the Masons and Elks. In politics he is a Republican.

Brother Z. Joseph.

BROTHER Z. JOSEPH.—As head of De La Salle Institute of Martinez, and also of the San Francisco Province of the Order of Christian Brothers and their several schools located on the Pacific Coast, Brother Joseph is carrying on a life work of far-reaching importance, and one which must leave a lasting imprint upon the future of the State. A native Californian himself, born in San Francisco on March 4, 1878, he attended the public schools of that city, and also Sacred Heart College and, later, St. Mary's College, receiving a most thorough training for his educational work.

De La Salle Institute is preeminently an educational institution, in which are imparted vital religious principles, and the curriculum of which embraces elementary, scientific and manual training for boys exclusively. Students are here trained for carrying on this wonderful work in the Order of the Christian Brothers. The school was founded in 1878 by Brother Justin, a conspicuous figure in the educational life of California, for he also established St. Mary's of Oakland; St. Joseph's of Berkeley; and Sacred Heart College, of San Francisco, in which city the Order also maintains the St. Peter's and Mission Dolores schools. The Christian Brothers have recently completed their new $200,000 school in Sacramento, and the "Christian Brothers High School" in Los Angeles. There are five Provinces of the Brothers, in all, in the United States, and three in Canada, with Brother Joseph at the head of the San Francisco Province, and with the aforementioned schools under his jurisdiction.

The "Brothers of the Christian Schools" was originally founded at Rheims, France, in 1680, by St. John Baptist de la Salle, who, at sixteen years of age, was elected a Canon of the Cathedral of his native city because of his exceptional ability and piety. It was while exercising his duties there that he became intensely interested in the educational problems then confronting France and the church; after much thought and tribulation he founded his first "free school," in 1679, and despite hardships of every kind lived to see his great work securely established. At his death, in 1719, he had given a new religious family to the church, had organized and prepared teachers for not less than twenty-five schools in all parts of France, had originated the idea of the "normal school," and had established forever the simultaneous, in place of the individual, system of teaching—the last two advances constituting a dual achievement for which the entire educational world, even if unconsciously, today honors his memory. In 1900 his great works and sanctity, following the most striking miracles through his intercession, were recognized by the Church, and he was placed in the calendar of the saints.

De La Salle Institute, Martinez, is a preparatory school for the Order. It trains and educates boys, not for the priesthood, but in the general aspects of a liberal education. Its purpose is to prepare leaders for fostering in the pupils of their schools high moral and spiritual manhood and exalted citizenship. The schools of the Brothers all along the Coast are well attended and have among their alumni many leading business men and teachers. J. Adolphus Graves, a non-Catholic, president of the Farmers and Merchants Bank of Los Angeles, was a student of the Brothers, and for two years following his graduation was a teacher at St. Mary's College. Ex-Governor Campbell of the State of Arizona; the late Judge Maurice Dooling; the late Thomas Lennon, president of the Alumni Association; the late Judge Frank Murasky; the late Judge Louis Ward; the late Garrett McEnerney, attorney; and many other well-known men along the Coast—clergy, professional men and business men—have been students of the Order. Martinez and Contra Costa County are fortunate in having so thorough a school right at their doors, and have shown every appreciation of that fact.

THEODORE M. NISSEN.—From that soil which has ever produced a hardy and industrious race of people comes Theodore M. Nissen, who was born October 8, 1870, in Denmark, the son of Soren and Christina (Sorenson) Nissen. There were four children in the family, two of whom came to America. The father was a farmer, versed in all of the agricultural lore that has been the heritage of the Danes for so many centuries, and it was from him that the son received the thorough training which was to be so valuable to him for the rest of his life. But news of a land of greater opportunities had reached the ears of the young man, and in 1888 he came to America, landing in New York, from which city he came direct to California, locating first in Dublin, where he remained for two years. In 1890 he came to Tassajara, where he worked for T. C. Johnston for six years. In 1896 he started farming for himself, renting at first, and finally, in 1900, moved to the ranch where he has since made his home. He rented the place at first, but by the exercise of industry and good judgment he was later enabled to buy it and has since added to his holdings from time to time, until now his ranch consists of 200 acres of excellent land, on which he does diversified farming. His brother, James Nissen, is the owner of a farm below the home place and resides with our subject, who rents all of his brother's interest.

Theodore Nissen became an American citizen in 1894. He has been road master for the past twenty years, starting with Mr. Casey when he first came into the office of supervisor, and he has built up all the roads in his district from cattle trails.

Since coming to America, Mr. Nissen has taken two trips to Europe. On his first trip he was accompanied by his childhood sweetheart, Caroline Hansen, daughter of L. P. Hansen, a fisherman who, as mate of a vessel, had visited America while following the sea. They visited their relatives and returned to San Francisco just after the fire and earthquake, and finding everything in confusion, were unable to locate Miss Hansen's relatives. They decided to be married at once, and after a great deal of trouble succeeded in locating the county clerk in an improvised office, where they were married on May 8, 1906. After a sumptuous wedding dinner, which cost fifty cents, in some unknown private place, they journeyed out to the ranch which was to be their future home. In 1922 they built a modern stucco residence on their ranch. In 1921 they journeyed to Europe again to celebrate the return of Schleswig to Denmark, and while there visited the battlefields of France and Belgium. They brought back with them to America, a niece, Caroline Erickson, and a nephew, Christen Erickson, both students in night school, preparing to become American citizens at an early date.

For more than thirty years Mr. Nissen has been an active member of the Odd Fellows. He is a charter member of Pleasanton Encampment, I. O. O. F., and belongs to Dania Lodge at Livermore, and to the Grange. He is fond of hunting and fishing and takes an extended camping trip each year. He is one of the leaders of his community, an active political worker, and a sterling citizen, highly esteemed by all who know him.

ANTONIO NICODEMO CODEGLIA.—A California pioneer of 1873, Antonio N. Codeglia has been closely identified with the best interests of his adopted State ever since that date, and with the passing of the years has made a name and place for himself in this commonwealth. He was born in Lucca, Italy, on September 14, 1857, the son of a merchant, Antonio Codeglia, who had married Miss Assunta Simi. They came to America in 1884, having been sent for by our subject. The family consisted of Ida, Mrs. Peter Freggario, now of Lodi; Angelina, Mrs. S. Lenzi, now of Stockton; and our subject.

Antonio N. Codeglia attended the Italian schools and in 1873 came to America and California. He found work as a ranch hand in the Sacramento Valley on the Sacramento River and on Grand Island for about eighteen months, and then went to Pescadero on Half Moon Bay and worked there one year. Tiring of farm work he decided he would try his hand in some commercial enterprise and found employment with Daniel Giovanini, wood and coal dealer. This was when he was about nineteen years old. Eighteen months later Antonio started a vegetable and fruit business, supplying the Presidio officers, and met with good success for the following three years. He was frugal and saved his money, and when he thought he had enough to start a fuel business he opened a place at 315 Broadway Street and built up a lucrative trade as a coal and wood merchant. He then enlarged his scope of operations, but after ten years sold out and entered the employ of the Geary Street and Ocean Park Railroad Company and for twenty-two years remained with them as a trusted workman. He still has the badge given him when he began working for this company, and says that in all the years he worked with the company there was not an accident to a passenger. He quit railroading in 1905. Later he traveled for F. Chevalier, a wholesale liquor dealer, and held this post until the Eighteenth Amendment went into effect by proclamation of the President of the United States. He had moved to Richmond in 1906, and two years previous to coming here he had spent two years as an employe of the Fugazi Popular Bank in San Francisco. In 1920 he opened a real estate and insurance office and became local agent for all lines of steamships and railroads, doing business especially with foreigners. His work has had a natural increase and he feels well satisfied with results thus far obtained, for while he has been building up a financial business he has also built up many strong and lasting friendships in this community. Mr. Codeglia was admitted to citizenship on July 31, 1886, by Judge J. R. Wilson in San Francisco, and exercises the right of franchise by supporting men and measures he considers best suited for the public good.

Mr. Codeglia was married on January 20, 1880, to Miss Mary Zawzi, born in New York City, a daughter of Peter and Teresa Zawzi, and one of eight children. This marriage resulted in the birth of the following children: A. J. Renaldo, who is the father of two children, Morgan and Lucile; Ernest J.; R. W.; Louise, who died aged eight years; Jennie, who died when seven; Albert, who passed away when he was eleven, and Florence, now connected with the Richmond public schools. During the World War two sons were in the United States Navy and one in the Army. E. J. and R. W. are employees of the Standard Oil Company. The sons are all members of the Masonic Lodge, and Mr. Codeglia belongs to McKinley Lodge No. 347, F. & A. M. He is a member of the Knights of Pythias, having joined in 1879, and is corresponding secretary and secretary of the insurance department, and a member of the Grand Lodge. He joined the Druids in 1881 and twice passed through the chairs of Golden Star Lodge No. 104, of San Francisco. While a student in the schools of his native country, Mr. Codeglia was an apt pupil and was often called upon to substitute as a teacher; he also had a private class of forty-one pupils, and some of those pupils call to see him when they happen to come to California. He studied French and English and was able to talk and understand the English language when he got to California. He speaks Italian, French and English, and is often called into court as an interpreter; and he often gives talks in lodge meetings. As a recreation, he enjoys hunting, but always keeps within the law. He is public-spirited and charitable, and always lends a helping hand to those less fortunate than himself. In 1884 he sent for his entire family to come to California, and is happy that he was able to put so much cheerfulnees in the lives of his parents. As a loyal citizen of the United States he believes in living and letting live.

HARRY BURDEWICK.—Identified with the agricultural interests of Contra Costa County, California, since his boyhood years, Harry Burdewick has gained a thorough knowledge of the occupation and has been a contributor to the development of that portion of the state where he was born and reared. He is one of the pioneer and successful alfalfa growers in the Byron-Brentwood section of eastern Contra Costa County, where he now operates about 200 acres. He was born in Byron Precinct on April 29, 1887, the only son of Peter and Emma (Kane) Burdewick, honored pioneers of this section, now living retired in Oakland, Cal.

Peter Burdewick, the father of our subject, was born in Hanover, Germany, November 7, 1847, and came to California via the Isthmus of Panama in 1866. For four years after arriving in California he lived with an uncle who owned a large stock range in the Sierra Nevada Mountains in the northern part of the State; later he went to Suisun and there engaged in grain and hay farming for a number of years. He then removed to Contra Costa County, rented land at first, and prospered as the years went by until he came to own some 800 acres; the greater part of it has been sold until there now remains about 200 acres which is all devoted to the raising of alfalfa. There are two children in this family, our subject and his sister Josephine, now Mrs. Sproule, who resides with her parents in Oakland.

Harry Burdewick attended school near the home farm and the Liberty High School in Brentwood. At the age of thirteen he was able to drive big teams of horses and help his father on the farm. He now has full charge of the large ranch of 200 acres which yields him a good return for his energy and industry.

At Redwood City on February 18, 1915, Mr. Burdewick was married to Miss Jasmine Galli, born in Bakersfield. Mr. Burdewick was drafted for service in the World War but the armistice intervened to keep him from going overseas. Mrs. Burdewick is a member of Byron Parlor No. 193, N. D. G. W.

ARCHIE V. McFAUL.—A former chairman of the board of trustees of the city of Pittsburg, Archie V. McFaul is a broad-minded, clear-visioned business man, thoroughly in sympathy with the progress of his municipality and the welfare of its citizenry. He is the owner and proprietor of McFaul's furniture store, one of the largest and oldest in Pittsburg, and is also the proprietor of an extensive plumbing business in the city. Born at Hampshire, Ill., on February 26, 1883, he is the son of J. R. and Frances (Davis) McFaul, the former a native of Kingston, Ontario, and the latter born on one of the Thousand Islands, Canada, and a daughter of Robert Davis, who owned and operated the Davis Dry Docks, at Kingston. J. R. McFaul followed mercantile pursuits both before and after coming to California, and he was well known in Pittsburg, where he located in 1904, coming from San Jose, and established himself in the furniture business. His death occurred in Pittsburg, November 6, 1912. He was an upright citizen and a successful business man. His wife was also well known here, though since her second marriage she resides in another city.

Archie V. McFaul came with his parents to California when ten years of age, and was reared in San Jose and Watsonville before coming to Pittsburg, his father being the proprietor of furniture stores in both cities. When the family came to Pittsburg he went to work in the mill of the Redwood Manufacturers Company, while his father opened a furniture store, which prospered from the start. By the exercise of industry and thrift, the son was soon able to buy a share in the father's store, and in 1907 the firm name became J. R. McFaul & Son. Their place of business from 1911 to 1918 was in the store building erected by the elder McFaul, at 105 Black Diamond Street. They added plumbing to the furniture line, and both branches prospered well, for both proprietors were men of intelligence and had a thorough knowledge of their lines.

After the death of the father, Archie V. McFaul became the managing head of the business, and since 1918, when he acquired his mother's interest in the business, he has been sole owner. In 1920 he moved to the large store building built by himself, and there he continues to supply the discriminating public of Pittsburg and surrounding territory with the best in furniture and plumbing.

The marriage of Mr. McFaul, occurring at Pittsburg, September 18, 1910, united him with Miss Lillian Rouner, a daughter of C. T. and Delia (Nash) Rouner, both well known in the county. The father still lives in Pittsburg, but Mrs. Rouner passed to her reward in 1924, at the age of sixty-three. She was a pianist and organist of note and a social favorite, active in lodge and church work, and for years was organist in the Congregational Church at Pittsburg. Both the Rouner and Nash families were early California pioneers, lured to the State by the gold excitement, and the Rouners were actively engaged in gold mining at Coloma, on the American River, for many years. Mrs. McFaul's father became an engineer, and has installed the mining machinery in many of California's mines. Mrs. McFaul is descended, on her mother's side, from the Mayflower families of Hopkins and Chipman, of the Massachusetts Bay Colony, while on the Rouner side she descends from Terrell, who was in charge of the King's Preserves in Virginia during early colonial days. One daughter, Janice, has been born to Mr. and Mrs. McFaul.

Mr. McFaul was elected to the high school board in 1916; since then he has served continuously, and he is now clerk of the board. He worked hard for the establishing of the union high school at Antioch; and as the three districts attending have grown, and Pittsburg's need for a local high school building is great, he is now interested, as a member of the board, in securing the passage of a bond issue for a high school building in the city of Pittsburg, where the high school classes are held in one of the grammar school buildings. He takes a very live interest in education at all times. In 1918 he was elected to the board of city trustees of Pittsburg, which in 1920 showed a population of 7000 and ranked as a city of the sixth class. In that year a bond issue of $440,000 was voted for the purpose of establishing a city water plant, paving streets, building municipal buildings and a municipal wharf, and carrying into effect other very necessary measures; and additional bonds aggregating $38,000 were subsequently voted for needed reforms, all of inestimable value to the city. The new library building is now completed, at a cost of $20,000. Mr. McFaul was active and interested in having the bond issue carried in 1920, and that same year he was made chairman of the board. The city found in him a very able and efficient executive, whole-heartedly devoted to its growth and development.

Fraternally, Mr. McFaul is active in Masonry; he is a Past Master of the lodge at Antioch, and is a charter member of the Masonic lodge which was organized in 1912, and was its first Master, and since 1913 has been its secretary. He is a member of the local advisory board of the Pittsburg branch of the Mercantile Trust Company of California, and is a prominent member of the Pittsburg Chamber of Commerce. Mrs. McFaul, who assists in keeping the books in their store, is also well known in Masonic circles, being a member of the Eastern Star; and she is also active in the order of Native Daughters of the Golden West.

WALTER S. VAN WINKLE.—There is probably no man residing in Bay Point that has taken a more active part in the upbuilding of the city and county than has Walter S. Van Winkle; and while not a native of California, he has made his home in this State for so many years that he is intimately associated with its progress and devoted to its development. Although still a young man, he is the owner of several business houses and residences, and is successfully operating a large department store at Bay Point, including hardware, furniture and a fine line of electrical fixtures. This store is attractive and up-to-date, and would do credit to a city several times the size of Bay Point. Mr. Van Winkle is the president of the Bay Point Light & Power Company, distributing electrical power to the citizens and manufactories of Bay Point and vicinity; and he is also agent for four of the best old-line insurance companies and does a thriving business along this line. He has recently platted a portion of his vacant property, and lots are being sold rapidly for homes. Another enterprise which he is successfully handling is the Highway Garage, together with the Ford agency; Harry Hines is the capable manager of these. Mr. Van Winkle predicts that Bay Point will be one of the lumber centers and manufacturing cities of California, and he is giving his best efforts along every line to help this prediction come true.

Walter S. Van Winkle was born at St. Louis, Mo., November 6, 1889, a son of W. D. and Emma (Krebs) Van Winkle, both parents being natives of Illinois. W. D. Van Winkle is a dentist by profession and practiced successfully in St. Louis until his removal in 1906 to Los Angeles, where he still follows his profession. Walter S. Van Winkle remained in St. Louis for a year after his parents came to Los Angeles, and during that year completed his high school course, graduating from the St. Louis High School, Class of 1907. In the fall of 1908 he matriculated at the University of California at Berkeley, where he pursued the course as prescribed by the Electrical Engineering Department, graduating with the Class of 1912. After his graduation he became connected with the Great Western Electric Power Company, and had charge of the power sales department for five years. In 1917 Mr. Van Winkle was one of the organizers of the Pacific Alloy & Steel Company; this company prospered exceedingly during the war period, manufacturing ferro-alloys for the government. Since the close of the war, the demand for these products having ceased, this company has had to close down; but they still retain the plant and property, which is leased to smaller manufactories.

W. S. Van Winkle was married at Berkeley in 1914 to Miss Eunice Beal, born in Calaveras County and a graduate of the classical course of the University of California, Class of 1912. Mr. and Mrs. Van Winkle are highly esteemed citizens of Bay Point. Fraternally Mr. Van Winkle is a member of the Bay Point Odd Fellows Lodge. In politics he is a consistent Republican. He is a member of the Congregational Church and serves as clerk of its board.

ANDREW HENRY ERICKSON.—The construction foreman of the Coos Bay Lumber Company at Bay Point, Contra Costa County, is Andrew Henry Erickson, a veteran construction man in his line of work. In 1908 he came to the C. A. Smith Lumber Company and assisted in the construction of the yards, sheds, lumber trucks, cranes, and dock, and thirty-three miles of tracks and tramways in their yards. When the fire of 1913 destroyed the greater part of the yards, Mr. Erickson rebuilt them. During his experience in construction work he has worked for various corporations in many places, and has built at least 1000 miles of tracks for these companies.

A native of Sweden, A. H. Erickson was born on January 17, 1862, a son of John Alvin and Augusta Erickson, farmer folk in their native land. The mother passed away in 1924 at the age of ninety-four years. His father was a large farmer and proprietor of an agricultural implement shop in Sweden. In their family were six boys and two girls, Andrew Henry being the third child. His father was killed in a runaway accident when he was sixty-two years old. The schools of Sweden furnished our subject his education, and at the age of seventeen he came to America and arrived in Chicago, where he secured a job in the car-building shop of Wells & French, builders of refrigerator cars. In 1882 he came to Minneapolis and was engaged in the construction department of the Twin-Cities Street Railway, and here he had his first experience in laying tracks. Desiring to see something of the country he had selected for his future home, he traveled through the Mississippi Valley to New Orleans, then returned to the North again and secured work on the Canadian Pacific, remaining four years and doing construction work through to the Rocky Mountains. He worked with the surveying crew and track-layers, and as mentioned has helped build 1000 miles of tracks. Three years of his time were spent as foreman of an extra gang on the Northern Pacific Railroad. He then came to Potlatch, Idaho, and went to work for the Weyerhouser Lumber Company, constructing yards and tracks, and afterwards was with the Humboldt Lumber Company at Sand Point, in that State. In his earlier days he had spent ten years at

Brainerd, Minn., in construction work for the Brainerd Lumber Company, gaining experience that prepared him for the work of his later years. At Potlatch he became acquainted with S. W. Rodgers, then the superintendent of the lumber company there, who came to Bay Point, Cal., in 1908 to establish the plant and yards for the C. A. Smith Lumber Company. Being familiar with the work done by our subject, he sent him a telegram to come to California to take the position of yard superintendent at Bay Point. Since coming to this State his services have been in demand. He constructed the yards at Stockton for the Stockton Lumber Company, and was employed in the same capacity in Sacramento and Oakland. He has spent four years in the Puget Sound country as a millwright for the North Mill Company at Everett, Wash., and one year at Bellingham; and he also spent four years in construction work at the iron mines in Michigan and Wisconsin. Thus it will be seen that Mr. Erickson has a thorough knowledge of every angle of his business, and is one of the most competent men in his line on the Pacific Coast.

The marriage of A. H. Erickson and Miss Florence Howard took place in Hurley, Wis., in 1887, and they have had four children, viz.: Sadie, who died when sixteen years old; George W., a carpenter employed by his father; Florence Mabel, wife of E. A. Dunning, of Oakland; and Alex, of Ironton, Minn. Fraternally, Mr. Erickson belongs to Odd Fellows Lodge No. 433, in Bay Point, and to the Modern Woodmen of America in that city. He was naturalized at Brainerd, Minn., and is a Republican. He owns a residence in Oakland and two in Bay Point.

ERNEST H. WARD.—Pittsburg has no more earnest or practical advocate of progress than Ernest H. Ward, popular junior member of the firm of Ward & Weigel, owners and operators of the W. & W. Garage. This business was started in 1915, when the first unit of its attractive buildings and various service departments was built. Two years later the second unit was completed; then, in 1919, another addition was built; and the final unit was completed in 1923. This gives to Pittsburg one of the best garages and automobile agencies in this section of the State. The W. & W. Garage handles the Buick cars, and in addition conducts a general service station, supplying everything required by motor-car owners: tires, tubes, accessories of all kinds, as well as oils, gasoline and other necessities. The repair department is one of the most modern in the State. Mr. Ward, a pioneer in the automobile industry, personally conducts the business of the W. & W. Garage, ably assisted by J. L. Adams, sales manager and one of the best-posted automobile authorities of this growing section of California.

Ernest H. Ward was born at Vallejo, April 24, 1876, a son of B. S. and Olive (Davidson) Ward, both natives of New York State. The father was eleven years old when he came to California with his parents in 1853. In 1881 the family removed to St. Helena, remaining there until 1890, when the residence was changed to San Francisco. The mother crossed the plains in a covered wagon in 1853, coming by way of the Emigrant Gap Road. B. S. Ward, the father of our subject, was a machinist by trade and was engaged as such at the Mare Island Navy Yard, where he assisted in laying the keel of the old Kearsarge battleship. He also owned and operated a blacksmith shop in San Francisco. He passed away in 1913, aged seventy-one years; the mother still makes her home in San Francisco.

Ernest H. Ward attended the Lincoln night school and also the San Francisco Business College. He then went to work for the W. P. Fuller Company and was with them until he enlisted as a volunteer in the Regular Army at San Francisco on June 9, 1898, and joined Battery G, 3rd U. S. Artillery. He sailed from San Francisco on June 27, of the same year, landed at Manila on August 1, and took part in the Battle of Manila Bay on August 13, 1898. One year later he was honorably discharged at Manila and shipped for home on the Steamer Newport, arriving in San Francisco on October 10, 1899. He again entered the employ of the W. P. Fuller Company, and remained with them until 1903.

At San Francisco on June 11, 1903, Mr. Ward was married to Miss Mattie Weigel, a daughter of J. Weigel, and they came to Pittsburg to make their home. Mr. Ward then entered the employ of the Redwood Manufacturers Company and worked up to be chief electrician, his term of employment covering a period of twelve years, when he opened the W. & W. Garage. Mr. Ward served for eight years on the city council of Pittsburg, and for the past three years has been president of the Chamber of Commerce, a position he still holds. He was from the first a firm believer in the Antioch bridge, which will mean more and more auto travel into the Pittsburg territory and will prove to be a big factor in development along the right lines. Mr. Ward is a real booster for Pittsburg and the surrounding section.

DANIEL COX.—Guardians of the public peace have, as a matter of course, lives filled with more thrills than are to be found in almost any other calling. Yet the very nature of their duties tends to make them reticent concerning these adventures. Daniel Cox, the highly respected chief of police of Richmond, during the several years of his service as an officer, has had many hazardous experiences which would make interesting reading indeed, but he modestly refuses to let them become a matter of public record.

Mr. Cox was born in Bolivar, Mo., on October 10, 1883, the son of Braxton and Sarah Cox, both natives of South Carolina. His early education was received in his native State, and at a very early age he started out to make his own way in the world. He arrived in California as a youth, and his first employment was on a farm near Woodland, Yolo County. Later he became an employee of the street railway company of San Francisco. On February 15, 1915, he joined the police force, and for two years he was patrolman, for two more years sergeant, for

Edwin Merrithew

five years inspector, and on May 15, 1924, he was appointed chief of police of Richmond, an office which he has filled most satisfactorily. During this period of service he has had many close calls, has engaged in several combats, and has been the recipient of some rewards as the result of his fidelity to duty.

Mr. Cox was united in marriage on January 27, 1904, to Miss Della Amme, a native of Cleveland, Ohio, and a daughter of a musician of that city. They are the parents of two children: Gladys, now a bookkeeper; and Frances, a pupil in Richmond High School.

In his private life Mr. Cox is fond of fishing and athletic sports, and also of motoring and camping. His vacations are generally spent on camping trips. He is a Knight Templar Mason and belongs to the Knights of Pythias.

EDWIN W. MERRITHEW, M. D.—Dr. Merrithew has been successfully engaged in the practice of medicine at Martinez since July, 1907, and is widely known as one of the ablest and most highly esteemed physicians of the county. A native son, he was born at Gold Run, Placer County, on November 23, 1880, a son of Moses W. and Annie Elizabeth (Hewitt) Merrithew, the former a native of Belfast, Maine, born on July 4, 1837, and the latter a native Californian, born in San Francisco in 1854. Moses W. Merrithew came out to California as a young man of fourteen, drawn here by the gold excitement, and for many years was engaged in gold mining in Placer County, in which he was fairly successful. His death occurred on July 30, 1917, at the age of eighty years. The mother is still living, at Gold Run, loved and honored by all who have the pleasure of knowing her.

Edwin W. Merrithew received his early education in Placer County, and then, having decided to become a physician, took a special preparatory course at the Stockton Normal, after which he entered Cooper Medical College at San Francisco, from which institution he was graduated in 1905. For the following two years he served as interne at Lane Hospital, San Francisco, and then for a brief period practiced his profession at Geyserville, in Sonoma County. In July, 1907, he located in Martinez, where he has since practiced with such success that he is considered one of the leading, if not the leading physician and surgeon, and enjoys the full confidence of the people throughout Contra Costa County. In November, 1911, he was appointed county physician, which office he held for many years with credit, and he has served as health officer for the city of Martinez since January 1, 1914. He is also local surgeon for the Southern Pacific Railway.

The marriage of Dr. Merrithew, which occurred at Martinez in 1910, united him with Miss Emma M. Kriner, also a native of the State, born at Dunsmuir. Two children have blessed their union, Wallace K. and Lois M. Both Dr. and Mrs. Merrithew are prominent in social circles in

20

Martinez, and are active participants in the work of the fraternal organizations, the doctor belonging to the Odd Fellows, the Knights of Pythias, and the Woodmen of the World, of which last-named order he is Camp physician. He is a member of the Native Sons, and is a Mason, belonging to the Scottish Rite Consistory and Aahmes Temple of Oakland, while his wife is a member of the Eastern Star. He is also a member of Vallejo Lodge No. 559, B. P. O. E. Dr. Merrithew belongs to the Contra Costa County Medical Society, the California State Medical Association, and the American Medical Association. In politics he is a consistent Republican, and both he and Mrs. Merrithew are active in all matters tending to promote the general welfare of the community and the growth and expansion of their home city.

JOHN A. ZOCHER.—One of the former proprietors of the Nord California Herold, the widely circulated and influential German-American newspaper of Sacramento, John A. Zocher is now giving his attention to agriculture and horticulture, on his ranch near Martinez, on the Pleasant Hill road. Born in Dresden, Saxony, Germany, on February 20, 1870, he came with a number of companions to America in 1886, landing at Castle Garden, New York, about October 1, 1886, and from there came right on through to San Francisco, where he landed on October 10, of that year. He is a son of Theodore Zocher, who was a theater manager in the city of Dresden, and who died when John A. was only ten years old. Reared in Saxony, the lad attended its schools, and then learned the printer's trade. His mother, Clara Schmidt before her marriage, is still living in Niederloessnitz, Saxony, and is now eighty-two years old. Of their four children, John A. was the third son and child. When he reached sixteen and one-half years of age, he sailed for America with a number of friends and after arriving at San Francisco took a job at three dollars per week on a German-American newspaper published in that city. He later went to Sacramento, and there, in association with Charles Schmidt, was engaged from 1908 until 1921 in journalistic work as co-proprietor of the Nord California Herold. In 1904, Mr. Zocher purchased a ranch of ninety-five acres in Contra Costa County, and his wife and sons moved there and operated the place while he continued at his newspaper work in Sacramento.

The marriage of Mr. Zocher, occurring in 1891 at San Francisco, united him with Miss Helen Zeidler, a native of his home town in Saxony, who had come to California previous to his arrival and had made a return trip back to Saxony and then another to California, when their marriage occurred. Four children have blessed their union: Walter F., Kurt, William and Carl. Kurt and William live on the home ranch, which has five acres in pears, ten planted to grapes and the balance to plums, peaches, prunes, apricots and almonds. These two sons are in business for themselves, owning and operating a threshing machine and two tractors, which they use on the home ranch and also for doing outside work on neighboring ranches. Walter F. is employed by the Shell Oil Company, in Martinez. He has one son, Walter Elton. Carl is working with his older brothers. All four sons are a credit to their parents and to the county in which they were reared, and all take an active interest in its development and prosperity, as do their parents. The family are known as self-reliant and industrious citizens of unquestioned integrity.

Mr. Zocher is a member of Sacramento Stamm No. 124, U. O. R. M., and of Sacramento Lodge No. 24, O. D. H. S., and has passed all the chairs of both orders.

JAMES FITZGERALD.—As city clerk and assessor, and formerly justice of the peace of Township No. 6, Contra Costa County, James Fitzgerald is well known in this part of the State as an honored pioneer, prominent citizen and upbuilder of this district. Born December 17, 1855, at Belvedere, N. J., he is the son of John and Mary Fitzgerald, and came to San Francisco with his parents in 1859. They lived in the Western Addition there when you could count all the residences on the fingers of two hands. He received his education in the bay city, and in 1876 he was in business at the corner of Devisadero and Sutter Streets, engaged in the grocery and butcher trade, and continued the same until 1900, twenty-four years in all. From 1900 to 1902, he was employed as deputy sheriff and deputy in the recorder's office, under Thomas J. Glynn, county recorder of San Francisco.

In 1902 Mr. Fitzgerald came to Pittsburg, and was employed by the F. E. Booth Company. That same year he was elected justice of the peace; and he was reelected five successive terms, making a total of twenty years in that office. He was also elected clerk and assessor for Pittsburg, in April, 1910, and has been reelected to that office continuously since that date, his present term to extend up to the year 1928. From 1913 to 1923, he was appointed and served Pittsburg as city recorder. His is an almost unequalled record of public service and one of which Pittsburg is proud. For it takes a big man to grow with the times, and that is the caliber of men who have made Pittsburg their home and have brought her to her present standard of growth and prosperity.

For the past twenty years, Mr. Fitzgerald has been in the real estate and insurance business in Pittsburg, dealing in real estate, loans and investments, and also executing legal documents. He has built several business blocks in Pittsburg, among them the Postoffice block, which was the first brick block erected on Railroad Street. He acts as agent for the Hartford Fire Insurance Company, and brings to every detail of his work the same careful and conscientious application which has made him so successful as a public official.

Mr. Fitzgerald was married in San Francisco, in July, 1895, and is the father of two sons: Edward D. and James J. He is a Republican in politics, and in fraternal life is a member of the B. P. O. Elks and the Fraternal Order of Eagles, being a Past President of the latter order.

LOUIS DE GREGORIO.—The leading painting and decorating contractor of Richmond, and dealer in the lines of goods a man of this calling uses in his business, is Louis De Gregorio, who is located at 321 Thirteenth Street, in that city. He owns 100 feet fronting on Thirteenth Street, and as his business increases he expects to expand accordingly, to facilitate his contracting operations and his retail trade. He was born in Italy on December 27, 1886, a son of Frank and Angelina (Virzi) De Gregorio. The father was a fish merchant in San Francisco, having settled there in 1888. There were eight children in the family, and two brothers and three sisters of our subject reside in Richmond.

Louis De Gregorio attended school in San Francisco and served an apprenticeship to learn the trade of the painter and decorator. After he had mastered the details of the business he worked as a journeyman for a time. In 1906, after having been burned out by the fire of that year, he came to Richmond to begin all over again. Since 1910 he has been carrying on an ever increasing business as a contracting painter and decorator; and he also handles paints, oils, varnishes, wall paper, brushes, etc., having established his store in 1923 at 321 Thirteenth Street. He keeps busy all the time, and specializes in residential work. Mr. Gregorio is a member of the Builders' Exchange, owns his own home and business property, and helped promote the new commercial hotel for Richmond, as well as taking a live interest in all civic matters.

On December 15, 1913, Louis De Gregorio was united in marriage with Miss Elizabeth Sorrentino, of San Francisco, daughter of Michael and Grace (Coccellato) Sorrentino, natives of Italy who came to California and are now living at Richmond. One child, Mary Angelina, has come to bless this happy union. For recreation, Mr. and Mrs. De Gregorio take week-end motoring trips. He became an American citizen in 1915, and by his vote and voice tries to put the best people in office.

MARION BRISCO BREWEN.—A descendant of early California pioneers, Marion Brisco Brewen was born in Kansas City, Mo., on December 9, 1850, and crossed the plains with his parents while a babe in his mother's arms, arriving at Mud Springs, Cal., in the fall of 1853. Eli and Caroline (Davis) Brewen, his parents, were both natives of Missouri, the father having been born near Jefferson City, and the mother at Independence, and both came from families that were early settlers and large landowners in that State. Eli Brewen was a blacksmith by trade, and after his arrival in California he followed that work at Mud Springs, Live Oak City, Mariposa, and San Ramon, in which latter place he died in 1873, aged forty-nine years, leaving a widow and eight children, of whom Marion Brisco was the oldest.

Marion Brisco Brewen had learned the blacksmith's trade, and on his father's death he became head of the family and continued to run the blacksmith shop at San Ramon until 1880, when he sold out and worked as a blacksmith at Squaw Canyon, Ariz., running a shop in connection with the building of the railroad. He later worked on the Railroad or Cook Ranch at Danville as blacksmith for three years, and also near Stockton for one year. An accident which occurred while he was shoeing a horse on the Railroad Ranch injured him so badly that he was incapacitated for work for six years, and during this time he spent thirteen months in Lake County and then went to Humbolt County for five years.

Coming to San Ramon, he worked there for a year, and then, in 1924, came to Martinez. For the first three years he rented a shop, and then ran a blacksmith shop in Franklin Canyon, where he owns a home place of one and one-half acres. This he purchased in 1898, and then moved his shop down there. Now, at seventy-five years of age, he is sturdy and active, and finds himself in comfortable circumstances as a result of a lifetime of hard work. Well-known in the county, he has many friends throughout this section who know him as a man of real worth. In these later years he rents out his blacksmith shop, and confines his activities to running the service station adjoining, where he also carries a line of automobile accessories.

The marriage of Mr. Brewen occurred in Humboldt County in 1888, and united him with Miss Melvina Sullenger, a sister of County Auditor Sullenger. Two children were born to them: Marion M., employed by the International Harvester Company in Fresno; and Nellie Irene, a telephone operator residing in San Francisco. Mrs. Brewen passed away in 1912, aged forty-seven years.

SAMUEL HOFFMAN.—One of the best-known business men in Martinez is Samuel Hoffman, proprietor of Hoffman's Cigar Store, on Ferry Street near the corner of Main Street, that city. He has been located in the Hook Building, which narrowly escaped destruction by fire on July 18, 1925, for the past quarter of a century. A man of unusual ability, full of energy and optimism, he has forged his way to the front as a cigar manufacturer, cigar dealer, financier and politician, since coming to this country as a lad of sixteen, and is today one of the most popular figures in the life of his home city.

Born in Hungary, on December 12, 1872, Mr. Hoffman came to New York in 1887, and there worked for eight months in a jewelry manu-factory. Coming to San Francisco, his objective point, in 1888, Mr. Hoffman took employment with a brother, Sandal Hoffman, who was already established as a cigar maker manufacturing the "O. K." cigar. This was San Francisco's first union cigar factory, and there our subject learned the cigar maker's trade thoroughly.

Samuel Hoffman was married in San Francisco, in 1896, to Miss Celia Lichtenstein, and soon thereafter came to Martinez and started in as a cigar manufacturer, making the celebrated "Blue Bird" ten-cent cigar, one of his leading brands, which reached a sale of 15,000 per week. While his cigar factory was running at its greatest capacity he employed eight cigar makers steadily. He now gives most of his time to his large and growing trade at his place of business, Hoffman's Cigar Store, where all the best brands of smoking materials and supplies are kept, as well as soft drinks, ice cream and confectionery. Hoffman's Cigar Store is a well-known gathering place in Martinez. Mr. Hoffman is recognized as a broad-minded and far-seeing man in public affairs, and is in a position to hear all sides of a question, and his counsel and advice are often sought. While not seeking political preferment for himself, he is interested in seeing the right men fill the right places in city management. He is a naturalized American citizen, and a Republican in political affiliation. As a stockholder in the First National Bank of Martinez, he is active in financial circles in his home town and county.

Four children make up the family of Mr. and Mrs Hoffman: Harry, who married Miss Leona Graham of Martinez, and is in business in Walnut Creek, where he resides; Mauritz, who married Miss Gladys Humberg of Martinez, in which city he conducts a radio shop; Joe, with his father in the cigar store; and Henry, at home.

JAMES COMAZZI.—One of the original ten men to organize the Martinez-Benicia Ferry, which has been of such inestimable value in the development of Martinez and Contra Costa County, James Comazzi has been a resident here for the past twenty-two years and has seen in actual fact the many changes his foresight visioned for this part of California; and during these two decades he has been an active factor in the development and expansion of the Bay region. A native of Piemonte, Italy, he was born on June 17, 1886, the son of Alexander and Angela (Colombo) Comazzi, of that country. The father was a farmer, and died in Italy; the mother was sent for by her son James and is now living with him at Martinez. Alexander and Angela Comazzi were the parents of six children, four girls and two boys, all now living. Two of the daughters are in Italy and two in Martinez, where the brother, Joseph, also resides after having served over seas in the World War.

James Comazzi is the fifth child in the family, and was reared on the home farm in Italy, attending the public schools there. When the lad was only eight years old his father died, and he had to shift for himself. He remained at home and assisted his mother until eleven years old, and then went to Basel, Switzerland, where he became assistant to a brick mason. When thirteen years old he went to Metz, Alsace-Lorraine and worked in the iron mines for one year, after which he returned to Italy and made preparations to come to the United States. His desire was to come to the Pacific Coast, and on March 25, 1902, he arrived in San Francisco, where he found employment in the stone quarries for three years. Coming then to Martinez, in 1905, he worked for the Mountain Copper Company for three years. In the meantime he was watching for an opportunity to work for himself, and he soon after became local agent for the Weiland Brewery Company, his territory including nearly all of Contra Costa County. He also took on the local agency for the Rainier Brewing Company of Tacoma, Wash., working hard and for long hours, and prospered accordingly. His work, carrying him all over the county, gave Mr. Comazzi ample opportunity to realize the real fertility and value of this wonderful region between the foothills and the bay; also that transportation facilities connecting it with both the principal bay cities and the northern inland territory would be the real starting point of development in this district. Consequently, when the Martinez-Benicia Ferry was organized he was one of the most earnest workers for its success. This ferry has been conceded to be one of the largest factors, if not the largest, in Contra Costa's steady growth in the past years. Mr. Comazzi was also one of the organizers of the National Bank of Martinez, and is a director in that institution. It is one of the flourishing financial houses in the county, and dedicated its new building on October 25, 1924.

The marriage of Mr. Comazzi, which occurred on December 3, 1910, at San Francisco, united him with Miss Lucy Canelli, also a native of Piemonte, Italy, and the daughter of George and Maria (Canale) Canelli, farmers of that country and the parents of eight children, three of whom live in California. The mother is now deceased, but the father still lives, in Italy. Mrs. Comazzi was reared and educated in Italy, and came to San Francisco in 1907. In 1920, Mr. and Mrs. Comazzi made an extended trip to their native home and the Continent, on the way viewing some of the battle fields in France, and remaining six months abroad. Fraternally, Mr. Comazzi belongs to Martinez Aerie No. 725, F. O. E., and is a charter member of the Moose and president of the Dante Society of that city. He became a naturalized citizen in Judge Latimer's court in Martinez in 1913. Since his first arrival here he has been more than satisfied with his selection of California and Contra Costa County as a place for his home; he is always loyal to its best interests, and being a man of progressive ideas, he has been a real worker for the welfare of the county and the commonwealth.

PATRICK JOSEPH NUGENT.—The substantial and well-to-do citizens of Richmond have no better representative than Patrick Joseph Nugent, who occupies an assured position among the keen, progressive and businesslike industrial men of this community, ably holding the important position of superintendent of sheet metal work for the Santa Fe Railroad Company. His birth occurred in the County of West Meath, Ireland, October 21, 1875, and he is one of a family of fifteen children born to Patrick and Annie (McNamara) Nugent, natives also of Ireland, where they were farmer folk. Four sons of this family came to America of whom one settled in Ohio and three in California; then there are also three sisters in California: one in Bakersfield, one in Newman, and one in Rodeo.

Patrick J. Nugent did not have much time to acquire an education in the usual way, but he had plenty of experience in earning his own way in the world. He began his apprenticeship in New York City and finished after he came to California in 1890. For eleven years he was an employee of the California Powder Works. For two years he worked for the Standard Oil Company, having charge of a crew of men in steam-fitting work; but twenty-three years of his life have been spent in the employ of the Santa Fe Railway Company.

On November 27, 1904, Mr. Nugent was married to Miss Annie May Maloney, a daughter of Michael and Bridget Maloney, all natives of Ireland. There were ten children in Mrs. Nugent's family, three of whom died in infancy. Mrs. Nugent is the youngest of the family. She has one sister living in San Francisco, Mrs. Katherine Brennen, whose husband is a nephew of Father Brennen, among the oldest and most esteemed Catholic priests in San Francisco. Mr. and Mrs. Nugent are the parents of two children: Nicholas, a student in the law department of St. Mary's College in Oakland; and Mary Anita, now in the high school. The family are members of the Catholic Church.

GEORGE LANDON SPAULDING.—A successful hardwood floor layer of Richmond is George L. Spaulding, who has had a varied life since the age of fifteen and has passed through some thrilling experiences in Indian warfare while in the army. He was born at Erie, Pa., on June 4, 1856, a son of Dr. Almond and Catherine (Landon) Spaulding, both natives of the Keystone State and now deceased. On the maternal side he is descended from German and Scotch ancestry. The brothers and sisters are: Julia, who married M. Weindorf and is deceased; Elizabeth I., also deceased; Frank P., a pensioner of the Standard Oil Company, living in Richmond; and George L., of this review. Dr. Almond Spaulding was a commissioned officer during the Civil War.

After finishing his schooling at the age of fifteen, George L. Spaulding entered the United States Navy on the S. S. Michigan, which is still doing duty on the Great Lakes. One year later he entered the regular army and served for five years, being stationed at Fort Apache, Arizona, where he was a non-commissioned officer. While he was at Fort Apache the fort was attacked by the Indians and several officers, privates, mail-carriers and emigrants were killed in a battle. Colonel Carr, commanding the Sixth Regiment at the fort, went out after the medicine man who had incited the fight and he was brought in dead. Around his neck was found a medal larger than three silver dollars, with the image of Grant on it with the words "Peace on Earth Good Will towards Man." He had told the Indians that the bullets of the white men would not kill the Indians, hence the attack. After Mr. Spaulding's experience he sailed the Great Lakes for a time, and then sold insurance for the Prudential Insurance Company. He also was in the life-saving service at Cleveland, Ohio.

Upon his arrival in California in 1908, Mr. Spaulding went to work for the Standard Oil Company for a year. He then began laying hardwood

John Ott.

floors, and ever since has been carrying on a prosperous and successful business. He has done work in nearly all of the business blocks and in many of the residences erected in the city since he started. His work is thorough, and he has gained the confidence of the contractors of the city, as well as of the citizens. He is a member of the Odd Fellows Lodge and Encampment back in Erie, Pa., and has represented his lodge at the Grand Lodge.

On July 5, 1899, Mr. Spaulding and Miss Laura P. Feightner were made man and wife. In her parents' family there were six girls and three boys. Mr. and Mrs. Spaulding own their own home at No. 595 Eighth Street, Richmond. Mr. Spaulding enjoys a game of baseball and is an ardent fan. He also enjoys hunting and fishing.

JOHN OTT.—For more than twenty years the constable of Township 5 of Contra Costa County has been John Ott. He was first elected in 1906 and has been re-elected every four years since. This gives some idea of the esteem in which he is held as an officer and as a citizen by his neighbors. Mr. Ott is also senior member of the Concord Building Material & Transfer Company, dealing in lime, cement, plaster, sand, gravel, crushed rock, brick, wood and coal. In addition to his official duties as constable, he was appointed deputy sheriff under Sheriff Veale in 1898 and has served the community in that capacity ever since.

John Ott was born in Pacheco, Cal., on December 25, 1873, the son of the late John N. Ott, a highly respected citizen who died in 1907. The father was a baker, and also engaged in the undertaking business at Pacheco for many years. He was born in Germany and came to San Francisco during the pioneer days of the early sixties. Later he removed to Pacheco, where he engaged in business and also in farming. He had learned the baker's trade in Germany, and he also followed carpentry. By the exercise of his various talents he prospered and became a substantial landowner, planting out a vineyard of fifteen acres. Then he made a trip to Germany, where he married a childhood sweetheart, Wilhelminia Fuhrman; and to them three children were born: Frederick, now in business in Seattle; Tillie, deceased at the age of twenty-six, who married Alfred Roeder and resided in Los Angeles; and John, the subject of this sketch.

John Ott received his education in the grammar school of Pacheco. When he was nine years old his mother died, and a few years later he left Pacheco and went up into Oregon. For a time he worked for the Union Pacific Railway as a brakeman, and on going to San Francisco he was employed on the Market Street Railway as a motorman. In 1889 he returned to his old home, and he has been a resident of Pacheco and Concord ever since.

Mr. Ott was married in San Francisco in 1898 to Mrs. Annie Hagen (nee Neilan), whom he had met in Oregon. Her daughter, Hattie Hagen, is now the wife of Frank Newman of San Diego. Mr. and Mrs. Ott are the parents of one child, Wilhelminia, now the wife of Edgar Bacon of

Concord, and the mother of one child, Betty Bacon, six years old. Mr. and Mrs. Ott moved to Concord from Pacheco. Mr. Ott was elected constable shortly afterward, and at about the same time founded his business, which has prospered. He is a charter member of the Pittsburg Lodge No. 1474, B. P. O. E., having joined the order in Richmond. He was a member of the first board of trustees and has always taken an active interest in the order. He is also a member of both the Odd Fellows and the Red Men of Concord. In politics Mr. Ott is a Republican.

JOHN PITT WOODS. — A capable executive and a citizen of worth, highly esteemed by all who know him, is John Pitt Woods, the superintendent of the Alhambra Cemetery Association, which was organized in the early sixties. The park contains between seven and eight acres of land, and under the able supervision of Mr. Woods a system of lots and blocks has been established whereby correct data regarding every interment can be obtained. He has carefully preserved all the old records and put them in such shape that anyone desiring information regarding any burial can obtain it at a moment's notice. Mr. Woods became superintendent of the Association on April 11, 1909, and since that time has devoted his entire attention to the work connected with his responsible position.

His birth occurred in Madison County, Mo., May 8, 1864, and he was fourth in a family of eight children born to D. N. and Mary A. (Pitt) Woods, natives of Kentucky and Indiana, respectively. D. N. Woods was a farmer and also engaged in carpenter work; he married Miss Pitt in Indiana and then removed to Randolph County, Ill., where he bought a farm between the Ohio and Mississippi Rivers in what was known as the American Bottom, noted for the exceptional fertility of its soil. After his death, the mother of our subject was married the second time, to a Mr. Kirby. Mrs. Kirby spent the latter part of her life in California, coming here in 1901; and from 1908 until the time of her death, on January 19, 1924, she lived in Sacramento. She lacked but nine months of reaching the advanced age of ninety years when she passed on to her reward.

John P. Woods was united in marriage with Miss Nannie E. Burrow, born in Lawrence County, Mo., a daughter of Richard R. and Lovonia Burrow, Missouri farmer folk, now both deceased. Mr. Woods at first rented land in Missouri, which he farmed; then he bought forty acres in Lawrence County, which he afterward sold, and then rented land and farmed on shares, continuing thus until 1899, when he came to California. Settling in San Francisco, he worked for a contracting firm until 1901, when he removed to Contra Costa County and settled at Franklin Canyon, where he was employed in a nursery. In 1903 Mr. Woods moved to Martinez, primarily for the purpose of educating his children. The family home since 1912 has been located at 848 Talbart Street. Mr. and Mrs. Woods have had ten children, four of whom are now deceased. Glen

Ellen is the wife of Russell Scott, an attorney in Salinas, Cal.; they have two children, Burrow and Shirley June. Fred L. is assistant manager of the Stadium Garage in Berkeley, Cal.; he married Miss Geneva Trojan and they have one child, Fred L., Jr. Fern is the wife of Joe Keller, and they reside in Martinez; John Melvin is in the garage business at Crockett, Cal.; and the others are Dell and Richard Milton. Mr. Woods is prominent in the I. O. O. F., being Past District Deputy Grand Master of District 49, Martinez, and a member of Benicia Encampment No. 96. He is also a member of Laurie Camp No. 145, W. O. W., of Martinez, and of Fraternal Brotherhood No. 443, of the same place. Mrs. Woods is an active member of the Rebekah Lodge of Martinez. Politically Mr. Woods prefers to vote independently, casting his ballot for men of principle and capability.

HARRY McNULTY BEEDE.—A member of the board of directors and a valued employee of the Antioch Lumber Company, Harry McNulty Beede is easily recognized as a leader in the business and financial circles in his home city. He was born in Antioch on April 13, 1873, the son of the late Henry Fuller Beede, who is mentioned on another page of this history. The middle name of our subject recalls that pioneer J. J. McNulty, who served for many years as a justice of the peace when his district covered the entire eastern part of Contra Costa County. He was of Scotch-Irish birth and came to California in 1852 from Louisiana, where he owned a sugar plantation. Upon his arrival in California he engaged in mining at Columbia, Tuolumne County, later coming to Antioch. His daughter, the mother of our subject, taught school at Nortonville in 1868, when she was about eighteen years old, and also taught in Antioch.

Harry McNulty Beede is the oldest son and child of the nine living children of his parents and he grew to young manhood in Antioch and here attended the public schools, later taking a commercial course at Healds Business College in San Francisco. During his spare time while he was going to the local schools he worked in the yards of the Antioch Lumber Company, learning the business. In 1889 he was a clerk in the office of the Hartford Fire Insurance Company and continued there until 1896. From that date until 1898 he worked for the Antioch Lumber Company. The latter year gold was discovered in Alaska and Mr. Beede quit his position and went over the Chilcoot Pass to Dawson, where he prospected and mined, sometimes for himself and sometimes for others, and during the six years he was in Alaska met with a fair degree of success. Upon returning to California he went to Bakersfield where he put in a year with the Bakersfield Sandstone Brick Company, but since 1906 he has been steadily engaged with the Antioch Lumber Company.

In 1907, at Antioch, Harry McNulty Beede was united in marriage with Miss Leonora Scott, a native daughter, born in Red Bluff, where she grew up and later taught school, and also taught in Kings County, and in Seattle, Wash. She takes an active interest in the Eastern Star, in which she is a Past Matron. Mr. Beede is a Past Master of Antioch Lodge No. 175, F. & A. M.; Past High Priest of Antioch Chapter No. 65, R. A. M.; Past Patron of the Eastern Star; and a member of the Sciots, all in Antioch.

ORVILLE E. HAYWARD.—One of the particularly well-known ranchers and horticulturists of Contra Costa County is Orville E. Hayward, whose ancestry dates back to the small band of sturdy pioneers who came over in the Mayflower and established a new country where they could have the freedom of their religious convictions. Born near Medora, Macoupin County, Ill., on September 10, 1852, he is the son of Ansel and Rebecca (Silsby) Hayward, the former a native of Massachusetts and the latter of Vermont. The parents were married in Illinois, and both died when Orville E. was a boy, the father's death occurring in 1862, and the mother following him the next year. The years of his youth and young manhood were somewhat shadowed by these two events, and he had to make his own way in life from an early age.

Ambitious to gain a good education, young Hayward attended the public schools, and entered Blackburn University, where he was a senior student when he left for California in 1875. After his arrival here he took a business course at the Pacific Business College, in San Francisco, and then entered employment as a bookkeeper with a wholesale fruit company. His state of health forced him to go to Alameda County, and later to Napa County for a season. The next two seasons he spent at Sonora, Tuolumne County, and from there he went to the Yosemite Valley for five or six months; but finally, in 1881, he came to Martinez and purchased ten acres of land, the nucleus of his present thirty-acre fruit ranch, situated about two miles south of Martinez. Here he has followed fruit growing with success, and through intelligent operation of the acreage has become one of Contra Costa County's foremost horticulturists, using intensive, modern methods in his fruit cultivation.

The marriage of Mr. Hayward, occurring at Oakland on March 28, 1883, united him with Miss Mary E. Bagge, a native of that city, and daughter of the late Christian E. and Emilie (Sultow) Bagge, highly honored California pioneers, who came to Oakland in 1852. Christian E. Bagge was a prominent man of his time in Oakland, where he was a large owner of realty, in both city and county. He served as land agent for the San Francisco Savings Union for a period of twenty-five years, and was considered an authority on land values in this section of the State. He owned a large tract of land, then devoted to ranching, near San Leandro, where Elmhurst is now located, in Alameda County, and was active in the building up of central California. His death occurred on May 17, 1901, and his good wife died in 1907.

Two children were born to Mr. and Mrs. Hayward, Emilie and Orville Ansel. Emilie is the wife of Frederick T. Slack, a resident of Oakland, and one child has been born to them, Hayward Childs Slack. Orville Ansel is now with the General Chemical Company at El Segundo. His marriage, in 1924, unted him with Miss Gladys West, of Redlands, and they reside at Hermosa Beach. Mr. Hayward has served for many years as clerk of the school board for his district. Both he and his wife are prominent in Masonic circles, Mr. Hayward having joined that order in 1896. He is a Past Master of Martinez Lodge No. 41, F. & A. M., the oldest lodge in Contra Costa County, and has served as its secretary for fourteen years; and he has served as secretary of Martinez Chapter No. 31, R. A. M., since 1913. Mrs. Hayward is a Past Matron of Los Ceritos Chapter No. 234, O. E. S., and for eighteen years served as secretary for that order. Prominent socially as well as fraternally, Mr. and Mrs. Hayward are among the most highly respected citizens of Contra Costa County, and have been actively interested in its advancement for several decades past. Mr. Hayward is a member of the Society of Mayflower Descendants, one of the most highly prized distinctions in America, holding membership at San Francisco.

ALBERT H. JONGENEEL.—An outstanding figure in the industrial and commercial circles of Pittsburg, Cal., is Albert H. Jongeneel, who for eighteen years was the vice-president and general manager of the Redwood Manufacturers Company, one of the largest enterprises of its kind in the West. It was organized by the late C. A. Hooper and the plant now covers 100 acres of land and employs from 600 to 700 persons in the manufacturing of doors, sash, frames, interior and exterior finish, cabinet work, tanks, water pipes, etc. It makes a specialty of using redwood, although it handles great quantities of pine and hardwood, shipping its products to all parts of the world. Mr. Jongeneel is now the general manager of the C. A. Hooper Company, which enterprise has done much to foster and develop home building in the prosperous and fast growing industrial city of Pittsburg.

Albert H. Jongeneel was born on April 5, 1872, in Holland, the son of A. W. M. and Gretta Jongeneel. The family came to California in 1889 and settled in Sacramento County, on the Sacramento River near Walnut Grove, where they engaged in horticulture, and they also had an orchard in Santa Clara County, near San Jose. Albert H. Jongeneel attended Gardner Business College at San Jose and when his course was finished found employment with the C. A. Hooper Company. He soon rose from a mediocre position to the important office of vice-president and general manager of the Redwood Manufacturers Company, which position he held from 1903 to 1921. Mr. Jongeneel has always been active in the promotion of the educational interests of the community and for eighteen years has been a member of the board of education of the city of Pittsburg, and secretary of the high and grammar schools. When he first became a member of the board of education there were only two teachers and one principal. The Roosevelt Union High School was located at Antioch, but the extraordinary growth of Pittsburg neces-

sitated the building of a separate high school at Pittsburg. Mr. Jongeneel
is keenly interested in the advancement of education and has seen to it
that Pittsburg's educational facilities have kept pace with the rapid growth
of the city's population.

On October 11, 1903, A. H. Jongeneel and Miss Berta Smyth were
united in marriage. She is a daughter of an old pioneer family from Vacaville, Cal. Their family consists of two children: Francis, a student at
Stanford University; and Elizabeth, attending the Berkeley High School.
Fraternally, he is a member of Pittsburg Lodge No. 429, F. & A. M., at
Pittsburg; and of Aahmes Temple, A. A. O. N. M. S., of Oakland. He is
a very active member of the Pittsburg Chamber of Commerce. Mr.
Jongeneel is a most progressive and enterprising citizen, whose sound
business judgment and ability have aided greatly in the development of
the industrial and financial interests of Pittsburg. Mr. Jongeneel resides
in Berkeley but keeps in close touch with business affairs in Pittsburg by
trips every two or three days.

REV. CHARLES C. CHAMPLIN.—In Rev. Charles C. Champlin,
Pittsburg has a citizen whom all take pleasure in honoring and than whom
no more earnest worker in the cause of Christianity, civic righteousness
and well being, can be found. He is always in favor of any movement calculated to be of material assistance to his adopted town and county, and
is an active member of the Pittsburg Chamber of Commerce, the Lions
Club and the Masons. A man of wide travel and broad intellect, he is
adding immeasurably to the moral and spiritual welfare of this section.

Charles C. Champlin was born in Sonoma County, Cal., December 21,
1876, the elder of two children born to Asahel W. and Adeline Bradford
(Park) Champlin. Grandfather Charles C. Champlin crossed the plains
from Illinois with his wife and several small children, one of whom,
Asahel W., rode a horse all the way across to California. Great-great-
grandfather John Champlin served in the War of 1812. Grandfather
Champlin purchased 300 acres of land in 1856 from M. J. Vallejo, and
this ranch has always remained in the family. The mother of our subject
was born in Boston, Mass., and was a descendant of Gov. William Bradford of Massachusetts Bay Colony. Rev. Champlin has one sister, Mrs.
Grace Champlin-Adams, now a resident of Antioch. The father, Asahel
W. Champlin, died in Martinez on August 24, 1926, at the age of eighty-
one years. He crossed the plains to California in 1850.

Charles C. Champlin began his preliminary education in Sonoma
County, and in 1902 he was graduated from the University of California,
in the social science course, with the degree of B. L. He then went to
Japan, where he was lecturer on English literature and professor of
French at the University of Tokio for two years. Rev. Champlin speaks
Japanese and French and can readily read Greek, Spanish and Latin.
Returning to California, he entered the Pacific School of Religion at
Berkeley and during his college term was student pastor at Pittsburg. In

1909 he was ordained by an Ecclesiastical Council a minister of the Congregational Church and thereafter continued his ministry until his graduation in 1910, when he received the degree of B. D.

Rev. Charles C. Champlin was married in 1910 at Alameda to Miss Maude Frazer, a graduate of the University of California, Class of 1901. They had two sons, Frazer Bradford and Malcolm Ross. During 1912 and 1913 Rev. Champlin took a trip around the world in order to study non-Christian religions, and the knowledge gained at that time gave the world the book entitled "The Non-Christian Religions." Returning to California, he became the pastor of the Congregational Church at San Rafael and remained there two years, when he was called back to Pittsburg. During the World War he served as chaplain and was active in army Y. M. C. A. work until after the armistice was signed. The family then moved to their ranch in Sonoma County, hoping that the out-door life would benefit Mrs. Champlin's health; but she passed away in March, 1923. Rev. Champlin continued to live on his ranch until he received a call to return to Pittsburg after the death of Reverend Muir in 1925. This makes the third time he has ministered to this congregation. On December 21, 1925, Rev. C. C. Champlin was united in marriage with Cordia Zimmerman Brown, of Pittsburg.

JOSEPH F. MATHERON.—Among the many fine people residing in Clayton Precinct of Contra Costa County are Mr. and Mrs. Joseph F. Matheron, both of whom are representatives of old pioneer families who contributed much toward the upbuilding of the county. They take a proper and justifiable pride in the preservation of the history of the pioneer period, realizing its influence upon the present generation and generations yet to come. Mr. Matheron holds the responsible position of manager of the old Kirkwood ranch, which is now owned by I. L. Borden, after whom the Borden Highway was named. Mr. Borden, who is a wealthy man of many business interests, resides in San Francisco, and he selects his executives with considerable care, hence Mr. Matheron is holding his present position only because he is a man of exceptional ability in that branch of management.

Joseph F. Matheron was born in Clayton Precinct, December 25, 1888, the son of Frank Matheron, now a retired farmer residing at Martinez, and Annie (Loring) Matheron, who was born in San Francisco. Both parents are still living, the father seventy-two years old and the mother sixty-seven. Joseph was the eldest of a family of six children, four boys and two girls. He grew up in Clayton and married on September 6, 1919, in Oakland, May Rumgay, who is a native of Concord and a descendant of Andrew and Martha (Lewis) Rumgay, natives of England and California respectively, and one of the California families of 1882. Mr. and Mrs. Matheron are the parents of two children: Andrew Newell and Franklin Loring. Politically Mr. Matheron is a Democrat. He became manager of the Kirkwood ranch of 407 acres in 1920. It is one of the show places in Clayton Precinct, producing principally oats and hay and feeding some cattle. Mr. Matheron is a fine example of the native born Clayton Precinct boy, of a type of citizenry of which any community may well feel proud.

ERNEST H. HIGGINS.—Since October 20, 1912, Ernest H. Higgins has been a resident of Richmond, where he is looked upon as a very public-spirited citizen and enterprising business man. He first saw the light of day at Point Arena, Mendocino County, on November 6, 1882, a son of Archibald and Alice Higgins, pioneer dairy folk of Mendocino County. The father died in 1905, but the mother is living and makes her home in Santa Rosa. The boyhood and youth of Ernest H. Higgins were spent on the ranch and he attended the common schools of the neighborhood and worked with his father on the dairy ranch. After he had grown to manhood he carried on a dairy on his own account for seven years in his native county. Working early and late and seldom having any vacation, Mr. Higgins decided that he would seek a location where he might make a living without such arduous labor. Coming to Richmond, where his brother Leland was the pioneer blacksmith at the Point, having the first shop there, he found employment with a street contractor and for three years did about as hard manual work as he had ever done, working early and late. He saved his money, however, and in 1916 was able to buy the transfer business carried on by Johnston and Brain, who also handled some material for building purposes. By giving his entire time and attention to the enterprise, Mr. Higgins began to build up a large trade in plaster, lime, gravel and cement, and for seven years he had this field with no competition. He has supplied material for half the buildings in the city of Richmond since he embarked in business, and has prospered accordingly. Now he has four competitors in his line of industry, but retains all of his old customers and gets his share of new accounts.

On November 4, 1903, Mr. Higgins married Miss Lillie Viola Gilmore, born in Mendocino County, the daughter of Emmett Gilmore, whose father, Hiram Gilmore, was an early pioneer of California and a pioneer dairyman and rancher in Mendocino County. Of this union two sons have been born: Archie, a graduate from the Richmond High School, Class of 1924; and Roy, a pupil in the high school. They were both born in Mendocino County. Mr. Higgins believes in progress and takes an active part in civic affairs as a member of the Chamber of Commerce and of the Builders' Exchange, of which he was elected president in 1924, and which has a membership of 100. He belongs to Richmond Lodge, No. 1251, B. P. O. E., and to Harbor Lodge No. 502, F. & A. M. He has seen the gradual growth of Richmond and vicinity, and is doing all in his power to foster the advancement of all industries that make for a better and bigger city. He belongs to the Lions Club and takes an active part in all its activities. Mr. Higgins has built up a lucrative business and a firm position in the commercial circles of his adopted city and county.

August Harder,

Mrs. A. Harder

AUGUST HARDER.—One of the prominent alfalfa growers of the Byron-Bethany Irrigation District in east Contra Costa County is August Harder, a native of California and the son of John and Lena (Peters) Harder, who were natives of Germany, in which country they were married before coming to America and settling at Banta, in the San Joaquin Velley. John Harder died when August was four years old and circumstances were such that August was compelled, at an early age, to work on ranches, and when he grew older and stronger he was employed on the great stock ranch of Miller & Lux. Later he and his brother Paul engaged in farming and running a meat market, but the enterprise did not prove a financial success and was abandoned. Afterwards Mr. Harder secured work at the Sperry Flour Mills at Stockton, and later was employed by the Southern Pacific Railway in San Francisco and Oakland, remaining in and around the Bay Cities for about two years.

In 1900, at Stockton, August Harder was united in marriage with Mrs. Florence (Philhower) Johnson, widow of Alfred Johnson. By her first marriage she had two children: Ernest, who resides in Oakland, where he is an employee of the Pacific Gas and Electric Company; and Jessie, wife of Harold Woods, who is a partner with August Harder in raising alfalfa in the Byron-Bethany section. In addition to the twenty-five acre home place, they rent about eighty acres of the Peter Burdewick ranch, all of which is in alfalfa except the twenty-five-acre home place. For several years before coming to their present home place, Mr. Harder tried dry farming in the Marsh Creek district, but the canceling of his lease forced him to give it up. Since coming to the Byron-Bethany Irrigation District he has won success in raising alfalfa, and as the result of his prosperity has built a home on the twenty-five-acre place. Mr. and Mrs. Harder are actively interested in fraternal circles, Mr. Harder being a member of Brentwood Lodge No. 345, F. & A. M.; the Scottish Rite Consistory at Oakland; and Aahmes Temple, A. A. O. N. M. S., also at Oakland. He is Past Grand of Byron Lodge No. 355, I. O. O. F., at Byron; and both he and his wife are members of the Rebekahs and of the Maspha Chapter, Order of the Eastern Star, at Brentwood. They enjoy their large circle of warm friendships in fraternal and social circles.

FRANK MARTENS.—One of the enterprising and successful business men of Martinez, Frank Martens has reached an assured position in life solely through his own efforts, for his career has been one of industry and thrift, and through good management he has accumulated a competence while carrying on conservative business enterprises. He is a native of Holland, born on February 22, 1876, and learned the butcher's trade in his old home, for he comes of a family of butchers; both his father and grandfather before him were engaged in that same line of business, and he absorbed its rudiments with his early training.

As a young man, Mr. Martens was chief butcher on transatlantic liners, for the Red Star and the American Line of steamships. Later, he worked at his trade in New York City, and from there came to California in 1905 and worked as a butcher in San Francisco and Oakland. In 1916 he came to Martinez, and for a time operated the Washington Market. He now owns and operates the Martinez Market, in the Hotel Scott building. This market he has fitted with the latest equipment for an up-to-date meat market, and here he is carrying the best supplies obtainable and catering to a discriminating patronage. Having been in the business all his life, he has a thorough knowledge of "what is what" in the buying of and caring for meats, and this has made his success assured.

The marriage of Mr. Martens, occurring May 1, 1896, at Antwerp, Belgium, united him with Maria Creamer, a native of Germany, and one son, Ferdinand, has been born to them. With a firm belief in the growth and development of Martinez, Mr. Martens has wisely invested in the building of houses and apartments. He owns a number of residences in Martinez, and in 1923 erected the Martinez Apartments, a new and modern apartment-house building, with the latest improvements and equipment, comprising eight apartments and being the only strictly modern apartment-house in the city. Fraternally, Mr. Martens is a member of Richmond Lodge No. 1251, B. P. O. E. A genial and well-liked man, his friends are many in Contra Costa County, as well as in his home city, where he is recognized as a supporter of all worthy projects for civic betterment and community upbuilding.

FOREST H. WRIGHT.—A prominent city official, who is also a pioneer of El Cerrito, is found in the person of Forest H. Wright, a native son of the Golden State, born in Tehama County on June 21, 1873. His parents, Forest M. and Harriet (Crouse) Wright, were both born and reared in Indiana, where Mr. Wright was engaged in railroading. He had the distinction of having piloted the first train over the Pittsburgh, Ft. Wayne and Chicago Railroad as an engineer on the construction train. He served in the Civil War, after which he went with his family to Muscatine County, Iowa, where he engaged in farming and also railroaded for a time. There were eight children in the family, three born in Iowa and five in California, to which State they migrated in 1871 to avoid the severe winters of the Middle West. They homesteaded a ranch in Tehama County, where the father made all the improvements and carried on general farming until his death in 1905, at the age of sixty-nine. The wife and mother died at Orland, Glenn County. Of their eight children, four are living, viz.: Anna, a trained nurse, who makes her home in El Cerrito; Forest H., of this review; Mrs. J. H. Warmoth, of El Cerrito; and Mrs. W. P. Burroughs, of Oakland. Mr. Wright was an enterprising man and took an active interest in all that promoted the welfare of the people and the State.

Forest H. Wright attended the public schools in Tehama County and took a commercial course in Atkinson's Business College in Sacramento, entering that institution in 1892. After completing his course he returned to the home ranch and assisted his father for a time, and then engaged in ranching for himself in Tehama, and later in Glenn County, his ranch being located nine miles southwest from Orland.

In 1897, in Glenn County, Mr. Wright was united in marriage with Miss Nellie Apperson, born of pioneer parents in Colusa (now Glenn) County. Her father was a first cousin to Mrs. Phoebe A. Hearst. Of this happy union seven children have been born. Vaughn F., a chief petty officer in the medical corps of the United States Navy at Mare Island, is married and the father of two children, Beverly and Virginia. Otto H. is at home. Pearl, a graduate of the Richmond High School and the State Teachers' College in San Jose, is now teaching at Manteca, San Joaquin County. The others are Apperson, Harriet, Margaret and James, all born, reared and educated in this state. After ranching for several years in Glenn County, the family decided to come to Oakland and Mr. Wright disposed of his interests and moved there in 1906. For a while he followed teaming, as he had brought a fine team of draft horses from the ranch; then for seven years he was in the employ of a large creamery company. He then engaged in buying, delivering and selling milk and cream on his own account, and built up a good paying business. Soon after his removal to Oakland he came to the Tapscott tract in what is now El Cerrito, bought two lots and erected his home, and upon its completion moved his family into it and traveled back and forth to his business every day. The family liked their surroundings, and in 1911 Mr. Wright began selling property for Mr. Tapscott. From 1911 to 1914 he was tract manager for him, and during that time located many families here. He has seen the locality gradually build up into a fine residential district, much of which he helped to accomplish, for he was employed as a builder in this section until 1924. That year he was appointed to the office of city marshal and tax collector, and he also holds the office of superintendent of streets; so his time is fully occupied. He takes a lively interest in the welfare of his home city, is a very efficient officer, and tries in every way to do his full duty. The improvement of the streets is a notable achievement. When he located in this section there were no paved streets and hardly any passable streets of any kind, and the street car line ran from Oakland to the county line and there was met by the East Shore Suburban, which carried passengers to Richmond. A believer in good schools, Mr. Wright served as a trustee of the Stege school for several years. Fraternally, he belongs to the Independent Order of Foresters, Court No. 1893, El Cerrito.

BIAGIO F. FERRARIO.—As the superintendent of the Port Costa Brick Works, near Port Costa, Biagio F. Ferrario is demonstrating his usefulness as a citizen of Contra Costa County, which has been the scene of his activity for many years. Twenty-one years ago he established the Port Costa Brick Works, made the first test bricks by hand himself, and personally tried out and tested the clay, thus demonstrating the value of such an enterprise to the county of his adoption. He was born in Oleggio, in the Province of Novara, Italy, on September 22, 1880, a son of John and Mary Ferrario, both of whom were born, lived and died in that province. In early life the father was a contractor and engaged in leveling land, building dams, highways, ditches, levees, etc.; but during the latter part of his life he was engaged in raising, buying and selling stock. There were three children in the family: Catherine, wife of Carlo Mossina, living in Italy, though three of her boys are working for the Port Costa Brick Works; Biagio F.; and Josephine, wife of Joseph Franchini, also residing in Italy.

B. F. Ferrario was reared in Italy and there went to the schools of his native province until he was fifteen years of age. Then he went to Basel, Switzerland, where he learned brick-making and bricklaying, remaining for three years, and while there acquired a speaking knowledge of German. He then went to Alsace-Lorraine and worked for nearly a year making brick. Since he was a lad in school he had had an ambition to come to America. California had always seemed a land of wonder to him, and now he decided to see the land of his dreams. He visited his parents, and then embarked from Havre, and landed in New York on March 11, 1900, and immediately coming to San Rafael, Cal., arrived there on March 19. Three days later he had secured work at gardening but he soon got a job in the brick yard in that city and was there four years, becoming a foreman. In 1904 he came to Richmond, Cal., and found employment as assistant superintendent in a brick yard there; then with the superintendent he organized the Wilson-Lyon Brick Company of Richmond and carried on the business for fourteen months.

Mr. Ferrario came to Port Costa and organized the Port Costa Brick Works on April 17, 1905, and this establishment has been a decided success from the start. It was organized with a capital stock of $25,000, and now has many thousands of dollars in equipment and buildings and employs forty-eight men in its different departments. It has a capacity of 60,000 bricks and from fifty to one hundred tons of building tile per day. The company holds 2700 acres under a twenty-five-year lease for clay privileges only. The business offices are at 808 Sharon Building, San Francisco. The company have the best of facilities for shipping, by rail over the Southern Pacific, which has a spur track and switch at the works, and also by boat from their own wharf on Carquinez Straits. The officers of this concern are: C. G. Berg, of San Francisco, president; John Beck, of Los Angeles, vice-president; and H. S. Hoyt of Berkeley, secretary and treasurer. Mr. Ferrario was one of the first to utilize electric power in Contra Costa County when he installed an eighty-five h. p. motor. He now uses 900 h. p. electric energy, besides coal and crude oil for burning brick in the kilns, using some 3000 tons of coal and 20,000 barrels or more of crude oil per annum. From a small beginning this company has grown with the passing of the years until it takes rank with the largest concerns of its kind in the State.

B. F. Ferrario was united in marriage in Martinez, on October 26, 1907, to Miss Pierina Mattachini, who was born in the same town in Italy as Mr. Ferrario, in which place they became acquainted. They have two children: Margaret Ellen, a graduate of the John Swett Union High School at Crockett, Class of 1926, and now a student at the University of California; and Mary Elizabeth, attending the Union High School. Mr. Ferrario received his naturalization papers in Judge Latimer's court in Martinez on March 28, 1913, and votes with the Republicans. He is a man with an excellent memory and can speak and understand German, Italian, French and English, having acquired the latter since landing in this country in 1900. He believes in progress, helps in every way to make Contra Costa County the banner county in the State, and has a large circle of friends and business associates among whom his word is considered as good as his bond.

A. F. CHRISTIAN.—A native son of the county in which he lives and labors, A. F. Christian is descended from a pioneer family of the State and was born at Concord, Contra Costa County, on July 13, 1885. His parents, John B. and Caroline (Lewis) Christian, are still living at Concord. There were five sons born in their family. Grandfather Lewis was a sea captain for thirty-six years, during which time he was wrecked in the Indian Ocean, doubled Cape Horn many times, and came to California the first time in 1852. He finally settled in Concord in 1879. He was born in Long Island, N. Y.

A. F. Christian attended the public schools of Concord and grew up there until he was fifteen, when he went to Oakland and entered the employ of the Crane Company and for five years served them in various capacities, in the machine shops, in the sales department, and as price clerk, shipping clerk, and city salesman for Oakland. Leaving there with a great deal of practical experience, he worked for several firms until 1900, when he entered the employ of the California Construction Company, and during 1901 and 1902 traveled over California erecting mining stamp mills and machinery of various kinds for his company until they failed. Hume & Bennett Lumber Company were his next employers, at Sanger; and he remained there until coming to Bay Point in 1912 to the C. A. Smith Lumber Company, as a millwright, the position he now holds. His work is exacting, but he is fortified with much practical experience and careful study in his line. For six years he took a course in Engineering and Machinery in the American Correspondence School of Chicago.

Mr. Christian was married in Martinez, in 1908, to Miss Lillian Chapman, daughter of George O. and Nancy Chapman, pioneers of Clayton, where Mrs. Christian was born and reared. They have become the parents of six children, viz.: Austin, Melvin, Helen, Tracy, Robert

K., who died aged fifteen months, and Lloyd. Mr. Christian is a member of the Bay Point Odd Fellows Lodge No. 433, of which he is a Past Grand, having passed through the chairs twice; and he is a member of the Antioch Encampment, I. O. O. F. The family belong to the Congregational Church. They have a home in Berkeley, now leased, and reside in Bay Point. Mr. Christian and his family stand high in their social set in Contra Costa County, where they are well and favorably known.

OSCAR F. OLSSON.—Among the active men of the Danville section of Contra Costa County is Oscar F. Olsson, supervisor from the Second District and proprietor of one of the best-equipped modern garages in this section. A splendid line of accessories is carried in stock, including tires. Auto repairs for all makes of machines are given particular attention. The equipment includes a recharging outfit, lathe machine, welding tools, and such devices as are needed for capable work. This garage is also distributing agent for the Nash automobile. Mr. Olsson is enthusiastic, as are all other residents of the Danville district, for the building of the highway along the south base line of Mount Diablo, that will establish a circuit of this great mountain sentinel, and bring into this section thousands of motoring tourists. He has ever been a booster for the building of good roads.

Oscar F. Olsson was born in Sweden, on August 19, 1882, the oldest in a family of three boys and three girls born to Andrew and Caroline (Anderson) Olsson. The father was a blacksmith by trade but after the family came to California he went into the garage business with our subject. Edwin, the youngest of the family, is also associated with our subject; Ruben lives in San Francisco; Astrid, now Mrs. Lawrence Humburg, resides in Alamo; Josephine runs a dressmaking parlor in Berkeley; and Ella is a school nurse in the Health Department in Oakland. The father passed away in November, 1921; the mother makes her home in Danville.

On July 22, 1916, Mr. Olsson was married to Miss Ella Boucher, of Alamo, a daughter of Josiah Boucher, a rancher in the Alamo section. Mrs. Olsson is a graduate of the San Francisco Normal School and was engaged in teaching at the time of her marriage. Four sons have been born of this union: David Edwin, Robert Frederick, John Westley, and James Russell.

Mr. Olsson came into the Danville country in 1917 from San Ramon, where he had been engaged in the blacksmith trade with his father. He at once took an interest in public matters and worked for progressive developments; he was constable of the Fourth Township for eight years, resigning to devote his time to his growing garage interests. The splendid record Mr. Olsson made as constable served to endear him to the people, and the demand became insistent that he make the race for supervisor of the Second District. Mr. Olsson had been appointed by Governor

Richardson to fill the vacancy caused by the death of Supervisor J. P. Casey; and he was elected to the office at the regular election in November, 1924, and is now serving on the hospital committee of the board. After assuming the duties of supervisor of his district, Mr. Olsson put through a road building project that had been talked of for twenty years. During 1924-1925 he built the road over Moore Hill through Crow Canyon, giving an excellent highway with a five-per-cent grade over into Alameda County, practically paralleling the Tunnel Road and thus giving an outlet for the people of the southern end of the county. It is considered a fine piece of engineering and road work, and cost about $17,000; and Alameda County will spend $75,000 to complete it on their side of the line. This is one of the outstanding accomplishments of Mr. Olsson's work as a member of the board of supervisors.

Fraternally, Mr. Olsson is a member of Alamo Lodge, Masons, of which he is a Past Master; and belongs to the Richmond Elks, No. 1251; the Woodmen of the World; the U. P. E. C.; the Eastern Star; and the Foresters of America. Locally he is an active member of the Danville Chamber of Commerce. Mrs. Olsson is a member and officer in the Eastern Star Chapter. The Olsson family go to the same camp in the mountains every year, where they enjoy hunting and fishing.

KIRK ELSWORTH GRAY.—A resident of California since 1874 and of Contra Costa County since 1911, Kirk Elsworth Gray has seen much of the development of the northern part of the State since reaching manhood's estate. He was born in Stark County, Ill., on May 6, 1873, and was brought to California by his mother and grandfather, Henry Beck, who settled at Fall River. His father had died when the subject of this sketch was a babe. From Fall River they went to Yreka, and later the lad attended the public school at Dunnigan, Yolo County, for four years. His mother died when he was about ten years old, and from that time to the present he has shifted for himself. He grew up to ranch work and was handy with horses at the age of ten, even driving plow teams at that early age. When a lad of fifteen he left the ranch and started to learn the carpenter's trade, which he followed for some time. However, at the age of nineteen he went back to ranching on his own hook and controlled 1800 acres in Siskiyou County, where he raised stock and also bought and shipped large numbers of cattle to the San Francisco and Oakland markets. Four years of this experience and he quit, "broke," and then went to Redding and worked in a mercantile store three years to get back on his feet. Two years were spent in road building as a subcontractor in Idaho, when he built the road from Boise City to Atlanta. While in that section he experienced many of the pioneer difficulties and found the country very primitive. He then went to Ely, Nev., in 1907, and followed the building business, going thence to Eureka, Nev., and continuing at his trade for about a year. In 1908 he came back to California, located at Vallejo, and contracted there for three years until things got pretty dull in his line. In 1911 he located on the tract now embraced in El Cerrito and was engaged for two weeks to work for the Standard Oil Company at Point Richmond. He is still there, and for years has been carpenter foreman; and much of the development of that immense plant has been done under the direction of Mr. Gray. In 1908 he had purchased a lot, and soon after erected a shanty in which he lived on the site of his present home. In 1911 he completed his residence and moved his family into it.

In 1907 Mr. Gray was united in marriage with Miss Cordelia Neel, the ceremony taking place in Boise City. Mrs. Gray is a native of Idaho, and comes of a pioneer family. They have a son, Gerald Kirk Gray, who graduated from the Richmond High School and is now employed in Oakland. Mr. Gray tells of the fine hunting he enjoyed, while engaged in his building operations for the Standard Oil Company, in the tules. Wild ducks and geese were plentiful and easily secured. At the time he came here the old street car line ran from the Point to the county line, and the Oakland cars stopped there. Ever since locating here he has been interested in having the community grow and has fostered every movement tending to that end. In 1917 a meeting was called to try to establish a lighting district; but upon examination it was found to be too expensive and the meeting virtually turned into one for the incorporation of a city, and resulted in the incorporation of El Cerrito. He was presiding as chairman of that meeting. When the city was incorporated, then he earnestly worked for lights, good streets, and such improvements as are essential to life in a modern city. At the first election Mr. Gray was elected a trustee and chosen chairman of the board, or mayor. In 1918 he was succeeded by P. A. Lee, but with the exception of two years since 1917 he has served the city as councilman. He owns his home property and a lot on Elm Street, thus giving him a strip clear through the block. Politically he is a Democrat in national affairs, but in local matters he considers men and measures rather than party. Fraternally he belongs to the Knights of Pythias of Richmond. He finds his recreation in camping, hunting and fishing. He believes there is a great future in store for this section of Contra Costa County and is always working to benefit the community.

JOHN A. BELL.—An important place among the substantial citizens of Richmond is justly accorded to John A. Bell, who came here almost a quarter of a century ago and whose strongest interests and associations are centered in this city. He was born in Franklin, Pa., on December 10, 1882, a son of Allen and Anna Elizabeth (Allen) Bell, natives of Canada and Wisconsin, respectively. The father came to Franklin, Pa., shortly after the Civil War, and there the family of three sons were born, two of whom died while still young.

John A. Bell received a grammar school education and then went to business college in Pittsburgh, Pa., After finishing school he worked for several firms as salesman. In 1903 he came to California and settled in

Frank Listek

Richmond, where he became an employe of the Standard Oil Company; he worked in several departments, and his promotions have been steady until he now fills the position of foreman of the Inspection Department.

On March 24, 1913, Mr. Bell was married to Miss Irma Adams, a daughter of William and Lydia (Pitzer) Adams. William Adams was a pioneer in Merced, Cal., where he was in the contracting business. Mrs. Bell has one brother living at El Cerrito. Mr. and Mrs. Bell are the parents of one son, Russell Allen. Mrs. Bell is an active member of the Parent-Teachers' Association in Richmond, and with her husband is a member of the Methodist Church. During 1916-1917 Mr. Bell was Exalted Ruler of the Elks in Richmond. He is a charter member of the Gun Club, his number being 11; the club now has a thousand members.

FRANK LISTEK.—A valued employe of the Columbia Steel Corporation in Pittsburg, Cal., Frank Listek enjoys the confidence of those whom he serves. He comes from a family of steel puddlers in Austria, where he was born at Vienna, on October 1, 1873. His father was Rudolph Listek, a steel puddler, and his mother was Elouise Listek. The family moved to Wilkowitz, Mororya, Austria, when Frank was a lad of six years, and it was there he received his education, attending the Gewerbe school, a technical school where he learned drafting. After he had completed his term he was apprenticed as a steel roller for two years. When seventeen he became a roll turner, at which he worked a year, and then began traveling about the country as a journeyman. He put in three years, from twenty-one until he was twenty-four, as a soldier in the Austrian army, after which he went back to the Wilkowitz steel works, where 26,000 men were employed during the day, and the same number at night.

It was while he was living in Wilkowitz that Mr. Listek was married, on February 13, 1898, to Bertha Kojetinsky, who was born in Silesia, of Polish parents, but who attended the German schools. After their marriage the Listeks remained in their home city for about four years, and then emigrated to Old Mexico, where Mr. Listek was employed at the Fumdidora de Fiero y Ocero de Monterey Nuer Leon, Mexico City. Being a very competent designer, he worked there from 1902 until 1906. He has a record of 500 tons in eight hours, and came nearly getting discharged because he did not do more. His old grandfather had a record in the old country of making four rails in twelve hours, for which he was treated to cigars and drinks free. Quite a contrast to these modern times.

When the Mexican revolution was at its height most of the Americans were forced to flee the country, and Mr. Listek with the rest of them. He had met N. A. Becker in Mexico City, where Mr. Becker was engaged in building mills, and he at once recognized a superior workman in Mr. Listek. When he had to leave Mexico he decided to come to California and join Mr. Becker. Accordingly he came to San Francisco, February 27, 1916, and entered the employ of Mr. Becker as a roll turner. Eleven months later he was made roll designer, continuing in South San

Francisco for eleven months. When Mr. Becker came to Pittsburg in 1919, Mr. Listek joined him and helped to build the roller and rod mill, and ever since he has found employment in this great steel manufacturing plant, where he is highly esteemed by his fellow workers. His work is exacting and requires much skill. He designs the rolls for rolling steel bars, rods, etc., produced in this mill.

Of the marriage of Mr. and Mrs. Listek nine children have been born, of whom five are now living, viz.: Josephine, the wife of John Moretti, a machinist in the San Francisco Steel Works, and the mother of two children, George and Albert; Frank, a roll turner with the Columbia Steel Corporation, who married Henrietta Diaz; Irene, the wife of Manuel Weidel, a bank clerk in the Bank of Newman at Crows Landing; and Elsie and Emma, who are attending the grammar school in Pittsburg. Mrs. Listek and the children had a harrowing experience while in Mexico, and suffered many privations. They were unable to join Mr. Listek when he left there, but as soon as possible they came to San Francisco. There the family resided for sixteen months, and then moved to Pittsburg, where they are residing at 129 West 10th Street.

HENRY HOLLMAN.—For more than half a century a resident of California, Henry Hollman is now living retired on the competence gained through many years of hard work; his residence is located at 525 South Sixteenth Street, Richmond, Cal. He has always been an honorable and well-disposed citizen, and as a consequence has won the regard and respect of his neighbors and friends. A son of William Hollman, he was born on October 10, 1852, in Hanover, Germany. His grandfather, John Hollman, was an Englishman, and lived at the time of the Napoleonic wars. William Hollman married Anna Bohling, also of German birth and parentage; her people were farmers in Germany. There were four sons in this family, one of whom died while still young.

Henry Hollman received a common-school education in Germany and there learned the trade of the groceryman. On May 7, 1870, he came to America and settled in New York, where he was in the grocery business for four years. He left New York via the Isthmus of Panama for California in 1874, and soon found employment as a clerk and a representative of wholesale houses in San Francisco, where he remained for three years. In 1880 he opened a grocery store for himself which he operated for the next fourteen years. In 1894 he went to Vallejo, and there he operated a hotel and liquor business, to which he gave his best efforts for eighteen years. In 1912 he removed to Oakland, where he purchased and operated the Pioneer Wine Depot and was in this business until the 18th Amendment was passed, when he retired and lived for a time afterward in Oakland. He purchased property in Richmond and erected buildings for rent; and for some time he has made his residence in this city.

Mr. Hollman was married the first time in 1879 to Adella Rhodes, a native of San Francisco. The following children were born to them:

Adella May, now Mrs. E. Thomas, of San Francisco; Laura, now Mrs. John Costello, of San Francisco, and the mother of three children; Lillie, Mrs. James Pygeorge, who has two children and resides in Alameda; Alice, Mrs. V. Berg, residing in San Francisco; Henry W.; and Alfred Richard, who was in the transport service during the war. Mrs. Hollman passed away in 1905. On February 28, 1908, Mr. Hollman married Mrs. Minnie Kohler, a native of Oakland. She is the daughter of Charles and Dorothea (Apel) Loyn, both natives of Hamburg, Germany. Mrs. Hollman's mother came around the Horn in 1849 on the first German sailing ship Johanes. She built the first brick house in Oakland at the corner of Second Street and Broadway. Charles Loyn built and operated the first brewery in Oakland, which was called the Washington Brewery. He also erected the Loyn Building in Hayward. Mrs. Hollman had four children by her first husband: Olga, Mrs. William Quigley, living in Oakland; Harriet, Mrs. C. Sobrero, who has four children; Frank, battalion chief of the Oakland fire department; and Jack, in business in Los Angeles. Mr. Hollman is Past Chancellor of the Knights of Pythias and a member of the Red Men and Sons of Herman. He is past president of the Retail Grocers' Association of San Francisco. Mr. Hollman spends much of his leisure time in gardening and raising chickens, and is a great lover of all animals.

FRANKLIN P. GRIMSLEY.—Having followed merchandising, and especially the selling of furniture, all of his adult life, and even beginning when but a small boy to learn the merchandising business, it is not surprising that Franklin P. Grimsley has made a success of his furnishing establishment in Richmond. He knows values, and his many years in the business have given him a knowledge of house furnishings which is unique, and which is at the service of his many patrons in Contra Costa County. A native of the Blue Grass State, Mr. Grimsley was born in Lawrence County, Ky., on August 11, 1873. His parents died when he was a baby, and he was obliged to shift for himself at an early age. Raised in the mountains of Kentucky, his schooling was of the log-cabin variety of that period, and was mostly gained in Boyd County, and his early environment built up a sturdy and self-reliant character that has stood him in good stead in later life.

His first place of business was a small country general store in Lawrence County, Ky., and later he ran the same type of store in Carter County, that State. His next step was taken when he conducted a produce business in Ashland, Ky. In June, 1908, Mr. Grimsley arrived in California, first locating on a ranch in Kings County, near Lemoore. After one year on the ranch, he moved into Lemoore and worked as a clerk in stores there for four years. Coming to Berkeley in 1913, he met B. B. McGinnis, and was interested with him in his Merced Store for about four years. Returning to Berkeley with $800 capital, Mr. Grimsley established a second-hand furniture store in South Berkeley. On June 15, 1917, he arrived in Richmond, and was with the LaSalle Company for a time. Leaving that concern, in March, 1922, he established the Richmond Furniture Company. Selling out his interest in that business, he then established the Richmond Furnishing Company, in March, 1923, in a new building built expressly for the purpose, at 320 Ninth Street. Here he specializes in a credit business, and has met with unqualified success. The establishment is the newest and most modern furniture store in Richmond, fully and completely stocked with home furnishings, and is decidedly a growing concern, under capable and up-to-the-minute management.

Mr. Grimsley married Alberta Patterson, also a Kentuckian, born in Ashland, and two daughters have blessed their union, Mary Catherine and Sarah Lucile. Fraternally, Mr. Grimsley is a member of Willard Lodge No. 626, F. & A. M., of Willard, Ky., and both he and Mrs. Grimsley are members of the Richmond Chapter of the Eastern Star. Mrs. Grimsley is a very efficient business woman, and an able assistant to her husband in carrying on his establishment.

COL. M. M. GARRETT.—One of the prettiest country places to be found in Contra Costa County is the home of Colonel Manuel Mordecai Garrett, where this veteran of four wars has retired to lead the quiet life necessary for his complete recuperation from the military campaigns in which he has taken an active part. Colonel Garrett was born in Booneville, Mo., on July 26, 1878, a son of John Smith Garrett, who was born September 2, 1833, in Frankfort, Ky. The grandfather, Robert Garrett, was born in Baltimore, Md., in 1786, and the great-grandfather was a native of Edinburgh, Scotland, where his father, Robert Garrett, was an agriculturist. Colonel Garrett's father and all of his brothers were members of the Confederate Army during the Civil War, the father serving as a lieutenant under Colonel McCullough. He was captured at Wilson Creek, near Springfield, Mo., and was placed on parole by General Lyons and so remained throughout the period of the war. Mary Schroeder Garrett, mother of John Smith Garrett, was of Dutch descent and was born in Harrodsburg, Ky. His wife was Rachel Clover of Belleville, Ill., daughter of James and Mary (Lane) Clover, natives of Ireland and England, respectively. John Smith Garrett remained in Missouri, locating in Cooper County, where he purchased land, engaged in agriculture, and reared a family. He died in 1892. There were seven children in the family, five of whom are still living.

Colonel Garrett was educated in the public schools and at Cooper Institute of Booneville. Leaving his studies to enlist in the 6th Missouri Volunteers for service in the Spanish-American War, on May 17, 1898, he was mustered into the Federal service on July 23, of that year, and remained in the 6th Missouri Volunteers till January 26, 1899, at which time he was discharged therefrom and enlisted in the 16th Infantry on February 1, 1899. He served with the 16th Infantry throughout the Philippine campaign, returning home in March, 1902, when he enlisted in the Coast

Artillery. He was commissioned second lieutenant of the infantry on October 9, 1903, and this was followed by regular promotions of various grades up to captain. He was then transferred to the Quartermaster's Corps in May, 1916, and detailed as paymaster on the Pershing expedition of 1916 to Mexico, serving with the Pershing staff until the return in March, 1917. He was then transferred to El Paso, Texas, as construction quartermaster, and upon the entrance of the United States into the World War was ordered to Camp Custer, Mich., for duty in the construction of the divisional cantonment. Upon the arrival of troops at Camp Custer he was detailed as camp quartermaster in addition to construction quartermaster, serving in both capacities until the completion of the camp. On August 5, 1917, he received a commission as Major of the Quartermaster Corps. Early in 1918 he was ordered to Newport News, Va., to relieve the congestion of that port, and was detailed to become Expeditionary Quartermaster. While here he received the commission of Lieutenant-Colonel and was ordered to sail for France. Upon his arrival in France he was ordered to duty at Le Havre, where he was made Base Quartermaster, Section No. 4 (Normandy Section). He remained at this station until his health failed as the result of his strenuous duties and he was ordered to the base hospital at Le Havre, and was sent back to the United States for an operation and retired on July 26, 1920, on account of disability incurred in line of duty.

Due to outdoor and country life, Colonel Garrett has practically recovered from his disability. In 1921 he entered the real estate business; but, on account of the state of his health at that time, he was forced to give it up and come to the country. He located in Happy Valley, near Lafayette, where he conducts a ranch in connection with his real estate and insurance business. His real estate transactions involve everything from large ranches to small home lots. His own ranch of 100 acres in Happy Valley is devoted to the growing of walnuts and pears and is one of the show places of that section. He is president of the Contra Costa County Farm Bureau, is a member of the Army & Navy Club of San Francisco, belongs to the American Legion, and is a member of the County Central Republican Committee. Colonel Garrett is a gifted speaker and a born leader of men. He also does some writing for various publications.

On August 26, 1906, Colonel Garrett married Miss Edith Spalding, of Honolulu, Hawaiian Islands. She is the daughter of E. I. Spalding, a banker and sugar man of the Islands, and his wife, Marie Kaler (Long) Spalding, formerly of Vallejo. Mrs. Garrett is a graduate of Oahu College and is a gifted musician. She is fond of flowers and gardening, and during her college days was a champion tennis player. Colonel and Mrs. Garrett are the parents of two children: Edith Marie, now attending the Anna Head School, a private institution in Berkeley, and Robert Spalding, a sophomore in Danville High School. Colonel Garrett is interested in all forms of athletics, and in his younger days was a wrestler and boxer.

ACHILLE CAVAGNOLO.—One of the most enterprising and successful bakers of Contra Costa County is Achille Cavagnolo, of Pittsburg, proprietor of the French-Italian Bakery located on East Seventh Street. Beginning on a small scale, he has gradually built up one of the best businesses of its kind in the county and does a strictly wholesale bakery business. He was born on May 22, 1886, at Rosignano, Monferrao, Italy, the son of Louis and Caroline Cavagnolo, the latter still living. The father has passed away.

Achille Cavagnolo spent his boyhood and youth in Italy, and after he had completed his schooling he learned the art of making cement decorations. Being ambitious to achieve success in life, he realized that America offered better and greater opportunities for honest, energetic and courageous young men, and in 1909 he sailed from Genoa for New York City, landing on June 3, that same year. His destination was San Francisco and he continued his journey westward and arrived on June 10. His brother Emelio had preceded him to California by about three years and was engaged in the pastry business in San Francisco. Achille found employment as shipping clerk for Swift & Company from 1909 to 1914. Then he engaged in business as a window cleaner and carried on that enterprise until 1918, when he sold out and came to Pittsburg and purchased the nucleus of his present business. It was not long before he had begun to make himself known to the public and to create a good demand for his various kinds of American, French and Italian breads, pies and pastries. The success of his business venture was made more apparent when he purchased real estate on East Seventh Street, in 1921. Here he built a store room, with living quarters, and also an up-to-date sanitary bakery on the rear of the lot; and here he operates his model bakery under strict sanitary conditions. Because of the use of the best ingredients in his bakery goods, and his courteous treatment of customers, his business continues to grow.

In San Francisco, on September 20, 1912, Mr. Cavagnolo was united in marriage with Miss Inez Carbonelli, a native of Frassmoro, Modena, Italy, where her parents still reside. This union has been blessed with two children: Lillian and Evelyn. Fraternally, Mr. Cavagnolo is a member of the Loyal Order of Moose and the Foresters. He belongs to the Pittsburg Chamber of Commerce and to the Lions Club.

WILLIAM G. MAYER.—One of the flourishing business enterprises of Richmond is the cleaning and dyeing establishment of William G. Mayer, one of the most substantial citizens of the community. Mr. Mayer was born in San Jose, on March 12, 1876, the son of B. E. and Dolores (Castanea) Mayer. B. E. Mayer was a shoemaker and a native of Germany. There were five children in the family, four boys and one girl, two of whom are now living in San Francisco and one in Redwood City, and one is deceased.

William G. Mayer received his early education in the grammar school of San Jose, and at the age of fifteen he started to work as salesman in his father's shoe store, which position he held for five years. His next venture was as a traveling salesman for the wholesale house of Cohn, Nicklesburg & Company of San Francisco, in whose employ he was for two years. Following this he went into business with his brothers in San Jose, where he remained until the time of the earthquake on April 18, 1906. The business was then discontinued, and he came to Richmond in 1909 and established his cleaning and dyeing business, which is now housed in a commodious building, which he owns. Twelve people are kept constantly employed, and the whole city and surrounding territory are covered by his wagons. The Glover system of cleaning, consisting of a continuous flow of chemicals, is used. Mr. Mayer also has other business interests in the city and is financially interested in a hog ranch, located on the San Pablo Dam road, where nine people are employed and 3000 to 3500 head of hogs are fed. He is a member of the Moose Lodge, in which he has been much interested for a long time, and also of the Red Men and the Native Sons of the Golden West. He is also a member of the Chamber of Commerce and the Merchants' Association of Richmond.

Mr. Mayer was married on June 9, 1904, to Miss Katherine Malovos, the ceremony being performed by Rev. Father Kenna, president of the Santa Clara University. Her father, Andrea Malovos, was an orchardist; and the mother, Maria J. (Alviso) Malovos, was one of the family for which the town of Alviso was named. Mrs. Mayer's mother and father are both now deceased. She is one of a family of twelve children. To Mr. and Mrs. Mayer four children have been born: William G. Jr., Lloyd Richard, and Marie Kathryn, all in high school; and Robert Anthony, in the junior high school.

JAMES W. HAMMOND, M. D.—Among the professional men of Contra Costa County, none is more in touch with the general spirit of progress in the West than James W. Hammond of Byron, widely known as a proficient exponent of the best principles of medical science and a conscientious physician and surgeon devoted to the amelioration of human suffering. To have practiced in one of the best communities of the State for more than a quarter of a century is an honor accorded to but few doctors in California, yet this is the honor enjoyed by Doctor Hammond. During the number of years he has pursued the practice of his profession in Byron, he has been known, not only for his skill and assiduity as a physician, but also for his culture, genial manners and optimistic spirit, which have made him one of the most beloved and highly esteemed citizens of the community.

Doctor Hammond is a native of Rock County, Wis., born September 8, 1856, a son of W. P. and Emily (Barrett) Hammond, the former a native of Connecticut, the latter of New York State. When James W. was but four years of age his parents migrated to California, settling at Napa where the father opened a shop as an expert cabinet maker, gunsmith and mechanic. He died at the age of seventy-six; the mother died when she was fifty-six. They were the parents of five children: James W., Oliver P., Harry, the well known editor and publisher of the Byron Times; Mrs. Lydia Turner of Long Beach, Cal.; and Fred, who died at the age of one year. Doctor Hammond graduated from the California Medical College at San Francisco, in 1897, and for some time practiced in that city before moving to Byron in 1898, where he has continuously followed his chosen profession. He is a prominent leader in the Seventh Day Adventist Church, at Byron, being one of the founders and builders of the attractive church edifice situated on the highway.

In 1894 J. W. Hammond was united in marriage with Miss Ida Hiserman, born in Salinas, Cal., and they are the parents of two children: William, now living at Stockton; and Mervyn. Doctor Hammond is a member of the San Francisco Society of the College of Physicians & Surgeons, and is affiliated with the Morton Hospital of that city; is medical examiner for several fraternal insurance and social organizations, and is the resident physician for the Southern Pacific Company at Byron. He holds membership in the State Medical Society and the National Medical Association. The name of Dr. James W. Hammond will be long and honorably associated with the history of Contra Costa County.

ALBERT C. TRETTE.—One of the prominent residents of Clayton is Albert C. Trette, assistant operator at the "Edelaine" plant of the Associated Oil Company at Avon. Mr. Trette's duties are of an exacting nature calling for great mechanical skill and scientific technical knowledge, hence it is a position of considerable responsibility. It is in this plant that "Burn-brite" kerosene is manufactured according to a recently adopted German formula which gives a product making a bright, clear light when used for illumination, and intense heat, free from odor, when used in oil heating stoves or ranges. Mr. Trette takes the delight of a true craftsman in his work and is a fine example of the right man in the right place.

He comes from a long line of machinists and mechanical experts. His father, Charles Henry Trette, conducted the village smithy in Clayton for thirty-four years and was noted throughout the county for his mechanical skill. He is still living and conducts an apartment house at Piedmont, a suburb of Oakland. Charles H. Trette was born in Germany and came to America while a young man. He married Emma Jane Robinson, a native daughter of California, who died in Clayton on November 4, 1914. They were the parents of seven children, three sons and four daughters, as follows: Rudolph, a machinist, resides in Clayton; Albert C., subject of this sketch; Orville, a machinist, in the employ of the Santa Fe Railroad; Ramona, resides in Richmond; Mabel, resides in Pixley; Pearl, resides in Richmond; and Wilhelmina, resides near San Francisco.

Albert C. Trette, the second son, was born in Clayton, on July 20, 1888, attended the public school of Clayton and as a boy and youth worked in his father's blacksmith shop, greatly enjoying the work. As a young man he secured a position on the old Kirkwood ranch near Clayton,

MR. AND MRS. GEORGE W. ATCHINSON

where he was employed for eleven years, being finally promoted to the position of foreman. During this period he married Miss Ada Jane Myrick, daughter of the pioneer farmer, Walter Myrick, of Clayton Precinct. To Mr. and Mrs. Trette two children were born, Albert C., Jr., and Reginald Benjamin. About 1923 Mr. Trette became connected with the Associated Oil Company, starting as a pipe fitter. It was apparent from the start that he had found his true vocation and he was rapidly promoted until finally transferred to his present responsible position.

MR. AND MRS. GEORGE W. ATCHINSON.—One of the venerable pioneer women of Clayton Precinct, Contra Costa County, is Mrs. Elizabeth Atchinson, widow of the late George Washington Atchinson, who died in Berkeley on November 22, 1925, at the age of eighty-seven years and fourteen days. Mr. Atchinson had made three trips across the plains to California and had witnessed much of its subsequent growth. For many years Mr. and Mrs. Atchinson were rated among the most industrious ranchers of this county, and their home was a model of its kind, where a real hospitality was dispensed. Both Mr. and Mrs. Atchinson were born in Fulton, Greene County, Ill., and there they were married. Their parents were among the pioneer settlers there when that section was considered as being on the Western frontier. Mrs. Atchinson was born on August 2, 1850, and was united in marriage with Mr. Atchinson on August 24, 1871.

Their marriage resulted in the birth of four boys: Alonzo W., of Berkeley, who is married and the father of one daughter living, Mamie, and two children deceased, Martin and Viola; John W., of Clayton Precinct, who is the parent of two children, Wilbur and Mrs. Mildred Edlen, the latter the mother of a son, Kenneth; Arthur B., who resides in Berkeley and has a son Arthur, Jr.; and George A., who lives on his own place, which was a part of the original home ranch, and has two boys, Marvin and Elden.

After going through the usual experiences of the prospector and miner, the father finally decided to settle down to agricultural pursuits and in 1895 bought a ranch near Clayton. His experience as a farmer in Iowa, whither he had moved with his wife and two boys before settling in California, now stood him in good stead; he began with bare land, and added every improvement seen on it today. With the help of his boys and his wife he made a success of his farming and finally retired to Berkeley, where he passed away. The property consists of fifty-five and three-quarters acres of fine land and is devoted to the raising of fruit and to general farming.

Mrs. Atchinson has first-hand knowledge of the hardships and struggles of the pioneer women, for she pioneered in Iowa before settling in California. Both she and her husband were honored residents of this

21

county, and by their kindly and neighborly acts to those in distress they drew around them a warm circle of devoted friends. Mrs. Atchinson divides her time between her four sons and their families, and is hale and hearty despite her many years of struggle and deprivation. She still owns the home ranch, and her visits there are looked forward to with joy by her children and grandchildren.

THOMAS D. WALKER.—Thomas D. Walker is one of the most widely known men of Walnut Creek, where he has been postmaster since 1922. Born in Kings County, Ireland, February 11, 1860, he is the son of Joseph James and Margaret (Dawson) Walker, both natives of the same country. There were six children in this family: James, deceased; Dawson, deceased; Joseph; Thomas D., our subject; Henry; and Cranston, deceased. Joseph James Walker lived to be seventy-four years old, and his wife was sixty-nine years old when she passed away.

Thomas D. Walker was reared and educated in his native country, attending first a private elementary school and later the University of Dublin. At the age of twenty years he left Ireland for Canada, settling at Winnipeg, where he spent four years farming and working for the Hudson Bay Trading Company. In 1885 he came to the United States and settled at Minneapolis, where he was employed by the Northern Pacific Railroad, serving as yardman and switchman for three years, and then becoming cashier at the Minneapolis station. On account of his dependability this company sent him to Portland, Ore., as claim agent, and he occupied this position for the following ten years. Mr. Walker was also outside auditor for Ladd & Tilton, of Portland. He then removed to San Francisco and accepted the position of secretary for the Phoenix Savings & Loan Society, continuing there until the opportunity came to enter the real estate business with Breed & Bancroft, a venture which proved of particular benefit financially. In 1906 Mr. Walker sold his home in Oakland and removed to Contra Costa County, where he was one of the first to purchase a portion of the Larkey Homestead subdivision. On this tract of land he engaged in farming successfully until 1911, when he took charge of the construction work for the Walnut Creek Development Company. During his three years of service in this capacity he helped to put through the Mount Diablo Boulevard and the Tunnel Road from Berkeley. Mr. Walker then became bookkeeper for the First National Bank of Walnut Creek, and later was advanced to assistant cashier of this institution, with which he remained until 1922, when he was appointed postmaster at Walnut Creek.

On December 26, 1884, at Moose Jaw, Canada, Mr. Walker was united in marriage to Miss Edith Welsh, a native of Liverpool, England, daughter of Robert A. and Elizabeth (Bowman) Welsh, and fifth child in a family of six children. Robert A. Welsh was manager of one of England's largest banks. When the financial panic hit London he lost heavily, and then went to South America, hoping to regain his former fortune; there he passed away while still a young man. Six children have been born to Mr. and Mrs. Walker: Robert Lawrence; Margaret, Mrs. Culver, residing in Oakland; Grace, Mrs. Harry M. Stow, residing in Walnut Creek; Christina, Mrs. Armand Stow, of Pittsburg, Cal.; Cranston; and Eva. There are twelve grandchildren in the family. Mr. Walker is a Republican in politics; and fraternally he is a member of the Masonic order in Oakland and the Sciots of San Francisco. Mrs. Walker is a member of the Eastern Star chapter of Walnut Creek. Mr. Walker holds the position of honorary treasurer of the city of Walnut Creek, and with his influence and means has liberally supported all projects that would advance the interests of its citizens.

ANTONIO F. MASSA.—A highly respected citizen of the Richmond district, and a hard-working man, Antonio F. Massa has seen much of the development of this section since he settled here in 1909. He was born in Italy on June 16, 1864, the son of G. Batiste Massa, a pioneer of California of 1856. In that early day the elder Massa arrived in the Golden State and went to prospecting and mining in Calaveras County continuing thus for six years. He did not get the expected fortune, but he did get enough money to return to his native land, where he married the girl of his choice in 1863. Her name was Madelina Zanoni, and she was a native of his locality. Their oldest child, our subject, was born there, and soon afterwards the father again came to California to follow his work on his placer claims in Calaveras County. He worked to gain the necessary money and in 1880 sent for wife, son and daughter, who were glad to join him in his new home. Two more years were spent in mining, and then his wife induced him to sell out and go to San Francisco and make another start. He died in Napa County at the age of seventy-seven, and his good wife died in Fresno County at the home of her daughter, Mrs. Victoria Perazzo, at the age of sixty-seven years.

Antonio F. Massa attended the Italian schools and came with his mother and sister to California in 1880. In San Francisco, when he was eighteen, he was apprenticed to Mr. O'Connor to learn the carpenter's trade and remained with him for six years, becoming one of his best workmen. When he started at the trade he received fifty cents a day for his services, and Mr. O'Connor told his father that he ought to charge him something to have the lad about instead of having to pay him anything. After six months he was paid one dollar a day, and later he was advanced to one dollar and fifty cents. Upon the death of Mr. O'Connor he went out on his own hook and worked at the trade in various localities. He was naturalized in 1886, when he was twenty-one, in the superior court in San Francisco. He never attended an English school, but had a hobby of going to theaters and in that way picked up the language, as also by reading papers and good books. To hear him talk, it would be difficult to comprehend that he had not attended schools in America. He followed the carpenter's trade for six more years in San Francisco, and then was in the employ of the United States Government at Mare Island Navy Yard for a number of years. He also spent two and one-half years for the Government in the Samoan Islands, but came back to California to join his family in 1895. They lived in Vallejo for thirteen years, and then moved back to San Francisco eight days before the great fire and earthquake, in which he lost all he possessed. He also followed his trade in San Mateo County for a time. In 1907 he went to Colusa and spent two years, coming to Contra Costa County in 1909.

In 1888 Mr. Massa was married in San Francisco to Theresa Vermi, a native of Chile, born of Italian parents, but reared and educated in San Francisco from the age of six months. Of this union eleven children were born, seven of whom are living, viz.: Charles; Alfred; Antonio, Jr.; Elwin; Edna, who married John Bogardo; Mabel; and Mildred. The children attended the local schools and the sons are associated with their father in his nursery business. Charles and Alfred served in the World War. Charles was in the Engineers' Corps of the 91st Division and saw service in France; Alfred's command were under marching orders to embark, but the following day the armistice was signed.

Coming to Contra Costa County in 1909, Mr. Massa met John Ryan, who put the tract where Mr. Massa now lives on the market. Mr. Massa bought two lots and erected their home. He followed the carpenter's trade for some years, and then was engaged in raising mushrooms for the market for eight years, losing some $18,000 in the business. He had as his friend and backer Frank Rossi, of Colma, San Mateo County. He began on a small scale, knowing nothing about the business; but he began to get ahead and every cent he made he put back into improvements and added to his capacity, even buying additional land to operate on. Having the property on his hands, he saw it opportune to erect greenhouses in place of the mushroom houses, and now has some 80,000 square feet under glass and with the aid of his sons is engaged in raising roses for the San Francisco markets. In 1926 a modern heating system was installed with an 80 horse-power boiler and a modern system of irrigation of his own planning, for watering and fertilizing at the same time, and sanitary in every way. He is one of the organizers and the president of the San Francisco Flower Growers' Association, and the American Rosarian Association count him a member. The firm of A. F. Massa & Sons is well equipped to do a fine business, and is noted for honesty and square dealings in all business transactions. Mr. Massa is a Republican in national affairs, but in local matters considers men and measures in preference to party. The family are well and favorably known in the bay region for their many fine traits of character.

LOUIS DELLA ROSA.—Among the successful business men of Martinez must be mentioned Louis Della Rosa, a son of Italy who came here in 1903, and has since that time been identified with the business life of the city. Born at Romanea, Messina, Italy, January 29, 1877, he is the oldest of three children born to his parents, who were farmer folk of that country and are still living there, the father now seventy-nine years old. The only member of the family to come to California, Louis Della Rosa grew up on the home farm, and attended the public schools of his native land. In addition to farming, as a youth and young man he learned the trade of the carpenter, bricklayer and plasterer. When twenty years of age, he entered the Italian Army as a member of Artillery Regiment No. 7, and served the regular two years prescribed by the Italian government, receiving at the end of that time his honorable discharge.

With the desire to see the new world and seek his fortunes there, in 1903 Mr. Della Rosa came to the United States, and after two months spent in Pennsylvania came on to California and settled in Martinez. For two years after his arrival he was in the employ of the Peyton Chemical Works, and from there he went to the Mountain Copper Company and worked for them steadily for the next five years. He then entered the employ of Mr. Lottman, then the agent of the San Francisco Brewery; and eighteen months later he established the Marconi Hotel, at the corner of Castro and Escobar Streets, Martinez, and continued as the Martinez agent for the San Francisco Brewery, which position he has held ever since. He prospered in his hotel business, continuing there until 1920, during which time he enlarged the building at two different times. In 1920, he opened the Liberty Hotel, on Pacheco Boulevard, and also built the garage across the street, known as the Ordway Garage. The hotel is provided with a fine ballroom and is the center for many balls, banquets, and other social functions. Mr. Della Rosa also owns and operates an extensive express business, with headquarters at Martinez, under the firm name of L. Della Rosa & Son. This company owns three large automobile trucks, and they also operate a number of large moving vans and dump trucks, doing a general express and freight business in the Bay region.

The marriage of Mr. Della Rosa, which occurred in Italy, united him with Rosa DeLucca, also a native of that country, and four children have blessed their union: Eugene, in active charge of the express business, and Constantina, Dorothy and Katherine; all are graduates of the Alhambra Union High School. Fraternally, Mr. Della Rosa is a member of the Dante Society, the Moose and the Druids, all of Martinez. His success in life has been reached through the application of the habits of work and thrift which he acquired in his youth, and he is a well-liked man in the community which has been his home for so many years.

FRANK J. CARDINALLI.—The efficient manager of the Pittsburg branch of the well-known firm of A. Paladini, Inc., of San Francisco, fish dealers, is Frank J. Cardinalli, born in Pittsburg when the place was known as Black Diamond. The corporation which he so ably represents is one of the largest and most important in the State, and Pittsburg is its most important branch. Some 750 fishermen are employed in catching fish for the various packing houses and canneries in Pittsburg, and the scenes of their activity are the Sacramento and San Joaquin Rivers, the San Pablo, Suisun and San Francisco Bays, and the Carquinez Straits.

Frank Cardinalli's father, Arasimo Cardinalli, was one of the pioneer fishermen upon the bays and rivers, beginning his operations here when this city was known as New York Landing. He built the first power launch, about 1902, and used it to visit the fishermen in order to buy their catches from their little fishing boats. In later years he operated on the Columbia River and its tributaries, in all his operations meeting with such success that he has been able to retire and enjoy the competence he has earned. He and his good wife became the parents of five children. Frank J., the oldest, was born on September 22, 1892. When only eleven years of age he accompanied his father in his power launch and wrote out the fish tags for the fish purchased, for his father could neither read nor write. When he was fifteen he had charge of one of the power launches owned by his father and bought fish himself, having learned every detail of the business as conducted by his father. After his father sold his packing plant to A. Paladini, Inc., Frank became manager for the new company, and he still holds that important position.

The seasons for fishing are from April 1 to June 15, and from August 15 to September 17, and during these periods Mr. Cardinalli finds plenty to occupy his time and attention. The corporation employs twenty-five men in and about the Pittsburg plant, and contracts for the catch of fish from about 150 fishermen. During the season from April 1 to June 15, 1925, this branch handled 1,000,000 pounds of salmon and striped bass and catfish; and during the season from August 1 to September 17, some 400,000 pounds, mostly salmon. This plant mild-cures shad and salmon in large quantities, the latter being used for smoking. The product finds ready market in New York and in Germany, while the shad is consumed in the United States.

Frank J. Cardinalli was married in San Francisco on June 17, 1912, to Miss Fannie Murzi, who was born in Santa Cruz, the daughter of Paul Murzi, pioneer fisherman of Santa Cruz and Monterey. One child has come to bless this happy union, Arasimo. The family are members of the Catholic Church and are popular in their social set in Pittsburg. In politics Mr. Cardinalli supports the candidates of the Republican party.

FRANK GANZERT.—A veteran of the Civil War, having seen service in California and Oregon, Frank Ganzert was born at Frankfort, Germany, on July 4, 1849, the son of Jacob Ganzert, who was also born in that city. Jacob Ganzert was a musician, and served for twelve years as musician in the German Army. He came to the United States, and soon entered the United States Army, serving twenty-one years as a musician. During this period he came to California with General Wright, taking part in the Indian Wars in Oregon. After his time was served, he decided to remain in California and lived retired in San Francisco. His death occurred at the Soldiers' Home at Yountville.

Frank Ganzert was brought to this country when eighteen months old, by his parents, and soon the father went to Fort Monroe and joined the government service. In 1852 they came in a sailing vessel around Cape Horn to San Francisco. From here the family went north to Vancouver, Wash., then to The Dalles, Ore., and from there to Walla Walla, and young Ganzert's education was obtained at these different places, through instructors supplied by the government. It was natural that he should first decide on a military career. After the family came down to the Presidio in San Francisco, he volunteered in Company E, 9th California Infantry, during the Civil War, and served under Capt. Edward Pollock. He was sent to Fort Point, and then to Fort Gaston, on the Klamath River, and served his country with patriotic zeal for four years, receiving his honorable discharge in 1866 at Fort Gaston Indian Reservation. These valiant old soldiers are given all honor by the citizens of a reunited country, and their thinning ranks serve to remind us of how much we owe to their unselfish and sacrificing patriotism.

After resuming civil life, Mr. Ganzert came to Walnut Creek, Contra Costa County, and then to San Francisco for a time; and from there he started on a prospecting and mining tour, going to Placer, Nevada, and Sierra Counties, California. Meantime, however, each winter was spent at Walnut Creek, where he had established his home soon after the close of the Civil War.

Mr. Ganzert's marriage, at Martinez, united him with Mrs. Lizzie Logan, a native of Missouri. She was the mother of one child by her first marriage, to John Logan. One child was born of their union, a daughter, Allie, who married Joe Marshall and has two children. Mrs. Ganzert died in 1919. An old-timer in Contra Costa County, Mr. Ganzert has seen the many changes which have taken place here, the remarkable growth of the past two decades and the even more remarkable projects which are now getting under way, and he has never regretted that he decided to locate here. He is a Republican in politics, and has the honor of having cast a vote for Abraham Lincoln.

JOSEPH STOCKFLETH.—Representatives of nearly all of the races of the earth have contributed their share toward the upbuilding and development of California. In this program of colonization and progress the Scandinavian racial strain has played a most important part. One of the leading citizens of Clayton Precinct in Contra Costa County is Joseph Stockfleth who is justly proud of the Danish blood which flows in his veins, and of the Swedish blood of his loyal wife. They are an industrious couple, deeply interested in their home, children and the common welfare—the brand of citizenship which is a valuable addition to any community. Mr. Stockfleth is a man of sound business judgment and a good manager, one of the leading farmers and stockmen of the vicinity. He was clerk of the school board in his district and takes a keen interest in all things pertaining to making the district a better place in which to live and rear a family.

Mr. Stockfleth is a native son, having been born in San Francisco on October 18, 1880. His father, Capt. John Stockfleth, was one of the best known sea captains of the Bay City and sailed the West Coast for thirty-seven years, a picturesque figure accustomed to facing calmly the perils and hardships of "those who go down to sea in ships." Captain Stockfleth was born in Schleswig-Holstein, which at that time was a province of Denmark. Like so many of his race he took to the sea at an early age and in time became a sea captain. Hearing of the opportunities to be found in America he came to San Francisco and became a member of the firm of Hobbs, Wall & Co., a steamship concern. For many years he was a commander of an ocean-going vessel of which he was part owner. As a boy Joseph Stockfleth often accompanied his father on these voyages and had many interesting experiences. In 1892 Captain Stockfleth, having grown weary of the sea, purchased land in Clayton Precinct and made many improvements. An almond orchard of twenty-five acres, which he set out, is now full bearing and one of the finest to be found in Contra Costa County. Captain Stockfleth married Isabel Wilkie, who was born in Nevada while her parents were on their way to California. They became the parents of seven children, Joseph being their second son and child. Captain Stockfleth lived to be seventy-seven years old. His wife died at the age of fifty-six years.

Joseph Stockfleth attended the public schools in San Francisco and was fourteen years old when he accompanied his parents to the farm in Clayton Precinct. As he became a young man he went to the mother-lode country and worked at quartz mining for several years with but indifferent success. Returning to Clayton Precinct he resumed farming and stock-raising which he found to be a more profitable calling than mining was for him. He is a well-known stockman, raising some of his cattle, but usually buys stockers and feeders in Nevada, Utah, Wyoming and Oregon. These he ships to his Clayton farms, in the fall of the year, where they feed upon the rich wild oats and other grasses. By spring they are ready for shipment to San Francisco markets where they command highest prices. He owns the old Stockfleth home ranch of eighty acres, the Wetmore ranch of 175 acres, a third ranch of forty acres, and he rents 1455 acres, making a total of 1750 acres which he controls.

On August 1, 1909, Mr. Stockfleth married Miss Laura Olofson, daughter of John P. and Clarissa Olofson. Her father was a native of Sweden, and the mother was born in England and came to California, where they married, settling in Oakland. Mr. and Mrs. Stockfleth have two children; Laura May, attending high school; and John, in the grammar school.

Alva S Sherlock

ALVA SHERMAN SHERLOCK.—One of the foremost of the leading citizens of Concord is Alva Sherman Sherlock, city attorney, who has most ably handled the legal affairs of the thriving community since 1916, when he was first appointed to that position, having been reappointed each consecutive year since.   Mr. Sherlock is a self-made man, a brilliant barrister, and enjoys the complete confidence of a large and constantly growing number of clients.

The branch of the Sherlock family from which Mr. Sherlock is a descendant, is an old and honorable one, originating in England and migrating to Ireland during the turbulent Cromwellian period, which changed the lives and fortunes of so many English families.   The family settled in County Antrim, Ireland, at some time prior to 1700.   The American progenitors, who were Protestants, arrived in this country in pre-Revolutionary days.   Hugh Sherlock, founder of this branch of the family, after his arrival from Ireland, settled in Muskingum County, Ohio, where he became a successful farmer and landowner, residing there until his death at the age of eighty-eight years.   It was on this farm that Abraham Sherlock was born; and he, too, became a successful farmer and landowner.   He married Adeline Sandel, who died in 1926 at the age of eighty-one; and they became the parents of Alva Sherman Sherlock, who was born on September 26, 1869.

In 1875 the family removed to Poweshiek County, Iowa, where Abraham Sherlock became the owner of 160 acres of land on which he raised cattle.   The early days of young Alva Sherlock were spent in herding cattle on the range, an occupation not without its thrills and, frequently, actual perils.   He had five brothers and one sister, being the second son and third child of the family.   The sister, Margaret V. Sherlock, lives with the mother in Oakland; Louis is a fruit grower in Santa Clara County; Hugh is employed by the Pacific Gas & Electric Company in Santa Cruz; Elmer is a successful attorney in Chicago; Edmund V. has been admitted to the bar, but is now engaged in real estate in Chicago; while the youngest brother, Roy W., is a fruit grower in San Luis Obispo County.   The mother of this family, now eighty-one years old, is still living, but the father died in Iowa some forty-six years ago.

As already mentioned, the early years of Alva Sherman Sherlock were spent on the range in Iowa, his education being received in the near-by country school.   But while still quite young he determined that he would become a lawyer, and this unwavering thought he kept in mind until his ambition was finally attained.   He attended night school in Chicago and studied law in the office of attorney H. A. Haines.   In 1897 he successfully passed the Illinois State Bar examinations and became a full-fledged attorney.   He continued his studies in Mr. Haines' office, however, and was employed in the Newberry Library in the evenings.   In 1898 came the call for volunteers for the Spanish-American War and he enlisted in the 1st Illinois Volunteer Cavalry, serving throughout the war until he was mustered out with an honorable discharge at Fort Sheridan, Chicago, October 11, 1898. After his discharge from the army he opened a law office in Chicago, where he practiced for several years.

On September 26, 1901, Mr. Sherlock was united in marriage with Miss May P. Kent, who was born in Circleville, Ohio, and graduated from the high school of Wellington, Kans. They moved to the State of Washington in 1906 and settled in Newport, which was then in Stevens County but is now in Pend Oreille County. Mr. Sherlock practiced there until 1913, being city attorney of Newport and also of Deer Park, Wash. During this period he assisted in the incorporation of the town of Ione. In 1913 he removed to Spokane, where he practiced for two years. In 1915 he came to Concord and opened a law office, after having been admitted to the California Bar in June, 1915. Later he was admitted to the United States District and Circuit Courts. Mr. and Mrs. Sherlock had a daughter, May Ruth, who graduated from the University of California and married Martin C. F. Graeber, of Long Beach. Mrs. Sherlock died on April 29, 1925, aged forty-two years.

Mr. Sherlock is a member of the American Bar Association, the California Bar Association, and the Bar Association of Contra Costa County. He is also a member of Camp Liscomb, of Oakland, Spanish-American War Veterans, and a member of the Royal Arcanum. He is attorney for the Bank of Concord and the Concord Branch of the American Bank.

JAMES A. McVITTIE.—As city manager of Richmond, Contra Costa County, the career of James A. McVittie has been almost phenomenal, for its record of civic accomplishment in the successful promotion of municipal improvements in the city under his direction. He worked so energetically and proved so successful in his management that there can be no doubt in anyone's mind that he is the right man in the right place. Born in Parkersburg, W. Va., February 5, 1885, he is the son of George and Florence McVittie. He was reared and educated in Hamilton, Ontario, and in 1903 came to Richmond, Cal., and entered the employ of the Standard Oil Company, doing clerical work. He remained with that company until July 1, 1910, and was then made city auditor of Richmond, which office he filled until July 15, 1920, when he was appointed city manager of Richmond.

Under his able management Richmond has grown and prospered to a really marvelous extent, and with the help of his fellow citizens he has tackled and brought to completion projects which much larger cities have hesitated to undertake. An electrolier lighting system has been installed in the business district, a series of parks and playgrounds laid out, and a bond issue of $150,000 voted for the purchase of land for this purpose. In 1912 a bond issue was passed for $730,000 for developing and dredging a canal for a harbor, and for buildings, docks, etc. The United States Government appropriated an additional amount of $428,000 for this work, and in 1920, $150,000 more was voted by the city for wharf improvements, etc. The city also passed a bond issue of $440,000 to build a highway and tunnel through the hills, from the water front, and in 1920 a $400,000 issue was passed for additional work on the harbor. Since 1920 the city has grown from a population of 16,843 to over 25,500.

A new Chamber of Commerce was formed in 1924, with new officials at the helm, and $20,000 was raised to carry on the work of that body, which comprises some of the ablest and most prominent men of the city. The work of the Chamber is to be carried out along strictly business lines and will be an important factor in the future advancement of Richmond, and the city which fifteen years ago was only a village will soon, at the present rate of growth, rank with the larger cities of the State. Mr. Mc-Vittie is a charter member and a director of the Chamber of Commerce, and a member of the State City Managers' Association and of the Central Section of California City Managers' Association, and keeps in touch with the most modern city improvements being adopted in other localities.

The marriage of Mr. McVittie, which occurred on December 25, 1917, at Ontario, Cal., united him with Della M. Wilsey, a native of Illinois, and two daughters have been born to them, Mary Elizabeth and Florence Eleanore. Fraternally Mr. McVittie is a member of McKinley Lodge No. 347, F. & A. M.; Richmond Lodge No. 1251, B. P. O. E.; Twilight Lodge No. 119, I. O. O. F.; and Contra Costa Encampment No. 99, of the last-named order.

EDGAR F. SLATTERY.—One of the best-known citizens of Concord, who has been active in business and public life for more than twenty years, is Edgar F. Slattery. Among other public services, Mr. Slattery was elected city marshal in 1919 and has held the office ever since. This particular office also involves a variety of civic duties (although it pays but one salary), but Mr. Slattery has taken care of them all in a most satisfactory manner and has had the distinction of taking in more city funds during his tenure of office than have any of his predecessors. In addition to his other duties Mr. Slattery is a deputy sheriff under Sheriff Veale. He is a member of the Concord Chamber of Commerce, and takes a keen interest in everything pertaining to the development of the city.

Mr. Slattery was born in San Francisco, May 16, 1870, a son of Dennis F. and Eliza (Jackson) Slattery, and one of three children. The father, a native of Ireland, was a railroad man and in his younger days was engaged in the shipping business. Young Edgar was educated in the grammar schools of San Francisco, and after leaving school he was connected for a time with several of the leading drygoods stores of his native city, such as the White House and O'Connor & Moffitt. He has the record of never having lost a job. For some time, also, he was connected with the license department at the San Francisco City Hall as an auditor. After the earthquake and fire in 1906 he went to Concord, where he has since made his home. For a number of years he engaged in the drygoods business in Concord and was partner in two stores which were finally destroyed by fire. One of these stores, a gents' furnishing store, is still under his management. Mr. Slattery is a member of the Elks, Native Sons, Woodmen of the World, and the U. P. E. C., and is a member and a Past Sachem of the Red Men.

On February 15, 1899, Mr. Slattery was united in marriage to Miss Katherine Hughes of Nevada County, a daughter of Joseph and Katherine (Gleason) Hughes. Her father was a miner and a California pioneer. She is one of six children. Mrs. Slattery has been active in the social life of Concord, and both she and Mr. Slattery have a wide circle of friends. Mr. Slattery is fond of hunting and fishing, and both he and his wife derive great pleasure from camping and motoring.

RICHARD DANIEL MAPLESDEN.—One of the well-known and successful horticulturists and nurserymen of Central and Northern California, R. D. Maplesden has been in business in Walnut Creek, Contra Costa County, since 1906. First coming to California in 1903, he located his residence in Oakland, but for the past twenty years he has made Walnut Creek his business headquarters. Of old New England ancestry, Mr. Maplesden was born in Derby, Orleans County, Vt., on August 1, 1858. His father, Richard Maplesden, was a native of England who came to Vermont when a young man and was there married to Alice Perkins, a native of Plymouth, Mass., of Puritan stock, the progenitor of her family having come from England to Massachusetts in the Mayflower; and members of the family were prominent in Colonial history, as well as serving in the Revolutionary War. Richard Maplesden was a farmer in Vermont, but in 1859 sold his New England farm and came around Cape Horn to California. Arriving in Sacramento, this old pioneer made his way by pack train to Yreka, Siskiyou County, locating on Doggett Creek, a branch of the Klamath River, where he engaged in mining. Losing his all the first year, he returned to Vermont in 1860, via Panama, and once more engaged in farming, this time taking up land in the spruce and fir forests, which he cleared and improved; and as he prospered he added to his acreage and in time became a very successful farmer. He passed away at eighty-six years of age, having never been sick a day in his life, but dying suddenly while resting, waiting for his noon meal. His good wife also died in Vermont. Of their three children, Richard Daniel is the third in order of birth and the only one now living.

R. D. Maplesden was brought up on the Vermont farm and educated in the local schools. His father was a horticulturist and nurseryman, and under his guidance he learned both pursuits. When twenty-one years old he came west as far as Boone County, Nebr., locating a homestead on the Platte River, and engaged in cattle-raising; but after three years of drouth he found himself with less than when he started the venture, and decided to come to California. His first work in the Golden State was mining, and he started with placer mining, continuing for six years, but with no success. In 1899 he began the nursery business, in which he has since been continuously engaged. In the beginning he represented the Oregon Nursery Company, of Portland, Ore., continuing with them for the following twelve years, during which time he traveled by team over eastern Oregon and Northern California, gaining valuable experience and becoming thoroughly familiar with the country; so much so, in fact, that he knew every cow-path in his territory. In 1913, he began using an automobile for traveling and selling nursery stock, and he still owns and drives the original Ford car with which he began in 1913 and which has traveled over 300,000 miles.

Mr. Maplesden resided in Siskiyou County until 1903, when he located in Oakland, in which city he still makes his home, while maintaining his business interests in Walnut Creek. He represented the Chico Nursery Company for ten years, and in 1922 bought the interests of this company at Walnut Creek and engaged in business on his own account. During the season, while taking orders, he calls at more than 3000 homes, and he has gained an acquaintance with thousands of people. Having made a study of horticulture and nursery stock since a boy, Mr. Maplesden is thoroughly informed and has become an expert in selecting trees suitable to soil and climatic conditions.

Mr. Maplesden was first married in Vermont, when twenty-one years of age, to Miss Linnie Moulton, born in that State of an old Colonial family. One year later they moved to Nebraska, and there, six years later, her death occurred. This union was blessed with one daughter, now Mrs. Fannie Judell, of Oakland. It was after the death of his wife that, discouraged and disappointed by the misfortunes Nebraska had shown him, Mr. Maplesden came to California. Eight years later he was married again, at Scott River, Siskiyou County, to Minnie A. Marfeldt, a native of that place and the daughter of an old settler of Siskiyou County. Her parents came to Scott River in 1849 and were prominent pioneers there until their deaths. Mr. and Mrs. Maplesden make their residence at 41 Linda Avenue, Oakland. Mr. Maplesden was made a Mason in North Star Lodge No. 91, at Fort Jones, Siskiyou County; he demitted and is now a member of Standard Lodge No. 440, Oakland. He is a thirty-second-degree Scottish Rite Mason, belonging to the Oakland Consistory; and with his wife he is a member of Golden Chain Chapter, Eastern Star, of Oakland. He is also a member of Fort Jones Lodge No. 115, I. O. O. F., and belongs to the Encampment, being a past officer in both orders. For many years he has been a member of the California Nurserymen's Association. In religious belief he is a member of Plymouth Congregational Church of Oakland.

ALBERT H. SCHUH.—In the musical life of Concord and vicinity, Albert H. Schuh has occupied an important place since locating here many years ago and has contributed largely to the social and musical life of the city, where he is now head of the School of Music; he also maintains a studio in San Francisco. He comes from a musical family. His father, Joseph Schuh, a native of Germany, where he spent his whole life, was a composer of note and in consequence the son was born and reared in a highly musical atmosphere.

Albert H. Schuh was born in Baden, Germany, on February 15, 1868, and his earliest recollections centered around music. He had the privilege of being an exchange student with other nations and in this way had the advantage of visiting such cities as Moscow, St. Petersburg, Vilna, Paris, London, besides other large cities. He has traveled practically all over the world and has become personally acquainted with the great musicians of his day. He studied in many of the leading conservatories of the world, which was of especial advantage to him, as the various nations emphasized different points of efficiency in musical attainment. Mr. Schuh, after finishing his work, opened a studio in London; and from there he went to Glasgow, Scotland, where he taught successfully for seven years. He then came to New York City, and got in touch with several opera companies with whom he served as director, and for the next fifteen years he was in and out of New York serving as director for various companies. After this he located in Los Angeles, California, and then in Seattle and Tacoma, Wash., and in these various places he taught music and directed various musical organizations. Mr. Schuh is also a fine organist and has played in many of the leading churches of the Coast. He devotes most of his time to teaching but finds pleasure and profit during his leisure time in composing music. He has completed a series of California compositions which were accepted by one of the largest music publishing concerns, and a handsome revenue is expected to result therefrom. The following numbers comprise the series: Yosemite, Santa Cruz, Catalina, Coronado, Mount Lassen, Diablo. Each place mentioned has been visited personally and the composition written on the spot.

Mr. Schuh is married and has three children, Edward, Clara and Bill. Mr. Schuh is a member of the American Federation of Musicians. He is public spirited and energetic, and has a host of friends in this and adjoining counties.

CARUSA BROTHERS.—The firm of Carusa Brothers of Pittsburg, Contra Costa County, is composed of the two brothers, Stephen and Vincent Carusa, both men of good business judgment who have met with success in their many undertakings. They are large owners of real estate; operate the Pittsburg Ice and Fuel Company and the S. Carusa & Brother Truck and Transfer Company; own the Central Hotel building, a pressed brick structure costing $65,000; and are agents for the National Ice Company. Carusa Brothers were the first undertakers in Black Diamond, but sold out their business in 1914 to George Higgins. They were also owners of a successful livery business until the automobile and truck came along, when, in keeping with their up-to-date methods, they turned their livery stable into a garage and started the first automobile-renting service in Pittsburg, in 1909. Carusa Brothers are up-to-date in all things and are very public-spirited when the welfare of their city is concerned. Frank Vincent and Concetta (Petralia) Carusa, their parents, were born at Catania, Italy, the city at the base of Mount Ætna that has twice been destroyed. Frank V. Carusa, like many of his name, was a seafaring man. At the age of seventeen he was mate of a vessel; and three of his brothers were sea captains. He came to San Francisco the first time in 1850 and was a miner for several years, but finally went back to Italy, was married there, and after a while brought his family to California and settled in Collinsville, in 1874. Later they moved to Black Diamond. There were six boys and two girls in the Carusa family.

Stephen Carusa was the first child in their family to be born at Black Diamond, and he first saw the light on June 19, 1882. Vincent was born at the same place on May 9, 1888. Both went to the public schools and from early boyhood began to take an interest in business matters. Stephen has twice been elected a member of the board of trustees of Pittsburg, and in 1911 was chairman of the street committee when the name of the place was changed to Pittsburg. An efficient officer, he was a credit to his friends and himself. The firm of Carusa Brothers was first composed of Stephen and Salvatore, but when the latter died Vincent was admitted to the firm.

Stephen Carusa and Miss Mabel Edstrom were married in Pittsburg on November 15, 1908. She was born in Chicago, Ill. They have two children: Etta and Evelyn. Stephen is a member of Pittsburg Lodge No. 436, I. O. O. F.; the Antioch Encampment, I. O. O. F.; Pittsburg Aerie, F. O. E.; and Pittsburg Lodge No. 1475, L. O. O. M. He also belongs to the Lions Club.

Vincent Carusa was married in San Francisco on July 19, 1914, to Miss Mary Mazzone, and they have three children: Walter, Irving and Bernice. He is a member of Pittsburg Lodge No. 1475, L. O. O. M.; Diamond Parlor, N. S. G. W.; and the I. D. E. S. of Antioch. Carusa Brothers are boosters for Pittsburg and believe firmly in its future, as shown by their wise investments in property. They give of their time and money to help all worthy projects that forward the growth and development of their native city and county.

CHARLES SCUDERO.—Under the able management of Charles Scudero, the popular chief of the fire department of the city of Pittsburg, Cal., this rapidly growing city is said to possess one of the most efficient fire departments, of its class, in the State. Charles Scudero was born at Black Diamond, now Pittsburg, Cal., on November 29, 1874, a son of Andrew and Rosie (Romeo) Scudero, both natives of Catania, Province of Sicily, Italy. Andrew Scudero came around the Horn to California in 1849, and Miss Rosie Romeo, who later became his wife, made her advent into the Golden State the following year, also sailing around the Horn; and both settled in San Francisco, where they were afterwards married. This union was blessed with eleven children, Charles being the fifth in order of birth. Andrew Scudero engaged in fishing and was one of the first commercial fishermen of San Francisco Bay. He died about twenty years ago, at Pittsburg, at the age of sixty-seven; his good wife passed away about two years later at the age of fifty-seven.

Charles Scudero attended the public schools at Black Diamond, now Pittsburg, and helped his father in the fish business. Being a strong and virile young man, he gained quite a reputation as an athlete and expert swimmer and has to his credit the rescue of thirty-seven bodies from the San Joaquin and Sacramento Rivers and the Carquinez Straits. He made a contrivance for use in the recovery of drowned persons, and by its use the number of recovered bodies has been greatly increased. His first employment was with the Redwood Manufacturers Company at Black Diamond, where he became foreman of the lumber yard, and he had at one time as high as 160 men to oversee. In the meantime he kept up his connection with the volunteer fire department and in 1901 became fire chief, serving in this capacity for five years without pay, and he has served continuously as chief ever since. After six years with the Redwood Manufacturers Company he accepted a position with the F. E. Booth Company, where for five years he served as watchman of their cannery. Six years ago he became a member of the Pittsburg police force, and is still an active member, as well as a deputy sheriff, having been appointed to the latter position by Sheriff R. R. Veale eighteen years ago.

On May 18, 1899, at Black Diamond, Charles Scudero was united in marriage with Miss Cora Belle Eggleston, a native of Collinsville, Cal., a daughter of Edward and Anna (Rogers) Eggleston and a granddaughter of the pioneer, Judge Rogers. Mr. and Mrs. Charles Scudero have five children living: Charles Edward, a member of the Pittsburg fire department; Andrew Clarence, an employee of the Columbia Steel Corporation; Sarah, the wife of Dr. Arthur Herman, at Los Angeles; Camille, living at home; and Williard, a pupil of the grammar school. Mr. Scudero is a member of the International, the California and the Pacific Coast Associations of Fire Chiefs, and has a large circle of warm friends who hold him in high esteem.

JOHN GEORGE BISHOP.—The capable foreman of the pattern-making shop of the Columbia Steel Corporation, John George Bishop, was born in Toronto, Canada, on December 21, 1884. When he was a babe of two years his parents moved to Nottingham, England, and in that city he grew to manhood, receiving his education in the elementary and high schools and graduating from the latter in due time, after which he was at once apprenticed to learn the cabinet-maker's trade. In 1904 he came to Boston, Mass., and entered upon an apprenticeship as a machinist with the Saco Pettee Machine Shop in Boston, continuing there for seven years. During this time he pursued his studies in a night school and thus completed his technical training. In the fall of 1911 he went to Spokane, Wash., and entered the employ of the Northwest Harvester

Beck Curry

Company, with whom he remained about seven years as a patternmaker, rising to become shop superintendent. Then he came to California and was employed at the Holt Manufacturing Company's plant in Stockton, after which he located in Pittsburg, in the fall of 1916. He entered upon his duties with the Columbia Steel Corporation as patternmaker, and succeeded the retiring foreman in 1921, since which time he has remained in this responsible position. He is well liked by his fellow employees and is discharging his duties as foreman with credit to himself and to the corporaton which employs him.

Mr. Bishop was married in Spokane, Wash., in 1912 to Miss Katherine McCarthy, and they had five children: Joseph Thomas, John George, Robert Arthur, Mary Katherine, and Annie Ruth. The wife and mother died in 1920. For his second wife Mr. Bishop married Miss Beatrice Amelia Raynor, a native of Nottingham, England. The family attend the Congregational Church. Their home is in Pittsburg, where they have a wide circle of friends. In all movements for the betterment of general conditions, Mr. Bishop is always found on the progressive side. Fraternally he is a Moose.

BERT CURRY.—One of the most highly esteemed citizens of Richmond is Bert Curry, mortician, whose never failing sympathy and tactful, intelligent services in the trying hours of bereavement have endeared him to the hearts of many families. He is a self-made man and a native of California and of Contra Costa County, having been born in Clayton, at the foot of Mount Diablo, on June 1, 1882. His father, James Curry, was one of the early pioneers, a resident of Tennessee, who crossed the plains and established the first stage line between Clayton and Oakland, also to Nortonville and along the coal-mining regions. He made two trips back to his native home with an ox-team. The mother was Helen (Callahan) Curry. There were eight children in the family, seven boys and one girl. The eldest brother, C. E. Curry, now deceased, was a grain dealer of Portland, Ore.; Sam R., an old resident of Richmond, was a liveryman; H. J. Curry, of Martinez, is an undertaker in that city; T. R. Curry resides at El Cerrito.

Bert Curry was educated in the grammar schools of Clayton and the Polytechnic High School of Oakland. At the age of nineteen he became associated with his brother in the undertaking business at Martinez, remaining there about five years. From there he came to Richmond and started in business for himself in 1906. His business has prospered, due to his professional skill, and he covers the whole surrounding territory, having something like $40,000 invested in equipment and stock. He was the pioneer undertaker of Richmond; and his close attention to every detail and conscientious, upright business methods have been responsible for his success. Mr. Curry served one year as coroner, and in 1926 as chief deputy under Mr. Donnelly.

In July, 1900, Mr. Curry was married to Henrietta Hartsinck of El Cerrito, whose father is still living and is foreman of the Pullman Car shops. They are the parents of three children: William, Henrietta Claire, and Bert, Jr. Mr. Curry is one of the early members of Elks Lodge No. 1251, of Richmond; a charter member of the Eagles; and a member of other fraternal organizations, including the Red Men and the Daughters of Pocahontas. He is also an active member of the Richmond Chamber of Commerce. Mr. Curry is fond of athletic games and of hunting, fishing and swimming; and his vacations are spent in the mountains. He is also fond of dancing and other social diversions.

GEORGE W. ADAMS.—A native son of the Golden State who represents an early pioneer family, George W. Adams was born in Merced, Cal., on October 22, 1884, a son of William Adams, an Englishman who came from his native land to California by way of Cape Horn in 1848. He settled in Mariposa County and followed the trade of the carpenter there; and when the railroad was being built through the San Joaquin Valley, he with many others moved down to the new town of Merced and there plied his trade, helping to build up a city. He was married at Hornitos to Lydia Pitzer, born in that town of pioneer parents, who came from Missouri with ox-teams across the plains. Both these old pioneers are living in Merced in the enjoyment of good health. William Adams, grandfather of our subject, served as superior judge for Mariposa County and for many years was a justice of the peace in Hornitos, and a large landowner in that county. He was a musician in England, emigrated from there to Canada, where he was leader of a large band, and then came to the United States and to California. He owned a gold cornet, which is still in the family. He was a thirty-third-degree Mason, and died at the age of ninety-two years. In the family of William and Lydia (Pitzer) Adams were three children: George W.; Irma, now Mrs. J. W. Bell, of Richmond; and Ernest, who died at the age of eighteen in Oakland.

George W. Adams attended the Merced schools and was the first baby to take a ride from Merced to Stockton on the San Joaquin Valley Road at the time of its completion to that point. His school days ended, he entered the employ of the Western Union Telegraph Company in Merced as a messenger. In 1901 he went to Brentwood as assistant agent for the Southern Pacific Railroad. The following year he was sent to Atwater, in his native county, and in 1903 opened the first telegraph office there. From Atwater he was shifted around by the company, and for two and one-half years was a relief man and served in many places throughout the northern part of the State, one year as ticket agent in Merced. His acquaintance is wide, and he has many warm friends throughout this section of California. During the fire and earthquake in San Francisco he was one of the wire inspectors for the government.

In all, Mr. Adams spent eleven years with the Southern Pacific. Then he was with the Standard Oil Company in Richmond for two years, after which he was for three years traffic manager for Borax Smith. He spent five and one-half years with the Union Oil Company at Oleum and organized their traffic department, and then came back to the Standard Oil Company for a time. His next move took him to San Francisco, in 1920, where he was with the Retail Furniture Association as secretary and developed their traffic department. In 1921 he organized the Furniture Traffic Bureau, doing business for the furniture manufacturer, wholesaler, and dealer. In 1923 he took in a partner, and thereafter continued thus until they dissolved partnership, on July 1, 1926. He then helped to organize the Retail Furniture Association Traffic Department, of California, with a membership of 400, with offices in the Furniture Exchange Building, San Francisco. He is assistant manager and traffic expert of the furniture industry of California.

Mr. Adams has been twice married. His first wife, whom he married in Martinez, on June 30, 1908, was Marie Cunningham, who was born in Henderson, Ky., in 1888; and by her he had a daughter, Ramona. Mrs. Adams died on July 9, 1911. In 1914 he married Flora O. (Boyd) Rodriguez, whose parents were pioneers of 1907 in what is now the El Cerrito district, then called Rust, after the first settler here. In 1917, when the incorporation of a city was considered, Mr. Adams worked hard to bring the matter to a successful conclusion, and on being chosen a member of the first board of trustees began at once to work for improvements of every kind. Like his father, he is a stanch Republican in national affairs, while locally he supports the best man regardless of party. The family home has been in El Cerrito since 1914. While in Concord in the employ of the railroad he became a charter member of the local Parlor of the Native Sons, but he is not now affiliated with the order. He belongs to Richmond Lodge No. 1251, B. P. O. E.; to the San Francisco Transportation Club; and to the East Bay Country Club. Mr. Adams has always worked hard for civic betterment, and gives to the women of El Cerrito great credit for making of the city the modern residential center it is today.

FRED LUTZ.—A well-known and prominent citizen of El Cerrito, a member of its board of trustees and a hard worker for the upbuilding of El Cerrito and Contra Costa County, is Fred Lutz, a native of California, born in San Francisco on December 26, 1882, a son of Ludwig and Eliza Lutz, of Alameda. The elder Lutz is a butcher by trade, and is still active at the age of seventy-seven years. He has worked at his trade for over sixty years. Three sons and one daughter were born in the Lutz family: Fred, of this review; Carl, in the employ of the United States Government at Panama; Mrs. Anita Cavaneer, of Berkeley; and Herman, a wireless operator at sea.

Fred Lutz attended the public school, and as soon as he was old enough went to work for the Union Pacific at Evanston, Wyo., as a call boy and brass polisher. He came back to California, entered the employ of the Southern Pacific and gradually worked his way to the front. He soon became a fireman on the road, working all over the Western division, and in 1900 he was promoted to be an engineer. He quit this work however, and went to braking, but did not take to that end of railroading and went to work for the street car company in Oakland as motorman. At that time the line ran to the county line. In 1916 he entered the employ of the Standard Oil Company and was labor foreman for a time, but is now in the welding department.

While railroading in Utah, Mr. Lutz was married to Miss Myrtle Bennett, a native of Kansas City, Mo. They have had four children: Fred died in infancy; Harrison Bennett, born in Utah, attended the grammar school in Richmond and the Vocational High School in Oakland, and is now an apprentice in the boiler shop at the Standard refinery; Robert Herman, born in Oakland, and Raymond Carl, born in Richmond, are attending the El Cerrito school. Mrs. Lutz is active in the work of the El Cerrito Improvement Club and in civic affairs.

Mr. Lutz belongs to Richmond Lodge No. 1251, B. P. O. E., and is a Republican in national affairs. In 1921 he was elected a member of the Stege Sanitary Board, serving as secretary and president during his incumbency. In May, 1924, he was elected a member of the board of trustees of El Cerrito, and is serving on the police and fire committee and the light and water and finance committees. He is deeply interested in the progress of the community and favors all worthy projects having that end in view.

HENRY H. SUMMER.—To build up such a business as that of the Summer Lumber Company requires a great amount of hard labor and much business acumen; but in face of the many obstacles he has had to overcome, Henry H. Summer has gained for himself an enviable reputation, has made a host of friends, and is considered one of the ruling business men of Pittsburg. A native of Tennessee, he was born at Harriman, August 17, 1882, a son of S. N. and Mary (Williams) Summer. The father was county treasurer of Morgan County, Tenn., for several years, and became a prosperous farmer in Roane County, that State.

Henry H. Summer was educated at the American Temperance University at Harriman, and at the age of twenty-three came West. Settling at Pittsburg, he became the traveling representative of the Redwood Manufacturers Company and for fifteen years traveled throughout the States of the East, Middle West and South in their interest.

Mr. Summer has made discerning investments in real estate in Pittsburg, having great confidence in the city he chose for his permanent home. Besides being at the head of the Summer Lumber Company, he is a member of the firm of Lanzafame & Summer, dealers in furniture; and he is vice-president of the Industrial Finance Company. The Summer Lumber Company has offices in the First National Bank Building and conducts an exclusively wholesale business, consigning in carload lots. This company receives its redwood supply largely from the lumber mills of Humboldt and Mendocino Counties, and Douglas Fir and its manufactured products are shipped direct from a number of large mills located in Oregon and Washington. Mr. Summer enjoys a wide acquaintance, both business and personal, among the principal lumber dealers in the United States.

In 1910, Mr. Summer was married to Miss Mary Viscuso, a daughter of the Pittsburg pioneer, G. Viscuso, now deceased. To Mr. and Mrs. Summer have been born two children, Henry and Marie. He is a member of Richmond Lodge No. 1251, B. P. O. E., at Richmond, and of the Eagles at Pittsburg.

WILLIAM H. CARPENTER.— The successful fruit grower, buyer and shipper, William H. Carpenter, living on Live Oak Avenue in the Oakley district in Contra Costa County, is accounted one of the most successful men in his neighborhood. He has three ranches: the home place of thirty-three acres on Live Oak Avenue, fifty-two acres in the Oakley precinct, and thirty-two acres in Lone Tree precinct, all devoted to apricots and almonds. The home place is irrigated from his own wells, which are equipped with pumps with a capacity of 2000 gallons per minute, and the water is piped to different parts of his orchard through a mile of pipe, all installed and planned by himself. On his fifty-two acres he has wells and pump with capacity of 1800 gallons per minute. Besides his own land he leases from others, and through his experience in raising almonds and apricots he is making a very good success of his fruit industry. His many years of practical experience in fruit growing have been of great benefit to him from a financial standpoint, for his fruits and nuts command a higher price in the market than the products of others. He knows just when and how to prune and trim his trees so that the sun can get to the fruit and give it that wonderful color so necessary for beauty, just how to thin the growing fruit so the strength will be given to what he leaves on the trees, and just when to irrigate the trees that yield all this fine quality of fruits and nuts. He is always willing to pass this knowledge along to those who ask for it and in other ways to assist the home-maker to make a success of his own work. Besides his own fruit he buys and dries fruit from other ranchers, and ships independently. His own dry yard is ample to accommodate and meet all requirements, and he is planning to erect his own shipping and packing sheds on the Southern Pacific Railroad.

Mr. Carpenter was born in Dayton, Rockingham County, Va., on August 18, 1881, and attended school until he accompanied his parents, William H. and Mary (Von Baer) Carpenter, to California in 1895. They went to Humboldt County and settled at Hydesville for thirteen months, and then came to Antioch by boat and lived there from 1896 until 1901. At that time Mr. Carpenter and his brother, C. F. Carpenter, opened the first general merchandise store in Oakley. The first passenger train passed through this station on July 1, 1901, at noon, at which time there was great rejoicing by the people living in this section of the county. This partnership continued until the fall of 1904, when Mr. Carpenter turned his attention to raising apricots and to the fruit business.

Mr. Carpenter married Miss Nellie M. Erickson, a native of Humboldt County, born in Eureka; and they have had the following children: Stanley Russell, studying engineering at the University of California; Wilford Howard, attending the College of the Pacific at Stockton; and Virginia Elizabeth and Ruth, at home. Mr. Carpenter has served as a school trustee and belongs to the Chamber of Commerce. He takes an active part in the Methodist Church of Oakley, of which he was one of the organizers. He is well-liked and has many friends in this section.

C. GEORGE BARBIKAS.—The president of the company known as Barbikas Brothers, Inc., is C. George Barbikas, who is making his influence felt in financial circles in Richmond. He was born in Vytina, near Athens, Greece, on November 22, 1880, a son of George and P. (Livana) Barbikas, the former a merchant and prominent citizen of his community. C. George Barbikas remained in his native country until he was twenty-one, arriving in New York in 1901, after receiving a good education and a training along business lines that enabled him to care for large interests successfully in later years. After a few months in New York he went to New Mexico, and in 1902 he came to Oakland, Cal., and was employed by a commission merchant for a time. He then went to Agnews and took charge of a hotel until he located in San Jose, where he was connected with Woodward and Bennett until they sold to Lesser Brothers, after which he remained with the latter proprietors one year. Leaving Lesser Brothers, he started a restaurant on his own account and remained there from 1903 to 1912. While in San Jose Mr. Barbikas was on friendly terms with many prominent men, among them Thomas Montgomery, banker and capitalist of that city. Disposing of his holdings in San Jose, he traveled over the State; and finally deciding that Richmond offered the best opportunities for him, he located here and has developed with the city. In 1910 Mr. Barbikas became a naturalized citizen of the United States, receiving his final naturalization papers.

After coming to Richmond Mr. Barbikas located at the Hotel Richmond, later leased the hotel, and in 1924 purchased the property. Barbikas Brothers' interests are varied. There are four brothers interested in the corporation: C. George, Steve G., John and Theodore. They conduct Hotel Richmond, S. Barbikas being the manager; the Richmond Wholesale Company, with C. George Barbikas as manager; the B-B Shoe Store, with Theodore Barbikas as manager; and the Palace Candy Store. They are owners of considerable valuable property in Richmond, all being carried on successfully under the direct management of C. G. Barbikas, president and manager of the concern. Their various enterprises are growing and expanding with the growth of Richmond, as they aim to keep abreast of the times in all things. C. G. Barbikas is one of Richmond's stanch boosters. He takes an intelligent part in political affairs and wants to see the offices filled by those best qualified rather than in accordance with party affiliations. He belongs to the local Chamber of Commerce and his public spirit is always shown in his support of all civic projects for the betterment of conditions in the city. During the World War he was chairman of the Red Cross drives. Personally, he is well liked and highly thought of by his many friends.

On December 20, 1905, at San Juan, Cal., C. G. Barbikas was united in marriage with Miss Myrtle Brown, daughter of William J. and Cynthia A. Brown, of Waverly, Ohio. Her father was a veteran of the Civil War, as were several of her uncles, one of whom was killed at the Battle of Gettysburg. In the Brown family there were the following children besides Mrs. Barbikas: Mrs. Laura Van Gundy, of the Hawaiian Islands; Mrs. Mary Wright; Mrs. Ida Pearce, deceased; and Corey, Will, and Isaac (deceased). The home of Mr. and Mrs. Barbikas has been blessed with six children. Leo, age nineteen, is a student in St. Mary's College, where he is making a study of commerce. He graduated from the Richmond Union High School with the Class of June, 1925. While in high school he was vice-president of the Boys' Hi Y Club and a first lieutenant in the high school cadet corps, and took part in other activities and club doings. He is a member of Richmond Chapter, Order of De Molay. Dorothy, age seventeen, is a sophomore at the University of California, registered in the School of Letters and Science. She is popular in college circles and takes part in many of its activities. She is a member of the University of California Masonic Club and the Masonic Girls' Glee Club, is on the staff of the Daily Californian, and is prominent in Y. W. C. A. work. She enjoys sports and takes particular interest in swimming and rifle-shooting. Besides her regular college work and activities, she also teaches a class in the Presbyterian Sunday School in Richmond. In her freshman year she was a member of the Freshman Women's Commission of the university. She also is a graduate of the Richmond High School, Class of 1925, and while in high school took part in its various activities, acting as vice-president of the Honor Society and helping to organize the Girls' Hi-Y Club, of which she was chosen first president. Mildred, aged sixteen, is a member of the senior class at the Richmond High School, an officer of the Student Body Commission, and a member of the Honor Society, Girl Reserves and other organizations in the school. Leroy is thirteen, and is attending the Roosevelt Junior High School. Paul, aged ten, attends the Grant School; and Harold, aged eight, is also a pupil in the Grant School. All the children are studying music, are meeting with success in all their educational work, are well-liked, and have a bright future before them.

C. G. Barbikas made an extended trip East and to Europe in 1925, visiting France, Italy, Greece and the other Balkan States. Upon his return to the United States he spent a month in New York City, studying various conditions, especially that of business. He also toured the southeastern part of the United States, spending considerable time in Florida and New Orleans. At Columbus, Ohio, he was entertained by relatives of his wife. Mrs. Barbikas is a cousin of Charles Warner, of the court of common pleas at Columbus.

JOHN P. LODGE.—To the expert superintendent of the rolling-mill department of the Columbia Steel Corporation, John P. Lodge, or "Jack" Lodge, as he is familiarly called, belongs the distinction of being the employee that rolled the first steel ingot ever made into steel bars at the corporation's plant at Pittsburg, Cal.

John P. Lodge was born at Ironton, Ohio, February 4, 1863, the son of Patrick and Mary (Mackey) Lodge, and when but eleven years of age left home to make his own way in the world. His first employment was with a steel mill at Ironton, Ohio, where he carried water to the workmen engaged in the hot and grimy tasks in the rolling-mill. Being an industrious lad and anxious to learn the steel business, he soon was advanced to positions of greater responsibility and in time became an expert. He has been employed by steel mills in several States, including Alabama, Ohio, Virginia, Pennsylvania, Maryland and New Jersey, as also in Canada. His reputation as an expert steel man became so well known that it was Jack Lodge who was sought out as the man to tear down the steel mill at Wyandotte, Mich., and to remove and reconstruct the same at Guelph, now called Royal City, in the Province of Ontario, Canada. Later he built the steel mills at Muskegon, Mich., and also those at Bessemer, Ala. He was made superintendent of the steel mill at Elim, B. C., a suburb of Vancouver, and was the first superintendent of the mill at Guelph. He was also superintendent of the mill at Connellsville, Pa., and constructed mills at Terre Haute, Ind., and Fort Dodge, Iowa. In 1913 Mr. Lodge came from Youngstown, Ohio, to San Francisco, where he became the head roller for the South San Francisco Steel Rolling Mills of the Pacific Coast Steel Company.

In February, 1920, Jack Lodge was the man selected to install the rolling mill machinery for the Columbia Steel Corporation at Pittsburg, Cal. He is a skilled workman, an expert mechanic, and possesses a genial personality, with the happy faculty of making and retaining many friends. He counts his friends by the thousand in the steel plants of this country and Canada, and many have come to Pittsburg to be associated with him in his work at the Columbia plant. To him great credit is due for the successful work achieved by the rolling-mill department of this great steel mill. After being connected with most of the important steel mills of this country, Mr. Lodge believes there are none better equipped to handle so great a tonnage as is handled by the Columbia.

On September 22, 1917, in Chicago, Ill., Mr. Lodge was united in marriage with Mrs. Beam of Oakland, Cal. She is the mother of two children by a former marriage. Mr. Lodge is the father of two sons by his first wife, whose maiden name was Julia Tomerlin. She passed away in Birmingham, Ala. The two sons are: John, a resident of Portsmouth,

Ohio, who is a locomotive engineer on the Norfolk & Western Railroad; and Clifford, who is a hotel man at Salt Lake City, Utah. Mrs. Lodge is a sister of the late Victor H. Metcalf, who was a member of Roosevelt's cabinet.

Since coming to Pittsburg Mr. Lodge has been very successful and has wisely invested in real estate in Pittsburg; and he also has a ranch in Sacramento County. He is deeply devoted to the advancement of the best interests of the community.

EDWARD P. JACKSON.—One of the most valued citizens of Concord is Edward P. Jackson, who has served his community not only as a progressive and substantial business man, but also as a dispenser of justice and an active worker in the fraternal orders which have done so much for the advancement of the common welfare. Mr. Jackson is the proprietor of a thoroughly modern and well-stocked furniture store which does a thriving business. He was appointed justice of the peace in 1911, was elected for a four-year term in 1914, and has held the office continuously ever since. Prior to that he had been town clerk, and in both capacities he has served in a manner which has won and held the esteem of his fellow townsmen. Mr. Jackson is a self-made man who has had a fair amount of the struggles incident to the attainment of success, and his never-failing courtesy and willingness to help any worthy project have made him one of the most highly respected citizens of Concord and vicinity.

Edward P. Jackson was born in Cincinnati, Ohio, on January 12, 1871, the son of Charles and Mary Elizabeth (Parris) Jackson. The Jackson family was of Welsh and Scotch ancestry; the Parris family was of French origin. The father, Charles Jackson, a native of Cincinnati, was a successful farmer and florist, and lived to be eighty-seven years old. He was the son of Thomas M. Jackson, who came from Pennsylvania and established the Hamilton County Bank, of which institution he was cashier for many years. His wife lived to be ninety-seven years old.

The family of Mr. and Mrs. Charles Jackson consisted of seven children, five boys and two girls. Edward P. Jackson was the fourth child, and when he was but eight years old the mother died. Two years later the family removed to Newton, Kans., where he received his schooling. After leaving school he became a messenger for the Wells-Fargo Express Company on the road and doing office work. In January, 1895, he came to Concord and opened an upholstery shop, remaining for a year, after which he went to San Francisco and there pursued the same occupation. Some time later he returned to Concord and was constable for three years, resigning in 1901. He then went to Livermore, where he resided for six years while engaging in business as a purchasing agent. After the San Francisco fire he returned to Concord, founding his present furniture business in February, 1907; and here he has since resided.

Mr. Jackson was married August 4, 1902, to Jettie Jaquith, a native of Canada. They have one child, Lloyd, aged twenty-one years, a graduate of the Mount Diablo Union High School. In politics Mr. Jackson is a Republican. Outside of his business his keenest interest, perhaps, is in the various fraternal orders in which he has been an active worker. He recently was made a life member of the Pittsburg Lodge of Elks of which he is a former Exalted Ruler. He was elected delegate to the National Convention, B. P. O. E., which convened in Chicago on July 12, 1926, and was accompanied to the gathering by Mrs. Jackson. Mr. Jackson is also a member of the Red Men, Odd Fellows, I. D. E. S., U. P. E. C., and Rebekahs, and has been treasurer of the Red Men's Lodge of Concord for fourteen years, and also served as secretary of the Odd Fellows. Mrs. Jackson is a member of the Rebekahs and the Eastern Star, and is greatly interested in fraternal work.

MRS. MARY E. LACASSIE. — The family represented by Mrs. Mary Lacassie has been identified with the history of California for a long period of time, and she herself is a native of this State, born at San Francisco. Her parents, John and Mary (Dwyer) Roche, were natives of New York and Wisconsin, respectively, and crossed the plains together in 1861 with ox-teams. During the greater part of his life, John Roche was engaged in the wholesale butcher business in San Francisco. Seven children were born in the Roche family: James, deceased; Mrs. Katherine Barreilles, of San Francisco; Mary E., our subject; Mrs. Margaret Marillo, of Oakland; and John, George and Frances, who are deceased. The father was seventy-one years old when he passed away, and the mother was sixty-three years old when she died.

The education of Mary E. Roche was obtained in the San Francisco schools. In September, 1879, she was first married to Frank Casaurang, a native of France, who was seventeen years old when he came to San Francisco. In 1883 Mr. and Mrs. Casaurang removed to Oakland, where Mr. Casaurang was engaged in the wholesale butcher business; and later he was in the dairy business. They were the parents of ten children: Marie, now Mrs. Joseph Coigdarripe, of Los Angeles; Rosella, Mrs. Charles Irwin, of Oakland; Lillian, Mrs. William Miller, of New York; William, of Monterey; Agnes, now Mrs. Guy Nottingham, of Walnut Creek, Charles, of Oakland; Dewey; Louis; Victorine, Mrs. James Speros, of Walnut Creek; and John, of Modesto. There are fourteen grandchildren.

Mrs. Casaurang was married the second time in 1902, to Samuel Lacassie, a native of France. For a number of years Mr. Lacassie was in the dairy business. In 1907 the family settled in Walnut Creek and purchased 250 acres of general farming land from James Stow. In 1922 Mrs. Lacassie purchased the Walnut Creek garage, which is operated by her sons. Mrs. Lacassie owns five lots within the town limits and she also owns the city water works, the tanks built in 1907 being filled from springs on her home place, and the water delivered by gravity to the consumers from the tanks on the hill. In politics Mrs. Lacassie adheres to the principles of the Republican party.

HENRY G. KRUMLAND.—A leader in fraternal circles, and for the past sixteen years justice of the peace of Byron Township, Contra Costa County, Henry G. Krumland is recognized as a man of affairs in Byron. In the judicial offices in the Byron Postoffice building, where Justice Krumland holds court, numerous local cases are tried, often with well-known lawyers caring for the interests of the clients. Henry G. Krumland is a valued assistant to L. G. Plumley, the well-known merchant of Byron, having been an employee of this store for twenty years. He is one of the general lodgemen of his home town; is a past officer and active member of Byron Lodge, No. 335, I. O. O. F.; is a member of Byron Parlor No. 170, N. S. G. W., and has served many times as delegate to State conventions, in which he takes active part; is a member of Brentwood Masons, and a recognized figure in his home community.

Judge Krumland comes from one of the pioneer families of the Byron section, and resides on his five-acre ranch on the State Highway, where, with his beloved mother, now seventy-six years of age, he enjoys the comforts of home. His birth occurred at Byron, on February 9, 1880, a son of George and Johanna (Dohrs) Krumland, the former a native of Germany and the latter of Maryland. George Krumland left his native country for America in 1848, and in 1850 came via Cape Horn to California, and engaged in mining for about ten years. He then removed to Contra Costa County where he found employment on ranches; later he leased land and engaged in farming and stock raising. He passed away on July 17, 1904.

Henry G. Krumland began his education in the grammar school in Byron, then went through high school and afterwards took a business course; upon his return to Byron he entered the employ of L. G. Plumley, where he has been ever since. In politics Judge Krumland is a Democrat.

MILLARD F. CHRISTOPHER.—For nearly a third of a century two well-known and popular figures of the church and social life of Concord have been Millard F. Christopher and his estimable wife. Both have been residents of California since the pioneer days and within the space of their lifetimes have witnessed many of the marvelous changes which have been a part of the development of this great commonwealth.

Mr. Christopher was born in Louisville, Ky., on August 7, 1856, the son of Henry and Mary (Henry) Christopher, both now deceased. There were six children in the family, and when Millard was a lad of ten his father, who was a farmer, died. The mother removed with her children to Washington in 1870, when that state was still a territory. Three years afterwards she died, leaving six children. Young Millard's education was received in the grammar school, and in 1877 he came to California and secured work on a farm. Farming has been his only occupation. His first residence in California was at Salinas in Monterey County, where he made his home for nine years; from there he removed to San Miguel, where he resided for about the same length of time. At this location he leased land and grew wheat.   From there he removed to Lafayette in 1895, and here he made his home for a year, finally locating between Walnut Creek and Concord in 1896.   He later became the owner of a farm near Pacheco which he sold and bought the Downing ranch.   In 1918 he sold to the Port Costa Water Company and became the owner of a home and other city property in Concord.

On November 1, 1883, Mr. Christopher married Miss Emily Porterfield, daughter of one of the early California pioneers, James Harvey Porterfield.   The father was born in Tennessee and came to California from Missouri in 1845.   He was a soldier in the Mexican War and was one of the courageous band that raised the Bear Flag in Sonoma before Mexico relinquished her claims to California.   He married Martha Elizabeth Alexander, also a native of Tennessee, and they became the parents of four children.   Mr. and Mrs. Christopher have one daughter, Mary Martha, now Mrs. William Bucholz of Bay Point, and the mother of a daughter, Beverly Thissell, by her marriage to Charles Thissell.   Both Mr. and Mrs. Christopher are active in the Christian Church of Concord, of which they are prominent members.   Mr. Christopher is a deacon of this church, and Mrs. Christopher served for five years as treasurer of the Missionary Society.   Mr. Christopher is a member of the Woodmen of the World.   He is fond of fishing and motoring.

BENJAMIN BRIGNONE.—A pioneer of Richmond since 1902, Benjamin Brignone has carried on a hotel business with increasing success since that date, in what is now known as West Richmond.   He has seen all of the development of Richmond, the building of the Standard Oil refinery, the development of the Santa Fe Railroad, and all of the other industrial and business places that have risen where once were hunting preserves and marsh and farming lands.   He was born in Italy on July 8, 1874, attended the schools of his own community, and at the age of eighteen landed in America to make his fortune.   He went to Tulare County and worked as a ranch hand for two years, and then tried his hand in a sawmill near Truckee for a couple of years, after which he was engaged as a miner near Nevada City for a year.   All this time he was picking up the English language and learning the methods of the American business man.   Having saved some money, Mr. Brignone then went to Rocklin, Placer County, and for eighteen months conducted an eating house; then he spent two years in the liquor business in Sacramento.   This brings us to 1902 when he arrived in Point Richmond, opened a hotel, which he named The Standard Hotel, and catered to the men who were doing the development work for the Santa Fe and Standard Oil Companies.   Mr. Brignone sold out in 1906, and in the fall of 1907 made a trip back to Italy to visit his family and friends.   Returning to Richmond, he built his present hotel, The Columbo, on land he had purchased for the purpose.   Ever since that time he has been "Mine Host" at this place.   He has always shown his public spirit and cooperated with various committees and civic bodies for the betterment of conditions and the advancing of the best interests of Richmond. He took out his citizenship papers in 1898, and ever since that time has been loyal to the land of his adoption.

In December, 1898, Benjamin Brignone was married to Miss Theresa Matroni, also a native of Italy. Her parents, Mr. and Mrs. Joseph Matroni, are deceased, as are the parents of Mr. Brignone, Giacamo and Madalena Brignone. Three children have been born to Mr. and Mrs. Benjamin Brignone. Mildred married John Patrick and lives at Giant; George E., now deceased, served over seas in the World War, was gassed, and died soon after he came home. He enlisted and was a member of the Ambulance Corps, Company 57. Albert, aged thirteen, is now attending the public school. Mr. Brignone belongs to the Odd Fellows and the Druids, having passed all the chairs in the latter order and served as treasurer for fourteen years; and he also belongs to the Fratellanza, an Italian lodge, in which he has also held office. He has been an ardent baseball fan and still enjoys a spirited game.

FRANK W. HUTCHINSON.—As president of the First National Bank of Crockett Frank W. Hutchinson holds a secure position in financial circles of the Bay district. A native son, he was born and reared in California and attended the public schools. During the Spanish-American War he was in the government service, in all spending ten years in the paymaster's department in the United States Army. Leaving the army he engaged in business and continued till the organization of the First National Bank of Crockett in 1919, in which Mr. Hutchinson took an active part. He is a conservative banker and a public spirited citizen, doing all he can in his position to assist in building up California. He is an active member of the State Bankers' Association; is Past Exalted Ruler of the Elks and attended their convention in Boston in 1924; he belongs to the Native Sons, and is an influential member of the Crockett-Valona Business Men's Association, always on the alert to take advantage of every movement for the best interests of his community. He is married and has a son, Francis Hutchinson.

The First National Bank of Crockett was granted its charter March 29, 1919, and opened its doors in its own modern concrete building at the corner of Loring Avenue and West Street on June 4. Its first president was T. J. O'Leary, and the cashier was J. B. Ledbetter. The original capital stock was $25,000, later this was doubled. The organizers of the bank were: F. W. Hutchinson, now its president; M. D. Parker, now cashier; and Albert Aljets, P. Murphy, P. Lucey, B. H. Zuppan, C. P. Thomas, August Berger, A. Boehm, B. Ferrario and C. Giumini were the officers and directors.

The furnishings and fixtures of the bank are of most modern construction, and the vault, with its safety-deposit boxes, is burglar and fireproof. Every consideration is shown the customers to make them feel at home and to guide them wisely in making investments. The growth has been phenomenal from the beginning and today it stands with the best banks in the county. It is a member of the Federal Reserve System and a depository for Postal Savings. Through the president and board of directors every encouragement is given to home builders and business extension of a safe and sane character. At the close of 1925 the resources were $703,531.76; surplus $10,000, deposits, $580,062.23. This shows a remarkable increase since the beginning and gives the bank an assured position in financial circles in California.

TOWNSEND T. CRAMER.—The history of Mr. Cramer's life is a good illustration of what one may accomplish if he but possess the determination to succeed. In young manhood he had no special advantages, but as a result of his industry and perseverance he is today a worthy and respected citizen of Richmond, Cal., where he has lived for the past twenty-five years. He is a native of Edenton, Ohio, born October 4, 1876, a son of Samuel and Matilda A. (Thompson) Cramer, also natives of Ohio. Samuel Cramer was a carpenter and a farmer; he passed his last days in Oklahoma, where his widow and three daughters now make their home. There were five children in this family, two sons and three daughters: Townsend T., of this review; another son passed away in boyhood; and Cora, Mrs. Charles Andrews; Lillie, Mrs. William Sackett; and Neoma, Mrs. Joe Sackett.

Townsend T. Cramer was only seventeen years old when he started out for himself; what education he had received was acquired in the public schools. He first went to Douglas, Kans., and from there to Florence, the same State, where he found work with the Santa Fe Railroad Company and remained until 1898, when he entered the Spanish-American War. The following year, in December, he returned from the war and came West to Winslow, Ariz. There he remained seven months, and then was transferred to Stockton, Cal. In February, 1901, he settled at Point Richmond, where he has been ever since. In 1904 he was promoted to the position of engineer. He has made an enviable record, in that he has had but one serious accident during his many years of piloting a train from place to place.

On January 19, 1900, Mr. Cramer was united in marriage with Miss Elizabeth Conry of Florence, Kans. Her father, Thomas J. Conry, was a surgeon for the Santa Fe system for thirty-three years; he married Miss Margaret Nivin, a native of Ohio, and to them were born seven children, four of whom are now deceased. The surviving brother of Mrs. Cramer, William H. Conry, lives in Emporia, Kans.; and a sister, Daisy, now Mrs. J. M. Bell, is living with Mrs. Cramer. The Conry family are of Scotch lineage, but for many generations have been in America; representatives of this family have been in all the wars fought on American soil. To Mr. and Mrs. Cramer has been born one son, Arthur Conry, now a student in California School of Arts and Crafts. Mrs. Cramer is a prominent club woman, being a member of the Westside Improvement Club.

She is Past Matron of the Eastern Star and Past President of the Ladies' Auxiliary to the Spanish-American War Veterans; and she has represented these lodges in various conventions. She has also been a trustee of the City Library for the past ten years; the board of trustees is made up of one trustee from each of five districts represented in the territory served by this circulating school library. Mr. Cramer is a member of the Brotherhood of Locomotive Engineers and the Spanish-American War Veterans.

SEWARD BRYAN MERRY.—The president of the Republic Steel Package Company of California at Richmond is Seward Bryan Merry, who has taken an active and intelligent interest in the industrial affairs of the East Bay region since he came here in 1921. He was born in Hays City, Kan., on January 12, 1889, the son of Theron T. and Rowena A. (Moore) Merry, natives of Burghill and Lorain, Ohio, respectively, whose family consisted of four sons. The youngest of the four children was Seward Bryan Merry, who attended the public schools of Cleveland, whither the family removed in 1894 and lived till 1921. While going to school he delivered newspapers, took care of a lamp route, worked in a baseball park, and also worked for a butcher, to earn money that he needed for his personal use. He secured his first important position with the American Steel and Wire Company, subsidiary to the United Steel Corporation, and was with them eight years. He then went to the Cleveland branch of the Republic Steel Package Company and remained there nine years, after which he was transferred to the Richmond branch of the company in 1921, and for two years had the management of the concern, or until the present corporation was organized under the State laws of California, since which time Mr. Merry has been the president of the company at Richmond.

The Republic Steel Package Company first began business in 1921, as a branch of the Eastern company in Ohio. On May 15, 1923, it was incorporated as mentioned above with S. B. Merry, president; H. H. Mylander, secretary and treasurer; and L. W. Evans, superintendent. It manufactures all kinds of steel containers for gasoline, oil, paint, chemicals, and insecticides, and also manufactuers underground storage tanks, lubricating oil tank outfits, etc. The employees work the usual eight-hour day, with over-time when needed. The daily capacity is 1000 steel oil barrels and 2000 light-gage packages, and from fifty to eighty-five men are regularly employed. The territory covered takes in the entire Pacific Coast, with branches at Portland, Seattle and Los Angeles. Four to six traveling salesmen are kept busy the year round, and an equal number of men are in their offices in San Francisco. Some of the articles manufactured are patented, but all are of standard make. Mr. Merry believes in paying a man what he is worth, and with their bonus system the production of some articles has been raised 400 per cent.

At the age of nineteen, on December 31, 1908, Mr. Merry was united in marriage with Miss Birdie E. Smith, born in Madison, Ohio, but living in Cleveland at the time of their marriage. They have one son, Theodore, aged fifteen and a student in the high school. Mr. Merry helped organize the present Chamber of Commerce in Richmond and served as director and vice-president for a time. He is a member of the Lodge and Chapter of Masonry in Cleveland, the Consistory of the Scottish Rite in Omaha, the Knights Templars in Richmond, and Aahmes Temple in Oakland. He belongs to the Berkeley Country Club and to the Richmond Rotary Club, is an enthusiastic golfer and a baseball fan, and enjoys all kinds of outdoor athletics.

JOSEPH B. WILLIS.—A highly esteemed citizen of the Richmond Annex who has always put forth his best efforts for the advancement of his community is Joseph B. Willis, who took up his residence here in 1923. He was born in Springfield, Ill., on August 31, 1883, of old Virginian ancestry. Grandfather Willis came from Virginia and homesteaded land near what is now Centralia, Ill., and this same property is still in possession of the Willis family. After graduating from the high school in Springfield, Joseph B. Willis was bound out by his father to learn the trade of the machinist in the railroad shops, and he served four years, from seventeen till he was twenty-one. Later he went to Milwaukee as a journeyman machinist and went to work with the Chalmers people, thus becoming familiar with automobile work. He came out to the Coast in 1905 and was employed at the Union Iron Works until the earthquake and fire; then he went to Fresno, and later to Bakersfield, where he was employed as an oil worker.

While working at his trade in the oil fields in Oklahoma, Mr. Willis was united in marriage with Miss Ida Hensley, on March 27, 1912. She was born in Texas. Some time after their marriage they began traveling from place to place in search of health for Mrs. Willis, and they have lived in many places since that time but never have found their ideal until settling in their present home. They traveled through the Southern States and throughout California, living at Dinuba, Oakland, and other places. Coming to the Annex in search of a home, they bought lots and built their house. At that time there were only five homes in sight, the locality having been a pasture. There were no electric lights here then, but now electricity is used for every purpose for which it is supposed to be used. Mr. and Mrs. Willis helped organize the Annex Improvement Club. This club, starting with twelve members, has grown to about 100 and they all work in harmony for the advancement of their community. Mr. and Mrs. Willis have a son, Jack Price Willis, born in Oklahoma. Mr. Willis is a Scottish Rite Mason and a Shriner, holding his membership in Ardmore, Okla. He is employed as a machinist at Berkeley and belongs to Machinists' Union No. 1546, in Oakland. He is thoroughly alive to the possibilities of this community and favors every project for its advancement.

Frank J. Silva

FRANK J. SILVA.—The senior member of the firm of Silva & Hornback, proprietors of the Community Market at Antioch, is Frank J. Silva. Mr. Silva was born in Contra Costa County, on November 25, 1879, on the site where the present Contra Costa County span of the Antioch bridge is built. His father, the late Joseph Silva, was one of the early ranchers in this district; and his mother, Annie Silva, is still living, makng her home at Oakley.

Frank J. Silva grew up on the home ranch and went to the local school until he was fifteen, after which he went to work in the general merchandise store run by J. Ross, where he learned the ins and outs of the business. He has been connected with the retail business all of his life since leaving school, and has built up a fine reputation in his home community. For two years he worked for the Antioch Hardware Company, and then was in the employ of the Paraffine Companies, Inc., in the administration department, for a time, after which he worked for L. Meyer and Company, pioneer merchants of Antioch, until he formed his present partnership. He was a member of the firm of Silva & O'Meara in Oakley from 1905 to 1911, and then was in the hardware trade, as already mentioned. In 1920, with C. W. Hornback, he began his present business at the corner of Third and G Streets. In time the business outgrew its quarters and they moved to their present location, which was remodeled to suit their needs, and under the name of Community Market they are here doing a thriving business. They sell for cash, keep no books, give very prompt delivery, and can give their customers actual bargains in prices on all their stock. The store is kept in the most cleanly manner, its equipment is up-to-date, and everything is handled in the most sanitary manner. Their four modern refrigerators, counters, shelving, cooling plant, and display space were built to the order of the proprietors, who wanted to make their store one of the most attractive in town; and their stock consists of the choicest and best selected foodstuffs it is possible to get.

Mr. Silva makes his home with his mother in Oakley. He is a director in the Contra Costa County Retail Grocers' Association and was one of its organizers, and he is a charter member of the East Contra Costa County Chamber of Commerce. He belongs to the Native Sons and holds a medal presented to him as Past President by the local parlor, of which he is now a trustee; and the Red Men, the Young Men's Institute, and the U. P. E. C. of Antioch, and the Moose of Pittsburg, claim him as a valued member. He is a director in the Antioch Development Company and is always ready and willing to lend a helping hand to all worthy projects. The slogan of the Community Market is "Service," and the aim of the two proprietors is to see that service is rendered. Mr. Silva takes a decided interest in the various associations of which he is a member, and has won a host of good friends throughout eastern Contra Costa County.

22

R. C. GRIFFITH.—Under the management of R. C. Griffith the O. K. Garage of Brentwood is doing a thriving business. He is dealer for the Star, the Chandler and the Cleveland automobiles, handles the Shell and Standard Oil Companies' products, and also maintains a battery service and deals in accessories.

R. C. Griffith was brought up on a Wisconsin farm. His first independent business after leaving the farm was connected with a cheese factory, of which he finally became the proprietor, at Spencer, Wis. Whatever he undertook to do was carried through with intelligence and well-directed energy and he continued in business there until 1909, when he landed in California and entered the employ of the Standard Oil Company as a mechanical engineer on construction of pipe lines. He next worked for the Shell Oil Company and became their chief mechanical engineer in pipe line construction through the San Joaquin Valley. He then decided he would have a business of his own and with his savings opened a tire and battery shop in Antioch. Coming to Brentwood in September, 1920, he opened his business in an old garage that now stands across the street from his present place of business, and in 1925 moved into his modern and up-to-date garage building. It is a two-story brick structure, the lower floor being devoted to his garage business and the upper floor to offices and apartments.

Mr. Griffith was married in Wisconsin in 1906 to Miss Rosalie Smith, of Spencer, Wis., and they have three children: Lowell, of the class of 1926, in the Brentwood High School, and Bella and Rex, in the grammar school. Mr. Griffith belongs to the Elks, the Odd Fellows and the Masons. In all matters pertaining to the development and progress of the county he takes a very active and discriminating interest.

MATHIAS C. ANDERSEN.—Among the many worthy citizens and capable and industrious farmers of Contra Costa County is Mathias C. Andersen, residing on his fine ranch of 160 acres in the vicinity of Danville. He purchased this place in 1920, has improved it with good buildings, and here he raises grain and runs a dairy. His stock is of the best, and he is a thorough, systematic agriculturist and progressive citizen. He was born in Schleswig-Holstein on November 24, 1869, a son of Andrew J. and Anna M. (Nicolaisen) Anderson, both natives of the same country. Andrew J. Andersen was a carpenter and builder and traveled from place to place plying his trade.

Mathias C. Andersen was educated in the public schools of his own country, and when twenty years of age came to America, landing at Halifax. His destination was California, however, and on arriving in the Golden State he immediately hunted around for a place to settle. For two years he worked on a farm near Black Diamond, now Pittsburg, Contra Costa County, and then went to San Francisco where he worked as a motorman on the street cars for six years. During this time he went to night school to study English and completed grammar school courses and two years of high school work. His next move took him to Livermore, and he remained there for four years; then he came to Danville in 1907, and was on a leased ranch for thirteen years, until he bought his present home, which he has since steadily improved to its present high state of productivity.

Mathias C. Andersen was married on November 2, 1895, to Miss Thyra H. Gram, a native of Denmark, the daughter of Nels Gram, a large farmer in Denmark. She attended private school and afterwards decided she would visit some of her relatives, a great many of whom were seafaring folks who had settled in various countries. She selected those in California and came hither, and has since lived here. One son, Andrew J., has blessed this union. He is a graduate of the San Ramon Union High School at Danville and assists his father with the work on the ranch. He is a Mason. Mr. Andersen is also a member of the Masonic Lodge. He is a trustee of the Sycamore Grammar School and of the San Ramon Union High School, and has been a member of the Danville Grange for many years, taking an active interest in agricultural and general economic development of the county.

PHARCELLUS K. BIGLOW.—The name Biglow is well known in Contra Costa County, where for many years the family have resided, and Pharcellus K. Biglow is considered one of the substantial dairy farmers of the Antioch section of the county. His well-kept and sanitary dairy is located on his ten-acre tract on Wilbur Avenue, two and a half miles east of Antioch. Most of this tract of land is devoted to raising alfalfa, besides Mr. Biglow rents an additional 100 acres for pasture. He maintains a choice herd of about thirty-six cows and delivers milk to the Pioneer Dairy Company in Pittsburg.

Pharcellus K. Biglow was born in Antioch on October 31, 1896, a son of Franklin J. and Mary (Jones) Biglow, both of Antioch. The grandfather of our subject, Adoniram Judson Biglow was born at Perkinsville, Vt., on April 20, 1821, and there grew to manhood. He came around the Horn to California in 1849 and settled in San Francisco, where he engaged in the draying business. He was married in San Jose, on October 25, 1857, to Miss Martha Jane Monroe, a native of Augusta, Maine, who came to California via Panama in 1854. The family then removed to Sacramento and there engaged in the bee business and had the distinction of being the first to bring Italian bees into California. The family remained in Sacramento until the great flood of 1862, when they moved to San Francisco and two years later moved to Sherman Island. Grandfather Biglow and his brother Pharcellus K. were pioneers in raising Early-Rose Potatoes and Palmetto asparagus, and planting grapes, apricots and peaches. There were four children in the family. Elizabeth Louise married John Newton Logan; Mr. Logan died June 26, 1924, and his widow now makes her home on Middle River near Holt, Cal. Franklin Judson is the father of our subject; Pharcellus Monroe was a farmer at Antioch and died May 3, 1915; and David Carlton Orvis is superintendent of the Upper and Lower Jones tracts of the Ringe Land Company in the Delta of San Joaquin County. Grandfather Biglow died in 1892, and grandmother Biglow in 1891.

Pharcellus K. Biglow is the fifth child in a family of six, born to Franklin K. and Mary Biglow, the others being W. A., who assists our subject in the dairy business; Frank Judson, in the grocery business in Antioch; Harold O., residing in Antioch; Mrs. A. Hodgson; and Mrs. A. Meehan. The father of our subject was accidentally killed in August, 1925, aged sixty-three years. Our subject attended the grammar school in Antioch. During the World War he was placed in Class-A-4 but the signing of the armistice kept him from being called to serve his country. Mr. Biglow has been in the dairy business for the past three years and has made a distinct success of it; he has installed the most modern equipment that insures perfect sanitation in every respect.

At Antioch on February 14, 1917, Mr. Biglow was married to Miss Irma E. Vanderhorst, a native of Ohio and daughter of Jacob P. and Josephine (Mack) Vanderhorst, both natives of Ohio. In 1910 the family left Ohio and settled at Antioch, Mr. Vanderhorst being employed at the chemical works in Pittsburg. They have three children: Mildred Irma, Thelma Dorothy and Vernon Cellus. Fraternally, Mr. Biglow is a member of the Eagles of Antioch, and in political affiliations he is a Republican.

SILAS BECKWITH ROBERSON.—A successful contractor and builder in Richmond is Silas B. Roberson, who resides with his family at No. 5142 Nevin Avenue in the Mira Vista section of Richmond. He was born at English, Crawford County, Ind., on December 16, 1888. His father, Frank H. Roberson, was a prominent and successful builder in Crawford County, Ind., and in Kansas City, Mo., having lived in the latter place since 1908. The mother was Mary S. Wright before her marriage, and she was also born in Indiana. There were seven children in the family. S. B. Roberson, of this review; and J. W. Roberson, who is employed by him and lives in Richmond, are the only ones in California. The others are Nolan, in Kansas City; Victor, deceased; Ada, Mrs. Grover Belcher, of Houston, Texas; Viola, Mrs. A. Shepard, of Kansas City; and Katie, Mrs. H. Stratton, also in Kansas City.

S. B. Roberson received his early education in the public schools in Indiana, and this foundation he has supplemented with correspondence courses. His first work was done at St. Louis, Mo., then he worked at Princeton, Ind., and next at Columbus, Ohio. In 1906 he enlisted in the United States Army and came to the Presidio in San Francisco, and remained till he was honorably discharged in 1911. He then took up the barber business in San Francisco, and worked at the trade for seven years, part of the time in Redwood City. He took up the building trade, spent one year in Redwood City, and then came to Richmond. For

a short time he was employed at Crockett by the C. & H. Sugar Refining Company and helped put in some foundation work, after which
he settled in Richmond and began taking contracts, with only $100 cap-
ital, and that borrowed money. He specializes in residences and has
erected some of the best in Richmond, among them one for Howard
Flint in Mira Vista.

Mr. Roberson was married on May 4, 1914, in San Francisco, to Miss
Claire Richel, of that city. She is the daughter of George and Minnie
(Schrader) Richel, natives of Germany and Kings City, Nev., respectively.
The father spent thirty-two years in the American Army as a band leader.
Besides Mrs. Roberson there were the following children in the Richel
family: Minnie, who married W. C. Dooley and lives in Richmond;
Gladys, Mrs. C. M. Curley, of Oakland; and Fred, at home in Oakland
with his parents. Mr. and Mrs. Roberson have three interesting children: Frank Leroy, Eleanor Lorraine, and Varney Hubbard. The two
oldest are in grammar school. The oldest son has a natural bent for
music. Mr. and Mrs. Roberson have considerable musical ability and
their children have inherited a fondness for music. Mr. Roberson has
served on various committees for the advancement of the community,
and is a member of the Builders' Exchange. He belongs to Harbor Lodge
No. 502, F. & A. M., and to the Eastern Star. He finds his recreation in
deer hunting and being in the open.

HENRY EICHER.—One of the pioneer residents of Pacheco, Cal.,
who first came to the town in 1882, is Henry Eicher, a man of marked
business ability and keen judgment in financial affairs. Mr. Eicher is a
native of Germany, born on February 9, 1855, in Hessen-Darmstadt.
As a young boy he attended a technical trade school for three years, after
which he was apprenticed to a large mercantile establishment in Germany,
where he was most thoroughly trained for business. At the age of seventeen he emigrated to America and for eight years was employed in the
mercantile business in New York City. Desiring to see more of the country
he joined the surveying corps of the Santa Fe Railway, at the time this
road was being constructed across the Western plains and mountains,
remaining in this service for two years while surveying in Arizona. In
1881 Mr. Eicher arrived in California, and for a short time thereafter
he was engaged in storekeeping in San Francisco. It was in the summer of
1882 that he arrived in Pacheco, Contra Costa County, where he became
the local agent for the Albany Brewery of San Francisco; and later he was
the agent for the Fredericksburg Brewery, also of San Francisco. Being
a man of keen business foresight and executive ability, he saved his money
and invested in lands. His sound judgment in business affairs led him to
success, and today he is regarded as Pacheco's most substantial citizen.
He has bought and sold farms in the vicinity, and is still interested in
real estate. His ability as a keen financier has been recognized, as is
evidenced by his appointment on the advisory board of the Concord

Branch of the American Bank. Mr. Eicher was one of the organizers of the First National Bank of Concord, the predecessor of the American Bank. He is active in the advancement of the best interests of Pacheco and gives his special attention to the betterment of educational facilities. For many years he has been a school trustee of his district; and for fifteen years he has been a member of the board of trustees of the Mount Diablo Union High School at Concord, serving eight years of that period as secretary. He is especially proud of the fact that during the time he has been a member of the board of trustees all the new school buildings have been constructed.

On December 25, 1885, Henry Eicher was united in marriage with Miss Louise Woodford, of Pacheco; and they became the parents of six children: Clarence, Loleta, Evelyn, Ray, Herman Theodore, and Louise Jeanette. Mrs. Eicher died in 1906, at the age of thirty-seven years. Fraternally, Mr. Eicher is a member and a Past Grand of Pacheco Lodge No. 117, I. O. O. F., and has been a member of the order for forty years.

LOUIS R. GINOCHIO.—Well known as a sturdy, industrious and successful stockman, Louis R. Ginochio has spent his entire lifetime in Contra Costa County. Twelve years ago he succeeded his father in the sheep business, and two and a half years ago he bought the beautiful residence on the highway just south of Antioch. He rents a tract of land consisting of 5000 acres in the vicinity of the old coal mines south of Antioch, where he pastures his large flock of sheep; at present he has 2000 lambs, some 1800 ewes, and 46 registered Shropshire bucks. He was born at Nortonville, Cal., on March 7, 1889, a son of John and Angeline Ginochio, both natives of Italy, where they grew up and were married. There are five children in their family: Mrs. Marie Cunningham, of San Francisco; John, in the roofing business in Oakland; Mrs. Lizzie Lougher, of Oakland; Louis R., of this review; and Mrs. Amelia Peel, of Oakland. Mr. Ginochio, now seventy-four years of age, makes his home in Oakland, retired from business cares after a residence of more than fifty years in California. His wife died at the age of seventy-two, in 1922.

Louis R. Ginochio attended public school in Carbondale, and while a very small boy began tending sheep for his father, who became a very successful sheep man of Contra Costa County. The lessons he learned in youth have followed him throughout his business career, and his industry and thrift have insured him a comfortable competence for the balance of his life time.

On November 4, 1911, Mr. Ginochio was married to Miss Marguerite Hunter, daughter of James and Almira (Snively) Hunter, the former a native of Pennsylvania and the latter of California. Five children were born to Mr. and Mrs. Hunter: Marguerite, Mrs. Ginochio; Mrs. Elsie Shumert; D. O. Hunter; Mrs. Ermyl Lewis; and Vernon. James Hunter had four children by a former marriage: John, James, Walter and Mrs. Rose Daly. By her first husband Mrs. Hunter had four children:

Charles Kingsley, now deceased; and Mrs. Mabel Baker, Mrs. Dorothy Bobo, and Mrs. Maude White. Mr. Hunter died in 1918, but Mrs. Hunter is still living. Mr. and Mrs. Ginochio are the parents of six children: Lauretta A., Anetta E., Lois M., Louis J., Viola E., and Lloyd Ralph. Mr. Ginochio is a Republican.

ARTHUR BURR MINTER.—A pioneer automobile mechanic and dealer is found in the person of Arthur Burr Minter, of the Twenty-second Street Garage, Richmond, Cal. He was born on the old Wicks place in Allegan, Mich., on April 26, 1876, a son of William B. Minter, an Englishman born at Ramsgate, Kent, who came to Chicago in the fifties. He operated three tugs on Lake Michigan and adjoining lakes and was a lumber speculator in the northern part of Michigan. He was married in Allegan, Mich., to Miss Charlotta Piper, who was born there, the daughter of Dr. Piper, one of the first dentists in southern Michigan. Dr. Piper had a son, Giles A. Piper, also a dentist, who was prominent in Masonic circles, and who served in the Civil War, and was taken prisoner and confined in Libby prison until he was exchanged. This was the second marriage of William B. Minter. He had three children by his first wife.

The only child by his father's second marriage, A. B. Minter received his education in the schools in St. Louis up to the age of eleven. He was always handy with tools, and accordingly learned the machinist's trade and ever since then has been working with engines and machinery. Since 1898 he has been interested in the automobile industry. Mr. Minter built the first fire engine of local manufacture, while with the Gorham Engineering Company, in Oakland. This fire engine was purchased by the city of Oakland and was the largest fire engine ever built west of the Mississippi River, of the gas engine type, up to that time. Mr. Minter was selected from among fifty machinists for this particular work, which required great engineering skill. It was built in 1912-1913 and is still in service. He worked in several gas-engine shops in Oakland and did experimental work making electrical score boards. In 1919 he wanted a valve lifter and was unable to procure what he wanted; so he made one that filled the bill and had it patented. This was the second valve lifter patent, of its kind, applied for in the United States.

In 1913 Mr. Minter came to Richmond as shop foreman for the Miles Standish Automobile Company. After one year here he bought out one of the partners owning the business, and the following year bought out the Standish interest and established himself in his present location at No. 325-327 Twenty-second Street. This is the only garage in the city of Richmond that has remained in the hands of the original owner through all the various changes; and it was also one of the first Richmond garages.

Mr. Minter has been uniformly successful and has shown his faith in the city of his adoption by investing in local property. He owns his garage and other property adjoining. He came here with only his bare hands and a good trade—and ill health; now he weighs 206 pounds and is more firmly convinced than ever that this is a "land of promise." He does all kinds of repair work on automobiles and engines and maintains a corps of skilled mechanics. He gives considerable personal attention to his sales department, and up to 1927, he had sold $200,000 worth of automobiles. He sticks to business and believes in giving service regardless of hours spent on a job.

Mr. Minter has been twice married. His first wife was Miss Mary Rickley, of St. Louis, Mo.; and they had four children, two of whom are living: Jesse Burr of Chicago; and Grace, wife of Peter McLaughlin, of San Francisco. For his second wife he chose Miss Augusta Voigt, who was born in West Bend, Wis., the daughter of a farmer; and they have two children: Edith and Ruth, pupils in the Richmond schools. Mr. Minter is a member of Richmond Lodge No. 1251, B. P. O. E., having joined the order on December 14, 1915. He is a member of Alpha Lodge No. 431, F. & A. M.; the Oakland Consistory No. 2, of the Scottish Rite; and Aahmes Temple, A. A. O. N. M. S. He is an honorary member of the Sons of Herman, and belonged to the Merchants' Association in former years. Mr. Minter is a crack marksman and has many trophies as the result of his skill with the rifle. For recreation he goes deer hunting every year, and usually brings game home.

FRANK ARTHUR WENN.—Another native son of the Golden State who is making his influence felt for the general good of the people in Crockett is Frank Arthur Wenn. He was born in Visalia, Tulare County, on September 20, 1885, a son of Stephen and Jennie (Hernandez) Wenn, natives of Italy and Los Angeles, Cal., respectively. His mother was a singer of more than ordinary ability. His father was a brick maker. Besides Frank there were Carmen, Joseph and Stephen in the family. Carmen is an accountant, Joseph is a violinist of note, and Stephen is a carpenter. Frank Arthur Wenn was educated in Tulare County and learned the trade of house painter. He came to Crockett in 1908 and engaged in the building business, then for seven years was the local agent for the Metropolitan Life Insurance Company and had a newspaper agency, later embarked in the candy business, and has since followed his trade.

Mr. Wenn is deeply interested in the cause of education and has done yeoman work in promotion of good school buildings, in organizing the grammar school district at Crockett and in the erection of the modern buildings. His hobby is the manual training of the young and the development of character in them. He has worked to protect the children at grade crossings, and he served as trustee of the grammar school in 1920, when the condition of the school building was deplorable, but through the efforts of the citizens, bonds were voted for modern structures.

On June 28, 1908, Mr. Wenn married Eugenia Gerz, a native of Germany, and they have three children: Viola, gifted with musical ability on the piano, in the high school; Frank, a graduate in the manual arts;

and Joseph, in kindergarten. Mr. Wenn belongs to the Young Men's Institute; the Knights of Columbus; is Past Sachem of Carquinez Tribe, No. 98, I. O. R. M.; is Past President of Carquinez Parlor No. 205, N. S. G. W.; Secretary of Crockett Aerie No. 774, F. O. E.; and in civic affairs is active in the Crockett-Valona Business Men's Association and identified with all progressive movements in the county. The family attend the Catholic Church.

RICHARD R. VEALE.—In thirty-two years of service in public office, and holding an office which calls for more real character, initiative and integrity of purpose than perhaps any other in public life, Sheriff Richard R. Veale, of Contra Costa County, during this long period of active duty has built up a reputation which is a matter of pride to his many friends in the district, and to the county as a whole. As a prominent resident of the county once said, "the school, the church, and the home have all found Richard R. Veale a bulwark of strength, a monument of untiring energy, dependable at all times, and first to the front when duty calls; yet ever kind, consistent and considerate—a real man." A native son, his birth occurred near Petaluma, Sonoma County, on March 27, 1864, the son of Richard R. and Martha (Rains) Veale. The father was born in Illinois and came to California via the Isthmus in the early fifties. He was married in 1863, at Petaluma, to Martha Rains, a native of Missouri and daughter of Gallant Rains, an influential Southern gentleman of means who with his family, including Martha, crossed the plains in charge of three wagon trains composed of many wagons and horses, and became a stock-raiser, rancher and a man of much influence in California, for he had an unusual strength of character, a characteristic no doubt inherited by his descendants. Grandfather Veale was also a highly respected and able man; he located at Penn's Grove, in Sonoma County, and became an extensive stock-raiser and rancher and a large land owner there.

Sheriff Veale attended the Cinnibar school in Petaluma during his grammar school days, and later pursued courses at the Petaluma High School and at a business college at Stockton. He came to Contra Costa County with his parents in 1868, but upon his mother's death, in 1871, he went to live with his Grandmother Rains, and so had his schooling mostly in Sonoma County. He entered politics very early in life, being selected as a local committeeman, and took an active interest in the doings of the Republican party. In the meantime he worked for his father on the farm, and for G. W. T. Carter on threshing machines, and also learned the blacksmith trade, at Brentwood. He farmed for a time on the Los Medanos ranch near Antioch, and later went to Brentwood, where he became an extensive rancher, and with his brother, W. W. Veale, operated 4000 acres, raising grain, cattle, horses and hogs.

It was while running this ranch that R. R. Veale was first elected to office as sheriff of Contra Costa County, in 1894, since which time he has been reelected nine times, and it is safe to say that he is the best-known peace officer on the Pacific Coast and over a large portion of the United States as well, as during his incumbency he has acquired a wide acquaintance with sheriffs, police officers and judges in almost every State in the Union. In all the public affairs of Contra Costa County his influence has been felt. The people of Richmond sent him to Washington to help Hon. Franklin P. Lane and Chas. F. Curry put over the reclamation district, known as the Richmond Harbor project. And it was largely through his efforts that the U. S. government was induced to clean out the shoals between Martinez and Pittsburg which had made navigation difficult. Deep going vessels can now go up as far as Antioch in safety. This water commerce is of inestimable value to the county. He is an ardent advocate of good roads, and was largely instrumental in the State highway being built between Martinez and Crockett, and from Crockett to the Alameda County line. Letters from N. D. Darlington, a member of the California Highway Commission, and from Charles D. Blaney, chairman of the California Highway Comission, were written in September, 1922, commending him most highly for the service rendered both the State and his county in helping to secure the necessary rights of way and public cooperation in the highway projects, now conceded to have been a most important factor in the remarkable upbuilding of the county.

And as sheriff of the county R. R. Veale has been so eminently the man for the place that his terms in office have been uninterrupted. In the early days, when Contra Costa was decidedly "Western" territory, he passed through many adventures and had numerous miraculous escapes, and while he arrested many desperate characters, and sent many of them to the penitentiary, he has never yet found it necessary to kill a man in the discharge of his duty, although he has captured many at the point of a gun; the Sheriff getting the "draw" first! His life has been so marked by characteristics of firmness, determination and courage, that these have controlled the situation without recourse to desperate measures, for he feels that it is his duty not to kill a criminal, but to arrest him, and then let the law take its course. He has always landed his man and been successful in getting national and international extradition of his prisoner. In the Mechanics Bank robbery at Richmond, which occurred one morning in November, 1926, at 8:30 o'clock, the next evening at 5 o'clock one of the defendants was in San Quentin, and over $8000 recovered. As custodian of the courthouse at Martinez, he has proved a real humanitarian. He installed the furniture and fixtures of the present jail, which is a model of cleanliness. The mattresses are kept cleanly and carefully in covers; and an abundance of both hot and cold water is provided for baths. Sheriff Veale takes a humane interest in the jail and its inmates, insisting on regular bathing and clean quarters; and every person committed to his keeping is given individual attention and medical aid when required; as a result of which many prisoners emerge from their confinement in a better condition of mind and body than when committed, and with a much greater chance of again becoming useful citizens. The courthouse, built in 1901, is overtaxed for room and additional buildings have been required. The same careful management is brought to bear throughout the buildings, and nothing destroyed which can be put to some use, or sold to help in county expenses. In covering the county under his charge as peace officer, Sheriff Veale has become so well acquainted with the wonderful fertility of the delta section, and the advantages of having seventy miles of waterfront, that he feels a deep loyalty toward doing everything in his power to further its best interests, and during the past years there has not been a worthy public project for development put forward in Contra Costa that Richard R. Veale did not take an active part in aiding, both as an efficient public officer and as a loyal citizen to his home district.

In 1884, at Oakland, occurred the marriage of Richard R. Veale and Miss Elizabeth Martin, a native daughter of San Francisco, and six children blessed their union: Robert Howard, superintendent of Hercules Powder Company at Kenosha, Wis.; William Minor, under-sheriff at Martinez; Leila, who is the wife of Absalom F. Bray, member of the law firm of Rodgers and Bray, of Martinez, and the mother of a son, Junior Bray; Mortimer Belshaw, an attorney at Antioch; Miriam E., wife of Francis McMahon, of the Shell Oil Company at Martinez; and Leola, Mrs. Bernard McDonald, of Los Angeles, who has a daughter, Nancy Elizabeth.

Fraternally, Sheriff Veale is a prominent Mason, and Shriner, a member of Aahmes Temple in Oakland; and he belongs to the Eastern Star, Odd Fellows, Knights of Pythias, Moose, Elks, the Native Sons, Rebekahs, Pythian Sisters, Neighbors of Woodcraft, Eagles, Woodmen of the World, U. P. E. C., etc. Since 1895 he has been secretary of the Sheriffs' Association of California. He is, and has been for many years, secretary of the Contra Costa Chamber of Commerce. During the World War he organized a Home Guard of 1200 men, and could send 250 armed men to any point in the county at short notice; they all served without pay or a dollar of expense to the taxpayers of the county. Always able to meet every situation in this industrial county of $26,424,500 annual payrolls, and $404,123,620 annual output—it is this ability which has won him such far-reaching respect. During the hoof and mouth disease in the county, he had photographs taken of infected cattle, which Congressman Curry used to excellent advantage in getting damages for Contra Costa stockmen. When he was first elected to office Richmond was not in existence, Pittsburg was but a fishing village, and other towns were small places. The growth of the county has necessitated the gradual increasing of police protection throughout the county, all of which has been done under the supervision of the sheriff. In 1923 Sheriff Veale received a very complimentary letter from R. A. Haynes, federal prohibition commissioner, in appreciation of his activities in that line, especially the receipt of padlock posters from Sheriff Veale, and copies of places closed under the Padlock provision, which Mr. Haynes wrote he was transmitting to the United States District Attorney in New York for his information and as a demonstration of what local officials may accomplish in coordination with Federal agents.

A trustworthy public official, and a man of remarkable attributes of mind and energy, Mr. Veale has been a decided factor in the upbuilding of Contra Costa County during the past third of a century.

FRANK H. ROSA.—Now in his third term as a member of the Sanitary Board of the San Pablo District, Frank H. Rosa is serving the public with the true spirit of a responsible official whose wish it is to work for the benefit of his community and to render unselfish service to those whose franchise has confided to him a public trust. He was born in the Azores Islands on June 8, 1886, a son of Manuel and Mary (Garcier) Rosa, both natives of the Azores. There were thirteen children in the Rosa family, and when the parents came to California three were still living in their native land.

Frank H. Rosa attended the schools on his native island and was the first of the family to migrate to America. He left home in 1904 and arrived at New Bedford, Conn., whence he came direct to San Pablo, Cal. He secured employment in the Pullman shops and later went to work at the refinery of the Standard Oil Company in Richmond, and has been with that firm ever since. After he had saved some money he sent back and helped his folks to get to the land of promise, and his parents are still living in Contra Costa County. As he has prospered he has invested his savings in property, and now owns a house in Richmond and two in San Pablo; and he also has stock in the Standard Oil Company. He is well pleased with Richmond and feels that in no other place could he have succeeded as well in so short a time. He has entered into the spirit of the community and was elected to the Sanitary Board, and twice reelected, which is evidence of his popularity and efficiency as a public official. At one time Mr. Rosa was a partner in an apartment house in San Francisco, but sold out after three years.

Mr. Rosa was married on April 25, 1914, in Oakland, to Miss Josephine Frega, of that city. There were three children born to them, only one of whom is living, a daughter, Genevieve E., aged eleven and a pupil in the local grammar school. Two children died in infancy, and on October 31, 1918, Mrs. Rosa died of the flu. Mr. Rosa is a member, and for sixteen years has been secretary, of the U. P. E. C.; is a member and the president of the I. D. E. S.; and is president of the Holy Ghost Society of San Pablo. For fifteen years he has represented the U. P. E. C. Society at the State conventions. The family are active workers in the Catholic Church of San Pablo, and are leaders in their social circle. Mr. Rosa has a host of good friends in his locality.

JOSEPH FREITAS.—The greater part of the life of Joseph Freitas has been spent in the Live Oak district of Contra Costa County, where he owns a productive twenty-acre ranch; fifteen acres are in grapes and the balance is set to almonds, all in full bearing. This ranch is one of the pioneer ranches of the community. It is under a high state of cultivation and on it is a comfortable residence and good improvements.

Joseph Freitas was born on the Island of Flores, October 15, 1869, and when nine years of age he came to America with his parents, Frank and Anna J. (Machada) Freitas. After a few months' stop in New Bedford, Mass. the Freitas family arrived at Half Moon Bay, Cal., in the month of May, 1879. One year later they located in the Oakley Precinct near what was then known as the Iron House school district, and in 1883 they located in the Live Oak district, on their present home place. This ranch was cleared of the chaparral and live-oak trees and was then planted to fruit and nut trees and vines. Many were the hardships and privations of these sturdy pioneers, but they never tired of striving for better things for their posterity. The mother passed away in 1924, aged eighty-two years; the father survived her until January 31, 1926, when he too passed away, aged eighty-eight years.

Joseph Freitas received a common school education, and since fourteen years of age has made his own way in the world. For sixteen years he worked on a hay-press. He saved his money through all the years, and today he is living in comfortable circumstances, enjoying the fruits of his labors.

In 1896 Mr. Freitas was married to Miss Frances Minta, a native daughter of California; and to them have been born five daughters; Rosaline; Frances; Evelyn, Mrs. Thomas De Maggio; Minnie, Mrs. Joseph McCurrio; and Marie. Mr. Freitas helped to organize and is a director in the Bridgeport Shipping Corporation. For twenty years he has served as a member of the Live Oak school board. In politics he is a Republican. He is a charter member of the I. D. E. S. No. 7, and belongs to Antioch Aerie No. 785, F. O. E., both of Antioch.

ROY E. EDSTROM.—One of the efficient and capable workmen for the F. E. Booth Company is Roy E. Edstrom, who has long been recognized by the company as a most valuable and dependable employee. He was born on New Year's Day, 1895, in Chicago, Ill., a son of Andrew and Evelyn Edstrom, and in 1900 came with his parents to San Francisco, where he spent his boyhood days and attended school. After graduating from grammar school he found employment with a theatrical booking company. In 1911 his mother died and he then severed his connection with the theatrical business and obtained employment with the F. E. Booth Company, San Francisco branch, in the canning department. His services were so loyal and efficient that his ability was soon recognized and by January, 1917, he had been advanced to the responsible post of warehouse foreman at Pittsburg, Cal. Few people outside of Pittsburg have an adequate idea of the magnitude of the varied output of the F. E. Booth Company's plant. Fruits, vegetables and fish are canned in carload and shipload lots. This company has experienced a healthy growth until now it ranks among the largest in the world.

Roy E. Edstrom has an enviable record for service during the World War. On September 19, 1917, he was assigned to the Depot Brigade and sent to Camp Lewis, and from there was transferred to Camp Mills, N. Y., where he was placed in the 41st Division. On December 12, 1917, he sailed from New York for St. Nazaire, France, where he arrived on December 26. He says he will always remember December 25, 1917, as their convoy, consisting of fourteen ships, destroyed two German submarines on Christmas Day. As a machine-gun man, Mr. Edstrom saw service in France at Bordeaux. His company volunteered on St. Patrick's Day to go to the front, where they fought side by side with the French in Flanders. He was with the 1st Division as a machine-gun man. He also fought in the Toul sector, and at Soissons, where he was severely wounded three times in the left leg and once in the left arm. After nine months in a French army hospital he was returned to the United States on October 10, 1918, and honorably discharged from Camp Kearney, Cal., on January 8, 1919.

Roy E. Edstrom was united in marriage on June 5, 1920, with Mamie Belleci, the daughter of Joe and Sarah Belleci. This union has been blessed with two children, Evelyn and Irvin. Mr. Edstrom belongs to the Pittsburg Chamber of Commerce, and is a member of the Loyal Order of Moose.

SALVATORE AND SYLVESTER ENEA.—Two brothers doing business under the name of S. Enea & Brother erected, own and operate the California Theater, the only first-class moving picture house in Pittsburg, Cal. They also own and operate the Palace Theater on Black Diamond Street. It is quite appropriate to mention in some detail the advancement of the moving picture business in this thriving city. In the early days of the moving pictures, when 4000 feet of film, then unperfected, was called a wonderful show, David Solari and Sylvester and Salvatore Enea saw in the motion picture good business possibilities. In 1908 these gentlemen operated and controlled the old opera house, giving the town of Black Diamond the best that the motion picture industry afforded. Six months later they opened the Diamond Theater on Railroad Avenue. Others also saw possibilities and the old opera house on York Street was remodeled and opened as a first-class motion picture theater. These young men were not satisfied, however, and in 1910 they built the Palace Theater, proclaimed by all the most magnificent structure in Black Diamond. In 1914 Mr. Solari sold his interest in the Palace and looked for larger fields, operating in Napa, Stockton, Hayward and Eureka.

On May 4, 1920, after every line of the motion picture had been perfected, Enea Brothers erected the California Theater, one of the finest motion picture palaces in any interior city in Northern California. Nearly $200,000 have been expended in building and equipping this building. It has a seating capacity of 1200 and there is a Leatherby-Smith Orchestral organ costing $20,000 to supply the music. A modern water pre-cooling system keeps atmospheric conditions perfect in all kinds of weather. The building is fire-proof, has numerous exits, and is modern in all its appointments. Amusement lovers of Pittsburg and vicinity have derived much pleasure from this theater, and Enea Brothers are very highly complimented for their excellent management and the high grade of pictures shown. The residents of this vicinity have shown their appreciation by a liberal patronage of this magnificent playhouse. The proprietors have shown their firm faith in the city, and make this their slogan: "When better pictures are made, we show them." They are very loyal boosters for Pittsburg and are accounted among the representative business men of Contra Costa County.

Salvatore Enea was born in Italy on January 25, 1885. His father had died, leaving his widow with several small children. She brought her family to California and settled at Black Diamond, as Pittsburg was then called, and nobly kept her little family together until her death, which occurred in this city. The children grew up in this environment and have proven themselves worthy of their parents. Salvatore Enea was married in San Francisco on December 3, 1905, to Miss Mary Solari, a representative of a pioneer family of this city, and they have four children: Stella, Rose, Frances and Virginia. Mr. Enea is a member of the Loyal Order of Moose in Pittsburg.

Sylvester Enea was born in Italy on January 13, 1888, grew to maturity in Pittsburg, and early became interested in the moving picture industry, as has already been mentioned. He was married in Pittsburg on October 18, 1914, to Miss Mary Partenico, of this city, where she grew up from the age of two. They have three children, Sammie, Salvatore and John.

LESTER G. LAWRENCE.—For the practice of his calling Lester G. Lawrence received a thorough preparatory training. Before he had finished his high school course he took up the machinist's trade, and he was prepared, at the opening of the World War, for a position as a mechanic in the department of air service. He enlisted in the Army on October 7, 1917, and was sent to Camp Lewis; from there he was transferred to Camp Hancock, Ga., and on February 8, 1918, sailed for France. His regiment repaired airplanes at Epinal, France, in the Vosges district, until the signing of the Armistice, and he then returned to the United States and his home in Walnut Creek, where he has continued his work as a mechanic.

Lester G. Lawrence was born at Half Moon Bay, Cal., October 27, 1894, and is the youngest of nine children born to J. C. and Lena (Frates) Lawrence, natives of Portugal and Massachusetts, respectively. The father, J. C. Lawrence, was a young man when he came to California. He engaged in mining in Idaho and California for a number of years after his arrival in the West, and then homesteaded land at Half Moon Bay. Here the family of nine children were born, as follows: Rose, now the wife of G. F. Womersley; Adaline, now Mrs. Board; Elizabeth, Mrs. Walsh; Louise, Mrs. Stephan; Mayme, Mrs. Wilcox; Fred; Joseph; Harry; and Lester, our subject. J. C. Lawrence was a butcher by trade, and besides looking after his homestead he operated a butcher shop in Half Moon Bay. When Lester was but a babe in arms, the family removed to Haywards and there the father ran a butcher shop for two years. Another move was made to Danville, and the father ran a shop there until he retired from active business cares and settled at Walnut Creek, where he passed away in March, 1923, at the age of eighty-four years. The mother of the family lived to be sixty-seven years old, and also died in March, 1923, and was buried on the same day as her husband. Lester G. Lawrence attended grammar school in Danville and after finishing the course entered the high school; then he attended the Concord High School, but left before finishing the course in order to learn the machinist's trade. He now owns a thriving garage business and is agent for the Buick and Star automobiles.

On September 8, 1922, Mr. Lawrence was united in marriage with Miss Jean Rogerson, who was born in Los Angeles, Cal., and they are the parents of one daughter, Barbara Jean. Mr. Lawrence's political views favor the policies of the Republican party. Fraternally, he is a member of the American Legion and the Woodmen of the World, both of Walnut Creek, and belongs to Richmond Lodge No. 1251, B. P. O. E.

FRANK G. IACONA.—Numbered among the successful growers of Pittsburg is Frank G. Iacona, an enterprising citizen whose adherence to right principles of business and courteous treatment of customers have developed the growing business enjoyed by the grocery department of the National Market, of which he is the owner and manager. The life which this narrative sketches began on August 19, 1880, in Licata, Province of Girgenti, Italy, when Frank G. Iacona was born in the family of Guiseppe and Maria Iacona. There were five children in the family: Vincenzo, Antonino, Frank G., Carmelo, and Angelo, four of whom reside in Pittsburg and one at Antioch. Carmelo, Vincenzo and Antonino are employed in the Pioneer Rubber Works at Pittsburg. The father is now deceased, but the mother is still living in Italy.

Frank G. Iacona attended the public school at Palermo, where his grandmother, Carmela Bonfiglio lived. The first one of the boys to emigrate to America was Vincenzo, who came over in 1898. Frank G. Iacona arrived in San Francisco in June, 1903, and found employment in the San Germain Restaurant in that city, where he remained over nine years. In 1911 he returned to Italy and was married on April 29 of that year to Catherine Taormina, a native of Trabia, Italy. He returned with his bride to San Francisco, where they resided until 1916. Mr. Iacona located

in Pittsburg in August, 1917, and is now operating the grocery department of the National Market. In 1922, in partnership with A. C. Cardinale, owner of the meat market department of the National Market, he built the two-story brick building at the corner of Railroad Avenue and East Third Street, Pittsburg, which is occupied by the National Market.

Mr. and Mrs. Iacona are the parents of two children, Maria and Teresa. In 1908 Mr. Iacona became a naturalized citizen of the United States. In national affairs he supports the Republican party. Fraternally, he is a member of the American Order of Foresters in Pittsburg.

ELLWOOD F. HERBERT, D. D. S.—Since 1919 Ellwood F. Herbert has practiced the dental profession in Pittsburg, and during that period he has gained an enviable reputation as a careful and skilled dental surgeon, so that he now draws his clientele from a wide radius. He was born in Solano County, Cal., on October 11, 1876, a son of William B. and Susan (Barnes) Herbert, the former a pioneer of 1850 and the latter of 1854, in this State.

William B. Herbert was born in Harford County, Md., in 1817, and comes from Revolutionary stock through relationship with General Herbert. After reaching young manhood he went to New Orleans and was engaged in the trading and transportation business between that city and St. Louis. In this way he heard a great deal about California from those going and coming over this route, and he decided that he would see the country for himself. Accordingly he outfitted for the trip across the plains in 1850, and walked all the way, suffering many privations. He mined for a time; but finding it was not productive of satisfactory returns, he looked about for some land, and in Solano County, three miles from what is now Davis, purchased a ranch and began general farming on it. After he became assured that a prosperous future awaited him here, he went back East, in 1854, and on May 5 of that year married Miss Susan Barnes. With his bride he returned to California via Panama and for a time after his arrival followed mercantile pursuits in San Francisco. He then went back to Solano County and engaged in farming and stock-raising until 1876, when he bought 2000 acres near Cambria, San Luis Obispo County, and carried on the stock business until 1881. As his children were attaining the age when they should have good school facilities, Mr. Herbert disposed of his ranch and stock and located near San Jose. He began the cultivation of his newly acquired property by setting out an orchard, being among the very first to engage in horticulture on a commercial scale. In 1894 he sold out and settled in San Jose, and there he died on June 13, 1901, aged eighty-four years. Mrs. Herbert is still living in San Jose, and at the age of ninety-two is enjoying life to its full.

Ellwood F. Herbert is the youngest son in a family of nine children. He attended the public schools of San Jose and the College of the Pacific, and then, in preparation for the profession he chose for a life work, he entered the University of California Dental College and was graduated with the Class of 1901. He began his practice in Santa Barbara and remained there for the following seventeen years. During the World War he was located in Vallejo, and then went to Richmond and followed his profession until November, 1919, when he located in Pittsburg, and since that date he has built up a lucrative practice and enlarged his already wide circle of friends.

On July 24, 1920, Dr. Herbert was united in marriage with Miss Catherine Clary, born in San Francisco, in which city their marriage was celebrated. Two sons, William Marden and Ellwood F., Jr., have blessed this union. Dr. Herbert is prominent in fraternal circles, being a Past Exalted Ruler of the Benevolent Protective Order of Elks, Past President of the Fraternal Order of Eagles, and Past President of the Native Sons of the Golden West, all of Santa Barbara. He has gained a reputation as an eloquent speaker and is frequently called upon to officiate at public gatherings. Since becoming a resident of Pittsburg he has entered heartily into the civic life of the city, and he is to be found on the side of progress at all times, giving of his time and means to help promote worthy projects for the upbuilding of his city and county.

CHARLES B. WEEKS.—The efficient ranch foreman for the Balfour-Guthrie Company, Charles B. Weeks, supervises some 4000 acres owned by the company in the Brentwood district of Contra Costa County. This is what remains of the original 13,000 acres of the holdings of Balfour-Guthrie Company, and it is capably managed by Mr. Weeks. The property is divided into several parts. Camp No. 1 is devoted to apricots, prunes, peaches and pears and a large acreage of alfalfa; Camp No. 2 is devoted to alfalfa and dairying; and Camp No. 3 is given over to sheep-raising and producing tomatoes. Camps No. 4, No. 5 and No. 6 have been sold off. Mr. Weeks makes his home at Camp No. 1. 1926 finds him putting in 350 acres of tomatoes and 100 acres of lettuce. There are some forty men employed as ranch hands and also fifteen dairy workers, all under the supervision of Mr. Weeks who keeps in close touch with every department at all times.

Charles B. Weeks was born at Kinsley, Edwards County, Kans., on July 7, 1884, and is a son of James P. and Florence G. (Blanchard) Weeks. The family came to California in 1894 and settled at Red Bluff, where the father began the cultivation of a peach orchard. He died the following year, leaving a widow with three children: Fred, now ranching near Red Bluff; Charles Blanchard, of this review; and James Pascal, of Dunsmuir, an employee of the Southern Pacific Railway. The mother still maintains the home in Red Bluff. During his attendance at the public schools our subject made himself generally useful around the ranch, and he early took up agricultural and horticultural pursuits, taking an extension course in the latter at the University of California. In time he was appointed horticultural commissioner of Tehama County, serving from 1910 to 1918, and giving general satisfaction to all concerned. He saw many changes in Tehama County as its products were changing from grain to fruits, and he did his share as an official. In 1918 he left Tehama County and engaged with the United States Smelting and Refining Company at Redding as field agent for their agricultural department, remaining till 1921, when he became field agent for the Nurserymen's Bud Selection Association, which position he held one year. In 1922 he came to Brentwood to take charge of the Kirkman Nursery and planted about 1500 acres to trees. In 1924 he assumed his present position with Balfour-Guthrie Company.

Charles B. Weeks was united in marriage at Red Bluff on December 6, 1910, with Miss Myrtle Edna Yancy, born in Colusa County, the daughter of Oliver Yancy, one of the early settlers of Colusa County. Two children have blessed this union: Charles Blanchard, Jr., and Mary Rideout. Mr. Weeks is a member of Vesper Lodge No. 84, F. & A. M., at Red Bluff, and also of the Eastern Star of that city, to which Mrs. Weeks also belongs. They are Republicans. Both Mr. and Mrs. Weeks have made many close friends in their new home district and are highly esteemed by all who know them.

CHARLES B. WIGHTMAN.—A descendant of an honored pioneer, Charles B. Wightman, owner of the Diablo Auto Park Service Station and Tourist Camp Grounds, located at the junction of Borden Highway and the Brentwood-Byron Highway, is the son of Joel D. Wightman an early pioneer settler of California, a man of high ideals and many sterling characteristics; an interesting sketch of his life will be found on another page of this work.

Charles B. Wightman was born at Antioch, Cal., November 7, 1882, the second son and child of Joel D. Wightman. He learned the trade of carpenter from his father and followed it for twelve years. In 1909 he and his brother Percy engaged in the garage business at Byron, Cal. In 1924 he purchased a two-acre tract of land on the highway which he has transformed into a beautiful auto park and camping grounds, erected an up-to-date service station, a modern residence, four cottages for campers and tourists and has tenting space for automobile tourists. He has spared no pains to make Diablo Auto Park attractive to the traveling public. It is supplied with plenty of water, which is pumped from a well by electric power, into a steel tank, and atop of the tank is an electric tower that furnishes light for the park. In addition to these necessities he has installed an electric water heater, and an electric stove, two shower baths and toilets; and the park is also supplied with a refreshment stand. Such a modern caravansary as this is indeed doubly welcomed by the tired and dusty auto tourists. Here they can enjoy the comforts of home amid the joys of out-of-door life. Although it is a new place it is well patronized by the traveling public.

On August 9, 1906, Charles B. Wightman was united in marriage with Miss Beatrice Wisdom, and this union has been blessed by two children:

Emma, Mrs. Raymond Parke, resides at Tracy, Cal.; and Sadie, a student at the Brentwood Liberty Union High School. Fraternally Mr. Wightman is a member of Byron Parlor No. 170, N. S. G. W.; Byron Lodge No. 355 I. O. O. F.; Brentwood Lodge No. 345 F. & A. M.; and of the Woodmen of the World. He is an enthusiastic worker for the East Contra Costa County Chamber of Commerce and gives his aid to all movements that have as their aim the betterment of social, educational, moral and commercial interests of his community.

JOE CESA.—The leading contractor and builder in eastern Contra Costa County is Joe Cesa, of Antioch. Mr. Cesa was born in Venice, Italy, on October 19, 1893, a son of Andreas and Theresa Cesa. Andreas Cesa was a prominent contractor in Italy and did much work for the Italian government. The parents are still in Italy, enjoying their prosperity there. They had four children. Two sisters of Joe Cesa still remain in their native land. His brother, Henry Cesa, was the first of the family to come to California. He was a contractor and builder and was prominent in Antioch up to the time of his death from the flu in 1918. He was married and had two children, but his wife and baby boy both passed away, leaving a little daughter, Theresa. She was adopted into the family of Joe Cesa and is now eleven years old.

Joe Cesa attended his home schools and there learned the trade of the plasterer, cement worker and brick mason. He left home on September 11, 1912, to join his brother at Antioch, Cal., arriving in October. His brother was rebuilding the Paraffine Companies, Inc., building just after their fire in 1912, and he was put at work laying brick and continued at work for eight months. He continued at his trade until the war broke out and then tendered his services to the United States government and was sent where he was most needed. His ability as a builder was soon noted and he was placed in charge in the erection of Y. M. C. A. and other buildings for the government, with fifteen men under his direction. At the close of the war he returned to Antioch from Camp Kearny.

His handiwork is seen on the Cardinalli, the Lanzafame and the National Market, in Pittsburg; the American Legion Memorial in Brentwood, and some of the finest homes there; the Pioneer Rubber Works, and homes in Walnut Creek and Martinez. He was the first to do concrete work on the new Antioch bridge, and he erects buildings for the C. A. Hooper Company. He is an expert workman and is always busily engaged in work. In his home town he erected the garage which he owns at the corner of Fourth and K Streets, doing the work nights and Sundays; and he has just completed his new home at Fifth and K Streets.

Mr. Cesa has perfected an ingenious arrangement for heating several rooms, or the entire house, from a fireplace, and has secured letters patent on the device, which is known as the Cesa Fireplace Heater. This is also a ventilator as well, and is operated by a small electric motor. This motor drives or draws the heat from the fireplace through pipes into the rooms to be heated, and thus saves the expense of a basement furnace. In summer the rooms can be ventilated through the same pipes and in the same manner. There is a vacuum attachment that works from the same motor from the furnace. This is the first of its kind in the United States and bids fair to become a household necessity. Mr. Cesa is an expert furnace builder and worker in cement of all kinds.

On August 22, 1921, Joe Cesa was married to Miss Lena Mattei, who was born in Boston, Mass., but grew up at Antioch. They have had one child, Ramona, now going on two years old, besides their adopted daughter, Theresa. Mr. Cesa is a member of Harding Post No. 161, American Legion, at Antioch, and belongs to the Loyal Order of Moose, the Fraternal Order of Eagles, and Columbus Lodge, Sons of Italy. In all civic affairs he stands ready and willing to do his share, and is loyal to the country of his adoption. He and his wife have many friends throughout eastern Contra Costa County.

JAMES L. CLAGHORN.—James L. Claghorn has every reason to be pleased with Contra Costa County, for a proper use of its opportunities has resulted in a competence for him. In partnership with Dr. H. R. Green, of Palo Alto, he owns 106 acres in the Lone Tree District of the county. For the past four years he has personally supervised the development of this ranch. Eighty acres have been planted to the Blenheim and Tilton varieties of apricots, and a considerable acreage is devoted to growing cantaloupes, lettuce, spinach, etc. Mr. Claghorn was born in New York City on June 10, 1889, a son of C. R. and Margaret (Montgomery) Claghorn. His father was a mining engineer by profession and was engaged along this line until his demise; the mother is still living. There are two sons in their family: James L., our subject; and D. M., an engineer residing in Pittsburgh, Pa.

James L. Claghorn attended the Hill School for boys in New York City, and when ready to enter college became a student at Columbia University, taking the mining engineering course, and was graduated with the Class of 1912. After finishing school he went to Alaska, where he engaged in the practice of his profession until 1915, when he came to California and was in the employ of various mining companies, especially at Grass Valley, Nevada County, and in Siskiyou County. Mr. Claghorn enlisted in the aviation section during the World War and became instructor at Ellington Field, in Houston, Texas; he served throughout the war and was commissioned first lieutenant.

James L. Claghorn was married in Houston, Texas, in 1918, to Miss Yvonne Lloyd, born in San Francisco, a daughter of J. C. Lloyd. Mr. Claghorn became interested in the oil fields of Texas and remained there until 1923, when he removed to California. He is now serving as secretary of the recently-organized Lone Tree Shipping Corporation; this company takes care of all the produce raised in this vicinity and is of great benefit to the farmers and fruit growers.

GEORGE CHRISTENSON.—An assured position among the prosperous agriculturists and respected citizens of Contra Costa County is held by George Christenson, who, with his good wife, resides on their ten-acre home place in the Oakley Precinct. Mr. Christenson was born in Neenah, Wis., on October 5, 1856, a son of Godfrid Christenson, a native of Norway who came to America and settled at Neenah, where he engaged in the mercantile business. George Christenson grew up and attended the public schools in Wisconsin; and after finishing the grade schools he entered a business college in Oshkosh, the same State, became an accountant, and was associated with his father in the grocery business in Neenah.

In 1892 Mr. Christenson was married to Mrs. Mary Spaulding, widow of Augustus Spaulding, a decorator of Neenah, Wis. Mrs. Christenson's maiden name was Mary Madison. She was born in Denmark, a daughter of Mrs. Anna Madison, who afterwards became Mrs. Jensen. Mrs. Madison was the mother of three children, Mrs. Christenson being the only one now living. Mrs. Christenson grew up in her native country until thirteen and then, with her mother and two sisters, came to Wisconsin. She was first married to Mr. Spaulding in Neenah; and one daughter, Augusta, was born of this union. She is now the wife of Clyde Olney, residing in Oakley, where she and her husband own and operate a general merchandise store; they also have a store in Richmond, Cal. In 1919 Mrs. Christenson and her daughter purchased the present home ranch of ten acres, which is devoted to the raising of almonds. The orchard is now in full bearing and is bringing in a good income to its owners. Mr. and Mrs. Olney stand high in Masonic circles, and Mrs. Olney is a pianist of note. They are the parents of three daughters: Mary Belle, Jane Elizabeth, and Grace. Mrs. Christenson was brought up in the Lutheran Church, but is now an attendant at the Presbyterian Church. Mr. Christenson is almost seventy years old, but retains his youthful vigor and enjoys keeping the home place in good order. By his industry and frugality a comfortable competence has been assured. He and his wife came to California in 1911 to join their daughter in Oakland, later went to Richmond, and then settled at Oakley.

LOUIS ANTONE.—A native son of Contra Costa County, who has made a success of his chosen business at Pittsburg, Cal., is Louis Antone, the popular proprietor of the Faultless Cleaners establishment located at 319 Los Medanos Street. Mr. Antone was born at Martinez on November 21, 1893, the son of John and Delphina Antone; the mother still resides in Martinez but the father is deceased.

Louis Antone is a self-made man. His success has been due to his own efforts since he was sixteen years of age, at which time he left school to seek his own way in the world. His first employment was that of working on a hay press, for which he received one dollar per day. In 1915, he started a clothes cleaning business at Martinez, but when the World War was declared his patriotic spirit would not allow him to remain at home and in November, 1918, he enlisted in the Aviation Service, being assigned to Squad No. 836, and entered training at Fort McDowell, Kelly Field, Waco, Texas, whence he was transferred to Garden City Camp, N. Y. In May, 1919, he sailed from New York City on the Aquitania under convoy, landing at Liverpool, England. There he remained two months, and then sailed from Southampton to Bordeaux, France. After seven months of service over seas he was returned to the United States and at San Diego, Cal., was honorably discharged. Afterwards he worked at the shipyards in San Francisco for four months and then returned to his old home at Martinez, where he resumed the cleaning business for six months. In May, 1921, he located at Pittsburg, formed a partnership, and entered into the cleaning business; but he soon sold his interest and left Pittsburg. After a short absence, however, he returned and again opened a cleaning business, this time establishing his shop under the name of the Faultless Cleaners; and since then he has been successful in building up a growing and profitable business. He attributes his success to good workmanship, courteous treatment of patrons, and close attention to details.

Fraternally, Mr. Antone is a member of the David A. Solari Post, American Legion, at Pittsburg; is Noble Grand of Pittsburg Lodge No. 436, I. O. O. F., and also belongs to the Rebekahs and the Encampment at Crockett; is a Past Sachem of Minatonka Tribe No. 243, I. O. R. M., at Pittsburg, and is a member of Pocahontas. He has a wide circle of friends and is highly esteemed in both Pittsburg and Martinez.

JOSEPH CHAPOT.—With the energy characteristic of the race from which he springs, J. Chapot has hewn his way to a prominent place in the affairs of Contra Costa County, eliciting approval as the senior member of the firm leasing and operating Hotel Martinez, at Martinez. This hotel is first-class in every detail, with seventy-five steam-heated rooms with private baths and showers. The hotel is in the heart of the city, and the proprietors make every effort to please their patrons.

The youth of Joseph Chapot was spent in his native province in France, that of Basses Pyrenees, where he was born on May 22, 1891, a son of Henry and Eugene Chapot. The father is a stone-cutter by trade, which he plies at Oloron, France. Both parents are still residents of Basses Pyrenees. As a boy, J. Chapot attended the public schools of Oloron, but when only sixteen years of age, in 1907, he left home for America, and came direct to Los Angeles, Cal., where he worked in a laundry. When the World War came on, he was in the first draft and was assigned to the infantry and trained at Camp Fremont. With the 12th Infantry he was sent to Siberia and spent a year and a half in that frigid country. At the end of his service he returned to the United States and was honorably discharged at San Francisco, on January 8, 1920.

During the summer of 1920, J. Chapot leased the Glasgow Hotel in San Francisco, which he operated until 1922; then he ran the Alvarado in the same city. With S. Bourrague, whom he had known in France, Mr. Chapot removed to Martinez; and together they assumed management of Hotel Martinez on November 8, 1923. This venture has proven a financial success, and the satisfaction of the public has been a stimulus to these energetic soldier boys.

The marriage of J. Chapot occurred in San Francisco in 1920, when he was united with Miss Margaret Malendres, also a native of France; to them have been born two children, Raymond and Jean. Mr. Chapot is a Democrat in politics, and fraternally he belongs to the Elks and the Parfaite Union No. 17, of San Francisco.

SAVIN BOURRAGUE.—Always a believer in the adage that "A rolling stone gathers no moss," Savin Bourrague presents an example of what steady and continuous effort in one channel of endeavor will accomplish, having devoted his time since reaching his majority to catering to the comforts of the traveling public. Mr. Bourrague, after reaching the United States, became a pastry cook at the Golden Pheasant Restaurant in San Francisco; and later he was with Christopher in Los Angeles. After his return from France in the service of the Government, he ran the Hotel Del Monte in San Francisco for three years. He gave this business his best thought and energy, and as a reward for this singleness of purpose and capable management was able to bring to the present partnership with Joseph Chapot, as joint manager with him of Hotel Martinez, a business sagacity that has brought success in a large degree.

Savin Bourrague was born at Villa Segure, Basses-Pyrenees Province, France, September 11, 1891. His father is a cabinet-maker, and is still engaged at his trade. As a boy Mr. Bourrague learned this trade with his father, and was thus occupied until he was twenty-one years of age, when he left his home in France and came to the United States. When the United States went into the World War, Mr. Bourrague was assigned first to the infantry; then he was transferred to the Bakery Division of the Quartermaster's Department and served for fifteen months at Camp Lewis and Camp Fremont. He was assigned to Bakery Company 340 and was sent to France, where he served for fifteen months, returning to the United States on July 12, 1919; he was honorably discharged at the Presidio, San Francisco, on July 14, 1919.

At Santa Cruz, Cal., in 1920, Mr. Bourrague was married to Miss Philomene Buros, also a native of France.

On November 8, 1923, the partnership of Chapot & Bourrague was formed and a lease was taken of Hotel Martinez. This hotel contains seventy-five rooms, steam-heated, with private baths and showers, and is first-class in every particular. The well-directed energy of these two French-American soldier boys not only has been productive of financial success, but has also set a standard of efficient and gratifying service to travelers from all parts of the world.

M. Johnson

MARTIN JOHNSEN.—A very capable blacksmith and dealer in agricultural implements at Antioch is Martin Johnsen, owner and proprietor of Peterson's Plow and Agricultural Works at the corner of Third and H Streets. He handles the International Harvester line of goods and has been steadily forging to the front in his particular field. His smithy is equipped with the modern appliances, and here from morning until night Mr. Johnsen is to be found hard at work. He finds plenty to do at all seasons of the year and is seldom idle, being an expert operator on any of the various machines in his shop. He has been a familiar figure in business circles in Antioch since 1914.

He was born in Denmark fifty-two years ago and began to learn the blacksmith's trade from his brother, but while still a youth he came to the United States and for a time worked in the Middle West. The lure of California was strong on him, for he knew better opportunities were awaiting him here. Upon his arrival in the State he went to Petaluma and worked at what he could find to do, but he soon secured a place in a blacksmith shop and there found his opportunity. He came to Contra Costa County in 1896 and worked at ranch work and carpentering in several places, finally coming to Antioch, where he opened a blacksmith shop. He soon demonstrated his superior workmanship, and his trade came to him, so that now he does the principal business in this entire section; and no job is too difficult for him to undertake. He believes in the precept of the Golden Rule and counts his friends by the score.

JOHN ZUBERBUHLER.—Now living practically retired from hard work, John Zuberbuhler and his good wife are enjoying the evening of their days as residents of the Knightsen district in Contra Costa County, where they have made many friends. Mr. Zuberbuhler was born in Canton Appenzell, Switzerland, on March 3, 1849, and there he was united in marriage with Miss Louisa Bosch, who was born in Leyden, Holland, but was taken to St. Gallens, Switzerland, by her parents and there grew up in the same canton as did Mr. Zuberbuhler, and learned the trade of the dressmaker and modiste, which she followed until her marriage. They both had the advantages of the good Swiss schools, and Mr. Zuberbuhler learned the miller's trade and followed it during the time he lived in Switzerland. With his wife and two children, John and Louisa, he arrived in New York on July 23, 1879, and journeyed to Webster County, Nebr., where Mrs. Zuberbuhler had a brother living. They leased land and began farming and built a sod house or dugout in which to live. Mrs. Zuberbuhler did some millinery work for neighbors and took chickens in payment, and sometimes a pig, there being no money to speak of in circulation among these pioneers. The land leased was owned by the B. & M. Railroad and located in Republican Valley. Mr. Zuberbuhler helped to build the B. & M. Railroad and was the second section foreman in that section, and he served five years. In 1886 the family came out to California and Mr. Zuberbuhler secured work with the Southern Pacific Railroad as section foreman at Volcano Springs, in what is now the Imperial Valley, then simply a waste of sand. He stayed there seven months and then came north to Los Angeles, being there during the building of the Arcade Depot. He was section foreman for the section between Los Angeles and Compton. In 1890 they went back to Nebraska and he bought 480 acres of land and again farmed. In 1893 the family took in, the World's Fair in Chicago; and in 1900 Mr. and Mrs. Zuberbuhler went to Switzerland for a visit and attended the Paris Exposition while there. He sold his farm in 1903.

California had such a hold upon Mr. and Mrs. Zuberbuhler that they decided they would make this their permanent home; and accordingly they came and located in Sonoma County, where Mrs. Zuberbuhler's brother, John D. Bosch, was living. They bought a vineyard near Geyserville; but this they sold out in 1907, and in 1910 they came to Knightsen. Here they own 200 acres of fine grain land, most of which is leased to tenants, Mr. Zuberbuhler retaining a small plot of ground and the home place, where they have a small chicken ranch with white Leghorn fowls. They have had four children, two of whom died in Nebraska. John married Minnie Fry, and they have three children—Clarence, Opal and Nelma—and are farming in Nebraska. Louisa is the wife of Gottlieb Somerhalder of Knightsen and has four children living: Paul, Arthur, Erwin and Samuel. Mr. Zuberbuhler and his good wife have worked together, and whatever of success has come to them has been the result of their combined efforts. They are adherents of the Zwingli religious faith.

RAY S. WIGHTMAN.—A highly respected and well-known citizen of eastern Contra Costa County is Ray S. Wightman, now living on his well-improved and productive ranch near Oakley. He was born in Antioch on November 18, 1885, the son of Joel D. and Sarah Jane (Snead) Wightman, the latter a native of New Jersey and still living. The father was in the contracting business in Antioch for many years, served as a member of the board of supervisors, and was on the building committee during the construction of the Court House in Martinez in 1901-1903. He bought twenty-five acres of land near the Live Oak schoolhouse and set twenty acres of it to olives. This ranch is now occupied by C. E. Wightman, a son, who is mentioned on another page of this history.

Ray S. Wightman attended the schools of Antioch and grew up and helped his father with his olive orchard until he went to work for Lauritzen Brothers in the carrying of passengers on the rivers from Antioch to Stockton and to Sacramento. He rose to be captain of the new boats operated in the passenger service, the Princess, the Ellen and the Gwendolin. He followed the river for eleven years, until 1920, when he bought a thirty-acre ranch near the new bridgehead and developed sixteen acres of it to a vineyard of wine grapes. This property was sold and Mr. Wightman bought his present home place of two and one-half acres four miles west of Oakley and erected his present comfortable and modern home.

He was one of the organizers and is a stockholder in the Bridgehead Shipping Corporation and serves as its secretary. He is acting as agent for the American Toll Bridge Company at the Antioch Bridge.

Ray S. Wightman was united in marriage at Yreka, Cal., on August 8, 1917, with Miss Ruth C. Davis, born in Chico, Cal., the daughter of J. L. and Elizabeth Davis, now residing at Wallace, Calaveras County, where Mr. Davis is engaged in stock-raising. Mrs. Wightman attended the schools of her home district, a private normal, and Heald's Business College in Stockton. She began teaching school in 1911 and is a very successful educator, now teaching in the Riverside school in Sacramento County. She is a talented and highly educated lady and has a wide circle of friends. Two children have blessed this marriage, Ray P. and George Davis. Mr. Wightman belongs to the East Contra Costa County Chamber of Commerce and is a live wire in all projects for the upbuilding of his community and county. In politics he is a Democrat.

CHARLES STANLEY DIMM.—A representative citizen of Richmond, and one who is prominently associated with the Standard Oil Refinery, is Charles S. Dimm, residing at No. 560 Key Boulevard. He is a native of Indiana, born at Whiting on March 18, 1895. His father, Luther D. Dimm, was born in Pennsylvania and from an early date has been connected with the oil industry. For a number of years he was manager of the Richmond refinery, and he is now manager of the refinery at El Segundo, Los Angeles County. The mother was Miss Lula Jennie Rickenbaugh, also born in Pennsylvania, the daughter of an old and highly respected family of the Keystone State. Charles S. Dimm is an only child. He attended the Richmond Union High School, and was graduated from the University of California in 1917 with the B. S. degree. He majored in economics, chemistry and general business. He was prominent in college life and was presented with a key for scholarship, in the Beta Gama Sigma scholarship society. He was president of the Glee Club and a member of the Delta Tau Delta Fraternity.

After his graduation from college Charles S. Dimm entered the employ of the Standard Oil Company at El Segundo and was there at the breaking out of the World War. He was in the government service at the aviation field at Lake Charles, La., and was honorably discharged in December, 1918. He then took a trip through the Eastern States, being absent for two months, and then came back to his work at El Segundo. On February 28, 1921, he came to Richmond, and has been at the Richmond Refinery since that date.

On February 10, 1923, Mr. Dimm was united in marriage with Miss Dorothy Dukes, of Berkeley. She is the daughter of Dr. Charles A. and Mabel (Saxe) Dukes, and took a three-year course in the University of California. They have a son, Stanley Dukes Dimm, born May 30, 1925. Mrs. Dimm is an efficient cellist and is well and favorably known in San Francisco, Oakland, Berkeley and other parts of the Bay section. Mr.

Dimm is a thirty-second degree Mason and a Shriner. He is a member of the University Club of Los Angeles. Both Mr. and Mrs. Dimm have a wide circle of friends throughout the Bay section.

PETER H. WIND.—Coming from good farming stock in Denmark, Peter H. Wind has chosen to make Crockett his home and the scene of his activities. He was born in Denmark on September 15, 1868, a son of Loren and Anna E. (Paulsen) Wind, both natives of Denmark where they were among the highly respected farmer folk. He has a sister in Burlingame and one in San Francisco. After going to the schools in his home locality until he was thirteen, Peter H. Wind set out for America. He stopped in New York but a short time, then made his way to Savanna, Ill., where he found work on the railroad and remained thus employed for ten years. During that period he saved his money and stored up a great deal of valuable information that has stood him in good stead since taking up his home in California.

When he first landed in Crockett he went to work with his brother-in-law, Christian Larsen, at the building trade. The latter is now a dealer in real estate and a builder in Burlingame. In 1896 Mr. Wind took to contracting for himself, and has erected many homes in Crockett and vicinity since then; also has contracted for business blocks and done considerable remodeling. His business has had a steady growth and he has given his patrons the best efforts in his line. One of the homes he built was that first occupied by George M. Rolph, when he came here as superintendent of the refinery; he also erected the first clubhouse. He operates under the name of P. H. Wind & Son, the latter is Fred Wind.

Mr. Wind was married in 1888 to Miss Anna M. Neilsen, a native of Denmark, who came in young womanhood to America, and is the only one of her family now living here. Her mother is still living and is ninety-four years old. Five children have been born to this union: Fred, a partner in the building business with his father; Berthel, died in young manhood; Anna J., bookkeeper in San Francisco; Lila E., Mrs. Renato Suscipi, of Rome, Italy; and the youngest, Charles, a high school graduate, who also spent two years at the University of California. The family attend the Presbyterian Church. Mr. Wind is an Odd Fellow and is a Past Grand in the order. He is a Republican in politics.

WALTER COOTS.—Among the native sons of Contra Costa County who have risen to important positions is Walter Coots, assistant manager of the mercantile establishment of L. M. Lasell Company, the Emporium of Contra Costa County. He resides in his beautiful home at 119 Pacheco Boulevard, Martinez. Mr. Coots is in charge of the following departments: dry goods, gents' furnishings, ladies' ready-to-wear, shoes, and the furniture department. He was born at Concord, Cal., June 10, 1886, a son of the late James Coots, who passed away at Concord in 1911, at the age of seventy-six, after a long and useful career. James

Coots was a native of Ireland, who immigrated to Canada while a young man, and in 1867 arrived in California. He was married at Pacheco, Cal., to Miss Winnifred Grant, a relative of Gen. U. S. Grant, who was a cousin of her father. Mrs. Coots' great-aunt, Lottie Grant, furnished the data for the Grant family history as recorded in "General Grant's Memoirs." The Coots family are of Scotch-Irish descent and lived in the northern part of Ireland. The mother of our subject was born at Walnut Creek, Cal. She is still in the enjoyment of health and happiness and now makes her home in Martinez. Two children were born of this union: Walter, our subject, and Robert, who is a bookkeeper for the Shell Corporation of California, at Martinez.

Walter Coots' early life was spent at Concord and vicinity, attending the public schools of his home district and assisting his father in the operation of two farms, a responsibility all the greater because of the fact that his father also operated a threshing outfit, threshing thousands of sacks of grain every year. His services were in great demand in the fertile grain growing section near Brentwood and Byron. Walter Coots was fourteen years old when he went to work for Geary & Company at Concord. Later he clerked in the store of Randall Brothers for two years. He entered the employ of L. M. Lasell on July 1, 1907, and he has continued there steadily ever since, having risen to his present position by sheer force of merit.

The marriage of Walter Coots occurred at San Jose, Cal., and united him with Miss Nina Claire Fenton. Her father was a locomotive engineer on the Siskiyou mountain division of the Southern Pacific system and was killed in a railway accident when Mrs. Coots was only three weeks old. His widow makes her home with her daughter, Mrs. Coots. Fraternally, Mr. Coots is affiliated with the Native Sons of the Golden West and the Woodmen of the World, both of Martinez. In politics he is a stanch Republican.

BERNARD DAL PORTO.—Known by his intimate friends as "Ben" Dal Porto, our subject was born at Jackson, Amador County, on June 27, 1895, the son of Salvatore and Mary (Frediani) Dal Porto, both born and reared in Italy. The father was born near Lucca on November 5, 1865, came to America and California in 1889, and was married in San Francisco in 1892. His wife was born on May 14, 1868. They had the following children: Frank, of the Oakley Garage, who served in the United States Navy during the World War, doing convoy duty; Edith, who married E. A. Silva of San Francisco; Lena, wife of Dr. C. H. Lindner, of San Francisco; Bernard, of this review; and Tony, a machinist in the Oakley Garage, who was in the motor vehicle department during the World War. Salvatore Dal Porto was a pioneer of Jackson and conducted a boarding house for the Kennedy Mining Company for several years. He saved his money and in 1908 came to Contra Costa County and invested in property at Oakley, and became the foremost upbuilder of the new town. He built the post office building at a cost of $8000; the Oakley Garage, costing $15,000; Oakley Theatre Block, also costing $15,000; and the Oakley Hotel at an expense of $50,000. The latter was completed in 1925 and is a modern building in all of its appointments.

Ben Dal Porto grew up in Jackson and attended the public schools there and in Oakley, coming here when he was thirteen years old. He helped his father on the ranch, and the boys and father have all worked together to bring about their present prosperity. Ben conducts a soft drink parlor and pool hall in the hotel building, which is also under his management. In 1917 Ben Dal Porto was in the draft for the World War and on December 10 of that year he was in France and was first assigned to the signal corps of the 41st Division. He was transferred from one department to another in the service, and when he was returned to California he was mustered out and honorably discharged at the Presidio in San Francisco on April 7, 1919, as sergeant of the first class from the Base Hospital. He belongs to the American Legion at Antioch.

On November 22, 1920, Mr. Dal Porto was married at Antioch to Miss Irma Lynn, daughter of John Lynn, one of the old settlers and a butcher in Antioch. Two children have blessed this marriage, Bernard, Jr., and Lynn. In politics Mr. Dal Porto votes the Republican ticket. Fraternally, he is a member of the Young Men's Institute of Antioch. Mrs. Dal Porto belongs to the Native Daughters in Antioch.

J. R. BUNDESEN.—A very competent machinist who is meeting with merited success is J. R. Bundesen, of the firm of Bundesen and Lauritzen, shipbuilders, machinists and dredging contractors of Pittsburg. Mr. Bundesen was born in San Francisco on November 19, 1892, the son of Boy and Annie (Lauritzen) Bundesen. The father, familiarly known among the boatmen as "Pete" Bundesen, was for years a ship painter in San Francisco.

After his school days were over J. R. Bundesen learned the trade of the machinist and applied himself to his calling with diligence. He served in the World War in the United States Navy and was in Germany during 1918 and part of 1919. He served as a machinist, was promoted to chief machinist and engineer, and was honorably discharged at Mare Island in 1919. He then located in Antioch and started the Bundesen Machine Shop, and soon became known as an expert in his line, specializing in work on Diesel Engines, so much used on river boats and water craft. On December 18, 1925, a partnership was formed with H. F. Lauritzen. The company bought the Lanteri Ship Yards at Pittsburg, and the new organization is known as Bundesen and Lauritzen Ship Yards and Machine Works. They are prepared to construct barges of all sizes, dredges, and all kinds of craft for river use. They have remodeled the Pittsburg plant, installing modern machinery, have erected a new machine shop, and now make their headquarters at the Pittsburg plant, Mr. Bundesen having discontinued the Antioch establishment. The new location has a 250-foot frontage in the heart of the manufacturing district, and they are executing orders for craft for use as far north as Oregon. They are both expert workmen and are able to make repairs on any and all kinds of river and harbor vessels. The firm took over the Delta Dredging Company, a Lanteri corporation, on April 1, 1926.

Mr. Bundesen was married in April, 1924, to Miss Nellie Eunice Higgins, daughter of Lee Higgins, rancher and sheep grower of Contra Costa County. The family home is at Antioch, where both Mr. and Mrs. Bundesen are leaders in their social circle. Mr. Bundesen is a member of Harding Post, No. 161, American Legion, of Antioch; Antioch Lodge No. 175, F. & A. M.; and the Loyal Order of Moose, of Pittsburg.

LAWRENCE NICOL.—A man of strong personality and good education, Lawrence Nicol holds an assured place among the prominent ranchers and citizens of eastern Contra Costa County, where he is managing the ranch owned by Nicol & Smith, Inc. This ranch comprises 640 acres of fine land, with 300 acres in alfalfa, 200 acres in twenty-five-year-old almond trees, and fifty acres in Blenheim and Tilton apricots. In 1920, when Mr. Nicol came here, this land was a grain field with the exception of the almond orchard. Since that date, as manager of the property, he has carefully planned and executed his improvements until the property has no equal in this part of the county. No expense has been spared to bring about this change and to place the ranch on a remunerative and productive basis equal to any in the Delta region.

Lawrence Nicol is a native Californian, born on September 17, 1888, in Stockton, where he was reared and where his father, Frank Nicol, was a leading lawyer for more than thirty years as the senior member of the firm of Nicol & Orr. The elder Nicol was born in Illinois, and in an early day crossed the plains with his parents in a covered wagon drawn by ox-teams. Upon arriving in California they settled at Columbia, Tuolumne County, where the older members of the family followed mining for a time. Frank Nicol studied law in Tuolumne County, and after being admitted to the bar moved to Stockton in 1880. He was married in Sonora to Adelaide Dodge, daughter of a pioneer family and herself born in this State. Her mother was a pioneer of 1854. Four children resulted from this union: Edwin E., in the insurance business in San Francisco; Mrs. Robert A. Smith, capitalist; Lawrence, of this review; and Mrs. Joseph Nielsen, of San Francisco. Frank Nicol died in Stockton in 1910, aged fifty-one years. Mrs. Nicol, now in her sixty-third year, makes her home in San Francisco.

Lawrence Nicol attended the Stockton public schools and was graduated from the high school in 1907. That year he entered the University of California, pursuing a natural science course; and after he was graduated he entered law school, from which he was graduated in 1911, and then took two postgraduate courses in law, receiving the degree of Doctor of Jurisprudence. He then entered the law firm of Goodfellow, Ells &

Orrick in San Francisco, and was following his profession at the time of the World War. In the fall of 1917 he answered the draft, trained at Camp Lewis, and went to France with the 41st Division, serving under General Alexander, and had charge of the military correspondence until the signing of the armistice. He then went to Paris and gained admission to the Sorbonne University of Paris, where he specialized in French, history and literature. Early in 1919 he came back to the United States and received his honorable discharge at Camp Mills, Long Island, as a corporal. In 1920 he again took up civil life and came to his present location, where he has built up a reputation for himself as a public-spirited citizen and successful rancher. He believes firmly in the future of the county, and is always found ready and willing to give of his best efforts to further every project for the advancement of those interests that make for a better and bigger prosperity for the people who select this county as their home.

At Ross, Marin County, on December 28, 1920, Lawrence Nicol was united in marriage with Miss Irene Hund. She was born and reared in Marin County and represents a prominent family of the north bay district. Three children have blessed this union: Frank David, Jean, and Walter Harry. Both Mr. and Mrs. Nicol have an ever widening circle of friends in this county, and it is a privilege to be counted among their personal acquaintances.

GIUSEPPE SPARACINO.—The standing attained by Giuseppe Sparacino, one of Contra Costa County's successful business men, is the result of well-directed effort accompanied by ability and energy. He has been a resident of Martinez since he was a very young man, and for several years has been the representative, in this city, for the San Francisco International Fish Company. He is a substantial citizen and willing at all times to assist in any movement for the welfare of the community.

Joe Sparacino, as he is familiarly known, was born at Santa Elia, Palermo, Italy, September 24, 1880, the second eldest in a family of five children born to Nunzio and Rosa (Belanti) Sparacino. Nunzio Sparacino was employed as a fireman for the Flavio Rubertino Company, now the Italian General Navigation Company, for more than twenty years; he came out to California for the first time in 1889 and engaged as a fisherman in the bay region. Returning to Italy on a visit to his family, he remained for one year and then returned to California, this time bringing our subject, who was then a lad of twelve years. They settled at Martinez and were there engaged as fishermen, and a few years later the rest of the family came to California to make their home. The father is now eighty years old, and the mother has reached her seventy-second year.

Giuseppe Sparacino attended public school in Italy up to his twelfth year, and after arriving in Martinez entered the public school, but only attended two terms, when he quit to assist his father in the fishing business, which had grown to such proportions that they owned several fishing boats. When his father retired from the business in 1907, Giuseppe,

Mr. and Mrs. Frank Seem

or Joe Sparacino succeeded to the business, which grew rapidly under his able management, so that he soon began to buy and market the catch of other local fishermen, and found himself in a lucrative wholesale business. Ten years ago his business was consolidated with the San Francisco International Fish Company, and Mr. Sparacino has since been the local manager of the Martinez branch.

On October 13, 1907, at Martinez, Mr. Sparacino was married to Miss Anna Belanti, born at Palermo, Italy, where she grew up and was educated. To them have been born seven children: Rosa, Nunzio, Joe, Nina, Peter, Frank, and an infant unnamed. Mr. Sparacino belongs to the Knights of Pythias and the Moose Lodges of Martinez and was made a Mason in Speranza Italiana Lodge No. 219, F. & A. M., San Francisco. In politics he is a Republican. Mr. Sparacino was one of the organizers of the National Bank of Martinez and is serving on its board of directors; he is also a director in the Richmond-Martinez Abstract Company.

FRANK SEENO.—Few residents of California outside of Pittsburg are aware of the fact that Pittsburg is one of the most important centers of the fishing industry in the State. It is estimated that about 700 persons are engaged in the fishing industry in the various capacities necessary to conduct the business in Pittsburg. The building of fishing boats, and motor boats for fishing, is considered a very important business here. Frank Seeno is one of the noted and successful boat builders in Pittsburg, where he has a well-equipped shop on the water front at the foot of Railroad Street. Here boats are built, launched, repaired and made ready for use on short notice. He began making sailboats, but now specializes in motor boats of from six to twelve horse-power gas engines.

Frank Seeno was born near Palermo, Italy, on the Island of Sicily, on August 5, 1873, the son of Erasmo and Rosa Seeno. The father lives in America, but the mother still resides in Italy. They had seven children: Frank, Gaetano, Angelo, Josephine, Rosa, Frances and Mary. The father was a stone mason by trade and Frank worked with him fifteen years, during which time they were engaged in building operations in Tunis and Algiers, Africa.

In 1902 Frank Seeno was married to Miss Rosa Cardinalli, the wedding taking place near Palermo. She died three years later. In 1906 he came to California and located at Black Diamond, now Pittsburg. He worked as a boat builder, and later satisfied a desire to see Alaska, where he spent three seasons working as a stevedore. Coming back to Pittsburg he leased a shop and began business, and later erected his own buildings and equipped them with modern wood-working machinery run by electric power. He has been successful, and is highly regarded in Pittsburg. In 1908 Mr. Seeno was again married, taking Miss Catherina Taormino, a native of Italy, as his wife. They have had five children: Rosa, Erasmo, Salvator, Vincent and Josephine.

23

WILLIAM LUTZ.—William Lutz is well and favorably known throughout Eastern Contra Costa County, and particularly in Oakley, where since 1922 he has operated the Oakley Pharmacy. In connection with his drug business, which includes a large and ever increasing prescription department, he handles newspapers, magazines and stationery. William Lutz was born in Geneva, N. Y., on September 18, 1898, his parents being John and Elizabeth Lutz, now honored citizens of Antioch. John Lutz, the father, is in the employ of the Pioneer Rubber Company at Pittsburg, but has his home in Antioch. The Lutz family came to California when our subject was six and a half years old. As a boy, William Lutz attended the grammar school in Antioch and later entered high school. He began to study pharmacy under Professor Flint, of the Physicians & Surgeons College in San Francisco, and then found employment in the Palace Drug Store in Antioch. During the World War he spent ten months in France in the Medical Department of the army, and prior to going to France he spent six months in training camps in the United States. Returning to the United States he resumed his position with the Palace Drug Store, after his discharge from the service on May 10, 1919, and in 1919 passed the State examination as a pharmacist. Three years later he opened his present drug store, where he has built up a prosperous business. He is thoroughly reliable and competent, and enjoys the confidence of the entire community.

On May 2, 1925, Mr. Lutz was married to Miss Verna Boyd, born in Butte County, Cal., and they are prominent in the best social circles of Antioch and Oakley. Mr. Lutz is a member of the American Legion, Harding Post No. 161, at Antioch.

GRIFFITH LLOYD.—A trusted employee of the Selby Smelting Company in Contra Costa County is found in Griffith Lloyd of Crockett. He was born in Wales on March 26, 1868, the son of Thomas and Catherine (Evans) Lloyd, both now deceased, the father died at the age of over ninety, in 1924. There were an even dozen children in the family of Thomas Lloyd. The oldest brother came to America when a young man and located in New York State, where also there is a sister now making her home.

After attending school up to the age of seventeen, Griffith Lloyd made up his mind he would come to America and join his brother, which he did in April, 1885, when he arrived in Utica where he had an aunt. That city did not impress the young man on account of its very muddy streets but he made the best of things and found work. He also went to school a couple of winters while in New York State and says the schools did not compare with those in his native country. For three years he worked out as a farm hand, then he went to Iowa and for the next ten years farmed there during the summers, usually working in the coal mines in winter. It was about 1897 that our subject arrived in Los Angeles; to thoroughly enjoy the climate he used to go to Santa Monica and lie in the sand and compare the eastern and western winter climates. In the spring of 1898 he came to San Francisco and felt an earthquake shock the first night. He traveled to the gravel mines and worked for eight months, then returned to San Francisco and worked as a laborer until he became connected with the Selby Smelter, where he has worked his way through the various positions until he is now a melter. He has the confidence of his superiors and of his fellow workers.

Mr. Lloyd was united in marriage on February 21, 1922, with Mrs. Annie (Roberts) Williams, born in North Wales, who came to California when young with an uncle and aunt. Her parents had eleven children, there being among them two pairs of twins, a boy and a girl and a boy and a girl. By her first marriage she has a daughter, Mrs. Elizabeth Elliott, of San Francisco. Mr. Lloyd belongs to the Masons in Crockett and the Odd Fellows in Iowa, and to the Crockett Eagles. The family are protestants. Since Mr. Lloyd has worked for the Selby Smelting Company he has witnessed many changes in the methods, particularly in the handling of materials. He is public-spirited and a booster for Contra Costa County where he has made many friends.

HENRY E. NEAR.—In the business which he conducts, that of a commercial plumber, Henry E. Near has been an active factor in the up-building of Walnut Creek, to which place he came after being honorably discharged from the United States Army, in which he distinguished himself in service during the World War, and was gradually promoted until he was Sergeant, 1st Class, in Company C of the 26th Engineers. Born on his father's farm near Hollister, Cal., April 15, 1885, he was the youngest in a family of five children born to John Henry and Alice A. (Barney) Near, the former a native of Iowa and the latter of California. Grandfather Barney was born in Illinois and came to California in 1851. He was among the first settlers of Sonoma County, where he farmed the greater part of his life. John Henry Near left home while still a young man and, coming to California, engaged in farming in Sonoma and San Benito Counties. He now makes his home at Lafayette, and is seventy-six years of age. The following children were born of this union: Edith and Pearl, deceased; Mrs. Nora Gilman, residing in Lafayette; Jesse, residing in Walnut Creek; and Henry E., of this review.

Henry E. Near attended grammar school in the cities of Santa Rosa and San Francisco. When sixteen years old he began to make his own way in the world and for three and a half years worked in the New York-Grassville Consolidated Mine on the old Perrin place. Following this, for four years, he worked for the Southern Pacific and Santa Fe Railroads. He then decided to learn the plumbing trade, and for a time thereafter was a journeyman plumber; then he established a plumbing business of his own in Walnut Creek. After the outbreak of the World War, however, he sold his business and on November 5, 1917, enlisted for service and was assigned to Company C of the 26th Engineers. He trained at

Camp Dix, N. J., for five months and was then sent over seas. He was in the Meuse-Argonne offensive from October 2 to November 11, 1918, and thereafter was with the Army of Occupation in France and Germany from November 17 to December 16, 1918. He then returned to the United States and on April 18, 1919, was honorably discharged at the Presidio. Following his discharge he worked at Mare Island for the Government as a steam-fitter and plumber for twenty-two months, after which he returned to Walnut Creek and established another plumbing shop. Fraternally, Mr. Near is affiliated with Richmond Lodge No. 1251, B. P. O. E. He is a member of the Lions Club, and of the Veterans of Foreign Wars. In politics he is a Republican.

On September 8, 1925, Mr. Near married Mrs. Erna Gallagher, and they reside at Walnut Creek.

GAETANO E. SEENO.—An able and successful contractor and builder is Gaetano E. Seeno, of Pittsburg, Cal., who has to his credit the erection of many of the best homes and business blocks in the city and is highly respected for his sterling manhood. He was born in the province of Sicily on April 20, 1885, the son of Erasmo and Rosa Seeno. The father resides in California and is in his eighty-third year; the mother lives in Italy and is seventy-one years old. There were three boys and four girls in the family, and two boys and two of the girls are in California.

In 1900 Gaetano E. Seeno came to America, sailing from Naples, and after landing in New York came direct to Pittsburg, Cal., arriving in March. He had a brother, Frank Seeno, in this city and for three years was employed by him in building boats for the fishing trade. Being a good carpenter he decided to enter upon a career for himself, and since making that decision he has become the leading contractor of Pittsburg. Among the more prominent buildings erected by him we mention the homes of J. J. Davi, C. Cautiello and S. Enea, the Lapori and Cardinelli apartments, the Continente and Liberty Hotels, the Columbia and Lincoln Grills, California Market, and Davi Financial Building. Mr. Seeno is a skilled workman and gives careful supervision to all his building operations. He keeps four men steadily employed.

On January 8, 1911, G. E. Seeno was united in marriage with Miss Rosa Di Maggio, daughter of Vincent and Rosa Di Maggio, and four children have blessed their union: Helen, Edith, Albert and Alvera. Mr. Seeno is a thirty-second-degree Scottish Rite Mason and a Shriner. He holds membership in Esperenza Lodge in San Francisco, the Oakland Consistory and Aahmes Temple, also of Oakland, the Pittsburg Knights of Pythias and Odd Fellows, and the Antioch Sciots. Mrs. Seeno belongs to Sterling Parlor N. D. G. W., of Pittsburg. He is interested in all progressive movements for town and county and can be counted upon for liberal support of the community's best interests.

FRANK LA MONTAGNE.—During the sixteen years that Frank La Montagne has resided in Antioch, he has been actively identified with its growth and prosperity. He is another of California's native sons, born at Clarksburg, Yolo County, seventeen miles from the capital city, on March 9, 1874, a son of Frank and Mary (Stave) La Montagne, the former a native of Quebec, Canada. As the name indicates, Frank La Montagne is of French ancestors, but several generations ago they emigrated to Canada. There were twelve children in this family, nine of whom are still living. The mother passed away in 1907, aged sixty-eight, and the father reached the age of eighty-three years, dying in 1919. A brother, George B. La Montagne, was mayor of Antioch when the new $60,000 City Hall was built in 1919; he is now superintendent of the Liberty Farms above Rio Vista.

Frank La Montagne grew up in Clarksburg and there attended the public schools. He became thoroughly familiar with the Delta country and as a boy was fond of fishing, swimming and boating, and thereby became intimately acquainted with river life. He learned the blacksmith's trade and operated a shop in Clarksburg for several years. Then he became a barge-man and later worked on a dredger for his brother, George B. La Montagne. Afterwards he became a captain on the river, and for three years was captain of the Shell Oil Company's river boat. Removing to Antioch in 1909 he opened a grocery store and began to build up a good business, continuing alone until 1924, when he took in a partner, Benjamin Olson. This company keeps a well-selected stock of staple and fancy groceries and enjoys a large and growing trade in Antioch and surrounding territory.

Mr. La Montagne was married at Sacramento to Miss Anna Nelson, a native of Sweden, and they have a family of seven children: Della, Dorothy, Myrtle, Esther, Frankie, Georgia and Grover B.

JOHN RASINO.—Representative of the enterprise and spirit of progress which have distinguished the industrial life of Contra Costa County, John Rasino is entitled to the respect and consideration accorded him by the citizens of Pittsburg. He came to California from his native country of Italy in 1920 and selected Pittsburg as the place for his permanent residence. Almost immediately he became connected with the Columbus Society of the Sons of Italy Lodge at Antioch, which was organized in 1909; and in 1923 he became president of this lodge. Later he served as vice-president, his term of office extending over three years; and in 1925 he was made Great Deputy, and in this capacity is doing valuable work for his fellow-countrymen who come as strangers from the foreign shores of Italy. He occupies the important and responsible position of dry-kiln operator for the Redwood Manufacturers Company at Pittsburg, in which capacity he has steadily worked for five years.

John Rasino was born in the town of Cercenasco, Province of Turin, Italy, October 8, 1890, the third son in a family of five boys born to

Fermino and Catharina Rasino, both natives of the same country. John attended the elementary schools of his native province, and when he reached military age entered the Italian army and served for eight years; he was in the war with Turkey in 1911; and from 1915 to 1919 served in the World War at the front as telephone operator, and twice was slightly wounded. He received his honorable discharge in Italy. When he arrived in California in 1920 he immediately applied for citizenship papers; and he is as loyal to his adopted country as he was to his native land. He is a valued employee of the company he has served for five years, showing marked aptitude for his special line of work in the dry-kiln.

Mr. Rasino has one brother still living in Italy, one in France, and two in the Argentine. With four other single Italian-Americans, Mr. Rasino occupies the second story of the building located at 850 West Street. Mr. Rasino is an accordion player of note, and his ability as a musician admits him to many social functions. Being of a genial and social disposition, he occupies a prominent position among the Italian-Americans of Pittsburg.

CHESTER ZENONE.—In no branch of agriculture is a more thorough knowledge and greater business capacity needed than in that pertaining to the breeding and raising of dairy cattle; and in this industry no one has met with more deserved success than Chester Zenone, a well-known dairyman and manager of the Dairy Deliveries Ranch of 237 acres in the heart of the Byron-Bethany alfalfa section of Contra Costa County. He was born at Locarno, Switzerland, December 1, 1892, the fourth child in a family of ten children born to Frank and Antoinette (Galzonia) Zenone, both natives of the same country. At one time the father was in business at Port Costa, Cal., and after several years spent there he returned to Switzerland, where he and his wife are now living. Chester's mother comes from a distinguished Swiss family. Her father reached the advanced age of 104 years. Chester Zenone made the most of his opportunity to obtain a good education in his native country and completed the high school course in Locarno. In 1910 he came to California and at once found employment upon dairy farms at La Honda, and later at Fort Ross in Sonoma County. He went to Stanislaus County and worked for four years on Cressy's dairy farm. In 1917 he came to Contra Costa County and went to work for the Balfour-Guthrie Company who later rented the place to Zenone and Smith. One hundred acres of this place were planted to tomatoes in 1926 preparatory to re-seeding to alfalfa.

Mr. Zenone is a Mason, a member of the Blue Lodge at Brentwood; Scottish Rite Consistory and Aahmes Temple, in Oakland. With all his hard work, Mr. Zenone is still a diligent student and progressive to a high degree. He has a thorough knowledge of the dairy business and is a recognized authority in this branch of agriculture.

ROLF NAAS.—A highly intelligent and successful civil engineer and surveyor of central California is Rolf Naas, city engineer of Antioch since 1923. Mr. Naas was born in Ostersand, Sweden, on April 12, 1890, the son of Magnus and Teckla (Naas) Mattsson. The father, born in 1854, is a noted civil engineer who spent his active life following his profession, most of the time in the employ of the Swedish government, running tunnels and surveying woods, railways, etc. He is now a pensioner.

Rolf Naas, who took his mother's name, grew up in his native land and was graduated from the Technical High School, Class of 1911, working with his father in the meantime from the age of fourteen. He then put in one year working under his father, learning what he could and getting practical training in his profession. He then resolved to try his fortunes in America, and landed in San Francisco in 1912. He immediately took up professional work as a civil engineer and was variously engaged in running tunnels, building roads, and mining engineering work in various places in this State, and in Alaska in 1915. In 1917 Mr. Naas voluteered his services for duty in the World War in the anti-aircraft artillery. After being trained he was sent to France and served from 1917 to 1919, during which time he designed the first fire control chart ever made for the United States forces in the anti-aircraft service. Returning to San Francisco, he was discharged at the Presidio in March, 1919.

Taking up civilian life once more, Mr. Naas was retained as a civil engineer on large reclamation projects in Colusa and Eldorado Counties. In 1922 he came to Antioch, and the following year he was made city engineer. In addition to his work for the city he has a general practice and is fast building up a lucrative business. As city engineer he built the reservoir for the Antioch Water Supply, which is now assured to the city for years to come. He is also city engineer for Isleton, Sacramento County, and acts in the same capacity for other nearby towns, and is doing some very important work for private firms and individuals.

Mr. Naas was married at Oakland on July 16, 1924, to Miss Maud Rhoades, who was born in Ohio but grew up in Los Angeles, Cal. They both have a large circle of friends, and are leaders in their social set in Antioch.

EDWARD MUSETTI.—Whoever labors, whether directly or indirectly, for the welfare of the community and by his efforts materially helps to maintain the life and health of its citizens, is a public benefactor. Such is the place of the modern, sanitary baker in the up-to-date city. Edward Musetti, the proprietor of the New Naples Bakery in Pittsburg, Cal., is a native of Italy, born about forty years ago in the province of Tuscany, a representative of one of the oldest families of the province.

Early in life he was obsessed with a desire to emigrate to America, where so many of his countrymen had achieved success in business. When seventeen years of age he arrived in New York, and, having heard so many alluring reports concerning California, continued his journey until he reached the Golden State and located in Jackson, Amador County, where he learned the trade of a baker, and remained until he removed to Pittsburg in 1922. Here he opened a bakery, specializing in French and Milk bread. By judicious management, courteous attention to his customers and the use of strict sanitary methods in baking, he soon built up a demand for his various kinds of bread, until today he averages about 1200 loaves each day of the week. He is doing his best to solve the bread question by making the "staff of life" of good, wholesome ingredients. As a result the New Naples Bakery is meeting with deserved success and in 1925 moved into their new quarters on West Fifth Street. Mr. Musetti employs only competent white bakers. He is an American citizen and a progressive business man.

On November 7, 1921, Edward Musetti was united in marriage with Miss Ermalinda de Mosecatelli, a native of Italy, and this union has been blessed with four children: Mary, Lena, Nancy, and Theressa. Fraternally, Mr. Musetti is a member of Pittsburg Lodge No. 18, K. of P., and Winchesters Lodge, I. O. O. F.; and he belongs to the Pittsburg Chamber of Commerce.

REV. J. W. McCLORY, O. P.—The resident pastor of Holy Rosary Catholic Church at Antioch is the Rev. Father J. W. McClory. This parish, which numbers some 300 parishioners, is more than seventy years old and was founded by Rev. Father Callahan. Father McClory was born in Chicago, Ill., on November 14, 1891, and is a son of Donald and Mary (Yenish) McClory, the former born in Quebec, Canada, and identified with the lumber business for many years. The mother was born in Traverse City, Mich. The family home is in Seattle, Wash.

The eldest of four children, J. W. McClory spent his life up to the age of ten in Traverse City, Mich., and then accompanied his parents to Seattle. He attended the public and parochial schools and had one year in the high school in Seattle; then he entered the Immaculate Conception College in Washington, D. C., in 1913, and remained a student there until 1920, except one year spent at St. Joseph's Seminary in Ohio. This is a college of the Dominican Order for teachers. He was graduated from the Immaculate Conception College in May, 1920. During the World War he did a great deal of missionary work about the army camps at Washington as auxiliary chaplain.

Coming to California, Father McClory spent five years in St. Dominic's Monastery in San Francisco and then came to Antioch to take charge of Holy Rosary Parish. The church was erected in 1905 and 1906, and the parish house was completed in 1924. Father McClory is doing good work in this locality and is well liked by his parshioners and by the general public at large, be they Catholics or Protestants. He heartily favors better civic conditions, and works for the social and moral uplift of the people of the community.

C. H. Guy. Amelia G. Guy

CHARLES HENRY GUY.—Self-educated and self-reliant, Charles Henry Guy has solved the vital problem of attaining success in the face of difficulties, and is today counted among the successful business men of Concord, Contra Costa County, and one whose highest ambition is to assist in the advancement and progress of his section. His birth occurred at Nortonville, Cal., December 22, 1879, and he is one of five children born to John W. and Lavinia Tennessee (McCain) Guy. Both parents were born in the South, the father in Alabama, the mother in Tennessee.

C. H. Guy received a grammar school education in the Concord schools; at the age of fourteen years he began to earn his own money, and for two years he worked in a drug store in Concord. About this time the wanderlust took possession of him and he traveled around a good deal for several years, and in 1900 took a trip to Honolulu. Returning to his native state, he took a position with the Utica Gold Mines at Angels Camp, where he worked for three years in their pipe line department. In 1903 he went to San Francisco and worked for a leading hardware firm; from this company he went to work in the stock room of the United Railways Company. Early in 1906, the year of the great earthquake, he went to Kokomo, Ind., and was there when the news of the great disaster was given to the world. Immediately he returned to California and resumed his old position with the United Railways Company; and later he was with the Pacific Gas & Electric Company. In 1882 his father had opened a mortuary establishment in Concord, and in 1909 Mr. Guy went into partnership with him in the business. In 1911 the father passed away and L. R. Palmer and A. Ford were taken into the partnership. In 1916 a new building with all modern equipment was erected on the corner of Fernando and Mount Diablo Streets.

On April 19, 1910 Mr. Guy was married to Miss Amelia Galindo, a daughter of John C. and Marina (Amador) Galindo. Mrs. Guy is a granddaughter of Salvio Pacheco, who obtained a grant of 18,000 acres in Contra Costa County and was one of the early pioneers of this section. Mr. and Mrs. Guy are the parents of one boy, Earl John. Mr. Guy is a director in the Bank of Concord and at the present time is city treasurer. He was serving as city clerk when he resigned to take the position of postmaster of Concord, and he served in that capacity from 1914 until 1923. Since 1910 Mr. Guy has served as deputy county coronor. He is an active member of the Concord Chamber of Commerce and has served on all of the important committees. Fraternally he belongs to the Masons, Elks, Native Sons, Odd Fellows, Woodmen of the World, I. D. E. S. and U. P. E. C. He is a member of the Lions Club recently organized in the city. Mr. Guy is a baseball enthusiast and has played some with the Concord baseball team.

WILLIAM A. SEARS, JR.—As the owner and proprietor of the Contra Costa Drug Store, at the corner of Ferry and Main Streets in Martinez, William A. Sears, Jr., is making his influence felt in business circles in Contra Costa County. He was interested in the opportunities offered in Martinez when he was looking for a permanent location in which to build up a business, and he purchased the drug business that had been established by Dr. Lawrence in 1850. Here he has built up a lucrative trade, owing to his conservative methods and his efficiency and knowledge of pharmacy. Since locating here, Mr. Sears has taken an intelligent interest in the development of both city and county; and he is accounted one of the public-spirited and successful men of Martinez.

William A. Sears, Jr., was born near Wright's Station, Santa Clara County, on June 17, 1890, the son of William A. and Sarah Bell (Loucks) Sears, now residents of Portersville, Tulare County. He obtained his education in the public schools of his native county and completed the high school course after the family located in Portersville. His ambition was to be a pharmacist, and he then entered the College of Pharmacy in San Francisco, from which he was graduated in 1911.

On September 8, 1915, in San Francisco, Mr. Sears and Miss Elsie Williams were united in marriage. They have two children: Elinore Belle and William Edgar.

HANS R. RASMUSSEN.—One of the most highly esteemed citizens of Clayton is Hans R. Rasmussen, the storekeeper. He is not only an able business man, but an individual who takes a keen interest in all the activities of the community. His reputation for honesty, square dealing and industry is unquestioned and the high esteem in which he is held is also shared by his loyal wife and devoted helpmeet. She is the daughter of J. G. Sargent, of Stanislaus County.

Mr. Rasmussen was born in Brown County, Wis., near Green Bay, February 28, 1880, (leap year), the son of Christensen and Annie Rasmussen, both of whom were born in Denmark. The mother died when Hans R. was but eleven years old, but the father, a venerable gentleman of eighty-five years, is still living and the owner of a farm south of Green Bay, Wis. As a boy, Hans Rasmussen attended the public schools of the community in which he was born and later was a student in the high school of Green Bay for two years. During his school years, and for some time after, Mr. Rasmussen was employed as a clerk in a general store of Brown County. In 1899, at the age of nineteen, he came to California and located at Crockett, where he was employed as clerk in a general store for twenty years. In 1919 he purchased the general store of G. E. Lindemann in Clayton, which has since been his home. For five years Mr. Rasmussen was the postmaster of Clayton. Politically he is a Democrat and in his fraternal affiliations is a member of the Knights of Pythias and Woodmen of the World at Crockett.

On February 22, 1901, Mr. Rasmussen was united in marriage to Miss Bertha Sargent at Knight's Ferry, Stanislaus County, of which locality she is a native. This union was blessed with three children: Albert G.; Marguerite, who married Andrew Berrendsen, a machinist at Nichols

Chemical Works, by whom she has one child, Alice; and Alma, wife of Clarence Frank, a resident of Clayton who is employed as a machinist at Avon, by whom she has one child, Robert David Frank.

THOMAS CHARLES PIMM.—A well-known and successful contractor and builder of Richmond is Thomas Charles Pimm, who was born in London, England, on July 8, 1876. His father, William Pimm, was a carpenter and builder in England; and he was married there to Ann Howcroft. They had eight children, of whom only one, John Pimm, besides our subject, ever came to America. They are: Ada, Lillie, Thomas C., William, Olvett, George, John and Grace.

Thomas Charles Pimm was educated in England and there served his apprenticeship at the carpenter's trade. In 1903 he came to California and stopped at Bakersfield, where he remained three years, and then came to San Francisco and worked as a journeyman, starting at $3.25 per day. In October, 1906, he came to Richmond, which just then was having a building boom. He continued working at his trade and in time began taking contracts; and now he does a general contracting and building business in Richmond and surrounding territory and keeps generally busy. He is satisfied with a living profit and believes in living and letting others live.

Mr. Pimm was married on July 1, 1905, to Miss Susan Harris, born in England, the daughter of George Harris, a painter by trade. The family came out to Cleveland, Ohio, but later returned to England. Mr. and Mrs. Pimm were acquainted with each other in England. They have three children. Chester Thomas is a student in high school preparing for entrance in the Y. M. C. A. University of Chicago; he is a leader in athletics, and is active in Y. M. C. A. work. Georgina, aged seventeen, is attending high school; Ivar, aged fourteen, is in the Roosevelt Junior High School. In 1910 Mr. Pimm made a trip back to his London home, and when he returned was accompanied by his brother, John E. Pimm, who is now employed at the Standard refinery in Richmond.

Mr. Pimm plays the pipe organ and is of a musical turn of mind. He believes Richmond has a great future and is satisfied that he selected it for his home. He is a member of the Sons of St. George, an organization designed to create good-fellowship between the Americans and the English, and has held various offices in the local order and represented it in conventions.

MRS. MARY STANDERSON.—Born in San Leandro on October 24, 1876, Mrs. Mary Standerson is the owner of a fine fruit ranch of about thirty acres in the Live Oak district of Oakley Precinct. Her parents, Manuel and Philomena Thomas, natives of Portugal, came to America when quite young and were married in Massachusetts, and there their oldest child was born. They decided to come to California, and in the early seventies had settled in San Leandro, where they remained eight years. Then they spent one year in Oakland, after which they removed to Oakley Precinct in Contra Costa County in 1885, where the father bought a home and worked at whatever he could find to do to make a living for his growing family. Mary attended the public schools in Alameda and Contra Costa Counties, and in 1893 was united in marriage with John Mello, a native of the Azores Islands. Together the young couple began the development of the ranch Mr. Mello had purchased, clearing it from the large live-oak trees that covered the country at that time and planting trees and vines. Mr. Mello met an accidental death in 1903. Of their union the following children were born: Joseph, married and now the father of two children, Muriel and Jacqueline; Mary, Mrs. Manuel Maderos; Flora, wife of Frank Fertado and the mother of four children, Wallace, Melba, Geraldine and Norman; Elizabeth, who married Emil Flossi and has one son, Eugene; John, married and the father of a daughter, Lorraine; and Jesse.

In 1904 Mrs. Mello married Joseph Azevedo. They had four children: Elaine; Grace, Mrs. Joseph Rodrigues; Clara, wife of Ralph Wilson and the mother of a son, Ralph W.; and Elsie. Mr. Azevedo died in 1918 of the flu.

On July 20, 1925, Mrs. Azevedo was united in marriage with her third husband, Michael Standerson, who has charge of the department of music in the Antioch schools. He is a musician and educator of note and also owns a ranch adjoining that of his wife's which is devoted to trees and vines. Professor Standerson has charge of the band music at the Antioch-Live Oak Grammar School and is a man well-liked by all who know him. Mr. and Mrs. Standerson are public-spirited and have a host of friends in this community. They are members of the Live Oak Farm Bureau.

MICHAEL M. PISTOCHINI.—A man of ability, enterprising and practical, Michael M. Pistochini is a prominent factor in the growth and prosperity of the county seat of Contra Costa County, as one of the proprietors of the Italian Hotel on Alhambra Avenue, Martinez. His birth occurred at Ologia, Piedmonte, Italy, April 25, 1874, the youngest in a family of six children born to Antonio and Savina (Colombo) Pistochini, also natives of Italy and farmer folk. The mother of the family passed away in 1915, aged sixty-five years; the father is still living in Italy, aged eighty-five years. Our subject is the only member of the family at present in America.

Michael M. Pistochini attended public school in his native land and assisted his father with the farm work until he was twenty-one years old, when he set out for California, arriving here in February, 1895. He located in San Francisco, where for five years he was in the employ of a street contractor. His one ambition was to get ahead and own a business of his own. He worked hard and saved his money, so that within a few years he had laid up enough to make the initial payment on the San Martinez Hotel, located at 309 Broadway, San Francisco. With his cousin, Antonio Pistochini, he operated this hotel until 1905, when they removed to Martinez and purchased the site on which the Italian Hotel now stands. They sold their property in San Francisco and invested the money in Martinez, where they have prospered year by year. Quick to see the prospects and advantages for a national bank in Martinez, Mr. Pistochini became one of the organizers of the National Bank of Martinez, and today is a member of its board of directors; he is also a stockholder in the Martinez-Benicia Auto Ferry.

At San Francisco, in 1903, Mr. Pistochini was married to Miss Mary Comazzi, born at Piedmonte, Italy. Mrs. Pistochini is the daughter of Alexander and Angeline (Colombo) Comazzi. The father passed away in Italy; the mother now makes her home in Martinez. Two children have blessed this union: Alfredo and Arturo. Mr. Pistochini is a Republican in politics, and fraternally he is a member of the Eagles Lodge at Martinez; he is also a member of the Dante Society in Martinez.

E. R. McCLELLAND.—As proprietor of the Brentwood Electric Company, E. R. McClelland is building a firm foundation for himself in Eastern Contra Costa County. He is an able workman, does the best kind of work, and keeps the best kind of electrical goods and supplies always on hand. He was born in Chicago, Ill., on May 14, 1885, and is a son of Joseph and Elizabeth Ann (Jones) McClelland. The McClellands are of old Scotch and Virginian ancestry, and distantly related to General McClellan. Joseph McClelland was a horseshoer and maintained a shop at Forty-third and State Streets in Chicago. Both himself and wife still make their home in Chicago.

E. R. McClelland attended the public schools of Englewood, a suburb of Chicago, graduating from the high school. At the age of twenty he entered the Armour School of Chicago and worked in the electrical department for Armour & Company, later becoming foreman of the department with Swift & Company. For a time he was in the service of the Public Service Company of Northern Illinois, being superintendent of construction. He went to Michigan and was connected with the Pierre Marquette Railroad Company as foreman of the electrical department, with headquarters at Grand Rapids. He had charge of the construction of the Southwest Land Tunnel in Chicago, and for a time was superintendent of construction for the Electric Service Engineering Company in that city. In 1923 he came to California and entered the employ of the Pacific Gas & Electric Company in San Francisco, but later moved to Brentwood and bought the L. Powell Electric Shop, changing the name to the Brentwood Electric Company. He enlarged the business, and now does all kinds of general electric contracting work and deals in general electric goods and supplies, as well as radios and accessories.

Mr. McClelland was married in San Francisco in 1924 to Miss Marguerite Bowers, a native of Chicago. Mrs. McClelland is a member of the Rebekahs. Mr. McClelland belongs to Kosmos Lodge No. 896, A. F. & A. M., of Chicago; to Pyramid No. 24, of the Sciots, in Antioch;

and to the Odd Fellows in Byron. He is a member of the American Institute of Electrical Engineers and of the National Electric Light Association. Mr. McClelland was in the second draft call for the World War, but on account of the armistice was not called to service. He is public-spirited and has an ever widening circle of friends.

CHARLES GARDNER GOOLD.—Few men are more inseparably associated with the history of Contra Costa County than Charles G. Goold, who, as rancher, stockman, bank director and general promoter of important enterprises, has proven the value of his citizenship and the integrity of his character. He was born in Centerville, Alameda County, on November 18, 1858, a son of Capt. Gardner and Elizabeth (Bradley) Goold, the latter a daughter of John and Mary Bradley of Brooklyn, N. Y.

Captain Gardner Goold was born at Eastport, Maine, in 1818. When he was thirteen he went to sea and from the post of cabin boy rose by degrees to become master of a vessel. He traveled over the world, aiming never to make two voyages to the same port. His first trip to California was made in 1848, by way of Cape Horn, in a sailing vessel; his second trip, in 1849. After his arrival he went to the mines near Marysville and tried his luck at mining. He found there was more money to be made at other occupations however, and he operated the first flat-bottom boat on the Sacramento River, running up to Marysville. It is said that he earned as much as $1000 a day in gold-dust for freight and passengers.

Captain Goold returned East to be married, and was united with Elizabeth Bradley on June 13, 1854. He came back to California, leaving Mrs. Goold at her home, but two years later went back to Maine and brought his wife back to California, coming via the Nicaragua route. They settled in Centerville, where he bought land from the Alviso family, securing a clear title to it. He built buildings with lumber that was shipped around the Horn, and so well were the buildings constructed that they are still standing. Captain Goold continued to follow the sea, carrying on trading in Alaska; and in 1854 he made a trip to Australia. In 1867 he bought land in the Livermore Valley, then known as Laddville, and farmed it in 1868; but that being a dry year, he got no crops. Then he came up to Mount Diablo and bought a squatter's title to 160 acres and the feed on it for $300, and brought his stock to his new ranch. This is now a part of the famous Blackhawk Ranch. In 1869 Mrs. Goold and family settled on the property. The ranch in Livermore Valley was looked after by a brother, Charles Gay Goold, while Captain Goold's sons cared for the Mount Diablo ranch. Captain Goold was forced to leave the sea on account of an accident, and he thereafter lived on his ranch until his death, in 1880.

Charles G. Goold was born in the home at Centerville and finished his education at Livermore College. He began life's battles when a lad of ten years, when he traveled by saddle horse from Centerville to Livermore buying hides of Mexican cattle, paying twenty-five cents each for them, and paying seventy-five cents for a hide full of tallow. He often carried as much as a thousand dollars in his saddlebags, yet was never molested, but always given the best of consideration by all with whom he came in contact. His father would take the hides and tallow back East with him on his trips, where they brought a good price. As he was growing up he worked the home ranch, and also worked with government surveyors as a flagger, signalling from one high point to another. He was given this job because he usually had good saddle horses and could get over the roughest of ground with dispatch. He lived on the home ranch for thirty-five years, and in 1903 bought seventy acres of land near Danville, where he now lives; he also owns a ranch in Sycamore Valley and range land in the Livermore mountains. Being a capable business man, it was quite natural that Mr. Goold should be sought as a director of the first San Ramon Valley Bank at Walnut Creek when it was organized; and he is also a director of the Danville Branch of the National Bank of Walnut Creek.

Mr. Goold has always taken an active interest in the development of those enterprises that would build up the business interests of the county, and has shown his personal interest in educational matters by serving for thirty years as a trustee of his school district. He was one of the chief promoters of the Sacramento Short Line Railroad and has witnessed the building of every railroad in the valley; the Southern Pacific being the first, which was constructed in 1869. When the Western Pacific was built, Mr. Goold was one of the contributors to the new enterprise.

On February 24, 1884, Charles G. Goold was united in marriage with Almira Johnson, a native of Contra Costa County and daughter of William and Annie (Shimpf) Johnson, honored pioneers of California, a sketch of whom will be found on another page of this history. Mr. and Mrs. Goold are the parents of one child, Helen W., who after her graduation from the high school at Danville entered college for one year, but owing to poor health she was obliged to discontinue her studies at college. Mrs. Goold, as a young lady, was considered one of the best horsewomen in the community, and it was her pride to have the best saddle horse in the valley. Active in community affairs, she is a past president of the Women's Club of Danville; has been for thirty years a member of Almona Chapter No. 214, O. E. S., at Walnut Creek; and is a Past Noble Grand and ex-District Deputy of the Daughters of the Rebekahs; an active worker in the Grange, and a member of the committee on history and landmarks of the Danville Club. Fraternally, Mr. Goold is a member of Alamo Lodge No. 122, F. & A. M.; a charter member of Danville Lodge No. 378, I. O. O. F.; and a former member of Old Mt. Diablo Parlor, N. S. G. W., Danville; and also a member of Danville Grange, Rebekahs and the Eastern Star.

He is very fond of out-of-door life, enjoys hunting and fishing, and has a game reserve on Trout Creek, on his land near Livermore, where he has made some improvements which make for greater comfort. He also enjoys motoring through the scenic sections of the State. In 1874, while looking for stock, he made a trip with a pack train through the Yosemite Valley, before any roads were built. He formerly raised thoroughbred running horses of the Glenco and Belmont stock. The original stock was brought across the plains by Grandfather Johnson. At present he has about fourteen head of splendid work horses. Mr. Goold has witnessed the most wonderful developments in this part of the State and remembers when Livermore, known as Laddville, consisted of only one store, a hotel and a blacksmith shop. The townsite was donated to the Southern Pacific Railroad by Philip Mendenhall and named Livermore.

FRED W. RAHLFS.—Among the successful vineyardists of Contra Costa County is Fred W. Rahlfs, whose twenty-acre farm is located one and one-half miles west of Oakley. Mr. Rahlfs has also been thoroughly trained as a brick and stone mason, as a cement worker, and as a plasterer; and his work along these lines is in great demand throughout his neighborhood. He was born in Hanover, Germany, on January 14, 1879. His early education was acquired in the public schools of his native country, and on reaching young manhood, he was apprenticed to learn the several branches of masonry, which includes working in brick, stone, cement and plaster. Before coming to America he served his time in the German army, spending two years. His good wife was also born in Hanover, Germany, and both were brought up in the German Lutheran Church. Mrs. Rahlfs, whose maiden name was Louisa Colling, comes from an excellent family and received a good education in her native land. She first came to America in 1896, but returned to Germany and in 1902, with Mr. Rahlfs and his sister, came back to America. Soon after reaching here they were married on March 6, 1903, and for a time thereafter lived in Stearns County, Minnesota. In October, 1904, they came to California, first settling in Oakland, where Mr. Rahlfs was engaged at his trade from 1904 until 1920. Then the family came to eastern Contra Costa County, where they purchased their present home of twenty acres. Mr. and Mrs. Rahlfs are the parents of four sons: Fred H., who is employed at Antioch with the Standard Oil Company; Gordon H., who works with his father; and Horace S. and John W.

Mr. Rahlfs employs several men besides himself and his son, and they have done the plastering on the Memorial Hall for the Harding Post, American Legion, at Antioch, and on many of the best cottages and bungalows in Oakley, Antioch and vicinity. They are equipped to do high-grade plastering and all kinds of interior decorating,

Mr. Rahlfs belongs to the Sons of Herman and the Red Men, of Oakland. Mrs. Rahlfs is a member of the Federation of Woman's Clubs at Oakley, the Farm Bureau, and the Parent-Teacher's Association, and both Mr. and Mrs. Rahlfs are members of the East Contra Costa County Chamber of Commerce. On December 26, 1912, Mr. Rahlfs was admitted to citizenship, and both he and his wife are stanch Republicans.

Michel Martin Dragon

✗ MICKEL MARTIN DRAGON. — Notwithstanding a few experiences of a somewhat discouraging nature, the business career of Mickel M. Dragon has been successful and he now occupies a position among the capable and resourceful business men of Antioch, Cal. He is of Italian birth and ancestry, a son of Peter and Concitta (Marasciulo) Dragon. In a family of thirteen children, five of whom are now deceased, Mickel M. is the oldest. He was born on October 30, 1884. The names of the living children are as follows: Frank, represented elsewhere in this volume; Dominick, a rancher in the vicinity of Antioch; James, who runs a grocery store on Long Island; Isabel, Mrs. Procino, in Italy; and Dan, Antoinetta and Mikel, all three in Italy.

The boyhood years of Mickel M. Dragon were uneventfully passed in his native province in Italy, where he had such educational advantages as the common schools afforded. In 1903 the father came to America and stopped for a time in New York State; six months later our subject joined him, and in 1904 they removed to California and settled in Oakland, where they found the climate much the same as in their native country. Peter Dragon later bought a ranch near Antioch, and also leased other farm lands in that vicinity and remained there until his death on August 6, 1909; the mother passed away in Italy about 1922, never having left her native shores.

Mickel M. Dragon found employment in a paper mill, first as a teamster's helper, then as a teamster, and finally rose to a finisher's position. Later he helped his father on his ranch. Following his father's death Mr. Dragon leased land from the Hooper Estate and for seven years successfully operated 500 acres; but two years of successive drouth proved his undoing and he turned his attention to his present occupation, that of special agent for the Western States Life Insurance Company, in which he is showing marked ability and meeting with success.

In Antioch on May 28, 1909, Mr. Dragon was married to Miss Antoinette Chiarolanza, also a native of Italy, who came to America as a young woman, first stopping in the East and then, in 1908, coming to California. They are the parents of four children: Peter M., Joseph A., Emma, and Frank D. In 1925 Mr. Dragon built a beautiful residence at 23 Sixth Street, Antioch, where the family live in happiness and contentment. Mr. Dragon was one of the five original members of the Columbus Association in Antioch, which is now affiliated with the Sons of Italy, and was a very active member until his insurance business claimed all of his attention. He is a member of the Young Men's Institute and the Chamber of Commerce. His wife belongs to the Young Ladies' Institute of Antioch. Mr. Dragon is a naturalized American citizen and is proud of his adopted country. In politics he is a Republican.

CORNELIUS L. KREIM.—The obliging station agent at Knightsen, Cornelius L. Kreim, is both an efficient employee of the Santa Fe Railroad Company and a successful vineyardist of the Knightsen district. Mr. Kreim takes an active interest in the advancement of this section of Contra Costa County, as is shown by his fifteen-acre vineyard of Flaming Tokay grapes, which he has developed from raw land. He has been in the employ of the Santa Fe Railroad Company for eighteen years in the Valley Division from Bakersfield to Ferry Point, and for the past eight years has served as station agent at Knightsen.

Mr. Kreim was born at Los Angeles on July 3, 1889, the son of Herman and Sarah (Kemble) Kreim, the former born in Iowa and the latter in Illinois. He grew up in Los Angeles and attended the public schools there. As soon as he had finished the grammar grades he began to learn operating, and in 1911, was sent to Waukena as telegraph operator. He then worked at various stations, and as relief man, until he came to Knightsen in 1918. During the World War he was exempted from military duty, as he was already an employee of the government, it having charge of all railroads.

Mr. Kreim was married at Stockton on August 3, 1917, to Miss Hazel Clair Kessel, a native of Oregon, born at Hood River; and they have two children, Hazel Clair and Mary Elizabeth. By a former marriage Mr. Kreim has a son, Lawrence Cornelius, fifteen years old, who is at Delano, Cal. Mr. Kreim is a member of the Order of Railroad Telegraphers. He is prominent in Masonic circles and belongs to Brentwood Lodge No. 345, F. & A. M., of which he is Master (1926), and to the Antioch Sciots. Both he and his wife belong to Maspha Chapter No. 198, O. E. S., of which Mrs. Kreim is a Past Matron.

HOWARD F. LAURITZEN.—The junior member of the firm of Bundesen & Lauritzen, Howard F. Lauritzen, is an expert boatman and substantial business man of Contra Costa County, who, besides his present business, has been active in river transportation service as a member of the firm of Lauritzen & Lauritzen, former owners of the Antioch-Sherman Island Ferry. He was born in Solano County on June 7, 1896, at the old river ferry then owned and operated by his father, located about two miles northeast of Rio Vista. His father, Frederick Christian Lauritzen, is a native of Denmark, who married Miss Anita Poole, a native of California. He emigrated with his parents to California when a child, and ever since has lived in this State.

Howard F. Lauritzen attended the public schools and lived with his parents at the old ferry until he went to live with his grandmother on Wood Island. He grew up to ranch work on the island, and to complete his education he spent one year at the Polytechnic High School in San Francisco and then returned to Wood Island and completed his schooling at the Rio Vista High School, graduating with the Class of 1916, the first to graduate from this high school. He then spent one year with his father and uncle in running their passenger boats on the Sacramento and San Joaquin Rivers. When the World War broke out he enlisted in the United States Navy as engine man and made one trip to France. Upon returning to this country he was honorably discharged as Ensign on July 1, 1919, in New York. Returning to his home he purchased a one-fifth interest in the ferry business and devoted his entire time to building up a good paying business, keeping abreast of the times in every way. In 1925 he purchased a half interest with Mr. Bundesen, and they bought the Lanteri Ship Yards at Pittsburg and have remodeled the entire plant. They are now equipped to do all kinds of repair work on water craft, and to build barges, dredges and river boats of all kinds and sizes. With the wide acquaintance of both partners, their new venture bids fair to become a very important enterprise, as it is located in the heart of the manufacturing district of Pittsburg. They also bought the Delta Dredging Company in April, 1926.

Mr. Lauritzen was married on May 5, 1924, at Antioch, to Miss Mary Faye Cox. The family home is located at No. 710 F Street, Antioch. He is a member of Harding Post No. 161, American Legion, at Antioch; and of Antioch Lodge No. 175, F. & A. M.; and is a thirty-second degree Scottish Rite Mason, holding membership in San Francisco Consistory No. 1. He also belongs to the Sciots in Antioch. Mr. Lauritzen is public-spirited and is popular in the community where he has made his home for so many years. He and his wife move in the best social circles in Contra Costa County.

E. J. SWANSON.—A resident of El Cerrito since 1920, E. J. Swanson has been very closely identified with the development of its varied interests and has taken an active part in civic affairs as a member of the El Cerrito Improvement Club. He was born in La Porte County, Ind., on April 23, 1876, and received his education in the public schools. At the age of seventeen he began working at the carpenter's trade, and as he was handy with tools, soon became a good workman and labored as a journeyman in Chicago for ten years prior to coming to California.

On May 24, 1906, Mr. Swanson was united in marriage with Miss Agnes Soderberg, a native of Sweden. She had been in San Francisco for some time and went through the great earthquake and fire of April, 1906, after which she went back to Chicago and there was married to Mr. Swanson. They have a son, Harold William, in the Richmond High School.

In 1917, on account of the ill health of Mrs. Swanson, Mr. Swanson decided he would come to the Pacific Coast and they arrived in San Francisco and made that city their home for three years, at the same time he was employed at carpenter work. He became tired of paying rent and living in flats and decided he would look for a place to buy a home. He found a fine location in El Cerrito and bought 200 feet on Stockton Street, just at the foot of the hills and overlooking the bay and valley below. When he moved into the little house that was on the land there was not a house on the hillside where now stand some 400 homes. Little by little Mr. and Mrs. Swanson have built up a very comfortable home and have a valuable property. He works at his trade and has been employed on buildings from Berkeley to Crockett. There has been no movement for the bettering of conditions in El Cerrito that has not found Mr. Swanson a champion of the cause. He takes an active part in church work and is a member of the Bethel Lutheran Church in Berkeley. In political matters he registers as a Democrat, but in local affairs he supports men and measures regardless of politics.

SAMUEL KIRKHOUSE.—An active member of the Crockett-Valona Business Men's Association, Samuel Kirkhouse is giving his best efforts to promote the welfare of his adopted city of Crockett. So far as he is able he contributes to all enterprises for the development of this section of Contra Costa County. Visible evidence of his work is seen on all sides for he has erected many homes and remodeled many buildings since he came to Crockett. He was born in England on July 21, 1871, a son of John and Susan (Price) Kirkhouse, the former still living in England, but the latter is deceased. His schooling was obtained in his native land and he lived there until July 20, 1911, the date of his arrival in this country. Arriving in California he worked at the building business in Vallejo, until he came to Crockett a few months later and established his own business as a contractor in house-painting and decorating. He tries to serve his patrons in a satisfactory manner, and by so doing has built up a substantial business in his line and is recognized as being dependable in all matters. He has an established credit for honest workmanship.

Mr. Kirkhouse married Miss Isabelle McLean and they have two boys: John Colin, a graduate from the high school, and with two sessions at the University of California to his credit; and William Reginald, also a graduate from the high school. In politics Mr. Kirkhouse is a Republican. He is a Scottish Rite Mason and a Shriner, belongs to the Elks, the Eagles, the Odd Fellows Lodge and Encampment, and also to the Eastern Star Chapter, and has held offices in some of these lodges. He is a Presbyterian in religious belief. Soon after coming to Crockett he purchased his own home, where he and his family now reside.

Mr. Kirkhouse has a brother, Ernest, and four sisters, Alice, Blanche, Susan and Julia, all married and living in England.

FRENCH McDONALD.—A resident of Contra Costa County since 1920, and an enterprising business man and citizen of El Cerrito since 1921, French McDonald is making his influence felt for the good of the community in civic matters as a member of the El Cerrito Improvement Association. He was born in Brown County, Kans., on June 30, 1879, and attended the public schools in Hiawatha, with two years in the high school there. At the age of nineteen he entered the employ of a large power company at its plant in Hiawatha. Beginning at the bottom, he gradually worked up to positions of trust and responsibility. From the age of nineteen until he came to California in 1920, Mr. McDonald was employed by various large power companies, water, steam and electric, in Kansas, Oklahoma, Iowa, Nebraska and Missouri. In the latter state, at Carrollton, he was chief engineer in an electric plant for seven years.

Thinking to better his condition and knowing that he would not make much advancement as long as he was working for wages, Mr. McDonald came to California looking for a place to engage in business. He entered the employ of the East Bay Water Company at the San Pablo Filter plant and remained one year, during which time he was studying the local conditions in El Cerrito. In 1921 he decided to embark in business and with his brother-in-law, H. P. Rude, started in the electrical contracting business and dealing in electrical supplies. From the first their business prospered and in 1923 Mr. McDonald bought out his partner and now carries on the business alone. He is located at 212 San Pablo Avenue and does everything in the electrical line. His handiwork shows in many of the homes erected here since he began business.

In 1903 Mr. McDonald was united in marriage at Winfield, Kans., to Daisy Rude, a native of that place, and they have three children: Thomas, a graduate of the Richmond High School and now a student in the Oakland Polytechnic College of Engineering; and Elizabeth and Mary, both in the Richmond High School. Mr. McDonald is a member of the Berkeley Chamber of Commerce; and also belongs to Wakenda Lodge No. 52, A. F. & A. M., at Carrollton, Mo. He is thoroughly equipped to handle any electrical job and is a very competent workman.

SAMUEL AND JOHN GIAMMONA.—The enterprising firm of wholesale dealers in fruits and produce at Pittsburg, Cal., is composed of two energetic and progressive young Italians, Sam and John Giammona, natives of Palermo, Island of Sicily, Italy. Sam was born on July 24, 1891, and John on January 15, 1895; their parents are both dead. Realizing that America offered a greater degree of independence and prosperity than the old home land, Sam preceded his brother to America by six years, locating at Grand Rapids, Mich. John joined his brother there in June, 1911. The two brothers have been closely associated in work and business ever since. At first they accepted work at anything that was honorable and by economical living saved their money until they had accumulated sufficient to enter the fruit and produce business at Grand Rapids, Mich. After the opening of the World War, Sam was drafted and served overseas about two years in France, where he was severely gassed and was in a French hospital for nine months. In the meantime John looked after the business at Grand Rapids. Upon Sam's return to America he reentered the business at Grand Rapids, although still feeling the ill effects of the gassing received during the war.

Samuel Giammona was married on June 21, 1915, to Miss Josephine Minardo, the ceremony occurring at Grand Rapids, Mich. John Giammona was united in marriage the following year, on September 11, 1916, to Lucy Minardo, a sister of Sam's wife. Both sisters are natives of

Michigan. The two brothers have each five children, and each family has chosen the same five names for the children: Frances, Pietro, Michael, Josephine, and Joseph.

For about three years the Giammona brothers conducted a fruit and produce business from wagons at Pittsburg. In June, 1925, they opened a large and commodious storeroom for the operating of a wholesale business, at No. 115 Black Diamond Street, where they are meeting with success, although this is a new enterprise for Pittsburg. The splendid executive and financial ability thus far shown by these two young men predicts for this firm an expanding business and a successful career.

CLARENCE ARCHER ODELL.—A pioneer of Richmond and a man who has been much interested in preserving its history is C. A. Odell, who, since March 4, 1918, has served as police judge of Richmond. He was born at Thorntown, Boone County, Ind., on November 4, 1868, a son of Alpheus Odell. He was also a native of Boone County, born there on February 7, 1836, and educated in the Thorntown Academy and Asbury University. After finishing college he began teaching school and followed that vocation practically the balance of his life. He married Julia Archer, at Spencer, Owen County, Ind., on November 26, 1862. She was born in Spencer on August 28, 1844, and became the mother of six children. The Odell family first came to Richmond in 1900, and established their residence in that place in 1901. A. Odell had the distinction of teaching the first school in Richmond. He was one of the first men to agitate the question of incorporating Richmond, wrote and circulated the first petition for that purpose; he also wrote the first petition for annexation and fixed the original boundaries of the city. He was one of the first to agitate boring a tunnel through the mountain for the municipal wharf; and was also the man who called the meeting for the organization of the first Masonic lodge. He died in Richmond on January 22, 1922. Mrs. Odell passed away on December 28, 1918.

C. A. Odell received a good education and then studied law and was admitted to practice, after passing the supreme court examination, at Sacramento, May 8, 1894. At San Francisco, on June 21, 1909, he was admitted to the United States District Court. Since taking up the law he has practiced uninterruptedly and has met with a flattering degree of success. He served as city recorder of Richmond from November 1, 1908, to August 1, 1909. When the freeholders charter went into effect on July 1, 1909, there was a change of administration and he was then appointed judge of the police court and has served continuously ever since. He has always taken a very active interest in development work and by his wide knowledge of conditions has been of much help in advancing the interest of the city of his adoption.

C. A. Odell was united in marriage on June 11, 1912, to Katherine R., daughter of Gersham D. and Jeanette R. Richardson. Mrs. Odell is a professional nurse, having graduated from the San Bernardino County Hospital, and the California Hospital in Los Angeles. They have three children: Clarence Archer, Jr., aged thirteen; Elizabeth T., aged eleven; and Lois E., aged one year. The Judge is a member of McKinley Lodge, F. & A. M., and the Eastern Star, and also of the Woodmen of the World.

RAYMOND HAYNES STANDISH.—The Pacific Coast manager of the United Cartridge Company is Raymond Haynes Standish, who is also serving the public as justice of the peace in the Twelfth Judicial Township, which comprises Crockett, Valona, Tormey and Selby. He is a native son and was born at Pacheco, on June 17, 1883, a son of George E. and Charlotte (Haynes) Standish, the former also having been born at Pacheco, the son of pioneer parents. He was a machinist by trade and for twenty-two years was superintendent of the cartridge factory of the Selby Smelter. He died at the age of fifty-two years, after a useful and honored career; the mother died in 1926, having reached the age of sixty-three years. She was the first librarian of the Crockett branch of the county free library and served for many years with marked efficiency. Mrs. Standish was born in the Willamette Valley in Oregon, and after settling at Crockett took an active interest in all matters pertaining to the general welfare of the people.

After graduating from the grammar school in Crockett, R. H. Standish became a student at the Wilmerding School of Architectural Arts, which is now a part of the Lick-Wilmerding School in San Francisco. After completing his course he entered upon a four-years apprenticeship as a machinist at the Union Iron Works. During this same time he pursued studies in the Humboldt Evening High School in San Francisco, majoring in mechanical arts for two years, and then served another apprenticeship as draftsman at the Union Iron Works for two years, when he received his certificate as master mechanic and draftsman. He then entered the employ of the Selby Smelter, where he worked as draftsman in remodeling the plant. When his father retired as superintendent of the cartridge factory in 1911, our subject succeeded to his position, having served as assistant superintendent from 1907 to 1911, under his father. In 1920 the Selby Smelter was sold to the United Cartridge Company, at which time Mr. Standish became manager on the Pacific Coast.

Raymond H. Standish was married first to Miss Flora McNeill, of San Francisco, and they had a son, Raymond Leslie, born March 11, 1907, who graduated from the John Swett Union High School and is now in the employ of the Bethlehem Steel Corporation in San Francisco. His second marriage united him with Miss Eva Rose, born in Kansas. In political affairs Judge Standish is a Republican and he was elected on that ticket to the office of justice of the peace of District No. 12 in 1914, and reelected twice since, thus showing the confidence his fellow citizens have in him. He has always taken an active interest in political matters that concern his county and community and counts his friends by the hundreds. He deals out justice to those brought before him without fear or favor and his administration of the office is very economical; he holds court at his office in Crockett every work-day evening except Saturday. Judge Standish is active in fraternal circles and belongs to the Odd Fellows, the Encampment, Improved Order of Red Men, the Knights of Pythias, the Vallejo Elks and the Native Sons, and has held various offices in these several orders. He is a booster for Contra Costa County and considers Crockett one of its favored sections; and accordingly he has invested his money in property in this city. He takes an active interest in civic matters and is considered a leader in all progressive movements for the upbuilding of town and county.

JAMES J. WHITE.—As chief of the Valona Fire Department, James J. White has proven himself a very efficient officer and all who know him are loud in the words of praise spoken in his behalf. He was born in Martinez on November 11, 1887, a son of Thomas and Mary (Tately) White, both natives of Ireland. The father came to America in young manhood and died in 1900. James J. attended the Martinez public schools and then was sent to St. Vincent's Home in San Rafael. His first work after leaving school was driving a milk wagon in Petaluma. One year later he went to work on the farm owned by James McKenna and remained there six years.

Mr. White was preparing himself physically for the position he had sometime hoped to hold, that of chief of a fire department. He took special training for the position he holds today. Entering the employ of the sugar refinery his adaptability was soon recognized and he was sent to San Francisco to enter the fire department to obtain all the instruction and information he could. The letters of commendation and the certificates of satisfactory work in the department of the bay city attest to his qualifications; that department also awarded him a medal for his efficiency.

On December 2, 1906, J. J. White married Miss Gertrude McVay, daughter of Hugh McVay of Prince Edward Island, who married Margaret Hughes. Mr. McVay was a grain merchant at Charlottestown, P. E. I., and with his wife is living in the enjoyment of good health. Of a family of two boys and twelve girls, one boy and five girls are living. Mr. and Mrs. White have had three children: William, who completed the courses at St. Vincent's Academy at Vallejo, where he took a special course in chemistry, and bears the distinction of being the first member of either side of the family to graduate from a high school. Florence died in infancy; and Althea is in the grammar school.

Immediately after their marriage, Mr. White started at boiler-making in 1906, and continued until 1911, when he came to the sugar refinery and took up his work there. At present he is a stationary fireman. He has been connected with the Valona Fire Department since 1914, and in 1918

Mr. & Mrs. Henry Bowman

was made chief, at which time he was sent to San Francisco as related. The department is equipped with a splendid chemical and hose wagon. This was converted from an ordinary truck automobile after Mr. White became chief. The water system has been extended and hydrants installed in various parts of the town to better serve the needs of the place. The apparatus is in first-class condition, with adequate hose for all requirements. He is a member of the National Fire Protection Association. By virtue of his position he serves as deputy sheriff under R. R. Veale. He belongs to the Knights of Columbus and the Red Men. In political affiliations their house is divided, Mr. White being a stanch believer in Democratic principles, while Mrs. White is a radical Republican. However, harmony reigns when it comes to voting for local officers for they both support the best men and measures. The family are members of the Catholic Church.

HENRY ROMAN.—Among the efficient planing mill superintendents on the Pacific Coast, one who understands the business, from the filing and running of saws and planers to the finest kind of work turned out by the mills, is Henry Roman, a whole-hearted man, self-made in the truest sense of the term. Mr. Roman has been a resident of Bay Point since 1908, when he came here at the request of S. W. Rodgers, the superintendent of the plant of the C. A. Smith Lumber Company. A native of Sweden, he was born on December 17, 1872. His father was a foreman in a limestone quarry in Sweden and died when our subject was only eight years old, since which time he has been self-supporting. His mother met with a serious accident, and for two years lingered in pain, finally dying in a hospital in their home town.

From the age of eight years Henry Roman worked at any kind of work his hands found to do. When he was eighteen, in 1890, he came to America to better his condition. He had had some experience in mill work in a planing mill in Sweden, becoming a fireman on one of their boats that plied in neighboring waters. Then he was an errand boy in a shoe factory, for a while, but went back to the planing mill, remaining in that work until he came to this country. He landed in New York on October 5, 1890, en route to Manson, Iowa, where he had a brother engaged in farming about twenty miles from Fort Dodge. This kind of work was not to his liking; so he went to Rhinelander, Wis., where there were eleven sawmills and fifteen planing mills operating, and secured work with Abner Connor & Son, remaining for two years. While living at Rhinelander Mr. Roman met with a very severe accident while working with a circular saw on August 5, 1895, and for months his life was despaired of. Later he engaged with the Underwood Lumber Company, continuing with that same plant until 1906, but under the successive ownership of Weeks, Bronson and French, and G. H. Queal, and meanwhile becoming thoroughly experienced in the various branches of planing mill work. In 1906 he went to Potlatch, Idaho, and worked there two years, becoming planing mill foreman under Superintendent S. W. Rodgers, who came to Bay Point to establish the yards and plant for the C. A. Smith Lumber Company. That same year Mr. Roman came to this State to join Mr. Rodgers and was made planing mill foreman. Under his direction all the machinery in the plant was set up, and his promotions have been well deserved. He became superintendent of the planing mill in 1921, and has one assistant, Henry Johnson, a competent workman.

At Rhinelander, Wis., on August 5, 1897, Mr. Roman was united in marriage with Miss Beda Olson, a native of Sweden, and they have had four children: Wilhelm, a tool and lock maker with the Sledge Lock Company, in San Francisco; Clarence H., proprietor of the Bay Point Garage; Anna, wife of L. Merrill, a fruit grower near Concord; and George, an employee of the Coos Bay Lumber Company in the planing mill. The family home is at Bay Point, where Mr. Roman owns two residences, and there the family are surrounded by a wide circle of friends. Mr. Roman is a member of the Odd Fellows at Bay Point and belongs to the Masonic Lodge in Martinez. In politics he supports the men and measures of the Republican party.

LEWIS B. WEATHERBEE, M. D.—Among the practicing physicians of Contra Costa County, none is more in touch with the general spirit of progress in his chosen profession than Dr. Lewis B. Weatherbee of Antioch, Cal., widely known as a proficient exponent of the latest principles of medical science. Antioch and the surrounding country are fortunate to have such an able and conscientious physician to care for the physical welfare of their citizens. Dr. Weatherbee was born at Lincoln, Maine, June 14, 1880, the son of A. W. and Lucinda (Butterfield) Weatherbee, both now deceased. The father was an honored member of the bar of Penobscot County, Maine, while the mother came from the well-known and highly esteemed Butterfield family of Maine.

Lewis B. Weatherbee spent his boyhood days in his native State and when twenty-one years old migrated to Baker, Ore., where he completed his high school studies and thereupon took up a special preparatory medical course at the University of Oregon, at Eugene. Later he entered the California Medical College at San Francisco, taking the regular four-year course. The great earthquake of 1906 caused the discontinuance of this college; so he took the last two years of his course at the California Eclectic Medical College at Los Angeles, graduating with the Class of 1909.

Dr. Weatherbee began practicing at Forest Hill, Placer County, Cal., where he remained one year. He then moved to Oakland, where he remained four years, afterwards locating at Oakley, in Contra Costa County, and also establishing an office at Brentwood. In 1918, Doctor Weatherbee moved to Antioch, where he has successfully practiced ever since. Being possessed of a vigorous mentality and endowed with an aptitude for learning, Dr. Weatherbee took advantage of several postgraduate courses under well-known national specialists, including the technique of X-Ray under Dr. E. C. Jermen of Chicago, and individual electric treatments under Dr. Waggoner, of Cleveland, Ohio. Although adhering to the methods of the eclectic school of medicine, he uses electricity very extensively in his practice, and his office is equipped with the latest X-Ray machine and electrical appliances that are equal to those found in the largest cities of the State. During the World War Dr. Weatherbee served in the Volunteer Medical Reserve Corps.

In Stockton, Cal., on June 20, 1923, L. B. Weatherbee was united in marriage with Miss Meda Andrews. They have adopted a daughter, Thelma, now thirteen years of age, who brightens their ideal home life. Dr. Weatherbee is a member of the National Eclectic Medical Association and State Medical Society. He is a member of Antioch Lodge No. 151, I. O. O. F., and also of the Encampment, and belongs to the Loyal Order of Moose at Pittsburg.

MATTHEW WARD.—To those who have succeeded in life solely by their own efforts much credit is due, and such an one is Judge Matthew Ward, justice of the peace of the eighth judicial township of Contra Costa County, who is in every way worthy of the success he has achieved. Judge Ward was born near Clayton, Contra Costa County, on September 24, 1883, the son of Matthew and Elizabeth (Dolan) Ward, the former a native of Ireland and the latter born in England, of Irish parentage. The father of Judge Ward emigrated to America, locating for a while in Pennsylvania and later removing to New York State, whence he came to California in 1868. He located and worked in the coal mines at Nortonville and it was at this place he was married to Miss Elizabeth Dolan in 1872. When the coal mines gave out he took up government land and became a sheep raiser and eventually a stockman, and the owner of about 500 acres of land in the Mount Diablo section. He passed away in 1906, at the age of sixty-one years; his wife died in 1884 when Matthew, Jr., was one year old, and he was reared by an older sister, Delia Ward, now deceased. There were five children in the family, only two of whom are now living: Robert E., a farmer living near Antioch; and the subject of this sketch.

Judge Matthew Ward worked on the home farm until eighteen years old. He had decided that to succeed in life he must obtain a good and thorough education along special lines. He took a course at the Stockton Business College, conducted by Professor Ramsey, and also took up a correspondence course, studying by himself; and so well did he succeed that at the age of eighteen he passed the teacher's examination. From that time until he was twenty-five he was engaged in teaching, his first school being at Clayton, this county, the community in which he first saw the light of day; afterwards he became the principal of the Port Costa school.

His youthful ambition was to become a lawyer; and to accomplish this aim he saved his money made from teaching and paid his way through the law school at Stanford University, graduating in July, 1913. He immediately took the State Bar examination and was admitted to practice in the same month. Locating at Antioch, Cal., he opened an office and was successful from the start. In November, 1922, Mr. Ward was elected to the office of justice of the peace for the eighth judicial township of Contra Costa County, and he is well and ably filling that responsible position. Judge Ward possesses an enviable reputation for sterling character and for the rendering of decrees that are strictly just and impartial. His self-reliance and persistency of purpose, coupled with a definite goal in life, have helped him to surmount difficulties that would have discouraged the faint-hearted, and to gain success and win achievements under adverse circumstances.

On April 18, 1916, Matthew Ward was united in marriage with Miss Minnie Barnes, a native of Kansas; and this union has been blessed with three children: Robert, Thomas, and Leonard. Judge Ward is a member of General Winn Parlor, N. S. G. W., at Antioch. He is a champion of all worthy movements that have as their aim the betterment of the educational, moral, and civic interests of the community.

EUGENE J. VIERA.—A native of Contra Costa County, Cal., Eugene J. Viera has been one of the active men of his section of the State, one who has at all times done his share toward the upbuilding of the community in which he has been reared. Every movement calculated to be of material benefit to the State or county has received his support, and today he is honored and respected by all who know him. Besides operating his sixty-acre ranch, located about two miles west of Oakley on the State Highway near Bridgehead Avenue, he is president of the Bridgehead Shipping Corporation and a large stockholder in it. This company maintains a shipping shed with a spur track, representing an investment of $7000, from which hundreds of carloads of fruits, grapes, nuts, celery, lettuce, asparagus, etc., are shipped to Eastern markets.

Eugene J. Viera was born on July 24, 1884, near Marsh Landing on the home ranch of his parents, Manuel and Elizabeth (Whelihan) Viera, natives of the Island of Pico, and San Francisco, Cal., respectively, and now honored and respected pioneers of Contra Costa County, who are represented on another page in this history. From the time when he was old enough to work, Eugene helped his father on the home place, which was virgin land covered with live-oaks when purchased. This place was cleared and planted by the Viera family, and today is among the most highly improved and productive places in the county. Mr. Viera raises grapes, almonds and walnuts on his own ranch, and is now interplanting his grape vines with walnuts. He erected the buildings at the corner of Bridgehead Avenue and Victory Highway and was the means of establishing the business center there.

On January 1, 1914, Mr. Viera was married to Miss Johanna Alma Mack, born at Minster, Ohio, a daughter of Charles August and Mary (Trimke) Mack, both deceased. She came to California with her sister and brother-in-law in 1902 when only eight years old and grew up in Contra Costa County. Four children have been born of this union: Edward, Dorothy, Donald and Betty Jean. Mr. Viera helped to organize the East Contra Costa County Chamber of Commerce; and he is also a member of the Live Oak Farm Bureau and of the board of trustees of the Antioch-Live Oak school district. He is one of the members of the organization known as the Industrial Survey of Eastern Contra Costa County. Fraternally, he belongs to the Native Sons. Mrs. Viera is active in the Oakley Woman's Club, the Live Oak Farm Center and the Live Oak Parent-Teacher's Association.

MRS. CORA E. VAUGHAN.—A woman of remarkable business ability, and at the same time a leader in social affairs, is found in the person of Mrs. Cora E. Vaughan, proprietor of the Home Bakery at Antioch and representative of a pioneer family from old American ancestry. Mrs. Vaughan is a native daughter of California, born at Upper Lake, Lake County, one of five children of Isaac and Sarah (Bucknell) Rice. Of these five children the following are living: Estelle, wife of Thomas Bourns, living at North Bend, Ore.; Cora E., of this review; and Frances, wife of Ray Marks, of Eureka, Cal. Isaac Rice was born in Missouri and was a neighbor and friend of ex-Governor Lilburn Boggs, of that State. When a young man he came to California and was here united in marriage with Sarah Bucknell, who was born in Stockton, a daughter of George Bucknell, a California pioneer of 1851, who moved from Stockton to Lake County in the early days. When Cora Rice was nine years old her parents moved into Mendocino County, settling in Willits, where Isaac Rice engaged in merchandising. Here the daughter grew up and attended the public schools, and imbibed the rules of business as laid down by her father.

At Willits, on April 16, 1896, Cora E. Rice and George Vaughan were united in marriage. Mr. Vaughan was born in Sonoma County and was an only child of a pioneer family of that county. From 1896 to 1898 Mr. and Mrs. Vaughan lived in San Francisco. When the Alaska gold excitement broke out, Mr. Vaughan decided to try his fortune in the northern country and his wife decided to accompany her husband. For the following twelve years they braved the dangers of the frontier. They spent the winter of 1898-1899 at Dyea, then went over Chilcoot Pass to Atlin, B. C., and then came back to Nome and other places, experiencing a life full of interest, which, if put into print, would fill a volume. Mr. Vaughan and Mr. Lindbloom, a Nome pioneer, accomplished the first trip ever made from Cook's Inlet to Nome over mountains of ice and snow. Mr. and Mrs. Vaughan's first child was born at Nome, while they were located there during the Nome development days. They became acquainted with Jack London and Alex. McKenzie, and also met Roald Amundsen, the Arctic explorer, who pulled up at Nome in the little schooner, Gjoa, now in Golden Gate Park Museum in San Francisco, after accomplishing the Northwest passage, a feat that had baffled all the Arctic explorers of the world for 300 years. A grand celebration was tendered Amundsen, Mr. Vaughan being on the entertainment committee. Coming back from Nome to California, Mr. and Mrs. Vaughan took up their residence in Oakland for a year. While there Mr. Vaughan became connected with the California Transportation Company and was sent to Antioch as local manager, continuing in this position until his death on May 22, 1922. Four children blessed their union; Avaloo Mary, a graduate from the Antioch High School, Class of 1925, and now in business for herself in Pittsburg with a branch of the Home Bakery; Mildred E., in Munson's secretarial school in San Francisco; and Cora Wilda and George William. After the death of Mr. Vaughan, his widow purchased the Home Bakery. She gives the business her personal attention and is rapidly building up a fine trade in Antioch and the surrounding country. She employs only the most experienced help and produces a superior product. She believes in the square deal in business; her experiences in the North have given her a broad outlook upon life, and she believes in the principle of the Golden Rule. Besides her bakery, Mrs. Vaughan owns a thirty-five acre ranch near Antioch, and her own home in town. She is a Past Matron of the Eastern Star, having served in 1923; is a Past President of the Improvement Club, which she served two years; and is prominent in all civic movements for the betterment of local conditions in Antioch.

LORENZO VALLI.—A successful and leading merchant in Valona, Lorenzo Valli was born in Italy on May 1, 1890. His parents were John and Rose (Cattini) Valli, the former a merchant in his native land. In 1901, the father came to America. A brother, Angelo Valli, is a carpenter in Italy; Antonio is a tailor in Crockett, and Joseph, who also lived in Crockett, was killed while serving in the Italian Army during the World War. Lorenzo went to the schools in Italy and completed his education in America. In 1907 he came to Crockett and worked at anything he could find to do that would give him an honest living until 1910, when he returned to Italy and served his required time in the Italian Army of a little more than two years. Returning to California he secured employment at the sugar refinery in Crockett in 1913 and continued there until November 5, 1917.

At that time he was called for duty in the United States Army, trained at Camp Lewis and was assigned to the 161st Infantry, Forty-first Division, later being transferred to the Second Division, and was sent to the firing line with the Twenty-third Infantry, Company M. He was in the battles of the Marne and Chateau Thierry, was wounded July 1, 1918, and spent seventy-eight days in the hospital at Bordeaux, from which he was transferred to the Casualty Company and remained until he was honorably discharged on July 9, 1919. Returning to Crockett he resumed work in the refinery and remained until February 22, 1920. With his savings he wanted to engage in the mercantile business and with a partner, Ambrogio Crivelli, purchased the store owned by Pete Verona, who had a gents' furnishing goods establishment, and opened the business under the firm name of Valli & Crivelli, and has since done a flourishing and lucrative business. Their business has increased and today they have a modern department store in Valona, with a branch in Crockett to better serve their increasing number of customers. They employ ten efficient salesmen and saleswomen.

Lorenzo Valli was married on December 16, 1920, to Miss Elena Cattini, a native of Italy, and they have a son, Joseph, born September 21, 1921. A bit of romance is connected with this marriage. During Mr. Valli's visit to Italy while on furlough he met Miss Cattini for the first time and during subsequent visits this acquaintance ripened into love and their marriage. She came to America on December 7, 1920, and they were married on December 16. They have hosts of warm friends in Valona and Crockett, who esteem them for their fine qualities of mind and heart. Mr. Valli takes an active interest in the Crockett-Valona Business Men's Association and supports all of its measures for better community interests. He belongs to the American Legion, the Foresters of America, the Ancient Order of Druids and the Elks. In his political views he favors Republican principles. He owns some valuable property in Oakland and his firm have property interests there also. The family are members of the Catholic Church in Valona.

WILLIAM HENRY WADMAN.—An eye-witness of the marvelous development of Crockett, which has taken place within the past two decades, has been William Henry Wadman, one of the best known citizens of that enterprising community. Although far from being aged Mr. Wadman is one of the pioneer residents and was one of the charter members of the fire department which he helped to organize in 1908. In earlier days the hose cart had to be pulled by hand to the top of the hill through what were then often muddy roads. When he arrived in the village in 1907 the water formed a lake around the depot and Loring Avenue ran in a horse shoe bend. The development of the parks has all occurred since then, for at that time not a single tree grew on the hill just above the post office, and the first house was being constructed there.

Mr. Wadman was born in Liverpool, England, on June 13, 1882, his father being William Henry Wadman, a sea captain and native of Canada, who died in England in 1889. His mother, Mary McLean, was a native of Nova Scotia, Canada, both she and her husband being of Scotch parentage. The subject of this sketch had two brothers and two sisters; two sisters and a brother now residing in New York City, and one brother in British Columbia. After the death of his father, Mr. Wadman, then seven years old, was taken to Canada to live with relatives. About five or six years later he went to New York City, where he received his education in the grammar schools. He resided in the metropolis from 1894 to

1907, being employed by the Arbuckle Sugar Refinery. In 1907, through the influence of some friends, he came to Crockett, where he has since made his home. When he first arrived he started in the evaporator and boiled sugar departments of the local refinery and has been steadily promoted until he is now head of the sugar boiling, with about twenty men in his department. Mr. Wadman is a studious type of man, reading many scientific books, and has an especial fondness for travel narratives. He is also a radio fan and takes much interest in everything relating to its development.

JAMES A. PURVIANCE.—The proprietors of the Den O' Sweets at 811-813 Macdonald Avenue, Richmond, are James A. Purviance & Sons, all working in harmony together since the organization of their business in 1919. Beginning on a small scale they have increased the size of their establishment from time to time and now give employment to fifteen people in the various departments. Their restaurant and ice-cream parlor are of the most modern construction, and they have their own ice-making machinery, supplying some 500 pounds daily, and this takes care of their soda fountain and storage rooms and candy making departments. The plans of the building they occupy were drawn by Frank Purviance, and the building erected by Mr. Berry of Oakland. The fixtures and all equipment have been installed at great expense and the establishment, with its various departments, is a credit to Richmond.

James A. Purviance was born in Illinois on January 19, 1859, a son of Walker and Perthena (Gudgell) Purviance, natives of Ohio and Indiana, respectively, and farmer folk. Our subject attended the schools of Illinois and Iowa, whither the family moved when he was yet quite small, and he finished his education in Cedar Rapids, and spent the most of his life there until coming to California in 1906. His brothers and sisters were also reared in Iowa but are now scattered: Charles, in Iowa; Lewis, in Louisiana; Robert, in Iowa; Clark, in Nebraska; John, in Arizona; Edward, in Iowa. One sister, Mrs. Anna Betzenheiser, is deceased.

On February 20, 1906, Mr. Purviance first came to California, located at Long Beach and worked at the carpenter trade some time, then came to Berkeley in January, 1907, and worked about the bay district during 1907-1908. Returning to Southern California he located in Orange and followed his trade of carpenter some ten years, coming to Richmond in 1918. Here he bought the business that is known as Den O' Sweets, installed his boys in the place and continued his carpenter work until February, 7, 1924, when he came into the store to assist his sons.

On December 31, 1885, James A. Purviance was united in marriage in Cedar Rapids, Iowa, with Miss Lettie Newton, daughter of Isaac and Sarah (Parker) Newton, the father a wagonmaker by trade in Maquoketa, Iowa, where Mrs. Purviance was born. They have three children: Frank, married Miss Vena Leona Jensen and has two children, Albert and Alberta; Glen, married Miss Mary Alice Gates; and Harold, married

Miss Nora L. Loveless, who now is in charge of the Richmond Health Center. The family are prominent in social circles and the father and sons take an active interest in all civic affairs and support all projects they believe will build up the city where they live and prosper.

EDWARD I. DE LAVEAGA.—A developer of the resources of Contra Costa County and a representative citizen of the Bay Cities is found in Edward I. de Laveaga, whose permanent home is at Orinda, Contra Costa County. He was born in San Francisco, on April 15, 1884, a son of Miguel A. and Marie (Le Breton) de Laveaga. His father was born at Rosario, Mexico, of Spanish parents; after locating in California he became one of the leading financiers in San Francisco. He also acquired considerable valuable property in Contra Costa County which is now being developed by our subject. The mother was born in San Francisco, in which city her brother, Albret Le Breton, was the first white male child born. The children of this family are: Joseph Vincent, of San Mateo, with business connections in San Francisco; Julia, who married Andrew P. Welch; and Edward I., of this review.

Edward I. de Laveaga received his education in private schools, Santa Clara College and the University of California. After he had completed his college courses, in 1907, he took charge of his father's property in San Benito County, which was known as the Quien Sabe Grant, one of the oldest and best known pieces of property in that county, and began his life work. During the World War he enlisted with the Red Cross and was awaiting orders of transportation to France when the Armistice was declared. After the war was over Mr. de Laveaga took up development work, at Orinda, on 1050 acres of the family holdings and began the work on a summer home place. His first work was with a subdivision to be put on sale for settlement. This was so successful that it encouraged him to start another subdivision and the establishment of a country club, the latter being situated between the two subdivisions. There are now nearly eighty homes in these two tracts, with houses costing from $3000 to $50,000 each. This settlement is known as Haciendas Del Orinda. He laid out a townsite, with a style of architecture to harmonize with his scheme of things, and there are now a fire house, equipped with the most modern fire-fighting apparatus, a general merchandise store, a block of four store buildings, garage and a riding academy. The club house cost $150,000, and there is a golf course of eighteen holes; also a lake a mile in circumference to supply water for domestic purposes, and to supply the golf course. Mr. de Laveaga's hobby is good riding horses and he has reserved eight acres for polo grounds and hurdling. He is a lover of flowers and birds and knows by name nearly all the various kinds found in California.

The marriage of Edward de Laveaga was celebrated on December 29, 1906, when he was united with Miss Delight Woodberry, daughter
24

of Charles J. and Lucia (Hall) Woodberry. Mr. Woodberry is a native of Beverly, Mass., and a graduate of Amherst College, and an author of some renown. Mr. and Mrs. de Laveaga have five children: Miguel A., aged eighteen, is a student in economics at the University of California; Lucia attends Miss Ransom's School; Edward Le Breton and Richard H. attend a private school; and Juliette, the youngest, is now eighteen months old. Mr. de Laveaga is a director in the East Bay Title Insurance Company; and also of the Orinda Country Club, which he organized. He occasionally appears in public as a speaker and is a contributor to newspapers on various topics. His hobby is hunting and fishing and in this way he finds recreation and relaxation from his arduous duties. It is through such energetic native sons, and men of their stamp, that the development of the present decade in California is being pushed through to completion, and to them is due a debt of gratitude for unselfish devotion to community affairs.

JAMES H. SHAW.—As the president of the Bank of Oakley, James H. Shaw is doing much to advance the agricultural interests of eastern Contra Costa County and other sound enterprises that naturally look to a bank for a solution of their difficulties. Mr. Shaw is a fruit grower and packer, and also packs and ships asparagus that is grown in the Delta country. He was born in Quincy, Ill., on April 5, 1883, a son of William L. and Elizabeth (Fleming) Shaw. The father was also born in Quincy and was a clothing merchant there for years, and now is living retired. The mother is deceased. There were six children in the Shaw family. Mrs. B. F. Lickey lives in San Francisco; Mrs. Elliott Shaw resides in New York City; Mrs. Ray Fuqua lives in Quincy, Ill.; James H., of this review, is the third child and oldest son; Joseph is a fruit shipper at Brawley, Cal.; and Francis is a wholesale clothing merchant at Quincy, Ill.

The early schooling of our subject was obtained in the schools in Quincy, Ill. At the age of seventeen he came out to Los Angeles, and soon after his arrival he engaged in the fruit business; and ever since that time he has been buying, packing and shipping fruits of various kinds. He has also made a specialty of growing fruit and asparagus. In 1912 Mr. Shaw came to Oakley as manager of the Miller & Cummings Packing House, and he was so well impressed with the conditions found here that he decided to make this his home. He moved his family here and has since devoted his time and talents to helping the community to grow. He now has fifteen packing plants of his own in Contra Costa, Alameda, Stanislaus, San Joaquin, Santa Clara, San Benito and Colusa Counties. He handles sixty cars of asparagus annually and also 100 cars of grapes, forty cars of apricots, and fifty cars of tomatoes. This large enterprise has gradually grown from a very small beginning, but under the personal supervision of Mr. Shaw it has proved a financial success and he feels amply rewarded for the efforts he has put forth to build up his business. His home ranch consists of twenty-three acres, which he bought in 1919

and which was then covered with live-oak trees. He cleared the timber
and set out a vineyard of wine grapes, and in 1921-1922 built his house.
The place is located about a half mile from Oakley on the State Highway.

Mr. Shaw is president of the Bank of Oakley, a State bank organized
under the State banking laws of 1920, with a paid-up capital of $25,000.
He was one of the organizers of the bank and was its first president. The
other officers are H. H. Hall, vice-president; F. C. Anderson, secretary;
and Paul Anderson, cashier.

Mr. Shaw has been married twice. His first wife, whom he married in
Los Angeles in 1905, became the mother of two children: Francis, attending school in New York City; and Robert M., attending the Santa Clara
Union High School. His second marriage occurred in Yuma, Ariz., in
1918, when he married Miss Ida S. Teale, born at Fullerton, Cal. They
have two children, Elizabeth and John H. Mr. Shaw takes a very active
interest in the development of eastern Contra Costa County and supports
all worthy movements that he thinks will help make this section a better
place in which to live and rear a family. He is strong for cooperation
and believes in the future of the county. He is a member of the East
Contra Costa Chamber of Commerce.

GEORGE WASHINGTON RYAN.—The editor of a city news-
paper should be a representative citizen, one who possesses an inherent
devotion to the welfare of the community. His chief concern should be
the directing of public thought into those channels that lead to the cooperation of the citizens with every movement that has as its aim the advancement of the educational, moral, and commercial interests of the city,
state and nation. The city of Richmond, Cal., is fortunate in having such
a man in the person of George W. Ryan, the editor of Albany Argus, at
Albany, and owner of the Terminal at Richmond, which he purchased in
1912. This paper originally was established in 1903 by Dr. Warren B.
Brown, and given the name Terminal by a prominent Santa Fe Railway
official because it advocated locating the Santa Fe at this point.

George W. Ryan was born at Albion, near Marshalltown, Iowa, on
July 30, 1857, a son of Samuel and Maria (Thompson) Ryan, both
natives of Pennsylvania. George and his sister Jennie, who is now Mrs.
Prizer, of Albany, Cal., are the only living members of the Ryan family.
George was educated in the splendid public schools of Iowa and after
leaving the high school supplemented his education with special courses in
newspaper work and printing, preparatory to entering upon his chosen
profession. At the age of twenty-one he started his career as a newspaper-
man and has followed this work in many different states of the union.
Mr. Ryan was a member of the staff of the Denver Tribune in 1881, when
the noted American poet, Eugene Field, was associated with this paper.
In 1897 Mr. Ryan made his first trip to California, and for three years
had charge of a syndicate newspaper at Holtville, after which he came to
Oakland. In 1912 he purchased the Terminal at Richmond, and in 1916

established the Albany Argus, at Albany, Cal., which has proved to be a very successful weekly paper. Politically, both of his papers are regarded as conservatively Republican; and at both plants he operates a job printing business. He is an ardent champion of the movement to make Richmond the leading harbor of the Pacific Coast. Its natural deep water harbor and superb location opposite the Golden Gate combine to make of it an ideal port for worldwide shipping.

On February 6, 1907, George W. Ryan was united in marriage with Mrs. Laura H. Codington, of Oakland, daughter of the late Rev. John B. Hill, formerly manager of the Methodist Book Concern, at San Francisco. Mr. and Mrs. Ryan have two sons: Sydney E., an athletic young man who attended the Leland Stanford University, and while a student was a member of the baseball team; and Thomas G., a student at the Richmond High School. Fraternally, Mr. Ryan is a member of Richmond Lodge No. 1251 B. P. O. Elks at Richmond, and is also a member of the Richmond Chamber of Commerce.

JAMES M. THOMPSON.—A resident of Richmond since 1906, and of California since 1901, James M. Thompson has been an eye witness to the wonderful growth and development of the entire state since he first came within its borders. He was born in Tennessee on January 30, 1879, and attended the public schools near their home farm. He had worked around machinery from early boyhood and was handy with tools, so at an early age he started out for himself, being the oldest of fourteen children in his parents' family. He worked in sawmills and lumber camps for several years, and when he arrived in California, went to Mariposa County and found employment in the mines and for practically five years worked underground.

This settling in Mariposa County was one of the best moves Mr. Thompson ever made, for it was here he met and in 1905 married Miss Lena Pettis, who was born in that county, the daughter of Charles and Celia (Collins) Pettis. Her grandparents came from Cornwall, England, to America in an early day and her grandfather was engaged in mining and ranching in Mariposa County. Members of the family have been prominently connected with community affairs for many years in the Mother Lode district. Mr. and Mrs. Thompson have a daughter Bernice, who married William E. Geach and has a son William Eugene.

Mr. Thompson came to Richmond to work for Edwin T. Blake, at the time he was opening up the quarry at Point Richmond for Blake Brothers and he remained with this firm until 1915, when he resigned to enter the employ of the Standard Oil Company. After having worked at various occupations he was placed in the power department at the salt water pumping station. This station has a capacity of 45,000,000 gallons every twenty-four hours. In 1907 Mr. Thompson moved his family to Richmond proper and they went through many pioneer experiences before the city assumed a place for itself in the county. Mrs. Thompson belongs to the Ladies of the Maccabees, and takes a live interest in community affairs. Mr. and Mrs. Thompson believe in Richmond and have faith in its growth and development and favor all projects to that end. Mr. Thompson finds his recreation in fishing.

PRESLEY MORGAN NEVILLE.—Descended from Revolutionary ancestors Presley Morgan Neville holds an assured position in the esteem of his friends in Richmond and the East Bay district, which has been his home since 1903. He was born in Chicago on January 4, 1889, the oldest of three sons of Frederick Morgan and Anna (Schreck) Neville, now living retired in Richmond.

Frederick M. Neville was born in West Virginia and is descended from General Daniel Morgan of Revolutionary fame. Mr. Neville is a man of good education and was master car builder for the Union Tank Line Car Company, of New York, continuing there until 1911, when he became their representative on the Pacific Coast. He was in charge of transport and shipping for the Union Tank Line Car Company until he was retired on a pension on January 15, 1926, after thirty-five years continuous service. He was married in 1888, and became the father of three sons: Presley M., Edgar and Way, all in Richmond.

Presley M. Neville attended the public schools and at the age of a little over fourteen, in June, 1903, entered the service of the Standard Oil Company in Richmond and since then he has witnessed the wonderful growth of this great concern. He started as a messenger boy in the laboratory and carried samples for a year, then was advanced to be inspector, and when he was only sixteen was night inspector; then for the next three and one-half years was in charge of that department. In November, 1906, he became connected with the transportation department, beginning at the bottom as a clerk to learn all the angles of that department so important to every large company; he worked up to be chief clerk, and in 1909 was promoted to be yardmaster, and in December, 1911, was advanced to general yardmaster, having charge of all incoming and outgoing shipments at the Richmond refinery. He has made a special study of transportation and is often sought by others for definite data along those lines. He has worked with the various officials and bodies in Richmond to perfect one of the best transportation systems for the city. Mr. Neville is the youngest man at the refinery with twenty-three years continuous service to his credit. He belongs to the San Francisco Transportation Club.

Presley M. Neville was married to Miss Neba Frances Miller on April 20, 1913. She was born at Savanna, Ill., an only child of Carl and Charlotte (Nymen) Miller, the latter born in Sweden. Carl Miller was the general foreign correspondent for the Northern Pacific Railroad Company for many years. When he retired he engaged in the real estate business in Chicago until his death. Mrs. Neville is a high school graduate and an accomplished musician. She has two children: Neba Charlotte, aged twelve, who is in the Junior High School, and Nancy Anne, four years old.

Mr. Neville is a pianist and formerly played in the churches. He was a member of the first band organized in Richmond. From 1911 until 1914 he was organist for the Modern Woodmen of America Camp in Richmond; and from 1914 till 1919 served in the same capacity for the Richmond Elks. He frequently is called upon to deliver addresses along his special line of work and has contributed to the Elks journal and other papers. He is a member of the Elks and the Modern Woodmen of America; and belongs to the Carquinez Golf Club. The Nevilles own their own home at 475 Carlston Avenue and take great pride in their beautiful lawn and garden. He enjoys motoring, golf and all sports.

J. E. QUINN, D. V. S.—The well-known and successful veterinarian, J. E. Quinn, of Antioch enjoys a wide practice which extends throughout the whole of eastern Contra Costa County. His office and hospital are located at 814 G Street, Antioch, and his equipment is of the most modern character. He was born in Franklin County, Ky., on August 3, 1861, the son of Alexander Quinn, a well-known carriage-maker at Frankfort, where he and a brother, John Quinn, built a factory and established a good business in their line. The elder Quinn was born in Ireland and married Margaret Hearn.

J. E. Quinn was sent to the public schools in Kentucky until he was sixteen. Then he left home and went to Missouri, and there was married on February 25, 1891, to Miss Clara Barr, daughter of James and Sarah (Case) Barr, natives of West Virginia and Michigan, respectively. Mrs. Quinn's grandfather Barr built the first railroad in West Virginia, where he was a wealthy contractor. When she was a child Mrs. Quinn left Iowa, where she was born, for Missouri with her parents, and there she grew up and attended school. After their marriage Mr. and Mrs. Quinn farmed in Missouri for a time and then went to Texas and continued farming for three years. Returning to Missouri, he thereafter acted as manager for several large farm owners. Mr. and Mrs. Quinn have five children: Margaret, wife of Martin Jensen, rancher near Antioch; James William, who served in the United States forces over seas during the World War and was wounded three times in various engagements, and who is now superintendent of the sub-station at Antioch for the Great Western Power Company; Norman, a fireman for the Standard Oil Company at the pumping plant at Helm, Fresno County; Emma, who died at the age of eighteen months; and Wallace, a cable splicer for the Great Western Power Company in Oakland.

In 1901 Mr. and Mrs. Quinn left Rich Hill, Mo., for Antioch, Cal. Mr. Quinn was employed on the Los Medanos Ranch by Mr. Hooper, who offered him the management of it, but he declined as he had decided to become a veterinary. He matriculated in the San Francisco Veterinary College in the fall of 1907, pursued the regular courses, and was graduated with the Class of 1910 with the degree of D. V. S. Locating in Antioch he began to build up a practice, and here has been the scene of his operations ever since. He is now serving as State meat inspector at Pittsburg and Brentwood, having been appointed in each city by the board of trustees. He is a member of the American Veterinary Association and of the California State Veterinary Association, and takes an active interest in each organization. He has made a success of his work, and is a good judge of stock values. Fraternally, Dr. Quinn belongs to the Modern Woodmen of America. The parents of Mrs. Quinn came to Contra Costa County in 1892, and took an active part in the development of the community. Mrs. Quinn has many friends in this community, who esteem her for her high ideals.

HERBERT T. KEYSER.—Numbered among the successful alfalfa growers of eastern Contra Costa County is the name of Herbert T. Keyser, who by his long and close identification with the agricultural interests of the county is looked up to as an authority on the subject of alfalfa growing. He has proven, by the results of his many years devoted to this special crop, that he thoroughly understands the requirements of raising alfalfa.

H. T. Keyser was born in Niagara County, N. Y., June 27, 1865, the son of Jacob and Amanda Keyser, both natives of New York State, where they were married. The family moved to Wisconsin, thence to Michigan and from there, in 1874, migrated to California, settling in the San Joaquin valley. Later they removed to El Dorado County, where Herbert T. Keyser remained three years; then he went to live with his aunt, Mrs. S. M. Wills, near Byron, Contra Costa County. After working for wages for several years Mr. Keyser became manager of the Butterwick place, owned by Vernon Taylor, and continued in this position for eleven years. In 1907 he purchased his present ranch of 162 acres on the Byron-Brentwood Highway and here he has developed one of the best alfalfa ranches in the county. In 1913 Mr. Keyser bought his home place of two and a half acres in Taylor Lane, and the following year built his home, where he now lives.

The first marriage of H. T. Keyser occurred in 1900 when he was united with Mary McKenzie. On September 10, 1919, he was married to Miss Jessie Rhoades, a native of England, who was brought to Tracy, Cal., when six months old, lived there until nine years of age, and then removed to Contra Costa County. The genealogy of the Keyser family dates back to pre-Revolutionary days when Great-grandfather Keyser emigrated from Holland to America; he had the distinction of being with General George Washington at Valley Forge. Herbert T. Keyser is a self-made man and his commendable success has been the result of his own efforts, as early in life he became dependent upon his own resources. By energetic, persistent and patient efforts, economical living, an optimistic and enterprising spirit, coupled with uprightness of character, he has won success in his chosen occupation, and has the esteem of the community where he has resided for so many years.

LEANDER JOHNSON.—A resident of the United States since 1900, and of Contra Costa County since 1901, when he located in Martinez, Leander Johnson there lived and labored for nine years, then moved to Richmond and made that his home for six years, after which he located in El Cerrito on the place he now occupies. Well he remembers the early condition of this section when he first saw the county. He has followed carpentering and building and house moving ever since he came here, his work taking him to the various bay cities and throughout Contra Costa County. For the easier conduct of his business he has a full equipment of tools, trucks, timbers, etc., and employs several men according to the size of his job. He believes in progress along all lines, especially good schools, and is giving his children the very best educations he can afford.

Born in Hapbaranda, Northern Sweden, on November 3, 1878, he attended the schools of his locality until he was fifteen. His father was a carpenter, boat builder and all-round workman and for several years followed the sea as a ship carpenter and touched at many ports. He and his wife spent their days in their native land. At the age of fifteen Leander joined a ship's crew as a ship carpenter, having followed in his father's footsteps; when he was twelve he had built a boat. During his time at sea he touched at Java and many ports of the Old World, worked in New Zealand for a time building boats, then went to Australia where he worked as a ship builder at Natural Park, some sixty miles from Sidney. He was a fine workman but could not understand English and consequently his employer paid him less than his worth; and when he asked for what was his due, it was denied him and he left and worked on his own hook in Sidney for a time. He then took ship and worked his way to the Hawaiian Islands, and after a time there came on a four-master to San Francisco. Leaving the deep water he took to the coasting trade. Then leaving the sea entirely he worked as a millwright in Oroville and in Santa Cruz. He had a friend in the chemical works in Martinez and came to join him and to find employment, which he did at the building business. It was in Martinez that he bought an equipment and began moving buildings. Selling out he came down to Richmond and followed contracting, later going back to house moving till 1913, when he located at his present home. He owns two houses in Richmond which he rents. He is well satisfied with his home in Contra Costa County.

Mr. Johnson was married in Sweden when he was twenty-one, in 1899, to Miss Emma Erickson and they have had six children. The oldest child, a son named John Hilmar, was born in Sweden and was six months old when his father left home; he grew up there, making his home with his mother's people; he is married and has a family, never having come to this country. It was while he was working at Oroville that Mr. Johnson sent for his wife, and she arrived in 1903. Five of their children are natives of Contra Costa County and are: Hilma, a graduate of the Richmond High School and now attending the University

Hans Jensing

of California at Berkeley; Herbert, a graduate of the Richmond High School, Class 1924, now assisting his father; Harve and Hugo, both students at the Richmond High School; and Signe, in the Union High at Richmond.

HANS JENSEN.—When Hans Jensen located in Contra Costa County, some thirty-seven years ago, there was little to suggest the prosperity which he himself has helped to bring about; for his influence has always been of a forceful and progressive nature. Though seventy-five years of age, Mr. Jensen is still strong and active, but he has now practically turned over the operation of his large landholdings to his son. For the past nine years he has been serving as a government reporter on weather, crops, etc., for this section of the county. He was born in Denmark on June 19, 1851, a son of Jens and Annie (Mortinsen) Jensen, who were born, reared, and married in Denmark, and died in their native land.

When eighteen years old, Hans Jensen entered the Danish army, and at that time was the youngest recruit in the service. On January 13, 1873, he landed in New York City; and from there he went to Racine, Wis., where he worked at various pursuits. While residing in Wisconsin he took out his first naturalization papers, in 1873. He went to Indianapolis in 1874 and worked in a spoke factory, and in 1875 he came to California, arriving in San Francisco on June 13. He was engaged for the next four years as a driver and street car conductor from Seventh Street to the Cemetery, and for eleven years he worked for A. K. P. Harmon as assistant gardener.

In 1876 Hans Jensen was married to Karen Christine Hansen, also a native of Denmark, and to them were born five children. Dorothea is at home with her father. Hannah, Mrs. Nilsen, is now deceased. Louise married Robert Kearns, an employe of the Southern Pacific in Oakland. Martin, a prosperous rancher, bought 160 acres from his father and rents and farms the balance of 300 acres; he married Miss Marguerite Quinn, daughter of J. E. Quinn, D. V. S., of Antioch, and they have one child, Clara. May married Alfred Miller and lives in Oakland. Mrs. Jensen passed away at the family home on March 3, 1921.

Mr. Jensen, as above stated, has sold 160 acres to his son, Martin. Besides this, he has sold ten acres to the East Bay Water Company and four and one-half acres to the Standard Oil Company, besides donating the right of way to the City of Antioch Water Company. Mr. Jensen completed his American citizenship in Oakland in 1879, and in politics is a stanch Republican.

CYRUS NEWLOVE.—Ever since establishing his home in Contra Costa County, Cyrus Newlove has made agriculture his chosen occupation. His speciality at first was the raising of grain, but for a number of years past he has devoted his attention to raising almonds. He was born in Wood County, Ohio, near Toledo, on March 27, 1866. His father,

James Newlove, was an Ohio pioneer, and served through the Civil War as a Union defender. He married Miss Catherine Stull. The family moved to Flora, Ill., when our subject was a lad of eight years, and he attended public school and in time became a teacher. He taught three years in Illinois before coming to California in 1892. He spent three years in Yolo County, and after settling in Contra Costa County, in 1895, he taught at Iron House for a while, but gave most of his attention to the development of his ranch, from which today he enjoys a comfortable livelihood. His ranch consists of 200 acres of fine productive soil, on which is a very highly cultivated almond orchard, while the balance is devoted to general farming. The Southern Pacific railroad runs through his ranch and the station of Neroly is near his residence, thus affording a fine shipping point for all produce raised on his ranch and others in the vicinity.

Mr. Newlove has never married, but by his quiet and efficient business methods he has won a host of friends and has come to be counted among the most highly esteemed citizens of his section, where he is deservedly popular. He is a consistent Republican in politics, and is a member of the Farm Bureau of Live Oak. Mr. Newlove was among the early settlers here. No improvements had been made in this district when he came, and he is among the pioneers who helped clear the land.

GEORGE ALBERT JOHNSON.—The progressive spirit, wise conservatism and keen foresight of George Albert Johnson have won for him a notable position among the best known and successful educators in Contra Costa County. He was born in Yuba County on September 13, 1877, and is a son of George W. and Louise (Sailor) Johnson, both of Missouri but who came to California early in life and established a home and reared their family of six children, of whom three sons and one daughter are living, George A. being the youngest son. He attended the public schools in Yuba County and completed his training in a private institution, where he pursued the normal course. To keep abreast of the times he has done post-graduate work in the University of California and is now specializing in law in Golden Gate College in San Francisco.

Mr. Johnson began his school work in Yuba County in 1898 as a teacher and was prominently connected with all educational affairs there, serving for two terms as president of the county board of education of Yuba County. To better his condition Mr. Johnson came to Crockett in 1913 to become principal of the grammar school, and ever since that period his whole time and attention have been directed along the lines of raising the standard of education in this growing community and he has taken a very aggressive part in all school activities all over Contra Costa County, serving at various times in positions of leadership, and now being president of the county board of education. One of the main projects with which Mr. Johnson has been identified has been the union of the Crockett and Valona grammar schools, for which bonds were voted for the erection of a modern school building at a cost of $250,000; also he was active in promoting the bond issue for $450,000 for the new John Swett Union High School building at Crockett. It has been his pleasure to witness the rapid growth of the schools in this community and the county board of education is now working on and perfecting a course of study best adapted to the needs of the pupils.

Mr. Johnson is closely associated with the boy-welfare movement, and for a number of years has served as scout master. During the World War, under his direction, the Boy Scouts and the grammar school pupils distinguished themselves in selling thrift stamps and otherwise promoting the war activities to win the struggle. He is in sympathy with all movements of town and county that tend to an upward growth, and higher community interests that make for better citizenship. As he has prospered Mr. Johnson has invested in property in Crockett and vicinity and owns his own home here.

It was on November 25, 1903, that George Albert Johnson took for his bride, Miss Ivy Kumle, born in California of parents who were also natives of the State. This marriage resulted in the birth of six children, one of whom is deceased. Alton is twenty-one, has graduated from high school and is employed in the First National Bank in Crockett. Audrey is nineteen, has completed the high school and is taking a special course in night school in Oakland, working in a store during the day. George Beverly is eighteen and a graduate of the Class of 1926, Crockett High School. Lola and Margaret attend the grammar school. A nephew of Mr. Johnson, Louis J. Blodgett, distinguished himself during the World War in the Marines and lost his life at the Battle of the Marne on October 4, 1917. Two brothers of Mr. Johnson still make their homes in Yuba County and there is a sister living in San Francisco.

C. L. LINDQUIST.—Apricots and prunes are the two resources to which C. L. Lindquist has devoted his energies since purchasing his sixty-acre home place nine years ago. As his name and personal characteristics indicate, Mr. Lindquist is of Swedish ancestry. He was born in central Sweden on October 2, 1870. His parents were well-to-do farmers who, at their death, left a good-sized estate to their two sons, our subject and his brother John Alfred, who also owns a farm of thirty acres in this same vicinity and now makes his home with our subject.

Mr. Lindquist attended the common schools in his native land, and when sixteen years of age came to America and for seven years lived in Hudson, Wis. In 1894 he came to California, settling at Vacaville, where he later bought land and was one of the original members of the Vacaville Fruit Company. Nine years ago he located in the Lone Tree District of Contra Costa County, purchasing sixty acres, but later sold off twenty acres. This ranch is in the section of the county where the land is known as heavy land and was considered unsuited for fruit-growing. Mr. Lindquist has demonstrated that this land will not only grow fruit trees, but that the trees are particularly productive. His young apricot trees yield from five to six tons per acre of the very finest fruit. Mr. Lindquist has made substantial improvements on his ranch, building a good house and other necessary buildings; and his orchard, which was one of the very first in this locality, is bringing him splendid returns for his careful labor. In 1921 he bought twenty acres one-half mile south of his home place, and this he set to apricots.

In 1895 Mr. Lindquist was married to Miss Annie Swanson, also a native of Sweden; and they are the parents of one daughter, Lillian Charlotte, a graduate of the Oakland High School. Mr. Lindquist became a naturalized citizen at Hudson, Wis., in 1894. He was brought up in the Lutheran faith. Fraternally, he belongs to the Masons at Vacaville, Cal.; and in politics he is a Republican. He is a member, and in 1925 was a director, of the East Contra Costa Chamber of Commerce; and is a director of the Lone Tree Irrigation District, and a director of the Lone Tree Shipping Association, which was organized in 1926.

MATTEO IMERONE.—A leading citizen and business man of Crockett is Matteo Imerone, who owns and operates one of the largest and most up-to-date bakeries in this part of Contra Costa County. He is a very progressive citizen and gives his support and cooperation to all worthy projects for the upbuilding of the county and State. Mr. Imerone was born in Italy, near the city of Touraine on October 8, 1880, a son of Giovanni Imerone, who was a baker by trade, as was his father before him, hence it is but natural that Matteo should follow in the footsteps of his sires. He was a pupil in the public schools of his native town and grew up in the bakery business, working with his father from the time he was old enough to do anything until he had mastered every detail of the trade and felt competent to go out into the world on his own responsibility. In 1902 he came to the New World and after arriving in New York came directly to San Francisco and found employment at once. He continued as a wage earner and attended night school in order better to carry out the tasks he was to undertake about two years later, when he came across the bay and opened a bakery in Oakland on Jefferson Street between Fifth and Sixth. From the beginning he met with good success and he carried on his business there until selling out in 1908. While he was carrying on his business he attended night school in Oakland and soon mastered English enough to express himself in that tongue.

In 1907 he was looking about the central part of the State for a growing town in which to locate, and after spending considerable time decided that Valona held just what he was looking for and he made a permanent location in the town and bought out a small bakery and began to build up a business. Four years later he was to lose considerable as his business was destroyed by fire. He next secured the property on the opposite side of the street where was located a grocery store. He bought the property, closed out the grocery stock, and installed the most modern machinery and appliances to carry on and develop a trade in bakery goods, and today his judgment has been justified, for he was able, with the help of seven employees, and the operation of three motor-driven machines and a truck, to extend his wholesale and retail business from Pinole to Bay Point. The capacity of the Valona Bakery is about 2500 loaves of bread per day, and he turns out all kinds of plain and fancy bakery goods that are noted for their wholesome qualities.

When Mr. Imerone married in 1902, in his home town in Italy, he chose for his wife Miss Theresa Gallo, who has proven a worthy helpmate. This marriage has resulted in three children: Eva, a graduate of Heald's Business College of Oakland, is assisting her father in his business; Lillie, a graduate of the Crockett High School, Class of 1926, is now taking a teacher's course in the Oakland Normal; Harry is attending the Valona John Swett High School. Mr. Imerone received his citizenship papers in 1908 in Oakland. Fraternally he is a member of the Eagles and the I. D. E. S., both of Crockett, and the Elks of Vallejo. Since coming to Crockett he has been identified with all movements for bettering the condition of the people and was at the front when the movement for incorporating Valona and Crockett was started, though it did not succeed at that time. He is a very active member of the Crockett-Valona Business Men's Association, and a fire commissioner of the Carquinez fire district. As he has prospered he has shown his faith in his adopted town by investing in property and owns some valuable business and residential property besides his own place of business, which is a two-story stucco building, erected in 1926, containing his bakery and residence. He is a shrewd business man and tries to live up to the Golden Rule as nearly as possible. In politics he is a stanch Republican. It is to such men as Mr. Imerone that Contra Costa County owes much of its prosperity.

WILLIAM W. HUTCHISON.—A well-known operator of dredges in the Delta country is W. W. Hutchison, of Antioch, who is one of the pioneers in reclamation work in this part of the State and has executed many large contracts in Contra Costa County. He was born in Stockton, January 26, 1892, the son of John D. and Annie Beatrice (Titherington) Hutchison. His father was born in Montreal, Canada, of English parents; the mother was born in England. Although they have a fine home in San Francisco, most of their time is spent on their ranch near Marysville, Cal. The father is aged sixty-five years, and the mother fifty-four years. There are three daughters: Dorothy, who married J. Goddard, a newspaper man in Fresno; Norma, wife of Shirley Truitt, a ship designer in San Francisco; and Melva, wife of Dr. J. Raphael, of Oakland. Both parents came to California when young, and were married in this State. J. D. Hutchison is a pioneer reclamation expert and was captain of the first dredger ever built in

California, which was used on Staten Island for Mr. Hagin. He was one of the first men to undertake the reclamation of land. At that time he was employed by J. B. Hagin in Staten Island and had 500 Chinamen under him, working with shovel and wheelbarrows, building levees. They were paid seventy-five cents per day of eleven hours and boarded themselves. He was very successful with the work in this way until the acreage became so large that other methods had to be used to build higher levees, and the dredges were then introduced. He led a very active life along the Sacramento and San Joaquin Rivers and is well-known by the early settlers of the Delta section. When he sold out his business to his son, he bought a fine piece of land on the Feather River bottoms and cleared it from the jungles, and now has 225 acres of fine productive land. His work as an independent dredger operator began in 1911 and continued till 1915, with headquarters at Antioch. This company was known as the Sacramento Dredging and Ditching Company, a close corporation, and in the latter year W. W. Hutchison succeeded to the business, his father retiring to his ranch in Yuba County.

W. W. Hutchison came to Antioch in 1901 and went through the grammar school, after which he spent two years at the Riverview High School. In the mornings and evenings, and on days when he was not in school, he worked as a chore boy on ranches in order to pay his way in school. On the ranch of Mrs. Von Baum part of his duties was to milk from four to ten cows and deliver the milk in Antioch to customers before school, and this he followed up for three years. In this way he earned his board and room when attending school. Suffice it to say that he appreciates the value of educational advantages. When older and with a little capital, our subject bought out the Peterson Plow and Agricultural Implement Works at Antioch, as the Hutchison and the Sacramento Dredging and Ditching Company had a great deal of blacksmithing to do and took it to this place. After getting possession of the plant Mr. Hutchison installed labor-saving machinery and equipped it in the most modern way, and for several years made $10,000 worth of plows and implements for the trade. When the tractors lessened the demand for the Peterson Plows the business was sold, in 1922.

In 1915 W. W. Hutchison bought out all the stockholders in the Sacramento Dredging and Ditching Company, and since then has been sole owner. He has two to four good outfits at work nearly all the time. Two outfits were at work for two years on the Arboga system, for the Fleishhacker interests. He constructed the irrigation and drainage system on the Pescadero Ranch near Tracy, reclaiming some 4000 acres and putting in fourteen miles of canals and twenty-six miles of laterals. In 1920 a partnership was formed with D. O. Jordan, who bought a half interest in one outfit, and operates under the name of Hutchison & Jordan, with headquarters at Stockton. During 1920, 1921, and 1922 they rebuilt the drainage system on Grand Island, a $25,000 contract which took ten months to complete. During 1923, 1924, and 1925

Mr. Hutchison did a great amount of work for the Edmonds Reclaimed Land Company on 2000 acres of Clear Lake in Lake County, handling 250,000 cubic yards of dirt. He reclaimed 1000 acres on Long Point Island for C. A. Lauritzen, now used as a gun club. He also dredged Ellis Lake at Marysville. Mr. Hutchison gives employment to from sixteen to fifty men, according to the size of his contracts.

On November 30, 1915, William W. Hutchison was married in San Francisco to Miss Teresa Bergantz, of Placerville, the daughter of an old pioneer of that place. They have had the following children: William W., Jr.; Marion Jean, who died at four years of age; and John Robert, Paul Clifford, and Charles Theodore. Mr. Hutchison is a member and Past Master of Antioch Lodge No. 175, F. & A. M. (1918), and belongs to the Royal Arch Masons, the Eastern Star and the Sciots, and also to the Vallejo Elks. Mrs. Hutchison is a member of the Eastern Star Chapter. Politically, Mr. Hutchison is a Republican. The family belong to the Congregational Church in Antioch. Like all native sons of this day and age, Mr. Hutchison is deeply interested in the preservation of the old landmarks and early history of California and the great Northwest.

PETER LARSEN.—A resident of El Cerrito since 1912, Peter Larsen has lived at the corner of Oak Street and Central Avenue for thirteen years and has watched the gradual growth of this district, indeed has aided very materially in its growth by following the building business. He was born at Trondhjem, Norway, on April 13, 1880, attended the public schools in the farming country where he lived, and worked on the farm until he was eighteen, then spent two years at the carpenter trade. He had remembered the description of various countries when he was studying history in school and decided he wanted to go to Australia, accordingly he shipped as a sailor before the mast and went around the world, but when the ship touched the Australian port the crew were not given any money and he did not want to desert the vessel, so he came with it to San Francisco, landing in 1902. During his life as a sailor he was employed on ships of almost every nation. Arriving in California he went into the coasting trade and worked on vessels plying from Puget Sound to San Diego. In 1905 Mr. Larsen entered the quartermaster's department of the U. S. Government on vessels plying between the Philippine Islands and Pacific Coast ports. Meeting with an accident that same year, he made San Francisco his headquarters, and when able to work returned to the carpenter's trade, which he has continued up to the present time, meeting with good success in his operations.

In 1911 Mr. Larsen was united in marriage at Oakland, with Miss Dagny Andersen, born at Christiania, Norway. Now that he had formed domestic ties Mr. Larson looked about for a suitable place to establish a home and decided upon Rust, at the county line. He bought property and erected his home and began to work for the betterment of local conditions and take an active interest in the community life. He worked hard for the incorporation of a city, which was called El Cerrito, was elected a member of the first board of trustees and put in four years on the board. The first two years he was a member of the Health and Safety Committee, and the second two years on Streets, Highways, Park and Sidewalk Committee. In 1912 he became an American citizen in San Francisco and ever since has voted the Republican ticket at national elections. He belongs to the Gustav Vasa society of Richmond. The marriage of Mr. and Mrs. Larsen has been blessed with one daughter, Clara Marie, a graduate of the Richmond Junior High School, Class of 1926.

CLARENCE M. SHOEMAKER.—The superintendent of the California Wharf & Warehouse Company at Brentwood is Clarence M. Shoemaker, one of the most highly esteemed men in eastern Contra Costa County. He is secretary and treasurer of the Brentwood Hall Association which erected the Masonic Temple in 1924. The officers besides Mr. Shoemaker are Judge Robert Wallace, Jr., president; O. C. Prewett, vice-president; and these with William Estes, comprise the board of trustees. Mr. Shoemaker is a member of Brentwood Lodge No. 345, F. & A. M., and serves as its treasurer; he also belongs to Pyramid No. 24, Sciots, in Antioch. He is an up-to-date rancher, with all his other interests, and is developing a sixty-acre tract of land near Brentwood. This is planted to walnuts, now coming into bearing.

C. M. Shoemaker was born at Bainbridge, Ohio, on January 7, 1885, and was graduated from the Bainbridge High School, after which he took a college course, in the meantime taking the United States Civil Service examination for first-class clerical work. Passing satisfactorily, he entered the government employ, spent two years in Iowa, and then came on to California. Six months were spent in the government offices in San Francisco, and then he was sent to Washington and from 1905 to 1907 was connected with the office end of the work done by the government on the jetties. One year was spent in the transfer work, and he then entered the forestry service in the office in Willows. In 1915 Mr. Shoemaker went to Idaho and improved a ranch, and at the same time was a court reporter at Gooding, Idaho, for two years. While there he became well acquainted with Governor Gooding. He returned to California in 1917, and has since been in charge of the Balfour-Guthrie interests at Brentwood. Besides his work for the company, Mr. Shoemaker finds time to assist in the development of worth-while projects for the advancement of his locality.

C. M. Shoemaker was united in marriage at Vallejo, Cal., on February 5, 1915, with Miss Estella Danner, born in Colusa of a family that came to this State from Ohio. They have a daughter, Eleanor E. The family live in Brentwood in a house owned by the Balfour-Guthrie Co.

Lulu L. Di Betta

LULU L. DI BETTA.—An accomplished and enterprising business woman, Lulu L. Di Betta is devoting her time and energies to the management of her drug store located at Main and Castro Streets, in Martinez. She is the eldest in a family of seven children born to John F. and Cecil (Musacchia) Di Betta, both natives of Italy. Her father was a barber by trade, being thus occupied for many years; but on account of his failing health, in 1918 the family removed to California from New Orleans and they now reside at Martinez.

Miss Lulu L. Di Betta was born in New Orleans, La., and there attended public school, finishing the eighth grade. Then she quit for the purpose of attending to her part of the business which the mother and three daughters had established, known as The Three Sisters' Store. In this business Miss Di Betta developed into a first-class drygoods and shoe buyer; and thus a foundation was laid for her success in future years. Adjoining The Three Sisters' Store in New Orleans was a drug store, and not content with her lot, she conceived the idea of becoming a pharmacist. In order to matriculate at the New Orleans College of Pharmacy she was required to have a high school education. Nothing daunted, she took the high school course at night school, passed her examinations creditably, and then entered the College of Pharmacy, from which she was duly graduated. She filled a number of positions in New Orleans, and when she came to Martinez in 1918 she took the state board examinations in pharmacy and was soon established in the responsible position of pharmacist in the Contra Costa Drug Store in Martinez, where she worked steadily for four and a half years. The close confinement began to tell on her health, however; so she gave up her position and took a trip back to her native city on a visit to friends and relatives. The following item taken from the New Orleans, La., "Modern Druggist" of March, 1920, gives an idea of the high esteem in which Miss Di Betta was held in her native city.

"A welcome visitor is Miss Lulu L. Di Betta, clever young New Orleans druggist, whom her confreres have missed since her departure to California. Her parents reside in Martinez, Cal., where Miss Di Betta is the owner of her own drug store. That town, only fifty miles from San Francisco, has a population of 4000, with only three drug stores, all of which are prosperous. One may be sure, with this attractive girl, the only woman druggist in the town, the Di Betta store is the most thriving of all! Miss Di Betta is a graduate of the New Orleans College of Pharmacy, 1917, and is registered in both Louisiana and California. She clerked at Mrs. Jahn's beautiful pharmacy in New Orleans for two years, where she made hosts of friends by her ingratiating manners, ready sympathy and skill. Her arrival in February created a general jubliee in drugdom."

Miss Di Betta adheres to the Catholic faith and is a member of the Young Ladies' Institute at Martinez. She belongs to the Rebekah Lodge, and in politics is a Republican.

JAMES HOBSON.—The accommodating proprietor of the auto service company in Antioch known as Chase's Stable, with headquarters at 241 I Street, is James Hobson, a native son of the county, born at Judsonville, at the Empire Coal Mine, of pioneer parents who are mentioned in the sketch of Mrs. Mary A. Dickinson on another page of this history. After attending the public schools, Jim Hobson, as he is familiarly called, started out to fight life's battles for himself; and he has worked at many kinds of labor during his active career. He farmed at Oakdale, in Stanislaus County, for a time, operating 5000 acres, raising wheat and grazing stock. He met with ordinary results in this field of activity and then went to Oakland and became foreman for the Spring Construction Company, and worked at macadamizing and grading the streets in Oakland in 1907. In 1908 he took his work stock and equipment and went to Pleasanton and graded the roadbed for the Western Pacific Railroad from Pleasanton to Sunol. His next work was done in building the levees on Old River near Tracy, working 100 head of stock, which he owned. He then began reclamation work on Tyler Island for Mr. McCormick, and the following year worked on Winters Island. He then came to Pittsburg and contracted for making the first streets in the town, and later became foreman for Mr. Swain, who was grading and macadamizing the streets in Antioch. His next venture was made in partnership with H. G. Preston in the Chase Livery Stable, which was then in its heyday of activity. They had seventy-five horses and sent out livery rigs of all kinds. It was Antioch's leading livery stable for many years. When the truck, tractor and automobile came into use to supplant the horse, Mr. Preston took up the undertaking business and Mr. Hobson began to build up his auto service business; and in this he has succeeded far beyond his expectations. He runs four auto busses that ply between Pittsburg and Antioch and runs on regular schedule to accommodate the employees of the various industrial plants who live at Antioch.

Mr. Hobson is well liked and has a host of friends. He is a member of the Antioch Odd Fellows Lodge and of the Stockton Elks.

JESSE CLARENCE HITCHCOCK.—A popular native son and the efficient manager of the Richmond office of the Pacific Gas & Electric Company, Jesse Clarence Hitchcock is looked upon as one of the leading citizens of Contra Costa County. He was born at Nevada City, Nevada County, on September 23, 1874, a son of Joseph B. and Rebecca (Sears) Hitchcock, natives of Illinois and Ohio, respectively. The father drove across the plains and arrived at Sacramento in 1851, and then went to the mines in Nevada County and followed prospecting and mining at Cement Hill and at Round Mountain. The mother came to California on one of the first through continental trains in 1869, and was married in California to Mr. Hitchcock. Their children were: Jesse C., of this review; Elmer Rich, lives in Oakland and is the father of a son; Sabra, Mrs. Fred Hallett, of Sacramento; William lives in Oakland and has a daughter; Alameda, Mrs. Charles Walker, of Sacramento has seven children; Clara, married William Sherman, has a son and a daughter and resides in Sacramento; Adella, became the wife of James Jackson and lives in Oakland; Josephine, married Edward Snell, a dentist in Hollister, and has a son; Grace, Mrs. Clarence Bond, has four children and lives at Woodland. These children were reared in California and have made names and places for themselves in their respective homes.

Jesse C. Hitchcock attended the public schools in Nevada County and took a course in power and lighting. His first work was in the West Harmony gravel mine, where he remained about four years and obtained considerable experience. He then went to the Ragon mines as hoist engineer and blacksmith for a year; then to the Milligan mines for another year; and then to the Home quartz mine on Deer Creek and remained four years. He was advanced from time to time and during the course of his mining experience filled many important posts, for a time being head timberman. A short time was spent in Tonopah, Nev., and also as an independent prospector on his own claim in Nevada County, Cal. Finding that the task of mining for precious metal was an uncertain quantity, Mr. Hitchcock went to Oakland and entered the employ of the Oakland Gas, Light & Heat Company in August, 1904. This company later became the California Gas & Electric Company and was finally merged with the Pacific Gas & Electric Company, one of the largest concerns of its kind in the State. Mr. Hitchcock has remained through the various changes and has become one of their dependable employees.

His first work with the Bay Counties Light & Power Company was in 1898, and consisted of the building of their dam that made Lake Vera, and the ditch down to the Rome powerhouse. He then was foreman of the crew putting in the pole line to Grass Valley, and also helped to install the second machine at the Rome Power plant. He next put in seven months at Bear Valley, then came back to Grass Valley, and later to Oakland, all in the interests of his company, then known as the Bay Counties Power Company. This brings him to the time of his arrival at Oakland, before mentioned. In 1905 he was made foreman of construction and in 1910 was transferred to Richmond, then a fast-growing city. In 1919 Mr. Hitchcock was promoted to the responsible position of agent for the P. G. & E. in Richmond, the position he now holds. When he came here there were only twenty-nine people and concerns being served by his company and this has increased until about 6000 are on their books and the number still increasing. The necessary office force has been enlarged to meet the demands of the business.

On September 20, 1896, Jesse C. Hitchcock and Miss Kathryn Hodge, of Grass Valley, were united in marriage. Her father and mother were Thomas and Delia Hodge, who had a family of twelve children, nine of them now living, viz.: Alex, John, Philip, Samuel, Louisa, Mary, Kathryn, Lavinia and Elizabeth. Sarah, Richard and Thomas Hodge are deceased. Of the marriage of Mr. and Mrs. Hitchcock two children have been born: Jesse C., Jr., married Miss Beatrice Phelps and they have a daughter, Lurline D.; Lurline is now Mrs. Daniel Bradley. Mr. Hitchcock is prominent in fraternal circles and is a member and Past Grand of the local lodge of Odd Fellows; and is a Past District Deputy Grand Master of the Grand Lodge; is a member of and served as president of the Odd Fellows Hall Association in 1924-1925; belongs to the Encampment and the Rebekahs of the I. O. O. F.; also to Richmond Lodge No. 1251, B. P. O. E.; McKinley Lodge No. 347, F. & A. M. He is a charter member of the Rotary Club in Richmond; also belongs to the Chamber of Commerce. Mr. Hitchcock takes an active part in all civic affairs and is a strong booster for Richmond and the Bay section. He is a good mixer and is prominent in social circles and athletics. He says "I have never quit a job that I could not go back to, nor quit working for a man without giving him due notice."

WILLIAM HAMMOND.—An enterprising ranchman of Contra Costa County, located in the Lone Tree District, is William Hammond, who was born near Marshall, Calhoun County, Mich., on November 20, 1862, a son of Gen. William Hammond. The latter was a native of New York, but a pioneer of Michigan, and during the Civil War was quartermaster general of Michigan. He married Miss Sarah L. Turner, born at Batavia, N. Y., and eight children were born to them. The father died in 1866 at the age of fifty-two years. In 1870 the mother, with five of the children, came to California and settled in Santa Clara. In 1915 she passed away in San Jose, having reached the advanced age of ninety-six.

William Hammond was a lad of eight years when he came to California. He attended the public school in Santa Clara and at the age of fifteen was apprenticed to learn the carriage-painting trade. After completing his apprenticeship he returned to Michigan and worked at his trade until 1892.

At Jackson, Mich., on April 25, 1889, Mr. Hammond was married to Miss Berta Landon, born near Rochester, N. Y., a daughter of Daniel Landon. In 1892 Mr. Hammond returned to California with his wife and daughter and settled in San Jose, where he was employed by the Santa Clara County Fruit Exchange as bookkeeper and general office man, remaining with them for thirteen years. In 1906 the family removed to Berkeley to give the daughter the advantage of a university education. In 1912 Mr. and Mrs. Hammond came to Contra Costa County and bought their present home place of ten acres, which is set to almonds. They rebuilt the house and barn, erected eight 8-pen poultry houses, incubator and brooder houses, etc., and now run from 1200 to 2000 pure-bred Rhode Island Reds. They have made a distinct success of their business; one cafeteria in Oakland takes all their dressed poultry, eggs and almonds.

Mr. and Mrs. Hammond have two children. Mrs. Sarah H. Kelley is in business in Santa Rosa; she has two children, Marion and Peter. William Landon is a rancher near Knightsen. He served in the 103rd

Ammunition Corps, 28th Division, during the World War, spending one year in France in active duty, and was honorably discharged in San Francisco in 1919. He also is married.

Both Mr. and Mrs. Hammond take a lively interest in all community work, Mr. Hammond serving as secretary of the Lone Tree Farm Center, while Mrs. Hammond is doing volunteer work in teaching sewing to the girls of the Brentwood Grammar School. They are both members of the Brentwood Methodist Episcopal Church.

SAM HILL.—Among the native sons of California, and since 1920 a resident in Contra Costa County, the name of Sam Hill stands prominent as that of a man who has rendered inestimable service toward the upbuilding and advancement of the community in which he makes his home. He is a man of good business principles, broad-minded and liberal, well versed on all current subjects, and enjoys to an exceptional degree the good will and appreciation of all who know him. As editor and publisher of the Brentwood News, a weekly paper which has a large circulation, he is giving to the community the most necessary adjunct toward growth and prosperity. He has had forty years experience in newspaper work and in all things he is progressive; his job and newspaper presses are the most modern obtainable, both electrically driven, and all the work he turns out is first class in every particular. In 1926 he put in a modern Mergenthaler Linotype Model No. 5 to add to his equipment.

Sam Hill was born at Downieville, Cal., January 27, 1876, a son of Harvey D. and Tryphena C. (Hall) Hill. Harvey D. Hill, Sr., was born in New Hampshire and was four years old when he was brought to California by his parents Samuel D. and Elizabeth (Giddings) Hill, natives of Vermont and England, respectively. Grandmother Hill was descended from the Peabody family of England and lived to be eighty-six years old; while grandfather Hill was eighty-four years old when he died. H. D. Hill, the father of our subject, followed mining at Downieville, then he became a telegraph operator, and for a time was publisher of a newspaper. He removed to Vallejo and became one of the head men in the Government's store, having charge of the refining of silver and other metals for the Government. He passed away in Vallejo on February 11, 1923, aged seventy-four years. Sam is the fourth child in a family of five children; Harvey D. Jr., lives in Dunsmuir; Charles A., conducts a battery shop in San Francisco; John C., resides in Vallejo; Sam; and May is now the wife of Harold McNeill, an electrician in Vallejo. The mother of this family makes her home with her son John C. Hill in Vallejo and she has reached the age of seventy-three years.

The schooling of Sam Hill was limited, for he was only ten years old when he entered upon his first position in a newspaper office as messenger boy in the office of the Mountain Messenger in Downieville, and was there for seven years. He was seventeen years old when he took charge of a newspaper in Sierraville, but disposed of it in a short time and went to Siskiyou County and worked on a paper at Etna Mills. Then he went to Sacramento and found employment in the State Printing Office. From Sacramento he went to Sisson, now called Shasta, and there he bought the Sisson Mirror, which he operated for the next eight years or until a destructive fire interrupted his operations and he removed to Dunsmuir. There he owned and operated the Dunsmuir News for fourteen and a half years when he sold out and went to Vallejo. For a time he worked on the Vallejo Chronicle, then went to Berkeley and bought a half interest in a job printing office, but remained there but a short time when he went to Antioch and worked on the Antioch Tribune for five months. In 1920 he purchased the Brentwood News and he has been successful in its operation ever since.

Sam Hill was first married to Miss Annie A. Beard on July 3, 1898. She was the daughter of Judge J. S. Beard, for eighteen years superior judge of Siskiyou County. To them were born four children: the first were twins who died at birth; Winona E. is now Mrs. Lorenz Inman of Oakland; and John S. is associated with his father on the Brentwood News and is in his last year in high school. Mrs. Hill passed away on June 2, 1922. Mr. Hill was married the second time on April 4, 1924, to Miss Edna Heidorn, a sister of Judge Heidorn of Knightsen. Mrs. Hill is a graduate of the State Teachers' College at San Jose. She was principal of the Knightsen school for seven years prior to her marriage, and is still teaching. She is attracting attention as a newspaper writer of considerable ability. Mr. Hill is prominent in fraternal circles, being a member of Brentwood Lodge No. 345, F. & A. M.; Byron Lodge No. 335, I. O. O. F., and Pyramid No. 24, Sciots at Antioch. Mr. and Mrs. Hill are members of Maspha Chapter No. 198, O. E. S., of Brentwood, of which Mrs. Hill is Past Matron; they also belong to the Florence Knight Rebekah Lodge No. 264 of Byron. Mr. Hill is an adherent of the Episcopalian faith and in politics is a Republican.

MOTT C. PRESTON.—A well-educated man and a worthy son of his father, Mott C. Preston is following the even tenor of his way and gradually working his way to a position of influence in his home community. He was born July 16, 1882, on a ranch owned by his father in eastern Contra Costa County and grew up to farm work. His father furnished the land, four acres, for the Union Cemetery, one of the oldest cemeteries in this section of the county. Mott C. attended the Excelsior school in his home district and a business college in Stockton. Returning to the home ranch, he engaged in ranching with his father. With the passing of time he has accumulated considerable farming property, which is devoted to alfalfa and almonds. In 1910 he had forty acres in alfalfa, which he let mature for the seed and when threshed it yielded fourteen tons. This was the first alfalfa seed raised for commercial purposes in this district. Mr. Preston was led to attempt this undertaking from the results obtained in 1909, when he let half an acre go to seed and threshed out 1000 pounds with a flail. He now leases his land to tenants and is devoting his attention to the duties of road overseer of the Brentwood District, the Fifth Supervisoral district of the county, which position he has filled since 1922 with credit to himself and satisfaction of those who gave him the appointment. Together with his present work he farms fifty-five acres belonging to Mrs. Preston, a part of the old Shafer holdings in Knightsen Precinct, which is devoted to seed production. He owns the old Preston place of 133 acres, and also 137 acres which he bought from Peter Burdewick.

On October 12, 1904, Mott C. Preston married Miss Winifred Shafer, daughter of an old pioneer family of this county. Her mother, Elizabeth Shafer, is mentioned on another page of this work. Mr. Preston was a hard worker for the Byron-Bethany Irrigation project and was employed in the office of the company as assessor, tax collector and treasurer for four years. He is a member of the Odd Fellows and Native Sons of the Golden West, and with Mrs. Preston belongs to the Rebekahs, all in Byron. Both are highly respected and have a wide circle of friends.

ARTHUR ALBERT HUGHES.—One of the prosperous merchants of Richmond is Arthur Albert Hughes, whose grocery store is located at No. 1094 Twenty-third Street. He was born in Humboldt, Nebr., on July 3, 1889, the son of Arthur Albert and Jennie (Fritz) Hughes, natives of Lexington, Ky., and Ohio, respectively. The father was a photographer. The Hughes children were: Faye, who married Dr. Seids and had one child; Arthur A.; Walter and Donald. Our subject attended the public schools in Oklahoma and then took a three-years course in engineering at the University of Missouri at Columbia. His first work upon leaving college was in a cyanide plant in Arizona, at the same time that he was continuing his studies. His next position was with the Standard Oil Company at Richmond, Cal., in the refining department, and he remained with the company from 1913 until 1923, when he resigned to engage in his present grocery business. The change was very agreeable to him and he has been steadily building up a good trade. He gives employment to two people and runs a delivery truck to Giant, San Pablo and the surrounding territory. He belongs to the Merchants Association and politically registers as a Democrat.

In August, 1917, Mr. Hughes entered the service of the United States with the 91st Division, 363rd Infantry, went over seas, and saw active duty in France with his Division, which distinguished itself in action. He participated in the battles of St. Mihiel, Argonne, Flanders, Ypres and Lys. He was honorably discharged in April 1919. Mr. Hughes says he "would not have missed the war experience, but does not think he would want to repeat it."

On March 14, 1925, Mr. Hughes married Mrs. Marie (Westdin) Moore, a native daughter, born at Arcata, Cal. She has one brother, Theodore Westdin, of Richmond. A sister Tillie, who married Herbert

Brown, a prominent real estate dealer of Richmond and who opened the Brown-Andrade tract, was associated with her husband until his death in May, 1919. She continued her interest in business affairs until she died on December 22, 1925. Mrs. Hughes' mother is living in Richmond. By the marriage with Joseph Moore three children were born: Barbara, Joseph and James. Mrs. Hughes takes a live interest in civic affairs and has a wide circle of friends in Richmond. Mr. Hughes is a Mason and a Shriner, and belongs to the Elks. He is fond of athletics and automobiling.

HENRY W. HEIDORN.—One of the prominent merchants and fruit growers in the Knightsen Precinct is Henry W. Heidorn, who has a general merchandise store in Knightsen, catering to a trade extending all over his district, and also owns and manages a fifty-acre fruit ranch, and is a one-third owner in 240 acres under development, besides being a stockholder in three banks in eastern Contra Costa County.

Henry W. Heidorn was born in Contra Costa County on July 16, 1876, a son of Christopher Heidorn, a native of Germany, who came to America when a young man and settled on the Alfred Ranch near Knightsen. Three years later he bought 240 acres and began general farming on it, and set out several acres to fruits of various kinds. He was active up to the time of his death, on November 21, 1906, and the success to which he attained was won through his own unaided efforts. He was highly esteemed as an honest and upright man and willingly gave a helping hand to all those less fortunate than himself.

Henry W. Heidorn attended the public schools and grew to manhood on the farm. He supplemented his public-school education with a course in a business college in San Francisco, and then entered a general merchandise store in that city. From there he went to Crockett where he was one of the pioneer merchants, and later to Antioch. In January, 1904, he opened his store at Knightsen; and here has built up a flourishing business and holds the respect and confidence of all who know him. No project has been put before Mr. Heidorn for the benefit of the community in general without receiving his cooperation. He favors good schools and served as a school trustee for many years. He also served as a deputy county assessor for the Fifth District. He is an active Republican and has been a delegate to many county and State conventions of his party, and served as a member of the County Central Committee of Contra Costa County. Mr. Heidorn has served as justice of the peace for the past eight years. He was formerly postmaster at Knightsen and was one of the leading spirits in organizing the Knightsen Irrigation District. He is still a member of its board, and is also a director in the Eastern Contra Costa County Irrigation District.

Henry W. Heidorn was married on September 27, 1905, to Miss Helen Sutherland Johnston, born in San Francisco, a daughter of James and Helen C. Johnston. James Johnston was a prominent contractor in

Frank Ketelhut

San Francisco and died in 1910. Mrs. Heidorn served as postmaster of Knightsen for several years and was filling that office at the time of her death, on January 4, 1926. She had a large circle of friends who miss her wise counsel and companionship. Mr. Heidorn succeeded his wife as postmaster, resigning as justice of the peace. Mr. Heidorn has met with a justifiable degree of success and stands out as a leader in eastern Contra Costa County, where he has done so much to bring it to its present state of productiveness.

FRANK KETELHUT.—The remarkably successful career of Frank Ketelhut, proprietor of Ketelhut Bakery at 1228 Macdonald Avenue, Richmond, is an example of what may be accomplished by a man who makes a specialty of one trade or occupation when his efforts are characterized by strict economy and courteous and conscientious dealings with the public, coupled with judicious management of his financial affairs.

Frank Ketelhut was born at Putzig, Germany, on December 24, 1860, a son of Frederick and Dorothea Ketelhut, whose family consisted of three children. The father was a master baker and miller by trade. After Frank had finished his schooling and apprenticeship, at the age of seventeen he left home to make his own way in the world and went to Hamburg, Germany, to perfect his trade. After six months he went to London and secured a position as a baker, working eighteen hours a day for seven shillings ($1.75) per week, and boarding himself. But he soon secured a place at fifteen shillings per week, and at the end of six weeks was getting as much pay as a London "Bobbie," thirty shillings, and was foreman of the shop. After three years spent as a baker he decided that he wanted to learn the butcher's trade and worked at that trade for a time.

Wanting to see something of the world, he then concluded to go to sea and secured a position as assistant steward on the S. S. Mona, in the wine trade. In this position he visited the various ports on the Mediterranean Sea and during his first trip the steward died and Mr. Ketelhut was promoted to the position of steward, and upon his return received his papers as a full-fledged steward. His next position was as steward on the S. S. Tossa, of the Red Star Line, plying between Antwerp and South American ports under the Spanish flag. His great ambition was to gain knowledge, and these various positions gave him the opportunity, and the experience gained through them has been of great value in his later life. He had always had a desire to visit San Francisco, and when the opportunity came he took a position as cook on a sailing vessel and came around Cape Horn from London, the trip consuming 124 days, and arrived in that city in 1890. Securing a position as a baker, after three months he was made foreman of the largest bakery in San Francisco. From there he went to Bakersfield and remained four years, during which time he operated a bakery and bought and located oil properties and oil wells. At one time he was worth a quarter million dollars, of which he says he was robbed by his good friends, whom he had left in charge while on a business and prospecting trip to Alaska, they having entered into a conspiracy not to do the assessment work required and then jump his claims. They in turn were robbed by one of their co-conspirators who jumped the claims in his own name and sold them to the Monte Cristo Oil Company for $250,000 and failed to divide the money with the others. While he was in Alaska, Mr. Ketelhut went through all the hardships of the early propector and found no gold, but did find oil seepages more than a mile in width, but too far inland to be of any commercial value, for the cost of getting oil to market would be so great that it could not be handled at a profit. He believes that some day, when Alaska is developed, there will be enough oil there to supply the world for a long time. He also found great ledges of native copper. He further believes there is a great future for Alaska, but says he would not go through the hardships again for all the gold in the world and wants to give some good advice to his fellow men: "Keep your hands off the mining game, both mining and mining stocks, unless you are an experienced miner, for it is the most hazardous of all business ventures." Upon his return from Alaska he soon discovered the situation he had been placed in by his supposed friends, and he then went to Tonopah, Nev., where he lived for the following twelve years. During this time he ran a chain of three hotels and earned the reputation of being the best friend of the prospector, for he never turned a man from his doors because of his lack of funds. Any man's credit was good for ten days' board and room, with the understanding, "Pay if you are lucky and make a strike." This made the Ketelhut hotels popular, and they seldom failed to come back and pay; even if they did not strike ore they usually secured a job and paid their benefactor what they owed him. When the World War came on, no powder or steel came for mining purposes and the miners left for the high war wages then being offered. So the hotel properties became worthless and Mr. Ketelhut was compelled to close out at a heavy loss. In addition to running his chain of hotels he was a heavy operator in mining, and because of his experience he was able to obtain some of the richest properties in Nevada, but through getting mixed up with promoters and corporations, and later through lawsuits, he lost control of his interests.

In 1917 Frank Ketelhut arrived in Richmond and started a small bake shop with an investment of about $200. The products of this bakery were so well liked by the patrons that his business grew rapidly, and that growth has continued to this day. As his business grew he kept adding to his equipment every modern device used in all first-class bakeries, until today he has one of the most complete and modern plants to be found in the Bay region. His display of bakery goods is complete and the capacity of the machinery is 40,000 loaves of bread daily. He employs ten people in his business and uses two motor trucks to accommodate the Richmond trade. He still adheres to his plans made in Nevada and never turns a person away from his store in want.

Like most successful men, Mr. Ketelhut has met with misfortunes, but with unbounded confidence in his own ability, and with untiring energy, he is overcoming all obstacles; and after losing two fortunes, at sixty-six years of age he has won an enviable position among the business men of Richmond and a gratifying financial independence for himself. He believes in progress and shows his public spirit at every opportunity. During the Santa Fe strike he gave away 150 loaves of bread daily to the families of the strikers for about eight months, and he is always willing to lend a helping hand.

On June 27, 1905, Frank Ketelhut was united in marriage with Miss Louise Gill, a native daughter of San Francisco; and this union has been blessed with two children: Albert Frank, a graduate of the Richmond High School, who is now learning the contracting business, and Edith Louise, a student in the high school, who is planning a business career. Mr. Ketelhut has always been an enthusiastic booster for Richmond, and thoroughly believes in the city's future; and he has been an active member of the Chamber of Commerce, the Merchants' Association, the Kiwanis Club, and the Sons of Herman.

CLIFFORD T. FALLON.—A worthy representative of the enterprising and progressive upbuilders of Richmond and vicinity is found in Clifford T. Fallon, a native son who has been most helpful towards the permanent development of Contra Costa County. He was born on a ranch about six miles from what is now Richmond, on June 15, 1886, a son of Thomas J. and Hannah (Clancy) Fallon, the former born in California and the latter born in New York but brought to California by her parents, Daniel and Mary Clancy, when she was four years of age. In 1859 her father arrived in California via Panama, soon after sending for his family. Thomas J. Fallon became the owner of two ranches, one in Wildcat Creek section and the other on San Pablo Creek. His last days were spent in Stege, where he died in 1902, aged about forty-eight; Mrs. Fallon died in 1922, aged about sixty-five. Grandfather Patrick Fallon was a California pioneer, having crossed the plains about 1850, with an ox-team train. He mined in the early days, then came to Contra Costa County and bought a ranch and farmed till his death. There were three children in the family of Thomas J. and Hannah Fallon, Clifford T., Harold F., and Mrs. Ida Christian, all now living in this vicinity.

Clifford T. Fallon received his education in the public schools of Berkeley and Contra Costa County, and four years later took a special course at the University of California. He was anxious to get into some business on his own account and chose that of general contractor. He began in 1910 and gradually built up a good business in copartnership with his brother Harold F. Being energetic young men they soon had a large volume of business, employing at times as high as 100 men. While they have done some railroad construction work, and work for the city of Richmond and also for the county supervisors, they have specialized in tract work, taking the contract to prepare the land for subdivision, from the engineering department to curbs, streets, sewers, water mains and sidewalks. Among tracts for which they have contracted, are: Coleman-Pullman, Coleman Park, Union, Pullman Park; Spaulding-Richmond-Pullman and Richmond-Pullman Home tracts, lying along Macdonald Avenue to San Pablo Avenue; Overland, Industrial Center, Syndicate Business Blocks, Syndicate, Inner Harbor Business Blocks and Keystone Business Blocks tracts, all in Richmond and vicinity. He owns his own equipment and shop and lives on Cypress Avenue in the Stege district.

On May 8, 1911, Clifford T. Fallon was united in marriage with Miss Doris J. Schmidt, daughter of Andrew and Katherine (Cook) Schmidt, both born in Germany. Andrew Schmidt was a landscape gardener and was educated along that line in Germany and became an expert. He was in the employ of the Park Department of the City of Oakland for many years and died in that city in 1913. Mr. and Mrs. Fallon have a son Clifford T. Jr., born on February 8, 1912, and now attending the Richmond Union High school. Mrs. Fallon has a sister, Mrs. Hourtane, in Berkeley, and a brother, William Schmidt, in Antioch. Mr. Fallon has always done his duty as a citizen and served as a roadmaster for his district for some time; he was the United States Census Bureau agent for the Stege district in 1910. Fraternally he is a member of Richmond Lodge No. 1251, B. P. O. E.

ELMER CHRISTENSEN.—As a one-hundred per cent American citizen Elmer Christensen is doing his duty as he sees it and is making a name and place for himself in western Contra Costa County. His home, one of the first houses to be erected in the Richmond Annex, is situated at No. 125 Panama Street. Mr. Christensen enters heartily into all movements for the development of his section and favors progress along every line of endeavor. He was born in Copenhagen, Denmark, on October 27, 1875, and educated in the public schools and confirmed when he was fourteen. His parents dying when he was small he began to make his own way at an early age and we find him in Shelby County, Iowa, working on a farm soon after leaving school and his native land. From the farm he went to Omaha, Nebr., and served an apprenticeship to learn the cooper's trade, after which he followed it as a journeyman in Omaha and began to save money.

In 1897, in Omaha, Mr. Christensen was united in marriage with Miss Nettie Bayles, a native of Iowa, and they have two children: Lloyd E., a graduate of the Fairmont school and living at home; and Mote, wife of Albert Wilson. Both children were born in Nebraska.

In 1911 Mr. Christensen left his family in Omaha and came to California. He came to Richmond and entered the employ of the Standard Oil Company, but became dissatisfied because he was not with his family, so he quit his job and returned to Omaha, sold his home there and with his wife and two children, and the parents and a sister of Mrs. Christensen, returned to California. Her father served in the Civil War, running away from home to join the army. After the death of his wife, in 1923, he went to Napa to live with a daughter. In 1912 the Christensen family settled at Richmond and two years later purchased their present home. The location is convenient to San Pablo Avenue and when he moved into his house there were but three other homes in the vicinity. The land had been a hay and grain field. He has since been employed in the barrel house of the refinery.

In March, 1925, Elmer Christensen was elected a member of the Stege Sanitary Board, which has about twenty-five miles of sewers under its jurisdiction. He gives the necessary time to the duties devolving on him and favors expansion, street improvement and such things as go towards making living more pleasant in his community. In 1892 he was admitted to full citizenship in Shelby County, Iowa, and has since voted the Republican ticket on national issues. In local affairs he selects the person for the office regardless of party lines. He belongs to the Independent Order of Foresters, Union Court, at El Cerrito. To further the best interests of the neighborhood he helped organize the Annex Improvement Club, which has done much towards social and civic betterment. He believes he has never seen a more attractive place to live than this section and is satisfied that he cast in his lot with California, for he had become tired of the severe winters and hot summers in the Middle West. His recreation is found in watching clean sports, wrestling and baseball. Both Mr. and Mrs. Christensen have an ever-widening circle of friends in their chosen home locality.

JOHN EKLUND.—Among the Swedish-Americans who have made their own way from a small beginning in the city of Richmond we mention John Eklund, proprietor of the Pacific Feed & Fuel Company. He was born in Sweden on November 15, 1872, the son of Andrew and Johanna (Johnson) Eklund, who had six children: Alma, Mrs. A. Enar; John; Gust, who came to America; Hilda, Mrs. Anderson; Selma and Fred. John went to the Swedish schools and, after he was confirmed, went to work as a farmer boy and continued in his native land until 1889, when he landed in America. He had learned the trade of iron molder and worked at that for a short time after arriving in this country. He remained in New York only a year and then tried his luck at mining in Alaska. He was in Chicago for fifteen years, following his trade with the Forbes Malleable Iron Works and with the National Iron Works, both of Chicago. The few years he spent in Alaska gave Mr. Eklund a wide experience and when he returned to San Francisco he found employment in foundries about San Francisco Bay. He has lived in Richmond fifteen years and has been closely identified with its gradual growth. He was in the grocery and feed business for a time, then devoted his time and work to build up a feed and fuel business under the name of the Pacific Feed & Fuel Company. His business has prospered from the beginning and he has a fine trade in Richmond and vicinity. He is continually making enlargements to accommodate his trade, and has bought and sold some property since he came here, always with the idea of bettering his condition. He employs four or more people and handles the Globe Mills feed, and the celebrated Dines coal.

On August 24, 1910, in San Francisco, Mr. Eklund married Miss Johanna Varmboldt, who was born in Germany. Mrs. Eklund had some relatives in Richmond and she came here to join them. Mr. Eklund is a member of Alpha Lodge No. 431, F. & A. M., and of the Richmond Swedish Lodge Gustav Vasa. As a young man he enjoyed football and swimming. His recreation is found in camping and he likes the out-door life. He is very progressive and is identified with movements for the upbuilding of the community in which he has made his money, and in which he has great faith for its future. All who know John Eklund speak well of him.

FRITZ CARLFIELD.—A competent stationary engineer in the employ of the Standard Oil Company, Fritz Carlfield enjoys the confidence and esteem of a wide circle of friends in Richmond and vicinity. He was born in Sweden on September 9, 1887, a son of Anders and Johannah (Erikson) Carlfield, both born in Fagersta, Sweden, where they spent their entire lives. The father was an expert mechanic and was superintendent of a tool factory until his death in 1892. There were nine children in the family, none of whom ever came to America except Fritz.

Fritz attended the Swedish schools and as soon as his school days were over learned the trade of an engineer, becoming very competent. At the age of nineteen he arrived in the United States, March 15, 1907, and traveled to Denver, Colo., where he spent about eighteen months in the mines, then went to Chicago. For some time he traveled over the country looking for a suitable place to establish himself and where he could find a suitable climate. He arrived in Richmond, Cal., in 1911 and entered the employ of the Standard Oil Company as a laborer, but it was soon discovered he was an engineer and his advancement was rapid and he was given a suitable position.

On January 1, 1914, Fritz Carlfield was united in marriage with Miss Eleanor Christina Petersen, the ceremony being performed at one minute past twelve o'clock of the new year at the Lutheran Church at Fifteenth and Dolores Streets in San Francisco, by Reverend Andrews. Her parents were natives of Denmark and died when Mrs. Carlfield was small. They had settled in Marydale, Kans. Three children have come to bless their home: Bernice Eleanor, Juanita Ruth and June Thelma, the eldest attending the grammar school. At the time of his marriage Mr. Carlfield was living in Richmond but he moved to his present location soon afterwards, purchasing some land and erecting their home in 1915. He has served as a trustee of the grammar school in San Pablo; also as secretary of the Sanitary District of San Pablo, which has put in thirty-seven miles of sewer pipes to the benefit of the entire district. Fraternally he is a member of the Knights of Pythias of Richmond, and is captain of the Uniform Rank K. of P.; and belongs to the Foresters. Mr. Carlfield secured his citizenship papers on December 2, 1918, in San Francisco in the Federal Court. He was disappointed when it came to answering the questions for he understood the examination would be difficult. There were two questions asked: "What does Congress consist of?" and "What does the State Legislature consist of?" He had prepared for a hard contest on many difficult questions but these were easy to answer. Since obtaining franchise he has worked for every civic enterprise that has been brought before the people that would be a credit to the community for he believes in progress.

CLINTON SYLVESTOR FORD.—The office of plumbing inspector for the city of Richmond is held by Clinton Sylvestor Ford, and is an appointive post by the city council. He was first appointed in 1919, and each succeeding two years has been returned to the office, thus showing his dependable qualities for public service. He was born in Fulton County, Ill., on December 22, 1865, a son of John Sylvestor Ford, born in Pennsylvania, reared in Ohio, who at an early age moved to Illinois. He married Phoebe Clark in Ohio, and their children were: Amos Henry, living at Blockton, Iowa; George W., deceased; Clinton S., of this review; Justin Orr, of Richmond; John Berton, in Omaha, Nebr.; Jennie May, wife of E. H. Streeter, in Ohio. In their younger days Mr. and Mrs. J. S. Ford moved to Missouri.

Clinton Sylvestor Ford attended the public school near their farm in Missouri and when twenty-one began farming near Blockton, Iowa, for himself and continued four and one-half years. He then went back to the home farm in Missouri and carried on agricultural pursuits for over seven years. His next venture was with the Waters-Pierce Oil Company in Oklahoma, where he continued seven years and gained considerable knowledge of the oil game. Desiring to engage in the plumbing business he took up the trade and went into business in Ponca City, Okla., and remained till 1913. He then served as county clerk in Kay County, Okla., two terms of two years each, and worked at the plumbing trade for two years. On December 28, 1918, Mr. Ford and his family moved to Richmond, Cal., and here he engaged in the plumbing business for a short time, when he received the appointment of city plumbing inspector and still holds the position, filling it to the satisfaction of nearly everyone interested. His duties include building plumbing inspection, as well as all sewers, there having been considerable addition to the latter since he took office.

Mr. Ford was married at Bedford, Iowa, on September 18, 1887, to Miss Sena, daughter of Samuel and Sena Raper, of Indiana, who had the following children besides Mrs. Ford: Edward and Silas, both in Iowa; Jesse, in Nebraska; Mrs. Amanda Sweat and Mrs. Alice Severns, both in Nebraska; Mrs. Maggie Adams, in Iowa; and Mary E., deceased. Of

the marriage of Mr. and Mrs. Ford the following children have been
born: Ida Floy, Mrs. Busic, of Los Angeles; Jennie Edith, married C. E.
Ramey and has three children, Addie, Edward and Barbara; George Edward, in Richmond; Clyde Sylvestor, who has a son Harry Clinton, and
lives in Los Angeles; Osmer Oren, married and resides in Oakland; Ella,
wife of K. J. Feudner and mother of a son Carl Edward, lives in Richmond; Addie, married Arthur Wurck of Oakland and has a daughter,
Corrine; and Claude Vernon, in school. Mr. Ford registers as a Democrat, but in local politics and affairs supports the candidates he deems best
fitted for the office. He belongs to the Masons, Odd Fellows, and Modern Woodmen of America. He is a Past Grand in the Odd Fellows lodge
and served as a delegate to the Grand Lodge, and belongs to the Encampment of the I. O. O. F. and has passed through all the chairs and
represented the Encampment in the Grand Encampment. He also belongs
to the Eastern Star Chapter and to the Rebekahs. He has many warm
friends in Richmond who appreciate his sterling citizenship.

RALPH MERRILL BEEDE.—A loyal native son of the Golden
State who is wielding a strong influence in social and business circles of
Antioch is Ralph Merrill Beede, son of the late Henry Fuller Beede,
who is mentioned at length on another page of this history. He was
born on January 14, 1879, in the city where he is now a leader in various
departments of activity, and here he attended the public schools. In
1898 he was graduated from the Lowell High School in San Francisco,
after which he put in one year at Stanford University, pursuing a general
science course. His college course was cut short because he went to
work in the office of the Antioch Lumber Company, with which concern
he has since been closely identified. He was one of the incorporators
of the company and became its first secretary in 1907, and has served
most efficiently ever since. Mr. Beede is also interested in the Casino
Theatre, his partner being F. Stamm. They started the first movie show
in Antioch in 1911, and at the present writing this is the only movie
show house in the city. Here all the high-grade films are shown every
night in the week, it being the aim of the proprietors of this theatre
to make every effort to satisfy their patrons. Their growing attendance
is proof that they are accomplishing their desires.

On August 28, 1901, occurred the marriage of Ralph Merrill Beede
and Miss Anna Hardy. She was born in Cheyenne, Wyo., but was brought
to this State when a small girl and here grew up. She was graduated from
the San Jose State Normal and taught school in Contra Costa and other
California counties until her marriage. This union has been blessed with
four children, three of them living. Merrill, a daughter, died at the
age of two years. Ruth and Henry Fuller are attending the Antioch
High School. Katherine is a pupil in the grammar school. Mrs. Beede
is very active in club work in Contra Costa County, and is a Past Matron
of Antioch Chapter of the Eastern Star and also prominent in civic move-

Edward A. Hoffman

ments in Antioch. Mr. Beede is a member and a Past Master of Antioch Lodge No. 175, F. & A. M., and belongs to Antioch Chapter No. 65, R. A. M., and to the Sciots. He is also a Past Patron of the Eastern Star Chapter in Antioch. Since 1914 he has served as treasurer of his native city, and he takes an active interest in all movements that aim to make Antioch a better place in which to live and prosper.

EDWARD A. HOFFMAN.—The city engineer and superintendent of streets of Richmond is Edward A. Hoffman, a native of San Francisco, where he was born on November 18, 1893, the son of Edward C. and Emily (Wacker) Hoffman, natives of Saxony and Wittenberg, Germany, respectively. They came to California and were married in San Francisco. There are three children in the family: Alma, wife of A. H. Campbell, superintendent of the California Cap Works; Walter, an attorney in San Francisco; and Edward A., of this review. The father is a master mechanic who moved to Stege in 1899 and for many years was master mechanic and superintendent of the Metropolitan Match Company at that place. The parents are now living practically retired in Richmond.

Edward A. Hoffman attended the schools of San Francisco and Richmond, graduating from the Richmond Union High School in 1911. He then entered the University of California and pursued a mining and civil engineering course, graduating with the B. S. degree in 1915. His first employment was with the Aurora Consolidated Mining Company at Aurora, Nev., where he started at the bottom. Before he had been there a year he was superintendent of their mill, and he gained a thorough knowledge of every department. Meeting with an accident, however, he came home and was laid up for several months. Upon his recovery he accepted a position as draftsman with the city of Richmond, and through his ability he worked his way to the position of city engineer. His department takes care of all the construction and maintenance work done by the city, including general construction work and street and sewer improvements. He was designing and supervising engineer during the construction of the Richmond Natatorium, and it was he who worked out most of the engineering and construction details of the project. The plunge is one of the most modern of its kind in the State and is an ornament to the city. Mr. Hoffman came to Richmond in 1899, at the time the Santa Fe Railroad was first prospected to this section, and he has been an eye-witness to the entire growth of the city and surrounding country. He takes an active interest in all that helps to build up the city and believes it has a great future as an industrial center.

Mr. Hoffman was united in marriage on September 15, 1921, with Miss Leonie Trautvetter, of Richmond. Her father, Andrew Trautvetter, is a native of San Francisco, and married Louise Janke, of one of the old pioneer families of San Mateo County. Their marriage has been blessed with one child, Enid Lou, fifteen months old. Mr. Hoffman is
25

one of the original stockholders in the California Guarantee Mortgage and Finance Company and a director in the Sierra Gold Mining Company, both local concerns. He belongs to the Richmond Chamber of Commerce, Lions Club, Sigma Phi Sigma Fraternity, and American Legion, and is a Scottish Rite Mason and a member of the Sciots. In 1917 he enlisted in the United States Navy and was commissioned an ensign on the U. S. S. Golden Gate. At the signing of the armistice he was honorably discharged.

In high school Mr. Hoffman was president of the student body and president of the Tennis Club, and took an active part in school athletics being their star sprinter and weight man. When he entered college he finished a five-year course in four years, and took an active part in the Mining Association. He is fond of hunting, fishing and camping, and finds his recreation in these pleasures.

EUGENE A. BYER.—The Byer family has been identified with the history and development of California since 1864, when the late honored pioneer John R. Byer, grandfather of Eugene A. Byer, crossed the plains with a covered wagon train from Illinois. Eugene A. Byer is a son of Allison Byer, and was born in Contra Costa County and reared on his father's ranch and attended the public school of the community. He supplemented this education with a course in a business college at Oakland, and with a correspondence course in architectural draftsmanship, the latter profession he followed for three years in Oakland. He and his brother Virgil own 110 acres of their father's ranch, situated northeast of Byron. In addition to this ranch Eugene Byer purchased forty acres which was originally a part of the Allison Byer ranch, and he rents the remainder of the Byer ranch, which gives him practically 200 acres for farming, the larger part of which he has planted to alfalfa; the rest of the land is allotted to grain and pasture. In addition to being one of eastern Contra Costa County's leading growers of alfalfa, Mr. Byer is breeding registered Holstein cattle of the strain Sir Aggie Mead, having obtained his start from prize-winning stock bought from the celebrated Toyon Farm at Los Altos, Cal.

Eugene A. Byer was united in marriage at Oakland, Cal., on October 13, 1915, with Miss Maude L. Gerrior, a daughter of the late Rev. John Gerrior, a well-known Presbyterian minister of Oakland, and for two years synodical missionary, and formerly an evangelist in the San Jose Presbytery. He died in 1920, at the age of sixty-seven years; his widow, Mrs. Sara A. (Harris) Gerrior, is making her home with her daughter, Mrs. Eugene Byer. Mr. Byer is a man of culture, a progressive and enterprising rancher who is well informed on agriculture and is a type of farmer whose presence in the community is helpful to its permanent welfare. He is a trustee of the Methodist Church at Byron, and is always interested in those movements that have as their goal the advancement of the moral, educational, and material interests of the community.

H. D. BUCKMANN, M. D.—Numbered among the successful members of the medical profession in Contra Costa County is H. D. Buckmann, of Martinez. Since taking up his residence and practice here he has demonstrated his ability and skill and has built up a very successful practice. His office and residence is located at 835 Escobar Street. He gives much of his time to the work at the county hospital. He was born in Bremen, Germany, on January 20, 1882, and is a son of John William and Catherine Buckmann. The family came direct from Bremen and located in Sacramento, where the parents live.

H. D. Buckmann attended the public schools in Sacramento, graduating from the high school there. Early in life he made up his mind he would become a physician and during vacation periods worked about the county hospital in Sacramento and thus laid a good foundation for his future work. He entered Cooper Medical College in San Francisco, affiliated with Stanford University since 1912, and was graduated therefrom in 1908 with his M. D. degree. He then spent one year as intern at the Sacramento County Hospital and in 1909 opened an office and began a general practice of his profession in Sacramento, remaining until 1921. He then took charge of the medical department of the Cowell Portland Cement Company at Cowell, this county, continuing there until 1924, when he located in Martinez and since then has been building up a fine and lucrative practice.

Doctor Buckmann was united in marriage on October 18, 1905, while attending medical college in San Francisco, with Miss Barbara Parsons, a native of Ireland, and they have had five children: Shelagh, Henrietta, Jack, Fred, and Patricia May. He belongs to the Masonic lodge in San Francisco. He is a member of the County and State medical societies and the National Medical Association.

EDWARD ALLEN FRANKLIN CARSON.—A very successful contractor and builder in Richmond is E. A. F. Carson, who resides with his wife and family at No. 542 Fourth Street. He was born at Grafton, Jersey County, Ill., on February 27, 1862, a son of Allen C. and Emily (Williams) Carson, natives of Posey County, Ind., and Jersey County, Ill., respectively. At an early day the family went to Russell County, Kans., in a covered wagon. The father died in 1923 at the age of eighty-six. The mother is still living and makes her home at Salina, Kans., and at the age of eighty-two is hale and hearty. The Carson family consisted of Augusta, who married F. Button and lives in Berkeley; Jennie, the wife of F. Lewis, of Pittsburg, Kans.; E. A. F., of this review; William H., in Kansas; and a boy and girl who died in childhood.

Our subject was educated in the common schools in Kansas and began working at the builders trade soon after leaving school. After he had mastered the carpenter's trade he worked as a journeyman and traveled about, finally arriving in San Francisco, via Spokane and Seattle. He worked at the trade in San Francisco two years, then spent 1891-1892 in the Hawaiian Islands doing carpenter work. Coming back to San Francisco he worked as a cabinet maker for three and one-half years and then began taking contracts to build houses. So thorough is he with his work that one job brings him another. He never asks a contract in writing, is always willing to accept verbal agreements and says he "never loses money by so doing." He contracted in the bay city from 1898 to 1917, when he came to Richmond and settled at Fifth and Nevin Streets, until moving to his present home place. He specializes in residences and apartments, gives all his contracts his personal attention and sees that his customers get value received. He is a member of the Chamber of Commerce and of the Builders Exchange in Richmond.

Mr. Carson was married on March 27, 1895, in San Francisco, to Miss Ann B. Skow, daughter of John H. and Ann Skow. John H. Skow was born in Denmark and after coming to California settled in Watsonville. The children are Chris, Emil and Ingward Skow, all living in Watsonville; Edna, Mrs. Jack Faville, also at Watsonville; and Gussie, Mrs. Charles Pardee, of San Jose. The Carson children are: Evelyn, a clerk in the office of the Southern Pacific in San Francisco; Edward, in the asphalt department of the Standard Oil refinery in Richmond; and Roy, attending the Roosevelt Junior High School. Mr. Carson's father was a soldier in the Civil War. And at the time of the Spanish-American War our subject tried to enlist but was rejected on account of his age and being a married man. He spends his spare time with his family, but enjoys a ball game.

MRS. LYDIA S. BURKHALTER.—The life which this narrative sketches began in Dampierre, Province of Doubs, in eastern France, where her parents, Pierre Louis and Emily Susan (DePuis) Cuonot, were also born and reared. Grandfather DePuis was an engineer by profession, as had been several of the ancestors before him. Both he and his good wife died at early ages.

Lydia S. Cuonot received her education in the schools of her native land and when twelve years of age was orphaned by the death of her parents. In the fall of 1886 she came to America alone and located in Philadelphia, where she secured employment as a maid in a wealthy family, with whom she traveled through Italy, France, England and Switzerland for nearly three years, thus rounding out her education by travel. She returned to the United States in 1889 and on June 5 of that year, came out to California, where she was united in marriage with Jacob Burkhalter, whom she had known in Philadelphia.

Mr. Burkhalter was born in the Province of Berne, Switzerland, on May 20, 1856. He received a good education and was employed in Switzerland as a railway clerk. He was not content to remain there, and in early manhood came to the United States and traveled from State to State for several years, always finding employment to suit his tastes. In 1890 he arrived in California, secured a position with the Southern

Pacific Railroad Company, and with his wife went to Port Costa for a year. From there he was sent to Vernalis, below Tracy, and remained eight years. In the meantime they saved their money and bought a home in Tracy as an investment, but this was sold in 1902. Mr. Burkhalter was transferred to Sacramento, and during his work there met with an injury when a switch engine ran him down while he was riding his bicycle, in the spring of 1901. He was severely injured and for five months was in a hospital, and for a year was an invalid. After his recovery he and his wife came to Contra Costa County again and bought a small ranch near the Live Oak school. This they improved by cutting out the live-oaks and the chapparal and setting out fruit and a vineyard. He died there on September 24, 1917. Mr. Burkhalter was a member of the Tracy Odd Fellows Lodge and Encampment, and had many friends who mourned his passing.

Mrs. Burkhalter recalls that when she came to this location Oakley had one blacksmith shop run by John Augusto, a box car for a depot, and Mr. Marsh was the postmaster. There were no roads, only trails through the sand; and she has watched with considerable interest the growth of this county as it has been cleared of live-oaks and chapparal to make new homes and productive ranches for the many incoming settlers. She continued to operate the ranch for two years following her husband's demise and then she removed to Oakley, where she purchased her present home. In 1925 she became custodian of the Oakley Public Library, a position she is filling with great satisfaction to the patrons. Mrs. Burkhalter is a Republican in politics. She counts her friends by the score in her home town of Oakley and vicinity.

HARRY H. HALL.—Adjoining Oakley on O'Hara Avenue is what is unquestionably one of the finest almond orchards in Contra Costa County. Its twelve acres are covered with finely developed and prolific trees, and the grove presents an aspect of thrift and attention rarely excelled in any part of the State. Its owner, Harry H. Hall, has always maintained that whatever was worth doing at all was worth doing well, and in confirmation of his theory his orchard shows studious care which results in unfailing production from year to year. On the Hall Ranch there is also a fine vineyard of Zinfandel grapes interplanted with Tragedy plums, and the other three acres are planted to Muir peaches—all testifying to the same studious attention characteristic of Mr. Hall's business methods.

Harry H. Hall was born in Cleveland, Ohio, August 17, 1855, a son of Sylvester C. and Nellie (De Graff) Hall. Two sons were born of this union, Harry H. and John C. The father was known as Capt. Charles Hall and was captain of a boat that plied Lake Superior in early days; and during a severe storm on the lake he was swept overboard and drowned, when Harry was a lad of nine years. The widow of Captain Hall, with her two boys, returned to the old home in Cleveland, where

Harry attended public school until he was twelve years old. He then struck out for himself and served an apprenticeship as a printer, and afterwards drifted from place to place, selling newspapers and working at his trade. In 1874 he was working in Cincinnati, when he decided to take a trip down the Ohio and Mississippi Rivers, going as far south as New Orleans. This experience was anything but pleasant, and in the dead of winter he finally succeeded in reaching his home in Cleveland and resumed work at his trade. He became pressman for the Williams Publishing Company of Cleveland, and was with that company for twelve years; and from there he went to New York State, working in New York City and other places until 1897, when he came to California. He entered the employ of the Union Lithograph Company in San Francisco as pressman, working for them for twelve years. Five years before he gave up his position he bought a place of seven and a half acres at Oakley, which he improved and in 1921 sold at a profit of $2900. He then purchased his present ranch of twenty acres, which he has so finely improved.

Mr. Hall was married in Cleveland, Ohio, to Miss Lizzie McBride; and of this union two sons were born. Mrs. Hall passed away in 1887, and Mr. Hall was later married a second time, being united with Miss Lizzie Huffman, also a native of Cleveland, Ohio. Her father, George Huffman, was a native of Germany and a wheelwright by trade; but later he became an insurance agent in Cleveland. Mr. and Mrs. Hall are the parents of three children. Edwin B. is a partner on the home ranch and is also leasing a nearby 50-acre ranch. George H. is a graduate of the University of California and is now assistant superintendent on Wright Tract No. 2, near Stockton. Calista is the wife of Fred Hudson, of Stockton; they have two children, Jesse and Doris. Mr. Hall is an independent Democrat in politics. He was brought up in the Dutch Reformed Church, while his wife was brought up in the German Reformed Church.

RICHARD EVANS.—For the past seven years Richard Evans has been chief engineer at the Selby Smelter, with which company he has been employed since 1908. He was born at Holyhead, Wales, on January 25, 1883, a son of Edward Evans, a locomotive engineer who met an accidental death while in the performance of his duty. The mother was Elizabeth Williams in maidenhood. They were both natives of Wales and never left that country. Richard had three brothers and four sisters, all of whom remained in their homeland, except one brother who went to Australia. They are all happily married.

Richard Evans attended the schools of his native town. Upon coming to America he made for California and entered the employ of the Southern Pacific in Oakland as a locomotive fireman, continuing for several months to become familiar with the country and conditions, and during this time he took the engine running course in the I. C. S. His next employment was with the Oakland Traction Company, remaining until 1908, when he came to Crockett to work in the smelter, first as fireman, then was promoted to be chief engineer through the various stages of advancement. Since he has been here many innovations have been made in the machinery at the smelter, from time to time the most modern has supplanted the old, and today the equipment is up-to-date.

On January 12, 1912, Mr. Evans and Miss Margaret Davies were united in marriage. She was born in the same town as he and arrived here in December, 1911. Her sister and three brothers are still living in Wales. Mr. and Mrs. Evans have two boys, Edward David and Richard John, both in the Crockett Grammar school. Mr. Evans owns his own home and shows his confidence in the community by investing in other realty and business interests in Crockett. He believes in protection, is a Republican and active in the workings of the party. For several years he has served as a trustee of the Presbyterian Church organization, while Mrs. Evans is a teacher in the Sunday School. She is also a club and fraternal woman, holding membership in the Eastern Star, the Rebekahs, the Woman's Club and the Ladies Aid Society of the church. Mr. Evans is an Odd Fellow since 1910, being a Past Grand; and belongs to the Encampment. He is a Mason and a member of the Eastern Star. He is a substantial citizen in every sense of the word.

BURROUGHS BROTHERS.—As the proprietors of the Burroughs Brothers' Creamery in the Knightsen precinct of Contra Costa County, B. R., W. P. and E. C. Burroughs have established a reputation for as pure products as can be produced by any dairy. Their milk is certified to by physicians as being pure and wholesome, and in consequence of this indorsement their trade is rapidly growing throughout this vicinity. The three brothers are among the leading dairymen in central California, and indeed, in the entire State. They were born near Quincy, Adams County, Ill., B. R. on October 7, 1875; W. P. on April 2, 1879; and E. C. on Christmas Day, 1882, and are the sons of Benjamin and Harriet Jane Burroughs, who came out from Illinois to California in 1895, settling on land in Tehama County, where the family engaged in horticultural pursuits and general farming. In 1898 the parents moved to Oakland and there they died. They had three sons and five daughters.

The Burroughs brothers came from Tehama County to Contra Costa County in 1907, purchased 320 acres of land in the Knightsen precinct, and began its development to alfalfa and a dairy. They have 165 cows, all high-grade Holsteins, and registered bulls for their herds. They market their certified milk not only in eastern Contra Costa County, but also in Oakland, San Francisco, Stockton, Fresno, Richmond, San Mateo, San Jose, Sacramento and Pittsburg. W. P. Burroughs looks after the distribution of their product in Oakland, where he is also interested in the disposition of the products of the Walnut Grove Creamery, in which he is financially interested. They carry on an increasingly successful enterprise, and their equipment is most modern and sanitary. They use the Universal Milking Machines and get the best of satisfaction from them. Their dairy barns are built after the latest designs for dairy purposes, and everything about their place shows a master hand at the helm to guide and direct the enterprise to ultimate success. They all believe in cooperation and do much towards promoting community interest in their section of the county. B. R. Burroughs makes his home in a modern residence erected on their ranch and oversees the ranch operations in person. E. C. Burroughs resides in Antioch, but spends his time on the ranch, assisting with the dairy enterprise.

B. R. Burroughs was married to Miss Edna Nelson, of Butte County, and they have five children: Rendale, Cynthia, Oscar, Philip and Ernest.

W. P. Burroughs was united in marriage with Harriet Wright, of Tehama County, and they have four children: Elizabeth, Katherine, Harriet and Willis.

E. C. Burroughs was united in marriage with Miss Clementine Clark, of Tennessee and they have three children: Mildred, Dorothy and Ernestine.

PASQUALLI BRUNO.—A splendid example of the honest, industrious, law-respecting Italian-American citizen is Pasqualli Bruno, who for many years has been rated among the prosperous ranchers of Contra Costa County. He was born in Italy on May 28, 1871, the son of Joseph and Anna Bruno, who were the parents of seven children. His father was a farmer and it was from him that the son received the training in the fundamentals of agriculture which he has since used so successfully during his residence in America. He came to the United States in 1896, landing in New York and came directly to California, which had long been the goal of his youthful ambition. He resided in Oakland for a year and a half then removed to Spruce Street, Berkeley, at the reservoir, where he resided with his family for fourteen years. During this period he had charge of the reservoir for the East Bay Water Company. About 1920 he gave up this position and commenced to branch out for himself by renting land from the water company. He raised cattle and fattened them for the market. Gradually he increased his leasehold until at one time he had 3000 acres of land leased on which he ran an average of from 300 to 400 head of cattle; now he has about 1100 acres. He fattens beef cattle exclusively and generally sells to the buyers and butchers on foot.

Mr. Bruno and his family are members of the Roman Catholic Church. He was married in Italy, at the age of twenty-one, on October 17, 1892, to Jennie Bruno (same family name but no relation). She is a native of Italy and her parents came to America and settled in Oakland. The parents of both Mr. and Mrs. Bruno are dead. Their children are: Anna, now Mrs. A. Denevi, of Richmond; Katherine, Mrs. J. Muratore, resides in Berkeley; Edward J. resides at home; and Edna J., a stenographer, also resides at home. Mr. Bruno is fond of athletic games, and

Arthur Spanshaw.

takes a keen interest in his adopted community and Contra Costa County generally. He is a property owner in both Richmond and Oakland. Both his wife and children are musically inclined and are proficient on several musical instruments. His son is a musical student and gives promise of a successful career in that line of endeavor.

ARTHUR GRANSHAW. — A successful florist of Martinez is Arthur Granshaw, whose slogan "Say it with Flowers" has come to be one of the most familiar signs to be seen in that city, as well as heralded throughout the county wherever his auto delivery cars are to be found. He thoroughly understands every branch of his business, having learned the details while living in Salt Lake City. Mr. Granshaw was born in London, England, on September 10, 1892, a son of Henry and Sarah Granshaw, the father being a furniture manufacturer. The tenth in order of birth in a family of twelve children, he attended the London city schools until he was eighteen. Then he went into the law office of Sharp & Prichard Company and was a law student for eighteen months. His health then failed and he had to seek employment that would take him out of doors and he decided to come to the United States.

In 1909 Mr. Granshaw came out to Utah and soon started a greenhouse in Salt Lake City. Selling out his greenhouse, he began clerking in a florist's shop in that city, and here he learned the business. In 1920 he went to Oakland and worked for Hogan & Evers, florists in that city. Coming to Martinez in August, 1922, he opened an establishment in the old Hook building on Main Street, but his business soon outgrew these quarters, and in 1924 he moved into the Martinez Hotel block. He is making a wonderful success of his enterprise, and by his genial manners and good nature is building up a fine trade as a florist. He delivers to all parts of Contra Costa County, supplying all kinds of floral offerings for all purposes, and now has the largest business of its kind in the entire county, and continually expanding.

Mr. Granshaw was married on April 3, 1921, in Salt Lake City, to Miss Olive Parsons, born in England, whom he knew as a girl in London. In his business he is ably assisted by his wife, who shares with him the esteem and good will of the citizens of the county. Fraternally, Mr. Granshaw belongs to the Masonic Lodge in Salt Lake City, and also to the W. O. W. He is a member of the Chamber of Commerce in Martinez.

GEORGE K. ANDERSON. — An enterprising and successful alfalfa grower, George K. Anderson enjoys to an unusual degree the esteem and confidence of his fellow citizens, who appreciate the ability and energy he has displayed in the cultivation and improvement of the property located one mile north of Byron. He was born in the university town of St. Andrews, Scotland, April 17, 1883, and obtained his education in his native city where, in 1909, he was married to Miss Margaret Wilson, born at Ladybank, Scotland, a daughter of Alexander and Margaret

(Nairn) Wilson, farmers in Scotland. The parents of our subject were William and Jane (Christian) Anderson and they were the parents of nine children, of whom our subject was next to the youngest. They were farmers in Scotland and both are now deceased.

Mr. Anderson brought his family to America in 1914 and came direct to California where he secured farm work, first as a farm laborer, then as a field foreman. He then went as manager for Volney Taylor and worked in that capacity for eight years. After Mr. Taylor's death in 1923, Mr. Anderson leased his land comprising 225 acres; besides operating this Mr. Anderson owns his own ranch property of thirty-five acres, all devoted to alfalfa. The average crop amounts to seven tons to the acre and there are six cuttings, making a desirable income to the man who is willing to give it time and attention.

Mr. and Mrs. Anderson are the parents of one son, Alexander; they have adopted a niece of Mrs. Anderson's, named Margaret Wilson, now six years old. Mr. Anderson became a naturalized citizen in 1920. Fraternally, he is a 32nd degree Scottish Rite Mason, and is a member of the Blue Lodge at Brentwood, Scottish Rite at Stockton, and a Shriner, being a member of Aahmes Temple in Oakland. Mr. Anderson is a member of the East Contra Costa County Chamber of Commerce. In 1924 the Anderson family made a trip to their old home in Scotland, which was a most enjoyable outing.

EDWARD C. EBSEN.—The editor of the Pinole Times at Pinole is Edward C. Ebsen, an experienced newspaper man and a native son of California. He was born at Rio Vista in 1874, the son of Edward C. Ebsen, Sr., who was born in Denmark and was a carpenter by trade. He came to America about 1865 and located in San Francisco, where he followed his trade with the Spreckels company until he located at Rio Vista. He next settled in Martinez, where he died. For many years he served as constable in Contra Costa County and voted with the Republicans. He married Jane Conlin, only daughter of Patrick Conlin, and a native of Ireland. She came to America with relatives about the same time Mr. Ebsen crossed the ocean. This marriage resulted in the birth of three children: Anna, who died in childhood; Edward C., of this review; and Emma, Mrs. Silvia De Cobas, of Argentine Republic; she was on the stage and took the name of Silvia Linden.

Edward C. Ebsen, Jr., attended the public schools and went to work in a printing office when a lad of sixteen; he worked on the Contra Costa Gazette for five years and learned the art of printing, then went to work on the Daily Item in Martinez, after which he came to Pinole and worked on the Pinole Times until the Spanish-American War broke out and he enlisted and saw service during the period of the war. After his discharge he returned to Pinole and worked on the Times two years, then went to the Daily Transcript in Nevada City. Again coming to Pinole he worked until 1916, then purchased the printing plant of the Pinole Times from

E. M. Downer and Dr. Fernandes. The paper had been started by Mr. Downer in 1894 and has been issued ever since. The policy of the paper is to present the news in a dignified manner, and its editorial page gives the views of the editor in a frank and straightforward style. The Times is a newsy and attractive paper and has a growing circulation. A general job printing is conducted by Mr. Ebsen, and for a time he printed papers for the smaller towns about. He is correspondent for the San Francisco papers and does all he can to help the community advance. He belongs to the Printers Union and has served on various committees; is a member of Pinole Lodge No. 353, F. & A. M. His recreation is found in hunting, fishing and camping and usually has fair luck in bringing down deer and other game. Mr. Ebsen is quiet and unassuming and holds a firm place in the estimation of his fellow citizens.

HUGH D. THOMASON.—Since establishing his home in Pittsburg in 1914, Hugh D. Thomason has given no little part of a busy life to the city's progress and upbuilding, and is now doing a general insurance business. He is a native of Fayetteville, Ark., born May 12, 1894, a grandson of Capt. T. W. Thomason, who was an officer in the Confederate Army and later served as a member of the Arkansas legislature, from 1892 to 1896. Our subject attended grammar school in his native State, and when he came to California, in 1910, attended high school in Madera for a time.

Six months prior to settling in Pittsburg, Mr. Thomason was agent at Concord, Cal., for the Sacramento Short Line; then he came to Pittsburg as station agent for the same company and served for the following fifteen months. He then entered the employ of the Columbia Steel Works at Pittsburg, first as a shipping clerk, and by subsequent promotions rose to be superintendent of the finishing department. He was with this company during the World War and his term of service covered eight years. On November 1, 1924, Mr. Thomason entered the general insurance field with offices at No. 333 Railroad Avenue, Pittsburg, where he is devoting his time and talents to his chosen field of endeavor.

At Martinez, on July 14, 1914, Mr. Thomason was married to Miss Hazel Whipple, a native of Duluth, Minn., but reared in Kansas. She is a descendant of William Whipple, one of the signers of the Declaration of Independence. They are the parents of three children: Raymond, Norine, and Eugene.

Mr. and Mrs. Thomason reside in their own home, located at 1240 York Street, and enjoy the respect and good-will of many friends and acquaintances. Mr. Thomason is a member of the Pittsburg Chamber of Commerce and a prominent member of the Improved Order of Red Men at Pittsburg, having been through all the chairs of that order. During 1924 he was President of the Past Sachems' Association for Alameda and Contra Costa Counties. Politically he is a Democrat.

BERNARD TAILLEFER.—Well and favorably known both in Antioch and Pittsburg, Bernard Taillefer is now the proprietor of the Antioch French Laundry and is exerting his best efforts to please a growing list of patrons. He was born in the Basses Pyrenees, France, on November 23, 1897, and in 1913 came with his parents to Pittsburg, Cal., where his father engaged in the laundry business.

As Bernard was growing up he worked with his father in the laundry for two years. In 1915 he enlisted for duty in the French Army as an infantryman and returned to his native land for service. He was in the engagements in Alsace-Lorraine, Colmar, Verdun, Champagne and Plateau Craonne; and while in the last-named battle he was wounded on June 17, 1918, and had a very narrow escape from death. He was in the hospitals at Blenfield and at Lyons, and later was assigned to duty as a carpenter. On May 1, 1919, he was honorably discharged from service and on May 1, 1920, returned to California.

Four months later Mr. Taillefer returned to France to marry the girl of his choice, Etenette Bordenave, daughter of John and Mary Louise Bordenave, of France. Mrs. Taillefer is the second in a family of five living children, six having passed away. Mr. and Mrs. Taillefer have had three children: Mary Madeline, with an aunt in France; and Jeannie and Jean, (twins) both deceased. In October, 1922, Mr. Taillefer again arrived in California where he was joined by his wife on January 2, 1923. On May 1, 1925, they embarked in business in Antioch under the name of the Antioch French Laundry. Mrs. Taillefer's father is a thoroughly experienced laundryman and operates the mechanical department of the plant. It is the purpose of Mr. Taillefer to open a branch in Pittsburg in the near future. All work turned out at his establishment is first class, and the prices are reasonable. An auto truck is used for delivery. The family are members of the Catholic Church, and are rapidly acquiring a wide circle of friends in this community. He belongs to the French Veterans, the French Hospital Association, and the Ancient Order of Druids No. 1., all of San Francisco, and to the French Union, of Oakland.

CHARLES A. FRENCH.—The accommodating postmaster at Brentwood is Charles A. French, a native of Tennessee, born on October 29, 1875. His father, Peter French, died in 1902; and his mother, Melinda French, passed away in 1910. Grandfather French was a pioneer of Knox County, Tenn., and was a highly respected citizen.

Charles A. French attended the public schools and later took a course in a college to better equip himself to make his way alone. He came West in May, 1903, and located at Brentwood, Cal., where he secured employment on a ranch with Mr. Grigsby. Later he bought a lease on the Marsh Grant, and in the fall of 1905 moved into Antioch, continuing to farm for a year. He next moved to Knightsen, but again came to Brentwood and for three more years carried on farming. He then became manager of the general mercantile store owned by R. E. LeMoine & Company for two years. Since its incorporation, Mr. French has been associated with the East Contra Costa Mercantile Company. In 1915 he was appointed postmaster of Brentwood, and has since been reappointed and serves the public in a most efficient manner.

Charles A. French was married on October 18, 1905, to Bertha Anna LeMoine; and they have two children, Bertha Anna, born May 15, 1909, and Floy Elsa, born August 21, 1913. In politics Mr. French is a Republican, and he takes an active interest in civic affairs. He serves on the board of education of the grammar school, acts as a deputy assessor under George O. Meese, and collects taxes in this district. Fraternally, he is a member of the Independent Order of Foresters. He is the Past State President of the National League of District Postmasters for the States of California and Nevada, and is the chairman of the Fifth District, comprising eleven Coast States. Mr. French can always be relied upon to do his duty in whatever he undertakes, and is a firm believer in progress and development.

C. W. SCHEDLER.—The vice-president in charge of operations of the Great Western Electro-Chemical Company in Pittsburg, Cal., C. W. Schedler, has made a name and place for himself in the history of this industrial city, where he is president of the Pittsburg Industrial Association and Water Users of Solano and Contra Costa Counties. Mr. Schedler has been a resident of the city since 1916, when he came out here to join John F. Bush, the vice-president and general manager of the Great Western Electro-Chemical Company, which Mr. Bush was instrumental in starting, with the assistance of Mr. Schedler. The plant represents an investment of over $2,000,000. The first officers were: Mortimer Fleishhacker, president; John F. Bush, vice-president; and Arthur Lillienthal, secretary and treasurer. During the World War the company executed several large government contracts, and its products are sold from San Diego to Vancouver, on the Pacific Coast. The products manufactured are bleaching powder, caustic soda, liquid chlorine, zinc chloride, muriatic acid and xanthate, a flotation used in the copper industry. This company buys its raw materials in the open market, but owns an interest in the limestone quarry at Sonora, Tuolumne County, Cal. When the plant was started on July 22, 1916, Mr. Schedler was the first superintendent, and he continued in this position until he was made general manager in 1919. The plant has trebled in size and employs some 200 men. This is considered one of the important enterprises of Pittsburg, and has done much to advertise the city's industrial possibilities wherever the products are sold. The rapid expansion of the company's business is in large measure due to the ability displayed by Mr. Schedler.

A native of Cleveland, Ohio, C. W. Schedler was born on December 6, 1888. He grew up in Ohio and New York States, and was graduated from the Rensselaer Polytechnic Institute of Troy, N. Y., after which, for five years, he was engaged in construction work of various kinds on twenty-five or thirty jobs, mainly with the Foundation Company in New York. He then drifted westward and was employed by the Hooker Chemical Company at Niagara Falls, New York, and while there became acquainted with John F. Bush, who conceived the idea of building an electro-chemical plant on the Pacific Coast, for which he selected Pittsburg, Cal., as the most favorable site. He accordingly sent for Mr. Schedler to join him as his superintendent, which he did in January, 1916. That his work has been satisfactory is evidenced by the success of the enterprise and by the esteem in which he is held by all who know him.

Mr. Schedler was united in marriage at Niagara Falls in 1916 with Miss Susan Hotchkiss, and they have two children, William F. and Elsie L. In 1917 the family moved to Berkeley. Mr. Schedler is a member of the American Society of Civil Engineers of New York City, and is also a member of several societies in the bay cities; of the State and National trade organizations; and of the Pittsburg Chamber of Commerce. He favors the Salt Water Dam project, desiring a complete survey with report on the proposition; and if that looks favorable to him the project will have his hearty support and cooperation.

HERMAN EDWIN YEATON.—Representing an old Colonial family of New England, Herman Edwin Yeaton, general night superintendent of the Columbia Steel Corporation at Pittsburg, Cal., worthily sustains the traditions of his forebears. He was born at Abington, half way between Plymouth and Boston, Mass., on July 24, 1882, the son of John Edwin and Harriet Velma (Richmond) Yeaton, both members of prominent families of that State. The mother was the only daughter of Benjamin Richmond, a highly respected farmer in the Green Mountain district of Vermont, and is still living, making her home with a daughter in Lometa Park, San Mateo County, Cal. Grandfather Charles Yeaton conducted a preparatory school in his younger days, and later was a pattern maker in a brass foundry in Portsmouth. John Edwin Yeaton was a blacksmith and carriage builder at Whitman, Mass., doing business in one shop for a quarter of a century; he was also well-known as a manufacturer of fire apparatus and hose wagons, and drew his trade from a wide radius. He died at the age of sixty-seven, in 1915. Various members of the Yeaton family have distinguished themselves in many lines of endeavor, in farming, mechanical pursuits and the professions, in New Hampshire, Vermont and Massachusetts.

Herman Edwin Yeaton attended the public school in Abington, and also took up mechanical engineering and metallurgy courses in the I. C. S. of Scranton, Pa. In 1909 he went to Chicago and found employment at Grand Crossing, with the Interstate Iron & Steel Company, remaining in their employ until 1917. He then went to Youngstown, Ohio, and was engaged with the Brier Hill Steel Company, making munitions of war for the U. S. Government, for use of the armies over seas. He came to

California in 1918, arriving in San Francisco, where he found employment with the Pacific Coast Steel Company as superintendent of the open hearth department for four and one-half years. Then he came to Pittsburg, on July 25, 1923, and took charge of the construction of furnaces 4 and 5, as night foreman, and is now general night superintendent.

The marriage of Mr. Yeaton, in Chicago, on March 12, 1911, united him with Ruth E. Weld, daughter of Newton Weld. Mr. Weld was born in Vermont, but later was a pioneer of Elgin, Ill., coming there when there was no Chicago, when the place was still known as Fort Dearborn. She was educated in Elgin, graduating from the high school, and from a business college; and she is also a graduate from the Chicago Conservatory of Music, being a pianist of much ability. Two children have blessed this union, Vivian and Edwin, both of whom are attending the public school. Mr. and Mrs. Yeaton own their own home in Pittsburg and have an ever widening circle of friends. Mr. Yeaton was a baritone singer in his younger days, being a member of some of the best male quartettes in New England. He belongs to the Masons, having been made a Mason in Portland, Maine; to the Berwick, Maine, Chapter; and to the Sciots in San Mateo. In national politics he is a Republican.

HENRY SHOWALTER.—The night superintendent of the sheet mill of the Columbia Steel Corporation at Pittsburg is Henry Showalter, a man of much experience and ability, his connection with the steel industry extending over a period of thirty-five years. He has the distinction of having started the steel sheet mill at Pittsburg, working as a roller the first day this mill was put in operation in 1922. Mr. Showalter was born in New York City, July 23, 1871, and is a son of Joseph and Jennie (Lawrence) Showalter, the former a native of Scotland and the latter of the Green Mountain district of Vermont, both now deceased. After his school days were over Henry Showalter began working in the steel works in Pittsburgh, Pa., and later went to Gary, Ind., and thence to Sharon, Pa.; Bethlehem, Pa.; and Youngstown, Ohio, getting a vast amount of experience in the steel industry and by contact adding to his knowledge of men.

In 1922 Mr. Showalter came to California to accept a position as assistant superintendent in the sheet mill, a very responsible position. He is thoroughly awake to the possibilities of the Columbia Steel Corporation, which is the most important steel mill on the Pacific Coast, taking rank with the best the United States has to offer. This mill turns out great quantities of material, plain, galvanized, and copper-coated sheets ranging from 12-gauge up to 30-gauge, and 144 inches long. Copper is used to improve the quality of their product, and nowhere is there a better product than is put out at Pittsburg, Cal. On August 24, 1926, Mr. Showalter was called upon by the superintendent of the Columbia Steel Corporation to experiment in rolling sheet tin. This he accomplished very successfully. The experiment was made to see if the quality of steel manufactured here could be rolled to the thinness desired, and by a process of his own this was done by Mr. Showalter. Plans are being made to increase the plant by adding a tin-rolling mill. The sample was 38-gauge. The mills run day and night, except Sunday.

Mr. Showalter stands for improvement in all lines, and believes in the future of Contra Costa County. He is the father of four children, and has a home in Pittsburg. Fraternally, Mr. Showalter is a member of the Knights of Pythias at Newcastle, Pa., and the Independent Order of Odd Fellows at St. Louis, Mo. He is a believer in the teachings and faith of the Desciples' Church. Politically, he is a Republican, and gives his undivided cooperation in forwarding all movements for the betterment of his adopted city and county.

ANDREW A. DEHN.—Among the thrifty farmers of Contra Costa County who are in every possible way aiding its agricultural growth and development, is Andrew A. Dehn, who is prosperously engaged in farming and stock-raising in Deer Valley, in the Lone Tree District of this county. He is a native of California, born at Antioch on March 5, 1869, a son of Charles and Katherine (Scheele) Thompson, the former a native of Denmark and the latter of Germany. His father was a sea captain and for many years ran a schooner from Antioch to Stockton; he passed away when our subject was about eleven years old. The mother of our subject is now seventy-seven years old and makes her home in San Francisco. Grandfather Scheele was a pioneer shoemaker of Antioch. There are four children in the family: Andrew A., our subject; Annie K., Mrs. Albert Lilley; Thomas, a carpenter in San Francisco; and Charles, the mate on the Santa Fe tug-boat. Andrew and his sister, Annie Katherine, were legally adopted by John and Rachel (McDonald) Dehn and brought up as their own children. Mrs. Dehn passed away in 1888, and her husband survived her until 1900, when he passed away, both dying in Contra Costa County.

Andrew A. Dehn grew up on the Dehn home place in Deer Valley and early learned to farm. He attended the country schools in the vicinity of his home, working mornings and evenings and during vacation, raising grain and stock. Some twenty-five years ago he planted an almond orchard on the Dehn ranch, where he now lives. This orchard is now among the finest in the county. The Dehn farm consists of 160 acres lying seven miles from Brentwood and eleven miles from Antioch, in the productive section of Contra Costa County known as Deer Valley, in the Lone Tree District.

On January 25, 1920, Mr. Dehn was married to Mrs. Frances Parsley, a daughter of David and Amanda (Hammond) Allen, natives of California and Arkansas, respectively. They were pioneers of Mariposa County, and David Allen was a member of the California State Legislature from that county. Mrs. Dehn was born in Kern County but was brought up in Mariposa County, and was the youngest of four children.

She is the mother of seven children by her former husband. David married Miss Blanche Olson and lives in San Francisco; Eva, the wife of Robert Ross, resides in Sausalito; Sylvester P. also lives in Sausalito; John P. married Margaret Baker, and they also live in Sausalito; Ruby is the wife of J. R. Mowbray; Blanche married Earl E. Thompson; and Raymond P. lives in San Francisco, where he is an employee of the Southern Pacific Railroad Company. Mrs. Dehn has four grandchildren. Fraternally, Mr. Dehn belongs to Antioch Lodge No. 161, I. O. O. F., at Antioch. In politics he is a Republican. He has done his duty as a juror many times.

JESSE V. ALLEN.—The proprietor of Allen's Garage, on the Pacheco Road out of Martinez, is Jesse V. Allen, one of the progressive business men of the county, a native Californian, and a descendant of the famous Ethan Allen of Revolutionary fame. Born at Round Mountain, Shasta County, on June 5, 1894, he is the son of Dr. Merrill C. Allen, a native of Montpelier, Vt., who was a practicing physician in Shasta County for many years. Dr. Allen married Stella Brown, a native of Baldwin, Wis.; she is still living, but the husband and father died in Los Angeles County in 1913, aged sixty-one years. They were the parents of two children who grew to maturity: Clinton, in the employ of the Associated Oil Company at Avon; and Jesse V., of this review.

Jesse V. Allen attended the public schools of Shasta and Eldorado Counties, moving to the latter county with his parents when eight years old. He grew up at Camino, that county, to the age of fourteen, and then went to Sacramento and attended the Polytechnic School. Here he specialized in the study of motors and motive power, including automobiles of electric, steam and gas motive power; and he also learned engineering along the same lines in Sacramento. Thereafter he was employed by the Brown Hoisting Machinery Company, of Cleveland, Ohio, as demonstrator, and introduced the Brown hoists to the Westwood Lumber Company in California, and the Verdi Lumber Company of Verdi, Nev. He remained with the Brown Company from 1913 to 1916, and after setting up the hoists for the Verdi Lumber Company in Nevada he took a position with them as locomotive engineer for one year.

In June, 1917, Mr. Allen went to San Francisco to enlist in the 18th Engineers for service in the World War; but he was needed at Moore and Scott's shipyards, where he went as an operator. He soon became crane foreman, and later became chief engineer and assistant master mechanic, having complete charge of all steam, gas and electric engineering in that immense plant where 10,000 men were employed. He was ushered into the government employ with the work of a chief engineer and assistant master mechanic, and received his honorable discharge in 1919.

In June of that same year Mr. Allen came to Martinez and built his present place of business, and the name Allen's Garage has become synonymous throughout the Bay region with first-class automobile service and repair work. He specializes in rebuilding and repairing motor cars of all kinds, and his place is the special service station of ten of the leading makes of cars. He also carries a full line of extras and accessories for all of these makes, and has the authorized tow service for Martinez and vicinity, owning and using a Chalmers tow car with crane and a complete wrecking equipment. Employing seven men, he has a completely equipped machine shop in connection with his garage. His success has been assured from the time of his establishing himself in business in Contra Costa County, and he is justly popular, both as a business man and as a worker for progress in his home community.

The marriage of Mr. Allen, on June 5, 1924, at Martinez, united him with Miss Louise M. Flood, daughter of Edward Flood, of Oakland. Fraternally, Mr. Allen is a Scottish Rite Mason, belonging to the Oakland Consistory and to Live Oak Lodge No. 61, F. & A. M., in that city. By the time this book goes to the press, he expects to have been initiated into Aahmes Temple, A. A. O. N. M. S., also in Oakland; and he belongs to the Sciots in Antioch and the Odd Fellows in Martinez, and to Martinez Parlor, N. S. G. W. Actively interested in civic affairs, he belongs to the Exchange Club and the Martinez Chamber of Commerce. In the latter he has served on the board of directors, and in 1926 was the president; and during his term he appointed the committee which successfully put over the $75,000 bond issue to develop the Martinez harbor. He is also president of the sanitary board of the Mountain View district of Martinez, the locality in which he lives, having erected his home here in 1924. In January, 1926, he received a commission as lieutenant in the Quartermaster Corps of the Officers' Reserve in the United States Army. He is a Republican in politics, and serves as a deputy under Sheriff Veale; and also as a deputy county clerk for the registration of voters of the Mountain View district.

WILLIAM EDGAR CUNNINGHAM, M. D.—To do one thing and to do that well has ever been the goal of William Edgar Cunningham, M. D., of Richmond, Cal. And the wisdom of his plan of life is attested to by the unostentatious, yet secure, success which has been his. As a skilful medical practitioner and surgeon he has gone about, in his quiet way, ministering to the sick and disabled of the community and proven himself of that sterling brand of citizenry of which the Golden State may well be proud.

Dr. Cunningham was born at Madera, Cal., February 14, 1878, the son of John and Sarah (Whiteford) Cunningham, both of whom were natives of Indiana. The father was both a merchant and a miner; there were five children in the family, three boys and two girls, all now located in California. Dr. Cunningham was educated in the grammar school and a private school of Madera County. Prior to graduation, however, he decided to take up the study of medicine and entered Cooper Medical College in San Francisco. In college he was known as a quiet "non-frat" man, but that he was thorough in his work is shown by the fact that after he received his degree he was assigned to one of the highly prized internships at Lane Hospital, where his studies were supplemented by practical experience for some time. He then practiced medicine in Oakdale for a short period, and in 1906 settled in Richmond, which locality has since been the scene of his labors. He has engaged in general practice, including surgery, and has been quite successful, being rated as one of the leading physicians of the county. The office building at corner of Macdonald Avenue and Ninth Street was erected by him.

Although he takes a keen interest in the welfare of his community Dr. Cunningham is not a politician and not a public man. Even at the medical meetings he is not a loquacious speaker, unless there is some special reason. He is a member of the Elks, the Rotary Club, and the State Medical Association, and the County Medical Society, having been president of the county organization for one year. His recreations are golf, hunting, autoing and outdoor life. He especially enjoys camping in the mountains with his family.

In 1908 Dr. Cunningham was united in marriage to Miss Edith Treanor of San Jose. Her father, Thomas Treanor, was a native of Ireland, a former recorder of Santa Clara County and a distributor of implements for the Studebaker Company. The mother, Matilda (Wehner) Treanor, was a native of Germany. Mrs. Cunningham, who is one of six children, is an accomplished musician. She has taught and composed music and is a graduate of the Pacific College of San Jose. Dr. and Mrs. Cunningham are the parents of two children: Jack and Helen, both are students in Richmond High School.

MORTIMER B. VEALE.—An attorney of marked ability and attainments, whose friends predict for him a very successful career, is Mortimer B. Veale, of the firm of Rodgers & Bray of Martinez. He is a native of Contra Costa County and was born on the Veale tract near Knightsen on November 18, 1893, a son of R. R. and Elizabeth (Martin) Veale, highly esteemed citizens of this county, where R. R. Veale has served as sheriff for thirty-two years. Mortimer Veale, who is the third son of his parents, attended the public schools of the county, graduating from the Alhambra Union High School with the Class of 1913. He then entered Stanford University and pursued the law course, graduating in December, 1919. His studies had been interrupted by the World War, during which he volunteered his services in the United States Navy. For three months he was stationed at San Pedro, and then was commissioned ensign on October 9, 1917, and served at sea until 1918, when he entered the United States Naval Academy at Annapolis, and was graduated in the Reserved Class in June, 1918. Receiving the commission of ensign, he was assigned to the Minnesota and served on her until March, 1919, when he was transferred to the United States Destroyer J. Fred Talbert and as radio officer did confidential communication for Vice-Admiral Grant. In June, 1919, Ensign Veale resigned from the navy and reentered Stanford University to complete his law course. Upon leaving the university he returned to Martinez and was connected with the sheriff's office one year. In June, 1921, he took the State Bar examination, and was admitted to practice on August 22 of that year. Mr. Veale at once opened an office in Martinez for the practice of his profession, continuing until he located in Antioch in 1923, where he became connected with the firm of Rodgers & Bray, the leading firm in Martinez and well known throughout the entire county.

On June 15, 1924, M. B. Veale was united in marriage at Martinez with Miss Ida Olive Honegger, of that city. Mr. Veale is a member of the Masons of Antioch and of the Eastern Star Chapter, to which Mrs. Veale also belongs. He belongs to the Elks of Richmond, and the Native Sons of Martinez, being a Past President of the latter, and also belongs to the Antioch Aërie of Eagles. He is Past Adjutant of Henry A. McNamara Post, American Legion, of which he served as Adjutant for more than two years, and is the present Adjutant of the County Council of the American Legion, as well as a member of the board of directors of the East Contra Costa County Chamber of Commerce and a member of the board of directors of the Bank of Antioch. Mr. Veale takes an active and enthusiastic interest in all movements that have as their special aim the advancement of the city of Antioch along commercial, educational and moral lines. He is a member of the board of trustees of the Congregational Church.

WILLIAM HAROLD ANDERSON.—An ambitious and energetic young man who holds a high place in the citizenship of Brentwood is W. H. Anderson, whose ability has already brought to him the responsibility for the discharge of various public duties. He is one of California's native sons, born in San Francisco on January 29, 1891. His father, R. K. Anderson, was a San Francisco contractor and builder, and is now deceased. The mother was in maidenhood Miss May Jane Carroll; she died when our subject was only four years old, and he then came to live with his aunt and uncle, Mr. and Mrs. John Geddes, in Brentwood for a time, but later was brought up by his stepmother, who still lives in San Francisco.

As a boy Harold Anderson, as he is familiarly known, attended public school in San Francisco, but on account of poor health he later came to Brentwood, where he attended the high school for two years. His health improved so that he could do ranch work, and thereafter for seven years he worked for one man. He then accepted a position with the Brentwood Lumber Company as yardman. When the war broke out he was called in the first draft and served with the 347th Field Artillery, 91st Division and was on the Verdun front for eleven days; and after the armistice was signed he was with the Army of Occupation for three months. Returning to the United States, he was honorably discharged at the Presidio in San Francisco on April 26, 1919, with the rank of corporal. After his discharge he again took up his work with the Brentwood Lumber Company, and in 1925 was promoted to the position of agent for the company. Mr. Anderson takes personal interest in every home erected in this section, stands ready to lend aid in every way, and enjoys prestige as an authority in building matters. He is ever alert to lend aid to projects that are put forward for the betterment of his home district, and is honored and esteemed by all who have had business relations with him through the Brentwood Lumber Company.

On March 8, 1920, Mr. Anderson was married to Mrs. Myrtle E. Watson, née Wristen, of a Brentwood pioneer family. Mr. and Mrs. Anderson are the parents of one child, Myrle Fern. Fraternally, Mr. Anderson is a member of the Brentwood Lodge No. 345, F. & A. M. He is (1926) adjutant of Roy Frerichs Post No. 202, American Legion, at Brentwood.

IRVINE SKEOCH.—That the Columbia Steel Corporation has been the means of bringing to Contra Costa County some of the most skilled artisans in the whole country there is no gainsaying. Their various departments require men of more than ordinary ability to carry out the policies of the great corporation, and among these men is Irvine Skeoch, superintendent of the wire and nail mills at the Pittsburg branch of this corporation. It is doubtful whether many people, even in Pittsburg, fully realize the importance this concern holds in the State. Nearly everything made of iron and steel is manufactured at Pittsburg in this plant. Each of the various departments are under the supervision of experts in their line, and no detail is overlooked in providing for the safety of the hundreds of employees that are necessary to keep the plant running. Of no little importance is the wire and nail mill where the ingot, which comes from the open hearth furnace, is taken and again heated and rolled into rods and then drawn into wire after proper chemical treatment. Nearly every size of wire on the market is produced in this department under the able supervision of Mr. Skeoch. Some 280 different sizes of nails are also made in the nail mill, which has fifty-four nail-making machines that turn out from 530 small nails to 150 seven-inch spikes per minute. These machines are operated by skilled workmen. By use of different dies each machine makes a certain sized nail. Sixteen hundred fifty 100-pound kegs of nails, brads and spikes are turned out every twenty-four hours, all machines running that number of hours each day. In the wire mill all kinds of wire, for every purpose, are made, from the copper-coated, steel and galvanized to baling wire. Products of this great corporation rank with any produced anywhere in the world.

Irvine Skeoch was born at Bellshill, ten miles from Glasgow, Scotland, on January 28, 1884, a son of Irvine and Janet (Baird) Skeoch. When he was eight years old he accompanied his parents to Carluke, where he grew up and attended school. While yet a youngster he served a five-years apprenticeship as a carpenter, at the same time attending night school, where he took up drafting. When he was competent to go out in the world for himself he returned to Bellshill and took a position in the Clydesdale Iron and Steel Mills. He also put in two years at the Technical College in Glasgow. He sailed for America on May 6, 1906, and arrived in New York on May 12. Remaining in New York two years, Mr. Skeoch followed construction work during that time, and then came to San Francisco by way of New Orleans. He followed construction work in the bay metropolis for various companies several years, after which he went into the South San Francisco Steel Rolling Mill and worked four years.. Prior to this, however, he was foreman of the trim in the building of the Oakland Auditorium in 1915, and also was construction foreman on the steel bridge built at Watsonville in 1915-1916. The name-plate on the structure fittingly commemorates our subject. In 1918, when the Steel Corporation in Pittsburg, Cal., decided to enlarge and rebuild their open-hearth furnaces, Mr. Skeoch was called there as construction engineer to take charge of the work. When the work had been successfully accomplished he was retained in the position of construction engineer on the rolling mill, and in 1923 to build the sheet mill, wire mill and nail mill. These were constructed after the plans of N. A. Becker. After the completion of these jobs Mr. Skeoch was retained as superintendent of the wire and nail mills, and has carried on the work to the entire satisfaction of his superiors.

Mr. Skeoch was married in Glasgow, Scotland, in 1905, to Miss Flora Jane McLachlan; and they have two children: Irvine, eighteen years old; and Thomas, sixteen years old. Mr. and Mrs. Skeoch were reared in the United Presbyterian Church. He is a member of the Masonic fraternity and a Sciot. He became a citizen of the United States in the Federal Court in San Francisco, and supports the best interests of the people at elections.

JOHN U. DIETHELM.—A resident of the Oakley precinct, Contra Costa County, since 1900, when the family came here to reside, Mr. Diethelm has improved his time and is now the owner of as fine a ranch as can be found in this section of the county. He is a self-made man, for ever since reaching man's estate he has made his own way in the world, and has accumulated a comfortable competency. He was born at St. Gallen, Switzerland, on September 19, 1863, a son of Jean Diethelm, who owned and operated a mill, a bakery, and a farm in and near St. Gallen.

John U. Diethelm was taught to work from the time he was old enough; and meantime he received a good common school education in his native city. He came to America in 1883, and that same year settled in San Francisco, where he found work of various kinds. Being of a thrifty nature, he saved his money and bought a hotel, which he operated for fifteen years. When Mr. Diethelm came to the Oakley precinct he found work on various ranches and in the meantime was looking for a place to buy. He first purchased 150 acres in 1893. This he knew to be extra good land and adapted to the raising of grapes and fruits. Mr. Diethelm cleared it from oak trees and planted sixty acres to almonds. In 1900 he began planting grapes and fruit. A portion of the place has been twice planted, changing from almonds to grapes. The fact that this ranch extends up to the water front makes it peculiarly adapted to the successful growing of nut trees, grapes and fruits. Mr. Diethelm did more perhaps than any other person to help establish the Antioch-Sherman Island Ferry, for he gave the use of land for approaches and roadways to the ferry. He is a stockholder in the American Toll Bridge Corporation, which promoted the Antioch-Sherman Island bridge; and he is also a stockholder, promoter and director in the Bridgehead Shipping Corporation, which has packing sheds on the Santa Fe Railway nearby and handles hundreds of carloads of green fruits, table grapes, asparagus, celery, etc., each year. Mr. Diethelm is content with only the best of everything, and his beautiful home and productive ranch are testimonials to this fact.

At San Francisco, Cal., on May 6, 1888, Mr. Diethelm was married to Miss Vinzentia Gamma, also a native of Switzerland; and they have had seven children, six of whom are now living, all doing well and a credit to their parents and community. They are: Ulrich; Emil, married and now at home; August F.; Emma, Mrs. Charles Ratto, of San Francisco; Charles; and Olga. Bertha died at the age of twenty-two, in October, 1924. All were born in San Francisco except the two youngest, who were born on the ranch, where the family settled in 1900. Mr. Diethelm is progressive and public-spirited, and cooperates with all projects for the upbuilding of the county.

WILLIAM B. SCHEFFER.—A self-made man, and one well qualified to fill the responsible position of superintendent of the National Chemical Company's plant at Pittsburg, is William B. Scheffer, who was born at Harrisburg, Pa., on October 15, 1895, the sixth and youngest son of Louis Kassouth Scheffer. The father was a printer by trade and owned a printing office in Harrisburg. He died in 1908. The mother was left a widow with six living children, but with the help of the older children she managed to keep the little family together until they were old enough to do for themselves. For seven generations the Scheffers have been leaders in philosophy and science in the Eastern States.

William B. Scheffer attended the public schools and since the age of thirteen has been practically self-supporting. He was graduated from the Harrisburg Technical High School, Class of 1915, helping to pay his way by carrying newspapers nights and mornings. He matriculated at the Gettysburg College in September, 1915, and was attending that institution when the World War broke out. He enlisted and entered the officers' training camp at Fort Niagara, N. Y., and commissioned second lieutenant in the 79th Division when he was twenty-one; seven months later he was promoted to first lieutenant, embarked at Philadelphia with the 304th French Mortar Battery (Artillery Company), and landed at Liverpool, England. The battery remained on English soil two weeks, and then was sent to France. There they concluded their training, and were on the train en route to the front when the Armistice was signed on November 11, 1918. Mr. Scheffer obtained permission from the proper military authorities to enter the University of Grenoble, France, and remained as a student of chemistry and French history from March 1 to July 1, 1919, when he received a certificate. He returned to New York City and was honorably discharged at Camp Dix on August 6, 1919, having served his country twenty-seven months. Re-entering Gettysburg College in September, 1919, he continued his studies in chemistry and was graduated in June, 1920. Two months prior to his graduation, however, he accepted a position in the chemical department of the Sherwin-Williams Company at Bound Brook, N. J. After continuing with that company one year, he became connected with the Standard Chemical Works at Reading, Pa., remaining there two years as chemist. The next year was spent as assistant superintendent of the Nitrate Agencies Company works at Bayonne, N. J. It was through the recommendation of Howard W. Ambruster, consulting engineer of New York City, under whom he had served in New York, that Mr. Scheffer came to the National Chemical Company in Pittsburg, on October 15, 1924; and he has acceptably filled the position of superintendent of their plant ever since. This plant employs some thirty-six men in the manufacture of its products, consisting of arsenical compounds, insecticides and weed killers of many varieties, and produced in large quantities.

The marriage of Mr. Scheffer and Miss Ida M. Krumboine, daughter of an acrobat of herculean strength and a leading performer in P. T. Barnum's circus, was solemnized at Womalsdorf, Pa., on September 28, 1923, and they have one child, a son born July 19, 1926. The family home is located at 640 East Street, Pittsburg, where they are surrounded by a large circle of friends. Mr. Scheffer was made a Mason at Bound Brook, N. J., and is a member of the Sciots at Antioch.

WILLIAM C. PURCHASE.—A member of the firm of Purchase & Biglow, grocers, of Antioch, William C. Purchase has been engaged in the grocery trade for nearly forty years and is one of the best-known men in Antioch, as also one of the most public-spirited. He was born in Herkimer County, New York, the son of James and Violetta (Belshaw) Purchase. The father is deceased, but the mother is now living in Jordanville, Herkimer County, N. Y. When a young man Mr. Purchase came to Antioch and began clerking, and from that time until the present he has been associated with the retail trade, either as a clerk or as proprietor of a business. From 1906 to February, 1920, he was back in Herkimer County, N. Y. He returned to California with his mother to settle the

John N Krislich

estate of the late Charles M. Belshaw, his cousin, his mother being the only heir of Mr. Belshaw, who met his death, with his wife, in an automobile accident in November of 1919. Mr. Purchase is popular with all who know him and has made and retained many friends in Contra Costa County. He belongs to the Lodge and Chapter of the Masons in Herkimer County, N. Y., and to the Odd Fellows in Antioch.

JOHN N. KRISTICH.—A prominent engineering contractor of central and northern California is John N. Kristich, who has two plants for the manufacture of cement pipe, one at King City and the other at Knightsen. He began on a very small scale in 1915 and has gradually enlarged the scope of his operations until he covers territory from King City, in Monterey County, to the Sacramento Valley. He has made an especial study of irrigation problems, manufactures all kinds of cement pipes, and does all kinds of cement work along lines of irrigation. His cement irrigating pipe is sold in all parts of California. Among the large orders he has filled we mention 250,000 feet of pipe for the California Orchard Company; 155,000 feet for the State Land Development Association at Delhi; some $170,000 worth of pipe for the Knightsen Irrigation District; and $25,000 worth for the Byron-Bethany Irrigation District. He makes pipe of all sizes by machines manufactured especially for that use, and no irrigation or reclamation job is too big for him to handle, as he has ample equipment for anything in the cement line.

John N. Kristich was born in Austria on May 21, 1891, and came to the United States when he was sixteen years old, landing in Los Angeles. There he secured work as a laborer with the Arthur S. Bent Construction Company and continued for about six years, during which time he worked in every department, from a pick-and-shovel man to foreman, learning all about cement work and contracting. He supplemented his early schooling by night study after arriving in Los Angeles, and has become a well-educated man, especially along technical lines. Desiring to begin work for himself, he went to King City, Monterey County, and began making pipe from concrete and cement and taking small contracts. From this small beginning he has developed one of the largest businesses of the kind in the State, and he has handled some of the largest contracts for irrigating and reclamation projects. He has a thorough knowledge of his work and gives his contract work his personal supervision, in consequence of which he is a very busy man. He located in Knightsen in 1920 and has been very active in the reclamation of the lands in eastern Contra Costa County, where he is well and favorably known. He is public-spirited and lends a helping hand to forward all upbuilding projects. He belongs to the Odd Fellows in King City.

ARNO FISCHER.—A resident of California for many years and a successful business man of Richmond since 1912, Arno Fischer has helped to build up the resources of this section of the State to the best of his ability.   He was born in Germany on December 29, 1868, a son of William and Henrietta (Brauer) Fischer.   There were seven in the Fischer family, three of the children having been born in America, and five are still living, viz.: Gus, living in San Jose; Alvin, makes his home in Richmond; Lou, is in Nevada County; Mrs. Annie Johnson, lives in Downieville; and Arno, of this review.

Arno Fischer attended the German schools and then came to America with his parents and his first employment was in the grocery business.   He then tried mining in Arizona for a time, also spent some time in the mines in Tuolumne County, 1890 to 1892.   Then he drifted back to the grocery business and in 1912 located a business in Richmond.   He began on a small scale at No. 335 Macdonald Avenue; in 1918 he opened a branch at No. 724 Macdonald Avenue; and in 1923 another at No. 634 Macdonald Avenue.   He carries a full line of staple and fancy groceries and not only aims to please his customers, but actually anticipates their wishes and keeps supplied with the best goods obtainable.

Mr. Fischer was married on June 3, 1902, to Miss Annie E. Black, born in Sierra City, the daughter of John F. and Annie (Curley) Black, and they have had three children: Anna, Mrs. Clyde M. Emery, is a graduate of the high school; Irene, a student in the University of California; and Francis, attending the high school.   The family home is in Berkeley, but Mr. Fischer gives his personal attention to his business in Richmond and is preparing to consolidate his three places into one for the convenience of his growing patronage.   He is satisfied with the progress made in the past years and predicts a bright future for Richmond and vicinity.   He is public spirited and supports all projects for the upbuilding of Richmond and the Bay district.

FRED P. NEVIUS, M. D.—During the years of his practice in medicine and surgery Fred P. Nevius, M. D., has ably demonstrated his ability and skill in diagnosis and operating and has built up a lucrative practice in eastern Contra Costa County, where he holds an assured position.   His work in surgery takes him to Martinez, Stockton and other places, where his operations have attracted wide attention.   As a surgeon during the World War he has an interesting history.

Fred P. Nevius was born at Benzonia, Benzie County, Mich., on November 22, 1883.   His father, Lot Nevius, is an attorney-at-law in Frankfort, Mich., and served two years in the Michigan State Senate at Lansing; he is a veteran of the Civil War who has reached the age of seventy-six years.   His wife, who in maidenhood was Henrietta Shattuck, died in 1898.   Fred P. Nevius completed the high school course and before entering college read medicine under Dr. McBain, of Port Huron.   Graduating from the Frankfort High School, Class of 1897, he then took a course in pharmacy at Big Rapids in the W. N. Ferris School of Pharmacy, graduating in 1899.   He then became a student at the Michigan College of Medicine and Surgery at Detroit and passed the regular courses, graduating with the M. D. degree in 1906. This college was merged with the Detroit College of Medicine in 1907. With this preparation Dr. Nevius became an intern in the Emergency Hospital in Detroit, serving one year. He then began the practice of his profession at Port Sanilac, Mich., soon going to the northern peninsula, where he remained till 1908. Going then to Paris, France, Dr. Nevius did postgraduate work during 1908 and 1909, specializing in abdominal surgery. He then opened an office in Detroit, and practiced at Grace hospital until 1916.

After the breaking out of the World War, Dr. Nevius enlisted as a French Army surgeon in 1916, went to France and served from April, 1916, until 1917, when he returned to the United States. Again enlisting, he entered the United States Army as a surgeon and served from July, 1917, to May, 1920. He was taken with the flu and was gassed severely. He saw active service at the front in the hospitals and on the firing line all during his time of active duty. After returning to the United States he spent some time traveling in search of health. In 1921 he arrived in California and became a surgeon at the San Joaquin County Hospital at French Camp, where he was also resident surgeon till 1922. Going then to New York he took a postgraduate course in the New York Post Graduate College of Medicine and afterwards returned to French Camp and worked as an assistant to Dr. Friedburger, the head physician. It was about this time that Dr. Nevius was severely injured in an auto accident and taken to the Stockton Hospital, where he remained from December, 1922, to March, 1923. As soon as he was able to be about he secured a berth as ship surgeon on the United States vessel then in the Coast and Geodetic Survey in Alaskan waters, and from this trip he came back to San Francisco practically a well man. On December 29, 1924, he located at Antioch, where he has since lived and where he is the leading physician and surgeon for eastern Contra Costa County.

Dr. Nevius was married in October, 1924, to Miss Blanche Cargile, a graduate nurse from San Francisco. She is proving of great assistance to him in his work in this community, being a woman of culture, refinement and sympathetic nature. He is the surgeon for the Paraffine Companies, Inc., at Antioch, and for the Santa Fe Railroad. Fraternally, Dr. Nevius is a Mason, having been elevated at Alpena, Mich., and he belongs to the Consistory in Detroit.

ANDRES MORENO.—A business man of Pittsburg, Cal. Andres Moreno is the proprietor of the National Pool Hall, the Mexican Hotel and the Golden Gate Restaurant, at 105 Black Diamond Street. He is also the Pittsburg agent for the Mexican Consulate in San Francisco. During the three years that he has lived in Pittsburg he has made his influence felt in social and business circles. He was born in Purepero, Micho, Mexico, on November 30, 1893, at the Hacienda Plan de las Rincones, his father's estate, and he was educated in private schools until he was able to make his own way. He has a command of the Mexican language and a speaking knowledge of Spanish and Italian, and learned to speak English after coming to the United States, when he landed in El Paso, Texas in 1918. After spending three years in El Paso he came to California and located at Sacramento, remaining there until he located in Pittsburg, Cal.

Prior to leaving Old Mexico Mr. Moreno conducted a clothing store, but when the Mexican revolution broke out it ruined his business and he was obliged to flee the country. During the sixteen years he was in business in his native country he failed twice; the second time was due to the depreciation of Mexican currency. He had sold two carloads of merchandise and took his pay, 52,000 pesos, in paper money and this decreased so much in value overnight that he found himself insolvent. Mr. Moreno is popular with the Latin contingent of Pittsburg and is rapidly building up his fortunes again. When General Obregon came to San Francisco Mr. Moreno was a member of the reception committee that greeted him.

Mr. Moreno was united in marriage at Martinez, in 1920, with Rosa Barreda, a native of Mexico, and they have three children; Lillian, Maria and Jose.

HARRY DE PIAZZA.—As the proprietor of the California Bakery, on Railroad Avenue, Pittsburg, Harry De Piazza is showing what perseverance and good business management can accomplish. His many years of work at his chosen trade has made him a good workman and a good business manager. He was born on December 23, 1887, at Valtellino, province of Sonotrio, Lombardy, Italy, the only child of Fidele and Jueditta De Piazza, the latter now making her home with her son in Pittsburg. Harry attended public and private schools until he was fourteen, then left home and began to make his own way. He went to London, England and served two years as an apprentice to learn the bakers trade, working from four a. m. until eleven p. m. for his room and board, his parents agreeing to furnish his clothes. The next two years he worked at the trade in Clifton, England, and here he attended night school to add to his education and learn English.

Young De Piazza had heard a great deal about California and he made up his mind to come here. He made a visit back to see his folks in Italy, then embarked from Havre, France on the S. S. Grossotto for New York City, arriving early in 1906. Upon his arrival in California he went to San Jose and found work at the New York Bakery for five years; then he had a bakery of his own at Watsonville and built up a fine trade and sold the business for $6000. He then invested in a bakery in San Francisco and operated it until 1917. When the call came for volunteers he enlisted for service for the World War and was assigned to the 56th Engineers, was transferred to the Searchlight Outfit and saw service over seas at St. Mihiel, the Argonne and at Verdun. He was wounded by a shell dropped from an airplane but did not go to a regular hospital. After the signing of the armistice he was returned to Newport News, Va., then sent to San Francisco, where he was honorably discharged at the presidio on December 3, 1919. He again took up the bakery business in San Francisco with Mrs. Briscoe for two years. In 1920 he came to Pittsburg, bought out a bakery and established his present business and is making it a great success by his thorough understanding of the trade in all its branches. He is courteous and obliging and tries to please his customers in every way. They believe in him, and his goods are the very best that can be manufactured, for he uses only the most wholesome ingredients.

On June 20, 1890, Harry De Piazza was married in San Francisco to Miss Rosa Quilici, also a native of Italy, but residing in San Francisco at the time of her marriage. They have a son, Fay Harry. Mr. De Piazza is a member of the Odd Fellows and is a Deputy Grand Master of the order; he also is a member of the Eagles, Moose, Druids, and active in David A. Solari Post of the American Legion in Pittsburg. He believes Pittsburg is one of the best business cities on the coast for its size and also that it has a great future and he is content to invest his money here.

WALTER AUSTIN ROGERS.—Although not a native of California, the earliest recollections of Walter Austin Rogers are associated with scenes of this then frontier region. Mr. Rogers was born at Ottumwa, Iowa, on December 10, 1851. His father, William Bolton Rogers, was born in Ohio; he married Miss Elizabeth Schaffer, and the year following the birth of our subject moved his family to California, crossing the plains and settling at Alamo, where he engaged in farming. This pursuit however did not hold him long for he went to Dry Town and Camp Seco and mined with fair success. The family then removed to San Francisco, where the father engaged in the draying and house moving business; he was also a member of the San Francisco police force at one time. He remained in business until 1878 when he located in Walnut Creek, Contra Costa County, and there built a hotel, which he and his son Charles W. Rogers operated until 1890. There were four children born of the marriage of Mr. and Mrs. Rogers: Walter Austin, our subject; Charles W.; Mary; and Nora. The mother passed away in 1867, while the father lived to be seventy-nine years old ere he died.

Walter Austin Rogers received his education at the old Lincoln Grammar School in San Francisco and in 1880 purchased his brother's interest in the hotel at Walnut Creek, and ten years later bought his father's interest and since that time conducted the business alone until leasing it.

At Walnut Creek, on April 2, 1902, Mr. Rogers was married to Miss Anna Buck, a native of Kansas, but reared in Montana. She is the daughter of Augustus Buck, now deceased. Mr. and Mrs. Rogers had one son, Walter A. Rogers. Mr. Rogers is a Republican.

PETER CLARY.—To be connected with an important industry as an employee at the Columbia Steel works in Pittsburg, and to have been advanced from an humble position to one of great responsibility, has been the lot of Peter Clary, assistant, under Superintendent Otto Kresse, as melter in the open hearth department of the plant. "Pete" Clary, as he is commonly known, is a native of Genoa, Italy, born on November 2, 1885, the son of Joseph Clary, who was for years in the employ of the Government on the railroad. The father is still living in Italy. The mother, Margaret Clary, died when Pete was a child of four years. As he was going through school he made a resolve to become a mechanic, and began working when he was nine years old as a mechanic's helper in a machine shop in his native town; but in accordance with the Italian law that age was too young for a mechanic, and so he went to learn the shoemaker's trade when he was fifteen. He continued at that trade until 1911, when he decided he would come to the New World; and he landed in New York on May 27 of that year.

His stay in the East was short, only for a visit with some friends. His cousin, Joe Bruno, was in San Francisco, and thither Pete headed and upon his arrival found a job in a steel and iron plant in that city. In July, 1911, he came to Pittsburg and went to work as a laborer in the foundry. Two months later he was detailed to the open hearth furnace department under Otto Kresse, as assistant melter, a position of much responsibility. The four furnaces have a capacity of 420 tons every twenty-four hours. It has been the pleasure of Mr. Clary to witness the growth of this wonderful plant, and he is proud to feel that he has a part in such a large and prosperous concern.

Mr. Clary was married on January 16, 1926, at Pittsburg, to Miss Emere Palmer, a native of Milwaukee, Wis. Fraternally, he is a member of the Pittsburg Aerie of Eagles.

SAM DELULIO.—Under the firm name of the Cooperative Shoe Store, Sam Delulio and his partner conduct an up-to-date establishment in Antioch. Mr. Delulio was born in Bangor, Pa., on May 16, 1879, where his father, Pasquale Delulio, was an anthracite coal miner. His mother was Assunta Farano before her marriage, and both parents were born in the province of Compobasso, Italy, where the father was a farmer. After living in America a number of years, in 1882 they moved back to Italy with their family of children, and there Sam grew up and attended school. In 1886 his parents came back to the United States, but left Sam in Italy with a sister, and they lived with their maternal grandparents. In 1892 Sam came to the land of his birth and joined his parents at Bangor, Pa. In 1894 they moved to Litchfield, Conn., and here the lad had four months of English schooling, but having some trouble with his teacher he left school and secured work in a shoe store in Torrington, Conn., and from there, in 1895, he went to

Newark, N. J. By this time he saw the folly of leaving his studies, and he therefore attended night school and worked during the daytime.

Returning to Torrington, Mr. Delulio was married, in 1900, to Miss A. Cistaro. In 1906 he came to California, leaving his wife and two children until he could make a home for them here. He arrived in San Francisco on January 4. Antioch was his destination, for he had a friend, R. Grananelli, who was a rancher near Antioch. It was not long before he had formed a liking for Antioch, and as the Belshaw building had just been erected on G Street, he entered the employ of C. M. Belshaw in the shoe department and continued there for eighteen months. Then he tried his luck at ranching, but went broke, as he found it was not to his liking. Coming back into town, he worked for five years for the Antioch Shoe Store. In 1913 he started the Cooperative Shoe Shop with a capital of sixty-six dollars, four children and a wife ill in the hospital at Martinez. Two of his children were sick from an attack of typhoid fever. His good friends came to his aid, knowing he was a good workman, and he secured enough work to keep things together and stuck to his business. By square dealing and hard work he succeeded and was sole owner of the business until 1923, when he took Thomas Rosetti in as a partner and moved to his present quarters at the corner of G and Third Streets. His shop is equipped with the best of modern appliances, all machinery being driven by electricity; and he carries a complete stock of shoes, such as to satisfy the most fastidious.

Although born in Bangor, Pa., Mr. Delulio could not find the record of his birth, and was naturalized in Torrington, Conn. Fraternally, he is a member of the Loyal Order of Moose and the Independent Order of Odd Fellows, both in Pittsburg. He is also secretary of Columbus Lodge No. 1315, Sons of Italy, which was instituted on September 5, 1909, as a club with eleven charter members. Up to August 31, 1924, it was conducted as a local society, but it then joined with the Sons of Italy and now has 150 members. Mr. Delulio takes an active part in all movements for the best interest of his fellow citizens.

ROBERT R. LEISHMAN.—A native son of the Golden State who has made good during his span of years is Robert R. Leishman, who is in charge of the millwork department of the Redwood Manufacturers Company at Pittsburg, Cal. This institution covers 100 acres of ground and is the largest of its kind in the West, employing 700 men and with a payroll of $790,000 annually. Approximately 80,000,-000 feet of lumber is worked up each year, and the products are shipped to all parts of the world. More than fifty per cent of the lumber arriving at this plant comes by ship from its own mills at Caspar, Mendocino County, and from the Greenwood plant of the Goodyear Lumber Company. This is supplemented by additional lumber from points in Northern California, Oregon and Washington. Every facility is used at the plant to simplify labor. The manufactured products include sash, doors, windows, cabinets, built-in fixtures, wooden pipe, tanks, silos, etc. It is next to the largest industrial plant in the city of Pittsburg, and has done much to advertise the possibilities of the Pacific Coast country.

Robert R. Leishman was born in Mendocino County on September 14, 1898, and is a son of John and Grace Leishman. The father has been engaged in the lumber industry at Caspar for thirty-five years and is a stockholder in the Caspar Lumber Company, and also in the Redwood Manufacturers Company. Robert Leishman has a sister, Verda, now a student in the College of the Pacific at Stockton. Our subject graduated from the Mendocino Union High School, Class of 1916, and then entered Pomona College, where he was a sophomore when he entered the service of the United States. He was in detached service for thirteen months, trained at the Fairmount school for non-commissioned officers, and received his commission as second lieutenant. He is a charter member of the Keith Powell Post of the American Legion at Claremont, which he helped to organize, and on coming to Pittsburg in 1921 was active in getting an appropriation from the supervisors for the memorial building for the David A. Solari Post in that city. He was elected the commander of the David A. Solari Post on January 1, 1925.

At Pomona, Cal., in 1922, Mr. Leishman was married to Miss Theda White, of Pomona, and they have a daughter Rhea Jane. He is a Mason, holding his membership in Mendocino County, and is a member of the commission on Americanization under the California State Department of the American Legion. The family home is at 625 East Twelfth Street, Pittsburg.

BERT W. LANZ.—The superintendent of the sheet mill of the Columbia Steel Corporation at Pittsburg, Cal., Bert W. Lanz is one of the ablest sheet rolling-mill men in the United States. He was born on April 27, 1890, in Western Pennsylvania, and comes from a family of steel workers, his father, grandfather and great-grandfather all having been steel workers. After his school days were over he also entered the steel business and was actively engaged in that industry in various capacities until he came to California. He was employed by the Zug Iron & Steel Co., in Pittsburgh, Pa.; the Berger Manufacturing Co. of Canton, Ohio; and the Otis Steel Co., at Cleveland, Ohio. Early in 1924 he came to Pittsburg, Cal., and succeeded W. A. Blockinger as superintendent of the sheet mill. With a thorough understanding of this branch of the steel industry he entered upon his career here with a confidence born of experience and his success speaks for itself.

The marriage of Mr. Lanz was celebrated in Pittsburgh, Pa., in 1909, when he was united with Miss Violet Blaichner, a native of that city. They have two children, William and James Francis. Mr. Lanz takes an active interest in the welfare of his adopted city and is a member of the Chamber of Commerce and of the Lions Club, in both of which organizations he exerts a helpful influence.

Frank Pratini

FRANK PRATINI.—An artist in designing granite and marble monuments, Frank Pratini has had years of practical experience in his specialty and is numbered among the substantial citizens of Antioch, where he has been located for many years as the proprietor of the Antioch Marble and Granite Works. As a sculptor and designer he has no equal in this section of the country. He was born in the province of Novarra, Italy, on December 1, 1883, and is descended from a family of sculptors. His father was Charles Pratini, a sculptor of note and a granite worker for many years in Barre, Vt., where he became a citizen of this country. David Pratini, grandfather of Frank, was also a noted sculptor in Italy. The mother was Josephine Pratini, who with her husband returned to Italy after being in America for several years, and it was then Frank was born. He grew up in Italy until he was fourteen, attending the schools of his locality, and then came to Barre, Vt., continuing his schooling there by studying drafting and sculpture in granite. At the age of eighteen he began a three-years apprenticeship in Young Brothers' Granite Shop, located at Barre.

In 1905 Mr. Pratini left the East and arrived in San Francisco on October 25, and at once secured work as a granite cutter. At the time of the earthquake and fire he lost all his tools. In 1907, with a partner, he opened a granite shop at 678 Broadway, San Francisco, but sold out after three years to his partner and went to Nevada and opened up a granite quarry. When the custom house in San Francisco was built, Mr. Pratini was selected to be one of the granite cutters to do the art work, cutting out eagles and lion heads from solid blocks of granite, and continued on the job for nine months.

In 1915 Frank Pratini came to Contra Costa County, located at Pittsburg, and became the proprietor of the Tivoli Hotel, remaining there till 1919. He then located in Antioch and started the Antioch Granite and Marble Works, where he has since executed many contracts for his growing patronage. When one wants an artistic monument, all that is necessary is to give Mr. Pratini an idea and he works out the design with dispatch. Samples of his work are to be found in the Byron Cemetery, Brentwood Cemetery, and Rio Vista Cemetery, as also at Antioch, Pittsburg and elsewhere, and even in Nevada and as far down the coast as Monterey. Six men are employed in his business, but he superintends the cutting, finishing and selling, always aiming to please the most exacting of his patrons.

In October, 1924, Frank Pratini was united in marriage with Mrs. Desolina Pratini, the widow of his brother Ernest, by whom she had two children: Evelyn, a graduate of the Pittsburg High School, class of 1926, and now attending the San Jose Teachers' College; and Inez, a student in the Pittsburg High School. The family make their home in Pittsburg, where Mr. Pratini is conducting a rooming house. He makes trips to

Antioch daily by automobile. Mr. Pratini belongs to several fraternal organizations and is active in the East Contra Costa Chamber of Commerce.

HARRY A. BARNES.—The genial and efficient secretary of the Pittsburg Chamber of Commerce, H. A. Barnes, was born at Detroit, Mich., on October 7, 1884, the son of Fred W. and Kate (Marion) Barnes, the former having been engaged as a logman in and around logging camps in Michigan during his lifetime. He died when our subject was only two years old. The mother, a native of Tivertown, England, died when he was six years of age; thus his early life was robbed of the usual joys of childhood. He early learned to rely upon himself, working for his living from boyhood, and realizing the value of an education obtained by means of night school. While pursuing his high school studies in this manner, he did work at odd times on the Detroit Free Press, receiving $3.50 per week for his services. He later took up advertising and editorial work on that same paper, and also worked for the Times and Journal at various times.

Leaving Detroit, Mr. Barnes went to the editorial department of the Toronto Globe, Toronto, Ont., in 1903, where he covered the police courts and stations. From there he went to Winnipeg, Manitoba, and took up feature story writing for the Free Press. He later became a special edition writer in connection with the Winnipeg papers, traveling over Manitoba, Saskatchawan, and Alberta. For a time in 1904, he worked for the Calgary Herald, and during the period he worked at times in connection with the well-known editorial writer, Bill Mack, in the northern Alberta country. Among other work, in the month of June, 1904, they took pictures, the first ever obtained, of the Stony Creek Indians; these primitive people had the superstition that taking their pictures robbed them of their God, and when a number of the tribe were taken sick soon after the pictures had been taken, Mr. Barnes and his friend were invited to leave, and this they were obliged to do, taking their departure on July 1, 1904, Dominion Day. Mr. Barnes also enjoys the distinction of having taken the first pictures of the fanatical Doukobors in the far Northwest country, sixty miles north of Edmonton, whose religious fanaticism led them to exposures on the verge of nudity, in that cold country.

Mr. Barnes then bought out the Ponoka Herald, in Alberta, and this venture was prospering, when the plant was burned out, in November, 1904, and he lost everything, including the little inheritance that had come to him as well as his savings. In the spring of 1905 he went to Seattle, Wash. and for a while worked on the Seattle Times, and later went to the advertising department of the Post Intelligencer. He remained in Seattle until May, 1905, when he went to Portland, Ore., at the time of the Lewis and Clark Exposition, and there worked on the Portland Oregonian for about four months; at the end of that time coming to San Francisco, and taking work on the San Francisco Examiner. In the early part of 1906 he had a call to go back to Detroit to do newspaper work, and arrived in that city just the day before the San Francisco earthquake and fire. California called him, however, and October 1, 1906, found him back in Sacramento, where he had charge of the classified advertising section of the Sacramento Bee for three years. He then engaged in the insurance business, continuing until he came to Pittsburg, in June, 1921. He has been connected with the Pittsburg Chamber of Commerce for the past two years, being first elected as part-time secretary on September 18, 1924, upon the resignation of D. C. Kelley. Mr. Barnes was elected full-time secretary and building director at the annual meeting held January 8, 1925. When he took office there were but eighty-two members; there are now 202.

Mr. Barnes married Alpha M. Selinger in San Francisco in 1915. She was born in Marysville, Cal. Two sons have blessed this union: Marion Francis and Harold Albert. Mr. Barnes is thoroughly and actively interested in helping Pittsburg expand to meet the requirements of a rapidly growing city; and also in promoting the best interests of Contra Costa County as a whole, for he realizes the natural advantages to be found here, his travels enabling him to make comparisons most favorable to this garden spot of the world. During the World War, he served as inspector in the shipyards of the Union Iron Works at San Francisco. California is now his home state, Contra Costa his county, and Pittsburg his home community. He is popular, and with Mrs. Barnes, is welcomed at social activities as well as business conferences. Mrs. Barnes is much interested in the development of Pittsburg and surrounding territory, and acts as assistant in the local Chamber of Commerce office.

MANUEL G. AZEVEDO.—Since 1921 Manuel G. Azevedo has been a special agent of the New York Life Insurance Company with offices at 505 Sixth Street, Antioch, where he and his family reside. Prior to that, from 1903 to the time he took up life insurance, he was the leading barber in Antioch, having a three-chair shop in the First National Bank Building. He is a man of unusual ability and easily makes friends and retains them. During 1916 he was the State President of the U. P. E. C. Lodge.

M. G. Azevedo was born in the Island of St. George, of the Azores group, on February 13, 1877, and grew up there until he was twelve. His parents were John and Isabel Azevedo, the former deceased and the latter still living. During his boyhood he attended the schools of his native island; and after arriving in California, in 1891, he went to Delano, Kern County, where he had an aunt, Miss Barbara Albert, and there lived two years and attended school to learn the English language. From Delano he went to Marin County and thence to San Francisco, finishing his schooling at the Lincoln School at Fifth and Mission Streets.

He spent eight years in that city, and one year and four months in Oakland, where he learned the barber's trade. In 1903 he came to Antioch to start a shop for himself, and since then has built up a popular and successful business.

At Antioch, on November 26, 1900, M. G. Azevedo was united in marriage with Emily Renas; and they have two children: Henry, who runs a barber shop in Antioch; and Maria, who attends the high school. Mr. Azevedo is a prominent member of the U. P. E. C., the Elks, and the Red Men, and belongs to the East Contra Costa County Chamber of Commerce. Politically he supports Republican men and measures. He served nearly four years as town trustee.

EDWARD V. CAMPBELL.—Holding the responsible position of yard superintendent at the Columbia Steel Corporation's plant at Pittsburg, E. V. Campbell has charge of all cranes, locomotives and all outside general labor. This place of responsibility has been gained by years of thorough preparation, beginning when a lad of sixteen, when he first went to work for the Union Steel Casting Company at Pittsburgh, Pa. A native of Pennsylvania, he was born at Oil City, March 4, 1889, the son of James and Rebecca (McMurtry) Campbell. The father was a pioneer oil man. Both parents are now deceased. Grandfather Campbell came to California in 1849, and in all made four trips to the Golden State, three times via the plains, when he was captain of a train that brought many miners here, and once via Cape Horn. The Campbells were originally from Virginia and were related to Alexander Campbell, the founder of the Christian Church. The parents of our subject followed the oil business in western Pennsylvania, and later moved to McDonald, Washington County, where E. V. Campbell grew to manhood. He attended the public schools, including two years at the Pittsburgh High School. At the age of sixteen he began working for the Union Steel Casting Company, and when nineteen he went to Moundsville, W. Va., and became timekeeper for the Manufacturers' Light and Heat Company, remaining there three years. He then spent five years with the Wheeling Mould and Foundry Company, as chief shipper. During the construction of the Panama Canal this company furnished the lifting and moving machinery for many of the locks and gates. Beginning in 1914, Mr. Campbell was with the Mesta Machine Company, of West Homestead, Pa., as chief shipper for two years, and then became superintendent of transportation for the ensuing six years. Leaving his position, he came direct to Pittsburg, Cal., and secured a position with the Columbia Steel Corporation, among whose trusted employees he has since been numbered.

Mr. Campbell has been twice married, first in Washington, Pa., where he was united with Miss Elma Ruth Gibson, of whom two children were born, Mary Virginia and Frank Kendall. Mrs. Campbell died of the flu in 1918. The second marriage took place at Greenburg, uniting him with Mrs. Mary (Gibson) Wineman, a sister of his first wife. She was a widow with one son, Louis Gibson Wineman. Mr. Campbell brought his family to Pittsburg, consisting of his wife and the three children, and Mrs. Campbell's mother, making the trip by automobile from Pittsburgh, Pa., to Pittsburg, Cal., where they are settled comfortably in a home among an ever widening circle of friends. The family attend the Christian Church. Mr. Campbell is looked upon as a progressive citizen, loyal to the best interests of his city and county, as well as of the corporation by whom he is employed.

CARLOS E. CORTES.—One of the leading men with the Shell Oil Company, at Martinez, and equally well-known in social and business circles, Carlos E. Cortes has been a resident here for the past decade, and in his responsible position is recognized as a man of authority. He was born at Guadalajara, Mexico, on June 14, 1881, the son of Mariano and Clarisa (Ortigoza) Cortes. Mariano Cortes was born in Mexico. He was a physician for many years at Guadalajara, his death occurring in 1908, at seventy years of age, which age is just now reached by his widow, who still resides in Guadalajara, Mexico's second largest city. One sister and one brother of Carlos also reside there.

Carlos Cortes grew to manhood in Guadalajara, and attended the schools there. Graduating from the high school at Notre Dame University, he went to Palo Alto, Cal., and entered Stanford University, where he studied the civil engineering course. When the great fire and earthquake of 1906 occurred and the subsequent necessity of rebuilding San Francisco called for engineers, he was offered a position as engineer with the San Francisco firm of architects, Shea & Lofquist. Making good, he was soon advanced to chief engineer of construction, and designed and supervised the steel construction of the Plaza Hotel, the Bank of Italy, St. Mary's Hospital, and many churches.

About 1907 he returned to Mexico and became a general building constructor in his native city; while there he was elected mayor of Guadalajara, and served with distinction. Returning to California in 1914, he engaged with the Shell Oil Company at Martinez. He has since advanced to his present position, that of construction engineer for the company, in connection with its great refinery at Martinez.

The marriage of Mr. Cortes, which occurred in San Francisco, in 1906, united him with Reine Alexandrine Blum, a daughter of Myrtle Blum, and granddaughter of Simon Blum, a pioneer merchant of Martinez. Six children have blessed their union: Carlos, graduate with the Class of 1924 from the Alhambra Union High School, and now in the university; Alejandro, Elena and Edwardo, all attending high school; Vincente, in grammar school; and Susana, three years old. Mr. Cortes is a Mason, holding membership in Mexico; and he belongs to the Moose.

PITTSBURG CHAMBER OF COMMERCE.—This institution, so active in promoting the best interests of the city of Pittsburg, was first started August 25, 1891. Joseph McAvoy was chosen president pro tem., and George P. Keller, secretary pro tem. On April 11, 1912, Dr. F. S. Gregory was elected president and Otis Loveridge vice president, with W. J. Buchanan as secretary. Interest waned, but this was revived when it was found that a professional publicity man was what was needed and at a meeting called September 11, 1917, Charles A. Vogelsang, who had acted as governor general of the Pacific-Panama Exposition, was endorsed for that office. Interest died down again. Then a meeting was called by the late B. P. Lanteri, at that time mayor of Pittsburg, to form a Chamber of Commerce. He acted as president pro tem. of the meeting, and R. N. Wolfe was appointed temporary secretary; then W. E. McDermott was nominated and elected president, Wade W. Moore elected secretary, and G. Todero elected treasurer, and a constitution and by-laws were drafted; but the Pittsburg Chamber of Commerce died down again.

November 10, 1921, the present Chamber of Commerce was formed, when, at the call of the Pittsburg city board of trustees, a meeting was held and W. J. Buchanan was elected president, Fred Mullins vice president, and R. M. Dorton secretary and treasurer; at this meeting thirty-two signed up as members. This was the real beginning of the Chamber. At the annual election held on January 5, 1922, the following officers and board of directors were elected; W. J. Buchanan, president; Fred Mullins, vice president; Otis Loveridge, secretary and treasurer; and Carl Lepori, Armand Stow, George McDonald, A. V. McFaul, Ernest Ward, Earl McDermott, directors. With all this influence the organization did not make much headway. Up to March 28, 1923, only part-time secretaries had been appointed; but this was changed at the meeting held on that date, when a motion was made and carried that a full-time secretary be appointed, and George C. Kelley was given the office. He resigned on April 23, 1924, and Harry A. Barnes was elected part-time secretary and served as such until September 18, 1924, when he was made full-time secretary. At the annual meeting held January 8, 1925, the following officers were elected: E. H. Ward, president; F. S. Ramsdell, first vice president; W. J. Buchanan, second vice president; Armand Stow, treasurer; Harry A. Barnes, secretary and building director. The following board of trustees were elected: E. H. Ward, J. E. Bankson, W. J. Buchanan, N. A. Becker, John L. Buffo, Arnold Linscheid, Fred S. Ramsdell, Otis Loveridge, A. V. McFaul, Armand Stow and R. M. Dorton; the latter resigned and moved to Monterey and was replaced by Oscar L. McQuiddy. There are now 202 members in the Chamber, as compared with eighty-two in September, 1924, and many worthwhile things have been accomplished.

The Chamber of Commerce of Pittsburg was instrumental in establishing the first union high school, known as the Riverview Union High

School, which is located at Antioch and embraces the Antioch, Pittsburg and Oakley districts. Then, seeing the need for a high school in Pittsburg, the Chamber advocated a school for the city, and organized a new high school district, which maintains a high school in the grammar school building, in Pittsburg; it is now agitating a bond issue for a new high school building.

The Chamber also cooperated with the new Library Club, and the Pittsburg Woman's Club, in passing a $20,000 bond issue for the new library building in Pittsburg, which is now completed; also in building the new city hall. The Chamber is doing effectual work in proclaiming to the world Pittsburg's advantages as a manufacturing city and Contra Costa County's great agricultural wealth, ranking as the richest county in the State, and leading in hay, grain, and dairy products. The value of a live Chamber of Commerce to a growing and up-to-date city, such as Pittsburg, can readily be seen and appreciated, and Pittsburg is indeed fortunate in having such capable and farseeing men at the helm in civic betterment.

BEN R. SERPA.—The junior member of the firm of Pacheco & Serpa, proprietors of the Crockett Creamery, Ben R. Serpa is a native of the Island of Pico, of the Azores group, and was born on December 11, 1881, a son of Joseph R. Serpa, a bricklayer in his native land and now deceased. The mother is still living in the Azores.

Ben R. Serpa attended the schools of his island and remained at home till he was sixteen. He was determined to come to America, the land that he had heard so much about as he was growing up; and arriving in California went to Turlock in 1908 and there followed farming until 1914, when he came to Crockett. He entered the employ of the C. & H. refinery, and for nine years worked steadily. In 1923 he went to work for Tony Pacheco in the Crockett Creamery, and so well did he satisfy his employer that on April 1, 1926, he was able to become a partner and bought a half interest in the business. The Crockett Creamery is one of the dependable businesses of Crockett, and the young men at the head of the concern have a high standing among the business men of the community. The products of the creamery are retailed in Crockett, Valona, Port Costa and near-by towns by motor vehicles. The milk is bought from the various dairies and is handled in the most sanitary manner to insure purity and give satisfaction to all customers.

Mr. Serpa was united in marriage on October 12, 1918, at Crockett, to Miss Clara Avellar, daughter of John J. and Mary Gloria (Machado) Avellar, natives of the Azores and California, respectively, now living in Valona. Mr. and Mrs. Serpa live in Valona, where they have a modern home. He is a member of the I. D. E. S. and U. P. E. C. lodges; has served several years as secretary, and later as president, of the former; and is a past president of the U. P. E. C.

WILLIAM JAMES BORLAND.—One of the solid, substantial business men of Contra Costa County is William James Borland, who has invaded the widely different callings of the rancher and contractor and attained considerable success at both. Mr. Borland is a native son, having been born in Oakland on July 21, 1878, the son of Archie and Agnes Borland. The father was a miner and head of a family of four children of whom the subject of this sketch was the youngest. A brother, Archie Borland, resides in Oakland; one sister, Agnes, now Mrs. W. M. Hart, makes her home in Berkeley; while the other sister, Mary, is Mrs. Van Odeling of Oakland. Mr. Borland received his education in the Oakland High School and the Hopkins Academy, which was on the site where the Merritt Hospital now stands. When a youth of twenty he started out for himself and worked as a cattleman in New Mexico. In 1906 he returned to California and embarked in the business of road grading and street contracting, a calling which he has followed ever since, building a number of important roads in different parts of the State.

In connection with his other activities, in 1921 Mr. Borland started a cattle ranch, leasing a tract of land containing 6400 acres from the East Bay Water Company on which he fattens several hundred head of cattle each year. He is a man of considerable means and influence in his community. In his fraternal affiliations he is a member of the Masons and the Elks. He is also a member of the San Francisco Chamber of Commerce and the Orinda Country Club; he is an ardent golfer and fond of hunting and outdoor life. In 1917 he married Miss Gertrude Jordon of Oakland, whose parents are both deceased. Mr. and Mrs. Borland are the parents of two daughters, Jane and Agnes.

ANTONE MELROSE.—A native Californian, Tony Melrose, as he is familiarly known, was born in San Francisco on August 8, 1893, a son of Antone and Mary Melrose, both born in Italy. The father was engaged as a fisherman, but is now deceased. The mother, now sixty years of age, still makes her home in Pittsburg. Tony grew up in the bay metropolis, remaining there until 1906. After the fire and earthquake the family moved to Pittsburg, where he finished the grammar school. His first work and business connection was with the Contra Costa Gas Company, in Pittsburg, now the Coast Counties Gas & Electric Company. Beginning as a laborer, he gradually worked his way towards the top until 1917, when he resigned his position to become local manager for the Pacific Gas & Electric Company, a position he still holds to the satisfaction of all concerned. This company has a large business in Pittsburg, furnishing power to the large manufacturing corporations doing business in that city.

Tony Melrose was married at Pittsburg in 1911 to Miss Patricia Rubina, and they have two children, Tony and Marion. Mr. Melrose is an active member of the Pittsburg Chamber of Commerce, and is a stanch booster for the city's best interests.

FRED E. GEORGE.—Favorably known in the milling business in California, Fred E. George, now superintendent of the California Bean Growers' Warehouse Association, with offices at Pittsburg, was born January 23, 1877, at Portland, Ore., a son of John L. and Fredricka L. George. The father was well-known in banking circles as vice-president of the First National Bank, and for years he was engaged in the wholesale barber supply business. Both parents are now deceased.

After leaving the public schools Fred E. George went to sea and for the following twelve years journeyed into various ports, in time becoming first mate. He spent one year in the shipyards of the Union Iron Works in San Francisco and then took up the milling business with the Crown Mills in Stockton and remained two years learning the business. The next two years were spent with the Globe Milling Company in Los Angeles, and he was then made superintendent of the warehouse for the Los Angeles Farm Milling Company for eighteen months. In each of these changes he was broadening his scope of knowledge and fitting himself for advancement. For seven years he was miller at the Del Monte Mills in San Francisco, and for five years was miller for the Globe Grain and Milling Company, also in that city. He was next with the Hazzard Warehouse Cleaners for seven years, remaining there until he accepted his present position as superintendent of the California Bean Growers' Warehouse Association. Mr. George is thoroughly competent to deal with men, and has always held the respect of those under his direction, as well as those whom he served. He is in touch with bean growers and brokers all over California, and is continually making a study of the business he follows, thus keeping abreast of the times in every way. He spends most of his time in Pittsburg looking after the interests of the business here, as this is one of the largest shipping points in the State.

Mr. George was married in San Francisco on June 15, 1906, to Miss Sarah Cochran, daughter of William and Anna Cochran. Her father was the veterinary for the E. J. (Lucky) Baldwin ranch, in charge of his racing stock, for a number of years. They have an adopted daughter, Agusta, now the wife of Harlan Howsley and the mother of two children, Harlan and Walter. Mr. George is a member of Oakland Lodge No. 171, B. P. O. E., and of Oakland Lodge No. 188, F. & A. M. Politically, he supports men and measures he thinks will be the best for the country regardless of party lines. His recreation is found in the out-of-doors, and he is very much interested in all kinds of athletic sports.

The Bean Growers' Warehouse Association erected a warehouse in Pittsburg in 1922 with a capacity of 100,000 sacks, and during the season it is a hive of industry. On November 18, 1925, the following article appeared in the Pittsburg Dispatch, which gives valuable information of the bean industry in the delta section of Central California:

"And now comes the lowly bean to soar to the pinnacle of eminence and share in the topmost honors of California's agricultural wealth. The praise of the bean is being seen in Pittsburg this week, with the arrival of no less than 70,000 sacks of beans of various varieties at the warehouse and processing plant of the California Bean Growers' Warehouse Corporation (up-to-date for the season of 1925.) They are the products of the Sacramento and San Joaquin delta districts and are brought here on barges and railroad trains from the bean fields for cleaning, grading, processing and repacking for shipment. A large tonnage is being made ready for export. The week's receipts, representing the first heavy shipments of the 1925 crop, will average 100 pounds to the sack, or approximately seven million pounds.

"By the time they reach the kitchen of Mr. and Mrs. Consumer they will have an average value of eight cents a pound and will hit the family budget for an aggregate of $560,000. The bean crop this year is seven weeks later than usual, according to Fred E. George, superintendent of the bean warehouse, but the lateness of the crop is proving a boon to bean growers. The result, he declares, is a heavier yield per acre, larger beans and better quality. Mr. George says the season now is sufficiently advanced to safely say that 1925 will be the banner bean year in California. A large crew has been employed at the bean warehouse to aid in sacking and handling of beans after they are cleaned and graded, which is largely automatic. Several barges are arriving daily from the bean fields, and export shipments are to be started within the next week."

WILLIAM H. BEASLEY.—The leading contracting plumber in Antioch is W. H. Beasley, who not only is a contractor, but also deals in all kinds of plumbing fixtures and accessories to his line. For the past ten years he has lived and worked in Antioch, and his shop on Third Street is usually a scene of busy industry. So thorough is he in executing his contracts that once a job is completed it is an advertisement for another bigger and better job.

W. H. Beasley was born on Squaw Creek, in Nevada County, Cal., on August 29, 1879. His father was Richard Beasley, who with his father and his father's family came from Boston, Mass., across the plains to California, the new Eldorado, in a covered wagon. Upon arriving here the father and grandfather engaged in mining for gold in Nevada County. They were both born in Ireland. It was in Nevada County that Richard Beasley married Miss Elizabeth Dugan, born in Boston, Mass. For many years the Beasleys followed mining and prospecting, eventually removing from Nevada City to Port Costa, and thence to San Francisco, where they ran the Metropolitan Hotel.

W. H. Beasley attended the public schools in San Francisco, finishing at the Polytechnic High School. He had to go to work early in life, and while serving his apprenticeship to the plumber's trade with W. F. Wilson, he attended night school. After completing his trade he worked as a journeyman, and upon coming to Antioch embarked in the business on his own account; and now he employs three and four men all the time. Some of the buildings that show his handiwork are the City Hall,

Bank of Antioch building, Bloomfield Apartments, Catholic rectory, Burroughs residence, and many other cottages and residences in and around Antioch. The reason for his popularity is that he gives not only service but also satisfaction to all his patrons.

On September 6, 1905, in Antioch, Mr. Beasley married Miss Estelle J. Sweeney, the talented daughter of C. A. Sweeney, one of the oldest officers in the town of Antioch, where he serves as city marshal. Mrs. Beasley is an only daughter and the second child in a family of three. Their family consists of two children: Ramona, attending the State Teachers' College in San Jose; and Billy, a high school pupil. The family are members of the Catholic Church in Antioch. Mr. Beasley belongs to the Eagles, the Native Sons, and the Young Men's Institute, in Antioch. Mrs. Beasley is a member of the Native Daughters and the Young Ladies' Institute. Their home is at Sixth and A Streets.

KARL J. HENNING.—One of the leading contractors and builders of fine homes and apartments in Richmond is Karl J. Henning, of No. 500 Key Boulevard. He has resided here since 1920 and since that time has revolutionized the building business in this locality. Before he began to erect his style of homes there were very few houses of any pretentions whatsoever. Up to 1926 he has built nearly 120 fine houses, most of them in the Mira Vista section, and costing from $5000 to $20,000. Among them we mention that for Edward Gray, assistant superintendent of the Standard Oil Company, on Eleventh Street; Dr. St. John Healy, on Thirteenth Street; the R. T. Osborn home; the Cecil Brunner Apartments, on Brooks Avenue near Twenty-third Street; the Casa Madrona Apartments at Barrett Avenue and Twenty-fourth Street. He specializes in home building and employs from twenty to fifty men, according to the job.

Mr. Henning was born in Saxony, Germany, on December 21, 1886, and received his education in the schools of his home community. He studied drafting in the advanced schools, specializing in bridge building and heavy construction work. He entered the employ of a company that had a patent on a composition flooring and he traveled over Italy, Russia, England and Africa, establishing branch agencies for his firm. At the age of twenty-three he was sent to St. Paul, Minn., to establish an agency; and later he became a contractor and builder in the Twin Cities on the Mississippi River and was prospering satisfactorily. He did not like the severe winters of that northern city and decided he would come to California to look after some real estate he had purchased in Richmond, in 1911, from a salesman who visited him. He had never seen the lots and bought from the map carried by the salesman. He was more fortunate than many others for his lots happened to be on high ground in the Grand View Terrace tract. He found no sale for his lots at that time and decided he would begin building homes on them to induce buyers to inspect and purchase. From the beginning he had difficulty in

914   CONTRA COSTA COUNTY

selling houses at the prices he asked, but soon the people began to become educated to owning a good home and he has since kept busy building. Most of his best structures are in the Mira Vista district, though he has done work in various parts of Richmond, and built some buildings at Crockett, and in El Cerrito. He feels well satisfied with conditions and believes Richmond has a bright future. Being of an observing nature he noticed that facilities had to be provided in other counties, where conditions had to be changed to suit, while here in Contra Costa County nature has provided the harbors and shipping facilities at no expense to the people. He has invested in lots in various sections of the city and is confident that in due time they will all be very valuable. He says that the main artery of travel, San Pablo Avenue, has no equal anywhere in the country and is bound to help build up from the county line through to Pinole.

On February 26, 1910 Mr. Henning married Mary Sommer, a native of Germany, who came to America at the age of eleven and was reared in St. Paul, Minn. They have two children: Erwin and Marjorie, both attending the Golden Gate Academy in Berkeley, of whose board of trustees Mr. Henning is a member. He belongs to the Seventh Day Adventist Church, in which he is an elder. This denomination controls the Golden Gate Academy. He is a member of the Builders Exchange and of the Lions Club, both of Richmond. He takes an active interest in the Chamber of Commerce, of which he is a member. In politics he supports the Republican party on national issues, but in local affairs he considers the candidate irrespective of party lines. To perfect himself in his work Mr. Henning took a correspondence course after coming to America. No civic improvement is ever brought to his notice but what he gives it his support and he is considered by all who know him as one of the leading citizens of Contra Costa County.

GEORGE H. CARR.—Among the most enterprising and progressive young business men of Pittsburg, Cal., is George H. Carr, whose keen business ability, sound judgment and fidelity to details have been recognized by the Columbia Steel Corporation, where he is ably filling the responsible position of paymaster and chief timekeeper.

Born on July 16, 1896, at Portland, Ore., he is the son of Frank and Elizabeth (Connors) Carr. His father was at one time county clerk of Multnomah County, Ore., and for several years was associated with the Frank Smith Lumber Company of Portland. He passed away in 1924 at the age of fifty-eight. The mother was born in Minnesota and was brought to California at the age of five years, being reared on the McDaniel ranch near Suisun.

George H. Carr spent his boyhood days in Portland, and after graduating from the Davis Grammar School he attended the Lincoln High School of that city for two years, after which, in 1913, he accepted a position with the parent plant of the Columbia Steel Corporation, at

Portland. This company now maintains plants at Pittsburg and Torrance, Cal., and in Carbon and Iron Counties, Utah, where they operate coke ovens and smelter works. In 1915 Mr. Carr was transferred to Pittsburg, Cal., to take over the responsible position of foundry clerk; and later he became an accountant in the general offices of the company at Pittsburg. During the World War he enlisted in the United States Government service as cost inspector at San Francisco, in the Bethlehem Ship Building Works, remaining at this post for thirteen months. After his honorable discharge he returned to Pittsburg, where he reentered the plant of the Columbia Steel Corporation as paymaster and chief timekeeper. The immense amount of detail incident to the careful oversight of this important position can be better understood when one realizes that the time and wages of 1250 employees must be accurately computed by this department before each pay day.

On February 19, 1918, George H. Carr was united in marriage with Miss Margaret Lynch, daughter of the pioneer rancher, Philip Lynch, who located at Antioch, Cal., when she was a little girl. Her education was received at St. Rose Academy, San Francisco.

Fraternally, Mr. Carr helped to organize Pittsburg Lodge No. 1474, B. P. O. E., the Lyons Club, and the David A. Solari Post of the American Legion at Pittsburg, Cal., and is active in each.

ROBERT T. OSBORN.—Among men of affairs connected with the Standard Oil Company at Richmond, Cal., is Robert T. Osborn, a man of high ideals of citizenship, and unquestioned business ability, which has been especially emphasized by him in the position he now occupies as manager of the refinery at Richmond. His record as an employee of the Standard Oil Company has been a continuous succession of promotions and advancements. Starting as an employee in 1913 he was assigned to the clerical force, later transferred to the laboratory department, and in time given charge of the physical laboratory. His next advancement made him chief refiner, and after successfully filling this position he became assistant superintendent of the refinery. His intelligent application of wise business methods, the exercise of superior judgment in overseeing men and his loyalty to the company's best interests in all former positions, so attracted the attention of higher officials of the corporation that Mr. Osborn was chosen, in February, 1924, superintendent of the refinery, with full charge of all manufacturing at the Richmond plant. On June 9, 1926, he became manager of the refinery.

Robert T. Osborn was born at Gallatin, Mo., on August 29, 1890, the son of William T. and Minnie (Higgins) Osborn, both of whom were born in Missouri. The father was a merchant at Gallatin and has spent all of his days in that place; his ancestors were English, those of his wife were from Ireland. Mr. and Mrs. W. T. Osborn are still living in the old home place at Gallatin. Their family consists of three children: Robert T., the subject of this review; Edwin, who lives in Oklahoma; and Mary, who resides with her parents. Robert T. Osborn was educated in the public schools at Gallatin, and held a most remarkable record for attendance, having never missed a day nor been tardy during his entire attendance in both the grammar and the high schools. After graduating from high school he attended the University of Missouri, from which institution he was graduated in June, 1912, with the degree of A. B. His business career with the Standard Oil Company at Richmond began in January, 1913, and he has remained with the company ever since. During this time he has achieved success in every position he has occupied and has won for himself a prominent position in the business circles of Richmond.

On October 20, 1919, Robert T. Osborn was united in marriage with Bessie Troy, of Richmond, a daughter of the late John and Mary (Hatch) Troy. Mrs. Osborn has two sisters and a brother in Richmond: Cary Troy, an employee of the Standard Oil Company; Marian, now Mrs. E. L. Schofield; and Helen, the wife of M. R. Burdick. Mr. Osborn is greatly interested in the welfare of the community and lends his aid to all worthy movements that aim to better the educational, moral, civic and commercial interests of Richmond. He is a member of Richmond Lodge No. 1251 B. P. O. E.

EDWARD W. CORDUA.—The obliging agent of the Santa Fe at Oakley is Edward W. Cordua, and he is also local agent for the American Railway Express Company. A native of Holland, he was born on June 22, 1890, and attended the schools of his native community until he was fifteen years old. In 1905 he came alone to the United States and stopped in Kansas City for two years. He was determined to see something of the West, and so sought work on the big cattle ranches in various parts of the Northwest and spent the time up to about 1910 in the saddle. Arriving in Denver, Colo., he took a course in telegraphy and then secured a position with the Denver & Rio Grande Railroad as an operator for one year. Having demonstrated his ability, Mr. Cordua became an employee of the Santa Fe and worked at various stations between Albuquerque and Raton on the New Mexico Division as a telegraph operator. On April 12, 1912, he came to California and became operator at Corcoran, and later at Bakersfield. He was next promoted to become station agent and operator at Planada, and in 1916 was transferred to Oakley as agent and telegraph operator, a position he is filling with satisfaction both to his employers and to the public.

Edward W. Cordua was married at Raton, N. M., to Miss Edith Marie Altman, a native of Indiana, but reared and educated in New Mexico. This union has been blessed with two boys: Harry T., aged thirteen, who is musically inclined and specializes with the saxophone and piano, taking an active part in musical circles in this vicinity, and with the Columbia Park Boys' Band in San Francisco, of which he is a member; and Edward George, another popular Oakley lad. In politics Mr.

Cordua is a Republican. He is a Mason, serving as Junior Warden of Antioch Lodge No. 175, F. & A. M.; and he is also a member of the Sciots, Antioch Pyramid No. 24, and both he and his wife are members of the Eastern Star Chapter at Antioch. Mr. Cordua is also a member of the Santa Fe Masonic Club of Los Angeles. Both Mr. and Mrs. Cordua are held in high esteem by their many friends in eastern Contra Costa County, and take an active part in social circles here.

GEORGE W. CARRICK.—A resident of Contra Costa County since October 22, 1911, George W. Carrick was born in Klamath Falls, Ore., on August 16, 1884, the son of Arthur Carrick, a native of California, born at Yreka, where he grew to manhood and learned the trade of the blacksmith. He started under Mr. Johnson, and shod the stage horses for the company running stages between Sisson and Red Bluff, when he was eighteen years old. He married Mollie George, who crossed the plains with her parents when she was eight years of age. Her father, Ben George, homesteaded land near Grants Pass, Ore. Both the Carrick and the George families were among the early pioneers of the northern part of California and saw much of the pioneer life of their period. Arthur Carrick and his wife located at Klamath Falls, Ore., where he was the blacksmith for the stage company running to that place. He owned forty acres in what is now the heart of Klamath Falls. There were five children born to Mr. and Mrs. Carrick: Fred W., who died in Los Angeles; Lela, who married William Humphrey of Klamath Falls; George W., of this review; Eva, Mrs. Steve Pollett, of Portland, Ore., and Sidney. Mr. Carrick sold lots 62 by 125 feet for twenty dollars each in Klamath Falls, and these same lots sold in 1910 for $480 per front foot. He was associated with the growth and development of the place and served as an early member of the city council. He met his death by lightning stroke on July 6, 1902. The wife and mother passed away on March 15, 1903, at the age of fifty years. Dave Carrick, a great-uncle of George W., came to California as a prospector and miner and later became one of the large stockmen near Weed, Cal.

George W. Carrick attended the public schools in Klamath Falls. When he was eighteen he began an apprenticeship to learn the plumber's trade, receiving for his services three dollars per week. After four years he went to Portland, Ore., to finish his trade, after which he worked as a journeyman in that city until 1910. He then bought an automobile, shipped it to The Dalles, and used it in the stage business, being the pioneer in staging between Shantico, Lake View, Madras, Bend, Burns and Klamath Falls. At some places he paid one dollar per gallon for gasoline. He operated one season and then quit and came to California, locating in Contra Costa County, and entered the employ of the Standard Oil Company at Richmond as a plumber, and he had charge of the plumbing of their large office building in San Francisco. He remained with the Standard for twelve years. He had saved his money, and now concluded that he could better his condition by being his own master; and accordingly he opened a plumbing business and gradually built up a good patronage. Two years of his time in this county he was a resident of Richmond; then he bought a place in the Richmond Annex and lived there until moving onto San Pablo Avenue. He still owns his Annex property. He built up a business in general plumbing and installing heating plants, his custom being drawn from a territory extending to Pinole and East Oakland. In 1926 he engaged in the grocery business at Mr. Miner's old stand, where he is catering to the needs of the public.

On July 28, 1910, Mr. Carrick was united in marriage at Portland, Ore., with Miss Jessie L. Dickerson, who was born in Oregon and lived there up to the time of her marriage. There are three children to brighten their home: Wilburn Lavern, born at Klamath Falls; and Barbara Jessie and George James, both born in Contra Costa County. In matters pertaining to the early history of California Mr. Carrick takes a great interest, his forebears having been among the trail-blazers here. In politics he is a Republican.

MORRIS PATANE.—Thrift and industry are illustrated in the career of Morris Patane, proprietor of the grocery department of the Grand Central Market, at 240 Railroad Street, Pittsburg. The subject of this sketch was born in the Province of Sicily, Italy, April 15, 1884, the son of Morris and Ida Patane. The mother is deceased, and the father still lives in the old homeland.

At the age of thirteen, Morris Patane became a sailor and visited the principal seaports of Italy, France, Albania and Greece. Being thrown upon his own resources so early in life his education was limited, but he was endowed with good health and self-reliance and determined to succeed in whatever line of work he undertook. Realizing that America offered better opportunities for an honest, hard-working young man, Morris Patane set sail for the United States in 1900, landing in New York City, where he was employed for four years. Hearing so many wonderful reports about the Golden State he journeyed to California and located in Pittsburg in 1910.

In 1913 he engaged in business for himself, opening the New Fish Market. Being successful in this venture, he opened a more extensive business in 1922, under the name of Grand Central Fruit Market, where he owns and operates the grocery department at 240 Railroad Street. Here he carries a good assortment of staple and fancy groceries, fresh fruit, vegetables and fish. By hard work, close attention to business details and square and courteous dealings with his customers he has established a good business and has the esteem of a large circle of friends.

In 1912 Mr. Patane returned to Italy, where, on November 12, he was united in marriage with Miss Sarin Ortolani, born in that country. They came to Pittsburg in 1913, when Mr. Patane opened his business. The family home is at No. 270 East Fourth Street.

N. S. NELSON.—The manager of the Pioneer Dairy Company, which also manufactures the Pioneer Ice Cream in Pittsburg, is N. S. Nelson, who holds an assured place in the business circles of Contra Costa County, and of Pittsburg in particular. A native of Sweden, Mr. Nelson was born in that country on July 2, 1863, and there received his education and his start in life, so that when he arrived in the United States, at the age of twenty-three, he was well equipped with a first-hand knowledge of farming, such as to enable him to carry on a successful business wherever he was located. After arriving in New York on May 20, 1886, he went direct to Galva, Ill. For two years he worked out on farms to acquaint himself with the American methods of agriculture, spending his time in Illinois, Minnesota and Dakota Territory. In 1889 he came to San Francisco and for seventeen months worked for the Safety-Nider Powder Company, where the Giant now is. With the savings of his few years of labor Mr. Nelson went to San Francisco and bought a milk route, and began delivering milk and cream to customers in that city. For two years he continued that business and prospered exceedingly, employing eighteen people in his business, which was conducted under the name of the San Carlos Dairy. In order to provide milk and cream for his business in San Francisco, Mr. Nelson came to Contra Costa County and bought a half interest in a lease of 2000 acres of land, and a small dairy thereon, from Joe Minice. The land was owned by the C. A. Hooper Company. The dairy was named the Diamond Dairy because the name of the town at that time was Black Diamond. After a partnership of one year Mr. Nelson bought the other's interest, thus becoming sole owner, and having as his manager John Helm. He carried on the San Francisco business for twenty-seven years, but lost considerable money because his first lease was not profitable. Relinquishing his business in 1919, he founded the Pittsburg Pioneer Dairy Company, which buys milk from the dairy farmers as far south as Byron and west to Lafayette, running eight big trucks and two teams to gather the product and bring it to his plant, where it is prepared for distribution and manufactured into various milk products. He sells milk and cream in Antioch, Brentwood, Oakley, Avon, Martinez, Concord, Cowell, Clyde, Nichols, Bay Point, and nearby localities, and he also sells his ice cream throughout these sections of the county. It might be fitting to mention that the superior product known as the Pioneer Ice Cream, manufactured by Mr. Nelson, is chemically pure and in great demand. An extensive business in milk, cream and milk products is also enjoyed in Pittsburg and vicinity, as well as in the various parts of Contra Costa County mentioned. These products are strictly pure and are recommended by physicians because of the sanitary methods of handling and preparing them for distribution. Mr. Nelson gives the business his personal attention, and since he is thoroughly competent as an experienced dairyman this personal oversight is in itself an assurance that every care has been given to produce nothing but the best of all kinds of milk and milk products distributed by the plant.

On March 14, 1896, in San Francisco, N. S. Nelson was united in marriage with Miss Sofina Blomquist, a native of Finland, and they have had three children, viz.: Carl, who married Miss Miller of Oakland and has two boys, Carl and Richard; Esther, who married Louis Rosenbloom and lives in Pittsburg; and Lillian, who is attending the Pittsburg High School. In political affiliations Mr. Nelson is a Republican. For many years he has been prominent in the Swedish Mission Church in San Francisco, and he is a member of the board of trustees of Mission Church, at Dolores and Dorland Streets. He belongs to the Pittsburg Chamber of Commerce, the East Contra Costa Chamber of Commerce, and the Credit Association. Ever since he has resided in this county, Mr. Nelson has been one of its upbuilders and has given freely of his time and means to assist all worthy projects. He is strictly a self-made man, and his word is considered as good as his bond.

YOUNG L. HARVILL.—The head of the police department and also of the general welfare work at the Columbia Steel Corporation's plant in Pittsburg, Cal., is Young L. Harvill, a man of wide acquaintance and much force of character. He was born at Centerville, Hickman County, Tenn., on March 16, 1886, and is one of a family of twelve children, all living, in the family of Young F. and Fannie (Williams) Harvill. The Harvills owned a large plantation in Tennessee, and the father served two terms in the legislature of that State, and for more than twenty-five years was justice of the peace in his county. The grandfather, Young J. Harvill, was a well-known Baptist preacher and a large landowner in Hickman County; he was prominent in all religious works, and served as a soldier in the Confederate Army during the Civil War. During the World War Young F. Harvill purchased a cotton plantation of 200 acres twelve miles north of Jackson, Miss., on the Illinois Central Railroad, and there he now makes his home.

Young L. Harvill attended the public schools of his native county, graduating from the high school in 1904, and soon after enlisted in the Third United States Cavalry at Fort Apache. He served in Arizona, and from there went to Fort Snelling, Minn., their troop being the first soldiers to occupy the new buildings at that fort. He was sent to the Philippines and served as a special assistant in the Headquarters Department under Major General McCarty and General Weston, and later under General Pershing. He received his honorable discharge at Luzon by special order of General Leonard Wood. After leaving the army, in 1908 he joined the Metropolitan Police Department in Manila, and remained there until 1912; then he was transferred to the Panama Canal Police Department and served at General Goethal's headquarters at Culebra. He was present when the dyke was blown up at Gamboa to admit the water into the canal at Panama. In 1915 he received an assignment to the detective department of the Government service and came to California to guard the Hercules Powder Works, officiating as the chief executive in the patrol department there. It was during the progress of the World War that he was assigned to the Columbia Steel Corporation's plant at Pittsburg, which was then engaged extensively in filling government contracts. Later Mr. Harvill was employed jointly by the Columbia Steel Corporation and the Electro-Chemical Company to organize the patrol for the two corporations in 1917.

In April, 1922, he was selected by S. F. Rutter, at that time California dry enforcement official, and was made a director of the prohibition forces in California. He continued in this work until in June, 1923, playing a major part in enforcing the Eighteenth Amendment and bringing to the bar of justice some of the most noted violators of the liquor law in the entire State. He has two honorable discharges from the United States service, and well merits the distinction he has won as a most efficient public servant.

Perhaps his most important work in Contra Costa County is the welfare work for the corporation he represents. There are 1250 men on the payroll of the Columbia Steel Corporation at Pittsburg, and Mr. Harvill looks after the safety of these men. The police department has made only nine arrests during the time Mr. Harvill has been at its head. The corporation has a hospital department with two nurses always on duty, an efficient fire department, a club room, including restaurant, reading room, pool hall and billiard room, and one hundred living rooms for the employees who prefer to live on the premises. As this population at the plant includes men of all nationalities, the position occupied by our subject represents one of great responsibility.

In 1916, at Pinole, Mr. Harvill was united in marriage with Miss Lillian M. Mills, daughter of the late Norman T. Mills. Mr. Harvill belongs to the Pittsburg Lions Club and is a member of the Knights of Pythias and the Pythian Sisters. He is a loyal booster for Pittsburg and Contra Costa County, and for all that makes for civic betterment. In politics he is a Republican.

MARTIN TOST.—The plant superintendent of the California & Hawaiian Sugar Refining Corporation is Martin Tost, of Crockett. A native of Germany, he was born on November 8, 1882, and was educated in the schools of his native country. On reaching manhood's estate, he came to America, landing in San Francisco in September, 1903. That same year marks his advent to Crockett and his entrance in the refinery as a day laborer. Since then Mr. Tost has gradually worked his way through the various departments until he reached his present position of trust in 1920. He is a most painstaking person, with an abundance of natural ability, and has won the respect of all.

Mr. Tost was married on May 27, 1916, to Miss Nora Helena Sanford, of Pacheco, Contra Costa County. In the month of March, 1926, Mr. and Mrs. Tost left on an extended visit to Europe. They were gone nearly four months, returning to Crockett on the 23rd of June.

They had a most delightful visit, especially at the home of Mr. Tost's mother at Hameln, Germany, where she still lives at the age of sixty-four. Mr. Tost's father died in 1918 at the age of sixty. It had been twenty-eight years since Mr. Tost had seen his mother, and it is needless to say that it was a most affectionate greeting. After two months spent at Hameln, Mr. and Mrs. Tost toured in other portions of Germany, and in France, Switzerland and England, returning to their home in Crockett much refreshed in body and spirit. Mr. Tost is a member of the Red Men and the Knights of Pythias. In politics he is a Republican on national issues, but in local affairs he considers the man rather than the party. He is a plain-spoken, generous-hearted man, and has a host of warm friends in his adopted home city and community.

CHARLES APPLETON HOOPER.—On July 12, 1914, at his home in Pittsburg, Cal., Charles Appleton Hooper passed away at the age of seventy-one years. He was one of the really great business men of California, and it is almost impossible adequately to write the story of his life without writing the history of the many industries with which he was connected, which space here forbids. Mr. Hooper came from sturdy New England stock, members of the family having participated in the Revolutionary War. He was born at Bangor, Maine, on March 14, 1843, and was graduated from the Hawes Grammar School in 1858, in South Boston, Mass., after which he attended the English High School for a short time. Upon leaving school he at once entered the employ of his uncle, William S. Perry, a lumber merchant, as a clerk and in two years rose to the position of bookkeeper and salesman, and then to active superintendent of the yard. At this time the Civil War swept over the country and young Hooper resigned his position to enlist, at the age of nineteen, in the 43rd Massachusetts Volunteers. After one year he received an honorable discharge, in 1863, and then decided to try his fortunes on the Pacific Coast, with his destination Amador County, whither his father, John Hooper, had migrated in 1851 and founded the town of Plymouth. Upon arriving there he worked at mining for his father in the Plymouth Mine one year.

Thinking that mining was not his forte, Mr. Hooper then went to San Francisco and established the firm of C. A. Hooper & Company at Fourth and Townsend Streets, and for several years did a thriving business in supplying lumber to the city and country districts around San Jose, and up the rivers tributary to San Francisco Bay. In 1867 he took as a partner William Lockerman, under the firm name of Hooper & Lockerman, but at the end of two years bought Lockerman's interest and resumed the old firm name. In 1869 George William Hooper, his brother, became a member of the firm, which had become enlarged into a wholesale, retail, and manufacturing business.

Mr. Hooper organized several lumber companies and invested heavily in California ranch lands and timber tracts, thus showing the firm

faith he had in the future of this great State.   He can justly be called
one of the lumber kings of this northwest territory.   Among the early
companies he organized were the Sacramento Lumber Company, of
which he was president.   In 1881 he organized the L. W. Blinn Lumber
Company at Los Angeles, for the Arizona business, and headed that
company also.   Then came the Southern California Lumber Company at
Los Angeles and the Russ Lumber and Mill Company at San Diego.   He
was also the founder of the California Lumber Company and the Redwood Manufacturers Company; and in 1907, of the Big Lagoon Lumber
Company of Humboldt County.   This latter he sold one year later for
more than $4,000,000.

The history of Pittsburg is almost a history of his life.   The Los
Médanos Rancho was granted to Jose Miguel and Antonio Mesa in
1836 by Mexican authority, and consisted of two square leagues, more
or less, of land.   The grant took its name from the heaps of sand or
sand dunes that originally lay upon the ground.   It comprised about
20,000 acres, running from the river on the front to the lomaries, or
small hills, at the back.   With the influx of Americans in 1848 disaster
overtook the owners, who mortgaged or sold some of the property, until
it was finally lost to them.   In 1849 Col. Jonathan D. Stevenson, who
came to California in 1847 in command of a regiment of soldiers to help
hold California for the United States, and Dr. William Parker jointly
bought the land and planned the creation of a great enterprise and the
building of a city to be known as the New York of the Pacific.   Lieut.
Gen. William T. Sherman, who later was made famous as a general by
his "march to the sea" in the Civil War, was hired to survey the townsite and make a plat of it.   This he did, receiving for his services $500
and ten city lots.   The place was called New York Landing and Colonel
Stevenson intended to make it the capital of California.   The Black
Diamond Coal Company were operating on a large scale a little later,
and were doing a thriving business until they got into litigation, and
from them the town took the name of Black Diamond.   Rather than
face a verdict against them they caused the mine to be flooded, and
mining ceased.   P. B. Cornwall, for many years a prominent citizen of
San Francisco, was president of this company and the railroad station
was named for him.

After the Mesas lost the property it fell into the hands of Col. L. L.
Robinson, but he lost it after long litigation.   He had erected a beautiful
home two miles from Black Diamond on ground covering forty acres,
and here he lived in splendid style.   When the Bank of California foreclosed, C. A. Hooper became the owner of some 8500 acres of the Los
Médanos Rancho; and subsequently he purchased additional holdings
until he owned about 11,000 acres, all told, in this locality.   Through
his experience in California he was able to foresee the possibilities of
this place as the site of a thriving industrial city.   Mr. Hooper maintained upon the site of the old Stevenson place a large and comfortable

residence which he made his country home. In 1903 he founded the Redwood Manufacturers Company, which covers 100 acres of ground. This is the largest manufacturing concern of its kind in the West, and its products are sent to every part of the world. He was liberal and donated sites for churches, parks, etc., and in time the town grew to considerable proportions and was given the name of Pittsburg, which it now bears. He was the means of establishing the Columbia Steel Corporation here, and also the Bowers Rubber Works, now the Pioneer Rubber Works, the Diamond Milling Company, the Pioneer Dairy, and other industrial concerns. In most of these organizations he was personally active and helpful, especially in capitalizing them. How well he succeeded can be seen from the fact that in 1925 said industrial concerns have a total capitalization of more than $30,000,000, with an annual payroll of $4,500,000 and with some 4000 people employed.

On June 7, 1880, at Grounsville, Maine, Mr. Hooper was united in marriage with Miss Ida Geneva Snow. They had two daughters, Mrs. Wigginton E. Creed, of Piedmont, and Mrs. Idalene H. Hale, of San Diego. The death of C. A. Hooper marked the passing of one of the most influential citizens of Contra Costa County. Every line of activity had felt the impetus of his large endeavors, notable among which is the C. A. Hooper Company, which has done much to foster the development of homebuilding in this thriving industrial city—a city that will always stand as a monument to his far-seeing vision and constructive enterprise.

JAMES L. McDONALD.—A fine type of Western self-made young manhood, James L. McDonald is now in charge of the pumping station for the Santa Fe Railway, at their Glen Frazer plant, about four miles south of Martinez on the Franklin Canyon highway. Having been in the railway service since the age of sixteen, he has had charge of their water plants at various stations since 1909, and through years of training is thoroughly capable in that line of work. Born in Ray County, Mo., he is the son of Alex and Cordelia (Mars) McDonald, both natives of that State and both now deceased. The father passed away in 1918, and the mother in 1919, both deaths occurring in Fresno. One brother and two sisters of James L. McDonald are residing in Yuba City, Cal., and one sister in Kansas. James L. is the youngest in the family, his birth having occurred on April 25, 1893.

The first marriage of Mr. McDonald united him with Miss Margaret Wright of Fresno. She died in 1919, leaving one child, Hazel, now attending grammar school. He was married a second time, in Fresno, choosing for his wife Miss Bernice Wright, a sister of Margaret; and three children have blessed their union: James and Harry, twins; and Margaret. The family reside in the cozy home provided for them by the railway company, and take an active part in the social life of their home community.

JOHN J. DAVI.—It would be hard to find a man or firm more actively in accord with the program of progress and advancement going forward in Pittsburg, Contra Costa County, than John J. Davi and the firm of John J. Davi & Bro., established by him in 1912. A native son of Pittsburg, John J. Davi was the first white boy born of Sicilian parents in that city, his birth occurring on July 15, 1892. He is a son of the well-known pioneers of Pittsburg, Girolamo and Angelina Davi, both born at Isolla, Della Femmine, Province de Palermo, Italy, where also they were married. The father came first to California, locating in Black Diamond, now Pittsburg, in 1888; and the mother joined him here in 1891. Both parents come from excellent Sicilian families, and the mother has been a woman of unusual ability, for years keeping the books for her husband's business at Black Diamond. Her maiden name was Angelina Siino, and she is the daughter of Giovanni Siino, who was justice of the peace, notary public and collector of port in his native country, as also the official appraiser of real estate. John J. Davi is named for him. On coming to Black Diamond, G. Davi engaged in fishing and kept a store there, and became the fish buyer for A. Palladini of San Francisco. He was both industrious and a good manager, and with the help of his capable wife he prospered in the new country. Both parents are still living in Pittsburg. Their children are: Salvatore T., born in Sicily and now employed by the Sacramento Short Line Railway, and John J., Bernard G., Horace D., Neno E., Victor, and David T.

After leaving school, in 1906, John J. Davi went to work for the Contra Costa Bank as office boy; and later he established a newspaper agency in Pittsburg, while working for the Redwood Manufacturers Company, where he also began as office boy. He worked on the Black Diamond Argus as reporter for a time, and then sold his newspaper agency to Jack Fisher. He then went back to the Contra Costa Bank for six months. In 1911 he went into the real estate business for himself, and one year later established in connection with it his insurance, investment and loan business. He took his brother Bernard George Davi as a partner in 1915. In April, 1921, they moved from the Continente Building, where the business was first located, to the Costanza Building; and again needing larger quarters, on January 3, 1925, the firm moved to its present place of business, on the ground floor of the Davi Finance Building, built in 1924 and owned by S. T. Davi. On the opening day 1017 people visited the new establishment, which had been brought to its present success by growing with the growth of the city, and was a concrete example of the prosperity and progress of Pittsburg and surrounding territory. The firm is one of the largest and most widely known insurance organizations in Contra Costa County, writing all forms of insurance—property, life, health, accident, fire, automobile, liability, grain and live stock—in fact, everything that can be legitimately insured. Enjoying the prestige founded on the confidence and loyalty of the people in the county, the firm handles much of the insurance written in Pittsburg and environs. In case of loss, adjustments are made promptly, a policy made possible by the confidential relations existing between the firm and the big companies. The real estate department is handled under the direction of B. G. Davi and is important and far-reaching in its work. Thoroughly informed through practical experience in regard to lands, locations and values in this district, including business properties, Mr. Davi places his knowledge at the service of the public, and the firm has a selected list of properties for sale, including industrial sites for large or small plants, desirable business properties, locations for homes, or land for any purpose. They also have improved properties, store buildings, warehouses, and homes, and several country estates adaptable for subdivision. One now being put on the market is known as West Pittsburg Park. Visitors are always welcome at the establishment, and are treated by Mr. Davi and his corps of assistants in the courteous manner that has had so much to do with establishing the splendid prestige enjoyed by the house of John J. Davi & Brother. This company represent the Western Loan and Building Company of Salt Lake City, act as agent for several steamship lines, and are headquarters of the touring bureau in connection with the National Automobile Club. John J. Davi is a deputy inspector for the State Motor Vehicle Department. He acts as advisor for the Italian people of this vicinity and is intrusted with much of their business; his judgment has proven sound and his position as their leader is easily recognized.

The marriage of John J. Davi, occurring in San Francisco, June 3, 1917, united him with Miss Lena Margaret Costanza, of Martinez. One child has been born to them, Rita. Always active in civic affairs, in 1912 Mr. Davi served as the first truant officer for the Pittsburg schools. He is an active member of the local Chamber of Commerce; president of the Industrial Finance Company; a director in the Richmond-Martinez Abstract and Title Company, the Contra Costa County Insurance Agents' Association, and the Contra Costa Realty Board; and president of the Eastern Contra Costa Agents' Association. In 1924 he served as secretary of the Coolidge-Dawes Club in Pittsburg. Fraternally, he belongs to Pittsburg Lodge No. 1474, B. P. O. E., and to Diamond Parlor No. 246, N. S. G. W., and served as financial secretary and trustee of the latter for some time. He is interested in local athletics, and acted as manager of the Sunset Ball Club of Pittsburg during 1912-1913.

In the establishment of his firm in Pittsburg, and in the personal endeavor he has put forth to help his community, Mr. Davi has been of signal service in aiding the growth and expansion of his native city, and he is known throughout the bay district as a man of unusually keen mind and foresight, both of which attributes have always been at the service of Pittsburg and Contra Costa County.

GEORGE MORRISON ROLPH.—Endowed by nature with those sterling traits of character that win the regard and esteem of mankind, George Morrison Rolph stands high in the estimation of the citizens of California, especially in the Bay section, where he has made a name and place for himself as the able and efficient president of the California & Hawaiian Sugar Refining Corporation, whose plant is located at Crockett, Contra Costa County. Mr. Rolph is a native son, born in San Francisco on February 6, 1873. His parents were James Rolph, Sr., and Margaret (Nicol) Rolph. The father came from Scotch ancestry, and was born on March 19, 1839. He came from London, England, to California in 1858, settled in the Mission district in San Francisco, and during all of his business life was associated with the Bank of California. He married Margaret Nicol on June 26, 1868, and they had the following children: James Rolph, Jr., mayor of San Francisco; William, connected with Griffith, Durney & Company, importers and exporters, in San Francisco; Ronald T., assistant manager of Alexander & Baldwin, Ltd., in San Francisco; Thomas, a member of the firm of Rolph, Mills & Company, exporters and importers, of San Francisco; George M., of this review; and Miss Elizabeth Rolph and Mrs. J. A. Moore, both of San Francisco. Mr. and Mrs. James Rolph, Sr., passed to their reward after having rounded out years filled with good deeds toward their fellow-men.

George M. Rolph attended the public schools in San Francisco. In order to earn money he peddled papers, in time working up a route of some 600 subscribers, who usually received their morning papers before breakfast. Young Rolph saved his money and enrolled at Stanford University, pursuing an elective course. He was a classmate of Herbert Hoover. Upon leaving college Mr. Rolph secured work in the Risdon Iron Works in San Francisco, and later went to Sanger, in Fresno County, and worked in a lumber mill. He continued at the hardest kinds of work in this connection for several years; in fact there was nothing connected with the lumber industry in the woods or mill that he was afraid to tackle, and he did the work with his accustomed efficiency. He always maintained his good nature and was liked by his superiors and fellow workmen.

In 1903 an opportunity came his way to go to the Hawaiian Islands to learn the fundamentals of the raising of sugar cane and the making of raw sugar. He did with enthusiasm the work set for him to do, and his energy attracted the attention of his employers, who soon advanced him to other duties and greater responsibilities. In 1904 the Sugar Factors Company, Ltd., was organized in the islands by a number of cane growers for the purpose of erecting a refinery in California to manufacture cane sugar, and the old beet sugar mill at Crockett was bought for the purpose. This old mill was formerly one of the earliest flour mills in the State, the Starr Flour Mill. The following year Mr. Rolph returned to California to manage the new venture. He has spent several millions of dollars in remodeling the plant and installing modern machinery and warehouses for refining and handling cane sugar. In 1906 the plant, owned by thirty-two of the largest cane growers in the islands, opened for business under the name of the California & Hawaiian Sugar Refining Company. Mr. Rolph has had wonderful success during the twenty years that he has been connected with this plant, and has kept abreast of the times in modernizing every department.

There have never been any labor troubles in this establishment. Mr. Rolph is humane, and looks upon the employees as human beings with feelings the same as his own. He keeps in close touch with their community life and their personal desires, and tries to be helpful to them in everything they do. In 1914 the company reduced the working hours from ten and twelve hours to eight hours a day, and with no reduction in pay. At the end of the first year the books showed that the unit of cost of refining sugar had not increased. This was because all the employees in the plant, from the general manager down, were "on their toes" all the time; no overtime was permitted unless absolutely necessary. Each employee had more time for recreation and for community and home life, and was therefore better qualified to put more energy into his work during the eight hours. After this experiment of Mr. Rolph's had shown such satisfactory results, the stockholders continued to expand these humane policies in other matters that have vital importance to their business, as well as to the health and the social and moral welfare of their workers.

One of the first progressive plans for the comfort of employees was the erection of a hotel with a view to renting rooms as reasonably as possible to the workers. There were deficiencies in the operating expenses of the hotel, and the company paid them. Then Mr. Rolph began to encourage the workers to build homes for their families. The company owned the land, upon which attractive residence subdivisions were graded and laid out, complete with streets, sidewalks and sewers, and with water, light and gas facilities. The local banks cooperated by taking sixty per cent of the mortgage, the company assuming thirty per cent of the second mortgage, while the employee who bought the home paid down ten per cent. The place was then paid for on the monthly installment plan. This plan has proved beneficial and has been fostered by the company ever since its inception. Many of the men with families own their own homes and have an active personal interest in the community in which their working day is spent.

A large men's clubhouse was built for the comfort of the men. It has a large gymnasium, billiard room, reading room, swimming pool and other conveniences, and is furnished in modern style. Later, a large athletic field was laid out by the company. This move prompted Wallace M. Alexander, an ex-president of the company, to donate two "tennis courts de-luxe," which are located in Alexander Park. The park also contains a large community auditorium which was built by the company for the use of the people of the community. The auditorium is equipped with a splendid floor for dancing, moving picture room, and banquet hall with full complement of utensils for the kitchen and dining room, as well as restrooms, locker rooms and shower rooms. There are two large out-of-door children's playgrounds in Crockett, fully equipped with apparatus, and two large parks, all with well-qualified attendants furnished by the company.

All of these humanizing ideas have emanated from the fertile brain of George M. Rolph, who feels that the future workers in the refinery are being trained in their own home town. The best of schools are maintained in Crockett, and all the buildings are kept adequate for the needs of the growing community. Night schools, part-time schools, and schools for the Americanization of the foreigner are conducted. From the kindergarten to the union high school there is developed a spirit of helpfulness. Mr. Rolph's faith in the employees of his company has never faltered, and Crockett is a typical community town. The company pays a very large percentage of the taxes, yet it insists upon the best obtainable, no matter for what purpose it is intended.

Crockett is thirty miles from San Francisco. The city has direct rail connections with the Southern Pacific, has deep water facilities, connects with the Western Pacific and the Santa Fe Railroads by shipping to their terminals by boat, and is a port of call for all ships that ply the San Joaquin and Sacramento Rivers, thus providing transportation facilities unsurpassed anywhere.

The Crockett refinery is the largest refinery in the world, and is also the cleanest. The interiors of the buildings are painted a battleship gray and white. The main buildings occupy a water frontage of nearly 3000 feet, erected on concrete piers and concrete piles set to bed rock. There are the melt and char houses, packinghouse, powerhouse and warehouses. The office fronts the main business street of the town and has a covered runway over the railroad tracks to the plant buildings. The capacity of the plant is 750,000 tons annually. The first year of operation only 67,000 tons of sugar was refined. In 1925, 640,000 tons were produced. In each of the 108 char filters in the plant 100,000 pounds of bone char is used. The entire plant is equipped with first-class fire protection, with a plant fire chief always on duty and a volunteer department among the employees to cooperate when needed. Both the company and the city take great pride in their fire departments and equipment.

Jared Smith writes: "Crockett is an unincorporated city built entirely on land owned by the company, and 'is the only municipality of its kind in California, if not in the United States', said Mr. Rolph, 'which has concrete streets and all the best and latest utilities to serve all residents, irrespective of their employment'. The community has a voice in its own affairs, but the company pays the taxes and foots the bills. Thereby Crockett escapes the waste and the loose disorganization which are so characteristic of American practical politics as exemplified in most town and cities. It is social cooperation, withal eminently pleasing to the workers who are so fortunate as to be citizens of this informal municipality."

The president and all his subordinates are always ready to cooperate with all progressive movements, and their social duties are many and exacting. Mr. Rolph is a member of the Pacific Union, the Bohemian and the Commercial Clubs in San Francisco. During the World War he was a Dollar-a-Year Man, serving on the Sugar Equalization Board under appointment by Herbert Hoover. Politically, Mr. Rolph is a Republican.

George M. Rolph was united in marriage on June 9, 1897, with Miss Lillian Ashton, daughter of Charles and Elizabeth (O'Mara) Ashton and a native of San Francisco. Mr. and Mrs. Rolph have two daughters, Mrs. Donald McKee and Mrs. George A. Stevenson.

CAPT. HANS P. LAURITZEN.—No history of Contra Costa County would be complete without a mention of the Richmond Navigation and Improvement Company, of Richmond, and its founder, Capt. H. P. Lauritzen. He was born in Denmark on February 14, 1870, and is the third son and fourth child of the late Hans P. and Adelhyte (Lorentzen) Lauritzen, pioneers of Wood's Island in the Sacramento River, and both now deceased.

The childhood and youth of H. P. Lauritzen, our subject, was anything but happy, for he had to help to clear the home farm of 250 acres, working in the malaria-infested country until he was compelled to take to his bed about four months each year. When he was eighteen he was six feet and one inch in height and weighed less than 100 pounds, and he realized that in order to live he would have to get away from that part of the country. Going to San Francisco, he shipped as a sailor before the mast on a schooner getting ready for a sealing expedition in the Behring and other northern seas. It was a rough life filled with hard work, but it was the means of working the malaria out of his system and the gaining of health. After an eight-months voyage he returned to San Francisco weighing 175 pounds and in perfect health. The following season he went out on another sealing expedition on the Helen Blum, and for two years he followed that business. He became so expert in the use of the rifle that he had the distinction of being the best shot on the Pacific Coast. In January of 1890 he was made captain of the Ivanhoe, a schooner owned by a stock company, he being interested in the vessel, which was purchased for $7000. After a six-months hunt in the North Pacific the vessel returned to San Francisco with $84,000 worth of furs. He was also one year on the C. G. White, and he made his last voyage as captain of this vessel, which hunted seals as far as the Japanese coast. He was caught in three typhoons, and had it not been for his dexterous seamanship, would have undoubtedly shared the fate of other wrecked American schooners he passed. At times the wind reached a velocity of

150 miles an hour. In one of these storms the C. G. White lost its rudder, some 1500 miles from Yokohama, the nearest shipyard. Captain Lauritzen sailed his vessel 1500 miles through the North Pacific to secure repairs, and the fact of its being rudderless is another proof of his seamanship. About this time difficulties arose and the United States government put a stop to further operations of vessels engaged in seal hunting. Captain Lauritzen still has damage suits pending amounting to $58,000 in the United States Court of Claims. After spending five years in seal hunting, and as a sailor and ship captain, our subject returned to California waters on December 25, 1893. It seemed that he was saved from harm by a veritable guardian angel, for the Ivanhoe was lost on the very next voyage after Captain Lauritzen transferred to another boat; the Helen Blum went down with all on board off the Semmoski Islands; and the C. G. White met a like fate. After being transferred to the C. G. Walker, the river boat belonging to the California Navigation & Improvement Company, he was made captain of her for a while and then went to the Mary Garrett. Two weeks later the Walker's steam drum exploded, killing the captain, the chief engineer and his wife, and two passengers.

On August 31, 1892, in San Francisco, Captain Lauritzen was united in marriage with Miss Maggie S. Cromwell, who was born in Canada but grew up in Solano County, where her parents had settled when she was a baby. The captain and his wife became the parents of two children: George B., who married Miss Ethel Eichbaum and has two children: George B., Jr., and Charles Philbrook; and Marguerite, who became the wife of Norbert B. Bush, a partner in the Richmond Navigation & Improvement Company. Throughout the various activities in which Captain Lauritzen has been interested he has had the hearty cooperation of his wife, and it was largely through her influence that Cutting Boulevard was transformed from a muddy road to one of the leading paved thoroughfares of Richmond.

After quitting the sea Captain Lauritzen entered the employ of the California Transportation Company as a pilot and captain on river boats for two years. Then for three years he was employed by the California Navigation & Improvement Company as captain of the fast steamer C. H. Cochran, making the round trip from Stockton to San Francisco each twenty-four hours. He was next employed by the Santa Fe Railroad Company, and as captain of their ferryboat, the Ocean Wave, operated the ferry service from Point Richmond to San Francisco, making the first trip on July 1, 1900, and carrying the first passengers landed at the wharf from the first passenger train entering Point Richmond. He continued with this work for ten years, and then established the Richmond Navigation & Improvement Company. From a humble beginning this concern has gradually expanded until it is among the important enterprises of Richmond. A general freight business is carried on, and also an express business. Gasoline launches, tug boats, and barges, as well as a fleet of express trucks, run on regular schedules. The company consists of H. P. Lauritzen, its founder; George B. Lauritzen, his son; and his son-in-law, N. B. Bush. They own thirteen and one-half acres on the inner harbor, which they have improved with modern concrete bunkers, warehouses and offices, for the conduct of their business; and they are prospering accordingly, in spite of keen competition. The company deals in sand, gravel, brick, lime, cement and crushed rock, and with their fleet of ten Fageol trucks for land distribution, and their fleet of barges, etc., serve their patrons with dispatch. Their freight and express business is a large item and is relied upon by many for quick delivery of various commodities.

Captain Lauritzen is a member of Occidental Lodge No. 22, F. & A. M. Politically he is a Republican. Both Captain and Mrs. Lauritzen are among the valued citizens of Richmond and always are to be found among those who work for progress along all lines. They have faith in the future of Richmond, as is shown by their investments; and with their family they hold an assured place in the esteem of the people.

MRS. ELLEN SLATE.—For almost a quarter of a century a resident of Rodeo, Mrs. Ellen Slate has, during that time, been a part of the social life of the community, and both she and her husband, the late James Edward Slate, have been prominent in its upbuilding. A native of Manchester, England, Mrs. Slate is the daughter of Joseph and Mary Ann Johnson, both of whom lived and died in Manchester, where the father was a brickmaker. Ellen Johnson came to California as a young lady, and married Mr. Slate in San Francisco, on June 30, 1889. James Edward Slate, or "Johnny," as he was more familiarly called, was born in Manchester, England, on June 11, 1869, a son of John and Ellen Slate. After their marriage, Mr. and Mrs. Slate lived for four years in San Francisco, then Mr. Slate was employed with the Selby Smelting Works, near Crockett, Contra Costa County, and for the next twenty-three years remained continuously in the employ of that firm, fifteen years of which he was their foreman.

During all these years the family resided in Rodeo, and their home, erected by Mr. Slate in 1911, has always been one where love and good cheer abide, the shelter of a devoted and filial family. They became the parents of six children: Alice, employed in San Francisco; William, a carpenter and builder, residing in Seattle; Ellen, now Mrs. Leo D. Laneving, and residing in Honolulu; Harold, living at home and employed in the laboratory of the Union Oil Company at Oleum; Dorothy, and LeRoy, attending school. Always a true wife and helpmate, Mrs. Slate was of great help to her husband, no little of his success in life being due to her efforts. His death, occurring February 6, 1922, was a decided loss to the community, for he was a man of sterling worth, holding a responsible position, and one of the substantial men of his town. Mrs. Slate is a member of the Presbyterian Church at Rodeo.

FLORIDO BALDINI.—The proprietor of the Antioch Dairy, Florido Baldini, was born in Portsmouth, N. H., on February 8, 1885, the son of F. and Clarice Baldini, who were both born in Italy and are now deceased. He has four sisters who are still residents of the East. Our subject grew up in New Hampshire and there received his schooling and learned the dairy business; and there he was married to Miss Josephine Farnacca. She was also born in New Hampshire, and is the daughter of Matteo and Cornea Farnacca, both residing at Antioch.

It was in 1919 that Mr. and Mrs. Baldini came to California and in August secured a lease on the Bonstell dairy ranch of eighty acres on Wilbur Avenue, where they run a dairy of twenty selected Holstein cows. These they have bred to registered Holstein bulls, and have thus developed a high-grade lot of stock. The dairy is clean and their product stands the high test necessary for their trade. Mr. Baldini delivers milk with a Ford delivery truck and makes a specialty of the finest product possible to obtain. With the assistance of his wife, he is doing a thriving and lucrative business.

Mrs. Baldini has an only brother, John Farnacca, who was educated at Dartmouth College. Though born in New Hampshire, he went to Italy and married and settled down at Florence, where he is the agent for the American Exchange. He has a son John.

Mr. and Mrs. Baldini are well-educated people and are leaders in their social circle.

CARL FREDERICK RUFF.—A very successful merchant and rancher is Carl Frederick Ruff, a highly esteemed citizen of Pinole. He was born in Bavaria, Germany, on February 19, 1872, the son of Konrad and Barbara (Pruegel) Ruff, who came to America in 1898, from their native Germany. Their family consisted of seven children, four of them sons, and our subject is the youngest. One brother and two sisters reside at San Jose.

Carl F. Ruff attended the schools of his native land and worked at various occupations until he was twenty-two; then, in 1894, he decided to seek a home and a fortune in the New World. Coming to California, he went to San Jose and for five years was employed in a brewery, then came to Pinole and found work as an acid maker at the Hercules Powder Works and was there six years. He met with an accident, which resulted in total blindness, but this did not discourage him for he knew he could still make a living. He started in business in a store ten by twelve feet in size and with the aid of his wife and children he began to build up a trade in the general merchandise business; in time he was able to erect his own brick building, the first one in the town, and he now has the leading grocery and confectionery store in Pinole. When he built his building many people in town considered Mr. Ruff very foolish to build such a large building; but he knew what he was doing and realized there was a future in store for this section of the country and his faith in local conditions has been amply rewarded. In 1912 the switchboard of the telephone company was installed in his store with twenty phones, since then it has increased to 160 and is still gaining ground. From one small board there are now two large switchboards.

In 1896 Mr. Ruff was united in marriage with Miss Anna Maria Widemann, who came from Germany to marry him and who was the sweetheart of his youth. They have had the following children: Katherine, at home; Maria, Mrs. Arthur Noyes; Barbara, Mrs. Bert Hock; Carl, of Pinole, and one of the town trustees. They also reared a nephew, who is employed in the store. Mr. Ruff has one hobby that is near to his heart and that is his 640-acre ranch in the mountains, which is stocked with cattle. This has been developed under his direction. He is a vigorous man and has a very cheerful disposition. He makes his way about town alone and enjoys the company of his friends. He is liked by all who know him.

CHARLES H. KELLER.—Of the many successful stockmen of Contra Costa County, Charles H. Keller may be reckoned among the foremost. He is the owner of three large cattle ranches, and of the home ranch, appropriately named "Casa del Sierra," one of the finest country homes to be found in the entire county. This ranch, purchased by Mr. Keller in 1910, was improved in 1912 by the erection of a luxurious and magnificent home, large barns, and cattle yards. The home is surrounded by beautiful rolling lawns, with flowers, shrubbery and trees, making it one of the show places in the county.

Mr. Keller is a member of one of the oldest pioneer families of this section of the State. His father, J. Henry Keller, was born in New Albany, Floyd County, Ind., on July 2, 1843, the son of John and Catherine (Graff) Keller, who were natives of Hesse-Darmstadt, Germany. John Keller was one of those hardy pioneers who crossed the plains with ox-teams in 1849. He was possessed of some capital and erected a canvas hotel on Front Street. The hotel was 30 by 60 feet in dimensions and was fitted up with bunks, four tiers high, which rented at one dollar each per day. One dollar was the price of a pie, and the same was charged for eggs; fifty cents was the price of a glass of liquor. In 1851, acting upon the advice of John Sutter of Sutter's Fort, John Keller engaged in raising vegetables. He died in 1882 at the age of forty years. J. Henry Keller, the second child in his family, was eleven years old at the time of his father's death, and he began helping his mother at that tender age. He rode and exercised race horses, and herded cattle for some of the pioneers of Yuba County; later he rode and won many races, being the rider of Peanut, Red Cloud, Colusa Sam, Patti and other famous horses of that day, altogether spending six years as a rider. In 1863 he was appointed to the responsible position of delivery clerk for Wells-Fargo Express Company, a post he held for six years with a record of great fidelity to his trusts. He removed to Concord, Contra

Costa County, where he engaged in ranching for a year, after which he embarked in the butcher business. He was married on May 24, 1864, to Celesta A. Collins, of Jamestown, Wis., and they became the parents of four sons and five daughters.

Charles H. Keller was born on the old Keller ranch above Clayton in 1875. His education was received in the public schools of Clayton and Concord. For many years he followed his father's occupation as a butcher. He has bought and sold many thousand head of cattle, buying in Oregon, Nevada, Idaho, Wyoming and Utah. For many years he has been one of the outstanding figures among the cattle men of the West.

R. E. CHILD.—One of California's native sons, R. E. Child was born at San Francisco on December 26, 1879, a son of the late Benjamin Wainwright Child, a civil engineer well-known in San Francisco and the San Joaquin Valley, where he was chief irrigation engineer for the Turlock Irrigation District during its pioneer days. Benjamin W. Child was a native of Michigan and was married in Honolulu to Miss Susan Helen Bovee, born in San Francisco, a daughter of James Samuel Bovee, who came to San Francisco from New York in 1850. Mr. Bovee was a miner by occupation and in early days acted as a member of the famous Vigilance Committee, in 1851 and 1856. Benjamin W. Child passed away at Turlock in 1922, aged sixty-nine years.

R. E. Child was reared in San Francisco and there attended the public schools and private preparatory schools. Under his father's able direction he began his preparatory work in civil engineering. His young manhood was spent in preparation for his life work, and step by step through the years he has been building up a successful career in his chosen field of endeavor. His war record is also of great interest, as he served in the Spanish-American War in Cuba and the Philippines, and also during the Boxer insurrection in China, and in the World War. At the beginning of the Spanish-American War he enlisted in the United States Navy as a seaman and began his service on the U. S. S. Mayflower, later being transferred to the U. S. S. Newark. Before returning to civil life he went to the Philippine Islands, and also saw service in China. In 1901 he was honorably discharged at Washington, D. C., and immediately returned to his home in San Francisco, where he again resumed his work as a civil engineer. In conjunction with his father, he worked on the Turlock irrigation system. Later, in Glenn County, Cal., he was engineer for the construction of the Central Canal. He was then solicited to become a member of the engineering department for the Spring Valley Water Company in San Francisco, and was chief assistant to Herman Schussler for nine years.

At the beginning of the World War Mr. Child enlisted as a captain of engineers, in August, 1917, and received his commission as a major. On January 9, 1918, he went over seas in command of the 523rd, 4th and

27

5th Engineers. Later he was stationed at the First Army European Headquarters in France, and then he was placed in command of the 4th Engineers, which served at St. Mihiel and in the Argonne. Following this he was assigned to the Second Army Headquarters at Toul, France. During May, 1919, he returned to the United States and assumed command of the 114th Engineers. On June 9, 1919, he received his honorable discharge, after which he served as hydraulic engineer with the California Railway Commission for seven months and then returned to private practice, taking up construction work for the Oregon and California Power Company at Keno, in southern Oregon. After the completion of this important work, he became superintendent of construction on the Snow Mountain dam, and from there went to Corcoran, Cal., as civil engineer on construction of irrigation canals. Then he returned again to San Francisco, where he conducted an office for a year and a half, meantime building the second section of the Skyline Boulevard below San Francisco. In 1924 he located in Pittsburg, first as superintendent for the Pittsburg Construction Company; but now he has a well established real estate and insurance business, which shows a decided increase month by month. His office is located at 186 East 4th Street.

Mr. Child was married at San Francisco, on April 18, 1907, to Miss Christine Engle Foster, also a native of the Bay City; and they have one daughter, Helen Engle. Mr. Child is a member of the David A. Solari Post, American Legion, at Pittsburg; the Chamber of Commerce; and the Lions Club. He is also a member on the advisory staff of General Leggett, of the Association of the Army of the United States, and a member of the Society of American Military Engineers.

EDWARD M. DOWNER.—One of the most prominent men in banking circles in Contra Costa County, and in fact throughout the East Bay region, is Edward M. Downer, president of the Bank of Pinole and of the Mechanics Bank of Richmond, and vice-president of the First National Bank of Richmond. Other financial interests claim his attention; and he is president of the Pinole Electric Light & Power Company, and many other companies number him among their stockholders and directors.

Edward M. Downer is a native son of California, born in Yuba County on April 28, 1869. His father was James Edward Downer, a native of New York who crossed the plains and engaged in mining in California in the days of the gold rush. He lived to reach the age of fifty-six. Edward M. Downer was educated in the schools of Nevada City and began his business career as a telegraph operator with the Southern Pacific Railroad Company. On February 1, 1890, he became station agent at Pinole, and served as postmaster also. In that same year he established the Pinole Times, the first and only paper printed in the town. On October 25, 1905, he was the means of the organizing of the Bank of Pinole with a capital stock of $25,000. J. Bermingham, Jr., was president; Patrick Tormey, vice-president; Louis Hart, secretary; and E. M. Downer, cashier. In 1907 a branch bank was established in Crockett, and in 1908 another was established at Rodeo. The capital stock was doubled in 1910, and has been increased several times since, being now $155,000, with a surplus of $75,000. In 1915 the bank erected its own building at Pinole, and in 1916 at Crockett. The Mechanics Bank of Richmond was organized on August 15, 1907, with a capital stock of $25,000, which was doubled in 1912 and again in 1916, and is now $200,000, with a surplus of $200,000. It has earned the distinction of being an honor bank, and is also the largest independent bank in Contra Costa County. Some time after Mr. Downer bought into this bank he was made its president. For more than twenty years he has served as mayor of Pinole, and he is deeply interested in all movements for the benefit of his home town.

The marriage of Edward M. Downer united him with Miss Lizzie Boquet, daughter of Frederick Boquet and a native of Contra Costa County. They became the parents of two children, viz.: Hazel I. and Edward M., Jr., the latter a law student at Leland Stanford, Jr., University. Mrs. Downer passed away on the 19th of October, 1924. Mr. Downer was again married at Oakland, on September 14, 1926, when he wedded Mrs. Edna McLean, nee Bultin, who was born near Calistoga, Cal. Fraternally, Mr. Downer is a Royal Arch Mason, and has served as an officer in the different branches of Masonry to which he belongs. He takes an active interest in all that tends toward the building up of Contra Costa County, and is always found ready to do his part to help promote every worthy project. He has never removed from Pinole, having maintained his home there ever since settling in Contra Costa County.

HUDSON FOLTZ.—A resident of Bay Point since 1919, during which time he has been in the employ of the Coos Bay Lumber Company, Hudson Foltz, more familiarly called John Foltz, holds the post of time-keeper with this corporation. Born in Janesville, Wis., on June 28, 1885, he was the only child of Harwood and Mollie C. (Lowry) Foltz. His father was a soldier in the Civil War; and his grandfather Foltz was a strong abolitionist. At the close of the war his father married, and soon after entered the retail store business in Janesville; but on account of failing health, he removed with his family to Pasadena, Cal., in 1887, just about the time the great boom in Southern California was over, and thereafter made this State his home until his death in 1903. The mother is still residing in Pasadena.

Hudson Foltz grew up in Pasadena and attended the public schools of that city, graduating from the high school in 1903. He then entered the employ of the Pacific Electric Railway and continued with them seven years as a clerk in the office of the construction department and in the store department. In 1911 he accepted a position with the Sugar

Pine Lumber Company, in Madera County, with whom he remained four years. Entering the University of California he then took special courses along cultural and business lines; and since coming to Bay Point he has given his entire time and attention to his duties with the Coos Bay Lumber Company.

Mr. Foltz is a Mason, holding membership in Corona Lodge No. 324, F. & A. M., in Pasadena; and he belongs to the Antioch Pyramid of Sciots.

HON. RANDALL H. LATIMER.—Among the representative men of Contra Costa County, none stood higher nor possessed a wider circle of friends than the late Hon. Randall H. Latimer, superior judge of California, in and for the County of Contra Costa. Judge Latimer was a self-made man who, by natural leadership, initiative and unswerving principles of honor, arose from a humble station through the several positions he held from drug clerk to the office of superior judge. As a judge, he was broad-minded, absolutely fair and impartial in his judicial decisions, and ever ready to mete out justice to all who were brought before him, rich and poor alike. His record on the bench was one that any judge might well be proud of, and his rulings were never reversed.

R. H. Latimer was born at Miami, Mo., on January 28, 1854, a son of Randolph and Nancy Latimer, both natives of Virginia. Randolph Latimer was born in 1800, in Virginia, where his ancestors had located generations ago. On the mother's side the family tree can be traced back to Revolutionary times. Randolph Latimer removed from Virginia to Missouri, where he engaged in farming. He became one of the prominent men of that State. He served two terms in the State legislature of Kentucky; and in the year of his death was nominated in Missouri for the legislature, but owing to ill-health was obliged to decline the honor. Fourteen children were born to Randolph Latimer and his wife, of whom Judge Latimer and a brother, Robert K., a prosperous real estate man living in Seattle, outlived all the others. Randolph Latimer passed away in August, 1861.

Randall H. Latimer was educated in the public and private schools of Missouri, later graduating from Mt. Pleasant College of Huntsville with the Class of 1877. Two years later he came to California, locating in Concord, this county, and while there served as justice of the peace two years; afterward he removed to Walnut Creek, where he was employed in a drug store. It was about this time that he decided to adopt the law as a profession. Accordingly he began reading law while working in the drug store, and was admitted to the bar in August, 1884. He opened a law office in Walnut Creek and practiced there for two years, after which he removed to Martinez. In the larger place his legal talent soon won recognition and he became prominent in many big cases, gaining a prestige among the leading jurists of the county. In 1908 he was urged by his friends to become a candidate for superior judge for Contra Costa

County and was elected by a flattering majority, and thereafter he was repeatedly reelected. Judge Latimer served as district attorney three years. He was active in the legal profession for upwards of a third of a century, and arose to the pinnacle of his profession. Judge Latimer was often called upon to preside over the superior courts in other counties, and decided many noted cases. As a leading man of affairs, a trained lawyer, and a superior court judge, he established a name of which the people of Contra Costa County and of California will always be proud. His brilliant career was cut short by his tragic death, which occurred on May 29, 1923, as a result of a stroke of apoplexy while in court; he was removed to his home, where he passed away on the same day.

The marriage of Judge Latimer occurred in 1889, and united him with Miss Madora Garner, of Los Gatos, Cal., a lady of education, refinement and culture. Fraternally, Judge Latimer was a member of the Masonic Lodge in Martinez; he was also an active member of the Independent Order of Odd Fellows at Martinez, and had passed the chairs in that lodge. He was an officer in the California State Iroquois Club. Mrs. Latimer was a most loving and devoted wife, and a true helpmate to her husband. She is a member of the Eastern Star and the Woman's Improvement Club of Martinez, and takes an active part in club work and social events.

JOSEPH & PETER LOPEZ.—Varied experiences and associations with diversified occupations have given the Lopez Brothers, successful grocers of Pittsburg, a broad knowledge of the great West. The firm of Lopez Brothers is a co-partnership composed of Joseph and Peter Lopez, natives of Spain. They are sons of Juan Lopez, who was a trusted employee of the Spanish Government for many years, being employed as a railroad section boss.

Joseph Lopez was born at Guadix, Grenada, Spain, October 12, 1890; Peter is four years younger, and was born at Malaga on January 23, 1894. Their boyhood days were spent in Spain, but with the advent of young manhood their thoughts turned towards the betterment of their financial condition and the making for themselves a career that would bring them a degree of prosperity and independence impossible in the old home land. The two brothers sailed from Gibraltar, Spain, on a British steamer for the Hawaiian Islands, landing at Honolulu on December 3, 1912. They found work on sugar plantations and remained on the Islands eleven months; after which they emigrated to America, landing at San Francisco, Cal., on November 10, 1913.

Upon their arrival in the Golden State the brothers went to Santa Rosa, where they secured work on the State Highway and continued in this employment three years. In 1916 they came to Contra Costa County and were employed on asparagus ranches, for which the county is especially noted. In time Joseph was advanced to the position of foreman for the F. E. Booth Company and had charge of sixty men for two years. Afterwards he went to Pittsburg, where he was employed by the same company in their large cannery, remaining another two years. As the result of good habits, combined with thrift, frugality, perseverance and steady employment, together with good business management, the brothers succeeded in saving enough money to engage in business for themselves. In 1920 they purchased the grocery store of L. Fontana, and since then have built up a profitable and growing business at the corner of Second and Railroad Streets, Pittsburg.

On December 31, 1917, Joseph Lopez was united in marriage with Miss Maria Lopez, a native of Spain, the ceremony taking place at San Jose, Cal. Although her surname was the same, they were not related. This union has been blessed with four children: John, Michael, Marina, and Anthony.

Peter Lopez was married in San Francisco, Cal., January 23, 1920, taking as his bride Miss Isabella Sanchez, a native of Spain; and they have three children: Marina, Michael and Isabella. Both families are attendants of the Catholic Church and have a large circle of friends in Pittsburg.

FRANK WILLIAM BAUER, SR.—The late Frank William Bauer, Sr., was a well-known character along the water front of Contra Costa County and around San Francisco Bay. He was born in Holland on November 11, 1836, and died at Crockett in 1919. Between these dates, his was a life full of hard work, and of good deeds to those less fortunate than himself. His early education was obtained in the land of his birth; but at the age of fourteen he left home, and when sixteen landed in America. For a time he followed the life of a sailor in New York, continuing thus until he arrived in California. After his arrival he came to Port Costa and became captain of a barkentine sailing vessel named Edward May, and he also was a stevedore in the employ of the Port Costa Lumber Company; then he came to the sugar refinery and was employed there until he became ill. He packed the lumber for the first building at Crockett on the east end of the water front, which was a hotel or eating house. He often spoke of how the Eckleys swam cattle across the straits, and deplored the cruelty to the animals when he saw their condition after having landed on the opposite shore. The Eckleys would take large logs and tie the heads of the cattle to the logs, then fasten the logs to a sailing boat, and in that way cross the straits. They used the boat Vollante, later owned by the Edwards brothers.

Mr. Bauer was married twice, and by his first wife he had a son. His second wife was Rosena Stangle, a native of Germany, and they were married in 1890. She had three children by a previous marriage, one of whom was killed by the earthquake, at San Francisco in 1906; and one daughter is in San Francisco. Of this second union Frank William, Jr., is the only child. Mr. Bauer, Sr., was a well-read man, a good conversationalist, and of a very sympathetic nature.

MICHELE EVOLA.—To be recognized as a self-made man is an honor of which any man should be proud. Without anyone to assist him in securing a start in the business world, by persistent labor, good health, and the constant exercise of economy, Mike Evola brought himself to the financial position in life where he possessed the means necessary for the building of a splendid residence, in which his family reside, and the well-known Evola Apartments of Pittsburg, both being valuable city properties.

Mike Evola, as he is familiarly called by his many friends, is a native of the Island of Sicily, Italy, where he was born on July 15, 1886, the son of John and Anna Evola; the father still lives in Italy, but the mother passed away in 1911. The father was a small farmer and market gardener, and Mike had to work from early boyhood; consequently his opportunities for attending school were few and his education necessarily meager. When fifteen years old he decided to emigrate to America, where he believed there were many opportunities for a young man who possessed a strong constitution, was hopeful, honest and industrious, and possessed a firm determination to surmount all obstacles. After landing in the United States he went to Detroit, Mich., where he secured employment in the iron works. After remaining there five years, he came to San Francisco soon after the great fire, and there worked at building. In 1909 Mr. Evola located in Pittsburg and was first employed as a day laborer. After gaining some experience in excavating, he secured a team of horses and a wagon and began business for himself, hauling and excavating. His business soon increased and he became able to accept larger contracts and employ more men. The accumulation of valuable real estate in the city of Pittsburg is evident proof of his rapid and substantial prosperity.

On October 10, 1910, Michele Evola was united in marriage with Miss Mary Vitalie, born at Collinsville, Solano County, a daughter of Vincent Vitalie. Mr. and Mrs. Evola are the parents of four children, Mary, John, Nauvrine and Bessie, who are the life and happiness of their beautiful home. The family are members of the Catholic Church. Fraternally, Mike Evola belongs to the Moose and the American Foresters. He is a member of the Pittsburg Chamber of Commerce.

GIUSEPPE CIPOLLINA.—Born in the province of Torino, Italy, on July 18, 1889, Giuseppe Cipollina received his education in the schools of his native land and served an apprenticeship at the plasterer's trade in his own country, where a man is thoroughly grounded in all branches of the calling, so that he is able to put up a brick or stone wall or to do cement work, being in fact equipped by his training for the allied trades of brick and stone mason. After learning his trade, Mr. Cipollina desired to branch out into broader fields than he could find in Italy; and accordingly he came to the United States, arriving in Buffalo, N. Y., on August 3, 1913. There he followed his trade, and also worked in Chicago and Denver, making his way gradually towards the Pacific Coast country. He and two others built the railroad station at Gunnison, Colo., and a very creditable structure it was. Mr. Cipollina also worked at mining in the Black Rock Mine and others in Butte, Mont.

Mr. Cipollina made his next important move when he came to California and to Pittsburg, where he arrived the week before Christmas in 1917. He immediately found work as a riveter on the dredger, Neptune, then being built for the Olympia Dredging Company. This job completed, Mr. Cipollina took up his regular trade, and the plastering on many of the best buildings in the city show his handiwork. Among them we mention the Contra Costa Bank Building and the Los Medanos Garage. His opportunity came when he became the proprietor of the old Union Hotel in 1921. As he prospered, he looked about for expansion and secured the Tivoli Hotel, and in 1922 took in for a partner Theodoro Ferre. Together they worked and prospered, and on July 1, 1925, closed the hotel and divided their interests, Mr. Ferre leasing the Italian Hotel. Mr. Cipollina developed into a first-class chef, and follows his old trade of cement worker also.

On November 24, 1921, Mr. Cipollina and Miss Louisa Barasso were married at Martinez. Mrs. Cipollina was born in Italy and has proven a worthy helpmate to her husband. They have one child, Joseph Mission Cipollina, born on Admission Day in 1922. Much of the success to which our subject has attained he credits to the cooperation of his good wife.

MANUEL LEWIS FORTADO.—A native of Contra Costa County who takes an active interest in all projects for the advancement of the county in general and of the Crockett section in particular is Manuel L. Fortado. He was born at Concord on June 8, 1886, a son of Lorain E. and Gillimina (Ignacia) Fortado. His father came from the Azores Islands when he was eighteen, and coming to California he worked as a laborer. He became a citizen of the United States at the earliest time possible. The lady whom he married left her home in the Azores when she was eighteen and came to California and they were married in the Catholic Church at Concord, Mr. Fortado being twenty-three, and his bride eighteen. They celebrated their golden wedding anniversary in May, 1926. Mrs. L. E. Fortado had two sisters come here at a later date; and seven boys and one girl were left in the Azores, of whom four boys have died. Of this marriage these children were born: Frank, in Berkeley; Anthony, in San Francisco; Lucy, Mrs. L. J. Arrighi, in Concord; and Manuel, in Crockett.

Manuel L. attended the public schools and during vacations worked in the fruit orchards. At the age of fifteen he went into the Selby smelter and did a man's work at the blast furnace for about a year, then went back to Concord and worked in H. Ivey's livery stable two years. At the age of eighteen, on October 19, 1904, he was married to Miss Gladys Pauline

Jones, niece of Robert Jones, a former assistant county surveyor, and a grand-daughter of Nathaniel Jones, one of the early pioneers of the Walnut Creek section. Her father was Wallace Lee Jones and her mother was Barbara Crow Jones, both died when Mrs. Fortado was a small child and she was reared in the home of her grandfather and grandmother Jones; the latter died in Crockett in 1908 at the age of eighty-three, and claimed to be the first white woman to cross the Carquinez Straits. Of the marriage of Mr. and Mrs. Fortado there is a son, Richard, who finished grammar school and is now working in the sheet metal department of the refinery. He married Helen Suchowaski and they have one child, Richard L., Jr.

For a time Mr. Fortado worked in a mercantile store in Walnut Creek; and also was in business for himself for about a year, and was employed by the California Wine Association for a time. Coming to Selby he worked in the cartridge factory from 1906 to 1911 and became inspector. He entered the sugar refinery as tallyman, then was promoted to be weigher.

Mr. Fortado was married the second time on October 19, 1921, at Crockett, when he was united with Miss Pauline Myra Suchowaski, born in Pueblo, Colo., but at the time of her marriage was living at Rodeo with her parents, Stephen and Anna (Orynicz) Suchowaski, borth born in Galacia. Her father was a watchman at the Selby smelter. Mr. Fortado is a member of the Eagles and the Red Men. He has been an active member of the volunteer fire department and for ten years was interested in baseball as an umpire. He is a strong advocate of all healthy and clean out door sports, believes in getting close to nature by going camping, fishing and hunting. Few know the various parts of the mountains of northern California better than does Mr. and Mrs. Fortado, who always spend their vacations in different localities.

GIOVANNI CONTINENTE.—Among the successful men of Pittsburg we find the name of Giovanni Continente, who for nearly twenty years has lived in this place, from the time when it was called Black Diamond, and has seen the many changes since that time. He was born on May 12, 1881, in Naples, Italy, a son of Antonio and Rose Continente, and he attended the schools of his native land. When he was twenty-five years old he made up his mind he would come to America; and after landing in Brooklyn, N. Y., he worked for two years and saved money enough to bring him to California. Arriving in 1908, he came at once to Black Diamond and made a permanent location, and since that year he has been actively engaged in business and has invested in real estate, thus helping to build up the present city. He is a very quiet and reserved man, but does what he can for the good of the town when called upon, and has many friends here.

On June 20, 1909, Mr. Continente was married to Miss Rosa Billeci, who was born in the Province of Sicily, Italy. She is a splendid business woman and gives her whole attention to looking after their many interests. To her good management Mr. Continente attributes much of their present financial success. Mr. and Mrs. Continente conduct the Continente Hotel, erected in 1924, a modern building, built of brick, three stories high with fifty-one guest rooms. These rooms are nicely furnished with up-to-date steel furniture; and there is hot and cold water in each room. The building is steam-heated throughout and has tub and shower baths and every convenience for the traveler. It is advertised as "A good place to stop when in Pittsburg," and the name and slogan tell the story of this modern hotel. Mr. and Mrs. Continente give their guests every attention, endeavoring to make them comfortable; and as a result they have a good patronage, including both tourists and traveling salesmen. Besides the hotel, the proprietors conduct the Continente Market on the ground floor of their building, where they handle a full line of staple and fancy groceries, vegetables and fruits. A meat market is operated by John and Joe Buffo in connection with the grocery. Mrs. Continente manages both the hotel and market and is a good business woman. Besides this building they also own other real estate in Pittsburg, and have shown their faith in its future by investing heavily in property here. They are both well liked and have many friends in the community.

OWEN O'CONNOR.—Although not a native of California, Owen O'Connor has made his home here for so many years that he is intimately acquainted with the State's progress and devoted to its development. Mr. O'Connor is an intelligent and hardworking citizen and owns a beautiful twenty-acre ranch home on the State Highway about one mile west of the town of Oakley. This ranch is set to almonds, grapes and apricots, and his trim acres and fine residence testify to his energy and industry.

Owen O'Connor was born in Ottawa, Canada, June 26, 1858, a son of John and Bridget O'Connor. John O'Connor was a shoemaker by trade. Owen was brought up to work, and learned the tinner's and sheet metal worker's trade in his home city. He then went to Manitoba and there followed his trade, but the climate was so severe that within a year he returned to Ottawa. In 1886 he left Ottawa and came to California. He homesteaded land near Coalinga, in Fresno County, and also had a tree-claim, on both of which he proved up, but the land turned out to be of little value. He removed then to Hanford and there worked at his trade until coming to this locality about a quarter of a century ago. On removing to Contra Costa County, he purchased his present home place of twenty acres, where he has since resided. He put up all the buildings and set out the orchard on the ranch, and is prospering in his operations.

At Fresno, on January 20, 1900, Mr. O'Connor was married to Miss Josephine Pirhensil, a native of Illinois, who came to California while a young lady. In politics Mr. O'Connor is a consistent Republican.

JOSEPH FRAY.—An honest, industrious and hard-working citizen of Richmond is Joseph Fray, who has tried his hand at many things in his eventful life. He was born in San Pablo, on August 10, 1880, a son of Frank Fray, a farmer and native of Portugal. His mother, Mary Gloria (Ferria) Fray, was one of the oldest women in Contra Costa county, residing in San Pablo, at the corner of Alvarado and Twenty-third Streets, until she passed away on June 16, 1926.

Mr. Fray was educated in the San Pablo public schools, after which he was employed by Maloney Brothers, San Pablo butchers, for a period of four years. For a time he worked on a hay press, and then he became an employee of the Giant Powder Works at the time Mr. Roller was superintendent and Mr. Level was foreman. When the Standard Oil Company entered this territory he was one of their first employees, remaining with them for a considerable time. Later he became associated with the Whale Oil plant, but returned to the Standard, where he was employed in the pipe line department for six years. After his marriage to Miss Katie Moitoza, his first wife, he became an employee of the Peoples Water Company at their pumping station. His wife became ill and it was necessary to send her to the mountains. Later her condition became so serious that he was forced to resign his position in order to give her the needed attention. Three months after she returned home she died, their only child, a son of three years, preceding her to the grave.

Mr. Fray was for a time an employee of the saloon at Stege, known as the Hunters' Horn, and drove a beer wagon for Tony Rigalio. Later he again entered the employ of the Standard Oil Company in a pumping station. In 1924 he became an employee of the Santa Fe Railroad, starting as a laborer. Because of his knowledge of Spanish he was soon promoted to a position as foreman over about twenty-five Mexicans. He was a hotel-keeper in San Pablo for a time, and an employee of the porcelain works, and he is now car inspector and repairer for the Union Tank Line. In addition to the activities mentioned, Mr. Fray has been a prize-fighter and fought with the well-known boxer Joe Moitoza, and others. He is found of hunting and fishing and has played amateur baseball with the San Pablo team.

Mr. Fray's second marriage occurred on September 2, 1915, when he was united with Mrs. Nancy (Ming) Matteri, of Swiss-German parentage. Her father, Julius Ming, opened the Pullman Hotel; and her mother was Mary (Tresch) Ming. The family numbered nine children. Mr. and Mrs. Fray are the parents of four children, two of whom are deceased. The two living are Lorine Gloria, born July 10, 1920, and Albert Joseph, born August 3, 1923.

EMIL GUSTAV GEBAUER.—A resident of Crockett since 1898, with the exception of two years spent in Colorado, Emil G. Gebauer is recognized as a man of honesty of purpose and high moral character. He was born in Dresden, Germany, in 1876, and educated in the schools of that country, and in 1893 came to America to better his financial condition. He landed in Chicago, where he remained for a year, and then came West to the State of Washington and spent four years there, working at whatever he could find to do that would bring him an honest living. In 1898 he arrived in Crockett to take up employment in the sugar refinery. In 1904 he went to Colorado for two years, returning then to Crockett to resume his former employment.

Mr. Gebauer was united in marriage at Crockett, on May 5, 1912, with Miss Mary Frances Glancy, daughter of John Charles Glancy, a sketch of whose life will be found in this history. She was born in Crockett on January 3, 1884, and is credited with being the first girl baby born here; while the first boy born in Crockett was Louis Berg, born in November, 1883. She attended the Crockett schools in pursuit of an education. The children born of this marriage are: Clement E., Mary Dolores, Leo Anthony, Ruth Bernadette and Catherine Bertha. Mrs. Gebauer is a member of the Young Ladies' Institute and of the Native Daughters, in which she is a Past President. Mr. Gebauer belongs to the Woodmen of the World. They are essentially home folks, but deeply interested in all that pertains to the civic and social advancement of Contra Costa County. They attend the Catholic Church, of which Mr. Gebauer was organist at one time.

CASPER T. CAUTIELLO.—A very progressive and enterprising citizen of Pittsburg, Cal., who possesses sound judgment and keen business ability, is Casper T. Cautiello, the proprietor of the oldest hardware store in the city. During his lifetime he has faced business reverses and seemingly insurmountable difficulties, but with a courageous and indomitable spirit has overcome all obstacles and by persisting in a straight-forward course of dealing in all of his business transactions has eventually gained a gratifying degree of success and prosperity. In 1906 he was engaged in the hardware business in San Francisco. This was the year of the great catastrophe in that city, and he lost the entire contents of his store in the fire that followed the earthquake; unfortunately he had no fire insurance. Undaunted by the loss of his earnings of fourteen years, however, he soon entered business again. He visited Pittsburg, Cal., where he purchased the oldest hardware store in the city, then owned by G. Viscuso. He also bought a store in San Francisco, which he operated successfully for one year, after which he decided to remove to Pittsburg and manage his store there. He has since concentrated his best efforts on this enterprise, which he has developed into a large and growing business.

Casper T. Cautiello was born in Singapore, Straits Settlements, Malay Peninsula, India, on May 10, 1883, the son of Louis and Amelia Cautiello, natives of Italy. The parents were operating a hotel in Singapore when their son was born. Afterwards they returned to Italy, but soon sailed to Sydney, Australia. In 1889 they removed to San Francisco, Cal., where they engaged in the hotel business. Both parents are now deceased. The migratory life of the parents brought their young son in contact with people of many lands and languages; and thus he learned, in a limited way, of their language and customs. This has been very helpful to him since he became a business man, as he can speak in French, Italian, Spanish or Chinese. The hardware business seemed to appeal to Mr. Cautiello at an unusually early age, as he was but eight years old when he first began clerking in the store of Isadore Merle, in San Francisco. For fourteen years he continued to work for Mr. Merle; and then, when twenty-two years of age, in February, 1906, he opened business for himself in San Francisco, where, as stated above, he lost all during the great fire of that year.

On May 1, 1904, Casper T. Cautiello was united in marriage with Miss Theresa Viscuso, daughter of G. and Aquilina Viscuso, early settlers of Contra Costa County. This union has been blessed with three children: Amelia, Angelina and Eleanor. Fraternally, Mr. Cautiello is a member of the Loyal Order of Moose. He is deeply interested in the advancement of the city's interests, and is an active member of the Pittsburg Chamber of Commerce.

CHARLES ALBERT STAEHLE.—A resident of California since early childhood, Charles Albert Staehle has seen the development of a wonderful region in the past forty years. He was born in New York City on January 4, 1872, the son of Charles A. and Ida (Wesley) Staehle, natives of Germany and New York, respectively. The father came from Germany to New York at an early age, married there, and in 1874 arrived in San Francisco. He died in 1878, in Oakland, where he was in the hotel business. Besides our subject, there are four brothers and three sisters still living in the family, one sister being in Crockett.

Our subject attended the public schools in Oakland and Crockett, completing his schooling in the building that stood on the hill in the southern part of town. At the age of sixteen he commenced working in the grain warehouses along the water front, and he continued at this work for four years. Preferring to become a producer, he accordingly went to the Sacramento Valley and began ranching, and also bought grain for Dave Levy until the breaking out of the Spanish-American War, when he enlisted for service and was assigned to the Eighth Regiment under Colonel Henshaw. He spent six months in the army and then was discharged. His services were in California, and he liked the experience. Returning to his ranching and grain-buying operations, Mr. Staehle continued until 1900, when he came to Crockett and secured work in the warehouses of the refinery until the plant closed. When it reopened he entered the employ of the company as a millwright, and he is still in this position.

Mr. Staehle was united in marriage on March 31, 1899, with Miss May Gertrude Reister, born at Williams, Colusa County, the daughter of Casper and Margaret (Martin) Reister. They have one daughter, Miss Melba Margaret Staehle. She is a graduate of the high school, the

State Teachers' College at San Francisco, and the San Francisco Institute of Music, with a special diploma, having specialized on stringed instruments. Having a natural talent for music, at the age of twelve she directed the first orchestra ever organized in the Crockett Grammar School. Her great-grandfather, George Martin, was a great musician and played in concerts throughout Europe. While attending the State Teachers' College she organized the first orchestra in the institution, and directed it while attending the school. At Concord, Miss Staehle organized the first orchestra in the town. She specializes in concert work for the benefit of poor children, and in buying instruments to be used in school orchestras. She teaches violin as a specialty, although she is competent on other stringed instruments. She wrote an operetta entitled Mothergoose Land, all music original; it is the story of the Woman Who Lived in a Shoe and it will be used by the C. & H. for their 1927 Christmas Festival at Crockett.

Mr. Staehle belongs to the Masons, the Red Men, and the Knights of Pythias, and has been chosen the representative of the Red Men and the Knights of Pythias at county and State meets. He has some very interesting stories to tell of the early days along the water front, one of them being of the night the McNear Warehouses at the straits were burning, when a figurehead from one of the vessels was seen floating in the water. He, with other young men, ran along with it and finally captured it as it came towards the shore, brought it to the Grangers' Warehouse, and set it up; and there it remained until about two years ago, when it was taken to Hollywood—where it likely has found a resting place in some movie studio.

WILLIAM WHITAKER.—A man endowed with a large amount of vim and energy, William Whitaker of Richmond has won for himself a notable position in the industrial world. Born in Florida, February 13, 1882, he is the son of Hamlin V. and Ella (Drew) Whitaker, the former a native of Florida and the latter of Alabama. The father is an enterprising farmer and fruit grower in Florida. There are three children in this family: Mary at home with her parents; William, of this review; and Charles B.

William Whitaker came to California in 1901 and spent one year as street car conductor in San Francisco; then he went to San Bernardino as a fireman for the Santa Fe Railroad Company; he was promoted to the position of engineer in 1909 and was running on the Los Angeles division; later in 1911 he was transferred to the Valley division, and in 1917 removed with his family to Richmond where they have since resided.

Mr. Whitaker's first marriage occurred on June 20, 1905, when he was united with Miss Alberta Rousseau of San Bernardino. This marriage resulted in the birth of two children: Flora Alberta and Frances Edith. On July 1, 1914, Mr. Whitaker was married the second time, Miss Edith Leslie Creason of Los Gatos, a daughter of William Jefferson and Gertrude Leslie (Walker) Creason, becoming his wife. Mrs. Whitaker is one of the three living children in a family of eight, born to Mr. and Mrs. Creason. A. F. lives in Richmond; and Fred and Frank reside in King City. Mr. and Mrs. Whitaker are the parents of one daughter, Gertrude Christine. Mr. Whitaker belongs to the Brotherhood of Locomotive Engineers of Richmond and with his family is a member of the Christian Church.

CHARLES COPLE.—As a highly intelligent and prosperous farmer of Contra Costa County, residing in Byron Precinct No. 1, Charles Cople is well-known in this vicinity, where he and his wife are held in high esteem as people of worth and integrity. A son of the late George Cople, an honored pioneer of this section of the county, he was born on February 17, 1871. George Cople was a successful agriculturist, and was a man of sterling worth to the community where he lived for many years; he passed away on October 27, 1923, at the age of eighty-seven years.

Charles Cople attended the Excelsior district school, and then took a business course at the San Jose Business College. After completing his studies he returned to the home place, where he became engrossed in agricultural and horticultural pursuits which have given him a competence well worth the time and labor spent.

The Byron-Bethany Irrigation District was largely established through an experiment made by Mr. Cople in 1909, when he put in a pump to raise the water from Kellogg Creek up onto the higher land, where he had planted fifteen acres to alfalfa. He knew that if water could be put on the high lands at a minimum of expense, it would induce the planting of hundreds of acres of alfalfa. Mr. Cople cut four crops from his acreage; and then others, who had laughed at him for trying the experiment, put in pumping plants along the creek until there was no more water to be used. This was the nucleus of what is now the present system, and Mr. Cople has served as a member of the board of directors ever since the organization.

On December 27, 1899, Mr. Cople was married to Miss Elsie Johnston, daughter of John and Mary Johnston of San Mateo County, where they were pioneers in farming and extensive landowners. Her father died in 1893, the mother surviving until 1911. Mr. and Mrs. Cople have a son, Kenneth D., born on August 2, 1901. Kenneth D. Cople married Miss Eva Champion. He is at the head of the commercial department and is also instructor in shorthand and typewriting in the Lodi Academy, conducted by the Seventh Day Adventists at Lodi, Cal.

Charles Cople is a member of Byron Parlor, Native Sons of the Golden West. Mr. and Mrs. Cople stand for temperance in all things and are strongly in favor of the Eighteenth Amendment. Mrs. Cople is a member of the Seventh Day Adventist Church at Byron.

GEORGE W. CRINKLAW, D. C.—Numbered among the most representative members of the chiropractic profession in Contra Costa County are Dr. George W. Crinklaw and his wife, who are co-partners in the practice of their chosen profession at Pittsburg under the firm name of Crinklaw and Crinklaw. Both are held in high esteem in the community and are making many friends for their profession by their careful and sympathetic application of the latest methods of chiropractic science and the helpful spirit in which they minister to the suffering. Almost every new fact or theory advanced, whether in science, religion, or new methods of therapeutics, meets with opposition at first, especially from the older and long-established cults and creeds. Chiropractic has been no exception, although today it is licensed and recognized as a helpful therapeutic agency for suffering humanity.

Dr. Crinklaw is a native of Illinois, born in Belvidere, Boone County, on June 29, 1866. His wife was born in Owosso, Mich., and it was in Owosso on May 28, 1890, that George W. Crinklaw was united in marriage with Miss Winnie Belle Wright. This happy union has been blessed with two daughters: Mrs. Dr. A. B. Hinkley, residing at Richmond, Cal., and Mrs. Dr. E. B. Lewman of San Rafael, Cal., both of whom are successful chiropractors.

Before taking up the study of chiropractic, Mr. Crinklaw was for thirteen years steadily employed by the Toledo, Ann Arbor & Northern Michigan Railroad as a locomotive engineer. This is the railroad now owned and operated by Henry Ford. In 1920 Mr. Crinklaw and his wife became students of chiropractic at the well-known Palmer School located at Davenport, Iowa, and were graduated with the Class of 1923. After graduating they located at Los Angeles, for a short time, then removed to Oakland, and from Oakland moved to St. Helena, Napa County, where they remained until September, 1924. They then located at Pittsburg, Cal., where they have been successful in their chosen work. They are members of the Federated Chiropractors of California, and the Universal Chiropractors' Association.

WARREN EDMOND HASELTINE.—The assistant sugar inspector at the California-Hawaiian Sugar Refinery at Crockett, Warren Edmond Haseltine, has won the respect of all who know him, for his upright character and strict integrity. He was born in Bureau County, Ill., on June 14, 1878, the son of Theodore Harris and Mary Elizabeth (Edmond) Haseltine. The father was a Methodist preacher, as was also Grandfather Haseltine, and both lived lives full of usefulness to their neighbors and friends.

Warren Edmond Haseltine attended the public schools in his home town and then spent two years at Northwestern University, at Evanston, Ill. He then entered the University of Illinois and was graduated in 1899 with the B. S. degree. He had majored in chemistry throughout his entire college courses, and also took special interest in sociology and political economy. He was a member of the college track team, the only athletics in the college at that time; and he was a member of the literary society and took an active part in all its activities. He is a member of the Delta Tau Delta fraternity.

After his graduation, Mr. Haseltine secured a position in the laboratory of the Chicago and Northwestern Railroad Company and remained in the testing department two and one-half years. His next move was to Aurora, Ill., where he was chief chemist for the William F. Jabbins Company, manufacturing and analytical chemists; and this position he held for fourteen years. Going to Kansas City, Mo., he became the superintendent of the glycerine refinery of Peet Brothers Soap Company. This company sent him to Berkeley, Cal., to one of their branch plants, and he spent three years there. He then came to Crockett, in 1917, and was made a foreman of the Sweetland press, one of a series of thirty-four presses in the refinery. He rose to be assistant sugar inspector. During all of his wanderings about the country, Mr. Haseltine has kept up his studies. He declares the profits in manufacturing in the future will depend upon the handling of by-products.

Mr. Haseltine's first wife was Miss Ruth Cleveland Raymond, born in Illinois. She became the mother of two boys: Theodore Raymond, twenty-three years of age, a graduate of Stanford University and now with Burns & McDonald, engineers in Kansas City, Mo.; and Stuart Edmond, aged twenty, who is taking an agricultural course in the University of Illinois. Mrs. Haseltine died on March 7, 1921. The second marriage united Mr. Haseltine with Miss Ruth Lillian Baker, daughter of Rev. L. H. Baker, a minister in the Methodist Church in Berkeley, but now in Long Beach, Cal. Rev. Baker was for a number of years pastor in Berkeley. Mrs. Baker is deceased. Mrs. Haseltine has one brother living in Santa Rosa. Mr. Haseltine belongs to the Elks Lodge in Vallejo, and to the Crockett Lodge of Masons, and the Consistory in Oakland. He owns his own home in Crockett and is surrounded with every convenience and many of the luxuries of this day and age. For recreation Mr. and Mrs. Haseltine enjoy camping and outdoor sports. Mr. Haseltine is much interested in the Boy Scout movement. He is a man of fine personality, cultured and well-read.

JOHN CHARLES GLANCY.—An early pioneer of the Crockett-Valona section of Contra Costa County, John Charles Glancy was privileged to see much of the development of this part of the county and was closely identified with the industrial advancement of the community. He was born in Harrisburg, Pa., on August 23, 1844, attended the common schools of his day and place, and learned the iron moulder's trade, which he followed in the East and after coming to the Pacific Coast. He landed in Sacramento in 1873 and entered the employ of the Southern Pacific Railroad Company at their shops, and there he remained until 1882, when he came to Crockett. Mr. Heald had just started his manufacturing establishment, on the present site of the sugar refinery, and Mr. Glancy came to take charge of the foundry; and he continued at this work until the business closed down. It was Mr. Heald, in partnership with Thomas Edwards, who laid out the town of Crockett on land owned by Judge Crockett, he having received several hundred acres as a fee in settlement of a lawsuit in early days.

Mr. Glancy was married in Harrisburg, Pa., to Miss Catherine Helt, who was born on January 18, 1846, in Harrisburg, Pa. They had the following children: Charles, who died by accident when thirteen years old; Mrs. Ellen Dempsey; Mrs. Catherine Hunt; Mrs. Eva Abel, of Berkeley; William F. Glancy, of Elk Grove; Mrs. Mary Gebauer, of Crockett; Eugene J.; Leo A., of San Francisco; and Albert H. Mrs. Glancy conducted a store in Crockett, and the family remained here; and Mr. Glancy returned to Sacramento to resume work in the foundry for the railroad company. He died in Crockett on January 18, 1910. The mother died on March 22, 1924, active to the last in the store. They owned the store building and erected the second house in Crockett, the first one having burned. Mrs. Gebauer assisted her mother in the store until she married. Mr. Glancy always took an active interest in the maintenance of good schools and saw wonderful development here along educational lines, as he did in every other line of endeavor. In politics he was a Democrat. The family are Catholics.

ADOLPH GUSTAVE BOEHM.—One of the successful restaurant and cafe men of the Bay region, A. G. Boehm has been in business in Port Costa since 1914 and during that time has made hosts of friends throughout the district, where he has become known as one of its substantial and progressive citizens. Born at Breslau, Silesia, Germany, on March 1, 1871, he is descended from an old German family, the full name of which was Von Boehm. His father, Lieutenant Herman Boehm, was a member of the famous Green Huzzars; and outside of army life he was a wholesale druggist in Gelsinkirchan Province, Westphalen, and in Essen. He married in Breslau, Pauline Ernestine Von Bulow. Both parents lived and died in Germany, the father dying in 1888, when a little over sixty-five years of age, as a result of wounds received in the Franco-German War; and the mother on November 7, 1922, at seventy-nine years, both deaths occurring in Essen. They were the parents of five children: Adolph Gustave, of this review; Conrad, formerly in the drug business in Germany, but now making his home in Essen, with his wife and three children; Herman Carl, a lieutenant on the German warship Embden, who went down with the ship when she sank during the World War, leaving a widow and three children; Pauline, wife of Carl Lux, residing at Dartmouth and the mother of two children; and Eliza, the mother of two children, residing at Wanne, Germany.

The eldest in the family, A. G. Boehm attended the grammar and high school in his native land. When seventeen he volunteered in the

German Army, but after serving eight months made his way to New York City, landing at Castle Garden on March 8, 1888, without money or friends. He went to work at anything he could find to make an honest dollar, and learned the trade of the pastry cook. For four years he served in Company K, 4th Illinois Regulars of the U. S. Army, doing duty mostly in Illinois. Since then he has always been in the hotel and restaurant business. He came to California in 1914, from San Antonio, Texas, where he had been the proprietor of a hotel and cafe, and stopped in San Francisco for a short time. He came to Port Costa in the latter part of 1914 and obtained a lease of the Burlington Hotel and Restaurant, and from the beginning he has made a success of the business. He is also the lessee of the Annex, with an additional thirty rooms.

The marriage of Mr. Boehm, which occurred in Flora, Ill., united him with Miss Maude Bryan, a daughter of Henry Bryan, who was a third cousin of the Hon. William Jennings Bryan. She has been a true helpmate to him, a capable wife and mother, and a woman of good sense and business ability who has been of much help to him in every business venture. They are the parents of two boys and a girl: Bryan, Herman, and Elizabeth. Fraternally, Mr. Boehm is a Mason, belonging to the Blue Lodge of Benicia. He is a Republican in politics, and adheres to the Lutheran faith in religion. In addition to his business affairs, he finds time for civic service, and is a deputy under Sheriff R. R. Veale. He is a director in both the First National Bank of Crockett and the First National Bank of Rodeo, and is also a director of the Crockett Investment Company. An affable and whole-hearted man, he has a genius for making and holding friends, perhaps because he is a loyal friend himself, and is filled with a desire to help others to help themselves. He believes thoroughly in the future of this part of the State, and as a patriotic citizen he does all in his power to help in the movements which have its best interests in view. Although of German birth, he yields to no man in patriotism for his adopted country; coming here as a boy of seventeen in order to live in a democracy and benefit by its laws, he has appreciated his opportunities and is grateful for them.

FRANK WILLIAM BAUER, JR.—Frank William Bauer, Jr., attended the schools in Crockett and San Francisco, and also night school. He learned the trade of the painter and has followed it all his active career. He is now employed in the sugar refinery as a painter, and has been with this firm since February, 1914.

The marriage uniting Mr. Bauer with Miss Esther Eriksen, a native of Michigan, took place on October 25, 1916. They have two children: Jack Francis and Francis William. Mr. Bauer is a member of the Knights of Pythias and the Red Men, and has held offices in these lodges. He is fond of camping and outdoor sports. Both Mr. and Mrs. Bauer are interested in Christian Science. They own their own home and have a large circle of friends.

PETER HENRY NANCETT.—In point of service, Peter Henry Nancett is one of the oldest employees of the Oleum Refinery, and is a highly trustworthy man. He has worked hard and has combined such good management with his industry that he now owns his own home and other income property in Rodeo, where he makes his home. Mr. and Mrs. Nancett first came to Oleum in 1897, and he immediately found employment at the Union Oil refinery. It is an historic fact that their oldest son, Harry, was the first boy baby born at Oleum.

P. H. Nancett was born at New Bedford, Mass., on August 4, 1869, the son of Henry L. and Louise (Rose) Nancett, both natives of Portugal. Grandfather Nancett was of half French blood, his father having been sent by the government from Lisbon to the Cape Verde Islands, where for many years he was a magistrate. Henry L. Nancett became a seafaring man and was a whaler out of New Bedford, and Peter Henry grew up at that place. His mother having died when he was only two years old, his stepmother reared him to maturity. He early became familiar with the sea, and went to Australia, where he lived for nine years, attending school there for about one year, and also worked as a marine fireman.

His stepmother preceeded him to San Francisco in 1893, and that same year he joined her and continued to follow the sea for some time after coming to California, making a trip to Alaska in the fishing industry. Returning to San Francisco he was married on September 5, 1895, to Miss M. Victoria Perry, a native of Chile, South America, and daughter of Manuel A. and Augusta Perry, she being now the only one living of their three children. Her father was a merchant in Chile. Her mother having died, father and daughter sailed in a whaling ship around Cape Horn to Providence, R. I., and when Mrs. Nancett was a girl of ten years, they came to California. She attended the public schools in San Benito and Mendocino Counties and in Sausalito, and was a schoolmate of Sheriff Burns of Mendocino County. After their marriage, Mr. and Mrs. Nancett lived in Alameda County until they came to Oleum in 1897. After this date Mr. Nancett followed the sea for two and one-half years, and during this time he had an experience which determined him to live on land for the rest of his days. He was shipwrecked off the coast of Cape Mendocino in 1900, when his ship, the Walla Walla, collided with the French freighter, Max, and for thirty-six hours battled the waves in a small boat, trying to land. He was one of nine out of thirty-six that escaped with their lives from the experience.

Five children blessed the marriage of Mr. and Mrs. Nancett: Emalinda, died when eighteen years old; Henry, or "Harry," in the employ of the Union Oil Company, married Miss Emma Hill, and is the father of three children, Rita, Victor, and Robert; Leo, a painter in the employ of the Shell Oil Company at Martinez; Arthur, with the Union Oil Company at Oleum, married Miss Anna Pezzuto of Crockett; and Peter

Anthony. The family are members of St. Patrick's Church, at Rodeo. Fraternally Mr. Nancett belongs to the I. D. E. S., the Moose, and the Druids. He votes the Republican ticket, and is interested in the growth and advancement of his home community. Mrs. Nancett is interested in Americanization work and taught the Portuguese who came from the old country, in her own home in Rodeo, before the public schools took up that work. Three of her pupils were World War heroes.

ARASIMO CARDINALLI.—Among the pioneer citizens of Pittsburg is Arasimo Cardinalli, now living retired at 421 East Fourth Street. Not only is he a pioneer, but he is rated among the wealthy men of this place. He erected the A. Cardinalli building on Black Diamond Street in 1919, and he and his wife conducted the Cardinalli Hotel, located on the second floor of his building. Mr. Cardinalli built and operated the first power launch on the rivers, using it to take him to and from the fishermen in smaller boats, from whom he bought fish. He had firm faith in the future of the town of his adoption and built several buildings on property he had purchased, one of which he and his family occupied as a home. He installed the first telephone to be used in this locality. Jealousy and his firm refusal to meet unreasonable demands on him led to black-hand methods, and this building was dynamited; but the family miraculously escaped, although the entire front of the building was blown out. Misfortunes never come singly; and in 1918 he consigned his pack of fish to the Talcot Grant Company of Astoria, Ore., and through their failure he lost heavily and was obliged to borrow $56,000. He paid every cent in time, and he was glad to get back on his feet once more, although he had to sacrifice much of his Pittsburg holdings.

Mr. Cardinalli was born in Palermo, Island of Sicily, Italy, on November 5, 1861. He grew up in that place and early engaged in the fishing industry. When a young man he came to America, settled in New Orleans, and engaged in fishing for oysters for three years. Then he came on to California and located at Pittsburg Landing, where he became a buyer and packer of fish and prospered accordingly, in time becoming the leading fish merchant here. He built and operated a fleet of motor boats, the first boat is still in operation and is in good condition.

Mr. Cardinalli was married in the old City Hall, in San Francisco, on June 2, 1890, to Miss Frances Junta, of Pittsburg. She is the oldest of nine children of Rasmo Junta, the pioneer boat and ship builder in Pittsburg. Mr. and Mrs. Cardinalli have had nine children born to them. Frank J. is mentioned at length on another page in this history. Jennie is the wife of Philip Crerello of Oakland and the mother of Dante, William and Minna Crerello. Susie is the widow of Robert McGrath, and is a teacher in the Pittsburg schools; she has a son, Robert. Vincent is married to Catherine Rossi of Pittsburg, and they have a son named Arasimo. Jack is employed by the Paladini Fish Company and married Miss

Ann Francois. The other children died in infancy. Through all his trials and tribulations, Mr. Cardinalli has had the loyal support and cooperation of his good wife, to whom he gives much credit for the success he has won and the position he holds in the esteem of his friends and associates.

OSCAR OTTO PRYTZ.—Descended from a pioneer of the sixties in California, Oscar Otto Prytz was born in Crockett, Cal., on May 23, 1883, a son of the late John Prytz, who was a native of Norway and a well educated man. Early in life he became a sailor and traveled to many ports until he finally rounded Cape Horn and arrived in San Francisco, where he sought employment in the coast lumber trade and worked for the A. C. Freese Steamboat Company. There is now a boat named Freese running in the coasting trade, which was named after the owner of this company. John Prytz married Miss Katherine Wickerson, a native of Germany, who had come to California a young woman and met Mr. Prytz in Redwood City. They lived in Redwood City while Mr. Prytz was running in the coast lumber trade. Then the little family moved to Stockton, and from there to Crockett in 1887, where the father worked on the water front and in boating. He had tried out his fortunes in Crockett during 1886, then was joined by his family the following year. This remained his home and place of business until his death in 1914. There were four boys in this family, viz.: William Ward, employed in the yards of Port Costa Lumber Company in Crockett; George Grover, engaged in the fuel business in Oakland; Edwin Edison, also living in Crockett; and Otto, of this review. The mother makes her home in Crockett where she is surrounded by her children and grandchildren.

Oscar Otto Prytz attended the public schools in Crockett and then went to Santa Clara, where he served an apprenticeship in the plumbing and sheet metal trade, and remained for five years, then came to Crockett and in 1909 established a plumbing and sheet metal business. He equipped his shop with all modern machinery and began to build up a business for himself and has met with uniform success from a financial point of view, and at the same time made a name and place for himself in business circles in Contra Costa County. Besides giving his personal attention to his business affairs and carefully looking after his family, Mr. Prytz has taken a very active part in civic affairs. He became a member of the Crockett fire department and during 1916-1917 served as its chief. During his term in that position he gave especial attention to developing the department and was the means of having the town buy its first truck, extend the water system and purchase new hose. He has found the work very interesting and feels that he has done his share in building the foundation for the present department. He belongs to the Crockett-Valona Business Men's Association and is always to be found on the side of progress. In line with his business he holds membership in the Master Plumbers Association of Upper Contra Costa County. Politically he believes in supporting men and measures he thinks will be most beneficial to the people.

Mr. Prytz is the father of two children, Lorraine and Mabel, both pupils in the John Swett Union High School in Crockett. He belongs to the Masons, the Odd Fellows, and the Encampment I. O. O. F., the Red Men, Native Sons and the Foresters, and has held some offices at various times. He is one of the substantial citizens of Contra Costa County and encourages all safe and sound development.

CHARLES W. ZIMMERMAN.—A man prominent in the political life of El Cerrito, Charles W. Zimmerman is making his influence felt for the good of the community by his persistent efforts to advance the general welfare and make his city a pleasant place in which to live. He was born in Kansas on December 17, 1873, and when a babe in arms was taken by his mother to Cambridge, Ohio, where he grew to years of maturity and attended the local public schools. At the age of eighteen he came to California, and for a number of years was employed at various occupations in the southern part of the State. In 1900 he entered the employ of the Pacific Creamery Company in Buena Park, where he remained for six years, and then went to Tempe, Ariz., for the same company, working his way from one post to another until he became assistant manager. In all, he remained with this company twenty years, the last six of which it was subsidiary to Armour & Company. The business grew to such proportions in Arizona that his firm had twenty-two trucks gathering raw milk throughout that section of the State. In 1919 he came back to California, and engaged in the dairy business on the Bixby ranch near Long Beach for seven months. Having a brother in Richmond, with whom he engaged in the bicycle business for a short time after leaving the ranch, he sold out and established an oil service station on San Pablo Avenue in El Cerrito. This was his first real venture in an independent business for himself. His was the first oil service station from University Avenue in Berkeley to his present place of business along the avenue. His home has been in El Cerrito since 1920, he having purchased a residence here at that time. He owns the land where his station is located and three lots farther to the north from his station.

The marriage of Mr. Zimmerman occurred in Honey Lake Valley, Lassen County, in 1895, while he was ranching in that county, where his brother was a pioneer of 1880. Mrs. Zimmerman was one of eleven sisters, five of whom are living. She was Minnie A. Tunnison, a native of Lassen County and the daughter of a California pioneer of 1850 in Honey Lake Valley, who farmed there all his life. Active to the last, he died at the age of seventy-seven years at the home of Mr. Zimmerman in Buena Park. Mr. Tunnison was active and enterprising, and a remarkable man in many ways. He kept a diary of daily happenings up to the day of his death. Mr. and Mrs. Zimmerman have three children: Erma, a graduate of the Tempe Normal School and now principal of the schools in Superior, Ariz.; Erdene, also a graduate of the Tempe Normal and now the wife of C. E. Ellsworth and mother of one daughter, Shirley; and Wesley L., who attended the Tempe High School and is now assisting his father.

Mr. Zimmerman entered into local politics in 1923, when he was appointed a member of the board of trustees of El Cerrito to fill a vacancy caused by the resignation of a member of that body. At the general election in 1924 he was a candidate for office and was elected. An active worker for civic betterment, he helped put over the $65,000 bond election for a new city fire house and hall; the installation of a Gamewell fire alarm system sufficient to take care of eighty boxes, of which eighteen alone cost $12,450; and the purchase of a modern American La France fire engine. Since he has been in office $119,000 has been spent in laying a complete system of six-inch water mains to all parts of the city of El Cerrito; and some $500,000 worth of modern street paving has been laid, to be paid for by the property owners benefited. In 1926 he became chairman of the board of trustees, succeeding Frank McDermott. Mr. Zimmerman supports the Republican candidates in national matters, but in local politics he prefers to vote for the men best suited for the office rather than hew to party lines. Fraternally, he is a member of Tempe Lodge No. 8, I. O. O. F., in which he is a Past Grand and a Past Deputy Grand Master. Both he and his wife are members of the Rebekahs. He enjoys the confidence and esteem of a wide circle of friends and business associates in this locality.

THOMAS HUGHES.—A pioneer of 1895 in Contra Costa County, Thomas Hughes has seen and been a part of the wonderful development of the Western part of this productive and important county. But few of the original settlers are now living; among them are the Edwards', Pat Murphy, J. J. Glancy, Pat Lucey, and a few others. The growth of the town has been safe and sure, and the incoming population have been the means of having parks established, playgrounds laid out and equipped, and some of the finest schools in the county erected, all of which have had our subject's most hearty cooperation and support. He was born in Ireland on August 31, 1873, the son of Patrick and Delia (Brown) Hughes, who sent their boy to the local schools of his native land; and when his school days were over he made up his mind that he would see something of the world, and accordingly made for California in 1895. He landed in San Benito County and worked on a ranch near Hollister a few months, and then sought employment in the big grain warehouses at Port Costa when this section was one of the most important grain-shipping centers in the State. One year later we find young Hughes in Crockett; and here he has been ever since, and has been a factor in its present growth and development. He holds the position of foreman of twenty men in the C. & H. warehouse, and is a trusted and efficient employee. As he has prospered he has bought property, and owns his own home and other interests here.

Mr. Hughes was married in 1900 to Miss Mary Hopkins, and they have four children: Catherine, Theresa, Thomas Jr., and Peter. Mr. Hughes casts his vote for the men he considers best fitted for office, and best able to serve the people. The family belong to the Catholic Church.

W. A. CHRISTIANSEN.—Ably representing the younger generation of men who are counted leaders in every community, W. A. Christiansen is making his influence felt in civic, fraternal and business circles in eastern Contra Costa County. He is an expert automobile mechanic, agent for the Willys-Knight and Overland cars for eastern Contra Costa County, and is a member of the board of trustees in Antioch. He was born in Portland, Ore., on March 5, 1888, a son of W. A. and Carrie (Jasperson) Christiansen, and the second in a family of seven children, five of whom are still living. His father is a marine engineer of more than ordinary ability; and when our subject was a lad of five years his parents located in San Francisco, where his father followed his calling and where the son attended the grammar school and later took a course in Van der Nailen's Polytechnic School. After he had finished his schooling, young Christiansen began an apprenticeship of three years with the Union Machine Works. When he had mastered the trade, then being nineteen years of age, he sought work with the Fageol truck and auto manufacturer in Oakland. Frank Fageol then had the agency for the Rambler automobile. After serving this concern four years Mr. Christiansen came to Concord and found work in an automobile machine shop, and remained three years. He then came to Antioch and began business for himself, establishing himself as an expert machinist and automobile repairer and securing the agency for the Chevrolet automobile. So well has he succeeded that today he owns his own place of business and his home, and wields a strong influence for the public good. He deals in auto accessories, tires, and tubes, and also stores cars and maintains the Willys-Knight and Overland agencies, his establishment being located at First and I Streets.

At Concord, on July 10, 1909, W. A. Christiansen married Miss Victorina Matheson, born in Chico, Cal.; and they have two children: Alice, a pupil in the high school; and Melvin. Fraternally, Mr. Christiansen is a thirty-second-degree Mason, belonging to San Francisco Consistory No. 1, and to Islam Temple in that city; he holds membership in Antioch Lodge No. 175, F. & A. M.; and with his wife is a member of the Eastern Star. He and his wife are members of the Congregational Church. He has served as city trustee since 1922, being now in his second term, during which time many developments have been made.

ERNEST NAVELLIER.—One of the pioneer residents of this section of Contra Costa County is Ernest Navellier of El Cerrito, where he resides on his poultry ranch on the hills overlooking the city. From his home can be seen seven of the counties bordering the Bay of San Francisco. Mr. Navellier was born in the Basses-Pyrenees, Southern France, on February 1, 1864. When he was sixteen he had graduated from the normal school, and soon thereafter he passed the examination for a teacher at Rodez, and taught for about two years prior to coming to California, when he was eighteen. He had sisters in San Francisco engaged in the laundry business, and thither he migrated to join them. Two hours after landing in the metropolis he had a job as driver of a laundry wagon; and in that line of business he continued for many years, both as an employee and later in the business for himself.

While Mr. Navellier was employed as driver of wagon No. 1, for an Oakland firm, he was given inside information that the Santa Fe Railroad was surveying rights of way for its terminal at what is now Richmond; so thither he came, with what ready cash he could get together, to look for a location where he might enter the laundry business for himself. Men were drilling test holes for water where the Standard Oil plant now stands. He gave $50 for an option on five acres where now stands Dr. Abbott's Sanitarium and the Point Richmond Bank, bargaining to buy this land for $150 per acre. After getting samples of the water from the wells, to see if it was suitable for laundry purposes he submitted it to chemists at the University in Berkeley, who pronounced it highly impregnated with alkali. He forfeited his option and looked further, and finally found springs of soft water at the top of the hill where he now lives. Here he purchased five acres of land at $125 an acre, erected his house and other buildings, and started to build up a laundry business, taking in all the small towns as far as Franklin Canyon, and going as far east to meet the construction camps of the railroad then building. He continued this business for years. When he was looking for his location the only habitation on the site of what is now Richmond was one house. A scow was anchored in the bay for the convenience of Messrs. Miller and Smith, caretakers of the gun club grounds where the Standard Oil plant is now situated. There were no settlements on the flat to amount to anything, and only seventeen pupils were going to the school where now stands St. John's Catholic Church. He named his laundry the Richmond Laundry, being the first to carry that name around among the people of the community. Later, Mr. Navellier spent three years in Tacoma, Wash., in the laundry business; then he came back to his Contra Costa home.

Mr. Navellier was employed at the California Cap Works for about sixteen years as a foreman and shipping clerk. He established what was known as Lafayette Park, a resort which he improved and where he built up a good business, retaining control of the property for six years, the first two of which he was with the California Cap Company, before leaving to give his entire time to his business at the park. In the meantime he was gradually building up a poultry business at his home place. He now has 2200 birds on his ranch, where he is raising birds for breeding purposes as well as for the eggs. He has his own incubators and is doing a prosperous business. Some of his fowls are pedigreed, and cost him from $10 to $85 each. His trade is among the people of the immediate vicinity, and he cannot supply the demand.

The lady Mr. Navellier married in 1888 was in maidenhood Josephine Pontacq, born in Basses-Pyrenees, France. She came to California when she was sixteen, to make her home with two brothers in San Francisco. Mr. and Mrs. Navellier's union has been blessed with four children. Victor, born in Tacoma, Wash., married Edith Bartel and has two children, Anna and Charlotte; Lucy, born in San Francisco, is the wife of Ernest Brensel and the mother of two children, Ernest and Eleanor; Louis married Gladys MacGregor and has a son, Ernest; and Ida is the wife of Arthur Bray and mother of a son, Arthur, Jr. Louis and Ida were born in Contra Costa County and, with the other children, attended the public schools here. Mr. Navellier was a member of the Sanitary Board of the Seventh District while the sewers were being installed. He served as a school trustee in the Stege district when the two schoolhouses, costing $40,000, were being built, and has always done his full duty as a citizen of his adopted country, taking out his citizenship papers when he became of age. He favored the incorporation of El Cerrito and helped put the issue through, and it is now a city of homes. Mr. Navellier is a member of the Berkeley Aërie of Eagles. He is a good-natured, whole-souled, public-spirited pioneer of this district, and with his wife and family he enjoys a wide circle of friends.

CHRISTIAN AUGUST LAURITZEN.—The descendant of pioneer parents who arrived in California in 1872, C. A. Lauritzen first saw the light on Wood Island, Sacramento County, on March 17, 1882. His father, Hans P. Lauritzen, married Adelhyte Lorentsen in Denmark, where they were both born and reared and where their first four children were born. In 1872 this family left their native shores to join a brother of Mrs. Lauritzen in California. They made the voyage via Panama and endured many hardships and privations, so much so that the children suffered very much. This brother, A. P. Lorentsen, was engaged in the lumber trade, shipping to and from Fisk Mill in Mendocino County, and upon the arrival of the family in this State they went to Mendocino County and the father secured work in the logging camps for the Fisk Mill, continuing there until 1874. It was soon after locating at Fisk Mill that the Lauritzen children began to show the results of the privations endured on board ship, where they did not have the proper food. Their mother knew they needed milk, but milk was not to be had, for the cattle were all wild. She persisted in trying to tame some of them and by kindness and perseverance succeeded in being able to milk them. At once, upon securing the nourishment they needed, the children began to recuperate and soon were entirely well. Mrs. Lauritzen still continued to milk her cows and found no trouble in selling the surplus milk and butter to neighbors. She also took in washing to help support their family. While living at Fisk Mill another child was born. There were many Indians in the county and some were their nearest neighbors. The women became much attached to this little white baby, with its blue eyes and fair skin, and were continually in evidence at the Lauritzen home. The mill manager began to be afraid that these Indian women might kidnap the little baby and advised the Lauritzen family to seek some other place for a home. Accordingly they went to Sacramento County and settled on Wood Island, where the father took up land, cleared it and began ranching, adding to his holdings until he owned the whole island of 250 acres. The hardships endured in time of floods can better be imagined than described, but Mr Lauritzen and his good wife stuck to their tasks and finally won out. When the State decided it needed this island for purposes of its own, Mr. Lauritzen sold it to the State of California. They had seven children, viz.: Robert, who died, leaving six children: Hans P., Lena, Niolcine, Tinca, Roland and Catherine; Lena, married B. Bundesen and died leaving one daughter, Lena; Frederick C., a rancher in the Delta country; Hans P., now lives in Richmond and is manager of the Richmond Navigation and Improvement Company; Annie, who became the third wife of B. Bundesen and died, leaving three children: Rudolph, Elise and Adelhyte; Andrew, of Rio Vista; and Christian August, the subject of this sketch. The father died at the age of seventy-two and the mother at seventy-eight years of age, leaving a blessed memory of a pioneer couple with a work well done.

Christian August attended the public schools of Rio Vista, crossing the river every school day in a row-boat, which he and his brothers made into a sail-boat, the sails being made from three flour sacks. He grew up on Wood Island and helped his father to clear and till the land. Needless to say this pioneer experience has meant a great deal to our subject in his later years. He and his brother Frederick early engaged in carrying passengers to points on the river, their first boat plying between Rio Vista and Antioch, where it made connections with the Santa Fe Railroad. The second boat they built was put on the run from Rio Vista to Sacramento, while the third and fourth boats made regular runs between Sacramento and Stockton and back to Sacramento. Their fifth boat was kept in reserve. With the building of the State Highway and the advent of the automobiles the river passenger traffic diminished; so the brothers divided their boats, Christian A. taking the three smaller boats. These he sold, and in 1917 established the ferry business known as the Antioch-Sherman Island Ferry. It was located at the point on the river where the new Antioch-Sherman Island Toll Bridge has just been completed. With his intimate knowledge of the Delta country, Mr. Lauritzen could forsee the logical site for his terminal for the Sacramento and Oakland automobile traffic, and the growth of his business was proof of his good judgment; and in locating their site the Toll Bridge Company made the same selection. Mr. Lauritzen had a partner, H. F. Lauritzen, his nephew, in his enterprise but he was the manager of the business. They ran the Victory and the Sherman boats and operated daily schedules until selling out to the American Toll Bridge Company on July 1, 1926. Mr. Lauritzen is equipped for building wharves and for doing pile-driving and kindred work. He has one sixty-foot and one seventy-five foot pile-driver. This branch of the business is carried on under the firm name of Lauritzen & Legg, and has been meeting with good success.

In 1926 Mr. Lauritzen established a ferry business from Jersey Island to Bradford Island, the Webb Tract, and the Frank Tract, and return, to open up the Delta country for transportation.

C. A. Lauritzen was united in marriage on March 19, 1924, with Miss Irene Thomas, who was born at Antioch of pioneer parents. They have a son, Christian August, Jr. The family home is a comfortable bungalow at the ferry landing. The building was formerly located in Antioch, but was moved to the ferry landing and remodeled into a comfortable residence. Mr. Lauritzen serves as a deputy under sheriff R. R. Veale. He is a very dependable man at all times, is public-spirited, and believes in progress on every hand. He has made many friends, who hold him in high esteem.

WILBUR S. PIERCE.—A man of liberal views, energetic, and progressive, Wilbur S. Pierce came to Richmond in 1914. Mr. Pierce is a lawyer of ability, being a member of the law firm of Pierce & Carlson, one of the leading firms of the East Bay section. A native son of California, he was born on March 12, 1891, a son of Charles E. and Virginia Alexander Pierce, the former a native of Iowa, and the latter of California. He is one of five children born to his parents, the others being Mrs. C. F. Robenson, Carl, Wirt E., and Harold D. Pierce.

Wilbur S. Pierce received his early education in Yolo County and was admitted to the bar on January 1, 1914. Coming to Richmond in the latter part of 1914, he was appointed assistant district attorney of Contra Costa County, in which capacity he served two years, and then entered into private practice.

During the World War, Mr. Pierce was first sent to American Lake, and from there was transferred to Washington, D. C., where he served as an attorney for the War Industries Board. During the time he was in Washington, he prosecuted several important cases concerning the violation of war relief, and emergency measures. He was in the audience when President Wilson presented to Congress and the Foreign Diplomats the conditions under which Germany had signed the armistice, which audience was generally reckoned as an assemblage of the greatest number of distinguished men ever held in the history of the world.

Mr. Pierce is prominent fraternally, being identified with most of the leading clubs and organizations. He is a member of the American

Legion, and at the present time is President of the Lions Club of Richmond. He is recognized as a trial lawyer of exceptional ability, and has distinguished himself as an eloquent forensic and public speaker. Mr. Pierce is a married man and the father of one child, five and one-half years of age, named Wilbur Barrett Pierce.

MRS. GERTRUDE BARNARD.—Taking her place in the business life of Contra Costa as assistant cashier of the Rodeo Branch of the Bank of Pinole, Mrs. Barnard is well known in her home county. A native of Crockett, she is the daughter of Edward Kearney, now residing in Oakland, but who was for many years an employee of the Selby Smelting Works; Grandfather Kearney was the owner of the Kearney Ranch on the Sobrante in western Contra Costa County, which is now the site of the Giant Powder Works. After finishing her grammar school courses, Mrs. Barnard attended the John Swett Union High School three years.

Her marriage, at Selby, Cal., united her with L. Barnard, an employee of the Selby Smelting Works, and one child blessed their union, a daughter, Cleo, who now makes her home with her mother in Oakland, Mrs. Barnard motoring to and from her work at the bank each day. She has proven herself to be a plucky and capable woman, both in her business duties and in the management of her personal affairs, and is deserving of much credit as a native daughter of Contra Costa County, who is interested in its advancement and willing to do all in her power to help the work of progress.

WILLIAM R. SHARKEY.—He who labors to secure the development of the section in which he lives, striving to bring out its latent resources and devoting his time to the general welfare of its people by championing those measures that advance the best interests of education, agriculture, commerce and finance, is accounted a public benefactor. Such a man is the Hon. William R. Sharkey, native son, loyal citizen, editor of the Martinez Daily Standard and Contra Costa Standard, at Martinez, and State senator for the Ninth District of California, comprising Contra Costa and Marin Counties.

William R. Sharkey was born in Sierra County on June 6, 1876, a son of Richard and Mary Sharkey. His education was obtained in the public schools—and in the school of hard knocks in learning the printing business. His first work was done on the Sierra County Tribune; then he was connected with the Mountain Mirror at Sierraville until he went to Amadee and worked on the Amadee Geyser in Lassen County. Later he returned to Sierraville and accepted a position with the Sierra Valley Leader, remaining there for one year. His health becoming impaired, he then resigned his post and took up riding the range as an ordinary cowboy until 1896, until he recovered his normal state of health and returned to newspaper work with the Sierra County Enterprise at Downieville. In 1899 Mr. Sharkey bought the Sierra Valley Record at Sierraville. He ran this paper until 1902, when he sold out and accepted a position with the Calkins Syndicate as coast manager. One year later he became city editor of the Morning Miner of Nevada City, and in 1905 he opened an office in Reno, Nev., for the Calkins Syndicate, representing the Orchard and Farm and Pacific Miner. His chief venture in the newspaper field was made in Martinez on April 1, 1906, when he became manager of the Contra Costa Standard. He greatly increased the circulation of the paper by his wise and business-like management and five years later established the Martinez Daily Standard, now one of the leading daily papers of the county. With the passing of the years these papers have succeeded financially, and in 1926 Mr. Sharkey erected a modern structure to house his plant, in which every convenience is to be found to facilitate the printing of a modern newspaper. This paper was established in 1874 at Pacheco, and was known as the Contra Costa News, then as the County Paper, and in 1906 as the Contra Costa Standard. In 1911 the Daily Standard was established; and today, through the judicious efforts of Mr. Sharkey and his corps of able assistants, both papers wield a healthy influence for progress in the county.

On September 6, 1899, William R. Sharkey and Miss Nannie Elizabeth Gott, a native of Plumas County, were united in marriage; and their union has been blessed with two children. Mary Muriel is a graduate of the Alhambra Union High School and of Heald's Business College, of Oakland. She is now the wife of Harold F. Hexner and the mother of a son, William Harold. William R. Sharkey, Jr., is a student in electrical engineering at the College of the Pacific at Stockton, Class of 1927.

Mr. Sharkey has always been interested in politics, and in 1915 served a term as assemblyman from the Eighteenth District. In 1916 he was elected State senator from the Ninth District, being then made chairman of the Rivers and Harbors Committee. So successful was he in the performance of his duties at the capital, that his constituents returned him to the senate at the general election in 1920, and again in 1924. Through his influence Mount Diablo State Park was established in Contra Costa County in 1921. He has always had at heart the best interests of his home county, and also of Marin, and has striven to bring about legislation for the good of the entire State.

Fraternally, Mr. Sharkey is a Past Master of Martinez Lodge No. 41, F. & A. M., and a member of Martinez Chapter No. 31, R. A. M.; Richmond Commandery No. 59, K. T.; Aahmes Temple, A. A. O. N. M. S., of Oakland; Los Ceritos Chapter No. 234, O. E. S., of Martinez; and Antioch Pyramid of Sciots. He also belongs to Richmond Lodge No. 1251, B. P. O. E.; Martinez Lodge, L. O. O. M.; and Golden Key Lodge, K. of P., and is a Past President of Mount Diablo Parlor, N. S. G. W.; a Past Council Commander of Laurel Camp No. 145, W. O. W.; and a member of California Camp, M. W. A. He belongs to the Kiwanis Club of Martinez.

EDWIN MARMADUKE TILDEN.—A progressive and enterprising citizen of Richmond who possesses sound judgment and keen business ability, those indispensable adjuncts to the successful operation of large business enterprises, E. M. Tilden is the leading spirit and business head of the Tilden Lumber Companies, located in various sections of California, and an able financier of the San Francisco Bay section. He was born at St. Michaels, Talbot County, Maryland, on July 2, 1866, a son of Dr. Thomas W. and Helen (Dawson) Tilden, both born in Maryland of English extraction. They were married in 1858 and became the parents of two sons and two daughters, viz.: Mary Ridgley, Mrs. Waverley Stairley, of Richmond; James Dawson, of Sacramento; Edwin M., of this review; and Mrs. Louise Wasley, of Chico. Dr. Tilden served in the Jefferson Davis Regiment during the Mexican War and as wounded in action. He died in 1874, in Butte County, Cal., whither the family came and settled in 1858. Mrs. Tilden is living, making her home in Oakland.

Edwin Marmaduke Tilden received his education in the public schools and the Woodman Academy in Chico. On account of his father's death, when E. M. was but eight years old, the lad worked at such jobs as a boy could during his school days, viz.: selling and delivering papers and as errand boy for various stores, to earn something towards his support and to aid in the support of the family. As soon as he had finished high school he went to work for the Sierra Lumber Company, at Red Bluff, and remained with this firm thirteen years. He entered the employ of the company as an office boy, passed through the various departments, each change being an advancement, and when he left it was as the manager of the plant at Woodland. With his knowledge of the business, and the money he had saved, Mr. Tilden went to Woodland and carried on a lumber business for himself for three years. In 1900 he came to Point Richmond and was the pioneer lumber man of this place. He had two or three carloads of lumber and a span of horses and in this way began his retail lumber business. He prospered from the start and as the community grew, he expanded with it, lending a helping hand to every enterprise that he thought would help to develop the new district. This was the beginning of the Tilden Lumber Company, since then its expansion has been brought about by the indefatigable energy and business acumen of Mr. Tilden.

In 1912 E. M. Tilden purchased the Berkeley Lumber Company; in 1917 he bought the Hogan Lumber Company in Oakland; in 1924 added the fifteen lumber yards of the Sunset Lumber Company, located in the principal towns and cities in Central California, to his holdings; and in 1925 took over the Pacific Pipe and Tank Company and the National Mill and Lumber Company, both in Oakland. Now the Tilden Lumber Company's interests include thirty lumber yards and mills in the State, with offices in New York, Salt Lake City and Honolulu; and with agents in nearly all of the South American States. The business receives the undivided attention of E. M. Tilden, who realizes that every successful enterprise must have a recognized head and leader.

As early as 1902 Mr. Tilden began to be interested in the banking business. He could see the necessity of establishing a bank at Point Richmond. It was largely through his solicitation that Waverley Stairley, then located at Red Bluff, came down here and soon afterward the Bank of Richmond, the pioneer financial institution of this city, was established. Mr. Tilden served as a director for ten years. With others he established the First National Bank of Richmond and is its president, and he is vice-president of the Mechanics Bank of Richmond. His interests are many and large, for in addition to those already mentioned he is president of all the Tilden Lumber companies; president of the Elks Hall in Richmond; president of the Builders Exchange of Alameda County; a director in the East Bay Industrial Association, the East Bay Title Insurance Company of Oakland, besides some other interests of lesser magnitude. Notwithstanding his many connections and large interests Mr. Tilden drops business cares when he leaves his office and thoroughly enjoys the hours between with his friends and his family. He has never aspired to political preference although solicited many times to become a candidate for office. He has helped promote every community interest in Richmond, the Elks Hall, City Hall, Richmond's new commercial hotel, etc. The volume of business of the Tilden Lumber Companies exceeds five million dollars annually, being the largest retail lumber business in the State. Over 1100 men, nearly all Americans, are employed in various capacities by this organization and the East Bay district is Mr. Tilden's particular field. His companies also do a considerable export business.

On February 17, 1892, E. M. Tilden was united in marriage with Miss Jane Eakle, of Woodland. She was one of twelve children in the family of Christian and Margaret Jane (Edrington) Eakle, Kentuckians. The father crossed the plains in the early days, driving an ox-team, and did his part to help maintain the great commonwealth of California. Mr. and Mrs. Tilden have the following children: Waverley, born March 18, 1893, now manager of the Tilden Lumber and Mill Company in Oakland, is married and has a daughter, Barbara; Helen, died at the age of thirteen; Edwin, born April 18, 1906, works in the Berkeley office of the Tilden Lumber Company. Waverley served in the World War and saw eighteen months service in France. Mr. Tilden is an Elk, a Mason and a Shriner. Mrs. Tilden is active in church work.

During the World War Mr. Tilden operated his mill and lumber yard night and day executing government contracts. He built the main office for the Bethlehem Ship Building Company known as the administration building. The building was planned and erected and ready for occupancy in one week's time. Mr. Tilden finds his recreation in traveling and at the various resorts, where he is free from business cares.

28

WARREN A. DAVIS.—Numbered among the successful business men of Crockett, whose excellent business judgment and untiring energy have contributed largely to the substantial growth of city and county, is Warren A. Davis. He was born at Somersville, Contra Costa County, on February 24, 1884, the son of William Augustus Davis, who was born in Schuykill County, Pa., April 25, 1859, and Libbie F. (Hughes) Davis, born in Bangor, Wis., July 22, 1860. The elder Davis accompanied his parents to California in 1861. They were William R., born May 14, 1816, and Ann (Parry) Davis, born July 1, 1824; and they had the following children: Hannah, Joseph A., Mrs. Lizzie .Morgans, William A., David A., Mary A., and John J. The Davis family settled in Calaveras County, and there lived until 1868, when they came to Contra Costa County and located at Nortonville.

William Augustus Davis received his education in the public schools, and was graduated from the Pacific Business College in 1877. He then entered the employ of W. W. Dodge in Nortonville, as a salesman, continuing there four years. In 1881 he went to Somersville and engaged in the general merchandise business with John Hughes as a partner. In 1883 he was married. Later he moved to Martinez and was associated with L. M. Lasell in business. In 1886 he went to Brentwood and started in business on his own account. Selling out, he went to Los Angeles in 1899, and thence came to Crockett in 1901. His brother, John J. Davis had started a business enterprise in Crockett in which William A. Davis was financially interested, and upon the latter's coming here he soon took an active part in the conduct of the store. John J. retiring from active participation, the business was incorporated under the name of Davis Brothers in 1904. William Davis continued active in the business until his death, which occurred on July 14, 1907. He was a member of Carquinez Lodge No. 337, F. & A. M., and of the Eastern Star; he also took an active part in church work. Besides our subject there is a daughter, Edna May Davis, who is a teacher of Spanish and French in a high school in Los Angeles. She is a graduate of Stanford. Mrs. Davis makes her home in Los Angeles, taking occasional trips to Contra Costa County.

There is some interesting pioneer history connected with the maternal side of the family. Warren A. Davis' grandfather was Rev. David Hughes, born in Bala, Wales, on December 28, 1832. He married Sarah Francis on Thanksgiving day, November 20, 1856, in Utica, N. Y. She was born in Trenton, N. Y., on May 3, 1834, and had several children. The Hughes family came to America in 1844 and settled in Deerfield, N. Y., where David Hughes was educated. David Hughes was a cousin of former Secretary of State, Charles Evan Hughes. In 1875 he was ordained to the ministry at Cambria, Wis., and his first pastorate was at Bangor, Wis. He remained there until 1881, when he came to California and located in Nortonville. After four years in Nortonville, he went to San Francisco and ministered to the Welsh people there for a number of years. His next field of endeavor was in Los Angeles, whither he went in 1888. In November of that year he organized the Welsh Presbyterian Church on Second Street and Broadway. In 1893 he organized the Bethesda Presbyterian Church, maintaining both churches until 1902, when he resigned because of failing health. He died on December 26, 1903. The Los Angeles papers said of him that he was a great Bible student and a learned man. He left a widow, one son, John F. Hughes, and the following daughters: Mrs. W. A. Davis, of Los Angeles; Mrs. B. F. Hicks, of Oakland, now deceased, whose daughter, Mrs. Will Jones, lives in Crockett; Mrs. Everett B. Thomas, of Los Angeles; Mrs. Jennie Rees, of San Francisco; Miss Sarah E. Hughes; and Mrs. Frances W. Mohlman, of Los Angeles. Mrs. Hughes died in 1915, mourned by many friends.

It will be noticed that the middle initial "A" is carried throughout the successive generations of the Davis family. Sometimes the name has only the letter, as in Warren A., simply to carry out the family characteristic. The Davis farm in Wales was named Warren, and Warren A. Davis was given his first name in honor of the old homestead.

Warren A. Davis accompanied his parents in their various removals, and attended the schools in Brentwood; Los Angeles, where he had two years of high school work; and Crockett, where he was graduated in the first class from the John Swett High School. He then entered Stanford University, majoring in electrical engineering, and was graduated in 1907 with the B. A. degree. His father's death soon after he came out of college did not permit him to follow his chosen career, and he took a place in the Davis Brothers' store as a clerk. C. L. Dodge, county treasurer, was then manager of the business, and he is still interested in it. A. N. Sullenger, county auditor, was also one of the original stockholders. Several now employed in the firm were connected with it at the beginning. In 1910 Warren A. Davis became manager, a position he still holds. In carrying on the business, many new innovations have been added to better serve customers, and also to simplify methods.

On June 16, 1909, Warren A. Davis and Miss Florence M. Linekin were united in marriage. Theirs was an old-fashioned home wedding in the house in which they now live. Mrs. Davis is a graduate of the State Teachers' College at San Jose, Class of 1907, and was teaching in the schools of Crockett at the time of their marriage. Her father, Warrington Young Linekin, was born in Maine, followed the sea for a time, and came to California at the time of the gold rush. Warrington Young Linekin was a horseman of note. He was a practical veterinarian, and was for many years the leading local authority on the horse and his diseases, and was called on from far and near, in and around Hayward, to treat sick horses. At the time of the severe earthquake of 1868, he was farming for Mr. Cunningham, and was taking a very heavy load of grain to the warehouse in Hayward on the Crow Canyon road with a twelve-horse team. The quake loosened many great rocks, which crashed down the hillsides and across the road; but he and his team and wagon miraculously escaped unhurt. For a time Mr. Linekin was a dealer in hardware in Hayward, and then held public office there. Mrs. Davis' mother was one of the neighborly women found in every locality, and nursed the sick, helped care for the dead, and extended sympathy to all who needed it. She was Anna Wrede in maidenhood, and was born in New Orleans and came to California in 1854, crossing the Isthmus of Panama with her parents. They settled in Sonora, Cal., where she married Mr. Linekin in 1867, after which they moved to Hayward. They had six children: Mrs. Alice LaBaree, teacher in the Crockett school; Mrs. Nellie L. Baldwin, of Danville; Mrs. Mary L. Reid, of Danville; Mrs. Sarah E. Hoyt, in Hayward; Kittie Adele, deceased; and Mrs. W. A. Davis. Mrs. Linekin died in 1916 at the age of sixty-seven, and Mr. Linekin died in 1904. Mr. and Mrs. Davis have two boys. Warren Alwyn was named by his great-grandmother Hughes, the middle name being taken from the Welsh, meaning "Loved by All." He is attending the California Polytechnic School at San Luis Obispo, where he has taken up agriculture. John Allison is in the Crockett Grammar School.

The activities of Mr. and Mrs. Davis have been many. He became a director in the Bank of Pinole upon its locating a branch in Crockett; is the chairman of the committee appointed to arrange for the numbering of houses in Crockett; was one of the live wires in the reorganization of the Business Men's Association; is secretary of the Contra Costa County Grocers' Association; was one of the exponents of the Community Church idea, which has proven successful, and was superintendent of Sunday school for several years. Upon the death of his father he was placed in his position as a trustee of the Congregational Church, and is now president of the board of the congregation group of trustees. At the time of the building of the Community Church in 1913-1914, he served on the building committee. He is active in the Young Men's Christian Association work, local and county, and in the work of the Boy Scouts, and has represented various organizations at outside conventions many times. Mrs. Davis has been active in church work, both as a teacher in the Sunday school and as a member of the Ladies' Aid and missionary societies of the church. She is a charter member and the corresponding secretary of the Carquinez Women's Club. During the World War she had charge of the Belgian Babies' Fund, working under Mrs. Spreckels of San Francisco in this district, and was presented a medal by the Belgian duchess who had charge of the work in Belgium. She is chairman of the Industrial and Social Relations Committee in the Alameda District C. F. W. C., comprising five counties, and especially interested in the social conditions in Contra Costa County. She has served as a member of the committee from the Contra Costa Federation of Women's Clubs that made the survey of condition at the old detention home and presented same to the supervisors, the result being the erection of a new and suitable building for this purpose. Being much interested in such work, Mrs. Davis hopes to see a Welfare Council organized here in the near future.

JAMES A. SILVAS.—A native of Contra Costa County James A. Silvas was born in the Briones Valley, the son of Cipriano Silvas, a native of Chile, S. A., who was born on September 26, 1823. His parents were Eusavia and Teresa (Henry) Silvas. Cipriano was a well educated man and a school teacher in his native country. He came to California with the gold rush, landed in the Pinole Valley and took up farming, raising grain, other farm products and stock, first in the southern part of the valley but later went to the upper end, which was called Briones Valley in honor of that old pioneer family, and there he lived and prospered until his death. He had married Mrs. Mary Acosta, whose maiden name was Alvarado and she was born in Los Angeles. Their children were: Henry B., born in 1862 and now living in Richmond. Joseph E. who was born on March 5, 1864, educated in the public schools of Briones Valley and reared to ranch life until reaching manhood, then learned the carpenter's trade, which he is still following; he married Miss Mary Maderas, Pinole, daughter of J. J. and Amelia Maderas and they have five children: Edward R., a machinist; Luella May, Lucille, Norbert Leslie and Harold Joseph are at home. Adella Silvas married F. Abrott and lives near Pinole; Cipriano, who lives in Pinole; Albert R., of Martinez; James A., of this review; Edward, in Berkeley, where he is a carpenter and builder; and Theresa, Mrs. John Curran, of Pinole. The father died on July 11, 1913, and the mother on February 19, 1924.

James A., attended the Briones school and at an early age began business as a saloonkeeper, continuing for twenty years, although part of the time he engaged in the haberdashery business, carrying on both lines of business at the same time until he sold the saloon and has since given his entire time to the other line and has been successful. He is a hale fellow well met and always ready to lend a helping hand to those less fortunate than himself. He is a good story-teller and of jovial disposition and likes to have people about him. He has a fondness for dogs and has owned some fine animals. He believes in progress and supports all progressive movements for the public good.

ALPHEUS RICHARDSON.—Numbered among the pioneers of the Golden State was the late Alpheus Richardson, who arrived here in 1852. He was born on October 3, 1830, and died on December 12, 1915. Between these two dates many years were spent by him in worthwhile endeavor. He was born in Marion County, Ohio, and was there reared, and received his education. In 1852 he came to California in a company under the leadership of Colonel Hollister. After his arrival he worked for a time near Marysville, and then engaged in placer mining in Placer County for one year, and "went broke." With the characteristic determination for which he was noted, he again went to work for wages, saved his earnings, and with them embarked in ranching; but this also proved a failure at that time. He reached Gilroy, Santa Clara County, and engaged in raising hogs, paying high prices for them. Unfortunately, when they were ready to sell the prices were low and again he did not make any money. He came to Contra Costa County and tried raising cattle for a couple of years, but then gave that up and went to Oregon in 1863. Again he tried mining in Alpine County, with the usual luck of the ordinary miner. In 1865 he again came to this county and settled in the Point of Timber section, where, with the experience of his former years as a rancher, he soon began to make headway, and on land that was once considered worthless made a success of his efforts. His principal crop was wheat, and by summer fallowing he made this pay, even in dry seasons. He took an active part in all movements for the best interests of the people among whom he lived, and in time became a well-to-do man. At the time of his death he was accounted a leader among the men of his community, and was mourned by a large concourse of friends.

Mr. Richardson married Miss Avyette Taylor, a sister of Volney Taylor. She was born on October 27, 1848, and died on May 29, 1907. Both Mr. and Mrs. Richardson are buried in the Point of Timber Cemetery about two miles north of Byron. They both became well and favorably known in Contra Costa County, and were always working to advance its best interests. Their home was one of the show places in the eastern section of the county. After making a success of his farming, Mr. and Mrs. Richardson took a trip, in 1876, throughout Canada and the Eastern and the Western States, and attended the Centennial Exposition at Philadelphia, traveling some 8000 miles. Their good works live after them.

JOHN FRANCIS O'NEILL, SR.—The subject of this sketch, John Francis O'Neill, Sr., was born in Ireland in 1842 and was a son of John Francis O'Neill, who brought his family to California in 1845 and settled in Calaveras County, where the father conducted a general merchandise store. Both our subject and his father died in the month of February, 1890, aged forty-eight and eighty-four years, respectively. From Calaveras County the family came to Contra Costa County and took up farming on the Sobrante grant of 18,000 acres owned by Victor Castro and his brother, Jose Castro. Our subject was educated in Santa Clara College and his life was spent as a rancher on the Castro property. He used to tell of having a job of driving a horse for twenty dollars a week, but lost it when the man got a mule that needed no driver.

Mr. O'Neill married Miss Isabella Castro, born in Stege, on July 10, 1848, the daughter of Victor and Louisa (Martinez) Castro, both pioneer Spanish families who owned thousands of acres of land in this county. Mrs. O'Neill was educated in a convent in San Francisco that stood where the Palace Hotel now is and said they could look out of the window and see the men dumping the dirt that filled in the bay from Montgomery Street. When she was eighteen years old Miss Castro came up to San Pablo Creek to keep house for her brother, Patricio, and remained there three years, or until her marriage. For a wedding trip they went to San Jose. They farmed on the grant till 1888, when they moved to Pinole, where she still lives. There were eight children in the family: John Francis, who is mentioned on another page of this work; Louise, Mrs. J. Walton, of Pinole; Edward, of Oakland; Josie, Mrs. Charles Poinsett, of Hercules; Jovita, Mrs. R. Robinson, of Hercules; William, a twin of Mrs. Robinson, died aged two years; Fred Lawrence, a machinist; Annie, Mrs. McDonald, was born two months after the death of her father. Point Isabella is where the Vigoret Powder Works was located and it was named in honor of Mrs. O'Neill, for it was from this point that her father corralled and shipped his cattle.

Isabella Castro, daughter of Victor Castro, was born in the adobe house that still stands near the county line in El Cerrito. Her father owned the Sobrante Grant in partnership with his brother, Jose. Victor Castro was the first white child born at the Presidio in San Francisco. The old adobe house was built by Mr. Castro and it can never pass from the Castro family. To keep Victor Castro from going to serve in the Mexican War the father of Miss Louisa Martinez suggested the marriage with his daughter and unite the fortunes of two prominent families. The wedding was a result. Mrs. J. F. O'Neill, Sr., lost her mother when she was but two years old and her father married Valecia Coriea, of Sonoma County and chartered a steamer to bring his bride to San Francisco. She lived only two years, dying at the age of twenty-two. The third wife of Victor Castro was Mrs. Julia Lupton. Victor Castro died aged eighty-five and is buried in the garden of the old adobe.

JAMES B. McCABE.—A man who has seen activity as a railroad employee since 1882 is James M. McCabe of Richmond. He was born in Toledo, Ohio, on October 8, 1861, and attended the public schools in pursuit of an education. When he was twenty-one he went to work as an engine wiper at Detroit, Mich., and in 1884 he began firing a locomotive on the road as an extra man. Mr. McCabe had two brothers with the Southern Pacific in California. In 1886 he came to California, stopping at Needles, and entered the employ of the Atlantic and Pacific Railroad. For fourteen years he ran out of Needles to Barstow, firing until his promotion in 1889 to engineer. When he first went to Needles there were but six houses in the town, and a lunch counter was operated by Stackpole and Lincoln where now the famous Harvey Houses on the Santa Fe system supply the demand for hotel and eating house. From Needles Mr. McCabe was transferred to Stockton and ran over the Valley Division until coming to East Yard, as Richmond was then called, in 1900. There was no place for a man to locate his family at that time, and the eating tent was conducted by Mrs. McNally at the place where the electric street car tracks cross the Santa Fe tracks. When Hotel Critchett was completed, in the fall, Mr. McCabe brought his family here. After coming here he worked on construction train filling the yard and then on the branch road into Oakland from Richmond. In 1903 he was able to move his family into a house just completed, which he had rented, and two years later they moved into a home he had erected at No. 77 Scenic Avenue. For the past twenty-six years Mr. McCabe has had a run out of Richmond. He says there have been many changes in railroading since he started, and especially is this true since he came to Richmond. There was no fresh water for engines then, and the salty water from the wells here was not good for boiler use. Mr. McCabe is very popular with his railroad associates, and with his many friends outside of railroad circles. He belongs to the Riverbank Division of the Brotherhood of Locomotive Engineers, No. 839.

Mr. McCabe married Mrs. Annie Stone at Needles, Cal. She was born at Walnut Creek, Contra Costa County, and has a son George by her first marriage. Mr. and Mrs. McCabe have a son, Melvin, born at Needles on March 23, 1896. He graduated from the Richmond High School and then entered the Agricultural College at Davis, but the World War interfered with the completion of his course. He enlisted in the Masonic Ambulance Corps and served eighteen months in France, and was in the Argonne campaign. After the war he returned home for a short time and then went to Washington, where he married a lady he had met while training at Camp Lewis. They have two children, Carol and Chester. He is engaged in the grocery business at Tenino, Wash. George Stone was reared by Mr. McCabe and learned the machinist's trade. He is now living in Los Angeles. He married and has a son, Burvel, who lives with Mr. and Mrs. McCabe. Mrs. McCabe has always taken an active part in all community affairs since locating here. She is a member of the Eastern Star. Mr. McCabe believes Richmond has a bright future marked out for it as a coming city on the Bay. His source of recreation and his hobby is fishing, and he indulges in this pastime upon every opportunity.

WARREN D. WOOD.—A resident of Richmond since 1912, when he came here to enter the engine service with the Santa Fe Railroad, Warren D. Wood has been much interested in watching the development of his chosen home locality. He was born in Jonesboro, Ark., on August 29, 1878, and he went to the public schools of his neighborhood. He had two brothers who served in the World War; Fred, who served in the engineer corps and was over seas for twenty-seven months; and Oliver, who served with the 20th Engineer Corps and was over seas for about a year.

In 1904 Mr. Wood made a trip to Southern California as a tourist; then after his marriage he and his wife made five trips. His first work as a railroad man was with the Frisco Line in the Ozark Mountains, and he fired a locomotive from 1902 to 1907, the latter year he was promoted to be an engineer and ran as extra man till 1912, when he got a regular run. He got tired of the mountainous country, so in 1912 he came to Los Angeles and hired out to the Santa Fe; later he went to Stockton and ran a switch engine two months then went to Riverbank. He found so many older men, in point of service ahead of him that he took a survey of conditions and when he was offered a job in the Richmond yards he took it immediately and has been in that part of the service ever since. There are now ten engines in the yards and five on the Belt Line. His first impressions of the town were unfavorable but he realizes there are few cities like Richmond and is contented and happy.

Mr. Wood and Miss Ora Ogle, daughter of Henry I. Ogle, who came to Pasadena in 1909, and who is now living at Haywards, were united in marriage in 1909. Their children are: Marion, Martha and Warren, all born in Richmond; and Gus, who was born in Missouri and died in Richmond in November, 1918, aged six years. Mr. Wood is a member of Alpha Lodge No. 431 F. & A. M., demitting from Arkansas Lodge No. 413; he belongs to Richmond Chapter No. 113, R. A. M. In line with his work he belongs to the B. of L. E. No. 839 at Riverbank; and to the Ozark No. 280 B. of L. F. & E. Mr. Wood owns his own home and property across the street. So enthusiastic is he over Richmond and its possibilities that he has influenced several to locate here.

MATTHEW WEIR.—Among the citizens who are deeply interested in church and religious movements in his locality we find Matthew Weir, whose home is situated at No. 301 Potrero Avenue, El Cerrito. He has been a valued resident of this locality since 1906, coming to Richmond in May of that year, and moving to his present location in 1915. He was born in Philadelphia, Pa., on December 6, 1870, and received his education in the common schools. At an early age he served an apprenticeship to learn to become a finisher of woolen and cotton goods. Desiring to see something of the world he left Pennsylvania and went to Chicago, where he found employment for two years. After the close of the Columbian Exposition in 1893, he came West to San Francisco, from there going to the gold mines in the northern part of the State, where he worked as a carpenter for various mining companies, and also did some prospecting on his own account and met with some success in searching for gold. He spent two years at mining in Tonopah and at Yerrington, Nev., during 1911-1912, when he again came to California. He had located in Richmond in 1906, after the earthquake and fire in San Francisco and entered the employ of the Standard Oil Company at their refinery as a carpenter. Later he was promoted to the power department, where he now is.

Mr. Weir was married in 1905, in Redding, Cal., to Mrs. Olive Haffey, daughter of Matthew Morrow, a pioneer miner. Mrs. Weir was born in Shasta County and has lived in California all her life. They have an adopted son, Jack Joseph Weir. Mr. Weir is a member of Alpha Lodge No. 431, F. & A. M., in Richmond, and belongs to the Oakland Consistory of the Scottish Rite. He has taken a very active interest in church work and is a member and an elder in the Stege Presbyterian chuch. Through his influence and leadership a new church, costing $15,000 was begun in January, 1923, and completed soon afterwards. Mr. Weir served on the building committee and was elected treasurer of the church board. The new church has a seating capacity of 650 when thrown open to the public; has a membership of 110, and a Sunday School attendance of 130. The building is modern in every respect, is lighted and heated by electricity, and has a fully equipped banquet hall and kitchen. It is conceded to rank with the best structures of its kind and size in the entire bay district and is a source of pride to all the members, who give due credit to Mr. Weir.

WILLIAM MURRAY LAIDLAW.—For nearly a quarter of a century the life of W. M. Laidlaw, editor and owner of the Crockett Signal, has been inseparably associated with the history of Crockett, Cal., he having located there in January of 1906. Prior to the advent of Mr. Laidlaw in Crockett, other newspapermen had ventured in the field, but meeting with varied experiences had departed. The Crockett Signal, under Mr. Laidlaw's management, made its first appearance on January 29, 1906, as a 4-column daily paper. It became apparent after a few months trial that the field would not support a daily and on September 14 of that year the Crockett Signal appeared as a 4-column folio weekly. Through the sufferance of the public it has continued ever since, the passing years witnessing its gradual growth until it is now published as a 7-column quarto paper.

William Murray Laidlaw was born January 2, 1876, in the little hamlet of Elmdale, St. Lawrence County, N. Y., the son of Robert Darling and Mary (Hall) Laidlaw. As the name implies, the family is of Scottish descent, tracing its origin far back into the history of Scotland.

In the year 1881 the parents of Mr. Laidlaw removed from New York State to Aberdeen, Brown County, S. D., a small prairie town, which at that period was the terminus of a new railroad then on its first lap in a construction program, which in later years carried it on to the Pacific Coast. The founder named the town after his home city in Scotland. In Aberdeen Mr. Laidlaw received the rudiments of an education in the grade school and when fifteen years of age began serving his apprenticeship as a printer. In the spring of 1901 he migrated to San Francisco and after a short residence there went to Richmond, Cal., entering the employ of the Santa Fe Railroad Company. His experiences finally convinced him he was not destined for a railroad career and he went back to printing, accepting a position on the Richmond Daily Leader, in time becoming manager and editor of this paper. In September, 1904, he disposed of his interests in the Daily Leader and went to Martinez, where he was employed on the Martinez Daily Gazette until January, 1906, when he chose Crockett as a place wherein to again embark in business.

In politics the Crockett Signal occupies a neutral position, its influence being exerted on behalf of issues deemed best for the interests of its contituents and supporting for public office, irrespective of party affiliation, those considered best qualified. In the advancement of the educational, moral, commercial and civic interests of the community, it has labored unceasingly.

In 1911 the parents of Mr. Laidlaw joined him at Crockett, the father being employed at the sugar refinery until his death in February of 1919. The mother returned to Aberdeen, S. D., to make her home with a daughter, Miss Clyde May Laidlaw. The latter for many years has held a responsible position in the office of registrar of deeds of Brown County. Another sister, Selina, is now Mrs. E. L. Milligan and resides in Illinois.

On September 11, 1904, W. M. Laidlaw was united in marriage with Miss Grace Anna Beach, a native of York, Nebr., and daughter of Dr. Morgan H. and Sarah M. (Walsworth) Beach, who came West in 1881 and located in Eastern Oregon; both of them are deceased. Mrs. Laidlaw has five brothers, all of whom are identified with the printing profession. A sister, Mrs. G. A. Follett, resides at Richmond. Mrs. Laidlaw was educated in the Oregon public schools and at the time of her mariage to Mr. Laidlaw resided at Ashland, Ore. She is an ideal helpmeet to her husband and the latter without hesitation ascribes the growth and popularity of the Crockett Signal to the influence for good wielded by his helpmeet and companion of nearly a quarter of a century.

Fraternally, Mr. Laidlaw has several affiliations. He is a member of Carquinez Lodge No. 337, F. & A. M. of Crockett; Crockett Chapter No. 184, O. E. S.; Oakland Consistory No. 2, M. R. S.; Aahmes Temple A. A. O. N. M. S. of Oakland; Vallejo Lodge No. 559, B. P. O. Elks; Selby Lodge No. 192, K. of P.; and Hollywood Camp No. 417, W. O. W. He is also a member of various clubs and business organizations and a stanch supporter of Boy Scout and Camp Fire Girl activities.

S. J. CLAEYS.—One of Contra Costa County's most influential citizens, and the leading spirit in the development of Rodeo and vicinity, is Mr. Claeys, president of the First National Bank of that city, and also one of the directors of the Rodeo-Vallejo Ferry. Mr. Claeys is in the foreground when movements are on foot for the further development of the county's resources, and he has been of inestimable value in the work of upbuilding this part of the State. Born in Oceania County, Mich., in the town of Hart, on March 13, 1879, he is the son of Campbell and Louise (Hasard) Claeys, both natives of Belgium, though they have made their home in the United States for the past fifty-six years. The parents took an active part in the agricultural development of Michigan, where they owned two large farms. There the father died in 1922, having reached the age of seventy-eight years; and there the good wife and mother is still residing, now also seventy-eight years old. Of their family of eleven children, Mr. Claeys is the only one residing in California. He attended the public schools of Michigan; but being one of a large family of children, he had to help in the farm work from the age of thirteen, and also do supplementary work in the lumber camps of Michigan during the winter months, working for wages from that early age. He assisted in the home farming and stock-raising in summer, and helped to clear the home acreage in winter, in the meantime driving teams to haul saw logs to the sawmill and working in the sawmills at odd times.

In 1904, Mr. Claeys came West to California, stopping on the way to visit the St. Louis Exposition, and from there coming on to Martinez, where his cousin, R. E. Claeys, was engaged in the grocery business. He went to work for McNamara & Winkleman for two years, in the butcher business at Martinez. In January, 1907, he came to Rodeo, and three months thereafter his marriage occurred, to Miss Henrietta Reder, a native of the Pinole Valley and daughter of Fred Reder, pioneer rancher. Five children have blessed their marriage: Josephine, Linus Francis, Reder, Margaret, and Milicent.

Mr. Claeys has engaged in ranching on an extensive scale, and is now the owner of 150 acres near Rodeo, besides being the renter of 1500 acres devoted to stock-raising. He is a cattle-raiser and dealer in live stock, and maintains a meat market at Rodeo, in the management of which he is assisted by his son. He is the owner of the Rodeo Water Works, which supply the city with water pumped from wells 200 feet deep, using electric power and a gravity system, thus giving the city the benefit of unusually good water for domestic purposes.

In 1918, when the First National Bank of Rodeo was started, Mr. Claeys helped to organize the institution and was on its first board of directors. He helped organize the Rodeo-Vallejo Ferry the same year. The First National Bank, of which he is now president, is capitalized at $50,000, and owns its own building, a two-story concrete structure erected in 1922. The Rodeo-Vallejo Ferry was capitalized at $500,000, with the late Avan J. Hanford as president; Oscar Klatt, secretary; and S. J. Claeys, treasurer. Mr. Claeys is also interested in the American Toll Bridge Company, capitalized at $6,000,000, which is constructing the toll bridge, to be completed in the spring of 1927 to span Carquinez Straits.

It would be hard to find a more thoroughly representative American citizen than Mr. Claeys, or one more in accord with the spirit of progress of the times. He firmly believes in aiding all worthy projects which have for their object the real advancement of his city, county, and state; and his worth is fully appreciated by his many friends in the community. Fraternally, he is a member of the Knights of Columbus of Berkeley, and of Richmond Lodge No. 1251, B. P. O. E., of Richmond. In politics he votes the Republican ticket.

GEORGE H. MILLER.—As head of the refining department for the Shell Oil Company at Martinez, George H. Miller takes rank among the foremost oil-refining experts in the United States. A practical man, he has learned the details of his line of work through long years of exprience. He was born and reared in one of the first oil fields of this country, and in point of service is the son of one of America's oldest oil refiners. Born on December 27, 1875, at Titusville, Pa., he is the son of G. R. Miller, who learned the oil refiner's business in Pennsylvania and became the first refining superintendent for the Pacific Coast Oil Company, at Alameda, Cal. This company was later taken over by the Standard Oil Company and removed to Richmond, and was thus the nucleus of one of the greatest, if not the greatest oil refining plant in the world. G. R. Miller was born in Pennsylvania, of Pennsylvania-Dutch and Scotch blood, and was refining superintendent for the Standard Oil Company at Olean, N. Y., for many years. He married Isadore Murray, who was a native of New York State and came from a long line of pioneer settlers of western New York. G. R. Miller retired from active business, in Alameda, a few years prior to his death, which occurred at the age of sixty-eight years.

George H. Miller was the second of seven children born to this worthy couple, and came to California with his mother in 1880, his father having preceded them two years before. He attended the public schools in Alameda, and later Heald's Business College in San Francisco. After finishing at the latter, like his father he took up the work of oil refining, first as stillman at the Pacific Coast Oil Company's station at Alameda; from there he went to the stockyards station of the Mercantile Oil Company at Oakland, and from there to the Capitol Refinery until it was taken over by the Shell. He then became superintendent of the Monarch Oil Company's refinery at West Berkeley for five years or more, spending one and one-half years at Maricopa, where his firm had another refinery. He next became superintendent of the Pinal Dome Oil Company, at Betteravia, Cal., and from there went to Salt Lake City, where he was connected with the Salt Lake City Utah Refinery eighteen months. On August 1, 1918, he came to Martinez, entering the employ of the Shell Oil Company, and soon after his arrival purchased his home on Pacheco Boulevard in that city, where he now resides. He was made head of the refining department for the Shell Company at Martinez in 1919, and still holds that important position, bringing to his work his varied and thorough experience and knowledge of oil refining which he has made his life work.

The marriage of Mr. Miller, at Alameda on April 26, 1905, united him with Miss Margaret Aitchison, a native of Nova Scotia of Scotch blood, whose ancestors for three generations have lived in Nova Scotia. She is the daughter of the former well-known Alameda contractor, Gavin Aitchison, who now resides at Buhach, Merced County. Mr. and Mrs. Miller are the parents of two children: George Reber, now a junior in the Alhambra High School; and Glen Aitchison, attending the Martinez Grammar School.

Fraternally Mr. Miller belongs to the Benevolent Protective Order of Elks, at Alameda. Primarily he is a home-loving man, and interested in everything that means the further upbuilding of his community, city and county.

PHILIP A. LEE.—One of the leading citizens of El Cerrito who has had much to do with the city in an official capacity, serving as chairman of the board of trustees from 1918 to 1924, is Philip A. Lee, known to his personal friends as "Phil". A native of Nevada, he was born in Pioche, on May 9, 1881, the son of Milton and Annie (Mathews) Lee, both of eastern birth, but who grew up in Nevada, where they were married. They had fourteen children, all still living; the father and mother having passed away on their ranch in that state when Phil was but eleven years old. The seventh in order of birth he attended the public schools until he was orphaned, when his school days were practically ended and he did such work about the ranch as a boy of his age was expected to do. At the age of eighteen he went to De Lamar and followed mining for many years, or until he came to California to live.

Mr. Lee was married in Tonopah, June 29, 1905, being united with Miss Olga Carling, born in Chemung, near Chicago, Ill. Her father, Benedict Carling, was born in Sweden, was well educated and a competent brick and stone mason and plasterer. He was always employed at his trade and traveled over considerable of the country after arriving in the United States. He met an accidental death on April 14, 1911, at the age of fifty-seven years. Of the eleven children born to Mr. and Mrs. Carling, five are still living. Mr. and Mrs. Lee are the parents of two children: P. Arthur and Olga Vilate, both born in El Cerrito and attending the El Cerrito public school.

Mr. Lee came to Contra Costa County in 1911, at the time his father-in-law was accidentally killed by a Southern Pacific train, intending to return to Nevada, but it was necessary for him to remain to settle the affairs of Mr. Carling, and in October of that year he secured work with the Standard Oil Company in their Richmond refinery and remained steadily employed until September 5, 1923. On the seventh of that month he took charge of an oil service station he had purchased at the corner of San Pablo and Fairmont Avenues, El Cerrito, and since then has gradually built up a very lucrative business, being assisted in his work by Mrs. Lee. This was his first business venture, he having always worked as a salaried man, and that he has more than made good is attested to by his friends.

While living in Nevada Mr. Lee was active in the Miners Union and was secretary of the Tonopah division of that order; also was a delegate to the national convention of that body held in Denver in 1909. While there a distinct honor was conferred upon him by his being chosen secretary of the convention of some 1600 delegates. He there made the acquaintance of "Mother" Jones and other celebrities in the mining world. Mr. Lee is a member of Point Lodge No. 503, F. & A. M.; Eclipse Lodge No. 403, I. O. O. F. and has taken an active interest in both organizations. His first entry into the political arena was when he was elected a trustee of El Cerrito on its incorporation in 1917. At the general election in 1918 he was again elected a member of that body and chosen chairman, and as such he served until 1923. In 1924 he was defeated by a small majority for reelection; again in 1926 he was a candidate for trustee and elected by the largest majority ever cast for any candidate in the city. He has implicit faith in the town and has invested all his savings in real estate, owning the corner on San Pablo and Fairmont Avenues, where his service station is located, and two houses, besides unimproved property. His recreation is found in healthful out of door sports and fishing.

Mr. Lee and his wife have always supported all progressive movements for the upbuilding of their city, the maintenance of good schools, (Mrs. Lee being a past president of the El Cerrito P. T. A.); good roads and for the best in civic development. Those who know Phil Lee make the statement that his word is as good as his bond, and his friends are legion in Contra Costa and Alameda Counties.

C. OTTO DAHLGREN.—Mr. Dahlgren can be called the veteran employee of the Oleum Refinery of the Union Oil Company, at Oleum, Cal., for it was he who broke ground for the company there, throwing the first shovelful of dirt, excavating for the foundation of the stills and boilers, in August, 1895. Born at Westby, Island of Gjotland, Sweden, on November 7, 1866, he is the son of Captain Lars Dahlgren, and comes from a line of seafaring men, his grandfather having also been a sea captain. His mother, who before her marriage was Caroline Nestrom, lived to be seventy-three years old; the father was accidentally drowned at sea. Of their five children, our subject was the third child, and attended the schools of Sweden, later being confirmed in the Lutheran Church. When fifteen years old he became a sailor before the mast, and has sailed around the world three times, doubled the Horn twice, and sailed to Australia, New Zealand, South America, West Indies, Siberia, and other points, on English merchant ships.

Landing in San Francisco in November, 1889, Mr. Dahlgren left the sea and engaged in carpenter work. In 1892 he came to Contra Costa County and worked for the Pacific Patent Plaster Company, and also for the Union Stock Yards Company at Rodeo. He was one of the first to go to work for the Union Oil Company at Oleum, in August, 1895, beginning as a laborer and being repeatedly promoted until he entered the laboratory and became laboratory foreman. The fumes of the chemicals impaired his health in time, and while recuperating he was made wharfinger for the company at Oleum, which position he now holds.

The marriage of Mr. Dahlgren, October 23, 1903, united him with Miss Marguerite Trainer, a native of San Francisco, and daughter of the late John William Trainer, contractor and builder of that city. John William Trainer was born in Maine, and married Elizabeth Cummings, who was a native of New York State; the former reached the age of eighty-two, while the mother died at sixty-two years. They were the parents of three children; Marguerite; Julia, now Mrs. C. E. Holt of Mill

Valley; and John W., of the firm of Trainer and Parson, Opticians, at San Francisco. Mr. and Mrs. Dahlgren are the parents of one child, John Victor, who graduated with the Class of 1923 from the John Swett Union High School at Crockett, and is now employed at San Pedro, Cal.

Fraternally Mr. Dahlgren belongs to the Odd Fellows, being Past Grand of Rodeo Lodge No. 193; Mrs. Dahlgren is a member of the I. D. E. S., and of the Druids, in Rodeo. A Republican in politics, Mr. Dahlgren cast his first vote for William McKinley. He believes in furthering the general welfare of his home community, doing his full share toward that end, in which effort his good wife joins him, for she is the descendant of one of California's pioneer families.

GUIDO TODARO.—A man of much business ability, thorough in all his undertakings and well qualified to hold the important position of vice-president of the First National Bank in Pittsburg, Guido Todaro is recognized today as one of the rising financiers of Central California. He was born on June 6, 1870, at Conselve, Padova, Italy, the son of Dr. Annibale and Philomena (Menegazzi) Todaro, the former a doctor in chemistry in Italy. The Todaro family are and have been druggists and chemists for generations. Dr. Todaro owns a house in which he has a store in Conselve, which is being carried on by one of his sons, who is a doctor of chemistry. The father was born in this house and has operated the drug store all his life. The grandfather was also born in the same house and conducted the same store during his lifetime. Thus it came that the family of Dr. Todaro were all born in the same home. The brother spoken of is now about sixty years old and has followed in the footsteps of his father and grandfather and is running the store. It is the plan of Guido Todaro to take his son to Italy and send him through the Padova University and in time he will take up the drug business in the same store above mentioned.

Guido Todaro was educated in Italy at the Lyceum and the University of Padova, but left the University before he received his diploma, to engage in the importing business at Calcutta, India. He left home in November, 1894, went to Bombay, crossed India and stopped at Calcutta. He then took trips throughout India until 1897, when he left Calcutta on account of the bubonic plague, and went to Hongkong, China, where he boarded the steamer Gaelic, went through Japan and thence to San Francisco, arriving on June 27, 1897. For seven years he was employed in the Italian-American Bank in San Francisco. In the latter part of 1903 he came to Pittsburg and opened the Contra Costa County Bank, as cashier and manager, and from the beginning until it was sold to the Mercantile Trust Company, of San Francisco, in 1923, was the leading factor in the operation of that bank which grew in importance each year under his guidance. In January, 1925, Mr. Todaro left the employ of the Mercantile Trust Company of California, and in April, 1925, accepted the vice-presidency of the First National Bank in Pittsburg. He was a director in the Contra Costa County Bank from January, 1905 until 1923; then a member of the advisory board of the Mercantile Trust Company from January, 1924 to January, 1925. Mr. Todaro is in every way the ideal banker, he has a wonderful personality, is a man of fine appearance with high ideals, and believes in the square deal in every business transaction. By following these lines in his business career he has won a large circle of close friends who hold him in the highest esteem. Mr. Todaro has made two trips back to Italy, one in 1923, when he took his two children with him, and the last one in 1926.

Guido Todaro was united in marriage in August, 1904, in San Jose, with Rose Williams, daughter of J. Williams. She passed away on November 11, 1922, leaving two children: Guido A., attending St. Mary's College in Oakland; and Mary K., attending Dominican College in San Rafael. Mr. Todaro holds membership in the Elks, Knights of Pythias and the Eagles. He attends the Catholic Church. Politically he is an admirer of Theodore Roosevelt's principles and is a strong progressive. Mr. Todaro is recognized by the banking fraternity of Central and Northern California as being a man of fine business acumen, and a leader in banking and financial circles who has a firm grasp of the financial problems confronting the successful banker of today.

WILLIAM ARTHUR ROWELL, M. D.—Only a few persons appreciate the patience, the self-denying application, the weight of care and anxiety and the enormous responsibility which attend the life of the conscientious physician. William Arthur Rowell was born on August 8, 1868, at San Francisco, Cal., a son of Rev. Joseph and Hannah (Cummings) Rowell, natives of New Hampshire and Maine, respectively. Reverend Rowell established the Mariners Church in San Francisco and maintained it until it was destroyed by the earthquake and fire of 1906. He was well-liked and favorably known in the Bay City. There were five children in this family: William A., of this review; Joseph C., who served as librarian at the University of California for many years and is now librarian emeritus of same; Edward F., who lives at Avon and is engaged in mining enterprises; and Mrs. Bertha L. Findlay, of Palo Alto; and Mrs. Grace W. Haynes, now deceased.

William A. Rowell received his elementary education in the public schools in San Francisco, after which he entered Cooper Medical College, now affiliated with Stanford University, from which he was graduated in 1891 with the degree of M. D. He served as intern in the hospitals in San Francisco, then became surgeon for the contractor's crew on the construction of the Southern Pacific for a brief period. He then went to Africa and traveled in central and southern parts, spending about seven years in that country as a frontiersman, studying and doing research work. While there he visited many places where white man had never set foot. His specialty was the study of tropical diseases and his headquarters were at Fort Jamison. After his return from Africa Dr.

Rowell spent four years in Mexico. His first practice in California was in Santa Barbara, where he hung out his shingle only a short time, when he once more returned to Africa and remained five years. While there this time he engaged in ranching with a partner, upon whose sudden death by attack of a wild elephant the doctor's plans were suddenly changed and he returned to America and practiced for a short period in Trinity County. The World War broke out and he tendered his services to the government, was commissioned Captain and connected with the Post Hospital at the Presidio in San Francisco, serving until the war was over. He is now ranking as Captain in the Officers Reserve Corps. The war over Dr. Rowell spent two years in South America as surgeon for a mining company. He came to Crockett in 1923 and by strenuous professional activity has succeeded in building up a lucrative practice, which is steadily growing as he enjoys the confidence and esteem of a wide circle of friends in this section of Contra Costa County.

On December 25, 1900, at Santa Barbara, Dr. Rowell was united in marriage with Miss Kate Campbell Higgins, of that city, and a woman of culture and refinement. Through all of his vicissitudes of fortune his wife has been his constant and cheerful companion. They celebrated their silver wedding in proper style on December 25, 1925. In politics the doctor is a Republican, though he takes very little active interest in political affairs. Fraternally, he is a Mason and an Elk, and he belongs to the American Legion Post at Crockett.

MANUEL R. SERPA.—A member of the painting firm of Serpa and Gistelli of Crockett, Manuel R. Serpa has established himself firmly in the business circles of this part of Contra Costa County. He is a native of the Azores Islands, where he was born on December 25, 1885. In 1904 he came to America and went to Glouster, Mass., where he had a sister living, and after making her a visit, continued his travels to the Pacific Coast, arriving in April, that year. He located in Kings County, going thence to Turlock, Stanislaus County, where he was engaged in ranching and in painting. In fact he has alternated painting with ranching several times, but is now engaged in contract painting. In the latter part of 1915 he came to Crockett and followed his trade, then spent two years in San Francisco, but returned to Crockett. In 1919 he entered the employ of the C. & H. Sugar Refinery. He is a member of the I. D. E. S. and the U. P. E. C. and the Druids.

On February 23, 1914, at Turlock, he married Miss Mary Avellar, born in Martinez. Her father, John J. Avellar, was born in the Azores on April 7, 1870, remained there until 1891, when he came to Lafayette, Cal. His father had died when John J. was about four years old. He remained at Lafayette for nine years, during which time he married, on October 14, 1896, Miss Mary Gloria Machado, of San Pablo. From Lafayette the Avellars farmed in Briones Valley, then went to Elmhurst, and next came to Tormey for eight years, and in 1905 settled in Valona. Three children have been born to Mr. and Mrs. Avellar: Mrs. Mary

Serpa; Mrs. Clara Serpa; and Elsie, still at home. Mr. Avellar belongs
to the I. D. E. S. and to the U.P. E. C. lodges. He has made an unusual
record as an employee of the Selby Smelter and enjoys the confidence of
his superiors. It was called the American Smelting and Refining Company when he first located in Valona. He is employed in the silver room,
a position of trust and honor he has held for twenty-eight years. The
family are members of the Catholic Church.

GAYLORD ROSERN DUNN.—A highly respected citizen of
Contra Costa County, and one who has watched with great interest the
development of parks, playgrounds, clubhouses, street improvements and
all other modern conveniences for the comfort of the citizens of Crockett,
is Gaylord R. Dunn, who was born in New York on December 22, 1855,
a son of Hiram G. and Mehitable (Hollister) Dunn. The father died
when Gaylord was nine years old. The lad attended the public schools
in his home section and afterwards learned telegraphy. His first position
was as operator with the Delaware, Lackawanna and Western Railroad,
with whom he remained five years. He then went to Chicago and was
in the employ of the Chicago and Northwestern Railway seven years on
various parts of their system. In 1878 Mr. Dunn came to San Francisco
and was employed by the Southern Pacific Railroad as station agent and
telegraph operator on their system, remaining in the employ of that company twenty-six years. He was sent to Crockett in 1905 and was station
agent and operator until 1913, when he quit railroad work and entered
the sugar refinery as an employee. His first work there was as a mingler
operator, but since that time he has worked at various tasks and in
various positions.

Mr. Dunn was united in marriage on April 29, 1879, with Miss Neil
Lakey, a native of New York State; and they have one daughter and one
son. The daughter, Mrs. F. R. George, of Oakland, is the mother of
two children: Roberta Jane, aged five, and one child who died in infancy.
Mr. George is an engineer in the employ of the P. G. & E. in San
Francisco. The son, F. Ross Dunn, died in 1918 in the flu epidemic, at
the age of thirty-four. He was in the last draft, had duly qualified, and
was ready to enter the service when the armistice was signed. He married Miss Georgia Stipes, of Snelling, Merced County, Cal. At the time
of his decease he was foreman in the California Warehouse Company's
warehouse at Crockett. He left three children, all daughters; viz.:
Dorothy, Kathleen, and Bernardine.

Mrs. G. R. Dunn is a Past President of the Carquinez Woman's
Club, having served two years; she is now vice-president. The club has
seventy-six members, all wide-awake to the topics of the day, and belongs
to the County, State and Interstate Federation of Women's Clubs. It is
a part of the Alameda District. Mrs. Dunn is also a member of the
Eastern Star, and of the Neighbors of Woodcraft. She just completed
her twentieth year as clerk of this organization and was presented an

appropriate gift of appreciation by the members for her efficient service. The local organization is called the Alhambra Circle, Neighbors of Woodcraft, and was instituted in 1899 with thirteen members, mostly residents on Alhambra Street; hence the name. Mrs. Dunn is also a member of the Druids, in which order she is a Past Arch Druidess, and is Past Pocahontas and now Keeper of Records. She belongs to the church missionary and aid societies. She has been chosen to represent various orders to which she belongs, at their Grand Conventions, and has acquitted herself with due regard for the best interests of all concerned. Mrs. Dunn, when president of the Woman's Club, arranged with a number of prominent speakers to speak at Crockett, among them Grace Palmer Craig, whom she entertained in the name of the C. & H. Company. This club offers prizes to the high school students for the best essay each year. Mrs. Dunn is descended from Revolutionary stock. Her great-grandfather was Col. Joshua Reynolds; and she is a cousin to Fanny Crosby. It will be seen that the activities of both Mr. and Mrs. Dunn in the interests of the community in which they are leaders have been many and varied, all for the public good.

Mr. Dunn is a member of the Masons and a Past Patron of the Eastern Star; and he belongs to the Ancient Order of Foresters. Mr. and Mrs. Dunn own their own home and take an active interest in all civic movements in Crockett. They were reared in the Episcopal Church, but as there is no church of that denomination in Crockett they attend the Community Church, in which Mrs. Dunn is a teacher in the Sunday School.

MRS. NETTIE GRISHAM AND MRS. MILDRED JOSEPHINE WHITCRAFT.—A native daughter of Contra Costa County, Mrs. Mildred Josephine Whitcraft held the position of postmaster at Rodeo from 1925 until her removal to Berkeley, where she now resides. She is the daughter of Mrs. Nettie Grisham, of Rodeo, and was born at Anaheim, Orange County, and there received her early schooling; later she entered the Richmond Union High School and was graduated with the Class of 1919. On March 9, 1925, she was appointed postmaster at Rodeo by President Coolidge, and she filled that office with satisfaction to her many friends until she resigned to make her home in Berkeley. Prior to accepting the postmastership of Rodeo she was connected with the United States Veteran's Bureau in San Francisco. She is a member of the Rodeo Rebekah Lodge and has a host of friends in Rodeo.

Mrs. Nettie Grisham was born in Missouri, and there she was reared until she was seventeen years old and then came to California. She was married at Pinole to John Grisham, now an employee of the Hercules Powder Works. This marriage resulted in the birth of three children: Mildred Josephine, who married George G. Whitcraft at Oakland on May 10, 1924; Roland Robert, who is in the John Sweet Union High School; and John Ward, now in the employ of the Union Oil Company at Oleum. Mrs. Grisham makes her home at Rodeo. She is a Past

Noble Grand of the Rebekah lodge at Rodeo and takes an active interest in the advancement of this section of the county. Both Mrs. Grisham and Mrs. Whitcraft are to be commended for their hospitable natures and their home has always been the center of a wide circle of friends.

CAPT. CHARLES N. NELSON.—A master mariner who has an enviable record in the merchant marine, as well as in the Government employ during the World War when he was enrolled as a volunteer and made master of a vessel, is Capt. Charles N. Nelson, a native of Bergen, Norway, born on June 27, 1864. His father was a successful business man, owning a large brewery in Bergen, and it was in that seaport town, with its beautiful fjord, that Charles N. was reared. He received a good education in the public schools of his native city, which is well-known as one of the large seaports on the west coast of Norway. As was the custom among the young men there, he went to sea soon after his confirmation in the Lutheran Church. Thus, at the age of fifteen, he was an apprentice on a barque and made a trip to the Mediterranean, and on his return, one to the Baltic Sea, ten months in all. Following these journeys, he sailed to New York City, and for a while worked on shore there. But the sea called him, and in 1883 he came to San Francisco via Cape Horn and followed the coasting trade. Attending a navigation school in that city, in due time he graduated and became second mate and later mate, and in 1891 captain with the Alaska Packers' Association. He continued as captain with various companies until he contracted with the California Sea Products Company, of San Francisco, and in 1922 went on a whaling voyage for them. Captain Nelson has been unusually successful as a navigator and very fortunate in his voyages, never losing a vessel. During the World War he volunteered his services with the United States Shipping Board as master, and served two years as captain on three different ships, the Mojave, Forsill and Olan, making trips across the Atlantic from New York and Newport, Mass., to France, England and Germany.

After making his residence for eleven years in San Francisco, and then for seven years in Fruitvale, in 1913 Captain Nelson came to Contra Costa County and built a comfortable home in Walnut Creek. His marriage, which occurred in 1886, in San Francisco, united him with Miss Bertha Geisler, who was born in Casper, Mendocino County. She was a woman of more than ordinary attainments and character, much endeared to her family and many friends. Captain Nelson was bereaved of his faithful wife in March, 1924. She left him two children: Ruth, who married Charles Miller, of Walnut Creek, and Beatrice, wife of George Edgar, of Walnut Creek. Having been reared in the Lutheran faith, Captain Nelson adheres to that church as a firm believer. He is a member of the Ship Masters' Association of the Pacific Coast, and of the San Francisco Tent, Independent Order of Red Men. In politics he is a Republican.

HON. ALBERT A. QUILL.—A native son of Crockett, where he was born on August 9, 1895, Albert A. Quill is a son of Dennis and Mary (Creedon) Quill, both natives of Ireland, who came to America in early life and in this country began making a name for themselves. They are both still living, though not enjoying good health. Albert A. attended the local public schools and after his graduation from the high school in Crockett entered the University of California and in due time was graduated with the degree of B. A. During his university course Mr. Quill specialized in law and was admitted to practice at the bar in California on March 7, 1922. He immediately came to his home town and opened an office and ever since then has been meeting with deserved success. His growing clientele is drawn from Crockett and Valona and he numbers among his clients the leading people of those two towns and the surrounding country. He is active in all affairs that have to do with the upbuilding of the county, is popular in business circles and belongs to the Vallejo lodge of Elks. He is active in Republican political circles and has before him the promise of a brilliant future.

EDWARD N. WUELZER.—Ever since he was eighteen months of age Edward N. Wuelzer, familiarly called Ed. Wuelzer, has lived in California. He was born in Cincinnati, Ohio, on October 20, 1885, a son of John W. and Catherine (Burkhardt) Wuelzer, both born in America of German parents. The father was a cigar-maker by trade and for twenty-five years served as secretary and treasurer of the Cigar Makers' Union. He died on October 31, 1895. There were seven children in the family, viz.: Mrs. Lillian Anderson, of Berkeley; Edward N., of this review; Benjamin H., a machinist in the employ of the Atlas Gas Engine Company; William J., employed by the Southern Pacific and a resident of El Cerrito; Frederick, also an employee of the Southern Pacific and a resident of Berkeley; Kathryn, wife of John Phillips, of San Francisco; and John, employed by the Virden Packing Company of Oakland. After the death of the father, the mother married Frank McDermott, ex-mayor of El Cerrito; and they have a daughter, Mrs. Frances Buckley. The family live on Liberty Street, El Cerrito.

The Wuelzer family first settled in San Francisco, and then moved to Oakland and remained there until 1911. Edward N. attended the Oakland grammar schools until he was fourteen, and then entered the employ of Taft & Pennoyer in Oakland as errand boy. He continued studying by himself during his employment, and has become a well-read man. For six years he remained with Taft & Pennoyer, becoming a valued employee of that firm. He then entered the office of the Southern Pacific Railway Company as assistant ticket agent and baggage master at their depot at First and Broadway, in Oakland, remaining there from April, 1905, until August, 1908. After this he entered the employ of the Home Telephone Company and installed all the underground cables in Oakland and San Francisco. In the spring of 1910 he began work with the Northern Commercial Company in Alaska. He saw a great deal of that country during the summer months and worked as far north as the Klondike. The winters were spent about the bay section. In 1915 he entered the employ of the Giant Powder Works as a pipe-fitter helper, and then became night engineer in the power house. He came to El Cerrito in the fall of 1911 and made his home with his mother until he established his own home. For a time he was employed by the Western Pipe and Steel Company in Richmond as acetylene welder. Since October, 1918, he has been in the employ of the Standard Oil Company at their refinery in Richmond, where he has charge of all barrel repairing as acetylene welder in their shops. He has made good in whatever position he has filled, is a man of broad experience and wide travel, and has a host of warm friends in the bay district.

In 1916 Edward N. Wuelzer was united in marriage with Miss Emma Margaret Mossman, who was born in Equality, Ill., and who came to California in 1913. They purchased property on Blake Street, El Cerrito, remodeled the house into a comfortable residence, and now make their home there at No. 700 Blake Street. Mrs. Wuelzer has been forelady in the Pullman Shops for the past twelve years. Mr. Wuelzer has always been interested in civic affairs, and in 1924 was elected a member and secretary of the Stege Sanitary District, serving with fidelity in this position. He serves on election boards and in many ways helps to promote the welfare of town and county. He is president of the El Cerrito Athletic Club, which occupies a fine club house erected by G. Rossi on Potrero Avenue, and which bids fair to become the center of healthful sports for this district. Mr. Wuelzer registers as a Republican, but in local matters votes for the men he considers best suited for the office, regardless of party lines. He holds membership with Richmond Lodge No. 1251, B. P. O. E.

CRAIN P. SANTOS.—A successful driller of water wells in the Bay district is C. P. Santos, who was born in the Island of Hawaii on November 1, 1885. He is one of nineteen children born to his parents. His father, Joseph Santos, was a sugar cane grower and was twice married.

C. P. Santos has been living in Richmond for the past fifteen years and has worked at well-drilling a great deal of the time, boring wells in various parts of Contra Costa and Alameda Counties. Some good wells have been brought in under his direction. He has drilled to the depth of 515 feet while working for others. He has two drilling outfits and has been quite successful in his operations. Both himself and his partner are well-known throughout the Bay district. Prior to coming to Richmond Mr. Santos worked in the gold and silver mines in Nevada for five years, but for the past five years he has carried on business for himself. Mr. Santos is able to speak Portuguese, Spanish and English, and this helps him greatly in his work. For pastime he enjoys fishing and camping; getting next to nature has alway been his hobby.

ANTONE SINCICH.—Self-made, in the best sense implied by the term, Antone Sincich, or Tony, as he is known by his friends, enjoys the confidence and esteem of all who have come to know him. Mr. Sincich located in Martinez in October, 1906, having come hither from his native country of Austria, and four years later he purchased his present business from his brother-in-law, Frank Robesa. His marble and granite works are located at 425 Main Street, his shop fronting on the street and his residence being in the rear. He is a master of his art, produces some exceptionally fine work, and has made a success of his trade as a stone and marble worker.

Antone Sincich's birth occurred at Istra, Austria, on April 26, 1879. He learned his trade from his father, John Sincich, a stone-cutter in his native town of Istra, and worked at stone cutting for fourteen years before he came to the United States. His destination was Martinez, Cal., where he has resided from that time to the present.

Mr. Sincich was married in Austria to Miss Francesca Robesa, also a native of that country, and to them have been born seven children, five now living: Dora, the wife of Mr. Davi, an expressman residing in Pittsburg, Cal.; and Tony, Otilia, Olga and Annie. Mr. and Mrs. Sincich are members of the Slavonian Lodge of Crockett, Cal., and he is also a member of a Slavonian Lodge in San Francisco. Mrs. Sincich belongs to the U. P. P. E. C. of Martinez. The family are members of the Catholic Church.

CHARLES HENRY SCHWAKE.—An experienced plumber in the Richmond district of Contra Costa County, and the son of a pioneer blacksmith of what was known as Rust, Charles Henry Schwake enjoys a good business and has a wide circle of friends in this locality. He was born in Gainesville, Texas, July 28, 1893, a son of Charles Henry and Louise (Scheele) Schwake, both born in Hanover, Germany, and there grew up and married; and there their first child, Fred Louis, was born. He became a draftsman and met death by drowning in Lake Merritt, Oakland, in 1913. Another son, William, was killed in a railroad accident in Yuma, Ariz., when he was only seventeen years old. The parents and one son came to Galveston, Texas, where Mrs. Schwake had some relatives living. Mr. Schwake engaged in blacksmithing and in building up a good trade, then would sell out to remove to some other place and do the same thing, continuing on his way until he landed in San Pablo, Cal., in 1895. There he bought the shop owned by the Kleinschmidts, but later sold it to buy the shop established by William Rust on San Pablo Avenue, at the county line between Alameda and Contra Costa Counties. He was a lover of fine horses and took pleasure in raising them. During the Spanish-American War he sold a good many head of horses to the United States Government. Removing to his new location at Rust he carried on the old Rust shop until Mr. Rust returned from a visit to Germany, then he was taken ill and passed away in 1902, aged about forty-eight years. His good wife died in 1909, at the age of fifty-two, both at the home place they had bought adjoining the Rust property, consisting of a square of land 150 by 150 feet for which they paid $219. After the death of the father the blacksmith shop was sold back to Mr. Rust. The elder Schwake was a prominent Odd Fellow in the Berkeley Lodge; and he also belonged to the U. P. E. C. He was a kindly man and had a wide circle of acquaintances and close friends.

Charles Henry Schwake, our subject, was the youngest of the family and attended the public schools of Alameda and Contra Costa Counties, walking to Berkeley every morning from their home at the county line. At the age of fifteen he went to work in the Du Pont Powder Works at Vigoret (Point Isabel) for one year. After this he went to Berkeley and apprenticed himself to learn the plumbing trade, which he learned very thoroughly, after which he worked as a journeyman in San Francisco, Oakland and Berkeley until 1916. At that time business was slack in his line and he went to work at the Standard Oil refinery in West Richmond and was in their employ for four and one-half years actual time. During these years he served his country during the World War, for eigtheen months at Camp Kearney, in the maintenance of plumbing etc at that camp. After his honorable discharge in 1919 he returned to the Standard refinery, holding the same rating he had when he entered his country's service. On May 23, 1923, he started in business for himself, establishing a general plumbing business at the old home place where his father and mother had lived and died. His scope of business includes the Richmond, Albany and El Cerrito districts, where he has built up a fine business. Mr. Schwake is the only survivor of the family name, that he knows anything about.

In 1913, in San Francisco, C. H. Schwake was united in marriage with Miss Queenie Lydia Evett, a native daughter, born in San Francisco, and they have a daughter, Frances Louise Schwake. Mr. Schwake is a Mason, belonging to Point Lodge No. 503, F. & A. M., of Richmond, and also to the Richmond Pyramid of Sciots No. 42. He also holds membership in the Berkeley Order of Owls. In earlier days he played ball with the Richmond Elks team, the Standard Oil team and in various teams throughout the State.

MRS. ROSE SCHAEFER.—As the leader in musical circles in Crockett and vicinity Mrs. Rose Schaefer holds an assured position. She was born in Iowa and was educated in the public schools and at the Nebraska Normal College at Wayne, Nebr., graduating with the Class of 1903. She at once began to teach in the grammar grades in the schools in Wausau, that state, continuing for five years; she also served as assistant superintendent of the Knox County schools for a time. Coming to California Mrs. Schaefer began her musical education, for which she has a natural aptitude, under the leading artists in San Francisco, among them Catherine Hertzog, Maud Wellendorff, and for the past three years has been a student under Benjamin Moore. During the years she has been studying she has also been teaching music. Mrs. Schaefer specializes in piano, and has given musical evenings, recitals and concerts and has taken an active part in promoting a musical interest in the community. She was chairman of the committee for music week in Crockett, which is now an annual affair, and is secretary of the County Music Week Committee at present; Mrs. Hanlon being chairman.

Mrs. Schaefer is the authorized teacher of the Perfield System of teaching music. This is a group system of instruction, employing established pedagogical principles, and through her activities has become very popular. It gives especial satisfaction with beginners as the quickest means of establishing an appreciation of harmony. Her studio is at her home, which is a modern bungalow in the western side of Crockett on the highway. She is an active member of the Carquinez Woman's Club.

Mrs. Schaefer and her husband are both lovers of the great out-of-doors and spend their vacations in the mountains where they study nature and forestry. They have accumulated many fine specimens from the various localities they have visited and have a wonderful store of information on this subject. They have a wide circle of close friends and are leaders in their social set in the East bay shore.

W. E. WATSON.—Among the most successful hotel men of Antioch is W. E. Watson, the genial and accommodating proprietor of the Commercial Hotel, whose services as a host are appreciated by the traveling public. He was born at Camden, Maine, September 22, 1867, a son of John E. and Ella (Cross) Watson, both of English extraction and old time State of Maine families. The Cross family took part in the Revolutionary struggle. The father, John E. Watson, was one of eleven brothers, ten of whom were seafaring men. The parents were married in Maine, and in 1870 the father came alone to California, settling in Oakland, where he was joined by his wife and our subject, then a lad of five years, two years later. A sister of our subject, Mrs. William Nichols resides at White Plains, N. Y. where her husband is a prominent lawyer. Mr. Watson's mother, Mrs. Farn Lam, resides in Oakland and is a member of the Pioneers Society of that city.

W. E. Watson was reared in Oakland and attended the public schools, and there learned the carpenter's trade. In 1887 he was married to Miss Kathryn Duddy, born in Oakland of pioneer parents. She passed away leaving two sons. Walter E. is in the taxicab business in Oakland; he saw service during the World War working in the Spruce Division in the Oregon woods cutting spruce lumber for the Government air planes; he is married and has two children, Claude and Francis. Arthur L. is proprietor of the Lorenz Hotel at Redding; he is married and has one child, Ann. Soon after his marriage W. E. Watson went to Arizona as carpenter for the Calumet-Heckla Mining Company and while in their employ helped to build their smelter. He continued there until August,

1905, when he went to Goldfield, Nev., and was there during its palmy days when they found gold ore that ran $28,000 to the ton. He remained in Goldfield until 1908, when he returned to Oakland and ran a cafe until 1915. Then he went to Ely, Nev., where he built and operated an apartment house. In 1924 Mr. Watson located in Antioch. Mr. Watson was married the second time in February, 1919, at Martinez, Cal., to Mrs. Palymer O'Hanlon, who was born in Lysle, France. Fraternally Mr. Watson is a member of the Eagle Lodge at Tucson, Ariz., and the Moose of Portland, Ore. He is a firm believer in the continued progress of Antioch and holds a five-year lease on the Commercial Hotel. He is a member of East Contra Costa County Chamber of Commerce.

HENRY J. GREGORY.—Among California's native sons, one who has made a success of the opportunities that have presented themselves to him is Henry J. Gregory, dealer in Ford products at Pittsburg, Contra Costa County, under the firm name of the Pittsburg Motor Company. He is a live wire booster for his native State and was born at San Luis Obispo, on January 4, 1893, the son of Frank and Mary (Conception) Gregory, now living in Santa Maria, this State. Frank Gregory came to California about 1880 and has been identified with its best interests ever since that year.

Henry J. Gregory received his early schooling in the grammar schools in San Luis Obispo and attended high school in Santa Maria, where his parents had settled. As soon as he took up the duties of life he became a salesman for the Studebaker automobile in Santa Maria, and was thus engaged when he entered the service of the government, enlisting in the Medical Department of the United States Army as an ambulance driver, and being stationed at Angel Island. He entered the army in the latter part of 1917 and received his honorable discharge on February 2, 1919.

On March 1, 1919, Mr. Gregory was united in marriage in San Francisco with Miss Bessie M. Gwin, born at Walla Walla, Wash., who was serving as a nurse in San Francisco and at Angel Island during the World War. After their marriage Mr. and Mrs. Gregory went to Santa Maria, where Mr. Gregory was agent for the Willys-Knight and Overland automobiles during 1920 and 1921. He was then given the management of the Willys-Knight and Overland branch agency in San Luis Obispo and moved to that city, remaining there until in May, 1924, when he went to Oakland as district representative of the Peerless Motor Company. On August 1, 1925, he was appointed dealer for the Ford products in Pittsburg and came here to make his home. On March 10, 1926, he moved into the building at the corner of Third and Cumberland Streets that had been expressly built for him, and here he has the most modern fireproof building and equipment to be found in this county. He has over 14,000 square feet of floor space on the two floors and is able to handle anything that may come to him in the line of repairs and battery work. He gives night and day service, and also has storage space for cars. His partner is Ernest J. Parrish, formerly with the Union Sugar Company. A bright future is predicted for these young and energetic men. Mr. Gregory is a charter member of the American Legion at Spokane, and belongs to the Lions Club and Chamber of Commerce in Pittsburg. He fully realizes the bright future in store for his adopted city and is ready to aid any worthy project for the good of the people and community.

RALPH NORTON.—A resident of Port Costa since early boyhood, Ralph Norton has, for the greater part of that time, been in the employ of the Associated Pipe Line Company and has risen to a responsible position with the company through his long years of service. Born in Hyde Park, Los Angeles, on June 6, 1893, he is the eldest of eight children born to Fred U. and Mary V. (Leuzinger) Norton, and obtained his education in the southern city, where he remained to finish his schooling until fifteen years old, and then joined his parents, who had located in Port Costa in 1906. After coming to join his parents, he went to work as a machinist in the Port Costa Brick and Tile Company's yard, in which his father was employed, and there young Norton remained for four and one-half years. At the end of that time, finding that he could better his position, he found employment with the Associated Pipe Line Company at Port Costa. Starting in as a laborer on construction work, and advancing step by step by his own ability, in time he reached his present position as superintendent of the Associated Pipe Line Company's plant at Port Costa, which includes the loading wharf where fuel oil is shipped to Northern California, Washington, Oregon, Honolulu, and Eastern ports. This oil is pumped to the loading wharf at Port Costa from Bakersfield, and also from Avon, from which latter place Diesel oil is pumped and shipped for use on Diesel engines. Vessels are here supplied with fuel oil for their own purposes; and tankers are also loaded for export shipment, making Port Costa a very important point in the fuel shipping trade, about 13,000,000 barrels being handled annually.

The only interruption in his service for the company occurred in 1918 when he entered the army for service during the World War as a member of Battery 374. He was stationed at Camp Lewis and received his honorable discharge as a corporal, at the Presidio, January 17, 1919. On doffing his uniform he immediately resumed his position, then a gauger, for the pipe line company.

The marriage of Mr. Norton, at Port Costa on July 28, 1919, united him with Miss Juanita Florence Soto, a daughter of J. A. and Manuella (Higuera) Soto, of Port Costa, both parents native Californians and descendants of early Spanish families in the history of the State. Mrs. Norton was born in Oakland, and reared and has lived in Port Costa and Crockett since she was five years old. Two daughters have blessed the union of Mr. and Mrs. Norton; Manuella Juanita and Verena Mary. Mr. Norton is a member of the Loyal Order of Moose in Martinez and the American Legion Post No. 33, at Crockett.

WARREN ARTHUR ORDWAY.—On the Pacheco Road just out from Martinez is located the Ordway Garage, where some of the best repair work on automobiles is done under the supervision of the proprietor, W. A. Ordway, who is a fine mechanic and auto-machinist. Warren Arthur Ordway was born in Cambridge, Mass., on November 23, 1888, and attended the public schools in pursuit of his education. He early learned the trade of the machinist in Boston, Mass., and did work in garages handling the Pierce-Arrow and Hudson cars. In 1918 he came out to California and stopped in Los Angeles, from there going to San Francisco, where he was employed in the J. J. Shueer auto machine shop. After he had learned the routine in this shop he went to Pittsburg, Cal., and had charge of the W. & W. Auto Machine Shop for three years, after which he worked for the Los Medanos Garage in that city for two years. He then came to Martinez in 1923 and became proprietor of his present place of business, known as Ordway Garage; and here he is fast building up a fine business, doing repair work on all kinds of automobiles, as well as tractors and other machinery.

Mr. Ordway was married on September 8, 1917, in Boston, Mass., to Miss Sarah Tinker; and they have two children, Warren A. Jr., and Lloyd James. Mr. Ordway is a self-made man, having begun at an early age to be self-supporting, as his father died when he was a lad of fifteen. He is a Republican in politics.

GEORGE VINCENT.—A resident of Contra Costa County for the past twenty-six years, George Vincent is well-known throughout the county as the proprietor of the Club House Cafe, on the Pacheco highway between Martinez and Walnut Creek. Born in New Orleans, La., in 1862, he is the son of George and Elizabeth (Goldsock) Vincent, both natives of England. George Vincent, Sr., was a sailor, and rose steadily until he became a master mariner. He resided for a time in New Orleans, where the son, George, Jr., was born, and in 1878 he brought his family around Cape Horn to San Francisco and there settled down. With his wife he afterwards made a trip to England on business, and there both parents passed away.

George Vincent, our subject was a delicate child and was left in San Francisco with Duncan McVicar. He received his education in the public schools of that city, and at the age of thirteen entered the employ of Peter Hopkins, in the Grand Hotel Saloon, continuing there until 1882, when he fulfilled a long-felt desire to travel. He shipped before the mast on the Carnarvon Castle, making the trip to Europe and back to New York. Then came a voyage to Australia on a sailing vessel, and he became acting second mate in the Australian trade, carrying horses from that country to the English Army at Madras, India, then sailing on to Rangoon and back to England. Following this, Mr. Vincent made a trip back to New York, and on to New Orleans, remaining in the latter city for ten years, during which time he engaged in business. In 1896, he returned to San Francisco, in the employ of the Matson Steamship Company, with whom he continued for the following two years. For a like period of time thereafter he was proprietor of the Bungalow, a resort cafe at Millbrae, in Marin County. In 1900, Mr. Vincent came to Martinez and established the Club House Cafe, about four miles out of Martinez, adjoining what is now the Martinez Gun Club, though at that time the gun club was not yet formed, nor was the highway built. And here he has remained in business ever since, catering to the patronage of the traveling public and to his many friends in the surrounding country, who appreciate his well-managed inn.

The marriage of Mr. Vincent, which occurred in San Francisco, united him with Miss Libby Hauge, a native of Denver, Colo. Her death occurred in 1920. Mr. Vincent was made a Mason in Union Lodge No. 172, F. & A. M., of New Orleans, of which he is a life member, as he is also of Concord Chapter No. 2, R. A. M. In politics he is a Republican. A well-informed man, of wide travels, he is an interesting conversationalist, and his friends are legion.

MIRO SINCICH.—An intelligent and able horticulturist, who for fifteen years was employed as foreman on the F. K. Burnham fruit ranch in the Alhambra Valley, is Miro Sincich, a native of Austria, born at Kastav on April 10, 1889, a son of John and Veronica (Paulinich) Sincich. The father is still living in that country, aged eighty-three; and the mother died there in 1919, aged seventy-two years.

Miro Sincich was the eighth in a family of eleven children born to his parents. When eighteen years old he came to California, and soon found employment as a ranch hand, in time becoming foreman on the Burnham fruit ranch, where he gained a thorough knowledge of horticulture and of the special advantages offered for horticultural work in this part of the state; and when he decided to ranch for himself, he located in the same neighborhood, and is now developing a ranch of fifty acres four and one-half miles south of Martinez. Eight acres of this ranch is devoted to vineyard, and the balance to fruits, pasture, and general farming.

The marriage of Mr. Sincich, which took place in Martinez on July 21, 1912, united him with Miss Maria Robesa, a native of his home town in Australia, who came to California in 1912. Three children have blessed their union: Emily R., John M., and Marion, all born in Contra Costa County. A Republican in political adherence, Mr. Sincich was naturalized in Judge McKenzie's court at Martinez in 1921. He is progressive in his ideas, with a full knowledge of the opportunites to be found in his adopted country, and the ability to take advantage of them. Two of his brothers are also located in Contra Costa County: Tony Sincich, in the marble business at Martinez, and Alex Sincich, a cooper employed by the Union Oil Company at Oleum, but living in Martinez. Mr. Sincich belongs to St. Joseph Lodge, in Crockett.

JOHN NIENBURG.—As superintendent of the Contra Costa County garage in Martinez, John Nienburg is making good. Included in the responsibilities of his position are the looking after all tractors, trucks, concrete mixers, road rollers, automobiles and one clamshell unloader, owned and operated by and for Contra Costa County. John Nienburg was born in Alameda County in the Tassajara Valley, on February 29, 1892, and is the son of Frank and Catherine (Wehling) Nienburg, both natives of Germany, who came to California when they were young and were here united in marriage. They became successful ranchers and fruit-raisers, and also were in the chicken business for a time on their twenty-two acres near Livermore, Alameda County. They had twelve children, all living, John being the sixth in order of birth. He grew up on the ranch and attended the grammar schools in Livermore, after which he went to work in a bicycle, gun and automobile shop in that town, learning the business from the ground up and remaining at that work for nine and one-half years. He was appointed to his present position on December 15, 1919, by the board of supervisors because of his ability as an all-round mechanic. The garage which is owned by the county, is located on Shell Avenue, just outside of Martinez, and here all repairs are looked after on all equipment in the engineering department of the county.

Mr. Nienburg has been a resident of Martinez since 1917, and since that time he has entered heartily into all movements tending towards making Contra Costa the banner county in the State. He is popular with all with whom he comes in contact, and his work is performed in a very thorough manner. Fraternally, he belongs to the Independent Order of Odd Fellows at Livermore.

GEORGES P. PINEAUX.—A worthy exponent of the modern science of healing is Georges P. Pineaux, chiropractor, with offices in the National Bank Building of Crockett. He is a native of Pennsylvania, having been born in Williamsport, a son of Thomas L. and Adele (Gstalder) Pineaux, both living. The father was born in Canada, of French extraction, and the mother was born in Paris. They now reside in Albuquerque, N. M. Dr. Pineaux attended the public schools in Williamsport, Pa., graduating from the high school with honors. When the family moved to New Mexico he accompanied them and from there came to California, matriculating in the West Coast Chiropractic College, obtaining the degree of D. of C. His first location was in Oakland, where he built up a successful practice in his profession, continuing there until 1923, when he came to Crockett. When he located here this branch of healing science was scarcely known and many were prejudiced against it. But by steadily keeping his eyes to the front and giving the best efforts to heal the sick and afflicted, he has gradually won a lucrative clientele and his benefitted patients are his best advertisements. Those who have been treated by him in Crockett and vicinity are loud in the praise of his drugless methods. He is now firmly established in this locality and has proven a valuable acquisition to the community through his public-spirited participation in all forward movements for the upbuilding of Crockett. He believes in the future greatness of California and of this section in particular. He is a member of the Federated Chiropractic Association of San Francisco, and is enthusiastic over the possibilities of his profession and keeps up with every modern thought and action to promote its interests.

Dr. Pineaux was married in March, 1920, to Miss Emma Fisher, of New Mexico, and they have two children: Georges P. Jr., born October 10, 1922, and Charles Armand, born December 4, 1924. The Doctor is a member of the Elks and the Masons and in politics is a Republican. In consideration of his services during the World War he is a member of the Veterans of Foreign Wars and of the American Legion, and active in all their endeavors to maintain the prestige of the soldiers.

MRS. ERNA (GALLAGHER) NEAR.—One of the successful business women of Walnut Creek is Mrs. Erna Near, a native daughter of California, born in Oakland, who has spent her entire life in the central part of the State. Her father, Martin Rohrbacher, was a native of Germany, and there received his education. As a young man he came to California, located at Oakland, and was employed by Scriber's Furniture Company, and afterwards by the Anderson Furniture Company. Later, he engaged in business for himself until his death. Martin Rohrbacher married Margaret Wilkins, also born in Germany, who came to California in her youth. She now resides in Oakland. Four children of the family born to this worthy couple are now living. Of the entire family, two sons served in the Spanish-American War, and one in the World War.

Erna Rohrbacher was reared in Oakland, attending the public schools, and was married in that city in 1901 to Edward R. Gallagher. In 1917 she located in Walnut Creek and leased the Walnut Creek Hotel, of which she continued as proprietor for two years. She then established the Ramona Grill, on Main Street, Walnut Creek, which she is now conducting. Her skill in cooking is well-known, and the grill has become the most popular eating place in town. Mrs. Near does all the cooking herself, even to the baking and pastries, and she personally supervises the service and sees to it that a high standard of both cleanliness and comfort is afforded her guests. Her establishment is very well patronized, and is known throughout Contra Costa County for the excellence of its cuisine.

Mrs. Near is the mother of three children: Erna, now Mrs. J. Mathieson, of Concord; Dorothy V., Mrs. Vearl Buckner, of Merced; and James Gallagher, who resides with his mother. In September, 1925, Mrs. Gallagher was married to Henry E. Near, of whom mention is made on another page in this history. A Republican in politics, Mrs. Near is interested in civic betterment. Fraternally she is a member of Fruitvale Parlor, No. 171, N. D. G. W.

MICHAEL PERINO.—A resident of California since 1907, Michael Perino has since that date become well and favorably known in the building business, both in Santa Clara County and in Richmond and vicinity. He was born on March 20, 1882, in Italy, attended the grammar school, and later studied architectural drawing to perfect himself as a builder and contractor. After the great fire and earthquake in San Francisco Mr. Perino decided to come here, and upon the advice of a friend came straight to San Francisco. The first six months he worked at the building business, and then he began taking contracts himself. He met with success and built good buildings, so that one job was a good advertisement for another. From San Francisco he went down to San Jose and followed his calling there with good financial results. Having a friend, Charles Faccini, who owned property in El Cerrito and wished to erect a home, he came to this place and built the home at 215 Fairmont Avenue.

Mr. Perino could see the advantages of this district and decided that he, too, would locate here. This he did in 1923, and ever since he has been busy at his contracting business both in Richmond and in El Cerrito. He erected the postoffice building in El Cerrito, and a fine business and apartment building at Thirty-ninth and Macdonald in Richmond, as well as many homes costing from $2500 to $5000. While living in San Jose he was a member of the Builders' Exchange. The six years he spent there gave him a wide experience in American methods, and he is now able to cope with almost any condition that arises.

Mr. Perino is unmarried. He belongs to the Richmond Aërie of Eagles and is gradually enlarging his circle of friends. He believes in progress and is ready to assist all worthy enterprises for the upbuilding of county and State.

MANUEL G. MOITOZA.—The agent for the Ford automobile at San Pablo, Manuel G. Moitoza, is well and favorably known in Contra Costa County. He was born at Suisun, Solano County, on September 6, 1884, the son of M. G. and Ignacia (Gularte) Moitoza, both natives of Portugal, who came to California when they were young folks. Manuel G. Moitoza attended the San Pablo schools, the family having removed here in 1890, where the father followed his trade as a carpenter. He died in 1893, but the mother is still living.

Manuel, known in his home locality by the nickname of "Mose" Moitoza, opened a blacksmith shop in San Pablo in partnership with his brother in 1905, and did all kinds of blacksmithing and wagon repairing. They were both good mechanics and their shop was up-to-date in appliances and equipment. During their spare time they built a farm tractor out of such material as they found at hand, and it did the work of four horses; but they did not follow up the manufacture of tractors. The partnership continued until 1920; after this Mose Moitoza ran the shop and business, and about that time secured the agency for the Ford auto-
29

mobile. Business fairly blew his way, and soon he needed more room and more help. He gave up blacksmithing and devoted his entire time to selling Ford cars, and his profits were invested in San Pablo property. Soon he erected his present building, fifty by one hundred feet, and here his stock of machines are on display. He handles the Ford and the Lincoln cars, and the Fordson tractor, as well as all accessories. His business has grown by leaps and bounds, and he is counted among the prosperous men of his community.

M. G. Moitoza was married in October, 1909, to Miss Ida Flohs, of San Pablo, and they have four children: Clarice, attending high school; George, Paul and Ruth, in the grammar school. Fraternally, Mr. Moitoza is a member of the Modern Woodmen of America and the Fraternal Order of Eagles. He has served on the sanitary board and the board of education of San Pablo, and is a constable and deputy sheriff. He takes great pride in the civic development of his community and is always ready to do his share in every way.

WILLIAM G. SELLICK.—The business methods of William G. Sellick are such as to win for him the commendation of all who have occasion to deal with him. His bakery, located at 649 Main Street in Martinez, is modern in all its appointments, is thoroughly equipped, and up-to-date in every respect; he supplies Martinez with the very best there is in bread and pastry of all kinds. Since buying the business in March, 1923, Mr. Sellick has made a host of friends who appreciate good bread and pastry. He was born in Cardiff, Wales, June 10, 1892, a son of W. A. and Margaret (Johnson) Sellick. The parents were married in England and came to America when our subject was only ten months old. The family came direct to California and settled first at Stockton, and there W. A. Sellick engaged in the bakery business; then he removed to Martinez and for eight years ran the Purity Bakery. He is now located in Walnut Creek and there operates the Walnut Creek Bakery. Our subject is the eldest in a family of twelve children, eight of whom are living in Contra Costa County. One son is living in Stockton and runs the Curnow Bakery. The father has reached the age of fifty-five, and the mother is fifty-three years old.

William G. Sellick attended public school in Stockton, and at an early age entered his father's bakery and learned the trade; he then became a journeyman baker, and before he was twenty-one years old had traveled twice around the world. He spent three years in the service of his country during the World War, serving in the 17th Field Artillery, 2nd Division; he was sixteen months over seas, where he was in engagements on five different battle fronts: Soissons, Champagne, the Meuse, Argonne, and St. Mihiel. In 1919 he returned to the United States and was honorably discharged at the Presidio, San Francisco.

At Santa Rosa, in February, 1920, Mr. Sellick was married to Miss Regna Rakestrow, a native of Iowa, but reared and educated in Colorado. She came to California with her parents and the family settled in

Live Oak, Yuba County, where her father, Charles Rakestrow, ran a grocery store for several years. The father is now living at Long Beach, Cal., but the mother has passed away. Mr. and Mrs. Sellick are the parents of one son, Charles Ernest. Mr. Sellick is a charter member of the Martinez Post of the Veterans of Foreign Wars, and is also a member of the Knights of Pythias and the Knights of Khorassan, both of Martinez. Although believing in the principles of the Republican party, Mr. Sellick is liberal in his political preferences.

LORENZO F. BUFFO.—A native son of Contra Costa County, Lorenzo F. Buffo, or "Link" Buffo, as he is more familiarly known by his friends, was born in Somersville, on March 5, 1892, the son of Ferminino and Margarita Buffo, both living in Pittsburg. The father was born in Italy and was one of the early coal miners at Somersville when coal mining was the principal industry in the county. Link grew up in Somersville and attended the public schools there, coming to Pittsburg in 1906. His first employment was with the Pioneer Rubber Works, and there he remained for eight or nine years before coming to the Columbia Steel Corporation's plant, where he is engaged as a melter and an assistant superintendent of the open hearth furnaces.

Mr. Buffo was married in Pittsburg on August 27, 1914, being united with Miss Louise De Stefano, who was born and reared in this city. They have one son, Melvin. Mr. Buffo is a member of Diamond Parlor No. 246, N. S. G. W., being a Past President; he is also a member of the Moose and the Foresters of America, both in Pittsburg. The family reside at 747 York Street, Pittsburg, where they have a wide circle of friends.

JOHN FRANCIS O'NEILL, JR.—A native son of the Golden State, John Francis O'Neill is meeting with success as a contractor in building golf links and excavations. He was born in this county on March 15, 1873, a son of the late John Francis O'Neill, a California pioneer. At an early age our subject left school and began working at ranch work on the home place. Owing to the death of his father he took charge of operations and remained there till 1903, when he went to Oakland and engaged in the hay business. Two years later he returned to Pinole and was employed by the Hercules Powder Works as a grading contractor and worked as high as thirty-five men. He still handles all grading contracts for the powder company. Mr. O'Neill specializes in golf links and built the Berkeley Country Club links, the snappiest course in the county; the Burlingame Country Club in San Mateo County; the Municipal Golf Links of San Francisco; and the Contra Costa Club links at Pacheco. His reputation for good work is his best advertisement and he finds plenty to do.

On October 2, 1901, Mr. O'Neill married Miss Edith Christine Beck, of Hayward. Her father, Peter J. Beck, was born in Denmark and was married to Miss Katherine Johnson, also of that country, where they were married. They came to California in the sixties where Mr. Beck worked as a brick-mason and contractor. There were four girls and one boy in the Beck family: Marie, Mrs. Wm. F. Boyd, of San Francisco; George P., of Redwood City; Katherine M., now Mrs. Frank Slater, of Walnut Creek; and her twin Anna C., Mrs. E. M. Bullock, of Occidental; and Mrs. Edith C. O'Neill. Mr. and Mrs. O'Neill have three children: John Milton, a graduate of the Richmond High School, married Vivian E. Vogel and they have a son Eugene Milton; Lawrence Gordon and Edith Marie are attending the grammar school. Mr. O'Neill is a member of the Woodmen of the World, the Native Sons of the Golden West and the Young Men's Institute. He owns his own home in Pinole and always works for the best interests of his community as a loyal native son. A sketch of Mr. O'Neill's parents and family will be found on another page in this history.

GEORGE J. WINKELMAN.—Thirty-five years have brought more than the average realization of expectations to George J. Winkelman, a resident of Martinez for that period. He is the owner of much valuable real estate in the city; part owner and a director in the Martinez-Benicia Auto Ferry; and organizer and a director in the National Bank of Martinez. He is the manager of the Alhambra Market, located at 707 Main Street, and part owner in the apartments known as the City Hall Building on Main Street. No better indication could be exhibited of the confidence in the future of his home city than has been demonstrated by Mr. Winkelman in the investments that he has made in Martinez. In partnership with the late J. J. McNamara the Alhambra Market was established in 1904. Mr. McNamara passed away on December 9, 1922, and Mr. Winkelman since then has succeeded to the ownership of the properties jointly owned by them.

George J. Winkelman was born in Erie County, N. Y., on July 4, 1867, and there he grew up and attended school. After he left school he worked around on farms until coming to California. Arriving in the Golden State he began looking about for farm work and for ten years was the manager of the fruit farm owned by Charles S. Deal; later he successfully managed the Grace Allen farm in Contra Costa County.

Mr. Winkelman has been married twice. His first wife was Miss Josephine Hittman, who passed away in 1906 and left two children: Welford, now assistant manager of the Alhambra Market, married Miss Germina Mazuppa; and Raymond, who married Marie Ruh, of Oakland, is a salesman for the Chanslor & Lyon Company, traveling out of Oakland where he resides. Mr. Winkelman was married the second time to Miss Martha Powers of Martinez, who passed away in January, 1921, leaving a son, George Joseph, Jr., only fifteen days old. In September, 1924, Mr. Winkelman and his son Raymond, purchased twenty acres of land in Big Valley, Lake County, Cal., which they have planted to Bartlett pears. Mr. Winkelman and his son Welford conduct the Alhambra Market at 707 Main Street, Martinez; it is clean and sanitary and has become one of the leading markets of Contra Costa County. Fraternally Mr. Winkelman is affiliated with the Knights of Columbus, Loyal Order of Moose and the Eagles, all of Martinez. With his family he is a communicant of the Catholic Church. Since the death of Mr. McNamara, Mr. Winkelman has taken his place on directorates and in the ownership of the properties owned in common. He is now serving on the board of trustees of the City of Martinez, having been appointed to fill the vacancy caused by the death of Councilman Brunscher.

GIULIO ROSSI.—A highly respected citizen of Contra Costa County and a resident of El Cerrito is found in Giulio Rossi, dealer in real estate and insurance, with his office and residence on Potrero Avenue, near San Pablo Avenue. A native of Italy, he was born on May 12, 1873, at Lonate Pozzolo, in the province of Milano. As a lad he attended the public schools in his native town and from the age of fourteen began to be self-supporting, as a handy lad for a flouring mill, doing any and every kind of work about the place. He was energetic and advanced rapidly and when he was twenty-four was a foreman of a construction crew of 114 men, from his own village, in the building of a canal to bring water down from the high Alps to generate electric power for the industrial plants in his native province. It was by his persistency of purpose in demanding employment for the men of his village that he was at last given a foremanship and thereafter kept busy with his work, continuing for three years.

In 1901 Mr. Rossi came to California. He had some friends in Stege and at once secured employment with the Stauffer Chemical Company, continuing there for seven years and being advanced from time to time to better pay and a more responsible position. He had married in Italy, in February, 1899, Miss Mary Bossetti, born in his native province and they had one son, Joseph, who is now associated with his father in the real estate and insurance business, under the firm name of G. Rossi & Son. In 1907 Mr. Rossi sent for his wife and boy and they arrived here on April 17, of that year. He had purchased property where he now lives and on it erected a house, into which he moved his family; he also had a store building, which he stocked with general merchandise and for two years carried on a very good business. He lost his building and stock by fire in 1909, causing him a loss of some $4,000, the accumulations of his seven years work in the chemical plant. Nothing daunted he rebuilt and opened a liquor store, continuing until the Eighteenth Amendment went into effect, at which time he was appointed by the government to look after the wine under bond in his place of business. The court decided in 1925 that the tax should be paid, which amounted to $1265, and the wine was destroyed. Then Mr. Rossi embarked in the real estate and insurance business and handles property anywhere in this district. At one time he owned a ranch in San Joaquin County which was sold some time ago. In 1925 Mr. Rossi remodeled one of his buildings and his son opened an athletic club, the district being well suited for that sort of an entertainment hall. A good future is in prospect for the business. It has been the aim of Mr. Rossi to reinvest every cent he has made here for he knows that in the near future the advance in price will justify his investments.

In 1908 a daughter was born to Mr. and Mrs. Rossi whom they named Edith M. She and her brother Joseph are graduates of the Richmond High School; she is a bookkeeper and was employed by the North El Cerrito General Merchandise Corporation, in which her father is interested and was its president four years. Joseph is a mechanic by trade. While in Italy Mr. Rossi served eighteen months in the Italian Army at Genova. In 1910 he was made a citizen of the United States in Martinez, is a Republican and a stanch supporter of Hiram Johnson and his policies. Fraternally he is a member of the Order of Owls in El Cerrito, and also belongs to an Italian mutual benefit association of Albany. He is a man of his word, believes in treating others as he would have them treat him, and has made a host of warm friends by so doing. He has a firm belief in his county and is a true citizen of America.

E. A. CRIVELLI.—The proprietor of Milano Hotel, corner of Second Avenue and Ceres Street, in Valona, is E. A. Crivelli, an Italian-American of sterling worth. He comes from a family of prominence in the province of Milano, Italy, where he was born near Milano, on February 18, 1888, a son of Felice and Giovanni Crivelli, both of whom are now deceased. The father was for many years in the employ of the Italian government. There were but two children in the family: Mary, who married Orpillo Orlando, formerly of Valona but now of Milano, Italy; and our subject. The public schools of Italy furnished our subject his education, and he has a command of the Italian, Spanish, French and English languages. While he studied the latter in the Italian schools, most of his English has been acquired since he came to America, through business connections and by reading. At the age of nineteen he left his native land and sailed from Havre, France, on July 25, 1907, arriving in New York on August 2, and in San Francisco on August 10. The very next day he came to Valona, where his sister was living, and it was not long before he secured a job as a day laborer at the Selby Smelter. After continuing thus for two years, he was then promoted to be a foreman and remained with the concern for fourteen years. In 1925 he became the proprietor of the Milano Hotel, which has eighteen rooms and is a clean and sanitary hostelry. It has a reputation as the home of real Italian cooking, and the tables are supplied with the best the markets afford.

Mr. Crivelli was married at Martinez, in 1913, to Miss Carolina Mazza, also a native of Milano province. She came to California at the age of seventeen. They have two children, Raymond and Beatrice. Mr. Crivelli is a member of the Foresters and the Druids. The family attend the Catholic Church. Both Mr. and Mrs. Crivelli are naturalized citizens and Republicans. On all occasions they show their public spirit and their faith in Crockett.

TOM F. TREZONA.—One of the proprietors of the Superior Service Stations located at the corner of Fourth and Black Diamond Streets and at Tenth Street and Railroad Avenue in Pittsburg is Tom F. Trezona. These service stations handle the Associated products and various oils and auto accessories, and also do battery work under the name of the Pittsburg Battery Company, specializing in the Willard Batteries. The company sell, rebuild and charge batteries. Prompt attention is given patrons of these stations, and obliging attendants are always on hand to see that customers are satisfied.

Tom F. Trezona was born in Virginia City, Nev., July 6, 1894, and his partner, F. T. Bastian, was born in Kansas City, Mo. They came to Pittsburg in 1922 and began their present business, and they now have two of the best stations in the city. They are both able and efficient men, attend strictly to their business, and give a square deal to everybody. Both are men of family and are a welcome addition to the business circles of Pittsburg. They show their public spirit by supporting worthy projects for the advancement of their adopted community. Tom F. Trezona is a member of the Masons, the Odd Fellows, Lions Club and Chamber of Commerce, all in Pittsburg.

I. P. TIKIOB.—Often referred to as the father of the Farm Bureau of Contra Costa County, and well-known throughout the county as an important factor in water development in this section of California, I. P. Tikiob is recognized as having had great influence on the agricultural and horticultural development of Contra Costa County. Born in Middleboro, Mass., July 29, 1884, he is a son of I. E. Tikiob, who was born in the Danish West Indies, of English and Danish descent. His grandfather, I. P. Tikiob, was a well-educated man who spoke several languages and was a sea captain. I. E. Tikiob married Maria Roberts, a native of Fayette City, Pa., on the Monongahela River. Her death occurred in Massachusetts. Seven children were born to them, our subject being the fourth in order of birth. The father, a contractor and builder in Massachusetts, came to Los Angeles, Cal., and died in 1925.

I. P. Tikiob was reared in Massachusetts and attended the grammar school and high school there. He worked at well-boring and also as an electrician, and followed that trade in Massachusetts until 1912, when he came to California and located in Oakland for a time, working as an electrician. In 1913 Mr. Tikiob came to Walnut Creek and bought a ranch, and in 1917 established himself in business as a well-borer. Since that time he has been steadily engaged in water development and has found that his former experience in that work, both in California and in the East, gives him an excellent understanding of water formations and conditions wherever found. He operates two rigs, both of them built by himself, one being of the percussion, or standard type, and the other a rotary rig. He has been unusually successful in the development of wells for irrigation purposes as well as for domestic use. He had made a close study of geological conditions in Contra Costa County, using former surveys of formations, and checking carefully by logs of wells previously drilled; and the data thus obtained, together with the results of his own experience, have all combined to insure his success. In this work he has helped greatly in forwarding the county's development, for with an abundance of water and the wonderful soil conditions found in Contra Costa County, its future prosperity is assured.

Mr. Tikiob was one of the prime movers in organizing the Farm Bureau of Contra Costa County, and perhaps the man most instrumental in bringing it to a reality; and he also helped to organize all the Farm Centers in the County, in all of which work he had the loyal support of the local press. He was director at large the first year, and then, because his hearing became impaired, declined further service in that office; but the good work he started has kept growing and expanding, and will always be a monument to his foresight and public spirit.

The marriage of Mr. Tikiob occurred on June 19, 1907, in New Haven, Conn. and united him with Miss Mabel Cummings, a graduate of the normal school there and for several years before her marriage a successful educator. Two children have blessed their union, Marcia and Ruth. The family residence is in the Pleasant Hill district, while Mr. Tikiob maintains his business office on Main Street, in Walnut Creek. Made a Mason in Rising Sun Lodge No. 27, A. F. & A. M., at Washington Depot, Conn., Mr. Tikiob still retains his membership there. In political belief he is a stanch Republican.

ALEX RONALD.—The proprietor of the Pioneer Coal and Transfer Company, Alex Ronald is a highly respected citizen of Richmond. In the operation of his business he runs three trucks and employs three men, and the growth of the enterprise has been gradual and satisfactory. Mr. Ronald was born at Moingona, Boone County, Iowa, August 23, 1878, a son of Harry and Lizzie (Drydale) Ronald. The father came from his native country of England with his parents when he was but three years old, and they settled at Roslyn, Wash., where the grandparents of our subject were among the pioneers. Their family consisted of the following children: Alex, James, Robert, Harry, Raymond, Mitchell, Mrs. Annie Dellahan, Mrs. Emma Lumley, and Mrs. Hettie Dunn.

Alex Ronald attended the common schools and grew up in Washington, and his first work was mining, at which he continued for six years. He next worked at railroading for about eighteen years, and then took a contract to operate the coal mines in Vancouver Island for three years, handling from 110 to 115 men. Leaving there, he came direct to Richmond in 1925 and bought the coal and transfer business owned and operated by R. E. Schrader; and he is continuing the broad policies of the former owner. Mr. Ronald knows his business and always keeps in close touch with its details. With the growth of Richmond, he plans to enlarge the capacity of his plant and to better handle the volume of business from an economic point of view. The territory over which he operates covers considerable ground and his trucks are busy all the time.

Mr. Ronald was married at Roslyn, Wash., on June 25, 1900, to Miss Jennie Toner, daughter of Ambhurst Toner. She has one sister, Mrs. Mary Dailey, in San Francisco. There are two children to brighten the home circle: Nellie, a graduate from the high school and Heald's Business College; and Thelma, attending grammar school. Mr. Ronald's hobby is to "stay on the job." He is fond of hunting and fishing, and when in Washington went out to shoot big game, deer and bear. He mentions the abundance of game on Vancouver Island and the excellent hunting it offered.

AUGUSTUS BESSENT.—A man who has made a really outstanding success in a business way in Contra Costa County, Mr. Bessent is well-known throughout the Bay district and is recognized as a business man of strict integrity and unusual ability, with a real interest in the advancement of his adopted country. Born in Pontypool, England, on February 11, 1882, he was reared in that country, the son of Alfred and Jeanette (Deer) Bessent. The father was for thirty-seven years a policeman in Pontypool, where both parents' death occurred.

The youngest of a family of four children born to his parents, "Gus" Bessent, as he is familiarly called, learned the furniture business in his home community, and also worked for the Dunlop Tire factory in Manchester, England, where he learned tire making in every detail and laid the foundation for future success in life. He came to the United States in 1914 and first located in San Francisco, where he started a retreading tire shop, but only remained in that city for a short time. That same year, with $110 as capital, he came to Contra Costa County, and bought one acre of ground on the Pacheco Road, at Vine Hill. Here he built a shack and started retreading tires, and he has enjoyed almost phenomenal success. In 1924 he did a gross business of $124,000, handling more tires than the aggregate of other dealers in the county (see mention in the Tire Magazine for December, 1924). He is now vulcanizing, retreading and distributing tires, wholesale as well as retail, and handles Star, Royal, Lancaster, Savage, Brunswick, and Spreckels cord and fabric tires, and the same makes of tubes, carrying an immense stock on hand at all times and employing two men besides himself, while Mrs. Bessent does her share as bookkeeper for the shop. He attends many tire conventions as representative of the tire concerns, and is the best-known individual tire man in the United States.

The marriage of Mr. Bessent, at Martinez, united him with Miss Emily Eggleston of Vine Hill, daughter of William and Catherine (Linskey) Eggleston, the former a native of Ottringham, England, and the latter also a native of that country, though their marriage occurred in Detroit, Mich. They became the parents of three children: Kate Ellen; Lilly May; and Emily Jane, now Mrs. Bessent. Mr. and Mrs. Eggleston came to California and the former became one of the well-known pioneer ranchers of the Alhambra Valley, in Contra Costa County. He is now living retired in Berkeley, having reached seventy-eight years in life's span. Mrs. Bessent has been a true helpmate to her husband. Before her marriage she was a successful business woman, having served for fourteen years as deputy auditor for Contra Costa County. One child has blessed their marriage, Trent.

In addition to his tire business, Mr. Bessent wholesales and retails Bessent's Batteries, and is connected with the Standard Battery Company of San Francisco, as a stockholder; and he is also a stockholder in the Pacific Gas and Electric Company of Pittsburg, the Sierra Pacific of Columbia Hill, and other companies. He was naturalized in Judge McKenzie's court at Martinez, and votes for the men and measures he deems best calculated to further the progress of Contra Costa County.

During 1917 Mr. Bessent's shop was robbed and $1100 worth of merchandise was stolen. Sheriff Veale became acquainted with him at this time and appointed him a deputy sheriff, in which office he is now serving. He is thoroughly well liked, both in his home community and throughout the county. Mr. Bessent is proud of his possession of medals won in the Crimean War by his father, who served as a sergeant during that conflict.

G. W. VAN DER BUNDT.—G. W. van der Bundt is a substantial representative of the industrious citizens of the Antioch section of Contra Costa County. He is a native of Holland, born on September 6, 1882, the fourth in order of birth in a family of seven children, all born and reared in Holland. He attended grammar school, and at the age of thirteen began working for wages, but lived at home, and at the same time entered upon an apprenticeship to become a landscape gardener. He studied at night in order to enter the Royal Academy at The Hague, pursuing the preparatory branches such as English, grammar and algebra; and used his meager earnings for private teachers. After completing his apprenticeship he entered the Royal Academy, taking up agriculture and horticulture for the next five years, when he was made head gardener at The Hague.

On November 1, 1909, Mr. van der Bundt was married to Miss Edith Julina Smythe, a native of England, and to them were born three children: Livinus G. W. and Walter Sydney were born in Holland; and Harriet Edith was born after the family came to America.

In October, 1912, Mr. van der Bundt and his family arrived in the United States, settling first at Herbster, Wis., where he was unfortunately victimized by an unscrupulous real estate agent who sold him land which took all of his savings, and had to be given up because it was land owned by Indians. The family then went to Minneapolis, where he soon found work as a gardener on a large estate on the shore of Lake Calhoun. Mrs. van der Bundt was then in frail health and her doctor advised coming West to a milder climate. They then came to California and located at Salinas, where Mr. van der Bundt had charge of the nursery and flower department of the Salinas Nursery Company; while his brother L. J. took charge of the bulbs. This connection, however, proved unsatisfactory and the family removed to Oakland, where Mrs. van der Bundt passed away on February 12, 1919. The task of rearing his three children was of great concern to Mr. van der Bundt and in order to give them better advantages he came to Antioch, where he became gardener for the Great Western Power Company, a position he held for two years; then he went to the Paraffine Company, Inc., and still occupies the position of superintendent of its gardens. In addition to his work as gardener he is operating a poultry farm of twenty-eight acres on the State Highway, two and a half miles east of Antioch; he keeps about 500 pullets and 250 two-year old hens of single comb White Leghorns.

L. J. van der Bundt, the brother of our subject was born in Holland November 1, 1885, and came to America in 1911. He is a landscape gardener and his specialty is the caring for and raising of bulbous plants. The van der Bundt brothers are successful poultrymen and are members of the Poultry Producers Association of California. They are both well trained and well educated and are a valuable addition to the population of Antioch and Contra Costa County.

WILLIAM CHARLES RICHARDS.—One of the leading feed and fuel merchants in Richmond is William Charles Richards, whose place of business is located at 1316 Macdonald Avenue. He is a native son of the State, born at Sonora, Tuolumne County, on February 9, 1875. His parents, William T. and Mary Elizabeth (Lanyon) Richards, were born in Wisconsin and England, respectively. When a child of three years the mother was brought to America and her parents settled at Hazelgreen, Wis., where she grew up and later married Mr. Richards. Soon after, they decided to come to California and on reaching here located at Sonora. Their children were: Eliza Ann, Mrs. J. Ferguson, of Sonora; James H., of Hughson, Stanislaus County; an infant that died; William C. of this review; and Cyrus, a rancher in Tuolumne County.

After finishing his education in the public schools of his birthplace, William Charles Richards started out to make his own way in the world. With his father as a partner he carried on a farm at Sonora until 1923. Disposing of his interests, he then came to Richmond and for six months worked for W. J. McCarthy, after which he established his present business at 1316 Macdonald Avenue. He handles feed, fuel, seeds, poultry supplies, bird foods and sprays and spray material, delivering to all parts of Richmond and throughout the surrounding country by auto truck. He owns his home and other property in Richmond and is accounted among the public-spirited citizens of the county; and he still owns a ranch in Sonora.

Mr. Richards was married on September 12, 1900, to Miss Margery Neighbor, of Snelling, Merced County. She is a daughter of the late Gilbert and Matilda (Smith) Neighbor, the former of New Jersey and the latter a native daughter of California, born in Jamestown. The children in the Neighbor household are: Charles Grant, in Oakland; Mrs. Richards; Mrs. Fred Robinson, of Merced County; Mrs. R. H. Allen, of Tracy; Melvin W., of Snelling; Ethel, Mrs. J. East, of Snelling; Pearl and Josephine, both deceased. Mrs. Neighbor still makes her home in Snelling. Mr. and Mrs. Richards have four children. Mary A., wife of J. Rihn, of Richmond, is a teacher and has a son, Richard. She attended the high school and took two terms in the University of California. Elmer L. was educated at high school, specialized in manual training, and is employed by the Santa Fe as a machinist. Gertrude and William Gilbert are in grammar school.

HENRY DEWEY MASON.—A prominent man in business and fraternal circles in Richmond is Henry Dewey Mason, proprietor of the Richmond Ice Delivery Company. He is a native of California, born in Merced County, on November 28, 1872, the son of Ezra C. and Clara (Dewey) Mason, natives of Elizabethtown, N. J. and Worcester, Mass., respectively. The father came to California as a sailor in 1864, and settling in Merced County, engaged in ranching for many years. He came to Point Richmond in 1901 and opened a saloon. For a time the family lived in a tent because there were but few houses here and all occupied. Mr. and Mrs. E. C. Mason were married in Monterey in 1871, and their children were: Henry D., of this review; Lulu, married J. R. Johnson and lives in Richmond; Elvina, married T. D. Wilson of Le Grand, Cal.; Walter G., also lives in Merced County; George and Charles are deceased.

Henry D. Mason attended the Merced public schools and his first employment was in a drug store in that city. Two years later he went to Coalinga as superintendent for the Merced Oil Company, but after two years there he went to ranching, continuing for three years. Leaving that occupation he came to Richmond and secured employment with the Standard Oil Company at the refinery; then was employed with the Santa Fe Railroad about two years. Meantime he engaged in the ice business, beginning on a moderately small scale; and now by giving the business his entire attention he has built up a lucrative trade. His place of business is No. 11, Sixth Street, where he began in October, 1903. His father was a partner until 1918, when Henry D. took it over and has since conducted it alone.

On October 26, 1910, Henry Dewey Mason and Miss Mabel Nystrom were united in marriage. She is the daughter of the late John R. Nystrom, who is mentioned elsewhere in this history. Mr. and Mrs. Mason have six children: Laurel and Lloyd are in the high schools in Richmond; Clyde and Edwin are grammar school pupils; Clara and Mabel Louise are the youngest. Mr. Mason served three years as secretary of the Eagles, of which he is an active member and a Past President; also is a Past President and secretary of the Native Sons. He belongs to the Odd Fellows, the Encampment and the Rebekahs; and to the Elks. Mrs. Mason belongs to the Eastern Star, the Rebekahs and the Native Daughters, and is a Past President of the latter. Mr. Mason is a member of the Chamber of Commerce and takes an active interest in all civic movements. His recreation is found in camping and motoring.

JOHN E. STALLINGS.—The chief engineer of the Coos Bay Lumber Company at Bay Point, Cal., John E. Stallings, thoroughly understands both electrical and steam engineering, and by study and practice has equipped himself for the important position he has been filling with much credit to himself and to the company. He was born in Pike County, Miss., on October 4, 1870, a son of John and Lucy (King) Stallings. His father was a mechanic in the employ of the Illinois Central Railroad at Tylertown, Miss., and in that State both his father and mother were born and married. Thus it was that early in life, after his school days were over, young Stallings took to mechanics and worked with machinery till he had mastered the business fairly well, when he changed and became a stationary engineer with the Big Creek Lumber Company, a subsidiary of the Missouri Pacific Railway Company, and for ten years was stationed at Pollock, La., until the mill was destroyed by fire in 1906. His next move was to Rochelle, La., and there he was engaged with the Louisiana Lumber Company, installing their engines and boilers. When this company was sold to the Fremont Lumber Company, Mr. Stallings remained with the new owners until 1920. He arrived at Bay Point on February 1, 1921, for his work with the present company.

The Coos Bay Lumber Company operate one of the largest lumber manufacturing plants on the Pacific Coast. Their main power is a 600 h. p. Allis-Chalmers Corliss steam engine for the planing mill. This same engine runs a 200-kilowatt generator for additional power, and the company also buys additional power. The water supply comes from four deep wells with two 75 h.p. pumps, electrically driven and supplying water to the lumber company's plant and to Bay Point for domestic use, as also to the Pacific Coast Shipbuilding plant. There are four boilers with a total of 750 h.p. to generate steam for the Corliss engine that also supplies power. The duties devolving upon the chief engineer are exacting, but he has proved himself able to give entire satisfaction to his employers. He is a kindly man and able to look upon both sides of questions before making any decision. While working in Louisiana he met with a serious accident that unfortunately crippled him for life, but notwithstanding this he fulfills every duty his position necessitates.

When Mr. Stallings came to marry he chose for his wife Miss Louisa Lucas, daughter of Ed. Lucas, a Louisiana planter. Their wedding was celebrated at Alexandria, La., on October 11, 1888; and they have four sons. John Oliver is head filer for the Euwona Lumber Company, at Klamath Falls, Ore. He was married at Rochelle, La., to Marguerite Heartbunnier; and they have three children: Geraldine, Jewell, and

Juanita. James Augustus, known as "Gust," is the proprietor of a garage at McNeary, Ariz. He was married at Rochelle, La., to Miss Ellen Taylor; and they have two children, Dorothy and Doris. William is head filer for the Shaw-Bertrand Lumber Company, at Klamath Falls, Ore. He was married at Rochelle, La., to Miss Lillie Belle Nash. Luther Edgar is in the sales department of the Pelican Bay Lumber Company, with general offices at Klamath Falls, Ore. He also was married in Rochelle, La., his wife's maiden name being Mary Cole; and they have two children, Edgar, Jr., and Zachrie. Fraternally, Mr. Stallings is a member of the Odd Fellows at Bay Point, and of the Woodmen of the World at Rochelle, La. Mr. and Mrs. Stallings hold to the Baptist Church and support its work, although there is no church of that denomination at Bay Point. Politically, he votes with the Democrats.

MICHAEL LOUIS DEL MONTE.—A native son of Contra Costa County, Mr. Del Monte has lived practically his entire life here, and is now enjoying the fruits of a life of industry and intelligent cooperation. Born at Black Diamond, now Pittsburg, on December 5, 1885, he is the son of Frank and Ida (Scudero) Del Monte, the former a native of Italy, and the latter of Pittsburg, where she passed away at the early age of forty-one years. Of their ten children, Michael Louis is the second, and when the family moved from Pittsburg to Rodeo, in 1892, he came with them and finished his schooling there. Leaving grammar school to go to work for the Union Oil Company, he learned the steam-fitting and plumbing trade, and worked at different jobs for that company and for the Hercules Powder Works and the Selby Smelting Company. For a time he was engaged, with his father as a partner, in running the Hotel Rodeo, at Rodeo. His father, now seventy-five years old, is in the furniture business in Pittsburg, still active and hearty.

Returning to work for the Union Oil Company in 1907, Mr. Del Monte has been with them since that date and is now the head of the pipe line department at Oleum, with thirty-five men under him. He has served as deputy sheriff under Sheriff Veale since 1906, and has won the confidence of the people of the county by his strict adherence to duty, under all circumstances, some of them exceedingly hazardous, and stands in line for political preferment.

The marriage of Mr. Del Monte, occurring at Richmond on September 7, 1910, united him with Miss Mary Wasco, a native of McKeesport, Pa., who was reared from the age of fourteen in California. Her father, Andy Wasco, is a pipe-fitter, now employed at El Segundo, Cal. Two children have blessed the union of Mr. and Mrs. Del Monte, Bernice and Jeanette.

Fraternally, Mr. Del Monte is a Mason, a member of the Pinole lodge of that order. Politically he is a Republican. In all walks of life he is an upright and public-spirited man, with the best interests of his community at heart.

JAMES E. RIAL.—A self-made man now residing in Richmond and an employee of the Standard Oil Company, at their refinery, is James E. Rial who lives at No. 510 Washington Avenue. He was born at Emlenton, Pa., and was orphaned at a tender age by the death of his parents, after which he was adopted into the family of Edward Rial, by whom he was reared. He attended the public schools at Franklin, Pa., and at the age of twenty-two started out in life on his own account and entered the book and stationery business in Franklin, remaining about eight years. He then went to New York and was employed by Lord and Taylor for two years, after which he returned to Franklin, Pa., and found work with a brass manufacturing company for two more years. Thus equipped with a firm foundation he came to California and to Richmond and here entered the refinery, starting in the manufacturing department and is still in that part of the work in this great institution, where he is fuel man.

On April 11, 1898, Mr. Rial was united in marriage with Miss Alice Parker, of Oil City, Pa., daughter of the late Henry Parker and his wife, who is also deceased. They have one child Catherine, Mrs. Ross Stewart, of Houston, Texas, who has a son and a daughter. Mr. Rial is a member of the Masonic Lodge. He was reared a Presbyterian. They own their own home in Richmond and take an active interest in all civic affairs. Mr. Rial enjoys automobiling as his recreation.

GIUSEPPE TROIA.—Persistency of purpose, coupled with a definite aim in life, has helped Giuseppe Troia to reach the goal set before him when a lad in far off Italy; and that is a plumbing establishment of his own. On January 1, 1890, he was born at Palermo, Island of Sicily, Italy, the son and the fifth child of Giuseppe and Pietra Troia. The father has been for years in the service of the railway managed by the Italian government; the mother passed away in the spring of 1925 at the age of sixty years.

Giuseppe Troia received a good education in the public schools of Palermo and when only thirteen years of age was apprenticed to the plumbing trade. In 1905 he emigrated to America and for a while worked at the plumber's trade in Chicago. About 1913 he made his first trip to California, but later returned to Chicago and from there returned to Italy and enlisted in the Italian Army, being assigned to the Infantry. He served twenty-two months, thirteen of which he was actively engaged in battle-front service, including Piave, Monte Ciamissi, Monte Grappa, Camp Elonda, and from there marched to Triento, after which he was honorably discharged from service. In 1919 he returned to America and for two years was in San Francisco, employed at his trade as a plumber. In July, 1921, Mr. Troia located in Pittsburg, where he again engaged in plumbing. That year he opened a plumbing establishment at 327 Black Diamond Street, and this he has successfully managed and operated ever since. During this time he has done the plumbing in twenty bungalows in Pittsburg and conducted a general plumbing business. He is a member of the Pittsburg Chamber of Commerce and is keenly interested in the advancement of the city.

On October 22, 1922, Giuseppe Troia was united in marriage with Mrs. Angelina Milta, whose maiden name was Angelina Camara, a daughter of the late Alfonso Camara, a veteran sailor who had visited many ports throughout the world. Mr. and Mrs. Troia are the parents of one son, Giuseppe Troia, Jr. Mrs. Troia has a daughter by her first husband, Lucy Milta.

D. G. STATHAKIS.—Another intelligently enterprising and energetic business man who has made good in Martinez is D. G. Stathakis, proprietor of the Martinez Candy Store and one of the substantial men of the community. He was born near Sparta, Greece, on February 24, 1887. His father, now deceased, was a farmer by occupation, and died before his young son was five years old; the mother, Georgia (Sinadinou) Stathakis, is still living in the old home in Greece. Educated in the public schools of his native country, and reared in the Greek Orthodox Church, Mr. Stathakis was ambitious to make his way in the world and left home when a youth of seventeen, sailing from Piraeus, Greece, and landing at Ellis Island, New York City, on April 14, 1904. He came on to Sioux City, Iowa, where he had a cousin, and remained there three months. From there he went to Chicago, thence to Springfield, Ill., then back to Chicago, and in 1905 to Terre Haute, Ind., where he remained until July, 1907. During most of this time he was engaged in the confectionery business.

From Terre Haute Mr. Stathakis bought a ticket to Redding, Cal., and there he worked in a sawmill for a time. In the fall of 1907 he came to San Francisco, remaining in that city until August, 1909; and on August 6 of that year he located in Martinez. For a time he worked for John Magulas, the pioneer confectioner of Martinez; and then, on May 6, 1911, he started his own confectionery store at 719 Main Street. He spent thousands of dollars in putting in modern fixtures, marble counters, soda fountain, and up-to-date dining booths finished in mahogany, for besides his confectionery store he engaged in a complete fountain and restaurant service, equal to any found in the largest cities. His confidence in Martinez as a place in which to start such a business met with immediate response from his fellow townspeople, and he has prospered exceedingly. In September, 1921, he purchased the building, known as the Dr. Rattan Building, in which his store is housed, on the main business street in Martinez.

Mr. Stathakis was married in 1925 to Miss Dragica Ellen Andratich, of Martinez. He was made an American citizen on April 17, 1913, in the United States District Court at San Francisco, before Judge Van Fleet. He served in the World War in the 12th Infantry, getting as far as New York, after having trained at Camp Fremont, before the armistice was signed, and he was honorably discharged at Newport News. He had a manager in charge of his business while away, and returned to civilian life once more to take up his business affairs, on February 4, 1919. Fraternally, Mr. Stathakis is a member of the Martinez Lodge of the Knights of Pythias, the Loyal Order of Moose, and the American Legion. In politics he is a Republican.

BEN EDWARD STOTTS.—Numbered among the Spanish-American War Veterans in Contra Costa is Ben E. Stotts of Martinez. He is connected with the Gazette Publishing Company and is an all-round practical printer, having followed that trade practically all his life since leaving school. He was born on November 23, 1877, in Wichita, Kans., the son of Ben Bell and Sarah Catherine (Pennington) Stotts. The father was a native of Kentucky and served during the Civil War with the Kansas Volunteer Battery.

Ben Edward Stotts was sent to the grammar schools in Colorado, where the family were then living, and as soon as he had finished the work there he entered a printing office to learn the business from the ground up. Starting as "printer's devil" he has risen through the ranks till he is accounted one of the old-time experienced printers, able to hold down any kind of a job to be found in a printing office. During the Spanish-American War he enlisted and served in the Philippines with Company C, First Colorado Volunteers. He belongs to the Spanish War Veterans, the Veterans of Foreign Wars, and the Veterans Service Club. In his political views Ben is a Republican.

On January 25, 1915, Ben E. Stotts was united in marriage with Miss Mackie May Shelby, daughter of William Reed and Fannie D. Shelby, and they are the parents of a son Ben Edward Stotts, Jr. For recreation Ben goes trout fishing, a sport he greatly enjoys.

OSWALD HARRY REBER.—An employee of the Columbia Steel Corporation who is making a name and place for himself in the steel business is Oswald Harry Reber, more familiarly called Harry Reber by his many friends. He was born on July 20, 1891, at Angels Camp, Calaveras County, where his father, Godfrey Reber, was a jeweler. Godfrey Reber is numbered among the pioneers of Calveras County, but is now living in San Pedro.

Oswald Harry Reber attended the public schools in Calveras County until he was ten years old, then accompanied the family to Petaluma, and from there came to Richmond in 1911. He found employment at the great winery at Winehaven, and from that position went to work for the Pioneer Rubber Works in Pittsburg, remaining there four years. His connection with the steel company dates from this period, when he entered the furnace department as second helper in the open-hearth furnaces. He continued at his work until he joined the army, in the 1st Division of the 26th Infantry. He trained at Camp Lewis, and at Camp Mills for three weeks, and then went over seas on the Leviathan and landed in Liverpool on December 25, 1917. He trained at Gonder-court, in France, from which place he was assigned to the Soissons front and took part in the first skirmish. He was taken with the flu and was in the hospital and evacuation camp when the armistice was signed. He was sent to Brest, where he embarked for New York, and landed on his home shores on July 25, 1919. He received his honorable discharge at Mitchell's Field, Long Island. Arriving in Pittsburg, Cal., he resumed his position with the Columbia Steel Corporation as first helper at the open-hearth furnace. From this position he became a melter, and then an assistant foreman in 1924.

Mr. Reber was married in Stockton in February, 1925, to Miss Mary Leckie, who was born in Stewartsville, Contra Costa County, the daughter of David Leckie, a coal miner who is now living retired in Pittsburg. This union has been blessed with two children: Margaret and Janet. Mr. Reber belongs to Diamond Parlor, N. S. G. W., and to the Masonic order. In politics he is a Republican. The family reside in their own home, which Mr. Reber erected in the Home Acre Tract.

WALLACE SNELGROVE.—As a successful contractor and builder of the Bay district, Wallace Snelgrove holds a substantial position among the representative business men of Richmond. He was born at Lancaster, N. H., February 11, 1886, a son of Thomas George and Elizabeth (Booth) Snelgrove. The mother came originally from Sheffield, England, accompanying her parents to America and settling in New Hampshire, where she met and married the father of our subject.

Wallace Snelgrove began his education in the public schools of his native city, and as time passed took special courses to fit him for his chosen line of work. For several years he worked in a sash and door factory; and then he went to Manchester, N. H., where he worked at his trade. He then removed to Butte, Mont., and for six years was an employee of the Anaconda Copper Company. Following this he came to California and worked for several companies before settling at Richmond, where he has resided since 1920 and has become an essential factor in the development and growth of this city. Mr. Snelgrove built the Galina Signal Oil Company's plant and many of the finest residences in Richmond and the surrounding country. He built the Odd Fellows' Building and Richmond Syndicate Building, and also the Galvin and the Richmond Daily Independent Buildings.

On September 4, 1918, Mr. Snelgrove was married to Miss Mary Willard of Santa Rosa, daughter of Wiley Willard, a farmer of that vicinity. Mr. Snelgrove has three sisters: Elizabeth, Mrs. Harry Longley, in Vermont; Mary, Mrs. James Lomby, in Massachusetts; and Ethel, Mrs. McIntire, in New York State. Mr. Snelgrove is a member and director of the Builders' Exchange and a member and formerly a director of the Lions Club of Richmond. Fraternally, he is a member and Past Noble Grand of the Independent Order of Odd Fellows and a director of the Odd Fellows' Hall Association.

CLARENCE H. ROMAN.—Among the successful young business men of Bay Point, Contra Costa County, Cal., there are none possessing greater energy and enterprise than Clarence H. Roman, proprietor of the Bay Point Garage. His birth occurred at Rhinelander, Wis., on May 5, 1900, the second child in a family of four born to Mr. and Mrs. Henry Roman. From Wisconsin the family moved to Potlatch, Idaho, and in this lumber town Clarence began his schooling. Then the family removed to Bay Point, Cal., where Henry Roman became the superintendent of the C. A. Smith Planing Mill, now known as the Coos Bay Lumber Company, and here the son continued his grammar school courses. Being of an ambitious turn of mind, he soon found employment with the Coos Bay Lumber Company, first as a laborer and then as a machinist, his employment with the company covering a period of seven years. He was caught in the 18 to 45 draft in 1918 and placed in Class A-1, and was ready to go to the front when the armistice was signed on November 11, 1918. He then decided to become an automobile mechanic and entered Sweeney's Automobile School at Kansas City, Mo., receiving his certificate from that institution in 1920. Upon his return to Bay Point he formed a partnership with Plino Rigolli, and together they operated the Bay Point Garage and Automobile Machine Shop until 1924, when Mr. Roman became the sole owner. Mr. Roman is a first-class mechanic and works on all makes of automobiles and trucks. He owns a good tow-car, which brings in wrecks and disabled cars; and repairs are made on short notice. Two mechanics assist Mr. Roman, and they have an excellent reputation for good and careful work.

Mr. Roman was married at Bay Point on November 16, 1921, to Miss Mary Brazz, of Concord, where she was born and where her grandparents were among the early pioneers. Mr. and Mrs. Roman have one child, Russell. Mr. Roman is a Past Grand of the Bay Point Lodge of Odd Fellows.

BATTISTA ARDIZZOIA.—The subject of this sketch, Battista Ardizzoia, is a man of ability and an efficient workman and foreman, well-liked both by his employers and by the men under him in the Port Costa Brick Company's plant, where he is machinist and head foreman. A native of Oleggio, Italy, he was born on November 9, 1887, the son of Francisco and Nattalina Ardizzoia, farmer folk in the province of Navara, Italy, where both are still living. Battista is the only son living, but he has six sisters, two of whom are in California; Giovanni, the wife of Pete Franzetti, and Teressa, wife of Joe Cardanni, both in Port Costa.

Mr. Ardizzoia attended the schools of Italy and grew up on the home farm, raising grapes, making wine, and helping in the dairy and other farm work. When nearly twenty years of age he came to the United States, having decided to seek his fortunes in the new world, and with him on the same steamer came his cousin, Miss Pierina Mattachini, now the wife of Biagio F. Ferrario, the superintendent of the Port Costa Brick Works. Arriving in Port Costa on October 12, 1907, Mr. Ardizzoia lost no time, but went to work as a common laborer. He worked hard and steadily, and has risen to the important and responsible position he holds as foreman in one of the largest brick and tile works in California, 60,000 bricks being the average daily output.

The marriage of Mr. Ardizzoia, in St. Catherine's Church, at Martinez, Cal., on April 16, 1912, united him with Miss Paolina Fortina, a native of the same village as her husband, and one child was born to them, Frank L., now attending the grammar school at Port Costa. The wife and mother died at Port Costa on April 15, 1925, after having been ill for several years, part of which time was spent in Italy in an effort to regain her health. Mr. Ardizzoia made one visit back to his home in Italy, in 1908, returning to Port Costa one year later. He has taken out his first naturalization papers and intends to become a citizen of the country where he has been so successful.

SEVERIN FERCHE.—A striking example of what energy and resourcefulness can accomplish when wisely directed is furnished in the career of Severin Ferche, contractor and builder of Crockett and the district in the west end of Contra Costa County. He is a man of natural ability and was born at St. Stephens, Minn., on January 8, 1895, where he attended school and learned the trade of carpenter. He has four brothers; Stephen, Joseph, Cyril and Frank, living in St. Stephen.

When Severin Ferche came to California in 1916 he joined the United States Army and spent four years at Mare Island. So important was his work there for the government that he was not permitted to go elsewhere as he had charge of the shops at headquarters in all construction work. On April 16, 1920, he received an honorable discharge from the Army, then made a visit back to his home folks in Minnesota, returning to Crockett in 1921. He took up hotel keeping at the Union Hotel for a few months, but resigned his position and took up general contracting and building and ever since has made his influence felt along that line in this part of the county. The business and his fame grew steadily and soon he took in a partner and as Ferche and Childs the firm has won a name for dependable work throughout this section. Among the outstanding contracts they have been awarded are the municipal firehouse and the library at Pinole, the Doctor Horne residence in Crockett Heights, and many other fine homes in this district that is so rapidly being built up in Crockett. To further promote the best interests of his adopted city he holds membership in the Crockett-Valona Business Men's Association.

Severin Ferche was married on September 15, 1921, to Miss Elizabeth Rossman, of St. Cloud, Minn., where her father, John Rossman, was prominent in political circles. Two children have been born of this union: Madeline and Dorothy. He belongs to the American Legion Post No. 33, at Crockett; is a Knight of Columbus, Fourth Degree; and a member of the Ancient Order of Druids. He is independent in politics and attends the Catholic Church.

FRANK L. RISON.—A resident of Richmond since 1905 who has earned the good will and esteem of a wide circle of close friends is Frank L. Rison. A native son of the State, he was born in Lake County, near Lakeport, on May 2, 1883. His father was the late Hiram G. Rison who came from Wisconsin to California in 1877. He was born in Ohio, and was married in Lake County, Cal., to Miss Elizabeth Ingram, who was born in Lake County, whither her father, Jonas Ingram, had located in 1849. Mr. Ingram was born in Jackson County, Ill., April 17, 1823, and died April 1, 1908. Some of the land that he homesteaded near Lakeport is still owned by members of his family. When Jonas Ingram came to Lakeport he was a single man; when he married he and his wife had to go on horseback to Napa, where the ceremony was performed. Besides farming Mr. Ingram made cheese, which he carried to Napa to sell, that being their nearest market place. Those were pioneer times before much improvement had been made in ranch development. Mrs. Elizabeth Rison's mother, Martha Hammock, crossed the plains in 1849, being then sixteen years old. The party lost some of their oxen through an Indian raid while en route from Missouri. Her grandfather, father and uncles took up government land in Lake County and were among the earliest pioneers of that section. In the Ingram family were two boys and four girls, all of whom grew up. Sarah Hammock, a daughter of Mrs. Elizabeth Rison's uncle, was the first white child born in Lake County. There were seven of the Hammock family in the train of forty wagons that arrived safely in the Golden State. In those early days in Lake County eggs sold for one dollar each and chickens were twenty dollars each. Middletown was then an active mining center and some of the men of the families tried their luck at mining until they took to farming. Bear and deer were plentiful in Lake County in those early days. Mr. and Mrs. Hiram Rison were married at the home of Mr. Ingram in 1880. They had four girls and one boy: Nellie, wife of William Carter of Santa Rosa; Frank L., of this review; Edna, Mrs. Walter W. Haggler, of Berkeley; Elsie, who married Dean Asdell of Portland, Ore.; and Ethel, of Richmond. Mr. Rison came to Richmond in 1905; and here he died nineteen years later, in 1924, at the age of seventy-seven. He had one sister living in Oregon.

Frank L. Rison attended the public schools in Lake County and grew up amidst the pioneer conditions of that county. In 1900 he left the ranch and went to Willits and found work in the Redwoods. His father and himself worked at carpenter work, rebuilding Willits after a fire had wiped out the town. That fall Frank went back to the home ranch and operated it for a year, then returned to the Redwoods and remained till 1905, when he came to Richmond to try his luck. In Willits he had an uncle that was one of the pioneer freighters from Willits to the grading camps along the Northwestern Pacific Railroad during its construction, and for a time Frank tried his luck at railroad construction, then went back to the lumber camps. He has seen much of frontier life in grading camps and lumber camps and was innured to hard work from early life. In 1905, with his father and some friends, he came to Richmond and found work with the Standard Oil Company. He has seen many changes in the plant and in the development of the city, but is satisfied that he cast in his lot in such a prosperous locality.

Frank L. Rison was united in marriage at Berkeley, on May 22, 1913, with Miss Amy Rose Turnbull, a native of East Liverpool, Ohio, who came to California and was here married. They have two children: Bernice Florence and Dorothy Alice. For four years the Risons lived at Point Richmond, but moved to their present place in 1914. Frank's mother makes her home with her son and they all have a wide circle of close friends in Richmond.

FRANK DRAGON.—Many desirable personal characteristics are contributing to the success of Frank Dragon, not the least of which is his determination to succeed in his chosen line of work. He is steadily forging to the front as a contractor and builder and his ability is fast becoming known throughout the environs of Antioch. His birth occurred in Italy on March 15, 1886, the second son of Peter and Concitta (Marasciulo) Dragon, now both deceased. He remained at home until he was eighteen years of age, then accompanied an uncle to the United States, where he joined his father and eldest brother, and with them came to California. Knowing nothing of the English language, Frank Dragon procured an English-Italian grammar and with the help of friends and attending night school, soon became able to read the daily papers. It was a difficult matter to find employment without a speaking knowledge of English; however he had the good fortune to meet Carmino Didio who piloted them to Antioch in 1904, where the father became a successful rancher and Frank helped his father; later he worked in a paper mill, then in a brick yard, but he never lost sight of the fact that he was determined to reach a higher plane; he had kept up his night studies, has completed the correspondence course in drafting and architecture in the International Correspondence School at Scranton, Pa., and has become a good draftsman.

In 1916 he began contracting for himself and makes a specialty of moderate priced homes. His work has been centered about Antioch, where he has built many houses. In 1926 he completed four magnesite houses for Louis Arata; he erected a rooming house of twenty-six rooms for Louis Fontana in Pittsburg; also an apartment house for M. Valente; and several residences. He built the Oakley Garage and several homes throughout the country.

At Antioch, on September 12, 1910, Frank Dragon was united in marriage to Miss Rose Didio, daughter of Carmino Didio, and they have three children: Peter F., born September 13, 1911; Carmen M., born July 28, 1914; and Roland M., born July 20, 1918. Mr. and Mrs. Dragon reside in their home on Wilbur Avenue, where they own two and one-half acres of fine productive land. One acre is planted to almonds and one acre to muscat and wine grapes. He belongs to the Young Men's Institute.

EDWARD ESLEY EVANS.—A representative of a pioneer California family, and a business man of El Cerrito, Edward E. Evans has a wide circle of friends and business associates in Contra Costa County and vicinity. A native of the State, he was born in Petaluma, Sonoma County, January 21, 1886, the oldest son of E. W. M. Evans, well known as the senior member of the firm of E. W. M. Evans & Sons, marble and stone workers. The great-grandfather was a Douglas, and came around the Horn to California in 1850, bringing with him material for a ready-made hotel and dwelling house. He landed at what is now Antioch and set up his house and hotel, but not liking the location, took them down and moved to Petaluma, where he again put up his buildings and made a permanent home. The dwelling house is still standing, but the hotel occupied the site of the new Petaluma Hotel building. Members of the Douglas family still reside in Petaluma and vicinity. Grandfather Tupper landed in California from a whaling vessel in 1848. He finally settled in Petaluma, and there he died at the age of eighty-eight. He was married in Petaluma, and the first child born of a marriage of white persons in that city was his daughter Ellen Tupper, mother of our subject. Both the Douglas and Tupper families had much to do with the upbuilding of Petaluma.

E. W. M. Evans was born in Ireland, in County Tyrone, in 1862, attended the schools of his native land and came with his father, in 1870, to California. The family lived in Alameda for several years, where E. W. M. Evans attended school. He learned the trade of the marble worker in Petaluma and began the business for himself when he bought out his former employer in 1889. He built up a fine trade and continued alone until 1919, when the firm was incorporated under the name of E. W. M. Evans & Sons, owning the Petaluma Granite and Marble Works in that city, and the Fairmont Monument Works in El Cerrito, Contra Costa County. Since its incorporation the firm has made a specialty of mantel and tile work, handling the products of the California Art Tile Company of Richmond. Mr. Evans was married in 1882 to Ellen Tupper, and they have had seven children: Mrs. F. J. Tolburg, of Sacramento; Edward E., of this review; Arthur B.; and Roy M.; Mrs. H. H. Cluver, of Petaluma; Mrs. Al Zimmerman, of Petaluma; and Roscoe D. The four sons are all members of the firm of E. W. M. Evans & Sons. The father is still actively engaged in his trade, and is found at the bench every day.

Edward E. Evans attended the public schools in Petaluma and at the age of sixteen began to learn the trade of the marble worker from his father. He has been through every department of the work, from the quarry to the finishing and setting-up of monuments. There being an opening for marble works at the Sunset View Cemetery in Contra Costa County, he came to this place and opened a branch of their Petaluma establishment on Fairmont Avenue where the El Cerrito library building stands, later moving to his present location at the gates of the cemetery. At the beginning it was real pioneer work. Labor was scarce and teamsters almost unknown, and many times the finished monument was hauled in a wheelbarrow to its resting place. The corporation represented by our subject is among the well-known firms in California. A splendid business has been the result of the pioneer efforts of Mr. Evans, and today he ranks among the leading citizens of El Cerrito, being a strong booster for his adopted city.

When Mr. Evans married he chose for his life companion Miss Anna Koch, also born in Petaluma, and they have one daughter, Esley Ann Evans. The family occupy their own home, which was built in 1915. Mr. Evans believes in civic betterment whenever and wherever possible and supports all movements having this in view. In politics he is a Republican. Socially, he is a member of the Exchange Club in Berkeley. Besides looking after his monument business and the interests of E. W. M. Evans & Sons, he represents some old-line fire insurance companies and handles considerable of that kind of business.

WILLIAM O'HARA.—A native son of California who has lived in Contra Costa County and vicinity nearly all his life, is William O'Hara. He was born in Solano County, a son of Michael and Julia O'Hara, both natives of Ireland, but who were married after reaching America. Michael O'Hara ran threshing machines for many years and threshed thousands of bushels of grain annually for the grain growers in the State.

Our subject attended the public schools in the localities where the family lived, but had to go to work at an early age, for his father died when the lad was only seven. He came to the Rodeo Valley and engaged in the cattle business and did some general ranching along with cattle raising for eighteen years; also was in the dairy business. He then moved to the Alhambra Valley, thence to a ranch near Walnut Creek, spending in all seventeen years in those sections of Contra Costa County. All these years he has followed the dairy and stock business, which has always stood him in good stead, especially at the present time, when he is carrying on the dairy business on a large scale in this section of the county. In 1922 he came to Crockett to live. Mr. O'Hara is a man of strong determination, is not afraid to work with his hands, and is an authority on cattle. He erected a large dairy barn with a capacity for 200 milch cows, which will meet all legal requirements, and is going to install milking machines. He has about 1400 acres of land at Tormey, where he pastures his stock, has his silos and mixing machines to prepare the feed for his cattle. He is building up a very modern dairy, sanitary in every particular and retails and delivers his milk by means of trucks. His cattle are high grade Holsteins and tested by the State veterinarian.

In his dairy business Mr. O'Hara is assisted by three sisters, who are partners with him in the enterprise. They share and share alike in the responsibilities and profits. Mr. O'Hara gives his personal time and attention to the business and therefore feels that it surely will continue to be a success. He stands for the "square deal" in business affairs, as well as in his contact with his fellow citizens.

JOHN GIACOSA.—An active and successful young Italian-American business man of Martinez, John Giacosa is well known in his home community. Born in Italy, on March 20, 1894, he is the son of Antonio and Filomena Giacosa, both natives of Italy who came to California when John was sixteen years old, in 1910, and have since made their home here. The first of five children born to his parents, he received his early education in Italy and also attended private and night schools after coming to Martinez, gaining most of his knowledge through self-application.

For three years Mr. Giacosa was in the ice and fuel business in Martinez, as a partner with S. J. Pongrace in the People's Ice and Fuel Company; but he sold his interest to his partner in the early part of 1925, and since that time has engaged as wholesale distributor of soft drinks, acting as wholesale agent for this district.

During the World War Mr. Giacosa served as a machine gunner with the 144th Machine Gun Battalion, 40th Division, and saw service in France for nine months. He was honorably discharged at Camp Kearny, San Diego, in May, 1919, and some time later went into the ice business in Martinez. He is a member of the American Legion at Martinez, and belongs to the Loyal Order of Moose.

LLEWELLYN W. EVANS.—An industrious, enterprising citizen of Richmond, who holds a responsible position with the Republic Steel Package Company, is Llewellyn W. Evans. Mr. Evans was born in Pinole on August 6, 1896, the son of L. P. Evans, a native of Wales who came to America in 1885. The father is still living and is connected with the Standard Oil Company. The mother, Bertha (Wilkie) Evans, was born in San Pablo. Two other children in their family were Bertha, now Mrs. F. Shubat of Richmond; Gwendollyn, Mrs. J. Carlisle of San Jose.

Mr. Evans received his early education in the grammar school of Pinole, and then took a course in the Engineering College of Oakland. After finishing his schooling he secured a position with the Larkin Machine Works of San Francisco, where he was employed for four years. During this period of apprenticeship he arose early every morning and traveled from San Pablo to San Francisco, traveling six hours daily to work eight hours, and made the exceptional record of never being late and never missing a day from labor. He next held a position with the Standard Oil Company for a year, and then took a position with the Pacific Gear & Tool Works of San Francisco. From there he went to Seattle, where he was employed by the Paragon Tool Company for three years. This was followed by a period of employment, lasting two years, with the Smith Can Machinery Company of Seattle. His next move was a business venture for himself in manufacturing tools and auto parts in Seattle for a year and a half. Selling out his plant, he removed to Eugene, Ore., and worked in the same line of business for a year. From there he came to San Pablo and opened a garage and machine shop. While engaged in this work he met Mr. Merry, of the Republic Steel Package Company, for whom he made some dies and did some machine work. This led to his being asked to take the position which he now holds, and he took up his duties in June, 1922. Since that time the plant has enjoyed a wonderful growth, and Mr. Evans has devoted himself strenuously to making such improvements in his department as the needs of the plant and the demands of the trade warrants.

On June 1, 1923, Mr. Evans married Miss Agnes Walters of Richmond, daughter of John Walters of San Jose, a brick manufacturer, who is still living. Mrs. Evans has one brother. Mr. and Mrs. Evans are the parents of two children, Luella Agnes and Catherine Viola. Mr. Evans is a member of the Masons. He is fond of fishing and hunting, and is interested in all forms of athletics. During the war he did valuable work in the navy in the construction of motors.

ANTONIO FILOMEO.—An energetic and successful man of Italian birth, but who was brought to San Francisco when a mere babe and reared in California, Antonio Filomeo has made good in his adopted country, where he has held various public offices and reached a substantial position in life. Born in Concenso, near Naples, Italy, on November 16, 1871, he is the son of John and Rosa Filomeo. The father came to San Francisco and for a time engaged in working for the Southern Pacific Railway, and later at ranching near Vacaville. Two of their four children were born in Italy. The mother and two children joined Mr. Filomeo here in California, where the two youngest children were born. Their names follow: Agnes, wife of Peter Dito, residing in San Francisco; Antonio, of this review; Frank, of Oakland; and Mary, wife of George Dalto, a business man of Vacaville. The good wife and mother died in Oakland, in 1918, having reached seventy-two in life's span; the father passed to his reward in 1896, his death occurring at Vacaville when he was fifty-five years old.

Antonio Filomeo was reared in San Francisco and attended the public schools of that city until thirteen years old, when the family moved to Vacaville, where he continued his schooling, and passed his boyhood on the home ranch of thirty-six acres. He helped in the ranch work until reaching twenty-one years, when he bought a ranch of his own, near Vacaville, and raised hay and fruit. Since then he has owned and farmed several ranches, at one time owning and operating 500 acres near Vacaville. An exceptionally public-spirited man, for sixteen years he was road master at Vacaville, and also served on the high school board of that city for eight years, being twice elected.

In 1920 Mr. Filomeo purchased his 196-acre ranch in Contra Costa County, situated about three and one-half miles south of Martinez, and has met with deserved success in its operation. The property has sixty acres planted to grapes; apricots, peaches and prunes on twenty additional acres; and the balance is devoted to hay, grain and pasture, making it one of the most valuable ranches in Contra Costa County. The ranch is operated by the son John Filomeo. Mr. Filomeo is now a resident of Oakland, where he is in the real estate business. Mr. Filomeo is a stockholder in the Oakland branch of the Banca Papolan Fugazi. He is a man of fine business acumen, making his industry count for something, and profiting by his investments.

The marriage of Mr. Filomeo, which occurred at San Francisco, September 16, 1895, united him with Miss Severia Dalto, a native of Italy, who was brought to the United States when she was eleven months old, by her parents, Joseph and Conchica Dalto. After living one year in New York City, the family came west to California and became ranchers at Vacaville, and there the young people met and were married. Mr. Filomeo ranched in Vacaville from 1884 until 1916, and is still largely interested in ranch lands at that place. Seven children were born to Mr. and Mrs. Filomeo: John, married Miss Madalene Corabello and is the father of five children, John, Vivian, Bobby, Elma and Donald; Joseph, married Miss Mamia Alexander and has one child, Leonard; Edward, married Vittie Jacoso; William, married Hazel Johnson and has one child; Rosa, wife of Brazil Sobasco, is the mother of two children; Alvira and Lucile.

MISS AGNES M. DRISCOLL.—The institution known as the Cottage Hospital, in Richmond, is owned and presided over by Miss Agnes M. Driscoll, a very competent nurse and good business woman who located in this industrial city in 1918. The principal work here is emergency surgical cases coming from the various industrial plants located in Richmond and its environs. The hospital is equipped with the most modern appliances to be found in the realm of surgery, and has a capacity for the accommodation of twenty patients. This humanitarian institution fills a long-felt need in Richmond, and is patronized by practitioners of the medical profession in the city, who here find ample accommodations and competent nurses for their patients.

Miss Driscoll was born in Newfoundland, Canada, in 1884, a daughter of Edward and Sarah Driscoll, who were farmers and merchants in Canada. The daughter attended the public schools in Newfoundland, and after finishing high school entered a nurse's training school, in 1906, at the Massachusetts State Infirmary, graduating three years later. For the next two years she did tubercular work in charge of a sanitarium at Redding, Mass.; then for two more years she was in the contagious department of the Municipal Hospital in Philadelphia. A call came to go to Texas, and she spent two years in San Antonio. In 1917 she came to San Francisco and started private nursing, continuing thus until she moved to Richmond to locate her own hospital here. She found a favorable field for such an institution and from the beginning was successful. She employs five nurses, has an X-ray laboratory, and gives every detail of the work brought to her hospital her personal supervision.

The Cottage Hospital is one of the leading hospitals in Contra Costa County, and Miss Driscoll stands high in the esteem of the physicians of Richmond, as well as of her many friends, who know her as a woman of keen perception, humanitarian instincts and warm sympathy. The hospital is located at Ninth Street and Barrett Avenue, Richmond. Miss Driscoll takes a live interest in civic matters relating to the progress of Richmond, and supports all projects of merit that are brought to her notice. She was reared in the Catholic faith.

HERBERT E. SULLIVAN.—A loyal native son of the Golden State is found in Herbert E. Sullivan, contractor and builder now living in El Cerrito. He was born on Wild Cat Creek, Contra Costa County, on September 3, 1873, the son of Eugene Owen Sullivan, a native of County Cork, Ireland, born in 1833. He came to America when a lad of seventeen and for a time lived and worked in Somerset County, N. J.; from there he went to Australia and engaged in farming. He was married in Australia to Mary Ellen Dowd, a native of County Kerry, Ireland, and soon thereafter they started for California where Mr. Sullivan had a brother, Patrick, living on Wild Cat Creek. Upon his arrival here he was in partnership with his brother for a year, then leased the Hurstel ranch, near what is now Orinda, and as he prospered he bought the ranch adjoining from W. W. Cameron and carried on ranching with considerable success until he retired to Oakland, where he spent the remainder of his days, dying on October 20, 1921, aged eighty-eight years. He was a man who showed his public spirit in all things and with others helped to build the first school house near his ranch and there educated his children. He served as a school trustee for many years. Mrs. Sullivan, now aged eighty-six, is making her home in Oakland and is hale and hearty and surrounded by her children, grandchildren and many warm friends. Their children are as follows: Frederick, who was born under the British flag while they were en route to California, died at the age of seventeen. Herbert E., the subject of this sketch. John L., now of Berkeley, is engaged in the building business; he is married and has two children, Robert and John L., Jr. Elizabeth married D. S. Barack and had one son Dion, and a daughter Aloha, before she died. Isabella Geerdts Petersen lives in Oakland; she had two children, Albert and Edgar Geerdts, by her first hubsand. James E. still owns the 250 acres at Orinda; he is married and has a son Bert and a daughter Kathleen and lives in Oakland where he is a builder.

Herbert E. left home when he was about twenty years old and went to San Francisco and learned the trade of boilermaker at the Risdon Iron Works, the Dundan Iron Works and the United Engine Works, becoming proficient at the trade. His brother, John L., had spent some time in Los Angeles at the carpenter's trade, but in 1905 came north and he and our subject joined forces and began building houses. Herbert E. picked up the carpenter trade quickly and for a time they carried on contracting and building under the name of Sullivan Brothers. At one time James was associated with them. In 1907 Herbert E. moved to Oakland and carried on business until 1914, when he moved to the Stege district in Contra Costa County. From 1911 until 1924 he carried on contracting under the name of H. E. Sullivan, but at that time he enlarged his scope of business and does business under the name of the Sullivan Building Company. He has erected some seventy-five homes in Richmond and El Cerrito. He was active in the incorporation of El Cerrito in 1917. As a young man while working on the home ranch he was engaged in baling hay and worked all over the district that now is embraced in El Cerrito and Richmond before either city was started.

In 1909 Mr. Sullivan was united in marriage with Buelah May Martin, born in Wichita, Kans., and they have two children: Bryon, attending the Richmond High School, and Herbert, in the El Cerrito Grammar School. Mr. Sullivan registers as a Democrat, but in all local matters supports the men and measures he thinks best suited to the welfare of the people and community. He favors good roads and good streets, as well as good schools, for he realizes that to the latter is due the education of the men and women of the future. He believes in preserving the old landmarks in California as well as its history and has a host of warm friends in Contra Costa and Alameda Counties, who esteem him for his worth as a citizen.

ERNEST FLORES.—A well-known and prominent architect of Richmond, Ernest Flores was born in San Francisco, on November 8, 1884. His parents were Daniel and Magdalena Flores, the father born in Chile and the mother in Los Angeles. An only child, our subject attended the grade and polytechnic schools in San Francisco and took a special course in the John Hopkins School of Fine Arts, now known as the California School of Fine Arts, in his native city. He studied architecture under Shea and Shea, who are the architects for the new St. Mary's College in Oakland. He was with this firm four years and then was with L. B. Sutton three years. Next he went to Sacramento and was with R. A. Harold for two years, and afterwards he spent five years in San Diego with T. C. Kistner. Coming to Richmond, he was with J. T. Narbett about five years, and then spent two years with John Reid, Jr., city architect of San Francisco.

In May, 1925, Mr. Flores came back to Richmond and engaged in business for himself. He feels that this city offers great inducements for men of worth and ability and is satisfied with the growth of his business. He is erecting a building of his own at 810-814 Chanslor Avenue. He has been connected with some important structures in the various places where he has been employed, among them the State Capital at Sacramento, and the Roosevelt Junior High School, City Hall and city buildings in Richmond. Mr. Flores has specialized in school architecture, and has served on some very important committees

Mr. Flores married Miss Edna Davies, of Richmond, on July 10, 1922, and they have a daughter, Barbara, aged three years, and an infant son, David Ernest. Mrs. Flores has a sister, Mrs. Hazel Yarnell, of El Cerrito. Mr. Flores is fond of landscape drawing, indulges in swimming and golf, and enjoys camping for a rest. He is highly esteemed by all who know him and has a bright future before him in his profession.

STEVE J. PONGRACE.—An intelligent, energetic and farseeing young man, who has worked his way to the front in Martinez business circles, Steve J. Pongrace is now proprietor of the People's Ice and Fuel Company of that city, making prompt deliveries of these great necessities of life. Born in Bohemia, on April 8, 1893, he is the son of John and Anna Pongrace, and came to the United States in 1910. He received his education in the public schools of Martinez, and also attended a private school there. His father's death occurred in Bohemia, but his mother came to this country and located in Pennsylvania.

Young Steve first began to work for C. Borghesani, in the ice and soda-water business, and gradually acquired the business which he now owns and which he has built up to a thriving establishment. During the World War he served at Camp Fort McDonald and was honorably discharged at the Presidio, November 18, 1918. His marriage, occurring May 19, 1917, united him with Miss Frances Borghesani, daughter of C. Borghesani, and three children have been born to them; Frances, Pauline, and Anita.

Mr. Pongrace realizes the advantages to be obtained in his adopted country, and became a citizen in Judge McKenzie's court at Martinez a year before the World War. He is a Republican in political belief, and fraternally belongs to the Loyal Order of Moose, the Woodmen, and the Y. M. I., all in Martinez.

EARL D. McCADDAM.—To be recognized as a self-made man is an honor that Earl D. McCaddam, owner of the Antioch Sand Company, is justly proud. He is the owner of thirteen acres of sand hills near Antioch, which extend back to the water front on the river, and from which an excellent quality of sand, especially adapted for making a high grade of asphalt concrete for street paving, is secured. This sand is used for street paving in Richmond, Oakland, San Francisco and other cities. The Santa Fe Railway has constructed a spur track into the sand pits which facilitates the shipping to all points; the annual amount shipped by Mr. McCaddam amounts to about 800 cars. The excavating and loading machinery are operated by electric power. Mr. McCaddam is an excellent business manager and personally superintends the loading of the cars. With his keen foresight he can visualize the appearance of his thirteen acres after the sand has been removed, which he estimates will be about fifteen years, at that time he believes he will possess a valuable site for a manufacturing plant, located on the water front of the San Joaquin River. The Antioch Sand Company maintains offices in the Lowe Building in San Francisco.

Earl D. McCaddam was born at Roswell, Miner County, S. Dak. on August 22, 1884, the son of John and Ellen (Bates) McCaddam, both natives of Scotland, who were married in Iowa. Earl D., their only child, was reared in South Dakota until he was fourteen years of age, when he started out to make his own way in the world. His various employments and experiences, if put into print, would read like a fairy tale. In 1906, two weeks after the great fire and earthquake in California, he came to the Golden State and was engaged by the Peninsular Teaming Company, at 62 Duboce Avenue, San Francisco, where he became foreman. The company failed in business and Mr. McCaddam was appointed assistant receiver for the company; but it was extricated from its financial difficulties largely through the keen business ability of Mr. McCaddam. Afterwards he began business for himself by accepting small contracts for grading, using horses and mules. He was successful in his contracts for macadamizing streets, and by living economically and saving his money, in time he had sufficient capital to purchase caterpillar tractors of the best well-known makes, which he rented to contractors. By industrious efforts, wise and judicious management of his financial affairs, he has succeeded in building up a splendid business. He possesses those sterling traits of character, honesty, integrity, and industry, which he inherited from his Scotch ancestors, and is the type of business man whose presence is helpful to the welfare of any community. He resides at 579 Haight Street, San Francisco.

DOMINICK CAMPAGLIA.—With the energy and resourcefulness characteristic of the race from which he springs, Dominick Campaglia has hewn his way to a prominent place in the business life of Martinez, eliciting approval as the successful proprietor of the Palm Garden Grill on Ferry Street. For many years Mr. Campaglia was the chef in the Palm Garden Grill, and during that time made that restaurant famous for its French and Italian meals. Later he established a grill at the corner of Main and Court Streets, which was known as Dominick's Place; still later he owned the Court House Cafe, which he sold in October, 1924, and immediately leased the Marconi Hotel which he remodeled and improved at considerable cost. He bought the Palm Garden Grill in August, 1926, which he now conducts.

Dominick Campaglia was born in the province of Vincenza, Italy, and grew up and received his education in that city, where his father, Giuseppi Campaglia was a merchant and innkeeper from young manhood to the day of his death; he was an honored citizen and prominent politically, serving as a member of the board of trustees of Vincenza; he married Miss Angela Todeschini and they were the parents of eight children, of whom our subject is the eldest. The father passed away aged fifty-six years. The mother of this family still runs the place established by her husband so many years ago.

Dominick Campaglia assisted his father in business until he was nineteen years old, when he entered the Italian army serving the required term of three years. Returning to his home in Vincenza he began preparations to come to America. On December 28, 1909, he sailed from Havre, France, landing in New York on January 6, 1910. His first job was as assistant chef in the Nelson Hotel at Rockford, Ill., where he remained for nine months; then going to Omaha, Nebr., he became chef for the Country Club Hotel; later was chef in Hotel Cafe, in Omaha, and still later chef at the Chesapeake Restaurant in Omaha. From Omaha he removed to San Francisco, where he was employed by the Southern Pacific Railroad Company for six months; then for a time he was chef at the Palace Hotel in San Francisco; from there he went to Santa Rosa. He located in Martinez in 1918, where from the first he has been gratifyingly successful in his calling.

At Santa Rosa, Cal., Mr. Campaglia was married to Miss Anna Rux, one of California's native daughters, born in Sonoma County, and they had one son, Albert; he was married to his present wife June 17, 1926. Mr. Campaglia is affiliated with the Woodman of the World and B. P. O. Elks of Martinez.

HENRY H. GOODFELLOW.—An adventurous and eventful career has characterized the life of Henry H. Goodfellow, now a resident of Richmond, Cal., after having ventured far in many lands. He is a veteran of the Spanish-American War, and during the campaign in which he took part in the Philippine Islands he gave tangible proof of his loyalty to the country of his adoption.

Mr. Goodfellow was born in England on July 27, 1878, the son of William and Elizabeth (Wilson) Goodfellow, both natives of England. His father was a butcher, and his mother died while he was an infant. They were the parents of four children, three boys and a girl, Elizabeth, who resides in Troy, New York. One of the boys, George, lives in Vermont. At the age of ten young Henry was sent by the Orphan's Home to Prince Edward Island, where he was educated in the grammar school. His first employment was on a farm. At the age of seventeen he left Prince Edward Island and settled at Barton, Vt., where he remained for two years. At the call for volunteers at the outbreak of the Spanish-American War he enlisted for the Philippine expedition, being a member of the 43rd U. S. Volunteers and going to Burlington, Vt., to mobilize. From there he was sent to New York and then to the Philippines via the Suez Canal. His first location was back of Manila, where he engaged in a skirmish. From there his regiment proceeded to the Island of Luzon, where it took part in several engagements, and then to the Island of Laitite. Here, after another engagement Mr. Goodfellow was discharged from service. For a time he engaged in the restaurant business in Manila and also worked for the government in the fire department, being in the Philippines about six years all together.

After leaving the Islands he came to California and was connected with the Redwood Lumber Company in Mendocino County for a time. In 1905 he came to Richmond and for sixteen years was an employee of the Standard Oil Company. For two years he was on a ranch in San Pablo, and for the past three years he has been employed by the Certainteed Company as a stillman.

On September 1, 1917, Mr. Goodfellow married Mrs. Celina Glaser of Richmond, the daughter of Louis and Chotilda Leloy, both natives of France. By her former marriage Mrs. Goodfellow has one son, George

Glaser, now a student in the Richmond High School. Mr. Goodfellow is a member of the Spanish War Veterans. His chief recreations are gardening and camping. He owns a nice home at 203 South Thirteenth Street, Richmond, and other property.

CAESAR BORGHESANI.—A highly intelligent and prosperous business man of Martinez is found in Caesar Borghesani, who owns and operates a soda works near his residence on F Street; in this same locality he has fourteen acres of rich land, and also owns considerable valuable real estate in Martinez. Mr. Borghesani is well-known in this vicinity and is held in high esteem as a man of worth and integrity. He was born in the Province of Bologna, Italy, on December 26, 1867, and at the age of twenty-four came to the United States and settled first at Springfield, Mass., where he was employed as animal keeper at Forest Park.

From Springfield, Mass., Mr. Borghesani came to San Francisco and was engaged as an engineer for the Fontana Company. Thirty years ago he located in Martinez, where he has continuously lived ever since. Mr. Borghesani is fraternally affiliated with the Dante Society, the Knights of Pythias, Loyal Order of Moose, Odd Fellows, I. D. E. S., and Eagles all of Martinez. In politics he is a Republican.

Mr. Borghesani's first marriage was in Italy and by this union there were two children. Everisto is now living with his father in Martinez. Frances, or Fannie as she is familiarly known, is now the wife of S. J. Pongrace, one of the proprietors of the people's Ice Company in Martinez. Mr. Borghesani was married the second time, in Martinez, to Miss Mary Mathos, and of this union there are three children living; Louis, Henry and Jennie. Martin died at Mare Island at the age of eighteen while serving in the marines. Mrs. Borghesani passed away at the family home in Martinez several years ago.

K. LOUIS DOUGHERTY.—The enterprising and efficient manager of the Concord Branch of the Tilden Lumber Company, K. Louis Dougherty is a native of Arizona, where he was born on October 3, 1899, the son of Frank and Esther Dougherty; the father being a school teacher in Arizona. When Louis was quite young the family moved to Texas, and from the Lone Star State, where they resided for nine years, they migrated to California, locating for a while at Los Angeles, but later settling at Oakland. By the time the family located at Oakland Louis was ready to enter the high school. Being a very ambitious boy he found employment at various occupations while not in school, which aided him financially to complete his education. He worked at one time in a lumber camp and at another time for the American Express Company; also at dredging. After leaving high school Mr. Dougherty attended Gallagher and Morris Business College at Oakland, and in that city was employed by the Sunset Lumber Company as an estimater and checker, from this position he was advanced to the auditing department;

30

later he accepted a position as salesman, but only followed it six months when he resigned to enter the automobile business. Mr. Dougherty's experience in the lumber business gained by his energetic efforts and progressive business methods made it possible for him to secure his present position as manager of the Concord yard of the Tilden Lumber Company, to which place he was appointed in April, 1926. His many friends predict for him a prosperous business career and feel assured that his intelligent application of wise business methods, loyalty to his employer's best interests at all times, will eventually lead him to a larger and more responsible position with the company.

In June, 1922, K. Louis Dougherty was united in marriage with Estella Mae Harvey, of Oakland, daughter of Roy and Susie A. Harvey, and this union has been blessed with one child, James Louis Dougherty. During his school days Mr. Dougherty was very fond of athletics and was considered a star in football and on track teams.

SOREN PEDERSEN SKOW.—A prominent dairyman, cattle raiser and rancher on San Pablo Creek, Contra Costa County, is found in the public-spirited citizen, Soren Pedersen Skow. He was born in Denmark on February 22, 1869, the son of Hans C. and Christina Skow, both natives of Denmark, who have spent their entire lives in that country. Soren P. attended the Danish schools until he was fourteen and then was confirmed. He at once decided he would go to sea and, after serving an apprenticeship, sailed as a sailor before the mast until he came around Cape Horn to California in 1887 and landed in San Francisco. He concluded he could better his condition as a landsman and therefore left the sea and secured work with the street car campany, driving on the horse car lines then in that city; he also did some carpenter work. In 1889 he came to San Pablo Creek, leased land and began raising cattle and horses. Success crowned his efforts from the start and he gradually enlarged his scope of operations until he now has 900 acres of land under his control. He established the Richmond Farm Creamery and has about 150 head of dairy cattle. During the hoof and mouth disease he lost 367 head of good stock, but nothing daunted, he once more embarked in the business and has since built up a fine herd. He runs three wagons, and with two hired men and his own boys, carries on a lucrative business. He is an intelligent and influential citizen and believes in lending a helping hand to those less fortunate than himself. He has served as a school trustee for years. Mr. Skow is a naturalized American citizen, upholding the laws of his country to the best of his ability and doing what he can to make his community a better place in which to live and prosper.

Mr. Skow was married on January 9, 1892, to Miss Anna Rasmussen, who was born in Denmark, the daughter of Mads and Maren (Monk) Rasmussen, both born and reared in Denmark. They came out to Dakota Territory and farmed, and there her father passed away several years ago. Her mother survived until 1925, when she died in Viborg, Turner County, S. Dak. The Rasmussen family had come to

California and were living in Oakland at the time of their daughter's marriage. Mr. and Mrs. Skow had six children: Harold C., living near his father; Eda, Mrs. George Lehmkule, keeping house for her father; Wilbur, also ranching near by; Lester, at home; Ellis, also at home; and Erma, a graduate from the high school and at home. In 1921 Mr. Skow moved from his former location to his present ranch and has an up-to-date dairy barn with all modern equipment. He belongs to all the branches in Odd Fellowship, and is a member of the Odd Fellows' Hall Association in Richmond. His sons and daughters all are members of the various branches of the Odd Fellows. Mrs. Skow passed away on August 22, 1923, leaving her family and friends to mourn her loss. Mr. Skow is an ardent baseball enthusiast and in that sport finds his recreation.

CHARLES ROBERT BLAKE, M. D.—A native son of California who has made good in his chosen profession is Charles Robert Blake, of Richmond. He was born in Visalia, Tulare County, on September 9, 1869, and moved to San Francisco when four years of age and attended the public schools there as he was growing up. His greatest ambition was to follow in the footsteps of his father and be a physician, and in later years his studies were directed along these lines. He entered the Medical Department of the University of California and later graduated with the degree of M. D. His first practice was as resident physician of the County Hospital in San Francisco. He afterwards spent seven years in Honolulu as government physician and practiced with success. In 1902 he came to Contra Costa County at a time when the city now known as Richmond was but a veritable infant. But in the future of the little city he manifested great faith and confidence for its progress and cast in his lot with this community, and with the passing of each year has endeared himself to the people by his sterling worth as a citizen and his unusual ability as a physician and surgeon; a position gained through his profound knowledge of his profession. His interest in the city has always been shown by his active participation in its affairs; the object of which was the betterment of every condition that exists in a thriving city. He has served as county and city health officer for years, being one of the best known health officers of California. He believes that Richmond of today is the most promising city of the Pacific Coast for home and industry. Dr. Blake belongs to the County Medical Society; the State and American Medical Associations, and keeps abreast of the times in medical science. He took post graduate courses in eye, ear, nose and throat diseases at the San Francisco Polyclinic.

In 1898 Dr. Blake was married to Miss Lillian M. Hoogs of Oakland. They have a son, Herbert, born December 30, 1900. The doctor is a member of the Richmond Elks, Odd Fellows, Eagles, and other fraternities. He is a Knight Templar Mason and a Shriner. He belongs to the Lions Club of Richmond and the University of California Club. During the World War Dr. Blake held the rank of first lieutenant and served on the examining board. He was commissioned for service on November 11, 1918, and ordered to Rockwell Field for duty, but owing to the armistice being declared the same day, his orders were countermanded. Politically Dr. Blake is a Republican. He maintains his home on Cutting Boulevard and his offices are at 629 Macdonald Avenue, Richmond.

JOHN HOWARD GREENE.—One of the rising and successful young business men of Martinez, who has taken advantage of the opportunities he found awaiting him on his arrival in the West, is J. Howard Greene, proprietor of the Martinez Garage. He was born in Leesburg, Loudoun County, Va., on January 2, 1890, and was reared on the home farm. At the age of seventeen he went to Wilkesbarre, Pa., and there learned the trade of the automobile mechanic with the Matthewson Motor Company. From there he went to different cities in the East and Canada, and also down South to Tennessee, working at his trade.

In 1914 the young traveler decided to come West, primarily to attend the San Francisco Exposition. That same year he located in Martinez and found work in the W. J. Johnson Garage; and later he became manager of the service department for the Chandler Automobile Company, of San Francisco. He is now proprietor of the Martinez Garage on Ferry Street, Martinez. He has been agent for the Chandler, Cleveland and Star cars, and in 1923 he sold 100 Star cars, more than half the number sold by all the dealers of the entire county of Contra Costa. All this has not been accomplished without hard and steady work, combined with good business management. Mr. Greene arrived in the city with just "four bits" in his pocket, and had to rely entirely upon his own resources, which consisted of a strong right arm and willingness to use it, coupled with keen foresight and business acumen.

In 1923 Mr. Greene married Miss Lillian George, born in Wisconsin, but a resident of Martinez at the time of her marriage. In 1926 he completed a residence at Pine and Jones Streets, and he is the owner of other valuable real estate in Martinez.

JOSEPH PIZIO.—The proprietor of the Piedmont Hotel in Antioch, Joseph Pizio, was born in Italy on September 15, 1884. As a lad he attended the local schools, but at an early age he went to work in a glass factory in Torino. Then, when he was old enough, he entered the Italian Army and soldiered for two years, returning to the glass factory after his discharge and continuing there until his marriage.

The wedding that united the lives of Joseph Pizio and Miss Rosa Chiesa was celebrated in September, 1908, at Torino. In 1909 they came to the United States and to California, and after arriving here Mr. Pizio worked in the brickyards at Tesla until 1911, when he settled in Antioch and engaged in the hotel business at the corner of J and Second Streets. Of the union of Mr. and Mrs. Pizio three children have been born: Catherine, Carlo and Edith. Fraternally, Mr. Pizio is a member of the Pittsburg Lodge of Odd Fellows, and the Eagles of Antioch, and the treasurer of Columbus Lodge of the Sons of Italy, which he helped to organize and which now has 150 members. He is highly esteemed by a large circle of friends in this part of the county and he and his wife are doing a fine business at their hotel.

JOHN F. GALVIN.—John F. Galvin, publisher of the Richmond Daily Independent, is a native of Minnesota, where he was born in 1882. His boyhood was spent in Oregon, and there he attended the Grant's Pass and Portland high schools, later completing his education at St. Mary's College, Oakland. He had his first newspaper experience at Grant's Pass, where he established and published a weekly newspaper when he was fourteen years of age. He left St. Mary's College in 1901 and went to work for the San Francisco Examiner. There he learned the rudiments of the publishing business. He later owned or managed newspapers at Vallejo, Martinez, Suisun, Marysville, Oroville, Fresno, Modesto and Bakersfield. He came to Richmond in 1912 as editor and part owner of the Daily Independent. Two years later he purchased the controlling interest in the Independent Publishing Company.

Mr. Galvin has taken an active interest in politics, and has served as a member of the State Civil Service Commission, as secretary of the California Highway Commission, and as treasurer of the Mendocino State Hospital. In 1908 he married Miss Jewel Harris in Vallejo.

CHARLES FACCINI.—A native of Contra Costa County, Charles Faccini was born at Collinsville on July 14, 1878, the oldest of six living children of Henry and Camille Faccini. The parents were both born in Italy and when quite young emigrated to California and were married at Black Diamond, where Mr. Faccini was engaged as a fisherman. Later he moved to San Francisco, where he continued his work about the Bay. He died at the age of about fifty-six, and his good wife passed away when she was about forty-five, both in San Francisco.

Charles Faccini at the age of five accompanied his parents to San Francisco. He went to the public schools, and when a young lad began fishing; and he has continued in the fish business in one way and another up to the present time. While engaged in the fishing industry he also was in the employ of Wells Fargo Express Company as a deliveryman for five years. In 1914 he located in Oakland, and he is still employed there in the fish market at Ninth and Clay Streets.

On March 2, 1907, Mr. Faccini was united in marriage with Miss Mary Buzzotto, a native of San Francisco and a daughter of Frank and Nellie Buzzotto. Her father came direct from France to California and became well known as a fisherman, at which occupation he still continues. Her mother died at the age of thirty-nine years. There were five children in the Buzzotto family, and they are all living. Mr. and Mrs. Faccini have had three children: Leslie, who died at the age of sixteen years; and Achilles and Barbara Jane. Mr. Faccini has always been active in civic affairs in El Cerrito, whither he moved in 1920 and erected his home at 215 Fairmont Avenue. In 1925 he completed a modern stucco bungalow at 217 Fairmont Avenue, where he is now living. In 1922 he was elected a member of the Stege Sanitary Board, and served two years. He is a candidate for the same office in 1926. Fraternally, Mr. Faccini is a member of the Independent Order of Foresters at El Cerrito. Politically, he registers as a Republican. Both Mr. and Mrs. Faccini have many warm friends in this community, and they show their public spirit at all times for the good of the whole community.

W. H. BLOOMFIELD.—An experienced man in his particular line of business is W. H. Bloomfield, car loader for the celery growers of the Delta country, whose business stands second to none among the agricultural producers in Contra Costa and adjoining counties in the Delta District. The celery is transported to Antioch by means of four river barges, each with a capacity of eight carloads, and is then loaded from the barges into refrigerator cars and shipped to the principal cities of the United States and Canada. About 1300 carloads of celery are shipped each year over the Santa Fe Railroad. By reason of his responsible position, Mr. Bloomfield is accounted one of the leading men of Antioch. A brother, W. G. Bloomfield, attends to the unloading of the barges. The business runs from November until February.

W. H. Bloomfield was born in San Francisco on January 20, 1886. His father, W. J. Bloomfield, was also born in San Francisco, in 1862, and now resides at Antioch with his wife, Martha (Hammond) Bloomfield. W. H. Bloomfield obtained his education in the public schools, and also attended evening school, in his home city. In 1907 he came to Antioch, and has ever since made this his home town.

Mr. Bloomfield married Miss Nettie Peters, and they have two children, Nyla and William F. The family attend the Catholic Church.

LOUIS E. HART.—Recognized as one of the progressive bankers of Northern California as well as a public-spirited citizen of Contra Costa County, Louis E. Hart holds the responsible position of cashier and manager of the Crockett Branch of the Bank of Pinole.

The Bank of Pinole was established on October 25, 1905, at Pinole, by E. M. Downer and L. E. Hart, with a capital stock of $25,000. The board of directors and officers were: J. Bermingham, Jr., president; P. Tormey, vice-president; Louis E. Hart, secretary; and E. M. Downer, cashier, and these together with L. Kavanaugh, W. A. Ray, Henry Boysen and Mrs. Sara Bermingham made up the directorate. So well did this financial institution fit into the scheme of things in this part of Contra Costa County that it was found expedient to establish a branch at Crockett in 1908, and when this was done, Louis E. Hart was made the resident cashier and manager. In 1917 a second branch was established at Rodeo. In 1910 the capital stock was increased to $50,000. In 1925 the capital stock was $125,000, with a surplus of $70,000, and with undivided profits of $35,000. The deposits are more than $2,100,000, which shows the confidence of the people in this bank. The present board of directors are: E. M. Downer, president, L. E. Hart, J. P. Connors, S. S. MacKinlay, Dr. M. L. Fernandes, E. D. Armstrong, L. G. Metcalf, Dr. J. H. Adams, J. H. Martin, W. A. Davis and John A. Fraser.

The development of the Bank of Pinole has been substantial, helpful and rapid. In 1915 it erected its own building at Pinole, and in 1916 one at Crockett. The Bank of Pinole serves a territory extending from Giant to Port Costa. Their equipment is modern in every way and facilitates the handling of their large and growing business. The interests of the patrons of the Bank of Pinole and its branches are carefully looked after by the directors and officers, all of whom exert a strong influence in their respective localities. The influence for good of the institution is keenly felt in industrial circles, home building, and in the carrying-on of business along all safe and sane lines. The policy of the directors is a conservative one and in every way they safeguard the interests of all with whom they have business dealings. The Bank of Pinole is recognized as one of the sound and leading banking institutions of Contra Costa County, due to the unceasing efforts of E. M. Downer, L. E. Hart and associates.

A résumé of the life of Louis E. Hart, known by his intimates as "Lou" Hart, is here given. He was born in San Francisco, on June 20, 1872, the son of Jesse B. and Sallie (Coleman) Hart, natives of Ohio and Louisiana, respectively. Jesse B. Hart came to California early in life and took up the practice of law in San Francisco, continuing thus engaged until he died in 1888. Four years later, in 1892, his widow passed away. They were parents of three children.

Lou Hart attended the public schools in San Francisco and his first venture in business was in a land brokerage establishment. In 1900 he became connected with the California Powder Works, as a clerk, and there remained until the organization of the Bank of Pinole, in which he took a leading and active part. When the Crockett Branch was established he became cashier and manager, a position he has since held. During his residence in this section he has been closely allied with every progressive movement in Crockett and western Contra Costa County. He is a stockholder in the East Richmond Land Company; he served as city clerk of Hercules; he is a Mason and an Elk, and has made a large circle of close friends in this section.

Mr. Hart has been twice married. His first union was in 1898, when he married Miss Augusta Ayres, of Petaluma, Sonoma County. She died in 1913, and on September 5, 1915, he married Miss Minnie DeKay, who was born in Rock Island, Ill., but who was a resident of San Francisco at the time of their marriage. Mr. and Mrs. Hart are highly esteemed by all who know them and both take an active part in the civic development of Crockett and vicinity. Mr. Hart is a member of the Crockett-Valona Business Men's Association.

FRANK H. ROBERTS.—The different cities of Contra Costa County are unusually fortunate in the class of men that have been attracted here to engage in business or to fill positions with the various oil companies that figure so largely in the wealth and enterprise of the county. Among these may be mentioned Frank H. Roberts, mayor of Martinez, and head office manager and refinery auditor for the Shell Oil Company at its refinery, one mile east of Martinez. Born at Dodgeville, Wis., on September 21, 1886, he is the son of H. J. Roberts, a substantial farmer and stockman of Iowa County, that State; and there he was reared. Finishing high school at the age of nineteen, he left home to make his own way in the world. Going to the great northern country, he made good in the United States Reclamation Service, beginning as a rodman and working in North Dakota and Montana. Thence he came to California in 1907, and passing the rigid civil service examinations, was engaged in the United States Navy Yard at Mare Island. He next became connected with one of the contractors on the Northwestern Pacific Railway; and on January 1, 1915, he came to Martinez.

Soon after his arrival, he entered the Shell Refinery office as a clerk; and by rapid promotions he has reached his present responsible position. He has twice been elected to the Martinez city board of trustees and is now serving his second term and sixth year in that office, the only Shell Company man on the board. He was elected mayor in January, 1926.

The marriage of Mr. Roberts, at Richmond, united him with Miss Fay Gott, daughter of J. T. Gott, of Downieville, Cal. Both Mr. and Mrs. Roberts take an active part in the social and civic life of Martinez. Mr. Roberts finds his recreation on the links of the Martinez Golf Club, of which he is a member.

REV. FR. JOSEPH PORTA.—To Reverend Joseph Porta, pastor of St. Paul's Catholic Church at San Pablo, the members of that parish owe much for the good that he has brought into their lives. It has been possible for him to beautify the church, rectory and grounds of the church property, to make them the most inviting of any to be found in Contra Costa County. Born at Tarragona, Spain, on April 6, 1875, Joseph Porta had the best educational advantages possible; he prepared for the priesthood and received his degree of Doctor of Divinity in the university in his native city. He was ordained to the priesthood there in 1898, and for the following nine years served as a priest in Spain, two years in his native town. At the call of Archbishop Riordan, he came to California and for a year was stationed in Tomales, Marin County, to master the Italian language; then he was sent to Hayward to do likewise with the Portuguese—all too short a time in either place. These steps were preparing him for his greatest work, that of pastor of St. Paul's Church in San Pablo. This property was in a very much run-down condition and the buildings and grounds badly neglected. Still unfamiliar with the language of the majority of his followers, Father Porta set to work under every disadvantage to accomplish something, he knew not what. Working with pick and shovel in his own hands to show what he wanted done, he began to put the grounds in shape, trimming trees and setting out more trees and shrubbery, and planting flowers, until today the grounds about the church and other buildings show the work of a master's hand. He also remodeled the interior of the church, at a cost of $5000, asking no money until the work was completed in order that his people would have visible evidence of what he had done. Then he remodeled the parish house with the same end in view; and later the clubhouse adjoining. During this same time he had charge of the work of building the church at Rodeo; and remodeling the one at Pinole, thus it will be seen that his has been a busy life during the fourteen years he has been here in Contra Costa County.

A little history of the parish will be told here. San Pablo was a mission to St. Mary's Church of Oakland and was looked after by Father King, who was the first pastor. It was in 1864 that the church was built, the cemetery established and the priests' house erected. The latter was burned in 1880, together with all the church records. The Parish was established by Bishop Alemany, and Father Gualco was installed as priest. After Father Gualco came Fathers Valentini, A. De-Campos, P. Commins, R. DeCaroles, J. G. Conlon, Thomas McNabo, J. J. Pimentel, Edward Nollen and Joseph Porta. At the time of the earthquake, in 1906, the church was badly damaged and it was Father Nollen who made the repairs on the exterior as seen today. What Father Porta has done has already been mentioned.

In the early days the parish took in all the territory from Oakland to Port Costa but, as the population increased, various parishes were cut off and priests established in them. In 1911, when Father Porta took charge the parish included San Pablo, Pinole and Rodeo. He set about beautifying the building and grounds at Pinole and in 1918 he built the Rodeo church, the land being donated by Patrick Tormey, and the name of St. Patrick given to the church in his honor. This was the first church built in the diocese without incurring indebtedness to be paid off at a later period. In 1923 the Pinole church was included in the Rodeo parish, leaving San Pablo by itself, which included Giant, East Richmond, San Pablo Creek, Grand Canyon and North Richmond. There are now 417 families in the parish and there is not a dollar of indebtedness.

When the San Pablo parish was organized Juan B. Alvarado donated the two acres of ground for the church and cemetery and other buildings. In 1914 Father Porta celebrated the golden jubilee of the establishment of the church and some 1500 people were present. Since taking charge over $35,000 has been spent on improvements by Father Porta. The Sunday School has over 200 children and in this he is assisted by Sisters of the Holy Family of Piedmont. There are athletic exercises arranged for the boys and girls. Where now stands the church hall, there stood the first parish school in the diocese. Plans are being formulated for an expenditure in the next five years of some $150,000, for a new and modern church and other improvements, to make St. Paul's parish an equal of any in this section of California. It is the desire of Father Porta to be granted to live long enough to see his dream fulfilled. He believes in progressing with the times and is enthusiastic over the possibilities of this section of the State.

MRS. CAROLINE PIODA GIUMINI.—That women are holding their own in commercial circles is amply demonstrated in the success achieved by Mrs. Caroline Pioda Giumini, of Valona, who not only is successful in business, but takes an especial interest in assisting foreigners who locate in this community to become good American citizens. She was born in Locarno, Canton Ticino, Switzerland, in 1872. Her father was James Pioda and her mother Innocentina (Tappa) Pioda. The Piodas represent a very prominent family in Switzerland, and her father held a government position nearly all his active life, at one time being judge of the court. One of his brothers was chief postmaster, or postmaster general, of that republic. Mrs. Giumini enjoys the distinction of being related to Giovanni Battista Pioda, who for a number of years was Minister from Switzerland to Washington, D. C., and she called upon him twice when he was visiting in San Francisco and dined with him.

Mrs. Giumini is a well educated woman, having graduated from the University of Lasone, and comes from a family of well-trained people. She came to America on October 31, 1890; and on October 22, 1892, she was married to S. Giumini, at the San Luis Obispo Mission. They began life together on a ranch of 3000 acres in San Luis Obispo County near San Luis Obispo, and for seven years carried on a successful dairy business. At this time Mrs. Giumini took a trip back to visit her family in Switzerland; meantime her father had died. Upon her return to California she began a mercantile business on a small scale and with modest means in Valona. This was on May 10, 1901, since which time her establishment has grown in prestige and size until she has found it necessary to take her son and only child, Olindo J., into partnership. He is rapidly coming to the front and is recognized as a rising young business man and banker. When he became a partner the firm became Mrs. S. Giumini and Son; their establishment is one of the leading ones in the community. Mrs. Giumini has made a name for herself among the prominent women of this locality and takes an active and intelligent interest in civic affairs. The firm belongs to the Crockett-Valona Business Men's Association. She owns her own home and other realty in this county. She is active in Catholic Church circles, especially among the poor foreign element in the church. She has a sister living in Oakland, formerly connected with the schools; also an older sister in Locarno, where friends of Mrs. Giumini have visited and received a hearty welcome at Villa Trinita.

Mrs. Giumini returned to Valona on November 8, 1926, after an extended trip to Europe, which included a visit to her girlhood home. She left Valona on May 2, and returned much refreshed in body and spririt. She reports a very pleasant visit and enjoys the distinction of having been a guest of Prince and Princess Borromeo, at Isola Bella, Lago Maggiore, Italy, on October 15 and 16, as the specially invited guest of the Princess, who received Mrs. Giumini in the Throne-room of the Prince's palace. She found the Prince and Princess greatly interested in America and thoroughly democratic in their manner. She also had the pleasure of attending the anniversary session of the Peace Conference at Locarno. The pleasant recollections of the many delightful incidents of her visit will linger with her until her dying day.

HARRY EUGENE AINE, JR.—A very efficient construction engineer employed by the Standard Oil Company at the Richmond refinery is Harry Eugene Aine, Jr., whose home is located at No. 341 Dimm Street in the Mira Vista Section. He is a son of Harry Eugene Aine, Sr., of French descent and a carpenter and builder of Richmond, who is now deceased. The father was born on the high sea, while the vessel in which his parents were coming to the Pacific Coast was rounding Cape Horn. The family settled at Virginia City, Nev., where Harry's grandfather and father were both engaged in mining for a time, and where the grandfather owned considerable valuable property. In 1871 the father went back to Chicago to help in rebuilding that city after the great fire of that year, but he failed to make the right business connecions and turned his face westward again. He went to Omaha, Nebr., and there made connection with a railroad company and for some months was engaged in bridge building. In 1873 he brought his family to Berkeley, Cal., where his wife and children remained and where the latter were reared and educated. Mrs. Aine was in maidenhood Miss Elizabeth Geissberger, and her parents came from New York to California in an early day and were farmers on the San Pablo grant. The old Geissberger homestead is still standing at San Pablo.

Harry Eugene Aine, Jr., was born at Omaha, Neb., on May 13, 1872, and was educated in the Berkeley schools, his parents coming to this State when he was only about eighteen months old. At the age of fourteen he began working at the carpenter's trade with his father. Three years later he entered the employ of the Giant Powder Works, and when he was twenty-one he was a foreman in that plant and remained there several years. His next position was with the Southern Pacific Railroad, in their shops, in Sacramento and he remained there until 1901, when he came to Richmond and entered the employ of the Standard Oil Company as a carpenter at the beginning of the construction of their great plant in this city. Soon he was promoted to be foreman, and later was placed on general construction work. The workmen labored under great difficulties, especially in wet weather, as there was nothing but heavy adobe mud in the flat lands. Standard Avenue in Point Richmond had to be paved before material for the plant could be landed where it was to be used. Often the men had to be pulled out of the mud, losing their rubber boots in the operation. One entire hill had to be scraped into the bay in the plant construction. At one time Mr. Aine had two-thirds of the workmen about the plant under his supervision. In 1914 he was assigned to the engineering department and is now assistant engineer, also acting in an advisory capacity about the plant. He has had much to do with perfecting the salt water plant, the largest of its kind in the world. In 1908 he was head of construction during the building of the tanker Benicia, which is still doing duty on the bay. Take it all in all he has been a valuable man in building up the greatest of oil refineries in the world.

In 1907 Mr. Aine was united in marriage with Miss Nettie Dawson. By a former marriage he has a son, Everett Eugene, who was educated in the schools of Richmond and graduated from the University of Nevada, at Reno, and who is now employed at the El Segundo refinery in Southern California. Mr. Aine is a member of the Richmond Elks and the Masonic lodge; he belongs to the Berkeley Country Club, was one of the organizers and is its president, and has served as chairman of the road committee. He also belongs to the Standard Oil Rod and Gun Club, which he helped organize in 1921, and ever since has served as president. When the first street car line was installed in Richmond Mr. Aine acted in an advisory capacity in the construction of the road and purchasing its equipment. Being a competent construction engineer his advice is often sought on construction problems; and he willingly gives of his time to help promote all worthy projects for the advancement of his home city. He is active in civic affairs and with his wife has a wide acquaintance in the bay region. He is a golf enthusiast and enjoys camping in the mountains. He and his wife are lovers of the esthetic and he spends much leisure time in beautifying their home place.

WILLIAM H. GEORGE.—A native son of California who has made a name and place for himself in the business world of the State is W. H. George, secretary of the Cowell Portland Cement Company, one of the principal industries of Contra Costa County that has helped to spread the name and fame of this section of the State. He was born in San Francisco on July 11, 1872, a son of Henry C. and Eliza (Baker) George, pioneers of the State.

William H. George attended the public schools of San Francisco, graduating from the grammar school in 1886. Immediately upon leaving the school room he went to work for the Henry Cowell Lime and Cement Company and has remained with this company ever since, working his way through the various departments of their business until he reached his present position. He has been so closely associated with the business that he has become an integral part of it and has helped to develop the plant to its present magnitude. He is also secretary of the Henry Cowell Lime and Cement Company; secretary and manager of the Bay Point and Clayton Railroad Company; and president of the Builders' Exchange of San Francisco. The company he represents maintain their business offices at No. 2 Market Street, San Francisco. Mr. George is actively interested in promulgating the principles of the "Open

Shop," which means the right of a man to work as he sees fit and to maintain harmony in industrial circles. His position of president of the Builders' Exchange for the past five years shows his fitness for such an important position.

W. H. George was married in San Francisco on October 7, 1896, to Miss Lillie Isabel Daly, a daughter of John D. and Lillie Frances Daly, and they have a daughter, Isabelle Cowell George. Mr. George is a Republican in politics. Fraternally he is a Knight Templar Mason and a Shriner; he also belongs to the Woodmen of the World. He is active in club life and holds membership in the National Union, the Olympic, the Press and the San Francisco Commercial Clubs. In every movement for the upbuilding of his native State W. H. George has always shown his public spirit by co-operating with every project for the best interests of the people and the State.

THEO. WEISSICH.—The superintendent of the Pittsburg branch of the Western California Fish Company is Theo. Weissich, a native of San Francisco, where he was born on January 12, 1898. His father, William O. Weissich, Jr., was born at Live Oak, Sutter County, Cal., and was a son of William O. Weissich, Sr., a California pioneer of 1849, and Augusta, his wife. W. O. Weissich, Jr., is said to be the first American-born man to engage in the wholesale fish business in California; and he is now the president of the Western California Fish Company, the largest exclusively fish company in San Francisco, and is prominent in business circles in the bay cities. This fish company and packing concern has become the largest of its kind by purchase of the American Fish and Oyster Company and the California Fish Company at Pittsburg, and maintains plants in Monterey, Santa Cruz, San Francisco, Oakland, Point Reyes, Bodega Bay, Shelter Cove, Eureka, Trinidad, Crescent City and Pittsburg, and also at Smith River, Ore. They have their own brand, CAL-PAC, which is a guarantee of quality and has a high standing in commercial circles. They specialize in Zalon, which is smoked shad cured in Russian style; Bloaters; Barbecued Sable Fish, commercially known as Kippered Cod; and Smoked Salmon. The brands are well-known to the trade all over the country, and also in foreign climes.

Theo. Weissich attended the public schools in San Francisco and worked in and about the fish plant operated by his father, where he learned the details of the business from the bottom up and fitted himself for the responsible position he now holds, that of superintendent of the Pittsburg plant for this large fish concern. That he is looked upon as an able business man is attested to by his standing in business circles in Pittsburg. He is enterprising, and takes an active interest in matters pertaining to the development of city, county and State.

On May 25, 1919, Mr. Weissich was united in marriage with Miss Shirley Paulsen, of Santa Cruz. Mr. and Mrs. Weissich reside at No. 1092 Black Diamond Street, Pittsburg, and move in the best social circles of this fast-growing city.

ROY AVERY WATKINS.—Among the younger generation in California, as well as elsewhere, we find men who have demonstrated both tact and capacity for business and have met with gratifying success. Of this class we mention Roy Avery Watkins, who, since 1925 has held the responsible position of city manager of Pittsburg. This plan was adopted by the city in August, 1919, and R. M. Dorton was the first city manager. Mr. Dorton resigned in 1925, on account of his removal to Monterey, and Mr. Watkins was appointed to succeed him, and entered upon his duties on July 1, 1925. He has demonstrated his ability to hold such a position of trust and responsibility and the city has been greatly benefitted by his systematic and economical management.

Born in Eldora, Iowa, March 20, 1892, R. A. Watkins is the son of O. H. and Mattie Jane (Fitzgerald) Watkins, both of whom are now residing in Glendale, Cal. Mr. Watkins was reared and educated in Eldora, Iowa, until attaining the age of fourteen years, when he decided to make his own way in the world. He went to Clinton, Iowa, where he began serving an apprenticeship in a machine shop; he also attended night school, where he completed his high school course. We next find him in Milwaukee, Wis., where he continued his apprenticeship as a machinist and where, during his spare time, he completed a course in accounting at a business college in Milwaukee. Determined to equip himself thoroughly for his life work, he entered the Engineering College at Ames, Iowa, where he spent two profitable years. His first position was with the Waterloo Gas Engine Company, at Waterloo, Iowa; where he rose to be head foreman. A better position was offered him with the American Machine Products Company, at Marshalltown, Iowa, and in 1915 he was serving as general works manager for this company. When war was declared he answered the call by enlisting in the U. S. Navy in June, 1917, at Philadelphia. He became engineering officer on the U. S. Submarine L. 4, of which the late General Hancock was the commanding officer. Later Mr. Watkins was transferred to the Aviation Department of the Navy, with the rank of lieutenant, his especial work being that of director of the field service, engineering and purchasing. Supervising the purchases of the Naval Departments he traveled all over the United States, and during his term of service was stationed at New York City, Washington, D. C., and Pensacola, Fla. During his stay in Pensacola he was detailed to go across to France, but the signing of the armistice intervened. He was released from active service in 1919, and received his honorable discharge in 1923. In 1919 he accepted the position of general works manager for the Clarinda Lawn Mower Company, at Clarinda, Iowa, holding this position until November, 1920, when he removed to Sacramento, Cal., and there accepted the position as superintendent of equipment for the California State Highway Commission, which he filled until 1925, when he settled in Pittsburg.

At Marshalltown, Iowa, June 5, 1916, Mr. Watkins was married to Miss Helen Gundlach, who was born and reared in Marshalltown. They are the parents of one daughter, Geraldine Helen. Mrs. Watkins was for some time society editor on the Long Beach Press, and was advanced to the position of circulation manager. Mr. and Mrs. Watkins are active members of the Masonic fraternity; both belong to the Eastern Star in Sacramento; Mr. Watkins is a member of Nodaway (Iowa) Lodge No. 140, A. F. & A. M.; Long Beach Chapter, R. A. M., and the Knights Templars at Sacramento. He is a member of the American Society of Mechanical Engineers; he is also a member of the Lions Club of Sacramento. Mr. Watkins was one of the first boys to join the Boy Scout movement in Iowa, and is still very much interested in that great movement. He is a member of the City Managers Association of America.

HERBERT WALLACE PHILLIPS.—An efficient employe of the Santa Fe Railroad Company is Herbert Wallace Phillips of Richmond. He was born in St. James, Minn., on January 5, 1882, a son of Nelson F. Phillips, who was a railway conductor and died in Los Angeles in July, 1920. The mother was in maidenhood Clara Jane Herrick, whose father, Seth Herrick was English. She died at Santa Ana, Cal., in March, 1921. The family are a mixture of Welsh, Scotch and English.

Herbert W. attended school in Glendive, Mont., but had lived in Minneapolis three years previous to going to Montana. In May, 1894, with his mother, he landed in Santa Ana, Cal., where she had relatives, and for a time the lad attended the school at Tustin, also in Santa Ana. He worked in a store for three years and in the meantime took a night course in business. He learned the trade of plumber in Santa Ana, finishing in Los Angeles, where he took up steam fitting. Later he was a motorman on the Los Angeles Street Railway for seven years. In the meantime his father had come to Los Angeles and was employed by the Salt Lake Railroad. Herbert W. thought he would like railroading and with a friend went to the Santa Fe office and applied for a job. On July 1, 1909, he was sent to Winslow, Ariz., where he worked on one of the coal burners, then alternated on an oil burner, and ran on the road four years. He was on the coal chute eighteen months, then stationary engineer, and finally got into the roundhouse as hostler for eighteen months. With this experience he was sent to Richmond, where he has since lived. He believes in the future of Richmond and has strengthened that belief by investing in property here. He is satisfied with his job and knows the railroad company always give their employees a square deal. Mr. Phillips first trip to Richmond was in 1914, when he came to visit a friend, and he was strongly impressed with the outlook for a large city and when he had an opportunity to settle here jumped at the chance.

Mr. Phillips married Sara Jane Neville, born in Baltimore, Md., but reared in Texas. Her mother now resides with Mrs. Phillips. Her father, William R. Neville was a doctor and pharmacist and died in 1920. Their children are Elma Jane, born in Texas January 4, 1919, while Mrs. Phillips was making a visit to her home there; and Neville Edward, born February 8, 1924, in Richmond. While Mrs. Phillips was on a visit to Texas the call came for Mr. Phillips to go to Richmond and he had their household belongings packed and ready to ship when she returned from her visit. Mr. Phillips was an only child and when his mother passed away he inherited her property, which consisted of some property at Signal Hill, which he sold and with the proceeds of this sale and his back pay, he bought his first home in Richmond. As he has prospered he built his present home in 1921 at No. 1619 Clinton Street, where he has a modern bungalow. Mr. Phillips belongs to the Association of Stationary Engineers and Firemen of the Santa Fe system. His recreation is found in motoring.

MRS. MATTIE CHANDLER.—Prominent in the civic life of Richmond, where she is serving very acceptably as mayor, Mrs. Mattie Chandler has been a resident of the city since 1911, when she accompanied her husband to this place. She was born in Iowa, a daughter of John Wagner, also born in that State, where he was a merchant and stock dealer at Knoxville. On account of better opportunities in the West he sold out and started for California, via New York City and the Horn, being accompanied by his wife and six children. The ship they were on, which was carrying the gold with which to pay off the soldiers in California, was wrecked by the captain near the coast of a small island, the captain getting away with that money, as well as considerable belonging to the passengers who had intrusted their money to his care. Mr. Wagner lost about $20,000. While waiting for a vessel to pick up the survivors of the wreck from this island a daughter was born to Mrs. Wagner. A British vessel rescued the people and brought them to San Francisco, where the Wagner family spent only a few weeks. The father once more turned his face towards Iowa and upon arriving at his old home, closed out his holdings and moved to Joplin, Mo., where he died at the age of fifty-seven years. They had thirteen children in their family.

Mattie Wagner was the twelfth child and was educated in the public schools in Joplin. She was united in marriage at Neosha, Mo., with James H. Chandler, born in Jefferson, Mo., and a barber by trade. When a young girl Miss Wagner came to California and made her home with an aunt in San Francisco, remaining with her until her death, when she went to the State of Washington, thence back to Iowa. In 1910 Mr. and Mrs. Chandler came to California and located in Stockton, where they made their home for a year, then moved to Richmond, where Mr. Chandler carried on a barber shop for years. They have a daughter, Glessner M., a graduate from the Richmond High School and a business college, now in the employ of the City of Richmond in the health department.

The first office ever held by Mrs. Chandler was when she served as a member of the school board in Joplin. She has always taken an active part in all progressive movements and is an active member of the Richmond Women's Improvement Club. She belongs to Acantha Chapter No. 249, O. E. S,. in which she is a Past Matron; she is also a Past Deputy Grand Matron, having served in 1920 for Contra Costa County.

In 1924 she was appointed a member of the city council to fill a vacancy occasioned by the death of Mr. Carey, and in 1925 she was duly elected to the office, leading the field with 3300 votes; in 1926 she is serving as mayor, and as such she is an ex-officio member of the various committees of the city board of trustees. Mrs. Chandler belongs to the Wesleyan Methodist Episcopal Church and is president of the Ladies' Aid. As a city official she works for the greatest good for the greatest number and by her square dealing has won a host of warm friends. To Mrs. Chandler belongs the honor of being the first woman mayor of any California City.

FRANK McDERMOTT.—Since the incorporation of El Cerrito (Little Hill) as a city, in 1917, it has been the aim of the officials to make it an attractive residential city and to that end there has been a continuous movement towards improvement. In 1924-1925 about $500,000 were spent in street paving; $65,000 bonds were voted for a fire hall and a fire alarm system; and one of the best and most systematic water systems has also been installed. Taking it all in all the one holding the office of mayor of such an enterprising city must needs have plenty to do. Frank McDermott, with the cooperation of the entire board of trustees made wonderful strides towards rendering the citizens of this commonwealth every satisfaction while serving in the office of president of the board of trustees. He came to this location in 1911 and ever since that date has been a booster for improvements of every kind that would benefit the majority of the people.

A native of San Francisco, he was born July 4, 1876, the son of John McDermott, a landscape gardener of that city, who came from his native Ireland to make a home in the West, traveling via Panama to San Francisco. He had married in Ireland and with his wife, Mary McDermott, who was born in Scotland, came to make their home here. The mother died in 1879 and the father in 1905. Frank attended the public schools in Oakland, working as he went along to pay his own way. As a youngster he recalls having hunted over the hills where today hundreds of homes dot the landscape. He learned the trade of butcher and worked for P. Swords at Temescal, now a part of Oakland, until 1915. Then he went to work to learn a mechanical trade with the Byron-Jackson Pump Works, and from that time to the present has gradually worked his way up with this company and is now rated as a specialist. Since 1915 he has lived in El Cerrito, which he considers one of the best residential cities in the bay section. In 1921 he was elected a member of the board of trustees, reelected in 1925 and chosen chairman or mayor to serve one year. In politics he is a Republican in national affairs.

Mr. McDermott was married in 1896, to Katherine Burkhardt, born in Maysville, Ky., but reared in Sidney, Ohio. They have one daughter, Frances, the wife of Ralph Buckley, a salesman for the Webber Company of San Francisco. Mrs. Buckley attended the schools of Oakland and El Cerrito. While a resident of Oakland Mr. McDermott was foreman of streets under Mayor Mott for eighteen months and always took an active part in the political life of the city as a member of the James G. Quinn Republican Club. Besides his home place on Liberty Street he owns a house and two lots on Curtis Street, and property in North Berkeley Terrace. He is a member of Richmond Lodge No. 1251, B. P. O. E.; Golden Gate Lodge, Foresters of America; the Butchers Associaton of Oakland; and the Machinists Union No. 284, also of Oakland. Mr. McDermott has served his constituents faithfully and well and is held in high esteem by all who know him for he is a "hail fellow well met" and popular with all classes. Mr. McDermott erected a comfortable home on Liberty Street, near Potrero Avenue, in 1926, where he resides with his family.

N. A. BECKER.—A man of wide experience and unusual ability, whose life from early youth has been spent in the iron and steel industry, is N. A. Becker, general superintendent of the Pittsburg plant of the Columbia Steel Company, where he has been employed since 1919. He was born in Belleville, St. Claire County, Ill., on January 25, 1874, a son of N. A. Becker, Sr., a pioneer manufacturer of Belleville. The son attended the public schools of his native town and grew up in the iron and steel business, his father being the master mechanic of the steel mills in that city, and the son was with him a great deal of the time. His education was completed in Chicago, where he attended the chemical laboratories and chemical school conducted by C. C. Hall. His school work ended, young Becker returned home and began working in the rolling mill for fifty-five cents a day of twelve hours. Here he stored up some very valuable experience that has been worth-while in his later operations. He worked in various steel and iron plants in the East and Middle West, among them Cleveland, Ohio; Pittsburgh, Pa.; Birmingham, Ala.; Youngstown, Ohio; Milwaukee, Wis.; South Chicago and Joliet, Ill. He has assisted in installing machinery in every mill in which he has worked, and has built many furnaces. In 1902 he came to the Pacific Coast, then went to Old Mexico, where he built three different steel plants, remaining until he was driven out by the revolution in that country.

Coming to San Francisco Mr. Becker took charge of the Pacific Coast Steel Company's plant on February 1, 1914, remaining there for five years, during which time many improvements were made by him; and during the World War several large contracts were executed by this plant. In 1919 he came to Pittsburg as superintendent of the Columbia Steel Company's plant and since then has given his undivided attention to its successful management and has rebuilt considerable of the plant according to his own ideas. The manufacture of almost everything in the iron and steel line is carried on in this great institution.

N. A. Becker was married at Joliet, Ill., on Thanksgiving day, 1899, to Miss Rose Donlon, born in Will County, Ill., a daughter of Will Donlon, superintendent of the Joliet rail mills. This union has been blessed by the birth of two children: Thomas, a graduate of Santa Clara University, served the government during the World War; and Rose, a student in Santa Clara University. Mr. Becker is a stanch supporter of the projects that help to build up the western coast and believes in the future possibilities of Contra Costa County. He is president of the Pittsburg Lions Club, which he helped to organize, and takes an active interest in all progressive movements for the advancement of Pittsburg. In all matters pertaining to the iron and steel industry he is an authority and his advice is eagerly sought by many.

VEREGGE BROTHERS.—The proprietors of the Pittsburg Sheet Metal Works, doing business at 129 Black Diamond Street, are Harry C. and Roy S. Vergge, known to the trade as Veregge Brothers. This enterprising firm has been established in Pittsburg since 1920 and since that date has been a factor in the business life of this section of Contra Costa County. Both are excellent workmen, energetic and reliable. Harry C. was born in Indianapolis, Ind., on October 28, 1893, and Roy S. first saw the light in the same city on October 3, 1899. They were educated in the public schools and early entered the sheet metal trade as journeymen. They owned a shop in Stockton, where they carried on their business with good success. It was the spirit of expansion that brought them to Pittsburg in 1920, and the move has never been regretted. They employ four experienced men and have built up a good patronage. By giving of the best that is in them to turn out satisfactory jobs, they have been enabled to make good headway towards success. Among some of the jobs they have executed we mention the Columbia Steel Plant, Continente Block, and indeed practically all of the sheet metal work done in Pittsburg since they located here. They are upstanding business men and good citizens, of whom any community might well be proud.

Harry C. Veregge was married in Stockton to Miss Geraldine Rimington, and they have three children, Harry C., Jr., Helen and Gerald. The family reside at 1020 York Street, Pittsburg. Mr. Veregge is a member of the Pittsburg Lodge of Odd Fellows and of David A. Solari Post of the American Legion. He saw eighteen months of service in France in the World War.

Roy S. Veregge was married in Sacramento to Miss Grace Zent, of Stockton, and they have two children, June and Ellwood. He resides with his family in a comfortable residence on Eighth Street, Pittsburg. He is also a member of the Odd Fellows.

JOHN JAMES COWARD.—A good citizen, as well as a good railroad man, John James Coward enjoys the good will of his many friends. He was born in England, on June 30, 1879, of English parents, who came to America to better their condition. The family settled in New York and there the lad was reared and remained until 1890. His father was a blacksmith by trade and was foreman of the shop in the steel plant at Troy, N. Y., till his death. This affliction left a widow with six children, therefore, J. J. had to go to work to help his mother support the rest of the family. He worked at odd jobs about his home town and then went to Cripple Creek, Colo., in 1890, to work in the mines and while there learned considerable about the mining game. He worked in various places and at various occupations and at the same time added to this fund of information by coming in contact with people and conditions until he is a well-informed man. Mining, lumbering and kindred occupations fell to his lot until he began his railroad work with the Colorado Southern; he became a fireman and worked seven years for that company.

On September 8, 1910, Mr. Coward came to California from Cheyenne, Wyo. He had a cousin in Richmond, so when he got to San Francisco he came on this side of the bay to find his relative, and was persuaded to stay. Being short of money he took any job that offered till a better one showed up. Soon he entered the employ of the Santa Fe, after having taken the examination, in July, 1911, as engineer on the switch engine. At that time the company was using two engines, one for day work and one for night, now this has increased to eight crews besides those employed on the Belt Line. He feels that he made no mistake in selecting this city for his home for it has afforded him advantages he never would have been able to grasp had he selected a road job. He joined McKinley Lodge of Masons and has passed through the chairs; and is also a member of Richmond Chapter No. 113, R. A. M.

Mr. Coward was married in Colorado, in December, 1904, to Anna Maxwell, a native of Scotland who was reared in Colorado. They have two children: John Gilbert, who graduated from the Richmond High, Class of 1924, is now working for the Standard Oil Company; Nellie Isabel, a member of Class of 1925 in the Richmond High, is majoring in chemistry at the University of California. Mrs. Coward belongs to the P. T. A., of which she is treasurer; she is a Past Matron of Mira Mar Chapter, O. E. S., and active in all civic, church and community affairs. The family home is at No. 60 Terrace Avenue, West Richmond, which Mr. Coward bought upon moving his family here.

JAMES LEE BARNAMAN.—The well-known business man, James Lee Barnaman, of Richmond, has made his influence felt for the best interests of the people with whom he has been associated ever since coming to California. He was born in Missouri on June 18, 1863, a son of William C. and Mildred Jane Barnaman, natives of Missouri and Kentucky, respectively. The father was a wagon and carriage maker by trade and they spent their married life in Missouri. James L. attended the grammar and high schools in his home town and early began working with his father and learning the trade of wagon maker; he also learned to make furniture. In 1888 Mr. Barnaman left Missouri and went to Montana, where he spent twenty years at his trade. In 1908 he came to California and located at Oakland; and five years later came to Richmond, Contra Costa County, and opened up a retail furniture store at 328 Nineteenth Street; he also had another store nearby. He still carries on business at this same place. He owns the building, which has apartments on the second floor for rental purposes. As he succeeded in business Mr. Barnaman thought it time to branch out and on March 15, 1924, began manufacturing furniture at Shattuck and Ashby Avenues in Berkeley, continuing until July, 1926, when he returned to Richmond. He specializes in bedroom sets and makes some of the best to be found in the State. The ivory, French gray and walnut are his special finishes. Several employees are kept busy to fill the orders secured in Oakland and San Frnacisco. Since entering the manufacturing field Mr. Barnaman gives his personal time and attention to all the detail work about his store and plant and finds that he has a gradually increasing trade. His goods are so satisfactory to purchasers that they advertise themselves and he is planning for greater business enlargement in the future.

On March 10, 1885, James L. Barnaman and Miss Sarah E. McMillan, a native of Missouri, were united in marriage. Her parents were John and Mary (Anderson) McMillan. This union resulted in the birth of five children. Jennie married Lester Burright and they have five children and live in San Jose. Mary S. married M. J. Snyder and is deceased. The three sons, Irvine, Wiliam T. and Arthur F. are associated with their father in business and are highly respected among their business associates. Mrs. Baraman passed away on March 16, 1926. A brother Wesley Barnaman is associated in business with him; and a sister, Mrs. N. E. Royce makes her home with him. Being much interested in music, Mr. Barnaman plays the violin, and is a member of a quartette in Richmond. He likes to fish and camp for his recreation.

LOUIS F. SOLARI.—A native Son of the Golden State, Louis F. Solari was born in Redwood City on February 23, 1885, and died on Sunday, November 29, 1925, by an accidental shot from a gun while he was hunting ducks. When he was a lad of five years his parents moved to Contra Costa County and settled on Marsh Creek, where the father followed market gardening. Later they removed to Pittsburg, where the family are well and favorably known. A more detailed account of the family is given in the sketch of Mrs. Rosa Solari, mother of Louis F.

Louis F. Solari attended the public schools of this county and then, having a liking for things mechanical, went to San Francisco and entered the shops of the Union Iron Works as an apprentice, later going to the Risdon Iron Works in that city. He also took a course in the International Correspondence School in mechanical engineering. Having mastered the trade, Mr. Solari began for himself immediately after the fire and earthquake, in 1906, in San Francisco, and there met with well-deserved success. Seeing a better opening in Pittsburg, however, he removed to this city and established the Pittsburg Machine Works, and built up a good paying business, the company making a specialty of marine and stationary gas engines. He was also the proprietor of the

Pittsburg Boat House, at Dock 1, where all kinds of small craft can be secured for business or pleasure. So competent a machinist was he, that the company came to draw customers from long distances, as well as from his home city and vicinity. The establishment is the local agency of the Fairbanks-Morse & Company's products, and installs all kinds of pumps and pumping machinery.

Mr. Solari was a booster for his home city and county and gave his support to all progressive measures. He made his home with his mother in Pittsburg. His brother, David A. Solari, for whom the American Legion Post in Pittsburg was named, was the only Pittsburg soldier who met his death in France during the World War. The family are highly esteemed and are among the best citizens in Pittsburg.

ALEXANDER H. MacKINNON.—There is no man more favorably known in El Cerrito than Alexander H. MacKinnon, justice of the peace of the Seventh Township, Contra Costa County. He was born on Prince Edward Island, Canada, on August 1, 1880, on a homestead that has been in the MacKinnon family since 1790; a younger brother now residing there, where the father and mother both passed their last days. A. H. attended the public schools and a commercial college. At the age of twenty-three years he came to Boston, Mass., and entered the employ of his brother-in-law, who was engaged in the hardware, plumbing and kindred lines of business. Beginning at the bottom he worked in various departments and learned the plumbers and sheet metal trades, also furnace work, etc., in time becoming a very efficient workman. Thinking he could better his condition and desiring to see something of California and the West, he came to San Francisco, where he was employed at his trade, making his home in Oakland in the meantime. He soon saw an opening near the county line in Contra Costa County, the locality then being known as Rust, and he located here and continued at his trade until he became associated with the Richmond Annex Land Company, which owned and promoted the Annex and the El Cerrito townsites. Since 1912 he has been engaged in the real estate business at El Cerrito. In 1914-1915 he was tract manager for his firm; and it is not questioned when the statement is made that Mr. MacKinnon has placed more people on property in this section than any other man.

Mr. MacKinnon early established his home in this locality and has taken an active interest in the upbuilding of the community, doing all in his power to further its best interests by serving in official capacity when called upon. Upon the incorporation of El Cerrito he was appointed, by the board of trustees, the first city recorder, and held office until May, 1924. In 1912 he became a naturalized citizen of this country, and in 1914 was elected justice of the peace of Township 7, serving until 1918, when he relinquished the office to give his services to his country, and was assigned to Troop Train Service in New York City and Newport News, Va., until 1919, when he was discharged and returned home to resume the duties of a private citizen. He was appointed justice of the peace by the board of supervisors and continues to hold that office to the satisfaction of all concerned.

Mr. MacKinnon was united in marriage in Boston, Mass., in 1906, with Miss Jennie Cochrane, a native of New Brunswick, and they have two children: Jean, in the Class of 1926 of the Richmond High School, and Hector, attending the El Cerrito Grammar School. In his political affiliations Mr. MacKinnon is a Republican. Fraternally, he is a member of Eclipse Lodge No. 403, I. O. O. F., of Richmond, having joined the Odd Fellows in Prince Edward Island in 1901; he demitted to Oakland Lodge No. 118, I. O. O. F., and passed the chairs in that lodge in 1909; he belongs to Richmond Lodge No. 1251, B. P. O. E.; and the Richmond Lions Club. He also holds membership in the Independent Order of Foresters, a Canadian Order; and in The Praetorians. Besides his real estate business Mr. MacKinnon writes fire insurance, having the agency of some of the best known companies; and he is a notary public. In 1925 he built a service station in El Cerrito and began building up a trade in that business. Mr. MacKinnon is of a jovial temperament and has a host of friends who look forward to a prosperous future for him.

HORACE A. DAVI.—A self-made man, well worthy of mention in these pages, is Horace A. Davi, bookkeeper for the well-known corporation of F. E. Booth & Company at their Pittsburg branch. At this place are canned salmon, sardines, peaches, tomatoes, asparagus, etc.; also large quantities of salmon and shad are packed here. Mr. Davi was born in Pittsburg on January 24, 1902, the son of Antone and Maria (Di Maggio) Davi, the former now deceased, while the latter is still living at their home in Pittsburg. Antone Davi had made his home at this place for thirty-two years before he met an accidental death, on August 20, 1912, when his fishing boat was run down by a hay barge and Mr. Davi was drowned. This worthy couple had eight children, viz.: Antone, Joseph, Marie, Rose, Horace A., Vincent, Bert and Neno. The parents were married in Italy and soon after came to the United States and to California, and in Contra Costa County Mr. Davi engaged in fishing for the canneries and packing plants at Black Diamond, as the place was known before it was given the name of Pittsburg.

Horace A. Davi had the advantage of studying in the grammar schools, but is otherwise largely self-taught. When a lad he entered the employ of the Wells Fargo Express Company as errand boy, working mornings, evenings and holidays; and it was here he picked up the rudiments of bookkeeping. In December, 1917, he entered the employ of the F. F. Booth Company as bo bookkeeper at their Pittsburg branch, and since that time he has given satisfaction to his employers. Mr. Davi is a member of Pittsburg Parlor, N. S. G. W., and is a young man whom it is a pleasure to meet and to call a friend.

GEORGE L. CHANEY.—Since the future growth and progress of any city and county depends upon the caliber of men who elect to live there and engage in business or professional pursuits, Martinez and Contra Costa County are especially fortunate in the class of men who have come here to locate and to help carry on constructive work. Among such men mention must be made of George L. Chaney, who has proven such a "live wire" and booster for the district and has established himself as a very real factor in its growth.

Born at Colorado Springs, Colo., on June 10, 1894, Mr. Chaney is descended from a family who, in spite of serious handicaps, accomplished some wonderful things in the world, for Frank H. and Emma A. (Kennedy) Chaney were both deaf mutes; and Grandfather and Grandmother Kennedy were the founders of the Deaf and Blind Institute at Lawrence, Kans., and also the institute at Colorado Springs, for the help of those so afflicted. His parents were the first deaf mute couple to be married in the State of Colorado, where the father was a personal friend of W. S. Stratton, the discoverer of the great gold deposits at Cripple Creek; and his brother, Silas O. Chaney, was a pioneer grain dealer and capitalist at Denver. The Chaney family originally came from Ohio, and they have been very active in developing the West, especially in Kansas and Colorado. Emma A. (Kennedy) Chaney died in Colorado, aged fifty-two years; but the father, Frank H. Chaney, is still living in Southern California, and is now seventy-five years old. Their other son, the brother of George L., is Lon F. Chaney, the celebrated moving picture star of Hollywood, who is conceded to be the greatest character actor in the world, with some truly marvelous characterizations to his credit, among them The Miracle Man, the Hunchback of Notre Dame, the Phantom of the Opera, and many others in which he starred.

George L. Chaney has been "on his own" since early boyhood, for he left home when twelve years old, and has been making his own way in the world ever since. He learned the paper ruling trade in San Francisco. When the World War came he enlisted in the 364th Ambulance Corps, otherwise known as the Masonic Ambulance Corps, in the 91st Division, and served in France and Belgium, taking part in four battles in the St. Mihiel, Argonne, Lys, and Scheldt sectors. Returning to the United States as a first-class private, he was honorably discharged at the Presidio on May 13, 1920. He then became traveling salesman for San Francisco paper houses, A. Carlisle, and H. S. Crocker, dealers in stationery and printer's supplies, and covered the State from Oakland to Bakersfield.

Deciding to locate in Martinez, in 1923 Mr. Chaney bought out the G. W. Hoffman job printing office and he is building up a very lucrative business, employing six experienced people, his rule being that they are always 100-per-cent ex-service men. He was elected Commander of the American Legion at Martinez in 1924. During his incumbency the membership increased from 32 to 175 men, and the new Memorial Building on Court Street, costing $30,000 was built. This is a two-story brick and concrete structure, 80 by 100 feet, with a swimming pool 30 by 60 feet, club rooms, and everything necessary to make an up-to-date club building. The Memorial Building is used for community affairs and is a distinct adjunct to the social life of the city.

The marriage of Mr. Chaney, occurring at Martinez, on February 1, 1920, united him with Miss Mae Sullenger, a daughter of A. N. Sullenger, county auditor of Contra Costa County. They have one son, George Clifton Chaney. Fraternally, Mr. Chaney is a member of the Masons, at Berkeley, and of the Richmond Lodge of Elks. He is a director in the Red Cross, and past president of the Exchange Club of Martinez. A Republican in politics, he was manager of President Coolidge's campaign in Martinez in 1924.

FRANK DEL ROSSO.—The proprietor of the Lucca Hotel, corner of I and Second Streets, Antioch, is Frank Del Rosso, who is justly popular among the Italian-American contingent in eastern Contra Costa County. The Lucca Hotel is run Italian style and in its operation he is assisted by his good wife. He was born at Bientina, Province of Pisa, Tuscany, Italy, on April 12, 1878, a son of Francisco and Madeline (Benardoni) Del Rosso. The parents were born and married in Italy. The father passed away in Italy at the age of seventy-five years; the mother is still living there and has attained to the age of ninety-three.

The Del Rosso family were very poor, the father earning the livelihood for the support of his family by day's labor. While still a very young boy, Frank Del Rosso went to work and when only thirteen years old he went to South America; eight years later he returned to his home in Italy and then, being twenty-one, he enlisted in the Italian Army in the Bersaglieri and served three years in China. After his term of enlistment had expired he came to the United States.

Mr. Del Rosso, after being discharged from the army, was married on September 12, 1902, to Miss Evelyn Masini, who was born and brought up in the same town as her husband. She is the daughter of Angelo and Laura (Stefanini) Masini. Her father died in Italy in 1923, seventy-four years old, and her mother passed away aged fifty-five years. Two weeks after their marriage Mr. and Mrs. Del Rosso sailed for the United States. They spent one year in the East where their oldest daughter was born, then came to Antioch, California, and for a number of years he worked at any work he found to do, and five years ran a grocery store. They have been the proprietors of the Lucca Hotel since November, 1923. This property belongs to Alfred Ferranti, a brother-in-law of Mrs. Del Rosso. Mr. and Mrs. Del Rosso are the parents of five children: Irene L. is the wife of Angelo Finato, a carpenter of Antioch, and they have two boys, Angelo and George; Josephine M., is the wife of Arthur Wring of Antioch, an employee of the Columbia Steel Corporation in Pittsburg; Frank, Jr., is a machinist in Antioch; Angelo, died at the age of twelve; and Pietro was four months at time of his death. Mr. Del Rosso is an active member of the Columbus Society of the Sons of Italy, which he helped to organize; he has been a member of the Antioch Aerie of Eagles for the past sixteen years. Both his sons-in-law and son, also are members of the Eagles.

CHARLES EDWIN CUMMINGS.—A native son of California who has made a name and place for himself in business circles in the Bay district is Charles Edwin Cummings, treasurer of the California Art Tile Company of Richmond. He was born in Rohnerville, Humboldt County, on January 10, 1876. His father was Elliott Carrol Cummings, a native of New York who was a school teacher by profession and came to California via Panama in 1862, and at one time served as superintendent of schools in Humboldt County; he was also engaged in the furniture business for a time. The mother was in maidenhood Miss Delia Hill, a native of Oregon, and their marriage occurred in Humboldt County, Cal. The five children who came to bless their union are: Mrs. May Gardner of Sacramento; George, living in Chicago; Charles E., of this review; William, of Sacramento; Joseph, of Guatemala. The father died in 1916, aged seventy-two. Mrs. Cummings lives in Oakland.

Charles Edwin Cummings attended the public schools of his native county and worked at such jobs as a lad usually tackles while going to school to make a little money for himself. In 1900 he began working on a gold dredger at Oroville and remained at that place for the following five years. He next spent one year in British Columbia at the same business, then came back to California and worked on Bear River a year. In 1907 he went to Dawson, Yukon Territory, and spent ten years, making several trips back to California in the meantime to spend the winter months. In 1917 he came back to California and went to mining on the American River, above Auburn, for a year. During the years in Dawson he was in the employ of the Yukon Gold Company; he was dredgemaster at Oroville for the Pacific Gold Dredge Company, as the company was known in California. After following the gold dredging business several years his health began to fail and he left that business and went to Livermore and entered the employ of the Livermore Fire Brick Company and remained with this concern until 1922, when he came to Richmond and became one of the organizers of, and an officer in the California Art Tile Company. He has charge of all manufacturing for the concern, which has a world-wide reputation and turns out a fine product. A more extended mention of the company will be found in the sketch of J. W. Hislop on another page of this work.

On June 15, 1903, Mr. Cummings was united in marriage with Miss Laura Evelyn Chase, of Oroville. She was born at Abilene, Kans., a daughter of George Francis and Mary Ann (Burr) Chase. Her father was born in Iowa but went to Michigan in early life; he was a soldier in the Civil War and ranked as sergeant. Her mother was born at Belleville, Ill. The children in the Chase family were: Edith, married E. K.

Brown and is dead; Alfred, of Oroville; Jessie, Mrs. W. E. Denny of Sacramento; Estelle, married Luther Hadley of Oroville; Sarah, Mrs. L. L. Lindsey, also in Oroville; Laura E., Mrs. Cummings; Mary, wife of J. J. Simonson of Orland; Clara, Mrs. George C. Wilson of Hammonton; Bruce E., deceased; and Chester H., of Oroville. Mr. and Mrs. Cummings had a son who died in infancy; they have a daughter Doris Jean. Mr. Cummings belongs to the Native Sons, the Masons and the Eastern Star. He enjoys fishing as a recreation and sport.

DAVID MENDEL.—One of the leading merchants of Martinez, David Mendel has made good in California and especially in Contra Costa County, where he has become a highly respected citizen and is recognized as one who has done his full share in building up his home city, and in furthering all projects which have this end in view. Born in 1872, in that part of Hungary which since the World War is included in Rumania, he attended the Hebrew schools and received a good education. His parents intended him for a Rabbi, but he took to mercantile pursuits instead. His worthy ambitions for himself and family led him to the decision to come to America, and in 1903 he made the journey alone, leaving in Hungary his wife and four children. He had been a merchant in the old country, and also had engaged in farming and stock-raising. Arriving in San Francisco, he engaged in merchandising, and did so well that in 1905 his wife and family joined him. In 1906, however, he lost everything he had, in the earthquake and fire of that year. Nothing daunted, he started in storekeeping again, but owing to a poor location, had to give up the business.

In 1914 Mr. Mendel came to Martinez in search for a more favorable location, and here he has succeeded beyond his most sanguine expectations and has become one of the city's substantial men, owning valuable business and residence properties. His business methods met with the approval of his fellow townsmen, and the sturdy character displayed in building up his fortunes anew from a double setback gave visible proof of his caliber as a man and as a real asset to the community where he had chosen to make his home. He owns the corner where his store was located, at Main and Castro Streets, Martinez, and he also owns the brick garage building on Alhambra Street, now the Buick and the Hudson and Essex Garage, and his residence property at 534 Talbert Street, where he makes his home, as well as other property. Mendel's Department Store, at 602 Main treet, was one of the dependable places to shop in Martinez, and he closed out his store in July, 1926, to improve the property with a modern building.

In Hungary, at the age of sixteen, Mr. Mendel married Goldie Fiege, also a native of Hungary; and four children have blessed their union. Albert S. is a clothing merchant in San Francisco; he married Frieda Thu, and they have two children, Bernard and Sarah. Rosa is the wife of Leon Snyder, and the mother of two children, Lillian and David. Mr. Snyder is a partner of Albert S. Mendel in the clothing store. Annie, the third child, is the wife of Mendell Blackfield, an accountant for the Southern Pacific, and is the mother of two children, Ethel and Irving. Sigmund is a realtor in San Francisco, and is married to Ruth Greenback. Mr. and Mrs. Mendel belong to the Jewish Orthodox Synagogue in San Francisco. In politics Mr. Mendel is a Republican. He was naturalized in San Francisco, and he has always been a loyal citizen of his adopted country.

G. LOMBARDO.—Perhaps there is no resident of Pittsburg better known than G. Lombardo, the genial shoemaker who has an up-to-date shoe-repairing shop on Railroad Avenue, where he does a good business. When not making or repairing shoes he makes gloves and mittens, having installed first-class machinery for both lines of work. His forefathers were shoemakers, as were his father and brother, all expert workmen in their native land. He was born in Tropani, Italy, on September 5, 1877, a son of Antonio and Crescezia (Ancoma) Lombardo. The father is dead, but the mother is still alive and is seventy-four years old.

Mr. Lombardo was married in Italy on April 30, 1909, to Miss Madalina Scalisa, a native of his own province; and they have had five children: Nino, Salvador, and Maria were born in Italy; Frank and Peter are native sons of California. In 1911 Mr. Lombardo and family came to California and located in Martinez, where he conducted a shoe-repairing business for six years. Then he found a better location in Pittsburg and moved here, and since then has built up a very good business in his line. He has made many friends in this city and is usually a busy man. Fraternally, he is a member of the Foresters and the Italian Lodge of Odd Fellows in Pittsburg. He has secured his first papers, showing his intention of becoming a citizen of the United States.

RAYMOND E. CLAEYS.—A city trustee and prominent business man of Martinez, Raymond E. Claeys is a native of Oceana County, Mich., born on September 13, 1893, the son of Alphonse and Theresa (Van De Walla) Claeys, both natives of Belgium and both still living. The father, a farmer in Michigan, came to California and settled in Contra Costa County in 1903, buying a ranch at Muir and there engaging in farming. Later he came to Martinez and bought the grocery store of J. J. McNamara, on Main Street. He has now retired from active business.

Raymond E. Claeys received his education in the Martinez schools, and clerked in the J. J. McNamara store for his first business experience. He later managed the business for his father, which expanded under his management until it became the largest store in Martinez, housed in a new building owned and erected by himself, which included both a complete grocery establishment, and also a coal, hay and grain department. Mr. Claeys bought a warehouse and spur railway track for the rapid handling of his merchandise, and has brought modern ideas to bear in the management of the concern, whose growth has been so rapid as to seem almost phenomenal; but in back of all the growth is the steady hand and head of a man brought up in the business, and every seemingly radical move is carefully planned from a background of practical experience; and with a view to expansion with the growth of Martinez and the surrounding country.

The mariage of Mr. Claeys united him with Ethel Kleiber, a native daughter of California, and four children have been born to them: Edward, Coulter, Vernon and Vivian. Elected city trustee in April, 1922, and re-elected in 1926, Mr. Claeys also has served his city as chairman of the finance committee. He knows the future in store for Contra Costa County, and believes in working with that knowledge in view, planning civic improvements with a broad yet practical vision, and in supporting this policy he has proved an invaluable man to the community, and a factor in its progress. Mr. Claeys is a director of the National Bank of Martinez, and a member of the Martinez Chamber of Commerce. Fraternally, he belongs to the Richmond lodge of Elks, and to the Eagles, Maccabees, Woodmen of the World, and the Young Men's Institute in Martinez.

WILLIAM A. CAPELLE.—The proprietor of the successful Richmond Hatchery located at No. 312 Thirty-ninth Street is William A. Capelle. He was born at Rockingham, N. C., on December 11, 1882, a son of William Edward and Elizabeth (Benton) Capele, wealthy retired folk in Rockingham. (It will be noted that the spelling of the name varies. The younger generations use the old original spelling as found in the old family records.) The Capelle children are: William A., of this review; Mary Jessie, wife of W. Nash, of Little Rock, Ark.; Nannie Benton, who married Dave Garrett, also of Little Rock; Archie B., also in that city; and Stella, who died in childhood. The Capelle family have always been prominent in religious work, and there were two very prominent physicians of that name. The grandfathers on both sides of the family were captains in the Confederate Army; Captain Benton led the fight at Gettysburg and had a citation from Gen. Robert E. Lee for bravery and distinguished services. Captain Benton was a large slave owner, having some 180 on his large plantation. After the slaves were freed, he deeded to those who were the heads of families five acres of land for their future homes.

William A. Capelle attended the grammar school and a commercial school and at the age of nineteen began an apprenticeship as a painter and decorator, serving five years, after which he worked as a journeyman in various places until 1920. He was with the Thomas Cusack Sign Company in Chicago for fourteen years, and then came to California and spent two years in San Francisco. In 1920 he entered the employ of the Standard Oil Company at the Richmond refinery, and when he left the company he was in the power department. He purchased his present property and erected his house and suitable accommodations for the establishment of a chicken hatchery; and he equipped the plant with most modern incubators and with a capacity of 7000 eggs. He covers the bay region and specializes in White Leghorns and Rhode Island Reds. No order is too small or too large for him to fill with efficiency and dispatch, and he gives his personal attention to all details of his business, which is expanding every mnth.

On March 31, 1907, Mr. Capelle was united in marriage with Miss Lucile Garland, of Prescott, Ark., daughter of Rufus K. Garland, attorney general of Arkansas. The mother was Isabella Walker in maidenhood, and all were born in Arkansas. An only brother is H. W. Garland, an oil man in Los Angeles; and a sister is Mrs. H. M. Hanna, of Hattiesburg, Miss. Mr. Capelle belongs to the Independent Order of Odd Fellows and the Knights of Pythias, and their auxiliaries. He has the honor of having been presented with the emblematic ring of the Knights of Pythias of the State of California by the Grand Master of the State in 1923, at the convention held in Oakland. Mr. Capelle takes an active interest in civic matters, stands for progress along all lines, and shows his public spirit at all times. For recreation he takes rod and reel and seeks the best-known fishing grounds.

FRED BUSBY.—A man of good business acumen, industrious and active, Fred Busby occupies a well-established place among the successful business men of Brentwood. Hard-working, persevering, and thinking for himself, he has met with success as the proprietor of the only exclusive shoe store in Brentwood and has gained the respect and confidence of the community. A native of Avalon, Mo., he was born March 4, 1881, a son of William and Martha Busby, southern people. The father was a shoemaker by trade in Avalon, where the family lived for several years, but he is now living retired in Stockton, Cal.; the mother died in 1923.

Fred Busby received a common school education. In Kansas City, Mo., he learned the shoemakers trade and traveled about from state to state working at his calling, finally coming to California about 1895, and is willing to remain here the balance of his life. For a number of years he worked as a journeyman shoemaker, then, in 1920, came to Brentwood where he has since made his home. He has installed a full equipment of up-to-date electrically-driven machinery for repairing shoes; also carries a full line of the best makes of men's, women's and children's shoes to suit his fast-growing trade.

In Stockton, June 19, 1919, Mr. Busby was married to Mrs. Mattie (Chamberlin) Cowan, born at Dinuba, Cal. By her first mariage she had three children, the only one now living being Reed Cowan. Mr. and Mrs. Busby have had four children, three of whom are living, Eugene, Sophia, and Lola. Mrs. Busby is a member of Rainbow Rebekah Lodge; Neighbors of Woodcraft, and the Maccabees, all in Stockton. Mr. Busby is a member of Tehama Tribe No. 203, I. O. R. M. in Corning, Cal. Locally he is an active member of the East Contra Costa Chamber of Commerce of Brentwood.

VICTOR D. AND ALBERT D. GIBERTI.—The Giberti brothers, native sons of Contra Costa County, and able business men and loyal citizens of Martinez, were reared on one of the county's fertile ranches, their parents being prominent ranchers about five miles south of Martinez, where they own a valuable ranch.

Victor D. Giberti, now the pioneer automobile mechanic and garage man in Martinez, was born in that city on July 7, 1899, the son of John and Alphonsa Giberti. After finishing the grammar school, he took a course in the International Correspondence School in automotive machinery and electricity, and after graduating, when seventeen years old, he started to work in the garage he now owns with a partner. His employer was C. C. Corkett, then the proprietor of the garage; but after working there for four years, Mr. Giberti took a lease of the premises and established the Giberti Garage.

Albert D. Giberti was born on October 5, 1905. He graduated from the Alhambra Union High School, and then joined his brother Victor in business, under the firm name of Giberti Bros.; and they have since conducted the garage together, doing a general storage and repair business and dealing in automobile accessories, as well as in Shell gasoline and Shell and Standard lubricating oils. They carry genuine Ford parts and other accessories. Their repair work has been extensive, and they have gained many patrons in the county by reason of their painstaking and conscientious work. They devote their entire time to the business and are meeting with merited success. The brothers are interested in civic advancement, and take an active part in progressive movements directed toward that end. Victor D. Giberti is a member of the Pittsburg lodge of Elks, Red Men, and the Dante Society.

GUNNAR HOLLEDAY.—As a contractor and builder, drawing his own designs and plans of architecture, Mr. Holleday is well known in Martinez and Contra Costa County, where he has been in business for the past decade and has planned and erected many buildings during that time. Born near Stockholm, Sweden, on January 7, 1879, he is the son of Gustav and Emma (Johnson) Holleday, farmer folk of Sweden and the parents of ten children, seven of whom are now living, three being in California.

The fourth youngest in the family, Gunnar Holleday was brought up on the home farm, and when thirteen years of age went to sea as a sailor before the mast. On his sailing voyages he visited the principal seaport cities of the Atlantic coast, and also the various North and South American ports washed by the waters of the Atlantic. In 1899 he came to California, but for the following year continued to go to sea, this time on the Pacific. At the end of that time he settled on land and took up the carpenter's trade in San Francisco, where he continued to work as a carpenter and builder for five years, during which time he helped erect many large buildings in the Bay city. In 1915, Mr. Holleday came to Martinez and entered upon his career as a contractor and builder, in which work he has met with deserved success. Among the buildings he has put up are the Dean Apartments, the Fitzpatrick residence, and three residences on his own account, on Talbert Street. Drawing his own plans and specifications, he is able to meet the wishes of his patrons in carrying on his work, and he is known as a conscientious builder and an able workman.

The marriage of Mr. Holleday, occurring in San Francisco, united him with Miss Ida Larson, a native of Dalarme, Sweden, and daughter of John and Christine Magnuson, who were farmers in that country. A woman of unusual charm and ability, Mrs. Holleday is a favorite in social and fraternal circles in Martinez, and especially in the Rebekah Lodge No. 292, in which she is serving as the First Guard of Pocahontas. Mr. Holleday was made an Odd Fellow in 1906, becoming a member of Odin Lodge No. 293, in San Francisco. While learning his trade, after leaving the sea, he attended night school in Oakland. He has always been a believer in self advancement and in working toward high ideals.

JOHN CREELY.—A substantial business man of Richmond is John Creely, dealer in feed, fuel and groceries at 4700 Potrero Avenue. He was born in Ireland on March 27, 1875, a son of William and Martha (Hughes) Creely. The father was a worker in the textile mills in his native land and only come on a visit to California. There were three sons in the family: William, in Philadelphia; Jacob, deceased; and John, of this review. He attended the schools of his native land and in 1890 landed in New York, remaining only a short time. He then went to Philadelphia and started in as a workman for a paint manufacturer as a mixer of dry colors, remaining at that business until 1913, when he landed in California. During this time he attended night school and prepared himself for the future as he might find it. Arriving here he entered the employ of the Stauffer Chemical Company at Stege, the oldest concern of its kind in California. When they ceased making dry colors the California Ink Company of Berkeley took over that branch and the work was continued under the head chemist Mr. Hulett. Mr. Creely quit on account of ill health and in 1919 opened a fuel and feed store and began to build up a good business. As he prospered he added groceries to his line and now does a thriving business and carries a staple line of the very best good. He delivers by motor and has a wide range of customers.

Mr. Creely was married on April 15, 1905, to Miss Letitia Taylor, also a native of Ireland and a daughter of Richard and Mary (Martin) Taylor, the former a textile worker. They have three children: Mary, Mrs. Leo Davidson, who has a son John and make their home with Mr. Creely; Marguerite, a grammar school pupil; and Helen, also in school. Mr. Creely is a member and an officer in the Presbyterian Church at Stege and was one of the promoters of the new building. He is a most loyal American and loves his adopted country. He is highly esteemed by all who know him and his word is considered as good as his bond.

HUGH H. DONOVAN.—A prominent attorney of Pittsburg, and a leader in all movements for the upbuilding of the city and county of his adoption, is Hugh H. Donovan, with offices in the First National Bank Building. Since coming to Pittsburg he has taken an active interest in civic affairs and can always be counted upon to give of his time and means for the betterment of the community and the people. A native of texas, he was born in Austin, in 1894, and attended the common schools of that city. He supplemented his primary education with studies at the Dublin University and at Queen's University in Belfast, Ireland. Upon returning to the United States he entered Stanford University and was graduated from that institution in June, 1923, with the degree of Juris Doctor. In seeking for a promising location in which he could find a field for his labors, Mr. Donovan selected Pittsburg; and in November, 1923, he opened an office for the practice of law in the First National Bank Building. He has served as a city trustee, and as such was always to be found on the side of progress. He is secretary of the Health Center Association and a director of the Chamber of Commerce.

During the World War Hugh H. Donovan enlisted from San Francisco and served in the Field Artillery, spending one year in France, where he was when the armistice was signed on November 11, 1918. He is a member of the David A. Solari Post of the American Legion in Pittsburg, and in 1926 served as Commander; in 1925 he was a delegate to the convention held at Catalina. He is a director of the Lions Club and secretary of the Contra Costa Golf Club. Fraternally, he is a member and the Chaplain of Pittsburg Lodge No. 1474, B. P. O. E. Prominent in politics, he is a stanch Democrat on national issues, and is a member of the University Democratic Club. His financial interests are large; he is a director in the First National Bank of Pittsburg and vice-president of the First National Bank of Bay Point. He believes in the future of Pittsburg and is looked upon as a leader in the various organizations to which he belongs that work for the general good.

EDWARD OLIVEIRI.—Born in Venice, Italy, on June 29, 1886, Edward Oliveiri is a son of Vincent and Rosina (De Mas) Oliveiri, natives of Italy and the parents of three children, viz.: Edward; Mrs. Elba Toniti, postmaster at Belluno, Italy; and Mrs. Louise Scossel, of Vallejo, Cal. Both parents are now deceased, the father having lived to be eighty-two years old, dying in 1922. He was a farmer and sausage maker in Italy, and was well known there.

Edward Oliveiri was educated in the schools of Venice and at the college in Treviso, receiving a good education up to the time he was seventeen years old, when he came to America, landing in New York City in November, 1905. His destination was California, where he had an uncle, who for twenty-eight years had been mayor of Sonoma, and his intention was to go to work for him; but unfortunately this uncle died before the arrival of our subject, and so he went to work in the quartz

31

mines in Shasta County. Several years later he went into Nevada, and then into Montana and Washington, following mining with more or less success, and in the meantime gaining some knowledge of the Pacific Northwest. In 1917 he came to Napa, Cal., and started a meat market and a sausage factory, for he had learned sausage-making from his father. Three years later he arrived in Martinez, established a sausage factory, meat market and grocery, and from the very beginning succeeded beyond his expectations. In 1924 he was enabled to erect his own factory, a brick structure, and his bungalow residence.

In 1918, on Thanksgiving day, Mr. Oliveiri was united in marriage at Santa Rosa, Cal., with Miss Rosina Marinoni, the only daughter of G. Marinoni, a prosperous business man and sausage maker now living in Petaluma. Of this union two children have been born, Elleanoro and Edward W. After Mr. Oliveiri became an American citizen he enrolled as a Republican, and now votes with that party. Fraternally, he is a member of the Moose of Martinez.

WILLIAM STONE DAVIS.—Descended from the old Western Sharon family, and himself a native son of California, William Stone Davis is now a valued employee of the Standard Oil Company at their refinery at Richmond, being connected with the department which has the final word as to the quality of the product before it is put on the market. He was born at San Jose on September 1, 1894. His father, William Sharon Davis, was born in Ohio and was a farmer. He came to California in early manhood, and on his mother's side was related to United States Senator Sharon of Nevada. The mother of our subject was named Susan Stone before her marriage, and was born in California. Her people came from Kentucky to California in 1850, her father being a physician in San Jose for many years, and an active man in civic affairs. There were four children in the Davis family. Susan Kirk, a graduate in agriculture at the University of California, is a landscape gardener in Berkeley. Pauline was a nurse, and served during the World War; she contracted the flu and died from its effects. William S. Davis of this review, is the next in order of birth. George Erwin W. is employed in the National City Bank in San Francisco. During the time when Benjamin Ide Wheeler was president of the University of California, Mrs. Susan Davis had the first dormitory for girls erected at the University of California. She is making her home in Berkeley, whither the family removed in 1909.

William S. Davis attended the Berkeley High School and from 1916 to 1917 was a student at the University of Nevada. After the entrance of the United States into the World War he enlisted, in August, 1917, and was with the aëro squadron at Fort McDowell and then at Kelley Field in Texas. He then went to Mitchell Field and left New York for England, on December 17, 1917, landing at Greenwich Harbor. They trained at Winchester for eight months and then were sent to France in

August, 1918. He participated in the St. Mihiel drive on September 12, 1918, and was in the Argonne-Meuse, September 18 to November 11, being attached to the First Army Corps. On May 1, 1919, he was returned to the United States and on May 26 was honorably discharged at Camp Kearny. Returning home to Berkeley, Mr. Davis entered the University of California in August, 1920, majoring in Economics and graduating with the degree of A. B. in 1922. He is a member of the Sigma Alpha Epsilon Fraternity and was a member of its baseball team. His first work after leaving college was with the Matson Navigation Company. Then he came to Richmond, in 1922, and entered the employ of the Standard Oil Company in the pipe shop. Next he was in the inspection department; and being a keen observer and an apt pupil, he was advanced from one department to another until he reached his present responsible position.

On April 30, 1924, Mr. Davis and Miss Penelope Allen Boden were united in marriage, the ceremony being performed at her home by Rev. Henry Ohlhoff. She was born in San Francisco and is a graduate of the University of California, Class of 1923. She majored in Anthropology. She was the first girl to be president of the Alpha Epsilon Society, and was also a member of the Alpha Xi Delta Sorority. Her parents are Frederick C. and Helen A. (Macdonald) Boden. Mr. Boden was in government service and spent much time abroad. Of this marriage one child has been born, Sherrod Stone Davis, aged ten months. Mr. Davis belongs to the Richmond Elks and to the American Legion Post. Both Mr. and Mrs. Davis are identified with the Episcopal Church. He owns his own home property and takes keen pleasure in gardening and beautifying his home. His recreation is found in hunting and fishing and in golf.

LEONARDO CANCIAMILLA.—In the career of Leonardo Canciamilla are illustrated the results of hard work, thrift, and a determined effort to overcome obstacles to his success in business. Earlier in life he was an Italian fruit peddler; to day he is the proprietor of a fruit and grocery store at the corner of Seventh and Black Diamond Streets, in Pittsburg, Cal., where he is building up a nice business. He was born in the Province of Palermo, Island of Sicily, Italy, November 6, 1879, a son of Giuseppe and Giuseppa Canciamilla. The father is still living in Italy, at the age of eighty-three; the mother passed away at the age of sixty-five years. Their family consisted of three children: Mariano, a rancher at San Jose; Gracia, the widow of Nicholas Donna, who died in Pittsburg, leaving five children who are now living with their mother in Oakland; and Leonardo, the subject of this sketch.

Realizing that America offered to young men with little money greater opportunities than he could ever hope for in his native land, Leonardo Canciamilla emigrated to America, locating at Boston in 1903. After some time spent in this country he returned to his native land and on February 14, 1906, at Trabia, Province of Palermo, Sicily, was united in marriage with Miss Carmilla Landolina. The young couple emigrated to America, sailing from Naples and arriving in New York City, from whence they continued their journey to San Francisco, arriving August 15, 1906. At Stockton, Cal., he opened a little fruit and grocery store. After some years he moved to Pittsburg, in 1914, and opened a store on Second Street remaining in that locality four years, and then moved to the corner of Black Diamond and Seventh Streets. Here he is building up a good business, in the operation of which he is ably assisted by his good wife and the children. The family of Mr. and Mrs. Canciamilla consists of three children: Joe, Nicholas and Marian. The children show their loyalty to their parents by helping all they can in the work of the store. This cooperation of children and parents in the business affairs of the family is highly commendable upon the part of the children, and has been responsible for the growth and eventual development of many small stores and factories into what are today large and successful stores and business establishments. Mr. Canciamilla has taken out his first papers of naturalization and is looking forward with much pleasure to the day when he shall be a full-fledged American citizen.

JOHN RAYMOND PEMBROKE.—A native son of Port Costa and one of its successful young business men, Raymond Pembroke, as he is more familiarly called, is well and favorably known throughout the county. The son of William P. and Annie (Dolan) Pembroke, well-known Port Costans and natives of Ireland, he was born at Port Costa on June 25, 1899, and grew up in that city, where his father, now past seventy-four, has for many years worked in the grain warehouses. Both parents are highly respected in their community.

After attending the public schools of Port Costa, Raymond Pembroke early learned the meat market business in his native town, where he has been a steady worker since his youth. He is now the manager and a partner in the Port Costa Market, which has been built up as a modern sanitary market largely through his intelligent and energetic efforts, for he built the building occupied by the market in 1923 and has given his entire time to the development of the business. The firm was formerly known as McNamara & Pembroke, but on February 12, 1925, it became Shea & Pembroke, taking in as a partner Earl Shea, another well-known and successful young business man of Port Costa. Mr. Shea had been the proprietor of the Port Costa Garage, which he sold in order to give his attention to the market. With these two energetic and up-to-date men at the helm, the Port Costa Market has become one of the principal business houses of the city, carrying at all times a large stock of the best in fresh and salt meats, and in fruits and vegetables, and catering to their many patrons in the city.

The marriage of Mr. Pembroke, which occurred in Berkeley on October 8, 1923, united him with Miss Grace Hunt, also a native Californian, born in Sacramento, and their marriage has been blessed with two children, William Raymond and Phyllis Margaret. Mr. Pembroke takes an active interest in public affairs and good government, but is not an office seeker, preferring to do his share as a private citizen in advancing his home community.

THEODORO FERRE.—An artist of more than ordinary ability and the proprietor of the Italian Hotel in Pittsburg, Contra Costa County, Theodoro Ferre is making a name and place for himself in the business circles of this county. He was born on October 15, 1893, in the Province of Milan, at Magnago, Italy, and comes from a very talented family of that province. His father, now deceased, as an architect of ability and gave to his son every educational advantage possible. He attended the schools of his native city and took a course at the Academy of Belle Arte in Milan, where he prepared himself for the greater things in life that might come his way.

Mr. Ferre arrived in New York City on October 20, 1920, after having served his country for five years in the World War, and having been promoted to the rank of sergeant for his services to his country. Mr. Ferre came at once to Pittsburg, Cal., and for a time followed the business of the painter and decorator. In this work the talents of Mr. Ferre were given ample opportunity. He painted a portrait of the late President Theodore Roosevelt, which adorns the walls of the First National Bank in Pittsburg. A painting of the martyred President, Abraham Lincoln, and scenes from Venice and Spring Time adorn the walls of the dining room of the Italian Hotel. After having learned the ways of this country by his contact with the people in Pittsburg, Mr. Ferre and a partner engaged in the hotel business, operating the Tivoli Hotel until July 1, 1925, when he moved to the present location on Black Diamond Street; and here, at the Italian Hotel, he has built up a good business. The hotel is equipped to serve special parties and to arrange banquets to the satisfaction of its patrons. He has an efficient chef, the cuisine is unexcelled, and the rooms are modern in every respect.

Mr. Ferre has applied for his citizenship papers, and he is always ready to help promote any interest to benefit his home city of Pittsburg. Fraternally, he is a member of the Ancient Order of Druids and of the Odd Fellows in Pittsburg.

GEORGE ROBERT CALVERT.—The efficient manager of the Richmond exchange of the Pacific Telephone and Telegraph Company is George Robert Calvert. He was born at California, Washington County, Pa., the son of John W. and Margaret (McDonald) Calvert, natives of Virginia and Maryland, respectively. The mother is deceased.

Mr. Calvert received his education in the public and private schools, and also attended night school in Chicago. His first real job was with Montgomery Ward & Company in Chicago, and he remained with them seven years, or until he came to California. His first two years here were spent in the construction engineering department of the Southern Pacific

Railroad Company. From 1906 to 1908 he was in the shoe business, part of the time as manager of an Oakland store and part of the time on the road as salesman. His first work with the telephone company was as collector, and he made his home in Oakland for a year. His ability was soon demonstrated, and he was selected to be the manager of the Richmond exchange. In 1910 he came to this city to take charge of the plant, and ever since that time he has been busy keeping in advance of the times and enlarging the company's business. The territory has been enlarged and he is district manager for the Richmond district. There were 400 connections when Mr. Calvert came here, and the number has been growing until there are now more than 4000 telephones in service and fifty-five people employed.

On April 9, 1917, Mr. Calvert married Miss Isabell McPherson, daughter of William and Susan (Fleming) McPherson, natives of Scotland. Her brother, James McPherson, died in service during the World War as a member of the English Navy. Mr. Calvert belongs to the Richmond Elks, the Chamber of Commerce, and the Rotary Club. His recreation is found in deer hunting, fishing and camping. He is fond of all out-of-door sports, especially baseball. He owns his own home and takes an active interest in municipal affairs.

EDWARD J. BALL.—Having practically "grown up" in the fruit industry in Contra Costa County, Mr. Ball is one of its most competent men in that line; and since fruit growing and packing is one of the principal industries, he is a well-known figure throughout the bay territory. A native son, he was born at Pleasant Hill on June 7, 1900, the only son born to Thomas R. and Jennie Ball, pioneers of the county, and he now resides at the beautiful country home built on his father's ranch near Martinez. Here he was reared amid the orchards of growing fruit, and attended the public schools of Martinez, graduating from the high school there with the Class of 1920; and later he graduated from Heald's Business College, at San Francisco. He then was in the employ of the Pioneer Fruit Company, of which concern his father, Thomas R. Ball, was manager. In 1922 the son succeeded his father as manager, and has since carried on the operations of the plant. Their packing house is located at Muir Station, on the Santa Fe Railway, near Martinez, and they handle about $250,000 worth of fruit each year, the greater part of the output of the Alhambra Valley. This comprises, on the average, 150 cars of pears; 30 cars of grapes, and 20 cars of apricots and plums. During the season twenty-five men are employed to carry on the work. The company maintain headquarters in San Francisco, and it makes a specialty of deciduous fruits for table use.

Mr. Ball was married at Martinez on February 8, 1922, to Miss Mildred A. Lockard, also a native of Martinez, and the daughter of L. R. Lockard, senior engineer at the Standard Oil Company's pumping station at Avon. One child has blessed their union, Mildred June.

JOHN DI BETTA.—John Di Betta and a partner own and operate the Valley Home Ranch, consisting of sixty-five acres four miles south of Martinez. This ranch they have changed from a dairy ranch to a vineyard, having planted forty-five acres to grapes, now just coming into bearing and promising to be one of the most productive vineyards of the valley. Born in Contessa, Entellina, Italy, on September 16, 1868, John Di Betta is a son of Frank and Lunna Di Betta, who were married in Italy, and moved to New Orleans, La., when John was one and one-half years old. He was five years old when the family went back to Italy, and there he was reared, in his home town. There the father died in 1889, and the mother lived until 1916, when she died aged eighty years.

Returning to the United States when twenty-three years old, after having served for three years in the Italian army, from which he was discharged with the rank of high corporal, John Di Betta went to New Orleans and there learned the barber's trade. In that city his marriage occurred, uniting him with Miss Celia Musacchia, who was born in New Orleans, a daughter of Leonard and Lilly Musacchia. Mrs. Di Betta's mother died of yellow fever when Mrs. Di Betta was only one month old. That dread disease was raging in New Orleans at that time and wiped out hundreds of lives. Seven children have been born to Mr. and Mrs. Di Betta: Lulu L., a pharmacist and druggist at Martinez; Julia, a forewoman at the sugar refinery at Crockett; Lillian, a stenographer with the Shell Company at Martinez; Frank, on the home ranch; Leonard; and Helen. All the children were born in New Orleans with the exception of Helen, who was born in California.

In 1914, Mr. Di Betta brought his family out to California, seeking a more healthful climate, and for eight years worked as a barber in Martinez. On June 12, 1922, with a partner, he bought his present ranch; and there he makes his home, his family continuing to reside at their residence in Martinez. The ranch has been improved with a dwelling house and ranch buildings, and is being developed by the two partners to a productive ranch.

WILLIAM HENRY STEPHENS.—One of the men deeply interested in the Boy Scouts and who is one of the shift bosses at the sugar refinery in Crockett is William H. Stephens, who has been connected with the refinery since 1914. He was born at Grand Junction, Colo., on December 28, 1890, the son of W. J. and Jennie (Brown) Stephens. W. J. Stephens and his wife were both natives of Wisconsin. The father went to Colorado during the gold rush of the eighties; he met an accidental death in 1923, when he was seventy-four. Mrs. Stephens died in 1891, when her son was a babe in arms. The lad attended the Grand Junction schools, taking a special course in chemistry. At the age of twenty-three he came to California and for six months worked in the sugar refinery at Hamilton City. In fact, ever since coming out of high school in 1906, in Colorado, Mr. Stephens has worked in the sugar business. In 1914 he landed in Crockett and secured a position at the C. & H. refinery. He began at the bottom and gradually has been advanced because of his exceptional ability until he is now a shift boss with all the responsibilities of the position. He likes the company by whom he is employed, and the community in which he lives and prospers, and takes a live interest in furthering every movement for the good of the people. He feels it is some satisfaction to work for one of the largest concerns of its kind in the world and does his best to promote its interests.

On August 14, 1912, W. H. Stephens married Miss Bessie Hall, of Grand Junction, Colo. She is the daughter of Lee and Annie Hall, farmers and fruit growers there. One daughter has come to bless this union, Irene Elizabeth, aged eleven and a pupil in the grammar school. Mrs. Stephens has two brothers living in Oregon City, Ore., where they are engaged in the automobile business; one sister in Vallejo and another in San Francisco. Mr. Stephens has a sister, Mrs. E. C. Barnes. Golf is Mr. Stephens hobby, and he also enjoys the great out-of-doors on seasonal camping trips. His religious belief is in the Episcopal doctrines, while Mrs. Stephens is a Christian Church worker. The family are highly respected and have won an assured place in the community in which they live.

NELS J. MEYER.—A successful fuel and feed merchant, whose place of business is located on the Giant Highway in the San Pablo district, is Nels J. Meyer. He was born in Jutland, Denmark, on November 27, 1879, and attended the schools of his native land until he was about fifteen. He grew up on a farm and early in life became accustomed to farm life, continuing in that line of work until he came to America in 1901. He worked as a farm hand in Wisconsin and later went to Minnesota, where he engaged in the dairy business near St. Paul two years.

Having relatives in California, Mr. Meyer decided to come to this State. Accordingly he arrived in Oakland in 1906, and soon after engaged in the fuel and feed business in Oakland. Thinking to better his financial condition, he came to Contra Costa County in 1913 and for five years carried on farming in the vicinity of San Pablo. His next move was the establishing of a fuel and feed business at his present location. For two years he had his brother as a partner, until the brother left to enter the service of his country in the World War. The firm opened business under the name of Meyer Brothers; and this still continues, although Nels purchased his brother's interest and is now sole owner.

Mr. Meyer has met with well-deserved success in this enterprise and has a growing trade in this entire community. His aim is to have satisfied customers, and through his affable manners and good business integrity he has won a large circle of friends. He believes in progress and is always ready to assist any worthy enterprise that has for its aim the building up of the city and county. His fraternal relations are with the Danish Brotherhood, No. 39, of Oakland, where he finds a warm welcome from his many friends in that Bay city.

HARRY L. BRADY.—A representative citizen of Martinez, well-known for his sterling qualities, both as a business man and as a public official, Harry L. Brady was born in Alamo, Contra Costa County, on September 25, 1875, the son of John and Jennie Brady, both natives of Michigan. The father came to Contra Costa County in early days and followed grain ranching in the Moraga Valley all the rest of his life. Four children were born to him and his good wife: Harry L., E. L., W. A., and Mrs. Cora Baldwin.

After finishing his schooling, Harry L. Brady learned the blacksmith's trade and followed that work, also engaging in ranching. For the past eight years he has been deputy sheriff of the county, six years of which time were spent in active service. Some four years ago he started in the fuel and ice business, and two years later completed a modern $30,000 cold-storage and ice plant in which to carry on the business. This is fully equipped with all the facilities necessary for so large a plant, and is a decided addition to the industrial and economic growth of Martinez. Mr. Brady is also in the tow-boat business, owning and operating three boats on the river at Martinez, and one boat in San Pedro harbor.

The marriage of Mr. Brady, which occurred in 1899, united him with Mary Smith, a native daughter of Alameda County, and they have two adopted children, Norman Smith and Dorothy Smith. Fraternally, Mr. Brady belongs to the Martinez Parlor, N. S. G. W., and to the Loyal Order of Moose.

JAMES A. MONTEVERDE.—The identification of the Monteverde family with California dates back to 1862, when John Monteverde, the father of James A. Monteverde, arrived in California via Cape Horn. He came from Boston, Mass., and upon arriving in California became a gold miner, working in the old Eureka, Lincoln and Mahoney quartz mines, and was rated as the strongest man on the Mother Lode and an A-1 miner. He was a native of Genoa, Italy, and after his mining experience he settled at Sutter Creek, Amador County, and operated a general store for many years. He passed away in August, 1918; and his widow, Rosa (Levaggi) Monteverde, and three daughters and a son, are still living at Sutter Creek and managing the business left by the husband and father.

James A. Monteverde was born at Sutter Creek, May 11, 1875. He attended the public school of the community and later supplemented his education by taking a special business course at Atkinson's Business College, in Sacramento, from which school he was graduated on August 16, 1893, after which he returned to his home at Sutter Creek and assisted his father in the management of the store, remaining there until 1901. He became a commercial traveler and for twenty years traveled as a "knight of the grip" in central and northern California, Washington, Oregon, Idaho, Montana, Utah, Nevada and British Columbia. From 1901 to 1915 he traveled for Bertin and Lepori, wholesale liquor dealers at 520 Washington Street, San Francisco; and from 1915 to 1921 he represented the wholesale establishment of N. Dingley & Co., of Sacramento, dealers in coffees, teas, and spices. John Jackson Monteverde, his brother, being sole proprietor of said firm.

In 1922 Mr. Monteverde became associated with the First National Bank of Pittsburg, Cal., as acting vice-president, resigning in 1924, but still retaining his interest in the bank, of which Mr. C. Lepori is president. On January 26, 1924, the Industrial Finance Company was incorporated, and James A. Monteverde was made the secretary and treasurer of the corporation. At first the company was incorporated for $25,000, but the success of the business by 1925 warranted the increase of the capital stock to $75,000. The officers of the Industrial Finance Company, Inc., are: John J. Davi, president; H. H. Summer, vice-president; and James A. Monteverde, secretary and treasurer. Perhaps no other man in Pittsburg has so large a number of business acquaintances as Mr. Monteverde, his long experience as a commercial traveler having afforded him an opportunity to meet and greet a host of persons in the great Northwest. His happy faculty of making and retaining friends is a very valuable asset to every man in business, but all are not so fortunate in this respect as Mr. Monteverde. Fraternally he is a member of Lodge No. 1474, B. P. O. E., at Pittsburg; and he holds membership in the Illinois Commercial Travelers, and in Lodge No. 147 of the United Commercial Travelers, at Sacramento. His family consists of three children: Mrs. Alice Henckll, of San Francisco; Whitton C., a medical student at the University of St. Louis; and Miss Olive Monteverde, of San Francisco.

CARL R. ALEXANDER.—As owner of the Pioneer Battery Company of Richmond, Carl R. Alexander has been connected with the best interests of Richmond since 1918, but he has lived in the city since 1912. He was born at Garnett, Kans., on May 25, 1888, the son of John A. and Clara May (Roach) Alexander, the former a native of Ohio and a farmer. The mother was born in Indiana, and her marriage to Mr. Alexander took place on October 18, 1885. Their children are as follows: Archie A., who is married and with his wife and four children resides in Richmond; Carl R., of this review; Wilma, who married T. V. Robertson and lives in Topeka, Kans.; Donald R., who also is married and has a daughter; and Helen, Mrs. C. Hetherington, of Topeka, Kans.

Carl R. Alexander attended the public schools in Topeka, Kans., and his first work after leaving school was in the Santa Fe Railroad shops, where he stayed for two years; then he was transferred to the electrical engineering department and remained there two years, after which he was sent to Arkansas City as electrical inspector and spent two years there. His next move brought him to Richmond, where he came as foreman of the train-lighting department in the Santa Fe shops, in which he remained five years. On September 15, 1918, he bought his present business, which had been established in 1915 and is the oldest one of its kind in the city. All kinds of battery work is executed by Mr. Alexander and his assistants, and his business has had a steady increase from the first. As a specialty the company deals in radios.

Carl R. Alexander was married on December 7, 1910, to Miss Louie Patterson, daughter of William and Minnie (Hayson) Patterson, natives of Scotland and Missouri, respectively, but now residents of Richmond. She has two brothers, Harold A. and Homer W., living in Richmond. Mr. Alexander is a prominent Mason, being a member and Past Master of Harbor Lodge No. 502, F. & A. M.; Past High Priest of Richmond Chapter No. 113, R. A. M.; vice-president of the Masters and Past Masters Association of Alameda and Contra Costa Counties; Conductor of Oakland Council No. 12, R. & S. M.; and Past Patron of Acantha Chapter No. 249, O. E. S. He belongs to the Rotary Club and to the Chamber of Commerce, and is active in civic work for the city of Richmond.

AXEL T. ANDERSON.—Although born in Sweden on June 4, 1888, Axel T. Anderson was but two years old when, in 1890, he was brought to the United States and to Minnesota by his parents, Oscar and Anna Anderson, who settled at Cloquet, that State. Of their six children, two girls and four boys, Axel T. Anderson, is the oldest. He grew up and attended the public schools and a business college at Cloquet, and there entered the lumber business as a grader, working for the Northern Lumber Company, and for the Cloquet Lumber Company. Later, after he had mastered quite a little of the business by practical application, he was employed at various times with other companies in Minnesota and in Ontario, Canada. In 1918 he came West to Bay Point from Cloquet, Minn., and entered the employ of the C. A. Smith Lumber Company. He worked his way through the various positions with this company until he was promoted to his present position, that of dock foreman for the Coos Bay Lumber Company, successors to the C. A. Smith Lumber Company. Mr. Anderson is a competent workman and understands the handling of lumber and the operation of the machinery used in its loading and unloading.

The Coos Bay Lumber Company own and operate three sea-going vessels that transport the lumber from their mills at Coos Bay, Ore., points to the docks at Bay Point. The manufactured material is reloaded onto barges, of which they have three, and is taken to Oakland and San Francisco for distribution. About 120,000,000 feet of lumber is handled at the docks annually.

At Two Harbors, Minn., Mr. Anderson was united in marriage with Miss Augusta Jackson, a native of Minnesota; and they have two children: Clarice, a student in the Mount Diablo Union High School, and Raymond, in the grammar school at Bay Point. The family own their own home at Bay Point, where they are highly respected by all who know them. Mr. Anderson is a member of Dalles Lodge No. 181, A. F. & A. M., at Cloquet, Minn., and of the Woodmen of the World.

FRANK McGEE.—The second largest newspaper agency in Contra Costa County is that owned and operated by Frank McGee in Martinez, his location being at 607 Ferry Street. A native Californian, Frank McGee was born in San Francisco on February 14, 1897, the son of John and Margaret McGee, the former of whom is now deceased. Frank attended the schools in San Francisco, worked in his mother's grocery store, and sold papers on the streets. In time he took over the Bulletin route in Berkeley, and then came to Martinez in 1919 and established himself in business as the McGee News Agency; and since that time he has built up a good business. His careful attention to each subscriber's necessities, and his reliability and courteous manners, have been the important factors in his success.

Frank McGee was united in marriage in San Francisco, on June 18, 1922, with Miss Eleanor Smith, who was also born in San Francisco, and grew up together with Mr. McGee. Mrs. McGee is an able assistant to her husband, and they enjoy the esteem of a wide circle of friends in Martinez. If you want any kind of a newspaper delivered to your home or office in Martinez, the McGee's Martinez Newspaper Agency will look after your wants with dispatch and guarantee delivery.

FRANK R. BEEDE.—A loyal native son of Contra Costa County is found in the person of Frank R. Beede, of Antioch, in which city he was born on April 30, 1897, a son of the late H. F. Beede, pioneer lumber and business man, who is mentioned at length on another page of this history.

After finishing the public school courses, Frank Beede was graduated from the Antioch High School with the Class of 1914. He then entered the University of California and was in his third year when he was enrolled in the United States Navy. After about nine months spent at San Pedro, he was sent to the Massachusetts Institute of Technology for his ground training, and from there went to Bay Shore, L. I., and later to Pensacola, Fla. His training was ended with the signing of the armistice, when he received the commission of Ensign in Naval Aviation. Returning to California, he was connected with the Associated Oil Company at Avon for a time, and then spent a short period in Sacramento. In 1923, with Alden Sutton, he opened a repair shop in Pittsburg and had the agency for the Willys-Knight and Overland automobiles. This partnership continued until he disposed of his interest to go back to Antioch and enter the lumber business, in which he is now employed. He has been an untiring worker for all projects that have for their aim the building up of Contra Costa County, among them the Antioch-Sherman Island bridge project, which is now completed and means so much to this section of the State. His advocacy of good roads, schools and all civic improvements is well known, and he has a wide circle of friends in this part of the county.

On March 24, 1923, Frank R. Beede was united in marriage with Miss Marion Sutton, a graduate in the letters and science course at the

University of California at Berkeley, who holds an important position in the commercial department of the Antioch High School. She is a daughter of John and Myrtle (Wells) Sutton, pioneers of this State. Mr. Beede is a Thirty-second degree Scottish Rite Mason in San Francisco Consistory No. 1, and a Shriner in Islam Temple of San Francisco. He holds membership in Antioch Lodge No. 175, F. & A. M., and belongs to the Sciots; and both Mr. and Mrs. Beede belong to Pittsburg Chapter No. 353, O. E. S. In politics both he and his wife are Republicans.

GEORGE VICTOR McCAUSLAND.—The son of a contractor and builder, George Victor McCausland is following in the footsteps of his sire and is building up a good business in Richmond and vicinity. He was born in Minneapolis, Minn., on February 8, 1880, the son of Charles H. McCausland, a native of Portland, Me., and a builder. He served as a soldier in the Civil War and was a leader in Grand Army circles in later years, having served as commander of his Post. He also served seven years as a justice of the peace. He married Eunice Day, born near Portland, Me., having met her in Minneapolis, where they were married in September, 1867. Coming to California in 1897, the McCausland family settled in San Francisco and there Mr. McCausland followed contracting and building until 1908, when they located in Richmond. He served here for a number of years as a sanitary inspector in San Pablo Sanitary District. The children in the McCausland family are: Cora, Mrs. Robert English, of San Pablo; Ernest J., died in 1917; Frank A., lives in Cloverdale; Charles E., of Berkeley; Albert E., in Oregon City, Ore.; George Victor, of this review; and Harold, also living in Berkeley.

George Victor McCausland received his schooling in Oregon and San Francisco and has taken a special course in building construction. He began working at the trade of carpenter in San Francisco and continued four years, until he felt competent to start out on his own account. This he did and continued there for six years. During these years he was a hard worker for the prohibition movement. Going to Fresno in 1916, he carried on his business until 1924, when he located in San Pablo and continues general contracting work in this community, specializing in moderately-priced residences, and employing from eight to eighteen men, according to his work at hand.

While living in Oregon Mr. McCausland entered the services of the United States government with the Second Oregon Volunteers in 1898, for participation in the Spanish-American War and was with the first expedition taking part in the Battle of Guatemala on Guam Island, then on to the Philippines for one year, where he participated in thirty-two engagements. He was in the Battle of Manila when the city was captured. He said of his war experience that a man "feels most nervous at the beginning of an engagement but becomes calm after the first round of shots"; and that he "would not want to have missed the experience, but would not want to repeat it." The World War was the first war in which America has participated that there were not some members of the McCausland family represented. He belongs to Admiral Dewey Post of the Spanish-American War Veterans.

On March 24, 1901, Mr. McCausland and Miss Ellen Shroyer, a native of Parkersburg, W. Va., were united in marriage. Her family consisted of her father, Caleb, his wife Mary Ellen (Rector) Shroyer, and sisters, Mrs. Sarah Glenn, of Newark, Ohio; Mrs. Mattie Mc-Conaughey, of Berkeley; and a brother, George, in San Francisco. Mr. and Mrs. McCausland have six children: Violet, Mrs. Curtis Beacon; Lloyd G., learning bricklaying; Walter Arnold, with his father; Ivy May, Charles Victor and Pansy Ellen, in the public schools. Mrs. McCausland takes an active interest in Sunday School work and is a teacher. With his interesting family Mr. McCausland occupies a prominent position in his community.

HOWARD HENRY MYLANDER.—The aggressive secretary-treasurer of the large and rapidly growing manufacturing concern known as the Republic Steel Package Company of California, the plant of which is located in Richmond, is Howard H. Mylander, familiarly known as "Keach," a nickname handed down from his grandfather, who was once badly bested in a horse trade by a man of that name. Mr. Mylander was born in Oak Harbor, Ohio, on October 5, 1894. His native village was a town of 2000 inhabitants located between Sandusky and Toledo, Ohio, on the Portage River, nine miles from Lake Erie. He is the son of Henry Casper and Marion A. (Young) Mylander, both natives of Ohio, the father being a hardware merchant. The parents were married in Ohio in 1878. Eight children resulted from this union, one dying in early childhood.

Howard H. Mylander was the only boy in the family. He received his early education in his native village, graduating from the high school in 1911, after which he attended Oberlin College in 1912-1913. While in college he specialized in mathematics and chemistry, and took some vocal training. During his high school and college days he was a popular football player on the class teams, and he played professional football for four years after leaving college.

During 1913-1914 Mr. Mylander assisted in the construction of the Lorain, Ashland and Southern Railway, which later became a part of the Pennsylvania Railway system. In 1915 he entered the employ of the National Tube Company at Lorain, Ohio, in the engineering department. After working in this department for two months he was transferred to the blast furnace department, and started to learn the pig iron business from the ground up, so far as its manufacture was concerned. His first position was that of a hop blastman, which is all that the name implies. After three months of that work he was given extra turns as blower on the blast furnaces, in the fall of 1915 he was made foreman of the pig machine plant, and in 1916 he was given charge of the stock bins. In the fall of 1916 he was placed in the main boiler plant as assistant superintendent. In line with other rapid promotions, in the spring of 1917 he was made foreman of blast furnaces Nos. 1, 2 and 3, where he remained until the fall of 1918, at which time he was again transferred to the offices of the blast furnace department, becoming the research engineer.

In January, 1921, Mr. Mylander came to California to assist in the construction of the plant in Richmond. When the organization finally separated itself from the parent plant in Ohio and became an independent corporation, known as the Republic Steel Package Company of California, he was made secretary-treasurer of the new organization, a position which he has since continued to hold. Mr. Mylander has been prominent in every phase of the activity and development of the plant, which at the present time is doing a business which amounts to about $1,250,000 yearly. A constantly increasing volume of business makes additions to the factory necessary, and three additions are in process of construction at the time this is written. Much of this development is due to the business acumen and rare good judgment of the firm's secretary-treasurer.

Mr. Mylander is a member of the Blue Lodge Masons, the Elks and the Lions Club, at which club, and similar organizations, he is much in demand as a speaker. He is also a vocalist of considerable ability and makes occasional public appearances for the entertainment of his friends. His firm is a member of the Richmond Chamber of Commerce and also of the manufacturers' association known as the Steel Barrel Manufacturing Institute. Among other activities, Mr. Mylander is an ardent golfer, being a member of the Carquinez County Club.

Mr. Mylander was married on March 19, 1919, to Mrs. Nita L. (Stover) Merry of Cleveland, Ohio. They reside at 476 Carlston Street, Mira Vista, Richmond.

GIOVANNI ALLASIA.—The genial proprietor of the Liberty Hotel, at Pittsburg, Cal., Giovanni Allasia, was born in the Province of Cuneo, Italy, March 14, 1886, and spent his boyhood days in his native country, where he attended school and also learned the trade of a blacksmith. When twenty years of age he emigrated to America, locating at San Francisco in 1906.

In Stockton, Cal., on December 26, 1916, G. Allasia was united in marriage with Miss Amelia Pesciullo, a native of the province of Genoa, Italy. They have one child, a son, Alfred. In 1917 Mr. and Mrs. Allasia located in Pittsburg, where they operated the old Union Hotel for four years; and then they decided to engage in the hotel business for themselves. The year 1921 saw the starting of the new building which was to be the Liberty Hotel, and the following year marked its completion. It is a substantial two-story brick building on the corner of Third and Cumberland Streets. The hotel is up-to-date in its equipment and service, and is well lighted, heated and ventilated. Its dining room is very popular with the public and has a large patronage, being noted for its splendid meals and Italian cooking. Mr. and Mrs. Allasia are working together in the operation and management of the hotel and are meeting with deserved success. He ascribes much of his success to his loyal wife, who has proved an able helpmate. They both possess a genial personality, an important factor in the operation of a popular hotel. Their personal attention to the wants and whims of their patrons contributes largely to the home-like atmosphere of the Liberty Hotel, and make their patrons feel more like welcome guests.

ZONA R. BAGNALL.—For more than twenty years Zona R. Bagnall has been a valued employee of the Santa Fe Railway, with all the responsibilities that rest upon the shoulders of a railway engineer. In all that time he has had the distinction of never having had a serious accident on any train that has been entrusted to his care, a record of which he may be justly proud. Mr. Bagnall was born in Show Low, Ariz., on August 17, 1880, the son of George and Sarah (Rue) Bagnall. The father, a shoemaker by occupation, was a native of England who came to the United States during the period of the Civil War and joined the Union forces. The mother was born in Camden, N. J., and was reared in Philadelphia. In addition to the subject of this sketch, they were the parents of two other children, George, Jr., who resides in Idaho, and Mrs. Cornelia J. Monroe, deceased.

During the childhood of Zona R. Bagnall his parents lived in several localities, but his education was obtained in the Arizona public schools. At the age of fourteen he became self-supporting, his first employment being in a grocery store, where he was employed for four years. In 1900 he arrived in Richmond and went to work for the Santa Fe Railway, starting in the round house, where he did the calling to crews. From helper he was promoted to the position of fireman, which occupation he followed for about five years. In 1906 he became a full-fledged engineer, a position he has held ever since. Taking a deep interest in everything pertaining to his calling, Mr. Bagnall is an active member of the Brotherhood of Locomotive Engineers and has been a representative of the local body. He is also a member of the Masons and Woodmen of the World, having been a member of the latter organization ever since his arrival in California.

On October 23, 1906, Mr. Bagnall was united in marriage with Miss Bertha C. Juillerat, who was born in Ohio but came to California with her parents when she was but two months old. She is the daughter of Frederick William Juillerat, a cabinet maker and native of Switzerland, who came to America in 1881. His wife, who was Laura Matilda Vuilleumier, came to America a little later, and they were married here, settling first in Stockton. Both parents are still living and reside in Richmond. Mrs. Bagnall had three brothers; one was an engineer, and another was killed in an accident on the Northern Pacific Railway. Her father had two brothers, both of whom were Presbyterian ministers. Mrs. Bagnall is a member of the Eastern Star and Pythian Sisters. She is a Protestant in her religious beliefs. Mr. Bagnall's father died in Los Angeles in 1911, and his mother died in Richmond in 1924. Mr. and Mrs. Bagnall are the parents of one son, William Stanley, aged fifteen, and now in high school. They are property owners and highly esteemed residents of Richmond.

JAMES WHITE HISLOP.—An assured place in manufacturing circles on the Pacific Coast is held by James White Hislop, of Richmond, where he and his associates organized the California Art Tile Company. He was born on September 18, 1860, the only child of William and Agnes (Smith) Hislop, both of Scotch birth and ancestry. After attending the schools of his home community, at the age of eighteen he entered upon an apprenticeship with a local brick-maker, to learn the business. For two generations the Hislops were makers of brick, and it was but natural that the young man should follow in the footsteps of his father as a worker in clay. To better his condition he went to Canada in 1878 and there followed his trade for three years, at the same time getting an experience of the world that has proven of much value to him in his later years. He next was located in British Columbia for three years, and then came to California, his ultimate destination.

Arriving in California in 1884, Mr. Hislop went to Lincoln, Placer County, where he entered the employ of Gladding and McBean Company. For the following fourteen years he remained with them, working his way through various departments to foreman of the enamel department, and later to superintendent of the glaze department. Leaving this position, Mr. Hislop entered the service of the Carnegie Brick and Pottery Company as superintendent of their plant at Tesla, Alameda County. After the fire and earthquake in 1906, in San Francisco, Mr. Hislop left this company and in April, 1907, landed at Stockton. Soon after, with others he organized the Stockton Fire and Enamel Brick Company, capitalized for $50,000. This plant was one of the most modern and up-to-date plants of its character in the State at that time, and for two years he served as the superintendent. His next berth was at Tropico, near Los Angeles, where he spent three years in the brick and tile business. Returning again to Central California, Mr. Hislop stopped at Livermore and became superintendent of the brick plant owned by W. S. Dickey, of Kansas City, Mo. He here remained one year, and then moved his family to a home at Inglewood and became superintendent for the Enamel Brick and Stone Company, continuing there until he came to Richmond in 1922 to engage in business.

At Richmond, in association with A. C. Myers, C. E. Cummings, W. A. and L. J. Hislop, he organized the California Art Tile Company, he being elected president. The other officers are: W. A. Hislop, first vice-president; C. E. Cummings, second vice-president; A. C. Myers, secretary; L. J. Hislop, treasurer. In 1926 the California Art Tile Company moved into a very modernly built plant, with the most up-to-date machinery for the manufacture of clay products and with shipping facili-

ties over the Southern Pacific Railroad. The formula for the manufacture of art tile and brick has been known to Mr. Hislop for fifty years.
Their clay comes from the pits at Lincoln, and the sand from Ione; it is
ground, mixed and run into slabs in their plant, and then cut, dried,
glazed and burned. They make about 40,000 feet of tile monthly, increasing the output as their growing trade demands. Their field of shipment covers the United States, Canada and Hawaiian Islands. About
sixty men are employed, about half of them being skilled workmen, and
all are residents of Richmond. Mr. Hislop has always taken an active
interest in the affairs of the communities where he has lived and labored,
and is a booster for Richmond.

J. W. Hislop was united in marriage at Lincoln, Cal., with Miss
Louisa Ahart, born in that city, the second in a family of ten children.
They have become the parents of eight children, viz.: Alta, wife of W.
G. Maddox; Eva, Mrs. A. H. Robbins; William A.; Emma, who married
C. H. Rhodes of Los Angeles; Ruth, Mrs. E. A. Longwell, of Lancaster,
Cal.; Louis James; George W.; and Velda, still at home. Mr. Hislop is
a member of the Masons and Odd Fellows of Lincoln. He became a
citizen of the United States in California and votes the Republican ticket.
The family are Scotch Presbyterians.

MRS. EMMA ANN GROTHMAN.—Mrs. Emma Ann Grothman,
widow of Richard Grothman, a well-known business man of San Francisco,
lives on her fruit ranch of thirteen acres in the fertile Alhambra Valley,
one mile south of Martinez. This property was formerly owned by Dr.
John Strentzel and later known as the old Wolford home ranch, the
stately old country residence having been built some forty years ago on
the Pinole Grant. This is a very choice ranch, both as to location and
as to soil, and is devoted to pears, peaches, and grapes. It is unusually
productive, even for this locality. Mrs. Grothman is a native of New
York City, being the elder daughter of Franz R. and Helena Woerkin
Von Kitz, who were married in Berlin, Germany, the former a native of
Amsterdam, Holland, and the latter of Berlin. The young couple decided to cast in their fortunes with the newer country; and on arriving in
New York, Mr. Von Kitz engaged in the wholesale drygoods business.
When Emma Ann was six months old, the family came West on a sailing
vessel that was wrecked coming around the Horn. After being rescued
they were transferred to another ship and proceeded to San Francisco,
and there the father resumed business. Later they moved to Petaluma,
and there Mrs. Grothman's only sister, Louise, was born; she became the
wife of William Cassius, and is now deceased. Still later, the family
moved to Marysville, where the mother died, aged but thirty-five years,
when her oldest child was just seven years old.

Mrs. Grothman attended the Lincoln school, and the school which
used to stand at Post and King Streets in San Francisco; and she also
attended school at Petaluma and Marysville. Her public schooling was

supplemented by a course at the Sisters of Mercy Convent, at Nevada City, Cal. After the mother's death the family moved back to San Francisco, and in that city she was married on November 22, 1883, to Richard Grothman. He was born in Bremen, Germany, came to San Francisco with his parents at the age of seven, and obtained his education in the public schools of the metropolis. Mr. Grothman was successfully engaged in business in San Francisco until his death, which occurred on January 27, 1895, at the early age of thirty-four. Mr. and Mrs. Grothman became the parents of three children: Louise is the wife of E. O. Mitchell, head gauger for the Shell Oil Company, and resides at Martinez; they are the proud parents of a son Norwood O. Herman is a marine engineer residing in Los Angeles; he married Miss Sallie Dunn, and they have two children, Kathleen and Richard. Gertrude is the wife of William E. Russell, marine superintendent of the Munson Line of steamships, and resides in New York City; they have one child, Helen.

Mrs. Grothman bought her present home place in September, 1914, and finds great happiness in her surroundings, appreciating the beauties of this fertile valley, which is unsurpassed in the State for location and for the delights of its pastoral scenery. She affiliates with the Christian Science Church, being a member at Martinez. She is a most attractive and versatile woman, has many friends in the community, and is the center of affection in her own family.

CLARENCE WILLIAM JOHNSON.—A city is judged by the hotel accommodations it offers the public. By this standard, Hotel Veale demonstrates that Richmond is a hospitable place for the wayfarer to rest, and by its up-to-date appurtenances in hotel equipment gives a favorable impression of the city. The hotel is located at 1514 Macdonald Avenue and is fireproof in every way. The hotel takes its name from the popular sheriff of Contra Costa County, who is a personal friend of the owner of the building. It has thirty rooms and caters to the tourist trade as a specialty. The hotel was opened for business in December, 1923, and its manager is Clarence William Johnson, an experienced hotel man of California, who has made that business a life study.

Mr. Johnson was born in Stoughton, Wis., on March 24, 1879, and is a son of Andrew Johnson, who was born on the high seas while his parents were en route from Norway to the United States. They settled in Wisconsin and there reared a family of nine children, all but two of whom are still living. The mother was in maidenhood Katherine Patterson, and was born in Illinois of Norwegian parents. C. W. Johnson received his education in the public schools in Stoughton, and after leaving school learned the barber's trade, which he followed for several years. He did his first hotel work at Santa Cruz, Cal., and next he was at Uplands three years, and from there went to Loyalton, Sierra County, where he also remained three years, or till he was burned out and lost everything, not having as much as a hat left. This was in the summer of 1923.

He then came to Richmond and opened Hotel Veale, on December 15. Since that date Mr. Johnson has built up a reputation in the East Bay region and taken an active part in community affairs in Richmond. He is a member of the Chamber of Commerce and believes in enforcing the laws as laid down in the statutes. While at Loyalton he was a member of the city board of trustees.

On May 28, 1912, Mr. Johnson married Miss Caroline Dimmen, a native of Norway, where her mother is still living. He belongs to the Masons, the Sciots, the Elks, and the Modern Woodmen of America. His recreation is found in witnessing a good game of baseball and other out-of-door sports.

HIRAM ELNATHAN JACOBS.—A native son and an eminent lawyer, Hiram Elnathan Jacobs is ably serving Contra Costa County as a deputy district attorney and practicing his profession in Richmond. He was born at Butte City, Cal., on May 21, 1884, a son of Albert L. and Mary (McConnell) Jacobs, born in Illinois and Canada, respectively.

Hiram E. Jacobs attended the public schools in Butte City and was graduated from the Santa Rosa High School, Class of 1904. He studied for the bar and in 1906 entered the employ of the Southern Pacific Railroad Company as a clerk in their offices. One year later he was employed as a clerk in the shipping department of the Standard Oil refinery, where he continued for seven years. In the meantime he studied law at night school, and in 1914, resigning his position with the Standard Oil Company he entered Hastings College of Law, and in 1915 was admitted to practice in the courts of California. Coming to Richmond to begin practice, on February 1, 1916, he was appointed police judge. After serving for two years, he resigned to enter the district attorney's office under Tom D. Johnston, deputy district attorney, remaining until Mr. Johnston went out of the office; then he opened an office in Richmond. In June, 1923, Mr. Jacobs was appointed a deputy under A. B. Tinning. He is still serving Contra Costa County in that capacity, and also continues his private practice in Richmond. He has been connected with some very important cases in the county, cases that have attracted wide attention.

On December 31, 1921, Mr. Jacobs and Amy B. Siewert, of Chicago, were united in marriage, and they have two children, Mary Belle and Hiram Robert. There is also Charles R. Jacobs, attending the public school. Mr. Jacobs is a member of the Contra Costa County Bar Association, and of the American Bar Association. He is a member and Past Master of McKinley Lodge No. 347, F. & A. M.; Past Patron of Mira Mar Chapter, O. E. S.; Past Royal Patron of the Order of Amaranth; Past Exalted Ruler of Richmond Lodge No. 1251, B. P. O. E.; and Past District Deputy of Grand Exalted Rulers of the Bay District of California. He is also a member and the first president of the Lions Club of Richmond, and belongs to the Chamber of Commerce. Mr. Jacobs takes a live interest in the community in which he lives, and is ready to cooperate in all progressive movements.

F. C. HEYLMAN.—A native of Amsterdam, Holland, F. C. Heylman was early sent to the schools of his native city, and after leaving the Technical School there he went to study in Germany, where he received his degree of Mechanical Engineer.

In 1902 he entered the service of the Royal Dutch Petroleum Company and was stationed at various places in the Dutch East Indies until being transferred to California in 1914, where he has since been identified with the Shell Oil Company of California as mechanical superintendent of their refinery at Martinez.

He is a member of the American Society of Mechanical Engineers, and a member of the American Welding Society.

BENJAMIN E. MORRIS.—Few persons in Contra Costa County are fully informed what the great importance the sand industry is to Antioch, from which city some 2000 cars are shipped annually for the mixing of asphalt, a purpose for which this particular grade of sand is unexcelled. The Benjamin Morris Sand Company is the most important of the sand pits east of Antioch and the owner operates three pits with bunkers from which the sand is loaded into the cars by electrical machinery. Mr. Morris ships his product through the Western Rocks Products Company of San Francisco and it finds a market within a 200-mile radius from Antioch. About an average of 600 cars are dispatched annually from Mr. Morris' pits. The original pit was opened in 1914 by Capt. John Scheller and since that time the business has developed into one of the industries of Antioch.

Benjamin E. Morris is a native son, born at North San Juan, Nevada County, on June 10, 1877, a son of Frank and Maggie (Pierce) Morris. Frank Morris was one of the pioneer mining men of Nevada County and numbered among his associates all of the leading men of the Mother Lode district. He was a prominent Mason and had served as Master of three different lodges. He was born in Maine, was a veteran of the Civil War, and helped to lay the first railroad tracks in California after his arrival here. He died in San Francisco after a useful and eventful career. After attending the public school in Nevada County until he was thirteen, Benjamin E. went to San Francisco and began life as a cabin boy and during the thirty years he followed the sea he operated ships both on the Pacific and on the inland rivers in California. He gave up the sea in 1919 and has since been interested in the sand business, being the pioneer here.

Mr. Morris was united in marriage in 1919, with Mrs. Marian Scheller, who had a daughter Louise by her union with Captain Scheller and who is now attending the University of California. Mrs. Morris died in 1921, and in October of that year Mr. Morris married Mrs. Ruth (Bradbury) McCullough, who had four children, James, Harold, William and Adah Ruth, by her first marriage. The family live two and one-half miles east of Antioch on Wilbur Avenue. Mr. Morris is a member of Antioch Lodge No. 175, F. & A. M.; and of Antioch

Chapter No. 65, R. A. M.; also of Oakland Council No. 12, R. & S. M. He is a highly esteemed citizen of Antioch, is interested in every movement that has as its aim the betterment of the community and his residence in the county has been marked by strict integrity and probity of character.

G. GASPARDONE.—As the proprietor of the Columbia Hotel in Pittsburg, G. Gaspardone is making a success of his labors and at the same time building up a reputation for himself in the city of his adoption. He was born at Monte Chiaro, province of Alexandria, Italy, on July 24, 1885, a son of Giuseppe and Maria (Bezzio) Gaspardone, and is the eldest of four living children of this couple. His father was a farmer in Italy during his early life, but is now in the employ of the Italian government. He is now seventy-two years of age and hale and hearty. The mother came to California, spent seven years here, and then returned to her native land, where she died in July, 1924, at the age of sixty-seven.

Our subject grew to boyhood on his father's farm in Italy, and attended the public schools until he was eleven, at which time he made a decision that he would go to sea. After several voyages into the chief Mediteranean ports he shipped to the Orient, visiting Japan and China, and during the Russian-Japanese war, in 1903, he visited Chinese ports. His one ambition was to get to America, and when he was nineteen he bade good-bye to home and family and sailed from Havre, France, to New Haven, Conn., arriving on May 8, 1906. Leaving his ship, he went to work making brick in Connecticut, and when he had saved enough money to pay his expenses to California he came to San Francisco in 1907 and found employment as a cement worker, chiefly in decorating, art work and finishing. His services were in demand during the rebuilding of that city, and in 1910 he moved across the bay to Oakland, where he continued his cement work until 1912, at which time he sold out and bought a ranch near Richfield, Tehama County. While following ranching he was taken with malaria and was forced to sell out and seek other climes, and in doing so lost $6000 inside of six months. In July he was back in Oakland, following his old line of work. Some of his handiwork is seen at the Sixteenth Street depot for the Southern Pacific Railway, and at the Oakland pier. On September 12, 1918, he was registered for service in the World War and was placed in Class Five, entering the service as a cement finisher at the government ship yards in Fruitvale, where the cement ships Fate and Palo Alto were constructed, and remaining as a foreman for one year. In 1921 Mr. Gaspardone located in Pittsburg and purchased the Columbia Hotel, which he runs as a working man's hotel in the Italian style.

It was while living in Oakland, on June 10, 1909, that Mr. Gaspardone was united in marriage with Miss Louise Garbero, a native of the Province of Alexandria, Italy, and the daughter of Bartelomeo and Francisca Garbero, both living in Oakland, where Mrs. Garbero conducts a grocery store. Mr. Garbero has been in the employ of a banker of Oakland for twenty years. The children of the union of Mr. and Mrs. Gaspardone are: Mary, Josephine, Frances, Rosa and Frank; the last named died when two months old. The girls attend the Pittsburg schools. The Columbia Hotel has twelve guest rooms and is a home-like establishment, patronized by laboring people, who find the proprietors ready to make every effort to please their patrons. Mr. Gaspardone still suffers from the malaria, but is gradually regaining his normal health. He is a member of the Ancient Order of Druids, of San Francisco. The family attend the Catholic Church in Pittsburg.

CARLO LEPORI.—That the late Carlo Lepori, of Pittsburg, had a host of friends in the county and city of his adoption, was attested to by the universal signs of mourning when word was received that he had passed to the Great Beyond while on his honeymoon tour in the South. Carlo Lepori was a highly educated man, who not only spoke English fluently, but also spoke Spanish, French and Italian. He acquired his knowledge of French at the University of Neuchatel, Switzerland; of Italian at the School of Languages in Bellinzona, Switzerland; and of Spanish at the University of Barcelona, Spain, in all spending three years abroad, from 1912 to 1915. He was born in San Francisco on August 6, 1891, a son of Costantino Lepori, now a resident of Pittsburg and president of the First National Bank of Pittsburg, is also one of the organizers of the Citizen's Bank of Fruitvale, now merged with the Bank of Italy, and the Fugazi Bank of San Francisco, and one of the founders of the Italian Swiss Colony. His mother, Aurelia Oneto in maidenhood, was born in Sonora, Cal., where she was married. She died on December 24, 1924, in Oakland. Cecelia Lepori, the only sister, died August 11, 1922. Grandfather John Oneto was born in Genoa, Italy, came round the Horn, and landed in San Francisco in 1850, whence he went direct to the Southern Mines. He followed mining for a time, but later became a rancher and stockman in Tuolumne County, where he died at the age of seventy-five. His wife was born in Genoa, Italy, and came via the Isthmus of Panama to California in 1855. They had been married in Italy before John Oneto left there for California.

Carlo Lepori's childhood was spent in Sonora and he received his education in the public schools in Oakland, and in Santa Clara College, from 1906 to 1909, and later went abroad and pursued further studies, as mentioned above. Returning to America, at the outbreak of the World War he enlisted, July 4, 1917, at San Francisco, for service in the United States Navy and served in the cable censor's office in San Francisco as interpreter. In February, 1919, he was honorably discharged with the rank of assistant paymaster, and returned to Pittsburg, Cal. Here he became active in the organization of the First National Bank, serving as cashier, and on January 1, 1925, became first vice-president. He was also elected president of the First National Bank of Bay Point, in which he acquired an interest in 1922, this bank being affiliated with the First

National Bank of Pittsburg. He was largely responsible for the modern bank building now occupied by the bank in Pittsburg. Mr. Lepori was a member of the city council of Pittsburg, having been elected in 1923 for a four-year term. He was active in the ranks of the Republican party and was a member of the Contra Costa County Republican Central Committee.

Carlo Lepori was married at Ensenada, Mexico, on August 6, 1925, to Miss Marion A. Cutino, then a student at the Holy Name College of Oakland. She was born in Pittsburg, the daughter of Paolo Cutino, a pioneer fisherman, who died in Alaska in the twenty-fourth year of his service in Alaskan waters. One daughter was born to Mrs. Lepori, on July 4, 1926, and named Carla Cecelia. It was while on a honeymoon trip with his bride of three months that Carlo Lepori was stricken with appendicitis and died very suddenly at National City, Cal., November 12, 1925. When his body was brought back to Pittsburg, flags on all public buildings were placed at half-mast; and on the day of his funeral all schools were closed and business houses closed at eleven o'clock, during the funeral hour. It was a cosmopolitan population that turned out to mourn their fellow townsman and to pay tribute to his memory. Mr. Lepori was always ready to help the poor and needy, to give them a chance to help themselves. He was a member of David A. Solari Post, American Legion; of the Pittsburg Lions Club; Athens Club, of Oakland; Pittsburg Chamber of Commerce; the Alumni of Santa Clara College; and the Parfaite Union, French Masons, of San Francisco;and was also a trustee of the Veterans' Memorial building at Pittsburg.

WILLIAM AHART HISLOP.—A Richmond business man who is held in high esteem for his activity in community work is William Ahart Hislop, first vice-president of the California Art Tile Company, of Richmond. He was born in Lincoln, Placer County, on October 23, 1893, a son of J. W. Hislop, who is mentioned on another page in this history. His schooling was secured in the good schools of Stockton, and as a boy he began working with his father in the manufacture of tile and brick. For a time he was employed by W. S. Dickey at Livermore, but resigned to come to Richmond in 1922, and help organize the company in which he is an official and which was incorporated in 1923. Since the organization he has had charge of the glazing and mixing of materials. Salesmen are employed to cover the territory in which they find output, and to create new fields. The company is in a flourishing condition. In local affairs Mr. Hislop is much interested and was an honorary bond salesman when the new Carquinez Hotel building was being promoted.

On November 6, 1913, Mr. Hislop married Miss Mary S. Newell, daughter of Stephen and Lillie (Kent) Newell, natives of Kansas and Michigan, respectively, but resident of Redlands, Cal. In the Newell family are the following children: Laverne, of Oakland; Ethel, Mrs. H. Sbraggia, of Pasadena; Minerva, who married W. E. Konantz, of Fort

Scott, Kans.; also a half-brother of Mrs. Hislop is George Shinn, of Redlands, well-known in Richmond as a singer in the church. Mrs. Hislop
attended the high school at Fort Scott, Kans. She is a teacher of a Sunday School class in the Wesleyan Methodist Church in Richmond. Mr.
and Mrs. Hislop have a son, William James, born December 9, 1921.
Mr. Hislop belongs to the Masons in Livermore, Cal. For recreation he
enjoys deer hunting. His hobby is inventions in clay working machinery
and he has perfected two machines, one of which is being used extensively
by the California Art Tile Company, two men doing the work with this
machine that formerly was done by ten men by hand. The home of the
family is at No. 634 Eleventh Street.

ERNEST RANDOLPH LASELL.—As resident partner, in charge
of the extensive business of L. M. Lasell Company in Martinez, Ernest
R. Lasell is demonstrating his worth as a business man and citizen of
California. This business, known as the "Emporium of Contra Costa
County," was established in 1886 by L. M. Lasell and from a small beginning has developed into the largest department store in this section of
the State, outside of the large cities. It has fourteen completely stocked
departments, each under the supervision of competent salespeople.

Born in Martinez on March 26, 1889, Ernest Randolph Lasell is the
son of L. M. Lasell, who is mentioned at length on another page in this
history. When Ernest was six years of age the family moved to Berkeley, and there he attended the public schools, graduating from the high
school with the Class of 1910; and that same year he entered the University of California and took a commercial course. Leaving his school
days behind him, Mr. Lasell then entered the establishment of his father
and from the beginning demonstrated his excellent business ability, thus
relieving his parent of much of the worry incident to the details of such
a large and growing business. He took a decided interest in planning
the new and modern building now occupied by the company at 900-922
Castro Street, where every attention has been given to modernize business, safeguard the employees, and show consideration to the ever-grow-
ing patronage of satisfied customers. He gives close personal attention
to the business, and has been a factor in the fast-developing enterprise.

Mr. Lasell is also interested in 300 acres of land upon which is located the source of supply of the Alhambra Pure Spring Water, which is
marketed under the name of the Alhambra Natural Water Company,
with head office, bottling works, storage and distributing warehouses located on Ferry Street in Martinez, and with J. J. Robrecht in charge as
general manager in Martinez, L. Wight Lasell in charge of the Oakland
office, and E. R. Lasell as owner and in charge of the depot and interests
in San Francisco.

Ernest Randolph Lasell was united in marriage in San Francisco on
June 17, 1920, with Miss Elizabeth Stark, born in Oakland, a daughter
of G. J. W. Stark, a well-known retired wholesale grocer of San Francisco. Of this union one son has been born, Ernest Randolph, Jr. Mr.

Lasell is a Mason, belonging to the Martinez Lodge, to the Chapter and Commandery of Berkeley, and the Aahmes Temple in Oakland. He is a member of the Martinez Chamber of Commerce. When war was declared with Germany, Mr. Lasell enlisted with the Masonic Ambulance Corps, served eleven months at Camp Lewis, and then went over seas with the 91st Division and saw service at Argonne and in Belgium, be-eleven months on foreign soil. He was honorably discharged in San Francisco on May 12, 1919. Mr. Lasell and his estimable wife are leaders in the younger social set in Martinez. He takes an active part in all movements that have for their aim the upbuilding of his city, county and State.

Z. C. LYTLE.—Since no small amount of the prosperity of a district depends upon the railway service extended to the ranchers and producers, it is gratifying to know that the Santa Fe Railway gives most efficient attention to the needs of the fruit shippers and ranchers of the Alhambra Valley, in Contra Costa County, and well merits the large patronage given it by the growers of the valley, who give their shipping business almost exclusively to the Santa Fe, thus making Muir Station an important point on the road; and both the railway and the residents of the valley are fortunate in that they have in charge of Muir Station a man who has spent practically all of his working life in railroad work, and understands thoroughly the details of the business. A Southerner by birth, and a native of Asheville, N. C., where his birth occurred on January 18, 1878. Z. C. Lytle is a son of John and Amanda (Osborne) Lytle, both Southerners before him, and now deceased. He was reared in North Carolina, attending the public schools at Asheville, and at the age of sixteen started in as messenger boy in the office of the Western Union Telegraph Company at Asheville, and later became clerk, learning telegraphy and finally becoming telegraph operator there for the company. After two years as operator there he went to Union, S. C., and acted as operator there for two years. He then started West, working for different railways and telegraph companies. It was while he was at Minden, La., as operator for the Western Union, that his marriage occurred, at Longview, Texas, to Miss Daisy King, a native daughter of that place, where her father was a carpenter and builder. He was David King, and had married Iona Simms, who was born in Arkansas and is still living in Los Angeles; the husband and father having died in that city in 1916, aged fifty-eight years.

After his marriage, Mr. Lytle continued in the railway business with the exception of one year, when he worked for the Commercial Lumber Company at Gilmer, Texas. In 1913 they came to California, arriving on July 15 of that year, and here he went to work for the Santa Fe, and came to Muir Station in 1918. Mrs. Lytle operates the Alhambra Service Station on the Alhambra road, near Muir Station.

Five children blessed the marriage of Mr. and Mrs. Lytle: Alwyn, a clerk in the Bank of Martinez; Lois, cashier for the L. M. Lasell Company; and Charlie, Robert, and Virda, attending grammar school. Popular in both social and business circles, the family are well known throughout the county. Mr. Lytle is a member of the Odd Fellows, of many years standing, having joined the order in Bronte, Texas, and demitted to Martinez Lodge No. 297. In national politics he supports the Democratic platform, and locally he stands for the best man and the community's best interests. With his wife he is a member of the First Methodist Church at Martinez.

EDWARD R. GUINAN, M.D.—A native son of California who has attained to the front rank in the medical profession in the State is Edward R. Guinan, M. D., of Richmond, Contra Costa County, where he takes a live interest in all that pertains to making this city a better place in which to live and prosper. He was born in San Diego, on May 11, 1889, the son of Robert P. and Nora Guinan. The father came from Ireland when he was sixteen years of age, and landed in California in 1878 as one of the pioneers of San Diego, where he followed glass, sash and door work for many years.

Edward R. Guinan was educated at St. Mary's College in Oakland, and was graduated from Cooper Medical College, affiliated with Stanford University, with his M.D. degree in 1911. His first practical experience was obtained at St. Mary's Hospital in San Francisco, where he took his first year's internship. He was also engaged in his professional work in Sacramento County Hospital and for a year was resident physician at Providence Hospital in Oakland. At the time of the Mexican trouble Dr. Guinan was graduated from the Army Medical School, and in 1917 he was commissioned lieutenant, senior grade, in the United States Navy, and saw service in the Orient; he was in the Island of Guam Naval Hospital for two years, and for eighteen months he was stationed at Mare Island. He resigned from the United States service in 1920 and went to Kern County, and at Bakersfield was associated with the leading physician there for a year.

In 1921 Dr. Guinan made a permanent location in Richmond, establishing an office on Macdonald Avenue. At that time he was an absolute stranger; now he has the leading practice in the city and is recognized as one of the leading men in the medical profession in western Contra Costa County. He is a member of the staff of Providence Hospital in Oakland. Doctor Guinan makes a specialty of surgical cases and has met with the best of success since he came here. He believes in Richmond's future, and in 1926 completed one of the finest homes in Mira Vista, modern in every detail. Besides his professional duties he also has other outside interests that make him a very busy man. The confidence he has gained has been won through his thorough understanding of medical science and his willingness to give each patient the full benefit of his knowledge. His offices are located at No. 335 Tenth Street.

Edward R. Guinan was united in marriage in Oakland, in 1917, with Miss Margaret Clark, the daughter of Robert and Julia Clark, large landowners in Sonoma. She was born at Petaluma. Dr. and Mrs. Guinan are the parents of two children, Jewel Kathleen and Clark Edward. Dr. Guinan is a member of the Benevolent Protective Order of Elks; the Improved Order of Red Men; the Fraternal Order of Eagles, in which he serves as physician; the Fraternal Brotherhood; the Knights of Columbus; and the Athens Athletic Club of Oakland. He is also a member of the American Legion, the Lions Club, the Chamber of Commerce, the County and State Medical Societies, the American Medical Association, and the Stanford Alumni Association. Politically, he is a Republican on national issues; locally, he supports men and measures regardless of party lines. He is an enthusiastic football fan, and for recreation enjoys hunting and trout-fishing, and touring by automobile through the many beauty spots to be found in California.

H. A. LASELL.—As secretary and accountant of the "Emporium of Contra Costa County," the largest department store in the county, with its fourteen completely stocked departments catering to the trade of the people of the entire county, H. A. Lasell finds his time fully occupied with his ever-increasing duties of the fast-growing business established in Martinez in 1886 by L. M. Lasell, now the pioneer merchant of Martinez. A native of New York State, H. A. Lasell was born on June 25, 1894, near Ellenburg Depot, Clinton County, the son of Marshall M. and Addie (Bond) Lasell. The father is a brother of L. M. Lasell of Martinez, and is still living, aged about seventy years. He is a native of Vermont but was married in New York, his wife having been born near Ellenburg Depot.

H. A. Lasell is the youngest of five children and is the only one in California. He grew up in New York State and attended the grammar and high schools of Ellenburg Depot, and while in his senior year in 1910, he came out to California on a visit. He became interested in his uncle's store and entered the employ of L. M. Lasell and Company as office clerk when the store occupied the old wooden buildings, which are still standing at the corner of Castro and Thompson Streets. From bookkeeper he rose to his present position through the various channels of the business, and he is held in the highest esteem by all connected with the great establishment.

Mr. Lasell was married on October 16, 1915, at San Rafael, to Miss Elsie Burns, born in Oregon but reared in Sacramento, Cal. Mr. and Mrs. Lasell have two children, Margaret and Muriel. The family attend the Congregational Church and Mrs. Lasell is a member of the Ladies' Aid Society. Fraternally, Mr. Lasell is a member of the Woodmen of the World. He applies his whole time and energy to business during working hours, and for recreation he seeks the streams where are to be found the game fish for which California is noted; and he seldom returns without having caught the limit. The family reside in their comfortable home at 717 Arlington Way, in Martinez.

LEWIS JAMES HISLOP.—The secretary of the California Art Tile Company at Richmond is L. J. Hislop, a native son of the Golden State, born at Lincoln, Placer County, on June 4, 1899, a son of J. W. Hislop, president and founder of the corporation mentioned above. L. J. attended the public schools at Inglewood, Los Angeles County, and at an early age began working in clay until he has become a practical man in the manufacture of the products put out by this enterprising concern. After leaving school Mr. Hislop went to New York, where he spent about fourteen months, then was in Chicago for a year. Returning to California he became associated with his father in business and has been with him in his different removals ever since. Upon the organization of the California Art Tile Company Mr. Hislop was elected treasurer, later becoming secretary, and is giving his entire time and attention to the growing business of the firm. They now occupy a very modern structure in Richmond and turn out products that find a market in many parts of the world.

On July 19, 1923, Mr. Hislop was united in marriage with Miss Fay Anita Farley, born in Carpentersville, Ill., the only child of her parents, who now reside at Richmond. This happy union has been blessed with two children, Patricia Ruth and James Lewis. Mr. Hislop belongs to Alpha Lodge No. 431, F. & A. M., at Richmond, and both himself and wife are members of Mira Mar Chapter of the Eastern Star. They hold an assured place in their social set in Richmond, where they have an ever increasing circle of warm friends.

FRANK AUSEZ.—One of the leading cement contractors in Richmond and vicinity is Frank Ausez of No. 2100 Burbeck Avenue, Richmond. He was born in Austria on December 3, 1883, one of five children in the family of Frank and Catherine Ausez. His father was a builder and it was natural that Frank, Jr., should take to the building trade. After finishing his education in his native land, in 1905, Mr. Ausez landed in America and crossed the continent to Lafayette, Colo., where he spent three years. After this he traveled through the northwest looking for a suitable place to pitch his tent and in 1909 landed in Richmond. After some deliberation he concluded he would try his luck here and began work as a concrete and cement contractor, a business he had become competent to handle in every department. From the first he was successful and as the years have passed he has had his share of the cement and concrete work in this locality and has done considerable bridge and street work. As he has prospered he has invested in property and owns his own home and is well satisfied that he cast in his lot with Contra Costa County. He became a full-fledged American citizen in San Francisco in 1919.

Mr. Ausez was married on November 9, 1913, to Miss Mary Yanezich, also a native of Austria and a daughter of John and Annie Yanezich. She has one brother living in Richmond. Mr. and Mrs. Ausez have three children: Frankie C., Annie and Frances. Mr. Ausez is a member of the Builders' Exchange and takes an active interest in its meetings. He belongs to the Woodmen of the World, the Red Men and the Richmond Elks. To help boost the city of his choice he is a member of the Chamber of Comerce. For rest and recreation Mr. Ausez likes to hunt and fish and is fond of watching athletic sports of all kinds. He is a busy man but not too busy but that he can lend a helping hand, when necessary, to promote the best interests of Richmond and the East Bay District.

JAMES S. HIGUERA.—Endowed by nature with an active mind, a cheerful disposition, and a resolute will, James S. Higuera began life for himself when a mere lad, and has met with deserved success in his undertakings. He is well-known in the business circles of Martinez, and was an employee of the Alhambra Market for a period of thirteen years. Beginning his life work when only twelve years of age, Mr. Higuera first worked for A. B. Catt; then, in 1910, he came to Martinez, where he began working for the Alhambra Market. On April 16, 1924, he bought the Quality Market, at 737 Ferry Street, which was sold under the sheriff's hammer, its former owners having failed to make good. This he closed out about one year later.

Coming of Spanish ancestry, James S. Higuera was born on August 3, 1891, at Pinole, Contra Costa County, Cal., the youngest in a family of five children born to Frank and Virginia (Rojes) Higuera, both of early Spanish families of the Bay section of California. Frank Higuera was an expressman by occupation; he passed away in 1910, aged fifty-six years; the mother is now living in Martinez. James S. Higuera grew up at Rodeo, Cal., and there attended the public schools until he was twelve years old, when he began to make his own way in the world, beginning at the bottom of the ladder and steadily working toward the top.

Mr. Higuera's marriage occurred on September 9, 1911, and united him with Miss Ethel McDonald, born at Clayton, Contra Costa County. Of this union there are seven children: Velda and Verda (twins), Donald, Eleanor, Le Verne, John, and Edith. Mr. Higuera is a Republican in politics. With his family he belongs to the Catholic Church.

CAMILLO LANZAFAME.—The life which this brief narrative sketches began in Aci, Catania, Italy, in the Island of Sicily, April 30, 1889, when Camillo Lanzafame was born to Delpho and Rose Lanzafame. Their family consisted of thirteen children, eleven of whom are living, eight boys and three girls, Camillo being the only member of the family in America. Delpho Lanzafame, the father, was a wholesale dealer in groceries and provisions in Italy.

When Camillo Lanzafame was seventeen years of age, he started out to make his own way in the world, sailing in 1906 to New York City. His first employment in America was secured at Lawrence, Mass., where he remained one year. He then migrated to California, locating at

Pittsburg in 1907, and there worked as a barber for some time. In 1915 Mr. Lanzafame established his present furniture business, in which he has been quite successful. Being of a happy and genial nature, he possesses the faculty of making and keeping many friends, which is an asset of inestimable value in business. In 1919 H. H. Summer, of the Summer Lumber Company, a brother-in-law, became associated with Mr. Lanzafame as his partner in the furniture and household furnishing business; and by courteous treatment of their patrons, strict attention to the details of business and honorable dealings with all, they are together building up a large and growing business and enjoying the confidence of the community.

On February 25, 1917, Camillo Lanzafame was united in marriage with Miss Susie Viscuso, a daughter of the late G. Viscuso and his widow, Aquilina Viscuso honored pioneers of Pittsburg. Mr. and Mrs. Lanzafame had one child, a son, Delpho. Mrs. Lanzafame died on February 26, 1920. Mr. Lanzafame has illustrated by his success the results of energy, thrift, and wise and judicious management of business affairs.

JOHN N. ASMUSSEN.—The competent superintendent for the Blake Brothers Company at their quarry in Richmond is John N. Asmussen, a capable workman who has taken an active interest in developing the business for his company. He was born at Russell, Cal., on October 23, 1887, a son of Thomas and Johanna Asmussen, both born in Denmark. He has one brother, Andy Asmussen, in Russell, and two sisters, Annie, (Mrs. W. Fletcher) and May, (Mrs. Ollie Davis) living in San Francisco.

John N. Asmussen attended the Russell and San Francisco public schools, and a night school for a time, and then served an apprenticeship as a machinist. His first work was with the George E. Dow Pump Works, where he remained till April, 1907. In 1908 he began with Blake Brothers as a machinist and one year later was promoted to be foreman of their plant. On November 1, 1917, he was made superintendent, the position he still holds. Mr. Asmussen has been instrumental in the growth of the plant and served as a director for a year. The largest shot fired in blasting at the quarry was twenty-three tons of powder, and the longest cut was an eighty foot fill 220 feet across. Mr. Asmussen thoroughly understands his work and is popular with the men under his direction.

On March 9, 1909, Mr. Asmussen and Miss Anna McNamara were united in marriage of Russell. She is the daughter and only child of Michael and Theresa (Murray) McNamara. Mr. McNamara was born in Ireland and is an old employee of the Southern Pacific. Mrs. Asmussen attended the grammar and high schools, and Heald's Business College of Oakland. They have one son, Edward, now sixteen years old and a pupil in the high school in Richmond. Mrs. Asmussen is a member of the Alpha Lodge of Masons and the Richmond Elks. The family are well and favorably known in the East Bay section.

ELLWOOD ORMSBEE MITCHELL.—Holding the responsible position of head gauger for the Shell Oil Company, at their plant in Martinez, for the past ten years Mr. Mitchell has filled an important place in the business and social life of Contra Costa County. A native Californian, he was born in Pasadena on February 3, 1889, the son of Albert A. and Eva E., (Baty) Mitchell. The father was a native of Virginia, and was district agent for one of the large wholesale coffee houses in Los Angeles, in which city his death occurred in 1915. The mother is still living, residing in Oakland. They were the parents of four children, Ellwood being the only one residing in Contra Costa County.

Ellwood Ormsbee Mitchell attended the Los Angeles grammar schools, and later graduated from the high school at San Jose with the class of 1911, after which he took a special law course at Stanford University. Becoming interested in the oil industry, he went to work for the Pinal Dome Oil Company in the Santa Maria field, and remained with that company for three and one-half years. In 1916 he came to Martinez and became a gauger for the Shell Oil Company, and one year later was promoted to the position of head gauger, which position he now holds.

The marriage of Mr. Mitchell, in 1921, at Martinez, united him with Miss Louise Helen Grothman; and they are now the parents of a son, Norwood Ormsbee. Having taken an active interest in sports, both at high school and during his university training, Mr. Mitchell has maintained that interest and is still an enthusiastic tennis player and baseball fan; and he is a member of the Contra Costa Golf Club. He is a member of the Alumni Association of Stanford University, and is a man of broad and keen vision, taking a live interest in current events, and doing all in his power to help in general welfare work.

DUDLEY DEAN WATSON.—Among the men of Contra Costa County who are building up the horticultural and agricultural interests for future generations we find Dudley Dean Watson, of Brentwood, taking a leading part. He believes the possibilities are good for eastern Contra Costa County to become the greatest fruit growing center in the State, and to show his faith he has purchased raw land and is developing it. Mr. Watson owns 311 acres of land, which he has planted to alfalfa and orchards, and upon which he now raises vegetables; he also has 689 acres under a fifteen-year lease from Horace L. Hill, Jr., of San Francisco. In addition to developing his own property he deals in real estate and does a general development of property for those who wish such work done. He is caring for and developing 750 acres for the Blyth-Witter Company and the Brentwood Orchards Company. Mr. Watson has developed an organization, having the most experienced engineers and the best men available in their various lines to carry on property development, such as mentioned above, under his personal supervision. In 1926 he engineered the development work on fifty various parcels of land in this district. In selling property he endeavors to interest that class of settlers who will mean much to the county in the future, among whom we mention H. W. Poett, who bought forty acres, which Mr. Watson has developed to apricots; H. P. Garin, the largest vegetable shipper on the Pacific Coast, who purchased two tracts of 125 acres each, one-half of the property being planted to lettuce and the other half being set to apricots, peaches and standard nectarines.

Mr. Watson has about the most perfect organization for the development and managing of land and land improvement, to be found anywhere. In 1926 he erected one of the largest, if not the largest, packing and shipping house in this district on the Santa Fe Railroad at Bixler; he has plans under way for a dehydrating and sun drying plant, and for shipping green fruit to the markets and canneries from one unit, thereby cutting down the expenses of handling the products as they now are being handled. He also deals in nursery stock and represents the Silva-Berkholdt Nursery Company at Newcastle, Cal.; also the Gregory Brothers Nurseries of Brentwood and Marysville.

D. D. Watson was born in San Francisco, on December 5, 1895. His parents are W. A. and Margaret (Jones) Watson, natives of California and Kentucky, respectively. W. A. Watson owned ranches in Yolo and Colusa Counties, became a very successful farmer, and is now living retired in Berkeley. The son attended the schools in Colusa County, graduating from the joint high school with the Class of 1914. He soon after entered the employ of H. L. Hill, Jr., on his Toyon Farm near Los Altos, Santa Clara County, and had been advanced to purchasing agent when the World War broke out. He enlisted in the air service and served twenty-two months over seas, testing airplanes and motors, and doing repair work. He rose to be a first class flight sergeant and was on the front at the Meuse in a German airdrome when the armistice was signed. Returning to the United States he was honorably discharged at San Diego in April, 1919. Reentering the employ of Mr. Hill that same summer he signed a fifteen-year lease for Westwind Farms, Brentwood. In February, 1924, he bought the Estes ranch of 311 acres.

In August, 1919, D. D. Watson was married to Florence Grossman, daughter of Mrs. Lucy Grossman, and they have three children: Jeanne Marie, Dudley Dean, Jr., and Robert Hayden. He is a member of the American Legion Post at Brentwood, the Stockton Elks, and the Union League Club in San Francisco. He is a stanch supporter of the Chamber of Commerce and Farm Bureau.

INDEX OF NAMES

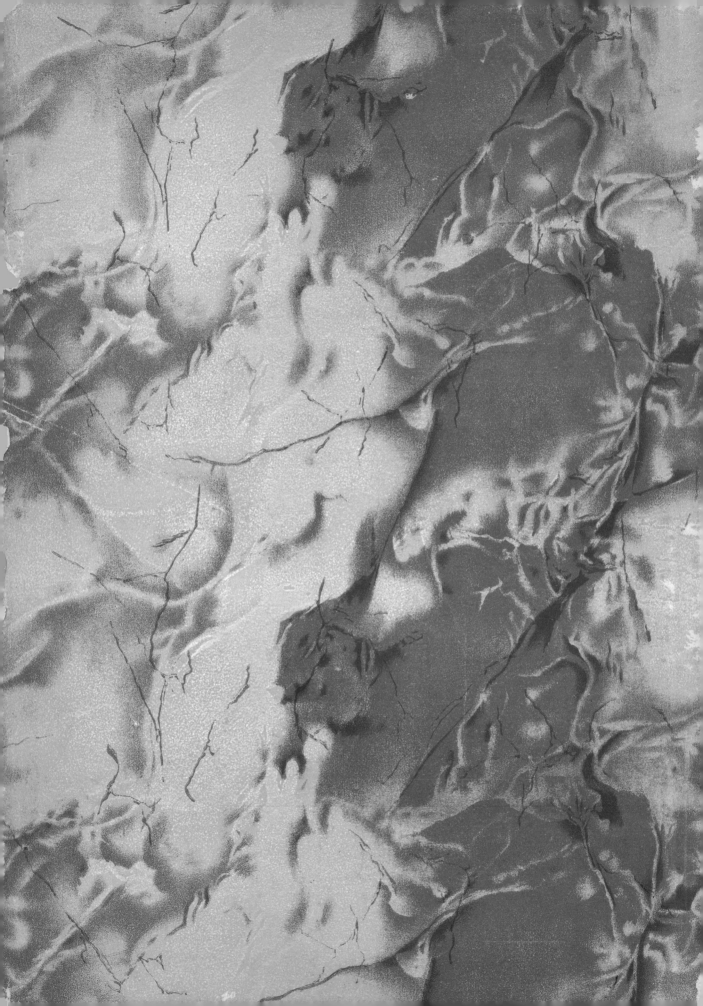